T-S
La.8 - P91
Pr-6

PRENTICE HALL
LITERATURE

Timeless Voices, Timeless Themes

COPPER LEVEL

PEARSON
Prentice Hall

Upper Saddle River, New Jersey

Needham, Massachusetts

Copyright © 2005 by Pearson Education, Inc., publishing as Pearson Prentice Hall, Upper Saddle River, New Jersey 07458. All rights reserved. Printed in the United States of America. This publication is protected by copyright, and permission should be obtained from the publisher prior to any prohibited reproduction, storage in a retrieval system, or transmission in any form or by any means, electronic, mechanical, photocopying, recording, or likewise. For information regarding permission(s), write to: Rights and Permissions Department.

Pearson Prentice Hall™ is a trademark of Pearson Education, Inc.
Pearson® is a registered trademark of Pearson plc.
Prentice Hall® is a registered trademark of Pearson Education, Inc.

ISBN 0-13-180430-8

1 2 3 4 5 6 7 8 9 10   07 06 05 04 03

Cover: *The Haystacks,* oil on canvas, Vincent van Gogh/Nationalmuseum, Stockholm, Sweden/Bridgeman Art Library, London/New York

ACKNOWLEDGMENTS

Grateful acknowledgment is made to the following for permission to reprint copyrighted material:

Airmont Publishing Company, Inc. "Water" from *The Story of My Life* by Helen Keller. Copyright © 1965 by Airmont Publishing Company, Inc. Reprinted by permission of Airmont Publishing Company, Inc.

Ricardo E. Alegría "The Three Wishes" from *The Three Wishes: A Collection of Puerto Rican Folktales,* selected and adapted by Ricardo E. Alegría, translated by Elizabeth Culbert. Reprinted by permission of the author.

Archaeological Institute of America (Newsbrief) "Human Footprints at Chauvet Cave" by Spencer P. M. Harrington, *Archaeology,* Volume 52, Number 5, 1999. Reprinted with the permission of *Archaeology* Magazine, Vol. 52, No. 5 (Copyright the Archaeological Institute of America, 1999).

A. H. Belo Corp., The Dallas Morning News From "Chinese immigrants remember detention at Angel Island" by Esther Wu, from *The Dallas Morning News,* May 19, 2000. Used by permission.

Susan Bergholz Literary Services From "Something to Declare to My Readers" by Julia Alvarez. Copyright © 1982, 1998 by Julia Alvarez. Published in *Something to Declare,* Algonquin Books of Chapel Hill, 1998. "Eleven" from *Woman Hollering Creek,* by Sandra Cisneros. Copyright © 1991 by Sandra Cisneros. Published by Vintage Books, a division of Random House, Inc., New York and originally in hardcover by Random House, Inc. New York. "Names/Nombres," by Julia Alvarez. Copyright © 1985 by Julia Alvarez. First published in *Nuestro.* March, 1985. Reprinted by permission of Susan Bergholz Literary Services, New York. All rights reserved.

Georges Borchardt, Inc., for the Estate of John Gardner "Dragon, Dragon" from *Dragon, Dragon and Other Tales* by John Gardner. Copyright © 1975 by Boskydell Artists Ltd. Reprinted by permission of Georges Borchardt, Inc., for the Estate of John Gardner.

Amanda Borden and ESPN Internet Group "Olympic Diary " by Amanda Borden, from ESPNET *Sportzone/1996 Olympic Diaries/Gymnastics.* Copyright © 1996, 1997 ESPN, Inc. Used by permission.

Brandt & Hochman Literary Agents, Inc. "Lob's Girl," from *A Whisper in the Night* by Joan Aiken, copyright © 1984 by Joan Aiken Enterprises, Ltd. "Wilbur Wright and Orville Wright" by Rosemary Benét and Stephen Vincent Benét, from *A Book of Americans* by Rosemary and Stephen Vincent Benét (Holt, Rinehart & Winston, Inc.). Copyright © 1933 by Rosemary and Stephen Vincent Benét. Copyright renewed © 1961 by Rosemary Benét. Reprinted by permission.

Candlewick Press From "Obie's Gift" by Martin Waddell, from *Little Obie and the Flood.* Text © 1991 by Martin Waddell. Reproduced by permission of the publisher Candlewick Press Inc., Cambridge, MA, on behalf of Walker Books Ltd., London.

Diana Chang "Saying Yes" by Diana Chang, copyright by Diana Chang. Reprinted by permission of the author.

Clarion Books, a division of Houghton Mifflin Company "A Backwoods Boy" from *Lincoln: A Photobiography.* Copyright © 1987 by Russell Freedman. Reprinted by permission of Clarion Books/Houghton Mifflin Company. All rights reserved.

(Acknowledgments continue on page R56, which constitutes an extension of this copyright page.)

PRENTICE HALL
LITERATURE

Timeless Voices, Timeless Themes

COPPER

BRONZE

SILVER

GOLD

PLATINUM

THE AMERICAN EXPERIENCE

THE BRITISH TRADITION

CONTRIBUTING AUTHORS

The contributing authors guided the direction and philosophy of *Prentice Hall Literature: Timeless Voices, Timeless Themes*. Working with the development team, they helped to build the pedagogical integrity of the program and to ensure its relevance for today's teachers and students.

Kate Kinsella

Kate Kinsella, Ed.D., is a faculty member in the Department of Secondary Education at San Francisco State University. A specialist in second-language acquisition and adolescent reading and writing, she teaches coursework addressing language and literacy development across the secondary curricula. She has taught high-school ESL and directed SFSU's *Intensive English Program* for first-generation bilingual college students. She maintains secondary classroom involvement by teaching an academic literacy class for second-language learners through the University's *Step to College* partnership program. A former Fulbright lecturer and perennial institute leader for TESOL, the California Reading Association, and the California League of Middle Schools, Dr. Kinsella provides professional development nationally on topics ranging from learning-style enhancement to second-language reading. Her scholarship has been published in journals such as the *TESOL Journal,* the *CATESOL Journal,* and the *Social Studies Review.* Dr. Kinsella earned her M.A. in TESOL from San Francisco State University and her Ed.D. in Second Language Acquisition from the University of San Francisco.

Kevin Feldman

Kevin Feldman, Ed.D., is the Director of Reading and Early Intervention with the Sonoma County Office of Education (SCOE). His career in education spans thirty-one years. As the Director of Reading and Early Intervention for SCOE, he develops, organizes, and monitors programs related to K–12 literacy and prevention of reading difficulties. He also serves as a Leadership Team Consultant to the California Reading and Literature Project and assists in the development and implementation of K–12 programs throughout California. Dr. Feldman earned his undergraduate degree in Psychology from Washington State University and has a Master's degree in Special Education, Learning Disabilities, and Instructional Design from U.C. Riverside. He earned his Ed.D. in Curriculum and Instruction from the University of San Francisco.

Colleen Shea Stump

Colleen Shea Stump, Ph.D., is a Special Education supervisor in the area of Resource and Inclusion for Seattle Public Schools. She served as a professor and chairperson for the Department of Special Education at San Francisco State University. She continues as a lead consultant in the area of collaboration for the California State Improvement Grant and travels the state of California providing professional development training in the areas of collaboration, content literacy instruction, and inclusive instruction. Dr. Stump earned her doctorate at the University of Washington, her M.A. in Special Education from the University of New Mexico, and her B.S. in Elementary Education from the University of Wisconsin–Eau Claire.

Joyce Armstrong Carroll

In her forty-year career, Joyce Armstrong Carroll, Ed. D., has taught on every grade level from primary to graduate school. In the past twenty years, she has trained teachers in the teaching of writing. A nationally known consultant, she has served as president of TCTE and on NCTE's Commission on Composition. More than fifty of her articles have appeared in journals such as *Curriculum Review, English Journal, Media & Methods, Southwest Philosophical Studies, English in Texas,* and the *Florida English Journal.* With Edward E. Wilson, Dr. Carroll co-authored *Acts of Teaching: How to Teach Writing* and co-edited *Poetry After Lunch: Poetry to Read Aloud.* She co-directs the New Jersey Writing Project in Texas.

Edward E. Wilson

A former editor of *English in Texas,* Edward E. Wilson has served as a high-school English teacher and a writing consultant in school districts nationwide. Wilson has served on both the Texas Teacher Professional Practices Commission and NCTE's Commission on Composition. Wilson's poetry appears in Paul Janeczko's anthology *The Music of What Happens.* With Dr. Carroll, he co-wrote *Acts of Teaching: How to Teach Writing* and co-edited *Poetry After Lunch: Poetry to Read Aloud.* Wilson co-directs the New Jersey Writing Project in Texas.

PROGRAM ADVISORS

The program advisors provided ongoing input throughout the development of *Prentice Hall Literature: Timeless Voices, Timeless Themes*. Their valuable insights ensure that the perspectives of the teachers throughout the country are represented within this literature series.

Diane Cappillo
English Department Chair
Barbara Goleman Senior High School
Miami, Florida

Anita Clay
Language Arts Instructor
Gateway Institute of Technology
St. Louis, Missouri

Ellen Eberly
Language Arts Instructor
Catholic Memorial High School
West Roxbury, Massachusetts

Nancy Fahner
L.A.M.P. Lansing Area Manufacturing
  Partnership
Ingham Intermediate School District
Mason, Michigan

Terri Fields
Instructor of Language Arts,
  Communication Arts, and Author
Sunnyslope High School
Phoenix, Arizona

Susan Goldberg
Language Arts Instructor
Westlake Middle School
Thornwood, New York

Margo L. Graf
English Department Chair, Speech,
  Yearbook, Journalism
Lane Middle School
Fort Wayne, Indiana

Christopher E. Guarraia
Language Arts Instructor
Lakewood High School
Saint Petersburg, Florida

V. Pauline Hodges
Teacher, Educational Consultant
Forgan High School
Forgan, Oklahoma

Karen Hurley
Language Arts Instructor
Perry Meridian Middle School
Indianapolis, Indiana

Lenore D. Hynes
Language Arts Coordinator
Sunman-Dearborn Community
  Schools
Sunman, Indiana

Linda Kramer
Language Arts Instructor
Norman High School North
Norman, Oklahoma

Thomas S. Lindsay
Assistant Superintendent of Schools
Mannheim District 83
Franklin Park, Illinois

Agathaniki (Niki) Locklear
English Department Chair
Simon Kenton High School
Independence, Kentucky

Ashley MacDonald
Language Arts Instructor
South Forsyth High School
Cumming, Georgia

Mary Ellen Mastej
Language Arts Instructor
Scott Middle School
Hammond, Indiana

Nancy L. Monroe
English, Speed Reading Teacher
Bolton High School
Alexandria, Louisiana

Jim Moody
Language Arts Instructor
Northside High School
Fort Smith, Arkansas

David Morris
Teacher of English, Writing,
  Publications, Yearbook
Washington High School
South Bend, Indiana

Rosemary A. Naab
English Department Chair
Ryan High School
Archdiocese of Philadelphia
Philadelphia, Pennsylvania

Ann Okamura
English Teacher
Laguna Creek High School
Elk Grove, California

Tucky Roger
Coordinator of Languages
Tulsa Public Schools
Tulsa, Oklahoma

Jonathan L. Schatz
English Teacher/Team Leader
Tappan Zee High School
Orangeburg, New York

John Scott
Assistant Principal
Middlesex High School
Saluda, Virginia

Ken Spurlock
Assistant Principal, Retired
Boone County High School
Florence, Kentucky

Dr. Jennifer Watson
Secondary Language Arts
  Coordinator
Putnam City Schools
Oklahoma City, Oklahoma

Joan West
Assistant Principal
Oliver Middle School
Broken Arrow, Oklahoma

Contents in Brief

Learn About Literature

Learn About Literature xxvi
Short Stories IN2
Nonfiction IN4
Drama IN6
Poetry IN8
Folk Literature IN10

Themes in Literature

Unit 1   Growing and Changing 1
Unit 2   Reaching Out 96
Unit 3   Proving Yourself 176
Unit 4   Seeing It Through 264
Unit 5   Mysterious Worlds 346

Literary Genres

Unit 6   Short Stories 428
Unit 7   Nonfiction 526
Unit 8   Drama 608
Unit 9   Poetry 700
Unit 10   The Oral Tradition 758

Resources

Suggestions for Sustained Reading R1
Glossary R7
Tips for Improving Reading Fluency R9
Literary Terms Handbook R12
Rubric Handbook R18
Writing Handbook R22
Citing Sources and Preparing Manuscript R24
Formatting Business Letters R26
Writing Friendly Letters R27
Internet Guide R28
Spelling Handbook R29
Grammar, Usage, and Mechanics Handbook R33
Grammar, Usage, and Mechanics Exercises R39
Speaking, Listening, and Viewing Handbook R47
Indexes R49
Acknowledgments (continued) R56
Credits R59

UNIT 1

THEME: *Growing and Changing*

Why Read Literature?..................................... 2

How to Read Literature: **Literal Comprehension Strategies** 3

Ray Bradbury | **The Sound of Summer Running** ....Short Story 6

Cynthia Rylant | **Stray** ....Short Story 18

Connections *Literature and the Media*
TV's Top Dogs ....Magazine Article 26

Comparing Literary Works

Robert Frost | **Dust of Snow**.............................Poem 30

Walt Whitman | **My Picture-Gallery** ....Poem 31

Diana Chang | **Saying Yes**...............................Poem 32

Walter Dean Myers | **Jeremiah's Song** ....Short Story 38

Jack London | **The King of Mazy May** ....Short Story 52

Comparing Literary Works

Francisco Jiménez | **The Circuit** ....Short Story 66

Russell Baker | **Hard as Nails** ....Nonfiction 72

Reading Informational Materials
Summer Hats ....Newspaper Article 82

Reading Informational Materials
An Astronaut's Answers........................Interview 86

SKILLS WORKSHOPS

Writing Workshop Narration: Autobiographical Writing 90

Listening and Speaking Workshop Organizing and Giving a Narrative Presentation......94

Assessment Workshop Distinguishing Multiple Meanings 95

THEME: *Reaching Out*

Why Read Literature?. 98

How to Read Literature: **Literal Comprehension Strategies** 99

Comparing Literary Works

Garrison Keillor | **How to Write a Letter**. . . . . Essay 102

Leslie Marmon Silko | **How to Write a Poem About the Sky** . . . . Poem 106

Comparing Literary Works

Myron Levoy | **Aaron's Gift** . . . . Short Story 112

Helen Keller | **Water**. . . . . Autobiography 120

Isaac Bashevis Singer | **Zlateh the Goat** . . . . Short Story 128

Comparing Literary Works

Charlotte Pomerantz | **Door Number Four**. . . . . Poem 140

George Eliot | **Count That Day Lost** . . . . Poem 141

Nikki Giovanni | **The World Is Not a Pleasant Place to Be** . . . . Poem 142

Connections *Literature Past and Present*

Jerry Spinelli | from **Stargirl**. . . . . Contemporary Fiction 146

Reading Informational Materials

Jerry Spinelli . . . . Interview 149

Comparing Literary Works

Jesse Stuart | **Old Ben** . . . . Autobiography 154

Arthur C. Clarke | **Feathered Friend**. . . . . Short Story 159

Reading Informational Materials

Carl Zebrowski | **As Close As We Can Get** . . . . Music Review 166

SKILLS WORKSHOPS

Writing Workshop Description: Descriptive Essay. 170

Listening and Speaking Workshop Evaluating Persuasive Messages. 174

Assessment Workshop Identifying and Supporting Main Ideas. 175

THEME: *Proving Yourself*

	Why Read Literature?		178
	How to Read Literature: **Interactive Reading Strategies**		179
Paul Zindel	*from* **The Pigman & Me**	Autobiography	182
Virginia Driving Hawk Sneve	**Thunder Butte**	Short Story	194
Rudyard Kipling	**Mowgli's Brothers**	Short Story	210

Comparing Literary Works

Julia Alvarez	**Names/Nombres**	Essay	224
Judith Viorst	**The Southpaw**	Short Story	229
Arnold Adoff	**Alone in the Nets**	Poem	232

Connections *Literature and Culture*

Women and Sports 238

Reading Informational Materials

Applications . . . . Applications 239

Comparing Literary Works

Ogden Nash	**Adventures of Isabel**	Poem	246
Gwendolyn Brooks	**I'll Stay**	Poem	247
Rosemary and Stephen Vincent Benét	**Wilbur Wright and Orville Wright**	Poem	248
Langston Hughes	**Dream Dust**	Poem	250

Reading Informational Materials

Gentle Giants in Trouble . . . . Cause-and-Effect Article 254

SKILLS WORKSHOPS

Writing Workshop Exposition: Problem-Solution Essay 258

Listening and Speaking Workshop Presenting a Problem-Solution Proposal 262

Assessment Workshop Identify Main Idea 263

UNIT 4

THEME: *Seeing It Through*

Why Read Literature?. 266

How to Read Literature: **Strategies for
Constructing Meaning** 267

Comparing Literary Works

Joan Aiken	**Lob's Girl**. Short Story	270
James Thurber	**The Tiger Who Would Be King** . . . . Fable	282
Aesop	**The Lion and the Bulls**. . . . . Fable	284

Jane Yolen	**Greyling** . . . . Short Story	290

Comparing Literary Works

Sandra Cisneros	**Abuelito Who** . . . . Poem	300
Walt Whitman	**The Open Road** . . . . Poem	302
Maya Angelou	**Life Doesn't Frighten Me**. . . . . Poem	304
E. E. Cummings	**who knows if the moon's**. . . . . Poem	306

Connections *Literature Past and Present*

Christopher Paul Curtis	*from* **Bud, Not Buddy** . . . . Historical Fiction	310

Comparing Literary Works

Russell Freedman	**A Backwoods Boy** . . . . Autobiography	316
Geoffrey C. Ward and Ken Burns	**Jackie Robinson: Justice at Last** . . . . Historical Account	325

Reading Informational Materials
Throw and Tell. . . . . Article 332

Reading Informational Materials
Preserving a Great American Symbol . . . . Persuasive Speech 336

SKILLS WORKSHOPS

Writing Workshop Persuasion: Persuasive Composition. 340

Listening and Speaking Workshop Delivering a Persuasive Speech. 344

Assessment Workshop Identifying Cause and Effect. 345

UNIT 5

THEME: *Mysterious Worlds*

	Why Read Literature?.....................................		348
	How to Read Literature: **Strategies for Reading Critically** ...		349
Isaac Asimov	**The Fun They Had**	Short Story	352

Connections *Science Fiction and Historical Fiction*

Pam Muñoz Ryan	*from* **Esperanza Rising**....................	Historical Fiction	360

Comparing Literary Works

Edgar Allan Poe	**A Dream Within a Dream**	Poem	366
Edna St. Vincent Millay	**The Spring and the Fall**	Poem	368
Jack Prelutsky	**Ankylosaurus**...	Poem	370

Reading Informational Materials

	Life and Times of Sue.........................	Web Page	374
Robert D. Ballard	*from* **Exploring the *Titanic****	Historical Account	380
Laurence Yep	**Breaker's Bridge**	Short Story	392

Comparing Literary Works

George Laycock	**The Loch Ness Monster**....................	Science Article	406
Chinua Achebe	**Why the Tortoise's Shell Is Not Smooth**	Folk Tale	411

Reading Informational Materials

	Human Footprints at Chauvet Cave ...	Social Studies Article	418

SKILLS WORKSHOPS

Writing Workshop Expository Writing: Cause-and-Effect Essay 422

Listening and Speaking Workshop Following Oral Directions 426

Assessment Workshop Draw Conclusions 427

GENRE: *Short Stories*

	Why Read Literature?....................................		430
	How to Read Literature: **Strategies for Reading Fiction** ...		431
John Gardner	**Dragon, Dragon**	Plot	434
James Berry	**Becky and the Wheels-and-Brake Boys**	Plot	448

Comparing Literary Works

Anton Chekhov	**Overdoing It**..	Character	460
Sandra Cisneros	**Eleven**	Character	465

Connections *Short Stories and Novels*

Martin Waddell	**Obie's Gift**	Contemporary Fiction	472

Comparing Literary Works

Charles Dickens	**The Lawyer and the Ghost**......................	Setting	478
Jean Craighead George	**The Wounded Wolf**	Setting	482

Reading Informational Materials

	Can Oiled Seabirds Be Rescued?	Magazine Article	490

Comparing Literary Works

Lensey Namioka	**The All-American Slurp**..........................	Theme	496
Lloyd Alexander	**The Stone**	Theme	505

Reading Informational Materials

	Snorkeling Tips...............................	Book Review	516

SKILLS WORKSHOPS

Writing Workshop Narration: Short Story.. 520

Listening and Speaking Workshop Identifying Tone, Mood, and Emotion 524

Assessment Workshop Describing Plot, Setting, Character, and Mood............... 525

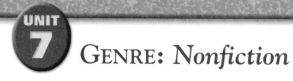

UNIT 7 GENRE: *Nonfiction*

Why Read Literature?...................................... 528

How to Read Literature: **Strategies for Reading Nonfiction** ... 529

Patricia McKissack and Frederick McKissack, Jr. **The Shutout** .... Historical Essay 532

Comparing Literary Works

F. Scott Fitzgerald **Letter to Scottie** .... Letter 542

Amanda Borden **Olympic Diary** .... Journal 545

Comparing Literary Works

Susy Clemens **My Papa, Mark Twain** .... Biography 554

Gary Soto **The Drive-In Movies** .... Autobiography 558

William Harwood **Space Shuttle *Challenger*** .... Eyewitness Account 562

Comparing Literary Works

Joseph Bruchac **Restoring the Circle** .... Persuasive Essay 572

Kerry Cochrane **How the Internet Works** .... Expository Essay 576

Bailey White **Turkeys** .... Narrative Essay 580

Connections *Literature and Science*
California's Much-Maligned Salton Sea .... Science Article 588

Reading Informational Materials
Populations and Communities .... Science 592

Reading Informational Materials
Sharks .... Research Report 596

SKILLS WORKSHOPS

Writing Workshop Research: Research Report 600

Listening and Speaking Workshop Delivering a Research Presentation 606

Assessment Workshop Distinguishing Fact and Opinion 607

UNIT 8

GENRE: *Drama*

Why Read Literature?...................................... 610

How to Read Literature: **Strategies for Reading Drama**.... 611

Susan Nanus   **The Phantom Tollbooth**
Act I... Drama 614
Act II .... Drama 637

Arthur Miller   **Grandpa and the Statue**.......................... Drama 666

Connections   *Themes in Drama and Nonfiction*
Julia Alvarez   *from* **Something to Declare** .... Essay 684

Reading Informational Materials
"Chinese Immigrants Remember
Detention at Angel Island" .... Article 686

Reading Informational Materials
Twist and Shout............................ How-to Essay 690

SKILLS WORKSHOPS

Writing Workshop   Response to Literature 694

Listening and Speaking Workshop   Delivering an Oral Response to Literature 698

Assessment Workshop   Sentence Construction....................................... 699

Why Read Literature?.................................... 702

How to Read Literature: **Strategies for Reading Poetry**.... 703

Comparing Literary Works

Richard Peck	**The Geese**.................................Lyric	706
Shel Silverstein	**Jimmy Jet and His TV Set**......................Narrative	707
Lewis Carroll	**The Walrus and the Carpenter**..................Narrative	708

Comparing Literary Works

Lillian Morrison	**The Sidewalk Racer**...........................Concrete	718
Bashō	**Haiku**.......................................Haiku	720
Anonymous	**Limerick**...................................Limerick	720

Comparing Literary Works

Octavio Paz	**Wind and water and stone**.......................Poem	726
Sara Teasdale	**February Twilight**..............................Lyric	727
William Shakespeare	**The Fairies' Lullaby**.......................Sound Devices	728
Gwendolyn Brooks	**Cynthia in the Snow**......................Sound Devices	729
Rachel Field	**Parade**...................................Sound Devices	730

Reading Informational Materials

Shakespeare's London . . . . Literary Background 734

Comparing Literary Works

Eve Merriam	**Simile: Willow and Ginkgo** . . . . Figurative Language 740
Emily Dickinson	**Fame Is a Bee** . . . . Figurative Language 741
Langston Hughes	**April Rain Song**. . . . . Figurative Language 742

Connections *Poetry and Nonfiction*

John Phillip
Santos **La Leña Buena** . . . . Nonfiction 746

Reading Informational Materials

More Than a Pinch . . . . Comparison-and-Contrast Article 748

SKILLS WORKSHOPS

Writing Workshop Exposition: Comparison-and-Contrast Essay 752

Listening and Speaking Workshop Engaging Listeners 756

Assessment Workshop Identifying Appropriate Usage 757

GENRE: *The Oral Tradition*

Why Read Literature?.................................... 760

How to Read Literature: **Strategies for
Reading Folk Literature**................................. 761

Comparing Literary Works

Leo Tolstoy	**The Ant and the Dove**........................... Folk Tale	764
Virginia Hamilton	**He Lion, Bruh Bear, and Bruh Rabbit**........... Folk Tale	765
I. G. Edmonds	**Señor Coyote and the Tricked Trickster**........ Folk Tale	770

Comparing Literary Works

Julius Lester	**Why Monkeys Live in Trees**..................... Folk Tale	780
Olivia E. Coolidge	**Arachne**.. Myth	784
Ricardo E. Alegría	**The Three Wishes** .... Folk Tale	789
My-Van Tran	**A Crippled Boy**.................................... Folk Tale	791

Connections *Literature and Social Studies*
from **Pericles' Funeral Oration**................................... 796

Reading Informational Materials
**Race to the End
of the Earth**............... Comparison-and-Contrast Article 798

Reading Informational Materials
National Geographic Web Site.................. Web Site 803

SKILLS WORKSHOPS

Writing Workshop Research: Multimedia Report..................................... 806

Listening and Speaking Workshop Using Visual Aids................................. 810

Assessment Workshop Spelling, Capitalization, Punctuation 811

COMPLETE CONTENTS BY GENRE

SHORT STORY

Plot

Stray
Cynthia Rylant 18

The King of Mazy May
Jack London 52

Aaron's Gift
Myron Levoy 112

Zlateh the Goat
Isaac Bashevis Singer 128

Feathered Friend
Arthur C. Clarke 159

Lob's Girl
Joan Aiken 270

Greyling
Jane Yolen 290

Dragon, Dragon
John Gardner 434

Becky and the Wheels-and-Brake Boys
James Berry 448

Character

The Sound of Summer Running
Ray Bradbury 6

Jeremiah's Song
Walter Dean Myers 38

Mowgli's Brothers
Rudyard Kipling 210

The Southpaw
Judith Viorst 229

Breaker's Bridge
Laurence Yep 392

Overdoing It
Anton Chekhov 460

Eleven
Sandra Cisneros 465

Setting

Thunder Butte
Virginia Driving Hawk Sneve 194

The Lawyer and the Ghost
Charles Dickens 478

The Wounded Wolf
Jean Craighead George 482

Theme

The Circuit
Francisco Jiménez 66

The Fun They Had
Isaac Asimov 352

The All-American Slurp
Lensey Namioka 496

The Stone
Lloyd Alexander 505

DRAMA

The Phantom Tollbooth
Susan Nanus 614

Grandpa and the Statue
Arthur Miller 666

NONFICTION

Essays and Articles

TV's Top Dogs
Deborah Starr Seibel. 26

How to Write a Letter
Garrison Keillor 102

from **Exploring the** *Titanic*
Robert D. Ballard. 380

The Loch Ness Monster
George Laycock 406

The Shutout
Patricia C. McKissack and Frederick McKissack, Jr. . . 532

Space Shuttle *Challenger*
William Harwood. 562

Restoring the Circle
Joseph Bruchac. 572

How the Internet Works
Kerry Cochrane 576

Turkeys
Bailey White. 580

Biographies and Autobiographies

Hard as Nails
Russell Baker 72

Water
Helen Keller 120

Old Ben
Jesse Stuart 154

from **The Pigman & Me**
Paul Zindel 182

Names/Nombres
Julia Alvarez. 224

A Backwoods Boy
Russell Freedman 316

Jackie Robinson: Justice at Last
Geoffrey C. Ward and Ken Burns. 325

My Papa, Mark Twain
Susy Clemens. 554

The Drive-In Movies
Gary Soto 558

Letters and Journals

Letter to Scottie
F. Scott Fitzgerald 542

Olympic Diary
Amanda Borden 545

THE ORAL TRADITION

Myths

Arachne
Olivia E. Coolidge 784

Fables

The Tiger Who Would Be King
James Thurber 282

The Lion and the Bulls
Aesop 284

Folk Tales

Why the Tortoise's Shell Is Not Smooth
Chinua Achebe 411

The Ant and the Dove
Leo Tolstoy 764

He Lion, Bruh Bear, and Bruh Rabbit
Virginia Hamilton 765

Señor Coyote and the Tricked Trickster
I. G. Edmonds 770

Why Monkeys Live in Trees
Julius Lester 780

The Three Wishes
Ricardo E. Alegría 789

A Crippled Boy
My-Van Tran 791

POETRY

Lyric Poetry

Door Number Four
Charlotte Pomerantz 140

Count That Day Lost
George Eliot 141

The World Is Not a Pleasant Place to Be
Nikki Giovanni 142

I'll Stay
Gwendolyn Brooks 247

Life Doesn't Frighten Me
Maya Angelou 304

who knows if the moon's
E. E. Cummings 306

The Open Road
Walt Whitman 302

The Spring and the Fall
Edna St. Vincent Millay 368

The Geese
Richard Peck 706

Wind and water and stone
Octavio Paz 726

February Twilight
Sara Teasdale.......................................727

Sound Devices

Saying Yes
Diana Chang...32

Ankylosaurus
Jack Prelutsky.......................................370

The Fairies' Lullaby
William Shakespeare 728

Cynthia in the Snow
Gwendolyn Brooks 729

Parade
Rachel Field 730

Narrative Poetry

Alone in the Nets
Arnold Adoff 232

Adventures of Isabel
Ogden Nash 246

Wilbur Wright and Orville Wright
Rosemary and Stephen Vincent Benét 248

Jimmy Jet and His TV Set
Shel Silverstein....................................707

The Walrus and the Carpenter
Lewis Carroll.......................................708

Sensory Language

Dust of Snow
Robert Frost 30

How to Write a Poem About the Sky
Leslie Marmon Silko 106

Abuelito Who
Sandra Cisneros....................................300

Other Forms

The Sidewalk Racer
Lillian Morrison 718

Haiku
Bashō..720

Limerick
Anonymous 720

Figurative Language

My Picture-Gallery
Walt Whitman...31

Dream Dust
Langston Hughes 250

A Dream Within a Dream
Edgar Allan Poe 366

Simile: Willow and Ginkgo
Eve Merriam...740

Fame Is a Bee
Emily Dickinson....................................741

April Rain Song
Langston Hughes 742

COMPARING LITERARY WORKS

Comparing Poems
Dust of Snow
Robert Frost.....................................30
My Picture-Gallery
Walt Whitman...................................31
Saying Yes
Diana Chang....................................32

Comparing Fiction and Nonfiction
The Circuit
Francisco Jiménez...........................66
Hard as Nails
Russell Baker..................................72

Comparing Nonfiction and Poetry
How to Write a Letter
Garrison Keillor.............................102
How to Write a Poem About the Sky
Leslie Marmon Silko........................106

Comparing Conflicts
Aaron's Gift
Myron Levoy..................................112
Water
Helen Keller..................................120

Comparing Speakers
Door Number Four
Charlotte Pomerantz........................140
Count That Day Lost
George Eliot..................................141
The World Is Not a Pleasant Place to Be
Nikki Giovanni...............................142

Comparing Nonfiction and Fiction
Old Ben
Jesse Stuart..................................154
Feathered Friend
Arthur C. Clarke.............................159

Comparing Speakers and Narrators
Names/Nombres
Julia Alvarez.................................224
The Southpaw
Judith Viorst.................................229
Alone in the Nets
Arnold Adoff.................................232

Comparing Stanzas
Adventures of Isabel
Ogden Nash..................................246
I'll Stay
Gwendolyn Brooks..........................247
Wilbur Wright and Orville Wright
Rosemary and Stephen Vincent Benét.......248
Dream Dust
Langston Hughes............................250

Comparing Foreshadowing
Lob's Girl
Joan Aiken...................................270
The Tiger Who Would Be King
James Thurber...............................282
The Lion and the Bulls
Aesop...284

Comparing Tone
Abuelito Who
Sandra Cisneros.............................300
The Open Road
Walt Whitman................................302
Life Doesn't Frighten Me
Maya Angelou................................304
who knows if the moon's
E. E. Cummings..............................306

Comparing Historical Accounts
A Backwoods Boy
Russell Freedman............................316
Jackie Robinson: Justice at Last
Geoffrey C. Ward and Ken Burns............325

Comparing Tone
A Dream Within a Dream
Edgar Allan Poe.............................366
The Spring and the Fall
Edna St. Vincent Millay......................368
Ankylosaurus
Jack Prelutsky...............................370

Comparing Fiction and Nonfiction
The Loch Ness Monster
George Laycock..............................406
Why the Tortoise's Shell Is Not Smooth
Chinua Achebe...............................411

Comparing Direct and Indirect Characterization
Overdoing It
Anton Chekhov 460
Eleven
Sandra Cisneros 465

Comparing Conflicts
The Lawyer and the Ghost
Charles Dickens 478
The Wounded Wolf
Jean Craighead George 482

Comparing Themes
The All-American Slurp
Lensey Namioka 496
The Stone
Lloyd Alexander 505

Comparing Intended Audiences
Letter to Scottie
F. Scott Fitzgerald 542
Olympic Diary
Amanda Borden 545

Comparing Narrators in Biography and Autobiography
My Papa, Mark Twain
Susy Clemens 554
The Drive-In Movies
Gary Soto 558
Space Shuttle *Challenger*
William Harwood 562

Comparing Purposes in Nonfiction
Restoring the Circle
Joseph Bruchac 572
How the Internet Works
Kerry Cochrane 576
Turkeys
Bailey White 580

Comparing Rhythm in Poetry
The Geese
Richard Peck 706
Jimmy Jet and His TV Set
Shel Silverstein 707
The Walrus and the Carpenter
Lewis Carroll 708

Comparing Forms of Poetry
The Sidewalk Racer
Lillian Morrison 718
Haiku
Bashō 720
Limerick
Anonymous 720

Comparing Sound Devices
Wind and water and stone
Octavio Paz 726
February Twilight
Sara Teasdale 727
The Fairies' Lullaby
William Shakespeare 728
Cynthia in the Snow
Gwendolyn Brooks 729
Parade
Rachel Field 730

Comparing Figurative Language
Simile: Willow and Ginkgo
Eve Merriam 740
Fame Is a Bee
Emily Dickinson 741
April Rain Song
Langston Hughes 742

Comparing Lessons in Folk Tales
The Ant and the Dove
Leo Tolstoy 764
He Lion, Bruh Bear, and Bruh Rabbit
Virginia Hamilton 765
Señor Coyote and the Tricked Trickster
I. G. Edmonds 770

Comparing Theme
Why Monkeys Live in Trees
Julius Lester 780
Arachne
Olivia Coolidge 784
The Three Wishes
Ricardo E. Alegría 789
A Crippled Boy
My-Van Tran 791

Writing Workshops

Narration: Autobiographical Writing......... 90

Description: Descriptive Essay 170

Exposition: Problem-Solution Essay 258

Persuasion: Persuasive Composition....... 340

Expository Writing:
Cause-and-Effect Essay 422

Narration: Short Story 520

Research: Research Report................. 600

Response to Literature..................... 694

Exposition: Comparison-and-Contrast Essay.. 752

Research: Multimedia Report.............. 806

Listening and Speaking Workshops

Organizing and Giving
a Narrative Presentation 94

Evaluating Persuasive Messages 174

Presenting a Problem-Solution Proposal.... 262

Delivering a Persuasive Speech 344

Following Oral Directions 426

Identifying Tone, Mood, and Emotion....... 524

Delivering a Research Presentation......... 606

Delivering an Oral Response to Literature... 698

Engaging Listeners........................ 756

Using Visual Aids.......................... 810

Assessment Workshops

Distinguishing Multiple Meanings 95

Identifying and Supporting Main Ideas 175

Identifying Main Idea 263

Identifying Cause and Effect 345

Draw Conclusions......................... 427

Describing Plot, Setting, Character,
and Mood.................................. 525

Distinguishing Fact and Opinion 607

Sentence Construction..................... 699

Identifying Appropriate Usage 757

Spelling, Capitalization, Punctuation 811

Reading Informational Materials

Summer Hats.......................... Newspaper Article   82

An Astronaut's Answers ....Interview   86

Jerry Spinelli ....Interview 149

Carl Zebrowski   **As Close As We Can Get** .... Music Review 166

Applications 239

Gentle Giants in Trouble.......... Cause-and-Effect Article 254

Throw and Tell....................................Article 332

Preserving a Great American Symbol ..... Persuasive Speech 336

Life and Times of Sue . . . . Web Page 374

Human Footprints at Chauvet Cave . . . . Article 418

Can Oiled Seabirds Be Rescued? . . . . Article 490

Snorkeling Tips . . . . Book Review 516

Populations and Communities . . . . Science 592

Sharks . . . . Research Report 596

**Chinese Immigrants Remember Detention
at Angel Island** . . . . Article 686

Twist and Shout . . . . How-to Essay 690

Shakespeare's London . . . . Literary Background 734

More Than a Pinch . . . . Comparison and Contrast 748

Race to the End of the Earth . . . Comparison and Contrast 798

National Geographic Web Site . . . . Web Site 803

CONNECTIONS

TV's Top Dogs . . . . Magazine Article 26

Jerry Spinelli   *from* **Stargirl** . . . . Fiction 146

Women in Sports . . . . Nonfiction 238

Christopher Paul Curtis   *from* **Bud, Not Buddy** . . . . Excerpt 310

Pam Muñoz Ryan   *from* **Esperanza Rising** . . . . Fiction 360

Martin Waddell   **Obie's Gift** . . . . Fiction 472

California's Much-Maligned Salton Sea . . . . Article 588

Julia Alvarez   *from* **Something to Declare** . . . . Essay 684

John Phillip Santos   **La Leña Buena** . . . . Nonfiction 746

from **Pericles' Funeral Oration** . . . . Speech 796

HOW TO READ LITERATURE

Literal Comprehension Strategies 3

Literal Comprehension Strategies 99

Interactive Reading Strategies 179

Strategies for Constructing Meaning 267

Strategies for Reading Critically 349

Strategies for Reading Fiction 431

Strategies for Reading Nonfiction 529

Strategies for Reading Drama 611

Strategies for Reading Poetry 703

Strategies for Reading Folk Literature 761

Forms of Literature

Novel and Novella • Short Story • Nonfiction • Poetry • Drama • The Oral Tradition

Each form of literature, called a genre (zhän´ rə), **has its own characteristics. In this introduction, you can learn about the genres of literature.**

● **Prose** is organized in sentences and paragraphs and does not have a regular rhythm. **Fiction** is prose writing that tells about imaginary characters and events. **Nonfiction** is prose writing that presents and explains ideas or that tells about real people, places, or events.

● **Poetry,** whose sentences appear in lines that do not always extend across the page, often has a regular beat or rhythm.

Novel and Novella

Novels and novellas are long works of fiction. They have a plot or a sequence of events that explores characters facing a problem in a specific time and place. These long works of fiction may introduce subplots or minor stories within the larger one. Novels and novellas address a theme or insight into life.

● **What does the opening of this novel reveal about the setting?**

The first week of August hangs at the very top of summer . . . At dawn, Mae Tuck set out on her horse for the wood at the edge of the village...

FROM *TUCK EVERLASTING*, NATALIE BABBITT, PRENTICE HALL LITERATURE LIBRARY

Short Story

A **short story** is a brief form of prose fiction with characters, a setting, and a plot. It resembles longer forms of fiction in exploring an insight into life.

● **What problem do you think will be solved in the course of this story?**

There was once a king whose kingdom was plagued by a dragon. The king did not know which way to turn. . . .

FROM "DRAGON, DRAGON," JOHN GARDNER, PAGE 434

Nonfiction

Nonfiction is literature that deals with the real world. It tells the story of actual events or people and addresses the world of ideas.

● **What is the subject of this nonfiction account?**

I witnessed the launch from the Kennedy Space Center press site just 4.2 miles from pad 39B. . . .

FROM "SPACE SHUTTLE *CHALLENGER*," WILLIAM HARWOOD, PAGE 562

> *"Just remember that reading is an art. . . . So please keep at it."*
>
> —Martin Amis

Poetry

Poetry is literature written in verse. Because the form uses comparatively few words, poets choose highly concise and emotionally packed language to convey their ideas. In addition, poetry includes rhythm and rhyme to make the writing musical.

● **Which characteristics identify the passage at right as poetry?**

My father was the first to hear
The passage of the geese each fall,
Passing above the house so near
He'd hear within his heart
their call. . . .

FROM "THE GEESE," RICHARD PECK, PAGE **706**

Drama

Drama tells a story through the words and actions of actors who impersonate the characters on stage. In the text of a drama, the characters' words are called the dialogue.

In addition to dialogue, a drama includes stage directions telling actors how to move and speak. Because a drama is usually written to be performed, you should imagine actors speaking the dialogue as you read it.

● **How does the text of this drama differ from the text of a short story?**

The Oral Tradition

Most literary works travel from the author's imagination to a page. Forms of fiction in the **oral tradition** make a different journey. They travel from the mouths of many tellers to the ears of many listeners. Such works include myths and folk tales that generations of storytellers shape for hundreds of years before people finally write them down. Telling and retelling tales ensures that they express the values of the culture from which they come.

● **In which part of the world was this tale told before it was written down?**

[LIGHTS UP *on the clock, a huge alarm clock. The clock reads 4:00. The lighting should make it appear that the clock is suspended in mid-air (if possible). The clock ticks for 30 seconds.*]

CLOCK. See that! Half a minute gone by. Seems like a long time when you're waiting for something to happen. . . .

FROM *THE PHANTOM TOLLBOOTH*, SUSAN NANUS, PAGE **614**

One day long ago in Mexico's land of sand and giant cactus *Señor Coyote* and *Señor Mouse* had a quarrel. . . .

FROM "SEÑOR COYOTE AND THE TRICKED TRICKSTER," RETOLD BY I. G. EDMONDS, PAGE **770**

Short Stories

Plot and Conflict • Character • Setting • Theme

The short stories in this book will take you to fictional worlds as far away as Russia and as close as the family next door. No two of these tales are exactly alike. However, they all share common characteristics. This introduction will help you understand these characteristics as you peek into some of the fictional worlds you will be exploring later.

Plot and Conflict

The **plot** of a story is a sequence of events linked by cause and effect—earlier events advance the plot by bringing about later ones. A typical plot, diagramed below, focuses on a **conflict** or problem between opposing forces. As the problem or conflict becomes worse, the story builds to the point of greatest tension, the climax. Then, there is a resolution, or solving, of the problem and the story ends.

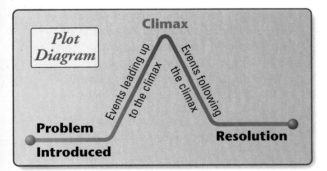

Plot Diagram

Climax

Events leading up to the climax

Events following the climax

Problem Introduced

Resolution

● **What problem does the person telling this story face?**

> . . . I only want to be with Nat, Aldo, Jimmy, and Ben. It's no fair reason they don't want to be with me. . . . A girl can not, not, let boys get away with it all the time. . . .
>
> FROM "BECKY AND THE WHEELS-AND-BRAKE BOYS," JAMES BERRY, PAGE **448**

Character

The **characters** in a story are the people or animals who take part in the action. Authors use characterization to bring characters to life. For example, authors can tell you directly about characters' qualities, such as courage or cowardice. Authors may also reveal these qualities indirectly, through characters' words and actions. In either case, the qualities that characters display influence the plot and the resolution of its problem or conflict.

● **What quality or qualities of the narrator do her opening words reveal? Explain.**

> What they don't understand about birthdays and what they never tell you is that when you're eleven, you're also ten, and nine, and eight, and seven, and six, and five, and four, and three, and two, and one. And when you wake up on your eleventh birthday you expect to feel eleven, but you don't. You open your eyes and everything's just like yesterday, only it's today. And you don't feel eleven at all. You feel like you're still ten. And you are—underneath the year that makes you eleven. . . .
>
> FROM "ELEVEN," SANDRA CISNEROS, PAGE **465**

> *"A short story is like a stripped-down racer; there's no room for anything extra in there."*
>
> —Robert Asprin

Setting

The plot and characters, which are the *what* and *who* of a story, must also have a *where* and *when*. That is why every story has a **setting**—the imaginary place and time of the action. In addition to details of time and place setting also includes information that shows a group's customs and beliefs.

- In a contemporary story, the made-up world of the setting usually includes details that are true to life.
- Historical fiction, which is partly based on events from history, may include a mixture of fact and fantasy.

In all types of stories, the setting can influence the plot and the resolution of the central problem.

● **"The Lawyer and the Ghost" is set in nineteenth-century London. What details of setting does the author provide in the opening of the story?**

I knew a man—let me see—it's forty years ago now—who took an old, damp, rotten set of chambers, in one of the most ancient Inns, that had been shut up and empty for years and years before. There were lots of old women's stories about the place, and it certainly was very far from being a cheerful one; but he was poor, and the rooms were cheap, and that would have been quite a sufficient reason for him, if they had been ten times worse than they really were. . . .

FROM "THE LAWYER AND THE GHOST,"
CHARLES DICKENS, PAGE 478

Theme

In short stories, authors use literary elements like character, plot, conflict, and setting to convey and explore a **theme,** an insight into life.

Authors sometimes state a theme directly at the beginning or end of a short story. More often, however, they imply or suggest the theme through what happens to the characters. To figure out an implied theme, think about how a character changes or solves a problem. Then, consider how this change or growth hints at a general idea about life.

● **In this story, which contrasting customs may suggest an insight into life?**

"As any respectable Chinese knows, the correct way to eat your soup is to slurp."

The first time our family was invited out to dinner in America, we disgraced ourselves while eating celery. We had emigrated to this country from China, and during our early days here we had a hard time with American table manners. . . ."

FROM "THE ALL-AMERICAN SLURP,"
LENSEY NAMIOKA, PAGE 496

Nonfiction

Historical Essay • Biography and Autobiography • Letters and Journals • Types of Essays • Informational Text

If fiction takes you on imaginative flights of fancy, nonfiction brings you back down to Earth. Nonfiction includes true stories about real people, places, experiences, and ideas. It also includes practical writing that informs, expository writing that explains, and persuasive writing meant to convince you to take action or change your beliefs. The terms defined on these pages will help you discover the characteristics of nonfiction.

Historical Essay

A **historical essay** is a short piece of nonfiction that gives you facts and ideas about an event or series of events in history. Historical essays often help you understand what life was like at a specific time in the past or help provide insight into why certain conditions existed.

The subject for such an essay might include anything from pyramid-building in ancient Egypt to Jackie Robinson and the integration of major league baseball.

● **What seems to be the subject of this historical essay?**

Baseball's development was slow during the Civil War years but teams continued to compete, and military records show that, sometimes between battles, Union soldiers chose up teams and played baseball games. It was during this time that records began mentioning African-American players. . . ."

FROM "THE SHUTOUT," PATRICIA C. MCKISSACK AND FREDERICK MCKISSACK, JR., PAGE 532

Biography and Autobiography

In a **biography**, an author tells the story of someone else's life. A biography is therefore a third-person narration. This means that the narrator or speaker refers to the subject by name or as "he" or "she." Usually, the subject of a biography is a person whose life has special meaning or value.

By contrast, an **autobiography** is the story of part or all of a person's life, written by that person. An autobiography is therefore a first-person narration. This means that the narrator or speaker is at the center of the action and refers to herself or himself as "I." The author's purpose may be to teach lessons in life, to tell how he or she developed, to entertain, or any combination of these.

● **Is this the beginning of a biography or an autobiography? Why?**

We are a very happy family. We consist of Papa, Mamma, Jean, Clara, and me. It is papa I am writing about, and I shall have no trouble in not knowing what to say about him, as he is a *very* striking character.

FROM "MY PAPA, MARK TWAIN," SUSY CLEMENS, PAGE 554

> *"Essays come in all shapes and sizes. . . ."*
>
> —John Gross

Letters and Journals

A **letter** is a written communication from one person to another, sharing information, thoughts, and feelings. A **journal** is a regular account of events and the writer's thoughts and feelings about them.

● **What events does this journal describe?**

> July 21, 1996
>
> What a whirlwind I've been on since the Olympic trials! We arrived in Atlanta at 1:30 P.M. and had processing, which took seven hours. . . .
>
> FROM *OLYMPIC DIARY*, AMANDA BORDEN, PAGE 545

Types of Essays

Essays share one common characteristic: They are brief prose works that are based on fact. However, essays can have different purposes, as follows.

- **Persuasive essays** try to convince you to think or act in a certain way.
- **Informational essays** convey and explain facts.
- **Narrative essays** tell a true story.

● **From which type of essay do you think this passage comes? Why?**

> Something about my mother attracts ornithologists. It all started years ago when a couple of them discovered she had a rare species of woodpecker coming to her bird feeder. They came in the house and sat around the window, exclaiming and taking pictures with big fancy cameras. . . .
>
> FROM "TURKEYS," BAILEY WHITE, PAGE 580

Informational Text

Informational texts are the written documents that help you manage your life in today's world. From bank applications and instructions for using a calculator to campaign speeches and magazine articles, informational texts can help you discover what is happening in the world, learn a subject, or master a sport.

● **In what type of publication would you expect to find an article like the one from which this passage is taken?**

> Like dozens of other volunteers, I felt compelled to help when a cargo ship spilled 5,000 gallons of fuel oil in the Humboldt Bay, near my home on California's north coast. When we released rehabilitated birds, we all felt great. Later, I learned that what we had done was controversial. Many biologists believe that rescuing oiled birds serves more to soothe human feelings than to help wildlife and some studies show that many cleaned birds survive for only a few days. But there are a number of encouraging success stories. . . .
>
> FROM "CAN OILED SEABIRDS BE RESCUED, OR ARE WE JUST FOOLING OURSELVES?" SHARON LEVY, PAGE 490

Drama

Elements of Drama • Dialogue • Theme

When you read a drama, you are likely to get completely swept up in the experience. This is because reading a play gives your imagination a full workout. You, the reader, have to picture the setting, the lighting, and the actors' movements. In addition, all the action unfolds through conversation and you have to imagine each character's thoughts and feelings. The terms defined on these pages will help you discover the characteristics of drama.

Elements of Drama

Like fiction, drama has literary elements such as characters, setting, and plot. However, fiction is meant to be read, while drama is meant to be performed.

At a performance, an audience sees the story coming to life as actors move across a stage and speak the words of the characters. The following elements make such a performance possible, whether it is on a real stage or in your imagination:

- **acts,** the units of the action in a drama. Acts are often divided into parts called scenes.
- **dialogue,** the words of the characters, which appear next to their names in scripts
- **stage directions,** bracketed information that tells what the set looks like and how the characters should move and speak
- **set,** a construction on the stage that suggests the time and place of the action
- **props,** movable items, like a book, a pencil, or a flashlight that the actors use to make their actions look realistic

● **What would you expect the stage and scenery to be for the scene shown here?**

A CT I, SCENE II The Road to Dictionopolis

[ENTER MILO *in his car.*]

MILO. This is weird! I don't recognize any of this scenery at all. [A SIGN *is held up before* MILO, *startling him.*] Huh? . . .

FROM *THE PHANTOM TOLLBOOTH*, SUSAN NANUS, PAGE **614**

> "There is no joy so great as that of reporting that a good play has come to town."
>
> —Brooks Atkinson

Dialogue

Dialogue—what characters say—is written next to their names in the text of a drama. Sometimes stage directions, written in brackets, tell actors how to speak their words, gesture, and move. By paying attention to what characters say and to what others say about them, you can figure out their qualities and predict their actions.

● **How do you think Monaghan's grandfather will react when he is asked to contribute to a fund for the Statue of Liberty? Why?**

MONAGHAN. Well. My grandfather was the stingiest man in Brooklyn. "Mercyless" Monaghan, they used to call him. He even used to save umbrella handles.

AUGUST. What for?

MONAGHAN. Just couldn't stand seeing anything go to waste. After a big windstorm there'd be a lot of broken umbrellas laying around in the streets.

AUGUST. Yeh?

MONAGHAN. He'd go around picking them up. . . .

FROM *GRANDPA AND THE STATUE*, ARTHUR MILLER, PAGE 666

Theme

Like a work of fiction, a play has a **theme**—an insight, idea, or a question about life—that it explores. Often the theme relates to the way in which the main character solves a problem or changes.

If you see a performance of a play, you can discuss its theme with others in the audience. If you read a play, you can test the theme against your own experience. You can also discuss the theme with classmates who have read the play.

● **Does the problem that the main character faces in this play seem easy to solve? Why or why not?**

HUMBUG. Well, all that he would have to do is cross the dangerous, unknown countryside between here and Digitopolis, where he would have to persuade the Mathemagician to release the Princesses, which we know to be impossible because the Mathemagician will never agree with Azaz about anything. . . .

FROM *THE PHANTOM TOLLBOOTH*, SUSAN NANUS, PAGE 614

Poetry

Narrative and Lyric Poetry •
Special Forms of Poetry • Sound Devices •
Figurative Language

In poetry, each word rings with meaning. In some poems, repetition and rhyme create musical rhythms. In other poems, fresh new language can help you see the world in a whole new way. The terms defined on these pages will help you discover the characteristics of poetry.

Narrative and Lyric Poetry

A **narrative poem** tells a story using plot, characters, dialogue, setting, and theme. However, a narrative poem tells a story more musically than prose fiction does. The poem uses sounds and regular rhythms to make the story memorable.

A **lyric poem** expresses the thoughts and feelings of the poem's speaker, the one who says its words. Once, lyric poems were actually sung to the accompaniment of a string instrument called a lyre. Today, these poems rely on their own music created through rhythm and sound.

⬤ **What makes the beginning of this narrative poem different from a prose narrative?**

I'll tell you the story of Jimmy Jet—
And you know what I tell you is true.
He loved to watch his TV set
Almost as much as you. . . .

FROM "JIMMY JET AND HIS TV SET,"
SHEL SILVERSTEIN, PAGE **707**

Special Forms of Poetry

A **poetic form** is a special way of arranging the lines and stanzas of a poem. Form includes not only the appearance of a poem on the page, but also the sound of its rhymes and rhythms. These are three examples of poetic forms:

- **Limerick** — a short, funny poem of five lines; the first, second, and fifth lines rhyme and have the same rhythm, and the third and fourth lines rhyme and have the same rhythm.
- **Haiku** — a Japanese verse form with three lines of five, seven, and five syllables each
- **Concrete poem** — a poem whose words take the shape of the poem's subject

⬤ **What is the form of this poem?**

A flea and a fly in a flue
Were caught, so what could they do?
　　　Said the fly, "Let us flee."
　　　"Let us fly," said the flea.
So they flew through a flaw in the flue.

FROM "A FLEA AND A FLY IN A FLUE," ANONYMOUS,
PAGE **720**

> *"The crown of literature is poetry."*
>
> —*Somerset Maugham*

Sound Devices

Sound devices are ways of adding music to poetry. Following are some common types of sound devices:

- **Rhyme** — the similarity of final sounds in accented syllables, as in *roar* and *before*
- **Onomatopoeia** (än´ ō mat´ ō pē´ ə) — the use of words like *hush* and *buzz* that sound like what they mean
- **Alliteration** — the repetition of consonant or vowel sounds in beginning or accented syllables of nearby words, as in "*wh*iteness,/ And *wh*itely *wh*irs away" (p. 729)

⬤ **Which sound devices are in these lines?**

> . . . Till leisurely and last of all
> Camels and elephants will pass
> Beneath our elms, along our grass.
>
> FROM "PARADE," RACHEL FIELD, PAGE 730

Tone

The **tone** is the author's attitude or feeling about the subject of the poem and the audience. An author's tone can be amused, angry, or superior, among many other possibilities.

⬤ **Would you describe the tone of this stanza as serious or amused? Why?**

> "The time has come," the Walrus said,
>   "To talk of many things:
> Of shoes—and ships—and sealing wax—
>   Of cabbages—and kings—
>
> FROM "THE WALRUS AND THE CARPENTER,"
> LEWIS CARROLL, PAGE 708

Figurative Language

Poems use **figurative language**, words not meant in their exact dictionary sense, to take you by surprise. Each type of figurative language is based on a comparison of apparently unlike items. However, when you think about the comparison, you will usually see that the items really are similar.

Type	Description	Example
Simile (sim´ ə lē)	Uses *like* or *as* to compare two apparently unlike items	"The will is like an etching, . . ."
Metaphor (met´ ə fər´)	Describes one thing as if it were another, apparently unlike thing	"Fame is a bee, . . ."
Personification (pər sän´ i fi kā´ shən)	Gives human qualities to something nonhuman	"Let the rain kiss you."

⬤ **What type of figurative language does this passage contain?**

> The rain makes running pools
>   in the gutter.
> The rain plays a little sleep-song on
>   our roof at night . . .
>
> FROM "APRIL RAIN SONG," LANGSTON
> HUGHES, PAGE 742

Folk Literature

Folk Tales • Characters in Folk Literature •
The Oral Tradition • Themes in Folk Literature

Imagine that instead of reading literature, you heard it told to you by storytellers around a campfire or a fireplace. Telling and listening to made-up stories, rather than writing them down, is part of the oral tradition. Individual tales in this tradition were usually told in different ways by storytellers entertaining different audiences. Eventually, versions of these tales were written down. As a result, you can join in the campfire circle and appreciate stories of animals, humans, and gods. These pages will teach you about the characteristics of works in the oral tradition.

Folk Tales

Folk tales are stories passed on by word of mouth among a group of people, the "folk." This type of literature often features talking animals or exaggerated situations to make a point. Their purpose may be not only to entertain, but also to teach a lesson or to explain something in nature. As you read the folk tales of a variety of cultures, you may see similarities in the lessons or values they teach.

● **What characteristic of folk tales does this passage demonstrate?**

Say that he Lion would get up each and every mornin. Stretch and walk around. He'd roar, ME AND MYSELF, ME AND MYSELF, like that. Scare all the little animals so they were afraid to come outside in the sunshine. . . .

FROM "HE LION, BRUH BEAR, AND BRUH RABBIT," RETOLD BY VIRGINIA HAMILTON, PAGE **766**

Characters in Folk Literature

Characters in folk literature usually do not have the same individuality as characters in stories and novels do. Whether they are people or animals, folk characters usually symbolize, or stand for, general qualities like cleverness, laziness, or courage. By focusing on what happens to these symbolic characters, listeners and readers can determine the message of the tale.

● **What quality do you think the dove in this story might represent?**

A thirsty ant went to the stream to drink. Suddenly it got caught in a whirlpool and was almost carried away.

At that moment a dove was passing by with a twig in its beak. The dove dropped the twig for the tiny insect to grab hold of. So it was that the ant was saved. . . .

FROM "THE ANT AND THE DOVE," RETOLD BY LEO TOLSTOY, PAGE **764**

"Folk tales travel wherever people travel."

—*Rudolfo Anaya*

The Oral Tradition

Stories passed down by word of mouth in the **oral tradition** reflect the beliefs, customs, and values of the culture that created them. In addition to folk tales, the oral tradition also includes myths, tales of gods, goddesses, and heroes that explain something in nature.

◉ **Judging by the beginning of this myth, what did the ancient Greeks value?**

Arachne [ä räk´ nē] was a maiden who became famous throughout Greece, though she was neither wellborn nor beautiful and came from no great city. She lived in an obscure little village, and her father was a humble dyer of wool. In this he was very skillful, producing many varied shades, while above all he was famous for the clear, bright scarlet which is made from shellfish, and this was the most glorious of all the colors used in ancient Greece. Even more skillful than her father was Arachne. It was her task to spin the fleecy wool into a fine, soft thread and to weave it into cloth on the high, standing loom within the cottage. . . . So soft and even was her thread, so fine her cloth, so gorgeous her embroidery, that soon her products were known all over Greece. . . .

FROM "ARACHNE," RETOLD BY OLIVIA E. COOLIDGE, PAGE **784**

Themes in Folk Literature

Like most other forms of literature, tales in the oral tradition also explore an idea about life called a **theme**. Usually the theme addresses the values or behaviors of a culture. These values may provide guidelines for living justly or honorably.

Sometimes the theme is stated directly at the end of the tale. Other times, you must use the characters' actions and the images, or word pictures, to figure out the theme.

◉ **What idea related to riches do you think this folk tale will explore? Why?**

Many years ago, there lived a woodsman and his wife. They were very poor but very happy in their little house in the forest. Poor as they were, they were always ready to share what little they had with anyone who came to their door. They loved each other very much and were quite content with their life together. Each evening, before eating, they gave thanks to God for their happiness. . . .

FROM "THE THREE WISHES," RETOLD BY RICARDO E. ALEGRÍA, PAGE 789

Growing and Changing

In the Garden, Joseph Raphael, The Redfern Gallery

Exploring the Theme

All around you, the world changes in large and small ways. The tree outside has more branches than it did last year. A new store opens on the next block. All growth involves change—especially in people. The literature in this unit will introduce you to people who grow and change through life's experiences. For example, in "Jeremiah's Song," music helps a young boy learn to listen to the cherished stories of his Grandpa. Poets such as Diana Chang and Walt Whitman express their experiences in verse.

◀ **Critical Viewing** In what ways does this picture suggest growing and changing? **[Connect]**

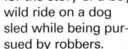

Why Read Literature?

You will find that, whenever you read, you have a purpose, or reason, for reading. Your purpose will vary depending on the content, style, and form of the work you will read. Preview three of the purposes you might see before reading the works in this unit.

1 Read for the love of literature.

Robert Frost is known as a "New England" poet, but he was born and raised in California! Read **"Dust of Snow,"** page 30, for a quick look at one of Frost's New England scenes.

Sometimes a life of high adventure leads an author to write action-packed fiction. Jack London is such a writer. At age seventeen, he went to sea to hunt seals. Several years later, feeling restless, he headed to the Klondike in search of gold. London wrote stories based on his adventures. Read London's **"The King of Mazy May,"** page 52, for the story of a boy's wild ride on a dog sled while being pursued by robbers.

2 Read to consider another viewpoint.

Russell Baker was a newspaper man when he was still a boy! Read **"Hard as Nails"** on page 72 to learn about his first job.

Science-fiction writer Ray Bradbury has a crater on the moon named after one of his books. When you read **"The Sound of Summer Running,"** page 6, you may be surprised to discover that Bradbury's character has both feet planted firmly on Earth.

3 Read for information.

For tips and guidance on how to find and choose a summer job, read **"Summer Hats,"** page 83.

Find out why John Glenn, the first American to orbit the Earth, returned to space at the age of seventy-seven. Read **"An Astronaut's Answers,"** page 86.

 Take It to the Net

Visit the Web site for online instruction and activities related to each selection in this unit.
www.phschool.com

How to Read Literature

Literal Comprehension Strategies

When you build a house, you first construct a foundation on which the other levels are built. In reading, too, you construct a foundation. This foundation is the literal meaning—the basic facts and details. The following strategies will help you understand a writer's words on a literal level.

1. Read fluently.

To read fluently means to read groups of words rather than one word at a time. Reading fluently helps you understand what you are reading. Improve your fluency in the following ways:

- Read aloud.
- Preview what you will read to check for unfamiliar words.
- Practice reading groups of words rather than individual words.

2. Use context to determine meaning.

Use the context, or the surroundings, of an unfamiliar word to find its meaning. In the following passage, words with similar meanings help you figure out that *timidly* means "showing shyness."

> The puppy stopped in the road, wagging its tail *timidly*, trembling with *shyness* and cold.

3. Recognize signal words.

Use signal words—*next* and *most important*, for example— to identify relationships, such as time or importance among ideas. The notepad shows commonly used signal words and what they indicate.

4. Reread to clarify.

If a word or phrase is unclear, reread the text in which it appears. The poem "My Picture-Gallery" seems to be describing a house. You may be confused about how a house could fit everything the poet says is in it. On rereading, however, you will discover the house is round and not fixed in place. These clues show that the house stands for something else.

5. Read accurately.

To read accurately, find the main parts of the sentence by breaking it down into meaningful sections. Note whom or what the sentence is about and what happens.

As you read the selections in this unit, review the reading strategies and look at the notes in the side columns. Use the suggestions to apply the strategies for literal comprehension.

Signal Words

That Show Time
while
then   next
              before

That Show Contrast
however
although   but

That Show Cause and Effect
because
consequently   as a result

Prepare to Read

The Sound of Summer Running

 Take It to the Net

Visit www.phschool.com for interactive activities and instruction related to "The Sound of Summer Running," including
- background
- graphic organizers
- literary elements
- reading strategies

Preview

Connecting to the Literature

For the boy in Ray Bradbury's "The Sound of Summer Running," a new pair of sneakers represents summer and all its possibilities. Think of all the sights, sounds, and experiences that you associate with summer.

Background

What you call something depends on where you live. In one place, you might ask for a *soda* and a *sub*. In another, you might ask for a *pop* and a *hoagie*. *Tennis shoes*, *sneakers*, and *running shoes* are terms used in different parts of the country to describe the same shoes. In "The Sound of Summer Running," set in the Midwest, Douglas refers to the shoes as *tennis shoes*.

Literary Analysis

Characters' Motives

Characters' motives are the impulses, emotions, or desires that cause characters to act in a certain way. In the following example, the character's motive for walking backward is that he wants the shoes he sees:

> Douglas walked backward, watching the tennis shoes in the midnight window left behind.

As you read "The Sound of Summer Running," fill in a chart for each character. List each important action a character takes, and indicate a motive for the action.

Connecting Literary Elements

Motives influence a character's actions. A character's actions, in turn, reveal a **character's qualities,** the personal traits that make up the character's personality. Douglas shows resourcefulness and independence. As you read, look for answers to the following focus questions.

1. What are two actions that show that Douglas is persistent?
2. What other qualities are shown in Douglas's solution to his problem?

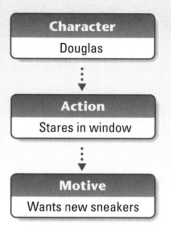

Reading Strategy

Reading Fluently

When walking or running, one foot follows the other smoothly. You do not stop after each step. When reading, do not pause after each word. **Read fluently,** that is, read groups of words together for meaning. Doing the following will help you improve your reading fluency.

- Preview the text to check for difficult or unfamiliar words.
- Practice reading aloud. Use punctuation to guide your pauses.

Read sections of "The Sound of Summer Running" aloud. Notice where your reading is smooth and practice sections where it is choppy.

Vocabulary Development

seized (sēzd) *v.* grabbed; taken hold of (p. 7)

suspended (sə spend′ id) *v.* stopped for a time (p. 7)

loam (lōm) *n.* rich soil (p. 7)

barometer (bə räm′ ət ər′) *n.* device to measure air pressure, to predict rain (p. 8)

alien (ā′ lē ən) *adj.* foreign; unfamiliar (p. 10)

limber (lim′ bər) *v.* loosen up (a muscle or limb); to make easy to bend (p. 11)

revelation (rev′ ə lā′ shən) *n.* sudden rush of understanding (p. 11)

The Sound of Summer Running

from **Dandelion Wine**   Ray Bradbury

Late that night, going home from the show with his mother and father and his brother Tom, Douglas saw the tennis shoes in the bright store window. He glanced quickly away, but his ankles were <u>seized</u>, his feet <u>suspended</u>, then rushed. The earth spun; the shop awnings slammed their canvas wings overhead with the thrust of his body running. His mother and father and brother walked quietly on both sides of him. Douglas walked backward, watching the tennis shoes in the midnight window left behind.

"It was a nice movie," said Mother.

Douglas murmured, "It was . . ."

It was June and long past time for buying the special shoes that were quiet as a summer rain falling on the walks. June and the earth full of raw power and everything everywhere in motion. The grass was still pouring in from the country, surrounding the sidewalks, stranding the houses. Any moment the town would capsize, go down and leave not a stir in the clover and weeds. And here Douglas stood, trapped on the dead cement and the red-brick streets, hardly able to move.

"Dad!" He blurted it out. "Back there in that window, those Cream-Sponge Para Litefoot Shoes . . ."

His father didn't even turn. "Suppose you tell me why you need a new pair of sneakers. Can you do that?"

"Well . . ."

It was because they felt the way it feels every summer when you take off your shoes for the first time and run in the grass. They felt like it feels sticking your feet out of the hot covers in wintertime to let the cold wind from the open window blow on them suddenly and you let them stay out a long time until you pull them back in under the covers again to feel them, like packed snow. The tennis shoes felt like it always feels the first time every year wading in the slow waters of the creek and seeing your feet below, half an inch further downstream, with refraction, than the real part of you above water.

"Dad," said Douglas, "it's hard to explain."

Somehow the people who made tennis shoes knew what boys needed and wanted. They put marshmallows and coiled springs in the soles and they wove the rest out of grasses bleached and fired in the wilderness. Somewhere deep in the soft <u>loam</u> of the shoes the thin hard sinews of the buck deer were hidden. The people that made the shoes must have watched a lot of winds blow the trees and a lot of rivers going down to the lakes. Whatever it was, it was in the shoes, and it was summer.

seized (sēzd) *v.* grabbed; taken hold of

suspended (sə spend′ id) *v.* stopped for a time

Literary Analysis
Characters' Motives
What do you think is Douglas's motive for talking to his father about the shoes?

loam (lōm) *n.* rich soil

☑ **Reading Check**

Why are the shoes so appealing?

◀ **Critical Viewing** What feelings do you think the boy in this picture might share with Douglas? **[Interpret]**

Douglas tried to get all this in words.

"Yes," said Father, "but what's wrong with last year's sneakers? Why can't you dig *them* out of the closet?"

Well, he felt sorry for boys who lived in California where they wore tennis shoes all year and never knew what it was to get winter off your feet, peel off the iron leather shoes all full of snow and rain and run barefoot for a day and then lace on the first new tennis shoes of the season, which was better than barefoot. The magic was always in the new pair of shoes. The magic might die by the first of September, but now in late June there was still plenty of magic, and shoes like these could jump you over trees and rivers and houses. And if you wanted, they could jump you over fences and sidewalks and dogs.

"Don't you see?" said Douglas. "I just *can't* use last year's pair."

For last year's pair were dead inside. They had been fine when he started them out, last year. But by the end of summer, every year, you always found out, you always knew, you couldn't really jump over rivers and trees and houses in them, and they were dead. But this was a new year, and he felt that this time, with this new pair of shoes, he could do anything, anything at all.

They walked up on the steps to their house. "Save your money," said Dad. "In five or six weeks—"

"Summer'll be over!"

Lights out, with Tom asleep, Douglas lay watching his feet, far away down there at the end of the bed in the moonlight, free of the heavy iron shoes, the big chunks of winter fallen away from them.

"Reason. I've got to think of reasons for the shoes."

Well, as anyone knew, the hills around town were wild with friends putting cows to riot, playing <u>barometer</u> to the atmospheric changes, taking sun, peeling like calendars each day to take more sun. To catch those friends, you must run much faster than foxes or squirrels. As for the town, it steamed with enemies grown irritable with heat, so remembering every winter argument and insult. *Find friends, ditch enemies!* That was the Cream-Sponge Para Litefoot motto. *Does the world run too fast? Want to catch up? Want to be alert, stay alert? Litefoot, then! Litefoot!*

He held his coin bank up and heard the faint small tinkling, the airy weight of money there.

Whatever you want, he thought, you got to make your own way. During the night now, let's find that path through the forest. . . .

Downtown, the store lights went out, one by one. A wind blew in the window. It was like a river going downstream and his feet wanting to go with it.

In his dreams he heard a rabbit running running running in the deep warm grass.

Old Mr. Sanderson moved through his shoe store as the proprietor

Reading Strategy
Reading Fluently
What tone of voice would you use to read Father's remarks to show how he felt?

Literary Analysis
Characters' Motives How do Douglas's motives differ from those of his father?

barometer (bə räm′ ət ər) *n.* device for measuring air pressure; used to predict rain

New Shoes for H, 1973-1974, Don Eddy, The Cleveland Museum of Art

◀ **Critical Viewing**
Do you think Douglas would be drawn to any of the items in this store window? Why or why not? **[Draw Conclusions]**

of a pet shop must move through his shop where are kenneled animals from everywhere in the world, touching each one briefly along the way. Mr. Sanderson brushed his hands over the shoes in the window, and some of them were like cats to him and some were like dogs; he touched each pair with concern, adjusting laces, fixing tongues. Then he stood in the exact center of the carpet and looked around, nodding.

There was a sound of growing thunder.

One moment, the door to Sanderson's Shoe Emporium was empty. The next, Douglas Spaulding stood clumsily there, staring down at his leather shoes as if these heavy things could not be pulled up out of the cement. The thunder had stopped when his shoes stopped. Now, with painful slowness, daring to look only at the money in his cupped hand, Douglas moved out of the bright sunlight of Saturday

Literary Analysis
Characters' Qualities
What do Mr. Sanderson's actions tell you about him?

✔ **Reading Check**

How does Douglas's father react when Douglas asks for the shoes?

noon. He made careful stacks of nickels, dimes, and quarters on the counter, like someone playing chess and worried if the next move carried him out into sun or deep into shadow.

"Don't say a word!" said Mr. Sanderson.

Douglas froze.

"First, I know just what you want to buy," said Mr. Sanderson. "Second, I see you every afternoon at my window; you think I don't see? You're wrong. Third, to give it its full name, you want the Royal Crown Cream-Sponge Para Litefoot Tennis Shoes: 'LIKE MENTHOL ON YOUR FEET!' Fourth, you want credit."

"No!" cried Douglas, breathing hard, as if he'd run all night in his dreams. "I got something better than credit to offer!" he gasped. "Before I tell, Mr. Sanderson, you got to do me one small favor. Can you remember when was the last time you yourself wore a pair of Litefoot sneakers, sir?"

Mr. Sanderson's face darkened. "Oh, ten, twenty, say, thirty years ago. Why . . . ?"

"Mr. Sanderson, don't you think you owe it to your customers, sir, to at least try the tennis shoes you sell, for just one minute, so you know how they feel? People forget if they don't keep testing things. United Cigar Store man smokes cigars, don't he? Candy-store man samples his own stuff, I should think. So . . ."

"You may have noticed," said the old man, "I'm wearing shoes."

"But not sneakers, sir! How you going to sell sneakers unless you can rave about them and how you going to rave about them unless you know them?"

Mr. Sanderson backed off a little distance from the boy's fever, one hand to his chin. "Well . . ."

"Mr. Sanderson," said Douglas, "you sell me something and I'll sell you something just as valuable."

"Is it absolutely necessary to the sale that I put on a pair of the sneakers, boy?" said the old man.

"I sure wish you could, sir!"

The old man sighed. A minute later, seated panting quietly, he laced the tennis shoes to his long narrow feet. They looked detached and <u>alien</u> down there next to the dark cuffs of his business suit. Mr. Sanderson stood up.

"How do they *feel*?" asked the boy.

"How do they feel, he asks; they feel fine." He started to sit down.

"Please!" Douglas held out his hand. "Mr. Sanderson, now could you kind of rock back and forth a little, sponge around, bounce kind of, while I tell you the rest? It's this: I give you my money, you give me the shoes, I owe you a dollar. But, Mr. Sanderson, *but*—soon as I get those shoes on, you know what *happens*?"

"What?"

Literary Analysis
Characters' Qualities
What character qualities does Douglas show in this paragraph?

alien (āʹ lē ən) *adj.* foreign; unfamiliar

Reading Strategy
Reading Fluently Read Douglas's remarks aloud, using the punctuation to help you read words in groups.

"Bang! I deliver your packages, pick up packages, bring you coffee, burn your trash, run to the post office, telegraph office, library! You'll see twelve of me in and out, in and out, every minute. Feel those shoes, Mr. Sanderson, *feel* how fast they'd take me? All those springs inside? Feel all the running inside? Feel how they kind of grab hold and can't let you alone and don't like you just *standing* there? Feel how quick I'd be doing the things you'd rather not bother with? You stay in the nice cool store while I'm jumping all around town! But it's not me really, it's the shoes. They're going like mad down alleys, cutting corners, and back! There they go!"

Mr. Sanderson stood amazed with the rush of words. When the words got going the flow carried him; he began to sink deep in the shoes, to flex his toes, <u>limber</u> his arches, test his ankles. He rocked softly, secretly, back and forth in a small breeze from the open door. The tennis shoes silently hushed themselves deep in the carpet, sank as in a jungle grass, in loam and resilient clay. He gave one solemn bounce of his heels in the yeasty dough, in the yielding and welcoming earth. Emotions hurried over his face as if many colored lights had been switched on and off. His mouth hung slightly open. Slowly he gentled and rocked himself to a halt, and the boy's voice faded and they stood there looking at each other in a tremendous and natural silence.

A few people drifted by on the sidewalk outside, in the hot sun.

Still the man and boy stood there, the boy glowing, the man with <u>revelation</u> in his face.

"Boy," said the old man at last, "in five years, how would you like a job selling shoes in this emporium?"

"Gosh, thanks, Mr. Sanderson, but I don't know what I'm going to be yet."

"Anything you want to be, son," said the old man, "you'll be. No one will ever stop you."

The old man walked lightly across the store to the wall of ten thousand boxes, came back with some shoes for the boy, and wrote up a list on some paper while the boy was lacing the shoes on his feet and then standing there, waiting.

The old man held out his list. "A dozen things you got to do for me this afternoon. Finish them, we're even Stephen, and you're fired."

"Thanks, Mr. Sanderson!" Douglas bounded away.

"Stop!" cried the old man.

Douglas pulled up and turned.

Mr. Sanderson leaned forward. "How do they *feel*?"

The boy looked down at his feet deep in the rivers, in the fields of wheat, in the wind that already was rushing him out of the town. He looked up at the old man, his eyes burning, his mouth moving, but no sound came out.

limber (lim´ bər) v. loosen up (a muscle or limb); to make easy to bend

revelation (rev´ ə lā´ shən) n. sudden rush of understanding

**Reading Check**

What does Douglas ask of Mr. Sanderson?

"Antelopes?" said the old man, looking from the boy's face to his shoes. "Gazelles?"

The boy thought about it, hesitated, and nodded a quick nod. Almost immediately he vanished. He just spun about with a whisper and went off. The door stood empty. The sound of the tennis shoes faded in the jungle heat.

Mr. Sanderson stood in the sun-blazed door, listening. From a long time ago, when he dreamed as a boy, he remembered the sound. Beautiful creatures leaping under the sky, gone through brush, under trees, away, and only the soft echo their running left behind.

"Antelopes," said Mr. Sanderson. "Gazelles."

He bent to pick up the boy's abandoned winter shoes, heavy with forgotten rains and long-melted snows. Moving out of the blazing sun, walking softly, lightly, slowly, he headed back toward civilization. . . .

Review and Assess

Thinking About the Selection

1. **Respond:** Is Douglas someone you admire? Why or why not?

2. **(a) Recall:** What are Douglas's feelings about last year's sneakers? **(b) Infer:** Why does he feel that way?

3. **(a) Recall:** What is Dad's reaction to Douglas's request? **(b) Contrast:** What difference between Douglas and his father does this reaction reveal? **(c) Speculate:** What are some possible reasons Douglas's father won't buy the new sneakers?

4. **(a) Recall:** What is Mr. Sanderson doing before Douglas arrives at the store? **(b) Infer:** How does Mr. Sanderson feel about his work?

5. **(a) Recall:** What is Mr. Sanderson's reaction when Douglas asks him to try on the sneakers? **(b) Deduce:** Why does he react this way? **(c) Analyze:** Explain the change in Mr. Sanderson when he is wearing the sneakers.

6. **(a) Synthesize:** In your own words, explain Douglas's plan, including his reasons for getting Mr. Sanderson to try on the sneakers. **(b) Evaluate:** Explain why you think this plan would or would not work on most store owners. **(c) Evaluate:** What other ways might Douglas have gone about getting the shoes and why would these methods have been more or less effective?

7. **(a) Analyze:** What do the tennis shoes represent to Douglas? **(b) Extend:** What do tennis shoes represent to you and others your age? **(c) Evaluate:** Why do you think tennis shoes often take on an important meaning for people your age?

Ray Bradbury

(b. 1920)

Athletes keep in shape by running or working out every day. Ray Bradbury exercises his mental muscles by drafting 2,000 to 3,000 words of manuscript a day!

As a boy, Ray Bradbury nourished his imagination by attending circuses, watching magicians, and reading the novels of science-fiction writer Edgar Rice Burroughs. At the age of twelve, Bradbury began writing his own stories, which were mostly about space travel. Although he is most famous for his science-fiction tales, he also writes down-to-earth stories, poetry, plays, and screen-plays. His childhood fears and dreams fill the pages of *Dandelion Wine*, the collection of short stories in which "The Sound of Summer Running" appears.

Review and Assess

Literary Analysis

Characters' Motives

1. What is Douglas's **motive** in asking Mr. Sanderson to try on the sneakers?
2. Explain Mr. Sanderson's motives for agreeing to Douglas's plan.
3. Use a chart like the one shown to map out Douglas's actions in the shoe store, the motives for his actions, and the consequences of his actions.

Connecting Literary Elements

4. What two actions show that Douglas is persistent?
5. What other qualities help Douglas solve his problem?
6. What are two of Mr. Sanderson's **character qualities**? Explain.
7. Use a Venn diagram like the one shown to compare and contrast Mr. Sanderson and Douglas's father. What personality traits do they share? How are they different?

Reading Strategy

Reading Fluently

8. Copy the following passage. Draw lines where you would pause. Circle the groups of words you would read together. Explain why you read the passage as you did.

    Bang! I deliver your packages, pick up packages, bring you coffee, burn your trash, run to the post office, telegraph office, library! You'll see twelve of me in and out, in and out, every minute.

9. Choose another passage from the text and repeat what you did in number 8.

Extending Understanding

10. **Career Connection:** What qualities does Douglas have that would make him a good salesperson?

Quick Review

Characters' motives are their reasons for thinking and acting in certain ways. To review character's motives, see page 5.

Characters' qualities are those traits that create the characters' personalities.

Reading fluently is reading groups of words together for meaning.

 Take It to the Net

www.phschool.com
Take the interactive self-test online to check your understanding of the selection.

Integrate Language Skills

Vocabulary Development Lesson

Word Analysis: Greek Root -meter-

Any word with the root -meter-, like *barometer*, has something to do with measurement.

On your paper, write the word from the list below that best completes each sentence.

chronometer   speedometer   thermometer

1. Dan checked his ___?___ to see how fast he was going.
2. A ___?___ measures time very precisely.
3. Sue could tell how hot it was by looking at the ___?___.

Spelling Strategy

When *e* and *i* appear together, the rule is "Use *i* before *e* except after *c* or when sounded like *a*, as in *neighbor* and *weigh*." The words *seized, either, leisure, weird, height*, and *protein* are exceptions to this rule. Unscramble the following words.

1. desize   2. efrig   3. wired

Grammar Lesson

Nouns

A **noun** names a person, place, or thing. Some nouns name what can be seen, such as *sneakers*. Other nouns name feelings or ideas, such as *happiness* or *memory*.

In this example, the noun that names a person is underlined; the noun that names a feeling is printed in boldface.

> **Example:** <u>Mr. Sanderson</u> rocked back and forth and remembered the **joys** of his youth.

Fluency: Clarify Word Meaning

Match each vocabulary word from the story with the song title that best fits the word's meaning.

1. seized   "Suddenly I Realize"
2. suspended   "How High Is the Air Pressure?"
3. alien   "All Caught Up"
4. limber   "This Rich Soil"
5. revelation   "Out of This World"
6. barometer   "Hanging On"
7. loam   "Aerobic Workout"

Practice Copy the following sentences and underline each noun.

1. Douglas stepped out of the sunlight.
2. The man felt a memory stir in his brain.
3. The sneakers made him feel like a gazelle.
4. The tennis shoes represented summer to him.

Writing Application Answer these questions with complete sentences. Underline the nouns in your answers.

1. What is your favorite season?
2. Who is your favorite singer?
3. What food don't you like?
4. What is your favorite animal?

W̶G Prentice Hall Writing and Grammar Connection: Chapter 14, Section 1

Writing Lesson

Sneaker Advertisement

Douglas uses vivid, precise words such as *packed snow* and *coiled springs* to create powerful impressions. Advertisers use words to create appealing impressions of a product. Write an advertisement for the sneakers Douglas longs for in the story.

Prewriting   Fold a sheet of paper into three panels as shown below. On the first panel, list the qualities of the sneakers. On the second panel, name something else that has that quality. On the third panel, list additional vivid words that describe or name qualities of the sneakers.

Model: Trifold to Identify Precise Language

Qualities of Sneakers	Things With Same Qualities	Describing Words

Drafting   Review the words you have listed. Use the ones you think are most appealing in a headline. Follow your headline with one or more paragraphs consisting of short sentences with words that capture how the sneakers look and feel.

Revising   Ask a peer to circle words in your draft that do not create a strong impression. Replace these words with more vivid, precise words.

W̶G̶ Prentice Hall Writing and Grammar Connection: Chapter 6, Section 1

Extension Activities

Listening and Speaking With a partner, perform a **dramatic reading** of the conversation between Douglas and Mr. Sanderson. Use your voice to help communicate meaning.

1. Pause before introducing an important point.
2. Speak quickly to show excitement, impatience, or eagerness. Speak slowly to show thoughtfulness or curiosity.
3. Speak clearly so that all your points are heard.

Research and Technology When Bradbury wrote this story, there were not many varieties of running shoes. Research different types of running shoes: their uses, purposes, durability, and benefits for feet. Use an electronic source such as a library database. Present your results in a graph or chart, using a computer, if possible, to create a **display of the information.**

 ***Take It to the Net***   www.phschool.com

Go online for an additional research activity using the Internet.

Prepare to Read

Stray

 Take It to the Net

Visit www.phschool.com for interactive activities and instruction related to "Stray," including
- background
- graphic organizers
- literary elements
- reading strategies

Preview

Connecting to the Literature

Sometimes, you cannot have what you want because there is not enough time, not enough space, or not enough money. The main character in this story knows her family cannot afford a pet. Words will not change the facts, so she keeps her feelings quiet.

Background

Animal shelters take in stray animals as well as pets that people can no longer keep. Although good animal shelters have the best interests of the animals at heart, many shelters at first appear frightening or depressing because of the noises, smells, and rows of cages.

Literary Analysis

Surprise Ending

When you read a story, the details lead you to expect a certain kind of ending. Sometimes, a story has a **surprise ending**— it ends differently from what you expected. Use a graphic like the one here to track details that lead you to expect "Stray" to end one way and details that lead to the actual ending.

Connecting Literary Elements

When you are surprised by the ending of a story, it is because the **plot,** or sequence of related events, did not turn out the way you expected. In most short stories, plot events are related to a single problem or situation. The events lead up to the moment when the problem is solved or the situation turns out one way or another.

Use these focus questions to help you think about the plot of "Stray."

1. What problem does Doris face in "Stray"?
2. What seems to be the most likely outcome of the situation?

Reading Strategy

Distinguishing Shades of Meaning

Many words have similar meanings. For example, *softly* and *quietly* have about the same meaning. However, each word conveys a shade of meaning, a slight difference, that makes it the best choice for a particular situation. To understand the effect of shades of meaning, notice how the following sentences would change if the italicized words were exchanged.

> It always wagged its tail, eyes all *sleepy*, when she found it there.

> Lying there, like stone, still *exhausted*, she wondered if she would ever in her life have anything.

When you come across a word that describes how a character thinks or feels, pause for a moment to identify the precise meaning of that word.

Vocabulary Development

timidly (tim´ id lē) *adv.* in a way that shows fear or shyness (p. 18)

trudged (trujd) *v.* walked as if tired or with effort (p. 18)

grudgingly (gruj´ iŋ lē) *adv.* in an unenthusiastic or resentful way (p. 19)

ignore (ig nôr´) *v.* pay no attention to (p. 20)

exhausted (eg zôs´ tid) *adj.* tired out (p. 21)

Stray

Cynthia Rylant

In January, a puppy wandered onto the property of Mr. Amos Lacey and his wife, Mamie, and their daughter, Doris. Icicles hung three feet or more from the eaves of houses, snowdrifts swallowed up automobiles and the birds were so fluffed up they looked comic.

The puppy had been abandoned, and it made its way down the road toward the Laceys' small house, its ears tucked, its tail between its legs, shivering.

Doris, whose school had been called off because of the snow, was out shoveling the cinderblock front steps when she spotted the pup on the road. She set down the shovel.

"Hey! Come on!" she called.

The puppy stopped in the road, wagging its tail <u>timidly</u>, trembling with shyness and cold.

Doris <u>trudged</u> through the yard, went up the shoveled drive and met the dog.

"Come on, Pooch."

Reading Strategy
Distinguish Shades of Meaning How is the meaning of *shivering* similar to and different from that of *trembling*?

timidly (tim´ id lē) *adv.* in a way that shows fear or shyness

trudged (trujd) *v.* walked as if tired or with effort

"Where did *that* come from?" Mrs. Lacey asked as soon as Doris put the dog down in the kitchen.

Mr. Lacey was at the table, cleaning his fingernails with his pocketknife. The snow was keeping him home from his job at the warehouse.

"I don't know where it came from," he said mildly, "but I know for sure where it's going."

Doris hugged the puppy hard against her. She said nothing.

Because the roads would be too bad for travel for many days, Mr. Lacey couldn't get out to take the puppy to the pound[1] in the city right away. He agreed to let it sleep in the basement while Mrs. Lacey <u>grudgingly</u> let Doris feed it table scraps. The woman was sensitive about throwing out food.

By the looks of it, Doris figured the puppy was about six months old, and on its way to being a big dog. She thought it might have some shepherd in it.

---

1. **pound** animal shelter.

grudgingly (gruj′ iŋ lē) *adv.* in an unenthusiastic or resentful way

☑ **Reading Check**

What does Mr. Lacey plan to do with the puppy?

Four days passed and the puppy did not complain. It never cried in the night or howled at the wind. It didn't tear up everything in the basement. It wouldn't even follow Doris up the basement steps unless it was invited.

It was a good dog.

Several times Doris had opened the door in the kitchen that led to the basement and the puppy had been there, all stretched out, on the top step. Doris knew it had wanted some company and that it had lain against the door, listening to the talk in the kitchen, smelling the food, being a part of things. It always wagged its tail, eyes all sleepy, when she found it there.

Even after a week had gone by, Doris didn't name the dog. She knew her parents wouldn't let her keep it, that her father made so little money any pets were out of the question, and that the pup would definitely go to the pound when the weather cleared.

Still, she tried talking to them about the dog at dinner one night.

"She's a good dog, isn't she?" Doris said, hoping one of them would agree with her.

Her parents glanced at each other and went on eating.

"She's not much trouble," Doris added. "I like her." She smiled at them, but they continued to <u>ignore</u> her.

"I figure she's real smart," Doris said to her mother. "I could teach her things."

Mrs. Lacey just shook her head and stuffed a forkful of sweet potato in her mouth. Doris fell silent, praying the weather would never clear.

But on Saturday, nine days after the dog had arrived, the sun was shining and the roads were plowed. Mr. Lacey opened up the trunk of his car and came into the house.

Doris was sitting alone in the living room, hugging a pillow and rocking back and forth on the edge of a chair. She was trying not to cry but she was not strong enough. Her face was wet and red, her eyes full of distress.

Mrs. Lacey looked into the room from the doorway.

"Mama," Doris said in a small voice. "Please."

Mrs. Lacey shook her head.

"You know we can't afford a dog, Doris. You try to act more grown-up about this."

Doris pressed her face into the pillow.

Outside, she heard the trunk of the car slam shut, one of the doors open and close, the old engine cough and choke and finally start up.

"Daddy," she whispered. "Please."

She heard the car travel down the road, and, though it was early afternoon, she could do nothing but go to her bed. She

ignore (ig nôr′) v. pay no attention to

cried herself to sleep, and her dreams were full of searching and searching for things lost.

It was nearly night when she finally woke up. Lying there, like stone, still <u>exhausted</u>, she wondered if she would ever in her life have anything. She stared at the wall for a while.

But she started feeling hungry, and she knew she'd have to make herself get out of bed and eat some dinner. She wanted not to go into the kitchen, past the basement door. She wanted not to face her parents.

But she rose up heavily.

Her parents were sitting at the table, dinner over, drinking coffee. They looked at her when she came in, but she kept her head down. No one spoke.

exhausted (eg zôs′ tid) *adj.* tired out

☑**Reading Check**

What does Doris do when Mr. Lacey takes the dog?

◀ **Critical Viewing** Why would a girl like Doris become attached to a dog like this? **[Analyze]**

Doris made herself a glass of powdered milk and drank it all down. Then she picked up a cold biscuit and started out of the room.

"You'd better feed that mutt before it dies of starvation," Mr. Lacey said.

Doris turned around.

"What?"

"I said, you'd better feed your dog. I figure it's looking for you."

Doris put her hand to her mouth.

"You didn't take her?" she asked.

"Oh, I took her all right," her father answered. "Worst looking place I've ever seen. Ten dogs to a cage. Smell was enough to knock you down. And they give an animal six days to live. Then they kill it with some kind of a shot."

Doris stared at her father.

"I wouldn't leave an *ant* in that place," he said. "So I brought the dog back."

Mrs. Lacey was smiling at him and shaking her head as if she would never, ever, understand him.

Mr. Lacey sipped his coffee.

"Well," he said, "are you going to feed it or not?"

Review and Assess

Thinking About the Selection

1. **Respond:** Do you think the Laceys care about Doris's feelings? Why or why not?

2. **(a) Recall:** Why do the Laceys wait before taking the dog to the pound? **(b) Evaluate:** How difficult is keeping the dog during this time? **(c) Analyze:** In what way does the waiting make giving the dog away more difficult for Doris?

3. **(a) Recall:** What does Doris do when her father tells her she can't keep the dog? **(b) Analyze:** Explain why Doris reacts this way.

4. **(a) Recall:** In your own words, restate Mr. Lacey's description of the pound. **(b) Analyze Cause and Effect:** Why does Mr. Lacey change his mind about keeping the dog?

5. **(a) Draw Conclusions:** For what reasons, other than the condition of the pound, might Mr. Lacey have brought the dog home? **(b) Interpret:** Which character(s) show love? Which character(s) show common sense? Explain.

6. **(a) Take a Position:** Do you feel like Doris should have made a stronger case for keeping the dog? Why or why not? **(b) Speculate:** What can Doris do in the future to make her father feel like he made the right decision?

Cynthia Rylant

(b. 1954)

As a child, Cynthia Rylant didn't think she would be a writer. "I always felt my life was too limited," she says. "Nothing to write about." At the age of twenty-four, however, she discovered that her life did in fact contain the seeds of many stories.

Her first book, *When I Was Young in the Mountains*, describes her childhood in the hills of West Virginia. Cynthia lived with her grandparents for four years in a tiny house without plumbing. This experience of hardship may be reflected in "Stray." Rylant has a special attachment to her young characters who, she feels, have more "possibilities": "They can get away with more love, more anger, more fear than adult characters . . ."

Review and Assess

Literary Analysis

Surprise Ending

1. Identify two facts about the family that make it unlikely they will keep the dog.
2. What details make you believe that the dog is gone forever?
3. How does Doris's father let her know that he kept the dog? Explain how this action makes the ending a surprise.

Connecting Literary Elements

4. What problem does Doris face in "Stray"?
5. What seems to be the most likely outcome of the situation?
6. On a diagram like the one below, identify **plot** events that lead up to the moment when the final decision seems to be made.
7. Identify the plot event that shows how the situation turns out.

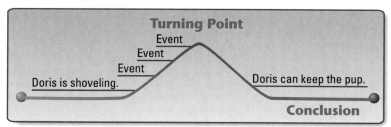

Turning Point
Event
Event
Event
Doris is shoveling.
Doris can keep the pup.
Conclusion

Reading Strategy

Distinguishing Shades of Meaning

8. Explain the different **shades of meaning** for the words in italics.
   It never *cried* in the night or *howled* at the wind.
9. Complete the following chart by supplying words that convey shades of meaning related to the word at the top of each column. Explain how each word you provide is different from the original word.

timid	trembling	hungry

Extending Understanding

10. **Make a Judgment:** Why might one person choose to have a pet and another choose not to?

Quick Review

A **surprise ending** occurs when the events of the story lead you to expect a different ending. To review surprise ending, see page 17.

Plot is the sequence of events that unfolds in the story. To review plot, see page 17.

Shades of meaning are the slight differences between words that have similar meanings.

 Take It to the Net
www.phschool.com
Take the interactive self-test online to check your understanding of the selection.

Integrate Language Skills

Vocabulary Development Lesson

Word Analysis: Suffix -ly

Words that end in the suffix -ly usually answer the question *how* or *in what way*. In "Stray," the puppy wags its tail *timidly*—in a shy and fearful way. Add the suffix -ly to each word below. Define each new word.

   1. beautiful   **2.** sad   **3.** immediate

Spelling Strategy

English words that end in the *j* sound, such as *grudge*, are spelled with a *ge* or *dge* at the end. Practice this unexpected consonant spelling. For each of the following phrases, write a synonym that spells the *j* sound with one of those letter combinations.

   1. walk slowly
   2. very big
   3. bravery
   4. building for parked cars

Concept Development: Connotations

Besides dictionary meanings, words have **connotations**—associations that they call to mind. The word *cheap*, for example, has a similar meaning to the word *inexpensive*. However, the word *cheap* may call to mind something that is shoddy.

Choose the word from this list that is similar in meaning to the italicized word. Then, explain the different connotations of the two words.

   exhausted   grudgingly   ignore
   trudged   timidly

   1. Darren was relieved that the strange dog approached him *shyly*.
   2. When Dad told Ryan to share the ball, he handed it to me *unenthusiastically*.
   3. Dreading the test, Maya *walked* up the hill.
   4. Taylor was *tired* after doing extra chores.
   5. Ms. Wolfson said to *disregard* the questions.

Grammar Lesson

Compound Nouns

Nouns—words that name people, places, or things—sometimes contain two or more words. Nouns made up of more than one word are called **compound nouns**. Compound nouns can be written as one word, as separate words, or as words linked by a hyphen.

> **Written as one word:**
>   thunderstorm   sunlight
> **Written with a hyphen between words:**
>   ten-year-old   mother-in-law
> **Written as separate words:**
>   ice cream   pen pal

Practice Copy the following sentences and underline each compound noun.

   1. Doris shoveled the driveway.
   2. Doris does a lot of work for an eleven-year-old.
   3. She had a sweet potato, meatloaf, and a milkshake for dinner.
   4. Mr. Lacey's sister is Mrs. Lacey's sister-in-law.
   5. Snowdrifts covered the treetops.

Writing Application Write a short paragraph about a favorite animal or pet. Include three compound nouns in your paragraph.

Writing Lesson

News Report

Doris's father has strong words to say about the local animal shelter. News reporters often respond to people's negative reactions by investigating. Write your own investigative news report about the problems facing animal shelters and the ways these problems are being addressed.

Prewriting   Use library resources or call animal shelters to gather details. Use the five W's—who, what, where, when, and why—to guide you.

Drafting   Begin with a lead sentence that contains a statistic, quotation, or other detail to capture readers' attention. Follow it with one or more short, clear sentences that sum up the basic facts. Continue with examples and details that illustrate your overall point.

Model: Beginning With an Effective Lead

"I wouldn't leave an ant in that place," said Amos Lacey.

Mr. Lacey is speaking about the animal shelter in his town, where animals are kept in overcrowded, unhealthy conditions. Other shelters, however, do fine work.

> Mr. Lacey's words make readers wonder why he wouldn't leave a dog there. This statement grabs readers' interest and leads them to read further.

Revising   Identify the question raised by your lead. If no question is raised, consider rewriting to build curiosity in your readers.

WG *Prentice Hall Writing and Grammar Connection: Chapter 9, Section 3*

Extension Activities

Listening and Speaking With a small group of students, organize a **presentation** about stray animals. Include a speaker from the local animal shelter. Group members may choose from the following tasks:

1. Call local shelters to find a speaker.
2. Prepare questions to ask the speaker.
3. Prepare an introduction to the speaker.
4. Lead a discussion of the problems facing shelters and possible solutions.

Research and Technology Create a **chart** showing the cost and time involved in owning a dog. Use prices from pet supply stores and do an Internet search for dog care information based on the type and size of dog. If possible, use a word processing or graphics program to create your chart.

 **Take It to the Net**   www.phschool.com

Go online for an additional research activity using the Internet.

More than one of the dogs you will read about in this article from *TV Guide* once lived in a pound as a stray—just like the puppy in "Stray." These dogs were lucky that humans saw something special in them—something that made each dog a star.

TV's Top Dogs
Deborah Starr Seibel

The star's handlers were clearly worried. Their anxiety had been filtering through phone and fax lines for more than a week over a request for an important photo session—known in the business as a "cover try." They were interested, but would their star be on the cover? No guarantee. Would their client have to share the spotlight with other celebrities? Maybe. Publicists conferred with other handlers, including studio executives in charge of the star's next big project. Suddenly, negotiations stalled.

Elizabeth Taylor? Julia Roberts? The women of "Melrose Place"? No, that little photo-shoot nightmare involved getting Lassie— Lassie!—to pose.

It epitomizes, however, the new pecking order among TV's top dogs, suddenly superbig, superhot. Superdogs. New power pooches—including Comet and Barkley from "Full House," Eddie from "Frasier," and Murray from "Mad About You"[1]—are forcing Lassie to make room as they paw their way into the ranks of Hollywood's power players.

How powerful? Well, their newfound clout[2] is propelling the canine craze into daytime. Vinnie, a lovable one-eared mutt, has the run of ABC's new daytime talk show "Mike & Maty." The dog often sits on Maty's lap during interviews. Another talk show is going even further by giving its bowwow top billing: On "Pet Department," on the fX channel, Jack the Dog is—hang onto your leash—the *co-host.* "The other host, Steve Walker, is human," explains the show's publicist.

It's a Cinderella story for many of these dogs. Vinnie was rescued from the pound.

---

1. **"Full House,"** . . . **"Frasier,"** . . . **"Mad About You"** television shows popular in the 1990s.
2. **clout** (klout) n. power; influence.

Eddie was given up by his owners because he was too much to handle. Seeing a certain something—energy, intelligence, or an unusual personality—Hollywood animal trainers adopt these dogs, refine their skills, and take them to casting calls. If they make the cut and the show is a hit, the transformation from house dog to superdog is complete.

Two-hundred-fifty dollars a day is the standard superdog rate (roughly $31 an hour, if you're doing the math). And then there are the extras. When Lassie makes out-of-town appearances, for example, she (he, really—all eight Lassies have been males) flies first class in a reserved seat. He also has his own traveling companion, a Jack Russell[3] named Mel Gibson. At their hotel, Lassie often drinks bottled water and indulges in gourmet biscuits.

Barkley, the sometimes ferocious-looking Jack Russell terrier with a two-picture deal at MGM, also flies first class, has his own director's chair, and demands ground transport worthy of a visiting dignitary.

Eddie, another scrappy Jack Russell, who regularly unnerves—and upstages—Dr. Frasier Crane with his persistent stare, sports Holiday cologne for dogs and eats "high-quality cooked chicken, hot dogs, and stew beef," according to his trainer, Mathilde deCagny. How good is the chow? "I eat it myself when I get hungry," she says, looking guilty.

It's a glam life. But these are special animals. At the *TV Guide* photo shoot, Barkley puts Murray and Eddie—and every other canine you've ever met—to shame. He's like a little old lady, full of dignity, never making noise or changing position until asked. The setup calls for the three dogs to ape the luxe life[4] in a convertible roadster. "Can you put his hands on the steering wheel?" asks the photographer, who, like the rest of us, has quickly mistaken this animal for a human being. "He doesn't have hands," says his trainer, laughing. So she poses his paws and he stays there—forever. When Murray gets out of position, when Eddie prematurely jumps out of the car for more food... Barkley drives on.

"That dog is incredible," says the photographer, staring at Barkley. "Easier than most of the people I work with."

---

3. **Jack Russell** small and energetic breed of dog.
4. **ape the luxe life** mimic (ape) the life of luxury.

Connecting Literature and the Media

1. What appealing qualities does the puppy in "Stray" share with the dogs in this article?
2. Why do you think people enjoy television programs with animal actors in them?
3. Do you think the puppy in "Stray" could be trained to become one of "TV's Top Dogs"? Why or why not?

Deborah Starr Seibel

Writer/ producer Deborah Starr Seibel has written extensively for *TV Guide* magazine. She has reviewed many television shows, including *Star Trek, the Next Generation*, and interviewed the stars of *Dr. Quinn, Medicine Woman* and *The Wonder Years*. She was also a co-producer of the 1998–1999 United Paramount Network science-fiction series, *Mercy Point*.

Prepare to Read

Dust of Snow ◆ My Picture-Gallery ◆ Saying Yes

Take It to the Net

Visit www.phschool.com
for interactive activities
and instruction related to
these selections, including
- background
- graphic organizers
- literary elements
- reading strategies

Preview

Connecting to the Literature

The poets in this group—Diana Chang, Walt Whitman, and Robert Frost—show how people look at the same things in different ways. Recall times when you and a friend have looked at the same thing in two ways. As you read these poems, you will see that things are not always what they at first seem to be.

Background

Reading poetry is sometimes like solving a riddle: The answer is not always obvious. Diana Chang's poem "Saying Yes" is a series of questions and answers about her Chinese American heritage. In Walt Whitman's poem "My Picture-Gallery," the speaker describes an art gallery, but this gallery is not what you might expect. In Robert Frost's poem "Dust of Snow," a seemingly unimportant event in nature turns the speaker's day completely around.

Literary Analysis

Images in Poetry

In general, poems tend to be more brief than works of prose. As a result, every word takes on increased importance. For this reason, poets make generous use of **images**—word pictures that appeal to the senses. A single image such as the "dust of snow" falling from a hemlock tree can make a memorable impression and stir up memories and associations in a reader's mind.

Comparing Literary Works

"My Picture-Gallery" and "Dust of Snow" are both built around a single, thought-provoking image. "Saying Yes," in contrast, conveys a meaningful message through **dialogue**—conversations among characters.

As you read, use these focus questions to examine the similarities and differences among the poems.

1. What do you picture in your mind as you read each poem?
2. Which poem creates the strongest impression and how does the poet create the impression?

Reading Strategy

Rereading to Clarify

At times, you may need to **reread to clarify,** or make clear, the meaning of expressions used in unusual ways or words with more than one meaning. In the following example, you may be confused by the word *fix'd.* Because *fix'd* can mean "repaired" or "stays in one place," you must clarify which is meant in this line.

> In a little house keep I pictures suspended, it is not a *fix'd* house,

Rereading helps you clarify that here, *fix'd* refers to a house that does not stay in one place. This detail, in turn, helps you clarify that Whitman is not talking about a real house.

As you read these poems, use a chart like the one shown to jot down words or phrases you do not understand on the first reading. Reread and write what you were able to clarify.

Passage with Unclear words

Clarification on Second Reading

Vocabulary Development

rued (rōōd) *v.* regretted (something) (p. 30)

suspended (sə spend´ id) *adj.* hung with a support from above (p. 31)

tableaus (ta blōz´) *n.* dramatic scenes or pictures (p. 31)

Dust of Snow

Robert Frost

The way a crow
Shook down on me
The dust of snow
From a hemlock tree

5   Has given my heart
A change of mood
And saved some part
Of a day I had <u>rued</u>.

rued (rood) *v.* regretted (something)

Robert Frost

(1874–1963)
Robert Frost began writing poetry as a high school student in New England. However, he wasn't recognized as a major poet until his book of poetry, *North of Boston*, became a bestseller. Before becoming a poet, Frost was a farmer.

My Picture-Gallery

Walt Whitman

In a little house keep I pictures <u>suspended</u>, it is not a
    fix'd house,
It is round, it is only a few inches from one side to the other;
Yet behold, it has room for all the shows of the world,
    all memories!
Here the <u>tableaus</u> of life, and here the groupings of death;
5   Here, do you know this? this is cicerone[1] himself,
With finger rais'd he points to the prodigal[2] pictures.

suspended (sə spend´ id)
adj. hung with a support
from above

tableaus (ta blōz´) *n.* dramatic scenes or pictures

---

1. **cicerone** (sis´ ə rō´ nē) *n.* guide who explains the history and important features
of a place to sightseers.
2. **prodigal** (präd´ i gəl) *adj.* very plentiful.

Review and Assess

Thinking About the Selection

1. **Respond:** In "Dust of Snow," Frost describes how he was
   changed by an event in nature. What other events in
   nature could change a person in some way?
2. **(a) Recall:** What action changes how the speaker feels?
   (b) Classify: Would you describe this action as
   deliberate or as occurring by chance? Explain.
3. **(a) Recall:** What effect does the crow's action have on
   the speaker? **(b) Draw Conclusions:** Why do you think
   the crow's action has the effect on the speaker that it does?
4. **(a) Recall:** How does the speaker feel before and after the
   crow's action? **(b) Generalize:** What lesson do you think the
   speaker learned from this experience?
5. **(a) Support:** What details in "My Picture-Gallery" reveal
   that the picture-gallery to which Whitman is referring is
   his own mind? **(b) Evaluate:** Do you think that a "picture-
   gallery" is a strong choice for an image to describe a person's
   mind? Why or why not? **(c) Extend:** If you were to choose an
   image to capture your own memories, what would it be? Why?

Walt Whitman

(1819–1892)

Walt Whitman
changed American
poetry. Before his
famous book
Leaves of Grass
came out in 1855,
American poets had
been imitating British
poets. With his unrhymed
verse and irregular rhythms,
Whitman burst on the
scene with a new and sometimes shocking voice. He
held many different jobs
and proudly declared in one
of his poems that he was
"an American, one of the
roughs . . ."

Saying Yes

Diana Chang

"Are you Chinese?"
"Yes."

"American?"
"Yes."

5 "*Really* Chinese?"
"No . . . not quite."

"*Really* American?"
"Well, actually, you see . . ."

But I would rather say
10 yes.
Not neither-nor,
not maybe,
but both, and not only

The homes I've had,
15 the ways I am

I'd rather say it
twice,
yes.

▲ **Critical Viewing**
Do you think the poet (pictured here) likes what she sees in the mirror? Explain. **[Infer]**

Diana Chang

(b. 1934)
Diana Chang admits that she is "preoccupied" with identity. Although she sometimes thinks of her Chinese American identity as confusing and lopsided, she also celebrates it by exploring it in her novels and poems. Chang's self-expression doesn't stop with writing. She also paints and has exhibited her paintings in art galleries.

Review and Assess

Thinking About the Selection

1. **Respond:** Have you ever asked or answered questions like the ones in "Saying Yes"? Explain.

2. **(a) Recall:** What questions is someone asking the speaker in "Saying Yes"? **(b) Infer:** Why do these questions make the poet feel uneasy?

3. **(a) Recall:** What would the poet rather say twice? **(b) Infer:** How does the poet feel about saying it? **(c) Extend:** What do the poet's responses reveal about her outlook on her own identity? **(d) Evaluate:** Do you feel that this is a good outlook? Why or why not?

Review and Assess

Literary Analysis

Images in Poetry

1. What are the key details of the **image** in "My Picture-Gallery"?
2. A **metaphor** is an implied comparison between two strikingly dissimilar things. Explain how Whitman uses the central image in "My Picture-Gallery" as part of a metaphor.
3. Although Robert Frost's poem contains only a single image, the image appeals to several senses. In a chart like the one below, write *yes* or *no* to indicate the senses to which Frost appeals. Provide an explanation for each answer.

Sight	Hearing	Smell	Taste	Touch

Comparing Literary Works

4. What do you picture in your mind as you read each poem?
5. Both "My Picture-Gallery" and "Dust of Snow" are built around a single image. What is different about the way the two poets present the images to readers?
6. All three poems present a vivid impression of the **speaker,** the voice behind the words in a poem. Explain how each speaker reveals information about herself or himself.

Reading Strategy

Rereading to Clarify

7. Which poem creates the strongest impression and how does the poet create the impression?
8. (a) What are two possible meanings of the word *dust*? (b) What does it mean in Frost's poem "Dust of Snow"?
9. (a) What does *suspended* mean in "My Picture-Gallery"? (b) How does this meaning help you clarify Whitman's description of his imagination and memory?

Extending Understanding

10. **Art Connection:** Compare and contrast the ways artists and poets capture images.

Quick Review

An **image** is a word picture that appeals to one or more of the senses. To review images in poetry, see page 29.

When you **reread to clarify,** you read a second time to better understand the meaning of words and phrases.

 Take It to the Net

www.phschool.com
Take the interactive self-test online to check your understanding of these selections.

Integrate Language Skills

Vocabulary Development Lesson

Concept Development: Homophones

Homophones sound alike but have different meanings and are often spelled differently. In "Dust of Snow," *rued* sounds like *rude*. Although the two words sound the same, one means *regret-ted* and the other means *not polite*. On your paper, write the correct homophone for each rhyme.

1. When asked who she *really* was, the poet (side, sighed). / She thought the ques-tioner was not on her (side, sighed).
2. The spot is (bear, bare) / Where I placed the sketch of the (bear, bare).
3. The crow in the hemlock was (rude, rued), / But he saved a day the poet had (rude, rued).

Fluency: Sentence Completions

Fill in each sentence with one of these words: *rued, suspended, tableaus*.

1. He saw paintings ____?____ from hooks.
2. The pictures included ____?____ of everyday life.
3. Whitman never ____?____ the time he spent in galleries.

Spelling Strategy

When adding *-ed* or *-ing* to words ending in *ue*, drop the *e*:

rue + *-ed* = rued   argue + *-ing* = arguing

1. issue + *-ing* = ____?____
2. sue + *-ed* = ____?____
3. glue + *-ing* = ____?____

Grammar Lesson

Common and Proper Nouns

A **common noun** names a category or type of person, place, or thing. A **proper noun** gives the name of a specific person, place, or thing.

Common nouns are capitalized only when they are the first word in a sentence. Proper nouns are always capitalized.

Common Nouns	book museum person
Proper Nouns	*The Poetry of Robert Frost* J. Paul Getty Museum Walt Whitman

Practice Copy each sentence. Underline the common nouns. Circle and capitalize the proper nouns.

1. The speaker talks about a little house.
2. The poem was written by walt whitman.
3. He was born in the united states.
4. Some people say he was the most influen-tial poet in our country.
5. In his poem, frost describes a funny moment.

Writing Application Use the information in the author biographies to answer the following ques-tions in complete sentences. Capitalize proper nouns. Underline any common nouns you use.

1. Where did Walt Whitman grow up?
2. Who wrote "Dust of Snow"?
3. Where did he live as a high-school student?

*W*G *Prentice Hall Writing and Grammar Connection: Chapter 14, Section 1*

Writing Lesson

Description of a Scene

Frost describes a scene in nature that made a difference to the speaker in the poem. Write a composition about a scene in nature that you remember well or that made some difference to you.

Prewriting Include **sensory details,** words that appeal to the senses, to bring your scene to life. To get started, list some of the sensory details in your scene in an organizer like the following.

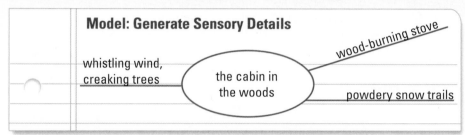

Model: Generate Sensory Details

whistling wind, creaking trees — the cabin in the woods — wood-burning stove — powdery snow trails

Drafting Include details that create a vivid picture of the scene and the impression it made on you. For example, use *refreshing* breeze, *oppressive* heat, *magnificent, towering* cliffs.

Revising Check that you included details to support what you claimed. If you say the scene was awe-inspiring, make sure you give details that show that it was. Add details, if necessary.

W̶G̶ Prentice Hall Writing and Grammar Connection: Chapter 6, Sections 1–6

Extension Activities

Listening and Speaking With two classmates, perform "Saying Yes" as a **brief drama**. Have one person ask the questions, another answer, and a third read lines 9–18. Rehearse the poem, adjusting your tone of voice to indicate what the speaker is feeling. For example:

- Speak forcefully to indicate confidence.
- Speak hesitantly to indicate uncertainty.
- Use nonverbal gestures, such as nodding your head, to reinforce positive responses.

Research and Technology Whitman describes the mind as a museum of memories. Find an actual diagram of the human brain and prepare your own **map or diagram** of the brain. Use labels and color-coding to indicate the function of each part. Call special attention to the area that controls memory. Include a list of sources on which you based your map.

 **Take It to the Net**   www.phschool.com

Go online for an additional research activity using the Internet.

Prepare to Read

Jeremiah's Song

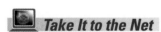 **Take It to the Net**

Visit www.phschool.com for interactive activities and instruction related to "Jeremiah's Song," including
- background
- graphic organizers
- literary elements
- reading strategies

Preview

Connecting to the Literature

In "Jeremiah's Song," characters use their talents in music and story-telling to express their feelings and their heritage. Think about the activities or talents that allow you to express yourself.

Background

The blues, the type of music played in "Jeremiah's Song," originated as folk music of African Americans. The people who "invented" the blues are not famous, but this musical form has influenced generations of musicians around the world.

Literary Analysis

First-Person Point of View

In a story told from the **first-person point of view,** the narrator, or person telling the story, participates in the action and refers to himself or herself as "I." Read the following example written in the first person.

> I was the one who loved Grandpa Jeremiah the most and she [Deacon Turner's wife] didn't hardly even know him so I didn't see why she was crying.

Notice that the narrator also includes details of his thoughts and feelings.

Connecting Literary Elements

In a story told from the **third-person point of view,** the narrator does not participate in the action and can tell things that the characters do not know. For example, a third-person narrator might tell why Deacon Turner's wife cries.

As you read "Jeremiah's Song," explore point of view by answering the following focus questions.

1. What details in "Jeremiah's Song" can only the first-person narrator know?

2. How might the story be different if it were told from a third-person point of view?

Reading Strategy

Using Context to Determine Meaning

When you encounter a word that looks familiar but is used in an unfamiliar way, the **context**—or surrounding words, sentences, and paragraphs—can help you figure out its meaning. In the following example, "fixing" is used in an unusual way.

Word	Clue	Meaning
fixing	"to die"	getting ready

> She didn't have no use for Macon even when things was going right, and with Grandpa Jeremiah *fixing* to die, I just knowed she wasn't gonna be liking him.

The context indicates that *fixing* means "getting ready" rather than "repairing." As you read, complete a chart to record clues that help you determine the meaning of an unfamiliar word or words.

Vocabulary Development

diagnosis (dī ag nō′ sis) *n.* explanation of or prediction about a person's medical condition (p. 40)

disinfect (dis′ in fekt′) *n.* dialect, or regional language, for disinfectant, a substance that kills germs (p. 41)

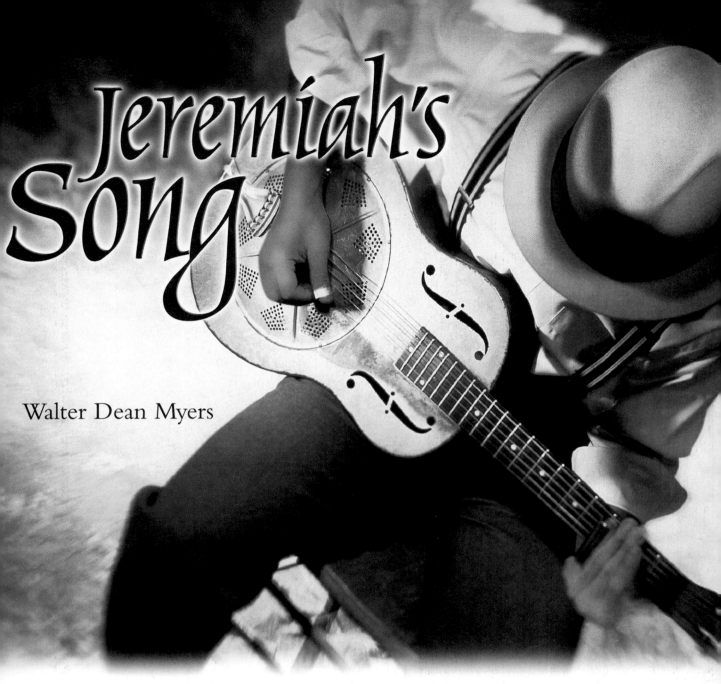

Jeremiah's Song

Walter Dean Myers

I knowed my cousin Ellie was gonna be mad when Macon Smith come around to the house. She didn't have no use for Macon even when things was going right, and when Grandpa Jeremiah was fixing to die I just knowed she wasn't gonna be liking him hanging around. Grandpa Jeremiah raised Ellie after her folks died and they used to be real close. Then she got to go on to college and when she come back the first year she was different. She didn't want to hear all them stories he used to tell her anymore. Ellie said the stories wasn't true, and that's why she didn't want to hear them.

Literary Analysis
First-Person Point of View
How do you know that the story is told from a first-person point of view?

I didn't know if they was true or not. Tell the truth I didn't think much on it either way, but I liked to hear them stories. Grandpa Jeremiah said they wasn't stories anyway, they was songs.

"They the songs of my people," he used to say.

I didn't see how they was songs, not regular songs anyway. Every little thing we did down in Curry seemed to matter to Ellie that first summer she come home from college. You couldn't do nothin' that was gonna please her. She didn't even come to church much. 'Course she come on Sunday or everybody would have had a regular fit, but she didn't come on Thursday nights and she didn't come on Saturday even though she used to sing in the gospel choir.

"I guess they teachin' her somethin' worthwhile up there at Greensboro," Grandpa Jeremiah said to Sister Todd. "I sure don't see what it is, though."

"You ain't never had no book learning, Jeremiah," Sister Todd shot back. She wiped at where a trickle of sweat made a little path through the white dusting powder she put on her chest to keep cool. "Them old ways you got ain't got nothing for these young folks."

"I guess you right," Grandpa Jeremiah said.

He said it but I could see he didn't like it none. He was a big man with a big head and had most all his hair even if it was white. All that summer, instead of sitting on the porch telling stories like he used to when I was real little, he would sit out there by himself while Ellie stayed in the house and watched the television or read a book. Sometimes I would think about asking him to tell me one of them stories he used to tell but they was too scary now that I didn't have nobody to sleep with but myself. I asked Ellie to sleep with me but she wouldn't.

"You're nine years old," she said, sounding real proper. "You're old enough to sleep alone."

I knew that. I just wanted her to sleep with me because I liked sleeping with her. Before she went off to college she used to put cocoa butter on her arms and face and it would smell real nice. When she come back from college she put something else on, but that smelled nice too.

It was right after Ellie went back to school that Grandpa Jeremiah had him a stroke and Macon started coming around. I think his mama probably made him come at first, but you could see he liked it. Macon had always been around, sitting over near the stuck window at church or going on the blueberry truck when we went picking down at Mister Gregory's place. For a long time he was just another kid, even though he was older'n me, but then, all of a sudden, he growed something fierce. I used to be up to his shoulder one time and then, before I could turn around good, I was only up to his shirt pocket. He changed too. When he used to

Reading Strategy
Using Context to Determine Meaning
How do the words "little path" provide a clue to the meaning of *trickle*?

Reading Check

How does the narrator feel about Grandpa's songs?

just hang around with the other boys and play ball or shoot at birds he would laugh a lot. He didn't laugh so much anymore and I figured he was just about grown. When Grandpa got sick he used to come around and help out with things around the house that was too hard for me to do. I mean, I could have done all the chores, but it would just take me longer.

When the work for the day was finished and the sows[1] fed, Grandpa would kind of ease into one of his stories and Macon, he would sit and listen to them and be real interested. I didn't mind listening to the stories when Grandpa told them to Macon because he would be telling them in the middle of the afternoon and they would be past my mind by the time I had to go to bed.

Macon had an old guitar he used to mess with, too. He wasn't too bad on it, and sometimes Grandpa would tell him to play us a tune. He could play something he called "the Delta Blues" real good, but when Sister Todd or somebody from the church come around he'd play "Precious Lord" or "Just a Closer Walk With Thee."

Grandpa Jeremiah had been feeling poorly from that stroke, and one of his legs got a little drag to it. Just about the time Ellie come from school the next summer he was real sick. He was breathing loud so you could hear it even in the next room and he would stay in bed a lot even when there was something that needed doing or fixing.

"I don't think he's going to make it much longer," Dr. Crawford said. "The only thing I can do is to give him something for the pain."

"Are you sure of your <u>diagnosis</u>?" Ellie asked. She was sitting around the table with Sister Todd, Deacon Turner, and his little skinny yellow wife.

Dr. Crawford looked at Ellie like he was surprised to hear her talking. "Yes, I'm sure," he said. "He had tests a few weeks ago and his condition was bad then."

"How much time he got?" Sister Todd asked.

"Maybe a week or two at best," Dr. Crawford said.

When he said that, Deacon Turner's wife started crying and goin' on and I give her a hard look but she just went on. I was the one who loved Grandpa Jeremiah the most and she didn't hardly even know him so I didn't see why she was crying.

Everybody started tiptoeing around the house after that. They would go in and ask Grandpa Jeremiah if he was comfortable and stuff like that or take him some food or a cold glass of lemonade. Sister Todd come over and stayed with us. Mostly what she did is make supper and do a lot of praying, which was good because I figured that maybe God would do something to make Grandpa Jeremiah well. When she wasn't doing that she was

Literary Analysis
First-Person Point of View What thoughts and feelings are shared by the narrator?

diagnosis (dĭ əg nō´ sis) *n.* explanation of or prediction about a person's medical condition

---

1. sows (souz) *n.* full-grown female pigs.

piecing on a fancy quilt she was making for some white people in Wilmington.

Ellie, she went around asking everybody how they felt about Dr. Crawford and then she went into town and asked about the tests and things. Sister Jenkins asked her if she thought she knowed more than Dr. Crawford, and Ellie rolled her eyes at her, but Sister Jenkins was reading out her Bible and didn't make no notice of it.

Then Macon come over.

He had been away on what he called "a little piece of a job" and hadn't heard how bad off Grandpa Jeremiah was. When he come over he talked to Ellie and she told him what was going on and then he got him a soft drink from the refrigerator and sat out on the porch and before you know it he was crying.

You could look at his face and tell the difference between him sweating and the tears. The sweat was close against his skin and shiny and the tears come down fatter and more sparkly.

Macon sat on the porch, without saying a word, until the sun went down and the crickets started chirping and carrying on. Then he went in to where Grandpa Jeremiah was and stayed in there for a long time.

Sister Todd was saying that Grandpa Jeremiah needed his rest and Ellie went in to see what Macon was doing. Then she come out real mad.

"He got Grandpa telling those old stories again," Ellie said. "I told him Grandpa needed his rest and for him not to be staying all night."

He did leave soon, but bright and early the next morning Macon was back again. This time he brought his guitar with him and he went on in to Grandpa Jeremiah's room. I went in, too.

Grandpa Jeremiah's room smelled terrible. It was all closed up so no drafts could get on him and the whole room was smelled down with <u>disinfect</u> and medicine. Grandpa Jeremiah lay propped up on the bed and he was so gray he looked scary. His hair wasn't combed down and his head on the pillow with his white hair sticking out was enough to send me flying if Macon hadn't been there. He was skinny, too. He looked like his skin got loose on his bones, and when he lifted his arms, it hung down like he was just wearing it instead of it being a part of him.

Macon sat slant-shouldered with his guitar across his lap. He was messin' with the guitar, not making any music, but just going over the strings as Grandpa talked.

"Old Carrie went around out back to where they kept the pigs penned up and she felt a cold wind across her face. . . ." Grandpa Jeremiah was telling the story about how a old woman out-tricked the Devil and got her son back. I had

disinfect (dis′ in fekt′) *n.* dialect, or regional language, for disinfectant, a substance that kills germs

Reading Check

Why is Ellie upset?

heard the story before, and I knew it was pretty scary. "When she felt the cold breeze she didn't blink nary an eye, but looked straight ahead. . . ."

All the time Grandpa Jeremiah was talking I could see Macon fingering his guitar. I tried to imagine what it would be like if he was actually plucking the strings. I tried to fix my mind on that because I didn't like the way the story went with the old woman wrestling with the Devil.

We sat there for nearly all the afternoon until Ellie and Sister Todd come in and said that supper was ready. Me and Macon went out and ate some collard greens, ham hocks,[2] and rice. Then Macon he went back in and listened to some more of Grandpa's stories until it was time for him to go home. I wasn't about to go in there and listen to no stories at night.

Dr. Crawford come around a few days later and said that Grandpa Jeremiah was doing a little better.

"You think the Good Lord gonna pull him through?" Sister Todd asked.

"I don't tell the Good Lord what He should or should not be doing," Dr. Crawford said, looking over at Sister Todd and at Ellie. "I just said that *my* patient seems to be doing okay for his condition."

"He been telling Macon all his stories," I said.

"Macon doesn't seem to understand that Grandpa Jeremiah needs his strength," Ellie said. "Now that he's improving, we don't want him to have a setback."

"No use in stopping him from telling his stories," Dr. Crawford said. "If it makes him feel good it's as good as any medicine I can give him."

I saw that this didn't set with Ellie, and when Dr. Crawford had left I asked her why.

"Dr. Crawford means well," she said, "but we have to get away from the kind of life that keeps us in the past."

She didn't say why we should be trying to get away from the stories and I really didn't care too much. All I knew was that when Macon was sitting in the room with Grandpa Jeremiah I wasn't nearly as scared as I used to be when it was just me and Ellie listening. I told that to Macon.

"You getting to be a big man, that's all," he said.

That was true. Me and Macon was getting to be good friends, too. I didn't even mind so much when he started being friends with Ellie later. It seemed kind of natural, almost like Macon was supposed to be there with us instead of just visiting.

Reading Strategy
Using Context to Determine Meaning
What context clues help you figure out the meaning of *fingering*?

Literary Analysis
First-Person Narrator
What does the narrator observe that no one else could observe?

---

2. **collard greens, ham hocks** leafy green vegetables and joints from a pig's leg; favorite southern dishes.

Harmonizing, 1979, Robert Gwathmey, Courtesy Terry Dintenfass Gallery, © Estate of Robert Gwathmey, Licensed by VAGA, New York, NY

◀ **Critical Viewing**
What story characters
might be represented
in this picture?

Grandpa wasn't getting no better, but he wasn't getting no worse, either.

"You liking Macon now?" I asked Ellie when we got to the middle of July. She was dishing out a plate of smothered chops for him and I hadn't even heard him ask for anything to eat.

"Macon's funny," Ellie said, not answering my question. "He's in there listening to all of those old stories like he's really interested in them. It's almost as if he and Grandpa Jeremiah are talking about something more than the stories, a secret language."

I didn't think I was supposed to say anything about that to Macon, but once, when Ellie, Sister Todd, and Macon were out on the porch shelling butter beans after Grandpa got tired and was resting, I went into his room and told him what Ellie had said.

"She said that?" Grandpa Jeremiah's face was skinny and old looking but his eyes looked like a baby's, they was so bright.

"Right there in the kitchen is where she said it," I said. "And I don't know what it mean but I was wondering about it."

✓**Reading Check**

What does the narrator
tell Macon?

"I didn't think she had any feeling for them stories," Grandpa Jeremiah said. "If she think we talking secrets, maybe she don't."

"I think she getting a feeling for Macon," I said,

"That's okay, too," Grandpa Jeremiah said. "They both young."

"Yeah, but them stories you be telling, Grandpa, they about old people who lived a long time ago," I said.

"Well, those the folks you got to know about," Grandpa Jeremiah said. "You think on what those folks been through, and what they was feeling, and you add it up with what you been through and what you been feeling, then you got you something."

"What you got Grandpa?"

"You got you a bridge," Grandpa said. "And a meaning. Then when things get so hard you about to break, you can sneak across that bridge and see some folks who went before you and see how they didn't break. Some got bent and some got twisted and a few fell along the way, but they didn't break."

"Am I going to break, Grandpa?"

Reading Strategy
Using Context to Determine Meaning
What context clues might help you figure out the meaning of *break* as it is used here?

Springtime Rain, 1975, Ogden M. Pleissner, Ogden M. Pleissner Estate Marion G. Pleissner Trust, Bankers Trust Company

▲ **Critical Viewing** Which characters from the story could be represented in this painting? **[Connect]**

"You? As strong as you is?" Grandpa Jeremiah pushed himself up on his elbow and give me a look. "No way you going to break, boy. You gonna be strong as they come. One day you gonna tell all them stories I told you to your young'uns and they'll be as strong as you."

"Suppose I ain't got no stories, can I make some up?"

"Sure you can, boy. You make 'em up and twist 'em around. Don't make no mind. Long as you got 'em."

"Is that what Macon is doing?" I asked. "Making up stories to play on his guitar?"

"He'll do with 'em what he see fit, I suppose," Grandpa Jeremiah said. "Can't ask more than that from a man."

It rained the first three days of August. It wasn't a hard rain but it rained anyway. The mailman said it was good for the crops over East but I didn't care about that so I didn't pay him no mind. What I did mind was when it rain like that the field mice come in and get in things like the flour bin and I always got the blame for leaving it open.

When the rain stopped I was pretty glad. Macon come over and sat with Grandpa and had something to eat with us. Sister Todd come over, too.

"How Grandpa doing?" Sister Todd asked. "They been asking about him in the church."

"He's doing all right," Ellie said.

"He's kind of quiet today," Macon said. "He was just talking about how the hogs needed breeding."

"He must have run out of stories to tell," Sister Todd said. "He'll be repeating on himself like my father used to do. That's the way I *hear* old folks get."

Everybody laughed at that because Sister Todd was pretty old, too. Maybe we was all happy because the sun was out after so much rain. When Sister Todd went in to take Grandpa Jeremiah a plate of potato salad with no mayonnaise like he liked it, she told him about how people was asking for him and he told her to tell them he was doing okay and to remember him in their prayers.

Sister Todd came over the next afternoon, too, with some rhubarb pie with cheese on it, which is my favorite pie. When she took a piece into Grandpa Jeremiah's room she come right out again and told Ellie to go fetch the Bible.

It was a hot day when they had the funeral. Mostly everybody was there. The church was hot as anything, even though they had the window open. Some yellowjacks flew in and buzzed around Sister Todd's niece and then around Deacon Turner's wife and settled right on her hat and stayed there until we all stood and sang "Soon-a Will Be Done."

At the graveyard Macon played "Precious Lord" and I cried hard

Literary Analysis
First-Person and Third-Person Point of View
How does the first-person point of view make this narration personal?

Reading Check
What does Grandpa explain about his stories?

even though I told myself that I wasn't going to cry the way Ellie and Sister Todd was, but it was such a sad thing when we left and Grandpa Jeremiah was still out to the grave that I couldn't help it.

During the funeral and all, Macon kind of told everybody where to go and where to sit and which of the three cars to ride in. After it was over he come by the house and sat on the front porch and played on his guitar. Ellie was standing leaning against the rail and she was crying but it wasn't a hard crying. It was a soft crying, the kind that last inside of you for a long time.

Macon was playing a tune I hadn't heard before. I thought it might have been what he was working at when Grandpa Jeremiah was telling him those stories and I watched his fingers but I couldn't tell if it was or not. It wasn't nothing special, that tune Macon was playing, maybe halfway between them Delta blues he would do when Sister Todd wasn't around and something you would play at church. It was something different and something the same at the same time. I watched his fingers go over that guitar and figured I could learn that tune one day if I had a mind to.

Review and Assess

Thinking About the Selection

1. **Respond:** What would you say to the narrator to comfort him after his grandfather's death?

2. **(a) Recall:** What is the relationship of Ellie to the narrator? **(b) Interpret:** Describe the narrator's feelings about Ellie.

3. **(a) Recall:** Why did Ellie like to hear Grandpa Jeremiah's songs? **(b) Speculate:** Why is Ellie's attitude different when she returns from college?

4. **(a) Recall:** Why doesn't Ellie want Macon around? **(b) Draw Conclusions:** Why does the narrator like Macon?

5. **(a) Recall:** How does Macon feel about Grandpa? **(b) Infer:** In what ways does Macon help Grandpa Jeremiah?

6. **Evaluate:** The narrator, Ellie, and Macon each behave differently toward Grandpa. Who do you think behaves most appropriately and why?

7. **Speculate:** Macon seems to understand Grandpa Jeremiah's "song." What role do you think these songs will play in the lives of Ellie, Macon, and the narrator?

8. **Take a Position:** How important do you think it is for traditional stories and songs like those of Grandpa Jeremiah to live on for future generations?

Walter Dean Myers

(b. 1937)

You would expect a preschooler to prefer picture books over other kinds of reading materials. Young Walter Dean Myers didn't. He was reading at age four. By age five, he was reading a newspaper every day. In spite of this impressive start with words, Myers didn't think that writing would be his career. Then, in his twenties, he won a writing contest. He hasn't stopped writing since—mostly about his heritage and his experiences growing up in Harlem, a part of New York City. Like the child in this story, Myers understands loss: He was three years old when his mother died.

Review and Assess

Literary Analysis

First-Person Point of View

1. Who is the narrator of "Jeremiah's Song"?
2. How does the **first-person** narration make this story more personal?
3. Describe the narrator's thoughts or feelings about two of the other characters. Use a chart like the following.

Character's name	What the narrator says	What the narrator thinks	What the narrator does

Connecting Literary Elements

4. Identify at least two details that only the narrator could tell you—that Macon or Ellie could not.
5. Explain how you think the story might be different if it had been told from a **third-person** point of view.
6. Do you think the story would have been more or less effective if it had been told from a third-person point of view? Why?

Reading Strategy

Using Context to Determine Meaning

7. Compare the meanings of the two italicized words in the following sentences.
   (a) Grandpa and Ellie used to be real *close* before Ellie went away.
   (b) Grandpa asked Macon to *close* the door.
8. Identify the clues in the sentences above that help you determine which way to say the italicized word and to know what it means.
9. Using the chart you created as you read, list at least three unfamiliar words you encountered in this story, and explain how context clues can be used to determine their meanings.

Extending Understanding

10. **Social Studies Connection:** What story do you know that preserves something from the past?
11. **Evaluate:** Are stories and songs a good way to pass culture along from generation to generation? Why or why not?

Quick Review

In **first-person point of view,** the narrator takes part in the action and tells the story from his or her perspective. To review first-person point of view, see page 37.

In **third-person point of view,** the narrator does not participate in the action.

The **context** of a word is the situation in which it is used—the words, sentences, and paragraphs around the word.

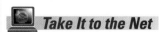 **Take It to the Net**

www.phschool.com
Take the interactive self-test online to check your understanding of the selection.

Integrate Language Skills

Vocabulary Development Lesson

Word Analysis: Latin Prefix *dis-*

The Latin prefix *dis-* changes the meaning of a word to its opposite meaning. On your paper, write the opposite of each word by adding or removing *dis-* from it.

1. agree, ____?____
2. displace, ____?____
3. respectful, ____?____
4. disservice, ____?____

Spelling Strategy

A prefix never changes the spelling of the original word—even when the word begins with a vowel. For example, when you add *dis-* to *infect*, you write *disinfect*, not *dissinfect*.

On your paper, add *dis-* to the following words:

1. trust
2. connect
3. obey
4. interested

Concept Development: Word Choice

On your paper, respond to each of the following questions containing vocabulary words from the story. Explain each response.

1. What might you do when you are given a *diagnosis*?
2. Why should a doctor *disinfect* his or her hands?
3. What are the similarities and differences between a *diagnosis* provided by a doctor and one given by an auto mechanic?
4. Why is it better to clean and *disinfect* a counter than to simply wipe it down with a cloth?

Grammar Lesson

Pronouns

A **pronoun** is a word that takes the place of a noun or another pronoun. Writers use pronouns to avoid the awkwardness of repeating the same noun over and over.

Personal pronouns refer to specific nouns that are named elsewhere in the sentence or paragraph. **Interrogative pronouns** are used in questions. **Indefinite pronouns** can be plural or singular, depending on how they are used.

Personal Pronouns	Interrogative pronouns	Indefinite pronouns
he, she, him, her, they, them, it	who, whom	some, other, none

Practice Copy the following sentences on your paper. Underline the pronoun(s). Identify the type of each pronoun.

1. After Ellie went to college, she didn't go to church much.
2. Grandpa was sick, so Macon visited him.
3. Who will learn the stories?
4. Some like to listen, others do not.
5. To whom did Grandpa tell the story?

Writing Application Revise the following paragraph by replacing nouns with pronouns.

The narrator is sometimes frightened by Grandpa's stories, but the narrator isn't scared when Macon listens, too. The narrator and Macon enjoy Grandpa's stories. Ellie used to enjoy the stories, but since Ellie went to college, Ellie doesn't listen anymore.

W̶G Prentice Hall Writing and Grammar Connection: Chapter 23

Writing Lesson

Character Description

In "Jeremiah's Song," the young grandson describes all the characters. Choose a character and write a brief description based on what you read in the story.

Prewriting Use a cluster diagram like the one shown to list details that describe the character—the character's appearance, actions, and personality.

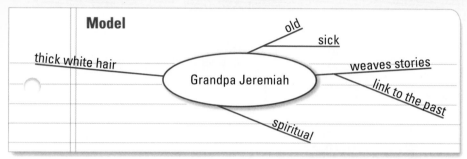

Model
old
sick
thick white hair
Grandpa Jeremiah
weaves stories
link to the past
spiritual

Drafting Start with a paragraph that introduces the character and sums up your overall impression. Follow with paragraphs that support your impression. Focus on using precise language to create a strong image. For example, "Grandpa looks bad" is not precise. "Grandpa's skin hung loosely from his body" paints an image that helps your reader see Grandpa.

Revising Look through your draft for vague words like *good* and *nice*. Replace them with words or phrases that describe the character more precisely.

W_G Prentice Hall Writing and Grammar Connection: Chapter 6, Section 2

Extension Activities

Listening and Speaking With two others, **role-play** a conversation among Ellie, the narrator, and Macon. Have each character tell how he or she feels about Grandpa's stories.

- Find details in the story that indicate how your character feels about the stories.
- Come up with a rough idea of how to get the conversation started.
- Role-play the conversation. Use facial expressions and gestures for emphasis.
- After the role-play, explain to one another what you thought each character was feeling.

Research and Technology Research the music of the "blues." Use print and media resources to find information about the people who made the "blues" famous. Then create a **timeline** including dates, names, and places for this music form. Include significant events such as

- birth years of musicians
- years musicians recorded
- other significant world events for context.

 **Take It to the Net**   www.phschool.com

Go online for an additional research activity using the Internet.

Prepare to Read

The King of Mazy May

 Take It to the Net

Visit www.phschool.com for interactive activities and instruction related to "The King of Mazy May," including
- background
- graphic organizers
- literary elements
- reading strategies

Preview

Connecting to the Literature

At times, you have probably stood up for a friend or defended someone who was being treated unfairly. In "The King of Mazy May" by Jack London, a young boy in the wilderness protects the property of a friend from thieves.

Background

In 1896, George Carmack found gold in the Klondike region of northwestern Canada. His find began with a quarter ounce of the precious metal—equal in value to what an average worker could earn in a week! Carmack was followed by thousands of others. Most found hardship, but no gold. In Jack London's short story, dangerous outlaws prey on gold-seekers in the Klondike.

Literary Analysis

Conflict Between Characters

A conflict is a struggle between opposing forces. A **conflict between characters** occurs when characters with different goals battle each other to achieve their goals.

In "The King of Mazy May," men who are desperate for gold battle a boy who is intent on justice. While reading "The King of Mazy May," identify the conflict by asking yourself the following focus questions:

1. How do different goals cause the strangers and Walt to clash?
2. What are two possible outcomes of the conflict?

Connecting Literary Elements

The **resolution** is the way the conflict turns out. In a story involving a conflict among characters, the resolution involves which character "wins." As you read "The King of Mazy May," try to predict how the conflict will be resolved. Use a chart like this one to track details that lead you to expect a specific resolution.

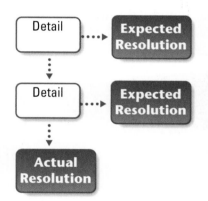

Reading Strategy

Recognizing Signal Words

Signal words indicate order of events and relationships among ideas and details. For example, the word *but* signals that the next idea differs from what you've just read. The word *next* indicates sequence of events.

- **Signal Words Indicating Time Use**
  first   then   after   before
- **Signal Words Indicating Cause and Effect**
  because   as a result
- **Signal Words Indicating Spatial Relationships**
  above   below   on top

As you read, pay close attention to signal words and note what they indicate about the relationships among details.

Vocabulary Development

toil (toil) *n.* hard work (p. 53)

endured (en doord´) *v.* suffered through (p. 53)

prospectors (prä´ spekt´ erz) *n.* people who make their living searching for valuable ores, such as gold (p. 53)

liable (lī´ ə bəl) *adj.* likely (to do something or have something happen to one) (p. 54)

poising (poiz´ iŋ) *adj.* balancing (p. 56)

declined (di klīnd´) *v.* refused (p. 57)

summit (sum´ it) *n.* highest part (p. 59)

The King of Mazy May

Jack London

Walt Masters is not a very large boy, but there is manliness in his make-up, and he himself, although he does not know a great deal that most boys know, knows much that other boys do not know. He has never seen a train of cars nor an elevator in his life, and for that matter he has never once looked upon a cornfield, a plow, a cow, or even a chicken. He has never had a pair of shoes on his feet, nor gone to a picnic or a party, nor talked to a girl. But he has seen the sun at midnight, watched the ice jams on one of the mightiest of rivers, and

▼ **Critical Viewing**
Why is it difficult to tell if these men are honest stakeholders or if they are claim jumpers?
[Generalize]

CLEAN-UP ON DISCOVERY = ANVIL CREEK

played beneath the northern lights,[1] the one white child in thousands of square miles of frozen wilderness.

Walt has walked all the fourteen years of his life in suntanned, moose-hide moccasins, and he can go to the Indian camps and "talk big" with the men, and trade calico and beads with them for their precious furs. He can make bread without baking powder, yeast, or hops, shoot a moose at three hundred yards, and drive the wild wolf dogs fifty miles a day on the packed trail.

Last of all, he has a good heart, and is not afraid of the darkness and loneliness, of man or beast or thing. His father is a good man, strong and brave, and Walt is growing up like him.

Walt was born a thousand miles or so down the Yukon,[2] in a trading post below the Ramparts. After his mother died, his father and he came up on the river, step by step, from camp to camp, till now they are settled down on the Mazy May Creek in the Klondike[3] country. Last year they and several others had spent much <u>toil</u> and time on the Mazy May, and <u>endured</u> great hardships; the creek, in turn, was just beginning to show up its richness and to reward them for their heavy labor. But with the news of their discoveries, strange men began to come and go through the short days and long nights, and many unjust things they did to the men who had worked so long upon the creek.

Si Hartman had gone away on a moose hunt, to return and find new stakes driven and his claim jumped.[4] George Lukens and his brother had lost their claims in a like manner, having delayed too long on the way to Dawson to record them. In short, it was the old story, and quite a number of the earnest, industrious <u>prospectors</u> had suffered similar losses.

But Walt Masters's father had recorded his claim at the start, so Walt had nothing to fear now that his father had gone on a short trip up the White River prospecting for quartz. Walt was well able to stay by himself in the cabin, cook his three meals a day, and look after things. Not only did he look after his father's claim, but he had agreed to keep an eye on the adjoining one of Loren Hall, who had started for Dawson to record it.

Loren Hall was an old man, and he had no dogs, so he had to travel very slowly. After he had been gone some time, word came up the river that he had broken through the ice at Rosebud Creek and frozen his feet so badly that he would not be able to travel for a

toil (toil) *n.* hard work

endured (en doord´) *v.* suffered through

prospectors (prä´ spekt´ erz) *n.* people who make their living searching for valuable ores, such as gold

✓**Reading Check**

Why did Walt stay behind?

---

1. northern lights glowing bands or streamers of light, sometimes appearing in the night sky of the Northern Hemisphere.
2. Yukon (yoo´ kän´) river flowing through the Yukon Territory of northwest Canada.
3. Klondike (klän´ dīk´) gold-mining region along a tributary of the Yukon River.
4. claim jumped a claim is a piece of land staked out by a miner (stakes are markers driven into the ground to show where the borders of the claim are). A claim that is jumped is stolen by someone else.

couple of weeks. Then Walt Masters received the news that old Loren was nearly all right again, and about to move on afoot for Dawson as fast as a weakened man could.

Walt was worried, however; the claim was <u>liable</u> to be jumped at any moment because of this delay, and a fresh stampede had started in on the Mazy May. He did not like the looks of the newcomers, and one day, when five of them came by with crack dog teams and the lightest of camping outfits, he could see that they were prepared to make speed, and resolved to keep an eye on them. So he locked up the cabin and followed them, being at the same time careful to remain hidden.

He had not watched them long before he was sure that they were professional stampeders, bent on jumping all the claims in sight. Walt crept along the snow at the rim of the creek and saw them change many stakes, destroy old ones, and set up new ones.

In the afternoon, with Walt always trailing on their heels, they came back down the creek, unharnessed their dogs, and went into camp within two claims of his cabin. When he saw them make preparations to cook, he hurried home to get something to eat himself, and then hurried back. He crept so close that he could hear them talking quite plainly, and by pushing the underbrush aside he could catch occasional glimpses of them. They had finished eating and were smoking around the fire.

"The creek is all right, boys," a large, black-bearded man, evidently the leader, said, "and I think the best thing we can do is to pull out tonight. The dogs can follow the trail; besides, it's going to be moonlight. What say you?"

"But it's going to be beastly cold," objected one of the party. "It's forty below zero now."

"An' sure, can't ye keep warm by jumpin' off the sleds an' runnin' after the dogs?" cried an Irishman. "An' who wouldn't? The creek's as rich as a United States mint! Faith, it's an ilegant chanst to be gettin' a run fer yer money! An' if ye don't run, it's mebbe you'll not get the money at all, at all."

"That's it," said the leader. "If we can get to Dawson and record, we're rich men; and there's no telling who's been sneaking along in our tracks, watching us, and perhaps now off to give the alarm. The thing for us to do is to rest the dogs a bit, and then hit the trail as hard as we can. What do you say?"

Evidently the men had agreed with their leader, for Walt Masters could hear nothing but the rattle of the tin dishes which were being washed. Peering out cautiously, he could see the leader studying a piece of paper. Walt knew what it was at a glance—a list of all the unrecorded claims on Mazy May. Any man could get these lists by applying to the gold commissioner at Dawson.

liable (līʹ ə bəl) *adj.* likely (to do something or have something happen to one)

Literary Analysis
Conflict Between Characters From what you know about Walt's character, what conflict might develop between him and these men?

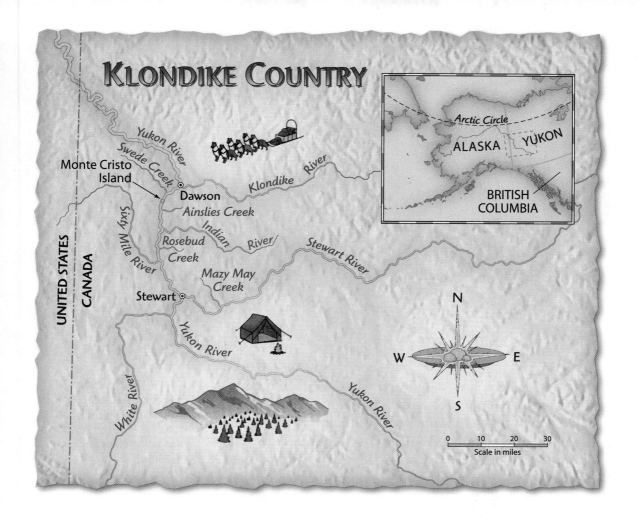

KLONDIKE COUNTRY

"Thirty-two," the leader said, lifting his face to the men. "Thirty-two isn't recorded, and this is thirty-three. Come on; let's take a look at it. I saw somebody had been working on it when we came up this morning."

Three of the men went with him, leaving one to remain in camp. Walt crept carefully after them till they came to Loren Hall's shaft. One of the men went down and built a fire on the bottom to thaw out the frozen gravel, while the others built another fire on the dump and melted water in a couple of gold pans. This they poured into a piece of canvas stretched between two logs, used by Loren Hall in which to wash his gold.

In a short time a couple of buckets of dirt were sent up by the man in the shaft, and Walt could see the others grouped anxiously about their leader as he proceeded to wash it. When this was finished, they stared at the broad streak of black sand and yellow gold grains on the bottom of the pan, and one of them called excitedly for the man who had remained in camp to come. Loren Hall had struck it rich and his claim was not yet recorded. It was plain that they were going to jump it.

▲ **Critical Viewing**
Based on what you have read, why do you think so few towns are settled in this area? **[Connect]**

✓**Reading Check**

What was Walt's reason for following the men?

The King of Mazy May ◆ 55

Walt lay in the snow, thinking rapidly. He was only a boy, but in the face of the threatened injustice to old lame Loren Hall he felt that he must do something. He waited and watched, with his mind made up, till he saw the men begin to square up new stakes. Then he crawled away till out of hearing, and broke into a run for the camp of the stampeders. Walt's father had taken their own dogs with him prospecting, and the boy knew how impossible it was for him to undertake the seventy miles to Dawson without the aid of dogs.

Gaining the camp, he picked out, with an experienced eye, the easiest running sled and started to harness up the stampeders' dogs. There were three teams of six each, and from these he chose ten of the best. Realizing how necessary it was to have a good head dog, he strove to discover a leader amongst them; but he had little time in which to do it, for he could hear the voices of the returning men. By the time the team was in shape and everything ready, the claim-jumpers came into sight in an open place not more than a hundred yards from the trail, which ran down the bed of the creek. They cried out to Walt, but instead of giving heed to them he grabbed up one of their fur sleeping robes, which lay loosely in the snow, and leaped upon the sled.

"Mush! Hi! Mush on!" he cried to the animals, snapping the keen-lashed whip among them.

The dogs sprang against the yoke straps, and the sled jerked under way so suddenly as to almost throw him off. Then it curved into the creek, <u>poising</u> perilously on the runner. He was almost breathless with suspense, when it finally righted with a bound and

▲ **Critical Viewing**
What do you think it would be like to live in this cabin with only these dogs for company? **[Relate]**

Reading Strategy
Recognizing Signal Words What contrasting ideas are connected with the word *but*?

poising (poiz′ iŋ) *adj.* balancing

After Dinner Music, 1988, Scott Kennedy, Courtesy of the Greenwich Workshop Inc.

sprang ahead again. The creek bank was high and he could not see the men, although he could hear their cries and knew they were running to cut him off. He did not dare to think what would happen if they caught him; he just clung to the sled, his heart beating wildly, and watched the snow rim of the bank above him.

Suddenly, over this snow rim came the flying body of the Irishman, who had leaped straight for the sled in a desperate attempt to capture it; but he was an instant too late. Striking on the very rear of it, he was thrown from his feet, backward, into the snow. Yet, with the quickness of a cat, he had clutched the end of the sled with one hand, turned over, and was dragging behind on his breast, swearing at the boy and threatening all kinds of terrible things if he did not stop the dogs; but Walt cracked him sharply across the knuckles with the butt of the dog whip till he let go.

It was eight miles from Walt's claim to the Yukon—eight very crooked miles, for the creek wound back and forth like a snake, "tying knots in itself," as George Lukens said. And because it was so crooked the dogs could not get up their best speed, while the sled ground heavily on its side against the curves, now to the right, now to the left.

Travelers who had come up and down the Mazy May on foot, with packs on their backs, had <u>declined</u> to go round all the bends, and instead had made shortcuts across the narrow necks of creek bottom. Two of his pursuers had gone back to harness the remaining dogs, but the others took advantage of these shortcuts, running on foot, and before he knew it they had almost overtaken him.

"Halt!" they cried after him. "Stop, or we'll shoot!"

But Walt only yelled the harder at the dogs, and dashed around the bend with a couple of revolver bullets singing after him. At the next bend they had drawn up closer still, and the bullets struck uncomfortably near him but at this point the Mazy May straightened out and ran for half a mile as the crow flies. Here the dogs stretched out in their long wolf swing, and the stampeders, quickly winded, slowed down and waited for their own sled to come up.

Looking over his shoulder, Walt reasoned that they had not given up the chase for good, and that they would soon be after him again. So he wrapped the fur robe about him to shut out the stinging air, and lay flat on the empty sled, encouraging the dogs, as he well knew how.

Literary Analysis
Conflict Between Characters What details show that both the Irishman and Walt are determined to achieve their goals?

declined (di klīnd′) *v.* refused

**Reading Check**

What did the men do when Walt did not stop?

At last, twisting abruptly between two river islands, he came upon the mighty Yukon sweeping grandly to the north. He could not see from bank to bank, and in the quick-falling twilight it loomed a great white sea of frozen stillness. There was not a sound, save the breathing of the dogs, and the churn of the steel-shod sled.

No snow had fallen for several weeks, and the traffic had packed the main river trail till it was hard and glassy as glare ice. Over this the sled flew along, and the dogs kept the trail fairly well, although Walt quickly discovered that he had made a mistake in choosing the leader. As they were driven in single file, without reins, he had to guide them by his voice, and it was evident the head dog had never learned the meaning of "gee" and "haw."[5] He hugged the inside of the curves too closely, often forcing his comrades behind him into the soft snow, while several times he thus capsized[6] the sled.

There was no wind, but the speed at which he traveled created a bitter blast, and with the thermometer down to forty below, this bit through fur and flesh to the very bones. Aware that if he remained constantly upon the sled he would freeze to death, and knowing the practice of Arctic travelers, Walt shortened up one of the lashing thongs, and whenever he felt chilled, seized hold of it, jumped off, and ran behind till warmth was restored. Then he would climb on and rest till the process had to be repeated.

Looking back he could see the sled of his pursuers, drawn by eight dogs, rising and falling over the ice hummocks like a boat in a seaway. The Irishman and the black-bearded leader were with it, taking turns in running and riding.

Night fell, and in the blackness of the first hour or so Walt toiled desperately with his dogs. On account of the poor lead dog, they were continually floundering off the beaten track into the soft snow, and the sled was as often riding on its side or top as it was in the proper way. This work and strain tried his strength sorely. Had he not been in such haste he could have avoided much of it, but he feared the stampeders would creep up in the darkness and overtake him. However, he could hear them yelling to their dogs, and knew from the sounds they were coming up very slowly.

When the moon rose he was off Sixty Mile, and Dawson was only fifty miles away. He was almost exhausted, and breathed a sigh of relief as he climbed on the sled again. Looking back, he saw his enemies had crawled up within four hundred yards. At this space they remained, a black speck of motion on the white river breast. Strive as they would, they could not shorten this distance, and strive as he would, he could not increase it.

Reading Strategy
Recognizing Signal Words
What do the signal words "On account of" tell you about the link between the "poor lead dog" and the "floundering" of the sled?

---

5. **"gee" and "haw"** (jē) and (hô) commands used to tell an animal to turn to the right or the left.
6. **capsized** (kap´ sīzd´) *v.* overturned.

Walt had now discovered the proper lead dog, and he knew he could easily run away from them if he could only change the bad leader for the good one. But this was impossible, for a moment's delay, at the speed they were running, would bring the men behind upon him.

When he was off the mouth of Rosebud Creek, just as he was topping a rise, the report of a gun and the ping of a bullet on the ice beside him told him that they were this time shooting at him with a rifle. And from then on, as he cleared the <u>summit</u> of each ice jam, he stretched flat on the leaping sled till the rifle shot from the rear warned him that he was safe till the next ice jam was reached.

Now it is very hard to lie on a moving sled, jumping and plunging and yawing[7] like a boat before the wind, and to shoot through the deceiving moonlight at an object four hundred yards away on another moving sled performing equally wild antics. So it is not to be wondered at that the black-bearded leader did not hit him.

After several hours of this, during which, perhaps, a score of bullets had struck about him, their ammunition began to give out and their fire slackened. They took greater care, and shot at him at the most favorable opportunities. He was also leaving them behind, the distance slowly increasing to six hundred yards.

Lifting clear on the crest of a great jam off Indian River, Walt Masters met with his first accident. A bullet sang past his ears, and struck the bad lead dog.

The poor brute plunged in a heap, with the rest of the team on top of him.

Like a flash Walt was by the leader. Cutting the traces with his hunting knife, he dragged the dying animal to one side and straightened out the team.

He glanced back. The other sled was coming up like an express train. With half the dogs still over their traces, he cried "Mush on!" and leaped upon the sled just as the pursuers dashed abreast[8] of him.

The Irishman was preparing to spring for him—they were so sure they had him that they did not shoot—when Walt turned fiercely upon them with his whip.

He struck at their faces, and men must save their faces with their hands. So there was no shooting just then. Before they could recover from the hot rain of blows, Walt reached out from his sled, catching their wheel dog by the forelegs in midspring, and throwing him heavily. This snarled the team, capsizing the sled and tangling his enemies up beautifully.

Away Walt flew, the runners of his sled fairly screaming as they bounded over the frozen surface. And what had seemed an accident

---

7. yawing (yô′ iŋ) *adj.* swinging from side to side.
8. abreast (ə brest′) *adv.* alongside.

summit (sum′ it) *n.* highest part

Literary Analysis
Conflict Between Characters and Resolution of Conflict
Who do you think will win this conflict? Why?

Reading Check

How did Walt stop the other sled?

proved to be a blessing in disguise. The proper lead dog was now to the fore, and he stretched low and whined with joy as he jerked his comrades along.

By the time he reached Ainslie's Creek, seventeen miles from Dawson, Walt had left his pursuers, a tiny speck, far behind. At Monte Cristo Island he could no longer see them. And at Swede Creek, just as daylight was silvering the pines, he ran plump into the camp of old Loren Hall.

Almost as quick as it takes to tell it, Loren had his sleeping furs rolled up, and had joined Walt on the sled. They permitted the dogs to travel more slowly, as there was no sign of the chase in the rear, and just as they pulled up at the gold commissioner's office in Dawson, Walt, who had kept his eyes open to the last, fell asleep.

And because of what Walt Masters did on this night, the men of the Yukon have become proud of him, and speak of him now as the King of Mazy May.

Review and Assess

Thinking About the Selection

1. **Respond:** Would you enjoy Walt's way of life? Why or why not?

2. **(a) Recall:** What are Walt's responsibilities while his father is away? **(b) Compare and Contrast:** How are Walt's responsibilities different from the responsibilities of other children his age?

3. **(a) Recall:** What are the stampeders planning to do? **(b) Infer:** Why does Walt want to stop them? **(c) Connect:** What do Walt's actions reveal about his beliefs?

4. **(a) Recall:** What does Walt do when his lead dog is shot? **(b) Infer:** What quality does Walt reveal through his actions in that situation? **(c) Synthesize:** Identify two other examples of Walt's actions or reactions that demonstrate the same quality.

5. **(a) Recall:** What does Walt do to defeat the stampeders' plan? **(b) Draw Conclusions:** In what way does this action make Walt's new title, "King of Mazy May," appropriate? **(c) Evaluate:** Do you consider Walt a hero? Why or why not?

6. **Evaluate:** This story suggests that "manliness" is based on strength and bravery. Explain whether you agree or disagree.

7. **(a) Extend:** As this story illustrates, the discovery of gold in the Klondike brought out both the best and the worst in people. Why do you think that the discovery of gold in the Klondike had such a major impact on people? **(b) Connect:** If you had lived during that time, would you have been tempted to travel to the Klondike in search of gold? Why or why not?

Jack London

(1876–1916)

Jack London lived an adventurous life. By the time he was barely out of his teens, this Californian had worked in a factory, traveled the United States as a hobo, captained a pirate ship, and prospected for gold.

London's love of reading and his own adventures inspired him to write. By the time he was thirty, London had written such classics as *The Call of the Wild* and *White Fang*. Altogether, he wrote more than fifty books.

The Story Behind the Story

In 1897, London went to northwestern Canada, where gold had just been discovered. He didn't find gold, but did have adventures on the way to Dawson City. Once, for instance, he made a boat from trees and ran the dangerous White Horse rapids. In this story, London writes about a young miner who also has a thrilling trip to Dawson.

Review and Assess

Literary Analysis

Conflict Between Characters

1. How do different goals cause the strangers and Walt to clash? Use a graphic organizer like the one below to show the **conflict**.

2. How does the **conflict** drive the story action and sustain interest?

Connecting Literary Elements

3. Using three examples from the story, explain how London keeps readers guessing about the **resolution** of the conflict.

4. Prepare a timeline that shows when the conflict is introduced and the key events in which the conflict is intensified. Indicate what each key event suggests about a possible resolution. Then, indicate which event makes clear the actual resolution.

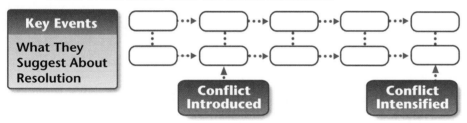

Reading Strategy

Recognizing Signal Words

5. Review the story and find five different signal words in sentences. Explain the relationship that each signal word indicates.

6. Reread the next-to-last sentence of the story. What word signals the cause for the dogs' being allowed to travel more slowly?

Extending Understanding

7. **Cultural Connection:** In what ways would life in a northern climate such as the Yukon differ from life in a southern climate?

Quick Review

A **conflict** is a struggle between opposing forces. To review conflict, see page 51.

The **resolution** of the conflict is the outcome.

Signal words are words and phrases such as *but, so, on account of,* and *because* that let you know that a different kind of information is coming next.

 Take It to the Net

www.phschool.com
Take the interactive self-test online to check your understanding of the selection.

Integrate Language Skills

Vocabulary Development Lesson

Word Analysis: Latin Suffix -or

The Latin suffix -or, as in *prospector,* means "a person or thing that does something." When you add the suffix -or to the end of an action word, you create a new word. The new word names the person or thing doing the action. For example, *prospect* means "to search." When you add -or to *prospect,* you create the word *prospector.* A *prospector* is "a person who searches for gold."

Before you add the suffix -or to a word ending in *e,* first drop the final *e.* For example, before you add -or to *create,* drop the final *e.* Then make *creator.*

Add the suffix -or to the following words to name the person who does these jobs.

1. sail
2. advise
3. edit
4. supervise

Fluency: Using New Words

Answer each question. Explain your answer.

1. Does gold mining require *toil?*
2. Was Walt a boy who had *endured* hardships?
3. Were the claim jumpers true *prospectors?*
4. When is your sled *poising* on its runner?
5. Were Klondike claims *liable* to be jumped?
6. Had Walt *declined* to battle the claim jumpers?
7. Can you climb higher than a mountain *summit?*

Spelling Strategy

The *oy* sound is spelled *oy* and *oi.* Use the letters *oi* in the middle of a single-syllable word, such as *toil.* Use the letters *oy* at the end of a word, such as *annoy.*

On your paper, spell these words correctly.

1. foyl
2. decoi
3. spoyl

Grammar Lesson

Pronouns and Antecedents

The noun or pronoun to which a pronoun refers is the pronoun's **antecedent.** Personal pronouns must have an antecedent to make sense. Interrogative pronouns do not have an antecedent. An indefinite pronoun may have an antecedent, but it does not have to have one.

In this sentence from "The King of Mazy May," Walt is the antecedent of the pronoun *he.*

> **Example:** <u>Walt</u> has walked all the fourteen years of his life in suntanned, moose-hide moccasins, and <u>he</u> can go to the Indian camps. . . .

Practice Copy these sentences on your paper. Underline the pronoun and circle its antecedent in each sentence.

1. Although Walt was not big, he was manly.
2. Walt's father was away, but he would be back soon.
3. The camp was new, but it was comfortable.
4. After the dogs started, they ran for hours.
5. Walt's mother had died, but Walt and his father remembered her with love.

Writing Application Write a brief account of an adventure story or a movie. Use each of the following pronouns at least once: *he, they, she, it.*

Prentice Hall Writing and Grammar Connection: Chapter 14, Section 2

Writing Lesson

Personal Narrative

You may not have foiled stampeders like Walt, but you have probably had the experience of struggling to meet a goal. Choose such an experience, and use it as the topic for a **personal narrative**—a story that captures the details of an experience, along with your thoughts and feelings about the experience.

Prewriting   Use a timeline like the one shown to list events in the order in which they occurred. Write the most important, or key, events first. Then, add other events and details to the timeline

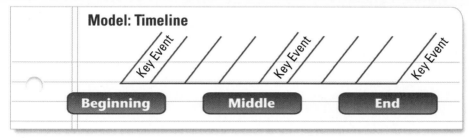

Model: Timeline

Key Event   Key Event   Key Event

Beginning   Middle   End

Drafting   Write a draft of your personal narrative, using the timeline. Include any problems you encountered in achieving your goal. Build tension by including thoughts or feelings of doubt or uncertainty about reaching your goal.

Revising   As you review each paragraph, circle sentences that do not appear in the order in which events occurred. Then, reorder your sentences as necessary. Also, look for places where you can add details to build tension about the outcome of the story.

Prentice Hall Writing and Grammar Connection: Chapter 5, Section 4

Extension Activities

Listening and Speaking   As Walt, give a **speech** accepting an award for courage from Dawson City.

1. Plan your speech. Make an outline to help you organize what you want to say.
2. Vary the volume, or loudness, of your voice. Increase the volume as you build toward an exciting moment or important idea. Call attention to important points by lowering your voice or pausing before making a statement.
3. Deliver your speech to classmates.

Research and Technology   In a small group, prepare a **presentation** on gold mining. Use resources such as the Internet and nonfiction books to research the life of a miner. Do a keyword search for gold in Canada. Use visuals to show where gold was mined. Make a diagram of the steps involved in gold mining. Share your findings.

 **Take It to the Net**   www.phschool.com

Go online for an additional research activity using the Internet.

Prepare to Read

The Circuit ◆ Hard as Nails

 Take It to the Net

Visit www.phschool.com for interactive activities and instruction related to these selections, including

- background
- graphic organizers
- literary elements
- reading strategies

Preview

Connecting to the Literature

The main characters in "The Circuit" and "Hard as Nails" experience significant changes in their lives. Connect to the story by thinking about how you react to changes.

Background

"The Circuit" is about a family of migrant farm workers. Most migrant workers in the United States move frequently to follow the seasonal demands of harvesting. The entire family usually travels together, with children helping adults work on the farms. Children may start school late in the fall or leave early in the spring to work around the harvest season.

Literary Analysis

Theme

The **theme,** or central idea, of a story is a thought about life that the story conveys. Sometimes a theme is directly stated. Other times you must figure it out yourself by considering the events in the story, the characters' thoughts and feelings, and the story's title. For example, this passage from "The Circuit" reveals that the character's life follows a pattern like that of the seasons—an important clue to the theme:

> Yes, it was that time of year. When I opened the front door to the shack, I stopped. Everything we owned was neatly packed in cardboard boxes.

Complete a graphic organizer like the one to the right to help you identify the theme of each selection.

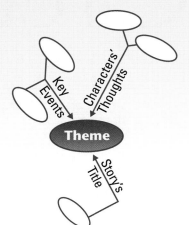

Comparing Literary Works

One of these selections is **fiction** (a work from imagination), and the other is **nonfiction** (a work that is true). Both deal with challenges faced by young people. Use these focus questions to compare the selections.

1. How do the experiences of the main characters compare?
2. Compare the boys' reactions to their experiences.

Reading Strategy

Reading With Expression

Reading with expression is using your voice to communicate the meaning of the words. To do this, break down long sentences into parts.

- First, identify the subject or what the sentence is about.
- Decide what the rest of the sentence tells you about the subject.

Read aloud the beginning of this sentence from "Hard as Nails":

> *"Watching the two of them in conversation, with Deems glancing at me now and then, I kept my shoulders drawn back. . . ."*

The subject of the sentence—*I*—is the teller of the story. The rest of the sentence tells how he behaved.

Vocabulary Development

drone (drōn) *n.* continuous humming sound (p. 68)

instinctively (in stiŋk′ tiv lē) *adv.* done by instinct, without thinking (p. 69)

savoring (sā′ vər iŋ) *v.* enjoying with appreciation; tasting; relishing (p. 69)

embedded (em bed′ əd) *adj.* firmly fixed in a material (p. 73)

exhaust (ig zôst′) *v.* use up (p. 73)

sublime (sə blīm′) *adj.* majestic; causing awe (p. 74)

immense (i mens′) *adj.* huge (p. 78)

The Circuit

Francisco Jiménez

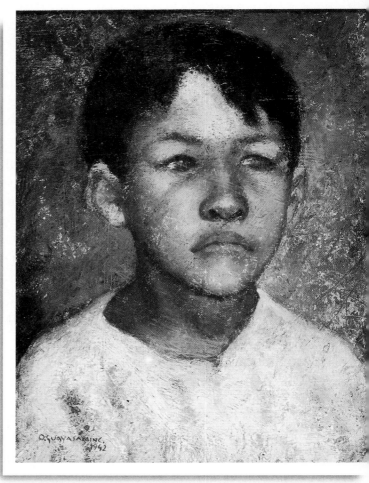

My Brother, 1942, Guayasamin (Oswaldo Guayasamin Calero) Collection, The Museum of Modern Art, New York

It was that time of year again. Ito, the strawberry sharecropper,[1] did not smile. It was natural. The peak of the strawberry season was over and the last few days the workers, most of them *braceros*,[2] were not picking as many boxes as they had during the months of June and July.

As the last days of August disappeared, so did the number of *braceros*. Sunday, only one—the best picker—came to work. I liked him. Sometimes we talked during our half-hour lunch break. That is how I found out he was from Jalisco, the same state in Mexico my family was from. That Sunday was the last time I saw him.

When the sun had tired and sunk behind the mountains, Ito signaled us that it was time to go home. "*Ya esora*,"[3] he yelled in his broken Spanish. Those were the words I waited for twelve hours a day, every day, seven days a week, week after week. And the thought of not hearing them again saddened me.

As we drove home Papá did not say a word. With both hands on the wheel, he stared at the dirt road. My older brother, Roberto, was also silent. He leaned his head back and closed his eyes. Once in a while he cleared from his throat the dust that blew in from outside.

---

1. **sharecropper** (sher′ kräp′ ər) *n.* one who works for a share of a crop; tenant farmer.
2. ***braceros*** (brä ser′ os) *n.* migrant Mexican farm laborers who harvest crops.
3. ***Ya esora*** (yä es ô rä) Spanish for "It's time" (*Ya es hora*).

Yes, it was that time of year. When I opened the front door to the shack, I stopped. Everything we owned was neatly packed in cardboard boxes. Suddenly I felt even more the weight of hours, days, weeks, and months of work. I sat down on a box. The thought of having to move to Fresno[4] and knowing what was in store for me there brought tears to my eyes.

That night I could not sleep. I lay in bed thinking about how much I hated this move.

A little before five o'clock in the morning, Papá woke everyone up. A few minutes later, the yelling and screaming of my little brothers and sisters, for whom the move was a great adventure, broke the silence of dawn. Shortly, the barking of the dogs accompanied them.

While we packed the breakfast dishes, Papá went outside to start the "Carcanchita."[5] That was the name Papá gave his old '38 black Plymouth. He bought it in a used-car lot in Santa Rosa in the winter of 1949. Papá was very proud of his little jalopy. He had a right to be proud of it. He spent a lot of time looking at other cars before buying this one. When he finally chose the "Carcanchita," he checked it thoroughly before driving it out of the car lot. He examined every inch of the car. He listened to the motor, tilting his head from side to side like a parrot, trying to detect any noises that spelled car trouble. After being satisfied with the looks and sounds of the car, Papá then insisted on knowing who the original owner was. He never did find out from the car salesman, but he bought the car anyway. Papá figured the original owner must have been an important man because behind the rear seat of the car he found a blue necktie.

Papá parked the car out in front and left the motor running. "*Listo*,"[6] he yelled. Without saying a word, Roberto and I began to carry the boxes out to the car. Roberto carried the two big boxes and I carried the two smaller ones. Papá then threw the mattress on top of the car roof and tied it with ropes to the front and rear bumpers.

Everything was packed except Mamá's pot. It was an old large galvanized[7] pot she had picked up at an army surplus store in Santa María the year I was born. The pot had many dents and nicks, and the more dents and nicks it acquired the more Mamá liked it. "*Mi olla*,"[8] she used to say proudly.

I held the front door open as Mamá carefully carried out her pot by both handles, making sure not to spill the cooked beans. When she got to the car, Papá reached out to help her with it. Roberto opened the rear car door and Papá gently placed it on the floor behind the

---

4. **Fresno** (frez´ nō) *n.* city in central California.
5. **Carcanchita** (kär kän chē´ tä) affectionate name for the car.
6. ***Listo*** (lēs to) Spanish for "Ready."
7. **galvanized** (gal´ və nīzd´) *adj.* coated with zinc to prevent rusting.
8. ***Mi olla*** (mē ō´ yä) Spanish for "My pot."

Literary Analysis
Theme In what way do this event and the narrator's actions give you a clue about the theme?

Reading Strategy
Reading With Expression What is being said about Papá in the sentence beginning "After being"? How would you read this sentence aloud?

Reading Check

How does the family feel about moving again?

front seat. All of us then climbed in. Papá sighed, wiped the sweat off his forehead with his sleeve, and said wearily: "*Es todo.*"[9]

As we drove away, I felt a lump in my throat. I turned around and looked at our little shack for the last time.

At sunset we drove into a labor camp near Fresno. Since Papá did not speak English, Mamá asked the camp foreman if he needed any more workers. "We don't need no more," said the foreman, scratching his head. "Check with Sullivan down the road. Can't miss him. He lives in a big white house with a fence around it."

When we got there, Mamá walked up to the house. She went through a white gate, past a row of rose bushes, up the stairs to the front door. She rang the doorbell. The porch light went on and a tall husky man came out. They exchanged a few words. After the man went in, Mamá clasped her hands and hurried back to the car. "We have work! Mr. Sullivan said we can stay there the whole season," she said, gasping and pointing to an old garage near the stables.

The garage was worn out by the years. It had no windows. The walls, eaten by termites, strained to support the roof full of holes. The dirt floor, populated by earthworms, looked like a gray road map.

That night, by the light of a kerosene lamp, we unpacked and cleaned our new home. Roberto swept away the loose dirt, leaving the hard ground. Papá plugged the holes in the walls with old newspapers and tin can tops. Mamá fed my little brothers and sisters. Papá and Roberto then brought in the mattress and placed it on the far corner of the garage. "Mamá, you and the little ones sleep on the mattress. Roberto, Panchito, and I will sleep outside under the trees," Papá said.

Early next morning Mr. Sullivan showed us where his crop was, and after breakfast, Papá, Roberto, and I headed for the vineyard to pick.

Around nine o'clock the temperature had risen to almost one hundred degrees. I was completely soaked in sweat and my mouth felt as if I had been chewing on a handkerchief. I walked over to the end of the row, picked up the jug of water we had brought, and began drinking. "Don't drink too much; you'll get sick," Roberto shouted. No sooner had he said that than I felt sick to my stomach. I dropped to my knees and let the jug roll off my hands. I remained motionless with my eyes glued on the hot sandy ground. All I could hear was the <u>drone</u> of insects. Slowly I began to recover. I poured water over my face and neck and watched the dirty water run down my arms to the ground.

I still felt a little dizzy when we took a break to eat lunch. It was

Reading Strategy
Reading With Expression
Who is the subject of the sentence beginning "That night"? What else does the sentence tell you?

Reading Strategy
Reading With Expression
Which part of the first sentence in this paragraph would you emphasize when reading it aloud?

drone (drōn) *n.* continuous humming sound

---

9. *Es todo* (es tō´ thō) Spanish for "That's everything."

past two o'clock and we sat underneath a large walnut tree that was on the side of the road. While we ate, Papá jotted down the number of boxes we had picked. Roberto drew designs on the ground with a stick. Suddenly I noticed Papá's face turn pale as he looked down the road. "Here comes the school bus," he whispered loudly in alarm. <u>Instinctively</u>, Roberto and I ran and hid in the vineyards. We did not want to get in trouble for not going to school. The neatly dressed boys about my age got off. They carried books under their arms. After they crossed the street, the bus drove away. Roberto and I came out from hiding and joined Papá. "*Tienen que tener cuidado*,"[10] he warned us.

After lunch we went back to work. The sun kept beating down. The buzzing insects, the wet sweat, and the hot dry dust made the afternoon seem to last forever. Finally the mountains around the valley reached out and swallowed the sun. Within an hour it was too dark to continue picking. The vines blanketed the grapes, making it difficult to see the bunches. "*Vámonos*,"[11] said Papá, signaling to us that it was time to quit work. Papá then took out a pencil and began to figure out how much we had earned our first day. He wrote down numbers, crossed some out, wrote down some more. "*Quince*,"[12] he murmured.

When we arrived home, we took a cold shower underneath a waterhose. We then sat down to eat dinner around some wooden crates that served as a table. Mamá had cooked a special meal for us. We had rice and tortillas with "*carne con chile*,"[13] my favorite dish.

The next morning I could hardly move. My body ached all over. I felt little control over my arms and legs. This feeling went on every morning for days until my muscles finally got used to the work.

It was Monday, the first week of November. The grape season was over and I could now go to school. I woke up early that morning and lay in bed, looking at the stars and <u>savoring</u> the thought of not going to work and of starting sixth grade for the first time that year. Since I could not sleep, I decided to get up and join

Literature
in context Geography Connection

Agricultural Seasons

With sunny weather and a favorable climate, California produces more crops than any other state. At every point in the year, there is a different crop ready to be harvested in some part of the state. Migrant workers, such as Panchito's family, migrate from place to place to harvest the available crop. Grapes are picked in the summer and fall in the lush valleys of central and northern California, peak strawberry season hits the southern coastal regions in spring, and cotton is harvested in the dry valleys of central and southern California during the winter.

instinctively (in stiŋk´ tiv lē) *adv.* done by instinct, without thinking

savoring (sā´ vər iŋ) *v.* enjoying with appreciation; tasting; relishing

✓Reading Check

When and why is Panchito finally able to go to school?

---

10. ***Tienen que tener cuidado*** (tē en´ en kā ten er´ kwē thä´ thō) Spanish for "You have to be careful."
11. ***Vámonos*** (vä´ mō nōs) Spanish for "Let's go."
12. ***Quince*** (kēn´ sā) Spanish for "fifteen."
13. ***carne con chile*** (kär´ nē kən chil´ ē) dish of ground meat, hot peppers, beans, and tomatoes.

Papá and Roberto at breakfast. I sat at the table across from Roberto, but I kept my head down. I did not want to look up and face him. I knew he was sad. He was not going to school today. He was not going tomorrow, or next week, or next month. He would not go until the cotton season was over, and that was sometime in February. I rubbed my hands together and watched the dry, acid stained skin fall to the floor in little rolls.

When Papá and Roberto left for work, I felt relief. I walked to the top of a small grade next to the shack and watched the "Carcanchita" disappear in the distance in a cloud of dust.

Two hours later, around eight o'clock, I stood by the side of the road waiting for school bus number twenty. When it arrived I climbed in. Everyone was busy either talking or yelling. I sat in an empty seat in the back.

When the bus stopped in front of the school, I felt very nervous. I looked out the bus window and saw boys and girls carrying books under their arms. I put my hands in my pant pockets and walked to the principal's office. When I entered I heard a woman's voice say: "May I help you?" I was startled. I had not heard English for months. For a few seconds I remained speechless. I looked at the lady who waited for my answer. My first instinct was to answer her in Spanish, but I held back. Finally, after struggling for English words, I managed to tell her that I wanted to enroll in the sixth grade. After answering many questions, I was led to the classroom.

Mr. Lema, the sixth-grade teacher, greeted me and assigned me a desk. He then introduced me to the class. I was so nervous and scared at that moment when everyone's eyes were on me that I wished I were with Papá and Roberto picking cotton. After taking roll, Mr. Lema gave the class the assignment for the first hour. "The first thing we have to do this morning is finish reading the story we began yesterday," he said enthusiastically. He walked up to me, handed me an English book, and asked me to read. "We are on page 125," he said politely. When I heard this, I felt my blood rush to my head; I felt dizzy. "Would you like to read?" he asked hesitantly. I opened the book to page 125. My mouth was dry. My eyes began to water. I could not begin. "You can read later," Mr. Lema said understandingly.

For the rest of the reading period I kept getting angrier and angrier at myself. I should have read, I thought to myself.

During recess I went into the restroom and opened my English book to page 125. I began to read in a low voice, pretending I was in class. There were many words I did not know. I closed the book and headed back to the classroom.

Mr. Lema was sitting at his desk correcting papers. When I entered he looked up at me and smiled. I felt better. I walked up to him and asked if he could help me with the new words. "Gladly," he said.

Literary Analysis
Theme How does the sentence that begins "He would not go" convey the idea that the family's life follows a cycle? How might this relate to the story's theme?

Reading Strategy
Reading With Expression Read aloud the sentence beginning *Finally*, and pause for punctuation. What is the sentence about?

The rest of the month I spent my lunch hours working on English with Mr. Lema, my best friend at school.

One Friday during lunch hour Mr. Lema asked me to take a walk with him to the music room. "Do you like music?" he asked me as we entered the building.

"Yes, I like *corridos*,"[14] I answered. He then picked up a trumpet, blew on it and handed it to me. The sound gave me goose bumps. I knew that sound. I had heard it in many *corridos*. "How would you like to learn how to play it?" he asked. He must have read my face because before I could answer, he added: "I'll teach you how to play it during our lunch hours."

That day I could hardly wait to get home to tell Papá and Mamá the great news. As I got off the bus, my little brothers and sisters ran up to meet me. They were yelling and screaming. I thought they were happy to see me, but when I opened the door to our shack, I saw that everything we owned was neatly packed in cardboard boxes.

---

14. *corridos* (kō rē′ thōs) *n.* ballads.

Review and Assess

Thinking About the Selection

1. **Respond:** What do you admire about Panchito? Why?
2. **(a) Recall:** What brings tears to Panchito's eyes at the beginning of "The Circuit"? **(b) Draw Conclusions:** Why does he react this way?
3. **(a) Recall:** What does Panchito do on his school lunch hours? **(b) Infer:** Why do you think Panchito calls Mr. Lema his "best friend at school"? **(c) Synthesize:** Based on what you learn in the story, how would you describe Panchito's personality?
4. **(a) Infer:** What is the best thing that happens on the last day of school? **(b) Infer:** What is the worst thing? **(c) Analyze:** What clues indicate that Panchito has been through this before?
5. **(a) Analyze:** In what way does the final paragraph bring Panchito back to where he was at the beginning? **(b) Interpret:** Explain how this return to the beginning is connected to the title.
6. **Generalize:** What are the main difficulties of constantly moving and attending new schools?
7. **Extend:** What might other students do to make Panchito feel more comfortable?
8. **Extend:** What, if anything, might be done to ease the hardships faced by families like Panchito's? Support your answer.

Francisco Jiménez

(b. 1943)
Born in Mexico, Francisco Jiménez (hē mā′ nez) came with his family to the United States when he was four. The Jiménez family settled in California, becoming migrant workers. Like the young man in "The Circuit," Jiménez couldn't go to school before the harvest ended.

In high school, Jiménez supported himself by working as a janitor. His excellent grades won him three college scholarships. He went on to become an outstanding teacher and college official. He has also won awards as a writer.

Hard as Nails

Russell Baker

My mother started me in newspaper work in 1937 right after my twelfth birthday. She would have started me younger, but there was a law against working before age twelve. She thought it was a silly law, and said so to Deems.

Deems was boss of a group of boys who worked home delivery routes for the *Baltimore News-Post*. She found out about him a few weeks after we got to Baltimore. She just went out on the street, stopped a paperboy, and asked how he'd got his job.

"There's this man Deems . . ."

Deems was short and plump and had curly brown hair. He owned a car and a light gray suit and always wore a necktie and white shirt. A real businessman, I thought the first time I saw him. My mother was talking to him on the sidewalk in front of the Union Square Methodist Church and I was standing as tall as I could, just out of earshot.

▼ **Critical Viewing**
Would you enjoy working in a group like this one? Why or why not?
[Support]

"Now, Buddy, when we get down there keep your shoulders back and stand up real straight," she had cautioned me after making sure my necktie was all right and my shirt clean.

Watching the two of them in conversation, with Deems glancing at me now and then, I kept my shoulders drawn back in the painful military style I'd seen in movies, trying to look a foot taller than I really was.

"Come over here, Russ, and meet Mister Deems," she finally said, and I did, managing to answer his greeting by saying, "The pleasure's all mine," which I'd heard people say in the movies. I probably blushed while saying it, because meeting strangers was painfully embarrassing to me.

"If that's the rule, it's the rule," my mother was telling Deems, "and we'll just have to put up with it, but it still doesn't make any sense to me."

As we walked back to the house she said I couldn't have a paper route until I was twelve. And all because of some foolish rule they had down here in Baltimore. You'd think if a boy wanted to work they would encourage him instead of making him stay idle so long that laziness got <u>embedded</u> in his bones.

That was April. We had barely finished the birthday cake in August before Deems came by the apartment and gave me the tools of the newspaper trade: an account book for keeping track of the customers' bills and a long, brown web belt. Slung around one shoulder and across the chest, the belt made it easy to balance fifteen or twenty pounds of papers against the hip. I had to buy my own wire cutters for opening the newspaper bundles the trucks dropped at Wisengoff's store on the corner of Stricker and West Lombard streets.

In February my mother had moved us down from New Jersey, where we had been living with her brother Allen ever since my father died in 1930. This move of hers to Baltimore was a step toward fulfilling a dream. More than almost anything else in the world, she wanted "a home of our own." I'd heard her talk of that "home of our own" all through those endless Depression years when we lived as poor relatives dependent on Uncle Allen's goodness. "A home of our own. One of these days, Buddy, we'll have a home of our own."

That winter she had finally saved just enough to make her move, and she came to Baltimore. There were several reasons for Baltimore. For one, there were people she knew in Baltimore, people she could go to if things got desperate. And desperation was possible, because the moving would <u>exhaust</u> her savings, and the apartment rent was twenty-four dollars a month. She would have to find a job quickly. My sister Doris was only nine, but I was old enough for an after-school job that could bring home a few dollars a week. So as soon as it was legal I went into newspaper work.

embedded (em bed´ əd) *adj.* firmly fixed in a sur- rounding material

Literary Analysis
Theme What do these events tell you about the theme of this essay?

exhaust (ig zôst´) v. use up

Reading Check

Why does Russ want a paper route?

The romance of it was almost unbearable on my first day as I trudged west along Lombard Street, then south along Gilmor, and east down Pratt Street with the bundle of newspapers strapped to my hip. I imagined people pausing to admire me as I performed this important work, spreading the news of the world, the city, and the racetracks onto doorsteps, through mail slots, and under door jambs. I had often gazed with envy at paperboys; to be one of them at last was happiness <u>sublime</u>.

Very soon, though, I discovered drawbacks. The worst of these was Deems. Though I had only forty customers, Deems sent papers for forty-five. Since I was billed for every paper left on Wisengoff's corner, I had to pay for the five extra copies out of income or try to hustle them on the street. I hated standing at streetcar stops yelling, "Paper! Paper!" at people getting off trolleys.[1] Usually, if my mother wasn't around to catch me, I stuck the extras in a dark closet and took the loss.

Deems was constantly baiting new traps to dump more papers on me. When I solved the problem of the five extras by getting five new subscribers for home delivery, Deems announced a competition with mouth-watering prizes for the newsboys who got the most new subscribers. Too innocent to cope with this sly master of private enterprise,[2] I took the bait.

"Look at these prizes I can get for signing up new customers," I told my mother. "A balloon-tire bicycle. A free pass to the movies for a whole year."

The temptation was too much. I reported my five new subscribers to help me in the competition.

Whereupon Deems promptly raised my order from forty-five to fifty papers, leaving me again with the choice of hustling to unload the five extras or losing money.

I won a free pass to the movies, though. It was good for a whole year. And to the magnificent Loew's Century located downtown on Lexington Street. The passes were good only for nights in the middle of the week when I usually had too much homework to allow for movies. Still, in the summer with school out, it was thrilling to go all the way downtown at night to sit in the Century's damask[3] and velvet splendor and see MGM's glamorous stars in their latest movies.

To collect my prize I had to go to a banquet the paper gave for its "honor carriers" at the Emerson Hotel. There were fifty of us, and I was sure the other forty-nine would all turn out to be slicksters

---

1. **trolleys** (träl´ ēz) *n.* electric passenger trains, also called streetcars, running on rails in the city streets; discontinued in many American cities after the mid-1900s.
2. **private enterprise** business run for profit.
3. **damask** (dam´ əsk) *adj.* decorated with the shiny cloth called damask.

Reading Strategy
Reading With Expression Determine the subject of the first sentence and what he does. Read the sentence aloud with expression.

sublime (sə blīm´) *adj.* majestic; causing awe

Literary Analysis
Theme Why do you think Deems comes up with schemes to get newsboys to sell more papers? How might his schemes relate to the theme?

▲ **Critical Viewing**
Why might it be difficult to concentrate in a room like this one? **[Infer]**

wised up to the ways of the world, who would laugh at my doltish ignorance of how to eat at a great hotel banquet. My fear of looking foolish at the banquet made me lie awake nights dreading it and imagining all the humiliating mistakes I could make.

I had seen banquets in movies. Every plate was surrounded by a baffling array of knives, forks, and spoons. I knew it would be the same at the Emerson Hotel. The Emerson was one of the swankiest hotels in Baltimore. It was not likely to hold down on the silverware. I talked to my mother.

"How will I know what to eat what with?"

The question did not interest her.

"Just watch what everybody else does, and enjoy yourself," she said.

I came back to the problem again and again.

"Do you use the same spoon for your coffee as you do for dessert?"

"Don't worry about it. Everybody isn't going to be staring at you."

"Is it all right to butter your bread with the same knife you use to cut the meat?"

"Just go and have a good time."

Close to panic, I showed up at the Emerson, found my way to the banquet, and was horrified to find that I had to sit beside Deems throughout the meal. We probably talked about something, but I was so busy sweating with terror and rolling my eyeballs sidewise to see what silverware Deems was using to eat with that I didn't hear a word all night. The following week, Deems started sending me another five extras.

✔**Reading Check**

What was Russ's challenge as a paperboy?

Now and then he also provided a treat. One day in 1938 he asked if I would like to join a small group of boys he was taking to visit the *News-Post* newsroom. My mother, in spite of believing that nothing came before homework at night, wasn't cold-hearted enough to deny me a chance to see the city room[4] of a great metropolitan newspaper. I had seen plenty of city rooms in the movies. They were glamorous places full of exciting people like Lee Tracey, Edmund Lowe, and Adolphe Menjou[5] trading wisecracks and making mayors and cops look like saps. To see such a place, to stand, actually stand, in the city room of a great newspaper and look at reporters who were in touch every day with killers and professional baseball players—that was a thrilling prospect.

Because the *News-Post* was an afternoon paper, almost everybody had left for the day when we got there that night. The building, located downtown near the harbor, was disappointing. It looked like a factory, and not a very big factory either. Inside there was a smell compounded of ink, pulp, chemicals, paste, oil, gasoline, greasy rags, and hot metal. We took an elevator up and came into a long room filled with dilapidated[6] desks, battered telephones, and big blocky typewriters. Almost nobody there, just two or three men in shirt-sleeves. It was the first time I'd ever seen Deems look awed.

"Boys, this is the nerve center of the newspaper," he said, his voice heavy and solemn like the voice of Westbrook Van Voorhis, the *March of Time*[7] man, when he said, "Time marches on."

I was confused. I had expected the newsroom to have glamour, but this place had nothing but squalor. The walls hadn't been painted for years. The windows were filthy. Desks were heaped with mounds of crumpled paper, torn sheets of newspaper, overturned paste pots, dog-eared telephone directories. The floor was ankle deep in newsprint, carbon paper, and crushed cigarette packages. Waist-high cans overflowed with trash. Ashtrays were buried under cigarette ashes and butts. Ugly old wooden chairs looked ready for the junk shop.

It looked to me like a place that probably had more cockroaches than we had back home on Lombard Street, but Deems was seeing it through rose-colored glasses.[8] As we stood looking

Reading Strategy
Reading With Expression
What is the main idea of the sentence beginning "To see such a place"?

Literary Analysis
Theme How do the realities of the newsroom conflict with Baker's previous ideas? Why might this contrast be a clue to the theme?

---

4. **city room** the office at a newspaper used by those who report on city events.
5. **Lee Tracey, Edmund Lowe, and Adolphe Menjou** actors in movies of the period.
6. **dilapidated** (də lap′ ə dāt′ əd) *adj.* run-down; in bad condition.
7. **the** *March of Time* the *March of Time* was a newsreel series that ran from 1935 to 1951, showing current news events along with interviews and dramatizations. Newsreels were shown between feature films at movie theaters.
8. **seeing it through rose-colored glasses** ignoring its unappealing features or drawbacks.

around at the ruins, he started telling us how lucky we were to be newsboys. Lucky to have a foot on the upward ladder so early in life. If we worked hard and kept expanding our paper routes we could make the men who ran this paper sit up and notice us. And when men like that noticed you, great things could happen, because they were important men, the most important of all being the man who owned our paper: Mr. Hearst Himself, William Randolph Hearst, founder of the greatest newspaper organization in America. A great man, Mr. Hearst, but not so great that he didn't appreciate his newsboys, who were the backbone of the business. Many of whom would someday grow up and work at big jobs on this paper. Did we realize that any of us, maybe all of us, could end up one of these days sitting right here in this vitally important room, the newsroom, the nerve center of the newspaper?

Yes, Deems was right. Riding home on the streetcar that night, I realized I was a lucky boy to be getting such an early start up the ladder of journalism. It was childish to feel let down because the city room looked like such a dump instead of like city rooms in the movies. Deems might be a slave driver, but he was doing it for my own good, and I ought to be grateful. In *News Selling*, the four-page special paper Mr. Hearst published just for his newsboys, they'd run a piece that put it almost as beautifully as Deems had.

YOU'RE A MEMBER OF THE FOURTH ESTATE was the headline on it. I was so impressed that I put the paper away in a safe place and often took it out to read when I needed inspiration. It told how "a great English orator" named Edmund Burke "started a new name for a new profession—the Fourth Estate . . . the press . . . NEWSPAPER MEN."[9]

And it went on to say:

"The Fourth Estate was then . . . and IS now . . . a great estate for HE-men . . . workers . . . those who are proud of the business they're in!"

(Mr. Hearst always liked plenty of exclamation marks, dots, and capital letters.)

"Get that kick of pride that comes from knowing you are a newspaper man. That means something!

Literature in context Humanities Connection

Journalism
Journalism is an important profession, responsible for informing people about local and world events. Journalists gather, write, and edit material for news stories. They work for newspapers, news services, magazines, radio, or television. In democracies such as the United States, journalists are free to report news without government interference. Reporters are responsible for accuracy and telling all sides of a news story. Editorial writers, meanwhile, express a news organization's views on issues.

✔ Reading Check
What did Russ learn about a newsroom during his visit?

---

9. **Edmund Burke . . . Fourth Estate** Edmund Burke (1729–1797) was an English political figure famous for his speeches and essays. He called the press the "Fourth Estate."

"A newspaper man never ducks a dare. YOU are a newspaper man. A salesman of newspapers . . . the final cog[10] in the <u>immense</u> machine of newspaper production—a SERVICE for any man to be proud of.

"So throw back the chest. Hit the route hard each day. Deliver fast and properly. Sell every day. Add to your route because you add to the NEWSPAPER field when you do. And YOU MAKE MONEY DOING IT. It is a great life—a grand opportunity. Don't boot it— build it up. Leave it better than when you came into it."

"It is a great life." I kept coming back to that sentence as I read and reread the thing. No matter how awful it got, and it sometimes got terrible, I never quit believing it was a great life. I kept at it until I was almost sixteen, chest thrown back, delivering fast and properly, selling every day and adding to my route. At the end I'd doubled its size and was making as much as four dollars a week from it.

A few months after he took us down to see the city room, Deems quit. My mother said he'd found a better job. Later, when I thought about him, I wondered if maybe it wasn't because he hated himself for having to make life hell for boys. I hoped that wasn't the reason because he was the first newspaperman I ever knew, and I wanted him to be the real thing. Hard as nails.

---

10. cog (käg) *n.* gear.

immense (i mens´) *adj.* huge

Review and Assess

Thinking About the Selection

1. **Respond:** Would you like to work for Deems? Why or why not?

2. **(a) Recall:** What does Russ's mother want her son to do?
   (b) Compare and Contrast: How are Russ's dreams for himself similar to and different from his mother's dreams for him?

3. **(a) Recall:** What did Russ think about newspaper work when he first started in the business? **(b) Support:** Find two examples that show the conflict between the realities of newspaper work and Baker's first ideas about it.

4. **(a) Recall:** What does Deems do when Russ sells all his papers?
   (b) Infer: What lesson do you think Deems is teaching Russ?
   (c) Draw Conclusions: At the end of "Hard as Nails," why does Russ want to believe that Deems really was "hard as nails"?
   (d) Speculate: Do you think this experience might help Baker in the future? Why or why not?

5. **Evaluate:** Do you think Deems treats the news boys fairly or unfairly? Why?

Russell Baker

(b. 1925)
Russell Baker grew up in Virginia, New Jersey, and Maryland. When he was in the seventh grade, he decided to become a writer. He thought that "making up stories must surely be almost as fun as reading them." As it turned out, Baker became a reporter. He won a Pulitzer Prize for his newspaper column in *The New York Times.* In "Hard as Nails," he describes his very first boss in the news business.

Review and Assess

Literary Analysis

Theme

1. In what two ways does the word "circuit" apply to Panchito's life?
2. What circumstances prevent Panchito from getting out?
3. What **theme**, or message, is Jiménez communicating through the title and the events in the story? To whom does the message apply? Explain.
4. Which people in "Hard as Nails" could be described by the words "hard as nails"?
5. What lessons does Baker learn and how might these lessons be applied to other people's lives?

Comparing Literary Works

6. Use a Venn diagram to compare and contrast Panchito and young Baker. Consider their circumstances, their experiences, their reactions to their experiences, and the personality traits they exhibit.

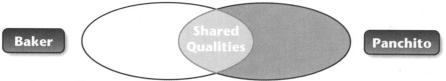

Baker — Shared Qualities — Panchito

Reading Strategy

Reading with Expression

For sentences 7 and 8, record the subject of each sentence and the key event on a chart like the one shown. Then read each sentence aloud with expression.

Subject	What happens	Additional details

7. I walked to the top of a small grade next to the shack and watched the "Carcanchita" disappear in the distance in a cloud of dust.
8. Because the *News-Post* was an afternoon paper, almost everybody had left for the day when we got there that night.

Extending Understanding

9. **Career Connection:** What qualities did young Russ learn that could be used in many jobs other than the newspaper business?

Quick Review

The **theme** is the central idea or thought about life that is expressed in a work of literature. To review theme, see page 65.

Reading with expression means using your voice to communicate, or express, the meaning of the words.

 Take It to the Net
www.phschool.com
Take the interactive self-test online to check your understanding of these selections.

Integrate Language Skills

Vocabulary Development Lesson

Word Analysis: Compound Nouns

A **compound noun** is a noun made up of two or more smaller words. Most compound nouns take their meaning from the two words in the compound. Explain how the words in each compound noun below contribute to its meaning.

1. streetcar   2. sidewalk   3. newsroom

Spelling Strategy

Copy each compound word above. Then, write each smaller word separately. Which word contains a silent letter? Which contain two vowels combining to make one sound?

Concept Development: Synonyms

Synonyms are words that have similar meanings, such as *journalist* and *reporter*. On your paper, write the letter for the word or phrase that is closest in meaning to each first word.

1. drone   a. very large
2. instinctively b. drain
3. savoring   c. hum
4. embedded   d. majestic
5. exhaust   e. naturally
6. sublime   f. enjoying
7. immense   g. fixed in

Grammar Lesson

Pronoun-Antecedent Agreement

Pronouns must agree with their antecedents (the words to which they refer).

Use a singular pronoun with a singular antecedent.
Example: *Tom* will lend Melissa *his* suitcase.

Use a plural pronoun with a plural antecedent.
Example: The *boys* have all brought *their* boots.

Use a singular pronoun with two or more singular antecedents joined by *or* or *nor*. Use a plural pronoun with two or more antecedents joined by *and*.
Example: Either *Andrew* or *Keith* will give *his* report.
          Joyce and *Bill* showed *their* father the drawing.

Use a singular pronoun to refer to a singular indefinite pronoun. Use a plural pronoun to refer to a plural indefinite pronoun.
Example: *One* of the boys will print *his* documents.

Example: *All* of the boys will print *their* documents.

Practice Copy the following sentences. Use pronouns that agree with their antecedents.

1. Panchito and Roberto worked in the fields, but ___?___ would have preferred to go to school.
2. Neither boy knows what ___?___ will say about the Yukon.
3. Fred and Tony are preparing ___?___ presentation.
4. Some of the reporters completed ___?___ stories on time.
5. One of the journalists rewrote ___?___ story.

Writing Application Write a brief explanation of how Mr. Lema influenced Panchito. Use each of the pronoun-antecedent agreement rules shown at the left.

W̶G̶ Prentice Hall Writing and Grammar Connection: Chapter 24, Section 2

Writing Lesson

Letter to a Character

Assume the role of Russell Baker and write a letter to Deems expressing your feelings about him and telling him what you learned from him.

Prewriting   Start by reviewing "Hard as Nails." Use a cluster diagram like the one below to note key experiences involving Baker and Deems, Baker's feelings about Deems, and what he learned from him.

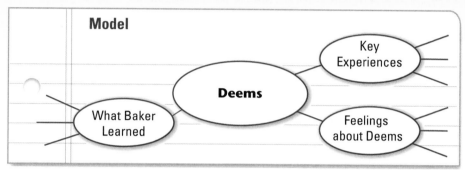

Model

- Key Experiences
- Deems
- What Baker Learned
- Feelings about Deems

Drafting   Using the details in your diagram, draft your letter. Begin with a paragraph reintroducing yourself. Then, follow with two or more paragraphs sharing your feelings and telling what you learned. Cite experiences involving Deems to back each point you make.

Revising   Review your draft to ensure that all of the content of your letter focuses on your feelings about Deems and what you learned from him. Each paragraph should focus on a single idea and contain details that support it.

*W*_G *Prentice Hall Writing and Grammar Connection: Chapter 12, Section 3*

Extension Activities

Listening and Speaking Russ was interested in the newspaper field, especially journalism. Take some time to **interview** an adult who works in a field that interests you. Prepare a list of questions about how to achieve success in that work.

- Be polite and speak clearly.
- Maintain eye contact with the person you are interviewing.
- Ask additional questions if something is unclear.

Tell the class about the results of your interview.

Research and Technology In a small group, research interesting jobs. Do a keyword search using a career or field such as *journalism*. Use Internet resources such as online news groups, newspapers, encyclopedias, and Web sites to gather statistics about each job, including education, skills, and salary ranges. Prepare a **report** to share your findings with the class.

 **Take It to the Net**   www.phschool.com

Go online for an additional research activity using the Internet.

READING INFORMATIONAL MATERIALS

Newspaper Articles

About Newspaper Articles

Newspapers are one kind of print medium. Most large-city newspapers are published daily. Newspapers keep people informed about local, national, and world events. Local or regional events, such as a fire or an election, make up most of a local paper, while daily papers published in cities include more national and world news. In addition, different sections of the paper cover specific subjects—for example, sports, business, the arts, and lifestyles. Usually, one or two pages are dedicated to editorial columns, with letters and essays written by people with opinions on current events.

Reading Strategy

Using Newspapers to Find Information

Few people read a newspaper from beginning to end. Instead, most people locate specific sections or articles and read only those that are of interest to them. Most large newspapers are divided into sections. Each section covers a particular category. The numbering of newspaper pages is usually a letter indicating the section followed by a numeral. This chart shows some of the structural features that can help you find information in a newspaper.

Feature	Function
Section heads, such as *Local News*, *Editorials*, or *Home*	Tell the focus of the articles within the section
Article titles are set on their own line in larger, heavier type than the article text.	Indicate topic of article
Run-in heads are printed in heavier type than the article but are not set on a separate line	Call out the key points in the article. The text that follows a run-in head gives more detail.
Pull-quotes	Highlight an important or interesting statement made by someone in the article
Photos and captions	Add visual information to be used with the text
Table of contents usually appears on the first page of the first section	Shows how the newspaper is broken into sections. Tells readers what page to turn to for regular features.

The article title
hints at the topic
and grabs
readers' interest.

Summer Hats

By Amy Lindgren

The pull-quote
calls attention to
the main idea of
the article.

If you're looking for work, different work, or more work, summertime is a great time to try a variety of jobs.

Summer's back! And our worker shortage prevails. These look like good conditions for a little experimenting with new jobs.

Of course, if you are a parent with school-age children, you may feel your summer "job" already has been chosen for you. Just arranging the kids' schedules for three months gives you training to be a high-level events planner.

Some of those kids are probably the right age for summer employment. Other people who might benefit from a short-term job include retirees; students; "winter workers," such as teachers and snowplow drivers; and, of course, the unemployed.

Summer employment is also a good option for the underemployed and dissatisfied workers who wonder what *else* they could do for a living. And, if you are struggling with a debt load, you might find relief by working to pay off a specific bill.

Some common summer jobs— for adults or kids—include farm work, lawn care, tourism work, anything in retail or food service, day-care/camp work, construction and some kinds of food production. Positions are available at all levels in most of these fields, although the short-term jobs tend to be at the entry level.

Be careful. As many of my readers have reminded me, it's possible to choose poorly. Indeed, bad summer jobs are almost a rite of passage in this country. To increase your chances of success, take these two simple steps:

First, define success. If you are taking a job purely for the money, figure out how much money you want to clear and establish a savings plan to safeguard the funds. If you are trying something new just for fun, how many hours a week can you spare? Perhaps you are trying to get experience in a new field so you can impress an employer later in your career; what kind of work would fit that bill?

Second, choose a job that meets the criteria you just established. You may have to approach employers instead of waiting for ads in the paper, but you'll be glad you took the initiative.

For example, if you would like to work at a garden center because you love plants and want to learn more about them (maybe you just want the discount!), don't hesitate to ask the manager of the center nearest you if the store needs help for the summer. If you can only work certain days, stick as close to that plan as possible. Otherwise, what started out to be fun will become a strain on your schedule.

Whatever your reasons for choosing a summer job, use these tips to make the experience a good one for you and your employer:

- **Take it seriously.** This may be just a summer fling for you, but it means everything to the employer. Your boss is counting on you to be dependable and to help keep the operation running.

- **Learn a new skill.** From corn detasseling to computer tutoring, every job has something to teach you. Perhaps you'll pick up some supervisory skills, or learn how to teach somebody else how to do what you're doing.

- **Learn about the business.** So you're delivering phone books? Why not ask a few questions about how the routes are created. Someday you may use that knowledge when you're setting up your own business as a product distributor. Working at an amusement park? How do they create promotions to attract visitors to the slow days? Ask questions and keep learning. If nothing else, it makes the time pass faster.

- **Get along with your co-workers and customers.** Whatever you do, make this a priority. After all, this is just a summer job. If you can't deal with difficult people for a few months, how will you ever manage it over the long haul?

- **Don't overwork.** Keep a balance between time off and your job so you don't collapse in September.

- **Leave on a good note.** There are several steps to take when leaving a short-term job. First, give plenty of notice. Ask for letters of recommendation and select a few samples of your work for your portfolio. For example, photos of you helping kids onto a carnival ride can work well later to demonstrate patience and responsibility. Give your contact information to anyone who might be able to connect you to more work later, and take down their names and numbers as well. Finally, thank your boss for the opportunity. Even if you hated the job, it's a classy touch.

Of course, don't forget to put your experiences on your resume. If you already have a career, you might include this job as a single line in an "Other" category. Workers just starting out will want to give this job higher billing and include more detail.

Have a good summer!

Run-in heads call out key points in the article.

The writer presents direct statements that offer practical advice for readers.

Check Your Comprehension

1. Who might be most interested in short-term jobs?
2. What might make summer employment advantageous?
3. List a few ways to ensure successful summer employment.
4. Why are summer jobs important to employers?

Applying the Reading Strategy

Using Text Features to Find Information

Use the text features in the chart on page 82 to find the information to answer these questions:

5. What is the topic of the article? Where did you find that information?
6. What are three key points about choosing a summer job that are called out by run-in heads?
7. In which section of the newspaper is this article most likely to be found? Why? **(a)** World News, **(b)** Living, **(c)** Entertainment

Activity

Use the text features of a newspaper to choose an article to read.

1. Begin by looking at the section heads. Choose one section that appeals to you.
2. Look over the article titles in that section. Choose three articles.
3. Read the run-in heads and the picture captions for each of the three articles. Choose and read the article that appears most interesting to you.
4. Explain why you made each choice. What information did you learn from section heads, article titles, run-in heads, and picture captions that guided you toward your final choice?

Comparing Informational Materials

Complete a chart like the one shown here to compare the structural features of a local newspaper and a national newspaper. Use newspapers that are printed on the same day.

	What are the sections?	What is the biggest section?	What is the first article on the first page?
Local			
National			

READING INFORMATIONAL MATERIALS

Interviews

About Interviews

An interview is an informational meeting that consists of questions asked by an interviewer and answers supplied by the person being interviewed. Interviews are a good way to gather people's opinions and knowledge of a subject or event.

To identify the kinds of information you will find in an interview, read the questions. (Questions are usually set off in a separate color or font.) "An Astronaut's Answers" is an interview with John Glenn on his memories of being the first American to orbit the Earth. The questions show that the interview contains the following information:

- Details about Glenn's first space mission
- Glenn's reasons for becoming an astronaut
- Glenn's reflections on space exploration

Reading Strategy

Using Prior Knowledge

To help you understand and connect to the main ideas or topic of an interview, draw on your prior knowledge. Your prior knowledge is the information, experiences, and thoughts you already have before you read any kind of written material. For example, you might already know that John Glenn was the first American to orbit the Earth. Use this prior knowledge to help you appreciate and understand Glenn's responses.

As you read the interview with John Glenn, use a graphic organizer like the one shown to think about what prior knowledge you have about astronauts and space travel. Then, when you have finished reading, write down what you learned from reading the interview.

My Prior Knowledge
astronauts:
John Glenn:
space travel:

What I Learned
astronauts:
John Glenn:
space travel:
Other:

An Astronaut's Answers

John Glenn

This interview was conducted shortly before Glenn returned to space at the age of seventy-seven on board the shuttle *Discovery*.

Questions are set off in red to distinguish them from Glenn's words.

The first time you went into space, how did it feel to be all alone except for communication through radio?

In 1962, I looked down from an orbit high above our planet and saw our beautiful Earth and its curved horizon against the vastness of space. I have never forgotten that sight nor the sense of wonder it engendered. Although I was alone in *Friendship 7*, I did not feel alone in space. I knew that I was supported by my family, my six fellow astronauts, thousands of NASA engineers and employees, and millions of people around the world.

These questions show that this section contains more opinions than facts.

Why did you want to be an astronaut? How did you fly around the Earth three times? Was it hard?

I served as a fighter pilot in World War II and the Korean conflict. After Korea, I graduated from the Naval Test Pilot School and worked as a fighter test pilot. I applied for the astronaut program because I thought it was a logical career step, a challenging opportunity and one in which I could help start a new area of research that would be very valuable to everyone here on Earth. I have always considered myself very fortunate to be selected in the first group of seven astronauts.

An Atlas rocket boosted me into space and I orbited the Earth in my space capsule, the *Friendship 7.* It certainly was a challenge but one for which I was well prepared. The National Aeronautics and Space Administration (NASA) wanted people who were test pilots and accustomed to working under very unusual conditions, including emergencies. During my first orbit I experienced some troubles with the automatic control system and so I had to take control of the capsule's movements by hand for the rest of the trip. Another problem developed when the signals showed that the heat shield was loose. To keep it secured during re-entry, I kept the retrorocket pack in place to steady the shield. When the *Friendship 7* entered the atmosphere, the retrorocket pack burned off and flew by my window, but the heat shield stayed in place. These were problems we could not have foreseen prior to the flight.

How long was your trip around the Earth?

My trip around the Earth lasted 4 hours and 55 minutes, and I flew about 81,000 miles.

What did you eat while you were in outer space?

I took along a number of different kinds of food, such as applesauce and a mixture of meat and vegetables, all emulsified like baby food. It was packaged in containers much like toothpaste tubes so I could squeeze food into my mouth. I had no trouble eating any of it, and it tasted fine.

Prior knowledge about weightlessness in a space vehicle helps you understand why the food is packaged as it is.

Why do astronauts go to the moon?

As adventurers of earlier eras crossed oceans and scaled mountains, astronauts in our time have flown to the moon and explored the heavens. The crucial hands-on experience of my flight in the Mercury program helped make the Gemini flights possible. The Gemini flights then helped make the Apollo missions to the moon a reality. Apollo gave us valuable information for the Shuttle missions, and the Shuttle/Mir program prepares us for the International Space Station. This is the nature of progress. Each of these missions has built on the knowledge gained from previous flights.

Use your knowledge that Glenn makes these comments before his return to space to increase your understanding of his thoughts.

We are curious, questing people and our research in this new laboratory of space represents an opportunity to benefit people right here on Earth and to increase our understanding of the universe. the potential scientific, medical, and economic benefits from space are beyond our wildest dreams. That's why astronauts went to the moon, and that's why we continue to pursue our dreams of space exploration.

Check Your Comprehension

1. How did John Glenn feel being alone in space?
2. How did John Glenn become an astronaut?
3. What kinds of problems did John Glenn face when he was orbiting the Earth?
4. What does John Glenn believe to be the reasons for astronauts going to the moon?
5. What did John Glenn eat while he was in space?

Applying the Reading Strategy

Using Prior Knowledge

6. What do you think is important to know before reading this interview?
7. What prior knowledge do you think the interviewer had before interviewing John Glenn?

Activity

Interview Questions

John Glenn is not only the first person to travel around the Earth; he is also the oldest person ever to travel in space. In 1998, John Glenn returned to space aboard the shuttle *Discovery*. Locate information about Glenn's journey aboard the shuttle *Discovery*. Create an article similar to "An Astronaut's Answers" by writing five interview questions. Answer the questions as John Glenn might by using the information you found in your research. Keep track of questions you want to find the answers to and the information you find while doing your research.

Interview Questions	Information Found
1.	
2.	
3.	
4.	
5.	

Contrasting Informational Materials

Interviews and News Articles

Find a news article that describes the launching of the shuttle *Discovery*. How does the reporting of the event differ from John Glenn's personal account? Which do you think gives more information? Which one is more appealing to readers? Write a brief comparison of the two different accounts.

Narration: Autobiographical Writing

Narrative writing is writing that tells a story. An **autobiographical narrative** tells the story of an event, a period, or a person in the writer's life. This workshop will give you the opportunity to write about an interesting experience in your life.

Assignment Criteria. Your autobiographical narrative should have the following characteristics:

- you, the writer, as a character in the story
- an interest-grabbing first sentence or opening paragraph
- a central problem or conflict that you or someone else resolves
- true events presented in logical order
- descriptive details about people, setting, and actions

To preview the criteria on which your autobiographical narrative will be assessed, see the Rubric on page 93.

Prewriting

Choose a topic. Use a **quicklist** to come up with a topic idea. Fold a piece of paper into three columns. In the first, list important people, places, and events. In the second, list words that describe those people, places, and events. In the third, jot down an action or event that illustrates the quality you have named. Choose one of the events in the last column as the topic for your narrative.

Narrow your topic. Once you have chosen your topic, narrow it to focus on the most interesting part. Identify the problem or the obstacle that you as the narrator (the person telling the story) will overcome.

Make a timeline. Use a timeline to plot events in your narrative. Note the most important things that happened and put them in chronological (time) order.

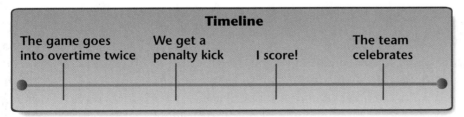

Timeline

| The game goes into overtime twice | We get a penalty kick | I score! | The team celebrates |

Add details about your thoughts and feelings. Review your timeline and add your reactions to events at different points in the narrative. Tell whether you were surprised, angry, joyous, or worried. If your reactions changed, tell how they changed in the narrative.

Student Model

Before you begin drafting your autobiographical narrative, read this student model and review the characteristics of a successful autobiographical narrative.

Christa Maikisch
Palos Verdes, CA

She Shoots! She Scores!

My heart was pounding in my ears, and sweat was running down my face. I was so nervous I couldn't feel my legs. Over and over in my imagination I sent the soccer ball flying over the net, completely missing the goal. I had just been through two overtimes and because of the heat, I didn't think I could last much longer. Sitting on the grass, waiting for my turn to make the penalty kick, I wandered back in my memory to my first years of soccer.

I started soccer when I was five. For my first two years, my mom was my coach. I played youth league for five years and club soccer for two. All those years had led up to this moment–when the whole team was depending on me. If I made this kick, we won. If I missed, we had to keep playing–and we were too hot and exhausted to play our best.

"Christa, you're up," said the coach.

"Uh, uh, OK . . ." I said.

"Relax, Christa, just relax," said the coach.

I took a deep breath and walked onto the field. "I can do this, I can do this" I told myself as I approached the referee. The ref checked the goalie, then nodded to me. The distance from the ball to the goal looked like an endless stretch of green. The goalie didn't look as tired as I felt. All these negative thoughts were not helping me! I shook my head to clear away the nerves. Then, I took five steps back . . . one more deep breath . . . I ran forward . . . kicked . . . and . . . it went in! The kick was good! Relief filled my heart because I knew I hadn't let my team down.

Suddenly, I saw my teammates rushing toward me. Just as I realized they were coming, I was mobbed. Everyone was screaming and laughing because we had won the game. Now, almost a year later, I look back on that day with pride and a smile on my face.

The writer grabs readers' interest by starting with details that create curiosity about why the writer is so nervous.

Because the writer is a character in the story, she can share her memories of what led up to this moment.

The conflict is the struggle between the writer's wish to make the goal and the possibility that she might miss.

These descriptive details help readers share the experience.

Drafting

Present the events in order. Present events in the order in which they happened. Tell enough about each event to give a clear picture. Stick to first-person point of view (use *I* to show that you are the narrator).

Create suspense. Build suspense in your narrative by focusing on the problem or conflict. If your story has little conflict, focus on what you learned or how the experience you are describing changed you. At the high point of your story, include details that tell how the conflict was resolved.

Use detail and dialogue. Include details from your timeline as you write. If it fits your narrative, add dialogue to show what people are thinking and feeling.

No dialogue: Ismail said that he wanted more cake.

With dialogue: "Oh please, please, puh-leez," begged Ismail, "I must have more triple-chocolate cake!"

Revising

Connect your paragraphs. Draw an arrow from each paragraph to the next. Label each arrow, telling the relationship between the paragraphs it links.

- Do events in one paragraph cause those in the next?
- Does a paragraph give more information about the previous one?
- Does a paragraph create curiosity about what will happen next?

   If a paragraph is not related to the ones before and after it, you might rewrite that paragraph, move it, or delete it.

Strengthen your lead. The start of a narrative—its **lead**—should make readers curious. Try these ideas:

- an exciting action
- a hint about a potential problem
- thought-provoking dialogue or a person's thoughts

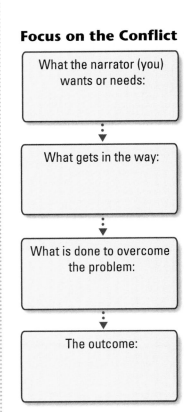

Focus on the Conflict

What the narrator (you) wants or needs:

What gets in the way:

What is done to overcome the problem:

The outcome:

The author creates more excitement with the revised lead.

Original Lead: I started soccer when I was five. For my first two years, my mom was my coach.

The author can provide this information later in the narrative.

Revised Lead: My heart was pounding in my ears, and sweat was running down my face.

Revise for word choice. Highlight the nouns in your draft. Evaluate each one, asking whether it might leave readers wondering *What kind?* Replace vague or general nouns with **precise nouns**.

Example: Eliza fed her *pet.*
Eliza fed her *hamster.*

Compare the model and the nonmodel. Why is the model more effective than the nonmodel?

Nonmodel	Model
Over and over in my head I completely missed the goal. I had just been through a long game and because of the heat, I didn't think I could last much longer. Sitting on the ground, I waited for my turn to make the penalty kick.	Over and over in my imagination I sent the soccer ball flying over the net, completely missing the goal. I had just been through two overtimes and because of the heat, I didn't think I could last much longer. Sitting on the grass, I waited for my turn to make the penalty kick.

Publishing and Presenting

Choose one of the following ways to share your writing with classmates or a wider audience.

Deliver a speech. Use your autobiographical narrative as the basis for a presentation.

Build an anthology. Use a word-processing program to create a neat final copy of your narrative. Gather narratives written by classmates, and compile them in an autobiographical anthology. Add art or photos to enhance each narrative.

 Prentice Hall Writing and Grammar Connection: Chapter 4

 *Speaking Connection*

To learn more about presenting an autobiographical narrative in a speech, see the **Listening and Speaking Workshop: Organizing and Giving a Narrative Presentation,** p. 94.

Rubric for Self-Assessment

Evaluate your autobiographical narrative, using the following criteria and rating scale:

Criteria	Rating Scale				
	Not very				Very
How consistently does the writer narrate events as someone who participates in the action?	1	2	3	4	5
How effective is the lead in grabbing your interest?	1	2	3	4	5
How clearly is the problem or conflict identified?	1	2	3	4	5
How clear is the order of events?	1	2	3	4	5
How detailed are the descriptions of the people, setting, and actions?	1	2	3	4	5

Listening and Speaking WORKSHOP

Organizing and Giving a Narrative Presentation

A **narrative presentation** is simply a story told aloud. The story may be real or made up. It may be about you or about someone else. In this workshop, you will organize and develop a narrative presentation. (To review the characteristics of autobiographical narratives, see the writing workshop, pp. 90–93. To preview the characteristics of a fictional narrative, see p. 520.) To deliver an effective account, organize and rehearse it first. The following strategies will help you give an effective presentation.

Organize and Rehearse

Like a written autobiographical narrative, an oral narrative account tells what happens in the story in chronological order, focusing on the central conflict, or struggle, in the story. Use the following guidelines to plan your spoken narrative.

Develop your plot. Use note cards to help you develop your plot. Write one narrative event on each card. Then, add dialogue that helps reveal your characters' personalities. Add concrete and sensory details about the people, setting, and actions.

Plan your delivery. Consider using some of the following techniques to add pep to your presentation. On each card, note the ones you might use.

- Change the pace. Slow down or speed up to emphasize the action in the narrative.
- Use gestures and movements that fit the story. You need only a few.
- Vary the pitch, raising or lowering your voice.

Rehearse. Practice your narrative in front of a mirror. Use your note cards to jog your memory, but put them aside when you no longer need them. Experiment with pace, pitch, and gestures.

> **Delivery Techniques**
>
> ### Pacing
> Speak slowly to build suspense: "Slowly, slowly, the footsteps grew louder. Angela and I waited. Who, who was coming up the stairs?"
>
> ### Gestures
> Wave, make a fist, clap, snap fingers, cover face with hands, shade eyes, beckon, put hands on hips, point
>
> ### Pitch
> - Try a high, squeaky voice to show excitement.
> - Try a low, rumbling voice to show anger.
> - Let your voice go up to end a question. Lower it slightly at the end of a statement.

(Activity:)
Presentation and Feedback Prepare and deliver a narrative presentation about a goal you have accomplished recently. Present your narrative to a partner and ask for constructive suggestions. Write down what they are. After your presentation, ask for audience feedback. Check the areas in which you improved your presentation.

Assessment WORKSHOP

Distinguishing Multiple Meanings

Some test questions ask you to choose the meaning of a word in a passage when the word has multiple meanings. The following methods will help you answer these types of questions.

- Read the passage to get the general meaning of the text.

- Locate the word that is set off in italics, boldface, or with an underscore.

- Ask yourself what the word must mean in order for the passage to make sense.

- Use the text surrounding the word to identify clues to the correct meaning.

Test-Taking Strategies

- Read the word in context before answering the question.
- Plug each word choice into the passage and cross out answers that do not make sense.

Sample Test Item

Directions: Read the following passage, and then choose the letter of the best answer to the question.

Sean's mother had asked him to clean out the garage, and he was happy to do it. As he put tools away, he thought about how hard his mother worked at the electronics **plant** to support the family.

1. The word **plant** in this passage means—

   A factory

   B leaf

   C hotel

   D flower

Answers and Explanations

The correct answer is **A**. If you place **B, C,** or **D** in the sentence, you realize that each one does not make sense within the context of the sentence.

▶ Practice

Directions: Answer these test questions based on the following passage.

Garrison Keillor reaches out to more than two million public radio listeners who **tune** in every week to hear his variety show, *A Prairie Home Companion.* Through songs, comedy, **sketches**, and stories, Keillor nudges listeners into thinking about the really important things in life—along with the really funny ones.

1. The word **tune** in this passage means—

   A melody

   B air

   C listen

   D prepare

2. In this passage, the word **sketches** means—

   A cartoons

   B designs

   C funny drawings

   D short plays

First Steps, Vincent van Gogh; Metropolitan Museum of Art

Exploring the Theme

The man in this picture reaches out to encourage the toddler to walk. In the same way, the stories, poems, and essays in this unit encourage you to move forward—to open new doors and discover new friends. By sharing the experiences of literary characters and considering the ideas expressed by the authors, you will recognize the many different ways people can reach out.

As you read, think about the ways in which writers and characters reach out in difficult situations and take steps toward understanding the world and the people in it.

◀ **Critical Viewing** What feelings do the actions of the characters in this painting express? **[Assess]**

Why Read Literature?

There are many specific purposes for reading. You might want to enjoy an adventure story, learn about a new invention, or consider how others feel about a particular issue. Preview three purposes you might have for reading the works in this unit.

1

Read for the love of literature.

A canary's heart races at about 1,000 beats per minute. Although this tiny bird may seem delicate and fragile, Arthur C. Clarke describes one tough canary in his science-fiction story **"Feathered Friend,"** page 159.

Polish American author Isaac Bashevis Singer was expected to follow in the family tradition and become a rabbi. Instead, he became a master short-story writer. Singer draws on people and scenes from his Polish heritage in many of his works. Follow Singer's exciting account of a young boy lost in the Polish countryside during a raging blizzard when you read **"Zlateh the Goat,"** page 128.

3

Read for information.

How does a deaf, blind toddler become a famous writer and lecturer? Learn about the breakthrough that set Helen Keller on the road to fame in **"Water,"** page 120.

2

Read to appreciate author's style.

Leslie Marmon Silko grew up at Laguna Pueblo in New Mexico where she listened to tales told by her great-grandmother. Share Silko's love for the beauty and power of words when you read her **"How to Write a Poem About the Sky,"** page 106.

Garrison Keillor is as well known for being a talker as he is for being a writer. Talking on the radio earned him a place in the Radio Hall of Fame. Enjoy the way Keillor makes writing seem like talking when you read his essay **"How to Write a Letter,"** page 102.

There are more than 2,700 types of snakes in the world, but only about 250 types are poisonous to humans. Learn other interesting and surprising facts when you read the true story of a friendly, helpful snake—**"Old Ben"**—by Jesse Stuart on page 154.

 Take It to the Net

Visit the Web site for online instruction and activities related to each selection in this unit.

www.phschool.com

How to Read Literature

Use Literal Comprehension Strategies

The first step in understanding a work of literature is to grasp its literal meaning—the basic facts and details the author is communicating. These strategies will help you understand a writer's words on a literal level:

1. Read words in groups.

When you read aloud, read words in groups. To do this, look ahead at the punctuation, which signals when to pause or stop and when to raise or lower your voice. Use expression to reflect the meaning of the words.

2. Use context to clarify meanings.

Use the context—or the surrounding words, sentences, and paragraphs—to find clues to the meaning of a familiar word that is used in a new or unusual way.

The surrounding words may include words that have similar or related meanings.

> . . . we had little trouble concealing our guest when VIP's from Earth came visiting. A space station has more hiding places than you can count; . . . —"Feathered Friend"

The word *concealing* may be unfamiliar to you, but the words *hiding places* are clues that *concealing* means "putting out of sight; hiding."

3. Summarize.

As you read, pause occasionally to think about and sum up the main points or events that have happened so far. Review the events in your mind, and then organize them in the sequence in which they occurred.

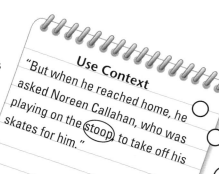

Use Context

"But when he reached home, he asked Noreen Callahan, who was playing on the *stoop* to take off his skates for him."

Noreen is playing on the stoop at home, so *stoop* cannot mean "to bend forward"; she is playing in front of Aaron's apartment house, so stoop must be part of the building. It's probably that little porch or set of steps in front of the building.

4. Paraphrase.

Restate a sentence or idea in your own words to make sure you understand it.

Longfellow's Words	Between the dark and the daylight, When the night is beginning to lower
Paraphrase	At twilight

As you read the selections in this unit, review the reading strategies and look at the notes in the side columns. Use the suggestions to apply the strategies for literal comprehension.

Prepare to Read

How to Write a Letter ◆ How to Write a Poem About the Sky

The Calm After the Storm, Edward Moran, Private Collection

 Take It to the Net

Visit www.phschool.com
for interactive activities
and instruction related to
these selections, including
• background
• graphic organizers
• literary elements
• reading strategies

Preview

Connecting to the Literature

In "How to Write a Letter" and "How to Write a Poem About the Sky," Garrison Keillor and Leslie Marmon Silko demonstrate how to create a beautiful gift out of an ordinary moment. How? Put the moment in writing. Before reading these selections, recall a moment or experience that you would like to share with someone else.

Background

Leslie Marmon Silko wrote "How to Write a Poem About the Sky" while teaching creative writing to schoolchildren in Alaska. Her poem captures the vast, uninhabited beauty of the landscape there.

Literary Analysis

Informal Essay

The titles of these two works suggest that they will be instructional essays—directions for writing. In fact, "How to Write a Letter" is an **informal essay**—a brief, nonfiction discussion of a topic, written in conversational language. It may contain humorous remarks. Although "How to Write a Poem About the Sky" is a poem, not an essay, it shares the informal conversational feeling of Keillor's essay. In this example, Keillor creates the feeling of conversation by using contractions and short sentences.

> Don't worry about form. It's not a term paper. When you come to the end of one episode, just start a new paragraph.

Comparing Literary Works

Although these two works are different genres (an essay and a poem), they share some common elements. Use a chart like the one here to compare and contrast the two works.

Use the chart to help you answer the following focus questions:

1. How are the topics of these works similar?
2. What is each writer's main point about writing?

How to Write a Letter		How to Write a Poem
Essay	Genre	Poem
	Topic	
	Language Style	
	Main point	

Reading Strategy

Reading Aloud with Expression

When you read aloud with expression, you use your voice to reflect the meaning of the words. As you read these works, practice reading sections with expression. Adjust your reading in the following ways:

1. **Pacing:** Pacing is the speed and rhythm of your reading. Read at a normal speed as the text builds to a point. Slow down for a key point. Pause before a fact or short sentence.

2. **Intonation:** Intonation is the volume, tone, and pitch of your voice. These vocal qualities can be used to express emotion or add emphasis. Depending on the feeling you want to communicate, make your voice higher, lower, louder, softer, firmer, or gentler.

Vocabulary Development

confidence (kän′ fi dəns′) *n.* belief in one's own abilities (p. 103)

anonymity (an′ ə nim′ ə tē) *adj.* the condition of being unknown (p. 103)

obligatory (əb lig′ ə tor′ ē) *adj.* required (p. 103)

episode (ep′ ə sōd′) *n.* one in a series of related events (p. 104)

sibling (sib′ liŋ) *n.* brother or sister (p. 104)

dense (dens) *adj.* tightly packed; difficult to see through (p. 106)

membranes (mem′ brānz) *n.* thin, flexible layers of tissue (p. 106)

How to Write a Letter

Garrison Keillor

We shy persons need to write a letter now and then, or else we'll dry up and blow away. It's true. And I speak as one who loves to reach for the phone, dial the number, and talk. I say, "Big Bopper here—what's shakin', babes?" The telephone is to shyness what Hawaii is to February, it's a way out of the woods, and yet: a letter is better.

Such a sweet gift—a piece of handmade writing, in an envelope that is not a bill, sitting in our friend's path when she trudges home from a long day spent among wahoos and savages, a day our

Literary Analysis
Informal Essay How is this paragraph of the essay like a friendly letter?

words will help repair. They don't need to be immortal, just sincere. She can read them twice and again tomorrow: *You're someone I care about, Corinne, and think of often and every time I do you make me smile.*

We need to write, otherwise nobody will know who we are. They will have only a vague impression of us as A Nice Person, because, frankly, we don't shine at conversation, we lack the <u>confidence</u> to thrust our faces forward and say, "Hi, I'm Heather Hooten; let me tell you about my week." Mostly we say "Uh-huh" and "Oh, really." People smile and look over our shoulder, looking for someone else to meet.

So a shy person sits down and writes a letter. To be known by another person—to meet and talk freely on the page—to be close despite distance. To escape from <u>anonymity</u> and be our own sweet selves and express the music of our souls.

Same thing that moves a giant rock star to sing his heart out in front of 123,000 people moves us to take ballpoint in hand and write a few lines to our dear Aunt Eleanor. *We want to be known.* We want her to know that we have fallen in love, that we quit our job, that we're moving to New York, and we want to say a few things that might not get said in casual conversation: *Thank you for what you've meant to me, I am very happy right now.*

The first step in writing letters is to get over the guilt of *not* writing. You don't "owe" anybody a letter. Letters are a gift. The burning shame you feel when you see unanswered mail makes it harder to pick up a pen and makes for a cheerless letter when you finally do. *I feel bad about not writing, but I've been so busy,* etc. Skip this. Few letters are <u>obligatory</u>, and they are *Thanks for the wonderful gift and I am terribly sorry to hear about George's death and Yes, you're welcome to stay with us next month,* and not many more than that. Write those promptly if you want to keep your friends. Don't worry about the others, except love letters, of course. When your true love writes, *Dear Light of My Life, Joy of My Heart, O Lovely Pulsating Core of My Sensate[1] Life,* some response is called for.

Some of the best letters are tossed off in a burst of inspiration, so keep your writing stuff in one place where you can sit down for a few minutes and (*Dear Roy, I am in the middle of a book entitled We Are Still Married but thought I'd drop you a line. Hi to your sweetie, too*) dash off a note to a pal. Envelopes, stamps, address book, everything in a drawer so you can write fast when the pen is hot.

A blank white eight-by-eleven sheet can look as big as Montana if the pen's not so hot—try a smaller page and write boldly. Or use a note card with a piece of fine art on the front; if your letter ain't

---

1. **sensate** (sen´ sāt) *adj.* having the power of sensory perception.

confidence (kän´ fi dəns´) *n.* belief in one's own abilities

anonymity (an´ ə nim´ ə tē) *n.* the condition of being unknown

Reading Strategy
Reading Aloud With Expression How would you adjust your intonation for the words *not* and "owe"?
obligatory (əb lig´ ə tor´ ē) *adj.* required

✔**Reading Check**
What is the first step in writing a letter?

good, at least they get the Matisse.[2] Get a pen that makes a sensuous[3] line, get a comfortable typewriter, a friendly word processor—whichever feels easy to the hand.

Sit for a few minutes with the blank sheet in front of you, and meditate on the person you will write to, let your friend come to mind until you can almost see her or him in the room with you. Remember the last time you saw each other and how your friend looked and what you said and what perhaps was unsaid between you, and when your friend becomes real to you, start to write.

Write the salutation—*Dear You*—and take a deep breath and plunge in. A simple declarative sentence will do, followed by another and another and another. Tell us what you're doing and tell it like you were talking to us. Don't think about grammar, don't think about lit'ry style, don't try to write dramatically, just give us your news. Where did you go, who did you see, what did they say, what do you think?

If you don't know where to begin, start with the present moment: *I'm sitting at the kitchen table on a rainy Saturday morning. Everyone is gone and the house is quiet.* Let your simple description of the present moment lead to something else, let the letter drift gently along.

The toughest letter to crank out is one that is meant to impress, as we all know from writing job applications; if it's hard work to slip off a letter to a friend, maybe you're trying too hard to be terrific. A letter is only a report to someone who already likes you for reasons other than your brilliance. Take it easy.

Don't worry about form. It's not a term paper. When you come to the end of one <u>episode</u>, just start a new paragraph. You can go from a few lines about the sad state of pro football to the fight with your mother to your fond memories of Mexico to your cat's urinary-tract infection to a few thoughts on personal indebtedness and on to the kitchen sink and what's in it. The more you write, the easier it gets, and when you have a True True Friend to write

▲ Critical Viewing
Judging from the expression on his face, who has written the letter this man is reading? **[Speculate]**

episode (ep′ ə sōd′) *n.* one in a series of related events

---

2. **Matisse** Henri Matisse (än rē mə tēs′)(1869–1954), a French painter.
3. **sensuous** (sen′ shoo əs) *adj.* readily grasped by the senses.

to, a compadre,[4] a soul <u>sibling</u>, then it's like driving a car down a country road, you just get behind the keyboard and press on the gas.

Don't tear up the page and start over when you write a bad line—try to write your way out of it. Make mistakes and plunge on. Let the letter cook along and let yourself be bold. Outrage, confusion, love—whatever is in your mind, let it find a way to the page. Writing is a means of discovery, always, and when you come to the end and write *Yours ever* or *Hugs and kisses*, you'll know something you didn't when you wrote *Dear Pal.*

Probably your friend will put your letter away, and it'll be read again a few years from now—and it will improve with age. And forty years from now, your friend's grandkids will dig it out of the attic and read it, a sweet and precious relic of the ancient eighties that gives them a sudden clear glimpse of you and her and the world we old-timers knew. You will then have created an object of art. Your simple lines about where you went, who you saw, what they said, will speak to those children and they will feel in their hearts the humanity of our times.

You can't pick up a phone and call the future and tell them about our times. You have to pick up a piece of paper.

---

4. **compadre** (kəm päd´ rä) *n.* Spanish for buddy; close friend.

sibling (sib´ liŋ) *n.* brother or sister

Review and Assess

Thinking About the Selection

1. **Respond:** Do you like writing letters? Why or why not?
2. **(a) Recall:** According to Keillor, why do people need to write letters? **(b) Analyze:** What can a writer accomplish in a letter that he or she cannot accomplish in everyday conversation? **(c) Distinguish:** Identify two situations for which a letter is the better form of communication and two situations for which a conversation is better.
3. **(a) Recall:** What does Keillor say is the first step in writing a letter? **(b) Analyze Cause and Effect:** How might following this suggestion result in a better letter?
4. **(a) Recall:** What are two kinds of letters you are obligated to write? **(b) Contrast:** How are these letters different from letters to close friends? **(c) Deduce:** How can you tell that Keillor has written many letters to friends?
5. **(a) Draw Conclusions:** In what ways is a letter more than just a good way to communicate? **(b) Evaluate:** Do you think letter writing is important in today's society? Explain.

Garrison Keillor

(b. 1942)
Over the years, Garrison Keillor's name has become a synonym for his public radio program called A *Prairie Home Companion*. In this award-winning variety show, Keillor uses songs, comedy sketches, and stories to nudge listeners into thinking about the really important things in life—along with the really funny ones. The highlight of the show is "News from Lake Wobegon," Keillor's monologue about doings in an imaginary midwestern town. Keillor is also the author of several books of humor and a member of the Radio Hall of Fame.

HOW TO WRITE A POEM ABOUT THE SKY

Leslie Marmon Silko

You see the sky now
colder than the frozen river
so <u>dense</u> and white
little birds
5   walk across it.

You see the sky now
but the earth
is lost in it
and there are no horizons.
10 It is all
a single breath.

You see the sky
but the earth is called
by the same name
15   the moment
              the wind shifts
sun splits it open
and bluish <u>membranes</u>
push through slits of skin.

20 You see the sky

dense (dens) *adj.* tightly packed; difficult to see through

membranes (mem´ brānz) *n.* thin, flexible layers of tissue

Leslie Marmon Silko

(b. 1948)
In addition to writing two well-received novels about Native American life (*Ceremony* and *Almanac of the Dead*), Leslie Marmon Silko has always been a poet and a lover of poetry.

Her work embraces her experiences growing up on a Laguna Pueblo reservation in New Mexico, as well as her love of landscape—such as the cold, barren region of Alaska, described in "How to Write a Poem About the Sky."

Review and Assess

Thinking About the Selection

1. **Respond:** Which verse in the poem seems most real to you?
2. **(a) Recall:** What color is the sky? **(b) Interpret:** In what way is the sky like the frozen river? **(c) Draw Conclusions:** Why is the speaker unable to see the horizon?
3. **(a) Synthesize:** In your own words, describe the change in the sky's appearance after the wind shifts. **(b) Interpret:** Why does the poet compare the sky to skin and membranes? **(c) Evaluate:** How effective is Silko in capturing true images of the sky?

Review and Assess

Literary Analysis

Informal Essay

1. Explain why "How to Write a Letter" can be categorized as an **informal essay.**
2. Explain which characteristics "How to Write a Poem About the Sky" shares with an informal essay.

Comparing Literary Works

3. Identify the topics, the points discussed, and the use of informal language in each work on a chart like the one shown below.

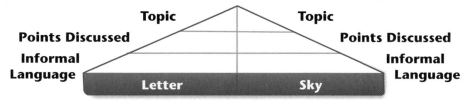

Topic   **Topic**

Points Discussed   **Points Discussed**

Informal Language   **Informal Language**

Letter   **Sky**

4. How much of each work focuses on how to do the writing?
5. How much does each work focus on the reason for writing or the writer's feelings about writing?
6. Which of these works most closely fits your image of "how to"?

Reading Strategy

Reading Aloud with Expression

7. Choose a paragraph from the essay and a verse from the poem to read aloud. On a chart like the one shown, identify specific words, phrases, or sentences for which you adjusted your pacing and intonation. Explain why you made adjustments.

Pacing   **Intonation**

Extending Understanding

8. **Career Connection:** How might Keillor's advice be different if he were explaining how to write a business letter?

Quick Review

An **essay** is a brief, non-fiction discussion of a topic.
An **informal essay** is an essay that uses casual, conversational language. To review informal essay, see page 101.

Pacing is the use of pauses and varied reading speeds.
Intonation is the use of a higher or lower voice. To review reading with expression, see page 101.

 Take It to the Net
www.phschool.com
Take the interactive self-test online to check your understanding of these selections.

Integrate Language Skills

Vocabulary Development Lesson

Word Analysis: Latin Suffix -ory

The Latin suffix -ory indicates "the quality or nature of." For example, *obligations* are *obligatory.* Copy the following items on your paper. Fill in the missing words.

1. Things related to the ___?___ are sensory.
2. Systems that ___?___ are regulatory.
3. You might use an accusatory tone when making an ___?___.

Spelling Strategy

The *ens* sound at the end of words like *confidence* is often spelled *ence.* You may need to memorize the spelling of words that end in *-ence.*

On your paper, write the ending for each word by adding *-ence.*

1. differ___?___
2. independ___?___
3. pres___?___

Fluency: Using Words in Context

On separate paper, answer these questions. Explain each answer.

1. Could someone call you a *sibling*?
2. How would you feel if someone called you a *sibling*?
3. Is one scene in a play an *episode*? Explain.
4. What is a common *episode* in the lunch-room at your school?
5. What increases your *confidence*?
6. When have you lost *confidence*?
7. Name one thing that is *obligatory* for staying alive.
8. Do you think a dress code should be *obligatory* at your school?
9. When would you wish for *anonymity*?
10. Why is *anonymity* important for a person who is accused of a crime but not yet tried?

Grammar Lesson

Verbs

A **verb** is a word that shows an action or state of being in a sentence. *Send, think,* and *run* are verbs that show action. *Was, am, became,* and *seem* are verbs that show state of being.

Practice Copy the following sentences on paper. Circle the verbs. (There may be more than one.)

1. A letter brightens a friend's day.
2. Take a deep breath and plunge in.
3. A blank piece of paper seems scary.
4. The letter becomes a precious relic.
5. It is not a report.

Writing Application Copy the following questions. Answer each with a complete sentence. Circle the verb or verbs in each question and each answer.

1. What does Keillor want you to do?
2. How old are you?
3. How often do you talk on the phone?
4. What did you eat for lunch yesterday?
5. What is something you want to do tomorrow?

W̲G *Prentice Hall Writing and Grammar Connection: Chapter 15, Section 1*

Writing Lesson

Letter

Use Keillor's suggestions in "How to Write a Letter" to write a letter to a friend.

Prewriting Think about a recent activity that you want to write about. Jot down what the activity was, whom you were with, and how you enjoyed it.

Drafting Open your letter with a friendly greeting and a sentence that tells your friend about the activity. The body of your letter should expand on the activity and how you felt about it. Include specific details that make it personal and informal, such as "The roller coaster has more loops than any other I've been on." The last paragraph of your letter should sum up your thoughts and feelings.

Revising Review your writing and add personal details that connect to your reader. Look for places where you can make your language more informal.

Model: Revising To Add Details

Dear Kaitlin,

It's even hotter than the last day of school!
It's very hot here. ^We don't mind because we swim in the

ocean all day anyway! The waves are huge!

> The writer uses contractions because a friendly letter is informal. She adds a personal detail here that the reader will appreciate.

WG Prentice Hall Writing and Grammar Connection: Chapter 4, Section 4

Extension Activities

Research and Technology Make an illustrated **timeline** that shows the history of mail. Use the Internet and other sources to get information about the milestones leading to the postal services we have today. To gather information, use a key word search on a search engine to find the Internet address for the U.S. Postal Service. Illustrate some of these milestones by including pictures on your timeline.

Listening and Speaking Choose a portion of Keillor's essay and present it as a **speech**. Practice delivering the speech. Slow down to emphasize the main points for your listeners. Give examples to emphasize the main points for your listeners. Deliver your speech to your class.

 **Take It to the Net**   www.phschool.com

Go online for an additional research activity using the Internet.

Prepare to Read

Aaron's Gift ◆ Water

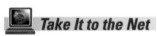
Take It to the Net

Visit www.phschool.com
for interactive activities
and instruction related to
these selections, including

- background
- graphic organizers
- literary elements
- reading strategies

Preview

Connecting to the Literature

The main characters in "Aaron's Gift" and "Water" find solutions to problems by explaining new approaches and new ways of looking at things. Connect your experience to the experiences of the characters by recalling a time when you have found a new approach or viewpoint that helped you solve a problem.

Background

The author of "Water," Helen Keller, became blind and deaf before she was two years old. When her teacher Annie Sullivan entered her life, Helen did not even know what "words" were. She had no idea that the people and things she felt with her hands had names.

Literary Analysis

Climax

A narrative starts with a problem or conflict. Each event in the narrative moves readers toward the moment when the outcome is decided. That moment is the **climax**, or turning point of the story. It is the high point of interest or suspense. As you read "Aaron's Gift," use a diagram like the one shown to record the events leading to the climax. Keep the following points in mind:

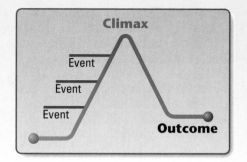

- All of the events before the climax help build tension in the story.
- All of the events following the climax lead to the resolution or final outcome.

Comparing Literary Works

Compare and contrast the types of problems or conflicts that Aaron and Helen Keller face. As you read both selections, use these focus questions to guide you:

1. Which character faces a problem with other characters?
2. Which character faces a problem within himself or herself?

Reading Strategy

Using Context to Clarify Meaning

Sometimes you may read a word you recognize, but the word is used in a way that is different from what you expected. Some words have more than one meaning. Clarify the meaning of such words by looking at the **context,** the situation in which the word is used. The word *dashed* commonly means "ran quickly." Here, the word has a different meaning.

> I became impatient at her repeated attempts and, seizing the new doll, I *dashed* it upon the floor. I was keenly delighted when I felt the fragments of the broken doll at my feet.

The writer's impatience, and the fact that the doll is broken, are clues that *dashed* probably means "threw down with force and anger."

Vocabulary Development

frenzied (fren´ zēd) *adj.* wild; frantic (p. 112)

mascot (mas´ kät) *n.* any person, animal, or thing adopted by a group; meant to bring good luck (p. 115)

coaxed (kōkst) *v.* tried to persuade (p. 115)

consoled (kän sōld´) *v.* comforted (p. 116)

Aaron's Gift

Myron Levoy

Aaron Kandel had come to Tompkins Square Park to roller-skate, for the streets near Second Avenue were always too crowded with children and peddlers and old ladies and baby buggies. Though few children had bicycles in those days, almost every child owned a pair of roller skates. And Aaron was, it must be said, a Class A, triple-fantastic roller skater.

Aaron skated back and forth on the wide walkway of the park, pretending he was an aviator in an air race zooming around pylons, which were actually two lampposts. During his third lap around the racecourse, he noticed a pigeon on the grass, behaving very strangely. Aaron skated to the line of benches, then climbed over onto the lawn.

The pigeon was trying to fly, but all it could manage was to flutter and turn round and round in a large circle, as if it were performing a <u>frenzied</u> dance. The left wing was only half open and was beating in a clumsy, jerking fashion; it was clearly broken.

▲ Critical Viewing
How would you compare this bird to Aaron's bird?
[Compare and Contrast]

frenzied (fren´ zēd) adj.
wild; frantic

Luckily, Aaron hadn't eaten the cookies he'd stuffed into his pocket before he'd gone clacking down the three flights of stairs from his apartment, his skates already on. He broke a cookie into small crumbs and tossed some toward the pigeon. "Here pidge, here pidge," he called. The pigeon spotted the cookie crumbs and, after a moment, stopped thrashing about. It folded its wings as best it could, but the broken wing still stuck half out. Then it strutted over to the crumbs, its head bobbing forth-back, forth-back, as if it were marching a little in front of the rest of the body—perfectly normal, except for that half-open wing which seemed to make the bird stagger sideways every so often.

The pigeon began eating the crumbs as Aaron quickly unbuttoned his shirt and pulled it off. Very slowly, he edged toward the bird, making little kissing sounds like the ones he heard his grandmother make when she fed the sparrows on the back fire escape.

Then suddenly Aaron plunged. The shirt, in both hands, came down like a torn parachute. The pigeon beat its wings, but Aaron held the shirt to the ground, and the bird couldn't escape. Aaron felt under the shirt, gently, and gently took hold of the wounded pigeon.

"Yes, yes, pidge," he said, very softly. "There's a good boy. Good pigeon, good."

The pigeon struggled in his hands, but little by little Aaron managed to soothe it. "Good boy, pidge. That's your new name. Pidge. I'm gonna take you home, Pidge. Yes, yes, *ssh.* Good boy. I'm gonna fix you up. Easy, Pidge, easy does it. Easy, boy."

Aaron squeezed through an opening between the row of benches and skated slowly out of the park, while holding the pigeon carefully with both hands as if it were one of his mother's rare, precious cups from the old country. How fast the pigeon's heart was beating! Was he afraid? Or did all pigeons' hearts beat fast?

It was fortunate that Aaron was an excellent skater, for he had to skate six blocks to his apartment, over broken pavement and sudden gratings and curbs and cobblestones. But when he reached home, he asked Noreen Callahan, who was playing on the stoop, to take off his skates for him. He would not chance going up three flights on roller skates this time.

"Is he sick?" asked Noreen.

"Broken wing," said Aaron. "I'm gonna fix him up and make him into a carrier pigeon or something."

"Can I watch?" asked Noreen.

"Watch what?"

"The operation. I'm gonna be a nurse when I grow up."

"OK," said Aaron. "You can even help. You can help hold him while I fix him up."

Literary Analysis
Climax What detail about the pigeon begins to build interest in the situation?

Reading Strategy
Using Context How does the word *escape* help you understand what *beat* means in this situation?

Reading Check

What is Aaron doing for the pigeon? Why?

Aaron wasn't quite certain what his mother would say about his new-found pet, but he was pretty sure he knew what his grandmother would think. His grandmother had lived with them ever since his grandfather had died three years ago. And she fed the sparrows and jays and crows and robins on the back fire escape with every spare crumb she could find. In fact, Aaron noticed that she sometimes created crumbs where they didn't exist, by squeezing and tearing pieces of her breakfast roll when his mother wasn't looking.

Aaron didn't really understand his grandmother, for he often saw her by the window having long conversations with the birds, telling them about her days as a little girl in the Ukraine.[1] And once he saw her take her mirror from her handbag and hold it out toward the birds. She told Aaron that she wanted them to see how beautiful they were. Very strange. But Aaron did know that she would love Pidge, because she loved everything.

Pigeons, John Sloan, The Hayden Collection, Courtesy, Museum of Fine Arts, Boston, Massachusetts

▲ **Critical Viewing**
What details in this painting suggest freedom? **[Interpret]**

To his surprise, his mother said he could keep the pigeon, temporarily, because it was sick, and we were all strangers in the land of Egypt,[2] and it might not be bad for Aaron to have a pet. *Temporarily.*

The wing was surprisingly easy to fix, for the break showed clearly and Pidge was remarkably patient and still, as if he knew he was being helped. Or perhaps he was just exhausted from all the thrashing about he had done. Two Popsicle sticks served as splints, and strips from an old undershirt were used to tie them in place. Another strip held the wing to the bird's body.

Aaron's father arrived home and stared at the pigeon. Aaron waited for the expected storm. But instead, Mr. Kandel asked, "Who *did* this?"

"Me," said Aaron. "And Noreen Callahan."

"Sophie!" he called to his wife. "Did you see this! Ten years old and it's better than Dr. Belasco could do. He's a genius!"

---

1. Ukraine (yo͞o krān´) country located in Eastern Europe. From 1924 to 1991, Ukraine was part of the Soviet Union.
2. we were all . . . land of Egypt a reference to the biblical story of the enslavement of the Hebrew people in Egypt. Around 1300 B.C., the Hebrews were led out of Egypt by Moses.

As the days passed, Aaron began training Pidge to be a carrier pigeon. He tied a little cardboard tube to Pidge's left leg and stuck tiny rolled-up sheets of paper with secret messages into it: THE ENEMY IS ATTACKING AT DAWN. Or: THE GUNS ARE HIDDEN IN THE TRUNK OF THE CAR. Or: VINCENT DEMARCO IS A BRITISH SPY. Then Aaron would set Pidge down at one end of the living room and put some popcorn at the other end. And Pidge would waddle slowly across the room, cooing softly, while the ends of his bandages trailed along the floor.

At the other end of the room, one of Aaron's friends would take out the message, stick a new one in, turn Pidge around, and aim him at the popcorn that Aaron put down on his side of the room.

And Pidge grew fat and contented on all the popcorn and crumbs and corn and crackers and Aaron's grandmother's breakfast rolls.

Aaron had told all the children about Pidge, but he only let his very best friends come up and play carrier-pigeon with him. But telling everyone had been a mistake. A group of older boys from down the block had a club—Aaron's mother called it a gang—and Aaron had longed to join as he had never longed for anything else. To be with them and share their secrets, the secrets of older boys. To be able to enter their clubhouse shack on the empty lot on the next street. To know the password and swear the secret oath. To belong.

About a month after Aaron had brought the pigeon home, Carl, the gang leader, walked over to Aaron in the street and told him he could be a member if he'd bring the pigeon down to be the club mascot. Aaron couldn't believe it; he immediately raced home to get Pidge. But his mother told Aaron to stay away from those boys, or else. And Aaron, miserable, argued with his mother and pleaded and cried and coaxed. It was no use. Not with those boys. No.

Aaron's mother tried to change the subject. She told him that it would soon be his grandmother's sixtieth birthday, a very special birthday indeed, and all the family from Brooklyn and the East Side would be coming to their apartment for a dinner and celebration. Would Aaron try to build something or make something for Grandma? A present made with his own hands would be nice. A decorated box for her hairpins or a crayon picture for her room or anything he liked.

In a flash Aaron knew what to give her: Pidge! Pidge would be her present! Pidge with his wing healed, who might be able to carry messages for her to the doctor or his Aunt Rachel or other people his grandmother seemed to go to a lot. It would be a surprise for everyone. And Pidge would make up for what had happened to Grandma

Reading Strategy
Using Context The most common meaning of "long" is to describe length. How do you know that *longed* is not related to length? What does it mean?

mascot (mas´ kät) *n.* a person or animal, adopted by a group for luck

coaxed (kōkst) *v.* tried to persuade

Reading Check

What group does Aaron want to join?

when she'd been a little girl in the Ukraine, wherever that was.

Often, in the evening, Aaron's grandmother would talk about the old days long ago in the Ukraine, in the same way that she talked to the birds on the back fire escape. She had lived in a village near a place called Kishinev with hundreds of other poor peasant families like her own. Things hadn't been too bad under someone called Czar Alexander the Second,[3] whom Aaron always pictured as a tall handsome man in a gold uniform. But Alexander the Second was assassinated, and Alexander the Third, whom Aaron pictured as an ugly man in a black cape, became the Czar. And the Jewish people of the Ukraine had no peace anymore.

One day, a thundering of horses was heard coming toward the village from the direction of Kishinev. *The Cossacks!* ◆ *The Cossacks!* someone had shouted. The Czar's horsemen! Quickly, quickly, everyone in Aaron's grandmother's family had climbed down to the cellar through a little trapdoor hidden under a mat in the big central room of their shack. But his grandmother's pet goat, whom she'd loved as much as Aaron loved Pidge and more, had to be left above, because if it had made a sound in the cellar, they would never have lived to see the next morning. They all hid under the wood in the woodbin and waited, hardly breathing.

Suddenly, from above, they heard shouts and calls and screams at a distance. And then the noise was in their house. Boots pounding on the floor, and everything breaking and crashing overhead. The smell of smoke and the shouts of a dozen men.

The terror went on for an hour and then the sound of horses' hooves faded into the distance. They waited another hour to make sure, and then the father went up out of the cellar and the rest of the family followed. The door to the house had been torn from its hinges and every piece of furniture was broken. Every window, every dish, every stitch of clothing was totally destroyed, and one wall had been completely bashed in. And on the floor was the goat, lying quietly. Aaron's grandmother, who was just a little girl of eight at the time, had wept over the goat all day and all night and could not be <u>consoled</u>.

But they had been lucky. For other houses had been burned to the ground. And everywhere, not goats alone, nor sheep, but men and women and children lay quietly on the ground. The word for this sort

in context **History Connection**

◆ *Cossacks*
Aaron's grandmother has a memory of Cossacks destroying her village. Cossacks were soldiers on horseback. At the time when Aaron's grandmother lived in the Ukraine, Cossacks held a special and privileged status. The Russian army used these soldiers to put down revolutionary activities. Sometimes, the Cossacks took the law into their own hands and attacked innocent people.

consoled (kən sōld´) *v.* comforted

---

3. **Czar Alexander the Second** leader of Russia from 1855 to 1881.

of massacre, Aaron had learned, was *pogrom*. It had been a pogrom. And the men on the horses were Cossacks. Hated word. Cossacks.

And so Pidge would replace that goat of long ago. A pigeon on Second Avenue where no one needed trapdoors or secret escape passages or woodpiles to hide under. A pigeon for his grandmother's sixtieth birthday. *Oh wing, heal quickly so my grandmother can send you flying to everywhere she wants!*

But a few days later, Aaron met Carl in the street again. And Carl told Aaron that there was going to be a meeting that afternoon in which a map was going to be drawn up to show where a secret treasure lay buried on the empty lot. "Bring the pigeon and you can come into the shack. We got a badge for you. A new kinda membership badge with a secret code on the back."

Aaron ran home, his heart pounding almost as fast as the pigeon's. He took Pidge in his hands and carried him out the door while his mother was busy in the kitchen making stuffed cabbage, his father's favorite dish. And by the time he reached the street, Aaron had decided to take the bandages off. Pidge would look like a real pigeon again, and none of the older boys would laugh or call him a bundle of rags.

Gently, gently he removed the bandages and the splints and put them in his pocket in case he should need them again. But Pidge seemed to hold his wing properly in place.

When he reached the empty lot, Aaron walked up to the shack, then hesitated. Four bigger boys were there. After a moment, Carl came out and commanded Aaron to hand Pidge over.

"Be careful," said Aaron. "I just took the bandages off."

"Oh sure, don't worry," said Carl. By now Pidge was used to people holding him, and he remained calm in Carl's hands.

"OK," said Carl. "Give him the badge." And one of the older boys handed Aaron his badge with the code on the back. "Now light the fire," said Carl.

"What . . . what fire?" asked Aaron.

"The fire. You'll see," Carl answered.

"You didn't say nothing about a fire," said Aaron. "You didn't say nothing to—"

"Hey!" said Carl. "I'm the leader here. And you don't talk unless I tell you that you have p'mission. Light the fire, Al."

The boy named Al went out to the side of the shack, where some wood and cardboard and old newspapers had been piled into a huge mound. He struck a match and held it to the newspapers.

"OK," said Carl. "Let's get 'er good and hot. Blow on it. Everybody blow."

Aaron's eyes stung from the smoke, but he blew alongside the others, going from side to side as the smoke shifted toward them and away.

Literary Analysis
Climax How does this event help to increase the tension and move the story toward a climax?

Literary Analysis
Climax Why does the fire increase the tension?

Reading Check

What happened to Aaron's grandmother's goat in the Ukraine?

"Let's fan it," said Al.

In a few minutes, the fire was crackling and glowing with a bright yellow-orange flame.

"Get me the rope," said Carl.

One of the boys brought Carl some cord and Carl, without a word, wound it twice around the pigeon, so that its wings were tight against its body.

"What . . . what are you *doing!*" shouted Aaron. "You're hurting his wing!"

"Don't worry about his wing," said Carl. "We're gonna throw him into the fire. And when we do, we're gonna swear an oath of loyalty to—"

"No! *No!*" shouted Aaron, moving toward Carl.

"Grab him!" called Carl. "Don't let him get the pigeon!"

But Aaron had leaped right across the fire at Carl, taking him completely by surprise. He threw Carl back against the shack and hit out at his face with both fists. Carl slid down to the ground and the pigeon rolled out of his hands. Aaron scooped up the pigeon and ran, pretending he was on roller skates so that he would go faster and faster. And as he ran across the lot he pulled the cord off Pidge and tried to find a place, *any* place, to hide him. But the boys were on top of him, and the pigeon slipped from Aaron's hands.

"Get him!" shouted Carl.

Aaron thought of the worst, the most horrible thing he could shout at the boys. "Cossacks!" he screamed. "You're all Cossacks!"

Two boys held Aaron back while the others tried to catch the pigeon. Pidge fluttered along the ground just out of reach, skittering one way and then the other. Then the boys came at him from two directions. But suddenly Pidge beat his wings in rhythm, and rose up, up over the roof of the nearest tenement, up over Second Avenue toward the park.

With the pigeon gone, the boys turned toward Aaron and tackled him to the ground and punched him and tore his clothes and punched him some more. Aaron twisted and turned and kicked and punched back, shouting "Cossacks! Cossacks!" And somehow the word gave him the strength to tear away from them.

When Aaron reached home, he tried to go past the kitchen quickly so his mother wouldn't see his bloody face and torn clothing. But it was no use; his father was home from work early that night and was seated in the living room. In a moment Aaron was surrounded by his mother, father, and grandmother, and in another moment he had told them everything that had happened, the words tumbling out between his broken sobs. Told them of the present he had planned, of the pigeon for a goat, of the gang, of the badge with the secret code on the back, of the shack, and the fire, and the pigeon's flight over the tenement roof.

And Aaron's grandmother kissed him and thanked him for his

present which was even better than the pigeon.

"What present?" asked Aaron, trying to stop the series of sobs.

And his grandmother opened her pocketbook and handed Aaron her mirror and asked him to look. But all Aaron saw was his dirty, bruised face and his torn shirt.

Aaron thought he understood and then, again, he thought he didn't. How could she be so happy when there really was no present? And why pretend that there was?

Later that night, just before he fell asleep, Aaron tried to imagine what his grandmother might have done with the pigeon. She would have fed it, and she certainly would have talked to it, as she did to all the birds, and . . . and then she would have let it go free. Yes, of course. Pidge's flight to freedom must have been the gift that had made his grandmother so happy. Her goat has escaped from the Cossacks at last, Aaron thought, half dreaming. And he fell asleep with a smile.

Review and Assess

Thinking About the Selection

1. **Respond:** What would you have done if Carl had asked you to join his club? Explain.

2. **(a) Recall:** How does Aaron find Pidge? **(b) Speculate:** Why does Aaron try to help Pidge? **(c) Infer:** What do Aaron's actions reveal about his personality?

3. **(a) Recall:** What is the reference to "strangers in the land of Egypt"? **(b) Interpret:** What does Aaron's mother mean when she says they are "all strangers in the land of Egypt"? **(c) Analyze Cause and Effect:** What does this saying have to do with her decision to allow Aaron to keep the injured bird until it recovers?

4. **(a) Recall:** What happened to Aaron's grandmother as a child? **(b) Analyze Cause and Effect:** How does the grandmother's childhood experience help Aaron decide what to give her for her birthday?

5. **(a) Recall:** What does Carl want to do with Pidge? **(b) Compare and Contrast:** How are Carl and the boys like the Cossacks?

6. **(a) Draw Conclusions:** Why is Aaron's grandmother happy that Pidge is set free? **(b) Evaluate:** Which is the better gift: the pigeon or the pigeon's freedom? Explain. **(c) Apply:** What are two other "gifts" that are not physical things that one person can give to another?

Myron Levoy

(b. 1930)

Myron Levoy has loved reading ever since he was a boy growing up in New York City. He studied to be a chemical engineer but soon turned to writing as a career. Most of his stories and novels focus on the teen or child who is somehow an outsider or a loner. These characters feel separation from what they think is the normal teen experience. Levoy's most well-known work, a novel called *Alan and Naomi*, has been made into a film. Levoy has also written works for adults.

Water

HELEN KELLER

▲ **Critical Viewing** In what way do the expressions on the faces of the woman and the girl show "discovery"? **[Analyze]**

he morning after my teacher came she led me into her room and gave me a doll. The little blind children at the Perkins Institution had sent it and Laura Bridgman had dressed it; but I did not know this until afterward. When I had played with it a little while, Miss Sullivan slowly spelled into my hand the word "d-o-l-l." I was at once interested in this finger play and tried to imitate it. When I finally succeeded in making the letters correctly I was flushed with childish pleasure and pride. Running downstairs to my mother I held up my hand and made the letters for doll. I did not know that I was spelling a word or even that words existed; I was simply making my fingers go in monkey-like imitation. In the days that followed I learned to spell in this uncomprehending way a great many words, among them *pin, hat, cup* and a few verbs like *sit, stand* and *walk*. But my teacher had been with me several weeks before I understood that everything has a name.

One day, while I was playing with my new doll, Miss Sullivan put my big rag doll into my lap also, spelled "d-o-l-l" and tried to make me understand that "d-o-l-l" applied to both. Earlier in the day we had had a tussle over the words "m-u-g" and "w-a-t-e-r." Miss Sullivan had tried to impress it upon me that "m-u-g" is *mug* and that "w-a-t-e-r" is *water*, but I persisted in confounding the two. In despair she had dropped the subject for the time, only to renew it at the first opportunity. I became impatient at her repeated attempts and, seizing the new doll, I dashed it upon the floor. I was keenly delighted when I felt the fragments of the broken doll at my feet. Neither sorrow nor regret followed my passionate outburst. I had not loved the doll. In the still, dark world in which I lived there was no strong sentiment or tenderness. I felt my teacher sweep the fragments to one side of the hearth,[1] and I had a sense of satisfaction that the cause of my discomfort was removed. She brought me my hat, and I knew I was going out into the warm sunshine. This thought, if a wordless sensation may be called a thought, made me hop and skip with pleasure.

We walked down the path to the well-house, attracted by the fragrance of the honeysuckle with which it was covered. Some one was drawing water and my teacher placed my hand under the spout. As the cool stream gushed over one hand she spelled into the other the

---

1. hearth (härth) *n.* stone or brick floor of a fireplace, sometimes stretching out into the room.

Literary Analysis
Climax In what way does this statement start building interest?

Reading Strategy
Using Context to Clarify Meaning How do you know that in this context, *drawing water* means making water come from the pump?

Reading Check

What is Miss Sullivan trying to teach Helen?

word *water,* first slowly, then rapidly. I stood still, my whole attention fixed upon the motions of her fingers. Suddenly I felt a misty consciousness as of something forgotten—a thrill of returning thought; and somehow the mystery of language was revealed to me. I knew then that "w-a-t-e-r" meant the wonderful cool something that was flowing over my hand. That living word awakened my soul, gave it light, hope, joy, set it free! There were barriers still, it is true, but barriers that could in time be swept away.

I left the well-house eager to learn. Everything had a name, and each name gave birth to a new thought. As we returned to the house every object which I touched seemed to quiver with life. That was because I saw everything with the strange, new sight that had come to me. On entering the door I remembered the doll I had broken. I felt my way to the hearth and picked up the pieces. I tried vainly to put them together. Then my eyes filled with tears; for I realized what I had done, and for the first time I felt repentance and sorrow.

I learned a great many new words that day. I do not remember what they all were; but I do know that *mother, father, sister, teacher* were among them—words that were to make the world blossom for me, "like Aaron's rod, with flowers." It would have been difficult to find a happier child than I was as I lay in my crib at the close of that eventful day and lived over the joys it had brought me, and for the first time longed for a new day to come.

Review and Assess

Thinking About the Selection

1. **Respond:** Do you think Helen should be excused for her behavior before she learned to communicate? Explain.

2. **(a) Recall:** What does Helen do to the doll? **(b) Infer:** Why does she do it?

3. **(a) Recall:** What event helps Helen recognize the meaning of "water"? **(b) Compare and Contrast:** How is the water from the pump different from the water in the mug? **(c) Draw Conclusions:** How does the difference between the water from the pump and the water in the mug make it possible for her finally to understand?

4. **(a) Recall:** What are two other words Helen remembers learning that day? **(b) Infer:** Why are those the words she remembers?

5. **(a) Recall:** How does Helen feel when she goes to bed that night? **(b) Infer:** Why does she feel that way? **(c) Evaluate:** What is the most valuable part of being able to communicate?

Helen Keller

(1880–1968)

Helen Keller was cut off from the world by an illness that left her deaf and blind at the age of one and one-half years.

In 1887, Helen was rescued from her darkness by a gifted teacher, Annie Sullivan, who came to live with her. Annie taught Helen the manual alphabet. Helen learned to communicate using this finger spelling. Eventually, Helen learned to speak by feeling the vibrations in Sullivan's throat with her hands and copying them. In "Water," from her autobiography, Helen describes the moment she learned to communicate.

Review and Assess

Literary Analysis

Climax

1. What event is the **climax**, or turning point, in "Aaron's Gift"?
2. What is the climax in "Water"?
3. Fill out a graphic organizer like the one shown here for "Water" to explore two possible outcomes for the climax of "Aaron's Gift." Circle the actual outcome.

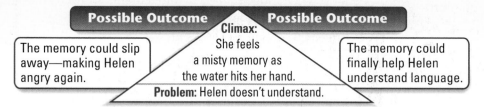

Possible Outcome | **Climax:** | **Possible Outcome**

The memory could slip away—making Helen angry again.

Climax: She feels a misty memory as the water hits her hand.

The memory could finally help Helen understand language.

Problem: Helen doesn't understand.

Comparing Literary Works

4. How is Aaron's problem different from Helen's?
5. In what way does each character solve his or her problem by reaching out?

Reading Strategy

Using Context to Clarify Meaning

Copy the numbered sentence. Then, copy the lettered sentence that uses the italicized word in the same way. Explain how **context** helps you make your choice.

6. The runners finished their last *lap*.

   (a) Miss Sullivan put my big rag doll into my *lap*.

   (b) During his third *lap* around the racecourse, he noticed a pigeon on the grass.

7. Miss Sullivan had tried to *impress* it upon me that m-u-g is mug.

   (a) Miss Sullivan wanted to *impress* me with her knowledge.

   (b) Miss Sullivan wanted to *impress* upon me the importance of language.

Extending Understanding

8. **Career Connection:** Based on what you know about Aaron's interests, actions, and personality, what careers do you think he should consider?

Quick Review

The **climax** of a story is the turning point at which the outcome of the conflict becomes clear. To review climax, see page 111.

Context is the situation in which a word is used: the surrounding words, sentences, and paragraphs.

 Take It to the Net

www.phschool.com

Take the interactive self-test online to check your understanding of these selections.

Integrate Language Skills

Vocabulary Development Lesson

Word Analysis: Forms of *console*

Console means "to comfort." On a piece of paper, match each form of *console* with its definition.

1. consolation   **a.** give comfort
2. console   **b.** unable to be comforted
3. inconsolable   **c.** comfort

Spelling Strategy

When adding an ending to a word that ends in y, usually follow these rules: If a consonant comes before the final y, change the y to *i* unless the ending begins with *i*, as in cry + -*ing* = crying. If a vowel comes before the final y, just add the ending, as in play + -*ed* = played.

Write the correct spelling for the following.

1. merry + -*ment*   3. reply + -*ed*
2. cry + -*ed*   4. journey + -*ing*

Fluency: Sentence Completions

On your paper, write the vocabulary word that belongs in each numbered sentence. Some words are used more than once.

1. Aaron ____?____ the pigeon to eat the crumbs.
2. Pidge's ____?____ movements showed the bird's fear.
3. They said a pigeon would be a good ____?____.
4. The smoke from the fire was ____?____ tears from Aaron's eyes.
5. If Pidge had died, could anyone have ____?____ Aaron?
6. Aaron slipped into a ____?____ anger when the boys attacked him.
7. In some ways, Aaron's grandmother ____?____ him on the loss of the pigeon.

Grammar Lesson

Verb Phrases

A **verb phrase** is a group of words made up of a main verb and one or more helping verbs. Verbs that can act as helping verbs include *do*, *will*, *should*, and the forms of *be*. The helping verb helps indicate the tense of the verb. In the example, the helping verb is underlined once. The main verb is underlined twice.

Helen <u>was</u> <u>playing</u> with a new doll.

The word *not* sometimes appears between a main verb and a helping verb.

She <u>did</u> *not* <u>know.</u>

Practice Copy these sentences. Underline each helping verb once and each main verb twice.

1. The pigeon's heart was beating fast.
2. The boys were waiting for Aaron.
3. You should have seen Helen's face.
4. He should not join.
5. She will remember.

Writing Application On separate paper, write three sentences about Aaron or Helen. Use each of the following verb phrases at least once. You may use the word *not* between parts of the verb phrase.

1. must have worried
2. could help
3. should have listened

W͠G *Prentice Hall Writing and Grammar Connection: Chapter 15, Section 2*

Writing Lesson

Interview

Aaron learned about his grandmother's past by talking to her. Interview an older person you know. An interview is a formal conversation in which one person asks questions, and the other person answers them. Write a record of your interview, including your comments.

Prewriting   Organize your questions in categories. Conduct the interview, taking careful notes. You might use a tape recorder as well.

Model: Organizing Questions by Category

People	Activities	School	Events
Who was the most popular celebrity?	What did you like to do on weekends?	What subjects did you study?	What is your most vivid memory?

> Use some of these sample categories and questions, but add your own as well. For examples of interview questions, see the interview with Jerry Spinelli, p. 150.

Drafting   Begin by introducing the subject of your interview. Then, write questions and answers from each category. Include your comments, such as why you asked a question. Use formatting or labels to distinguish between your words and the subject's.

Revising   When you revise, strengthen your organization by making sure information is presented in categories.

Prentice Hall Writing and Grammar Connection: Chapter 6, Section 4

Extension Activities

Listening and Speaking Annie Sullivan taught Helen Keller how to communicate with sign language. In small teams, conduct research on American Sign Language. Then, **present a program** on American Sign Language using these guidelines.

1. Select a focus for each team; for example, explain the development of sign language, demonstrate its use, and show diagrams.
2. Plan the organization of the presentation: what to include and in what order.
3. Adjust volume and pacing for your audience.

Practice the oral delivery before presenting.

Research and Technology As an adult, Helen Keller attended college and wrote her autobiography. Research the devices Keller used to read and write. Then, find out what devices are used by deaf and blind people today. Make a **chart** of some technological advances that have been made in tools for people with physical disabilities since Keller's time.

 **Take It to the Net**   www.phschool.com

Go online for an additional research activity using the Internet.

Prepare to Read

Zlateh the Goat

 Take It to the Net

Visit www.phschool.com for interactive activities and instruction related to "Zlateh the Goat," including

- background
- graphic organizers
- literary elements
- reading strategies

Preview

Connecting to the Literature

In "Zlateh the Goat," snow becomes a deadly enemy for a boy and a goat, who must help each other survive a snowstorm. Think about times when weather has created problems or dangerous situations for you or someone you know.

Background

Aaron in "Zlateh the Goat" is lost outdoors in a winter storm. He runs the risk of frostbite and hypothermia. When hypothermia occurs, the body temperature drops below normal and breathing slows. If the victim is not warmed, he or she becomes unconscious.

Literary Analysis

Conflict with Nature

Stories develop around a conflict, a struggle between opposing forces. In a **conflict with nature,** a character or characters struggle against a natural element. In "Zlateh the Goat," two characters battle a blizzard.

> Aaron did not want to admit the danger, but he knew just the same that if they did not find shelter they would freeze to death. This was no ordinary storm. It was a mighty blizzard.

How the conflict will turn out is a question of life and death.

Connecting Literary Elements

A story's **setting** is the time and place of the action. In many stories, especially stories about a conflict with nature, the setting contributes to the conflict. In "Zlateh the Goat," the time is winter in the days before cars. The place is rural Eastern Europe in an area where houses and villages are far apart. Think about these focus questions as you read.

1. What natural elements are a result of the time of the setting?
2. What details of the place add to Aaron's problems?

Reading Strategy

Summarizing

You can better understand what is going on in a story if you pause occasionally to **summarize**—to review what has happened so far. Summarize using the following steps:

1. Identify the main events.
2. Organize them in the order in which they happen.
3. Note when one event causes another event.

As you read "Zlateh the Goat," pause at the events indicated on the timeline. Summarize what has happened up to that point by noting main events on a timeline of your own.

Vocabulary Development

bound (bound) *v.* tied (p. 129)

conclusion (kən kloo′ zhən) *n.* belief or decision reached by reasoning (p. 129)

rapidly (rap′ id lē) *adv.* quickly (p. 129)

exuded (eg zyood′ əd) *v.* gave off; oozed; radiated (p. 131)

trace (trās) *n.* mark left behind by something (p. 133)

Beginning

1 ...

2 ...

3 ... Aaron and Zlateh leave for the butcher.

4 ...

5 ...

6 ... Aaron and Zlateh find the haystack.

7 ...

8 ...

9 ... The family decides to keep Zlateh.

End

ZLATEH
the Goat

Isaac Bashevis Singer

Illustration by Maurice Sendak, H:

At Hanukkah[1] time the road from the village to the town is usually covered with snow, but this year the winter had been a mild one. Hanukkah had almost come, yet little snow had fallen. The sun shone most of the time. The peasants complained that because of the dry weather there would be a poor harvest of winter grain. New grass sprouted, and the peasants sent their cattle out to pasture.

---

1. Hanukkah (khä´ noo kä) Jewish festival celebrated for eight days in early winter. Hanukkah is also called the "festival of lights" because a new candle is lit on each night of Hanukkah—one candle on the first night, two on the second night, and so on.

For Reuven the furrier it was a bad year, and after long hesitation he decided to sell Zlateh the goat. She was old and gave little milk. Feivel the town butcher had offered eight gulden[2] for her. Such a sum would buy Hanukkah candles, potatoes and oil for pancakes, gifts for the children, and other holiday necessaries for the house. Reuven told his oldest boy Aaron to take the goat to town.

Aaron understood what taking the goat to Feivel meant, but had to obey his father. Leah, his mother, wiped the tears from her eyes when she heard the news. Aaron's younger sisters, Anna and Miriam, cried loudly. Aaron put on his quilted jacket and a cap with earmuffs, <u>bound</u> a rope around Zlateh's neck, and took along two slices of bread with cheese to eat on the road. Aaron was supposed to deliver the goat by evening, spend the night at the butcher's, and return the next day with the money.

bound (bound) *v.* tied

While the family said goodbye to the goat, and Aaron placed the rope around her neck, Zlateh stood as patiently and good-naturedly as ever. She licked Reuven's hand. She shook her small white beard. Zlateh trusted human beings. She knew that they always fed her and never did her any harm.

When Aaron brought her out on the road to town, she seemed somewhat astonished. She'd never been led in that direction before. She looked back at him questioningly, as if to say, "Where are you taking me?" But after a while she seemed to come to the <u>conclusion</u> that a goat shouldn't ask questions. Still, the road was different. They passed new fields, pastures, and huts with thatched roofs. Here and there a dog barked and came running after them, but Aaron chased it away with his stick.

conclusion (kən kloo′ zhən) *n.* belief or decision reached by reasoning

The sun was shining when Aaron left the village. Suddenly the weather changed. A large black cloud with a bluish center appeared in the east and spread itself <u>rapidly</u> over the sky. A cold wind blew in with it. The crows flew low, croaking. At first it looked as if it would rain, but instead it began to hail as in summer. It was early in the day, but it became dark as dusk. After a while the hail turned to snow.

rapidly (rap′ id lē) *adv.* quickly

Literary Analysis
Conflict with Nature
In what two ways are the snow and wind in conflict with Aaron?

In his twelve years Aaron had seen all kinds of weather, but he had never experienced a snow like this one. It was so dense it shut out the light of the day. In a short time their path was completely covered. The wind became as cold as ice. The road to town was narrow and winding. Aaron no longer knew where he was. He could not see through the snow. The cold soon penetrated his quilted jacket.

✔Reading Check

Why is Aaron taking the goat to Feivel?

---

2. gulden (gool′ dən) *n.* unit of money.

At first Zlateh didn't seem to mind the change in weather. She, too, was twelve years old and knew what winter meant. But when her legs sank deeper and deeper into the snow, she began to turn her head and look at Aaron in wonderment. Her mild eyes seemed to ask, "Why are we out in such a storm?" Aaron hoped that a peasant would come along with his cart, but no one passed by.

The snow grew thicker, falling to the ground in large, whirling flakes. Beneath it Aaron's boots touched the softness of a plowed field. He realized that he was no longer on the road. He had gone astray. He could no longer figure out which was east or west, which way was the village, the town. The wind whistled, howled, whirled the snow about in eddies.[3] It looked as if white imps were playing tag on the fields. A white dust rose above the ground. Zlateh stopped. She could walk no longer. Stubbornly she anchored her cleft hooves in the earth and bleated as if pleading to be taken home. Icicles hung from her white beard, and her horns were glazed with frost.

Illustration by Maurice Sendak, HarperCollins

Aaron did not want to admit the danger, but he knew just the same that if they did not find shelter they would freeze to death. This was no ordinary storm. It was a mighty blizzard. The snow had reached his knees. His hands were numb, and he could no longer feel his toes. He choked when he breathed. His nose felt like wood, and he rubbed it with snow. Zlateh's bleating began to sound like crying. Those humans in whom she had so much confidence had dragged her into a trap. Aaron began to pray to God for himself and for the innocent animal.

Suddenly he made out the shape of a hill. He wondered what it could be. Who had piled snow into such a huge heap? He moved toward it, dragging Zlateh after him. When he came near it, he

▲ Critical Viewing
Why does Aaron look downcast in this picture?
[Connect]

---

3. eddies (ed´ ēz) *n.* currents of air moving in circular motions; little whirlwinds.

realized that it was a large haystack which the snow had blanketed.

Aaron realized immediately that they were saved. With great effort he dug his way through the snow. He was a village boy and knew what to do. When he reached the hay, he hollowed out a nest for himself and the goat. No matter how cold it may be outside, in the hay it is always warm. And hay was food for Zlateh. The moment she smelled it she became contented and began to eat. Outside, the snow continued to fall. It quickly covered the passageway Aaron had dug. But a boy and an animal need to breathe, and there was hardly any air in their hideout. Aaron bored a kind of a window through the hay and snow and carefully kept the passage clear.

Zlateh, having eaten her fill, sat down on her hind legs and seemed to have regained her confidence in man. Aaron ate his two slices of bread and cheese, but after the difficult journey he was still hungry. He looked at Zlateh and noticed her udders were full. He lay down next to her, placing himself so that when he milked her he could squirt the milk into his mouth. It was rich and sweet. Zlateh was not accustomed to being milked that way, but she did not resist. On the contrary, she seemed eager to reward Aaron for bringing her to a shelter whose very walls, floor, and ceiling were made of food.

Through the window Aaron could catch a glimpse of the chaos outside. The wind carried before it whole drifts of snow. It was completely dark, and he did not know whether night had already come or whether it was the darkness of the storm. Thank God that in the hay it was not cold. The dried hay, grass, and field flowers <u>exuded</u> the warmth of the summer sun. Zlateh ate frequently; she nibbled from above, below, from the left and right. Her body gave forth an animal warmth, and Aaron cuddled up to her. He had always loved Zlateh, but now she was like a sister. He was alone, cut off from his family, and wanted to talk. He began to talk to Zlateh. "Zlateh, what do you think about what has happened to us?" he asked.

"Maaaa," Zlateh answered.

"If we hadn't found this stack of hay, we would both be frozen stiff by now," Aaron said.

"Maaaa," was the goat's reply.

"If the snow keeps on falling like this, we may have to stay here for days," Aaron explained.

"Maaaa," Zlateh bleated.

"What does 'maaaa' mean?" Aaron asked. "You'd better speak up clearly."

"Maaaa, maaaa," Zlateh tried.

"Well, let it be 'maaaa' then," Aaron said patiently. "You can't

Reading Strategy
Summarizing Retell the two most important events since Aaron and Zlateh left home.

exuded (eg zyōōd′ əd) *v.* gave off; oozed; radiated

Reading Check

What food and shelter do Aaron and Zlateh have?

speak, but I know you understand. I need you and you need me. Isn't that right?"

"Maaaa."

Aaron became sleepy. He made a pillow out of some hay, leaned his head on it, and dozed off. Zlateh, too, fell asleep.

When Aaron opened his eyes, he didn't know whether it was morning or night. The snow had blocked up his window. He tried to clear it, but when he had bored through to the length of his arm, he still hadn't reached the outside. Luckily he had his stick with him and was able to break through to the open air. It was

Literary Analysis
Conflict with Nature In what way are Aaron and Zlateh still in danger from the storm?

Illustration by Maurice Sendak, HarperCollins

◀ **Critical Viewing**
What do you think the goat would say if she could speak? **[Speculate]**

still dark outside. The snow continued to fall and the wind wailed, first with one voice and then with many. Sometimes it had the sound of devilish laughter. Zlateh, too, awoke, and when Aaron greeted her, she answered, "Maaa." Yes, Zlateh's language consisted of only one word, but it meant many things. Now she was saying, "We must accept all that God gives us—heat, cold, hunger, satisfaction, light, and darkness."

Aaron had awakened hungry. He had eaten up his food, but Zlateh had plenty of milk.

For three days Aaron and Zlateh stayed in the haystack. Aaron had always loved Zlateh, but in these three days he loved her more and more. She fed him with her milk and helped him keep warm. She comforted him with her patience. He told her many stories, and she always cocked her ears and listened. When he patted her, she licked his hand and his face. Then she said, "Maaaa," and he knew it meant, I love you, too.

The snow fell for three days, though after the first day it was not as thick and the wind quieted down. Sometimes Aaron felt that there could never have been a summer, that the snow had always fallen, ever since he could remember. He, Aaron, never had a father or mother or sisters. He was a snow child, born of the snow, and so was Zlateh. It was so quiet in the hay that his ears rang in the stillness. Aaron and Zlateh slept all night and a good part of the day. As for Aaron's dreams, they were all about warm weather. He dreamed of green fields, trees covered with blossoms, clear brooks, and singing birds. By the third night the snow had stopped, but Aaron did not dare to find his way home in the darkness. The sky became clear and the moon shone, casting silvery nets on the snow. Aaron dug his way out and looked at the world. It was all white, quiet, dreaming dreams of heavenly splendor. The stars were large and close. The moon swam in the sky as in a sea.

On the morning of the fourth day Aaron heard the ringing of sleigh bells. The haystack was not far from the road. The peasant who drove the sleigh pointed out the way to him—not to the town and Feivel the butcher, but home to the village. Aaron had decided in the haystack that he would never part with Zlateh.

Aaron's family and their neighbors had searched for the boy and the goat but had found no <u>trace</u> of them during the storm. They feared they were lost. Aaron's mother and sisters cried for him; his father remained silent and gloomy. Suddenly one of the neighbors came running to their house with the news that Aaron and Zlateh were coming up the road.

Reading Strategy
Summarizing Review and summarize the events that have occurred so far.

trace (trās) *n.* mark left behind by something

✔**Reading Check**
How long does the blizzard last?

There was great joy in the family. Aaron told them how he had found the stack of hay and how Zlateh had fed him with her milk. Aaron's sisters kissed and hugged Zlateh and gave her a special treat of chopped carrots and potato peels, which Zlateh gobbled up hungrily.

Nobody ever again thought of selling Zlateh, and now that the cold weather had finally set in, the villagers needed the services of Reuven the furrier once more. When Hanukkah came, Aaron's mother was able to fry pancakes every evening, and Zlateh got her portion, too. Even though Zlateh had her own pen, she often came to the kitchen, knocking on the door with her horns to indicate that she was ready to visit, and she was always admitted. In the evening Aaron, Miriam, and Anna played dreidel.[4] Zlateh sat near the stove watching the children and the flickering of the Hanukkah candles.

Once in a while Aaron would ask her, "Zlateh, do you remember the three days we spent together?"

And Zlateh would scratch her neck with a horn, shake her white bearded head, and come out with the single sound which expressed all her thoughts, and all her love.

Reading Strategy
Summarizing How would you summarize the end of the story to include Zlateh?

---

4. **dreidel** (drā´ dəl) *n.* small top with Hebrew letters on each of four sides, spun in a game played by children.

Review and Assess

Thinking About the Selection

1. **Respond:** What do you think is the most frightening part of Aaron's experience?

2. **(a) Recall:** Why does Reuven decide to sell Zlateh? **(b) Infer:** Why is it a difficult decision for him?

3. **(a) Recall:** Where is Aaron supposed to spend the night after delivering the goat? **(b) Draw Conclusions:** Why doesn't Aaron plan to return from the butcher the same day?

4. **(a) Recall:** What happens to Aaron and Zlateh on the way to town? **(b) Deduce:** Why is their situation dangerous? **(c) Synthesize:** Explain how the haystack helps solve their problems.

5. **(a) Draw Conclusions:** Why does the stay in the haystack change Aaron's mind about what he must do with Zlateh? **(b) Apply:** What is this story's message about friendship and trust? **(c) Take a Position:** What is the limit on what one friend can ask of another?

Isaac Bashevis Singer

(1904–1991)

Isaac Bashevis Singer wrote many stories about Polish villages and neighborhoods like the ones he grew up in. Singer moved to the city of Warsaw when he left home. Faced with prejudice against Jews, Singer left Poland for New York City in 1935. Soon after, World War II devastated the Jews of Eastern Europe and their neighborhoods. Yet Singer kept writing stories about the places of his youth. "Zlateh the Goat" helps recapture this vanished world. Throughout his life, Singer wrote in Yiddish, translating his stories into English afterward.

Review and Assess

Literary Analysis

Conflict with Nature

1. What two problems do Aaron and Zlateh face in their **conflict with nature**?
2. Explain how the snowstorm both creates a problem and solves a problem.
3. Identify the conflicts with nature in the story using the chart shown. In the first column, record the conflict for Aaron. In the second column, write what nature does to create the conflict.

Aaron's Conflict	How Nature Creates Conflict

Connecting Literary Elements

4. How does the **setting** contribute to the dangerous and isolated position in which Aaron and Zlateh find themselves?
5. What details of the place add to Aaron's problems?
6. What influence does the setting have on the characters? In a diagram like the one shown, record the details that explain how the setting affects the characters' thoughts and actions.

Setting	Influences	Actions and Thoughts
snowstorm		
	Aaron and Zlateh	
haystack		

Reading Strategy

Summarizing

7. Identify two events that occurred before Aaron and Zlateh left for the butcher.
8. Tell three things that happened in the haystack.
9. Summarize the events that led to Zlateh's not being sold.

Extending Understanding

10. **Apply:** In what ways do weather, geography, and climate affect people's lives?

Quick Review

A **conflict with nature** is a struggle between a character and some forces of nature. To review conflict, see page 127.

The **setting** is the time and place in which the action of a story takes place. To review setting, see page 127.

When you **summarize,** you organize main events and ideas in order and identify the connections between them.

 Take It to the Net
www.phschool.com
Take the interactive self-test online to check your understanding of the selection.

Integrate Language Skills

Vocabulary Development Lesson

Word Analysis: Latin Prefix *ex-*

The Latin prefix *ex-* means "out" or "away from." Knowing the meaning of *ex-* can help you figure out the meaning of the italicized word in the following sentence.

The haystack *exuded* the warmth of the summer sun.

Use the meanings of *ex-* to define the italicized word in the following sentences. Write your answers on your paper. You may use a dictionary to check your responses.

1. Aaron and Zlateh *exerted* a great effort to trudge through the snow.
2. Aaron was *exhausted* when they reached the haystack.
3. Zlateh made one sound that *expressed* all her thoughts.

Fluency: Sentence Completions

On your paper, complete each sentence with one of these words:

bound   conclusion   rapidly   exuded   trace

1. The packages were ___?___ with string.
2. The goat ___?___ a strong smell.
3. What ___?___ have you reached?
4. The news spread ___?___ through town.
5. They found no ___?___ of the path.

Spelling Strategy

Sometimes you spell the *s* sound at the end of a word with *ce*, as in *trace*. On your paper, unscramble each word to match the definition.

1. ceir (a grainlike food)
2. icme (small furry animals)
3. pacle (a spot or location)

Grammar Lesson

Principal Parts of Verbs

Every verb has four main forms, or **principal parts**. These parts are used to form verb tenses that show time. The chart here shows the four principal parts. Notice that regular verbs form their past tense and past participles by adding *-ed* or *-d*. Irregular verbs, such as *be*, form their past tense and/or past participles in different ways.

Base (present)	Present Participle	Past	Past Participle
howl	(*am, are,* or *is*) howling	howled	(*have* or *has*) howled
be	(*am, are,* or *is*) being	been	(*have* or *has*) been
eat	(*am, are,* or *is*) eating	ate	(*have* or *has*) eaten

Practice Rewrite each sentence, replacing the italicized verb with the principal part indicated in parentheses.

1. I *look* for shelter. (present participle)
2. We *be* down this road before. (past participle)
3. The snow *change* the hay's shape. (past)
4. I think that hill *move*. (past participle)
5. We *start* to get cold. (present participle)

Writing Application Write four sentences about the story. In each sentence, use a different principal part of *snow*.

WG *Prentice Hall Writing and Grammar Connection: Chapter 22, Section 1*

Writing Lesson

Persuasive Speech

Write a short persuasive speech that Aaron might give to his father, with the purpose of changing Reuven's mind.

Prewriting   List the reasons for keeping the goat. Focus on reasons that will appeal to Reuven, because your purpose is to affect his decision. For example, Reuven would not be influenced by the fact that Zlateh is cute. He would be influenced by the fact that Zlateh saved Aaron.

Drafting   State your position clearly in the first paragraph and make your purpose known. Organize the reasons for your position.

Model: Establish a Clear Purpose

This goat has shown us great friendship. Reconsider your decision to sell her. No matter how much we need the money, *you must not sell her* . . .

> The first paragraph includes a clear statement of the writer's position: You must not sell her.

Revising   Revise your speech to remove details that will not influence Reuven.

*W*G *Prentice Hall Writing and Grammar Connection: Chapter 7, Section 3*

Extension Activities

Research and Technology With a small group, find out about *shtetls*, Jewish villages of Eastern Europe. Use the word *shtetl* as a key word to begin a search on the Internet. Prepare **charts** and make **dioramas** to show a setting similar to Aaron's home.

Find out about Aaron's day-to-day life by answering the following questions.

1. What are the homes like?
2. What responsibilities would a twelve-year-old boy have?
3. How do most people make a living?

Listening and Speaking Deliver a humorous **monologue,** a funny speech given by one person, in which you, as Zlateh, say what you think about the humans' behavior.

1. Use exaggerated facial expressions to reflect the meaning of your words.
2. Occasionally change your position on the stage or in the room.
3. Change the tone and volume of your voice to show happiness, fear, or annoyance.

 **Take It to the Net**   www.phschool.com

Go online for an additional research activity using the Internet.

Prepare to Read

Door Number Four ◆ Count That Day Lost
The World Is Not a Pleasant Place to Be

 Take It to the Net

Visit www.phschool.com
for interactive activities
and instruction related to
these selections, including

- background
- graphic organizers
- literary elements
- reading strategies

Preview

Connecting to the Literature

These three poems explore the importance of caring about others and having others who care about you. Connect to these poems by thinking about the important people in your life and the different ways you show one another you care.

Background

Friendship depends more on actions than on words. Language, therefore, should not be a barrier to friendship. Charlotte Pomerantz illustrates this point by using Indonesian words for *door, number, four,* and *friend* in her poem of friendship, "Door Number Four."

Literary Analysis

Speaker

The **speaker** is the imaginary voice a poet uses to "tell" a poem. The speaker may be the poet or a character the poet invents. The personality and age of the speaker are partly indicated through the way the speaker uses language. A young speaker would use simple language. Non-English words may be used to establish the culture of the speaker. In "Door Number Four," the Indonesian word *teman* is used for "friend." In a poem with a speaker from a Spanish-speaking culture, the speaker might use the word *amigo*.

Look for other kinds of details in each of the poems that give you clues about the speakers.

Comparing Literary Works

Each of these works communicates a message about the way people interact. However, the messages are conveyed in different ways. Compare the three poems by focusing on the following questions as you read:

1. How is the speaker of each poem similar to and different from the speakers of the other poems?
2. How is the message of each poem similar to and different from the messages of the other poems?

Reading Strategy

Paraphrasing

When you **paraphrase**, you put an author's sentences or ideas into your own words. By "saying back" what you have read (even if it is in your head), you make sure you understand what you read.

Use a chart like the one shown to help you paraphrase difficult or confusing lines from the poems. Write the words from the poem in one column. In the other column, use your own words to explain what is meant.

Lines From Poem	My Paraphrase
If you sit down at set of sun	If you sit down at the end of the day
That eased the heart of him who heard	That made someone feel better

Vocabulary Development

eased (ēzd) *v.* comforted; freed from pain or worry (p. 141)

One Child Between Doors, (Seorang Anak de Antara Pintu Ruang) 1984,
Dede Eri Supria, Courtesy of Joseph Fischer

Door Number Four

CHARLOTTE POMERANTZ

◀ **Critical Viewing** How
is starting a friendship like
opening a door? [**Relate**]

Above my uncle's grocery store
is a pintu,
is a door.
On the pintu
5 is a number,
nomer empat,
number four.
In the door
there is a key.
10 Turn it,
enter quietly.
Hush hush, diam-diam,
quietly.
There, in lamplight,
15 you will see
a friend,
teman,
a friend
who's me.

Charlotte Pomerantz

(b. 1930)
Charlotte
Pomerantz
has been
making
friends
with young
readers for
years. She won the Jane
Addams Children's Book
Award for *The Princess and
the Admiral.* You can see
her fascination with lan-
guage in her books, espe-
cially *If I Had a Paka*,
which is the source of
"Door Number Four."

COUNT THAT DAY LOST
George Eliot

If you sit down at set of sun
And count the acts that you have done,
  And, counting, find
One self-denying[1] deed, one word
5 That <u>eased</u> the heart of him who heard,
  One glance most kind
That fell like sunshine where it went—
Then you may count that day well spent.

But if, through all the livelong day,
10 You've cheered no heart, by yea or nay—
  If, through it all
You've nothing done that you can trace
That brought the sunshine to one face—
  No act most small
15 That helped some soul and nothing cost—
Then count that day as worse than lost.

---

1. **self-denying** *adj.* opposite of selfish; done without concern for one's own interests.

eased (ēzd) *v.* comforted; freed from pain or worry

Review and Assess
Thinking About the Selections

1. **Respond:** Which of these poems would you give to your best friend? Why?

2. **(a) Recall:** In "Door Number Four," where is the speaker? **(b) Infer:** At what time of day do you think "Door Number Four" takes place? **(c) Speculate:** Why do you think the speaker wants someone to visit?

3. **(a) Recall:** What does the speaker of "Count That Day Lost" say one needs to do in order to have a day well spent? **(b) Interpret:** Why does the speaker say that a day is lost if you haven't helped someone? **(c) Apply:** Give an example of a "self-denying deed" and words that might ease someone's heart.

4. **Make a Judgment:** Identify three qualities you value in a friend. Explain why each quality is important to you. Give examples.

George Eliot
(1819–1880)

The writer George Eliot (her real name was Mary Ann Evans) grew up in the English countryside. She describes the life there vividly in her very successful novels. Eliot was a friend of many important thinkers of her time, and she thought and wrote much about the ties between people.

The World Is Not a Pleasant Place to Be

NIKKI GIOVANNI

the world is not a pleasant place
to be without
someone to hold and be held by

a river would stop
5 its flow if only
a stream were there
to receive it

an ocean would never laugh
if clouds weren't there
10 to kiss her tears

the world is not
a pleasant place to be without
someone

Review and Assess

Thinking About the Selections

1. **Respond:** Do you think this poem is more or less effective than the other two at capturing the importance of caring? Explain.

2. **(a) Recall:** What two images does Nikki Giovanni use to show companionship in "The World Is Not a Pleasant Place to Be"? **(b) Support:** Explain why you do or do not think Giovanni uses good images for friendship. **(c) Extend:** Think of another image that could be used to describe companionship.

3. **(a) Compare and Contrast:** How are the last lines of the first and last stanzas (groups of lines) similar and different? **(b) Analyze:** What effect does the difference have on the way you read each stanza?

Nikki Giovanni

(b. 1943)
In her poems, Nikki Giovanni shares her thoughts and experiences. Born in Knoxville, Tennessee, and raised both there and in Cincinnati, Ohio, she has become one of America's most popular poets.

Review and Assess

Literary Analysis

Speaker

1. Describe the speaker of "Door Number Four." Provide details in each of the following categories:
   - age
   - language(s) spoken
   - where he or she lives
   - what matters to him or her

2. **(a)** How would "Door Number Four" be different if the speaker were from a country where Spanish, French, Chinese or another language was spoken? **(b)** What are some commonly used words for *friend*, or related to friendship, that come from other languages?

3. What do you think is the age of the speaker in "Count That Day Lost"? Explain.

4. What two clues does "The World Is Not a Pleasant Place to Be" give you about the feelings of the speaker?

Comparing Literary Works

5. Fill out a chart like the one shown here with quotations from the poems that show the speaker's personality, the mood or feeling of the poem, and the poem's message.

Poem	Personality	Mood	Message
"Door Number Four"			
"Count That Day Lost"			
"The World Is Not a Pleasant Place to Be"			

6. How is the speaker of each poem similar to and different from the speakers of the other poems?

7. How is the message of each poem similar to and different from the messages of the other poems?

Reading Strategy

Paraphrasing

8. Paraphrase lines 8–11 of "Door Number Four."

9. Paraphrase lines 11–16 of "Count That Day Lost."

Extending Understanding

10. **Social Studies Connection:** In what ways could the messages of these poems be applied to relationships between countries?

Quick Review

The **speaker** is the imaginary voice a poet uses when writing a poem. To review speaker, see page 139.

Paraphrasing is restating an author's ideas in your own words.

 Take It to the Net
www.phschool.com
Take the interactive self-test online to check your understanding of these selections.

Integrate Language Skills

Vocabulary Development Lesson

Concept Development: Analogies

An **analogy** makes a comparison between two or more things that are otherwise unalike. Analogies can be made between ideas, situations, or even single words. The relationship between the words in each pair will be similar. Look at the following example:

helped : aided :: glance : look

The relationship between *helped* and *aided* is similar to the relationship between the words *glance* and *look*: Both pairs are synonyms. The chart shows two types of word relationships.

Word Relationships

Synonyms		Antonyms	
helped	aided	cheerful	sullen
happy	joyful	sunny	rainy

Grammar Lesson

Verb Tenses

A **verb** is a word that expresses an action or a state of being. A **verb tense** shows the time of the action or state of being that is expressed by the verb.

Form the past tense of regular verbs with *-ed* or *-d*. Memorize the past tense of irregular verbs. All future tenses use the helping verb *will*.

Tenses	Regular verb: cheer	Irregular verb: sit	Irregular verb: be
Present	I cheer.	I sit.	I am.
Past	I cheered.	I sat.	I was.
Future	I will cheer.	I will sit.	I will be.

Word Analysis: Word Pairs

On your paper, complete each word pair analogy with a word from the list.

pause   pleasant   eased

1. angered : enraged :: comforted : ___?___
2. laugh : cry :: continue : ___?___
3. high : low :: nasty : ___?___

Spelling Strategy

Sometimes, you spell the *z* sound with the letter *s*, as in *eased*. Sometimes you spell it with a *z*, as in *prize*. On your paper, write the correct spelling of the word that contains the *z* sound.

1. Try to be (pleazant/pleasant) each day.
2. She (gazed/gased) at them kindly.
3. When angry, (pauze/pause) before you speak.
4. She was (surprized/surprised) at the party.
5. Don't be (confuzed/confused).

Practice On your paper, write each of the following sentences in the past, present, and future tense.

1. He (be).
2. You (sit).
3. You (ease).
4. It (be).
5. We (help).

Writing Application Write three sentences about school. Write one sentence in the past tense, one in the present tense, and one in the future tense. Check your writing for correct capitalization.

W_G *Prentice Hall Writing and Grammar Connection: Chapter 22, Section 2*

Writing Lesson

Friendly Letter

Write a letter to tell a friend, family member, or other special person why he or she is special to you.

Prewriting Make a list of special people. Write one word to describe each of those people. Then, write an example of how that person shows the quality you have identified. Choose a person from the list as the subject of your letter.

Drafting Organize the paragraphs of your letter by category. For example, list three or four qualities. Then, focus on a single quality.

Model: Organize by Category

Aunt Edna's Qualities

Generous

Funny

Good

How Aunt Edna Shows Generosity

to family

to friends

to others

> No matter what categories you use to organize your letter, be sure to give examples that support your statements.

Revising Revise your letter by moving any details that belong in a different category. Check your use of capital letters.

Prentice Hall Writing and Grammar Connection: Chapter 2, Section 1

Extension Activities

Research and Technology Some words are almost as familiar in other languages as they are in English. For instance, the Spanish *amigo* is widely recognized to mean "friend," even by people who do not speak Spanish.

1. Use a dictionary to find the languages from which these other two friendship words come: *confidante, comrade*.
2. Collect other words from other languages related to friends and friendship.
3. Use the words to make a **friendship dictionary** in which you categorize and define these words.

Listening and Speaking With a group, prepare and present a poetry reading and discussion. For each poem, have one group member do the following.

1. Read the poem aloud.
2. Explain its message.
3. Point out how the poet uses repeated words and phrases to emphasize the message.

 **Take It to the Net** www.phschool.com

Go online for an additional research activity using the Internet.

CONNECTIONS
Literature Past and Present

Themes of Giving and Caring

The importance of giving and the many ways people can give to one another are common themes in literature. In "Door Number Four," Charlotte Pomerantz shows that people from different backgrounds can share a friendship. Writing a century ago, poet and novelist George Eliot expressed the view that a day in which you do not do at least one kind deed is a lost day. In her poem "The World Is Not a Pleasant Place to Be," Nikki Giovanni captures the loneliness of being without at least one friend you can count on.

The related themes of these poems are also explored in other types of literature. In his novel *Stargirl*, contemporary author Jerry Spinelli tells the story of an unusual girl who gives to others for the joy of giving. The story is told from the viewpoint of a high-school boy who is at first frightened by the difference between this girl and the other students. Although he comes to appreciate her unique personality, he has trouble understanding the reasons she acts as she does. In this excerpt from *Stargirl*, the narrator and Stargirl have a conversation in which they discuss their very different ideas about doing nice things for other people.

Stargirl

Jerry Spinelli

I told her I wanted to be a TV director. She said she wanted to be a silver-lunch-truck driver.

"Huh?" I said.

"You know," she said, "people work all morning and then it's twelve o'clock. The secretaries in the offices walk out the door, the construction workers put down their hard hats and hammers, and everybody's hungry, and they look up and there I am! No matter where they are, no matter where they work, I'm there. I have a whole fleet of silver lunch trucks. They go everywhere. 'Let Lunch Come to You!' That's my slogan. Just seeing my silver lunch truck makes them happy." She described how she would roll up the side panels and everyone would practically faint at the cloud of wonderful smells. Hot food, cold food, Chinese, Italian, you name it. Even a salad bar. "They can't believe how much food I fit into my truck. No matter where you are—out in the desert, the mountains, even down in the mines—if you want my silver lunch service, I get it to you. I find a way."

I tagged along on missions. One day she bought a small plant, an African violet in a plastic pot on sale for ninety-nine cents at a drugstore.

"Who's it for?" I asked her.

"I'm not exactly sure," she said. "I just know that someone at an address on Marion Drive is in the hospital for surgery, so I thought whoever's back home could use a little cheering up."

"How do you know this stuff?" I said.

She gave me a mischievous grin. "I have my ways."

We went to the house on Marion Drive. She reached into the saddle pack behind her bicycle seat. She pulled out a handful of ribbons. She chose a pale violet one that matched the color of the tiny blossoms and stuffed the remaining ribbons back into the seat pack. She tied the violet ribbon around the pot. I held her bike while she set the plant by the front door.

Riding away, I said, "Why don't you leave a card or something with your name on it?"

Thematic Connection
What poem from the previous grouping do Stargirl's actions bring to mind?

Reading Check

What is special about Stargirl?

The question surprised her. "Why should I?"

Her question surprised me. "Well, I don't know, it's just the way people do things. They expect it. They get a gift, they expect to know where it came from."

"Is that important?"

"Yeah, I guess—"

I never finished that thought. My tires shuddered as I slammed my bike to a halt. She stopped ahead of me. She backed up. She stared.

"Leo, what is it?"

I wagged my head. I grinned. I pointed to her. "It was you."

"Me what?"

"Two years ago. My birthday. I found a package on my front step. A porcupine necktie. I never found out who gave it to me."

She walked her bike alongside mine. She grinned. "A mystery."

"Where did you find it?" I said.

"I didn't. I had my mother make it."

She didn't seem to want to dwell on the subject. She started pedaling and we continued on our way.

"Where were we?" she said.

"Getting credit," I said.

"What about it?"

"Well, it's nice to get credit."

The spokes of her rear wheel spun behind the curtain of her long skirt. She looked like a photograph from a hundred years ago. She turned her wide eyes on me. "Is it?" she said.

Connecting Literature Past and Present

1. How does the message in the excerpt from *Stargirl* compare with the message in George Eliot's poem "Count That Day Lost"?

2. Compare and contrast the narrator's and Stargirl's ideas about doing nice things for other people.

3. Which speaker in the three poems do you think would most appreciate Stargirl? Explain.

4. Which poem do you think Stargirl would like best? Explain.

5. Which poem do you think the narrator would like best? Explain.

6. What is another work you have read that addresses the themes of giving and caring? Explain how that work is similar to and different from *Stargirl* and the poems. Include in your answer the genre or form of the work, the message itself, and the time period and culture from which the work comes.

7. Which work do you think has the most useful or relevant message for people today? Explain.

Jerry Spinelli

(b. 1941)

Jerry Spinelli, the father of six children and grandfather of eleven, has written more than fifteen books for young readers. He has won many honors, among them the Newbery Medal.

A popular writer with young adults, Spinelli is best known for his fiction about the ups and downs of teenage life. Although most of his work is fiction, the characters are realistic and experience "real-life" situations to which readers can relate. Spinelli advises young writers to "write what you really care about."

READING INFORMATIONAL MATERIALS

Interviews

About Interviews

An interview is a formal conversation in which one person (the interviewer) asks questions, and another person (the subject of the interview, or interviewee) answers them. Interviews with writers, actors, sports figures, and other celebrities are often featured in newspapers and magazines. Initials, formatting, or other design elements are used to distinguish between the words of the interviewer and those of the interviewee. An interview usually has a limited scope—that is, the questions focus on a particular area or time period of the subject's life.

Reading Strategy

Connecting and Clarifying Main Ideas

An interview gives you a firsthand look at the subject's opinions and ideas. The types of questions and the answers the subject gives can help you identify a few main ideas about the subject. The interview itself, however, is not the whole picture. As an active reader, you will clarify these ideas by connecting them to what you already know about the subject from other sources. In addition, you can clarify main ideas by making connections to related topics. The chart shows other sources and topics related to different kinds of celebrities whose interviews you might read. Explore these sources and topics to clarify ideas you read in interviews.

	Actors	**Writers**	**Athletes**
Other Sources	Other interviews	Other interviews	Other interviews
	His or her performances	Themes in his or her written works	The athlete's performance in the sport
	Talk show appearances	Reviews of his or her works	Articles about the athlete
	Comments from other actors or directors	Biography or autobiography of the writer	Comments from coaches and teammates
Related Topics	Style of acting	Other writers' treatment of similar themes	The athlete's particular sport
	Topics related to specific references in interview	Topics related to specific comments in the interview	Topics related to specific comments in the interview

Interview with Jerry Spinelli

from
The Borzoi Young Reader 1998

The text of an interview begins with the identification of the interviewer (in this case, Borzoi Young Reader, or **BYR**) and the subject (in this case, the author **JS**).

Interview questions are usually specific and focused. Here, Jerry Spinelli answers the specific question of how he compares himself today to young Jerry in *Knots in My Yo-yo String.*

Jerry Spinelli gives us a glimpse of the artist as a (very) young man in *Knots in My Yo-yo String.*

Borzoi Young Reader: You have an incredible memory of your early childhood. Has this always been the case—or did you do a lot of research and conduct interviews to fill in the gaps?

JS: Memories of childhood seem to come naturally to me. Until I started writing books for kids, I thought that was the case with everybody. I did consult my mother and brother at length, and the family scrapbooks. Others I spoke with are listed in the "Acknowledgments."

BYR: Readers who know your books can find many seeds and details from your novels in your own childhood. Is there a character in one of your novels who's the most like you as a boy?

JS: No one character in any book is all me. I guess the one who comes closest is Jason in *Space Station Seventh Grade.* Others include Maniac Magee and Eddie Mott in the School Daze series.

BYR: We learn from your memoir that you weren't much of a reader (of books) all through your childhood. When did this change?

JS: I finally became a willing, enthusiastic reader during my year in graduate school at the Writing Seminars, Johns Hopkins University. Because I regret that it took me so long, I put a book in Maniac Magee's hand everywhere he goes.

BYR: What are you reading right now?

JS: A book about tuning into your life called *Callings* by Gregg Lavoy and a murder mystery, *Nocturne,* by Ed McBain.

BYR: How similar are you to the young Jerry in *Knots in My Yo-yo String?* Do movies, baseball, yo-yos, and fanatical neatness still have a place in your life?

JS: The game I play now is tennis rather than baseball; I haven't spun a yo-yo in years; and no father of six kids is fanatically neat. But I recently watched a bunch of Flash Gordon episodes on the AMC channel, and I still hate war and love cowboys and sports, and I still feel bad for not visiting Garfield Shainline, and I still swoon when I look at the night sky and try to imagine eternity. I finally learned to swim (a little) and eat hot peppers (a little), but I still can't blast an earsplitting, two-fingered whistle.

Check Your Comprehension

1. Whom did Jerry Spinelli consult about his childhood when he wrote his autobiography *Knots in My Yo-yo String*?
2. Which character from one of his novels does Spinelli think is most like himself as a young boy?

Applying the Reading Strategy

Connecting and Clarifying Main Ideas

3. Identify two main ideas from the interview.
4. What information in the author biography on page 148 helps you clarify information in this interview?
5. What else could you read to clarify the main ideas you have identified?

Activity

Interview Questions

Interviewers prepare for an interview by doing preliminary research about the interview subject. The researched information helps interviewers pose relevant questions—questions that are meaningful to the interviewee and questions that will interest the reader.

Choose a famous person of interest to you and about whom you know something. Write five questions you would ask this person in an interview. Use a graphic organizer like the one shown here to show the relationship between what you know about the subject and the questions you ask. The first row contains an example from the Spinelli interview.

What you know	What you want to know	Why you want to know
Jerry Spinelli's stories are often based on his life.	Which characters are most similar to him as a boy?	It will give insight into what he was like as a kid.

Comparing Informational Materials

Interviews and Biographical Writing

Reread the biographical information about Jerry Spinelli on page 148.

6. In what way does an interview look different from biographical writing?
7. What can you learn by reading a biography that you might not learn from an interview?

Prepare to Read

Old Ben ◆ Feathered Friend

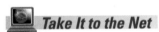 **Take It to the Net**

Visit www.phschool.com
for interactive activities
and instruction related to
these selections, including

- background
- graphic organizers
- literary elements
- reading strategies

Preview

Connecting to the Literature

The joys and sorrows of animal companions are the subject of Jesse Stuart's "Old Ben" and Arthur C. Clarke's "Feathered Friend." Connect to the selections by thinking about animals you have known or animal characters in movies, television, and literature.

Background

In "Feathered Friend," a canary travels into space. Historically, canaries have traveled down, rather than up. Miners used to bring these birds into mines to detect odorless but deadly fumes that sometimes accumulated. Because it is small, a canary would pass out long before the miners were affected. The early warning allowed miners to address the danger before there were tragic results.

Literary Analysis

Narratives

Each of these works is a **narrative**, that is, each work tells a series of events that make a story. Narratives can be fiction (made up) like "Feathered Friend" or nonfiction (true) like "Old Ben."

- **Fictional narratives:** short stories, novels, novellas
- **Nonfiction narratives:** Autobiography, biography, historical accounts

Use a chart like the one shown to track the events in each narrative.

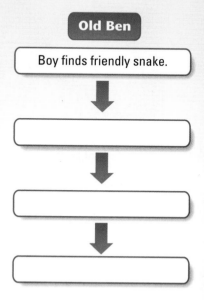

Comparing Literary Works

Although both of these works are narratives, they belong to different genres, or types, of literature.

"Old Ben" is **nonfiction**. The narrator is a real person telling a true story.

"Feathered Friend" is **fiction**, a made-up story about events and people that the writer creates.

As you compare the two works, think about the following focus questions:

1. In what ways do both selections seem as if they could be true stories?
2. In what ways do both selections seem as if they could be made-up stories?

Reading Strategy

Using Context Clues

When you come across an unknown word, or a word used in an unusual way, you can figure out the meaning by using **context clues**, information provided in the words, phrases, and sentences around the unfamiliar word. You can use context clues in all kinds of reading—short stories, nonfiction narratives, textbooks, and other materials. In the following example, you can use context clues to figure out the meaning of *garbs:*

> It was a skilled and difficult job, for a space suit is not the most convenient of *garbs* in which to work.

Since a space suit is a type of *garb,* you can figure out that *garbs* are things you wear.

Vocabulary Development

scarce (skers) *adj.* few in number or infrequent; not common (p. 157)

regulation (reg′ yə lā′ shən) *n.* rule (p. 159)

fusing (fyōō′ ziŋ) *adj.* joining permanently (p. 159)

ceased (sēsd) *v.* stopped (p. 160)

Old Ben

Jesse Stuart

One morning in July when I was walking across a clover field to a sweet-apple tree, I almost stepped on him. There he lay coiled like heavy strands of black rope. He was a big bull blacksnake. We looked at each other a minute, and then I stuck the toe of my shoe up to his mouth. He drew his head back in a friendly way. He didn't want trouble. Had he shown the least fight, I would have soon finished him. My father had always told me there was only one good snake—a dead one.

When the big fellow didn't show any fight, I reached down and picked him up by the neck. When I lifted him he was as long as I was tall. That was six feet. I started calling him Old Ben as I held him by the neck and rubbed his back. He enjoyed having his back rubbed and his head stroked. Then I lifted him into my arms. He was the first snake I'd ever been friendly with. I was afraid at first to let Old Ben wrap himself around me. I thought he might wrap himself around my neck and choke me.

Literary Analysis
Narratives What two important events occur in this paragraph?

The more I petted him, the more affectionate he became. He was so friendly I decided to trust him. I wrapped him around my neck a couple of times and let him loose. He crawled down one arm and went back to my neck, around and down the other arm and back again. He struck out his forked tongue to the sound of my voice as I talked to him.

"I wouldn't kill you at all," I said. "You're a friendly snake. I'm taking you home with me."

I headed home with Old Ben wrapped around my neck and shoulders. When I started over the hill by the pine grove, I met my cousin Wayne Holbrook coming up the hill. He stopped suddenly when he saw me. He started backing down the hill.

"He's a pet, Wayne," I said. "Don't be afraid of Old Ben."

It was a minute before Wayne could tell me what he wanted. He had come to borrow a plow. He kept a safe distance as we walked on together.

Before we reached the barn, Wayne got brave enough to touch Old Ben's long body.

"What are you going to do with him?" Wayne asked. "Uncle Mick won't let you keep him!"

"Put him in the corncrib," I said. "He'll have plenty of delicate food in there. The cats we keep at this barn have grown fat and lazy on the milk we feed 'em."

I opened the corncrib door and took Old Ben from around my neck because he was beginning to get warm and a little heavy.

"This will be your home," I said. "You'd better hide under the corn."

Besides my father, I knew Old Ben would have another enemy at our home. He was our hunting dog, Blackie, who would trail a snake, same as a possum or mink. He had treed blacksnakes, and my father had shot them from the trees. I knew Blackie would find Old Ben, because he followed us to the barn each morning.

The first morning after I'd put Old Ben in the corncrib, Blackie followed us. He started toward the corncrib holding his head high, sniffing. He stuck his nose up to a crack in the crib and began to bark. Then he tried to tear a plank off.

"Stop it, Blackie," Pa scolded him. "What's the matter with you? Have you taken to barking at mice?"

"Blackie is not barking at a mouse," I said. "I put a blacksnake in there yesterday!"

"A blacksnake?" Pa asked, looking unbelievingly. "A blacksnake?"

"Yes, a pet blacksnake," I said.

"Have you gone crazy?" he said. "I'll move a thousand bushels of corn to get that snake!"

"You won't mind this one," I said. "You and Mom will love him."

My father said a few unprintable words before we started back

Reading Strategy
Using Context Clues
What clues in these two sentences help tell you the meaning of *corncrib*?

✓ **Reading Check**

How do people react to Old Ben?

to the house. After breakfast, when Pa and Mom came to the barn, I was already there. I had opened the crib door and there was Old Ben. He'd crawled up front and was coiled on a sack. I put my hand down and he crawled up my arm to my neck and over my shoulder. When Mom and Pa reached the crib, I thought Pa was going to faint.

"He has a pet snake," Mom said.

"Won't be a bird or a young chicken left on this place," Pa said. "Every time I pick up an ear of corn in the crib, I'll be jumping."

"Pa, he won't hurt you," I said, patting the snake's head. "He's a natural pet, or somebody has tamed him. And he's not going to bother birds and young chickens when there are so many mice in this crib."

"Mick, let him keep the snake," Mom said. "I won't be afraid of it."

This was the beginning of a long friendship.

Mom went to the corncrib morning after morning and shelled corn for her geese and chickens. Often Old Ben would be lying in front on his burlap sack. Mom watched him at first from the corner of her eye. Later she didn't bother to watch him any more than she did a cat that came up for his milk.

Later it occurred to us that Old Ben might like milk, too. We started leaving milk for him. We never saw him drink it, but his pan was always empty when we returned. We know the mice didn't drink it, because he took care of them.

"One thing is certain," Mom said one morning when she went to shell corn. "We don't find any more corn chewed up by the mice and left on the floor."

July passed and August came. My father got used to Old Ben, but not until he had proved his worth. Ben had done something our nine cats couldn't. He had cleaned the corncrib of mice.

Then my father began to worry about Old Ben's going after water, and Blackie's finding his track. So he put water in the crib.

September came and went. We began wondering where our pet would go when days grew colder. One morning in early October we left milk for Old Ben, and it was there when we went back that afternoon. But Old Ben wasn't there.

"Old Ben's a good pet for the warm months," Pa said. "But in the winter months, my cats will have to do the work. Maybe Blackie got him!"

"He might have holed up for the winter in the hayloft,"[1] I told Pa after we had removed all the corn and didn't find him. "I'm worried about him. I've had a lot of pets—groundhogs, crows and hawks— but Old Ben's the best yet."

Reading Strategy
Using Context Clues
Name two context clues that help you figure out what *shelled* means in this sentence.

---

1. hayloft (hā´ lôft´) *n.* upper story in a barn or stable used for storing hay.

November, December, January, February, and March came and went. Of course we never expected to see Old Ben in one of those months. We doubted if we ever would see him again.

One day early in April I went to the corncrib, and Old Ben lay stretched across the floor. He looked taller than I was now. His skin was rough and his long body had a flabby appearance. I knew Old Ben needed mice and milk. I picked him up, petted him, and told him so. But the chill of early April was still with him. He got his tongue out slower to answer the kind words I was saying to him. He tried to crawl up my arm but he couldn't make it.

That spring and summer mice got <u>scarce</u> in the corncrib and Old Ben got daring. He went over to the barn and crawled up into the hayloft, where he had many feasts. But he made one mistake.

He crawled from the hayloft down into Fred's feed box, where it was cool. Old Fred was our horse.

There he lay coiled when the horse came in and put his nose down on top of Old Ben. Fred let out a big snort and started kicking. He kicked down a partition,[2] and then turned his heels on his feed box and kicked it down. Lucky for Old Ben that he got out in one piece. But he got back to his crib.

Old Ben became a part of our barnyard family, a pet and darling of all. When children came to play with my brother and sisters, they always went to the crib and got Old Ben. He enjoyed the children, who were afraid of him at first but later learned to pet this kind old reptile.

Summer passed and the late days of September were very humid. Old Ben failed one morning to drink his milk. We knew it wasn't time for him to hole up for the winter.

We knew something had happened.

Pa and I moved the corn searching for him. Mom made a couple of trips to the barn lot to see if we had found him. But all we found was the rough skin he had shed last spring.

"Fred's never been very sociable with Old Ben since he got in his box that time," Pa said. "I wonder if he could have stomped Old Ben to death. Old Ben could've been crawling over the barn lot, and Fred saw his chance to get even!"

"We'll see," I said.

Pa and I left the crib and walked to the barn lot. He went one way and I went the other, each searching the ground.

Literary Analysis
Narratives How do these details strengthen the impression that this is a nonfiction narrative?

scarce (skers) *adj.* few in number or infrequent; not common

✔**Reading Check**

Why does the family search for Old Ben?

---

2. partition (pär tish´ ən) *n.* something that separates or divides, such as an interior wall that separates one room from another.

Mom came through the gate and walked over where my father was looking. She started looking around, too.

"We think Fred might've got him," Pa said. "We're sure Fred's got it in for him over Old Ben getting in his feed box last summer."

"You're accusing Fred wrong," Mom said. "Here's Old Ben's track in the sand."

I ran over to where Mom had found the track. Pa went over to look, too.

"It's no use now," Pa said, softly. "Wouldn't have taken anything for that snake. I'll miss him on that burlap sack every morning when I come to feed the horses. Always looked up at me as if he understood."

The last trace Old Ben had left was in the corner of the lot near the hogpen. His track went straight to the woven wire fence and stopped.

"They've got him," Pa said. "Old Ben trusted everything and everybody. He went for a visit to the wrong place. He didn't last long among sixteen hogs. They go wild over a snake. Even a biting copperhead can't stop a hog. There won't be a trace of Old Ben left."

We stood silently for a minute looking at the broad, smooth track Old Ben had left in the sand.

Review and Assess

Thinking About the Selection

1. **Respond:** Have your feelings about snakes changed as a result of reading "Old Ben"? Explain why or why not.

2. **(a) Recall:** What kind of snake does the narrator's father say is the only good kind? **(b) Analyze Causes and Effects:** Why do Pa's feelings change? **(c) Draw Conclusions:** How do you know Pa's feelings have changed?

3. **(a) Recall:** List three examples of Old Ben's trusting, friendly nature. **(b) Deduce:** How does Ben's trusting nature get him into trouble with Fred?

4. **(a) Recall:** How does the family know something has happened to Ben? **(b) Infer:** How does Pa know that Ben went to the hog pen?

5. **(a) Recall:** How do the narrator and Old Ben meet?
   (b) Support: Explain how "Old Ben" illustrates the idea that friends can be found in the most unexpected places.
   (c) Extend: Explain another lesson this story teaches about expectations and making judgments.

Jesse Stuart

(1906–1984)

A writer for the *Chicago Tribune* once said that Jesse Stuart's stories "all have a heart." Stuart's narrative about an unusual pet—"Old Ben"— is no exception. The Kentucky-born novelist, poet, and short-story writer received a number of awards for his writing.

Feathered Friend

ARTHUR C. CLARKE

To the best of my knowledge, there's never been a <u>regulation</u> that forbids one to keep pets in a space station. No one ever thought it was necessary—and even had such a rule existed, I am quite certain that Sven Olsen would have ignored it.

With a name like that, you will picture Sven at once as a six-foot-six Nordic giant, built like a bull and with a voice to match. Had this been so, his chances of getting a job in space would have been very slim. Actually he was a wiry little fellow, like most of the early spacers, and managed to qualify easily for the 150-pound bonus[1] that kept so many of us on a reducing diet.

Sven was one of our best construction men, and excelled at the tricky and specialized work of collecting assorted girders[2] as they floated around in free fall, making them do the slow-motion, three-dimensional ballet that would get them into their right positions, and <u>fusing</u> the pieces together when they were precisely dovetailed into the intended pattern: it was a skilled and difficult job, for a space suit is not the most convenient of garbs in which to work. However, Sven's team had one great advantage over the construction gangs you see putting up skyscrapers down on Earth. They could step back and admire their handiwork without being abruptly parted from it by gravity. . . .

---

1. **150-pound bonus** extra money for being lightweight.
2. **girders** (gur´ dərz) *n.* long, thick pieces of metal.

regulation (reg´ yə lā´ shən) *n.* rule

fusing (fyo͞o´ ziŋ) *adj.* joining permanently

Reading Check

Where does Sven do his construction work?

Don't ask me why Sven wanted a pet, or why he chose the one he did. I'm not a psychologist, but I must admit that his selection was very sensible. Claribel weighed practically nothing, her food requirements were tiny—and she was not worried, as most animals would have been, by the absence of gravity.

I first became aware that Claribel was aboard when I was sitting in the little cubbyhole laughingly called my office, checking through my lists of technical stores to decide what items we'd be running out of next. When I heard the musical whistle beside my ear, I assumed that it had come over the station intercom, and waited for an announcement to follow. It didn't; instead, there was a long and involved pattern of melody that made me look up with such a start that I forgot all about the angle beam just behind my head. When the stars had <u>ceased</u> to explode before my eyes, I had my first view of Claribel.

She was a small yellow canary, hanging in the air as motionless as a hummingbird—and with much less effort, for her wings were quietly folded along her sides. We stared at each other for a minute; then, before I had quite recovered my wits, she did a curious kind of backward loop I'm sure no earthbound canary had ever managed, and departed with a few leisurely flicks. It was quite obvious that she'd already learned how to operate in the absence of gravity, and did not believe in doing unnecessary work.

Sven didn't confess to her ownership for several days, and by that time it no longer mattered, because Claribel was a general pet. He had smuggled her up on the last ferry from Earth, when he came back from leave—partly, he claimed, out of sheer scientific curiosity. He wanted to see just how a bird would operate when it had no weight but could still use its wings.

Claribel thrived and grew fat. On the whole, we had little trouble concealing our guest when VIP's from Earth came visiting. A space station has more hiding places than you can count; the only problem was that Claribel got rather noisy when she was upset, and we sometimes had to think fast to explain the curious peeps and whistles that came from ventilating shafts and storage bulkheads. There were a couple of narrow escapes—but then who would dream of looking for a canary in a space station?

We were now on twelve-hour watches, which was not as bad as it sounds, since you need little sleep in space. Though of course there is no "day" and "night" when you are floating in permanent sunlight, it was still convenient to stick to the terms. Certainly when I woke that "morning" it felt like 6:00 A.M. on Earth. I had a nagging headache, and vague memories of fitful, disturbed

ceased (sēsd) v. stopped

dreams. It took me ages to undo my bunk straps, and I was still only half awake when I joined the remainder of the duty crew in the mess. Breakfast was unusually quiet, and there was one seat vacant.

"Where's Sven?" I asked, not very much caring.

"He's looking for Claribel," someone answered. "Says he can't find her anywhere. She usually wakes him up."

Before I could retort that she usually woke me up, too, Sven came in through the doorway, and we could see at once that something was wrong. He slowly opened his hand, and there lay a tiny bundle of yellow feathers, with two clenched claws sticking pathetically up into the air.

"What happened?" we asked, all equally distressed.

"I don't know," said Sven mournfully. "I just found her like this."

"Let's have a look at her," said Jock Duncan, our cook-doctor-dietitian. We all waited in hushed silence while he held Claribel against his ear in an attempt to detect any heartbeat.

Presently he shook his head. "I can't hear anything, but that doesn't prove she's dead. I've never listened to a canary's heart," he added rather apologetically.

"Give her a shot of oxygen," suggested somebody, pointing to the green-banded emergency cylinder in its recess beside the door. Everyone agreed that this was an excellent idea, and Claribel was tucked snugly into a face mask that was large enough to serve as a complete oxygen tent for her.

To our delighted surprise, she revived at once. Beaming broadly, Sven removed the mask, and she hopped onto his finger. She gave her series of "Come to the cookhouse, boys" trills—then promptly keeled over again.

"I don't get it," lamented Sven. "What's wrong with her? She's never done this before."

For the last few minutes, something had been tugging at my memory. My mind seemed to be very sluggish that morning, as if I was still unable to cast off the burden of sleep. I felt that I could do with some of that oxygen—but before I could reach the mask, understanding exploded in my brain. I whirled on the duty engineer and said urgently:

▲ Critical Viewing
Do you think these crew members get along with one another? Explain. [Infer]

✓ Reading Check

What did the crew members do to wake up Claribel?

"Jim!" There's something wrong with the air! That's why Claribel's passed out. I've just remembered that miners used to carry canaries down to warn them of gas."

"Nonsense!" said Jim. "The alarms would have gone off. We've got duplicate circuits, operating independently."

"Er—the second alarm circuit isn't connected up yet," his assistant reminded him. That shook Jim; he left without a word, while we stood arguing and passing the oxygen bottle around like a pipe of peace.

He came back ten minutes later with a sheepish expression. It was one of those accidents that couldn't possibly happen; we'd had one of our rare eclipses by Earth's shadow that night; part of the air purifier had frozen up, and the single alarm in the circuit had failed to go off. Half a million dollars' worth of chemical and electronic engineering had let us down completely. Without Claribel, we should soon have been slightly dead.

So now, if you visit any space station, don't be surprised if you hear an inexplicable snatch of birdsong. There's no need to be alarmed; on the contrary, in fact. It will mean that you're being doubly safeguarded, at practically no extra expense.

Review and Assess

Thinking About the Selection

1. **Respond:** Do you think it was a good idea for Sven to bring Claribel into space? Why or why not?

2. **(a) Recall:** Where does the story take place? **(b) Compare and Contrast:** Name two features of life in the story that differ from life on Earth.

3. **(a) Recall:** What do the crew members do with Claribel when VIPs visit the space station? **(b) Infer:** How do the crew members feel about Claribel? **(c) Apply:** What is the benefit of having a pet in the space station?

4. **(a) Synthesize:** Explain at least three events or factors that help the narrator figure out that something is wrong with the air. **(b) Make a Judgment:** Who is responsible for saving the crew's lives: Claribel or the narrator?

5. **(a) Analyze Causes and Effects:** Explain reasons that the alarm did not warn the crew about the problem.
   (b) Speculate: What are some potential problems with using a canary instead of an electric alarm? **(c) Evaluate:** Which do you think is the better alarm? Why?

Arthur C. Clarke

(b. 1917)
When he first got his television set, noted science-fiction writer Arthur C. Clarke became the only television owner on Sri Lanka, the island off India where he lives.

Clarke holds another, more important television "first." He was the first to think of sending television and radio signals around the world by bouncing them off satellites. If not for his own idea, his television set would have no signals to pick up! Though "Feathered Friend" is science fiction, some of Clarke's dreams about the future have become "science fact."

Review and Assess

Literary Analysis

Narratives

1. Tell the sequence of events in "Old Ben."
2. Tell the sequence of events in "Feathered Friend."
3. Who tells the story in each narrative?

Comparing Literary Works

4. In what ways do both selections seem as if they could be true stories?
5. In what ways do both selections seem as if they could be made-up stories?
6. Complete an organizer like the one shown here to compare and contrast the works.

	Characters	Plot	Ending
"Old Ben"	Boy my age, friendly snake		
"Feathered Friend"		Bird is pet on spaceship. Astronauts don't know what's wrong.	

7. Which story did you prefer? Explain, using details from the chart.

Reading Strategy

Using Context Clues

8. Find each of the following words in the story. Use a graphic organizer like the one shown to list the context clues that help you figure out the meaning of each word.

   a. *stroked*, p. 154   **b.** *coiled*, p. 154   **c.** *corncrib*, p. 155

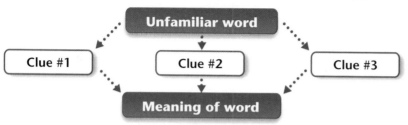

9. Use context clues to explain the meaning of *eclipses* below. We'd had one of our rare *eclipses* by Earth's shadow that night.

Extend Understanding

10. **Science Connection:** Name three reasons that space travelers might take plants and animals into space.

Quick Review

A **narrative** is a story. A **fictional narrative** is a made-up story from the writer's imagination. A **nonfictional narrative** is a true story about events that actually happened.
To review narratives, see page 153.

Context clues are words and phrases around an unfamiliar word that help you figure out its meaning. To review context clues, see page 153.

 Take It to the Net
www.phschool.com
Take the interactive self-test online to check your understanding of these selections.

Integrate Language Skills

Vocabulary Development Lesson

Word Analysis: Forms of *regulate*

You can form many new words by adding endings to certain verbs, or action words. For example, the verb *regulate* means "to govern according to a rule." When you add the ending *-tion* to *regulate* (after dropping the final *e*), you form the word *regulation*, meaning "rule." On your paper, use a form of *regulate* to fill in each blank.

> regulate   regulation   regulator   regulatory

Taisha was the ___?___ for quality control at a catcher's mitt factory. She knew every ___?___ in the book. One day, she received a memo from a ___?___ agency. Taisha now had to ___?___ the way workers checked gloves for holes.

Concept Development: Definition

On your paper, match each numbered word with its definition.

1. scarce
2. fusing
3. regulation
4. ceased

a. stopped
b. rule
c. infrequent
d. joining

Spelling Strategy

When a word ends in silent *e*, drop the *e* when adding a suffix, or ending, beginning with a vowel. Do not drop the *e* when adding a suffix beginning with a consonant. Add the suffix to each word.

1. precise + *-ly*
2. ventilate + *-ing*
3. peace + *-ful*
4. fake + *-er*

Grammar Lesson

Perfect Verb Tenses

The **perfect verb tenses** of verbs combine a form of *have* with the past participle.

- The **present perfect tense** shows an action that began in the past and continues into the present.
- The **past perfect tense** shows a past action or condition that ended before another past action began.
- The **future perfect tense** shows a future action or condition that will have ended before another begins.

Practice Identify the verbs and their tenses.

1. Pa had told me not to play with snakes.
2. He has noticed snakes before.
3. He had liked no snakes until now.
4. I have not seen a snake like that before.
5. By next year, it will have grown.

Writing Application Write three sentences about Old Ben. Use a different perfect tense in each. To review the principal parts of verbs, see page 136.

Present Perfect	Past Perfect	Future Perfect
have, has + past participle	*had* + past participle	*will have* + past participle
There *has been* no rule against pets in space.	Sven *had smuggled* his pet on the last ferry.	Before long, others *will have brought* pets, too.

WG Prentice Hall Writing and Grammar Connection: Chapter 22, Section 2

Writing Lesson

Feature Story

Write a brief feature story—a newspaper article about something that is not actually news but is interesting or unusual—about Claribel or Ben.

Prewriting   Think of the questions your readers will have, such as what makes this animal different from other animals of its kind? Gather details to answer those questions.

Drafting   Describe the interesting features, activities, or abilities of the animal. Organize each paragraph around a main idea. Then, supply examples, explanations, and details.

Revising   Revise your paragraph to improve the organization. Highlight the main idea in each paragraph. Delete any sentences in the paragraph that do not support, explain, or give details about that main idea.

Model: Deleting Unrelated Details

You might expect a bird to be timid or at least cautious. Although Claribel is tiny, she is not afraid of anything. ~~She can hide in the smallest space.~~ Whatever the crew is working on, no matter how noisy, Claribel wants to be part of the action.

> The detail about Claribel's ability to hide is deleted because it does not contribute to the main idea that she is not afraid.

 Prentice Hall Writing and Grammar Connection: Chapter 7, Section 4

Extension Activities

Listening and Speaking   Create a **multimedia presentation** about your own or someone else's experience with a pet. Identify the people involved and the events. Include details to make your story come alive, and use photos, recordings, charts, or other visuals. To tell your story,

- include your own thoughts and actions.
- tell listeners how you or the subject of the story feels about the pet.

After you make your presentation to your class, ask your classmates to share their experiences with a similiar pet.

Research and Technology   With a small group, choose a type of pet to research for a pet fair. Go online to get photos and gather information about the pet's habits, pet care (including training and feeding), and costs involved in having pets. Create **fact sheets** and hand them out at the fair. **[Group Activity]**

 Take It to the Net   www.phschool.com

Go online for an additional research activity using the Internet.

Reviews

About Reviews

A **review** describes and evaluates a product or performance. Reviews are one source of information you can use to find out about the following topics.

- a book
- a movie or television program
- a stage performance
- a music disc, collection, or performance
- a restaurant

By describing a product or performance, the reviewer gives the reader information that can be used to make a decision. If a reviewer likes something, he or she will rave about it and thereby influence readers positively. On the other hand, a negative review can discourage people from buying, visiting, reading, or viewing.

The following selection, "As Close As We Can Get," is a music review about the *Smithsonian Folkways' Anthology of American Folk Music*. As you read, think about whether you would or would not purchase the collection, based on the review.

Reading Strategy

Reading Accurately

To **read accurately** means to read each word correctly and to understand the meaning of each word. When you are reading informational texts, you are likely to encounter specialized vocabulary that is unfamiliar. To ensure that you read accurately, scan a text—run your eyes quickly over the words—before you read it closely.

- Identify unfamiliar words and terms.
- Look them up in a dictionary or other resource.
- Learn their pronunciations.

Each of these steps will help you read and comprehend more accurately during reading. Before you read the review, scan the text.

Use a chart like the one shown to write down any unfamiliar words you notice. Then, look up their pronunciations as well as their meanings and record them in the space provided. After reading, review new words so you will read them accurately when you see them again.

Unfamiliar Word	Meaning	Pronunciation
self-conscious	awkward or embarrassed in the presence of others; ill at ease	self´ känshəs

As Close As We Can Get

❧ Carl Zebrowski ❧

The Banjo Lesson, 1893, Henry Ossawa Tanner, Hampton University Museum, Hampton, Virginia

Scan the text to find the words *anthology, medium, pretensions, bowing, virtuosity,* and *era.* Look up each word in a dictionary, decide which definition fits in this situation, and make sure you can pronounce each word.

Listening to the recordings in *Smithsonian Folkways' Anthology of American Folk Music* is like looking at a photo of a Civil War soldier dressed in a crumpled uniform. Beneath the medium's time-worn surface you can sense the presence of a vibrant living person.

Music Review, *Civil War Times,* October 1999

What cuts through the mild surface noise of the anthology's 70-year-old recordings is people in all their joy and sorrow. These are plain folk, mostly from south of the Mason-Dixon Line. They have no pretensions. They are not self-conscious. Their music is earthy yet at the same time other-worldly.

There's plenty of sloppy string plucking and bowing here, and warbling voices, too, but surely that's what folk music sounded like in the 1860s (and often still does). It was a time when entertainment for a social gathering often meant a friend playing his banjo. He probably wasn't an accomplished musician by traditional standards, but his confident rhythm and enthusiasm made the music come alive in ways sheer virtuosity can't. This anthology is about as close as we can get to the music of that era.

The reviewer identifies the strengths and weaknesses of the collection.

Although the recordings here were, of course, not made during the war, the performances are timeless. The songs are even more so. Indeed, many of them have been around for hundreds of years. They were played in the 1860s and are still played today. As everything in history does, these simple tunes have picked up a little bit of all the generations they've passed through. That historical gold dust shows up on these recordings.

Music Review, *Civil War Times*, October 1999

Check Your Comprehension

1. How old are the recordings on the anthology?
2. Where are most of the people who made the recordings from?
3. In the 1860s, what kind of entertainment would there have been at a social gathering?

Applying the Reading Strategy

Reading Accurately

4. What is the meaning and pronunciation of the word "anthology"?
5. Which words did you look up for definition or pronunciation? Read aloud the sentences in which the words appear.

Activity

Radio Review

Prepare a reading of "As Close As We Can Get" as if you were giving a review on a radio broadcast. Make sure you know the meaning of each word in the text as well as how to pronounce it. When you are confident of your ability, perform your radio review for your class.

Contrasting Informational Materials

Music Reviews and Advertisements

Reviewers have the ability to influence readers positively or negatively, which may then sway readers to go out and buy, watch, visit, or read whatever is being reviewed. Although reviewers may influence people's decisions to buy something, the reviewer does not benefit from the reader's decision one way or another.

Like music reviews, advertisements use descriptive language and persuasion to influence their audience. However, the purpose of an advertisement is to persuade readers or listeners to buy the product.

In a newspaper or magazine, find a review of a movie, CD, or performance. Then, find an advertisement for the same movie, CD, or performance. (It does not have to appear in the same magazine or newspaper.) Then, using a chart like the one provided, compare the advertisement to the review.

	Advertisement	Music Review
Purpose		
Kinds of words used to persuade		
Biased or unbiased? How do you know?		
Would you buy the product? Why?		

Writing WORKSHOP

Description: Descriptive Essay

A **descriptive essay** creates a picture of a person, place, thing, or event. In this workshop, you will write a descriptive essay focused on a topic that interests you.

Assignment Criteria. Your descriptive essay should have the following characteristics:

- main impression to which each detail adds specific information
- rich sensory language that appeals to the five senses
- organizational pattern appropriate to the type of composition
- figurative language that creates vivid comparisons

See the Rubric on page 173 for the criteria on which your descriptive essay may be assessed.

Prewriting

Choose a topic. Use **trigger words** to help you think of a topic. Think of three general words, such as *vacation, family, memories.* Take a few minutes to list specific words that you associate with each general word. Then, review what you have written, circle descriptive words, and choose the most interesting topic from your list.

Narrow your topic. When you have chosen your topic, narrow it to focus on a part that is specific enough to be described in a single composition. For example, "the national park" is too broad. You could not give a clear picture of the whole park in one composition. However, "our campsite at the national park" and "the old pine next to our campsite" are narrowed topics that you could fully describe in one composition.

Use sensory details. Use a sensory details chart like the one shown to help you gather details about the sights, scents, textures, sounds, and tastes associated with a campsite.

	Model: Gathering Sensory Details				
	Taste	Touch	Smell	Sight	Hearing
	None	Rough tail	Hay	Star	Clopping

Student Model

Before you begin drafting your descriptive essay, read this student model and review the characteristics of successful description.

Jessica Kile

Short and Sweet

The day looked too gray and foggy to bother going outside. I looked out the window once more, then turned back toward the kitchen. Suddenly I realized I had seen something strange. My father was walking up the driveway with—a dog? No. What was that thing? It was mostly black, with a shaggy black coat that contrasted with the white mane and tail. Mane and tail? I realized that I was describing a horse, but this animal clopping up the driveway was too small to be a horse. Or was it?

Outside, where my father introduced Lucky, the miniature horse, I examined our new pet. I began by examining Lucky's face. Like a full-sized horse, Lucky had a broad forehead with a wisp of mane tossed down between his ears. His eyes were deep brown and peaceful. The black coat was not shaggy here. The hair on Lucky's head was soft, but a little bumpy, like a terry cloth towel. The smoothest, softest part of any horse's head is his nose—and Lucky was no exception. The hair around his nose was so short and soft it felt like velour. I gave his neck a hug and breathed in the horsy smell that seemed like a mix of warm hay and wet leaves. When I hugged him, he nickered—a sound like a little chuckle that moves from his throat to his nose.

I ran my hands across his back, noticing how much tinier it was than a full-sized horse. Here, his coat was rough and shaggy. I checked his legs, which seemed to be healthy and straight. The hooves, too, seemed in good shape. They were smooth with a thick "shell" that had no cracks.

His tail was thick and the hair here was much coarser and rougher than any human hair. It was strange because from a distance the tail looked smooth and flowing. When you touched it though, it became a rough rope. Lucky became impatient with my "health inspection." He nudged me with his velvety nose to get me back to scratching his ears.

"What do you think?" asked Dad after I had examined Lucky from head to toe.

"Well," I said, "I've never seen a horse like this! I like him though. He may be short, but he's sweet!"

The writer establishes a main impression of a horse—just a smaller horse than people expect.

Beginning with Lucky's head, the author will describe the horse, in spatial order.

The writer uses details that appeal to the senses. Here, smell and sound are described.

Through figurative language, the writer establishes the feel of the horse's tail.

Drafting

Organize the details. Arrange the details in an order that will help the reader picture your subject. Use the organization chart to decide which organization is most appropriate for a descriptive essay. Then, write the draft of your essay using that organization.

Use figurative language. Figurative language is writing that is not meant to be taken literally. In your description, use figurative language such as metaphors and similes to emphasize qualities of your subject.

- **Simile:** A comparison expressed using the word *like* or *as.*

  "His tail was like a rough rope."

- **Metaphor:** A comparison expressed without the words *like* or *as.* One thing is referred to as if it were another.

  "His tail was a rough rope."

  "The rough rope of his tail . . ."

Create a main impression. Make connections between the details to create a single impression—an idea or a feeling—about your subject. Focus mainly on details that contribute to that main impression.

Chronological Order

- Present events in the order in which they occur.
- Use for a remembrance or other description of an event.

Spatial Order

- Present details from left to right, top to bottom, or back to front.
- Use for descriptions of places or objects.

Order of Importance

- Present least important details at the beginning and the most important at the end.
- Use for descriptions that will be used to evaluate the thing being described or to show its significance.

Revising

Revise to vary sentence length. Revise in places where you have several sentences containing long lists of descriptive words. Group some related details in lists. Emphasize unusual or unique details by breaking them into individual sentences. Use the model on page 172 as a guide.

Model: Revising Sentence Length

Outside, where my father introduced Lucky, the miniature horse, I examined our new pet.

Draft: ~~I went outside. My father introduced Lucky, the minature horse. Lucky, the~~

~~miniature horse. I examined our new pet.~~ I began by examining Lucky's face. Like a

with

full-sized horse, Lucky had a broad forehead. ~~He had~~ a wisp of mane tossed down

between his ears.

> Because several short sentences in a row gave a choppy sound to the writing, the writer combined some sentences to create variety with two long sentences around one short one.

Revise word choice. Check your adjectives—the words that describe nouns—to make sure they add specific details to your description. Vague words like *great, nice,* and *good* do not add details that readers can identify. Vague adjectives leave readers wondering in what way the thing you are describing is *great, nice,* or *good.* Use precise adjectives like *exciting, helpful,* and *spicy* to give readers specific information.

Compare the nonmodel and the model. Why is the model stronger than the nonmodel?

Nonmodel	Model
Lucky was a nice horse. His coat was soft—especially around his nose. His legs and hooves looked good, and his coat was great.	Lucky was a friendly and curious horse. His coat was like velvet—especially around his nose. His legs and hooves looked solid, and his coat was shiny.

Publishing and Presenting

Choose one of the following ways to share your writing with classmates or a wider audience.

Record it. Make an audio recording of your description. Play the tape for a group of classmates or family members.

Mail it. Send your descriptive essay to a friend or relative by e-mail.

Save it for future use. Descriptive writing is used in almost all other forms of writing, including narration and persuasion. Save your description. You can use part or all of it in a story, persuasive essay, or speech. Depending on the topic of your description and the new writing, you might incorporate the whole description or only specific details.

WG Prentice Hall Writing and Grammar Connection: Chapter 5

Listening Connection

To learn to evaluate and make judgments about descriptions in advertisements and other persuasive messages, see the **Listening and Speaking Workshop** on page 174.

Rubric for Self-Assessment

Evaluate your descriptive essay using the following criteria and rating scale:

Criteria	Rating Scale				
	Not very				Very
How clear is the main impression?	1	2	3	4	5
Do details contribute to the main impression?	1	2	3	4	5
Is the description logically organized?	1	2	3	4	5
How vivid and varied is the sensory language?	1	2	3	4	5
How effective is the figurative language?	1	2	3	4	5

Listening and Speaking WORKSHOP

Evaluating Persuasive Messages

A **persuasive message** encourages the audience to think or act in a certain way. Many persuasive messages—such as political presentations, debates, editorials, advertisements, infomercials, and others—are communicated on television. Learn to evaluate persuasive messages.

Evaluate Information

Identify false and misleading information. Do not believe that everything stated as a fact is accurate.

- **Consider the source**. Facts supplied by the person or group that is selling or persuading may be slanted to favor a particular point of view.
- **Distinguish between fact and opinion**. Opinions can be supported, but not proved. A fact can be proved true.
- **Recognize propaganda**. Propaganda is the spreading of distorted or misleading ideas to promote a special interest or to damage a person, group, or cause.

Evaluate Delivery

A persuasive message on television may include speech, music, and visual images that add appeal but do not add factual content.

Notice persuasive techniques. Be aware of the persuasive techniques shown here that are sometimes used in place of factual information.

Recognize emotional appeals. An emotional appeal is a persuasive technique through which your choice is influenced with feelings rather than information. For example, an advertisement may be very entertaining but give very little information about the product. Images shown with the product can make it seem as if people who buy or use the product are more popular, happy, or successful. Always ask yourself if the associations made in an ad are valid—can the product really create a situation like the one shown in the ad?

Technique	Example
Bandwagon appeal	Every sixth-grader thinks this, so you should too.
Testimonial	Famous people use this product, so it must be good.
Loaded language (words meant to give a positive or negative slant to a statement)	My opponent is *wavering*. I am *considering the options*...

Activity: Advertisement Evaluation

Evaluate several television advertisements by asking these questions.

- How reliable and accurate is the information?
- What persuasive techniques are used?
- What associations are made? Are they valid?
- Is the advertisement entertaining or memorable?
- Are you persuaded? Why or why not?

Few persuasive messages are strictly factual. Evaluate each message, and use sound reasoning to make up your mind about the advertisement.

Assessment WORKSHOP

Identifying and Supporting Main Ideas

In the reading sections of some tests, you may be required to read a passage and answer multiple-choice questions about the main idea or supporting details in a passage. Use the strategies to help you answer test questions about details.

Read the question carefully to identify whether you are being asked for a main idea or a supporting detail. Then, read the answer choices to see if you can eliminate any answer that is not the kind of information being asked for.

Test-Taking Strategies

- Look over the questions before reading passages to help you focus on key points.
- Before choosing an answer, make sure you have identified whether the question asks for a main idea or a supporting detail.

Sample Test Item

A strong breeze made the leaves rustle. A twig snapped beneath his foot, and Martin jumped. He had never walked the woodsy path between his house and Andy's alone at night. An owl's hoot didn't exactly scare him, but it did make him nervous.

1. How does Martin feel about his walk?
   A He feels uneasy.
   B He is walking the path alone for the first time.
   C It is dark.
   D The owl's hoot doesn't frighten him.

Answer and Explanation

The question asks you to identify the main idea of how Martin feels about the walk. *B, C,* and *D* are incorrect because they are details that contribute to the main idea. The answer is *A*.

▶ Practice

Answer the questions based on this passage:

The world's tropical rain forests are filled with treasures more valuable than gold or jewels. Rain forests include many varieties of fruits, thousands of species of animals, and many plants with healing properties. The trees give off oxygen, which is necessary to humans. Rubber trees yield natural rubber, necessary for many products. The sap of one kind of tree is similar to diesel oil.

1. Treasures of the rain forests include
   A oxygen, fruits, gold.
   B fruits, rubber, oxygen.
   C diesel fuel, animals, jewels.
   D fruits, medicine, wheat.

2. Why are the rain forests important?
   A They have fruit.
   B The sap of one kind of tree is like diesel oil.
   C Plants have healing properties.
   D There are a wide variety of useful resources found only in the rain forest.

© Paul Schulenberg/Stock Illustration Source, Inc.

Exploring the Theme

Life is full of twists and turns, choices and challenges. Each choice leads to a different path that gives you the chance to test your abilities and find new strengths. The literature in this unit introduces you to authors and characters who are put to the test at significant points in their lives. As you read about the experiences of others—real people and fictional characters—think about how they test their skills and prove their abilities in challenging situations.

Why Read Literature?

There are a variety of reasons for reading literature. You might read to explore the theme in this unit—proving yourself—to see how others meet the challenge of adversity. You might read a poem aloud to enjoy the poet's rhythm and word choice. Preview three purposes you might have for reading the works in this unit.

1

Read for the love of literature.

In 1920, a missionary in Northern India raided a den of wolves and hauled out two children, aged three and five, who were being raised by wolves. Read Nobel Prize winner Rudyard Kipling's story **"Mowgli's Brothers,"** on page 210 for an imaginative fictional account of wolves raising a human child.

To see a line of poetry "bounce" in a poem about soccer, read **"Alone in the Nets,"** page 232.

2

Read to be inspired.

Growing up in the Dominican Republic, Julia Alvarez was a happy, lively child with lots of friends. Then, when she was 10, her family was forced to flee her native land. To learn what it was like to arrive as a new immigrant, at a new school, in a strange country, read **"Names/Nombres"** on page 224.

The first female Olympic champion was a Greek princess who rode to victory as a champion charioteer in the ancient Olympic Games in the fourth century B.C. In the modern Olympics Games, women began competing in 1900. Learn more about accomplished women athletes in **"Women in Sports,"** page 238.

It was not until 1974 that girls were allowed to play on Little League baseball and softball teams. Read a humorous fictional account of how one girl finds her place on a previously all-boy team in **"The Southpaw,"** page 229.

3

Read for information.

The inventors of the airplane worked as bicycle repairmen! Find out more about them when you read the poem **"Wilbur Wright and Orville Wright,"** p. 248.

Learn how to read and accurately fill out applications when you read the applications for a bank account, a library card, and a sports league, p. 239.

 Take It to the Net

Visit the Web site for online instruction and activities related to each selection in this unit.

www.phschool.com

How to Read Literature

Interactive Reading Strategies

Books do not come with plugs or batteries. To make a book work, you have to plug yourself in by interacting with the words on the page. The following strategies will help you make the connection that lights up your imagination.

1. Understand shades of meaning.

To get the most meaning from a word, recognize and react to its particular shade of meaning. In the following example, notice how the sentence would have a slightly different meaning if *sleepy* were replaced with *exhausted, tired,* or *drowsy.*

> "You must get an early start if you are going to go to the west side of the butte and return by supper," John said to the sleepy boy—*from* "Thunder Butte"

In this unit, you will learn to recognize shades of meaning and analyze your reaction to them.

2. Predicting characters' actions.

Increase your involvement in a narrative, or story, by making predictions—educated guesses based on story facts and your experience. Predicting what characters will do next leads you to get to know them better. As you read the works in this unit, you will develop skill in recognizing details that help you make predictions.

Details

Janet is a good player.

+

Richard's team is losing.

+

Several players are injured.

Prediction

Richard will ask Janet to play.

3. Set a purpose for reading.

Before you begin, set a purpose for reading. The following example shows you how the purpose you set determines the details you focus on.

Reading for Enjoyment	Reading for Insight
Janet really wants to be on Richard's team—I want to find out if she can convince him to let her play.	I wonder what would happen if Richard wanted to play on Janet's all-girls team.

4. Interpret meaning.

If you listened to people speaking another language, you would hear what they say but you would need an interpreter—someone to explain the meaning—to understand it. Be your own interpreter when you read literature. In this unit, you will learn to find the meanings of words that can be used in more than one way and the meaning of figurative language—words and phrases that are not meant to be interpreted literally.

As you read the selections in this unit, review the reading strategies and look at the notes in the side column. Use the suggestions to apply the strategies for interactive reading.

Prepare to Read

from The Pigman & Me

 Take It to the Net

Visit www.phschool.com
for interactive activities
and instruction related to
The Pigman & Me,
including

- background
- graphic organizers
- literary elements
- reading strategies

Preview

Connecting to the Literature

In this excerpt from *The Pigman & Me* by Paul Zindel, the author looks back with humor on one of his experiences as the new kid in school. Connect to the author's experience by recalling a blunder you have made in a new place or an unfamiliar situation.

Background

Different places have different rules. Usually rules are spelled out or written for everyone to read. Sometimes rules are unwritten and are just as important as the written ones. In the excerpt from *The Pigman & Me,* Paul Zindel recalls a time when, according to an unwritten rule, he was "not allowed" to back down from a fight.

Literary Analysis

Internal Conflict

An **internal conflict** is a struggle within a person or character. The character struggles with two different feelings, needs, or choices.

In *The Pigman & Me*, Paul wants to avoid a fight, but he also wants to prove he is not afraid. These feelings produce an internal conflict.

Record other details of Paul's internal conflict in a chart like the one shown here.

Connecting Literary Elements

Paul's internal conflict is connected to an **external conflict**—a conflict with a force outside himself. In this case, the outside force is another student.

As you read, use the following focus questions to explore Paul's internal and external conflicts:

1. What events lead to Paul's external conflict?
2. How is Paul's external conflict connected to his internal conflict?

1. Paul is ashamed to call off the fight.	**I n t e r n a l C o n f l i c t**	1. Paul is afraid to fight.
2.		2.
3.		3.

Reading Strategy

Recognizing Word Origins

Many words in English are borrowed from other languages. Some words have been used in English for so long that they are no longer considered to be a foreign language. Look at the examples below.

- pizza
- cliché
- siesta
- amigo

Other commonly used words from languages other than English appear in *The Pigman & Me*. Notice them as you read.

Vocabulary Development

exact (eg zakt´) *v.* take using force or authority (p. 183)

tactics (tak´ tiks) *n.* methods used for a particular purpose; tricks (p. 184)

undulating (un´ dyo͞o lā´ tiŋ) *adj.* moving in waves, like a snake (p. 187)

goading (gō´ diŋ) *v.* pushing a person into acting, especially by using pain or insults (p. 187)

distorted (di stôr´ tid) *adj.* twisted out of the normal shape (p. 187)

groveled (grä´ vəld) *v.* lay or crawled about before someone in hope of mercy (p. 187)

from
THE PIGMAN
& ME
Paul Zindel

When trouble came to me, it didn't involve anybody I thought it would. It involved the nice, normal, smart boy by the name of John Quinn. Life does that to us a lot. Just when we think something awful's going to happen one way, it throws you a curve and the something awful happens another way. This happened on the first Friday, during gym period, when we were allowed to play games in the school yard. A boy by the name of Richard Cahill, who lived near an old linoleum factory, asked me if I'd like to play paddle ball with him, and I said, "Yes." Some of the kids played softball, some played warball, and there were a few other games where you could sign out equipment and do what you wanted. What I didn't know was that you were allowed to sign out the paddles for only fifteen minutes per period so more kids could get a chance to use them. I just didn't happen to know that little rule, and Richard Cahill didn't think to tell me about it. Richard was getting a drink from the water fountain when John Quinn came up to me and told me I had to give him my paddle.

"No," I said, being a little paranoid about being the new kid and thinking everyone was going to try to take advantage of me.

"Look, you *have* to give it to me," John Quinn insisted.

That was when I did something berserk. I was so wound up and frightened that I didn't think, and I struck out at him with my right fist. I had forgotten I was holding the paddle, and it smacked into his face, giving him an instant black eye. John was shocked. I was shocked. Richard Cahill came running back and he was shocked.

"What's going on here?" Mr. Trellis, the gym teacher, growled.

"He hit me with the paddle," John moaned, holding his eye. He was red as a beet, as Little Frankfurter, Conehead, Moose, and lots of the others gathered around.

"He tried to take the paddle away from me!" I complained.

"His time was up," John said.

Mr. Trellis set me wise to the rules as he took John over to a supply locker and pulled out a first-aid kit.

"I'm sorry," I said, over and over again.

Then the bell rang, and all John Quinn whispered to me was that he was going to get even. He didn't say it like a nasty rotten kid, just more like an all-American boy who knew he'd have to regain his dignity about having to walk around school with a black eye. Before the end of school, Jennifer came running up to me in the halls and told me John Quinn had announced to everyone he was going to <u>exact</u> revenge on me after school on Monday. That was the note of disaster my first week at school ended on, and I was terrified because I didn't know how to fight. I had never even been in a fight. What had happened was all an accident. It really was.

When Nonno Frankie arrived on Saturday morning, he found me sitting in the apple tree alone. Mom had told him it was O.K. to walk around the whole yard now, as long as he didn't do any diggings or mutilations other than weed-pulling on her side. I was expecting him to notice right off the bat that I was white with fear, but instead he stood looking at the carvings Jennifer and I had made in the trunk of the tree. I thought he was just intensely curious about what "ESCAPE! PAUL & JENNIFER!" meant. Of course, the twins, being such copycats, had already added their names so the full carving away of the bark now read, "ESCAPE! PAUL & JENNIFER! & NICKY & JOEY!" And the letters circled halfway around the tree.

"You're killing it," Nonno Frankie said sadly.

"What?" I jumped down to his side.

"The tree will die if you cut any more."

I thought he was kidding, because all we had done was carve off the outer pieces of bark. We hadn't carved deep into the tree, not into the *heart* of the tree. The tree was too important to us. It was the most crucial place to me and Jennifer, and the last thing we'd want to do was hurt it.

"The heart of a tree isn't deep inside of it. Its heart and blood are on the *outside*, just under the bark," Nonno Frankie explained. "That's the living part of a tree. If you carve in a circle all around the trunk, it's like slitting its throat. The water and juices and life of the

exact (eg zakt´) *v.* take using force or authority

Reading Strategy
Recognizing Word Origins *Nonno* is the Italian word for "grandfather." *Nonna* is "grandmother." What English word for "grandmother" sounds similar to *Nonna*?

Reading Check

Why is Paul afraid?

tree can't move up from the roots!" I knew about the living layer of a tree, but I didn't know exposing it would kill the whole tree. I just never thought about it, or I figured trees patched themselves up.

"Now it can feed itself from only half its trunk," Nonno Frankie explained. "You must not cut any more."

"I won't," I promised. Then I felt worse than ever. Not only was I scheduled to get beat up by John Quinn after school on Monday, I was also a near tree-killer. Nonno Frankie finally looked closely at me.

"Your first week at school wasn't all juicy meatballs?" he asked.

That was all he had to say, and I spilled out each and every horrifying detail. Nonno Frankie let me babble on and on. He looked as if he understood exactly how I felt and wasn't going to call me stupid or demented or a big yellow coward. When I didn't have another word left in me, I just shut up and stared down at the ground.

"Stab nail at ill Italian bats!" Nonno Frankie finally said.

"What?"

He repeated the weird sentence and asked me what was special about it. I guessed, "It reads the same backward as forward?"

"Right! Ho! Ho! Ho! See, you learn! You remember things I teach you. So today I will teach you how to fight, and you will smack this John Quinn around like floured pizza dough."

"But I can't fight."

"I'll show you Sicilian combat <u>tactics</u>."

"Like what?"

"Everything about Italian fighting. It has to do with your mind and body. Things you have to know so you don't have to be afraid of bullies. Street smarts my father taught me. Like 'Never miss a good chance to shut up!'"

VAROOOOOOOOOOM!

A plane took off over our heads. We walked out beyond the yard to the great field overlooking the airport.

Nonno Frankie suddenly let out a yell. "*Aaeeeeeyaaaayeeeeeh!*" It was so blood-curdlingly weird, I decided to wait until he felt like explaining it.

"*Aaeeeeeyaaaayeeeeeh!*" he bellowed again. "It's good to be able to yell like Tarzan!" he said. "This confuses your enemy, and you can also yell it if you have to retreat. You run away roaring and everyone thinks you at least have guts! It confuses everybody!"

"Is that all I need to know?" I asked, now more afraid than ever of facing John Quinn in front of all the kids.

"No. Tonight I will cut your hair."

"Cut it?"

"Yes. It's too long!"

"It is?"

Reading Strategy
Recognizing Word Origins What word in this paragraph has its origin in Italian?

tactics (tak´ tiks) *n.* methods used for a particular purpose; tricks

"Ah," Nonno Frankie said, "you'd be surprised how many kids lose fights because of their hair. Alexander the Great always ordered his entire army to shave their heads. Long hair makes it easy for an enemy to grab it and cut off your head."

"John Quinn just wants to beat me up!"

"You can never be too sure. This boy might have the spirit of Genghis Khan!"

"Who was Genghis Khan?"

"Who? He once killed two million enemies in one hour. Some of them he killed with yo-yos."

"Yo-yos?"

"See, these are the things you need to know. The yo-yo was first invented as a weapon. Of course, they were as heavy as steel pipes and had long rope cords, but they were still yo-yos!"

"I didn't know that," I admitted.

"That's why I'm telling you. You should always ask about the rules when you go to a new place."

"I didn't think there'd be a time limit on hand-ball paddles."

"That's why you must ask."

"I can't ask everything," I complained.

"Then you *read*. You need to know all the rules wherever you go. Did you know it's illegal to hunt camels in Arizona?"

"No."

"See? These are little facts you pick up from books and teachers and parents as you grow older. Some facts and rules come in handy, some don't. You've got to be observant. Did you know that Mickey Mouse has only *four* fingers on each hand?"

"No."

"All you have to do is look. And rules change! You've got to remember that. In ancient Rome, my ancestors worshipped a god who ruled over mildew. Nobody does anymore, but it's an interesting thing to know. You have to be connected to the past and present and future. At NBC, when they put in a new cookie-cutting machine, I had to have an open mind. I had to prepare and draw upon everything I knew so that I didn't get hurt."

Nonno Frankie must have seen my mouth was open so wide a baseball could have flown into my throat and choked me to death. He stopped at the highest point in the rise of land above the airport. "I can see you want some meat and potatoes. You want to know exactly how to beat this vicious John Quinn."

"He's not vicious."

Elephant Tree, © 1996, Robert Vickrey/Licensed by VAGA, New York, NY

▲ **Critical Viewing**
What details express the way Paul feels during the first school week? **[Interpret]**

Reading Check

What does Nonno Frankie teach the narrator to do?

"Make believe he is. It'll give you more energy for the fight. When he comes at you, don't underestimate the power of negative thinking! You must have only positive thoughts in your heart that you're going to cripple this monster. Stick a piece of garlic in your pocket for good luck. A woman my mother knew in Palermo did this, and she was able to fight off a dozen three-foot-tall muscular Greeks who landed and tried to eat her. You think this is not true, but half her town saw it. The Greeks all had rough skin and wore backpacks and one-piece clothes. You have to go with what you feel in your heart. One of my teachers in Sicily believed the Portuguese man-of-war jellyfish originally came from England. He felt that in his heart, and he eventually proved it. He later went on to be awarded a government grant to study tourist swooning sickness in Florence."

"But how do I hold my hands to fight? How do I hold my fists?" I wanted to know.

"Like *this!*" Nonno Frankie demonstrated, taking a boxing stance with his left foot and fist forward.

"And then I just swing my right fist forward as hard as I can?"

"No. First you curse him."

"*Curse* him?"

"Yes, you curse this John Quinn. You tell him, 'May your left ear wither and fall into your right pocket!' And you tell him he looks like a fugitive from a brain gang! And tell him he has a face like a mattress! And that an espresso coffee cup would fit on his head like a sombrero. And then you just give him the big Sicilian surprise!"

"What?"

"You *kick* him in the shins!"

By the time Monday morning came, I was a nervous wreck. Nonno Frankie had gone back to New York the night before, but had left me a special bowl of pasta and steamed octopus that he said I should eat for breakfast so I'd have "gusto" for combat. I had asked him not to discuss my upcoming bout with my mother or sister, and Betty didn't say anything so I assumed she hadn't heard about it.

Jennifer had offered to get one of her older brothers to protect me, and, if I wanted, she was willing to tell Miss Haines so she could stop anything from happening. I told her, "No." I thought there was a chance John Quinn would have even forgotten the whole incident and wouldn't make good on his revenge threat. Nevertheless, my mind was numb with fear all day at school. In every class I went to, it seemed there were a dozen different kids coming over to me and telling me they heard John Quinn was going to beat me up after school.

At 3 P.M. sharp, the bell rang.

All the kids started to leave school.

I dawdled.

Reading Strategy
Recognizing Word Origins What are the meanings of the Italian word *espresso* and the Spanish word *sombrero*?

Literary Analysis
Internal Conflict Would Jennifer's offer solve Paul's problem?

I cleaned my desk and took time packing up my books. Jennifer was at my side as we left the main exit of the building. There, across the street in a field behind Ronkewitz's Candy Store, was a crowd of about 300 kids standing around like a big, <u>undulating</u> horseshoe, with John Quinn standing at the center bend glaring at me.

"You could *run*," Jennifer suggested, tossing her hair all to the left side of her face. She looked much more than pretty now. She looked loyal to the bone.

"No," I said. I just walked forward toward my fate, with the blood in my temples pounding so hard I thought I was going to pass out. Moose and Leon and Mike and Conehead and Little Frankfurter were sprinkled out in front of me, <u>goading</u> me forward. I didn't even hear what they said. I saw only their faces <u>distorted</u> in ecstasy and expectation. They looked like the mob I had seen in a sixteenth-century etching where folks in London had bought tickets to watch bulldogs attacking water buffalo.

John stood with his black eye, and his fists up.

I stopped a few feet from him and put my fists up. A lot of kids in the crowd started to shout, "Kill him, Johnny!" but I may have imagined that part.

John came closer. He started to dance on his feet like all father-trained fighters do. I danced, too, as best I could. The crowd began to scream for blood. Jennifer kept shouting, "Hey, there's no need to fight! You don't have to fight, guys!"

But John came in for the kill. He was close enough now so any punch he threw could hit me. All I thought of was Nonno Frankie, but I couldn't remember half of what he told me and I didn't think any of it would work anyway.

"Aaeeeeeyaaaayeeeeeh!" I suddenly screamed at John. He stopped in his tracks and the crowd froze in amazed silence. Instantly, I brought back my right foot, and shot it forward to kick John in his left shin. The crowd was shocked, and booed me with mass condemnation for my Sicilian fighting technique. I missed John's shin, and kicked vainly again. He threw a punch at me. It barely touched me, but I was so busy kicking, I tripped myself and fell down. The crowd cheered. I realized everyone including John thought his punch had floored me. I decided to go along with it. I <u>groveled</u> in the dirt for a few moments, and then stood up slowly holding my head as though I'd received a death blow. John put his fists down. He was satisfied justice had been done and his black eye had been avenged. He turned to leave, but Moose wasn't happy.

"Hey, ya didn't punch him enough," Moose complained to John.

"It's over," John said, like the decent kid he was.

"No, it's not," Moose yelled, and the crowd began to call for more blood. Now it was Moose coming toward me, and I figured I was dead

undulating (un′ dyoo lā′ tiŋ) *adj.* moving in waves, like a snake

goading (gō′ diŋ) *v.* pushing a person into acting, especially by using pain or insults

distorted (di stôr′ tid) *adj.* twisted out of the normal shape

groveled (grä′ vəld) *v.* lay or crawled about before someone in hope of mercy

**Reading Check**

What happens to the narrator during the fight?

meat. He came closer and closer. Jennifer shouted for him to stop and threatened to pull his eyeballs out, but he kept coming. And that was when something amazing happened. I was aware of a figure taller than me, running, charging. The figure had long blond hair, and it struck Moose from behind. I could see it was a girl and she had her hands right around Moose's neck, choking him. When she let him go, she threw him about ten feet, accidentally tearing off a religious medal from around his neck. Everyone stopped dead in their tracks, and I could see my savior was my sister.

"If any of you tries to hurt my brother again, I'll rip your guts out," she announced.

Moose was not happy. Conehead and Little Frankfurter were not happy. But the crowd broke up fast and everyone headed home. I guess that was the first day everybody learned that if nothing else, the Zindel kids stick together. As for Nonno Frankie's Sicilian fighting technique, I came to realize he was ahead of his time. In fact, these days it's called karate.

Paul Zindel

(b. 1936)

When he was growing up in Staten Island, New York, Paul Zindel met Nonno Frankie Vivona. Frankie gave him much advice, some of it unusual. Zindel describes Frankie in loving detail in the memoir, *The Pigman & Me.*

Frankie also inspired a character in Zindel's first novel, *The Pigman,* which draws on Zindel's confusing, lonely teenage days.

Before he wrote *The Pigman,* Zindel taught high-school science for ten years. After the success of this book and a play, he started writing full time. As one of his English teachers had predicted, Zindel had become a writer!

Review and Assess

Thinking About the Selection

1. **Respond:** Do you think Paul should have backed out of the fight? Why or why not?

2. **(a) Recall:** Whom does Paul not want to know about his planned fight? **(b) Infer:** Why do you think Paul asks Nonno Frankie not to tell them? **(c) Speculate:** How do you think they would have reacted?

3. **(a) Recall:** Identify two pieces of advice that Nonno Frankie gives Paul. **(b) Analyze:** Does the advice apply more to the fight or to life?

4. **(a) Recall:** What does Paul do after he falls down during the fight? **(b) Infer:** Why does he do this? **(c) Evaluate:** Is his strategy a good one? Explain.

5. **(a) Contrast:** Describe the difference in John's attitude and the attitude of the other students after Paul falls down. **(b) Analyze:** Why do they each react as they do? **(c) Apply:** What problems does the attitude of the other students create for John and for Paul? **(d) Speculate:** If Paul had fought Moose and won the fight, how do you think the other students would have reacted? Explain.

6. **(a) Deduce:** Why is the fight important to Paul? **(b) Synthesize:** What lesson does Paul learn?

7. **Take a Position:** Is it ever okay to resort to fighting? Explain.

Review and Assess

Literary Analysis

Internal Conflict

1. Explain the **internal conflict** that Paul experiences. Use a graphic organizer like this one to help you develop your answer.

Why Paul doesn't want to fight → **Paul must decide** ← **Why Paul does want to fight**

2. Is Paul's internal conflict settled at the end of the story? Support your answer with at least two details from the story.

3. What internal conflict might John have?

Connecting Literary Elements

4. What **external conflict** does Paul experience and what events lead to it?

5. How does Paul's external conflict lead to his internal conflict?

Reading Strategy

Recognizing Word Origins

6. Use your own knowledge and a dictionary to complete a chart like the one shown. In the last column, write a sentence that gives clues to the meaning of the word.

Word	Origin	Meaning	Sentence
pizza			
espresso			
cliché			The corny speech was full of clichés.
siesta	Spanish	rest	
adios			
bon voyage		"Have a good trip."	

7. Why can some words from languages other than English be understood and used by English speakers?

Extending Understanding

8. **Apply:** Explain why you think children fight and how fights can be avoided.

Quick Review

An **internal conflict** is a struggle that takes place within the mind of a person or character. To review internal conflict, see page 181.

An **external conflict** is a struggle that takes place between a character and an outside force. To review external conflict, see page 181.

Word origins are the original languages or uses of words. To review word origins, see page 181.

 Take It to the Net

www.phschool.com

Take the interactive self-test online to check your understanding of the selection.

Integrate Language Skills

Vocabulary Development Lesson

Word Analysis: Latin Suffix -tion

The Latin suffix -tion means "the act, condition, or result of." For example, to condemn is to judge someone as deserving punishment. Condemnation is the act of condemning. Define each of the following on your paper.

1. aggravation   **2.** hesitation   **3.** reduction

Spelling Strategy

Words that contain the shun sound are frequently misspelled because the shun sound can be spelled -tion, -ssion, or -sion. Learn words that spell the shun sound -tion. Unscramble the letters to write a word that ends in -tion.

1. snoibirscupt   **3.** paplicnatio

2. netnotini   **4.** treaconi

Concept Development: Connotations

The **connotation** of a word is the set of ideas associated with it in addition to its literal meaning. Some words, like confident, have positive connotations. Others, like aggressive, can have negative connotations. Some words are neutral—they have neither positive nor negative connotations or associations.

On your paper, write whether each of the following words has a positive, negative, or neutral connotation. Write a sentence explaining each of your answers.

1. distorted   **4.** groveled

2. tactics   **5.** goading

3. undulating   **6.** exact

Grammar Lesson

Adjectives

An **adjective** is a word that describes a person, place, or thing. An adjective answers one of the following questions: *What kind? Which one? How many? How much?*

Adjective	Answers the question . . .
a *black* eye	*What kind of eye? A black one.*
my *right* fist	*Which one? The right one.*
about *300* kids	*How many? 300.*
some meat and potatoes	*How much? Some.*

A special category of adjectives, called **articles,** includes *a, an,* and *the.*

Practice Write these sentences. Then, underline the adjectives and circle the articles.

1. Nonno Frankie took a boxing stance.

2. I stopped a few feet from him.

3. Everyone stopped dead in their tracks.

4. They looked like the mob I had seen in a sixteenth-century etching.

5. The crowd froze in amazed silence.

Writing Application For each noun below, write a sentence in which the noun is modified by an adjective. Underline the adjective.

Example: crowd: The <u>angry</u> crowd roared.

1. friend   **3.** tactics   **5.** pride

2. crowd   **4.** foe

W͞G Prentice Hall Writing and Grammar Connection: Chapter 16, Section 1

Writing Lesson

School Rules

Having a list of rules, including those for gym, might have helped Paul avoid a fight. Write the twenty most important rules that new students in your school need to know.

Prewriting Write as many of your school's rules as you can think of. Then, choose the twenty most important.

Drafting Write in imperative sentences—sentences that give an order. Use the positive rather than the negative. For instance, write "Put trash in trash barrels" instead of "Don't litter." Organize rules in order of importance, from most to least.

Model: Drafting Imperative Sentences
BAKER SCHOOL RULES

1. Be in your homeroom at **8 a.m.**
2. Call in absences. (*Absences must be reported by **8:30**.*)
3. Pay attention to dress code. (**NO** cutoffs!)
4. Use the library for studying. (*Talk Quietly!*)
5. Keep the halls clean—use the wastebaskets.

Revising Format your list of rules by using different sizes and types of letters, underlining, and arrangement of the text on the page. If possible, use a word-processing program to format your rules electronically. Find and use the commands for tabs, **boldface,** underscore, and *italics.*

WG Prentice Hall Writing and Grammar Connection: Chapter 11, Section 2

Extension Activities

Research and Technology Television often tries to "hook" consumers by suggesting that a product will make them happier, better looking, stronger, or more popular. **Identify emotional appeals** used in at least five television advertisements.

- Present an oral explanation of each ad.
- Tell which character—Paul, Nonno Frankie, Moose, or Jennifer—would be most influenced and why.

After presenting your findings to your class, ask them if they agree or disagree with you.

Listening and Speaking With others, present a **news report** on Paul's fight. Two students might act as anchors, while another gives a live report. [Group Activity]

Writing Write a brief **essay** in which you explain why children fight and how fights can be avoided. Use examples drawn from experience.

 **Take It to the Net**   www.phschool.com

Go online for an additional research activity using the Internet.

Prepare to Read

Thunder Butte

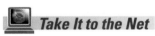 **Take It to the Net**

Visit www.phschool.com for interactive activities and instruction related to "Thunder Butte," including

- background
- graphic organizers
- literary elements
- reading strategies

Preview

Connecting to the Literature

You probably have privileges now that you did not have last year. However, you may also have had to let go of some old habits. The main character in "Thunder Butte" must find a way to balance new ideas with traditions from his Native American past.

Background

The Sioux are one of the many Native American peoples who once lived throughout the Midwest. In the plains of the Dakotas and Nebraska, steep, flat-topped hills appear suddenly, rising as if out of nowhere. These land formations are called *buttes* (byo͞ots) or *mesas* (mā′ səs). In the past, Native Americans climbed these buttes to scan the plains for miles around for enemies, animals, or other activity.

Literary Analysis
Atmosphere

Atmosphere is the feeling or mood of a work. Just as the atmosphere of the Earth can produce weather such as rain, wind, or snow, the atmosphere of a story can create emotional weather—fear, sadness, joy, or silliness. In "Thunder Butte," descriptive details produce a dark, threatening atmosphere.

> . . . the hill *looming* high above . . . was capped with *dark, low-hanging clouds*.

As you read, identify the story's atmosphere and the details that contribute to it.

Connecting Literary Elements

One element that shapes a story's atmosphere is **setting**—the time and place of the action. In "Thunder Butte," details of the setting—such as the stormy weather and the deserted butte—contribute to an atmosphere of tension and pressure. Use these focus questions to help you consider the setting and its impact on the story's atmosphere:

1. What details of the setting are dark and threatening?
2. How do these details influence your feelings about the story?

Reading Strategy
Understanding Shades of Meaning in Related Words

Although many words have similar definitions, most have different **shades of meaning**—variations in the intensity of the word or associations with the word.

Examples: old ⟶ ancient
clean ⟶ immaculate

Look at this chart showing the use of the word *old* in the story and providing closely related words with similar shades of meaning. As you read, pay close attention to the writer's use of descriptive words. Think about other words that could have been used, and how using these other words would have changed the shade of meaning.

Vocabulary Development

meanderings (mē an´ dər iŋz) *n.* aimless wanderings (p. 194)

diminutive (də min´ yōō tiv) *adj.* very small (p. 197)

variegated (ver´ ē ə gāt´ id) *adj.* streaked with different colors (p. 198)

heathen (hē´ thən) *adj.* uncivilized (p. 202)

adamant (ad´ ə mənt) *adj.* not flexible; not willing to give in (p. 202)

THUNDER BUTTE

Virginia Driving Hawk Sneve

The sun was just beginning to rise when John woke Norman the next morning.

"You must get an early start if you are going to go to the west side of the butte and return by supper," John said to the sleepy boy. "If you are not home by the time I get back from work, I'll come looking for you."

Norman reluctantly rose. Last night he had accepted his grandfather's command to go to the Thunder Butte without too many doubts. Yet now in the morning's chill light the boy wondered if his grandfather's dreams were the meaningless meanderings of an old mind, or if his grandfather was really worthy of the tribe's respect as one of the few remaining wise elders who understood the ancient ways.

Norman dressed in his oldest clothes and pulled on worn and scuffed boots to protect his feet from the rocks and snakes of the butte. He heard his parents talking in the other room and knew his father was telling his mother where Norman was going.

As the boy entered the room, which was kitchen and living room as well as his parents' bedroom, he heard his mother say, "What if there is a rock slide and Norman is hurt or buried on the butte? We won't know anything until you get home from work, John. I don't want Norman to go."

meanderings
(mē an´ dər iŋz) n.
aimless wanderings

"The boy is old enough to have learned to be careful on the butte. He'll be all right," John answered as he tried to reassure Sarah. "Besides," he added, "my father dreamed of this happening."

Sarah grunted scornfully, "No one believes in dreams or in any of those old superstitious ways anymore."

"I'll be okay, Mom," Norman said as he sat down at the table. "I should be able to find lots of agates[1] on the west side where there is all that loose rock. Maybe I can talk the trader into giving me money for them after all." He spoke bravely despite his own inner misgivings about going to the butte.

Sarah protested no more. Norman looked at her, but she lowered her head as she set a plate of pancakes in front of him. He knew she was hiding the worry she felt for him.

John put on his hat and went to the door. "Don't forget to take the willow branch with you," he said to Norman, "and be careful."

Norman nodded and ate his breakfast. When he was finished he stood up. "Guess I'll go," he said to his mother, who was pouring hot water from the tea kettle into her dish pan. When she didn't speak Norman took the willow cane from where he had propped it by the door and his hat from the nail above it.

"Wait," Sarah called and handed him a paper bag.

Reading Strategy
Understanding Shades of Meaning What words are related in meaning to *misgivings*?

Reading Check

Why is Norman going to the west side of the butte?

---

1. **agates** (ag´ its) *n.* hard, semiprecious stones with striped or clouded coloring.

"Here is a lunch for you. You'll need something to eat since you'll be gone all day." She gave him an affectionate shove. "Oh, go on. I know you'll be all right. Like your dad said, you're old enough to be careful."

Norman smiled at his mother. "Thanks," he said as he tucked the lunch into his shirt. He checked his back pocket to see if he'd remembered the salt bag to put the agates in.

He walked briskly across the open prairie and turned to wave at his mother, who had come outside to watch him leave. She waved back and Norman quickened his pace. He whistled, trying to echo the meadowlarks who were greeting the day with their happy song. He swiped the willow cane at the bushy sage and practiced spearing the pear cactus that dotted his path. The early morning air was cool, but the sun soon warmed the back of his neck and he knew it would be a hot day.

He crossed the creek south of where Matt Two Bull's tent was pitched and then he was climbing the gentle beginning slope of the butte. He stopped and studied the way before him and wondered if it wouldn't be easier to reach the west side by walking around the base of the butte even though it would be longer. Then Norman smiled as he remembered his grandfather's command to climb the south trail that wound to the top. He decided to do what the old man wanted.

Literary Analysis
Atmosphere What atmosphere is created by the details of whistling meadowlarks and Norman swiping at the sage and spearing the pear cactus?

▼ **Critical Viewing**
What is the atmosphere of this photo? **[Analyze]**

The ascent sharply steepened and the sun rose with him as Norman climbed. What looked like a smooth path from the prairie floor was rough rocky terrain. The trail spiraled up a sharp incline and Norman had to detour around fallen rocks. He paused to rest about half way up and then saw how sharply the overhanging ledge of the butte protruded. Getting to the top of it was going to be a difficult struggle. He climbed on. His foot slipped and his ankle twisted painfully. Small pebbles bounced down the slope and he saw a rattlesnake slither out of the way. He tightly clutched the willow branch and leaned panting against the butte. He sighed with relief as the snake crawled out of sight. He wiggled his foot until the pain left his ankle. Then he started to trudge up the incline again.

At last only the ledge of the butte loomed over him. There appeared to be no way up. Disgusted that his laborious climb seemed dead-ended he stubbornly tried to reach the top. Remembering the courage of the ancient young men who had struggled in this same place to gain the summit and seek their visions, he was determined not to go back. His fingers found tiny cracks to hold on to. The cane was cumbersome and in the way. He was tempted to drop it, but he thought of the snake he'd seen and struggled on with it awkwardly under his arm.

Finally Norman spied a narrow opening in the ledge which tapered down to only a few feet from where he clung. He inched his way up until he reached the base of the opening and then he found a use for the cane. He jammed the stout branch high into the boulders above him. Cautiously he pulled to see if it would hold his weight. It held. Using the cane as a lever he pulled himself to the top.

This final exertion winded the boy and he lay exhausted on the summit, boots hanging over the edge. Cautiously he pulled his feet under him, stood and looked around.

He gazed at a new world. The sun bathed the eastern valley in pale yellow which was spotted with dark clumps of sage. The creek was a green and silver serpent winding its way to the southeast. His grandfather's tent was a white shoe box in its clearing, and beside it stood a <u>diminutive</u> form waving a red flag. It was Matt Two Bull signaling with his shirt, and Norman knew that his grandfather had been watching him climb. He waved his hat in reply and then walked to the outer edge of the butte.

The summit was not as smoothly flat as it looked from below. Norman stepped warily over the many cracks and holes that pitted the surface. He was elated that he had successfully made the difficult ascent, but now as he surveyed the butte top he had a sense of discomfort.

Reading Strategy
Understanding Shades of Meaning Look at the words *slither* and *crawled*, which describe the rattle-snake's actions. What are the different shades of meaning each word conveys?

diminutive (də min′ yoo tiv) *adj.* very small

**Reading Check**

How does Norman get to the top of the butte?

There were burn scars on the rough summit, and Norman wondered if these spots were where the lightning had struck, or were they evidence of ancient man-made fires? He remembered that this was a sacred place to the old ones and his uneasiness increased. He longed to be back on the secure level of the plains.

On the west edge he saw that the butte cast a sharp shadow below because the rim protruded as sharply as it had on the slope he'd climbed. Two flat rocks jutted up on either side of a narrow opening, and Norman saw shallow steps hewn into the space between. This must be the trail of which his grandfather had spoken.

Norman stepped down and then quickly turned to hug the butte face as the steps ended abruptly in space. The rest of the rocky staircase lay broken and crumbled below. The only way down was to jump.

He cautiously let go of the willow branch and watched how it landed and bounced against the rocks. He took a deep breath as if to draw courage from the air. He lowered himself so that he was hanging by his fingertips to the last rough step, closed his eyes and dropped.

The impact of his landing stung the soles of his feet. He stumbled and felt the cut of the sharp rocks against one knee as he struggled to retain his balance. He did not fall and finally stood upright breathing deeply until the wild pounding of his heart slowed. "Wow," he said softly as he looked back up at the ledge, "that must have been at least a twenty foot drop."

He picked up the willow branch and started walking slowly down the steep slope. The trail Matt Two Bull had told him about had been obliterated by years of falling rock. Loose shale and gravel shifted under Norman's feet, and he probed cautiously ahead with the cane to test the firmness of each step.

He soon found stones which he thought were agates. He identified them by spitting on each rock and rubbing the wet spot with his finger. The dull rock seemed to come alive! Variegated hues of brown and gray glowed as if polished. They were agates all right. Quickly he had his salt bag half full.

It was almost noon and his stomach growled. He stopped to rest against a large boulder and pulled out his lunch from his shirt. But his mouth was too dry to chew the cheese sandwich. He couldn't swallow without water.

Thirsty and hungry, Norman decided to go straight down the butte and head for home.

Walking more confidently as the slope leveled out he thrust the pointed cane carelessly into the ground. He suddenly fell as the cane went deep into the soft shale.

Literary Analysis
Atmosphere and Setting
In what ways has the atmosphere changed?

variegated (ver′ ē ə gāt′ id)
adj. marked with different colors in spots or streaks

Norman slid several feet. Loose rocks rolled around him as he came to rest against a boulder. He lay still for a long time fearing that his tumble might cause a rock fall. But no thundering slide came, so he cautiously climbed back to where the tip of the willow branch protruded from the ground.

He was afraid that the cane may have plunged into a rattlesnake den. Carefully he pulled at the stout branch, wiggling it this way and that with one hand while he dug with the other. It came loose, sending a shower of rocks down the hill, and Norman saw that something else was sticking up in the hole he had uncovered.

Curious, and seeing no sign of snakes, he kept digging and soon found the tip of a leather-covered stick. Bits of leather and wood fell off in his hand as he gently pulled. The stick, almost as long as he was tall and curved on one end, emerged as he tugged. Holding it before him, his heart pounding with excitement, he realized that he had found a thing that once belonged to the old ones.

Norman shivered at the thought that he may have disturbed a grave, which was *tehinda* [tā khin′ dä], forbidden. He cleared more dirt away but saw no bones nor other sign that this was a burial place. Quickly he picked up the stick and his willow cane and hurried down the hill. When he reached the bottom he discovered that in his fall the salt bag of agates had pulled loose from his belt. But he did not return to search for it. It would take most of the afternoon to travel around the base of the butte to the east side.

The creek was in the deep shade of the butte when he reached it and thirstily flopped down and drank. He crossed the shallow stream and walked to his grandfather's tent.

"You have been gone a long time," Matt Two Bull greeted as Norman walked into the clearing where the old man was seated.

"I have come from the west side of the butte, Grandpa," Norman said wearily. He sat down on the ground and examined a tear in his jeans and the bruise on his knee.

"Was it difficult?" the old man asked.

"Yes," Norman nodded. He told of the rough climb up the south slope, the jump down and finally of his fall which led him to discover the long leather-covered stick. He held the stick out to his grandfather who took it and examined it carefully.

"Are you sure there was no body in the place where you found this?"

Norman shook his head. "No, I found nothing else but the stick. Do you know what it is, Grandpa?"

"You have found a *coup* [kōō] stick which belonged to the old ones."

"I know that it is old because the wood is brittle and the leather is peeling, but what is—was a *coup* stick?" Norman asked.

Literary Analysis
Atmosphere What details contribute to the atmosphere of suspense in this paragraph?

Reading Strategy
Shades of Meaning
What shade of meaning is communicated by *flopped* that would not be communicated by *sank*?

**Reading Check**
What does Norman find in the hole?

"In the days when the old ones roamed all of the plains," the old man swept his hand in a circle, "a courageous act of valor was thought to be more important than killing an enemy. When a warrior rode or ran up to his enemy, close enough to touch the man with a stick, without killing or being killed, the action was called *coup*.♦

"The French, the first white men in this part of the land, named this brave deed *coup*. In their language the word meant 'hit' or 'strike.' The special stick which was used to strike with came to be known as a *coup* stick.

"Some sticks were long like this one," Matt Two Bull held the stick upright. "Some were straight, and others had a curve on the end like the sheep herder's crook," he pointed to the curving end of the stick.

"The sticks were decorated with fur or painted leather strips. A warrior kept count of his coups by tying an eagle feather to the crook for each brave deed. See," he pointed to the staff end, "here is a remnant of a tie thong which must have once held a feather."

The old man and boy closely examined the *coup* stick. Matt Two Bull traced with his finger the faint zig zag design painted on the stick. "See," he said, "it is the thunderbolt."

"What does that mean?" Norman asked.

"The Thunders favored a certain few of the young men who sought their vision on the butte. The thunderbolt may have been part of a sacred dream sent as a token of the Thunders' favor. If this was so, the young man could use the thunderbolt symbol on his possessions."

"How do you suppose the stick came to be on the butte?" Norman asked.

His grandfather shook his head. "No one can say. Usually such a thing was buried with a dead warrior as were his weapons and other prized belongings."

"Is the *coup* stick what you dreamed about, Grandpa?"

"No. In my dream I only knew that you were to find a *Wakan*, [wä kän] a holy thing. But I did not know what it would be."

Norman laughed nervously. "What do you mean, *Wakan*? Is this stick haunted?"

Matt Two Bull smiled, "No, not like you mean in a fearful way. But in a sacred manner because it once had great meaning to the old ones."

"But why should I have been the one to find it?" Norman questioned.

His grandfather shrugged, "Perhaps to help you understand the ways—the values of the old ones."

♦ *Coup*

The word *coup* is a French word that is also used in English. In French, *coup* means "blow, hit, or strike." In English, *coup* has several meanings, including

- a brilliant or clever move that is often unexpected
- a sudden overthrow of a government (also called a *coup d'état*)
- among certain Native Americans, an act of bravery performed in battle, such as touching an enemy with a stick and then escaping unharmed

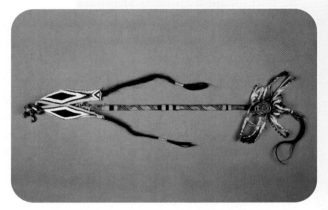

A *coup* stick

"But nobody believes in that kind of thing anymore," Norman scoffed. "And even if people did, I couldn't run out and hit my enemy with the stick and get away with it." He smiled thinking of Mr. Brannon. "No one would think I was brave. I'd probably just get thrown in jail."

Suddenly Norman felt compelled to stop talking. In the distance he heard a gentle rumble which seemed to come from the butte. He glanced up at the hill looming high above and saw that it was capped with dark, low-hanging clouds.

Matt Two Bull looked too and smiled. "The Thunders are displeased with your thoughts," he said to Norman. "Listen to their message."

A sharp streak of lightning split the clouds and the thunder cracked and echoed over the plains.

Norman was frightened but he answered with bravado, "The message I get is that a storm is coming," but his voice betrayed him by quavering. "Maybe you'd better come home with me, Grandpa. Your tent will get soaked through if it rains hard."

"No," murmured Matt Two Bull, "no rain will come. It is just the Thunders speaking." There was another spark of lightning, and an explosive reverberation sounded as if in agreement with the old man.

Norman jumped to his feet. "Well, I'm going home. Mom will be worried because I'm late now." He turned to leave.

"Wait!" Matt Two Bull commanded. "Take the *coup* stick with you."

Norman backed away, "No, I don't want it. You can have it."

The old man rose swiftly despite the stiffness of his years and sternly held out the stick to the boy. "You found it. It belongs to you. Take it!"

Norman slowly reached out his hands and took the stick.

"Even if you think the old ways are only superstition and the stick no longer has meaning, it is all that remains of an old life and must be treated with respect." Matt Two Bull smiled at the boy. "Take it," he repeated gently, "and hang it in the house where it will not be handled."

Norman hurried home as fast as he could carrying the long stick in one hand and the willow cane in the other. He felt vaguely uneasy and somehow a little frightened. It was only when he reached the security of his home that he realized the thunder had stopped and there had been no storm.

"Mom," he called as he went into the house, "I'm home."

His mother was standing at the stove. "Oh, Norman," she greeted him smiling. "I'm glad you're back. I was beginning to worry." Her welcoming smile turned to a frown as she saw the *coup* stick in Norman's hand. "What is that?"

Reading Strategy
Understanding Shades of Meaning How does the use of the words *sharp* and *cracked* create a vivid picture of the lightning?

**Reading Check**

Why does Matt Two Bull say the *coup* stick is important?

"Grandpa says it's a *coup* stick. Here," Norman handed it to her, "take a look at it. It's interesting the way it is made and decor—"

"No," Sarah interrupted and backed away from him. "I won't touch that <u>heathen</u> thing no matter what it is! Get it out of the house!"

heathen (hē´ thən) *adj.* uncivilized

"What?" Norman asked, surprised and puzzled. "There is nothing wrong with it. It's just an old stick I found up on the butte."

"I don't care," Sarah insisted. "I won't have such a thing in the house!"

"But, Mom," Norman protested, "it's not like we believe in those old ways the way Grandpa does."

But Sarah was <u>adamant</u>. "Take it out of the house!" she ordered, pointing to the door. "We'll talk about it when your dad gets home."

adamant (ad´ ə mənt) *adj.* not flexible; not willing to give in

Reluctantly Norman took the *coup* stick outside and gently propped it against the house and sat on the steps to wait for his father. He was confused. First by his grandfather's reverent treatment of the *coup* stick as if it were a sacred object and then by Sarah's rejection of it as a heathen symbol.

He looked at the stick where it leaned against the wall and shook his head. So much fuss over a brittle, rotten length of wood. Even though he had gone through a lot of hard, even dangerous, effort to get it he was now tempted to heave it out on the trash pile.

Norman wearily leaned his head against the house. He suddenly felt tired and his knee ached. As he sat wearily rubbing the bruise John Two Bull rode the old mare into the yard. Norman got up and walked back to the shed to help unsaddle the horse.

John climbed stiffly out of the saddle. His faded blue work shirt and jeans were stained with perspiration and dirt. His boots were worn and scuffed.

"Hard day, Dad?" Norman asked.

"Yeah," John answered, slipping the bridle over the mare's head. "Rustlers got away with twenty steers last night. I spent the day counting head and mending fences. Whoever the thief was cut the fence, drove a truck right onto the range and loaded the cattle without being seen." He began rubbing the mare down as she munched the hay in her manger.

"How did your day on the butte go?" John asked.

"Rough," Norman answered. "I'm beat too. The climb up the butte was tough and coming down was bad too." He told his father all that had happened on the butte, winding up with the climax of his falling and finding the old *coup* stick.

John listened attentively and did not interrupt until Norman told of Matt Two Bull's reaction to the stick. "I think Grandpa's mind has gotten weak," Norman said. "He really believes that the *coup* stick has some sort of mysterious power and that the Thunders were talking."

"Don't make fun of your grandfather," John reprimanded, "or of the old ways he believes in."

"Okay, okay," Norman said quickly, not wanting another scolding. "But Mom is just the opposite from Grandpa," he went on. "She doesn't want the *coup* stick in the house. Says it's heathen."

He walked to the house and handed the stick to his father. John examined it and then carried it into the house.

"John!" Sarah exclaimed as she saw her husband bring the stick into the room. "I told Norman, and I tell you, that I won't have that heathenish thing in the house!"

But John ignored her and propped the stick against the door while he pulled his tool box out from under the washstand to look for a hammer and nails.

"John," Sarah persisted, "did you hear me?"

"I heard," John answered quietly, but Norman knew his father was angry. "And I don't want to hear anymore."

Norman was surprised to hear his father speak in such a fashion. John was slow to anger, usually spoke quietly and tried to avoid conflict of any kind, but now he went on.

"This," he said holding the *coup* stick upright, "is a relic of our people's past glory when it was a good thing to be an Indian. It is a symbol of something that shall never be again."

Sarah gasped and stepped in front of her husband as he started to climb a chair to pound the nails in the wall above the window. "But that's what I mean," she said. "Those old ways were just superstition. They don't mean anything now—they can't because such a way of life can't be anymore. We don't need to have those old symbols of heathen ways hanging in the house!" She grabbed at the *coup* stick, but John jerked it out of her reach.

▲ **Critical Viewing**
How would you describe the atmosphere of this picture? **[Analyze]**

Literary Analysis
Atmosphere What details increase the atmosphere of tension?

Reading Check

What is Sarah's reaction to the *coup* stick?

"Don't touch it!" he shouted and Sarah fell back against the table in shocked surprise. Norman took a step forward as if to protect his mother. The boy had never seen his father so angry.

John shook his head as if to clear it. "Sarah, I'm sorry. I didn't mean to yell. It's just that the old ones would not permit a woman to touch such a thing as this." He handed Norman the stick to hold while he hammered the nails in the wall. Then he hung the stick above the window.

"Sarah," he said as he put the tools away, "think of the stick as an object that could be in a museum, a part of history. It's not like we were going to fall down on our knees and pray to it." His voice was light and teasing as he tried to make peace.

But Sarah stood stiffly at the stove preparing supper and would not answer. Norman felt sick. His appetite was gone. When his mother set a plate of food before him he excused himself saying, "I guess I'm too tired to eat," and went to his room.

But after he had undressed and crawled into bed he couldn't sleep. His mind whirled with the angry words his parents had spoken. They had never argued in such a way before. "I wish I had never brought that old stick home," he whispered and then pulled the pillow over his head to shut out the sound of the low rumble of thunder that came from the west.

Review and Assess

Thinking About the Selection

1. **Respond:** Do you agree with Norman's mother or his father? Why?

2. **(a) Recall:** Who tells Norman to climb the butte? **(b) Infer:** Why does Norman agree to climb the butte?
   (c) Draw Conclusions: What do his regrets about agreeing indicate about his feelings?

3. **(a) Recall:** What do Sioux warriors use a *coup* stick for?
   (b) Analyze: What does a *coup* stick represent to Norman's father and grandfather? **(c) Contrast:** What does the *coup* stick represent to Norman's mother?

4. **(a) Contrast:** In what way is Norman's mother's reaction to the *coup* stick different from his father's? **(b) Deduce:** Why is Norman unsure of his feelings about his heritage?

5. **Recall:** How does John react when Norman makes fun of his grandfather's beliefs? **(b) Infer:** Why does he react as he does?

6. **(a) Analyze:** In what ways do the past and present come into conflict at the end of "Thunder Butte"? **(b) Take a Position:** Which is more important: progress or tradition? Explain.

Virginia Driving Hawk Sneve

(b. 1933)
Virginia Driving Hawk Sneve was born on a Sioux Indian Reservation in South Dakota. As a teacher and a writer, she devotes herself to sharing Native American life as she has experienced it. She portrays Indians and their heritage from a Native American point of view. "Thunder Butte" (from the novel *When Thunders Spoke*) reflects conflicts that many Native Americans experience today. She works "to interpret history from the viewpoint of the American Indian" because she feels they have been misrepresented by historians who are not Native Americans.

Review and Assess

Literary Analysis

Atmosphere

1. Identify three details at the beginning of "Thunder Butte" that create an **atmosphere** of danger. Record them on a chart like the one shown.

2. How would you describe the atmosphere as Norman climbs the butte? List three details to support your answer.

3. How does the atmosphere at breakfast differ from the atmosphere at dinner?

Connecting Literary Elements

4. How do the changes in the weather affect the atmosphere in the story?

5. What other details of the **setting** contribute to the atmosphere of "Thunder Butte"?

6. Use a chart like the one shown to list ways in which details of the setting affect events in the story.

	Details of Setting	Story Events
Time		
Place		

Reading Strategy

Understanding Shades of Meaning in Related Words

7. Reread pages in the opening of the story and use the surrounding words to explain the difference in **shades of meaning** between *doubts* on page 194 and *misgivings* on page 195.

8. What is the difference in meaning between being *reprimanded*, as Norman is by his father, and being *scolded*, as he is by his mother? Which would be preferable? Why?

Extend Understanding

9. **Cultural Connection:** In what way are artifacts valuable to understanding past cultures? Why might it be important for you to understand your own heritage?

Quick Review

Atmosphere is the mood or feeling of a work. To review atmosphere, see page 193.

Setting is the time and place of the action. To review setting, see page 193.

Shades of meaning are the slight differences in the meanings of related words. To review shades of meaning, see page 193.

 Take It to the Net
www.phschool.com
Take the interactive self-test online to check your understanding of the selection.

Integrate Language Skills

Vocabulary Development Lesson

Word Analysis: Forms of *vary*

The word *vary* means "to make different." Forms of *vary* include the idea of difference in their meaning. For example, in "Thunder Butte," Norman finds *variegated* stones, or stones of different colors.

Use a form of *vary* to complete each sentence below.

variety	varied	various	variable

1. They offer a wide ___?___ of flowers.
2. An experiment should have only one ___?___.
3. He ___?___ the music by playing some fast tunes and some slow ones.
4. You can choose from ___?___ candies.

Fluency: Word Meanings

Explain why each statement is true or false.

1. Calling someone a *heathen* is a compliment.
2. A *variegated* leaf has a few different colors.
3. *Adamant* people are unsure of their beliefs.
4. A hut is a *diminutive* building.
5. *Meanderings* are paths in straight lines.

Spelling Strategy

Learn how spellings change when the form of a word changes. Write the words or word parts from the list at left that answer the following questions about forms of *vary*.

1. What letter is *y* changed to before an ending is added?
2. Which two forms have four syllables?
3. Which word part is the same in all forms?

Grammar Lesson

Possessive Adjectives

Adjectives are words that modify nouns or pronouns by answering the questions *What kind? Which one? How many?* and *How much?*

Nouns that show possession, or ownership—such as *mother's* or *Norman's*—function as **possessive adjectives.** They answer the question *whose?*

Pronouns are words that stand for a noun or take the place of a noun. **Possessive pronouns,** such as *my, your, his, her, its, our, your,* and *their,* function as adjectives. They also answer the question *whose?*

> **Example:** Last night he had accepted *his grandfather's* command . . .

Practice On your paper, circle the possessives that function as adjectives. Draw an arrow to the word each possessive modifies.

1. She lowered her head.
2. My father dreamed of this.
3. Norman's father spoke of the event.
4. The butte hid its secrets from his eyes.
5. The stick's meaning was not understood.

Writing Application Rewrite the following sentences so that they contain possessive adjectives.

1. Grandfather spoke of the past that belonged to him.
2. He wanted Norman to know the traditions that belonged to them.

W̶G Prentice Hall Writing and Grammar Connection: Chapter 16, Section 1

Writing Lesson

Opinion Paper

Each adult in Norman's family has an opinion about how the past and the future are related to the present. Do you think people benefit more from looking back or from looking forward? Write a few paragraphs to explain and support your ideas. Include examples from the story as well as from life to support your opinion.

Prewriting Use a graphic organizer such as the following to plan your writing. First, state your opinion. Then, list three main ideas on which you base your opinions. These ideas are the reasons you think as you do.

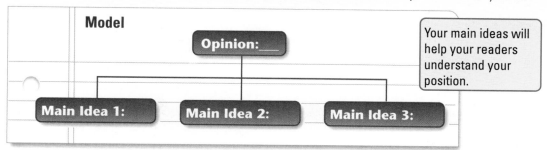

Model

Opinion:___

Your main ideas will help your readers understand your position.

Main Idea 1:   Main Idea 2:   Main Idea 3:

Drafting Begin by stating your position. Then, write a paragraph based on each of your main ideas. Include details and facts to support them. Conclude with a summary of your opinion and main ideas.

Revising Ask a classmate to read your paper and restate your opinion and three main ideas. If he or she cannot clearly restate any of these elements, revise the appropriate section.

*W*G *Prentice Hall Writing and Grammar Connection: Chapter 7, Section 3*

Extension Activities

Speaking and Listening With a small group, prepare an **informative presentation** on how the Sioux's lifestyle has changed from the 1800s to the present day. To begin, identify questions based on what you read in the story. Possible questions include

- What were the responsibilities of boys in a Native American family of the 1800s?
- Is Matt Two Bull's tent a common dwelling today?
- To what is John referring when he speaks of "our people's past glory"?

Research and Technology Conduct research to find out more about Sioux customs. Choose one and **write an explanation** of how Norman, Norman's mother, and Norman's father would feel about the custom.

Writing Write an **essay** in which you explain how the past and present come into conflict in the story.

Take It to the Net   www.phschool.com

Go online for an additional research activity using the Internet.

Prepare to Read

Mowgli's Brothers

 Take It to the Net

Visit www.phschool.com for interactive activities and instruction related to "Mowgli's Brothers," including

- background
- graphic organizers
- literary elements
- reading strategies

Preview

Connecting to the Literature

In "Mowgli's Brothers" by Rudyard Kipling, a little boy faces a life-or-death choice—but others make it for him. Think about the choices you make for yourself and those that are made for you by others.

Background

The behavior of the animals in "Mowgli's Brothers" is based on the real habits of animals in the jungle. Wolves live in packs, have a social structure, and obey a pack leader. Although they do not have a "council" as described in the story, wolves are known for working as a group. Tigers, on the other hand, like Shere Khan in the story, are solitary hunters.

Literary Analysis

Animal Characters

Characters in stories can be animals as well as humans. Most of the characters you will meet in "Mowgli's Brothers" are animals. **Animal characters** in fiction often behave according to their animal qualities, but they may also have human qualities, emotions, and abilities.

Connecting Literary Elements

Fictional animal characters are often brought to life through **personification.** Personification is the representation of an animal or an object as if it had a human personality, intelligence, or emotions.

In "Mowgli's Brothers," each animal shows at least one strong human quality. The human qualities of the animals affect the plot—the story's sequence of events. For example, Mother Wolf's compassion results in a boy being raised among wolves.

Use the following focus questions to help you analyze the story:

1. Which animals in the story have courage? Which are cowards?
2. What effect do the qualities of these characters have on story events and the way the story turns out?

Reading Strategy

Predicting Characters' Actions

When you **predict,** you make logical guesses about what characters will do or what events will occur. Predict characters' actions by thinking about whether a character is brave, cowardly, kind, honest, or sneaky. Then, decide how the character will act or what the character will do, based on what you have learned about him or her in the story. As you read, use a chart like the one shown to record predictions about characters' actions.

Vocabulary Development

scuttled (skut′ əld) v. scurried; scampered (p. 211)

quarry (kwôr′ ē) n. prey; anything being hunted or pursued (p. 214)

fostering (fôs′ tər iŋ) n. taking care of (p. 215)

veterans (vet′ ər enz′) n. those having experience (p. 216)

monotonous (mə nät′ n əs′) adj. unchanging; tiresome because it does not vary (p. 216)

dispute (di spyo͞ot′) n. argument; debate; quarrel (p. 217)

clamor (klam′ ər) n. loud demand or complaint (p. 217)

Character Qualities and Story Details

↓

Prediction
_____
_____
_____

MOWGLI'S BROTHERS

Rudyard Kipling

Now Chil the Kite[1] brings home the night
　　That Mang the Bat sets free—
The herds are shut in byre[2] and hut
　　For loosed till dawn are we.
This is the hour of pride and power,
　　Talon and tush[3] and claw.
Oh hear the call!—Good hunting all
　　That keep the Jungle Law!
　　　　　Night-Song in the Jungle

It was seven o'clock of a very warm evening in the Seeonee hills[4] when Father Wolf woke up from his day's rest, scratched himself, yawned, and spread out his paws one after the other to get rid of the sleepy feeling in their tips. Mother Wolf lay with her big gray nose dropped across her four tumbling, squealing cubs, and the moon shone into the mouth of the cave where they all lived. "Augrh!" said Father Wolf, "it is time to hunt again"; and he was going to spring downhill when a little shadow with a bushy tail crossed the threshold and whined: "Good luck go with you, O Chief of the Wolves; and good luck and strong white teeth go with the noble children, that they may never forget the hungry in this world."

It was the jackal—Tabaqui the Dishlicker—and the wolves of India despise Tabaqui because he runs about making mischief, and telling tales, and eating rags and pieces of leather from the village rubbish-heaps. But they are afraid of him too, because Tabaqui, more than anyone else in the jungle, is apt to go mad, and then he forgets that he was ever afraid of anyone, and runs through the forest biting everything in his way. Even the tiger runs and hides when little Tabaqui goes mad, for madness is the most disgraceful thing that can overtake a wild creature. We call it hydrophobia, but they call it *dewanee*—the madness—and run.

"Enter, then, and look," said Father Wolf, stiffly; "but there is no food here."

"For a wolf, no," said Tabaqui; "but for so mean a person as myself a dry bone is a good feast. Who are we, the Gidur-log [the jackal-people], to pick and choose?" He <u>scuttled</u> to the back of the cave, where he found the bone of a buck with some meat on it, and sat cracking the end merrily.

◀ **Critical Viewing** Do you think this tiger is friendly to humans? Why or why not? [**Speculate**]

---

1. **Kite** (kīt) *n.* bird of the hawk family.
2. **byre** (bīr) *n.* cow barn.
3. **tush** (tush) *n.* tusk.
4. **Seeonee** (sē ō′ nē) **hills** hills in central India.

Literary Analysis
Animal Characters
Which character has a trait that may lead to problems for other characters? What is the trait?

scuttled (skut′ əld) v. scurried; scampered

✔**Reading Check**

What is Mother Wolf doing?

"All thanks for this good meal," he said, licking his lips. "How beautiful are the noble children! How large are their eyes! And so young too! Indeed, indeed, I might have remembered that the children of Kings are men from the beginning."

Now, Tabaqui knew as well as anyone else that there is nothing so unlucky as to compliment children to their faces; and it pleases him to see Mother and Father Wolf look uncomfortable.

Tabaqui sat still, rejoicing in the mischief that he had made: then he said spitefully:

"Shere Khan, the Big One, has shifted his hunting-grounds. He will hunt among these hills for the next moon, so he has told me."

Shere Khan was the tiger who lived near the Waingunga River, twenty miles away.

"He has no right!" Father Wolf began angrily—"By the Law of the Jungle he has no right to change his quarters without due warning. He will frighten every head of game within ten miles, and I—I have to kill for two, these days."

"His mother did not call him Lungri [the Lame One] for nothing," said Mother Wolf, quietly. "He has been lame in one foot from his birth. That is why he has only killed cattle. Now the villagers of the Waingunga are angry with him, and he has come here to make our villagers angry. They will scour the Jungle for him when he is far away, and we and our children must run when the grass is set alight. Indeed, we are very grateful to Shere Khan!"

"Shall I tell him of your gratitude?" said Tabaqui.

"Out!" snapped Father Wolf. "Out and hunt with thy master. Thou hast done harm enough for one night."

"I go," said Tabaqui, quietly. "Ye can hear Shere Khan below in the thickets. I might have saved myself the message."

Father Wolf listened, and below in the valley that ran down to a little river, he heard the dry, angry, snarly, singsong whine of a tiger who has caught nothing and does not care if all the Jungle knows it.

"The fool!" said Father Wolf. "To begin a night's work with that noise! Does he think that our buck are like his fat Waingunga bullocks ?"[5]

"H'sh! It is neither bullock nor buck he hunts tonight," said Mother Wolf. "It is Man." The whine had changed to a sort of humming purr that seemed to come from every quarter of the compass. It was the noise that bewilders woodcutters and gypsies sleeping in the open, and makes them run sometimes into the very mouth of the tiger.

"Man!" said Father Wolf, showing all his white teeth. "Faugh! Are there not enough beetles and frogs in the tanks that he must eat Man and on our ground too!"

Reading Strategy
Predicting What character traits and story details help you predict that there will be a problem between Shere Kahn and the wolves?

---

5. bullocks (bool′ əks) *n.* steers.

The Law of the Jungle, which never orders anything without a reason, forbids every beast to eat Man except when he is killing to show his children how to kill, and then he must hunt outside the hunting-grounds of his pack or tribe. The real reason for this is that man-killing means, sooner or later, the arrival of white men on elephants, with guns, and hundreds of brown men with gongs and rockets and torches. Then everybody in the jungle suffers. The reason the beasts give among themselves is that Man is the weakest and most defenseless of all living things, and it is unsportsmanlike to touch him. They say too—and it is true—that man-eaters become mangy,[6] and lose their teeth.

The purr grew louder, and ended in the full-throated "Aaarh!" of the tiger's charge.

Then there was a howl—an untigerish howl—from Shere Khan. "He has missed," said Mother Wolf. "What is it?"

Father Wolf ran out a few paces and heard Shere Khan muttering and mumbling savagely, as he tumbled about in the scrub.

"The fool has had no more sense than to jump at a woodcutter's campfire, and has burned his feet," said Father Wolf, with a grunt. "Tabaqui is with him."

"Something is coming up hill," said Mother Wolf, twitching one ear. "Get ready."

The bushes rustled a little in the thicket, and Father Wolf dropped with his haunches under him, ready for his leap. Then, if you had been watching, you would have seen the most wonderful thing in the world—the wolf checked in mid-spring. He made his bound before he saw what it was he was jumping at, and then he tried to stop himself. The result was that he shot up straight into the air for four or five feet, landing almost where he left ground.

"Man!" he snapped. "A man's cub. Look!"

Directly in front of him, holding on by a low branch, stood a naked brown baby who could just walk—as soft and as dimpled a little atom[7] as ever came to a wolf's cave at night. He looked up into Father Wolf's face, and laughed.

"Is that a man's cub?" said Mother Wolf. "I have never seen one. Bring it here."

A wolf accustomed to moving his own cubs can, if necessary, mouth an egg without breaking it, and though Father Wolf's jaws closed right on the child's back not a tooth even scratched the skin, as he laid it down among the cubs.

"How little! How naked, and—how bold!" said Mother Wolf, softly. The baby was pushing his way between the cubs to get close to the

---

6. **mangy** (mān´ jē) adj. having the mange, a skin disease of mammals that causes sores and loss of hair.
7. **atom** (at´ əm) n. tiny piece of matter.

Literary Analysis
Animal Characters and Personification What human quality does Shere Khan demonstrate?

Reading Strategy
Predicting What do you predict will happen to the man's cub?

**Reading Check**

What surprises Father wolf?

warm hide. "Ahai! He is taking his meal with the others. And so this is a man's cub. Now, was there ever a wolf that could boast of a man's cub among her children?"

"I have heard now and again of such a thing, but never in our Pack or in my time," said Father Wolf. "He is altogether without hair, and I could kill him with a touch of my foot. But see, he looks up and is not afraid."

The moonlight was blocked out of the mouth of the cave, for Shere Khan's great square head and shoulders were thrust into the entrance. Tabaqui, behind him, was squeaking: "My lord, my lord, it went in here!"

"Shere Khan does us great honor," said Father Wolf, but his eyes were very angry. "What does Shere Khan need?"

"My quarry. A man's cub went this way," said Shere Khan. "Its parents have run off. Give it to me."

Shere Khan had jumped at a woodcutter's campfire, as Father Wolf had said, and was furious from the pain of his burned feet. But Father Wolf knew that the mouth of the cave was too narrow for a tiger to come in by. Even where he was, Shere Khan's shoulders and forepaws were cramped for want of room, as a man's would be if he tried to fight in a barrel.

"The Wolves are a free people," said Father Wolf. "They take orders from the Head of the Pack, and not from any striped cattle-killer. The man's cub is ours—to kill if we choose."

"Ye choose and ye do not choose! What talk is this of choosing? By the bull that I killed, am I to stand nosing into your dog's den for my fair dues? It is I, Shere Khan, who speak!"

The tiger's roar filled the cave with thunder. Mother Wolf shook herself

quarry (kwôr´ē) *n.* prey; anything being hunted or pursued

▼ **Critical Viewing**
What qualities of Mother Wolf do you see in this wolf? **[Connect]**

clear of the cubs and sprang forward, her eyes, like two green moons in the darkness, facing the blazing eyes of Shere Khan.

"And it is I, Raksha [The Demon], who answer. The man's cub is mine, Lungri—mine to me! He shall not be killed. He shall live to run with the Pack and to hunt with the Pack; and in the end, look you, hunter of little naked cubs—frog-eater—fish-killer—he shall hunt *thee*! Now get hence, or by the Sambhur that I killed (I eat no starved cattle), back thou goest to thy mother, burned beast of the Jungle, lamer than ever thou camest into the world! Go!"

Father Wolf looked on amazed. He had almost forgotten the days when he won Mother Wolf in fair fight from five other wolves, when she ran in the Pack and was not called The Demon for compliment's sake. Shere Khan might have faced Father Wolf, but he could not stand up against Mother Wolf, for he knew that where he was she had all the advantage of the ground, and would fight to the death. So he backed out of the cave-mouth growling, and when he was clear he shouted:

"Each dog barks in his own yard! We will see what the Pack will say to this <u>fostering</u> of man-cubs. The cub is mine, and to my teeth he will come in the end, O bush-tailed thieves!"

Mother Wolf threw herself down panting among the cubs, and Father Wolf said to her gravely:

"Shere Khan speaks this much truth. The cub must be shown to the Pack. Wilt thou still keep him, Mother?"

"Keep him!" she gasped. "He came naked, by night, alone and very hungry; yet he was not afraid! Look, he has pushed one of my babies to one side already. And that lame butcher would have killed him and would have run off to the Waingunga while the villagers here hunted through all our lairs in revenge! Keep him? Assuredly I will keep him. Lie still, little frog. O thou Mowgli—for Mowgli the Frog I will call thee—the time will come when thou wilt hunt Shere Khan as he has hunted thee."

"But what will our Pack say?" said Father Wolf. The Law of the Jungle lays down very clearly that any wolf may, when he marries, withdraw from the Pack he belongs to; but as soon as his cubs are old enough to stand on their feet he must bring them to the Pack Council, which is generally held once a month at full moon, in order that the other wolves may identify them. After that inspection the cubs are free to run where they please, and until they have killed their first buck no excuse is accepted if a grown wolf of the Pack kills one of them. The punishment is death where the murderer can be found; and if you think for a minute you will see that this must be so.

Father Wolf waited till his cubs could run a little, and then on the night of the Pack Meeting took them and Mowgli and Mother Wolf to the Council Rock—a hilltop covered with stones and boulders where a hundred wolves could hide. Akela, the great gray Lone Wolf, who

fostering (fŏs′ tər ĭŋ) *n.* taking care of

Literary Analysis
Animal Characters How does the author portray Mother Wolf as similar to a human mother?

Reading Strategy
Predicting What do you think the pack will say about Mowgli?

**Reading Check**

How does Mother Wolf respond to Shere Khan's demands?

led all the Pack by strength and cunning, lay out at full length on his rock, and below him sat forty or more wolves of every size and color, from badger-colored <u>veterans</u> who could handle a buck alone, to young black three-year-olds who thought they could. The Lone Wolf had led them for a year now. He had fallen twice into a wolf-trap in his youth, and once he had been beaten and left for dead; so he knew the manners and customs of men. There was very little talking at the Rock. The cubs tumbled over each other in the center of the circle where their mothers and fathers sat, and now and again a senior wolf would go quietly up to a cub, look at him carefully, and return to his place on noiseless feet. Sometimes a mother would push her cub far out into the moonlight, to be sure that he had not been overlooked. Akela from his rock would cry: "Ye know the Law—ye know the Law. Look well, O Wolves!" and the anxious mothers would take up the call: "Look—look well, O Wolves!"

At last—and Mother Wolf's neck-bristles lifted as the time came—Father Wolf pushed "Mowgli the Frog," as they called him, into the center, where he sat laughing and playing with some pebbles that glistened in the moonlight.

Akela never raised his head from his paws, but went on with the <u>monotonous</u> cry: "Look well!" A muffled roar came up from behind the rocks—the voice of Shere Khan crying: "The cub is mine. Give him to me. What have the Free People to do with a man's cub?" Akela never even twitched his ears: all he said was: "Look well, O Wolves! What have the Free People to do with the orders of any save the Free People? Look well!"

There was a chorus of deep growls, and a young wolf in his fourth year flung back Shere Khan's question to Akela: "What have the Free People to do with the man's cub?" Now the Law of the Jungle lays

veterans (vet′ ər enz′) *n.* those having experience

monotonous (mə nät′n əs′) *adj.* tiresome because it does not vary

down that if there is any <u>dispute</u> as to the right of a cub to be accepted by the Pack, he must be spoken for by at least two members of the Pack who are not his father and mother.

"Who speaks for this cub?" said Akela. "Among the Free People who speaks?" There was no answer, and Mother Wolf got ready for what she knew would be her last fight, if things came to fighting.

Then the only other creature who is allowed at the Pack Council—Baloo, the sleepy brown bear who teaches the wolf cubs the Law of the Jungle: old Baloo, who can come and go where he pleases because he eats only nuts and roots and honey—rose up on his hind quarters and grunted.

"The man's cub—the man's cub?" he said. "I speak for the man's cub. There is no harm in a man's cub. I have no gift of words, but I speak the truth. Let him run with the Pack, and be entered with the others. I myself will teach him.""We need yet another," said Akela. "Baloo has spoken, and he is our teacher for the young cubs. Who speaks besides Baloo?"

A black shadow dropped down into the circle. It was Bagheera the Black Panther, inky black all over, but with the panther marking showing up in certain lights like the pattern of watered silk. Everybody knew Bagheera, and nobody cared to cross his path; for he was as cunning as Tabaqui, as bold as the wild buffalo, and as reckless as the wounded elephant. But he had a voice as soft as wild honey dripping from a tree, and a skin softer than down.

"O Akela, and ye the Free People," he purred, "I have no right in your assembly; but the Law of the Jungle says that if there is a doubt which is not a killing matter in regard to a new cub, the life of that cub may be bought at a price. And the Law does not say who may or may not pay that price. Am I right?"

"Good! good!" said the young wolves, who are always hungry. "Listen to Bagheera. The cub can be bought for a price. It is the Law."

"Knowing that I have no right to speak here, I ask your leave."

"Speak then," cried twenty voices.

"To kill a naked cub is shame. Besides, he may make better sport for you when he is grown. Baloo has spoken in his behalf. Now to Baloo's word I will add one bull, and a fat one, newly killed, not half a mile from here, if ye will accept the man's cub according to the Law. Is it difficult?"

There was a <u>clamor</u> of scores of voices, saying: "What matter? He will die in the winter rains. He will scorch in the sun. What harm can a naked frog do us? Let him run with the Pack. Where is the bull, Bagheera? Let him be accepted." And then came Akela's deep bay, crying: "Look well—look well, O Wolves !"

Mowgli was still deeply interested in the pebbles, and he did not notice when the wolves came and looked at him one by one. At last

dispute (di spyo͞ot´) *n.* argument; debate; quarrel

Literary Analysis
Animal Characters and Personification Find three details from this scene that are examples of personification.

clamor (klam´ ər) *n.* loud demand or complaint

**Reading Check**

Why doesn't Shere Kahn get to take Mowgli?

Mowgli's Brothers ◆ 217

they all went down the hill for the dead bull, and only Akela, Bagheera, Baloo, and Mowgli's own wolves were left. Shere Khan roared still in the night, for he was very angry that Mowgli had not been handed over to him.

"Ay, roar well," said Bagheera, under his whiskers; "for the time comes when this naked thing will make thee roar to another tune, or I know nothing of man."

"It was well done," said Akela. "Men and their cubs are very wise. He may be a help in time."

"Truly, a help in time of need; for none can hope to lead the Pack forever," said Bagheera.

Akela said nothing. He was thinking of the time that comes to every leader of every pack when his strength goes from him and he gets feebler and feebler till at last he is killed by the wolves and a new leader comes up—to be killed in his turn.

"Take him away," he said to Father Wolf, "and train him as befits one of the Free People."

And that is how Mowgli was entered into the Seeonee wolf-pack at the price of a bull and on Baloo's good word.

Review and Assess

Thinking About the Selection

1. **Respond:** If you were a member of the Council, would you want Mowgli in the pack? Why or why not?

2. **(a) Recall:** What does Mother Wolf do when Shere Khan tries to take Mowgli from her? **(b) Infer:** Why does she react as she does? **(c) Interpret:** How do her actions show the meaning of her nickname?

3. **(a) Compare:** How is Mowgli similar to the wolf cubs? **(b) Contrast:** How is he different? **(c) Analyze:** Why do Mother Wolf and Shere Kahn have opposite reactions to the similarities and differences?

4. **(a) Recall:** At the council, what does Shere Khan say should be done with Mowgli? **(b) Infer:** Why doesn't Akela answer Shere Khan? **(c) Synthesize:** Why do the young wolves agree to let Mowgli join the pack?

5. **(a) Recall:** Who pays for Mowgli's life? **(b) Evaluate:** Are his reasons helpful or destructive? **(c) Support:** What examples from the story support your answer?

6. **Evaluate:** Describe the way the wolves in the pack make decisions. Is this a good way for a group to make a decision? Explain your answer.

Rudyard Kipling

(1865–1936)

Rudyard Kipling was born in India of British parents. When he was very little, his Indian nurses told him folk tales that featured talking animals. These stories provided inspiration for characters in Kipling's works, including *The Jungle Book,* in which "Mowgli's Brothers" appears. As a young boy, Kipling was sent to school in England. Not until 1882, at the age of seventeen, did he make his way back to India as a journalist. His work as a reporter, fiction writer, and poet earned him the 1907 Nobel Prize for Literature.

Review and Assess

Literary Analysis

Animal Characters

1. What two qualities of Shere Khan reflect his nature as a tiger?

2. In what way are the wolves in the story similar to and different from real wolves?

3. Complete a chart like the one shown for each of the following **animal characters:** Tabaqui, Akela, Bagheera.

Character's Name	
Animal Qualities_____	Human Qualities_____
_____	_____

Connecting Literary Elements

4. Which animals in the story have courage? Which are cowards? Explain your answers.

5. How do the qualities of these characters affect the way events turn out? Complete a graphic organizer like this one for each main character. In the first oval, list the character's most important qualities. In the ovals in the middle, list each event that was affected by these qualities. Include an explanation of each. In the cell on the right, explain how the character's qualities affected the outcome.

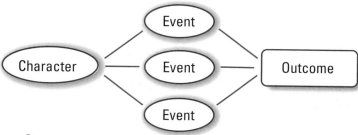

Reading Strategy

Predicting Characters' Actions

6. When Mowgli was discovered, what did you predict would happen to him? Why?

7. Which of Shere Khan's actions were you able to predict? Why?

8. Which of the wolves' actions were you able to predict? Why?

Extending Understanding

9. **Science Connection:** What do you learn about jungle habitats from this story? Explain.

Quick Review

Animal characters often have human as well as animal qualities. To review animal characters, see p. 209.

Personification is describing things that are nonhuman as if they had human abilities, qualities, and emotions.

When you **predict** characters' actions, you make educated guesses about what they will do, based on their qualities and the situation.

 Take It to the Net
www.phschool.com
Take the interactive self-test online to check your understanding of the selection.

Integrate Language Skills

Vocabulary Development Lesson

Word Analysis: Greek Prefix *mono-*

Monotonous means "unchanging." It contains the Greek prefix *mono-*, which means "one." Use this knowledge of the prefix *mono-* in your answer to each of the following questions.

1. What kind of speech is a *monologue*?
2. On what kind of track does a *monorail* train run?

Spelling Strategy

The words *there*, *their*, and *they're* sound alike but have different meanings and spellings. Remember, to spell *there*, begin with *here*.

Supply the correct spelling of *there*, *their*, or *they're* to complete each sentence.

1. Mowgli wandered in ___?___.
2. This is ___?___ cave.
3. The wolves agree because ___?___ hungry.
4. Bagheera says he has food over ___?___.

Concept Development: Synonyms

On your paper, match the numbered vocabulary word on the left with its **synonym,** or word with almost the same meaning, on the right. Then, come up with an additional synonym for two of the vocabulary words.

To help you, review the vocabulary words on page 209.

1. clamor	a. experts
2. dispute	b. argument
3. fostering	c. prey
4. monotonous	d. scampered
5. quarry	e. outcry
6. scuttled	f. aiding
7. veterans	g. unchanging

Grammar Lesson

Adverbs

An **adverb** is a word that modifies—or describes—a verb, an adjective, or another adverb. Adverbs answer the questions *when, how, where,* or *to what extent.*

Adverb	Answers the question
He spoke *spitefully.*	*How* did he speak?
The tiger hunts *now.*	*When* does the tiger hunt?
The wolf lives *here.*	*Where* does the wolf live?
Bagheera was *most* persuasive.	*To what extent* was Bagheera persuasive?

Practice Copy the following sentences. Circle each adverb and explain what question it answers.

1. Enter and look. There is no food here.
2. Tabaqui knew well that compliments are unlucky.
3. "I go," said Tabaqui, quietly.
4. The Council met yesterday.
5. Bagheera spoke longest.

Writing Application Rewrite this passage. Add adverbs to answer the questions.

Mother Wolf growled. (*How?*) Tabaqui waited. (*Where?*) He feared Father Wolf, but he feared Mother Wolf. (*To what extent?*)

W̸G Prentice Hall Writing and Grammar Connection: Chapter 16, Section 2

Writing Lesson

Comparison and Contrast of Characters

Write a brief composition in which you compare and contrast two animal characters in "Mowgli's Brothers."

Prewriting   Choose two characters to compare and contrast. Make a list of details about each character. Circle all the details about appearance in blue. Underline all the details about personality in red.

Drafting   Begin with an introductory paragraph that presents your general observations about the characters. For example, you might note that the characters have very similar personalities. Follow with body paragraphs, using one of the organizations shown below. End with a conclusion in which you restate your general observations.

Character by Character	Point by Point
Present all the details about one character first. Then, present all the details about the other.	Discuss each topic about each animal—for example, discuss the appearances of both animals, then go on to discuss the personalities of each animal.

Revising   Highlight the details about each animal in a different color. Use this to check that you followed the organization you chose and that you have about the same number of details for each character.

W *Prentice Hall Writing and Grammar Connection: Chapter 8, Section 2*

Extension Activities

Listening and Speaking   **Role-play** the conversation between Father Wolf and Shere Khan.

1. With a partner, read aloud sections of dialogue between the characters. Choose one of the dialogues as the starting point.

2. Begin where the written dialogue ends. Say the words that you think your character would say. Continue until each character has spoken at least five times.

3. Use postures, gestures, and facial expressions to indicate the emotions your character is feeling.

Research and Technology   Prepare a short **presentation** on communication in a real wolf pack. Use the Internet, CD-ROM encyclopedias, and magazines and newspapers found in the library. Use visual aids such as charts, maps, or graphs to represent statistics. Identify the sources of your information.

Take It to the Net   www.phschool.com

Go online for an additional research activity using the Internet.

Prepare to Read

Names/Nombres ◆ The Southpaw ◆ Alone in the Nets

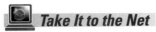 **Take It to the Net**

Visit www.phschool.com
for interactive activities
and instruction related to
these selections, including

- background
- graphic organizers
- literary elements
- reading strategies

Preview

Connecting to the Literature

The authors of "Names/Nombres," "The Southpaw," and "Alone in the Nets" write about group experiences. Connect to the selections by recalling your experiences as a member of groups such as family, friends, classes, clubs, and teams.

Background

In "Names/Nombres," Julia Alvarez tells how language differences make her feel like an outsider. In Spanish, the letter *j* is used for the sound English speakers associate with *h*. The letter *r* has a very different sound from its sound in English. Although many Spanish words have found their way into English, some of their pronunciations have changed over time, reflecting the influence of English speakers.

Literary Analysis

Narrator and Speaker

An author writes a story or a poem, but a **narrator** or **speaker** tells the story or "says" the poem. In works written in the first person, the narrator or speaker refers to himself or herself as *I*. The *I*, however, does not necessarily refer to the writer. Read the following example from "The Southpaw."

> If I'm not good enough to play on your team, I'm not good enough to be friends with.

Although the writer Judith Viorst uses the word *I*, she is referring to a character she invented to tell the story. (In fact, in "The Southpaw," two invented narrators tell the story.) As you read, use these focus questions to help you think about the narrator or speaker:

1. Who is telling the story?
2. How do his or her views shape how the story is told?

Comparing Literary Works

These three works are written in the first person, but the speakers and narrators have different qualities. In "Names/Nombres," the narrator is a real person—the author. Yet she shares some qualities with the made-up speaker of "Alone in the Nets." Use a Venn diagram like the one shown here to compare and contrast the qualities of the narrators or speakers. Use the overlapping portions of the circles for shared qualities. Include details for both narrators of "The Southpaw."

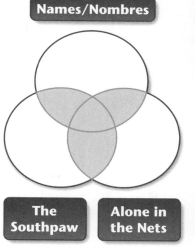

Reading Strategy

Setting a Purpose for Reading

When you set a purpose, you give yourself a focus. Here are a few purposes a reader might have for reading "The Southpaw."

- to be entertained by a funny story about baseball
- to gain insight into disagreements
- to look at a situation from two different sides

Set a purpose before reading each of these works.

Vocabulary Development

transport (trans pôrt´) *v.* carry from one place to another (p. 226)

inevitably (in ev´ i tə blē´) *adv.* unavoidably (p. 227)

chaotic (kā ät´ ik) *adj.* completely confused (p. 227)

inscribed (in skrībd´) *adj.* written on (p. 228)

opposition (äp´ ə zish´ ən) *n.* here, the other team (p. 233)

evaporate (i vap´ ə rāt´) *v.* disappear like vapor (p. 234)

Names
Nombres

Julia Alvarez

W hen we arrived in New York City, our names changed almost immediately. At Immigration,[1] the officer asked my father, *Mister Elbures*, if he had anything to declare. My father shook his head, "No," and we were waved through. I was too afraid we wouldn't be let in if I corrected the man's pronunciation, but I said our name to myself, opening my mouth wide for the organ blast of the *a*, trilling my tongue for the drum-roll of the *r*, *All-vah-rrr-es*! How could anyone get *Elbures* out of that orchestra of sound?

At the hotel my mother was *Missus Alburest*, and I was little girl, as in, "Hey, *little girl*, stop riding the elevator up and down. It's *not* a toy."

When we moved into our new apartment building, the super[2] called my father *Mister Alberase*, and the neighbors who became mother's friends pronounced her name *Jew-lee-ah* instead of *Hoo-lee-ah*. I, her namesake, was known as *Hoo-lee-tah* at home. But at school, I was *Judy* or *Judith*, and once an English teacher mistook me for *Juliet*.

It took awhile to get used to my new names. I wondered if I shouldn't correct my teachers and new friends. But my mother argued that it didn't matter. "You know what your friend Shakespeare said, '*A rose by any other name would smell as sweet.*' " My father had gotten into the habit of calling any famous author "my friend" because I had begun to write poems and stories in English class.

By the time I was in high school, I was a popular kid, and it showed in my name. Friends called me *Jules* or *Hey Jude*, and once a group of troublemaking friends my mother forbade me to hang out with called me *Alcatraz*. I was *Hoo-lee-tah* only to Mami and Papi and uncles and aunts who came over to eat *sancocho* on Sunday afternoons—old world folk whom I would just as soon go back to where they came from and leave me to pursue whatever mischief I wanted to in America. JUDY ALCATRAZ: the name on the Wanted Poster would read. Who would ever trace her to me?

My older sister had the hardest time getting an American name for herself because *Mauricia* did not translate into English. Ironically, although she had the most foreign-sounding name, she and I were the Americans in the family. We had been born in New York City when our parents had first tried immigration and then gone back "home,"

---

1. **Immigration** government agency that processes immigrants.
2. **super** superintendent; the person who manages an apartment building.

Literary Analysis
Narrator and Speaker
How does the detail about the author's life help you make the connection between the young Julia and the adult writer?

**Reading Check**

What does Julia experience when she arrives in New York City?

too homesick to stay. My mother often told the story of how she had almost changed my sister's name in the hospital.

After the delivery, Mami and some other new mothers were cooing over their new baby sons and daughters and exchanging names and weights and delivery stories. My mother was embarrassed among the Sallys and Janes and Georges and Johns to reveal the rich, noisy name of *Mauricia*, so when her turn came to brag, she gave her baby's name as *Maureen*.

"Why'd ya give her an Irish name with so many pretty Spanish names to choose from?" one of the women asked.

My mother blushed and admitted her baby's real name to the group. Her mother-in-law had recently died, she apologized, and her husband had insisted that the first daughter be named after his mother, *Mauran*. My mother thought it the ugliest name she had ever heard, and she talked my father into what she believed was an improvement, a combination of *Mauran* and her own mother's name, *Felicia*.

"Her name is *Mao-ree-shee-ah*," my mother said to the group of women.

"Why that's a beautiful name," the new mothers cried. "*Moor-ee-sha, Moor-ee-sha*," they cooed into the pink blanket. *Moor-ee-sha* it was when we returned to the States eleven years later. Sometimes, American tongues found even that mispronunciation tough to say and called her *Maria* or *Marsha* or *Maudy* from her nickname *Maury*. I pitied her. What an awful name to have to <u>transport</u> across borders!

My little sister, Ana, had the easiest time of all. She was plain *Anne*—that is, only her name was plain, for she turned out to be the pale, blond "American beauty" in the family. The only Hispanic thing about her was the affectionate nicknames her boyfriends sometimes gave her. *Anita*, or as one goofy guy used to sing to her to the tune of the banana advertisement, *Anita Banana*.[3]

Later, during her college years in the late '60s, there was a push to pronounce Third World names correctly. I remember calling her long distance at her group house and a roommate answering.

"Can I speak to Ana?" I asked, pronouncing her name the American way.

---

3. ***Anita Banana*** a play on the Chiquita Banana name.

Collage (detail), 1992, Juan Sanchez, Courtesy of Juan Sanchez and Guarighen, Inc. NYC

▼ **Critical Viewing**
How does the artist of this picture communicate "heritage"? **[Analyze]**

transport (trans pôrt') *v.* carry from one place to another

"Ana?" The man's voice hesitated. "Oh! you must mean *Ah-nah!*"

Our first few years in the States, though, ethnicity was not yet "in." Those were the blond, blue-eyed, bobby sock years of junior high and high school before the '60s ushered in peasant blouses, hoop earrings, serapes.[4] My initial desire to be known by my correct Dominican name faded. I just wanted to be Judy and merge with the Sallys and Janes in my class. But <u>inevitably</u>, my accent and coloring gave me away. "So where are you from, Judy?"

"New York," I told my classmates. After all, I had been born blocks away at Columbia Presbyterian Hospital.

"I mean, *originally.*"

"From the Caribbean," I answered vaguely, for if I specified, no one was quite sure on what continent our island was located.

"Really? I've been to Bermuda. We went last April for spring vacation. I got the worst sunburn! So, are you from Portoriko?"

"No," I sighed. "From the Dominican Republic."

"Where's that?"

"South of Bermuda."

They were just being curious, I knew, but I burned with shame whenever they singled me out as a "foreigner," a rare, exotic friend.

"Say your name in Spanish, oh please say it!" I had made mouths drop one day by rattling off my full name, which according to Dominican custom, included my middle names, Mother's and Father's surnames for four generations back.

"Julia Altagracia María Teresa Álvarez Tavares Perello Espaillat Julia Pérez Rochet González," I pronounced it slowly, a name as <u>chaotic</u> with sounds as a Middle Eastern bazaar[5] or market day in a South American village.

My Dominican heritage was never more apparent than when my extended family attended school occasions. For my graduation, they all came, the whole lot of aunts and uncles and the many little cousins who snuck in without tickets. They sat in the first row in order to better understand the Americans' fast-spoken English. But how could they listen when they were constantly speaking among themselves in florid-sounding phrases, rococo[6] consonants, rich, rhyming vowels?

Introducing them to my friends was a further trial to me. These relatives had such complicated names and there were so many of them, and their relationships to myself were so convoluted. There was my Tía Josefina, who was not really an aunt but a much older

---

inevitably (in ev′ i tə blē) *adv.* unavoidably

Literary Analysis
Narrator and Speaker
Why does the writer spell Puerto Rico this way? How does the spelling reveal the narrator's perspective?

chaotic (kā ät′ ik) *adj.* completely confused

**Reading Check**

Why does Julia try to hide her home country from her classmates?

---

4. **serapes** (sə rä′ pēz) *n.* colorful shawls worn in Latin America.
5. **bazaar** (bə zär′) *n.* marketplace; frequently, one held outdoors.
6. **rococo** (rə kō′ kō) fancy, ornate style of art of the early eighteenth century.

cousin. And her daughter, Aida Margarita, who was adopted, *una hija de crianza.* My uncle of affection, Tío José, brought my *madrina* Tía Amelia and her *comadre* Tía Pilar. My friends rarely had more than a "Mom and Dad" to introduce.

After the commencement ceremony my family waited outside in the parking lot while my friends and I signed yearbooks with nicknames which recalled our high school good times: "Beans" and "Pepperoni" and "Alcatraz." We hugged and cried and promised to keep in touch.

Our goodbyes went on too long. I heard my father's voice calling out across the parking lot, "*Hoo-lee-tah! Vamonos!*"

Back home, my *tíos* and *tías* and *primas,* Mami and Papi, and *mis hermanas* had a party for me with *sancocho* and a store-bought *pudín,* <u>inscribed</u> with *Happy Graduation, Julie.* There were many gifts—that was a plus to a large family! I got several wallets and a suitcase with my initials and a graduation charm from my godmother and money from my uncles. The biggest gift was a portable typewriter from my parents for writing my stories and poems.

Someday, the family predicted, my name would be well-known throughout the United States. I laughed to myself, wondering which one I would go by.

inscribed (in skrībd′) *adj.*
written on

Review and Assess

Thinking About the Selection

1. **Respond:** Which name do you think best fits the author? Why?

2. **(a) Recall:** How does Julia's family say her name? **(b) Analyze Cause and Effect:** Explain why some English speakers mispronounce her name. **(c) Connect:** What do you do or say when someone mispronounces your name?

3. **(a) Recall:** How does Julia respond when her classmates ask her where she's from? **(b) Draw Conclusions:** Why does she respond as she does? **(c) Evaluate:** Would you make the same decision in the same situation? Why or why not?

4. **(a) Interpret:** Explain how the title captures the focus of Alvarez's narrative. **(b) Analyze:** How do Alvarez's feelings about the topic change over time? **(c) Synthesize:** What do names represent for Alvarez and others?

5. **Assess:** How important are names in the way people view themselves and others? Support your answer with details from the selection.

Julia Alvarez

(b. 1950)
Like many immigrants, the Alvarez family came to the United States for political reasons. After working to overthrow the dictator of the Dominican Republic, Julia's father and his family fled the country. Julia was only ten years old when they arrived in the United States. Growing up here, Alvarez felt she had to "translate her experience in English." Sometimes, as she shows in "Names/Nombres," it was the Americans who did the "translating," blending the exotic-sounding syllables of her family's names into more familiar words.

The Southpaw

Judith Viorst

Dear Richard,

Don't invite me to your birthday party because I'm not coming. And give back the Disneyland sweatshirt I said you could wear.

If I'm not good enough to play on your team, I'm not good enough to be friends with.

Your former friend,
Janet

P.S. I hope when you go to the dentist he finds 20 cavities.

Dear Janet,

Here is your stupid Disneyland sweatshirt, if that's how you're going to be. I want my comic books now—finished or not. No girl has ever played on the Mapes Street baseball team, and as long as I'm captain, no girl ever will.
Your former friend,
Richard

P.S. I hope when you go for your checkup you need a tetanus shot.

Dear Richard,

I'm changing my goldfish's name from Richard to Stanley. Don't count on my vote for class president next year. Just because I'm a member of the ballet club doesn't mean I'm not a terrific ballplayer.
Your former friend,
Janet

P.S. I see you lost your first game 28–0.

Dear Janet,

I'm not saving any more seats for you on the bus. For all I care you can stand the whole way to school. Why don't you just forget about baseball and learn something nice like knitting?
Your former friend,
Richard

P.S. Wait until Wednesday.

▲ **Critical Viewing**
What details in this picture show team spirit? **[Analyze]**

Literary Analysis
Narrator and Speaker
Describe each narrator's point of view about the subject of the argument.

✓ **Reading Check**
What are Richard and Janet fighting about?

Dear Richard,
   My father said I could call someone to go with us for a ride and hot-fudge sundaes. In case you didn't notice, I didn't call you.
   Your former friend,
      Janet

P.S. I see you lost your second game, 34–0.

Dear Janet,
   Remember when I took the laces out of my blue-and-white sneakers and gave them to you? I want them back.
   Your former friend,
      Richard

P.S. Wait until Friday.

Dear Richard,
   Congratulations on your un-broken record. Eight straight losses, wow! I understand you're the laughingstock of New Jersey.
      Your former friend,
      Janet

   P.S. Why don't you and your team forget about baseball and learn something nice like knitting maybe?

Dear Janet,
   Here's the silver horseback riding trophy that you gave me. I don't think I want to keep it anymore.
   Your former friend,
      Richard

P.S. I didn't think you'd be the kind who'd kick a man when he's down.

Dear Richard,
   I wasn't kicking exactly. I was kicking back.
   Your former friend,
      Janet

P.S. In case you were wondering, my batting average is .345.

Dear Janet,
   Alfie is having his tonsils out tomorrow. We might be able to let you catch next week.
      Richard

Dear Richard,
   I pitch.
Janet

Dear Janet,
   Joel is moving to Kansas and Danny sprained his wrist. How about a permanent place in the outfield?
      Richard

Dear Richard,
*   I pitch.*
Richard

Dear Janet,
    Ronnie caught the chicken pox and Leo broke his toe and Elwood has these stupid violin lessons. I'll give you first base, and that's my final offer.
        Richard

Literary Analysis
Narrator and Speaker
What qualities do the narrators share?

Dear Richard,
*   Susan Reilly plays*
first base, Marilyn
Jackson catches, Ethel
Kahn plays center field,
I pitch. It's a package deal.
*   Janet*

P.S. Sorry about your 12-game losing streak.

Dear Janet,
    Please! Not Marilyn Jackson.
Richard

Dear Richard,
*   Nobody ever said that I was unreasonable. How about Lizzie Martindale instead?*
*   Janet*

Dear Janet,
    At least could you call your goldfish Richard again?
Your friend,
    Richard

Judith Viorst

(b. 1931)
Judith Viorst has had some practice choosing her own way. Her first job was modeling in New York City. She always wanted to be a writer, though, and kept writing until she became a successful writer of stories and poetry for adults and children. Her three sons—Alexander, Nick, and Anthony—sometimes pop up as characters in her books. Choosing her own way, says Viorst, is an ongoing process. " . . . [You discover that] this is who you are and you trust that . . ."

Review and Assess

Thinking About the Selections

1. **(a) Recall:** In "The Southpaw," why is Janet angry at Richard? **(b) Analyze:** Using two examples, explain how each friend shows anger.

2. **(a) Recall:** What reason does Richard give for not including Janet on the team? **(b) Contrast:** How does his attitude change? **(c) Analyze:** Why does his attitude change?

3. **(a) Recall:** What position does Janet want to play? **(b) Infer:** What agreement do Janet and Richard reach about Janet's demands? **(c) Evaluate:** Explain why the arrrangement is fair to both sides or unfair to one side.

Alone
in the Nets

Arnold Adoff

Alone in the Nets

I
am
alone of course,
5   in the nets, on this cold and raining afternoon,
and our best defending fullback
is lying on the wet ground out of position.
Half the <u>opposition</u> is pounding
down the field,
10   and their lead forward is gliding
so fast, she can just barely keep
the ball in front of her sliding
foot.

Her cleats are expensive.
15   and her hair b o u n c e s
neatly
like the after
girls   in the shampoo commercials.
There   is   a   big   grin
20   on her face.
Now: In This Frozen Moment On This Moving World Through Space
is the right time to ask why am I here just standing
in my frozen place?
Why did I get up on time this morning?
25   Why did I get up at all?
Why did I listen to the coach and agree to play
this strange position in a r e a l game
in a strange town on this wet and moving world?
Why is it raining?
30   Why is it raining so h a r d?
Where
are all of our defenders?
Why do all of our players
do all of the falling
35   down?
Why am I here?
But Frozen Moments Can Unfreeze And I Can Stretch
and reach for the ball flying to the corner of
our
goal.

opposition (ăp´ ə zish´ ən)
n. here, the other team

**Reading Check**

What happens to the
speaker when she sees
the ball coming her way?

Alone in the Nets ◆ 233

            I can reach and jump
                    and dive into the s p a c e
                              between my out
                                    stretched
45   hands
    and the outside poles
            of the nets.
    My fears <u>evaporate</u> like my sweat in this chilling
                                        breeze,
50 and I can move with this moving world
    and pace my steps
    like that old
            movie
            high
55   noon sheriff in his just
                            right
                            time.
    That grinning forward gets her shot away too soon,
    and I am there, on my own time, in the air,
60   to meet the ball,
    and fall on it
    for the save.
        I wave my happy ending wave and get up.
                    The game goes on.

evaporate (i vap′ ə rāt′) v.
disappear like vapor

Review and Assess

Thinking About the Selections

1. **Respond:** What advice would you give to the speaker of this poem?

2. **(a) Recall:** What position does the speaker play on the team? **(b) Support:** Which details indicate the position she plays?

3. **(a) Assess:** Do you think the speaker is an experienced player? Why or why not? **(b) Predict:** Will the speaker experience the same anxiety during every game? Explain.

4. **(a) Evaluate:** How well does the author of "Alone in the Nets" capture the tension of a goalie during a soccer game? **(b) Support:** What details indicate her tension?

5. **Evaluate:** What are some advantages and disadvantages to playing on an organized sports team? Use examples from the poem as well as from your own observations and experience.

Arnold Adoff

(b. 1935)

Poet, author, teacher, and lecturer, Arnold Adoff has been writing poetry since he was a boy! His own memories and his experiences as a teacher and a father help him understand the feelings and interests of young people. Adoff also benefits from the support of his wife, award-winning writer Virginia Hamilton.

Review and Assess

Literary Analysis

Narrator and Speaker

1. Which details indicate that the narrator of "Names/Nombres" is also the author?
2. Who are the narrators of "The Southpaw"?
3. Explain why "The Southpaw" would be more effective or less effective if it were told by just one of the two narrators or by a third-person narrator—one who does not participate in the story.
4. Who is the speaker of "Alone in the Nets"?
5. Explain how each of the narrators or speakers shapes your impression of the events in each selection.

Comparing Literary Works

6. Which two narrators or speakers are most similar? Explain.
7. Which two are most different? Explain.
8. What advice do you think Julia in "Names/Nombres" would have given to Janet in "The Southpaw"? Why?
9. What advice do you think Janet would have given to Julia? Why?

Reading Strategy

Setting a Purpose for Reading

10. On a chart like this one, record details from each selection that helped you achieve your purposes for reading.

Title	Purpose	Details
"Names/Nombres"		
"The Southpaw"		
"Alone in the Nets"		

11. Using details from the chart above, explain how setting a purpose increased your understanding of each selection.

Extending Understanding

12. **Media Connection:** Explain how a product's name can affect how people view that product.

Quick Review

The **narrator** or **speaker** is the one who tells the story or "says" the poem. To review narrator and speaker, see page 223.

Your **purpose for reading** is your reason.

Setting a purpose helps you focus your reading.

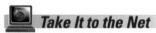 **Take It to the Net**
www.phschool.com
Take the interactive self-test online to check your understanding of these selections.

Integrate Language Skills

Vocabulary Development Lesson

Word Analysis: Latin Prefix *trans-*

The Latin prefix *trans-* means "over, through, or across." Define the italicized words below.

1. Ships *transport* immigrants across the ocean.
2. The radio *transmission* was unclear.
3. *Transatlantic* flights are long.

Spelling Strategy

Your shows belonging, as in "*your* sweater." *You're* is the contraction for *you are*, as in "*You're* a good friend." Copy the following passage. Proofread for misspelled *you're* and *your*.

You may not know it, but your name has a meaning. For example, if you're name is Arthur, then your name means "great" or "noble." If you're name is John, then youre "beloved." Your also sharing a name with Ian and Sean. These names are other versions of you're name.

Fluency: Complete the Sentences

Write these sentences, filling in the blanks with the correct vocabulary words from the list on page 223.

1. The ship will ___?___ passengers from island to island.
2. With an ace pitcher on the mound, the Sluggers ___?___ won the championship.
3. The long lines made the lobby seem ___?___.
4. The watch with my initials ___?___ on the back is missing.
5. In this heat, the water will ___?___ quickly.
6. We hoped to defeat the ___?___.

Grammar Lesson

Adverbs Modifying Adjectives and Adverbs

An **adverb** modifies—or describes—a verb, an adjective (a word that modifies a noun), or another adverb. *Almost, too, so, very, quite, rather, usually, much,* and *more* are some adverbs that modify adjectives and other adverbs.

Adverb	Modifies the word	Answers the question
The trip is *too* long.	*long* (adjective)	*To what extent?*
He walks *very* quickly.	*quickly* (adverb)	*How?*

Practice Write the following sentences. Underline each adverb and draw an arrow to the word it modifies.

1. Our names changed almost immediately.
2. Our goodbyes went on too long.
3. My heritage was never more apparent.
4. You don't think I'm good enough to play.
5. They settled their conflict, but not swiftly.

Writing Application To each sentence, add an adverb that answers the question in parentheses.

1. I was afraid we were late. (*How afraid?*)
2. They are crowded. (*To what extent?*)
3. Janet pitched fast. (*How fast?*)

W̶G̶ Prentice Hall Writing and Grammar Connection: Chapter 16, Section 2

Writing Lesson

Sports Scene

The form of writing you choose often depends as much on your purpose as on your topic. Because Arnold Adoff's purpose is to capture the goalie's thoughts, he writes a poem with the goalie as the speaker. Choose a different purpose. Then, write about the topic of the poem in a form that suits this different purpose.

Prewriting List possible purposes for writing. Choose one. Then, decide on the best form for achieving your purpose. Some common purposes and forms are suggested below.

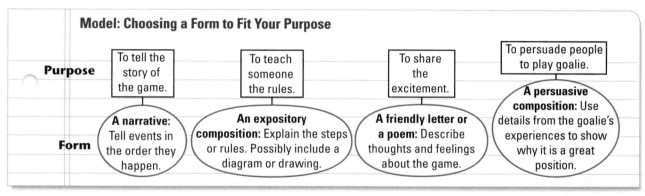

Model: Choosing a Form to Fit Your Purpose

Purpose

| To tell the story of the game. | To teach someone the rules. | To share the excitement. | To persuade people to play goalie. |

Form

A narrative: Tell events in the order they happen.

An expository composition: Explain the steps or rules. Possibly include a diagram or drawing.

A friendly letter or a poem: Describe thoughts and feelings about the game.

A persuasive composition: Use details from the goalie's experiences to show why it is a great position.

Drafting Consult the Writing Handbook on page R13 to learn more about the form of writing you have chosen. Then, as you write, focus on including details appropriate to your purpose and form.

Revising Delete details that do not help you achieve your writing purpose.

WG Prentice Hall Writing and Grammar Connection: Chapter 11, Section 3

Extension Activities

Listening and Speaking Invite a coach to your class to explain how to swing a bat, kick a soccer ball, or make a free throw. After the coach speaks, work in small groups to prepare instructional presentations of your own. **Give directions and demonstrate** the skill.

1. Restate the directions.
2. Demonstrate each step.
3. Use and explain any key terms.
4. Finish by summarizing any tips the coach gave for effective practice or drill.

Research and Technology In a group, prepare a **presentation** on the political and economic factors that caused Julia's family to leave the Dominican Republic.

Writing Before 1974, girls were not allowed to play with boys on Little League teams. Write a short **essay** explaining whether or not you think this rule was a good one.

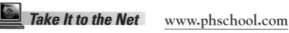 **Take It to the Net** www.phschool.com

Go online for an additional research activity using the Internet.

CONNECTIONS
Literature and Culture

Women in Sports

Both "The Southpaw" and "Alone in the Nets" present girls in active athletic roles, which many people take for granted today. However, in the United States as recently as 1971, only one in twenty-seven girls participated in high-school varsity sports. Today, one out of every three girls participates. The following athletes are just a few of the women who have earned a place in sports history.

Babe Didrickson In the Olympics of 1932, Babe Didrickson entered three competitions, setting a world record and winning two gold medals. She then went on to become a golfing legend, winning seventeen tournaments in a row. She was one of the founders of the Ladies Professional Golf Association in 1949. The LPGA exists to this day.

Wilma Rudolph In 1960, Wilma Rudolph became the first African American female athlete to set a world record in the 200 meters during the Olympic trials. In the Olympics, she became the first American woman to win three gold medals in track.

Nancy Lopez Lopez grew up in New Mexico, where her father taught her to play golf when she was eight years old. She became a national celebrity in 1978 when she won the LPGA National Championship.

Rebecca Lobo Basketball player Rebecca Lobo was the youngest member of the 1996 Olympic women's basketball team. She went on to play professional basketball, and contributed to her team's success and the sport's popularity. With her mother, she has co-written an autobiography called *Home Team*.

Tisha Venturini Along with her teammates, including Mia Hamm, soccer player Tisha Venturini won a gold medal at the 1996 Olympics. She scored two of the goals that helped the team win the game. A California native, she has a degree in physical education.

Connecting Literature and Culture

1. Which athlete do you think the speaker in "Alone in the Nets" would want to meet? Why?
2. Which athlete do you think Janet in "The Southpaw" would want to meet? Why?
3. Which athlete would you like to meet? Why?
4. What resources could you use to find out more information about these athletes or their sports?

Applications

About Applications

The purpose of an application is to provide specific information requested by a group or organization that will make a decision based on that information. At one time or another, you will probably fill out an application for one or more of the following reasons:

- to get a library card
- to get a job
- to be admitted to a school
- to open a savings account
- to join a club or sports league
- to get a driver's license

When preparing applications, read carefully to find out what information is needed, when and where the application should be turned in, and what, if any, other documents, payments, or paperwork should be included with the application.

Reading Strategy

Following Multiple-Step Directions

Applications often have **multiple-step directions**— instructions that have several steps or parts that must be done before the application is complete. On some applications, these directions are numbered and written in sentences. On other applications, the "directions" consist of brief labels that indicate what information is to be provided in each section.

To successfully complete multi-step directions on an application, preview and review the text and the form.

- **Preview** Before you begin following the directions to fill out the application, make sure you can answer the questions listed in the chart at the right.

- **Review** After you have filled out the application, review it. Check that you have completed all the necessary sections and that the information is legible, or readable.

Previewing an Application

1. What information is being asked for?
2. On which line or in which space is the information to be placed?
3. Does the information need to be typed, printed, or entered electronically?
4. Are there any places where I am not supposed to write?
5. What important dates do I need to know?
6. What do I need to include with the application?
7. What do I do with the completed application?

VILLA PARK PUBLIC LIBRARY

Library Card Application

To obtain a Villa Park Public Library card, you will need to bring the following to the Library:

- Two forms of identification with your Villa Park address (one of which includes a photograph).
- An <u>application form</u>, which must be signed at the Library's circulation desk.
- If you are under the age of 18, you will also need a parent to sign the form at the Library's circulation desk.
- For Oakbrook Terrace residents, a certificate of residence from the City of Oakbrook Terrace (available at the City Clerk's office).
- Other non-residents must pay a <u>fee</u> for a library card.

> These lines tell you what else you need to supply when you submit your application.

STAFF USE   **Expiration**

Date: _____   **Spec Designation** _____
                                                       OBT—1/4ly—Family Fee

Name typed _____
                                  Last, First, MI

New - Renew - Ex Rew

> Do not write in spaces marked "Office Use" or "Staff Use" or "Department Use."

REGISTRATION WORKSHEET

Today's Date _____

Name _____
        Please Print First, Middle Initial, Last

Address _____
              Street   City, State, Zip Code

Phone Number _____   Social Security Number_____

Reference _____   Phone Number _____

Address _____
              Street   City, State, Zip Code

Business Name _____   Phone Number _____

Business Address _____
              Street   City, State, Zip Code

Date of Birth (if under 18) _____

> A *reference* is an adult who will give you a recommendation—a statement saying they think you are responsible enough to have your application approved. Ask for permission before using someone's name as a reference.

The lines below must be signed in person at the Library's circulation desk:

I agree to be responsible for all materials checked out on my library card and fines and fees accrued.

Signed_____

If person signing this application is under 18, a parent's signature is needed.

I am responsible for all materials checked out on my child's library card and fines and fees accrued.

_____   _____
Please Print Parent's Name   Parent's Signature

> Watch for specific directions that tell you when and where a step must be completed.

SAVINGS ACCOUNT APPLICATION

Simply complete this short form to start your application process.

1. What type of account would you like to open?

   ❏ Young Investors' Club

   ❏ Statement Savings

   ❏ Holiday Savings

2. Would you like Internet banking?

   ❏ Yes ❏ No

3. Provide the following information. (Please print.)
   Name _____
   E-Mail _____
   Street Address _____
   Address (cont.) _____
   City _____ State _____ Zip code _____
   Work Phone _____
   Home Phone _____

4. Today's Date ⬚⬚⬚⬚⬚⬚ mm/dd/yy

5. Initial Deposit Amount _____
   You must make an initial deposit as required by the type of savings account you are opening.

6. Date of Birth ⬚⬚⬚⬚⬚⬚ mm/dd/yy

   Social Security Number_____

   Signature _____

These lines require a choice to be made. If you do not understand the choices on an application, ask someone. Do not leave choices blank.

Here, specific directions are given for how information is to be entered.

If the application asks for information in a category that does not apply to you, such as a work phone number, write N/A. N/A stands for *not applicable.*

When boxes are provided, write one letter or numeral in each box. The label *mm/dd/yy* indicates that you should write the month, date, and year. Write the number of the month, not the letters. Use a 0 before any single digit numbers. Use the last two numerals of the year. For example, March 5, 2002 would be written as 030502.

PASADENA YOUTH ROLLER HOCKEY
REGISTRATION FORM

REGISTRATION DEADLINE APRIL 6, 2002
COST $75.00 ($65.00 IF YOU REGISTER BY APRIL 6, 2002)

Player Tryout & Draft: Saturday, April 6, 2002
League Starts: Thursday, April 18, 2002

EQUIPMENT NEEDED:
Skates—In-line or Regular Quad
Helmet—MANDATORY with full face mask or shield. No Goalie Helmet
Stick—Regulation hockey stick, preferred to be no higher than nose
Gloves—Regulation hockey gloves
Elbow Pads/Shin Guards—Recommended, but not Mandatory

*ALL EQUIPMENT NEEDS ARE AVAILABLE
AT THE PASADENA ROLLER RINK, USUALLY CHEAPER THAN
OR EQUAL TO ATHLETIC STORE PRICES.*

**TO REGISTER—MAIL YOUR FORM(S) TO 4100 JANA LN,
PASADENA, TX 77505 OR COME BY THE PASADENA ROLLER
RINK AT 2602 CHERRYBROOK, PASADENA, TX.**

**PASADENA YOUTH ROLLER HOCKEY LEAGUE
Registration Form, 4100 Jana Ln, Pasadena, TX 77505
REGISTRATION DEADLINE APRIL 6, 2002**

PLAYER'S NAME_____ AGE _____ DOB _____

ADDRESS_____ CITY _____ ZIP _____

PARENTS' NAME (Mom)_____(Dad)_____

PHONE NUMBER (____)_____ SHIRT SIZE _____

The player listed above has my permission to participate in this activity.
I understand that the Pasadena Roller Rink and the Pasadena Youth Hockey
League do not provide insurance and are not responsible for accident coverage.

PARENT'S SIGNATURE_____ DATE __/__/__

Deadlines indicate the date after which the application will not be accepted. Other important dates are also indicated here.

This list indicates what players will be expected to purchase if they are accepted to the program. The word *mandatory* means required.

These lines indicate that there is more than one acceptable way to submit your application.

In this section, the lines are labeled to indicate what information you should provide in each space. The abbreviation DOB stands for Date of Birth.

Check Your Comprehension

1. What is a reference?
2. What does *mm/dd/yy* stand for?
3. Which of the following pieces of equipment are *required* to play roller hockey?   (a) shin guards   (b) helmets   (c) gloves

Applying the Reading Strategy

Following Multiple-Step Directions

4. What documents do you need to submit with a library card application?
5. What questions would you ask before choosing the type of savings account you would like to open?
6. What do you do with your completed registration form for youth roller hockey?
7. Choose one of the applications and write the answers to the Preview the Application questions on p. 239.

Activity

Complete Applications

Obtain from local groups or organizations an application for at least two of the following:

- a volunteer organization
- a checking account
- a health club
- a job in a store

Fill out the applications. Make a list of the documents you will need to provide, fees you will need to pay, and deadlines you will need to meet.

Comparing and Contrasting Informational Materials

Types of Applications

Make a chart like the one shown. Complete each section to find the similarities and differences in the different applications. Add a column to include one of the applications from the activity.

	Library Card	Savings Account	Roller Hockey
Is identification required?			
Are references required?			
Does the application need to be signed by anyone other than the applicant?			
Can the application be mailed in?			
Is your birthday required?			
Is your address required?			
Is money required?			

Prepare to Read

Adventures of Isabel ◆ I'll Stay
Wilbur Wright and Orville Wright ◆ Dream Dust

The Granger Collection, New York

 Take It to the Net

Visit www.phschool.com
for interactive activities
and instruction related to
these selections, including

- background
- graphic organizers
- literary elements
- reading strategies

Preview

Connecting to the Literature

The poems in this group describe success—real and imagined, small and large. Connect to the poems by considering how you feel on an "up" day—a day when you have achieved something or feel as if you could take on any challenge.

Background

"Wilbur Wright and Orville Wright," by Rosemary and Stephen Vincent Benét, tells the story of a success that affected the course of history. The Wright brothers, who spent years experimenting with gliders, flew the first power-driven, heavier-than-air machine on December 17, 1903, near Kitty Hawk, North Carolina. Their plane flew 120 feet and was in the air for twelve seconds.

Literary Analysis

Stanzas

A **stanza** is a group of lines of poetry that are usually similar in length and pattern and are separated by spaces. A stanza is like a paragraph of poetry—it develops one main idea. Poets use stanzas to organize their ideas, and they sometimes break from a stanza-pattern to emphasize certain ideas.

Comparing Literary Works

Two of the poems you are about to read have regular stanzas. One has stanzas of irregular length; the other consists of single lines, not stanzas. As you read, use the following focus questions to help you compare and contrast the four poets' different uses—or lack of use—of stanzas.

1. Which two poems have the most regular stanzas?
2. What is the effect of not having regular stanzas?

Reading Strategy

Interpreting Meaning

Interpreting the meaning of words is going beyond the pronunciation and expected meaning to figure out what is really meant. When you read these and other works, look for the following types of words that can cause confusion or misinterpretation:

- **Figurative language:** Words and phrases that are not meant to be read literally. For example, if a poet writes, "She was a rock," he or she is trying to convey that the person was strong.
- **Words with multiple meanings:** Words that can be used to mean different things in different situations. For example, the word *trying* often means "attempting." In the following lines, however, it means something else.

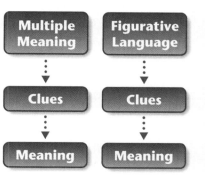

> "These birds are very trying.
> I'm sick of hearing them cheep-cheep . . ."

Because the speaker of the poem is sick of listening to the birds, you can figure out that trying means "annoying."

As you read, use a graphic organizer like this one to identify and interpret figurative language and words with multiple meanings.

Vocabulary Development

ravenous (rav´ ə nəs´) *adj.* greedily hungry (p. 246)

cavernous (kav´ ər nəs´) *adj.* deep and empty (p. 246)

rancor (raŋ´ kər) *n.* bitter hate (p. 246)

grant (grant) *v.* admit (p. 248)

ADVENTURES of ISABEL
OGDEN NASH

Isabel met an enormous bear,
Isabel, Isabel, didn't care;
The bear was hungry, the bear was <u>ravenous</u>,
The bear's big mouth was cruel and <u>cavernous</u>.
5 The bear said, Isabel, glad to meet you,
How do, Isabel, now I'll eat you!
Isabel, Isabel, didn't worry,
Isabel didn't scream or scurry.
She washed her hands and she straightened her hair up,
10 Then Isabel quietly ate the bear up.

Once in a night as black as pitch
Isabel met a wicked old witch.
The witch's face was cross and wrinkled,
The witch's gums with teeth were sprinkled.
15 Ho ho, Isabel! the old witch crowed,
I'll turn you into an ugly toad!
Isabel, Isabel, didn't worry,
Isabel didn't scream or scurry,
She showed no rage and she showed no <u>rancor</u>,
20 But she turned the witch into milk and drank her.

Isabel met a hideous giant,
Isabel continued self-reliant.
The giant was hairy, the giant was horrid,
He had one eye in the middle of his forehead.
25 Good morning Isabel, the giant said,
I'll grind your bones to make my bread.
Isabel, Isabel, didn't worry,
Isabel didn't scream or scurry.
She nibbled the zwieback that she always fed off,
30 And when it was gone, she cut the giant's head off.

Isabel met a troublesome doctor,
He punched and he poked till he really shocked her.
The doctor's talk was of coughs and chills
And the doctor's satchel bulged with pills.
35 The doctor said unto Isabel,
Swallow this, it will make you well.
Isabel, Isabel, didn't worry,
Isabel didn't scream or scurry.
She took those pills from the pill concocter,
40 And Isabel calmly cured the doctor.

ravenous (rav´ ə nəs´) *adj.* greedily hungry

cavernous (kav´ ər nəs´) *adj.* deep and empty

rancor (raŋ´ kər) *n.* bitter hate or ill will

Ogden Nash

(1902–1971)
Ogden Nash threw away his first poetry attempt. Luckily, he pulled it out of the trash and sent it to a magazine—which published it immediately! Nash wrote light, humorous verse collected in titles such as *Parents Keep Out: Elderly Poems for Youngerly Readers.*

I like the plates on the ledge
of the dining room wall (to the north)
standing on edge,
standing as if they thought they could stay.

5   Confident things can stand and stay!

I am confident.
I always thought there was something to be
     done about everything.
I'll stay.
I'll not go pouting and shouting out of the city.
10   I'll stay.
My name will be Up in Lights!
I believe it!
They will know me as Nora-the-Wonderful!
It will happen!
15   I'll stay.

Mother says "You rise in the morning—
You must be the Sun!
For wherever *you* are there is Light,
and those who are near you are warm,
20   feel Efficient."

I'll stay.

Review and Assess

Thinking About the Selection

1. **(a) Recall:** What are three challenges Isabel faces?
   (b) Infer: What is Nash's purpose in describing such unbelievable adventures for Isabel? **(c) Evaluate:** How effectively does he achieve this purpose?

2. **(a) Support:** Describe Isabel's personality using details from the poem to support your answer. **(b) Assess:** Explain why Isabel is or is not someone you would want to have in your class.

3. **(a) Recall:** What does the speaker in "I'll Stay" like about the plates? **(b) Apply:** How does the description of the plates apply to the speaker herself?

Gwendolyn Brooks

(1917–2000)

By age seven, Gwendolyn Brooks had convinced her parents that she would become a writer—a promise she fulfilled with many published poetry books and one novel. They probably didn't predict, however, that their daughter would become the first African American to win the Pulitzer Prize! Brooks also served as the Poet Laureate of Illinois.

Wilbur Wright AND Orville Wright

ROSEMARY AND STEPHEN VINCENT BENÉT

Said Orville Wright to Wilbur Wright,
"These birds are very trying.
I'm sick of hearing them cheep-cheep
About the fun of flying.
5 A bird has feathers, it is true.
That much I freely grant.
But, must that stop us, W?"
Said Wilbur Wright, "It shan't."

And so they built a glider, first,
10 And then they built another.
—There never were two brothers more
Devoted to each other.
They ran a dusty little shop

Literary Analysis
Stanzas What does the first stanza say about the Wright brothers?

grant (grant) *v.* admit

▼**Critical Viewing**
Compare this scene with a modern airport.
[**Compare and Contrast**]

For bicycle-repairing,
15 And bought each other soda-pop
and praised each other's daring.

They glided here, they glided there,
They sometimes skinned their noses.
—For learning how to rule the air
20 Was not a bed of roses—
But each would murmur, afterward,
While patching up his bro,
"Are we discouraged, W?"
"Of course we are not, O!"

25 And finally, at Kitty Hawk
In Nineteen-Three (let's cheer it!)
The first real airplane really flew
With Orville there to steer it!
—And kingdoms may forget their kings
30 And dogs forget their bites,
But, not till Man forgets his wings,
Will men forget the Wrights.

Reading Strategy
Interpreting Meaning
Explain the words "bed of roses." What is another way to convey the meaning?

Review and Assess

Thinking About the Selection

1. **Respond:** Would you have wanted to be the pilot in the Wright brothers' airplane? Why or why not?

2. **(a) Recall:** What kind of shop do the Wright brothers have? **(b) Infer:** What skills would they use in their work? **(c) Apply:** In what ways can the skills they use in their shop help them achieve their goal?

3. **(a) Recall:** In what year do the Wright brothers make their first successful airplane flight? **(b) Speculate:** What would their reaction be to airplanes and jets of today? **(c) Generalize:** What statement can you make about the Wright brothers' contribution to air travel?

4. **(a) Support:** What details in "Wilbur Wright and Orville Wright" reveal that the authors admire the Wright brothers? **(b) Evaluate:** Do you think the Wright brothers earned their fame? Why or why not?

Rosemary and Stephen Vincent Benét

Rosemary (1898–1962) and Stephen Vincent Benét (1898–1943)

This husband-and-wife team wrote a poetry collection, entitled *A Book of Americans*, from which "Wilbur Wright and Orville Wright" is taken. Rosemary Benét was a frequent contributor to many important magazines, including *The New Yorker*. Stephen Vincent Benét won the Pulitzer Prize for Poetry—twice!

Dream Dust

LANGSTON HUGHES

Gather out of star-dust

Earth-dust,

Cloud-dust,

Storm-dust,

5 And splinters of hail,

One handful of dream-dust

Not for sale.

Langston Hughes

(1902–1967)

As a young man, Langston Hughes traveled to Africa and Europe as part of the crew on merchant ships. When he returned to the United States, he settled in Harlem, a section of New York City. Hughes is best known for his work during the Harlem Renaissance—a period during the late 1920s and early 1930s when African American literature, visual arts, and performing arts flourished.

Review and Assess

Thinking About the Selection

1. **Respond:** To whom would you recommend this poem?
2. **(a) Recall:** In "Dream Dust," what are three kinds of dust that are mentioned? **(b) Interpret:** Why does the speaker mention these different kinds of dust? **(c) Synthesize:** What is dream dust made of?
3. **(a) Infer:** Why should at least one handful of dream dust not be for sale? **(b) Apply:** Explain how the message of this poem applies to the Wright brothers or someone else who has made a contribution to progress.

Review and Assess

Literary Analysis

Stanzas

1. Prepare a chart like the one shown to write the main idea for each stanza of these two poems: "Wilbur Wright and Orville Wright" and "Adventures of Isabel."

Stanza	Main Idea
1.	
2.	

Comparing Literary Works

2. In what ways are the stanzas of "I'll Stay" different from the stanzas of "Adventures of Isabel" and "Wilbur Wright and Orville Wright"?
3. Which poem has stanzas of irregular length?
4. What is the effect of the short stanzas in this poem?

Reading Strategy

Interpret Meaning

5. Make a chart like the one here to show interpretations of **figurative language.** Add three more examples of figurative language.

	"I'll Stay"	"Wilbur Wright and Orville Wright"	"Dream Dust"
Word or phrase	You must be the Sun!	not till Man forgets his wings,	One handful of dream-dust/Not for sale.
Describes, renames, or refers to	The speaker of the poem		
Probably means	The person the speaker is addressing is bright and warm		

6. Find three examples of words from the selections that have **multiple meanings.** Explain how each word is used and how the surrounding text makes the meaning clear.

Extending Understanding

7. **Social Studies Connection:** Identify three figures from American history that you would suggest as subjects of poems, and explain why.

Quick Review

A **stanza** is a group of lines of poetry, usually similar in length and pattern and separated by spaces. To review stanzas, see page 245.

Figurative language is language that is not meant to be interpreted literally. Words with **multiple meanings** have different meanings in different situations. To review strategies for interpreting meaning, see page 245.

 Take It to the Net
www.phschool.com
Take the interactive self-test online to check your understanding of these selections.

Integrate Language Skills

Vocabulary Development Lesson

Word Analysis: Latin Suffix -ous

The Latin suffix -ous means "having the qualities of " or "full of." Define each word below. Then, write the name of someone or something that fits each word. Explain your answers.

1. courageous **2.** dangerous **3.** virtuous

Concept Development: Antonyms

Antonyms are words with opposite meanings. Write the antonym of each vocabulary word.

1. ravenous: a. greedy, b. full, c. angry

2. cavernous: a. cramped, b. fast,
c. comfortable

3. rancor: a. comfort, b. exhaustion,
c. affection

4. grant: a. spend, b. harm, c. deny

Spelling Strategy

You cannot hear the *o* in -*ous*, but remember to include it when you spell words ending with this suffix. Copy the following paragraph, correcting -*ous* words that are incorrectly spelled. Use a dictionary to check your work.

The clown was wearing an outrageus costume. The whole costume party was very mysterios. The food, however, was scrumptius, and the decorations were luxuriuus.

Next, list at least five more words that end in -*ous*. Write the five words, but misspell at least two. Exchange papers with a classmate, and correct the spelling errors you each have introduced.

Grammar Lesson

Adjective or Adverb?

Though many adverbs end in -*ly*, not all words that end in -*ly* are adverbs.

Adverb: *quietly* ate   **Adjective:** *ugly* toad

Sometimes, the same word may be used as either an adjective or an adverb.

Adverb: worked *hard*   **Adjective:** *hard* work

	Answer the Question	Modify or Describe
Adjectives	Which? What kind? How many?	Nouns and pronouns
Adverbs	How? When? Where? To what extent?	Verbs, adjectives, and adverbs

Practice Copy the italicized words, identifying them as adjectives or adverbs. Then, tell what question each word answers and the part of speech of the word it modifies.

1. Isabel smiled *happily*.

2. The *silly* man left.

3. Bears move *fast*!

4. That bear is *fast*.

5. That was a *close* call.

Writing Application Write a paragraph about a confident, determined person. Use the words *confidently, early, straight, late,* and *last*. Explain whether you used each word as an adjective or an adverb.

W̶G̶ Prentice Hall Writing and Grammar Connection: Chapter 16, Section 2

Writing Lesson

Response to a Poem

The form of writing you choose for responding to literature depends on your audience and purpose. Choose a form of writing and use it to write a response to one of the poems in this group.

Prewriting Look at the possible audiences, purposes, and forms shown below. Then, pick a poem, identify your audience and purpose, and choose the form for your response.

Possible Audiences, Purposes, and Forms

Audience	Purpose	Form
Classmates	Tell them why they will like the poem	Review
Poet	Find out his or her reasons for writing	Letter
Teacher	Explain why I think the poem is or is not a good poem	Brief essay

Drafting Follow the format and conventions for the form of writing you choose. If you write a letter to an author, use a formal letter format (see p. R14). If you are writing an essay, begin with an introduction that states your main point. Then, follow with a series of body paragraphs, each on a single subpoint.

Revising Evaluate the language level of your response. In a letter to a friend, contractions and slang are acceptable. In a letter to an author or an essay for your teacher, use formal language—avoid contractions and slang.

Prentice Hall Writing and Grammar Connection: Chapter 12, Section 2

Extension Activities

Listening and Speaking With a partner, plan an **interview** with one of the Wright brothers. Ask questions from a particular point of view. For example, a contemporary pilot might ask how much the plane weighed.

1. Develop a list of questions to be asked.
2. Organize the questions into categories.
3. Do research to find the answers.
4. Act out the interview.

Research and Technology Make a **timeline** that shows major events in the history of flight—from the time the Wright brothers flew at Kitty Hawk to today. Combine text with electronic or visual displays in your presentation.

 **Take It to the Net** www.phschool.com

Go online for an additional research activity using the Internet.

Cause-and-Effect Articles

About Cause-and-Effect Articles

Exposition is writing that informs or explains. A **cause-and-effect article** explains the circumstances leading to an event or a situation. To get the most information from a cause-and-effect article, look for the following:

- a clear explanation of one or more causes or one or more effects
- a thorough presentation of facts, statistics, and other details that support each explanation
- transitions that clearly indicate the connections among the details

We read cause-and-effect articles to learn about events and their causes in politics, society, and the sciences. Such articles may be found in many newspapers and magazines, and in your textbooks.

Reading Strategy

Analyze Causes and Effects

Ancient peoples used fables, myths, and legends to explain events, but today we look for **causes**—the reasons behind events—and **effects**—the results produced by causes. As you read a cause-and-effect essay, first identify the topic event or effect—such as the decrease in the population of manatees—and then identify the causes and effects presented by the writer. Note the listed causes and effects in the chart below before you read "Gentle Giants in Trouble." As you read, notice how the author presents the causes and effects to the reader.

Manatee Cause-and-Effect Chart	
Causes	**Effects**
Construction	Manatees' feeding grounds disappeared
Pollution	Manatees injured or killed
Power boats	Manatees injured or killed

Gentle Giants in Trouble

Ross Bankson

They have no natural enemies, but they are in trouble anyway. West Indian manatees—large, gentle marine mammals—are in danger because of people…

Some manatee feeding grounds have disappeared, filled in for construction projects. Other feeding grounds have been damaged by pollution, which becomes worse as the number of people grows. Discarded plastic objects floating in waterways can kill a manatee that swallows them.

Causes are not necessarily always listed before effects in an article. The author begins his article with an effect—the endangerment of manatees—before giving the broad cause—people.

Boaters create the greatest hazard for West Indian manatees in the shallow water that the animals prefer. The slow-moving manatees often cannot get away from speeding boats. In a collision with a boat, a manatee may be killed or injured by the force of the hit or by cuts from the propeller. Of some 1,500 manatees in Florida today, nearly all adults bear scars from run-ins with propellers.

The good news for the West Indian manatee is this: People can help as well as harm. Many in fact are working to save manatees. Some Florida car owners pay extra money for a "Save the Manatee" license plate. By doing so they help fund the state's manatee protection program and other programs for environmental education. Florida laws regulate boating in areas where manatees live. Other laws protect the animal as an endangered species.

Still, the experts say, even more safeguards are needed. The manatee population is shrinking. "With public support," says Judith Valee, "we can bring the species back from the brink of extinction."

> Next, the writer presents the various reasons—or causes—for the manatee's near extinction.

> The last paragraphs encourage readers to support a solution to the problem—which is part of the writer's purpose.

Check Your Comprehension

1. What is the main cause of danger to the manatee?
2. Why are power boats so hazardous to manatees?
3. What is some good news for the manatee population?

Applying the Reading Strategy

Analyze Causes and Effects

4. How many causes for the decrease in the manatee population are listed in the article? Which is the greatest hazard? Why?
5. What might boaters do to lessen the effect of their boats on manatees? How could more public support cause the manatee population to grow?
6. What kind of magazine or textbook might you find this article in? In what other classes will reading require you to identify cause and effect? Explain your choice.

Activity

Find Cause-and-Effect Articles

Cause-and-effect articles are often found in periodicals—newspapers, magazines, and other printed materials—that are published at regular intervals, or periods. Periodicals may be issued daily, weekly, monthly, or at any other regular interval.

Choose a topic that interests you and find two articles about it that address cause and effect. Either conduct a search on the Internet, or go to the library and look in a periodical index such as the *Readers' Guide to Periodical Literature*. The *Readers' Guide* covers all types of periodicals. A sample listing from the *Readers' Guide* for a topic appears here. Note that the entries tell exactly where the article appears and when it was published. With this information, you can find the article in the library.

SAMPLE *READERS' GUIDE* ENTRY

Fruit ———————————————————— Main subject heading

　　See also
　　Cooking—Fruit ——————————— Cross references
　　individual names of fruit
　Fruit for all seasons. E.W. Stiles il *Nat Hist* —— Author of article
　　93:42—53 Ag '84 ——————————— Title of article
　Fruit selection. N. Nevins. il *South Living*
　　19:144
　　　　　　　　　　　——————————— Name of Periodical

Comparing Informational Materials

Cause-and-Effect Essays

Review the cause-and-effect articles you have found, and compare them. Note that the article on the previous page was organized around a single broad cause—people—and a single general effect—manatees are endangered. Below are two more common ways to organize cause-and-effect essays. Decide which kind of organization your articles use, and track the causes and effects in organizers like these.

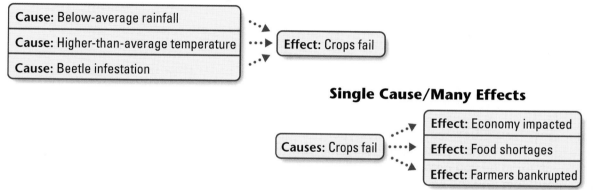

Many Causes/Single Effect

| Cause: Below-average rainfall |
| Cause: Higher-than-average temperature | ···▶ | **Effect: Crops fail** |
| Cause: Beetle infestation |

Single Cause/Many Effects

	Effect: Economy impacted
Causes: Crops fail	···▶	**Effect: Food shortages**
	Effect: Farmers bankrupted

Writing WORKSHOP

Exposition: Problem-Solution Essay

A **problem-solution essay** identifies and explains a problem and then presents one or more possible solutions to it. In this writing workshop, you will write about a problem that concerns you.

Assignment Criteria. Your problem-solution essay should have the following characteristics:

- a clearly stated problem and an explanation of the situation
- step-by-step solutions
- evidence that supports the suggested solution
- consistent, logical organization
- transitions that show the relationships between ideas

See the Rubric on page 261 for the criteria on which your problem-solution essay may be assessed.

Prewriting

Choose a topic. Scan a newspaper for stories about community problems that need to be solved. They might involve school policies, the environment, or your neighborhood. Make a list of problems. Brainstorm for solutions to each problem. Jot down all ideas. Then, review your list and choose a problem for which you have identified at least one practical or workable solution.

Gather details. Gather details that make clear what the causes and effects of the problem are as well as details that show why or how your solution will work.

Gathering Details

1. Use current newspaper and magazine articles to gather statistics and examples.

2. Interview people to find out how they are affected by the problem.

3. If possible, interview experts who can comment on your proposed solution.

Consider your audience. To achieve your purpose of persuading others to accept your proposed solution, keep your audience—your readers—in mind as you gather details. Choose details that will show how the problem and the solution affect your audience.

Student Model

Before you begin drafting your problem-solution composition, read this student model and review the characteristics of effective problem solving.

Shamus Cunningham
Daytona Beach, Florida

Panther Problems

The Florida Panther is one of our state's most interesting animals, but sadly it is also one of the rarest. There are currently only about sixty panthers in Florida. Panther numbers don't grow because of decreasing panther habitat and increasing traffic in areas populated by panthers. To save the panther from extinction, we must make sure there is enough land set aside for panthers to live on and that they have safe ways to move through the areas in which they live.

A grown panther needs approximately 275 square miles to roam and hunt. If too many adult panthers occupy the same territory, they fight and injure or kill one another. In addition, panthers hunt other wild animals, such as deer, for food. For an area to be a good habitat for a panther, the area must have enough prey animals for the panther to hunt. Because of development, the "wild" areas that panthers used to call home are now filled with houses and stores, rather than food and hiding places. It is unlikely that development will suddenly stop or even slow down. Therefore, experts must plan ahead and set aside one or two large protected areas where panthers can live, rather than many smaller areas.

Loss of habitat isn't the only problem caused by development. More houses mean more roads, and that means more problems for panthers. According to the Florida Freshwater Fish and Game Commission, 42% of panther deaths between 1973 and 1997 were road kills. Underpasses have been built to allow panthers and other animals to cross a territory without crossing a road. In the area known as Alligator Alley, one large underpass was built. Since then, there have been no reported killings of panthers by cars. The success of the underpass in this area shows that we can take steps to protect the panthers without completely halting progress.

The two solutions suggested here would allow the needs of humans and panthers to be met. The solutions are costly, but they have been proven effective, and they are the least disruptive to the human community. Saving the Florida panther is a complex issue, but if we just put our heads together, I'm confident we can make the right decisions.

> Because there are two main parts to the problem, a two-step solution is suggested.

> The problem is explained in more detail so that readers will have the information they need to understand the value of the solution being proposed.

> Transition words such as *because* and *therefore* show cause-and-effect relationships.

> Each part of the problem and its solution is addressed in a separate paragraph. Statistics provide evidence that a solution is needed and that the proposed solution is the right one.

Drafting

State the problem and solution. In the beginning of your composition, establish the problem and state your proposed solution. Then, make your problem clear by further explaining the situation. After you have explained the problem, develop your solution with examples and details.

Organize paragraphs to show causes and effects. When you explain the problem, show its causes and effects. Then, as you present each step in your proposed solution, show the effect it will have on the problem in general or on the next step that needs to be taken. Finally show the effects of your proposed solution.

Model: Emphasize Causes and Effects

Because of development, the "wild" areas that panthers used to call home are now filled with houses and stores, rather than food and hiding places. It is unlikely that development will suddenly stop or slow down. Therefore, experts must plan ahead and set aside one or two large protected areas.

> Causes are underlined in red. Effects are underlined in blue.

Revising

Revise for order. Make sure you present each step or part of your solution in the order in which tasks must be completed. Circle any step that is out of order, and use an arrow to show where it belongs. Add transition words such as *next, in addition,* or *after* to reinforce the order of steps and the connection between the steps or parts of your solution.

Revise for sentence structure. Review your composition to identify and correct run-on sentences. These are two separate and complete thoughts put together without a connecting word or punctuation mark.

Run-on: The traffic is terrible at the crossing of Main Street and Third Avenue I think something should be done about it.

There are several ways to correct run-on sentences.

- **Create two sentences:** The traffic is terrible at the crossing of Main Street and Third Avenue. I think something should be done about it.
- **Use a semicolon or a connecting word with a comma:** The traffic is terrible at the crossing, and I think something should be done about it.
- **Make one of the ideas dependent on the other one:** Because the traffic is terrible at the crossing, I think something should be done about it.

Compare the model and the nonmodel. Why is the model more effective than the nonmodel?

Nonmodel	Model
The Florida Panther is one of our state's most interesting animals it is also one of the rarest. There are currently only about sixty panthers in Florida. Panther numbers don't grow because of decreasing panther habitat and increasing traffic in areas populated by panthers. To save the panther from extinction, we must make sure there is enough land set aside for panthers to live on they to have safe ways to move through the areas in which they live.	The Florida Panther is one of our state's most interesting animals, but, sadly, it is also one of the rarest. There are currently only about sixty panthers in Florida. Panther numbers don't grow because of decreasing panther habitat and increasing traffic in areas populated by panthers. To save the panther from extinction, we must make sure there is enough land set aside for panthers to live on and that they have safe ways to move through the areas in which they live.

Publishing and Presenting

Choose one of the following ways to share your writing with classmates or a wider audience.

Present a proposal. Use your problem-solution composition as the basis of a presentation.

Submit your paper for publication. Send a clean copy to your school paper or local newspaper. Enclose a cover letter.

WG Prentice Hall Writing and Grammar Connection: Chapter 9 and Chapter 10

Speaking Connection

To learn more about presenting a problem-solution speech, see the **Listening and Speaking Workshop: Present a Proposal,** p. 262.

Rubric for Self-Assessment

Evaluate your problem-solution composition, using the following criteria and rating scale:

Criteria	Rating Scale				
	Not very				Very
How clearly is the problem stated and explained?	1	2	3	4	5
How organized are the steps or parts of the solution?	1	2	3	4	5
How strong and convincing is the support?	1	2	3	4	5
How effectively are transitions used to connect ideas?	1	2	3	4	5
How consistently does the writer avoid run-on sentences?	1	2	3	4	5

Listening and Speaking WORKSHOP

Presenting a Problem-Solution Proposal

A **problem-solution proposal** is a formal plan that suggests a course of action for solving a problem or improving a situation. A problem-solution proposal shares many of the characteristics of a problem-solution essay. (To review the guidelines for a problem-solution essay, see pp. 258–259.) The following strategies will help you present a spoken proposal persuasively and effectively.

Prepare Your Proposal

The following strategies will help you organize and prepare your presentation.

Organize your ideas. First, identify the problem and list the circumstances that you think cause the problem. Then, describe your proposed solution and list the reasons why you think it will work. Finally, add notes with statistics, examples, and other details that provide evidence for your points.

Establish connections and provide evidence. Use visual aids to show connections or provide evidence. A diagram can show the connection between the arrangement of streets and the need for a traffic light. A bar graph can show the connections between amounts. Look at the sample bar graph on this page. Notice how it captures the problem.

If you have access to a computer, use a presentation program to create your visual aids. As an alternative, you can draw them.

Deliver Your Proposal

Use delivery techniques to make your presentation more persuasive.

Adjust your speaking rate. Speak slowly enough that your audience will understand each word. Adjust your speaking rate by pausing after you make an important point. For example, pause for a few seconds after you state the problem to give the audience time to think about the problem. Pause more frequently as you present visuals. Your audience needs the time to "read" the visual as you speak.

Use gestures. Point to items on your visuals as you present the parts they are related to. When presenting a list of causes or steps, count them off on your fingers to focus your audience's attention on each item.

Activity:
Proposal to Solve a Local Problem

Prepare a proposal to solve a problem or improve a situation in your neighborhood or community. Present your proposal to a group of classmates. Use at least one visual aid.

Problem: Accidents have increased each year.

Solution: Replace stop signs with a traffic light.

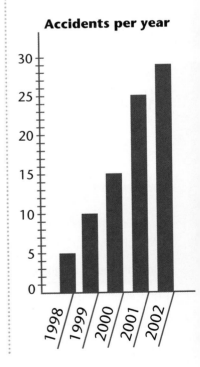

Accidents per year

Assessment WORKSHOP

Identifying the Main Idea

The reading sections of some tests require you to read a passage and answer multiple-choice questions about main ideas. Use the following strategies to help you answer such questions:

- Look for a sentence that ties together or unifies the other sentences.
- Avoid making the assumption that the first sentence of a paragraph always contains the main idea.

Test-Taking Strategies

- Read the questions before reading the passage.
- If you are unsure of an answer, try to eliminate items you are sure are incorrect.

Sample Test Item

Identify the Stated Main Idea A main idea is often stated in a topic sentence that summarizes the passage. The topic sentence may be located anywhere in the passage. In a test question, the correct answer choice sometimes restates the topic sentence in different words. Look at the following passage and question:

Every year hundreds of powwows are held all over the United States and Canada. A powwow is a celebration of Native American heritage. With drummers setting the rhythm, dancers compete in various categories, including fancy dances, grass dances, and jingle dances. Between the contests, dances called intertribals are open to anyone.

1. What is the main idea of this passage?
   A Dancers compete in different categories.
   B A powwow celebrates Native American heritage.
   C Every year hundreds of powwows are held.
   D Intertribals are open to anyone.

Answers and Explanations

A and D are details. C is a general comment, not the main idea. *B* is the main idea.

Practice

Apply the Strategies Answer the questions based on this passage.

While Maria's neighbors were on vacation, she went to their apartment every morning to take care of the cats. First, she put out fresh food and water. Next, she cleaned the litter box. Then, Maria played with the cats. Taking care of cats was the best job she ever had.

Maria hoped to convince her parents to let her have a cat. "You would not have extra work," she argued. " I can take care of a cat by myself."

1. What is the main idea of the first paragraph?
   A Maria went to her neighbor's apartment.
   B She put out fresh food and water for the cats.
   C Taking care of cats was her best job.
   D Maria played with the cats.
2. What is the main idea of the second paragraph?
   A Maria likes cats.
   B Her parents would not let her have a cat.
   C Cats make good pets.
   D Maria believes she can take care of a cat.

Seeing It Through

Emigrants Crossing the Plains, 1867, oil on canvas, 60 × 96 in. Albert Bierstadt, National Cowboy Hall of Fame Collection, Oklahoma City

Exploring the Theme

The travelers in this painting are choosing a new road. It will take all their strength and determination to see their journey through to the end. The stories, poems, and essays in this unit deal with the struggles and triumphs that story characters and real people encounter when they choose a new path in life.

Reading about other persevering characters and real people who "see it through" to reach their goals and dreams may help you look at some of your own experiences in a new light.

◀ **Critical Viewing** What details of this picture indicate that the end of the journey will be worth the struggle of reaching it? **[Analyze]**

Why Read Literature?

You will want to read the selections in this unit to learn how real people and story characters "see it through" difficult and challenging situations to reach their goals. Look ahead at some of the other purposes you will have for reading these selections.

1 Read for the love of literature.

After English, Spanish is the most commonly spoken language in the United States. Almost 20 million people in the U.S. claim Spanish as their native language. Experience the beauty of Spanish words in Sandra Cisneros's poem **"Abuelito Who,"** page 300.

Walt Whitman was turned down by every publisher he approached with *Leaves of Grass,* his now famous book of poetry. Read poetry from this book that changed the face of American poetry: **"The Open Road,"** page 302.

2 Read for information.

Jim Morris went from being a high-school science teacher and baseball coach to a major-league player, supported all the way by his hometown fans. Learn how Jim Morris realized his dream in **"Throw and Tell,"** page 333.

Jackie Robinson began his professional sports career as a football player before becoming a baseball player. In 1941, he played for the Los Angeles Bulldogs of the Pacific Coast League. Find out why this former pro football player is a baseball legend when you read **"Jackie Robinson: Justice at Last,"** page 325.

3 Read to be inspired.

As a boy, Abraham Lincoln attended school only when he could be spared from chores at home. His total days of formal schooling add up to approximately one year. Learn more about the early life of this inspiring president in **"A Backwoods Boy,"** page 316.

Maya Angelou toured Europe and Africa performing in the musical *Porgy and Bess.* She read her poetry at former president William Clinton's inauguration and has won a Grammy award. Read the brave words of this actress, poet, and songwriter in the poem **"Life Doesn't Frighten Me,"** page 304.

 Take It to the Net

Visit the Web site for online instruction and activities related to each selection in this unit.

www.phschool.com

How to Read Literature

Strategies to Construct Meaning

Constructing is building. In this unit, you will learn to construct, or build, meaning from the pieces provided in the literature. You will learn to construct meaning using the following strategies.

1. Determine main ideas.

Main ideas are the building blocks of meaning. In this unit, you will learn how to clearly identify and restate main ideas and how to put them together to construct meaning.

2. Compare and contrast characters.

A character's qualities will have more meaning when you compare and contrast one character with another. The similarities and differences will help you recognize the strengths and weaknesses in each. In this unit, you will meet a wide variety of characters that represent a range of good and bad qualities. As you notice what is alike and different about characters, consider why the author chose particular traits for individual characters and how these characters add to the story.

3. Predict.

To predict, you must make logical guesses about what will happen based on what you know. Predicting helps you construct meaning by focusing your attention on the significance of details and events.

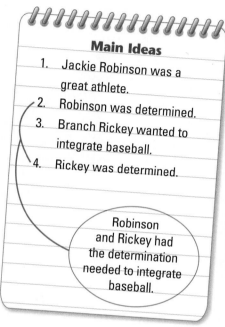

Main Ideas
1. Jackie Robinson was a great athlete.
2. Robinson was determined.
3. Branch Rickey wanted to integrate baseball.
4. Rickey was determined.

Robinson and Rickey had the determination needed to integrate baseball.

Details Facts Events ····▶ Prediction ····▶ NEW details, facts, events ····▶ NEW Prediction ····▶

4. Draw inferences.

Drawing inferences is like "reading between the lines." When you draw inferences, you draw conclusions based on the details the author provides. To draw inferences,

- Consider the details about characters or events the author includes or does not include.

- Think about what this choice of details might mean.

- Read ahead to find out if your inference is supported.

As you read the selections in this unit, review the reading strategies and look at the notes in the side columns. Use the suggestions to apply the strategies for reading critically.

Prepare to Read

Lob's Girl ◆ The Tiger Who Would Be King
The Lion and the Bulls

 Take It to the Net

Visit www.phschool.com
for interactive activities
and instruction related to
these selections, including

- background
- graphic organizers
- literary elements
- reading strategies

Preview

Connecting to the Literature

Through their experiences, the characters in "Lob's Girl," "The Tiger Who Would Be King," and "The Lion and the Bulls" learn—sometimes too late—lessons about love, power, and working together. Think of experiences in your own life that have taught you lessons similar to those learned by the characters.

Background

In "Lob's Girl," a dog travels from Liverpool to Cornwall, England. Liverpool is a city in England. Cornwall is a seaside village in England. To get from one to the other, the dog must travel more than 400 miles.

Literary Analysis

Foreshadowing

Foreshadowing is a word with two parts: *fore*, meaning "before," and *shadow*, meaning "image." **Foreshadowing** is a literary device in which the author gives clues to hint at what might happen later in a story. Authors give hints by including comments made by the narrator, experiences or feelings of characters, or events in the story. In "Lob's Girl," Joan Aiken includes this description to foreshadow that something bad is about to happen:

> The wind was howling through the shrouds of boats drawn up on the Hard.

As you read, look for hints and consider what they foreshadow.

Comparing Literary Works

Some examples of foreshadowing are more obvious than others. For example, by using the title "The Tiger Who Would Be King" rather than "The Tiger Who Is King," the author makes it obvious that the tiger probably will not succeed in becoming king. As you read, compare the different foreshadowing techniques and consider these focus questions:

1. Which story contains more examples of foreshadowing?
2. Which author uses more obvious examples of foreshadowing?

Reading Strategy

Comparing and Contrasting Characters

Analyzing characters' behaviors or personalities can help you understand them. One way to examine characters is to **compare and contrast** them—identify similarities in behavior and personality. When you examine differences in behavior and personality, you contrast them. As you read, use a Venn diagram like this one to compare and contrast characters.

Character 1

Unique qualities or actions

Similar qualities or actions

Unique qualities or actions

Character 2

Vocabulary Development

decisively (di sī′ siv lē′) *adv.* with determination (p. 271)

atone (a tōn′) *v.* make up for a wrong (p. 271)

resolutions (rez′ ə loo′ shənz) *n.* intentions; things decided (p. 273)

melancholy (mel′ ən käl′ ē) *adj.* sad; gloomy (p. 273)

intimated (in′ tə māt′ id) *v.* hinted; made known (p. 275)

aggrieved (ə grēvd′) *adj.* offended; wronged (p. 278)

prowled (prould) *v.* crawled quietly and secretly (p. 282)

repulse (ri puls′) *v.* drive back; repel an attack (p. 283)

slanderous (slan′ der əs′) *adj.* untrue and damaging (p. 284)

Lob's Girl

Joan Aiken

Some people choose their dogs, and some dogs choose their people. The Pengelly family had no say in the choosing of Lob; he came to them in the second way, and very <u>decisively</u>.

It began on the beach, the summer when Sandy was five, Don, her older brother, twelve, and the twins were three. Sandy was really Alexandra, because her grandmother had a beautiful picture of a queen in a diamond tiara and high collar of pearls. It hung by Granny Pearce's kitchen sink and was as familiar as the doormat. When Sandy was born everyone agreed that she was the living spit of the picture, and so she was called Alexandra and Sandy for short.

On this summer day she was lying peacefully reading a comic and not keeping an eye on the twins, who didn't need it because they were occupied in seeing which of them could wrap the most seaweed around the other one's legs. Father—Bert Pengelly—and Don were up on the Hard painting the bottom boards of the boat in which Father went fishing for pilchards. And Mother—Jean Pengelly—was getting ahead with making the Christmas puddings because she never felt easy in her mind if they weren't made and safely put away by the end of August. As usual, each member of the family was happily getting on with his or her own affairs. Little did they guess how soon this state of things would be changed by the large new member who was going to erupt into their midst.

Sandy rolled onto her back to make sure that the twins were not climbing on slippery rocks or getting cut off by the tide. At the same moment a large body struck her forcibly in the midriff and she was covered by flying sand. Instinctively she shut her eyes and felt the sand being wiped off her face by something that seemed like a warm, rough, damp flannel. She opened her eyes and looked. It was a tongue. Its owner was a large and bouncy young Alsatian, or German shepherd, with topaz eyes, black-tipped prick ears, a thick, soft coat, and a bushy black-tipped tail.

"*Lob!*" shouted a man farther up the beach. "Lob, come here!"

But Lob, as if trying to <u>atone</u> for the surprise he had given her, went on licking the sand off Sandy's face, wagging his tail so hard while he kept on knocking up more clouds of sand. His owner, a gray-haired man with a limp, walked over as quickly as he could and seized him by the collar.

"I hope he didn't give you a fright?" the man said to Sandy. "He meant it in play—he's only young."

"Oh, no, I think he's *beautiful*," said Sandy truly. She picked up a bit of driftwood and threw it. Lob, whisking easily out of his master's grip, was after it like a sand-colored bullet. He came back with the

decisively (di sī′ siv lē′)
adv. with determination

Literary Analysis
Foreshadowing Based on this hint, what do you think is going to happen?

atone (a tōn′) *v.* make up for a wrong

✔**Reading Check**

How does Sandy meet Lob?

◀ **Critical Viewing** What clue does this picture give you about the identity of "Lob" in the title? **[Connect]**

stick, beaming, and gave it to Sandy. At the same time he gave himself, though no one else was aware of this at the time. But with Sandy, too, it was love at first sight, and when, after a lot more stick-throwing, she and the twins joined Father and Don to go home for tea, they cast many a backward glance at Lob being led firmly away by his master.

"I wish we could play with him every day." Tess sighed.

"Why can't we?" said Tim.

Sandy explained. "Because Mr. Dodsworth, who owns him, is from Liverpool, and he is only staying at the Fisherman's Arms till Saturday."

"Is Liverpool a long way off?"

"Right at the other end of England from Cornwall, I'm afraid."

It was a Cornish fishing village where the Pengelly family lived, with rocks and cliffs and a strip of beach and a little round harbor, and palm trees growing in the gardens of the little whitewashed stone houses. The village was approached by a narrow, steep, twisting hill- road, and guarded by a notice that said LOW GEAR FOR 1½ MILES, DANGEROUS TO CYCLISTS.

The Pengelly children went home to scones with Cornish cream and jam, thinking they had seen the last of Lob. But they were much mistaken. The whole family was playing cards by the fire in the front room after supper when there was a loud thump and a crash of china in the kitchen.

"My Christmas puddings!" exclaimed Jean, and ran out.

"Did you put TNT in them, then?" her husband said.

But it was Lob, who, finding the front door shut, had gone around to the back and bounced in through the open kitchen window, where the puddings were cooling on the sill. Luckily only the smallest was knocked down and broken.

Lob stood on his hind legs and plastered Sandy's face with licks. Then he did the same for the twins, who shrieked with joy.

"Where does this friend of yours come from?" inquired Mr. Pengelly.

"He's staying at the Fisherman's Arms—I mean his owner is."

"Then he must go back there. Find a bit of string, Sandy, to tie to his collar."

▼ **Critical Viewing** What qualities of Lob do you see in this dog? **[Analyze]**

That's My Dog (German Shepherd) Jim Killen, Voyageur Art

"I wonder how he found his way here," Mrs. Pengelly said, when the reluctant Lob had been led whining away and Sandy had explained about their afternoon's game on the beach. "Fisherman's Arms is right around the other side of the harbor."

Lob's owner scolded him and thanked Mr. Pengelly for bringing him back. Jean Pengelly warned the children that they had better not encourage Lob any more if they met him on the beach, or it would only lead to more trouble. So they dutifully took no notice of him the next day until he spoiled their good <u>resolutions</u> by dashing up to them with joyful barks, wagging his tail so hard that he winded Tess and knocked Tim's legs from under him.

They had a happy day, playing on the sand.

The next day was Saturday. Sandy had found out that Mr. Dodsworth was to catch the half-past-nine train. She went out secretly, down to the station, nodded to Mr. Hoskins, the station-master, who wouldn't dream of charging any local for a platform ticket, and climbed up on the footbridge that led over the tracks. She didn't want to be seen, but she did want to see. She saw Mr. Dodsworth get on the train, accompanied by an unhappy-looking Lob with drooping ears and tail. Then she saw the train slide away out of sight around the next headland, with a <u>melancholy</u> wail that sounded like Lob's last good-bye.

Sandy wished she hadn't had the idea of coming to the station. She walked home miserably, with her shoulders hunched and her hands in her pockets. For the rest of the day she was so cross and unlike herself that Tess and Tim were quite surprised, and her mother gave her a dose of senna.

A week passed. Then, one evening, Mrs. Pengelly and the younger children were in the front room playing snakes and ladders. Mr. Pengelly and Don had gone fishing on the evening tide. If your father is a fisherman, he will never be home at the same time from one week to the next.

Suddenly, history repeating itself, there was a crash from the kitchen. Jean Pengelly leaped up, crying, "My blackberry jelly!" She and the children had spent the morning picking and the afternoon boiling fruit.

But Sandy was ahead of her mother. With flushed cheeks and eyes like stars she had darted into the kitchen, where she and Lob were hugging one another in a frenzy of joy. About a yard of his tongue was out, and he was licking every part of her that he could reach.

"Good heavens!" exclaimed Jean. "How in the world did *he* get here?"

"He must have walked," said Sandy. "Look at his feet."

They were worn, dusty, and tarry. One had a cut on the pad.

Literary Analysis
Foreshadowing What upcoming event might Mrs. Pengelly's questioning statement foreshadow?

resolutions
(rez´ ə lōō´ shənz) n. intentions; things decided

melancholy (mel´ ən käl´ ē) *adj.* sad; gloomy

✓**Reading Check**
What happens the week after Sandy watched the train pull out of the town station?

"They ought to be bathed," said Jean Pengelly. "Sandy, run a bowl of warm water while I get disinfectant."

"What'll we do about him, Mother?" said Sandy anxiously.

Mrs. Pengelly looked at her daughter's pleading eyes and sighed.

"He must go back to his owner, of course," she said, making her voice firm. "Your dad can get the address from the Fisherman's tomorrow, and phone him or send a telegram. In the meantime he'd better have a long drink and a good meal."

Lob was very grateful for the drink and the meal, and made no objection to having his feet washed. Then he flopped down on the hearthrug and slept in front of the fire they had lit because it was a cold, wet evening, with his head on Sandy's feet. He was a very tired dog. He had walked all the way from Liverpool to Cornwall, which is more than four hundred miles.

The next day Mr. Pengelly phoned Lob's owner, and the following morning Mr. Dodsworth arrived off the night train, decidedly put out, to take his pet home. That parting was worse than the first. Lob whined, Don walked out of the house, the twins burst out crying, and Sandy crept up to her bedroom afterward and lay with her face pressed into the quilt, feeling as if she were bruised all over.

Jean Pengelly took them all into Plymouth to see the circus on the next day and the twins cheered up a little, but even the hour's ride in the train each way and the Liberty horses and performing seals could not cure Sandy's sore heart.

She need not have bothered, though. In ten days' time Lob was back—limping this time, with a torn ear and a patch missing out of his furry coat, as if he had met and tangled with an enemy or two in the course of his four-hundred-mile walk.

Bert Pengelly rang up Liverpool again. Mr. Dodsworth, when he answered, sounded weary. He said, "That dog has already cost me two days that I can't spare away from my work—plus endless time in police stations and drafting newspaper advertisements. I'm too old for these ups and downs. I think we'd better face the fact, Mr. Pengelly, that it's your family he wants to stay with—that is, if you want to have him."

Bert Pengelly gulped. He was not a rich man; and Lob was a pedigreed dog. He said cautiously, "How much would you be asking for him?"

"Good heavens, man, I'm not suggesting I'd sell him to you. You must have him as a gift. Think of the train fares I'll be saving. You'll be doing me a good turn."

"Is he a big eater?" Bert asked doubtfully.

By this time the children, breathless in the background listening to one side of this conversation, had realized what was in the

Reading Strategy
Comparing and Contrasting Characters
Compare and contrast Sandy's and Mr. Dodsworth's feelings about Lob.

wind and were dancing up and down with their hands clasped beseechingly.

"Oh, not for his size," Lob's owner assured Bert. "Two or three pounds of meat a day and some vegetables and gravy and biscuits— he does very well on that."

Alexandra's father looked over the telephone at his daughter's swimming eyes and trembling lips. He reached a decision. "Well, then, Mr. Dodsworth," he said briskly, "we'll accept your offer and thank you very much. The children will be overjoyed and you can be sure Lob has come to a good home. They'll look after him and see he gets enough exercise. But I can tell you," he ended firmly, "if he wants to settle in with us he'll have to learn to eat a lot of fish."

So that was how Lob came to live with the Pengelly family. Everybody loved him and he loved them all. But there was never any question who came first with him. He was Sandy's dog. He slept by her bed and followed her everywhere he was allowed.

Nine years went by, and each summer Mr. Dodsworth came back to stay at the Fisherman's Arms and call on his erstwhile dog. Lob always met him with recognition and dignified pleasure, accompanied him for a walk or two—but showed no signs of wishing to return to Liverpool. His place, he <u>intimated</u>, was definitely with the Pengellys.

In the course of nine years Lob changed less than Sandy. As she went into her teens he became a little slower, a little stiffer, there was a touch of gray on his nose, but he was still a handsome dog. He and Sandy still loved one another devotedly.

One evening in October all the summer visitors had left, and the little fishing town looked empty and secretive. It was a wet, windy dusk. When the children came home from school—even the twins were at high school now, and Don was a full-fledged fisherman— Jean Pengelly said, "Sandy, your Aunt Rebecca says she's lonesome because Uncle Will Hoskins has gone out trawling, and she wants one of you to go and spend the evening with her. You go, dear; you can take your homework with you."

Sandy looked far from enthusiastic.

"Can I take Lob with me?"

"You know Aunt Becky doesn't really like dogs—Oh, very well." Mrs. Pengelly sighed. "I suppose she'll have to put up with him as well as you."

Reluctantly Sandy tidied herself, took her schoolbag, put on the damp raincoat she had just taken off, fastened Lob's lead to his collar, and set off to walk through the dusk to Aunt Becky's cottage, which was five minutes' climb up the steep hill.

The wind was howling through the shrouds of boats drawn up on the Hard.

Reading Strategy
Comparing and Contrasting Characters
Compare Mr. Dodsworth to Mr. Pengelly. What similar quality do their actions show?

intimated (in′ tə māt′ id) v. hinted; made known indirectly

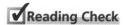**Reading Check**

What does Mr. Dodsworth offer to Mr. Pengelly?

"Put some cheerful music on, do," said Jean Pengelly to the nearest twin. "Anything to drown that wretched sound while I make your dad's supper." So Don, who had just come in, put on some rock music, loud. Which was why the Pengellys did not hear the truck hurtle down the hill and crash against the post office wall a few minutes later.

Dr. Travers was driving through Cornwall with his wife, taking a late holiday before patients began coming down with winter colds and flu. He saw the sign that said STEEP HILL. LOW GEAR FOR $1\frac{1}{2}$ MILES. Dutifully he changed into second gear.

"We must be nearly there," said his wife, looking out of her window. "I noticed a sign on the coast road that said the Fisherman's Arms was two miles. What a narrow, dangerous hill! But the cottages are very pretty—Oh, Frank, stop, *stop*! There's a child, I'm sure it's a child—by the wall over there!"

Dr. Travers jammed on his brakes and brought the car to a stop. A little stream ran down by the road in a shallow stone culvert, and half in the water lay something that looked, in the dusk, like a pile of clothes—or was it the body of the child? Mrs. Travers was out of the car in a flash, but her husband was quicker.

"Don't touch her, Emily!" he said sharply. "She's been hit. Can't be more than a few minutes. Remember that truck that overtook us half a mile back, speeding like the devil? Here, quick, go into that cottage and phone for an ambulance. The girl's in a bad way. I'll stay here and do what I can to stop the bleeding. Don't waste a minute."

Doctors are expert at stopping dangerous bleeding, for they know the right places to press. This Dr. Travers was able to do, but he didn't dare do more; the girl was lying in a queerly crumpled heap, and he guessed she had a number of bones broken and that it would be highly dangerous to move her. He watched her with great concentration, wondering where the truck had got to and what other damage it had done.

Mrs. Travers was very quick. She had seen plenty of accident cases and knew the importance of speed. The first cottage she tried had a phone; in four minutes she was back, and in six an ambulance was wailing down the hill.

Its attendants lifted the child onto a stretcher as carefully as if she were made of fine thistledown. The ambulance sped off to Plymouth—for the local cottage hospital did not take serious accident cases—and Dr. Travers went down to the police station to report what he had done.

He found that the police already knew about the speeding truck—which had suffered from loss of brakes and ended up with

◀ **Critical Viewing** What elements of danger do you see in this picture? **[Analyze]**

Literary Analysis
Foreshadowing What hints does this paragraph contain about events to come?

☑**Reading Check**

What happens to Sandy?

its radiator halfway through the post-office wall. The driver was concussed and shocked, but the police thought he was the only person injured—until Dr. Travers told his tale.

At half-past nine that night Aunt Rebecca Hoskins was sitting by her fire thinking <u>aggrieved</u> thoughts about the inconsiderateness of nieces who were asked to supper and never turned up, when she was startled by a neighbor, who burst in, exclaiming, "Have you heard about Sandy Pengelly, then, Mrs. Hoskins? Terrible thing, poor little soul, and they don't know if she's likely to live. Police have got the truck driver that hit her—ah, it didn't ought to be allowed, speeding through the place like that at umpty miles an hour, they ought to jail him for life—not that that'd be any comfort for poor Bert and Jean."

Horrified, Aunt Rebecca put on a coat and went down to her brother's house. She found the family with white shocked faces; Bert and Jean were about to drive off to the hospital where Sandy had been taken, and the twins were crying bitterly. Lob was nowhere to be seen. But Aunt Rebecca was not interested in dogs; she did not inquire about him.

"Thank the Lord you've come, Beck," said her brother. "Will you stay the night with Don and the twins? Don's out looking for Lob and heaven knows when we'll be back; we may get a bed with Jean's mother in Plymouth."

"Oh, if only I'd never invited the poor child," wailed Mrs. Hoskins. But Bert and Jean hardly heard her.

That night seemed to last forever. The twins cried themselves to sleep. Don came home very late and grim-faced. Bert and Jean sat in a waiting room of the Western Counties Hospital, but Sandy was unconscious, they were told, and she remained so. All that could be done for her was done. She was given transfusions to replace all the blood she had lost. The broken bones were set and put in slings and cradles.

"Is she a healthy girl? Has she a good constitution?" the emergency doctor asked.

"Aye, doctor, she is that," Bert said hoarsely. The lump in Jean's throat prevented her from answering; she merely nodded.

"Then she ought to have a chance. But I won't conceal from you that her condition is very serious, unless she shows signs of coming out from this coma."

But as hour succeeded hour, Sandy showed no signs of recovering consciousness. Her parents sat in the waiting room with haggard faces; sometimes one of them would go to telephone the family at home, or to try to get a little sleep at the home of Granny Pearce, not far away.

At noon next day Dr. and Mrs. Travers went to the Pengelly

aggrieved (ə grēvd´) *adj.* offended; wronged

Reading Strategy
Compare and Contrast Characters How do Bert and Jean act differently during the crisis?

cottage to inquire how Sandy was doing, but the report was gloomy: "Still in a very serious condition." The twins were miserably unhappy. They forgot that they had sometimes called their elder sister bossy and only remembered how often she had shared her pocket money with them, how she read to them and took them for picnics and helped with their homework. Now there was no Sandy, no Mother and Dad, Don went around with a gray, shuttered face, and worse still, there was no Lob.

The Western Counties Hospital is a large one, with dozens of different departments and five or six connected buildings, each with three or four entrances. By that afternoon it became noticeable that a dog seemed to have taken up position outside the hospital, with the fixed intention of getting in. Patiently he would try first one entrance and then another, all the way around, and then begin again. Sometimes he would get a little way inside, following a visitor, but animals were, of course, forbidden, and he was always kindly but firmly turned out again. Sometimes the guard at the main entrance gave him a pat or offered him a bit of sandwich—he looked so wet and beseeching and desperate. But he never ate the sandwich. No one seemed to own him or to know where he came from; Plymouth is a large city and he might have belonged to anybody.

At tea time Granny Pearce came through the pouring rain to bring a flask of hot tea with brandy in it to her daughter and son-in-law. Just as she reached the main entrance the guard was gently but forcibly shoving out a large, agitated, soaking-wet Alsatian dog.

"No, old fellow, you can *not* come in. Hospitals are for people, not for dogs."

"Why, bless me," exclaimed old Mrs. Pearce. "That's Lob! Here, Lob, Lobby boy!"

Lob ran to her, whining. Mrs. Pearce walked up to the desk.

"I'm sorry, madam, you can't bring that dog in here," the guard said.

Mrs. Pearce was a very determined old lady. She looked the porter in the eye.

"Now, see here, young man. That dog has walked twenty miles from St. Killan to get to my granddaughter. Heaven knows how he knew she was here, but it's plain he knows. And he ought to have his rights! He ought to get to see her! Do you know," she went on, bristling, "that dog has walked the length of England—*twice*—to be with that girl? And you think you can keep him out with your fiddling rules and regulations?"

"I'll have to ask the medical officer," the guard said weakly.

"You do that, young man." Granny Pearce sat down in a

Literary Analysis
Foreshadowing
What do you think is foreshadowed by the dog's mysterious appearance?

Reading Check
What is Lob trying to do?

determined manner, shutting her umbrella, and Lob sat patiently dripping at her feet. Every now and then he shook his head, as if to dislodge something heavy that was tied around his neck.

Presently a tired, thin, intelligent-looking man in a white coat came downstairs, with an impressive, silver-haired man in a dark suit, and there was a low-voiced discussion. Granny Pearce eyed them, biding her time.

"Frankly. . . not much to lose," said the older man. The man in the white coat approached Granny Pearce.

"It's strictly against every rule, but as it's such a serious case we are making an exception," he said to her quietly. "But only *outside* her bedroom door—and only for a moment or two."

Without a word, Granny Pearce rose and stumped upstairs. Lob followed close to her skirts, as if he knew his hope lay with her.

They waited in the green-floored corridor outside Sandy's room. The door was half shut. Bert and Jean were inside. Everything was terribly quiet. A nurse came out. The white-coated man asked her something and she shook her head. She had left the door ajar and through it could now be seen a high, narrow bed with a lot of gadgets around it. Sandy lay there, very flat under the covers, very still. Her head was turned away. All Lob's attention was riveted on the bed. He strained toward it, but Granny Pearce clasped his collar firmly.

"I've done a lot for you, my boy, now you behave yourself," she whispered grimly. Lob let out a faint whine, anxious and pleading.

At the sound of that whine Sandy stirred just a little. She sighed and moved her head the least fraction. Lob whined again. And then Sandy turned her head right over. Her eyes opened, looking at the door.

"Lob?" she murmured—no more than a breath of sound. "Lobby, boy?"

The doctor by Granny Pearce drew a quick, sharp breath. Sandy moved her left arm—the one that was not broken—from below the covers and let her hand dangle down, feeling, as she always did in the mornings, for Lob's furry head. The doctor nodded slowly.

"All right," he whispered. "Let him go to the bedside. But keep a hold of him."

Granny Pearce and Lob moved to the bedside. Now she could see Bert and Jean, white-faced and shocked, on the far side of the bed. But she didn't look at them. She looked at the smile on her granddaughter's face as the groping fingers found Lob's wet ears and gently pulled them. "Good boy," whispered Sandy, and fell asleep again.

Granny Pearce led Lob out into the passage again. There she let go of him and he ran off swiftly down the stairs. She would have

Literary Analysis
Foreshadowing
Why might Bert and Jean be shocked when Lob walks into the room?

followed him, but Bert and Jean had come out into the passage, and she spoke to Bert fiercely.

"*I* don't know why you were so foolish as not to bring the dog before! Leaving him to find the way here himself—"

"But, Mother!" said Jean Pengelly. "That can't have been Lob. What a chance to take! Suppose Sandy hadn't—" She stopped, with her handkerchief pressed to her mouth.

"Not Lob? I've known that dog nine years! I suppose I ought to know my own granddaughter's dog?"

"Listen, Mother," said Bert. "Lob was killed by the same truck that hit Sandy. Don found him—when he went to look for Sandy's schoolbag. He was—he was dead. Ribs all smashed. No question of that. Don told me on the phone—he and Will Hoskins rowed a half mile out to sea and sank the dog with a lump of concrete tied to his collar. Poor old boy. Still—he was getting on. Couldn't have lasted forever."

"*Sank him at sea?* Then what—?"

Slowly old Mrs. Pearce, and then the other two, turned to look at the trail of dripping-wet footprints that led down the hospital stairs.

In the Pengellys' garden they have a stone, under the palm tree. It says: "Lob. Sandy's dog. Buried at sea."

Review and Assess

Thinking About the Selection

1. **Respond:** Would you have ended this story differently than the author did? Why or why not?

2. **(a) Recall:** How do Sandy and her family first meet Lob? **(b) Speculate:** Why does Lob twice travel more than 400 miles to be with Sandy? **(c) Analyze:** How do Sandy and Lob feel about each other? Support your answer with evidence.

3. **(a) Recall:** What does Mr. Dodsworth say when he gives Lob to the Pengellys? **(b) Infer:** How do you think he feels when Lob chooses Sandy over him?

4. **(a) Recall:** What happens when Sandy goes to visit her aunt? **(b) Interpret:** Why does hearing Lob's whine help Sandy wake up? **(c) Generalize:** What might this say about the strength of people's relationships with their pets?

5. **(a) Recall:** According to Bert Pengelly, what actually happened to Lob? **(b) Speculate:** What does Lob's mysterious return at the end suggest about his bond with Sandy? **(c) Evaluate:** Why do you think the author chose to end the story in this unusual way?

Joan Aiken

(b. 1924)

Joan Aiken began her writing career early—at the age of five! By her teens, she was a published author. This is not surprising when you consider that she comes from a family of writers. Her father is poet Conrad Aiken, and two of her sisters are also professional writers. Fans of all ages enjoy reading her tales, most of which have an unusual twist or a mysterious turn of events.

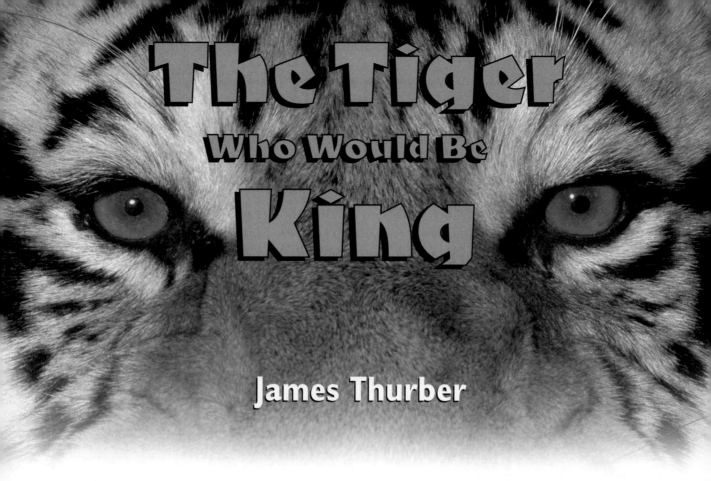

The Tiger Who Would Be King

James Thurber

One morning the tiger woke up in the jungle and told his mate that he was king of beasts.

"Leo, the lion, is king of beasts," she said.

"We need a change," said the tiger. "The creatures are crying for a change."

The tigress listened but she could hear no crying, except that of her cubs.

"I'll be king of beasts by the time the moon rises," said the tiger. "It will be a yellow moon with black stripes, in my honor."

"Oh, sure," said the tigress as she went to look after her young, one of whom, a male, very like his father, had got an imaginary thorn in his paw.

The tiger <u>prowled</u> through the jungle till he came to the lion's den. "Come out," he roared, "and greet the king of beasts! The king is dead, long live the king!"

Inside the den, the lioness woke her mate. "The king is here to see you," she said.

"What king?" he inquired, sleepily.

"The king of beasts," she said.

prowled (prould) *v.* crawled quietly and secretly

Literary Analysis
Foreshadowing
What events might be foreshadowed by the tiger's cry?

"I am the king of beasts," roared Leo, and he charged out of the den to defend his crown against the pretender.

It was a terrible fight, and it lasted until the setting of the sun. All the animals of the jungle joined in, some taking the side of the tiger and others the side of the lion. Every creature from the aardvark to the zebra took part in the struggle to overthrow the lion or to <u>repulse</u> the tiger, and some did not know which they were fighting for, and some fought for both, and some fought whoever was nearest, and some fought for the sake of fighting.

"What are we fighting for?" someone asked the aardvark.

"The old order," said the aardvark.

"What are we dying for?" someone asked the zebra.

"The new order," said the zebra.

When the moon rose, fevered and gibbous,[1] it shone upon a jungle in which nothing stirred except a macaw[2] and a cockatoo,[3] screaming in horror. All the beasts were dead except the tiger, and his days were numbered and his time was ticking away. He was monarch of all he surveyed, but it didn't seem to mean anything.

MORAL: You can't very well be king of beasts if there aren't any.

repulse (ri puls') *v.* drive back; repel an attack

---

1. gibbous (gib' əs) *adj.* more than half but less than completely illuminated.
2. macaw (mə kô') *n.* large parrot of Central or South America with bright colors and a harsh voice.
3. cockatoo (käk' ə tōō') *n.* crested parrot with white plumage tinged with yellow or pink.

Review and Assess

Thinking About the Selections

1. **Respond:** Do you find any parts of this story humorous? Explain.

2. **(a) Recall:** Which two animals fight to rule in "The Tiger Who Would Be King"? **(b) Infer:** Some of the animals join the fight for the sake of fighting. What does this suggest about the animals? **(c) Apply:** What human qualities does Thurber show in these animals?

3. **(a) Recall:** What is the result of the battle in "The Tiger Who Would Be King"? **(b) Interpret:** What is the meaning of the moral, "You can't very well be king of beasts if there aren't any"?

4. **(a) Connect:** To what human situation could you apply the lesson in this fable? **(b) Make a Judgment:** What, if anything, do you believe is worth fighting for?

James Thurber

(1894–1961)

James Thurber left college to become a clerk in the U.S. State Department. Thurber soon left this serious position to pursue his love of laughter through writing and cartooning. Much of his early work appeared in *The New Yorker* magazine. When failing eyesight forced him to give up drawing, Thurber kept making people laugh with his writing. Some of his funny stories, such as "The Tiger Who Would Be King," have a serious point behind the humor.

The LION and the BULLS

✳✳✳ A E S O P ✳✳✳

A lion often prowled about a pasture where three bulls grazed together. He had tried without success to lure one or the other of them to the edge of the pasture. He had even attempted a direct attack, only to see them form a ring so that from whatever direction he approached he was met by the horns of one of them.

Then a plan began to form in the lion's mind. Secretly he started spreading evil and <u>slanderous</u> reports of one bull against the other. The three bulls, distrustingly, began to avoid one another, and each withdrew to a different part of the pasture to graze. Of course, this was exactly what the lion wanted. One by one he fell upon the bulls, and so made easy prey of them all.

MORAL: United we stand; divided we fall.

slanderous (slan´ der əs´)
adj. untrue and damaging

Review and Assess

Thinking About the Selections

1. **Respond:** How did you feel when you read the last sentence of the fable?

2. **(a) Recall:** What do the bulls do when the lion makes a direct attack? **(b) Analyze:** Why is this an effective strategy? **(c) Apply:** How could this strategy be applied to a human situation?

3. **(a) Recall:** How does the lion get the bulls to separate? **(b) Interpret:** What is the meaning of the moral, "United we stand, divided we fall"? **(c) Apply:** How might you apply this idea to situations in your own life?

4. **(a) Speculate:** What kinds of lies do you think the lion tells the bulls? **(b) Infer:** Why are the bulls willing to believe the lion?

5. **(a) Infer:** What human qualities does Aesop show in the animals? **(b) Assess:** Is an animal fable more or less effective than one with human characters? Explain.

Aesop

(c. 620–560 B.C.)
According to tradition, Aesop was a Greek slave. He is known as the author of *Aesop's Fables*, a famous collection of short tales that teach lessons about human values and behavior.

Review and Assess

Literary Analysis

Foreshadowing

1. In "Lob's Girl," Joan Aiken uses details in the setting to hint at the upcoming accident. Explain how the details of setting shown below foreshadow the accident.

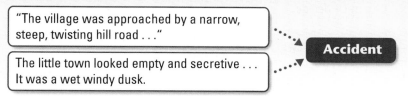

"The village was approached by a narrow, steep, twisting hill road . . ."

The little town looked empty and secretive . . . It was a wet windy dusk.

→ **Accident**

2. When Lob arrives at the hospital, he shakes his head as if to shake off something heavy. What does this mysterious detail foreshadow?
3. In "The Tiger Who Would Be King," what statement by the tiger foreshadows his hollow victory?

Comparing Literary Works

4. Which story contains more examples of foreshadowing?
5. In a chart like the one below, write the hints you found in each selection. Then, classify each hint as "obvious" or "not obvious."

Hint	Foreshadows	Obvious	Not Obvious
At the hospital, Lob shakes his head as if to remove something heavy.	It foreshadows Lob's burial at sea.		not obvious

6. Which author uses more obvious examples of foreshadowing?

Reading Strategy

Compare and Contrast Characters

7. In "Lob's Girl," in what ways are Sandy and Mr. Dodsworth similar and different?
8. Identify the ways in which the actions of the animals in "The Tiger Who Would Be King" are similar and different from the actions of the bulls in "The Lion and the Bulls."

Extending Understanding

9. **Evaluate:** Do you prefer stories in which animals behave realistically or in which they can speak? Explain using examples from the story.

Quick Review

Foreshadowing is the use of hints that suggest future story events. To review foreshadowing, see page 269.

Comparing characters means examining similarities in their behavior and personalities.
Contrasting characters means examining differences.

 Take It to the Net
www.phschool.com
Take the interactive self-test online to check your understanding of these selections.

Integrate Language Skills

Vocabulary Development Lesson

Word Analysis: Forms of *decide*

A character who speaks *decisively* has made a *decision*. Both *decisively* and *decision* are forms of *decide*. Copy the following sentences on your paper, replacing each blank with a form of *decide*.

1. Mr. Dodson spoke ___?___.
2. He had made his ___?___.
3. Now, Mr. Pengelly had to ___?___ what to do.

Spelling Strategy

Remember when spelling forms of a word that the root is the clue to spelling the form. Unscramble the letters to spell forms of *decide*. Begin by taking out *deci*, because all these forms will begin with those letters.

1. cisdenio
2. leedsciviy
3. diceed
4. cedviesi

Fluency: Word Meaning

On your paper, answer each of the following questions about the vocabulary words.

1. Which three words name or describe unpleasant feelings or ideas?
2. Which two words indicate determined actions?
3. Which word might be the action of a person who is sorry?
4. Which word might be the action of a person with a secret?
5. Which word describes the action of a sneaky character?
6. Which word might be the action of someone defending himself or herself from attack?

Grammar Lesson

Prepositional Phrases

A **preposition** relates a noun or a pronoun following it to another word in the sentence. Common prepositions include *on*, *between*, *from*, and *for*. A **prepositional phrase** is a group of words beginning with a preposition and ending with a noun or pronoun. The noun or pronoun in the phrase is called the object of the preposition.

Example: The dog jumped *into the* sea.
PREP PHRASE

The example shows that the preposition, *into*, relates the object of the preposition, *sea*, to the word *jumped*.

Practice On your paper, write the prepositional phrase in each sentence. Underline the preposition. Circle the object of the preposition.

1. The tiger woke up in the jungle.
2. Greet the king of beasts!
3. Some animals fought for the tiger.
4. A plan formed in the lion's mind.
5. He fell upon the bulls.

Writing Application On your paper, complete each sentence by adding a prepositional phrase. Begin the phrase with the preposition indicated.

1. One bull stood (between)
2. They were not safe (from)

WG Prentice Hall Writing and Grammar Connection: Chapter 17

Writing Lesson

Fable

"The Tiger Who Would Be King" and "The Lion and the Bulls" are **fables**—brief tales that teach a lesson. Write a fable of your own that teaches the same lesson as one of these.

Prewriting   Consider what situations might illustrate the moral you have chosen. Use an organizer like the one below to work out your characters and situation.

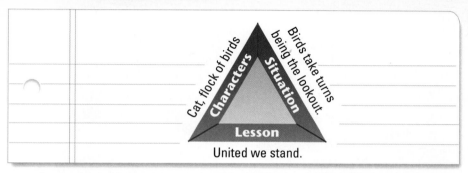

Drafting   Build up to the moral by describing events in climactic order. In other words, each event should lead closer and closer to the story's main event, or climax. Write the moral at the end.

Revising   Ask a partner whether the events you describe support the moral. Use his or her suggestions when you revise.

WG Prentice Hall Writing and Grammar Connection: Chapter 5, Section 2

Extension Activities

Listening and Speaking In small groups, plan a **television news feature** on "Lob's Girl." First, discuss what aspect or "angle" of the story would make a good news focus. Then, write the script, indicating

- the role of the anchor.
- the characters who will be interviewed.
- the visual aids you will include.

If possible, videotape your presentation. During your presentation, vary the volume, tone, and pitch of your voice to emphasize the important ideas. **[Group Activity]**

Research and Technology Using electronic resources, conduct author, subject, and title searches to find retellings of "The Lion and the Bulls." Prepare an **annotated list** of the retellings. Explain to a group how you used the subject, title, and author to find the other versions. Explain how the other versions compare and contrast with the one presented here.

 **Take It to the Net**   www.phschool.com

Go online for an additional research activity using the Internet.

Prepare to Read

Greyling

One, 1986, April Gornik, Edward Thorp Gallery

 Take It to the Net

Visit www.phschool.com for interactive activities and instruction related to "Greyling," including

- background
- graphic organizers
- literary elements
- reading strategies

Preview

Connecting to the Literature

When you meet a challenge or overcome an obstacle, you usually discover new talents or strengths that you did not know you had. The main character in this story not only discovers a hidden talent—he discovers a hidden identity!

Background

"Greyling" is the story of a selchie. Selchies (or silkies) are common in the folk traditions of England, Ireland, Scotland, and Wales. There are many versions of selchie stories, but they all agree on one point: The selchie, who appears as a person on land, changes to a seal in the water.

Literary Analysis

Conflict and Resolution

A **conflict** is a struggle between two opposing forces. The events in the story all move toward the **resolution**—the way in which the conflict is settled. In "Greyling," the main conflict is the struggle between the two sides of Greyling's character: seal and human. This conflict is resolved when another conflict arises.

As you read, use the following focus questions to help you analyze the conflicts in the story and the resolutions:

1. What is the conflict inside Greyling?
2. What is the conflict between Greyling's father and the sea?

Connecting Literary Elements

In this story, Greyling's **character traits**, the qualities that make up his personality, contribute to the conflict. This excerpt from the story shows how his love for the sea that he came from creates an inner struggle.

> ". . . he often stood by the shore or high in the town on the great grey cliffs, looking and longing and grieving in his heart for what he did not really know . . ."

At the end of the story, notice Greyling's character traits that contribute to the resolution.

Reading Strategy

Predicting

When you **predict,** you make logical guesses about upcoming events. To predict,

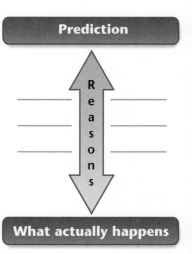

- think about what might happen based on a character's actions or words.
- pay attention to new information that might cause you to revise a prediction.
- keep track of your predictions and how accurate they were.

Use a graphic organizer like the one shown for each prediction you make.

Vocabulary Development

grief (grēf) *n.* deep sadness (p. 291)

sheared (shird) *v.* cut off sharply (p. 291)

slough (sluf) *v.* be cast off (p. 293)

wallowed (wäl´ ōd) *v.* rolled and tilted (p. 293)

Greyling

Jane Yolen

Once on a time when wishes were aplenty, a fisherman and his wife lived by the side of the sea. All that they ate came out of the sea. Their hut was covered with the finest mosses that kept them cool in the summer and warm in the winter. And there was nothing they needed or wanted except a child.

Each morning, when the moon touched down behind the water and the sun rose up behind the plains, the wife would say to the fisherman, "You have your boat and your nets and your lines. But I have no baby to hold in my arms." And again, in the evening, it was the same. She would weep and wail and rock the cradle that stood by the hearth. But year in and year out the cradle stayed empty.

Now the fisherman was also sad that they had no child. But he kept his sorrow to himself so that his wife would not know his <u>grief</u> and thus double her own. Indeed, he would leave the hut each morning with a breath of song and return each night with a whistle on his lips. His nets were full but his heart was empty, yet he never told his wife.

One sunny day, when the beach was a tan thread spun between sea and plain, the fisherman as usual went down to his boat. But this day he found a small grey seal stranded on the sandbar, crying for its own.

The fisherman looked up the beach and down. He looked in front of him and behind. And he looked to the town on the great grey cliffs that <u>sheared</u> off into the sea. But there were no other seals in sight.

So he shrugged his shoulders and took off his shirt. Then he dipped it into the water and wrapped the seal pup carefully in its folds.

"You have no father and you have no mother," he said. "And I have no child. So you shall come home with me."

And the fisherman did no fishing that day but brought the seal pup, wrapped in his shirt, straight home to his wife.

When she saw him coming home early with no shirt on, the fisherman's wife ran out of the hut, fear riding in her heart. Then she looked wonderingly at the bundle which he held in his arms.

"It's nothing," he said, "but a seal pup I found stranded in the shallows and longing for its own. I thought we could give it love and care until it is old enough to seek its kin."

The fisherman's wife nodded and took the bundle. Then she uncovered the wrapping and gave a loud cry. "Nothing!" she said. "You call this nothing?"

The fisherman looked. Instead of a seal lying in the folds, there

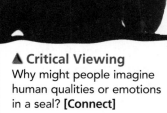

▲ Critical Viewing
Why might people imagine human qualities or emotions in a seal? **[Connect]**

grief (grēf) *n.* deep sadness

sheared (shird) *v.* cut off sharply

Reading Check

Why are the fisherman and his wife sad?

was a strange child with great grey eyes and silvery grey hair, smiling up at him.

The fisherman wrung his hands. "It is a selchie," he cried. "I have heard of them. They are men upon the land and seals in the sea. I thought it was but a tale."

"Then he shall remain a man upon the land," said the fisherman's wife, clasping the child in her arms, "for I shall never let him return to the sea."

"Never," agreed the fisherman, for he knew how his wife had wanted a child. And in his secret heart, he wanted one, too. Yet he felt, somehow, it was wrong.

"We shall call him Greyling," said the fisherman's wife, "for his eyes and hair are the color of a storm-coming sky. Greyling, though he has brought sunlight into our home."

And though they still lived by the side of the water in a hut covered with mosses that kept them warm in the winter and cool in the summer, the boy Greyling was never allowed into the sea.

He grew from a child to a lad. He grew from a lad to a young man. He gathered driftwood for his mother's hearth and searched the tide pools for shells for her mantel. He mended his father's nets and tended his father's boat. But though he often stood by the shore or high in the town on the great grey cliffs, looking and longing and grieving in his heart for what he did not really know, he never went into the sea.

Literary Analysis
Conflict and Character
What part of Greyling's character leads to the conflict he feels inside himself?

Then one wind-wailing morning just fifteen years from the day that Greyling had been found, a great storm blew up suddenly in the North. It was such a storm as had never been seen before: the sky turned nearly black and even the fish had trouble swimming. The wind pushed huge waves onto the shore. The waters gobbled up the little hut on the beach. And Greyling and the fisherman's wife were forced to flee to the town high on the great grey cliffs. There they looked down at the roiling, boiling, sea. Far from shore they spied the fisherman's boat, its sails flapping like the wings of a wounded gull. And clinging to the broken mast was the fisherman himself, sinking deeper with every wave.

The fisherman's wife gave a terrible cry. "Will no one save him?" she called to the people of the town who had gathered on the edge of the cliff. "Will no one save my own dear husband who is all of life to me?"

But the townsmen looked away. There was no man there who dared risk his life in that sea, even to save a drowning soul.

"Will no one at all save him?" she cried out again.

"Let the boy go," said one old man, pointing at Greyling with his stick. "He looks strong enough."

But the fisherman's wife clasped Greyling in her arms and held his ears with her hands. She did not want him to go into the sea. She was afraid he would never return.

"Will no one save my own dear heart?" cried the fisherman's wife for a third and last time.

But shaking their heads, the people of the town edged to their houses and shut their doors and locked their windows and set their backs to the ocean and their faces to the fires that glowed in every hearth.

"I will save him, Mother," cried Greyling, "or die as I try."

And before she could tell him no, he broke from her grasp and dived from the top of the great cliffs, down, down, down into the tumbling sea.

"He will surely sink," whispered the women as they ran from their warm fires to watch.

"He will certainly drown," called the men as they took down their spyglasses from the shelves.

They gathered on the cliffs and watched the boy dive down into the sea.

As Greyling disappeared beneath the waves, little fingers of foam tore at his clothes. They snatched his shirt and his pants and his shoes and sent them bubbling away to the shore. And as Greyling went deeper beneath the waves, even his skin seemed to <u>slough</u> off till he swam, free at last, in the sleek grey coat of a great grey seal.

The selchie had returned to the sea.

But the people of the town did not see this. All they saw was the diving boy disappearing under the waves and then, farther out, a large seal swimming toward the boat that <u>wallowed</u> in the sea. The sleek grey seal, with no effort at all, eased the fisherman to the shore though the waves were wild and bright with foam. And then, with a final salute, it turned its back on the land and headed joyously out to sea.

The fisherman's wife hurried down to the sand. And behind her followed the people of the town. They searched up the beach and down, but they did not find the boy.

Reading Strategy
Predicting What will happen when Greyling goes in the ocean?

slough (sluf) v. be cast off; be gotten rid of

wallowed (wäl′ ōd) v. rolled and tilted

Reading Check

Why doesn't the fisherman's wife want Greyling to go in the sea?

"A brave son," said the men when they found his shirt, for they thought he was certainly drowned.

"A very brave son," said the women when they found his shoes, for they thought him lost for sure.

"Has he really gone?" asked the fisherman's wife of her husband when at last they were alone.

"Yes, quite gone," the fisherman said to her. "Gone where his heart calls, gone to the great wide sea. And though my heart grieves at his leaving, it tells me this way is best."

The fisherman's wife sighed. And then she cried. But at last she agreed that, perhaps, it was best. "For he is both man and seal," she said. "And though we cared for him for a while, now he must care for himself." And she never cried again. So once more they lived alone by the side of the sea in a new little hut which was covered with mosses to keep them warm in the winter and cool in the summer.

Yet, once a year, a great grey seal is seen at night near the fisherman's home. And the people in town talk of it, and wonder. But seals do come to the shore and men do go to the sea; and so the townfolk do not dwell upon it very long.

But it is no ordinary seal. It is Greyling himself come home— come to tell his parents tales of the lands that lie far beyond the waters, and to sing them songs of the wonders that lie far beneath the sea.

Review and Assess

Thinking About the Selection

1. **Respond:** Do you agree that Greyling belongs in the sea? Why or why not?

2. **(a) Recall:** How do the fisherman and his wife come to have a son? **(b) Speculate:** What problems does raising this child involve?

3. **(a) Recall:** Why does the fisherman's wife name the boy Greyling? **(b)** What does this name show about his animal nature? **(c) Connect:** How does this name help predict what happens to him?

4. **(a) Recall:** Why does Greyling finally go into the water? **(b) Support:** Does Greyling know what will happen when he dives into the sea? Support your answer.

5. **(a) Recall:** What response do the fisherman and his wife have to Greyling's change? **(b) Draw Conclusions:** What main idea about parents and children does this tale present?

6. **Make a Judgment:** Should the fisherman and his wife have kept Greyling from the sea? Why or why not?

Jane Yolen

(b. 1939)
Jane Yolen reads aloud every sentence she writes to hear how it sounds. When she completes a paragraph, she reads that out loud, too. That's a lot of reading because Jane Yolen has written more than two hundred books, most of them for children or young adults. Because she loves the timeless feelings and values in so many folk tales, fables, and fairy tales, Yolen often bases her stories on them. "Greyling" is a story from Yolen's imagination, but its main character, a selchie, comes from the folklore of Scotland and Ireland.

Review and Assess

Literary Analysis

Conflict and Resolution

1. What is the **conflict** inside Greyling?
2. What is the **conflict** between Greyling's father and the sea?
3. How are the resolutions of these conflicts related? Fill out a graphic organizer like the one shown here before you answer.

Connecting Literary Elements

4. Fill out a Venn diagram like the one shown here to explore Greyling's character traits as a seal and as a human. In the center section, write the qualities that apply to the seal and the human, such as love for the fisherman.

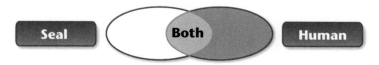

5. Which human traits lead Greyling to save the fisherman?
6. Which seal traits help Greyling save the fisherman?

Reading Strategy

Predict

7. When the man found the seal, what prediction did you make? Why?
8. When the seal became a baby, what prediction did you make? Why?
9. At which point, if any, in the story did you change your prediction? Why?

Extending Understanding

10. **Career Connection:** Explain how the lesson of this story could apply to the experiences of veterinarians (animal doctors) who work with wildlife.

Quick Review

The **conflict** is a struggle between two opposing forces.

The **resolution** is the way the conflict turns out. To review conflict and resolution, see page 289.

Character traits are a character's qualities. To review character traits, see page 289.

Predicting is making logical guesses about upcoming events by using information given in the story.

 Take It to the Net
www.phschool.com
Take the interactive self-test online to check your understanding of the selection.

Integrate Language Skills

Vocabulary Development Lesson

Word Analysis: Forms of *grief*

The fisherman in this story hides his *grief*—his deep sadness. In your notebook, write the form of grief next to its definition.

a. grief   **b.** grievous   **c.** grieve

1. feel deep sadness
2. deep sadness
3. bad enough to cause deep sadness

Spelling Strategy

Slough is one of the few words in English that spells the *uff* sound with *ough*. For each clue, write a word that rhymes with *slough* and is spelled with *ough*.

1. plenty   2. very strong or sturdy   3. not gentle

Grammar Lesson

Interjections

An **interjection** is a word or group of words that expresses emotion. A strong interjection is followed by an exclamation point, as in these examples from "Greyling."

Nothing! You call this nothing?

What! Do you expect me to believe that?

A comma follows a mild interjection.

Oh, you poor little thing.

Now, don't cry.

Fluency: Complete the Sentences

On your paper, write the vocabulary word that belongs in each numbered sentence. You will use some words twice.

1. The fisherman's little boat ____?____ in the waves.
2. The mountains rose above Greyling, but the cliffs ____?____ away.
3. At first, Greyling's mother felt ____?____ when her son left.
4. Did Greyling ____?____ off his old, human skin?
5. The fisherman's wife experienced ____?____ more than once in this story.
6. The fish ____?____ in the huge waves.
7. Was it Greyling's fate to ____?____ off his human life?

Practice Copy the sentences. Circle the interjection.

1. Please! Won't someone help him?
2. Well, maybe the boy should go.
3. No! I won't believe it.
4. He swims fast. Wow!
5. Oh no! I can't see him!

Writing Application Copy the following conversation. Add at least three interjections.

"He's such a good swimmer," said the fisherman's wife.
"He sure is," replied the fisherman. "Just look at him go."
"I wish he didn't have to leave."

Prentice Hall Writing and Grammar Connection: Chapter 18, Section 2

Writing Lesson

Letter

Write a letter from Greyling explaining why you returned to the sea after saving the fisherman. Use what you have learned about the mythical selchies to add details and reasons to your letter.

Prewriting   Gather details from the story that indicate that Greyling is not completely happy on land. Jot these down to include as examples in your letter. Review the background on p. 288 for details about selchies that will help explain why you needed to return to the sea.

Drafting   First, make clear that you have returned to the sea. Then, give an overall reason why, based on the details you will present. Finally, include the details and examples that support your reason.

Revising   Look for places where you have included details that are not related to your reasons for returning to the sea. Eliminate these irrelevant details.

Model: Eliminate Unnecessary Details

You know I have always felt that I did not belong on land. When I jumped in the water, ~~it was so cold.~~ I was amazed to discover how at home I felt.

> The detail of the water temperature is deleted because it has nothing to do with why Greyling returned to the sea.

Prentice Hall Writing and Grammar Connection: Chapter 7, Section 4

Extension Activities

Research and Technology   Use a key word search to find possible explanations for selchie legends. Once you have found several sites, scroll or search text in documents to find the answers to the following questions.

1. Are there true stories of seals rescuing people?
2. What physical features of seals might appear human?

After answering the questions, prepare a **report** and share it with your class.

Listening and Speaking   With other students, **role-play** the scene in which the villagers refuse to help. Use body language to show anger, fear, reluctance, or embarrassment. Communicate these emotions nonverbally—without words—through

- facial expressions.
- the way you stand.

As a group, discuss what each person's body language seemed to communicate. **[Group Activity]**

 **Take It to the Net**   www.phschool.com

Go online for an additional research activity using the Internet.

Prepare to Read

Abuelito Who ◆ The Open Road
Life Doesn't Frighten Me ◆ who knows if the moon's

 Take It to the Net

Visit www.phschool.com
for interactive activities
and instruction related to
these selections, including

- background
- graphic organizers
- literary elements
- reading strategies

Preview

Connecting to the Literature

The poets in this group—Sandra Cisneros, E. E. Cummings, Walt Whitman, and Maya Angelou—focus on change. Two of them—Cummings and Whitman—express the thrill and possibility of traveling new roads. What new roads do you look forward to traveling?

Background

E. E. Cummings created his own rules when writing poetry. By rarely using periods or capital letters, he let the rhythm of the words speak for itself. The lines "always/it's/Spring" would read more easily as one line—"it's always Spring"—but Cummings makes us slow down to appreciate the idea.

Literary Analysis

Free Verse

A poem written in **free verse** does not reflect traditional structures or rules. Its lines do not necessarily rhyme at the end or contain a set number of syllables. Still, the poem works with the sound, sense, and rhythm of the words. For instance, the poet may repeat words or put rhyming words close to each other. In the following lines from "Abuelito Who," Sandra Cisneros creates rhythm by using repeated words:

> who tells me in Spanish you are my diamond
> who tells me in English you are my sky

Comparing Literary Works

The **tone** of a poem is the writer's attitude toward the subject and the audience. Tone can often be described in a single word, such as *formal, informal, serious,* or *humorous.* You can determine a poem's tone by examining the writer's word choice and the length and arrangement of lines. For example, in these lines from "Life Doesn't Frighten Me," the short, slang words and the singsong rhythm create an informal, almost childlike tone:

> I go boo
> Make them shoo

Compare the tones of these poems. Keep the following focus questions in mind as you read.

1. Which two poems have the most similar tones?
2. Which two poems have the most different tones?

Reading Strategy

Drawing Inferences

When you **draw inferences,** you form ideas or come to conclusions based on the information you are given. The conclusion you form is usually not directly stated. For example, in "Abuelito Who" we learn that the grandfather calls his granddaughter a diamond. From this detail, we can infer that he loves his granddaughter. The chart shows another inference you can draw from details in "Abuelito Who."

Detail
Abuelito throws coins like rain.

Inference
Abuelito is generous.

Vocabulary Development

henceforth (hens fôrth´) *adv.* from now on (p. 302)

whimper (hwim´ pər) *v.* whine softly as in fear or pain (p. 302)

querulous (kwer´ yo͞o ləs) *adj.* inclined to find mistakes; complaining (p. 302)

Abuelito Who

Sandra Cisneros

Ezra Davenport, 1929, Clarence Holbrook Carter, Courtesy of the artist

▲ **Critical Viewing** Find two details in this painting that match the description of Abuelito. **[Connect]**

Abuelito[1] who throws coins like rain
and asks who loves him
who is dough and feathers
who is a watch and glass of water
5   whose hair is made of fur
is too sad to come downstairs today
who tells me in Spanish you are my diamond
who tells me in English you are my sky
whose little eyes are string
10   can't come out to play
sleeps in his little room all night and day
who used to laugh like the letter k
is sick
is a doorknob tied to a sour stick
15   is tired shut the door
doesn't live here anymore
is hiding underneath the bed
who talks to me inside my head
is blankets and spoons and big brown shoes
20   who snores up and down up and down up and down again
is the rain on the roof that falls like coins
asking who loves him
who loves him who?

---

1. **Abuelito** (ä bwe lē´ tō) in Spanish, an affectionate term for a grandfather.

Review and Assess

Thinking About the Selection

1. **Respond:** Would you like to have Abuelito as a grand-father? Explain.

2. **(a) Analyze:** Who is Abuelito? **(b) Analyze Cause and Effect:** Why can't Abuelito come downstairs?

3. **(a) Recall:** Name two things Abuelito has done often in the past. **(b) Draw Conclusions:** What do these things show about Abuelito's personality?

4. **(a) Recall:** Describe Abuelito today. **(b) Interpret:** Why does the speaker feel as if Abuelito is "hiding underneath the bed"? **(c) Compare and Contrast:** How is Abuelito different today from how he was in the past?

5. **(a) Interpret:** Name three ways in which the speaker is reminded of Abuelito. **(b) Support:** Based on the descriptions of Abuelito, how does the speaker feel about him? **(c) Extend:** In what ways does this poem honor all grandparents?

Sandra Cisneros

(b. 1954)
Growing up in a poor neighborhood in Chicago, Illinois, made for difficult times. Sandra Cisneros kept her focus, though. Drawing on her Mexican heritage, she has written short stories, poetry, and the book *The House on Mango Street*.

Cisneros believes that writers must make connections between their own lives and those of others. In "Abuelito Who," she shares her feelings about her grandfather.

The Open Road

Walt Whitman

Afoot and light-hearted, I take to the open road,
Healthy, free, the world before me,
The long brown path before me, leading wherever I choose.

Henceforth I ask not good-fortune, I myself am good-fortune,
5   Henceforth I whimper no more, postpone no more,
     need nothing,
Done with indoor complaints, libraries, querulous criticisms,
Strong and content, I travel the open road.

henceforth (hens fôrth´)
adv. from now on

whimper (hwim´ pər) *v.*
whine softly as in fear
or pain

querulous (kwer´ yoo ləs)
adj. complaining

Review and Assess

Thinking About the Selections

1. **Respond:** How did you feel reading this poem? Explain.

2. **(a) Recall:** At the beginning of "The Open Road," what is the speaker about to do? **(b) Analyze Cause and Effect:** Why does the speaker feel "light-hearted" at this moment?

3. **(a) Recall:** What decision does the speaker in "The Open Road" announce? **(b) Interpret:** Now that he "is" good fortune, how do you think the speaker will respond when things go wrong? **(c) Speculate:** Do you think this poem is about a road used for physical travel? What else might this "open road" be?

4. **(a) Recall:** What is the speaker done with? **(b) Interpret:** Give one example of each thing the speaker is done with. **(c) Deduce:** Why is the speaker done with these things?

5. **(a) Speculate:** What has led the speaker to this changed attitude? **(b) Evaluate:** Do you think that this is a good attitude for a person to have? Explain.

Walt Whitman

(1819–1892)

A poet, printer, and journalist, Walt Whitman considered himself first and foremost an American. In his book *Leaves of Grass*, he created a powerful vision of what democracy means. Around the time of the Civil War, when Whitman lived, writers in the United States thought they had much to learn from European writers. Whitman believed that they could find everything they needed to know in themselves and their fellow citizens.

Life Doesn't Frighten Me

Maya Angelou

Shadows on the wall
Noises down the hall
Life doesn't frighten me at all
Bad dogs barking loud
5   Big ghosts in a cloud
Life doesn't frighten me at all.

Mean old Mother Goose
Lions on the loose
They don't frighten me at all
10 Dragons breathing flame
On my counterpane[1]
That doesn't frighten me at all.

I go boo
Make them shoo
15 I make fun
Way they run
I won't cry
So they fly
I just smile
20 They go wild
Life doesn't frighten me at all.

Tough guys in a fight
All alone at night
Life doesn't frighten me at all.

25 Panthers in the park
Strangers in the dark
No, they don't frighten me at all.

▶ Critical Viewing
Identify the details of this picture that indicate the girl is confident and determined. [Compare and Contrast]

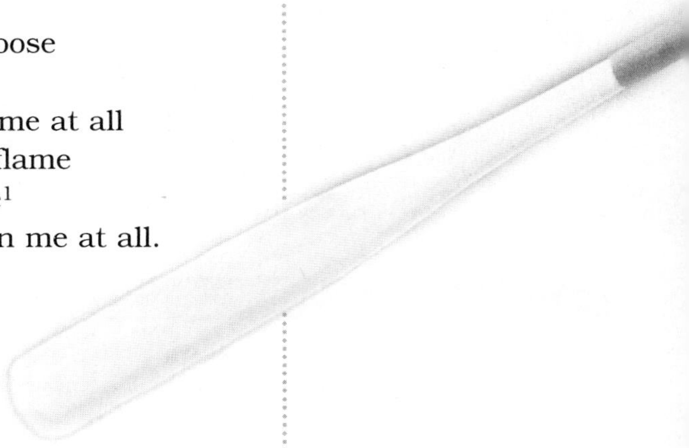

---

1. **counterpane** bedspread.

That new classroom where
Boys all pull my hair
30 (Kissy little girls
With their hair in curls)
They don't frighten me at all.

Don't show me frogs and snakes
And listen for my scream,
35 If I'm afraid at all
It's only in my dreams.

I've got a magic charm
That I keep up my sleeve,
I can walk the ocean floor
40 And never have to breathe.

Life doesn't frighten me at all
Not at all
Not at all.
Life doesn't frighten me at all.

Review and Assess

Thinking About the Selections

1. **Respond:** Would you like to meet the speaker of this poem?

2. **(a) Recall:** Name three things that do not frighten the speaker of this poem. **(b) Infer:** Why does the speaker smile at frightening things? **(c) Analyze:** What does this reveal about the speaker's personality?

3. **(a) Interpret:** What is the "magic charm" that the speaker keeps up her sleeve? **(b) Apply:** What "magic charms" do you have to help you in difficult situations?

4. **(a) Compare and Contrast:** Which things mentioned by the speaker are real and which are imaginary? **(b) Deduce:** Where does the speaker get the imaginary ideas?

5. **(a) Assess:** What effect is created by the repetition in the last four lines?

6. **Make a Judgment:** In what situations, if any, is it appropriate or useful to admit a fear?

Maya Angelou

(b. 1928)
Maya Angelou may have changed her childhood name, but she has never forgotten her childhood. Born Marguerite Johnson in St. Louis, Missouri, the adult Maya Angelou recalls the events and difficulties of her past in her autobiography, *I Know Why the Caged Bird Sings*. In "Life Doesn't Frighten Me," she explores the worries and concerns that a young person conquers as she moves toward adulthood.

who knows
if the moon's

E.E. Cummings

who knows if the moon's
a balloon, coming out of a keen[1] city
in the sky—filled with pretty people?
(and if you and i should

5   get into it, if they
should take me and take you into their balloon,
why then
we'd go up higher with all the pretty people

than houses and steeples and clouds:
10   go sailing
away and away sailing into a keen
city which nobody's ever visited, where

always
            it's
15   Spring) and everyone's
in love and flowers pick themselves

---

1. **keen** (kēn) *adj.* slang for sharp-looking.
Also, intensely felt.

Review and Assess

Thinking About the Selections

1. **Respond:** Would you like to visit the place Cummings describes? Explain.

2. **(a) Recall:** In Cummings's poem, what might happen if the moon were a balloon? **(b) Interpret:** Describe Cummings's "keen city." **(c) Compare and Contrast:** Name three differences between Cummings's "keen city" and the ordinary world.

3. **(a) Recall:** What would the speaker in Cummings's poem see as he traveled in the balloon? **(b) Infer:** Based on these details, what feelings does looking at the moon inspire in the speaker? **(c) Extend:** Do you think there are any places on earth that are similar to the city Cummings describes? Explain.

E.E. Cummings

(1894–1962)

E. E. Cummings celebrated freedom and quirkiness. Born in Cambridge, Massachusetts, he studied painting in Paris. It was his experiments with poetry, though, that made him famous. Cummings taught punctuation marks new tricks, using them as no one had before. He put lines on the page like a painter splashing color or a jazz player skipping around the beat. He gave poets new roads to follow.

Review and Assess

Literary Analysis

Free Verse

1. What are two examples of repeated words and rhymed words from "Abuelito Who"?
2. In what way does the visual structure of "who knows if the moon's" show that it does not follow a regular rhythm?
3. Why do you think Whitman wrote "The Open Road" in **free verse**?

Comparing Literary Works

4. In a chart like the one below, record words from each poem that reveal its **tone**.

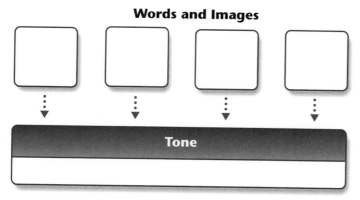

Words and Images

Tone

5. Which two poems have the most similar tones? Explain.
6. Which two poems have the most different tones? Explain.

Reading Strategy

Draw Inferences

7. How does the speaker in "Abuelito Who" feel about Abuelito?
8. Would the speaker in "who knows if the moon's" like to visit the "keen city"? Which detail in the poem supports your answer?
9. How does the speaker of "The Open Road" feel about his or her journey? How can you tell?
10. What inferences can you draw about the speaker of "Life Doesn't Frighten Me"?

Extending Understanding

11. **Health Connection:** What effects of aging does Abuelito show?

Quick Review

Free verse is poetry that does not follow traditional rules or fit traditional structures. To review free verse, see page 299.

Tone is the writer's attitude toward the subject and the audience.

Drawing inferences is forming ideas or coming to conclusions that are based on information you are given.

 Take It to the Net
www.phschool.com
Take the interactive self-test online to check your understanding of these selections.

Integrate Language Skills

Vocabulary Development Lesson

Word Analysis: Compound Transition Words

Compound words are made by joining two or more words. Compound transition words show a connection between ideas or events. Whitman uses the compound transition word *henceforth*, meaning "from this time on," to relate present and future events.

Fill in the blanks, using one of these compound transition words: *henceforth*, *nonetheless*.

1. Every day this week I got caught in the rain. ____?____, I will bring my umbrella.
2. The wind brought a great chill to the air. ____?____, she did not wear a jacket.

Concept Development: Connotations

A word's **connotation** is the associations that it brings to mind. Explain whether the connotation of each italicized vocabulary word is positive, negative, or neutral.

1. The *querulous* man frustrated the lecturer.
2. The nervous dog *whimpered* at the thunder.
3. *Henceforth* we will only stop at the store on our way home from school.

Spelling Strategy

When combined in a compound transition word, words usually keep the same spelling. For example, *hence + forth = henceforth*. Join the words in each item to spell a compound word.

1. how + ever
2. mean + while
3. never + the + less
4. more + over

Grammar Lesson

Conjunctions

Conjunctions connect words and groups of words. **Coordinating conjunctions** connect words or groups of words of a similar type: noun with noun or phrase with phrase, for example. The coordinating conjunctions are *and, but, for, or, nor, so,* and *yet*.

"Afoot *and* light-hearted, . . ."

Subordinating conjunctions connect ideas by making one dependent on the other. Common subordinating conjunctions are *after, although, as, because, before, if, since, when, where, whenever, wherever, while, unless,* and *until*.

She won't cry *because* she's not afraid.

Practice Copy these sentences. Circle the conjunctions and underline the words or word groups they connect. Then, tell whether each conjunction is coordinating or subordinating.

1. Abuelito is blankets and big, brown shoes.
2. It will be spring when we get there.
3. I am not frightened because I am strong.
4. She is young, yet wise.
5. She will travel, but he will stay home.

Writing Application Join each pair of sentences with a subordinating conjunction.

1. He threw coins like rain. He became sick.
2. We looked at houses and steeples and clouds. We rode in the balloon.

W͟G Prentice Hall Writing and Grammar Connection: Chapter 18, Section 1

Writing Lesson

Portrait

In "Abuelito Who," Sandra Cisneros uses words to paint a portrait of the speaker's grandfather. Choose an important person in your life, and create a portrait in words that captures his or her special qualities.

Prewriting   Use a cluster diagram like the one below to brainstorm for a list of your subject's qualities. Include precise nouns, verbs, and adjectives to paint a vivid image for your reader.

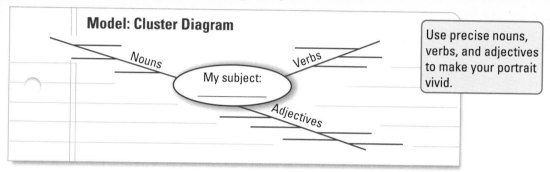

Model: Cluster Diagram

Nouns

Verbs

My subject:

Adjectives

Use precise nouns, verbs, and adjectives to make your portrait vivid.

Drafting   Use details to show the qualities of your subject. For example, to show height, you might write, "When we eat at a restaurant, he has to sit on two phone books."

Revising   Look for places where you can add specific details that show rather than tell. Proofread for errors in grammar and spelling.

W/G Prentice Hall Writing and Grammar Connection: Chapter 6, Section 2

Extension Activities

Listening and Speaking With a group, find a television advertisement that features either a family, an elderly person, or a child and write an **advertisement review.** Determine how the image is used to persuade. For example, a vitamin ad that shows an elderly woman riding a bicycle might persuade viewers that the vitamins will keep them healthy. Address these points:

- what ideas the image conveys
- how these ideas connect with the product
- whether the connection is true or false

[Group Activity]

Research and Technology Using the Internet and other resources, gather a variety of poems and stories about the moon. Organize them in a **booklet,** making sure to include visual aids such as photographs and drawings. Write an annotation—a helpful comment—on each poem, comparing or contrasting it with "who knows if the moon's."

 **Take It to the Net**   www.phschool.com

Go online for an additional research activity using the Internet.

In the 1930s, America was struggling through the Great Depression—an economic crisis that threatened the lives of most Americans. Millions of unemployed people, from farmers to factory workers, faced homelessness and hunger. People lost all their possessions, and parents were separated from their children. Optimism—a positive outlook in the face of difficulty or change—is a common theme in American literature. In the late 1800s, Walt Whitman expresses excitement at the prospect of traveling the open road with no possessions. In the 1980s, Maya Angelou presents a speaker who is not intimidated by contemporary dangers.

During the Depression around the country, "shantytowns" sprang up as people built shelter from cardboard boxes, old pieces of metal, and other found items. Many people traveled around looking for work or relatives to take them in. The easiest no-cost way to travel was to "hop a train," to jump onto a boxcar when train officials weren't looking.

Bud, the main character in *Bud, Not Buddy*, is a motherless boy trying to find his father. With only a suitcase and an optimistic outlook, Bud sets off. His first attempt to hop a train results in his being separated from a newfound friend. As you read, keep the context of the time period in mind.

from

BUD, NOT BUDDY
CHRISTOPHER PAUL CURTIS

We broke out of the woods and there in the dark sat the train. The locomotive was hissing and spitting coal-black smoke into the sky, every once in a while a big shower of sparks would glow up from inside the dark cloud, making it look like a gigantic black genie was trying to raise up out of the smokestack. The train went as far back as you could see, there must've been a thousand box-cars, but everyone had stopped and was just standing there watching. No one was trying to get on.

I pushed my way to the front to see if I could find Bugs and I saw why everyone had stopped. There were four cop cars and eight cops standing between the crowd and the train. The cops all had billy clubs and were spread out to protect the train.

The crowd kept getting bigger and bigger.

One of the cops yelled, "You men know you can't get on this train, just go on back to Shantytown and there won't be no trouble."

A white man said, "This is the only train going west for the next month, you know we got families to feed and have got to be on it. You go get back in your cars and you'll be right, there won't be no trouble."

The cop said, "I'm warning you, the Flint police are on the way, this here is private property and they have orders to shoot anyone who tries to get on this train."

A man next to me said, "I'd rather be shot than sit around and watch my kids go hungry."

The cop said, "This is America, boys, you're sounding like a bunch of Commies[1], you know I can't let you on this train. I got kids to feed too, and I'd lose my job."

Someone yelled, "Well, welcome to the club, brother."

Thematic Connection
What evidence does the author give that Bud can "see it through"?

---

1. **Commies** slang for Communists

It seemed like we stood looking at the cops and them looking at us for a whole hour. Our side was getting bigger and bigger and the other cops started looking nervous. The one who was doing all the talking saw them fidgeting and said, "Hold steady, men."

One of the cops said, "Jake, there's four hundred men out there and more coming, I don't like these odds. Mr. Pinkerton ain't paying me enough to do this," He threw his cop hat and his billy club on the ground.

▲ **Critical Viewing**
Based on what you see in the picture, what is one reason the police might have for preventing train-hopping? **[Connect]**

Everybody froze when the train whistle blew one long time and the engine started saying *shuh-shuh-shuh*. The big steel wheels creaked a couple of times, then started moving.

Four of the other cops threw their hats and billy clubs down too. The boss cop said, "You lily-livered rats," and it was like someone said, "On your mark, get set, go!"

The engine was saying *SHUHSHUHSHUHSHUHSHUH...* and a million boys and men broke for the train.

I got pushed from behind and fell on top of my suitcase. Someone reached down and pulled me up. I squeezed my bag to my stomach and ran. The train was going faster and faster. People were jumping on and reaching back to help others. I finally got to the tracks and was running as hard as I could. I looked up into the boxcar and saw Bugs.

He screamed, "Bud, throw your bag, throw me your bag!"

I used both hands to throw my suitcase at the train. Bugs caught it and when he set it behind him the blue flyer blew out of the twine and fluttered outside the door. But it was like a miracle, the flyer flipped over three times and landed right in my hand. I slowed down and put it in my pocket.

Bugs reached one arm out and screamed, "Bud, don't stop! Run!"

I started running again but it felt like my legs were gone. The car with Bugs in it was getting farther and farther away. Finally I stopped.

Bugs was leaning out of the door and stopped reaching back for me. He waved and disappeared into the boxcar. A second later my suitcase came flying out of the door.

I walked over to where it landed and picked it up. Man, this is one tough suitcase, you couldn't even tell what it had been through, it still looked exactly the same.

I sat on the side of the tracks and tried to catch my breath.

The train and my new pretend brother got farther and farther away, chugging to Chicago. Man, I'd found some family and he was gone before we could really get to know each other.

Connecting Literature Past and Present

1. In what way do Buddy's experiences relate to the poem "The Open Road"?
2. Do you think Buddy would get along with the speaker of "Life Doesn't Frighten Me"? Explain.
3. Which details of this excerpt give clues about life during the Depression?

Thematic Connection
How is the theme of optimism communicated here?

Christopher Paul Curtis

(b. 1954)
Like the characters in his books, Christopher Paul Curtis was raised in Flint, Michigan. While working in an automotive assembly plant, he began attending college classes at the University of Michigan. During that time, he won a prize for a draft of his first story. He then took a year off and, supported by his family, wrote his first book, *The Watsons Go to Birmingham*, which won the Coretta Scott King Award and was a Newbery Honor Book in 1996.

Bud, Not Buddy is Curtis's second book based on life in the difficult times of the Depression. Curtis's own background as the son of an auto worker gives him firsthand knowledge of families working in the auto plants. *Bud, Not Buddy* won both the Newbery Medal and the Coretta Scott King Text Honor in 2000.

Curtis is living in Canada with his wife and children.

Prepare to Read

A Backwoods Boy ◆ Jackie Robinson: Justice at Last

 Take It to the Net

Visit www.phschool.com for interactive activities and instruction related to these selections, including

- background
- graphic organizers
- literary elements
- reading strategies

Preview

Connecting to the Literature

Abraham Lincoln and Jackie Robinson were people who faced and overcame huge roadblocks on the road to success. What problems and roadblocks do you face as you try to achieve the things that mean the most to you?

Background

In the early 1900s, major league baseball clubs excluded African Americans. African American players formed their own teams, and in the 1920s, they organized the Negro leagues. Although they did not become as widely known as their white counterparts, some of the best players in baseball history played in the Negro leagues. Jackie Robinson began his professional baseball career on the Negro leagues' team, the Kansas City Monarchs.

Literary Analysis

Historical Account

A **historical account** tells about real people and events of the past. A historical account may tell a story, but it is not necessarily written in strict time order.

The details in the example below are drawn from various points in Lincoln's life to illustrate his lifelong love of reading.

> Mostly, he educated himself by borrowing books and newspapers. There are many stories about Lincoln's efforts to find enough books to satisfy him in that backwoods country. Those he liked he read again and again, losing himself in the adventures of *Robinson Crusoe* or the magical tales of *The Arabian Nights*.

Comparing Literary Works

These two historical accounts focus on important people in history whose actions changed the way people thought or acted. Compare and contrast the subjects of the accounts by thinking about the following focus questions.

1. In what way did each person affect history?
2. What qualities do you admire in each subject? Explain.

Reading Strategy

Determining Main Ideas

The **main ideas** are the core of a piece of writing. To determine main ideas, you look at how the details work together to suggest or point to a big idea. The graphic organizer shows four details from which you can determine that Jackie Robinson was a good athlete.

Organize details in your mind to determine main ideas as you read these two works.

Vocabulary Development

aptitude (ap′ te tood′) *n.* natural ability (p. 322)

intrigued (in trēgd′) *v.* fascinated (p. 323)

treacherous (trech′ ər əs) *adj.* dangerous (p. 324)

integrate (in′ tə grāt′) *v.* remove barriers and allow access to all (p. 326)

retaliated (ri tal′ ē at′ id) *v.* harmed or did wrong to someone in return for an injury or wrong he or she has done (p. 328)

A BACKWOODS BOY

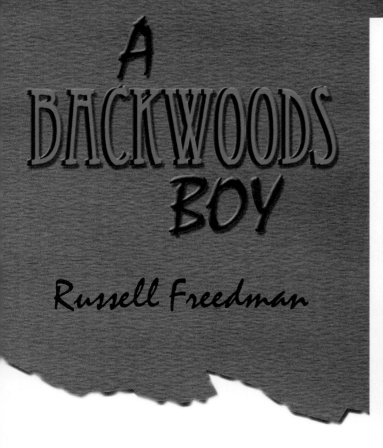

Russell Freedman

"It is a great piece of folly to attempt to make anything out of my early life. It can all be condensed into a simple sentence, and that sentence you will find in Gray's Elegy[1]—'the short and simple annals[2] of the poor.' That's my life, and that's all you or anyone else can make out of it."[3]

Abraham Lincoln never liked to talk much about his early life. A poor backwoods farm boy, he grew up swinging an ax on frontier homesteads in Kentucky, Indiana, and Illinois.

He was born near Hodgenville, Kentucky, on February 12, 1809, in a log cabin with one window, one door, a chimney, and a hardpacked dirt floor. His parents named him after his pioneer grandfather. The first Abraham Lincoln had been shot dead by hostile Indians

▲ **Critical Viewing** Is it surprising that one of the presidents of the United States was born in a house like this one? **[Assess]**

---

1. **elegy** (el′ ə jē) *n.* poem praising someone who has died.
2. **annals** (an′ əlz) *n.* historical records.
3. **"It is a great . . . out of it"** this is a quotation from Abraham Lincoln.

in 1786, while planting a field of corn in the Kentucky wilderness.

Young Abraham was still a toddler when his family packed their belongings and moved to another log-cabin farm a few miles north, on Knob Creek. That was the first home he could remember, the place where he ran and played as a barefoot boy.

He remembered the bright waters of Knob Creek as it tumbled past the Lincoln cabin and disappeared into the Kentucky hills. Once he fell into the rushing creek and almost drowned before he was pulled out by a neighbor boy. Another time he caught a fish and gave it to a passing soldier.

Lincoln never forgot the names of his first teachers—Zachariah Riney followed by Caleb Hazel—who ran a windowless log schoolhouse two miles away. It was called a "blab school." Pupils of all ages sat on rough wooden benches and bawled out their lessons aloud. Abraham went there with his sister Sarah, who was two years older, when they could be spared from their chores at home. Holding hands, they would walk through scrub trees and across creek bottoms to the schoolhouse door. They learned their numbers from one to ten, and a smattering of reading, writing, and spelling.

Their parents couldn't read or write at all. Abraham's mother, Nancy, signed her name by making a shakily drawn mark. He would remember her as a thin, sad-eyed woman who labored beside her husband in the fields. She liked to gather the children around her in the evening to recite prayers and Bible stories she had memorized.

His father, Thomas, was a burly, barrel-chested farmer and carpenter who had worked hard at homesteading since marrying Nancy Hanks in 1806. A sociable fellow, his greatest pleasure was to crack jokes and swap stories with his chums. With painful

Reading Strategy
Determining Main Idea
What is the main idea about Lincoln's schooling?

Reading Check

What did Lincoln learn in school?

effort, Thomas Lincoln could scrawl his name. Like his wife, he had grown up without education, but that wasn't unusual in those days. He supported his family by living off his own land, and he watched for a chance to better himself.

In 1816, Thomas decided to pull up stakes again and move north to Indiana, which was about to join the Union as the nation's nineteenth state. Abraham was seven. He remembered the one-hundred-mile journey as the hardest experience of his life. The family set out on a cold morning in December, loading all their possessions on two horses. They crossed the Ohio River on a makeshift ferry, traveled through towering forests, then hacked a path through tangled underbrush until they reached their new homesite near the backwoods community of Little Pigeon Creek.

Thomas put up a temporary winter shelter—a crude, three-sided lean-to of logs and branches. At the open end, he kept a fire burning to take the edge off the cold and scare off the wild animals. At night, wrapped in bearskins and huddled by the fire, Abraham and Sarah listened to wolves howl and panthers scream.

Abraham passed his eighth birthday in the lean-to. He was big for his age, "a tall spider of a boy," and old enough to handle an ax. He helped his father clear the land. They planted corn and pumpkin seeds between the tree stumps. And they built a new log cabin, the biggest one yet, where Abraham climbed a ladder and slept in a loft beneath the roof.

Soon after the cabin was finished, some of Nancy's kinfolk arrived. Her aunt and uncle with their adopted son Dennis had decided to follow the Lincolns to Indiana. Dennis Hanks became an extra hand to Thomas and a big brother to Abraham, someone to run and wrestle with.

A year later, Nancy's aunt and uncle lay dead, victims of the dreaded "milk sickness" (now known to be caused by a poisonous plant called white snake root). An epidemic of the disease swept through the Indiana woods in the summer of 1818. Nancy had nursed her relatives until the end, and then she too came down with the disease. Abraham watched his mother toss in bed with chills, fever, and pain for seven days before she died at the age of thirty-four. "She knew she was going to die," Dennis Hanks recalled. "She called up the children to her dying side and told them to be good and kind to their father, to one another, and to the world."

Thomas built a coffin from black cherry wood, and nine-year-old Abraham whittled the pegs that held the wooden planks together. They buried Nancy on a windswept hill, next to her aunt and uncle. Sarah, now eleven, took her mother's place, cooking, cleaning, and mending clothes for her father, brother, and cousin Dennis in the forlorn and lonely cabin.

Literary Analysis
Historical Account What comment does Freedman make on the facts he presents here?

Thomas Lincoln waited for a year. Then he went back to Kentucky to find himself a new wife. He returned in a four-horse wagon with a widow named Sarah Bush Johnston, her three children, and all her household goods. Abraham and his sister were fortunate, for their stepmother was a warm and loving person. She took the motherless children to her heart and raised them as her own. She also spruced up the neglected Lincoln cabin, now shared by eight people who lived, ate, and slept in a single smoky room with a loft.

Abraham was growing fast, shooting up like a sunflower, a spindly youngster with big bony hands, unruly black hair, a dark complexion, and luminous gray eyes. He became an expert with the ax, working alongside his father, who also hired him out to work for others. For twenty-five cents a day, the boy dug wells, built pigpens, split fence rails, felled trees. "My how he could chop!" exclaimed a friend. "His ax would flash and bite into a sugar tree or a sycamore, and down it would come. If you heard him felling trees in a clearing, you would say there were three men at work, the way the trees fell."

Reading Strategy
Determining Main Idea
What is the main idea of this paragraph?

Meanwhile, he went to school "by littles," a few weeks one winter, maybe a month the next. Lincoln said later that all his schooling together "did not amount to one year." Some fragments of his schoolwork still survive, including a verse that he wrote in his homemade arithmetic book: "Abraham Lincoln/his hand and pen/he will be good but/god knows When."

Mostly, he educated himself by borrowing books and newspapers. There are many stories about Lincoln's efforts to find enough books to satisfy him in that backwoods country. Those he liked he read again and again, losing himself in the adventures of *Robinson Crusoe* or the magical tales of *The Arabian Nights*. He was thrilled by a biography of George Washington, with its stirring account of the Revolutionary War. And he came to love the rhyme and rhythm of poetry, reciting passages from Shakespeare or the Scottish poet Robert Burns at the drop of a hat. He would carry a book out to the field with him, so he could read at the end of each plow furrow, while the horse was getting its breath. When noon came, he would sit under a tree and read while he ate. "I never saw Abe after he was twelve that he didn't have a book in his hand or in his pocket," Dennis Hanks remembered. "It didn't seem natural to see a feller read like that."

Literary Analysis
Historical Account
What interpretations of fact might Freedman be making here?

By the time he was sixteen, Abraham was six feet tall—"the gangliest awkwardest feller . . . he appeared to be all joints," said a neighbor. He may have looked awkward, but hard physical labor had given him a tough, lean body with muscular arms like steel cables. He could grab a woodsman's ax by the handle and hold it straight out at arm's length. And he was one of the best wrestlers and runners around.

✔**Reading Check**

How did Lincoln feel about reading?

He also had a reputation as a comic and storyteller. Like his father, Abraham was fond of talking and listening to talk. About this time he had found a book called *Lessons in Elocution*, which offered advice on public speaking. He practiced before his friends, standing on a tree stump as he entertained them with fiery imitations of the roving preachers and politicians who often visited Little Pigeon Creek.

Folks liked young Lincoln. They regarded him as a good-humored, easy-going boy—a bookworm maybe, but smart and willing to oblige. Yet even then, people noticed that he could be moody and withdrawn. As a friend put it, he was "witty, sad, and reflective by turns."

At the age of seventeen, Abraham left home for a few months to work as a ferryman's helper on the Ohio River. He was eighteen when his sister Sarah died early in 1828, while giving birth to her first child.

That spring, Abraham had a chance to get away from the backwoods and see something of the world. A local merchant named James Gentry hired Lincoln to accompany his son Allen on a twelve-hundred-mile flatboat voyage to New Orleans. With their cargo of country produce, the two boys floated down the Ohio River and into the Mississippi, maneuvering with long poles to avoid snags and sandbars, and to navigate in the busy river traffic.

New Orleans was the first real city they had ever seen. Their eyes must have popped as the great harbor came into view, jammed with the masts of sailing ships from distant ports all over the world. The city's cobblestone streets teemed with sailors, traders, and adventurers speaking strange languages. And there were gangs of slaves everywhere. Lincoln would never forget the sight of black men, women, and children being driven along in chains and auctioned off like cattle. In those days, New Orleans had more than two hundred slave dealers.

The boys sold their cargo and their flatboat and returned upriver by steamboat. Abraham earned twenty-four dollars—a good bit of money at the time—for the three-month trip. He handed the money over to his father, according to law and custom.

Thomas Lincoln was thinking about moving on again. Lately he had heard glowing reports about Illinois, where instead of forests there were endless prairies with plenty of rich black soil. Early in 1830, Thomas sold his Indiana farm. The Lincolns piled everything they owned into two ox-drawn wagons and set out over muddy roads, with Abraham, just turned twenty-one, driving one of the wagons himself. They traveled west to their new homesite in central Illinois, not far from Decatur. Once again, Abraham helped his father build a cabin and start a new farm.

▼ **Critical Viewing**
How does this image of Thomas Lincoln compare with your image of Abraham Lincoln? **[Compare]**

He stayed with his family through their first prairie winter, but he was getting restless. He had met an enterprising fellow named Denton Offutt, who wanted him to take another boatload of cargo down the river to New Orleans. Abraham agreed to make the trip with his stepbrother, John Johnston, and a cousin, John Hanks.

When he returned to Illinois three months later, he paid a quick farewell visit to his father and stepmother. Abraham was twenty-two now, of legal age, free to do what he wanted. His parents were settled and could get along without him. Denton Offutt was planning to open a general store in the flourishing village of New Salem, Illinois, and he had promised Lincoln a steady job.

Lincoln arrived in New Salem in July 1831 wearing a faded cotton shirt and blue jeans too short for his long legs—a "friendless, uneducated, penniless boy," as he later described himself. He tended the counter at Denton Offutt's store and slept in a room at the back.

The village stood in a wooded grove on a bluff above the Sangamon River. Founded just two years earlier, it had about one hundred people living in one- and two-room log houses. Cattle grazed behind split-rail fences, hogs snuffled along dusty lanes, and chickens and geese flapped about underfoot. New Salem was still a small place, but it was growing. The settlers expected it to become a frontier boom town.

With his gifts for swapping stories and making friends, Lincoln fit easily into the life of the village. He showed off his skill with an ax, competed in footraces, and got along with everyone from Mentor Graham, the schoolmaster, to Jack Armstrong, the leader of a rowdy gang called the Clary's Grove boys. Armstrong was the wrestling champion of New Salem. He quickly challenged Lincoln to a match.

On the appointed day, an excited crowd gathered down by the river, placing bets as the wrestlers stripped to the waist for combat. They circled each other, then came to grips, twisting and tugging until they crashed to the ground with Lincoln on top. As he pinned Armstrong's shoulders to the ground, the other Clary's Grove boys dived in to join the scuffle. Lincoln broke away, backed against a cliff, and defiantly offered to take them all on—one at a time. Impressed, Armstrong jumped to his feet and offered Lincoln his hand, declaring the match a draw. After that, they were fast friends.

Lincoln also found a place among the town's intellectuals. He joined the New Salem Debating Society, which met once a week in James Rutledge's tavern. The first time he debated, he seemed nervous. But as he began to speak in his high, reedy voice, he surprised everyone with the force and logic of his argument. "He was already a fine speaker," one debater recalled. "All he lacked was culture."

Lincoln was self-conscious about his meager education, and ambitious to improve himself. Mentor Graham, the schoolmaster and a

Reading Check

How does Denton Offutt change Lincoln's life?

fellow debater, took a liking to the young man, lent him books, and offered to coach him in the fine points of English grammar. Lincoln had plenty of time to study. There wasn't much business at Offutt's store, so he could spend long hours reading as he sat behind the counter.

When the store failed in 1832, Offutt moved on to other schemes. Lincoln had to find something else to do. At the age of twenty-three, he decided to run for the Illinois state legislature. Why not? He knew everyone in town, people liked him, and he was rapidly gaining confidence as a public speaker. His friends urged him to run, saying that a bright young man could go far in politics. So Lincoln announced his candidacy and his political platform. He was in favor of local improvements, like better roads and canals. He had made a study of the Sangamon River, and he proposed that it be dredged and cleared so steamboats could call at New Salem—insuring a glorious future for the town.

Reading Strategy
Determining Main Ideas
What is the main idea of this paragraph?

Before he could start his campaign, an Indian war flared up in northern Illinois. Chief Black Hawk of the Sauk and Fox tribes had crossed the Mississippi, intending, he said, to raise corn on land that had been taken from his people thirty years earlier. The white settlers were alarmed, and the governor called for volunteers to stop the invasion. Lincoln enlisted in a militia company made up of his friends and neighbors. He was surprised and pleased when the men elected him as their captain, with Jack Armstrong as first sergeant. His troops drilled and marched, but they never did sight any hostile Indians. Years later, Lincoln would joke about his three-month stint as a military man, telling how he survived "a good many bloody battles with mosquitoes."

By the time he returned to New Salem, election day was just two weeks off. He jumped into the campaign—pitching horseshoes with voters, speaking at barbecues, chatting with farmers in the fields, joking with customers at country stores. He lost, finishing eighth in a field of thirteen. But in his own precinct,[4] where folks knew him, he received 227 votes out of 300 cast.

Defeated as a politician, he decided to try his luck as a frontier merchant. With a fellow named William Berry as his partner, Lincoln operated a general store that sold everything from axes to beeswax. But the two men showed little aptitude for business, and their store finally "winked out," as Lincoln put it. Then Berry died, leaving Lincoln saddled with a $1,100 debt—a gigantic amount for someone who had never earned more than a few dollars a month. Lincoln called it "the National Debt," but he vowed to repay every cent. He spent the next fifteen years doing so.

aptitude (ap′ tə tōōd′) *n.* natural ability

---

4. precinct (prē′ siŋkt) *n.* election district.

To support himself, he worked at all sorts of odd jobs. He split fence rails, hired himself out as a farmhand, helped at the local gristmill.[5] With the help of friends, he was appointed postmaster of New Salem, a part-time job that paid about fifty dollars a year. Then he was offered a chance to become deputy to the local surveyor.[6] He knew nothing about surveying, so he bought a compass, a chain, and a couple of textbooks on the subject. Within six weeks, he had taught himself enough to start work—laying out roads and townsites, and marking off property boundaries.

As he traveled about the county, making surveys and delivering mail to faraway farms, people came to know him as an honest and dependable fellow. Lincoln could be counted on to witness a contract, settle a boundary dispute, or compose a letter for folks who couldn't write much themselves. For the first time, his neighbors began to call him "Abe."

In 1834, Lincoln ran for the state legislature again. This time he placed second in a field of thirteen candidates, and was one of four men elected to the Illinois House of Representatives from Sangamon County. In November, wearing a sixty-dollar tailor-made suit he had bought on credit, the first suit he had ever owned, the twenty-five-year-old legislator climbed into a stagecoach and set out for the state capital in Vandalia.

In those days, Illinois lawmakers were paid three dollars a day to cover their expenses, but only while the legislature was in session. Lincoln still had to earn a living. One of his fellow representatives, a rising young attorney named John Todd Stuart, urged Lincoln to take up the study of law. As Stuart pointed out, it was an ideal profession for anyone with political ambitions.

And in fact, Lincoln had been toying with the idea of becoming a lawyer. For years he had hung around frontier courthouses, watching country lawyers bluster and strut as they cross-examined witnesses and delivered impassioned speeches before juries. He had sat on juries himself, appeared as a witness, drawn up legal documents for his neighbors. He had even argued a few cases before the local justice of the peace.

Yes, the law <u>intrigued</u> him. It would give him a chance to rise in the world, to earn a respected place in the community, to live by his wits instead of by hard physical labor.

Yet Lincoln hesitated, unsure of himself because he had so little formal education. That was no great obstacle, his friend Stuart kept telling him. In the 1830's, few American lawyers had ever seen the inside of a law school. Instead, they "read law" in the office of a practicing attorney until they knew enough to pass their exams.

Literary Analysis
Historical Account
What background is provided here to show the significance of Lincoln's election?

intrigued (in trēgd') v. fascinated

**Reading Check**

Why does Lincoln buy his first suit?

---

5. **gristmill** (grist' mil') n. place where grain is ground into flour.
6. **surveyor** (sər vā' ər) n. person who determines the boundaries of land.

Lincoln decided to study entirely on his own. He borrowed some law books from Stuart, bought others at an auction, and began to read and memorize legal codes[7] and precedents.[8] Back in New Salem, folks would see him walking down the road, reciting aloud from one of his law books, or lying under a tree as he read, his long legs stretched up the trunk. He studied for nearly three years before passing his exams and being admitted to practice on March 1, 1837.

By then, the state legislature was planning to move from Vandalia to Springfield, which had been named the new capital of Illinois. Lincoln had been elected to a second term in the legislature. And he had accepted a job as junior partner in John Todd Stuart's Springfield law office.

In April, he went back to New Salem for the last time to pack his belongings and say goodbye to his friends. The little village was declining now. Its hopes for growth and prosperity had vanished when the Sangamon River proved too <u>treacherous</u> for steamboat travel. Settlers were moving away, seeking brighter prospects elsewhere.

By 1840, New Salem was a ghost town. It would have been forgotten completely if Abraham Lincoln hadn't gone there to live when he was young, penniless, and ambitious.

treacherous (trech' ər əs) *adj.* dangerous

---

7. **legal codes:** Body of law, as for a nation or a city, arranged systematically
8. **precedents** (pres' ə dənts) *n.*: Legal cases that may serve as a reference

Review and Assess

Thinking About the Selection

1. **Respond:** What was the most interesting fact you learned about young Abraham Lincoln?

2. **(a) Analyze:** What are two facts you recall about Lincoln before the age of eight? **(b) Generalize:** What generalization could you make about Lincoln's early life?

3. **(a) Recall:** What are two facts from Lincoln's life between the ages of eight and twenty-one? **(b) Classify:** What words would you use to describe Lincoln at this time in his life?

4. **(a) Recall:** Why did Lincoln move to New Salem? **(b) Analyze:** In what ways did his life change there? **(c) Connect:** In what ways is the Lincoln of New Salem similar to or different from the Lincoln that most people know in American history?

5. **(a) Recall:** What was Lincoln's first political office? **(b) Interpret:** How did Lincoln continue to develop and change after he was elected to office? **(c) Speculate:** In what ways did these experiences help form the great leader he would become?

Russell Freedman

(b. 1929)

When Russell Freedman was growing up in San Francisco, California, his mother had a job in a bookstore and his father worked in publishing. It's not surprising, then, that Freedman eventually became a writer. After working as a reporter for the Associated Press, he went on to write more than thirty books for young readers. These include *Immigrant Kids*, *Children of the Wild West*, and *Cowboys of the Wild West*. "A Backwoods Boy" is from Freedman's award-winning book *Lincoln: A Photobiography*.

Jackie Robinson:
Justice at Last

Geoffrey C. Ward and Ken Burns

It was 1945, and World War II had ended. Americans of all races had died for their country. Yet black men were still not allowed in the major leagues. The national pastime was loved by all America, but the major leagues were for white men only.

▲ **Critical Viewing** What details in this picture indicate that Jackie Robinson and his teammates shared team spirit? **[Analyze]**

Branch Rickey of the Brooklyn Dodgers thought that was wrong. He was the only team owner who believed blacks and whites should play together. Baseball, he felt, would become even more thrilling, and fans of all colors would swarm to his ballpark.

Rickey decided his team would be the first to <u>integrate</u>. There were plenty of brilliant Negro league players, but he knew the first black major leaguer would need much more than athletic ability.

Many fans and players were prejudiced—they didn't want the races to play together. Rickey knew the first black player would be cursed and booed. Pitchers would throw at him; runners

integrate (in´ tə grāt´) v. remove barriers and allow access to all

◀ **Critical Viewing**
What qualities of Jackie Robinson do you see demonstrated in this picture? **[Analyze]**

would spike him. Even his own teammates might try to pick a fight.

But somehow this man had to rise above that. No matter what happened, he must never lose his temper. No matter what was said to him, he must never answer back. If he had even one fight, people might say integration wouldn't work.

When Rickey met Jackie Robinson, he thought he'd found the right man. Robinson was 28 years old, and a superb athlete. In his first season in the Negro leagues, he hit .387. But just as importantly, he had great intelligence and sensitivity. Robinson was college-educated, and knew what joining the majors would mean for blacks. The grandson of a slave, he was proud of his race and wanted others to feel the same.

In the past, Robinson had always stood up for his rights. But now Rickey told him he would have to stop. The Dodgers needed "a man that will take abuse."

At first Robinson thought Rickey wanted someone who was afraid to defend himself. But as they talked, he realized that in this case a truly brave man would have to avoid fighting. He thought for a while, then promised Rickey he would not fight back.

Reading Strategy
Determining Main Ideas
What is the main idea of this paragraph?

Robinson signed with the Dodgers and went to play in the minors in 1946. Rickey was right—fans insulted him, and so did players. But he performed brilliantly and avoided fights. Then, in 1947, he came to the majors.

Many Dodgers were angry. Some signed a petition demanding to be traded. But Robinson and Rickey were determined to make their experiment work.

On April 15—Opening Day—26,623 fans came out to Ebbets Field. More than half of them were black—Robinson was already their hero. Now he was making history just by being on the field.

The afternoon was cold and wet, but no one left the ballpark. The Dodgers beat the Boston Braves, 5–3. Robinson went hitless, but the hometown fans didn't seem to care—they cheered his every move.

✔**Reading Check**

What does Branch Rickey do to change baseball?

Robinson's first season was difficult. Fans threatened to kill him; players tried to hurt him. The St. Louis Cardinals said they would strike if he took the field. And because of laws separating the races in certain states, he often couldn't eat or sleep in the same places as his teammates.

Yet through it all, he kept his promise to Rickey. No matter who insulted him, he never <u>retaliated</u>.

Robinson's dignity paid off. Thousands of fans jammed stadiums to see him play. The Dodgers set attendance records in a number of cities.

Slowly his teammates accepted him, realizing that he was the spark that made them a winning team. No one was more daring on the base paths or better with the glove. At the plate, he had great bat control—he could hit the ball anywhere. That season, he was named baseball's first Rookie of the Year.

Jackie Robinson went on to a glorious career. But he did more than play the game well—his bravery taught Americans a lesson. Branch Rickey opened a door, and Jackie Robinson stepped through it, making sure it could never be closed again. Something wonderful happened to baseball—and America—the day Jackie Robinson joined the Dodgers.

retaliated (ri tal´ ē at´ id) v. harmed or did wrong to someone in return for an injury or wrong he or she has done

Review and Assess

Thinking About the Selection

1. **Respond:** Would you have accepted a place on the team if you had been in Jackie Robinson's shoes? Why or why not?

2. **(a) Recall:** Who was Branch Rickey? **(b) Analyze:** Why do Ward and Burns give Rickey a great deal of credit in this article?

3. **(a) Recall:** Why did Jackie Robinson come to the attention of Branch Rickey? **(b) Analyze:** What did Rickey have to convince Robinson not to do? **(c) Connect:** How important was this advice?

4. **(a) Recall:** Name three difficult situations that Jackie Robinson and the Dodgers faced in Robinson's first season. **(b) Infer:** How did Robinson and the team overcome these difficulties?

5. **(a) Recall:** Why did Robinson's teammates eventually accept him? **(b) Speculate:** Why did everyone else eventually accept Robinson and integrate baseball?

Geoffrey C. Ward
Ken Burns

(b. 1940)
(b. 1953)

The creative team of Geoffrey C. Ward and Ken Burns is best known for documentaries, factual film presentations about real people and events. For example, Ward and Burns created an award-winning documentary on the United States Civil War. It told the story of that conflict using the words and photographs of those who lived it—from Abraham Lincoln to the soldier slogging through the mud. "Jackie Robinson: Justice at Last" is from a book based on their documentary *Baseball*, which presents the history of our national pastime.

Review and Assess

Literary Analysis

Historical Account

1. What facts do you learn in this account about Lincoln's first home, first school, and parents? Add more facts to a chart like this one:

First Home	First School	Parents
in Kentucky wilderness	two miles away	father—farmer and carpenter

2. What do you learn about how Lincoln got involved in politics?
3. What do you learn about Robinson before Branch Rickey met him?
4. What facts do you learn about baseball during the days that Jackie Robinson played the game?

Comparing Literary Works

5. For each work, complete an organizer like the one shown. Record the most significant or important points.

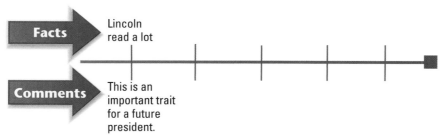

Facts — Lincoln read a lot

Comments — This is an important trait for a future president.

6. Which writer offers more opinions or comments on events?
7. Which writer provides more background information to show the significance of events?

Reading Strategy

Determining Main Ideas

8. List three main ideas about Abraham Lincoln that you identified while reading "A Backwoods Boy."
9. List two main ideas about the history of baseball that you identified while reading "Jackie Robinson: Justice at Last."

Extending Understanding

10. **History Connection:** What historical connection is there between Abraham Lincoln and Jackie Robinson?

Quick Review

A **historical account** tells about real people who lived in the past and real events that took place in the past. To review historical accounts, see page 315.

Main ideas are the most important points. To review main ideas, see page 315.

 Take It to the Net
www.phschool.com
Take the interactive self-test online to check your understanding of these selections.

Integrate Language Skills

Vocabulary Development Lesson

Word Analysis: Latin Prefix re-

The Latin prefix *re-* means "back," "again," or "against." You can see the meaning "back" in *retaliated*, which means "got revenge" or "paid back." Explain the meaning of each of these words.

1. remember   2. redesign   3. reverse

Spelling Strategy

Exaggerate your pronunciation before writing a word so that you don't leave syllables or letters out.

Example: ap–ti–tude

Pronounce each of the following words. Then choose the correct word for each sentence below.

at–ti–tude   grat–i–tude

1. You show your ____?____ by how you act.
2. You show your ____?____ by saying thank you.

Fluency: Using Words in Context

Answer the following questions with *yes* or *no.* Then, explain your responses.

1. Did Abraham Lincoln have an *aptitude* for public speaking?
2. Did the job of state representative *intrigue* Lincoln?
3. Was the Sangamon River a *treacherous* place for steamboats?
4. Did Jackie Robinson help baseball become *integrated*?
5. Did Branch Rickey convince Robinson not to *retaliate* against prejudice?
6. Did Jackie Robinson lack *aptitude* for the game of baseball?

Grammar Lesson

Conjunctions

A **conjunction** is a word that connects other words or groups of words. When conjunctions join sentences (complete thoughts), they show the relationship between the ideas in the complete thoughts that they join. The conjunction *and* shows addition. *But* and *yet* show a contrast between ideas. *For* and *so* show a cause-effect relationship between the sentences. When you join two complete thoughts with a conjunction, always use a comma before the conjunction.

> **Example:** The Lincoln children were fortunate, *for* their stepmother was loving.

Practice Copy these sentences. Underline the conjunctions, and explain the connection between ideas.

1. The afternoon was cold and wet, but no one left the ballpark.
2. He carried a book around the field, so he could read at the end of each plow furrow.

Writing Application Rewrite the following passage. Use commas and conjunctions to combine sentences and to show relationships between ideas.

Rickey understood Robinson's talent. He wanted Robinson on his team. Robinson agreed. He was worried about people's reactions.

Prentice Hall Writing and Grammar Connection: Chapter 18, Section 1

Writing Lesson

Writer's Choice

The authors of these selections wrote historical accounts of people they admired. Use what you have learned in one of these accounts to write about the subject in another form.

Prewriting   You might consider a poem, an essay, or a letter. The following chart shows some purposes and forms you might consider.

Model: Choose a Purpose and Form

Purpose	Possible Form
To imagine what you would like to tell the subject	Letter to the subject
To record feelings and impressions about the subject	Poem or journal entry
To persuade others to admire the subject	Persuasive speech, letter, or essay

Drafting   Follow the format of your chosen form. Incorporate details you learned in the historical accounts.

Revising   No matter what form of writing you choose, check that you have used correct spelling and have written legibly, or in a way that can be read.

W̲G Prentice Hall Writing and Grammar Connection: Chapter 11, Section 2

Extension Activities

Listening and Speaking With a partner, **role-play** the first conversation between Jackie Robinson and Branch Rickey.

1. Begin by rereading the text for details you can incorporate in your role play.
2. Discuss with your partner the appropriate emotions each speaker should show.
3. Experiment with using gestures or louder or softer voices to indicate the emotions behind the words.
4. Present your role play to the class. Ask for feedback on how effectively you communicated the emotions behind the words.

Research and Technology In a group, prepare a **visual timeline** to tell the story of Abraham Lincoln's life. Find information by using the Internet, databases, and CD-ROMs. Download and print out various forms of visual information, such as photographs, drawings, and reproductions of letters and documents to include in the timeline. Be sure to label every visual clearly and accurately. **[Group Activity]**

 **Take It to the Net**   www.phschool.com

Go online for an additional research activity using the Internet.

Magazine Articles

About Magazine Articles

Magazines may be published once a week, once a month, or every two months. Because they are published periodically, they are referred to as periodicals. One reference to use when looking for an article is the *Readers' Guide to Periodical Literature*. It is available electronically and in text form.

Magazine articles can be found on almost any subject you can name. Although each magazine article has unique characteristics, articles do share some common qualities.

- Articles give facts about a subject.
- Articles often include a comment by the writer on the subject.
- Articles are usually short enough to be read in one sitting.

One common type of article is a human-interest article. A human-interest article focuses on a single unique person, animal, or situation.

Reading Strategy

Evaluating Evidence for an Author's Conclusions

Authors of magazine articles can, and often do, draw conclusions based on the information they present. Do not let someone else do your thinking for you. Decide for yourself if you accept the author's conclusions. Evaluate the evidence. Then, evaluate whether the evidence actually supports the writer's claims.

1. What conclusion had the author drawn?
2. What reasons does the author give?
3. Does the evidence logically support the conclusion(s) the author has drawn?

Use an organizer like the one shown here to record and take notes on the information presented in this article. Put a star next to any facts or details you would like to check.

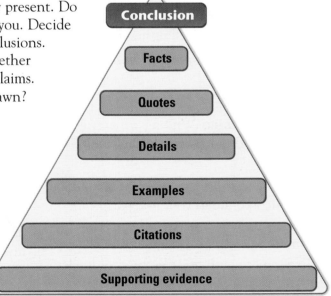

Conclusion
Facts
Quotes
Details
Examples
Citations
Supporting evidence

THROW
AND TELL

Gifted with a 98-mph fastball, teacher Jim Morris goes from a Texas classroom to baseball's big leagues.

The sentence in bold type is a summary of the article.

The magazine title (italics) identifies the subject, and the date tells the reader when the article was published.

People Weekly, OCTOBER 1, 1999

The Reagan County High School baseball team had a beef. Not about their field in Big Lake, Texas—where dust from a nearby rodeo arena sometimes stops games—but about batting practice. According to the kids, coach Jim Morris, a former minor leaguer forced out of the game a decade earlier by arm problems, was making pitches that they just couldn't hit. "The team used to tell me I was throwing too hard," says Morris, 35, who also taught science. "I thought they were complaining because they didn't want to take batting practice." Finally, he proposed a deal: If the team made the state play-offs, he would try out for the major leagues.

The kids did their part, and in mid-June, Morris did his, dazzling scouts with his 98-mph fastball. Within a week Morris had signed with the Tampa Bay Devil Rays and, with the blessing of wife Lorri, was launched on one of the most improbable baseball adventures this side of Kevin Costner. After posting a 3-1 record at the Devil Rays' Durham, N.C., farm club, the big lefthander got his call to the majors last month. On Sept. 18, against the Texas Rangers, Morris entered the game in the eighth inning, becoming the oldest big league rookie in nearly three decades. As Lorri, a college admissions officer, and the couple's three children looked on, Morris struck out Royce Clayton on four pitches. "My 8-year-old is ecstatic—he took that ball to school," says Morris. "My 5-year-old just wants me to come home."

Unfortunately for little Jessica, Daddy still has work to do. He's headed to the Arizona Fall League, where teams send their most promising prospects. "It's been an unbelievable journey," says Morris. "It's strange to go from signing report cards to signing autographs almost overnight."

When an article is about a person's very recent experience, it often includes quotations from that person.

■ ■ ■ ■

People Weekly, OCTOBER 1, 1999

Check Your Comprehension

1. Name three things you learned from the article about Jim Morris.
2. What led Jim Morris to try out for the major leagues?
3. What distinguished Morris from the other Tampa Bay Devil Rays?

Applying the Reading Strategy

Evaluating Evidence for an Author's Conclusions

4. What conclusion(s) has the author drawn about the likelihood of Morris's baseball career?
5. What reasons does the author give for his conclusion(s)?

Activity

Investigate a Conclusion

Do research to discover whether the author's conclusions turned out to be valid. Use the Internet to find online information. Use the *Readers' Guide to Periodical Literature* (print or electronic) to find magazine articles. If you don't know how to use the *Readers' Guide*, ask the reference librarian to help you. Compare what has happened in Jim Morris's baseball career with the author's conclusions.

Contrasting Informational Materials

Articles and Autobiographies

Autobiographical writing is writing in which the subject writes about all or part of his or her own life. In **biographical articles,** such as "Throw and Tell," the author writes about all or part of someone else's life. Look at the chart that shows characteristics of biographical articles and autobiographical writing. Contrast the two types of informational materials by answering the questions.

1. What is one reason a reader might choose an article over an autobiography?
2. What is one reason a reader might choose an autobiography over an article?
3. What details in "Throw and Tell" might not be included in an autobiographical account by Jim Morris?

	Biographical Article	Autobiography
Purpose	To tell about someone else's life	To tell about one's own life
Details	What the writer observes or is told about the subject	What the writer knows about his or her own actions, thoughts, and feelings
Audience	People interested in the person's life	People interested in the author's life

READING INFORMATIONAL MATERIALS

Persuasive Speeches

About Persuasive Speeches

A persuasive speech is a public presentation that argues for or against a particular position. People who use persuasive speeches to sway an audience's opinion include politicians and business people. A powerful persuasive speech can change the way an audience thinks and feels about an issue. Most persuasive speeches have the following characteristics:

- An issue with two sides
- A clear statement of the speaker's purpose and position
- Clear organization, including an introduction, a body, and a conclusion
- Powerful language intended to persuade

Reading Strategy

Understanding a Writer's Purpose

When a speaker writes and delivers a persuasive speech, the basic purpose is always the same. To understand a writer's purpose, consider these points:

- The speaker is trying to persuade you to accept his or her position.
- His or her position can usually be determined by reading the opening paragraphs of the speech.
- The rest of the speech is devoted to supporting the position with facts and arguments.

When reading the speech, determine the writer's possible purpose and whether the speech achieves this purpose.

Writer's Purpose	Was it achieved?
The writer was trying to persuade me to believe that _____ _____ _____ _____	Did the writer present accurate facts? Did the writer support a position with convincing arguments? Were the arguments presented clearly, in a logical order? Did the writer convince me to accept that position?

Preserving a Great American Symbol

Richard Durbin

Congressman Richard Durbin gave the following humorous speech in the House of Representatives on July 26, 1989. While most speeches to Congress are serious, Durbin's is humorous yet persuasive and "drives home" the point that wooden baseball bats should not be replaced with metal ones.

In his introduction, Durbin clearly introduces his topic and his purpose for delivering the speech.

Mr. Speaker, I rise to condemn the desecration of a great American symbol. No, I am not referring to flagburning; I am referring to the baseball bat.

Several experts tell us that the wooden baseball bat is doomed to extinction, that major league baseball players will soon be standing at home plate with aluminum bats in their hands.

Baseball fans have been forced to endure countless indignities by those who just cannot leave well enough alone: designated hitters,[1] plastic grass, uniforms that look like pajamas, chicken clowns dancing on the base lines, and, of course, the most heinous sacrilege, lights in Wrigley Field.[2]

Durbin uses humor to persuade and entertain.

Are we willing to hear the crack of a bat replaced by the dinky ping? Are we ready to see the Louisville Slugger replaced by the aluminum ping dinger? Is nothing sacred?

Please do not tell me that wooden bats are too expensive, when players who cannot hit their weight are being paid more money than the President of the United States.

Please do not try to sell me on the notion that these metal clubs will make better hitters.

What will be next? Teflon baseballs? Radar-enhanced gloves? I ask you.

I do not want to hear about saving trees. Any tree in America would gladly give its life for the glory of a day at home plate.

I do not know if it will take a constitutional amendment to keep our baseball traditions alive, but if we forsake the great Americana of broken-bat singles and pine tar,[3] we will have certainly lost our way as a nation.

Durbin closes with a dramatic statement, which serves as a final persuasive argument.

---

1. **designated hitter** player who bats in place of the pitcher and does not play any other position. The position was created in 1973 in the American League. Some fans argue it has changed the game for the worse.
2. **Wrigley Field** historic baseball field in Chicago. It did not have lights for night games until 1988. Some fans regretted the change.
3. **broken-bat singles . . . pine tar** When a batter breaks a wooden bat while hitting the ball and makes it to first base, it is a notable event in a baseball game. Pine tar is a substance used to improve the batter's grip on a wooden bat.

Check Your Comprehension

1. To which "American symbol" does Durbin refer in his opening statement?
2. Why does Durbin favor wooden bats and dislike aluminum bats?
3. How does the author tie baseball to America's national well-being?

Applying the Reading Strategy

Analyzing the Writer's Purpose

4. What is Richard Durbin's purpose in delivering this speech?
5. Summarize the arguments he uses to achieve his purpose.
6. Why do you think Durbin chose to use humor in his speech?
7. **(a)** Did Durbin persuade you with his arguments? Explain.
   (b) Did he leave out any details that would have been more persuasive? Explain.

Activity

Persuasive Speech

Write and present a persuasive speech that takes the opposite side of the position taken by Durbin. In other words, try to convince an audience that baseball teams should replace their wooden bats with aluminum ones.

- State your main position and purpose clearly in the opening and closing portions of the speech.
- Back up your main position with appropriate evidence and arguments that make sense.

To learn more about how to deliver a persuasive speech, see the Listening and Speaking Workshop on page 344.

Comparing Informational Materials

Political Speeches and Advertisements

Richard Durbin's persuasive speech supporting wooden bats is a political speech that uses humor as a persuasive tool. He also uses images that have emotional appeal and language that evokes strong emotions. Find examples of each persuasive technique in this speech and in an advertisement. Complete the chart with the examples you find.

	Political Speech	Advertisement
Purpose	(Persuasion) To convince enough voters to support a particular position.	(Persuasion) To convince customers to buy a particular product or service.
Methods		

Writing WORKSHOP

Persuasion: Persuasive Composition

A **persuasive composition** presents an argument for or against a particular position. In this workshop, you will write a persuasive composition in support of a proposition, or proposal.

Assignment Criteria. Your persuasive composition should have the following characteristics:

- An issue with two sides
- A clear thesis statement—a statement of your position on an issue, a proposition, or proposal
- Evidence that supports your position and anticipates the readers' concerns and counter-arguments
- A clear organization, including an introduction, a body, and a strong conclusion
- Powerful images and language

See the Rubric on page 343 for the criteria on which your persuasive composition may be assessed.

Prewriting

Choose a topic. Choose a topic that has at least two sides. Your purpose will be to show that your position, or side, is stronger than the opposing position.

Gather evidence. Identify facts, examples, statistics, quotations, and personal observations that support your position. Take notes on the sources of your information. You may need to recheck facts, and you will need to credit any ideas or words that are not your own.

Anticipate counterarguments. Anticipate readers' concerns, questions, and arguments against your position. Identify facts that can be included in the composition to address opposing positions.

Arguments	Counterarguments
It isn't music.	It is a group of organized sounds.
	It has a rhythmic pattern
There's no variety; all the same key.	The old standby key of E is gone.
	Guitarists are experimenting with techniques for changing keys.

Student Model

Before you begin drafting your persuasive composition, read this student model and review the characteristics of a successful persuasive composition.

Isaac Tetenbaum
Reseda, CA

Modern Rock Is Music, Too

Maybe you think Chopin is really cool—the blissful tones of the piano, played to serenade and mesmerize, the dazzling cadenzas and glistening high notes. For a change, though, why don't you pop in a modern rock CD? Contemporary music gets very little respect, yet most of the people who put it down haven't even listened to it. Modern rock deserves to be regarded and respected as music.

Music can be classified as any group of organized sounds. Yet while the roars of today's lead vocalists don't seem to make sense, even they are organized and related to the message of the song. Is it music? Yes. It follows a precise rhythmic pattern. It repeats. Just because howls from a modern vocalist don't follow any pitches doesn't mean they can't be classified as perfectly good music. You might not like the style, but you cannot deny it is music. Once you've accepted rock as music, you might say all rock songs are in the same key—E. Just because the lowest string of the guitar is an E doesn't mean modern rock musicians continuously strum that string and open and end a tune with it. Nowadays, as new musicians experiment with different pitches, the common E of rock has almost disappeared.

In a technique called "dropping," guitarists and bassists of modern rock bands have been able to use lower pitches in their songs. In fact, a well-known modern-style guitarist has successfully created a seven-string guitar. Its seventh string has the default pitch of a B. Although you might have to listen a little harder to hear the evidence, the musicians of contemporary bands know their music. How else could they come up with "dropping" and the seven-string guitar?

I think anyone, even the most classic of classical music lovers, can appreciate today's sounds if given a chance. (Notice I didn't say love, just appreciate.) I listen to Chopin and modern rock. I respect both kinds of music because each one has its place. Chopin is like elegant figure skating—rock is like snowboarding. I feel free when I listen to my favorite rock group. Why don't you listen with me?

The writer clearly established the two sides—those who like contemporary music and those who prefer classical.

The last sentence in the introduction is the thesis.

The writer provides evidence that contemporary artists would be considered musical even by classical definitions.

Here, the writer realizes that readers might argue that all rock music is written in the same key—an argument he says used to be true but isn't anymore.

A powerful image helps readers understand the difference in the effect of the two kinds of music and to recognize that one person can like two different things for two different occasions.

Drafting

Write a thesis statement. Review your notes, and write a strong one-sentence statement of your position. Include this sentence early in your composition.

Example: Our school should have a recycling bin next to every trash can.

Support each point. To support and clarify your points, use the following techniques.

- Find and use examples.
- Use facts or statistics.
- Make a specific observation.
- Include quotes and expert opinions.

Create a clear organization. Organize your thoughts clearly and concisely. Include your thesis statement in your introduction. Support your thesis statement in the body. Organize facts, details, and other support into paragraphs. Each paragraph should focus on one reason you give for your position. Conclude with a restatement of your thesis.

Revising

Revise to strengthen support. Look over your draft to find places where you can strengthen your support.

1. Underline your thesis statement in red.

2. Put a star next to each supporting point. Add more support if you have few stars.

Introduction

Thesis statement

Body

Main point followed by facts, details, arguments, statistics, expert opinions. Explanations and evidence for readers' concerns and counterarguments.

Conclusion

Summary of arguments Strong restatement of position

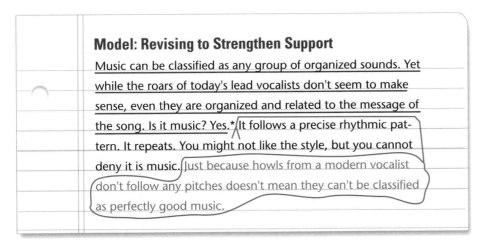

Model: Revising to Strengthen Support

Music can be classified as any group of organized sounds. Yet while the roars of today's lead vocalists don't seem to make sense, even they are organized and related to the message of the song. Is it music? Yes.* It follows a precise rhythmic pattern. It repeats. You might not like the style, but you cannot deny it is music. Just because howls from a modern vocalist don't follow any pitches doesn't mean they can't be classified as perfectly good music.

Revise to strengthen images. Look for places where you can add or improve an image that illustrates your point. Use words that call specific pictures or sensory details to mind.

Compare the model and the nonmodel. Why is the model more effective than the nonmodel?

Nonmodel	Model
I think anyone, even the most classic of classical music lovers, can appreciate today's sounds if given a chance. I listen to Chopin and modern rock. I respect both kinds of music because each one has its place.	I think anyone, even the most classic of classical music lovers, can appreciate today's sound if given a chance. (Notice I didn't say love, just appreciate.) I listen to Chopin and modern rock. I respect both kinds of music because each one has its place. Chopin is like elegant figure skating—rock is like snowboarding.

Publishing and Presenting

Choose one of these ways to share your writing with classmates or a larger audience.

Deliver a speech. Use your persuasive composition as the basis for a speech that you give to your classmates.

Post your essay. Use a word-processing program to format your composition. Post your persuasive composition on a class bulletin board so that classmates can read it and discuss your position.

WG *Prentice Hall Writing and Grammar Connection: Chapter 7, Section 6*

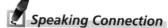
Speaking Connection
To learn more about delivering a persuasive composition as a speech, see the **Listening and Speaking Workshop: Delivering a Persuasive Speech**, page 344.

Rubric for Self-Assessment

Evaluate your persuasive composition using the following criteria and rating scale:

Criteria	Rating Scale Not very				Very
Does the issue have two sides?	1	2	3	4	5
How clear and focused is the thesis statement?	1	2	3	4	5
How well are readers' concerns anticipated and addressed?	1	2	3	4	5
How effectively are arguments organized?	1	2	3	4	5
How powerful is the persuasive language?	1	2	3	4	5

Listening and Speaking WORKSHOP

Delivering a Persuasive Speech

A **persuasive speech** shares many of the characteristics of a persuasive composition. (To review the characteristics of successful persuasive compositions, see the Writing Workshop, pp. 340–343.) The following speaking strategies will help you engage and convince your listeners.

Engage Listeners

Like compositions, persuasive speeches provide clear position statements and include supporting evidence in logical order. Follow these guidelines to plan and deliver a persuasive speech.

Start strong. Begin with a startling comparison or an anecdote that will capture your audience's attention.

> **Example:** Animal shelters across the country are full of unwanted pets that have been thrown away like garbage.

Make contact. Your audience will hear your presentation only once—make sure they hear each and every word.

● Speak loudly and slowly enough to be heard and understood.

● Make eye contact.

● Move around the room as you speak.

● Pause after key points.

Convince Listeners

To convince an audience of listeners, use speaking strategies that will highlight your strongest support.

Repeat key points. An audience of listeners cannot reread a point they have missed. As a speaker, make sure your audience does not miss your most important evidence and support. After explaining a key point, repeat it in a single sentence. After explaining several points, pause and restate the points in order.

Use visuals. A picture or chart can be a dramatic illustration of a point you are making. If you claim that overcrowding is a problem, show a picture of the overcrowding. If you say accidents are increasing, use a bar graph or a line graph to show the increase. The line graph at right shows how an increase can be shown to an audience rather than just described.

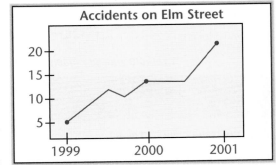

Accidents on Elm Street

(Activity:) Plan a Persuasive Speech Plan and deliver your speech to the class. Ask for feedback on how you can improve your delivery.

Assessment WORKSHOP

Identifying Cause and Effect

The reading sections of some tests require you to read a passage and answer multiple-choice questions about cause and effect. Use what you have learned about cause and effect to help you answer such questions.

To answer a cause-and-effect test item, ask yourself, "Why did something happen?" or "What happened as a result of something?"

Test-Taking Strategies

- Look for signal words such as *because, why, the reason for, as a result of, in order to,* and *so that.*
- Watch out for distractors—choices that state an event that is from the passage but that is not the cause or effect.

Sample Test Item

Directions: Read the passage and answer the questions.

The Cabrera children liked their new home in the United States. Their parents had good jobs, the neighbors were friendly, and their house was pleasant. Still, they missed their relatives in the Dominican Republic and looked forward to a long summer vacation on the island.

1. Why were the Cabrera children happy in the United States?
   A The neighbors were friendly.
   B They could go to the Dominican Republic for the summer.
   C Their mother didn't have to work.
   D Their new house was like their old one.

2. The children missed their relatives, so they—
   A planned to move back to the Dominican Republic
   B asked their parents to quit their jobs
   C looked forward to summer vacation
   D sold their new home in the United States

Answers and Explanations

1. **C** and **D** are not stated. **B** is not the reason they were happy. *A* is the answer.

2. **A** and **B** are not stated. **D** does not make sense in the sentence. *C* is the answer.

▶ Practice

Directions: Read the passage and answer the questions.

Immigrants have come to the United States for many reasons. Some have come to escape war, famine, or religious persecution. Others have come to make a better life for their families.

In the early twentieth century, millions of immigrants came from southern and eastern Europe. Many of them stayed in the coastal cities where they landed. As a result, these cities experienced growth and overcrowding.

1. Immigrants came to the United States to—
   A lose their old identity
   B escape war, famine, and persecution
   C avoid prosecution in their old country
   D escape political conditions

2. What contributed to the growth of cities in the United States in the early twentieth century?
   A overcrowding
   B famine
   C immigration
   D progress

Mysterious Worlds

This, That, There, 1993, Pat Adams, Courtesy of Eleanor Munro

Exploring the Theme

The picture on these pages could be a view of distant planets as seen through a telescope, or it could be a view of microorganisms as seen through a microscope. The stories, poems, and essays in this unit give you a lens through which you can examine mysteries near and far. Through the literature you can explore the mysteries of the past, search for answers to the unexplained, and appreciate the mysteries in the everyday world around you.

◀ **Critical Viewing** How does the artist suggest mystery and the unknown? **[Analyze]**

Why Read Literature?

This unit explores mysterious worlds—looking into the past and the future at unsolved mysteries and worlds to be discovered. While reading about the mysteries we can or cannot explain, you may have other purposes for reading these works. Preview three of the purposes you might set before reading the selections in this unit.

1 Read for information.

Sightings of the Loch Ness monster and monsters in other large lakes around the world have been reported for more than 1,400 years. Today, scientists use sonar, underwater photography, and other technological equipment to search for proof that these creatures do or do not exist. So far, clues found through technological means have only deepened the mystery. Learn what scientists have done to try to find "Nessie" when you read **"The Loch Ness Monster,"** page 406.

Only seven skeletons that are more than half complete of Tyrannosaurus Rex have ever been discovered. The most complete skeleton was discovered by an amateur fossil hunter. Learn interesting facts about this dinosaur discovery when you read information from the Web page **"The Life and Times of Sue,"** page 376.

The *Titanic* was one of three luxury liners in a fleet built by the White Star Line. The *Olympic,* one of the other two, survived four submarine attacks and made hundreds of transatlantic crossings without accident. Although the *Titanic* was the one people called "unsinkable," the *Olympic* eventually earned the nickname "Old Reliable." Find out why the *Titanic* could not live up to its unsinkable reputation when you read the excerpt from **"Exploring the *Titanic*,"** page 380.

2 Read for the love of literature.

When Jack Prelutsky was a boy, he hated poetry. When he grew up, he became a poet. Read a poem by this former poetry hater: **"Ankylosaurus,"** page 370.

A tortoise's shell has approximately fifty bones covered by twenty-six "scutes." The scutes are the separate sections that you can see on a tortoise's shell. Long before scientists came up with an explanation for these markings, storytellers in Africa were offering an entertaining explanation of their own. Read this humorous explanation in **"Why the Tortoise's Shell Is Not Smooth,"** page 411.

3 Read to be entertained.

The first general-purpose electronic digital computer was built in 1946. It was called ENIAC, for *E*lectronic *N*umerical *I*ntegrator *A*nd *C*omputer. It weighed thirty tons and took up more than 1,500 square feet. Isaac Asimov's story about computers, **"The Fun They Had,"** page 352, was written during ENIAC's time. Read it to see whether Asimov's vision of the future was accurate.

 Take It to the Net

Visit the Web site for online instruction and activities related to each selection in this unit.

www.phschool.com

How to Read Literature

Strategies for Reading Critically

Every day we receive countless messages through the media. In addition, we read texts that are fiction and nonfiction. To get the most from our reading, we need to read critically—to make decisions about what we believe and what we question. In this unit, you will learn strategies that will help you read critically.

1. Evaluate the author's message.

A good reader thinks about the writer's ideas and views and evaluates the author's message. Evaluating means making a critical judgment using questions like these:

- Does the writer present accurate information?
- Does the writer support opinions with sound reasons?
- Do I agree with the writer's message? Why or why not?

As you read the selections in this unit, you will practice asking and answering these questions to evaluate authors' messages.

2. Distinguish between fact and opinion.

Use the evidence the author presents to distinguish between fact and opinion. A fact can be proved. An opinion can be supported by facts, but a different opinion might also be supported. A statement of opinion is based on interpretation of evidence. A statement of fact is based on evidence alone.

Fact

Can be proved.

The radio room had received a total of seven ice warning messages in one day.

Opinion

Can be supported but not proved.

The atmosphere in the radio room was chaotic.

3. Evaluate logic and reasoning.

As you read, determine whether the author's conclusions are logical by identifying the specific facts that support each conclusion. Look for explanations, evidence, and arguments the author uses as reasons for statements about the topic.

4. Determine cause and effect.

Nonfiction writing, such as works about science and history, often explains the causes and effects of events. Fiction is also based on events with causes and effects. One way to determine cause and effect is to look for words that signal the cause—for example, *because, as a result, therefore,* and *so that.*

Example: The emperor asked Breaker to build a bridge *because* he believed that Breaker was a clever man.

As you read the selections in this unit, review the reading strategies and look at the notes in the side columns. Use the suggestions to apply the strategies for reading critically.

Prepare to Read

The Fun They Had

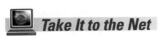 **Take It to the Net**

Visit www.phschool.com for interactive activities and instruction related to "The Fun They Had," including
- background
- graphic organizers
- literary elements
- reading strategies

Preview

Connecting to the Literature

In "The Fun They Had," by Isaac Asimov, two schoolchildren in the year 2155 find a relic of the past. Think about objects you associate with the past—such as record albums, which have been replaced by CDs. Read the story to find out what surprising item these children think of as outdated—in fact, antique!

Background

Isaac Asimov published "The Fun They Had" in 1957. At that time, the technology that led to the invention of computers was "science fiction." Personal computers were introduced in 1975, but it was not until 1992 that the World Wide Web was available to everyone. As you read "The Fun They Had," keep in mind that it was written long before computers were used in schools.

Literary Analysis

Science Fiction

Science fiction is writing that tells about imaginary events that involve science or technology. Often, science fiction is set in the future. In "The Fun They Had," Asimov takes an idea from the present—teaching—and imagines what it will be like in the future. In this excerpt, he describes a mechanical teacher of the future:

> . . . large and ugly, with a big screen on which all the lessons were shown and the questions were asked.

As you read, notice the elements of science fiction in this story by looking for answers to the following focus questions:

1. What elements of science does Asimov incorporate in his story?
2. What details did Asimov create from his imagination?

Connecting Literary Elements

Like other short stories, science fiction stories have the following elements:

- **plot**: a series of related events that tell a story
- **characters**: the "actors" in a story
- **setting**: the time and place of the story
- **theme**: the message or insight about life that the work conveys

Identify these elements in "The Fun They Had."

Reading Strategy

Evaluating the Author's Message

When you **evaluate the author's message,** you make a judgment. You decide whether the author's points are logical. As you read "The Fun They Had," consider what point Asimov is making. That point is his message. Then, evaluate whether his message makes sense and whether you agree or disagree. The graphic organizer at right shows some points you might consider as you evaluate Asimov's message in "The Fun They Had."

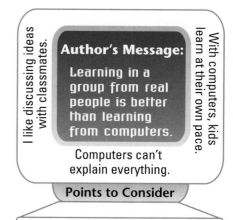

I like discussing ideas with classmates.

Author's Message:
Learning in a group from real people is better than learning from computers.

With computers, kids learn at their own pace.

Computers can't explain everything.

Points to Consider

Vocabulary Development

calculated (kal′ kyoo lāt′ id) v. determined by using math (p. 353)

loftily (lôf′ tə lē) adv. in a superior way (p. 355)

dispute (di spyoot′) v. argue; debate (p. 355)

nonchalantly (nän′ shə lant′ lē) adv. without concern or interest (p. 355)

The Fun They Had

Isaac Asimov

Margie even wrote about it that night in her diary. On the page headed May 17, 2155, she wrote, "Today Tommy found a real book."

It was a very old book. Margie's grandfather once said that when he was a little boy, *his* grandfather told him that there was a time when all stories were printed on paper.

They turned the pages, which were yellow and crinkly, and it was awfully funny to read words that stood still instead of moving the way they were supposed to—on a screen, you know. And then, when they turned back to the page before, it had the same words on it that it had had when they read it the first time.

"Gee," said Tommy, "what a waste. When you're through with the book, you just throw it away, I guess. Our television screen must have had a million books on it and it's good for plenty more. I wouldn't throw *it* away."

"Same with mine," said Margie. She was eleven and hadn't seen as many telebooks as Tommy had. He was thirteen.

She said, "Where did you find it?"

"In my house." He pointed without looking, because he was busy reading. "In the attic."

"What's it about?"

"School."

Margie was scornful. "School? What's there to write about school? I hate school." Margie always hated school, but now she hated it more than ever. The mechanical teacher had been giving her test after test in geography, and she had been doing worse and worse until her mother had shaken her head sorrowfully and sent for the county inspector.

He was a round little man with a red face and a whole box of tools with dials and wires. He smiled at her and gave her an apple, then took the teacher apart. Margie had hoped he wouldn't know how to put it together again, but he knew how all right, and after an hour or so, there it was again, large and ugly, with a big screen on which all the lessons were shown and the questions were asked. That wasn't so bad. The part she hated most was the slot where she had to put homework and test papers. She always had to write them out in a punch code they made her learn when she was six years old, and the mechanical teacher <u>calculated</u> the mark in no time.

◀ **Critical Viewing** In what ways does this picture combine imagination and technology? **[Analyze]**

Literary Analysis
Science Fiction This story was written in the mid-twentieth century. What detail at the opening suggests that it is science fiction?

calculated (kal´ kyōo lāt´ id) *v.* determined by using math

✔**Reading Check**

What does Tommy find?

The inspector had smiled after he was finished and patted her head. He said to her mother, "It's not the little girl's fault, Mrs. Jones. I think the geography sector was geared a little too quick. Those things happen sometimes. I've slowed it up to an average ten-year level. Actually, the overall pattern of her progress is quite satisfactory." And he patted Margie's head again.

Margie was disappointed. She had been hoping they would take the teacher away altogether. They had once taken Tommy's

Literary Analysis
Science Fiction and Setting How do these details indicate that the setting of the story is the future?

▼ **Critical Viewing** Do you think it would be fun to go to a school of the past, such as the one shown in the picture? **[Make a Judgment]**

teacher away for nearly a month because the history sector had blanked out completely.

So she said to Tommy, "Why would anyone write about school?"

Tommy looked at her with very superior eyes. "Because it's not our kind of school, stupid. This is the old kind of school that they had hundreds and hundreds of year ago." He added <u>loftily</u>, pronouncing the word carefully, "*Centuries* ago."

Margie was hurt. "Well, I don't know what kind of school they had all that time ago." She read the book over his shoulder for a while, then said, "Anyway, they had a teacher."

"Sure they had a teacher, but it wasn't a *regular* teacher. It was a man."

"A man? How could a man be a teacher?"

"Well, he just told the boys and girls things and gave them homework and asked them questions."

"A man isn't smart enough."

"Sure he is. My father knows as much as my teacher."

"He can't. A man can't know as much as a teacher."

"He knows almost as much I betcha."

Margie wasn't prepared to <u>dispute</u> that. She said, "I wouldn't want a strange man in my house to teach me."

Tommy screamed with laughter. "You don't know much, Margie. The teachers didn't live in the house. They had a special building and all the kids went there."

"And all the kids learned the same thing?"

"Sure, if they were the same age."

"But my mother says a teacher has to be adjusted to fit the mind of each boy and girl it teaches and that each kid has to be taught differently."

"Just the same, they didn't do it that way then. If you don't like it, you don't have to read the book."

"I didn't say I didn't like it," Margie said quickly. She wanted to read about those funny schools.

They weren't even half finished when Margie's mother called, "Margie! School!"

Margie looked up. "Not yet, Mamma."

"Now," said Mrs. Jones. "And it's probably time for Tommy, too."

Margie said to Tommy, "Can I read the book some more with you after school?"

"Maybe," he said, <u>nonchalantly</u>. He walked away whistling, the dusty old book tucked beneath his arm.

Margie went into the schoolroom. It was right next to her bedroom, and the mechanical teacher was on and waiting for her. It was always on at the same time every day except Saturday and

loftily (lof′ tə lē) *adv.* in a superior way

Literary Analysis
Science Fiction How can you tell that the school of the future is different from yours?

dispute (di spyo͞ot′) *v.* argue; debate

nonchalantly (nän′ shə lant′ lē) *adv.* without concern or interest

**Reading Check**

What do Tommy and Margot learn from the book?

Sunday, because her mother said little girls learned better if they learned at regular hours.

The screen was lit up, and it said: "Today's arithmetic lesson is on the addition of proper fractions. Please insert yesterday's homework in the proper slot."

Margie did so with a sigh. She was thinking about the old schools they had when her grandfather's grandfather was a little boy. All the kids from the whole neighborhood came, laughing and shouting in the schoolyard, sitting together in the schoolroom, going home together at the end of the day. They learned the same things so they could help one another on the homework and talk about it.

And the teachers were people. . . .

The mechanical teacher was flashing on the screen: "When we add the fractions $1/2$ and $1/4$ . . ."

Margie was thinking about how the kids must have loved it in the old days. She was thinking about the fun they had.

Review and Assess

Thinking About the Selection

1. **Respond:** Would you like to go to school the way Margie and Tommy do? Why or why not?

2. **(a) Recall:** What does Margie write in her diary about the book?
   (b) Infer: What does she think of the book?
   (c) Draw Conclusions: Why does she have such a strong reaction to the book?

3. **(a) Recall:** How does Margie hand in her homework?
   (b) Compare and Contrast: How is this activity different in 2155 than it is now? **(c) Speculate:** Do you think homework could be corrected mechanically in the future? Why or why not?

4. **(a) Recall:** Who are the main characters in this story? **(b) Infer:** Why do you think the author shows his ideas about the future through these characters? **(c) Assess:** Is the author successful in convincing you that his inventions of the future could really happen? Why or why not?

5. **(a) Recall:** Describe what school is like for the main characters.
   (b) Draw Conclusions: Why does Margie think that school in the past was fun? **(c) Compare and Contrast:** How is Margie's school the same as and different from your school?

6. **(a) Apply:** Describe the school of the future using science or technology. Give two examples of what the day will be like and what students will do. **(b) Make a Judgment:** Are human teachers or computerized teachers more effective? Why?

Isaac Asimov

(1920–1992)
Check any section of the library and you will probably find a book by Isaac Asimov. He wrote fiction, medical books, humor, autobiography, essays, a guide to Shakespeare, and science books. Although he was an expert in many subjects, his main interest was science. Asimov taught biochemistry at Boston University for thirteen years before becoming a full-time writer. He is best known for his science-fiction work, a kind of writing his father regarded as "trash" and would not—until convinced—allow the young Isaac to read as a child.

Review and Assess

Literary Analysis

Science Fiction

1. What are two uses of technology that Asimov imagines for the future?
2. How does technology change education by the year 2155?
3. Asimov creates **science fiction** with his imagination and technology. In the diagram shown, list details or events from the story to show how Asimov used his imagination and technology to create science fiction.

Imagination
1. _____
2. _____
3. _____

Technology
1. _____
2. _____
3. _____

Science Fiction

Connecting Literary Elements

4. What elements do science fiction stories share with other short stories?
5. Retell the plot of "The Fun They Had."
6. On an organizer like the one shown, write details from the story that indicate the time and the place.

Time	Place

Reading Strategy

Evaluating the Author's Message

7. What does Asimov appear to say is the main difference between the schools of the past and the schools of 2155?
8. Which methods of education does Asimov prefer: those of 2155 or those of the past? Which story details help you draw this conclusion?
9. Explain Asimov's **message.** Do you agree with him? Explain why or why not.

Extending Understanding

10. **Career Connection:** How do teachers today use computers in the classroom?

Quick Review

Science fiction is writing that tells about imaginary events that involve science or technology. It is often set in the future. To review science fiction, see page 351.

The elements of a **short story** are plot, characters, setting, and theme. To review these elements, see page 351.

The **author's message** is the point or lesson of the work.

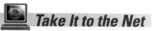 **Take It to the Net**
www.phschool.com
Take the interactive self-test online to check your understanding of the selection.

Integrate Language Skills

Vocabulary Development Lesson

Word Analysis: Latin Prefix *non-*

You can add the Latin prefix *non-* to many words in English to form words that mean "not" or "without." For example, *nonbreakable* means "not breakable," and the story word *nonchalant* means "without concern or interest." On your paper, write a meaning for each word.

1. nonviolent
2. nonsense
3. nontoxic
4. nonstop

Spelling Strategy

The *sh* sound has many different spellings. In some words the *sh* sound is spelled *ch*, as in *nonchalant*, a story word. For each definition, write a word on your paper that contains the *sh* sound spelled with a *ch*.

1. a type of nut: pi _ _ _ _ _ io
2. equipment that does work: m _ _ _ ine
3. a head cook: _ _ _ _
4. a driver: _ _ au _ _ eu _

Fluency: Definitions

On your paper, write the word in the first column that matches the meaning of each word in the second column.

1. calculated   a. proudly
2. loftily   b. argue
3. dispute   c. casually
4. nonchalantly   d. figured out

Use each word in one of the following sentences.

1. Tommy wanted to appear casual, so he spoke _____?_____.
2. As she added up one row of numbers, he _____?_____ the other.
3. Feeling superior, he spoke _____?_____.
4. There was no argument at recess, but a _____?_____ occurred after school.

Grammar Lesson

Simple Subjects and Predicates

A **simple subject** is the person, place, or thing about which a sentence is written. A **simple predicate** is the verb or verb phrase that tells the action or states the condition of the subject. Look at the examples below. The complete subject is underlined once and the complete predicate twice. The simple subject is highlighted in blue. The simple predicate is highlighted in green.

Margie even wrote about it in her diary.

The mechanical teacher had been giving her tests in geography.

▶ *For more practice, see page R28, Exercise A.*
Practice Copy these sentences. Underline the complete subject once and label it S. Underline the complete predicate twice and label it P. Circle the simple subject and the simple predicate.

1. It was a very old book.
2. They turned the pages of the book.
3. Tommy had been looking in the attic.
4. The inspector had smiled at Margie.
5. All the children learned the same thing.

Writing Application On your paper, write four or five sentences about your school day. Draw one line under the simple subject and two lines under the simple predicate in each sentence.

W̶G̶ Prentice Hall Writing and Grammar Connection: Chapter 19, Section 1

Writing Lesson

Comparison of School Then and Now

Learn more about school in the 1950s, when "The Fun They Had" was written. Write a comparison-and-contrast essay that shows how school then is similar to and different from school now.

Prewriting   Write a list of categories that relate to school, such as subjects taught, books used, rules, equipment in the classroom, teachers, homework, and sports. Review "The Fun They Had" to gather preliminary details in each category. Gather further information by asking older adults in your family and by using library resources.

Drafting   Organize details into paragraphs based on your categories. For each category, give the details of then and the details of now.

Revising   On a draft of your essay, highlight all the details of "Then" with one color and all the details of "Now" with another. If you have far more of one color than the other, revise to add details for a better balance.

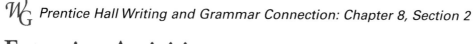

Model: Revising for Balance

Most students wrote with a fountain pen. They wrote their

Now many students do homework on a computer.

homework on paper. Most students today have never even seen a fountain pen.

> This paragraph should be revised for balance. Add a detail about "Now" to create balance.

W̶G Prentice Hall Writing and Grammar Connection: Chapter 8, Section 2

Extension Activities

Listening and Speaking   Give a **speech** presenting the advantages and disadvantages of technological advances.

1. Divide a paper into two columns, labeled *Advantages* and *Disadvantages*. List examples in each column.
2. Prepare a graph or chart to illustrate the growth of technology.
3. Give your speech.

Research and Technology   In a group, prepare a **multimedia report** that shows some of the major technological advances made during the past fifty years.

Writing   The story opens with one sentence from Margie's journal. As Margie, write the rest of the journal entry. Include details from the story about events and your reaction, as Margie, to these events.

 **Take It to the Net**   www.phschool.com

Go online for an additional research activity using the Internet.

Fact and Fantasy

Esperanza Rising is a novel about the past. "The Fun They Had" is a story about the future. What these two fictional works have in common is that the time of the setting and the circumstances of the characters make them completely unfamiliar with objects and a lifestyle that seems ordinary to most readers. In "The Fun They Had," the characters are unfamiliar with books. In *Esperanza Rising*, the character is unfamiliar with a broom.

Different but the same. When you read about characters in the past or in the future, you might think that their feelings and reactions would be very different from yours. In fact, if a writer does his or her job correctly, you can understand the feelings of story characters even if they are living on Mars! Although people and characters come from different backgrounds, cultures, and time periods, most people share a desire to feel as if they belong, as if they are part of a group. These common feelings make it possible for readers to relate to fictional characters who live in different times or places.

Find out more. When you read historical fiction, you might want to do a little background research to get an even greater understanding of a character's circumstances. For example, the political circumstances in Mexico during the early 1900s and the Great Depression in the United States have an impact on the way characters act and think in *Esperanza Rising*. Because of the upheaval caused by both sets of circumstances, it is believable that a character could go from riches to rags, as Esperanza does. This sudden change in her fortune provides a logical explanation for why she is unable to sweep. As you read, look for other details of Esperanza's circumstances that make it possible for you to understand and believe her feelings, actions, and reactions.

from Esperanza Rising

Pam Muñoz Ryan

Esperanza is the thirteen-year-old daughter of a wealthy Mexican rancher. When she emigrates to the United States, she is no longer a rich aristocrat, but a laborer in the fields. Esperanza struggles to learn how to work to be a support to her mother.

Isabel sat with the babies while Esperanza went to sweep the platform. The camp was quiet and even though it was late in the day, the sun was unrelenting. She retrieved the broom and stepped onto the wooden floor. Dried and brittle onion skins were everywhere.

In her entire life, Esperanza [es´pə rän´zə] had never held a broom in her hand. But she had seen Hortensia [hôr´ten sē ə] sweep and she tried to visualize the memory. It couldn't possibly be that hard. She put both hands near the middle of the broomstick and moved it back and forth. It swung wildly. The motion seemed awkward and the fine dirt on the wooden planks lifted into a cloud. Onion jackets[1] flew into the air instead of gathering together in a neat pile like Hortensia's. Esperanza's elbows did not know what to do. Neither did her arms. She felt streams of perspiration sliding down her neck. She stopped for a moment and stared at the broom, as if willing it to behave. Determined, she tried again. She hadn't noticed that several trucks were already unloading workers nearby. Then she heard it. First a small tittering and then louder. She turned around. A group of women were laughing at her. And in the middle of the group was Marta, pointing.

¡La Cenicienta! Cinderella!" she laughed.

Burning with humiliation,[2] Esperanza dropped the broom and ran back to the cabin.

In her room, she sat on the edge of the cot. Her face flushed again at the thought of the ridicule. She was still sitting there, staring at the wall, when Isabel found her.

Thematic Connection
To what extent is Esperanza's inability to sweep realistic? What details of the situation make her character believable?

---

1. **onion jackets** the outer skins of the onion
2. **humiliation** (hyōō mil´e ā shən) a feeling of hurt, or loss of pride or dignity

▲ Critical Viewing
What details in this
picture seem familiar and
recognizable to you?
Which seem strange and
unfamiliar? Explain.
[Compare and Contrast]

"I said I could work. I told Mama I could help. But I cannot even wash
clothes or sweep a floor. Does the whole camp know?"

Isabel sat down on the bed next to her and patted her back. "Yes."

Esperanza groaned. "I will never be able to show my face." She put her
head in her hands until she heard someone else come into the room.

Esperanza looked up to see Miguel, holding a broom and a dustpan.
But he wasn't laughing. She looked down and bit her lip so she wouldn't
cry in front of him.

He shut the door, then stood in front of her and said, "How would you
know how to sweep a floor? The only thing you ever learned was how to
give orders. That is not your fault. Anza, look at me."

She looked up.

"Pay attention," he said, his face serious. "You hold the broom like
this. One hand here and the other here."

Esperanza watched.

"Then you push like this. Or pull it toward you like this. Here, you
try," he said, holding out the broom.

Slowly, Esperanza got up and took the broom from him. He positioned her hands on the handle. She tried to copy him but her movements were too big.

"Smaller strokes," said Miguel, coaching. "And sweep all in one direction."

She did as he said.

"Now, when you get all the dirt into a pile, you hold the broom down here, near the bottom, and push the dirt into the pan."

Esperanza collected the dirt.

"See, you can do it." Miguel raised his thick eyebrows and smiled. "Someday, you just might make a very good servant."

Isabel giggled.

Esperanza could not yet find humor in the situation. Somberly[3] she said, "Thank you, Miguel."

He grinned and bowed. "At your service, *mi reina*." But this time, his voice was kind.

She remembered that he had gone to look for work at the railroad. "Did you get a job?"

His smile faded. He put his hands in his pockets and shrugged his shoulders. "It is frustrating. I can fix any engine. But they will only hire Mexicans to lay track and dig ditches, not as mechanics. I've decided to work in the fields until I can convince someone to give me a chance."

Esperanza nodded.

After he left the room, Isabel said, "He calls you *mi reina!* Will you tell me about your life as a queen?

Esperanza sat on the mattress and patted the spot next to her. Isabel sat down.

"Isabel, I will tell you all about how I used to live. About parties and private school and beautiful dresses. I will even show you the beautiful doll my papa bought me, if you will teach me how to pin diapers, how to wash, and . . ."

Isabel interrupted her. "But that is so easy!"

Esperanza stood up and carefully practiced with the broom. "It is not easy for me."

---

3. somberly (säm′bər lē) in a dark, gloomy, or dull way

Connecting Science Fiction and Historical Fiction

1. What kinds of challenges do you think Esperanza is going to face besides learning how to work?

2. Why does Esperanza find a different life difficult, but the characters in "The Fun They Had" find a different life appealing?

3. Do you find the characters in *Esperanza Rising* or in "The Fun They Had" more realistic and believable? Explain.

4. In what ways are Esperanza's challenges similar to and different from the challenges of the students in "The Fun They Had"?

Pam Muñoz Ryan

Pam Muñoz Ryan grew up in the San Joaquin Valley of California. She now lives with her family near San Diego. The story of *Esperanza Rising* is based on the experiences of her grandmother on her mother's side.

Prepare to Read

A Dream Within a Dream ◆
The Spring and the Fall ◆ Ankylosaurus

 Take It to the Net

Visit www.phschool.com
for interactive activities
and instruction related to
these selections, including

- background
- graphic organizers
- literary elements
- reading strategies

Preview

Connecting to the Literature

The poets in this group show that the past has a way of leaving its mark on the present. Your world may change unexpectedly when a friend moves or an event upsets you. Yet no friend or experience ever completely leaves you. Look back at past people and events in your life and think about what you have learned from them or what memories they have left with you.

Background

Fossil remains reveal the lives of dinosaurs, such as the Ankylosaurus in Prelutsky's poem. Ankylosaurus (aŋ′ kə lō sôr əs) had small jaws and weak teeth suitable only for chewing soft plants. For protection, an Ankylosaurus had tough, leathery skin and a heavy tail shaped like a club. Its short, stubby legs kept the ankylosaurus close to the ground, protecting its soft underbelly. The picture on page 370 shows what scientists believe an Ankylosaurus looked like.

Literary Analysis

Rhyme

Rhyme is the repetition of sounds at the ends of words. Many poems have rhyming words at the ends of lines. To identify the pattern of rhyme in a poem, use letters. For example, lines ending in *sing, last, ring, past* have an *abab* rhyme scheme, or pattern. The following lines from Prelutsky's poem shown below have an *aabb* pattern.

> Clankity Clankity Clankity Clank!
> Ankylosaurus was built like a tank,
> its hide was a fortress as sturdy as steel,
> it tended to be an inedible meal.

The choice of words that rhyme in this poem reinforces the writer's amused attitude toward the subject. As you read, notice the rhymes.

Comparing Literary Works

In addition to the words that rhyme, the poet's choice of words can also reveal the **tone**, or author's attitude toward the subject. In "A Dream Within a Dream," the formal word choice conveys a serious, dramatic tone.

> Take this kiss upon the brow!
> And, in parting from you now,
> Thus much let me avow—

Compare and contrast the tones of these poems. Think about these focus questions:

1. Which two of these three poems have a more serious tone?
2. Which poem has the most humorous tone?

Reading Strategy

Drawing Inferences

The poems in this group hint at past events and circumstances rather than directly stating them. You can **draw inferences** about past events, that is, make logical guesses about them, based on details that are provided in the poem. As you read, look for details that you can put together to draw inferences. The organizer shows one example of details that can be used to draw an inference.

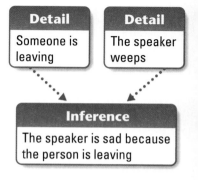

Detail	**Detail**
Someone is leaving	The speaker weeps

Inference

The speaker is sad because the person is leaving

Vocabulary Development

deem (dēm) *v.* judge (p. 367)

bough (bou) *n.* tree branch (p. 369)

raucous (rô′ kəs) *adj.* loud and rowdy (p. 369)

inedible (in ed′ ə bəl) *adj.* not fit to be eaten (p. 370)

cudgel (kuj′ əl) *n.* short, thick stick or club (p. 370)

A Dream Within a Dream

EDGAR ALLAN POE

Take this kiss upon the brow!
And, in parting from you now,
Thus much let me avow—
You are not wrong, who <u>deem</u>
5   That my days have been a dream;
Yet if hope has flown away
In a night, or in a day,
In a vision, or in none,
Is it therefore the less *gone*?
10   *All* that we see or seem
Is but a dream within a dream.
I stand amid the roar
Of a surf-tormented shore,
And I hold within my hand
15   Grains of the golden sand—
How few! yet how they creep
Through my fingers to the deep,
While I weep—while I weep!
O God! can I not grasp
20   Them with a tighter clasp?
O God! can I not save
One from the pitiless wave?
Is *all* that we see or seem
But a dream within a dream?

deem (dēm) *v.* judge

◄ **Critical Viewing** What does the sand running through the hourglass suggest about time? **[Interpret]**

Edgar Allan Poe

(1809–1849)
Edgar Allan Poe, one of America's best-known writers, led a troubled life plagued by poverty and the loss of people he loved. His father deserted him, his mother died before he was three, and his wife died while she was still young. Despite his problems, Poe produced a large body of work, including short stories, essays, and poems. He died in Baltimore at the age of forty, but his stories and poems live on, read by millions in America and around the world.

Review and Assess

Thinking About the Selections

1. **Respond:** Do you think you would enjoy meeting the speaker in Poe's poem?

2. **(a) Analyze:** What happens in the first two lines of "A Dream Within a Dream"? **(b) Interpret:** Who is *you* in lines 2 and 4? **(c) Connect:** What does the person in lines 2 and 4 have to do with the dream?

3. **(a) Analyze:** What is the speaker doing in lines 13–19? **(b) Connect:** How are these actions related to the idea of dreaming? **(c) Interpret:** Explain the title. What dream is within what dream?

4. **Interpret:** What is the "pitiless wave" that washes away the "grains" of experiences that the speaker tries to hold in his or her hand?

The Spring and the Fall

Edna St. Vincent Millay

In the spring of the year, in the spring of the year,
I walked the road beside my dear.
The trees were black where the bark was wet.
I see them yet, in the spring of the year.
5 He broke me a <u>bough</u> of the blossoming peach
That was out of the way and hard to reach.

In the fall of the year, in the fall of the year,
I walked the road beside my dear.
The rooks[1] went up with a <u>raucous</u> trill.
10 I hear them still, in the fall of the year.
He laughed at all I dared to praise,
And broke my heart, in little ways.

Year be springing or year be falling,
The bark will drip and the birds be calling.
15 There's much that's fine to see and hear
In the spring of a year, in the fall of a year.
'Tis not love's going hurts my days,
But that it went in little ways.

---

bough (bou) *n.* branch of a tree

raucous (rô´ kəs) *adj.* loud and rowdy

1. **rooks** (rŏŏks) *n.* European crows.

◀ **Critical Viewing** What emotions do you think this woman is feeling? **[Infer]**

Review and Assess

Thinking About the Selections

1. **Respond:** What questions would you like to ask Edna St. Vincent Millay about the poem?
2. **(a) Recall:** What happens to the couple in spring in this poem?
   (b) Connect: How does the idea of a new love connect with the idea of spring?
3. **(a) Recall:** What happens to the couple in fall in this poem?
   (b) Connect: How does the idea of love's departure connect with the idea of fall? **(c) Draw Conclusions:** Do you think "The Spring and the Fall" is an appropriate title? Why or why not?

Edna St. Vincent Millay

(1892–1950)
Edna St. Vincent Millay was born in Rockland, Maine. Raised by her mother, who encouraged her creativity, she published her first poem in a children's magazine when she was only fourteen. Her first book of poetry came out when she was twenty-five. Just six years later, in 1923, she won a Pulitzer Prize for poetry. Like "The Spring and the Fall," many of Millay's poems and sonnets are about love and the loss of love.

Ankylosaurus

Jack Prelutsky

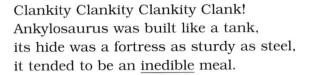

Clankity Clankity Clankity Clank!
Ankylosaurus was built like a tank,
its hide was a fortress as sturdy as steel,
it tended to be an <u>inedible</u> meal.

5   It was armored in front, it was armored behind,
there wasn't a thing on its minuscule mind,
it waddled about on its four stubby legs,
nibbling on plants with a mouthful of pegs.

Ankylosaurus was best left alone,
10 its tail was a <u>cudgel</u> of gristle and bone,
Clankity Clankity Clankity Clank!
Ankylosaurus was built like a tank.

inedible (in ed´ ə bəl) *adj.*
not fit to be eaten

cudgel (kuj´ əl) *n.*
short, thick stick or club

Jack Prelutsky

(b. 1940)
Jack Prelutsky was born in Brooklyn, New York. His writing career began when he showed a friend some poems he had written to accompany drawings of imaginary creatures. With his friend's encouragement, Prelutsky soon published his first book of poems. He went on to write many more books and to win numerous awards for his humorous verse.

Review and Assess

Thinking About the Selection

1. **Respond:** Do you find the description of Ankylosaurus amusing or frightening? Why?

2. **(a) Recall:** What was Ankylosaurus built like? **(b) Analyze:** Which sound words help reinforce this image? **(c) Speculate:** Why do you think Prelutsky begins the poem with these words and this image?

3. **(a) Recall:** What kind of meal did Ankylosaurus make? **(b) Hypothesize:** How did this help ensure the survival of Ankylosaurus?

4. **(a) Recall:** What was the tail of Ankylosaurus like? **(b) Speculate:** What was likely to happen in a fight between Ankylosaurus and another animal? **(c) Generalize:** Why was Ankylosaurus "best left alone"?

Review and Assess

Literary Analysis

Rhyme

1. Where do the rhyming words in these three poems usually fall?
2. Complete a chart like the one shown to give examples of rhyming words each poet uses.

Poem	Rhyming Words
"Dream Within a Dream"	
"The Spring and the Fall"	
"Ankylosaurus"	

3. Use letters to show the **rhyme scheme** of the first stanza of "The Spring and the Fall."

Comparing Literary Works

4. Which two of these three poems have the most serious **tone**? Explain.
5. Which poem has the most humorous tone? Explain.
6. Identify the similarities and differences in word choice that reveal the similarities and differences in tone.
7. How do the similarities and differences in tone affect your reactions to the poems?

Reading Strategy

Drawing Inferences

8. What inferences do you draw about the couple's relationship in "The Spring and the Fall"?
9. What details from "Ankylosaurus" help you make inferences about the world in which the dinosaur lived?

Extending Understanding

10. **Career Connection:** People who explore the past by studying dinosaurs are called paleontologists. What other careers are available to people who enjoy studying the past?

Quick Review

Rhyme is the repetition of sounds at the ends of words. Rhyme often occurs at the ends of lines of poetry. To review rhyme, see page 365.

Tone is the author's attitude toward the subject. To review tone, see page 365.

Drawing inferences is forming ideas or coming to conclusions that are based on the reading.

 Take It to the Net
www.phschool.com
Take the interactive self-test online to check your understanding of these selections.

Integrate Language Skills

Vocabulary Development Lesson

Word Analysis: Latin Prefix *in-*

The Latin prefix *in-* means "not" or "the opposite of." Combined with *edible*, which means "fit to eat," it forms a word that means "not fit to eat." Copy the following sentences. Add the Latin prefix *in-* to the italicized word to change its meaning to the opposite. Then, explain whether the rewritten sentence makes sense.

1. The speaker of "A Dream Within a Dream" feels *complete*.
2. A year is a(n) *definite* period of time.
3. Prelutsky's description of Ankylosaurus is *accurate*.

Fluency: Context

On your paper, answer the following questions, explaining your answers.

1. Does Prelutsky *deem* Ankylosaurus thoughtful?
2. Did Ankylosaurus find plants *inedible?*
3. Would a *raucous* song make a good lullaby?
4. Would a *bough* make a good *cudgel?*

Spelling Strategy

The word *bough* is one example of the *ow* sound spelled with *ough*. *Brow* is an example of the *ow* sound spelled with *ow*. On your paper, unscramble the letters to spell words that have the *ow* sound.

1. glopuh   2. dworc   3. dogruth   4. wronf

Grammar Lesson

Complete Sentences

A **complete sentence** is a group of words that expresses a complete thought and contains at least one subject and one predicate (verb).

>   S   P
> **Example:** I walked the road beside my dear.

The following is not a complete sentence: "While I weep—While I weep!" Although it contains a subject and predicate, it does not express a complete thought. "While I weep" is a subordinate thought. The following example is a complete sentence because it tells what happens.

>   S   P
> **Example:** The grains of sand run through my fingers while I weep.

▶ *For more practice, see page R28, Exercise B.*
Practice Copy the following sentences. If an item is a subordinate thought, add the information needed to make a complete sentence.

1. As it nibbled on plants.
2. You are not wrong.
3. If hope has flown away.
4. The bark will drip, and the birds will call.
5. Because it was an inedible meal.

Writing Application Add your own words to make each of the following complete sentences.

1. As I walked along the road
2. If he had stayed
3. Although it was strong and sturdy at first

W͟G *Prentice Hall Writing and Grammar Connection: Chapter 21, Section 4*

Writing Lesson

Dinosaur Description

Although Jack Prelutsky includes factual information in his poem, his primary purpose is to entertain. Describe another dinosaur. Decide what your primary purpose is, then choose the form of writing that best suits your purpose.

Prewriting   Do research to find facts that will help you achieve your purpose. For example, if your purpose is to entertain, look for unusual facts or details you can present in a humorous way. Use this chart to consider how to match your form to your purpose.

Model: Match Form to Purpose

Purpose	Possible Form
Entertain	poem, dialogue
Inform	essay, description, report
Explore ideas	imaginary journal entry, short story including dinosaurs

Drafting   If you write a poem, dialogue, or imaginary journal entry, you can use contractions and informal language. If you write a story, relate events in chronological or time order. If you write an essay, report, or description, structure your writing with an introduction, a body, and a conclusion.

Revising   Review your writing to make sure you have included descriptive details—no matter what your form or purpose. Circle words that you can make more exact.

WG Prentice Hall Writing and Grammar Connection: Chapter 2

Extension Activities

Listening and Speaking With a small group, prepare a **choral reading** of one of the poems. Read the poem together, deciding what you want to emphasize and where you want to add special effects. Evaluate each other's reading on

- rise and fall of the voice.
- emphasis on rhyme and rhythm.
- adjustment of pace to punctuation.

Perform the poem for the class. [**Group Activity**]

Research and Technology Write a **research summary** of an encyclopedia article about Ankylosaurus. Include points that are mentioned in the article and in the poem.

Writing Write an **interpretation** in which you explain in your own words the meaning of one of the poems.

 Take It to the Net   www.phschool.com

Go online for an additional research activity using the Internet.

READING INFORMATIONAL MATERIALS

Web Sites and Web Pages

About Web Sites

Web sites are specific locations on the Internet. If you think of the Internet as a giant library, Web sites are individual books within that library. As you explore a Web site on a computer, what you see on the screen is a part of the site called a Web page. A Web site can have many Web pages, just as a book has many pages. You can move from one Web page to another easily (or from one part of a long Web page to another) by using the mouse to click on a picture, a "button," or a highlighted or underlined word or phrase, called a *link*.

Reading Strategy

Using Structural Features of Web Sites

Use the special features of Web sites to move quickly around the site and find the information you need. Web sites and Web pages have some of the same structural features as textbooks and magazines, such as headings and graphics, but they have some special features unique to electronic texts as well. Learn to navigate, or find your way from place to place, in a Web site by using these special features. The features will make your searches for information more efficient by getting you to the right place in the shortest amount of time.

The chart shows some of the special features of Web sites and Web pages.

Web Site Features	
Link	A connection to another spot on the same Web page or to a different Web page or Web site. A link can be underlined or highlighted text, or an image or photograph. Links are what make the Web a "web."
Icon	An image or small drawing that may appear by itself or with accompanying text. Icons are often links as well.
Graphics	Pictures, maps, tables, and other graphic sources are often featured on a Web site. These graphics are often sources of information in themselves, but they may also be links to other Web pages.

Use bookmarks to "save" useful Web sites so that you can quickly return to them when you need to verify or find additional information. Most Web browsers—the software that allows you to get to the material on the Web—have a "bookmark" or "favorites" feature that creates an easy-to-access list of your favorite sites.

Museums, libraries, and other nonprofit organizations usually have the letters *org* at the end of their addresses.

http://www.fieldmuseum.org

Sue at The Field Museum

The Field Museum   home   search   sitemap

sue's home

Who is Sue?

- Who is Sue?
- What's New With Sue?
- The Preparation of Sue
- What Can We Learn from Sue?
- Sue and *T.rex* Relatives
- Life and Times of Sue
- Frequently Asked Questions
- Image Gallery

Dinosaur of the Month

Just for Kids

Who is Sue?

In 1990, Sue, the world's largest *Tyrannosaurus rex*, was found near Faith, South Dakota. In 1997, The Field Museum purchased it with generous financial support from McDonald's Corporation, Walt Disney World Resort, the California State University system, and private individuals.

Sue Home - Sue Public Programs - Geology Credits - Field Museum - Home

Questions about The Field Museum?
Technical Questions about The Field Museum Web site?

A list of links to other pages of the Web site often appears in a side column. Clicking on a link takes you directly to the new page.

"Back" and "Forward" buttons allow you to "turn" pages. They are navigational tools that allow you to retrace steps you have taken to reach a page.

http://www.fieldmuseum.org

The Field Museum

home   search   sitemap

sue's home

Life and Times of Sue

- Who is Sue?
- What's New With Sue?
- The Preparation of Sue
- What Can We Learn from Sue?
- Sue and *T. rex* Relatives
- Life and Times of Sue
- Frequently Asked Questions
- Image Gallery

Sue inhabited a world very different, yet in some ways similar to our own. Snakes, turtles, frogs, salamanders, shore birds, and opossums—all of which have relatives alive today—walked, swam and flew across the landscape. Present-day South Dakota, where Sue was found, was home to hardwood forests of oak, hickory, magnolia, and cycads. Swamps were present as well, with abundant cypresses, giant sequoias, and china firs.

This image shows Montana, 75 million years ago--a herd of *Parasaurolophus* is under attack from a *Tyrannosaurus rex*.

next

Sue Home - Sue Public Programs - Geology Credits - Field Museum - Home

Questions about The Field Museum?
Technical Questions about The Field Museum Web site?

The bottom of a Web page usually displays links to frequently used places on the site, such as the home page.

Check Your Comprehension

1. Where was Sue found?
2. When was Sue found?
3. Describe the environment in which Sue lived.

Applying the Reading Strategy

Using Web Site Features

4. To what page can you link to learn about the most recent findings on Sue?
5. How do you know that the star on the map of South Dakota will take you to a new page or section of the site?

Activity

Web Site Evaluation

With a partner or group, find two different Web sites related to a topic you are currently studying in social studies or science, or find two Web sites on an author whose work you have read. Evaluate the two Web sites based on the following criteria

- reliability of source
- amount of information
- navigability
  (how easy it is to find your way around)
- use of graphics

Give each Web site a rating in each category. Then, give each Web site an overall rating. Explain your ratings to the class.

Comparing Informational Materials

Web Sites and Encyclopedias

Compare the structural features of Web sites and pages to the structural features of an encyclopedia article. In an encyclopedia, find an article on a topic of interest. Find a Web site on the same or a very similar topic. Make a chart like the one shown. In each category, write brief notes that show how the encyclopedia and the Web site are similar and different.

Feature	Web Site	Encyclopedia Article
Links	10 hot links	5 cross references to other articles
Headings		
Bullets, Numerals, and Other Organizing Elements		
Icons		
Graphics		

Prepare to Read

from Exploring the *Titanic*

Take It to the Net

Visit www.phschool.com for interactive activities and instruction related to "*from* Exploring the *Titanic*," including
- background
- graphic organizers
- literary elements
- reading strategies

Preview

Connecting to the Literature

This excerpt from *Exploring the* Titanic by Robert D. Ballard narrates the events that led to one of the most famous disasters of all time. The sinking of the *Titanic* has been covered in movies, books, and documentaries. Think about what you already know about the *Titanic* from these and other sources. Then, read the selection to see if what you know is accurate and complete.

Background

The *Titanic* was the largest and most luxurious ocean liner of its time. Huge watertight doors between sections and a construction believed to be "unbreakable" made the *Titanic* seem safer than other ships. According to the publicity, it was "unsinkable." Perhaps the owners of the *Titanic* did not supply enough lifeboats for all the passengers because they were sure lifeboats would never be needed.

Literary Analysis

Suspense

Suspense is the feeling of anxious uncertainty about upcoming events. In literature, writers create suspense by keeping you wondering *what* will happen or *when* an event will happen.

When you read this excerpt from *Exploring the* Titanic, you know that the *Titanic* will hit an iceberg, but you do not know when. Ballard builds suspense by constantly reminding you that icebergs are out there and by keeping you wondering when the ship will hit one. Add details that increase the suspense to an organizer like the one shown.

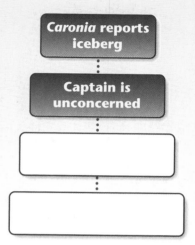

Connecting Literary Elements

Atmosphere, or mood, is the feeling created in a work or passage. One way writers create atmosphere is with images—words and phrases that appeal to one or more of the five senses. In the following example, the two details of *calm* and *cold* create an atmosphere of uncomfortable waiting, as if something is about to happen.

> The sea was dead calm. The air bitterly cold.

As you read, keep these focus questions in mind.

1. Why does Ballard include descriptions of the calm, moonless night?
2. What other details contribute to the atmosphere?

Reading Strategy

Distinguishing Between Fact and Opinion

Nonfiction works often include an author's opinions as well as facts.

- A **fact** is information that can be proved true or false: Harold Bride was only 22 years old.
- An **opinion** expresses a belief that can be supported, but not proved: He was quite pleased with himself . . .

Although the opinions Ballard includes cannot be proven, they are logical conclusions based on the facts. By including them, Ballard makes the characters and events more real to readers. As you read, distinguish between actual facts and the author's opinions.

Vocabulary Development

majestically (mə jes´ tik lē) *adv.* grandly (p. 381)

collision (kə lizh´ ən) *n.* coming together with a sudden violent force; a crash (p. 381)

novelty (näv´ əl tē) *n.* something new or unusual (p. 381)

watertight *adj.* put together so that no water can get through (p. 385)

from Exploring the TITANIC
Robert D. Ballard

At noon on Wednesday, April 10, the *Titanic* cast off. The whistles on her huge funnels were the biggest ever made. As she began her journey to the sea, they were heard for miles around.

Moving <u>majestically</u> down the River Test, and watched by a crowd that had turned out for the occasion, the *Titanic* slowly passed two ships tied up to a dock. All of a sudden, the mooring ropes holding the passenger liner *New York* snapped with a series of sharp cracks like fireworks going off. The enormous pull created by the *Titanic* moving past her had broken the *New York's* ropes and was now drawing her stern toward the *Titanic*. Jack Thayer watched in horror as the two ships came closer and closer. "It looked as though there surely would be a <u>collision</u>," he later wrote. "Her stern could not have been more than a yard or two from our side. It almost hit us." At the last moment, some quick action by Captain Smith and a tugboat captain nearby allowed the *Titanic* to slide past with only inches to spare.

It was not a good sign. Did it mean that the *Titanic* might be too big a ship to handle safely? Those who knew about the sea thought that such a close call at the beginning of a maiden voyage was a very bad omen.

Jack Phillips, the first wireless operator on the *Titanic*, quickly jotted down the message coming in over his headphones. "It's another iceberg warning," he said wearily to his young assistant, Harold Bride. "You'd better take it up to the bridge." Both men had been at work for hours in the *Titanic's* radio room trying to get caught up in sending out a large number of personal messages. In 1912, passengers on ocean liners thought it was a real <u>novelty</u> to send postcard-style messages to friends at home from the middle of the Atlantic.

Bride picked up the iceberg message and stepped out onto the boat deck. It was a sunny but cold Sunday morning, the fourth day of the *Titanic's* maiden voyage. The ship was steaming at full speed across a calm sea. Harold Bride was quite pleased with himself at having landed a job on such a magnificent new ship. After all, he was only twenty-two years old and had just nine months' experience at operating a "wireless set," as a ship's radio was then called. As he entered the bridge area, he could see one of the crewmen standing behind the ship's wheel steering her course toward New York.

Captain Smith was on duty in the bridge, so Bride handed the message to him. "It's from the *Caronia*, sir. She's reporting icebergs

majestically (mə jes´ tik lē) *adv.* grandly

collision (kə lizh´ ən) *n.* coming together with a sudden violent force; a crash

novelty (näv´ əl tē) *n.* something new or unusual

Reading Check

What happens to the *Titanic* at the beginning of her maiden voyage?

◀ **Critical Viewing** Why might an iceberg like this one be difficult to spot from far away? **[Analyze]**

and pack ice ahead." The captain thanked him, read the message, and then posted it on the bulletin board for other officers on watch to read. On his way back to the radio room, Bride thought the captain had seemed quite unconcerned by the message. But then again, he had been told that it was not unusual to have ice floating in the sea lanes during an April crossing. Besides, what danger could a few pieces of ice present to an unsinkable ship?

Elsewhere on board, passengers relaxed on deck chairs, reading or taking naps. Some played cards, some wrote letters, while

Literary Analysis
Suspense How does the question about an "unsinkable ship" increase suspense?

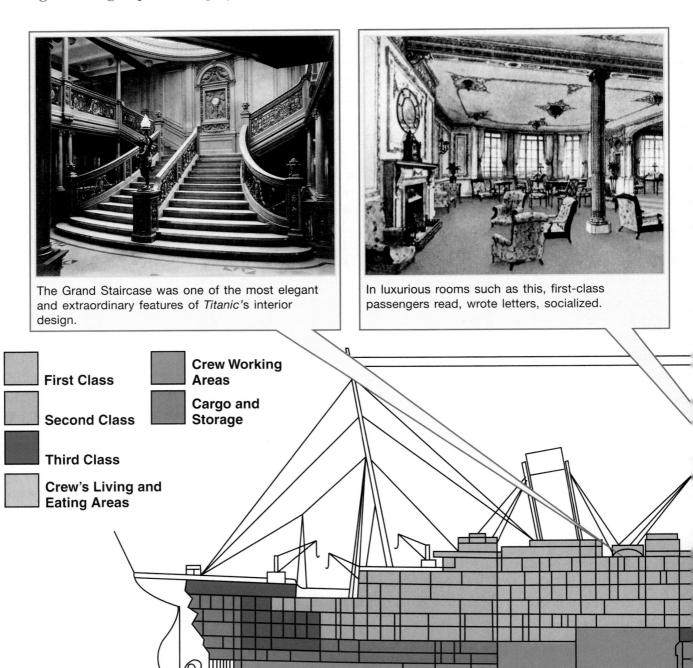

The Grand Staircase was one of the most elegant and extraordinary features of *Titanic*'s interior design.

In luxurious rooms such as this, first-class passengers read, wrote letters, socialized.

First Class

Second Class

Third Class

Crew's Living and Eating Areas

Crew Working Areas

Cargo and Storage

others chatted with friends. As it was Sunday, church services had been held in the morning, the first-class service led by Captain Smith. Jack Thayer spent most of the day walking about the decks getting some fresh air with his parents.

Two more ice warnings were received from nearby ships around lunch time. In the chaos of the radio room, Harold Bride only had time to take one of them to the bridge. The rest of the day passed quietly. Then, in the late afternoon, the temperature began to drop rapidly. Darkness approached as the bugle call announced dinner.

☑️**Reading Check**

What message does Bride give to the captain?

The "stokers" shoveled coal to feed the huge boilers that powered the ship. When water poured into the boiler rooms, the men rushed to escape, sealing watertight doors behind them.

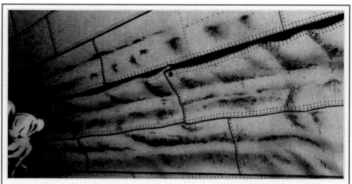

The pressure of the iceberg scraping the side of *Titanic*'s hull caused the plates to buckle, allowing huge amounts of water to flow into the ship.

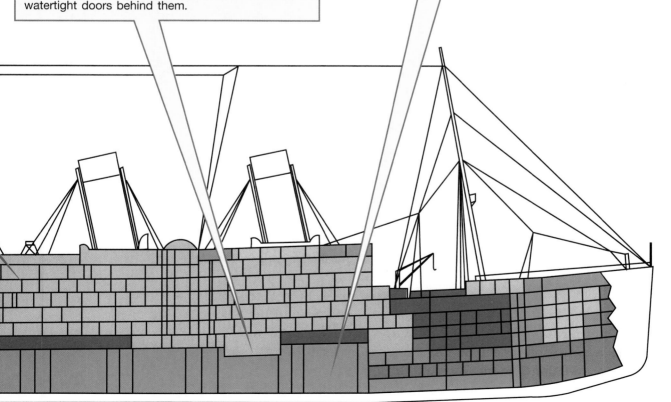

Jack Thayer's parents had been invited to a special dinner for Captain Smith, so Jack ate alone in the first-class dining room. After dinner, as he was having a cup of coffee, he was joined by Milton Long, another passenger going home to the States. Long was older than Jack, but in the easy-going atmosphere of shipboard travel, they struck up a conversation and talked together for an hour or so.

At 7:30 P.M., the radio room received three more warnings of ice about fifty miles ahead. One of them was from the steamer *Californian* reporting three large icebergs. Harold Bride took this message up to the bridge, and it was again politely received. Captain Smith was attending the dinner party being held for him when the warning was delivered. He never got to see it. Then, around 9:00 P.M., the captain excused himself and went up to the bridge. He and his officers talked about how difficult it was to spot icebergs on a calm, clear, moonless night like this with no wind to kick up white surf around them. Before going to bed, the captain ordered the lookouts to keep a sharp watch for ice.

After trading travel stories with Milton Long, Jack Thayer put on his coat and walked around the deck. "It had become very much colder," he said later. "It was a brilliant, starry night. There was no moon, and I have never seen the stars shine brighter . . . sparkling like diamonds. . . . It was the kind of night that made one feel glad to be alive." At eleven o'clock, he went below to his cabin, put on his pajamas, and got ready for bed.

In the radio room, Harold Bride was exhausted. The two operators were expected to keep the radio working twenty-four hours a day, and Bride lay down to take a much-needed nap. Phillips was so busy with the passenger messages that he actually brushed off the final ice warning of the night. It was from the *Californian*. Trapped in a field of ice, she had stopped for the night about nineteen miles north of the Titanic. She was so close that the message literally blasted in Phillips's ears. Annoyed by the loud interruption, he cut off the *Californian's* radio operator with the words, "Shut up, shut up, I'm busy."

The radio room had received a total of seven ice warning messages in one day. It was quite clear that floating icebergs lay ahead of the *Titanic*.

High up in the crow's nest on the forward mast, Fred Fleet had passed a quiet watch. It was now 11:40 P.M., and he and his fellow lookout were waiting to be relieved so they could head below, perhaps for a hot drink before hopping into their warm bunks. The sea was dead calm. The air bitterly cold.

▲ **Critical Viewing**
Based on this picture, explain why the first sign of a problem is sometimes referred to as "just the tip of the iceberg." **[Connect]**

Suddenly, Fleet saw something. A huge, dark shape loomed out of the night directly ahead of the *Titanic.* An iceberg! He quickly sounded the alarm bell three times and picked up the telephone.

"What did you see?" asked the duty officer.

"Iceberg right ahead," replied Fleet.

Immediately, the officer on the bridge ordered the wheel turned as far as it would go. The engine room was told to reverse the engines, while a button was pushed to close the doors to the <u>watertight</u> compartments in the bottom of the ship.

The lookouts in the crow's nest braced themselves for a collision. Slowly the ship started to turn. It looked as though they would miss it. But it was too late. They had avoided a head-on crash, but the iceberg had struck a glancing blow along the *Titanic's* starboard bow.[1] Several tons of ice fell on the ship's decks as the iceberg brushed along the side of the ship and passed into the night. A few minutes later, the *Titanic* came to a stop.

Many of the passengers didn't know the ship had hit anything. Because it was so cold, almost everyone was inside, and most people had already gone to bed. Ruth Becker and her mother were awakened by the dead silence. They could no longer hear the soothing hum of the vibrating engines from below. Jack Thayer was about to step into bed when he felt himself sway ever so slightly. The engines stopped. He was startled by the sudden quiet.

Sensing trouble, Ruth's mother looked out of the door of their second-class cabin and asked a steward[2] what had happened. He told her that nothing was the matter, so Mrs. Becker went back to bed. But as she lay there, she couldn't help feeling that something was very wrong.

Jack heard running feet and voices in the hallway outside his first-class cabin. "I hurried into my heavy overcoat and drew on my slippers. All excited, but not thinking anything serious had occurred, I called in to my father and mother that I was going up on deck to see the fun."

On deck, Jack watched some third-class passengers playing with the ice that had landed on the forward deck as the iceberg had brushed by. Some people were throwing chunks at each other, while a few skidded about playing football with pieces of ice.

Down in the very bottom of the ship, things were very different. When the iceberg had struck, there had been a noise like a big gun going off in one of the boiler rooms. A couple of stokers had been immediately hit by a jet of icy water. The noise and the shock of cold water had sent them running for safety.

---

1. **starboard bow** right side of the front of the ship.
2. **steward** worker on a ship who attends to the needs of the passengers.

**Literary Analysis
Suspense** What details here heighten the suspense?

watertight *adj.* put together so that no water can get through

**Reading Strategy
Distinguishing Between Fact and Opinion** Identify one fact and one opinion in this section.

**Reading Check**

What does Fred Fleet see in the ocean?

Twenty minutes after the crash, things looked very bad indeed to Captain Smith. He and the ship's builder, Thomas Andrews, had made a rapid tour below decks to inspect the damage. The mail room was filling up with water, and sacks of mail were floating about. Water was also pouring into some of the forward holds and two of the boiler rooms.

Captain Smith knew that the *Titanic*'s hull was divided into a number of watertight compartments. She had been designed so that she could still float if only the first four compartments were flooded, but not any more than that. But water was pouring into the first five compartments. And when the water filled them, it would spill over into the next compartment. One by one all the remaining compartments would flood, and the ship would eventually sink. Andrews told the captain that the ship could last an hour, an hour and a half at the most.

Harold Bride had just awakened in the radio room when Captain Smith stuck his head in the door. "Send the call for assistance," he ordered.

"What call should I send?" Phillips asked.

"The regulation international call for help. Just that." Then the captain was gone. Phillips began to send the Morse code "CQD" distress call, flashing away and joking as he did it. After all, they knew the ship was unsinkable.

Review and Assess

Thinking About the Selections

1. **Respond:** If you could interview one person aboard the *Titanic*, who would it be? Why?

2. **(a) Recall:** Why are the radio operators so busy and behind in their work? **(b) Analyze Cause and Effect:** What is the effect of their being so busy?

3. **(a) Recall:** What messages do other ships send to the *Titanic*? **(b) Draw Conclusions:** Why isn't Captain Smith concerned about the warnings he receives?

4. **(a) Infer:** Why do you think people are unprepared for the disaster? **(b) Compare and Contrast:** How does the scene on the deck contrast with the scene at the bottom of the ship following the crash?

5. **(a) Assess:** Who or what is responsible for the crash? **(b) Make a Judgment:** Who or what is responsible for the loss of so many lives? **(c) Distinguish:** Explain why this responsibility is or is not different from the responsibility for the crash.

Robert D. Ballard

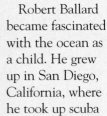

(b. 1942)
Robert Ballard became fascinated with the ocean as a child. He grew up in San Diego, California, where he took up scuba diving as a teenager. Ballard studied and worked as a marine geologist. He developed a special underwater camera and a remote-controlled robot that could take pictures underwater. Ballard's curiosity and inventions led him to find the famous *Titanic*, which rested more than two miles underwater on the floor of the North Atlantic Ocean. On September 1, 1985, he found the sunken ocean liner. It had been there 73 years!

Review and Assess

Literary Analysis

Suspense

1. What event at the beginning of the *Titanic*'s journey contributes to the **suspense** of the account?
2. In what way do the ice warnings add to the suspense?
3. Identify two other facts that add to the **suspense**.

Connecting Literary Elements

4. Why does Ballard include several descriptions of the calm, moonless night?
5. What other details contribute to the atmosphere?
6. Identify images that contribute to the atmosphere before and after the collision. Use a diagram like the one shown.

Before		After
1. huge, dark shape loomed	Atmosphere	1. noise like a big gun going off

Reading Strategy

Distinguishing Between Fact and Opinion

7. What **fact** tells what Captain Smith does after reading the *Caronia*'s ice warning?
8. What is Harold Bride's **opinion** of Captain Smith's reaction to the *Caronia*'s warning?
9. On organizers like the one shown here, record one fact and one opinion about each topic or event.

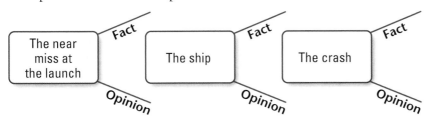

The near miss at the launch — Fact — Opinion

The ship — Fact — Opinion

The crash — Fact — Opinion

Extending Understanding

10. **Math Connection:** Why would the designer of a ship need strong math skills?

Quick Review

Suspense is the feeling of tension you experience as you wait to find out what will happen or when something will happen. To review suspense, see page 379.

Atmosphere is the feeling created in a reader by a literary work or passage. To review atmosphere, see page 379.

A **fact** is a statement that can be proved true.

An **opinion** can be supported but not proved. To review fact and opinion, see page 379.

 Take It to the Net
www.phschool.com
Take the interactive self-test online to check your understanding of the selection.

Integrate Language Skills

Vocabulary Development Lesson

Concept Development: Compound Adjectives

A **compound adjective** is made up of two or more words linked together as one word to modify, or describe, a noun or pronoun.

> water + tight = watertight

A *watertight* compartment does not let water in.

On your paper, match each compound adjective with the word it would best describe.

1. head-on
2. icebound
3. easy-going

   a. ship
   b. collision
   c. mood

Fluency: Sentence Completions

Copy the paragraph. Replace each blank with a vocabulary word.

The *Titanic* sailed ____?____ out to sea. To many on board this was a ____?____. No one expected the coming ____?____, or that the ____?____ compartments would fill so rapidly.

Spelling Strategy

The word *collision* in the story has the sound *zhun* and is spelled *sion*. Many words with the sound *zhun* end in *sion*. Write a word ending in *sion* for each clue.

1. the ability to see
2. the end
3. something that intrudes
4. attempts to persuade

Grammar Lesson

Types of Sentences

There are four types of sentences. Each kind has a purpose and a form that requires specific punctuation, as shown in this chart. All sentences, no matter what type, begin with a capital letter.

Type of Sentence	What It Does	Punctuation
Declarative	Makes a statement	Period (.)
Imperative	Gives a command or makes a request	Period. Exclamation point (!)
Interrogative	Asks a question	Question mark (?)
Exclamatory	Shows strong feeling	Exclamation point (!)

Declarative: Bride has awakened.
Imperative: Send the call.
Interrogative: What will you do?
Exclamatory: That's terrible!

▶ *For more practice, see page R28, Exercise A.*
Practice Copy each sentence, adding capitals and punctuation as needed. (For some sentences there may be more than one correct choice for punctuation.) Then, identify the sentence type.

1. daylight shone through the glass dome
2. did it mean that the *Titanic* was too big
3. what a cold night it is
4. send the call for assistance
5. what call should I send

Writing Application On your paper, write a short paragraph about the *Titanic*. Use at least one of each of the four kinds of sentences. Use the appropriate punctuation and capitalization.

W͟G *Prentice Hall Writing and Grammar Connection: Chapter 21, Section 1*

Writing Lesson

Investigative Report

Use details you have learned about from the selection to prepare an investigative report on the sinking of the *Titanic*. In your report, identify the sequence of events—the reasons things happen and the results of actions and decisions.

Prewriting   Identify what you know and what you want to know about the sinking of the *Titanic*. Use the library and computer resources to find the answers. Be sure to make source cards including the author, title, date of publication, or name of the Web site.

Drafting   Organize events in chronological or time order. As you relate each event, include descriptive details related to the event. Use words like *meanwhile* and *simultaneously* to indicate events that are happening at the same time.

Revising   Use a highlighter to call out dates, times, and words that indicate time. Review the order of your details. Revise if necessary to put events in correct time order.

Model: Organize Ideas Within and Between Paragraphs

(2) It was the largest ship built and carried 2200 people. (4) When it collided with an iceberg on its maiden voyage, it sank. (5) A nearby ship did not respond in time to save many passengers. (3) At the time, the <u>Titanic</u> was considered unsinkable. (1) In 1912, the <u>Titanic</u>, a huge luxury liner, sailed from England.

> Look for dates and words that indicate time. Then, number the sentences in chronological order. Revise the paragraph by putting the sentences in order.

Prentice Hall Writing and Grammar Connection: Chapter 11, Section 2

Extension Activities

Listening and Speaking The publicity for the *Titanic* included the word "unsinkable." This information turned out to be false.

- False information is simply not true.
- Misleading information is true, but is presented in such a way that it suggests other facts or circumstances that are not necessarily true.

Develop a **list of examples** of false or misleading information you find in advertising.

Research and Technology In a group, create a **timeline** to show the events in the sinking of the *Titanic*. Include the specific hours that events occurred. On the timeline, identify the decision points and the choices that were made. Add other choices that might have been considered.

 Take It to the Net   www.phschool.com

Go online for an additional research activity using the Internet.

Prepare to Read

Breaker's Bridge

The Kintai Bridge in Springtime (detail), Kawase Hasui

Take It to the Net

Visit www.phschool.com for interactive activities and instruction related to "Breaker's Bridge," including

- background
- graphic organizers
- literary elements
- reading strategies

Preview

Connecting to the Literature

At one time or another, you have probably been faced with what seems like an impossible job. In "Breaker's Bridge," by Laurence Yep, the main character must complete an overwhelming task set by the emperor. If he does not finish the job, he faces an enormous penalty.

Background

Most bridges must be built on piers—columns that support the weight of the bridge. Without piers, a bridge can cover only a short distance. Even with modern equipment and technology, building piers in deep water is extremely difficult and expensive. For Breaker, in ancient China, building piers in a deep, swift-moving river seems impossible.

Literary Analysis

Character Traits

Character traits are the qualities that determine a person's or character's personality and actions. A character's traits influence how the character acts. In "Breaker's Bridge," a once clumsy boy who earned the nickname "Breaker" demonstrates his traits of intelligence and determination when facing a difficult challenge. As you read the story, look for the connections between the characters' traits and characters' actions.

Connecting Literary Elements

In a story, the characters' traits and their actions are often a clue to the **theme**—the message of the work. For example, when a villain in a story commits a crime—and is caught—the theme suggested is "Crime doesn't pay." As you read "Breaker's Bridge," look for the theme conveyed, in part by the characters and their actions. Use the following focus questions to guide you:

1. What qualities are shown in Breaker's actions?

2. In what way do Breaker's character traits lead to Breaker's success?

Jot notes on an organizer like the one shown to identify other details that will help you connect the characters' traits and actions to the theme.

Reading Strategy

Determining Cause and Effect

The main character in this story is called Breaker because he is clumsy. His clumsiness is a **cause**—a reason why something happens. The **effect**, or result, is that people gave him a nickname. To understand the action in a story, identify causes-and-effects. Keep in mind that there is not necessarily a cause-and-effect relationship between events that follow one another.

Cause and effect: Because the river flooded, the bridge was washed away.

Not cause and effect: The bridge was washed away. Then, the floods increased.

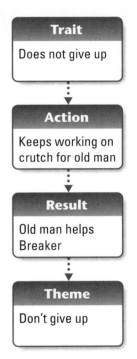

Trait
Does not give up

Action
Keeps working on crutch for old man

Result
Old man helps Breaker

Theme
Don't give up

Vocabulary Development

obstacle (äb′ stə kəl′) *n.* something that stands in the way (p. 393)

writhing (rīth′ iŋ) *adj.* twisting and turning (p. 394)

piers (pirz) *n.* heavy structures supporting the sections of a bridge (p. 394)

executioner (ek′ si kyo͞o′ shən ər) *n.* one who carries out a death penalty imposed by the courts or a ruler (p. 396)

immortals (im môrt′ əlz) *n.* beings who live forever (p. 400)

The Immortal, 1990, Chi-Fong Lei, Courtesy of the artist

Breaker's Bridge

LAURENCE YEP

There was once a boy who was always breaking things. He didn't do it on purpose. He just had very clumsy hands. No matter how careful he tried to be, he always dropped whatever he picked up. His family soon learned not to let him set the table or send him for eggs. Everyone in the village called him Breaker.

But Breaker was as clever as he was clumsy. When he grew up, he managed to outlive his nickname. He could design a bridge to cross any obstacle. No canyon was too wide. No river was too deep. Somehow the clever man always found a way to bridge them all.

Eventually the emperor heard about this clever builder and sent for him.

"There is a river in the hills," the emperor said to him. "Everyone tells me it is too swift and deep to span. So I have to go a long way around it to get to my hunting palace. But you're famous for doing the impossible."

The kneeling man bowed his head to the floor. "So far I have been lucky. But there is always a first time when you can't do something."

The emperor frowned. "I didn't think you were lazy like my other bridge builders. You can have all the workers and all the materials you need. Build the bridge and you'll have your weight in gold. Fail and I'll have your head."

There was nothing for Breaker to do but thank the emperor and leave. He went right away to see the river. He had to take a steep road that wound upward through the hills toward the emperor's hunting palace.

It was really more than a palace, for it included a park the size of a district, and only the emperor could hunt the wildlife. The road to it had to snake through high, steep mountains. Although the road was

obstacle (äb´ stə kəl´) *n.* something that stands in the way

Literary Analysis
Character Traits What character trait do Breaker and the emperor share?

✔**Reading Check**

What does the emperor want Breaker to do?

◀**Critical Viewing** How do you think this old man might help Breaker solve his problem? **[Speculate]**

well kept, the land became wilder and wilder. Pointed boulders thrust up like fangs, and the trees grew in twisted, <u>writhing</u> clumps.

Breaker became uneasy. "This is a place that doesn't like people very much."

The road twisted suddenly to the left when it came to a deep river gorge. On the other side of the gorge, the many trees of the palace looked like a dark-green sea. The yellow-tiled roofs looked like golden rafts floating on its top. Dark mountains, their tops capped with snow all year round, loomed behind the palace like monstrous guards.

Breaker carefully sidled to the edge of the gorge and looked down. Far below, he saw the river. When the snow melted in the distant mountains, the water flowed together to form this river. It raced faster than a tiger and stronger than a thousand buffalo. When it splashed against a rock, it threw up sheets of white spray like an ocean wave.

Breaker shook his head in dismay. "The emperor might as well have commanded me to bridge the sea."

But his failure would mean the loss of his head, so the next day Breaker set to work. The river was too wide to span with a simple bridge. Breaker would have to construct two <u>piers</u> in the middle of

writing (rĭthˊ ĭn) *adj.* twisting and turning

piers (pirz) *n.* heavy structures supporting the sections of a bridge

the river. The piers would support the bridge like miniature stone islands.

From the forests of the south came huge logs that were as tough and heavy as iron. From the quarries of the west came large, heavy stones of granite. The workers braved the cold water to sink the logs in the muddy riverbed. Breaker had to change the teams of workers often. The cold numbed anyone who stayed too long in the river.

Once the logs had been pounded into the mud, he tried to set the stones on top of the logs. But the river did not want to be tamed. It bucked and fought like a herd of wild stallions. It crushed the piles of stones into pebbles. It dug up the logs and smashed them against the rocky sides until they were mounds of soggy toothpicks.

Over the next month, Breaker tried every trick he knew; and each time the river defeated him. With each new failure, Breaker suspected more and more that he had met his match. The river flowed hard and strong and fast like the lifeblood of the earth itself. Breaker might as well have tried to tame the mountains.

In desperation, he finally tried to build a dam to hold back the river while he constructed the biggest and strongest piers yet. As he was supervising the construction, an official came by from the emperor.

Reading Strategy
Determining Cause and Effect What is the effect of the river's wild rushing?

Reading Check

How does Breaker feel about building the bridge when he sees the river?

◄**Critical Viewing**
What details of this scene seem magical and mysterious? [Analyze]

"This bridge has already cost a lot of money," he announced to the wrecker. "What do you have to show for it?"

Breaker pointed to the two piers.♦ They rose like twin towers toward the top of the gorge. "With a little luck, the emperor will have his bridge."

Suddenly, they heard a distant roar. The official looked up at the sky. "It sounds like thunder, but I don't see a cloud in the sky."

Breaker cupped his hands around his mouth to amplify his voice. "Get out," he shouted to his men. "Get out. The river must have broken our dam."

His men slipped and slid on the muddy riverbed, but they all managed to scramble out just as a wall of water rolled down the gorge. The river swept around the two piers, pulling and tugging at the stones.

Everyone held their breath. Slowly the two piers began to rock back and forth on their foundations until they toppled over with a crash into the river. Water splashed in huge sheets over everyone, and when the spray finally fell back into the river, not one sign of the piers remained.

"All this time and all this money, and you have nothing to show for it." The official took a soggy yellow envelope from his sleeve.

Breaker and the other workers recognized the imperial color of the emperor. They instantly dropped to their knees and bowed their heads.

Then, with difficulty, Breaker opened the damp envelope and unfolded the letter. "In one month," it said, "I will have a bridge or I will have your head." It was sealed in red ink with the official seal of the emperor.

Breaker returned the letter and bowed again. "I'll try," he promised.

"You will do more than try," the official snapped. "You will build that bridge for the emperor. Or the <u>executioner</u> will be sharpening his sword." And the official left.

Wet and cold and tired, Breaker made his way along a path toward the room he had taken in an inn. It was getting late, so the surrounding forest was black with shadows. As he walked, Breaker tried to come up with some kind of new scheme, but the dam had been his last resort. In a month's time, he would feel the "kiss" of the executioner's sword.

"Hee, hee, hee," an old man laughed in a creaky voice that

♦ Piers and Bridges

The **piers** of a bridge are the columns that support the bridge over the water. (The structure that supports the bridge where it touches land is an **abutment** or **anchorage**.) Most kinds of bridges require piers to keep them from collapsing. The Golden Gate Bridge, shown below, is one of the world's longest suspension bridges. Below the roadway it is supported by two piers. Above the piers rise the towers, which help to distribute the weight.

Golden Gate Bridge

Reading Strategy
Determining Cause and Effect What feeling about the emperor causes the workers to drop to their knees here?

executioner
(ek′ si kyōō′ shən ər) *n.* one who carries out a death penalty imposed by the courts or a ruler

sounded like feet on old, worn steps. "You never liked hats anyway. Now you'll have an excuse not to wear them."

Breaker turned and saw a crooked old man sitting by the side of the road. He was dressed in rags, and a gourd hung from a strap against his hip. One leg was shorter than the other.

"How did you know that, old man?" Breaker wondered.

"Hee, hee, hee. I know a lot of things: the softness of clouds underneath my feet, the sounds of souls inside bodies." And he shook his gourd so that it rattled as if there were beans inside. "It is the law of the universe that all things must change; and yet Nature hates change the most of all."

"The river certainly fits that description." Although he was exhausted and worried, Breaker squatted down beside the funny old man. "But you better get inside, old man. Night's coming on and it gets cold up in these mountains."

"Can't." The old man nodded to his broken crutch.

Breaker looked all around. It was growing dark, and his stomach was aching with hunger. But he couldn't leave the old man stranded in the mountains, so Breaker took out his knife. "If I make you a new crutch, can you reach your home?"

"If you make me a crutch, we'll all have what we want." It was getting so dim that Breaker could not be sure if the old man smiled.

Although it was hard to see, Breaker found a tall, straight sapling and tried to trim the branches from its sides; but being Breaker, he dropped his knife several times and lost it twice among the old leaves on the forest floor. He also cut each of his fingers. By the time he was ready to cut down the sapling, he couldn't see it. Of course, he cut his fingers even more. And just as he was trimming the last branch from the sapling, he cut the sapling right in two.

He tried to carve another sapling and broke that one. It was so dark by now that he could not see at all. He had to find the next sapling by feel. This time he managed to cut it down and began to trim it. But halfway through he dropped his knife and broke it. "He'll just have to take it as it is," Breaker said.

When he finally emerged from the forest, the moon had come out. Sucking on his cut fingers, Breaker presented the new crutch to the funny old man.

The old man looked at the branches that grew from the sides of his new crutch. "A little splintery."

Breaker angrily took his cut finger from his mouth. "Don't insult someone who's doing you a favor."

The crooked old man lifted his right arm with difficulty and managed to bring it behind his neck. "Keep that in mind yourself." He began to rub the back of his neck.

Literary Analysis
Character Traits What character trait shows in Breaker's concern for the old man?

☑ **Reading Check**

What will happen to Breaker if he does not finish constructing the bridge by the end of the month?

Breaker thrust the crutch at the old man. "Here, old man. This is what you wanted."

But the old man kept rubbing the back of his neck. "Rivers are like people: Every now and then, they have to be reminded that change is the law that binds us all."

"It's late. I'm tired and hungry and I have to come up with a new plan. Here's your crutch." And Breaker laid the crutch down beside the old man.

But before Breaker could straighten, the old man's left hand shot out and caught hold of Breaker's wrist. The old man's grip was as strong as iron. "Even the least word from me will remind that river of the law."

Breaker tried to pull away, but as strong as he was, he could not break the old man's hold. "Let me go."

But the crooked old man lowered his right hand so that Breaker could see that he had rubbed some of the dirt and sweat from his skin. "We are all bound together," the old man murmured, "and by the same laws." He murmured that over and over until he was almost humming like a bee. At the same time, his fingers quickly rolled the dirt and sweat into two round little pellets.

Frightened, Breaker could only stare at the old man. "Ar-ar-are you some mountain spirit?"* he stammered.

The old man turned Breaker's palm upward and deposited the two little pellets on it. Then he closed Breaker's fingers over them. "Leave one of these at each spot where you want a pier. Be sure not to lose them."

"Yes, all right, of course," Breaker promised quickly.

The old man picked up the crutch and thrust himself up from the ground. "Then you'll have what you want too." And he hobbled away quickly.

Breaker kept hold of the pellets until he reached the inn. Once he was among the inn's bright lights and could smell a hot meal, he began to laugh at himself. "You've let the emperor's letter upset you so much that you let a harmless old man scare you."

Even so, Breaker didn't throw away the pellets but put them in a little pouch. And the next morning when he returned to the gorge, he took along the pouch.

The canyon widened at one point so that there was a small beach. Breaker kept his supplies of stone and logs there. Figuring that he had nothing to lose, Breaker walked down the steep path. Then he took the boat and rowed out onto the river.

As he sat in the bobbing boat, he thought of the funny old man again. "You and I," he said to the river, "are both part of the same scheme of things. And it's time you faced up to it."

Literary Analysis
Character Traits and Theme What do the words of this mysterious character seem to be telling Breaker?

Although it was difficult to row at the same time, he got out the pouch with the two pellets. "I must be even crazier than that old man." He opened the pouch and shook one of the pellets into his hand.

When he was by the spot where the first pier should be, Breaker threw the pellet in. For a moment, nothing happened. There was only the sound of his oars slapping at the water.

And suddenly the surface began to boil. Frantically, he tried to row away, but the water began to whirl and whirl around in circles. Onshore, the workers shouted and ran to higher ground as waves splashed over the logs and stones.

From beneath the river came loud thumps and thuds and the grinding of stone on stone. A rock appeared above the surface. The water rose in another wave. On top of the wave another stone floated as if it were a block of wood. The river laid the first stone by the second.

Open-mouthed, Breaker watched the river lay stone after stone. The watery arms reached higher and higher until the first pier rose to the top of the gorge.

As the waters calmed, Breaker eagerly rowed the boat over to the second spot. At the same time that he tried to row enough to keep himself in the right place, Breaker reached for the pouch and opened it.

But in his hurry, his clumsy fingers crushed part of the pellet. He threw the remainder of the pellet into the water and then shook out the contents of the pouch. But this time, the river only swirled and rippled.

Breaker leaned over the side and peered below. He could just make out the pale, murky shape of a mound, but that was all. Even so, Breaker wasn't upset. His workers could easily build a second pier and meet the emperor's deadline.

So Breaker finished the bridge, and that summer the emperor reached his hunting palace with ease. When the emperor finished hunting and returned to his capital, he showered Breaker with gold and promised him all the work he could ever want.

However, winter brought deep snows once again to the mountains. That spring, when the snow thawed, the river grew strong and wild again. It roared down the gorge and smashed against the first pier. But the first pier was solid as a mountain.

Literature in context Cultural Connection

♦ **The Eight Immortals**

The old man in the story is one of the Eight Immortals, the Ba Xian of Chinese mythology. The Eight Immortals are symbols of good fortune. They are often featured in Chinese art and literature.

The Eight Immortals Crossing the Sea (detail), illustration from "Myths and Legends of China" by Edward T.C. Werner, pub. by George G. Harrap & Co., 1922, Private Collection

One of The Eight Immortals

Literary Analysis
Character Traits
How does Breaker's clumsiness affect what happens to the bridge?

✔**Reading Check**

What happens when Breaker throws the first pellet into the water?

However, the second pier had not been built with magic. The river swept away the second pier as if it were nothing but twigs.

The bridge was repaired before the summer hunting, but the emperor angrily summoned Breaker to his hunting palace. "You were supposed to build a bridge for me," the emperor declared.

"Hee, hee, hee," laughed a creaky old voice. "He did, but you didn't say how long it was supposed to stay up."

Breaker turned around and saw it was the crooked old man. He was leaning on the crutch that Breaker had made for him. "How did you get here?" he asked the old man. But from the corner of his eye, he could see all the court officials kneeling down. And when Breaker looked back at the throne, he saw even the emperor kneeling.

"How can we serve you and the other eight <u>immortals</u>?" the emperor asked the crooked old man.

"We are all bound by the same laws," the old man croaked again, and then vanished.

And then Breaker knew the old man for what he truly was—a saint and a powerful magician.

So the emperor spared Breaker and sent him to build other projects all over China. And the emperor never regretted that he had let Breaker keep his head. But every year, the river washed away part of the bridge and every year it was rebuilt. And so things change and yet do not change.

immortals (im môrt′ əlz) *n.* beings who live forever

Review and Assess

Thinking About the Selection

1. **Respond:** Do you think the emperor was fair to Breaker? Explain.

2. **(a) Recall:** Why did the emperor want Breaker instead of other builders to build the bridge? **(b) Infer:** Why does Breaker accept the challenge? **(c) Assess:** What are the advantages and disadvantages of his situation?

3. **(a) Recall:** How does the crooked old man first appear to Breaker? **(b) Analyze:** What clues indicate that the old man is more than he seems? **(c) Support:** What events prove that the old man is more than he seems?

4. **(a) Recall:** What does Breaker accomplish? **(b) Synthesize:** What do you think Breaker and the old man have in common?

5. **(a) Interpret:** In your own words, explain the meaning of "change is the law that binds us all." **(b) Assess:** Do you agree or disagree with this idea? **(c) Support:** Give examples from life, movies, and literature that support your position.

Laurence Yep

(b. 1948)

Laurence Yep was born and raised in San Francisco, California. A third-generation Chinese American, he began writing in high school, selling his first story when he was just eighteen years old. Since then, he has written many books for young people and won numerous honors and awards. Much of Yep's subject matter comes from his interest in other worlds. His books of science fiction and fantasy tell of strange events in mysterious lands. He has also researched and written novels about the experiences of Chinese immigrants and their descendants.

Review and Assess

Literary Analysis

Character Traits

1. What is one **character trait** of the emperor? Give an example of an action that demonstrates this trait.
2. What action shows that one of the old man's character traits is mischievousness?

Connecting Literary Elements

3. What qualities are shown in Breaker's actions?
4. Complete the organizer to connect character traits to actions to the message of the work.

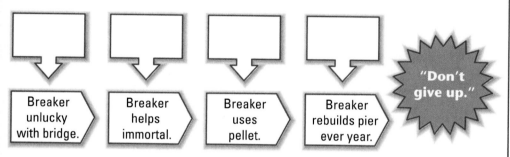

Breaker unlucky with bridge. → Breaker helps immortal. → Breaker uses pellet. → Breaker rebuilds pier ever year.

"Don't give up."

Reading Strategy

Determining Cause and Effect

5. What **effect** would take place if Breaker fails to build the bridge?
6. Copy the chart. Connect the **causes and effects** by drawing arrows between them. Do not connect events that simply follow each other.

| 1. Breaker tries to build bridge. | 2. River washes out first bridge. | 3. Breaker gets letter. | 4. Breaker makes crutch for old man. | 5. Old man gives Breaker pellets. |

Extending Understanding

7. **Make a Judgment:** Did Breaker meet the emperor's demands? Explain.
8. **Math Connection:** In what way would a bridge builder use measurements of distance and weight?

Quick Review

Character traits are the qualities that determine a person's or character's personality and actions. To review character traits, see page 391.

Theme is the message in a literary work. To review theme, see page 391.

A **cause** is the reason something happens. An effect is the result.

 Take It to the Net
www.phschool.com
Take the interactive self-test online to check your understanding of the selection.

Integrate Language Skills

Vocabulary Development Lesson

Word Analysis: Forms of *execute*

In your notebook, use a form of *execute* to complete each sentence. Choose from *execute*, *executive*, *execution*, or *executioner*.

1. Breaker did not want the ___?___ to carry out the emperor's threat.
2. An ___?___ carries out business plans.
3. This plan is not easy to ___?___.
4. The ___?___ of the plan is complicated.

Spelling Strategy

Words with the vowel combination *ie* such as *pier* follow this spelling rule: Use *i* before *e* except after *c* or when sounded like *a*, as in *neighbor* and *weigh*. Add letters to correctly spell words

1. A strong opinion: b_l_ _f
2. To trick or lie: d_c_ _ _e
3. How heavy something is: w_ _gh_

Concept Development: Analogies

Analogies are comparisons between things that are in most ways not alike, but which share one main quality. Word pairs are sometimes called analogies because the first pair and the second pair share one main quality. The quality may be that they both name opposites. It may be that the first word in each pair is a part and the second word names the whole. On your paper, write a vocabulary word that completes the second pair of words.

1. Bake is to baker as kill is to ___?___.
2. Natural is to mortal as supernatural is to ___?___.
3. Help is to assistance as problem is to ___?___.
4. Motionless is to still as twisting is to ___?___.
5. Table is to legs as bridge is to ___?___.

Grammar Lesson

Direct and Indirect Objects

A **direct object** is a noun or pronoun that receives the action of the verb and answers the question *what* or *whom*.

He could design a bridge to cross any obstacle. (Design what? a *bridge*)

An **indirect object** is a noun or pronoun that names the person or thing to whom or for whom an action is done. The indirect object immediately follows the verb and precedes the direct object.

If I make *you* a new crutch, can you reach your home? (Make what? *a crutch* For whom? *you*)

▶ *For more practice, see page R28, Exercise B*
Practice On your paper, copy the following sentences. Write DO over each direct object and IO over each indirect object.

1. The official handed Breaker the letter.
2. The old man gave him the pellets.
3. The emperor summoned Breaker.
4. Breaker found an unusual solution.
5. Breaker built the emperor a bridge.

Writing Application Write four sentences about the story. Two should include direct objects, and two should include indirect and direct objects.

*W*G *Prentice Hall Writing and Grammar Connection: Chapter 19, Section 5*

Writing Lesson

Proposal for Research

While reading "Breaker's Bridge," you might have wondered how bridge builders get the foundation for a bridge into the water. Write a **research proposal** to study a question about bridge building. A research proposal is an overview of what you want to learn, why you want to learn it, and what you will need to complete your research.

Prewriting   Make a chart like the one shown to plan the details of your proposal.

Model: Proposal

Question	Reason	Resources	Time
How do bridge builders get the foundation set into the water?	I have always wondered what holds a bridge in place.	Interviews with engineers	Two afternoons
	My research will teach me about practical applications of some principles of gravity, force, and matter.	Internet search	Two evenings
		Encyclopedia	One hour for encyclopedia review

Drafting   Use an excerpt from "Breaker's Bridge" to explain why your question interests you. Then, explain the resources and time you will need.

Revising   Look for places where you can be more specific about times and resources. Add the needed details.

W_G *Prentice Hall Writing and Grammar Connection: Chapter 11, Section 2*

Extension Activities

Listening and Speaking In a group, prepare a **dramatization** of "Breaker's Bridge" using these guidelines.

1. First, decide which scenes to enact and write a brief script.
2. Determine the mood of each scene and how it should be interpreted. Highlight parts of the script that can help create the mood.
3. Perform the dramatization for the class.

Research and Technology Conduct research on the "immortals" of Chinese lore. Use what you learn to write an **essay** giving background that will help readers understand the significance of the old man in the story.

Writing Write a **letter** from Breaker to the emperor explaining why it is difficult to complete the bridge.

 **Take It to the Net**   www.phschool.com

Go online for an additional research activity using the Internet.

Prepare to Read

The Loch Ness Monster ◆
Why the Tortoise's Shell Is Not Smooth

 Take It to the Net

Visit www.phschool.com
for interactive activities
and instruction related to
these selections, including

- background
- graphic organizers
- literary elements
- reading strategies

Preview

Connecting to the Literature

You know that it is important to think for yourself—to evaluate information and come to your own conclusion or decision. "The Loch Ness Monster" and "Why the Tortoise's Shell Is Not Smooth" both deal with the problems people and characters face when they must make judgments based on incomplete or faulty information.

Background

Some scientists believe that the depths of the ocean may still hold undiscovered species—or members of species thought to be extinct. Many wonder if Loch Ness, a deep murky lake that may be connected to the ocean by underwater tunnels, may also contain an unidentified species.

Literary Analysis

Oral tradition

Oral tradition is the passing along of songs, stories, and poems by word of mouth. For example, "Why the Tortoise's Shell Is Not Smooth" was originally told orally. Because oral storytelling is not as common as it was once, writers have preserved many of the works in written texts. Think about these focus questions as you read:

1. In what way is the story of the Loch Ness monster part of the oral tradition?
2. Which detail in "Why the Tortoise's Shell Is Not Smooth" indicates that it is part of the oral tradition?

Comparing Literary Works

Both of these works offer explanations of something in nature. However, "Why the Tortoise's Shell Is Not Smooth" is **fiction.** The details come from the storyteller's imagination. On the other hand, "The Loch Ness Monster" is **nonfiction.** While the Loch Ness monster itself may or may not be a creature of the imagination, the details are factual. Compare and contrast the two works by supplying specific examples of the description on the diagram.

Reading Strategy

Evaluating Logic and Reasoning

Faulty reasoning is reasoning that seems logical because it contains facts, but it uses or interprets the facts in an illogical way.

- **Unsupported inferences**: Conclusions that are based on too few examples or facts.
  Example: Mark was frowning when he walked out of math class. *Mark doesn't like math.*
  Sound reasoning: Mark was frowning when he walked out of math class. *Mark was unhappy about something that happened in math class.*
- **Fallacious reasoning:** False or incorrect interpretation of facts
  Example: Many people have dogs. *Dogs are the best pets.*

As you read, evaluate whether the reasoning in each work is logical or faulty.

Vocabulary Development

elusive (ē loo′ siv) *adj.* always escaping (p. 407)

abundant (ə bun′ dənt) *adj.* plentiful; more than enough (p. 407)

famine (fa′ min) *n.* shortage of food (p. 412)

orator (ôr′ ə ter) *n.* speaker (p. 412)

eloquent (el′ ə kwint) *adj.* persuasive and expressive (p. 413)

Tortoise

- imaginative details
- ancient story
- made up of events
- fantasy

Explanation of something in nature — **Both**

- scientific details
- contemporary author
- actual events
- facts

Loch Ness Monster

The Loch Ness Monster

GEORGE LAYCOCK

In 1938, a tugboat captain was steering his boat across Loch Ness. Everything seemed to be in order. The sky was cloudy just as it is much of the time around Loch Ness. The water was rough from the wind. The tug plowed on mile after mile, its engines laboring normally. The captain was not thinking about monsters. He didn't believe in Nessie anyhow. He made this plain enough to anyone who asked him if he'd ever seen the beast. Then, beside the boat, a creature like nothing the captain had ever seen before stuck its long humped back out of the water. It had a long, slender neck and a little head. The monster rushed ahead, gained speed on the tug, and disappeared far out in front of the boat. This was enough to change the captain's mind. As far as he was concerned, Nessie was real, after all.

Other sightings even included an observation by a driver who saw Nessie in the beam of his headlights on a dark night as the monster crossed the highway near the loch.

These stories were told and retold. Word of Nessie spread around the world. This did a marvelous thing for Scotland. Tourists began to visit Loch Ness, hoping for a glimpse of the <u>elusive</u> lake monster. Tourism can be good for a country's economy. Nessie, real or not, became the most valuable animal in all Scotland.

But the lecturer who was to tell us about the Loch Ness monster that night in Oxford, Ohio, had brought scientific methods to the search for Nessie, and people were eager to hear his message. All the seats were filled and students stood around the walls and sat in the aisles to listen to the story Robert H. Rines had to tell.

Dr. Rines, president of the Boston Academy of Applied Science, led his first scientific expedition to Loch Ness in 1970. He took along modern sonar equipment and used this to "see" into the murky depths. Sonar works by sending high-intensity sound impulses into the water and measuring the echoes sent back as the sound waves bounce off the bottom or off objects between it and the bottom. It can reveal the depth of objects in the water, their size, and whether or not they are moving. That summer the sonar equipment showed the researchers important facts. There were large moving objects in the loch. Also there were <u>abundant</u> fish to feed monsters.

Dr. Rines meanwhile was consulting with his colleagues, searching for still better equipment for gathering information about the monster of Loch Ness. He worked with Dr. Harold E. Edgerton, who, as a professor at Massachusetts Institute of Technology, had pioneered in the development of high-speed underwater photography. Dr. Edgerton

Literary Analysis
Oral Tradition How does news about Nessie spread?

elusive (ē loō´ siv) *adj.* always escaping

abundant (ə bun´ dənt) *adj.* plentiful; more than enough

✔**Reading Check**
Who is Nessie?

◀ **Critical Viewing** Describe the "creature" you see in the photographs. **[Describe]**

had also developed remarkable strobe lights for making pictures in dingy water. Now, he designed a system of lights Dr. Rines might use to obtain closeup pictures in Loch Ness.

Dr. Rines linked his camera to the sonar and set it so that it would begin making pictures automatically as soon as any large object passed through the sonar field. It would continue to make pictures every fifteen seconds as long as the sonar told it to.

For their first test, the crew of monster seekers chose the bay where Nessie had most often been sighted. They carefully cleaned the camera lens, then began lowering it gently toward the lake bottom. Divers checked it there and found it clean and ready to make monster pictures.

Another camera was suspended under the research boat and pointed downward into the dark water. All that was needed now was to wait for Nessie to come nosing around.

But a strange thing happened. The lens of the camera on the bottom of the loch was suddenly covered with sand, apparently kicked onto it by some large frightened creature. Had Nessie been there and kicked up the silt?

Reading Strategy
Evaluate Logic Explain why assuming that "Nessie had been there" would be an example of fallacious reasoning.

That camera, with its sand-covered lens, made no pictures. But the other camera, hanging beneath the boat, was still in working order. It yielded pictures that to some looked plainly like parts of a huge unknown monster swimming in the water. These color pictures were perhaps the best evidence yet that there really is a Nessie. In 1975 Dr. Rines and his crew were back in Scotland with still better photographic equipment, and the pictures they took were among those shown to the audience in Oxford.

One famous picture, believed by some to be Nessie, was made in 1934 by a noted physician who was vacationing on Loch Ness. It showed a large, dark creature swimming on the surface. Its long slender neck and small head stuck out of the water. No one was ever able to prove that this picture had been faked. Neither could anyone suggest a reason why the photographer would want to set up such a hoax. But this picture, like others made later, was rather indistinct. So, for that matter, were those made by Dr. Rines and his crew in 1972 and 1975.

But, sitting in the darkened auditorium, we saw the head of a monster in murky water as it filled the screen before us. It was lumpy and appeared to have a wide mouth where the mouth should be. It also seemed to have two small horns on the top of the head. But perhaps these were not horns. Some believe that they may, instead, have been breathing tubes. This supports the theory that Nessie is a huge reptile that must come to the surface to breathe.

Another picture revealed a large angular object that could have been a flipper, four to six feet across. It was attached to the side of what may have been the body of Nessie.

But the research team also wanted to know more about the nature of the lake deep below the surface. They hoped to learn whether there really were places where large creatures could hide.

This search was concentrated on Urquhart Bay, where Nessie has been most often reported. On the research vessel *Narwhal* the scientists cruised back and forth over the bay, taking soundings and pictures and transferring the information to a map.

For the first time they began to understand the truth about this arm of Loch Ness. Underwater, along both sides of the bay, were deep hidden ravines, rocky canyons and caves, dark recesses far below the surface. This excited the research team. The hiding places made the whole story of Nessie more believable. Nessie, it was agreed, could cruise about down there among those dark caves without sending a ripple to the surface.

This is also the area in which one earlier investigator heard strange underwater sounds the year before, tapping sounds that no biologist has yet been able to successfully identify.

These are the bits of evidence that help convince a growing number of people that there really is some "large animal" living deep in Loch Ness. Studying the accumulated evidence, Dr. George R. Zug, curator of amphibians and reptiles at the Smithsonian Institution in Washington, D.C., said, "I started as a skeptic. Now I believe there is a population of large animals in the loch. I don't have any idea of what they are." But he is convinced that research should continue and that the mystery of the Loch Ness monster should be solved.

Another scientist calling for more such research is Dr. Alfred W. Crompton, professor of biology at Harvard University. He, too, believes that the evidence points to a large aquatic animal living in Loch Ness.

What kind of animal this might be is little more than a guess. The most frequent speculation is that Nessie is an ancient reptile, a plesiosaur♦ believed extinct for fifty million years or more.

This is not the only such monster reported from deep lakes over the years. For more than half a century people around Montana's Flathead Lake have thought there might be something very large and unidentified living in the depths of that cold lake. Indians told

Literature in context   History Connection

♦**Plesiosaurs**
One theory about the creature in Loch Ness is that it is a plesiosaur: a large, long-necked water reptile with four paddle-like flippers. The problem with this theory is that plesiosaurs are believed to have become extinct millions of years ago. Although there are explanations for and against this theory, it has not been conclusively proved or disproved.

Picture of the unidentified creature photographed in Loch Ness

Reading Strategy
Evaluate Logic Explain whether the examples offered should be called evidence or not.

Reading Check

What evidence is used to convince people of Nessie's existence?

the earliest white people about this monster. The monster of Flathead Lake is said to be at least twenty-five feet long and uniformly black, and to swim on the surface, sometimes creating huge waves even when the rest of the lake is calm.

In 1922 scientists in Argentina were choosing sides on the question of whether there could be a similar monster in Patagonia. An American mining engineer was among those who had sighted such a creature. What he described had the size, outline, and features of the ancient plesiosaurs. But there has been little heard of this population of monsters in recent times, and if they were indeed there, they may by now have become extinct.

The mystery locked in the depths of Loch Ness may be closer to an answer than ever before. Dr. Rines and Sir Peter Scott of England have even given Nessie a proper scientific name, *Nessiteras rhombopteryx,* meaning "Ness marvel with a diamond-shaped fin." Some believe that science will soon solve the ancient mystery.

Meanwhile, officials in Scotland have taken steps to protect Nessie. They warn that their famous monsters, if they are really out there in the cold water of Loch Ness, must be among the world's most endangered wildlife. Anyone harming, or even teasing, a Loch Ness monster can be arrested.

Review and Assess

Thinking About the Selection

1. **Respond:** How would you feel if you saw a strange creature like Nessie? Explain.

2. **(a) Recall:** What techniques have scientists used to try to prove Nessie's existence? **(b) Apply:** What features of the loch prevent scientists from conclusively proving that Nessie does or does not exist?

3. **(a) Recall:** What is Nessie reported to look like? **(b) Distinguish:** Which parts of Nessie do the photographs seem to show? **(c) Synthesize:** Why don't people accept the photographs as evidence of Nessie's existence?

4. **(a) Make a Judgment:** Do you believe that an unidentified creature lives in Loch Ness? Why or why not? **(b) Predict:** What would happen to Loch Ness and Nessie if scientists prove that the creature exists? What would happen if scientists prove that the creature definitely does not exist? **(c) Take a Position:** If such a creature does exist, should it be captured or left in the lake? Explain.

George Laycock

(b. 1921)

George Laycock is an avid photographer who often illustrates his writing with his photographs. He lives in Cincinnati, Ohio, not far from the town of Zanesville, where he was born. His interest in nature, wildlife, and the environment is evident in the books and magazine articles he writes. As a professional writer, Laycock has received many honors, including five Science Teacher of America awards for outstanding books for young people.

Why the Tortoise's Shell Is Not Smooth

Chinua Achebe

Low voices, broken now and again by singing, reached Okonkwo (ō kŏn′ kwō) from his wives' huts as each woman and her children told folk stories. Ekwefi (e kwe′ fē) and her daughter, Ezinma (e zēn′ mä), sat on a mat on the floor. It was Ekwefi's turn to tell a story.

"Once upon a time," she began, "all the birds were invited to a feast in the sky. They were very happy and began to prepare themselves for the great day. They painted their bodies with red cam wood[1] and drew beautiful patterns on them with dye.

"Tortoise saw all these preparations and soon discovered what it all meant. Nothing that happened in the world of the animals ever escaped his notice; he was full of cunning. As

1. **red cam** (cam) **wood** hard West African wood that makes red dye.

▲ **Critical Viewing**
What details in this picture might lead to questions about a tortoise's appearance? **[Connect]**

☑ **Reading Check**

Who is telling stories?

▲ **Critical Viewing** What techniques might a storyteller like the one in this picture use to keep an audience interested? **[Speculate]**

soon as he heard of the great feast in the sky his throat began to itch at the very thought. There was a <u>famine</u> in those days and Tortoise had not eaten a good meal for two moons. His body rattled like a piece of dry stick in his empty shell. So he began to plan how he would go to the sky."

"But he had no wings," said Ezinma.

"Be patient," replied her mother. "That is the story. Tortoise had no wings, but he went to the birds and asked to be allowed to go with them.

"'We know you too well,' said the birds when they had heard him. 'You are full of cunning and you are ungrateful. If we allow you to come with us you will soon begin your mischief.'

"'You do not know me,' said Tortoise. 'I am a changed man. I have learned that a man who makes trouble for others is also making it for himself.'

"Tortoise had a sweet tongue, and within a short time all the birds agreed that he was a changed man, and they each gave him a feather, with which he made two wings.

"At last the great day came and Tortoise was the first to arrive at the meeting place. When all the birds had gathered together, they set off in a body. Tortoise was very happy as he flew among the birds, and he was soon chosen as the man to speak for the party because he was a great <u>orator</u>.

famine (fa′ min) *n.* shortage of food

orator (ôr′ ə ter) *n.*: speaker

"'There is one important thing which we must not forget,' he said as they flew on their way. 'When people are invited to a great feast like this, they take new names for the occasion. Our hosts in the sky will expect us to honor this age-old custom.'

"None of the birds had heard of this custom but they knew that Tortoise, in spite of his failings in other directions, was a widely traveled man who knew the customs of different peoples. And so they each took a new name. When they had all taken, Tortoise also took one. He was to be called *All of you.*

"At last the party arrived in the sky and their hosts were very happy to see them. Tortoise stood up in his many-colored plumage and thanked them for their invitation. His speech was so <u>eloquent</u> that all the birds were glad they had brought him, and nodded their heads in approval of all he said. Their hosts took him as the king of the birds, especially as he looked somewhat different from the others.

"After kola nuts[2] had been presented and eaten, the people of the sky set before their guests the most delectable dishes Tortoise had ever seen or dreamed of. The soup was brought out hot from the fire and in the very pot in which it had been cooked. It was full of meat and fish. Tortoise began to sniff aloud. There was pounded yam[3] and also yam pottage[4] cooked with palm oil and fresh fish. There were also pots of palm wine. When everything had been set before the guests, one of the people of the sky came forward and tasted a little from each pot. He then invited the birds to eat. But Tortoise jumped to his feet and asked: 'For whom have you pre-pared this feast?'

"'For all of you,' replied the man.

"Tortoise turned to the birds and said: 'You remember that my name is *All of you.* The custom here is to serve the spokesman first and the others later. They will serve you when I have eaten.'

"He began to eat and the birds grumbled angrily. The people of the sky thought it must be their custom to leave all the food for their king. And so Tortoise ate the best part of the food and then drank two pots of palm wine, so that he was full of food and drink and his body grew fat enough to fill out his shell.

"The birds gathered round to eat what was left and to peck at the bones he had thrown all about the floor. Some of them were too angry to eat. They chose to fly home on an empty stomach. But before they left, each took back the feather he had lent to Tortoise. And there he stood in his hard shell full of food and wine but without any wings to fly home. He asked the birds to take a

---

2. **kola** (kō′ lə) **nuts** the seeds of the African cola tree. These seeds contain caffeine and are used to make soft drinks and medicines.
3. **yam** (yam) *n.* sweet potato.
4. **pottage** (pät′ ij) *n.* thick soup or stew.

eloquent (el′ ə kwint) *adj.* persuasive and expressive

Literary Analysis
Oral Tradition Why might a storyteller include names of specific foods in a tale?

Reading Check

Why do the birds change their names?

message for his wife, but they all refused. In the end Parrot, who had felt more angry than the others, suddenly changed his mind and agreed to take the message.

"'Tell my wife,' said Tortoise, 'to bring out all the soft things in my house and cover the compound⁵ with them so that I can jump down from the sky without very great danger.'

"Parrot promised to deliver the message, and then flew away. But when he reached Tortoise's house he told his wife to bring out all the hard things in the house. And so she brought out her husband's hoes, machetes,⁶ spears, guns, and even his cannon. Tortoise looked down from the sky and saw his wife bringing things out, but it was too far to see what they were. When all seemed ready he let himself go. He fell and fell and fell until he began to fear that he would never stop falling. And then like the sound of his cannon he crashed on the compound."

"Did he die?" asked Ezinma.

"No," replied Ekwefi. "His shell broke into pieces. But there was a great medicine man in the neighborhood. Tortoise's wife sent for him and he gathered all the bits of shell and stuck them together. That is why Tortoise's shell is not smooth."

---

5. **compound** (käm′ pɔund) *n.* grounds surrounded by buildings.
6. **machetes** (mə shet′ ēz) *n.* large heavy-bladed knives.

Review and Assess

Thinking About the Selection

1. **Respond:** Do you think the tortoise got what he deserved? Why or why not?

2. **(a) Recall:** Why does the tortoise want to go to the great feast? **(b) Infer:** Why don't the birds want to take him?

3. **(a) Analyze:** Why do the birds decide to help Tortoise go to the feast? **(b) Deduce:** Why do they choose him to speak for the group? **(c) Assess:** How does Tortoise make use of this privilege?

4. **(a) Interpret:** Explain how Tortoise's new name allows him to eat before the birds. **(b) Apply:** What lesson have the birds learned about Tortoise? **(c) Speculate:** How might the story have ended if the Tortoise had behaved himself at the feast?

5. **(a) Make a Judgment:** Should the birds have helped Tortoise return home? Why or why not? **(b) Extend:** Do you consider the birds' actions to be revenge or justice? Explain. **(c) Apply:** Use a situation from real life to illustrate the difference between justice and revenge.

Chinua Achebe

(b. 1930)
Chinua Achebe likes to retell stories that originated in his native country of Nigeria many years ago. Achebe writes, "Our ancestors created their myths and legends and told their stories for a purpose. Any good story, any good novel, should have a message."

Achebe studied broadcasting in London after graduating from college. Then, he became a professional writer. Although he has written poetry, short stories, and essays, he is best known for his novels, which have won many honors and awards. His favorite topics for writing are Nigerian history and culture and African politics.

Review and Assess

Literary Analysis

Oral Tradition

1. Why can the story of the Loch Ness monster be considered part of the **oral tradition**?
2. What details at the beginning of "Why the Tortoise's Shell Is Not Smooth" indicate that it is part of the oral tradition?
3. Identify three details from "Why the Tortoise's Shell Is Not Smooth" that reflect ancient Nigerian customs and culture.

Comparing Literary Works

4. Use an organizer like the one shown to record details that reflect the difference between **fiction and nonfiction**. Explain your choices.

Nonfiction
1.
2.
3.

Loch Ness   Tortoise

Fiction
1.
2.
3.

Reading Strategy

Evaluating Logic and Reasoning

5. What examples of photographic evidence of Nessie's existence does George Laycock include in "The Loch Ness Monster"?
6. What are two possible interpretations of these pictures?
7. What is one example of **faulty reasoning** in "The Loch Ness Monster"?
8. Based on the fact that Tortoise eats first, the people of the sky infer that it is a custom to let the leader or spokesperson eat first. Explain whether this inference is supported or unsupported.

Extending Understanding

9. **Science Connection:** Explain how Dr. Rines proved that the food web in Loch Ness could support a creature such as Nessie.
10. **Take a Position:** Do you think scientists should continue to spend money and time searching for Nessie? Explain.

Quick Review

Oral tradition is the passing along of songs, stories, and poems by word of mouth. To review oral tradition, see page 405.

Fiction is prose writing that tells about imaginary characters and events. **Nonfiction** is prose writing that presents and explains ideas or that tells about real people, places, objects, or events. To review fiction and nonfiction, see page 405.

Faulty reasoning looks logical because it contains facts, but it uses or interprets the facts in an illogical way. To review faulty reasoning, see page 405.

 Take It to the Net
www.phschool.com
Take the interactive self-test online to check your understanding of these selections.

Integrate Language Skills

Vocabulary Development Lesson

Word Analysis: Forms of *orate*

The story word *orator* comes from the word *orate*, which means "deliver a speech." Other words that are forms of *orate* also relate to speaking.

On your paper, write each sentence and complete it with one of these forms of *orate*:

orator   oration   oratorical

1. Tortoise's _____?_____ skills were admired by all.
2. He is considered a great _____?_____ by the birds.
3. His eloquent _____?_____ was applauded.

Concept Development: Word Groups

Answer each question with a vocabulary word.

1. Which two words deal with speaking?
2. Which two words could describe opposite amounts of food?
3. Which word describes something that keeps escaping?

Spelling Strategy

The ending sound in the story words *eloquent* and *abundant* is the same, but the words have different spellings. Use *eloquent*, *abundant*, and *frequent* in these sentences to practice spelling the endings.

1. The Tortoise gave an _____?_____ speech.
2. _____?_____ fish were available in the loch.
3. There were _____?_____ sightings of the Loch Ness Monster.

Grammar Lesson

Subject Complements

A **subject complement** is a word that comes after a linking verb and identifies or describes the subject. A subject complement may be either a predicate noun or a predicate adjective.

A predicate noun (or pronoun) follows a linking verb and identifies or renames the subject.

I am a changed man. (*Man* renames *I*.)

A predicate adjective follows a linking verb and describes the subject.

Tortoise was very happy as he flew among the birds. (*Happy* describes *Tortoise*.)

▶ *For more practice, see page R28, Exercise B*

Practice Copy the following sentences. Underline each subject complement. Identify it as a predicate noun or predicate adjective. Then, draw an arrow to the word it renames or describes.

1. Tortoise is a great orator.
2. His speech was eloquent
3. Parrot seemed to be a bird of great intelligence.
4. The birds felt cheated.
5. That is the reason.

Writing Application Write four sentences about Tortoise. In the first two, use predicate nouns to rename him. In the second two, use predicate adjectives to describe him.

W͞G Prentice Hall Writing and Grammar Connection: Chapter 19, Section 5

Writing Lesson

Invitation to the Feast

Based on details from "Why the Tortoise's Shell Is Not Smooth," make an invitation to the feast. Use a word-processing program to make your invitation. Use tabs, spacing, special fonts, and page orientation to format your invitation.

Prewriting   Review the story to identify details that can be used in your invitation. Make up additional details, such as time and date, that are not provided in the story. The basic information to be included on any invitation is time, date, and place. Some invitations will tell whether the guest should RSVP (respond).

Drafting   Begin your invitation with a paragraph that describes the activities and food at the feast. Use vivid verbs that tell what guests will do and precise nouns to tell what things and foods will be at the feast. Use text formatting to highlight the words *date*, *time*, and *place*. Decide whether your page orientation will be vertical (called *portrait*) or horizontal (called *landscape*).

Come to the Feast

Celebrate with us! Stuff yourself with yams, kola nuts, and fish.

Date: March 26   *Place:* The Palace of the Sky People
Time: 4:00 p.m.   *RSVP:* The Sky King: 555-4141

Revising   If the date, time, and place are not the most noticeable information on your invitation, revise to make them more visible.

WG   Prentice Hall Writing and Grammar Connection: Chapter 6, Section 2

Extension Activities

Listening and Speaking Prepare and deliver a brief **presentation** on the history of and current research related to Nessie. Explain how it confirms or refutes the evidence in this selection.

1. Develop a sentence outline of your most important points.
2. Use this general organization to highlight the most important ideas and information in your presentation.

Research and Technology Write a one-page **summary** that updates the latest scientific information on the Loch Ness monster. Use electronic sources such as the Internet and electronic library catalogs to research current sightings and scientific theories.

 **Take It to the Net**   www.phschool.com

Go online for an additional research activity using the Internet.

READING INFORMATIONAL MATERIALS

Social Studies Texts

About Social Studies Texts

Information about social studies topics can be found in a variety of texts. For any given topic you can probably find a full-length nonfiction book, an anthology in which the writings of several experts are collected, magazine articles, and Web pages. You might consult social studies texts other than your social studies textbook for several reasons, including the following:

- **General interest**—to find out more about a specific topic you have studied in class.

- **Background**—to improve your understanding of a specific event or topic.

- **Perspective**—to look at an event or topic from several different angles or viewpoints to get a clear picture of it.

- **Research**—to find facts and details that support a thesis or proposition.

Reading Strategy

Watch for Unknown Words

When you read an article on a specialized topic, watch for unknown words, names, and terms. Decide which ones to look up immediately, which to check later, and which to take notes on.

- Knowing the pronunciation of a name will not affect your understanding of the text, so you can wait until you are done reading to look it up.

- Knowing the meaning of a specialized term may make a difference to the meaning of the text, so you might want to look it up right away.

- Take notes on unfamiliar words, names, and specialized terms. You may run into them again in related texts.

March 26, 20__

"Human Footprints at Chauvet Cave" by Spencer Harrington

Summary:
Scientists discover oldest human footprints in a cave in France. More than 447 paintings have also been found in this cave.

Names:
* Aldene, Montespan, Niaux, Pech Merle = other caves
* Jean-Marie Chauvet = He discovered the cave with the footprints

New Words:
* upper paleolithic— 40,000–10,000 BC
* "ca." = "circa" = about; approximately

Section of the paintings found in Chauvet Cave.

Human Footprints
at Chauvet Cave

Spencer P.M. Harrington

Recent exploration of the Chauvet [shō vä´] Cave near Vallon-Pont-d'Arc [valon´ pon dark] in southern France has yielded the oldest footprints of *Homo sapiens sapiens* and a cavern with a dozen new animal figures. The footprints appear to be those of an eight-year-old boy, according to prehistorian Michel-Alain Garcia [mē shel´ a lan´ gär sē´ ä] of the Centre National de la Recherche Scientifique, Nanterre.[1] They are between 20 and 30 thousand years old, perhaps twice as old as those discovered previously at Aldene, Montespan [mon tə span], Niaux [nē o], Pech Merle [pesh merl], and other Upper Palaeolithic sites.[2]

Garcia estimates that the boy was about four-and-a-half feet tall, his feet more than eight inches long and three-and-a-half inches wide. First spotted in 1994 by Jean-Marie [zhän mä rē´] Chauvet, the cave's discoverer,

---

1. Centre National de la Recherche Scientifique, Nanterre French for "National Center for Scientific Research [at] Nanterre."
2. Upper Palaeolithic sites places believed to have artifacts from the period of time between approximately 40,000 and 10,000 B.C.

The translation of this name does not affect your immediate understanding of the article. You can wait until you have finished reading to check the footnote.

The words "Upper Palaeolithic sites" affect your understanding of the significance and age of the footprints. You should read the footnote before continuing.

If you don't know the meaning of *ca.*, look it up to see how it affects the meaning of the number that follows. You will see *ca.* in many informational materials.

Make connections to other studies. In what other subject areas might you read articles containing the names of people and places mentioned in this article?

the footsteps stretch perhaps 150 feet and at times cross those of bears and wolves. The steps lead to the so-called room of skulls, where a number of bear skulls have been found. In a few places, there is evidence that the boy slipped on the soft clay floor, though Garcia says the prints show the boy was not running, but walking normally. The boy appears at one point to have stopped to clean his torch, charcoal from which has been dated to ca. 26,000 years ago. The prints from the Chauvet Cave, like nearly all footprints thus far discovered in Palaeolithic caves, are from bare feet, which has led scholars to speculate that people of the time either left footwear at cave entrances or carried them.

Meanwhile, a team of 15 specialists directed by French prehistorian Jean Clottes recently investigated an uninventoried room originally discovered by Chauvet. There they found a dozen new paintings of mammoth, bison, and horses, among other animals. Clottes' team has so far documented 447 animals of 14 different species. By comparison, Niaux Cave in the French Pyrenees, cited by the French Palaeolithic specialist Abbé Breuil [ä bā´ brool] as one of the half-dozen great caves containing prehistoric art, has 110 images of six species.

Check Your Comprehension

1. How much older are the footprints found in the Chauvet Cave compared to ones previously found?
2. Who do scientists believe made the footprints? How do you think they came to that conclusion?
3. Where do the footprints lead?
4. What do scientists believe is the reason for all the footprints found that were made by bare feet?
5. How many animal paintings have been found in Chauvet Cave?

Applying the Reading Strategy

Watch for Unknown Words

6. What are four significant place names in this text? Why are they significant?
7. What is one new word you noted that is not a place or person's name? Why did you take notes on it?
8. Compare your notes with a partner. Do your lists contain the same words or different words? Explain why you might have some of the same notes and some different notes.

Activity

Use one of the names of people or places that you took notes on as a key word in an Internet search or look the name up in an encyclopedia. Explain to a partner or small group what the significance of the person or place is beyond a connection with the Chauvet Cave.

Contrasting Informational Materials

Articles Written From Different Perspectives

Compare this social studies article to an article on the Chauvet Cave that is written for an art magazine or an art Web site. Use a Venn diagram to compare and contrast the types of information included in the two articles.

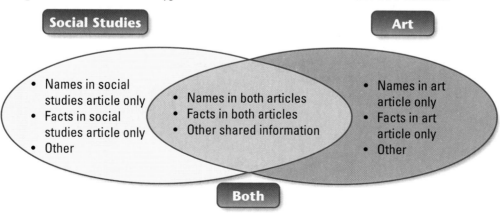

Social Studies
- Names in social studies article only
- Facts in social studies article only
- Other

Both
- Names in both articles
- Facts in both articles
- Other shared information

Art
- Names in art article only
- Facts in art article only
- Other

Writing WORKSHOP

Expository Writing: Cause-and-Effect Essay

Expository writing is writing that informs. In an expository composition, you explain, analyze, or describe. This workshop will give you tips and strategies for writing a **cause-and-effect essay**—a composition in which you explain and analyze the specific reasons for and results of an event or a situation.

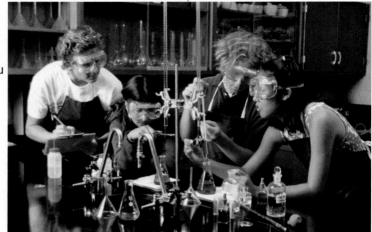

Assignment Criteria. Your expository composition should have the following characteristics:

- A clearly stated thesis about the causes and effects of a situation
- Facts and details that support the thesis statement
- An organizational pattern that emphasizes the cause-and-effect relationships
- Transitions that make connections between ideas

See the rubric on page 425 for the criteria on which your cause-and-effect essay may be assessed.

Prewriting

Choose a topic. Consider the following topic possibilities:

- an event or situation you are learning about in social studies
- a natural phenomenon such as erosion or lightning
- an event currently in the news

Write a thesis statement. Use your notes to write a clear statement that introduces the topic or purpose of your expository composition.

> In his thesis statement, Bryson identifies the cause-and-effect relationship he will analyze: The *effects* of the sun are a *cause* for wearing sunscreen.

Model: Thesis Statement

Sunscreen should always be worn when you are out in the sun because the effects of the sun can be dangerous to your skin.

Student Model

Before you begin drafting your composition, read this student model and review the characteristics of a successful explanation.

Bryson McCollum
Cumming, Georgia

Sunscreen should always be worn when you are out in the sun because the sun can be very dangerous to your skin. If your skin is exposed to the sun's ultraviolet rays without sunscreen, it will turn red, burn, and hurt. Many people believe that burning their skin is one step closer to their desire of getting a tan. They do not realize that both burning and tanning your skin can damage it. Once you burn or tan and the redness or color begins to fade, the damaged skin may begin to peel, leaving a new, unhealthy, thin, and sensitive layer of skin.

> The writer begins by stating his thesis, the cause-and-effect relationship he will show.

> Details about the sun's ability to damage the skin help support the writer's purpose.

What you do to your skin as a child and as a young adult will affect your skin in the future. Doctors recommend that children apply sunscreen often and at least 30 minutes before going out in the sun. Adults, children, and young adults will benefit from using sunscreens with sun protection factor (SPF) numbers 15 or more. The SPF number gives some idea of how long you can stay out in the sun without burning. For example, an SPF of 15 should protect you for approximately 150 minutes in the sun. While some sunscreens say they are waterproof, they do not give you total protection from water and sweat. As a result, it is also recommended that sunscreen be applied often.

> The writer uses examples to make doctor recommendations clear.

Nobody's skin is immune to skin cancer. If your skin is damaged a lot by the sun during your childhood and adult years, your chances of getting skin cancer are great. Some signs of skin cancer are leathery scab-like patches of skin that may be discolored, bleed, or burn. If you have been burned several times in a short period of time, you should be checked by a doctor because some forms of skin cancer cannot be detected.

> Each paragraph focuses on a cause or an effect related to Bryson's thesis.

So, next time you are at the beach or the pool without sunscreen, hoping to absorb the sun, be careful and apply sunscreen. Remember that even though a tan may look nice, it may cause you health problems and unhealthy looking skin in the future.

Drafting

Write from a plan. Use an organizer to plan the sections of your essay. As you draft, group details in paragraphs based on the sections of your organizer.

Develop paragraphs. Write a topic sentence, or main idea sentence, for each paragraph. Organize supporting information under each topic sentence.

Connect with transitions. Use transitional words and phrases to make cause-and-effect relationships clear.

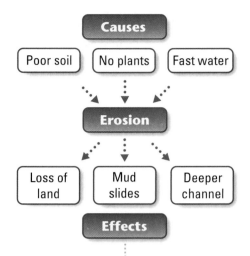

Words that indicate a cause:
due to, because, for this reason

Words that indicate effects:
as a result, consequently, so, therefore

Revising

Revise for logical organization. Check the overall organization of your essay by checking the connections between paragraphs as well as the order of your paragraphs.

1. Highlight the topic sentence of each paragraph.

2. Read the topic sentences in the order in which they appear.

3. Label each topic sentence's connection to the topic as cause or effect.

> **Model: Checking Topic Sentences**
>
> *Cause*   What you do to your skin as a child and young adult will affect your skin in the future. Doctors recommend that children apply sunscreen often. . . .
>
> *Effect*   Nobody's skin is immune to skin cancer. If your skin is damaged a lot by the sun during your childhood and adult years, your chances of getting skin cancer are great.

Revise for transitions. Look for places to add transitions to make connections between ideas. In the following example, *because* connects two related ideas.

Draft: We were late. We did not see the movie beginning.
Revision: We could not see the movie beginning *because* we were late.

Compare the model and the nonmodel. Why is the model more effective than the nonmodel?

Nonmodel	Model
If your skin is exposed to the sun's ultraviolet rays without sunscreen, it will turn red, burn, and hurt. The burning damages the skin. The top layers peel off. Thin, raw, unprotected skin is exposed.	Without sunscreen, your skin is exposed to the sun's ultraviolet rays. As a result, your skin will tun red, burn, and hurt. The burning damages the skin. Consequently, the top layers peel off.

Publishing and Presenting

Choose one of these ways to share your writing with classmates or a larger audience.

Make a movie. Treat your expository composition as if it were the script for a short film. Make a storyboard that shows the images that you would choose to go with it.

Deliver instructions. Read your composition to a small group as a way of having listeners follow multiple-step oral directions.

*W*G *Prentice Hall Writing and Grammar Connection: Chapter 9*

Speaking Connection

To learn how to get information from an expository presentation, see **Listening and Speaking Workshop: Following Oral Directions,** page 426.

Rubric for Self-Assessment

Evaluate your expository composition using the following criteria and rating scale:

Criteria	Rating Scale				
	Not very				Very
How clearly is the cause-and-effect relationship identified in the thesis statement?	1	2	3	4	5
How well do the facts and details support the thesis?	1	2	3	4	5
How clearly does the organization link cause-and-effect relationships?	1	2	3	4	5
How well do transitions connect related ideas?	1	2	3	4	5

Listening and Speaking WORKSHOP

Following Oral Directions

Every day, you hear and follow oral directions and instructions. To understand and carry out **multiple-step oral directions**, or spoken directions with several steps, you need to listen carefully to the speaker and restate the directions in the correct sequence. The following strategies will help you demonstrate effective listening skills.

Listen Carefully

Following oral directions correctly requires understanding the speaker's message. To understand directions, follow these guidelines.

Notice action words and time-order words. Pay special attention to the key action word in each step. The key action words will help you remember what to do. For example, in these directions for a fire drill, the action words are underlined.

> First, <u>close</u> the doors and windows. Then, <u>walk</u> to the nearest exit. When you are outside, <u>stand</u> with your class until the teacher counts the group.

Most directions are stated in chronological order and include words such as *first, then, next, finally,* and *last.*

Ask questions. Do not assume that the speaker will give you all the information you need. Identify missing information and ask questions to clarify. Some questions you might ask to clarify information are

- How far?
- How much?
- How long?
- How many?

Restate Directions

Repeating the directions allows the directions-giver to correct any misunderstanding.

Use the action words and transition words. Repeat or restate the directions in your own words using the action words to recall the action required. Use the transition words at the beginning of each step to restate multiple-step directions. The example below shows a restatement of the fire drill directions in the example above.

> First, shut the windows. After the windows are shut, walk to the closest door. Once you get out, stand with the rest of the class. Don't move until the teacher counts you.

Checklist for Restating and Following Directions

Listen Carefully

- ☑ Focus on the speaker. Listen for main ideas and details.
- ☑ Notice the action word in each step of the directions.
- ☑ Notice words that tell time order.
- ☑ Ask questions.

Restate Directions

- ☑ Repeat the directions using the action words.
- ☑ Use words that tell chronological order.

Activity:
Directions
Ask a partner to give you oral directions for an unfamiliar activity, such as a new sports technique or a way of getting from school to another place. Restate the directions. With adult permission, follow the directions to check your understanding.

Assessment WORKSHOP

Draw Conclusions

The reading sections of some tests require you to read a passage and answer multiple-choice questions about inferences and conclusions. Use what you have learned in this unit about evaluating logic and reasoning to answer these questions.

Test-Taking Strategies

- Read the questions related to a passage before reading the passage.
- After making your choice, quickly scan the passage to make sure your choice is logically supported.

Sample Test Items

Directions: Read the passage and answer the questions that follow.

Sam checked his backpack once again. He didn't want to arrive too early at the bus stop to stand with kids he didn't know. After fidgeting for five more minutes, Sam said good-bye to his mother and walked out the front door. Seven or eight boys and girls were waiting at the corner. "Hi," said one of them. "Are you new in town?"

1. Which word best describes Sam?

   A cheerful

   B nervous

   C relaxed

   D sloppy

2. The passage gives you reason to believe that—

   A Sam is unfriendly

   B Sam and his mother don't communicate well

   C Sam lives near his new school

   D this is Sam's first day at a new school

Answers and Explanations

1. There are no details to support choices **A, C,** or **D**. Answer **B** is correct.

2. There is no evidence to support choices **A** or **B**. Sam is taking a bus, so **C** is not correct. **D** is the correct answer.

▶ Practice

Directions: Read the passage and answer the questions that follow.

For years, people have dreamed of having robots to do household chores. While this has not happened, robots are doing many important jobs. Surgeons use robots to make precise movements that are difficult for a human hand. Robots pick apples from the tops of trees without bruising them. Security robots warn of fires and intruders. Scientists have used robots to explore places too dangerous for humans, for example, inside active volcanoes, on the ocean floor, and on the surface of Mars.

1. Information in the passage suggests that—

   A robots are cheaper than human surgeons

   B Mars is too cold for humans

   C robots are not as reliable as humans

   D robots can survive higher temperatures than humans

2. From this passage, you can conclude that—

   A robots will never do household chores

   B robots have expanded scientific knowledge

   C the idea for robots came from science fiction

   D robots would not be useful in schools

Short Stories

The Storyteller, Adolphe Tidemand, Christie's, London

Exploring the Genre

A short story is a doorway into another world. The world of a short story may be another town or city similar to yours or it may be a distant planet. A short story may introduce you to new ideas or remind you of events in your own life. Although short stories cover a wide range of possibilities, they all share certain elements.

- **Plot:** the sequence of events that keeps the story moving.
- **Characters:** the people or animals in the story.
- **Setting:** the time and place in which the characters live and the events occur.
- **Theme:** the central message expressed in the story.

You will learn more about these elements as you read the short stories in this unit.

◀ **Critical Viewing** Which person in this picture is telling a story? How do you know? **[Analyze]**

Why Read Literature?

This unit presents a variety of short stories by authors from different cultures. Your purpose for reading each selection may be different, depending on the content. You might want to read to consider another point of view, read for information, or read for the love of literature. Preview the three purposes you might set before reading the works in this unit.

1 Read for the love of literature.

Charles Dickens is one of the "Top Ten" authors of all time. Along with Shakespeare, Dickens is one of the five authors who have had more books published about them than any other authors. Read a sample of the work the world finds so fascinating and enjoy a tale of ghostly humor when you read **"The Lawyer and the Ghost,"** page 476.

You may think a nineteenth-century Russian author who suffered from disease much of his life would have a poor sense of humor, but you would be wrong. Discover the laughter in literature when you read Anton Chekhov's humorous story **"Overdoing It,"** page 460.

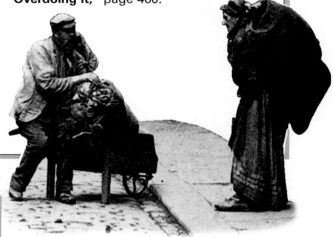

2 Read for information.

You have probably heard about the devastating effects of oil spills on wildlife. Find out what can and cannot be done to help water birds that have been covered with oil during a spill. Read **"Can Oiled Seabirds Be Rescued?"** page 491.

Wolves have been observed "decorating" the outsides of their dens with flowers. Jean Craighead George spent months in Alaska studying the behavior of wolves before writing her novel *Julie of the Wolves.* During her study, she once saw a wolf bring a bunch of flowers to the outside of its den and carefully place them at the entrance. Find out more about the unexpected qualities of wolves when you read **"The Wounded Wolf,"** page 482.

3 Read to consider another point of view.

You may think that all dragon slayers are strong and brave and that all birthdays are happy. Read two stories that consider other possibilities. Read about a meek and humble dragon slayer in **"Dragon, Dragon,"** page 434, and an unhappy birthday in **"Eleven,"** page 465.

 Take It to the Net
Visit the Web site for online instruction and activities related to each selection in this unit.
www.phschool.com

How to Read Literature

Strategies for Reading Fiction

Fiction, which includes short stories and novels, is filled with made-up characters and events. Reading a work of fiction is like exploring a new world. As you read, your imagination creates a map of this world. The following strategies will help you find your way in a work of fiction.

1. Compare and contrast characters.

Looking at the similarities and differences between characters can help you understand them more fully. This unit will give you opportunities to compare and contrast characters from a variety of cultures and time periods.

2. Predict.

A map tells you what you will see around the next turn. As you read, make predictions about what might happen farther along the "road" of the story. Base predictions on your experience or on information in the story. In the same way that a rock in the road may cause you to choose a new path, new information can lead to new predictions.

3. Draw inferences.

Draw inferences, that is, make logical guesses or assumptions, based on details in a story. Strategies you will learn in this unit will help you "read between the lines" of fiction, to understand both what is stated and what is implied or suggested.

4. Picture the setting.

Use details provided in the story to create an image in your mind of a setting—the time and place in which the action of a story occurs.

- In this unit, you will learn to notice sensory details—words that appeal to the senses of sight, sound, smell, taste, and touch. These details will help you picture a variety of settings, including historical time periods and distant places.

As you read the selections in this unit, review the reading strategies and look at the notes in the side columns. Use the suggestions to apply the strategies for reading fiction.

Prepare to Read

Dragon, Dragon

 Take It to the Net

Visit www.phschool.com
for interactive activities
and instruction related
to "Dragon, Dragon,"
including
- background
- graphic organizers
- literary elements
- reading strategies

Preview

Connecting to the Literature

In "Dragon, Dragon," author John Gardner illustrates the power of
advice—even advice that does not seem at first to make much sense. How
has advice helped you work through problems?

Background

Since ancient times, dragon stories have been told all over the world.
Different cultures have different beliefs about these imaginary creatures.
Although Asian dragons are believed to be wise and good, in other
cultures, dragons are greedy, evil creatures. In most Western folklore, the
hero who kills a dragon is a brave, strong warrior who is rewarded with
marriage to the king's daughter.

Literary Analysis

Plot

The **plot** of a story is the sequence of events arranged around a problem, or conflict. In "Dragon, Dragon," the problem is introduced in the first sentence:

> There was once a king whose kingdom was plagued by a dragon.

As characters attempt to solve the problem, events build to a climax, or turning point. The resolution, or conclusion, of the story follows the climax. As you read "Dragon, Dragon," identify the following parts of the plot:

- **Exposition** (introduction of the problem)
- **Rising Action** (development of the problem)
- **Climax** (turning point)
- **Falling Action** (after the problem is solved)
- **Resolution** (how the problem turns out)

Connecting Literary Elements

The **theme**, or central idea, of a story is an insight about life or human nature. Sometimes, the theme is stated directly. Other times, you must figure it out for yourself by thinking about the characters and their actions. Determine the theme of "Dragon, Dragon" by looking for the lesson behind the outcome of each character's actions. While reading, keep the following focus questions in mind.

1. Which of the sons is successful at solving the problem, and why?
2. What theme, or message, is suggested by his success?

Reading Strategy

Comparing and Contrasting

When you **compare and contrast**, you examine similarities and differences. Comparing and contrasting characters and their actions can provide a clue to the meaning of a story. As you read, make an organizer like this one. Then, compare and contrast the three brothers in this story, all of whom act differently when given the chance to become a hero.

Vocabulary Development

plagued (plāgd) *v.* tormented (p. 435)

ravaged (rav′ ijd) *v.* violently destroyed; ruined (p. 435)

tyrant (tī′ rənt) *n.* cruel, unjust ruler (p. 436)

reflecting (ri flekt′ iŋ) *adj.* thinking seriously (p. 440)

craned (krānd) *v.* stretched out (one's neck) for a better view (p. 441)

Dragon,

John Gardner

DAN MITRA

Dragon

There was once a king whose kingdom was <u>plagued</u> by a dragon. The king did not know which way to turn. The king's knights were all cowards who hid under their beds whenever the dragon came in sight, so they were of no use to the king at all. And the king's wizard could not help either because, being old, he had forgotten his magic spells. Nor could the wizard look up the spells that had slipped his mind, for he had unfortunately misplaced his wizard's book many years before. The king was at his wit's end.

Every time there was a full moon the dragon came out of his lair and <u>ravaged</u> the countryside. He frightened maidens and stopped up chimneys and broke store windows and set people's clocks back and made dogs bark until no one could hear himself think.

He tipped over fences and robbed graves and put frogs in people's drinking water and tore the last chapters out of novels and changed house numbers around so that people crawled into bed with their neighbors.

He stole spark plugs out of people's cars and put firecrackers in people's cigars and stole the clappers from all the church bells and sprung every bear trap for miles around so the bears could wander wherever they pleased.

And to top it all off, he changed around all the roads in the kingdom so that people could not get anywhere except by starting out in the wrong direction.

"That," said the king in a fury, "is enough!" And he called a meeting of everyone in the kingdom.

Now it happened that there lived in the kingdom a wise old cobbler who had a wife and three sons. The cobbler and his family came to the king's meeting and stood way in back by the door, for the cobbler had a feeling that since he was nobody important there had probably been some mistake, and no doubt the king had intended the meeting for everyone in the kingdom except his family and him.

"Ladies and gentlemen," said the king when everyone was present, "I've put up with that dragon as long as I can. He has got to be stopped."

plagued (plāgd) *v.* tormented

ravaged (rav´ ijd) *v.* violently destroyed; ruined

**Reading Check**

What is the problem in the kingdom?

All the people whispered amongst themselves, and the king smiled, pleased with the impression he had made.

But the wise cobbler said gloomily, "It's all very well to talk about it—but how are you going to do it?"

And now all the people smiled and winked as if to say, "Well, King, he's got you there!"

The king frowned.

"It's not that His Majesty hasn't tried," the queen spoke up loyally.

"Yes," said the king, "I've told my knights again and again that they ought to slay that dragon. But I can't *force* them to go. I'm not a <u>tyrant</u>."

"Why doesn't the wizard say a magic spell?" asked the cobbler.

"He's done the best he can," said the king.

The wizard blushed and everyone looked embarrassed. "I used to do all sorts of spells and chants when I was younger," the wizard explained. "But I've lost my spell book, and I begin to fear I'm losing my memory too. For instance, I've been trying for days to recall one spell I used to do. I forget, just now, what the deuce it was for. It went something like—

Bimble,
Wimble,
Cha, cha
CHOOMPF!

Suddenly, to everyone's surprise, the queen turned into a rosebush.

"Oh dear," said the wizard.

"Now you've done it," groaned the king.

"Poor Mother," said the princess.

"I don't know what can have happened," the wizard said nervously, "but don't worry, I'll have her changed back in a jiffy." He shut his eyes and racked his brain for a spell that would change her back.

But the king said quickly, "You'd better leave well enough alone. If you change her into a rattlesnake we'll have to chop off her head."

Meanwhile the cobbler stood with his hands in his pockets, sighing at the waste of time. "About the dragon . . . " he began.

"Oh yes," said the king. "I'll tell you what I'll do. I'll give the princess's hand in marriage to anyone who can make the dragon stop."

"It's not enough," said the cobbler. "She's a nice enough girl, you understand. But how would an ordinary person support her?

_L_iterature
in context Humanities Connection

Traditional Dragon Stories

Much of the humor in "Dragon, Dragon" comes from the way it turns traditional dragon stories upside down. For example, in one of the most famous dragon stories of all time, *Beowulf*, the king is a wise and noble man. A terrible dragon has been attacking his hall and killing his warriors. When brave Beowulf, a true hero, learns the king needs help, he sails quickly to the rescue, humbly yet courageously presenting himself as the man for the job.

Frontispiece of The Boy's King Arthur, N.C. Wyeth

tyrant (tī′ rənt) *n.* cruel, unjust ruler

Also, what about those of us that are already married?"

"In that case," said the king, "I'll offer the princess's hand or half the kingdom or both—whichever is most convenient."

The cobbler scratched his chin and considered it. "It's not enough," he said at last. "It's a good enough kingdom, you understand, but it's too much responsibility."

"Take it or leave it," the king said.

"I'll leave it," said the cobbler. And he shrugged and went home.

But the cobbler's eldest son thought the bargain was a good one, for the princess was very beautiful and he liked the idea of having half the kingdom to run as he pleased. So he said to the king, "I'll accept those terms, Your Majesty. By tomorrow morning the dragon will be slain."

"Bless you!" cried the king.

"Hooray, hooray, hooray!" cried all the people, throwing their hats in the air.

The cobbler's eldest son beamed with pride, and the second eldest looked at him enviously. The youngest son said timidly, "Excuse me, Your Majesty, but don't you think the queen looks a little unwell? If I were you I think I'd water her."

"Good heavens," cried the king, glancing at the queen who had been changed into a rosebush, "I'm glad you mentioned it!"

Now the cobbler's eldest son was very clever and was known far and wide for how quickly he could multiply fractions in his head. He was perfectly sure he could slay the dragon by somehow or other playing a trick on him, and he didn't feel that he needed his wise old father's advice. But he thought it was only polite to ask, and so he went to his father, who was working as usual at his cobbler's bench, and said, "Well, Father, I'm off to slay the dragon. Have you any advice to give me?"

The cobbler thought a moment and replied, "When and if you come to the dragon's lair, recite the following poem:
Dragon, dragon, how do you do?
I've come from the king to murder you.
Say it very loudly and firmly and the dragon will fall, God willing, at your feet."

"How curious!" said the eldest son. And he thought to himself, "The old man is not as wise as I thought. If I say something like that to the dragon, he will eat me up in an instant. The way to kill a dragon is to out-fox him." And keeping his opinion to himself, the eldest son set forth on his quest.

When he came at last to the dragon's lair, which was a cave, the eldest son slyly disguised himself as a peddler and knocked on the door and called out, "Hello there!"

"There's nobody home!" roared a voice.

Reading Strategy
Comparing and Contrasting Which character, the cobbler or his eldest son, seems more sensible? **[Explain]**

Reading Check

What does the father tell his eldest son to do when he gets to the dragon's lair?

The voice was as loud as an earthquake, and the eldest son's knees knocked together in terror.

"I don't come to trouble you," the eldest son said meekly. "I merely thought you might be interested in looking at some of our brushes. Or if you'd prefer," he added quickly, "I could leave our catalogue with you and I could drop by again, say, early next week."

"I don't want any brushes," the voice roared, "and I especially don't want any brushes next week."

"Oh," said the eldest son. By now his knees were knocking together so badly that he had to sit down.

Suddenly a great shadow fell over him, and the eldest son looked up. It was the dragon. The eldest son drew his sword, but the dragon lunged and swallowed him in a single gulp, sword and all, and the eldest son found himself in the dark of the dragon's belly. "What a fool I was not to listen to my wise old father!" thought the eldest son. And he began to weep bitterly.

"Well," sighed the king the next morning, "I see the dragon has not been slain yet."

"I'm just as glad, personally," said the princess, sprinkling the queen. "I would have had to marry that eldest son, and he had warts."

Now the cobbler's middle son decided it was his turn to try. The middle son was very strong and he was known far and wide for being able to lift up the corner of a church. He felt perfectly sure he could slay the dragon by simply laying into him, but he thought it would be only polite to ask his father's advice. So he went to his father and said to him, "Well, Father, I'm off to slay the dragon. Have you any advice for me?"

The cobbler told the middle son exactly what he'd told the eldest.

"When and if you come to the dragon's lair, recite the following poem:

Dragon, dragon, how do you do?
I've come from the king to murder you.

Say it very loudly and firmly, and the dragon will fall, God willing, at your feet."

"What an odd thing to say," thought the middle son. "The old man is not as wise as I thought. You have to take these dragons by surprise." But he kept his opinion to himself and set forth.

When he came in sight of the dragon's lair, the middle son spurred his horse to a gallop and thundered into the entrance swinging his sword with all his might.

But the dragon had seen him while he was still a long way off, and being very clever, the dragon had crawled up on top of the door so that when the son came charging in he went under the

Literary Analysis
Plot and Theme What lesson does the cobbler's son learn as events unfold?

Dick Whittington on his way to London from My Nursery Story Book, Private Collection

◀ **Critical Viewing**
Does the boy in this picture look like a dragon slayer? Explain.
[Evaluate]

dragon and on to the back of the cave and slammed into the wall. Then the dragon chuckled and got down off the door, taking his time, and strolled back to where the man and the horse lay unconscious from the terrific blow. Opening his mouth as if for a yawn, the dragon swallowed the middle son in a single gulp and put the horse in the freezer to eat another day.

✔ **Reading Check**

What happens to the middle son when he arrives at the dragon's lair?

"What a fool I was not to listen to my wise old father," thought the middle son when he came to in the dragon's belly. And he too began to weep bitterly.

That night there was a full moon, and the dragon ravaged the countryside so terribly that several families moved to another kingdom.

"Well," sighed the king in the morning, "still no luck in this dragon business, I see."

"I'm just as glad, myself," said the princess, moving her mother, pot and all, to the window where the sun could get at her. "The cobbler's middle son was a kind of humpback."

Now the cobbler's youngest son saw that his turn had come. He was very upset and nervous, and he wished he had never been born. He was not clever, like his eldest brother, and he was not strong, like his second-eldest brother. He was a decent, honest boy who always minded his elders.

He borrowed a suit of armor from a friend of his who was a knight, and when the youngest son put the armor on it was so heavy he could hardly walk. From another knight he borrowed a sword, and that was so heavy that the only way the youngest son could get it to the dragon's lair was to drag it along behind his horse like a plow.

When everything was in readiness, the youngest son went for a last conversation with his father.

"Father, have you any advice to give me?" he asked.

"Only this," said the cobbler. "When and if you come to the dragon's lair, recite the following poem:

Dragon, dragon, how do you do?
I've come from the king to murder you.

Say it very loudly and firmly, and the dragon will fall, God willing, at your feet."

"Are you certain?" asked the youngest son uneasily.

"As certain as one can ever be in these matters," said the wise old cobbler.

And so the youngest son set forth on his quest. He traveled over hill and dale and at last came to the dragon's cave.

The dragon, who had seen the cobbler's youngest son while he was still a long way off, was seated up above the door, inside the cave, waiting and smiling to himself. But minutes passed and no one came thundering in. The dragon frowned, puzzled, and was tempted to peek out. However, <u>reflecting</u> that patience seldom goes unrewarded, the dragon kept his head up out of sight and went on waiting. At last, when he could stand it no longer, the dragon

Reading Strategy
Comparing and Contrasting What is the most important difference between the youngest son and his brothers?

reflecting (ri flekt' iŋ) *adj.* thinking seriously

<u>craned</u> his neck and looked. There at the entrance of the cave stood a trembling young man in a suit of armor twice his size, struggling with a sword so heavy he could lift only one end of it at a time.

At sight of the dragon, the cobbler's youngest son began to tremble so violently that his armor rattled like a house caving in. He heaved with all his might at the sword and got the handle up level with his chest, but even now the point was down in the dirt. As loudly and firmly as he could manage, the youngest son cried—

Dragon, dragon, how do you do?
I've come from the king to murder you.

"What?" cried the dragon, flabbergasted. "You? *You?* Murder *Me???*" All at once he began to laugh, pointing at the little cobbler's son. "*He he he ho ha!*" he roared, shaking all over, and tears filled his eyes. "*He he he ho ho ho ha ha!*" laughed the dragon. He was laughing so hard he had to hang onto his sides, and he fell off the door and landed on his back, still laughing, kicking his legs helplessly, rolling from side to side, laughing and laughing and laughing.

The cobbler's son was annoyed, "I *do* come from the king to murder you," he said. "A person doesn't like to be laughed at for a thing like that."

"*He he he!*" wailed the dragon, almost sobbing, gasping for breath. "Of course not, poor dear boy! But really, *he he,* the *idea* of it, *ha, ha, ha!* And that simply ridiculous *poem!*" Tears streamed from the dragon's eyes and he lay on his back perfectly helpless with laughter.

"It's a good poem," said the cobbler's youngest son loyally. "My father made it up." And growing angrier he shouted, "I want you to stop that laughing, or I'll—I'll—" But the dragon could not stop for the life of him. And suddenly, in a terrific rage, the cobbler's son began flopping the sword end over end in the direction of the dragon. Sweat ran off the youngest son's forehead, but he labored on, blistering mad, and at last, with one supreme heave, he had the sword standing on its handle a foot from the dragon's throat. Of its own weight the sword fell, slicing the dragon's head off.

"*He he ho huk,*" went the dragon—and then he lay dead.

The two older brothers crawled out and thanked their younger brother for saving their lives. "We have learned our lesson," they said.

Then the three brothers gathered all the treasures from the dragon's cave and tied them to the back end of the youngest brother's horse, and tied the dragon's head on behind the treasures, and started home. "I'm glad I listened to my father," the youngest son thought. "Now I'll be the richest man in the kingdom."

craned (krānd) *v.* stretched out (one's neck) for a better view

Literary Analysis
Plot and Theme What message is suggested by the way the problem is resolved?

 **Reading Check**

What happens when the youngest brother meets the dragon?

There were hand-carved picture frames and silver spoons and boxes of jewels and chests of money and silver compasses and maps telling where there were more treasures buried when these ran out. There was also a curious old book with a picture of an owl on the cover, and inside, poems and odd sentences and recipes that seemed to make no sense.

When they reached the king's castle the people all leaped for joy to see that the dragon was dead, and the princess ran out and kissed the youngest brother on the forehead, for secretly she had hoped it would be him.

"Well," said the king, "which half of the kingdom do you want?"

"My wizard's book!" exclaimed the wizard. "He's found my wizard's book!" He opened the book and ran his finger along under the words and then said in a loud voice, "Glmuzk, shkzmlp, blam!"

Instantly the queen stood before them in her natural shape, except she was soaking wet from being sprinkled too often. She glared at the king.

"Oh dear," said the king, hurrying toward the door.

Review and Assess

Thinking About the Selection

1. **Respond:** Do you think the cobbler is wise? Explain.

2. **(a) Recall:** Name two reasons the king has been unable to get rid of the dragon. **(b) Describe:** How would you describe the king, the knights, and the wizard? **(c) Distinguish:** In what ways are these characters different from kings, knights, and wizards typically found in fairy tales?

3. **(a) Recall:** What advice does the cobbler give his sons? **(b) Describe:** How do the two elder sons respond to their father's advice? **(c) Analyze:** What quality leads the two elder sons to respond this way?

4. **(a) Recall:** What happens to the two elder sons when they attempt to slay the dragon? **(b) Interpret:** What might their fate say about people who refuse to consider the advice of others?

5. **(a) Recall:** How does the youngest son succeed in slaying the dragon? **(b) Interpret:** What quality leads the youngest son to accept his father's advice? **(c) Deduce:** What did the cobbler seem to know all along about his sons and about the dragon?

6. **Distinguish:** What is the difference between listening to advice and letting others do your thinking for you?

John Gardner

(1933–1982)

John Gardner loved tales of heroes and other old-fashioned stories. In a few different ways, he devoted his life to keeping the old stories fresh.

Born in upstate New York, Gardner became a professor and taught at a number of universities. He made new translations of poems from the Middle Ages, such as the tales of King Arthur.

Gardner brought a few old stories to life in his own writing. His first successful novel, *Grendel*, retells the Old English story of Beowulf, one of the most famous monster-slaying heroes—but Gardner tells his legend from the monster's point of view! His stories for younger readers, such as "Dragon, Dragon," also twist the familiar patterns of fairy tales into humorous new shapes.

Review and Assess

Literary Analysis

Plot

1. Complete an organizer like the one below to show the **plot** of "Dragon, Dragon."

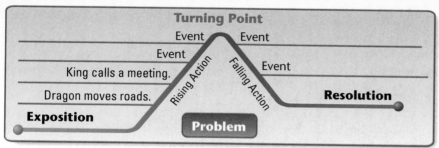

Turning Point

Event   Event

Event

King calls a meeting.

Dragon moves roads.

Rising Action   Falling Action

Event

Resolution

Exposition

Problem

2. What events are part of the rising action?
3. How is the problem or conflict resolved?

Connecting Literary Elements

4. Which of the sons is successful at solving the problem, and why?
5. On a chart like the one below, list the qualities of each son that ultimately lead to his success or failure.

Character	Main Qualities	Results of These Qualities

6. What **theme,** or message, is suggested by the youngest son's success?

Reading Strategy

Comparing and Contrasting

7. How is the dragon in this story similar to or different from other dragons you have read about?
8. How is the cobbler's advice similar to or different from the advice you would expect to hear for killing a dragon?

Extend Understanding

9. **Community Connection:** What processes or methods do modern communities use to identify and choose solutions to problems?

Quick Review

The **plot** of a story is the sequence of events arranged around a problem or conflict. It includes the exposition, the rising action, the climax, the falling action, and the resolution. To review plot, see page 433.

The **theme** of a story is its central insight about life or human nature. To review theme, see page 433.

Comparing and contrasting is examining similarities and differences in order to better understand the plot, characters, or theme of a literary work.

 Take It to the Net

www.phschool.com

Take the interactive self-test online to check your understanding of the selection.

Integrate Language Skills

Vocabulary Development Lesson

Word Analysis: Using Forms of *tyrant*

When the king in "Dragon, Dragon" says that he is no *tyrant*, he is saying that he is not "a cruel, unjust ruler." Use the meaning of *tyrant* to help you explain the meaning of the forms of *tyrant* used in the following sentences.

1. His *tyranny* made him an unpopular ruler.
2. His *tyrannous* behavior made his subjects angry.
3. He *tyrannized* the people.
4. He rules *tyrannically*.
5. The people overthrew the *tyrannical* leader.

Concept Development: Definitions

Match each numbered word with its meaning.

1. plagued   a. ruined
2. ravaged   b. stretched to get a view
3. reflecting   c. cruel, unjust ruler
4. tyrant   d. thinking seriously
5. craned   e. tormented

Spelling Strategy

The long *i* sound is sometimes spelled with a y, as in the word *tyrant*. On your paper, write the correct word in which the long *i* sound is spelled with a y.

1. A street fixture firefighters use to get water
2. Overly energetic
3. A doglike animal from Africa

Grammar Lesson

Clauses

A **clause** is any group of words that contains a subject and a verb. An **independent clause** can stand on its own as a complete sentence.

> Subject   Verb
> He chased the dragon.

A **subordinate clause** cannot stand alone.

> Subject Verb
> while the dragon ran away from him

A subordinate clause depends on an independent clause to complete its meaning.

> He chased the dragon while the dragon ran away from him.

▶ *For more practice, see page R28, Exercise C.*
Practice Copy the sentences. Underline each clause and identify it as independent or subordinate.

1. There was once a king whose kingdom was plagued by a dragon.
2. The youngest son began to shake so violently that his armor rattled.
3. Recite a poem when you reach the dragon's lair.
4. Although the youngest brother was not strong, he was brave.
5. His hands shook when he saw the dragon.

Writing Application Use each clause in a sentence to express a complete thought.

1. as he came near the end of the cave
2. while the dragon laughed
3. when the treasure ran out

W̶G̶ Prentice Hall Writing and Grammar Connection: Chapter 20, Section 2

Writing Lesson

Help-Wanted Ad

Write a newspaper advertisement for a dragon slayer based on the qualities of the successful dragon slayer in "Dragon, Dragon." Use formatting to call attention to key points.

Prewriting Review the story, and make a list of the characteristics your hero needs to have. Identify details of the reward as well.

Drafting Include a brief paragraph describing the position. Then, use the position and appearance of the text to emphasize key points. If possible, use a word-processing program with tabs and formatting.

Model: Format an Advertisement

> **HELP WANTED: Dragon Slayer**
>
> Must be willing to take advice . . . .
>
> **Qualifications**
> -
> -
> -
>
> **REWARD:**

Revising Remember that ads are limited to a small space. Use your word processor to format the text so it fits within the limits.

𝒲G Prentice Hall Writing and Grammar Connection: Chapter 7, Section 3

Extension Activities

Listening and Speaking In a group, present a **dramatic reading** of the scene in which the youngest son approaches the cave.

1. Act out the parts of the boy and the dragon using exact words from the text.
2. Vary volume and tone of voice to show different levels of feeling, such as "annoyed" and "blistering mad."
3. For each reading, have other group members determine which feelings are being shown. Revise the reading to incorporate group feedback.

Research and Technology Make a **compare-and-contrast chart** about dragons in world literature. Using the word *dragon*, perform key word searches in online databases to find information about dragons in many cultures. In your chart, explore some of the following characteristics: physical features, potential for good and evil, and the types of tales in which they typically appear.

 Take It to the Net   www.phschool.com

Go online for an additional research activity using the Internet.

Prepare to Read

Becky and the Wheels-and-Brake Boys

Biking for Fun, 1992, Carlton Murrell, Courtesy of the artist

 Take It to the Net

Visit www.phschool.com
for interactive activities
and instruction related to
"Becky and the Wheels-
and-Brake Boys,"
including

- background
- graphic organizers
- literary elements
- reading strategies

Preview

Connecting to the Literature

In this story, the main character's mother cannot understand why a
bicycle is so important to a girl. As you read, notice how this mother and
daughter come to understand one another. Think of a time that you
worked with a friend or family member to find common ground.

Background

People who speak the same language may come from different countries and regions, have different accents, use different words for the same
thing, or have different ways of using the same words. These language
variations are called *dialects*. In this story, Becky and her friends and
family speak a West Indian dialect of English.

Literary Analysis

Conflict

The **conflict** in a story is the struggle between two opposing forces. It may be an **internal conflict,** a character in conflict with himself or herself, or an **external conflict,** a character struggling with an outside force. As you read "Becky and the Wheels-and-Brake Boys," examine the conflict by answering these focus questions:

1. What does Becky want, and why?
2. What characters or conditions prevent Becky from getting what she wants?

Connecting Literary Elements

All the events in a short story contribute either to the conflict or to the **resolution**—the way the story turns out, one way or another. The resolution can be that a decision is made, a battle is won or lost, a character accepts defeat, or a character conquers an obstacle. The following passage from this story increases the intensity of the conflict by making it seem as if the conflict is about to be resolved. Then an interruption postpones the resolution.

> I knew Mum was just about to give in. Then my granny had to come out on the veranda and interfere. Listen to that Granny-Liz. "Becky, I heard your mother tell you over and over she cahn [can't] afford to buy you a bike . . ."

As you read, look for other events that contribute to the conflict and the resolution.

Reading Strategy

Predicting

When you **predict,** you make a logical guess based on information in the story and past experience. Make predictions as you read "Becky and the Wheels-and-Brake Boys." As new information is revealed, adjust your predictions or make new ones. Use a chart like this one to record your predictions and check how often you predicted correctly.

What I Predict	What Happens
1. Becky will make a plan to earn money.	1.
2.	2.
3.	3.

Vocabulary Development

veranda (və ran′ də) *n.* open porch, usually with a roof, along the outside of a building (p. 449)

menace (men′ əs) *n.* threat; a troublesome or annoying person (p. 450)

reckless (rek′ lis) *adj.* not careful; taking chances (p. 452)

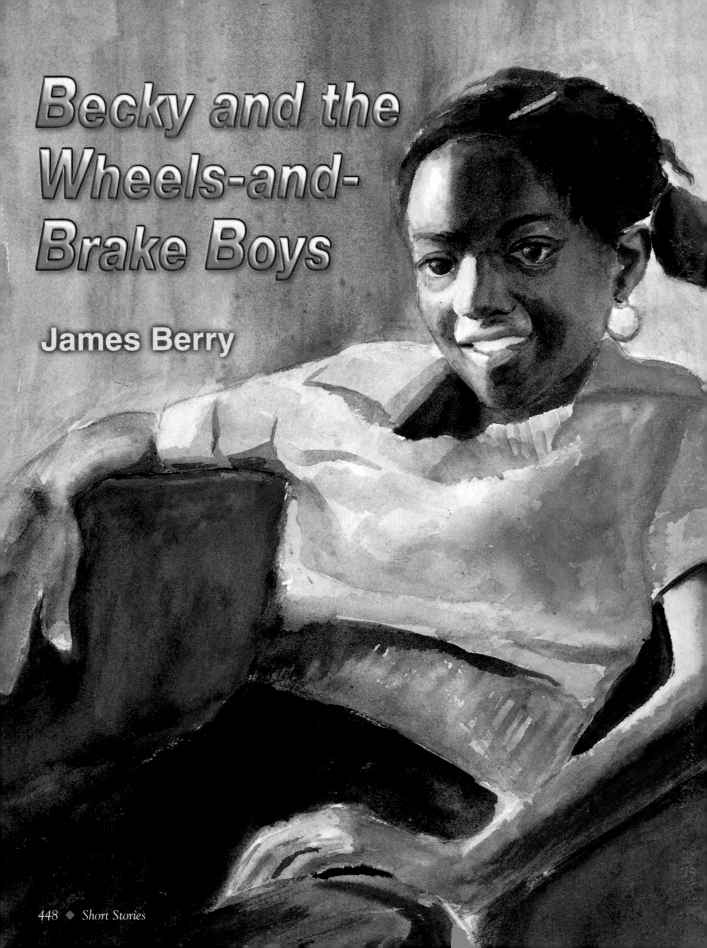

Becky and the Wheels-and-Brake Boys

James Berry

Even my own cousin Ben was there—riding away, in the ringing of bicycle bells down the road. Every time I came to watch them— see them riding round and round enjoying themselves—they scooted off like crazy on their bikes.

They can't keep doing that. They'll see!

I only want to be with Nat, Aldo, Jimmy, and Ben. It's no fair reason they don't want to be with me. Anybody could go off their head for that. Anybody! A girl can not, not, let boys get away with it all the time.

Bother! I have to walk back home, alone.

I know total-total that if I had my own bike, the Wheels-and-Brake Boys wouldn't treat me like that. I'd just ride away with them, wouldn't I?

Over and over I told my mum I wanted a bike. Over and over she looked at me as if I was crazy. "Becky, d'you think you're a boy? Eh? D'you think you're a boy? In any case, where's the money to come from? Eh?"

Of course I know I'm not a boy. Of course I know I'm not crazy. Of course I know all that's no reason why I can't have a bike. No reason! As soon as I get indoors I'll just have to ask again— ask Mum once more.

At home, indoors, I didn't ask my mum.

It was evening time, but sunshine was still big patches in yards and on housetops. My two younger brothers, Lenny and Vin, played marbles in the road. Mum was taking measurements of a boy I knew, for his new trousers and shirt. Mum made clothes for people. Meggie, my sister two years younger than me, was helping Mum on the <u>veranda</u>. Nobody would be pleased with me not helping. I began to help.

Granny-Liz would always stop fanning herself to drink up a glass of ice water. I gave my granny a glass of ice water, there in her rocking chair. I looked in the kitchen to find shelled coconut pieces to cut into small cubes for the fowls' morning feed. But Granny-Liz had done it. I came and started tidying up bits and pieces of cut-off material around my mum on the floor. My sister got nasty, saying she was already helping Mum. Not a single good thing was happening for me.

With me even being all so thoughtful of Granny's need of a cool drink, she started up some botheration[1] against me.

---

1. **botheration** (bäth′ ər ā′ shən) *n.* trouble.

◀ **Critical Viewing** Based on the expression and posture of the girl in this picture, what kind of personality do you think she has? **[Analyze]**

Opposite page: ***Daddy's Girl,*** 1992, Carlton Murrell, Courtesy of the artist

Literary Analysis
Conflict What is the conflict in the story?

veranda (və ran′ də) *n.* open porch, usually with a roof, along the outside of a building

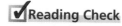**Reading Check**

What does Becky want and what are some reasons she cannot have it?

Listen to Granny-Liz: "Becky, with you moving about me here on the veranda, I hope you dohn have any centipedes or scorpions[2] in a jam jar in your pocket."

"No, mam," I said sighing, trying to be calm. "Granny-Liz," I went on, "you forgot. My centipede and scorpion died." All the same, storm broke against me.

"Becky," my mum said. "You know I don't like you wandering off after dinner. Haven't I told you I don't want you keeping company with those awful riding-about bicycle boys? Eh?"

"Yes, mam."

"Those boys are a <u>menace</u>. Riding bicycles on sidewalks and narrow paths together, ringing bicycle bells and braking at people's feet like wild bulls charging anybody, they're heading for trouble."

"They're the Wheels-and-Brake Boys, mam."

"The what?"

"The Wheels-and-Brake Boys."

"Oh! Given themselves a name as well, have they? Well, Becky, answer this. How d'you always manage to look like you just escaped from a hair-pulling battle? Eh? And don't I tell you not to break the backs down and wear your canvas shoes like slippers? Don't you ever hear what I say?"

"Yes, mam."

"D'you want to end up a field laborer? Like where your father used to be overseer?"[3]

"No, mam."

"Well, Becky, will you please go off and do your homework?"

Everybody did everything to stop me. I was allowed no chance whatsoever. No chance to talk to Mum about the bike I dream of day and night! And I knew exactly the bike I wanted. I wanted a bike like Ben's bike. Oh, I wished I still had even my scorpion on a string to run up and down somebody's back!

I answered my mum. "Yes, mam." I went off into Meg's and my bedroom.

I sat down at the little table, as well as I might. Could homework stay in anybody's head in broad daylight outside? No. Could I keep a bike like Ben's out of my head? Not one bit. That bike took me all over the place. My beautiful bike jumped every log, every rock, every fence. My beautiful bike did everything cleverer than a clever cowboy's horse, with me in the saddle. And the bell, the bell was such a glorious gong of a ring!

If Dad was alive, I could talk to him. If Dad was alive, he'd give me money for the bike like a shot.

menace (men´ əs) n. threat; a troublesome or annoying person

Reading Strategy
Predicting Do you think Becky will give up her idea of getting a bike? Why or why not?

---

2. **scorpions** (skôr´ pē ənz) *n.* close relatives of spiders, with a poisonous stinger at the end of their tails; found in warm regions.
3. **overseer** (ō´ vər sē´ ər) *n.* supervisor of laborers.

Mother, I Love to Ride, 1992, Carlton Murrell, Courtesy of the artist

I sighed. It was amazing what a sigh could do. I sighed and tumbled on a great idea. Tomorrow evening I'd get Shirnette to come with me. Both of us together would be sure to get the boys interested to teach us to ride. Wow! With Shirnette they can't just ride away!

Next day at school, everything went sour. For the first time, Shirnette and me had a real fight, because of what I hated most.

Shirnette brought a cockroach to school in a shoe-polish tin. At playtime she opened the tin and let the cockroach fly into my blouse. Pure panic and disgust nearly killed me. I crushed up the cockroach in my clothes and practically ripped my blouse off, there in open sunlight. Oh, the smell of a cockroach is the nastiest ever to block your nose! I started running with my blouse to go and wash it. Twice I had to stop and be sick.

▲ **Critical Viewing**
What do you think the girl in this picture would tell Becky's mother about riding a bike?
[Speculate]

✔**Reading Check**

How does Becky's mother feel about the Wheels-and-Brake Boys?

Becky and the Wheels-and-Brake Boys ◆ 451

I washed away the crushed cockroach stain from my blouse. Then the stupid Shirnette had to come into the toilet, falling about laughing. All right, I knew the cockroach treatment was for the time when I made my centipede on a string crawl up Shirnette's back. But you put fair-is-fair aside. I just barged into Shirnette.

When it was all over, I had on a wet blouse, but Shirnette had one on, too.

Then, going home with the noisy flock of children from school, I had such a new, new idea. If Mum thought I was scruffy, Nat, Aldo, Jimmy, and Ben might think so, too. I didn't like that.

After dinner I combed my hair in the bedroom. Mum did her machining[4] on the veranda. Meggie helped Mum. Granny sat there, wishing she could take on any job, as usual.

I told Mum I was going to make up a quarrel with Shirnette. I went, but my friend wouldn't speak to me, let alone come out to keep my company. I stood alone and watched the Wheels-and-Brake Boys again.

This time the boys didn't race away past me. I stood leaning against the tall coconut palm tree. People passed up and down. The nearby main road was busy with traffic. But I didn't mind. I watched the boys. Riding round and round the big flame tree, Nat, Aldo, Jimmy, and Ben looked marvelous.

At first each boy rode round the tree alone. Then each boy raced each other round the tree, going round three times. As he won, the winner rang his bell on and on, till he stopped panting and could laugh and talk properly. Next, most <u>reckless</u> and fierce, all the boys raced against each other. And, leaning against their bicycles, talking and joking, the boys popped soft drinks open, drank, and ate chipped bananas.

I walked up to Nat, Aldo, Jimmy, and Ben and said, "Can somebody teach me to ride?"

"Why don't you stay indoors and learn to cook and sew and wash clothes?" Jimmy said.

I grinned. "I know all that already," I said. "And one day perhaps I'll even be mum to a boy child, like all of you. Can you cook and sew and wash clothes, Jimmy? All I want is to learn to ride. I want you to teach me."

I didn't know why I said what I said. But everybody went silent and serious.

One after the other, Nat, Aldo, Jimmy, and Ben got on their bikes and rode off. I wasn't at all cross with them. I only wanted to be riding out of the playground with them. I knew they'd be heading into the town to have ice cream and things and talk and laugh.

---

4. **machining** (mə shēn′ iŋ) v. sewing.

reckless (rek′ lis) adj. not careful; taking chances

Mum was sitting alone on the veranda. She sewed buttons onto a white shirt she'd made. I sat down next to Mum. Straightaway, "Mum," I said, "I still want to have a bike badly."

"Oh, Becky, you still have that foolishness in your head? What am I going to do?"

Mum talked with some sympathy. Mum knew I was honest. "I can't get rid of it, mam," I said.

Mum stopped sewing. "Becky," she said, staring in my face, "how many girls around here do you see with bicycles?"

"Janice Gordon has a bike," I reminded her.

"Janice Gordon's dad has acres and acres of coconuts and bananas, with a business in the town as well."

I knew Mum was just about to give in. Then my granny had to come out onto the veranda and interfere. Listen to that Granny-Liz. "Becky, I heard your mother tell you over and over she cahn[5] afford to buy you a bike. Yet you keep on and on. Child, you're a girl."

"But I don't want a bike because I'm a girl."

"D'you want it because you feel like a bwoy?" Granny said.

"No. I only want a bike because I want it and want it and want it."

Granny just carried on. "A tomboy's like a whistling woman and a crowing hen, who can only come to a bad end. D'you understand?"

I didn't want to understand. I knew Granny's speech was an awful speech. I went and sat down with Lenny and Vin, who were making a kite.

By Saturday morning I felt real sorry for Mum. I could see Mum really had it hard for money. I had to try and help. I knew anything of Dad's—anything—would be worth a great mighty hundred dollars.

I found myself in the center of town, going through the busy Saturday crowd. I hoped Mum wouldn't be too cross. I went into the fire station. With lots of luck I came face to face with a round-faced man in uniform. He talked to me. "Little miss, can I help you?"

I told him I'd like to talk to the head man. He took me into the office and gave me a chair. I sat down. I opened out my brown paper parcel. I showed him my dad's sun helmet. I told him I thought it would make a good fireman's hat. I wanted to sell the helmet for some money toward a bike, I told him.

The fireman laughed a lot. I began to laugh, too. The fireman put me in a car and drove me back home.

Mum's eyes popped to see me bringing home the fireman. The round-faced fireman laughed at my adventure. Mum laughed, too, which was really good. The fireman gave Mum my dad's hat back. Then—mystery, mystery—Mum sent me outside while they talked.

5. **cahn** can't.

Literary Analysis
Conflict and Resolution
In what way does Becky try to resolve the conflict on her own?

 **Reading Check**

What does Becky do to try to get money for a bike?

My mum was only a little cross with me. Then—mystery and more mystery—my mum took me with the fireman in his car to his house.

The fireman brought out what? A bicycle! A beautiful, shining bicycle! His nephew's bike. His nephew had been taken away, all the way to America. The bike had been left with the fireman-uncle for him to sell it. And the good, kind fireman-uncle decided we could have the bike—on small payments. My mum looked uncertain. But in a big, big way, the fireman knew it was all right. And Mum smiled a little. My mum had good sense to know it was all right. My mum took the bike from the fireman Mr. Dean.

And guess what? Seeing my bike much, much newer than his, my cousin Ben's eyes popped with envy. But he took on the big job. He taught me to ride. Then he taught Shirnette.

I ride into town with the Wheels-and-Brake Boys now. When she can borrow a bike, Shirnette comes too. We all sit together. We have patties and ice cream and drink drinks together. We talk and joke. We ride about, all over the place.

And, again, guess what? Fireman Mr. Dean became our best friend, and Mum's especially. He started coming around almost every day.

Review and Assess

Thinking About the Selection

1. **Respond:** Do you think Becky should have taken her father's sun helmet to sell? Why or why not?

2. **(a) Recall:** Who are the Wheels-and-Brake Boys? **(b) Interpret:** Why does Becky want to join them? **(c) Analyze:** For Becky, what do the Wheels-and-Brake Boys represent?

3. **(a) Recall:** What do Becky's mother and grandmother think of the Wheels-and-Brake Boys? **(b) Infer:** Why don't they want Becky to get a bike and join the group? **(c) Analyze:** What additional reasons keep Becky from getting a bike?

4. **(a) Recall:** Who offers to sell Becky a bicycle? **(b) Infer:** Why does Becky's mother finally consent to buying Becky a bike? **(c) Analyze:** In what ways does the story end happily for both Becky and her mother?

5. **(a) Infer:** How would you describe Becky's personality? **(b) Analyze:** Which parts of Becky's personality help her to achieve her goal?

6. **Distinguish:** What is the difference between being determined and being stubborn? Use details from the story to illustrate your points.

James Berry

(b. 1925)

In his writing, James Berry often celebrates the richness of his West Indian heritage. His characters speak with the sounds and rhythms of Jamaican dialects, and many of his stories are set in his island birthplace.

Although he moved to England as an adult, James Berry's imagination seems to live in Jamaica. His young-adult fiction includes a novel called *Ajeemah and His Son*, the story of an African man and his son who are snatched by slave traders and taken to Jamaica. Another book, *A Thief in the Village and Other Stories*, is a collection of stories about life in Jamaica. "Becky and the Wheels-and-Brake Boys" comes from this collection.

Review and Assess

Literary Analysis

Conflict

1. What does Becky want, and why?
2. What characters or conditions prevent Becky from getting what she wants?
3. How does the **conflict** intensify, and how is it solved? Show your answer on an organizer like this one.

Connecting Literary Elements

4. What is the **resolution** of the story? In other words, how is the conflict resolved?
5. On a web like the one below, list some of Becky's qualities that contribute to the resolution of the story.

6. Which other characters influence the resolution? How?

Reading Strategy

Predicting

7. **(a)** What **prediction** did you make about Becky's getting a bike? **(b)** On what details did you base your prediction?
8. Did you change any predictions? Why or why not?

Extend Understanding

9. **Science Connection:** Explain the relationship between the pedals on a bike and the wheels.

Quick Review

The **conflict** in a story is the struggle between two opposing forces. To review conflict, see page 447.

The **resolution** is the way the story turns out. To review resolution, see page 447.

A **prediction** is a logical guess based on past experience and information in the story.

 Take It to the Net
www.phschool.com
Take the interactive self-test online to check your understanding of the selection.

Integrate Language Skills

Vocabulary Development Lesson

Concept Development: Regional Synonyms

Regional synonyms are the words used in different places to describe or name the same thing. For example, Becky uses the word *veranda* to refer to a porch. On your paper, match the regional synonyms.

1. soda   **a.** pants
2. trousers   **b.** hero
3. hoagie   **c.** soft drink

Spelling Strategy

The *is* sound at the end of a word is sometimes spelled *ace*. Unscramble the letters to spell words that end in *ace*.

1. lanckece   2. secrauf   3. ceneam

Concept Development: Analogies

In word **analogies**, the pairs of words have the same relationship. In the following example, both first words are opposites of the second words.

    fear : courage   joy : sadness

Complete each analogy to create word pairs that are synonyms.

1. certain : sure :: menace : _____
2. happy : glad :: careless : _____

Use a vocabulary word from the list on page 447 to complete each sentence.

3. *Precipice* is to *danger* as *wildfire* is to __?__.
4. *Prudent* is to *sensible* as *irresponsible* is to __?__.
5. *Basement* is to *cellar* as *porch* is to __?__.

Grammar Lesson

Independent Clauses

An **independent clause** is a group of words that has a subject and a verb and that can stand on its own. A **simple sentence** consists of a single independent clause:

The boys ride their bikes.

A **compound sentence** consists of two or more independent clauses. To join two independent clauses, use a comma and a coordinating conjunction or a semicolon:

I will ask, but she might say no.
He has a bike; I do not.

Practice Complete each of the following sentences with an independent clause. If the resulting sentence has two independent clauses, be sure to join them correctly.

1. When I open my book again, __?__.
2. __?__ because she wanted a bike.
3. Becky went to see Mr. Dean __?__.
4. __?__ as they rode.
5. Becky smiled at her new bike __?__.

Writing Application Add an independent clause to each independent clause below. Connect your new sentences with semicolons.

1. Becky played a trick on Shirnette.
2. Those two girls are best friends.

𝒲𝒢 *Prentice Hall Writing and Grammar Connection: Chapter 20, Section 2*

Writing Lesson

Journal Entry

Write a journal entry as one of the characters in "Becky and the Wheels-and-Brake Boys." In the journal entry, describe an event from the story and include your own thoughts and feelings (as the character) about the event.

Prewriting   Choose a moment in the story as the topic of your journal entry. Review the story, and jot down notes about your character's reaction to the occurrences.

Drafting   Tell what happened, but do not stop there. Explain how you feel about the events, rather than just reporting them.

Model: Include Thoughts and Feelings

I sat down at the little table, as well as I might. Could homework stay in anybody's head in broad daylight outside? No. Could I keep a bike like Ben's out of my head? Not one bit.

> Becky tells how she cannot keep her mind off her bike. She does this by asking and answering questions.

Revising   Ask a partner to comment on whether your journal entry reflects the feelings of the character you have chosen. Keep your partner's suggestions in mind as you revise.

𝒲ᵍ Prentice Hall Writing and Grammar Connection: Chapter 5, Section 4

Extension Activities

Research and Technology Imagine that Becky has asked you to recommend a bicycle. Prepare a **chart** that compares and contrasts at least three different kinds of bikes.

1. To begin finding information, use the word *bicycle* to do a keyword search on the Internet.
2. Prepare a chart with the following categories: price, features, and condition.
3. Do comparisons in each category on retail Web sites. Then, based on your data, decide which one is the best buy.

Listening and Speaking Becky will need to learn how to take care of her bike. Present a set of **directions** for good bicycle maintenance. Obtain information in books or magazines about bikes. In your presentation, include the following:

- a list of materials needed
- a series of steps explained in logical order
- details that tell *when, how much, how often,* or *to what extent*

 **Take It to the Net**   www.phschool.com

Go online for an additional research activity using the Internet.

Prepare to Read

Overdoing It ◆ Eleven

Take It to the Net

Visit www.phschool.com
for interactive activities
and instruction related to
these selections, including
- background
- graphic organizers
- literary elements
- reading strategies

Preview

Connecting to the Literature

Sometimes, it seems that nothing goes well, and you just have to hope that tomorrow will be better. As you read these stories, ask yourself how you would react to the difficulties the characters face.

Background

In Anton Chekov's story "Overdoing It," a character's fear leads him to say and do foolish things. Fear caused many problems for Russians in the late nineteenth century. Because the czars (rulers of Russia) feared losing their power, they passed harsh laws prohibiting people from disagreeing with them. Sometimes people were imprisoned for suspected rather than real crimes.

Literary Analysis

Characterization

Characterization is the art of developing a character. Authors reveal characters' traits or qualities through their words, thoughts, and actions. Here, Chekhov uses the words and actions of the surveyor in "Overdoing It" to reveal the surveyor's faultfinding nature:

> "What kind of a wagon do you have here!" grumbled the surveyor as he climbed into the wagon. "You can't tell the front from the rear."

Comparing Literary Works

With **direct characterization**, a writer makes direct statements about a character. With **indirect characterization,** a writer reveals a character's traits through his or her thoughts, words, and actions and through what other characters say and think about the character. Use the focus questions to compare and contrast characterization in "Overdoing It" and "Eleven":

1. How much direct characterization does each writer use?
2. In which story did you learn more about a character?

Reading Strategy

Recognizing Word Origins

Word origins are a word's roots—where a word comes from. English words often share origins with words from other languages. Some words used in English were borrowed from foreign languages and have changed over time. Others are spelled and used in their original form. The chart shows English and French for some travel-related words you will read in "Overdoing It." Notice similarities that indicate shared origins or borrowed words. Look for the English words in the story.

English	French
vehicle	véhicule
passenger	passager
station	station
mile	mille

Vocabulary Development

prolonged (prō lōŋd) *adj.* long and drawn out (p. 461)

emaciated (ē mā′ shē āt id) *adj.* thin and bony as a result of starvation or disease (p. 461)

wry (rī) *adj.* twisted (p. 462)

foresee (fôr sē′) *v.* know beforehand (p. 463)

emerged (ē merjd′) *v.* came out from; came into view (p. 464)

meditated (med′ i tāt id) *v.* thought deeply (p. 464)

Overdoing It

Anton Chekhov

Old Man's Head, Study, 1955, Yuri Alexeevich Dryakhlov, Courtesy of Overland Gallery of Fine Art, Scottsdale, Arizona

The land surveyor[1] Gleb Smirnov got off the train at Gnilushka. The station was some twenty miles from the estate he came to survey, and he had to cover that distance in a horse-drawn vehicle of some sort.

"Tell me, please, where could I find post horses and a carriage around here?" the surveyor said to the station guard.

"What kind? . . . Post horses? . . . Here for fifty miles around you couldn't even find a sled dog, let alone post horses. . . . Where are you bound for?"

"For Devkino—the estate of General Khokhotov."

"Well," the guard yawned, "try on the other side of the station. You may find some peasants over there who haul passengers."

The land surveyor made his way across from the station. After looking for some time, then after <u>prolonged</u> negotiations and hesitations, he engaged a husky peasant—glum, pockmarked, and dressed in a tattered gray coarse wool coat and bast-bark shoes.

"What kind of a wagon do you have here!" grumbled the surveyor as he climbed into the wagon. "You can't tell the front from the rear."

"What is there to tell? Near the horse's tail it's the front, and where your lordship is now sitting is the rear."

The horse was young but <u>emaciated</u>, with splayed hoofs and nicked ears. When the driver, raising himself, struck her with his hemp whip, she merely shook her head. When he cursed and struck her a second time, the wagon creaked and shook as if with a bad chill. After the third stroke, the wagon lurched and swayed from side to side, and after the fourth, it moved.

"Is this how we'll proceed all the way?" the surveyor asked, feeling a violent jolting and amazed at the ability of Russian drivers to combine a snail's pace with a jolting that turned one's insides upside down.

"We-e-'ll get there . . . ," the driver assured him. "The mare is a young one, and spirited. Just let her get started at her own pace, then there'll be no stopping her . . . . Giddy-up, you accursed one!"

It was dusk when the wagon drew away from the station. To the right of the surveyor stretched the dark, frozen plain—broad and endless. Try to cross it and you'll come to the end of the world. On the horizon, where the plain merged with the sky and disappeared, the autumn sun was lazily sinking in the mist. To the left of the road, in the darkening space, loomed oddly shaped mounds, and it was hard to tell whether they were last year's haystacks or the

prolonged (prō lôŋd) *adj.* long and drawn out

emaciated (ē mā´ shē āt id) *adj.* thin and bony as a result of starvation or disease

**Reading Check**

Who are the two men and why are they traveling together?

---

1. **land surveyor** one who measures land boundaries.

huts of a village. What there was ahead of them the surveyor could not tell because his field of vision was completely obstructed by the massive back of the driver. It was still, cold, frosty.

"What a God-forsaken place this is!" thought the surveyor as he tried to cover his ears with the collar of his greatcoat. "Not a man or beast in sight! Who knows what could happen in a place like this—they can attack you and rob you and no one will be the wiser for it. And this driver—he's not very reassuring. . . . Some husky back he's got! And he has the mug of a beast . . . yes, it's all very frightening."

"Tell me, my dear man," the surveyor asked, "what is your name?"

"Mine? Klim."

"Well, tell me, Klim, is it safe around here? No ruffians?"

"No, thank God! What kind of ruffians could there be here?"

"That's good that there are none. But, just the same, to play it safe, I brought along three revolvers," the surveyor lied. "And with a gun, as you know, it's bad business to joke. I can handle ten cutthroats with them!"

It grew dark. The wagon suddenly creaked, squeaked, shook, and, as though against its will, turned left.

"Where is he taking me?" the surveyor thought. "He's driving straight ahead and suddenly he turns left. What is he up to? He'll take me, the wretch, into some thicket and . . . and. . . . One hears of such things happening!"

"Listen here," he called to the driver. "You say there's no danger around here? That's too bad! I like to fight off cutthroats. In appearance I'm thin, sickly looking, but I have the strength of a bull! Once three highwaymen threw themselves upon me. And what do you think happened? One of them I socked so hard that he gave up his soul to the Lord, and the other two were sentenced to Siberia to do hard labor because of me. And where I get all this power, I really couldn't tell you. I can grab a husky fellow—like you—and knock him down flat!"

Klim looked around at the surveyor, made a <u>wry</u> face, and struck the horse with the whip.

"Yes, brother . . . ," continued the surveyor, "may God help those who tangle with me! Not only will the cutthroat remain without arms and without legs, but he will be dragged off to court as well. I'm acquainted with every district judge and police inspector. I'm a civil servant, you know, and an important one at that. I'm in transit now, but the officials know about this journey . . . they're watching that no one does me any harm. Everywhere along the way, behind the bushes over there, are deputized village police inspectors and policemen. St-o-o-o-p!" the surveyor suddenly screamed. "Where did you drive into now? Where are you taking me?"

Literary Analysis
Characterization What do the surveyor's words reveal about him?

wry (rī) *adj.* twisted

"Can't you see? Into the forest."

"That's right—it's a forest . . . ," thought the surveyor. "And I got scared! However, I must not show my fear. He's noticed already that I'm scared. Why has he been looking around at me so much? He's probably planning something. . . . Before he crawled along, and now look at him speed!"

"Listen, Klim, why are you hurrying your horse this way?"

"I'm not hurrying her. She is speeding of her own free will. I suppose she herself isn't pleased to have legs that make her go that fast."

"You're lying! I can see that you're lying! But I'd advise you not to rush that way. Rein in your horse! Do you hear me? Rein it in!"

"Why?"

"Because . . . because four pals of mine are joining me here . . . from the station. We must let them catch up with us. They promised to catch up with me in this forest. . . . It will be merrier to travel with them. . . . They are tough fellows, thick-set . . . each one is armed with a pistol. . . . Why do you keep looking around and fidgeting as if you were on pins and needles? Why? There is nothing to look at . . . there is nothing especially interesting about me . . . just my guns, perhaps . . . if you want me to, I'll get them out and show them to you . . . if you want . . ."

The surveyor dug into his pockets for the imaginary guns. And then something unexpected, something that he did not <u>foresee</u> in all his cowardice, happened. Klim suddenly rolled off the wagon and almost on all fours rushed into a thicket.

"Help!" he wailed. "Help! Take the horse and the wagon, but don't kill me! Help!"

The surveyor heard the departing steps of the driver, the crackling of the underbrush—then complete silence. Not expecting such a verbal attack, the surveyor first of all stopped the horse, then sat back more comfortably in the wagon and gave himself over to thought.

"He ran off . . . got scared, the fool! What'll I do now? I can't go on by myself because I don't know the way, and also, I might be suspected of stealing his horse. . . . What had I better do?"

"Klim! Klim!"

"Klim!" answered the echo.

The thought that he might have to spend the night sitting there in the cold dark forest, hearing only the wolves, their echo, and the neighing of the emaciated mare, sent shivers up and down the surveyor's spine, as though it were being scraped with a cold file.

"Klimushka!" he cried. "My dear man! Where are you, Klimushka?"

The surveyor called for about two hours, and only after he

Reading Strategy
Recognizing Word Origins
Why do you think the word *station* has the same meaning and spelling in French and English?

foresee (fôr sē´) *v.* know beforehand

Reading Check

What does Klim think the surveyor will do?

became hoarse and resigned himself to spending the night in the forest, did a soft wind carry to him the sound of someone's groaning.

"Klim! Is that you, my dear man? Let's go on!"

"You'll ki-i-i-ill me!"

"I was just joking, my man! May God punish me if I wasn't joking! I have no guns! I lied because I was scared! Do me a favor, let's go on! I'm freezing to death!"

Klim, having perhaps decided that a real cutthroat would have long since got away with his horse and wagon, <u>emerged</u> from the thicket and hesitantly approached his passenger.

"What was there to get scared about, you fool? I . . . I was just kidding, and got scared. . . . Get in!"

"I'll have nothing more to do with you, master," Klim muttered, climbing up into the wagon. "Had I known, I wouldn't have taken you on, not for a hundred rubles. You nearly made me die of fright."

Klim struck the horse with his whip. The wagon trembled. Klim struck again, and the wagon lurched. After the fourth time, when the wagon moved, the surveyor covered his ears with his collar, and <u>meditated</u>. The road and Klim no longer seemed to him threatening.

emerged (ē merjd´) v. came out from; came into view

meditated (med´ i tāt id) v. thought deeply

Anton Chekhov

(1860–1904)

Anton Chekhov was born in the middle of a family of six children. The family lived in a small coastal town of Southern Russia, where Chekhov's father ran a grocery business. When the business failed, the family moved to Moscow. There, Chekhov enrolled in medical school. By writing short stories and humorous articles, he earned enough money to help support his family.

Although Chekhov had tuberculosis for most of his adult life, he didn't allow his struggles against illness to limit him. In Chekhov's short lifetime, he wrote more than 400 short stories. He is considered one of Russia's greatest writers.

Review and Assess

Thinking About the Selection

1. **Respond:** What was your reaction when the driver ran into the woods?

2. **(a) Recall:** What is the surveyor looking for when he gets off the train? **(b) Interpret:** What do you learn about the surveyor before he meets the driver? **(c) Support:** Which of his words and actions support your answer?

3. **(a) Recall:** What is the surveyor's reaction to the isolated setting? **(b) Interpret:** Why is the surveyor so fearful? **(c) Analyze Cause and Effect:** How does the surveyor cope with his fear?

4. **(a) Recall:** How does the driver react to the surveyor's bragging? **(b) Infer:** Why is the surveyor surprised by the driver's reaction? **(c) Deduce:** What assumptions do you think the surveyor had made about the driver?

5. **(a) Recall:** What happens at the end of the story? **(b) Evaluate:** Does the surveyor benefit from bragging? **(c) Speculate:** What do you think the surveyor has learned from this experience?

Eleven

Sandra Cisneros

Orange Sweater, 1955, Elmer Bischoff, San Francisco Museum of Modern Art, San Francisco, California

What they don't understand about birthdays and what they never tell you is that when you're eleven, you're also ten, and nine, and eight, and seven, and six, and five, and four, and three, and two, and one. And when you wake up on your eleventh birthday you expect to feel eleven, but you don't. You open your eyes and everything's just like yesterday, only it's today. And you don't feel eleven at all. You feel like you're still ten. And you are—underneath the year that makes you eleven.

▲ Critical Viewing
Why might the girl in the picture be sitting alone?

✔ Reading Check
How does the narrator feel about her eleventh birthday?

Like some days you might say something stupid, and that's the part of you that's still ten. Or maybe some days you might need to sit on your mama's lap because you're scared, and that's the part of you that's five. And one day when you're all grown up maybe you will need to cry like if you're three, and that's okay. That's what I tell Mama when she's sad and needs to cry. Maybe she's feeling three.

Because the way you grow old is kind of like an onion or like the rings inside a tree trunk or like my little wooden dolls that fit one inside the other, each year inside the next one. That's how being eleven years old is.

You don't feel eleven. Not right away. It takes a few days, weeks even, sometimes even months before you say eleven when they ask you. And you don't feel smart eleven, not until you're almost twelve. That's the way it is.

Only today I wish I didn't have just eleven years rattling inside me like pennies in a tin Band-Aid box. Today I wish I was one-hundred-and-two instead of eleven because if I was one-hundred-and-two I'd have known what to say when Mrs. Price put the red sweater on my desk. I would've known how to tell her it wasn't mine instead of just sitting there with that look on my face and nothing coming out of my mouth.

"Whose is this?" Mrs. Price says, and she holds the red sweater up in the air for all the class to see. "Whose? It's been sitting in the coatroom for a month."

"Not mine," says everybody. "Not me."

"It has to belong to somebody," Mrs. Price keeps saying, but nobody can remember. It's an ugly sweater with red plastic buttons and a collar and sleeves all stretched out like you could use it for a jump rope. It's maybe a thousand years old and even if it belonged to me I wouldn't say so.

Maybe because I'm skinny, maybe because she doesn't like me, that stupid Felice Garcia says, "I think it belongs to Rachel." An ugly sweater like that, all raggedy and old, but Mrs. Price believes her. Mrs. Price takes the sweater and puts it

Portrait, From the Estate of Eloy Blanco, Collection of El Museo del Barrio, New York, NY

right on my desk, but when I open my mouth nothing comes out.

"That's not, I don't, you're not . . . not mine," I finally say in a little voice that was maybe me when I was four.

"Of course it's yours," Mrs. Price says, "I remember you wearing it once." Because she's older and the teacher, she's right and I'm not.

Not mine, not mine, not mine, but Mrs. Price is already turning to page 32, and math problem number four. I don't know why but all of a sudden I'm feeling sick inside, like the part of me that's three wants to come out of my eyes, only I squeeze them shut tight and bite down on my teeth real hard and try to remember today I am eleven, eleven. Mama is making a cake for me for tonight, and when Papa comes home everybody will sing happy birthday, happy birthday to you.

But when the sick feeling goes away and I open my eyes, the red sweater's still sitting there like a big red mountain. I move the red sweater to the corner of my desk with my ruler. I move my pencil and books and eraser as far from it as possible. I even move my chair a little to the right. Not mine, not mine, not mine.

In my head I'm thinking how long till lunch time, how long till I can take the red sweater and throw it over the schoolyard fence, or leave it hanging on a parking meter, or bunch it up into a little ball and toss it in the alley. Except when math period ends Mrs. Price says loud and in front of everybody, "Now, Rachel, that's enough," because she sees I've shoved the red sweater to the tippy-tip corner of my desk and it's hanging all over the edge like a waterfall, but I don't care.

"Rachel," Mrs. Price says. She says it like she's getting mad. "You put that sweater on right now and no more nonsense."

"But it's not . . ."

"Now!" Mrs. Price says.

This is when I wish I wasn't eleven, because all the years inside of me—ten, nine, eight, seven, six, five, four, three, two, and one—are all pushing at the back of my eyes when I put one arm through one sleeve of the sweater that smells like cottage cheese, and then the other arm through the other and stand there with my arms apart as if the sweater hurts me and it does, all itchy and full of germs that aren't even mine.

That's when everything I've been holding in since this morning, since when Mrs. Price put the sweater on my desk, finally lets go, and all of a sudden I'm crying in front of everybody. I wish I was invisible but I'm not. I'm eleven and it's my birthday today and I'm crying like I'm three in front of everybody. I put my head down on the desk and bury my face in my stupid clown sweater arms. My face all hot and spit coming out of my mouth because I can't stop the little animal noises from coming out of me, until there aren't

Literary Analysis
Characterization How do Mrs. Price's actions show that she is not a patient or sympathetic character?

Reading Check
What does Rachel do after putting on the sweater?

any more tears left in my eyes, and it's just my body shaking like when you have the hiccups, and my whole head hurts like when you drink milk too fast.

But the worst part is right before the bell rings for lunch. That stupid Phyllis Lopez, who is even dumber than Felice Garcia, says she remembers the red sweater is hers! I take it off right away and give it to her, only Mrs. Price pretends like everything's okay.

Today I'm eleven. There's a cake Mama's making for tonight, and when Papa comes home from work we'll eat it. There'll be candles and presents and everybody will sing happy birthday, happy birthday to you, Rachel, only it's too late.

I'm eleven today. I'm eleven, ten, nine, eight, seven, six, five, four, three, two, and one, but I wish I was one-hundred-and-two. I wish I was anything but eleven, because I want today to be far away already, far away like a tiny kite in the sky, so tiny-tiny you have to close your eyes to see it.

Review and Assess

Thinking About the Selection

1. **Respond:** What would you like to say to Rachel? To Mrs. Price? To Felice Garcia?

2. **(a) Recall:** What is special about the day in this story? **(b) Interpret:** What is Rachel's theory about a person's age? **(c) Analyze:** Explain how Rachel can be eleven, but also all her younger ages as well.

3. **(a) Recall:** How do Mrs. Price and Rachel react differently to the red sweater? **(b) Infer:** Why can't Rachel speak up to tell Mrs. Price that the sweater is not hers? **(c) Analyze:** Why does Rachel react so strongly to being given the sweater?

4. **(a) Recall:** How is the mix-up straightened out? **(b) Describe:** How does Rachel feel after the problem is solved? **(c) Distinguish:** In what ways is this a satisfactory or unsatisfactory solution?

5. **(a) Analyze:** Why does Rachel wish she were "anything but eleven"? **(b) Connect:** In what way do the story events suggest that Rachel's theory about ages has some truth to it?

6. **(a) Assess:** What are some advantages and disadvantages to "growing up"? **(b) Apply:** What disadvantages do Rachel's experiences illustrate? **(c) Make a Judgment:** Are Rachel's reactions understandable? Explain.

Sandra Cisneros

(b. 1954)

Sandra Cisneros was born in Chicago and stayed in her hometown through college. Then, she moved to Iowa and began to write about her life, her family, and her Mexican heritage. She writes about real-life experiences.

Cisneros creates characters who are distinctly Hispanic and who are often isolated from mainstream culture. The themes of isolation, divided cultural loyalties, and alienation appear in many of her works. They reflect Cisneros's own feeling of being an "outsider" as a Hispanic American youth growing up in the United States.

Review and Assess

Literary Analysis

Characterization

1. On a chart like the one shown, identify some of the key details of **characterization** for each character.

Character	Words	Thoughts	Actions
Klim			
Surveyor			
Rachel			
Mrs. Price			

2. Describe each character in your own words.

Comparing Literary Works

3. Use organizers like these to record details of **direct** and **indirect** characterization of Klim, the surveyor, Rachel, and Mrs. Price.

4. How much direct characterization does each writer use?
5. Which character from these stories seems the most believable? Explain why.
6. In which story did you learn more about a character? Why?

Reading Strategy

Recognizing Word Origins

7. Use a dictionary to find the **origins** of the following words:
   (a) mile (b) station (c) vehicle (d) passenger.
8. The French word *bon* means *good*. Explain the meaning of *bon voyage*.
9. If Rachel invited classmates to a birthday party, the invitation would probably say *RSVP*. Use a dictionary to find the origin and meaning of this expression. Explain what language it comes from, what the full expression is, and what it means.

Extend Understanding

10. **Career Connection:** The land surveyor's job requires that he visit unfamiliar places. In what other careers do people often travel to unfamiliar places?

Quick Review

Characterization is the art of creating and developing a character. To review characterization, see page 463.

Direct characterization results when an author directly states information about a character.

Indirect characterization results when the character's traits are revealed through what the character does, says, and thinks, as well as through the words and thoughts of other characters.

Word origins are a word's roots—where a word comes from. To review word origins, see page 463.

Take It to the Net
www.phschool.com
Take the interactive self-test online to check your understanding of these selections.

Integrate Language Skills

Vocabulary Development Lesson

Word Analysis: Recognizing Commonly Used Foreign Words

Many words used by English speakers are words from other languages. For example, *cliché* (which means "unoriginal") is from the French verb *clicher*, meaning "to stereotype." Use a dictionary to determine the origins and meanings of the following foreign words commonly used in English.

1. faux pas **2.** rendezvous **3.** siesta **4.** mañana

Spelling Strategy

Sometimes, the *r* sound is spelled *wr*, as in *wry*. For each word below, write the homophone—another word that sounds the same but has a different meaning and spelling—that begins with *wr*.

1. rap **2.** ring **3.** rest **4.** right **5.** rye

Fluency: Sentence Completions

Copy each sentence on your paper. Use one of the following words to complete each one.

prolonged	meditated
emaciated	wry
foresee	emerged

1. The hungry dog looked ____?____.
2. The ceremony was ____?____ by lengthy speeches.
3. He made a ____?____ face.
4. The butterfly ____?____ from its cocoon.
5. The professor ____?____ on the question.
6. I cannot ____?____ the future.

Grammar Lesson

Subordinate Clauses

A **subordinate clause** is a group of words that has a subject and a verb but cannot stand alone as a sentence. It is dependent on an independent clause to complete its meaning. Subordinate clauses usually begin with words such as *who*, *which*, *that*, *after*, *because*, *before*, *when*, and *until*. In the following examples, the subordinate clauses are shown in italics. Notice that they do not express complete thoughts.

"You may find some peasants over there *who haul passengers*."

When Papa comes home from work, we will eat cake.

▶ *For more practice, see page R29, Exercise C.*

Practice Copy these sentences on your paper. Underline the subordinate clause in each sentence.

1. It was dusk when the wagon left the station.
2. He's noticed already that I'm scared.
3. It takes a few days before you say eleven.
4. She was not upset until she saw the sweater.
5. After Rachel left school, she went home.

Writing Application In your notebook, complete each sentence with a subordinate clause. The first word in the clause is given in parentheses.

1. The wagon lurched (because) ____?____.
2. Kim hid (until) ____?____.
3. It was clear (that) ____?____.

𝒲𝒢 *Prentice Hall Writing and Grammar Connection: Chapter 20, Section 2*

Writing Lesson

Character Description

A **character description** is a written sketch of a character. It conveys a main impression about a character by focusing on his or her major traits. Write a character description about one of the characters in "Overdoing It" or "Eleven."

Prewriting   Choose your character, and then review the story to find his or her three main character traits. Support each trait with details from the text. Use a web like the one below to organize your thoughts.

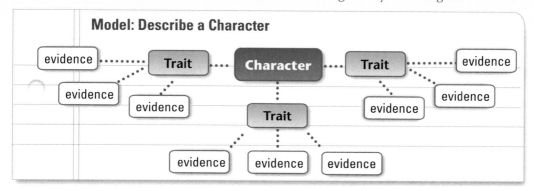

Model: Describe a Character

Drafting   Write your description, discussing the three traits you listed above. Include brief quotations as part of the evidence that illustrates your points.

Revising   Make sure you have provided evidence for all three traits. Then, proofread for spelling, grammar, and mechanics.

WG Prentice Hall Writing and Grammar Connection: Chapter 6, Sections 3

Extension Activities

Listening and Speaking   In "Overdoing It," the surveyor's fear leads him to believe false information. When people intentionally mislead others by playing on their fears, the false information is called **propaganda**. With a group, research an example of propaganda in history or current events. In a **group discussion**, talk about the following:

- the example of propaganda
- the fear that fuels people's acceptance of it
- the results of this acceptance

Research and Technology   Make a **chart** comparing and contrasting modern-day Russia with nineteenth-century Russia—the setting of "Overdoing It." Use electronic resources to find information about the country and its people during both time periods. Discuss with your class how the story might have turned out differently in a modern setting. **[Group Activity]**

 **Take It to the Net**   www.phschool.com

Go online for an additional research activity using the Internet.

Birthdays are a time when people can measure the changes in their lives and in themselves since the previous year. In the short story "Eleven," Rachel is confused because, although her age is changing, she still feels all the fears and insecurities of a younger child. "Obie's Gift" is an excerpt from the novel *Little Obie and the Flood*. The characters have more time to grow and change because a novel is longer than a short story. Both forms of fiction, however, communicate messages, or themes, through events and actions. In this excerpt from *Little Obie and the Flood*, a grandson's birthday gift lovingly illustrates the changes in the family.

Obie's Gift

Martin Waddell

The following selection is from the book Little Obie and the Flood. *The story begins on the day of Effie's birthday. Effie's grandson has been working very hard on a present for her. He has made a puppet that consists of four wooden dolls that are connected together. The dolls' hips and knees are also connected by string; when you move the dolls, they look like they are dancing. Each doll represents a member of the family, including Marty, an orphan who lives with Effie's family.*

The next day Effie got her presents.

"Well, I declare!" said Effie, when she saw the spread.

"That's from Marty and me," said Grandad.

"Not from me," said Little Obie. "I made you something all by myself. I made it 'cause I haven't got no money."

And he gave it to her.

"That's you," said Little Obie, "the one with the big nose. The one with the humpy sort of back is Grandad, and the two little ones, either side, are me and Marty."

"Is that so?" said Effie, fingering her nose and wondering.

And he fitted the stick from the creek in the back of the figures, put the barrel-plank on his knee and put the figures on it, and then . . .

Tap-tap-tap he tapped the plank with his knuckles, and . . . *tap-tap-tap* the four figures danced, all stiff in a row, with their legs jerking up and down. Little Obie had jointed the knees with yarn, and the ankles and the hips, so that all eight wooden legs skipped around just like people dancing.

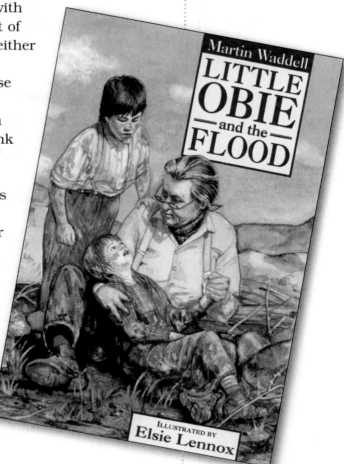

"That's real nice, Little Obie," Effie said, and she was so pleased she forgot all about having a big nose.

Effie took the plank and put it on her knee and danced the doll family.

Then Grandad did it.

Then Marty did it.

Then Effie did it again.

"Thank you!" she said, and she gave Little Obie a hug, which was something she didn't often do.

"They're us," Little Obie explained again, in case Effie hadn't understood. "That one is me and this one is Marty . . ."

"And that's me! "said Effie. "And the big one is Obadiah!"

"Don't look like me," said Grandad, holding his old bones as straight as he could, because no one had ever called him humpy before.

"It's got your wooden head!" said Effie.

When it was late and all the family had gone to bed, Effie heard a noise coming from the big room.

Tap-tap-tap.

She put on her wrap and went to look.

Marty was out of bed, sitting in Grandad's old chair in the fire-light, with Effie's new stitched spread around her to keep her warm.

She had the barrel-plank on her knee and she was *tap-tap-tapping* to make the dolls dance.

▲**Critical Viewing** Based on this picture, during what time period
do you think "Obie's Gift" is set? [**Speculate**]

"Marty?" Effie said, but she said it very softly because she didn't want to frighten her.

Marty never heard her. She was talking to the dolls.

"You're our family," she said. "You're me, and that one's Grandma with her big nose, and that one is Grandad with the humpy back, and the little skinny one down at the end, that's Little Obie."

"A-hem!" said Effie, clearing her throat.

Marty looked up.

"Back to bed, Marty!" Effie said.

Marty went back to bed.

Effie didn't.

She sat down in the firelight in her own chair, with the new spread around her to keep the hog-bite warm. She picked up the barrel-plank, and rested it on her knee. Then she stuck the stick in the back and let the doll family dance and dance.

Tap-tap-tap. Tap-tap-tap.

The Marty doll danced, and the Effie doll danced, and the Obadiah doll danced, and the Little Obie doll danced.

Tap-tap-tap. Tap-tap-tap.

Then Effie stopped tapping the plank and the doll family stopped dancing.

"Time we was all in bed!" Effie told them, and then she looked up, quick-like, to make sure no one had heard her.

No one had, so she laid the dolls on the table and, gathering her new, all-the-colors-of-the-rainbow spread around her, she went back to bed, a year older but years younger as well.

Effie went to sleep.

Everybody slept.

A whole family, together in their cabin at Cold Creek on the Rock River.

Martin Waddell

(b. 1941)

Martin Waddell was born in Belfast, Ireland, in 1941 during the bombing of that city by the Germans. He grew up in Newcastle, County Down, where he still lives today. Waddell is a successful author of children's books, having written more than ninety books—both picture books and novels. *Can't You Sleep, Little Bear?* won the Smarties Grand Prix in 1988. *The Park in the Dark* was awarded the Kurt Maschler/Emil Award in 1989, and *Farmer Duck* won the Smarties Grand Prix in 1991. Waddell has written a number of books for older children on the situation in Northern Ireland. Waddell's advice for budding writers is "to write about things that you feel passionate about."

Connecting Short Stories and Novels

1. In what ways does Effie's family try to make her feel special on her birthday?

2. How are Effie's feelings about her birthday different from Rachel's in "Eleven"?

3. Compare the realizations Effie and Rachel come to on their birthdays.

4. In what ways does this novel excerpt seem like a short story? In what ways is it different?

5. Would you like to read more about these characters? Why or why not?

Prepare to Read

The Lawyer and the Ghost ◆ The Wounded Wolf

 Take It to the Net

Visit www.phschool.com for interactive activities and instruction related to these selections, including

- background
- graphic organizers
- literary elements
- reading strategies

Preview

Connecting to the Literature

Anything that takes away your healthy appearance, such as worry or illness, can make you seem pale, weak, and ghostly. These stories show how worry and injury make "ghosts." When has worry or injury made you a ghost?

Background

In "The Lawyer and the Ghost," the lawyer lives in nineteenth-century London in a centuries-old building known as an Inn of Court. Lawyers ate, slept, and studied in these buildings. Lawsuits could last for years, leaving only papers and a ghostly memory of the original complaint.

Literary Analysis

Setting

The **setting** is the time and place of a story's events. The "time" may be established as a historical era, the present, or the future, the season of the year, or the hour of the day. The "place" can be as general as "outer space" or as specific as a particular street. The following line from "The Lawyer and the Ghost" describes the gloomy building in which the story takes place.

> "I knew a man . . . who took an old, damp, rotten set of chambers, in one of the most ancient Inns, that had been shut up and empty for years and years before."

Comparing Literary Works

In many stories, the setting influences the **conflict,** or problem, and its **resolution,** or the way the problem is settled. In "The Wounded Wolf," the harsh winter setting contributes to the problem, but some physical features of the setting also contribute to the solution.

Compare and contrast the settings of these two stories and the ways each setting influences the problem and its solution. Think about the following focus questions as you read.

1. In what ways are the two settings similar and different?
2. Do the settings make problems or solutions?

Reading Strategy

Picturing the Setting

You can see the setting of a movie because the director has filmed the right details. When you read, be your own director. **Picture the setting** by making a movie of the story in your mind. With your senses, try to see, hear, touch, taste, and smell the surroundings. Use an organizer like this one to help you.

Detail	Sense
"damp, rotten rooms"	touch, smell

Vocabulary Development

sufficient (sə fish′ ənt) *adj.* enough, satisfactory (p. 479)

expend (ek spend′) *v.* spend (p. 480)

inconsistent (in′ kən sis′ tənt) *n.* contradictory; not making sense (p. 480)

massive (mass′ iv) *adj.* huge; large and impressive (p. 483)

stoic (stō ik) *adj.* showing no reaction to good or bad events; calm and unaffected by hardship (p. 485)

gnashes (nash′ iz) *v.* bites with grinding teeth (p. 486)

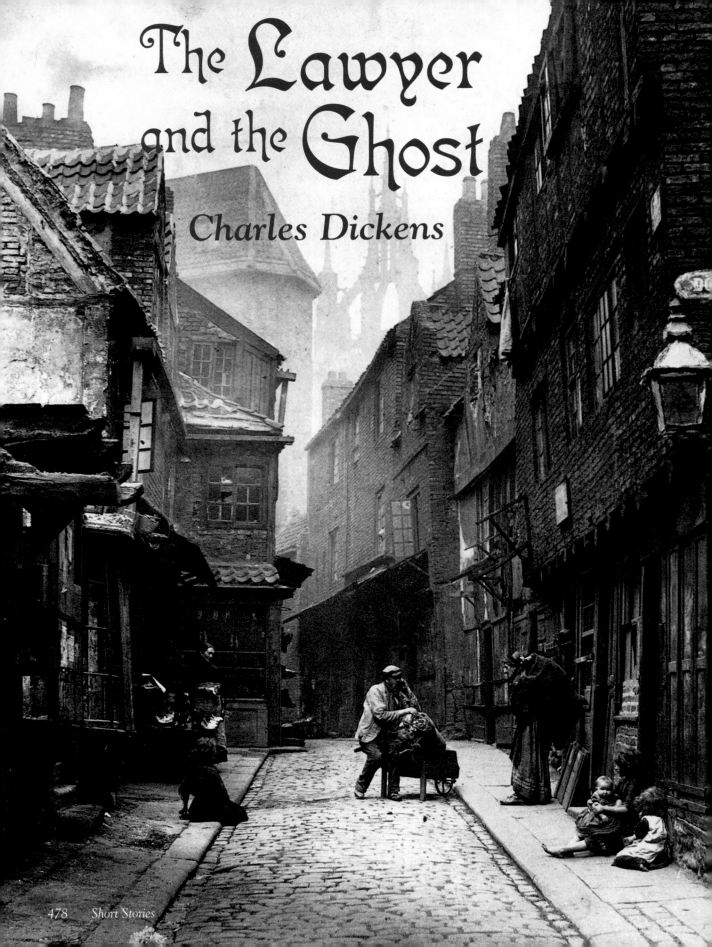

The Lawyer
and the Ghost

Charles Dickens

𝒢 knew [a] man—let me see—it's forty years ago now—who took an old, damp, rotten set of chambers, in one of the most ancient Inns, that had been shut up and empty for years and years before. There were lots of old women's stories about the place, and it certainly was very far from being a cheerful one; but he was poor, and the rooms were cheap, and that would have been quite a sufficient reason for him, if they had been ten times worse than they really were. He was obliged to take some moldering fixtures that were on the place, and, among the rest, was a great lumbering wooden press for papers, with large glass doors, and a green curtain inside; a pretty useless thing for him, for he had no papers to put in it; and as to his clothes, he carried them about with him, and that wasn't very hard work, either.

Well, he had moved in all his furniture—it wasn't quite a truck-full—and sprinkled it about the room, so as to make the four chairs look as much like a dozen as possible, and was sitting down before the fire at night, . . . when his eyes encountered the glass doors of the wooden press. "Ah!" says he— "If I hadn't been obliged to take that ugly article at the old broker's valuation, I might have got something comfortable for the money. I'll tell you what it is, old fellow," he said, speaking aloud to the press, just because he had got nothing else to speak to— "If it wouldn't cost more to break up your old carcass, than it would ever be worth afterwards, I'd have a fire out of you, in less than no time."

He had hardly spoken the words, when a sound resembling a faint groan, appeared to issue from the interior of the case. It startled him at first, but thinking, on a moment's reflection, that it must be some young fellow in the next chambers, who had been dining out, he put his feet on the fender, and raised the poker to stir the fire. At that moment, the sound was repeated: and one of the glass doors slowly opening, disclosed a pale and emaciated figure in soiled and worn apparel, standing erect in the press. The figure was tall and thin, and the countenance expressive of care and anxiety; but there was something in the hue of the skin, and gaunt and unearthly appearance of the whole form, which no being of this world was ever seen to wear.

"Who are you?" said the new tenant, turning very pale, poising the poker in his hand, however, and taking a very decent aim at the countenance[1] of the figure— "Who are you?"

"Don't throw that poker at me," replied the form— "If you hurled

---

1. **countenance** (koun′ tə nəns) n. face; also, the look on a person's face.

◀ **Critical Viewing** Does this photograph of nineteenth-century London capture the same mood as the story? Explain using details. **[Support]**

sufficient (sə fish′ ənt) *adj.* enough; satisfactory

Reading Strategy
Picturing the Setting
What details help you picture the time and place of the story?

✔**Reading Check**

What does the man see coming out of the old wooden press?

it with ever so sure an aim, it would pass through me, without resistance, and <u>expend</u> its force on the wood behind. I am a spirit."

"And, pray, what do you want here?" faltered the tenant.

"In this room," replied the apparition, "my worldly ruin was worked, and I and my children beggared. In this press, the papers in a long, long suit,[2] which accumulated for years, were deposited. In this room, when I had died of grief, and long-deferred hope, two wily harpies[3] divided the wealth for which I had contested during a wretched existence, and of which, at last, not one farthing was left for my unhappy descendants. I terrified them from the spot, and since that day have prowled by night—the only period at which I can re-visit the earth—about the scenes of my long-protracted misery. This apartment is mine: leave it to me."

"If you insist upon making your appearance here," said the tenant, who had had time to collect his presence of mind during this prosy statement of the ghost's— "I shall give up possession with greatest pleasure; but I should like to ask you one question, if you will allow me."

"Say on," said the apparition, sternly.

"Well," said the tenant, "I don't apply the observation personally to you, because it is equally applicable to all the ghosts I ever heard of; but it does appear to me, somewhat <u>inconsistent</u>, that when you have an opportunity of visiting the fairest spots of earth—for I suppose space is nothing to

◄ **Critical Viewing**
What adjectives used to describe the apparition in the story could be used to describe the ghost in this picture? **[Compare and Contrast]**

expend (ek spend´) v. spend

inconsistent (in´ kən sis´ tənt) n. contradictory; not making sense

---

2. suit (sōot) n. lawsuit; a court case in which two or more persons or businesses argue over a matter.
3. harpies (här´ pēz) n. greedy people (originally the name of hideous mythological monsters with women's heads and birds' wings and claws).

you—you should always return exactly to the very places where you have been most miserable."

"Egad, that's very true; I never thought of that before," said the ghost.

"You see, Sir," pursued the tenant, "this is a very uncomfortable room. From the appearance of that press, I should be disposed to say that it is not wholly free from bugs; and I really think you might find much more comfortable quarters: to say nothing of the climate of London, which is extremely disagreeable."

"You are very right, Sir," said the ghost, politely, "it never struck me till now; I'll try a change of air directly"—and, in fact, he began to vanish as he spoke: his legs, indeed, had quite disappeared.

"And if, Sir," said the tenant, calling after him, "if you *would* have the goodness to suggest to the other ladies and gentlemen who are now engaged in haunting old empty houses, that they might be much more comfortable elsewhere, you will confer a very great benefit on society."

"I will," replied the ghost; "we must be dull fellows—very dull fellows, indeed; I can't imagine how we can have been so stupid." With these words, the spirit disappeared; and what is rather remarkable, . . . he never came back again.

Literary Analysis
Setting What details of the setting help the man solve the problem?

Charles Dickens

(1812–1870)

The stories of English author Charles Dickens remain popular today. You may be familiar with *A Christmas Carol* and its main character, Ebenezer Scrooge.

Dickens's early life was difficult. When Dickens was just a boy, his father went to prison, and Dickens had to work long hours pasting labels on bottles.

At fourteen, Dickens became a law clerk. He taught himself shorthand and became a court reporter. His observations of lawyers helped him to write novels such as *Great Expectations*. They also helped him describe the damp, dusty lawyer's room in "The Lawyer and the Ghost."

Review and Assess

Thinking About the Selection

1. **Respond:** What would you have said to the ghost if it asked you to leave?

2. **(a) Recall:** What piece of furniture comes with the room?
   (b) Describe: What is the condition of the piece?

3. **(a) Recall:** Who is the ghost that haunts these rooms?
   (b) Infer: What does the ghost want? **(c) Analyze:** Why do you think the ghost returns to the scene of his "misery"?

4. **(a) Recall:** What question does the man ask the ghost?
   (b) Infer: For what purpose does he ask the question?
   (c) Compare and Contrast: How is the man's behavior with the ghost similar to or different from what you expected?

5. **(a) Recall:** How does the ghost respond to the man's question? **(b) Analyze:** What is surprising about the end of this story? **(c) Draw Conclusions:** How does the interaction between the man and the ghost make this story a humorous one?

The Wounded Wolf

Jean Craighead George

▲ **Critical Viewing** What physical features help this wolf survive in a cold, harsh environment? **[Analyze]**

A wounded wolf climbs Toklat Ridge, a <u>massive</u> spine of rock and ice. As he limps, dawn strikes the ridge and lights it up with sparks and stars. Roko, the wounded wolf, blinks in the ice fire, then stops to rest and watch his pack run the thawing Arctic valley.

They plunge and turn. They fight the mighty caribou that struck young Roko with his hoof and wounded him. He jumped between the beast and Kiglo, leader of the Toklat pack. Young Roko spun and fell. Hooves, paws, and teeth roared over him. And then his pack and the beast were gone.

Gravely injured, Roko pulls himself toward the shelter rock. Weakness overcomes him. He stops. He and his pack are thin and hungry. This is the season of starvation. The winter's harvest has been taken. The produce of spring has not begun.

Young Roko glances down the valley. He droops his head and stiffens his tail to signal to his pack that he is badly hurt. Winds wail. A frigid blast picks up long shawls of snow and drapes them between young Roko and his pack. And so his message is not read.

A raven scouting Toklat Ridge sees Roko's signal. "Kong, kong, kong," he bells—death is coming to the ridge; there will be flesh and bone for all. His voice rolls out across the valley. It penetrates the rocky cracks where the Toklat ravens rest. One by one they hear and spread their wings. They beat their way to Toklat Ridge. They alight upon the snow and walk behind the wounded wolf.

"Kong," they toll[1] with keen excitement, for the raven clan is hungry, too. "Kong, kong"—there will be flesh and bone for all.

Roko snarls and hurries toward the shelter rock. A cloud of snow envelops him. He limps in blinding whiteness now.

A ghostly presence flits around. "Hahahahahahaha," the white fox states—death is coming to the Ridge. Roko smells the fox tagging at his heels.

The cloud whirls off. Two golden eyes look up at Roko. The snowy owl has heard the ravens and joined the deathwatch.

Roko limps along. The ravens walk. The white fox leaps. The snowy owl flies and hops along the rim of Toklat Ridge. Roko stops. Below the ledge out on the flats the musk-ox herd is circling. They form a ring and all face out, a fort of heads and horns and fur that sweeps down to their hooves. Their circle means to Roko that an enemy is present. He squints and smells the wind. It carries scents of thawing ice, broken grass—and earth. The grizzly bear is up! He has awakened from his winter's sleep. A craving need for flesh will drive him.

---

1. **toll** (tōl) *v.* announce.

Literary Analysis
Setting In what region of the world and at what time of year is the story set?

✔**Reading Check**
What is Roko's problem?

Roko sees the shelter rock. He strains to reach it. He stumbles. The ravens move in closer. The white fox boldly walks beside him. "Hahaha," he yaps. The snowy owl flies ahead, alights, and waits.

The grizzly hears the eager fox and rises on his flat hind feet. He twists his powerful neck and head. His great paws dangle at his

▼ **Critical Viewing**
The wolf in the photograph is howling. Given what you learn in the story, what can you infer about the number of wolves in the area? **[Infer]**

chest. He sees the animal procession and hears the ravens' knell[2] of death. Dropping to all fours, he joins the march up Toklat Ridge.

Roko stops; his breath comes hard. A raven alights upon his back and picks the open wound. Roko snaps. The raven flies and circles back. The white fox nips at Roko's toes. The snowy owl inches closer. The grizzly bear, still dulled by sleep, stumbles onto Toklat Ridge.

Only yards from the shelter rock, Roko falls.

Instantly the ravens mob him. They scream and peck and stab at his eyes. The white fox leaps upon his wound. The snowy owl sits and waits.

Young Roko struggles to his feet. He bites the ravens. Snaps the fox. And lunges at the <u>stoic</u> owl. He turns and warns the grizzly bear. Then he bursts into a run and falls against the shelter rock. The wounded wolf wedges down between the rock and barren ground. Now protected on three sides, he turns and faces all his foes.

The ravens step a few feet closer. The fox slides toward him on his belly. The snowy owl blinks and waits, and on the ridge rim roars the hungry grizzly bear.

Roko growls.

The sun comes up. Far across the Toklat Valley, Roko hears his pack's "hunt's end" song. The music wails and sobs, wilder than the bleating wind. The hunt song ends. Next comes the roll call. Each member of the Toklat pack barks to say that he is home and well.

"Kiglo here," Roko hears his leader bark. There is a pause. It is young Roko's turn. He cannot lift his head to answer. The pack is silent. The leader starts the count once more. "Kiglo here."—A pause. Roko cannot answer.

The wounded wolf whimpers softly. A mindful raven hears. "Kong, kong, kong," he tolls—this is the end. His booming sounds across the valley. The wolf pack hears the raven's message that something is dying. They know it is Roko, who has not answered roll call.

The hours pass. The wind slams snow on Toklat Ridge. Massive clouds blot out the sun. In their gloom Roko sees the deathwatch move in closer. Suddenly he hears the musk-oxen thundering into their circle. The ice cracks as the grizzly leaves. The ravens burst into the air. The white fox runs. The snowy owl flaps to the top of the shelter rock. And Kiglo rounds the knoll.

In his mouth he carries meat. He drops it close to Roko's head and wags his tail excitedly. Roko licks Kiglo's chin to honor him. Then Kiglo puts his mouth around Roko's nose. This gesture says "I am your leader." And by mouthing Roko, he binds him and all the wolves together.

---

2. **knell** (nel) *n.* mournful sound, like a slowly ringing bell—usually indicating a death.

stoic (stō′ ik) *adj.* showing no reaction to good or bad events; calm and unaffected by hardship

Literary Analysis
Setting Which features of the setting create a problem, and which features help solve a problem?

**Reading Check**

What makes the animals run away from Roko?

The wounded wolf wags his tail. Kiglo trots away.

Already Roko's wound feels better. He gulps the food and feels his strength return. He shatters bone, flesh, and gristle and shakes the scraps out on the snow. The hungry ravens swoop upon them. The white fox snatches up a bone. The snowy owl gulps down flesh and fur. And Roko wags his tail and watches.

For days Kiglo brings young Roko food. He <u>gnashes</u>, gorges, and shatters bits upon the snow.

A purple sandpiper winging north sees ravens, owl, and fox. And he drops in upon the feast. The long-tailed jaeger gull flies down and joins the crowd on Toklat Ridge. Roko wags his tail.

One dawn he moves his wounded leg. He stretches it and pulls himself into the sunlight. He walks—he romps. He runs in circles. He leaps and plays with chunks of ice. Suddenly he stops. The "hunt's end" song rings out. Next comes the roll call.

"Kiglo here."

"Roko here," he barks out strongly.

The pack is silent.

"Kiglo here," the leader repeats.

"Roko here."

Across the distance comes the sound of whoops and yips and barks and howls. They fill the dawn with celebration. And Roko prances down the Ridge.

gnashes (nash´ iz) v. bites with grinding teeth

Review and Assess

Thinking About the Selection

1. **Respond:** Do you admire the wolves in this story? Why?

2. **(a) Recall:** What action did Roko take that caused him to be wounded? **(b) Infer:** Why does he climb the ridge? **(c) Draw Conclusions:** Based on these actions, how would you describe Roko's personality?

3. **(a) Recall:** Describe the threats that Roko faces.
(b) Compare and Contrast: In what way are animals that follow Roko similar to the wolves? **(c) Evaluate:** Are there "good-guy" and "bad-guy" animals in this story? Explain.

4. **(a) Recall:** How does Kiglo learn that Roko is hurt?
(b) Infer: What does Kiglo do when he finds out Roko is hurt?
(c) Synthesize: How do the wolves demonstrate "teamwork"?

5. **(a) Recall:** What happens at the end of the story?
(b) Interpret: What does the celebration at the end mean?
(c) Generalize: Based on what you have read, what general statement can you make about wolf relationships?

Jean Craighead George

(b. 1919)

Jean Craighead George has been a reporter, illustrator, teacher, and editor. She is the author of more than 100 books, including *My Side of the Mountain* and *Julie of the Wolves.*

Nearly all of George's books are about nature. She grew up on land that her family had farmed since the 1700s. Her experiences of rural life, wild animals, and family pets fostered the love of nature shown in her writing. George calls her fiction "documentary novels" because the facts about nature that they contain are scientifically accurate.

Review and Assess

Literary Analysis

Setting

1. List four details in "The Wounded Wolf" that reveal the amount of time that passes. Record them on a chart like the one shown.

Setting: Details that show the passage of time
1.
2.
3.
4.

2. In "The Lawyer and the Ghost," what are three clues that suggest the story does not take place in contemporary London?

Comparing Literary Works

3. In what ways are the settings similar and different?
4. Do the settings make problems or solutions? Explain.
5. Make a chart to show how setting influences the problem and the resolution.

Story:_____

Problem		Setting		Resolution
	◀·····		····▶	

6. Which setting do you think is more important to the resolution of the story? Explain why.

Reading Strategy

Picturing the Setting

7. In your own words, describe the place where "The Lawyer and the Ghost" occurs.
8. What sensory details do you associate with the setting of "The Wounded Wolf?"

Extend Understanding

9. **Cultural Connection:** What does "The Lawyer and the Ghost" suggest about lawyers and law in Dickens's England?

Quick Review

The **setting** is the time and place of a story's events. To review setting, see page 477.

The **conflict** is the problem in a story. The **resolution** is the way the problem is settled. To review conflict and resolution, see page 477.

When **picturing the setting** of a story, you use sensory details to experience it.

 Take It to the Net
www.phschool.com
Take the interactive self-test online to check your understanding of these selections.

Integrate Language Skills

Vocabulary Development Lesson

Word Analysis: Latin Prefix *in-*

The Latin prefix *in-* can mean "no, not, without, the lack of, or the opposite of." In "The Lawyer and the Ghost," for example, *inconsistent* means "not consistent." On your paper, add *in-* to the first word in each phrase. Then, explain the change in meaning.

1. expensive room
2. consistent reason
3. digestible food
4. efficient methods

Spelling Strategy

The *shent* sound is often spelled *cient*, as in *sufficient*. On your paper, correct the following misspelled words.

1. profishent (skillful in doing something)
2. defishent (lacking in something)

Fluency: Definitions

On your paper, match each word in the first column with its lettered meaning in the second column. Then, write a sentence in which you use each word.

1. sufficient
2. expend
3. inconsistent
4. massive
5. stoic
6. gnashes

a. not reacting to good or bad events
b. not making sense
c. bites with grinding teeth
d. enough
e. large and impressive
f. use up; spend

Grammar Lesson

Simple and Compound Sentences

A **simple sentence** is made of a single independent clause—a group of words that contains a subject and a verb and can stand by itself as a sentence. A simple sentence can contain a **compound subject** (a subject made up of two or more nouns) or a **compound verb** (two or more verbs that name actions done by the same subject) and still be a simple sentence.

> **Compound subject**
> The ghost and the lawyer talked about the situation.
> **Compound verb**
> Kiglo watched and waited.

▶ *For more practice, see page R29, Exercise F.*
Practice Copy the sentences on your paper. Circle each subject. Underline each verb. Then, label the compound subjects and verbs.

1. He stops and looks.
2. Kiglo and the other wolves helped Roko.
3. Hooves, paws, and teeth roared over him.
4. The raven hops and flaps its wings.
5. The snowy owl has heard the ravens and joined the deathwatch.

Writing Application Write five sentences to describe a scene from "The Wounded Wolf." Include two sentences with compound verbs and one sentence with a compound subject.

W̦G *Prentice Hall Writing and Grammar Connection: Chapter 20, Section 2*

Writing Lesson

Annotated Bibliography

An **annotated bibliography** is a list of materials on a given topic, along with publication information and summaries. Write down five questions about wolves that you have after reading "The Wounded Wolf." Then, compile an **annotated bibliography**—a source list with comments—of materials that could answer these questions.

Prewriting Write your questions and then go to the library to gather useful sources. Record the publication information and write a summary of each source.

Drafting After writing your summaries, write a bibliography entry for each source. See the model for help in formatting your bibliography.

Model: Bibliography Format

Full-Length Book: Carpenter, Albert, *Football, Now and Then.* Upper Saddle River, NJ: Prentice Hall, 1997.

Encyclopedia Entry: "Football." World Book. Vol. 7, pp. 365, 366.

Magazine Article: Taylor, Beth. "Glory Days." *Football Journal,* July 1995, pp. 40–45.

Revising Make sure all of your publication information is accurate and that you have used the correct format.

W̧G Prentice Hall Writing and Grammar Connection: Chapter 11, Section 5

Extension Activities

Listening and Speaking Prepare a **persuasive presentation** in which you state and support an opinion on the issue of whether or not efforts should be made to protect wolves. Do research to learn about both sides of the issue. Support your opinion with detailed evidence arranged in a visual display. For example, you might

- make a graph that shows the declining population of wolves.
- use photographs to show the damage caused by wolves.

Check your facts for accuracy, and then present your findings.

Research and Technology With a partner, research what London was like during Charles Dickens's life. What details from "The Lawyer and the Ghost" are historically accurate? To show what you learned, give your class **an oral report on the historical setting** of the story. In your oral report, include visuals such as diagrams, drawings, or reproductions of photographs. Try to find representations of the Inns of Court and the paper press that are described in the story. [**Group Activity**]

 **Take It to the Net**   www.phschool.com

Go online for an additional research activity using the Internet.

Magazine Articles

About Magazine Articles

Magazine articles are nonfiction texts written for various reasons: to inform readers about a person or topic, to state a viewpoint, or to convince readers to take a specific action. Whatever the purpose, the writer should include statements that support the claims made in the text. When you read magazine articles, evaluate whether claims are supported and whether they are logically presented.

Reading Strategy

Recognizing Supported and Unsupported Claims

To reach your own conclusions about the information in a magazine article, read carefully, noting claims unsupported by the text. As you read, ask yourself these questions:

- Does the writer support the statement with facts (information that can be proved to be true) or with opinions (the writer's or someone else's viewpoint)?
- Are citations (quotes and sources of information) accurate and related to the claims?
- Is the reasoning logical and appropriate to the claims made by the writer?

As you read the article on the next two pages, use a chart like the one shown to identify and analyze the writer's statements that are not supported by the text. Write the statement and the supporting text. If there is no supporting text, explain the support that is needed.

Analyzing Support

Statement	Support	Support Needed
Rehabilitation techniques have come a long way in the past quarter century.	None	The writer needs to tell *how* techniques have improved.

Can Oiled Seabirds Be Rescued, Or Are We Just Fooling Ourselves?

Sharon Levy

Like dozens of other volunteers, I felt compelled to help when a cargo ship spilled 5,000 gallons of fuel oil in Humboldt Bay, near my home on California's north coast. When we released rehabilitated birds, we all felt great. Later, I learned that what we had done was controversial. Many biologists believe that rescuing oiled birds serves more to soothe human feelings than to help wildlife and some studies show that many cleaned birds survive for only a few days. But there are a number of encouraging success stories.

Plumage normally keeps a seabird warm and dry even as it dives far below the surface. When oil coats feathers, the plumage loses its ability to insulate, leaving a bird susceptible to hypothermia. Beached birds also suffer from dehydration, anemia and pneumonia.

Rehabilitation techniques have come a long way in the past quarter century. But critics contend that the surviving birds represent an insignificant proportion

National Wildlife Feb-Mar 1999

Look for examples in the article that support the claim that there are encouraging success stories.

of the bird populations affected in most spills. "Future oil company support for bird rescue should be considered a public relations effort to counteract negative public opinion," wrote Oregon biologist Brian Sharp in a 1995 report. He estimates that only 4 percent of cleaned birds live for a year in the wild.

Here, an opinion is quoted. Do not mistake quoted opinions for factual support.

"Bird survival will be quite different from spill to spill," says David Jessup, a veterinarian with the California Department of Fish and Game's Office of Spill Prevention and Response, which has established regional facilities to provide rapid response during such catastrophes. "The species involved, the toxicity of the oil, the weather and length of time between oiling and being picked up, all influence survival."

After the Platform Irene oil spill near Santa Barbara last winter, researchers conducted one of the first studies using radiotelemetry to directly compare the survival of oiled and unoiled western gulls. "It was a sticky, nasty crude oil that pasted the birds' feathers, wings and legs to their bodies," recalls veterinarian Jonna Mazet, director of the state's Oiled Wildlife Care Network. "Following release, all of the rehabilitated gulls survived for the life of their radio transmitters [more than eight months] and did as well or better than a control group of unoiled birds."

A specific example of a scientific study directly supports the earlier claim of success stories.

The most successful cases of oiled-bird rescue have occurred at the tip of South Africa, where African penguin colonies have suffered from several serious oil spills over the last decade. Penguins have a better chance of surviving oiling and rehabilitation then most other seabirds. They have a layer of blubber to keep them warm. And their normal life cycle involves periods of fasting. Following a spill in 1994, more than 65 percent of the 4,076 penguins that were cleaned were later resighted in good health.

Dee Boersma, a University of Washington biologist who works with Magellanic penguins in Argentina, hasn't experienced the same success. "The reason South Africa worked is they had a huge aquarium and fire department that delivered water free so that they could really wash the birds. In Argentina, it's a desert. The nearest town is many miles from the large penguin colonies and there's no water."

During a major spill off Argentina in 1991, Boersma estimates 17,000 birds were oiled. "Perhaps 360 birds were recovered, giving a false impression that the population was being rescued," she says.

Here, the writer presents facts about a failure and the reasons for the failure.

At the Humboldt spill, I experienced the joy of seeing birds recover as well as the sorrow of seeing them suffer. If an oil spill does hit here again, chances are I'll go back to the wildlife care center to help out. I'll do this for some good reasons and for some bad ones. I'll do it because I know action is an effective antidote to the grief I'll feel. I'll do it in the hope that a majority of the birds that go through rehabilitation will survive. That's a goal that seems far more attainable here than on the remote beaches of Argentina.

This conclusion is logical, because conditions in California more closely resemble conditions in successful areas than conditions in Argentina.

Yes, I'd work at the center again. But I'd know as I started up my car engine to go there that I was applying a Band-Aid, not solving the problem of oil pollution. Like everyone else in our oil-addicted society, I am still part of that dilemma.

Californian Sharon Levy specializes in topics relating to science and nature.

National Wildlife Feb-Mar 1999

Check Your Comprehension

1. Where did the writer volunteer to help out with the oil spill?
2. Using details from the article, explain the phrase "rehabilitated birds."
3. How does oil affect a bird's plumage?
4. What species of bird has a better chance of surviving oiling than most other seabirds? Why?
5. Why does the writer feel that she is part of the oil-spill problem?

Applying the Reading Strategy

Recognizing Supported and Unsupported Claims

6. Identify one claim that is not supported by the text. Tell what kind of information is needed to support the claim.
7. Choose a claim made by the writer that is supported by the text. Write the statement and the supporting text.

Activity

Support Search

With a group, conduct a "support search" to analyze both sides of the question this article explores. Prepare two empty bulletin boards or display areas to represent the two possible answers. Over the course of a week, look for articles, studies, and examples that support either answer. Post photocopies of your findings on the bulletin boards. At the end of the week, discuss and evaluate the evidence the group has found.

Comparing Informational Materials

Magazine and Online Articles

Find an article on the Internet about rescuing oiled seabirds. Compare and contrast the amount, type, and presentation of information in the online article and "Oiled Seabirds." Use a chart like the one at right. After you have completed your chart, write a one-paragraph evaluation explaining which medium you found to be more effective. Use details from your chart for support.

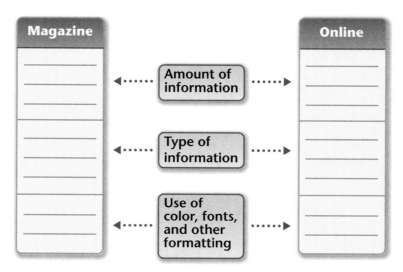

Prepare to Read

The All-American Slurp ◆ The Stone

 Take It to the Net

Visit www.phschool.com
for interactive activities
and instruction related to
these selections, including

- background
- graphic organizers
- literary elements
- reading strategies

Preview

Connecting to the Literature

These selections share insights into growth and change. As you read, notice how the characters deal with the challenges that change brings. Then, consider how you might have reacted to similar situations.

Background

In "The All-American Slurp," a Chinese family newly arrived in the United States must deal with unfamiliar eating habits. The following are some Chinese customs concerning food that the family in this story observes:

- Food is usually served "family style" on large platters in the center of the table.
- Food is scooped up or handled with slender sticks called chopsticks.

Literary Analysis

Theme

The theme is the central message of a literary work. The theme of a story can be either stated or implied.

- A **stated theme** is expressed directly by the author.
- An **implied theme** is suggested, or stated indirectly.

Often, you can figure out the implied theme by paying attention to the characters' actions. To figure out the implied theme in these stories, think about the following:

- The ways in which the Lin family changes
- What Maibon learns from getting his wish

Comparing Literary Works

As you read these stories, think about what each one says about change.

Compare and contrast the themes in these selections by answering these focus questions as you read:

1. What does each story say about change?
2. What themes do these stories share? What themes are unique to each story?

Reading Strategy

Drawing Inferences

Sometimes you need to figure out an implied theme by **drawing inferences**, or reaching conclusions based on evidence. Evidence may include unusual events, as well as characters' words, actions, and reactions. Use a chart like the one here to help you draw inferences about the important details in these stories.

Vocabulary Development

emigrated (em i grāt´ id) *v.* left one country to settle in another (p. 496)

etiquette (et´ i ket) *n.* acceptable social manners (p. 501)

consumption (kən sump´ shen) *n.* eating; drinking; using up (p. 501)

plight (plīt) *n.* awkward, sad, or dangerous situation (p. 507)

jubilation (jōō bə lā´ shen) *n.* great joy; triumph (p. 508)

rue (rōō) *v.* regret (p. 508)

fallow (fal´ ō) *adj.* inactive; unproductive (p. 512)

Story Detail

The Lins sit "stiffly in a row" on the Gleasons' couch.

⋮
▼

My Thoughts

People sit stiffly when they are nervous.

⋮
▼

My Inference

New to the United States, the Lins are afraid of making a mistake.

The All-American Slurp

Lensey Namioka

The first time our family was invited out to dinner in America, we disgraced ourselves while eating celery. We had <u>emigrated</u> to this country from China, and during our early days here we had a hard time with American table manners.

In China we never ate celery raw, or any other kind of vegetable raw. We always had to disinfect the vegetables in boiling water first. When we were presented with our first relish tray, the raw celery caught us unprepared.

We had been invited to dinner by our neighbors, the Gleasons. After arriving at the house, we shook hands with our hosts and packed ourselves into a sofa. As our family of four sat stiffly in a row, my younger brother and I stole glances at our parents for a clue as to what to do next.

Mrs. Gleason offered the relish tray to Mother. The tray looked pretty, with its tiny red radishes, curly sticks of carrots, and long, slender stalks of pale green celery. "Do try some of the celery, Mrs. Lin," she said. "It's from a local farmer, and it's sweet."

Mother picked up one of the green stalks, and Father followed suit. Then I picked up a stalk, and my brother did too. So there we sat, each with a stalk of celery in our right hand.

Mrs. Gleason kept smiling. "Would you like to try some of the dip, Mrs. Lin? It's my own recipe: sour cream and onion flakes, with a dash of Tabasco sauce."

Most Chinese don't care for dairy products, and in those days I wasn't even ready to drink fresh milk. Sour cream sounded perfectly revolting. Our family shook our heads in unison.

emigrated (em´ i grāt´ id) v. left one country to settle in another

Mrs. Gleason went off with the relish tray to the other guests, and we carefully watched to see what they did. Everyone seemed to eat the raw vegetables quite happily.

Mother took a bite of her celery. *Crunch.* "It's not bad!" she whispered.

Father took a bite of his celery. *Crunch.* "Yes, it is good," he said, looking surprised.

I took a bite, and then my brother. *Crunch, crunch.* It was more than good; it was delicious.

Raw celery has a slight sparkle, a zingy taste that you don't get in cooked celery. When Mrs. Gleason came around with the relish tray, we each took another stalk of celery, except my brother. He took two.

There was only one problem: long strings ran through the length of the stalk, and they got caught in my teeth. When I help my mother in the kitchen, I always pull the string out before slicing celery.

I pulled the strings out of my stalk. *Z-z-zip, z-z-zip.* My brother followed suit. *Z-z-zip, z-z-zip, z-z-zip.* To my left, my parents were taking care of their own stalks. *Z-z-zip, z-z-zip, z-z-zip.*

Suddenly I realized that there was dead silence except for our zipping. Looking up, I saw that the eyes of everyone in the room were on our family. Mr. and Mrs. Gleason, their daughter Meg, who was my friend, and their neighbors the Badels—they were all staring at us as we busily pulled the strings of our celery.

That wasn't the end of it. Mrs. Gleason announced that dinner was served and invited us to the dining table. It was lavishly covered with platters of food, but we couldn't see any chairs around the table. So we helpfully carried over some dining chairs and sat down. All the other guests just stood there.

Mrs. Gleason bent down and whispered to us, "This is a buffet dinner. You help yourselves to some food and eat it in the living room."

Our family beat a retreat back to the sofa as if chased by enemy soldiers. For the rest of the evening, too mortified to go back to the dining table, I nursed a bit of potato salad on my plate.

Reading Strategy
Drawing Inferences
What can you infer based on the Lins' surprised reactions to the raw vegetables?

Reading Check

Why is the narrator embarrassed?

Next day Meg and I got on the school bus together. I wasn't sure how she would feel about me after the spectacle our family made at the party. But she was just the same as usual, and the only reference she made to the party was, "Hope you and your folks got enough to eat last night. You certainly didn't take very much. Mom never tries to figure out how much food to prepare. She just puts everything on the table and hopes for the best."

I began to relax. The Gleasons' dinner party wasn't so different from a Chinese meal after all. My mother also puts everything on the table and hopes for the best.

Meg was the first friend I had made after we came to America. I eventually got acquainted with a few other kids in school, but Meg was still the only real friend I had.

My brother didn't have any problems making friends. He spent all his time with some boys who were teaching him baseball, and in no time he could speak English much faster than I could—not better, but faster.

I worried more about making mistakes, and I spoke carefully, making sure I could say everything right before opening my mouth. At least I had a better accent than my parents, who never really got rid of their Chinese accent, even years later. My parents had both studied English in school before coming to America, but what they had studied was mostly written English, not spoken.

Father's approach to English was a scientific one. Since Chinese verbs have no tense, he was fascinated by the way English verbs changed form according to whether they were in the present, past imperfect, perfect, pluperfect,[1] future, or future perfect tense. He was always making diagrams of verbs and their inflections,[2] and he looked for opportunities to show off his mastery of the pluperfect and future perfect tenses, his two favorites. "I shall have finished my project by Monday," he would say smugly.[3]

Mother's approach was to memorize lists of polite phrases that would cover all possible social situations. She was constantly muttering things like "I'm fine, thank you. And you?" Once she accidentally stepped on someone's foot, and hurriedly blurted, "Oh, that's quite all right!" Embarrassed by her slip, she resolved to do better next time. So when someone stepped on *her* foot, she cried, "You're welcome!"

Reading Strategy
Drawing Inferences
What can you infer about the narrator after reading this paragraph?

---

1. **pluperfect** (plo͞o′ pʉr′ fikt) *adj.* the past perfect tense of verbs in English.
2. **inflections** (in flek′ shən) *n.* the changes in the forms of words to show different tenses.
3. **smugly** (smug′ lē) *adv.* in a way that shows satisfaction with oneself.

In our own different ways, we made progress in learning English. But I had another worry, and that was my appearance. My brother didn't have to worry, since Mother bought him blue jeans for school, and he dressed like all the other boys. But she insisted that girls had to wear skirts. By the time she saw that Meg and the other girls were wearing jeans, it was too late. My school clothes were bought already, and we didn't have money left to buy new outfits for me. We had too many other things to buy first, like furniture, pots, and pans.

The first time I visited Meg's house, she took me upstairs to her room, and I wound up trying on her clothes. We were pretty much the same size, since Meg was shorter and thinner than average. Maybe that's how we became friends in the first place. Wearing Meg's jeans and T-shirt, I looked at myself in the mirror. I could almost pass for an American—from the back, anyway. At least the kids in school wouldn't stop and stare at me in my white blouse and navy blue skirt that went a couple of inches below the knees.

Literary Analysis
Theme What does the narrator's statement about almost passing for an American suggest that the theme might revolve around?

When Meg came to my house, I invited her to try on my Chinese dresses, the ones with a high collar and slits up the sides. Meg's eyes were bright as she looked at herself in the mirror. She struck several sultry poses, and we nearly fell over laughing.

The dinner party at the Gleasons' didn't stop my growing friendship with Meg. Things were getting better for me in other ways too. Mother finally bought me some jeans at the end of the month, when Father got his paycheck. She wasn't in any hurry about buying them at first, until I worked on her. This is what I did. Since we didn't have a car in those days, I often ran down to the neighborhood store to pick up things for her. The groceries cost less at a big supermarket, but the closest one was many blocks away. One day, when she ran out of flour, I offered to borrow a bike from our neighbor's son and buy a ten-pound bag of flour at the supermarket. I mounted the boy's bike and waved to Mother. "I'll be back in five minutes!"

Before I started pedaling, I heard her voice behind me. "You can't go out in public like that! People can see all the way up to your thighs!"

"I'm sorry," I said innocently. "I thought you were in a hurry to get the flour." For dinner we were going to have pot-stickers (fried Chinese dumplings), and we needed a lot of flour.

"Couldn't you borrow a girl's bicycle?" complained Mother. "That way your skirt won't be pushed up."

"There aren't too many of those around," I said. "Almost all the girls wear jeans while riding a bike, so they don't see any point buying a girl's bike."

☑**Reading Check**

What does the speaker think is wrong with her appearance?

We didn't eat pot-stickers that evening, and Mother was thoughtful. Next day we took the bus downtown and she bought me a pair of jeans. In the same week, my brother made the baseball team of his junior high school, Father started taking driving lessons, and Mother discovered rummage sales.

We soon got all the furniture we needed, plus a dart board and a 1,000-piece jigsaw puzzle (fourteen hours later, we discovered that it was a 999-piece jigsaw puzzle). There was hope that the Lins might become a normal American family after all.

Then came our dinner at the Lakeview restaurant.

The Lakeview was an expensive restaurant, one of those places where a headwaiter dressed in tails conducted you to your seat, and the only light came from candles and flaming desserts. In one corner of the room a lady harpist played tinkling melodies.

Father wanted to celebrate, because he had just been promoted. He worked for an electronics company, and after his English started improving, his superiors decided to appoint him to a position more suited to his training. The promotion not only brought a higher salary but was also a tremendous boost to his pride.

Up to then we had eaten only in Chinese restaurants. Although my brother and I were becoming fond of hamburgers, my parents didn't care much for western food, other than chow mein.[4] But this was a special occasion, and Father asked his coworkers to recommend a really elegant restaurant. So there we were at the Lakeview, stumbling after the headwaiter in the murky dining room.

At our table we were handed our menus, and they were so big that to read mine I almost had to stand up again. But why bother? It was mostly in French, anyway.

Father, being an engineer, was always systematic.[5] He took out a pocket French dictionary. "They told me that most of the items would be in French, so I came prepared." He even had a pocket flashlight, the size of a marking pen. While Mother held the flashlight over the menu, he looked up the items that were in French.

"*Pâté en croûte*," (pä tā´ än krōōt) he muttered. "Let's see . . . *pâté* is paste . . . *croûte* is crust . . . hmm . . . a paste in crust."

---

4. chow mein (chou´ mān´) *n.* thick stew of meat, celery, and Chinese vegetables.
5. systematic (sis´ tə mat´ ik) *adj.* orderly.

The waiter stood looking patient. I squirmed and died at least fifty times.

At long last Father gave up. "Why don't we just order four complete dinners at random?" he suggested.

"Isn't that risky?" asked Mother. "The French eat some rather peculiar things, I've heard."

"A Chinese can eat anything a Frenchman can eat," Father declared.

The soup arrived in a plate. How do you get soup up from a plate? I glanced at the other diners, but the ones at the nearby tables were not on their soup course, while the more distant ones were invisible in the darkness.

Fortunately my parents had studied books on western etiquette before they came to America. "Tilt your plate," whispered my mother. "It's easier to spoon the soup up that way."

She was right. Tilting the plate did the trick. But the etiquette book didn't say anything about what you did after the soup reached your lips. As any respectable Chinese knows, the correct way to eat your soup is to slurp. This helps to cool the liquid and prevent you from burning your lips. It also shows your appreciation.

We showed our appreciation. *Shloop*, went my father. *Shloop* went my mother. *Shloop, shloop*, went my brother, who was the hungriest.

The lady harpist stopped playing to take a rest. And in the silence, our family's consumption of soup suddenly seemed unnaturally loud. You know how it sounds on a rocky beach when the tide goes out and the water drains from all those little pools? They go *shloop, shloop, shloop*. That was the Lin family, eating soup.

At the next table a waiter was pouring wine. When a large *shloop* reached him, he froze. The bottle continued to pour, and red wine flooded the tabletop and into the lap of a customer. Even the customer didn't notice anything at first, being also hypnotized by the *shloop, shloop, shloop*.

It was too much. "I need to go to the toilet," I mumbled, jumping to my feet. A waiter, sensing my urgency, quickly directed me to the ladies' room.

I splashed cold water on my burning face, and as I dried myself with a paper towel, I stared into the mirror. In this perfumed ladies' room, with its pink-and-silver wallpaper and marbled sinks, I looked completely out of place. What was I doing here? What was our family doing in the Lakeview restaurant? In America?

etiquette (et′ i ket) *n.* acceptable social manners

consumption (kən sump′ shen) *n.* eating; drinking; using up

**Reading Check**

Why does the Lin family slurp their soup?

The door to the ladies' room opened. A woman came in and glanced curiously at me. I retreated into one of the toilet cubicles and latched the door.

Time passed—maybe half an hour, maybe an hour. Then I heard the door open again, and my mother's voice. "Are you in there? You're not sick, are you?"

There was real concern in her voice. A girl can't leave her family just because they slurp their soup. Besides, the toilet cubicle had a few drawbacks as a permanent residence. "I'm all right," I said, undoing the latch.

Mother didn't tell me how the rest of the dinner went, and I didn't want to know. In the weeks following, I managed to push the whole thing into the back of my mind, where it jumped out at me only a few times a day. Even now, I turn hot all over when I think of the Lakeview restaurant.

But by the time we had been in this country for three months, our family was definitely making progress toward becoming Americanized. I remember my parents' first PTA meeting. Father wore a neat suit and tie, and Mother put on her first pair of high heels. She stumbled only once. They met my homeroom teacher and beamed as she told them that I would make honor roll soon at the rate I was going. Of course Chinese etiquette forced Father to say that I was a very stupid girl and Mother to protest that the teacher was showing favoritism toward me. But I could tell they were both very proud.

The day came when my parents announced that they wanted to give a dinner party. We had invited Chinese friends to eat with us before, but this dinner was going to be different. In addition to a Chinese-American family, we were going to invite the Gleasons.

"Gee, I can hardly wait to have dinner at your house," Meg said to me. "I just *love* Chinese food."

That was a relief. Mother was a good cook, but I wasn't sure if people who ate sour cream would also eat chicken gizzards stewed in soy sauce.

Mother decided not to take a chance with chicken gizzards. Since we had western guests, she set the table with large dinner plates, which we never used in Chinese meals. In fact we didn't use individual plates at all, but picked up food from the platters in the middle of the table and brought it directly to our rice bowls. Following the practice of Chinese-American restaurants, Mother also placed large serving spoons on the platters.

Reading Strategy
Drawing Inferences
How does the narrator feel about her family's behavior?

The dinner started well. Mrs. Gleason exclaimed at the beautifully arranged dishes of food: the colorful candied fruit in the sweet-and-sour pork dish, the noodle-thin shreds of chicken meat stir-fried with tiny peas, and the glistening pink prawns in a ginger sauce.

At first I was too busy enjoying my food to notice how the guests were doing. But soon I remembered my duties. Sometimes guests were too polite to help themselves and you had to serve them with more food.

I glanced at Meg, to see if she needed more food, and my eyes nearly popped out at the sight of her plate. It was piled with food: the sweet-and-sour meat pushed right against the chicken shreds, and the chicken sauce ran into the prawns. She had been taking food from a second dish before she finished eating her helping from the first!

Horrified, I turned to look at Mrs. Gleason. She was dumping rice out of her bowl and putting it on her dinner plate. Then she ladled prawns and gravy on top of the rice and mixed everything together, the way you mix sand, gravel, and cement to make concrete.

I couldn't bear to look any longer, and I turned to Mr. Gleason. He was chasing a pea around his plate. Several times he got it to the edge, but when he tried to pick it up with his chopsticks, it rolled back toward the center of the plate again. Finally he put down his chopsticks and picked up the pea with his fingers. He really did! A grown man!

All of us, our family and the Chinese guests, stopped eating to watch the activities of the Gleasons. I wanted to giggle. Then I caught my mother's eyes on me. She frowned and shook her head slightly, and I understood the message: the Gleasons were not used to Chinese ways, and they were just coping the best they could. For some reason I thought of celery strings.

When the main courses were finished, Mother brought out a platter of fruit. "I hope you weren't expecting a sweet dessert," she said. "Since the Chinese don't eat dessert, I didn't think to prepare any."

"Oh, I couldn't possibly eat

Reading Strategy
Drawing Inferences What can you infer about the Lins' dinner customs based on the narrator's reaction to the Gleasons' actions?

Literary Analysis
Theme What lesson is the narrator learning about people's experiences?

✔**Reading Check**

What happens when the Gleasons come over to the Lins' for dinner?

dessert!" cried Mrs. Gleason. "I'm simply stuffed!"

Meg had different ideas. When the table was cleared, she announced that she and I were going for a walk. "I don't know about you, but I feel like dessert," she told me, when we were outside. "Come on, there's a Dairy Queen down the street. I could use a big chocolate milkshake!"

Although I didn't really want anything more to eat, I insisted on paying for the milkshakes. After all, I was still hostess.

Meg got her large chocolate milkshake and I had a small one. Even so, she was finishing hers while I was only half done. Toward the end she pulled hard on her straws and went *shloop, shloop.*

"Do you always slurp when you eat a milkshake?" I asked, before I could stop myself.

Meg grinned. "Sure. All Americans slurp."

Review and Assess

Thinking About the Selection

1. **Respond:** What advice would you give the narrator about adjusting to life in the United States? Why?

2. **(a) Recall:** Describe the way in which each family member learns English. **(b) Infer:** What does each person's way of learning English reveal about his or her personality?

3. **(a) Recall:** How does the narrator convince her mother to buy jeans? **(b) Infer:** Why are jeans so important to the narrator? **(c) Compare and Contrast:** How is the narrator's experience in adjusting to life in the U.S. different from her mother's experience?

4. **(a) Recall:** What do the Lins do with their soup at a restaurant? **(b) Interpret:** Why does the narrator run to the ladies' room?

5. **(a) Recall:** Name two things the Gleasons do at the Lins' dinner party that shock the narrator. **(b) Compare and Contrast:** In what way are the Gleasons' actions at the Lins' dinner party similar to the Lins' actions at the Gleasons' party?

6. **(a) Recall:** What does Meg say that all Americans do? **(b) Infer:** Why does Meg's comment seem funny and reassuring to the narrator? **(c) Evaluate:** Do you think the narrator has a good sense of humor about her family's difficulties in adjusting to life in the U.S.? Why?

Lensey Namioka

(b. 1929)

Lensey Namioka is a Chinese American who uses her Chinese heritage in her writing. Her novel *Who's Hu?*, the story of a Chinese girl learning the ways of Americans, is among her most popular works. The novel's heroine, Emma Hu, is a math whiz who has to battle prejudice against girls in math.

Namioka's main character in "The All-American Slurp" is based on Namioka herself. Like her character, she was born in China and moved with her family to the United States as a teenager. Also like her character, she discovered big differences between Chinese and American eating habits.

The Stone

Lloyd Alexander

Walk in the Country, Javran

▲ **Critical Viewing**
What impression of old age does the picture give? **[Support]**

✔ **Reading Check**

Who is Maibon?

There was a cottager named Maibon, and one day he was driving down the road in his horse and cart when he saw an old man hobbling along, so frail and feeble he doubted the poor soul could go many more steps. Though Maibon offered to take him in the cart, the old man refused; and Maibon went his way home, shaking his head over such a pitiful sight, and said to his wife, Modrona:

"Ah, ah, what a sorry thing it is to have your bones creaking and cracking, and dim eyes, and dull wits. When I think this might come to me, too! A fine, strong-armed, sturdy-legged fellow like me?

One day to go tottering, and have his teeth rattling in his head, and live on porridge, like a baby? There's no fate worse in all the world."

"There is," answered Modrona, "and that would be to have neither teeth nor porridge. Get on with you, Maibon, and stop borrowing trouble. Hoe your field or you'll have no crop to harvest, and no food for you, nor me, nor the little ones."

Sighing and grumbling, Maibon did as his wife bade him. Although the day was fair and cloudless, he took no pleasure in it. His ax-blade was notched, the wooden handle splintery; his saw had lost its edge; and his hoe, once shining new, had begun to rust. None of his tools, it seemed to him, cut or chopped or delved[1] as well as they once had done.

"They're as worn out as that old codger I saw on the road," Maibon said to himself. He squinted up at the sky. "Even the sun isn't as bright as it used to be, and doesn't warm me half as well. It's gone threadbare as my cloak. And no wonder, for it's been there longer than I can remember. Come to think of it, the moon's been looking a little wilted around the edges, too.

"As for me," went on Maibon, in dismay, "I'm in even a worse state. My appetite's faded, especially after meals. Mornings, when I wake, I can hardly keep myself from yawning. And at night, when I go to bed, my eyes are so heavy I can't hold them open. If that's the way things are now, the older I grow, the worse it will be!"

In the midst of his complaining, Maibon glimpsed something bouncing and tossing back and forth beside a fallen tree in a corner of the field. Wondering if one of his piglets had squeezed out of the sty and gone rooting for acorns, Maibon hurried across the turf. Then he dropped his ax and gaped in astonishment.

There, struggling to free his leg which had been caught under the log, lay a short, thickset figure: a dwarf with red hair bristling in all directions beneath his round, close-fitting leather cap. At the sight of Maibon, the dwarf squeezed shut his bright red eyes and began holding his breath. After a moment, the dwarf's face went redder than his hair; his cheeks puffed out and soon turned purple. Then he opened one eye and blinked rapidly at Maibon, who was staring at him, speechless.

"What," snapped the dwarf, "you can still see me?"

"That I can," replied Maibon, more than ever puzzled, "and I can see very well you've got yourself tight as a wedge under that log, and all your kicking only makes it worse."

At this, the dwarf blew out his breath and shook his fists. "I can't do it!" he shouted. "No matter how I try! I can't make myself invisible! Everyone in my family can disappear—Poof! Gone! Vanished! But not

Reading Strategy
Drawing Inferences What can you infer about Maibon's feelings about growing old? Explain.

---

1. **delved** (delvd) *v.* dug.

me! Not Doli! Believe me, if I could have done, you never would have found me in such a <u>plight</u>. Worse luck! Well, come on. Don't stand there goggling like an idiot. Help me get loose!"

plight (plīt) *n.* awkward, sad, or dangerous situation

At this sharp command, Maibon began tugging and heaving at the log. Then he stopped, wrinkled his brow, and scratched his head, saying:

"Well, now, just a moment, friend. The way you look, and all your talk about turning yourself invisible—I'm thinking you might be one of the Fair Folk."

"Oh, clever!" Doli retorted. "Oh, brilliant! Great clodhopper! Giant beanpole! Of course I am! What else! Enough gabbling. Get a move on. My leg's going to sleep."

"If a man does the Fair Folk a good turn," cried Maibon, his excitement growing, "it's told they must do one for him."

"I knew sooner or later you'd come round to that," grumbled the dwarf. "That's the way of it with you ham-handed, heavy-footed oafs. Time was, you humans got along well with us. But nowadays, you no sooner see a Fair Folk than it's grab, grab, grab! Gobble, gobble, gobble! Grant my wish! Give me this, give me that! As if we had nothing better to do!

"Yes, I'll give you a favor," Doli went on. "That's the rule, I'm obliged to. Now, get on with it."

Hearing this, Maibon pulled and pried and chopped away at the log as fast as he could, and soon freed the dwarf.

Doli heaved a sigh of relief, rubbed his shin, and cocked a red eye at Maibon, saying:

"All right. You've done your work, you'll have your reward. What do you want? Gold, I suppose. That's the usual. Jewels? Fine clothes? Take my advice, go for something practical. A hazelwood twig to help you find water if your well ever goes dry? An ax that never needs sharpening? A cook pot always brimming with food?"

"None of those!" cried Maibon. He bent down to the dwarf and whispered eagerly, "But I've heard tell that you Fair Folk have magic stones that can keep a man young forever. That's what I want. I claim one for my reward."

Doli snorted. "I might have known you'd pick something like that. As to be expected, you humans have it all muddled. There's nothing can make a man young again. That's even beyond the best of our skills. Those stones you're babbling about? Well, yes, there are such things. But greatly overrated. All they'll do is keep you from growing any older."

"Just as good!" Maibon exclaimed. "I want no more than that!"

Doli hesitated and frowned. "Ah—between the two of us, take the cook pot. Better all around. Those stones—we'd sooner not give them away. There's a difficulty—"

Literary Analysis
Theme What kind of lesson do stories about wishes usually teach?

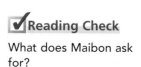

Reading Check

What does Maibon ask for?

"Because you'd rather keep them for yourselves," Maibon broke in. "No, no, you shan't cheat me of my due. Don't put me off with excuses. I told you what I want, and that's what I'll have. Come, hand it over and not another word."

Doli shrugged and opened a leather pouch that hung from his belt. He spilled a number of brightly colored pebbles into his palm, picked out one of the larger stones, and handed it to Maibon. The dwarf then jumped up, took to his heels, raced across the field, and disappeared into a thicket.

Laughing and crowing over his good fortune and his cleverness, Maibon hurried back to the cottage. There, he told his wife what had happened, and showed her the stone he had claimed from the Fair Folk.

"As I am now, so I'll always be!" Maibon declared, flexing his arms and thumping his chest. "A fine figure of a man! Oho, no gray beard and wrinkled brow for me!"

Instead of sharing her husband's <u>jubilation</u>, Modrona flung up her hands and burst out:

"Maibon, you're a greater fool than ever I supposed! And selfish into the bargain! You've turned down treasures! You didn't even ask that dwarf for so much as new jackets for the children! Nor a new apron for me! You could have had the roof mended. Or the walls plastered. No, a stone is what you ask for! A bit of rock no better than you'll dig up in the cow pasture!"

Crestfallen[2] and sheepish, Maibon began thinking his wife was right, and the dwarf had indeed given him no more than a common field stone.

"Eh, well, it's true," he stammered, "I feel no different than I did this morning, no better nor worse, but every way the same. That redheaded little wretch! He'll <u>rue</u> the day if I ever find him again!"

So saying, Maibon threw the stone into the fireplace. That night he grumbled his way to bed, dreaming revenge on the dishonest dwarf.

Next morning, after a restless night, he yawned, rubbed his eyes, and scratched his chin. Then he sat bolt upright in bed, patting his cheeks in amazement.

"My beard!" he cried, tumbling out and hurrying to tell his wife. "It hasn't grown! Not by a hair! Can it be the dwarf didn't cheat me after all?"

"Don't talk to me about beards," declared his wife as Maibon went to the fireplace, picked out the stone, and clutched it safely in both hands. "There's trouble enough in the chicken roost. Those eggs should have hatched by now, but the hen is still brooding on her nest."

jubilation (jo͞o′ bə lā′ shen) *n.* great joy; triumph

rue (ro͞o) *v.* regret

---

2. **crestfallen** (krest′ fôl′ ən) *adj.* made sad or humble; disheartened.

Harvesting the Fruit Crop, Javran

"Let the chickens worry about that," answered Maibon. "Wife, don't you see what a grand thing's happened to me? I'm not a minute older than I was yesterday. Bless that generous-hearted dwarf!"

"Let me lay hands on him and I'll bless him," retorted Modrona. "That's all well and good for you. But what of me? You'll stay as you are, but I'll turn old and gray, and worn and wrinkled, and go doddering into my grave! And what of our little ones? They'll grow up and have children of their own. And grandchildren, and great-grandchildren. And you, younger than any of them. What a foolish sight you'll be!"

But Maibon, gleeful over his good luck, paid his wife no heed, and only tucked the stone deeper into his pocket. Next day, however, the eggs had still not hatched.

"And the cow!" Modrona cried. "She's long past due to calve, and no sign of a young one ready to be born!"

▲ Critical Viewing
Find three details that suggest the people in the painting live a life similar to that of Maibon and his wife. [Support]

✔ Reading Check
What does Maibon realize when he wakes up in the morning?

The Stone ◆ 509

"Don't bother me with cows and chickens," replied Maibon. "They'll all come right, in time. As for time, I've got all the time in the world!"

Having no appetite for breakfast, Maibon went out into the field. Of all the seeds he had sown there, however, he was surprised to see not one had sprouted. The field, which by now should have been covered with green shoots, lay bare and empty.

"Eh, things do seem a little late these days," Maibon said to himself. "Well, no hurry. It's that much less for me to do. The wheat isn't growing, but neither are the weeds."

Some days went by and still the eggs had not hatched, the cow had not calved, the wheat had not sprouted. And now Maibon saw that his apple tree showed no sign of even the smallest, greenest fruit.

"Maibon, it's the fault of that stone!" wailed his wife. "Get rid of the thing!"

"Nonsense," replied Maibon "The season's slow, that's all."

Nevertheless, his wife kept at him and kept at him so much that Maibon at last, and very reluctantly, threw the stone out the cottage window. Not too far, though, for he had it in the back of his mind to go later and find it again.

Next morning he had no need to go looking for it, for there was the stone sitting on the window ledge.

"You see?" said Maibon to his wife. "Here it is back again. So, it's a gift meant for me to keep."

"Maibon!" cried his wife. "Will you get rid of it! We've had nothing but trouble since you brought it into the house. Now the baby's fretting and fuming. Teething, poor little thing. But not a tooth to be seen! Maibon, that stone's bad luck and I want no part of it!"

Protesting it was none of his doing that the stone had come back, Maibon carried it into the vegetable patch. He dug a hole, not a very deep one, and put the stone into it.

Next day, there was the stone above ground, winking and glittering.

"Maibon!" cried his wife. "Once and for all, if you care for your family, get rid of that cursed thing!"

Seeing no other way to keep peace in the household, Maibon regretfully and unwillingly took the stone and threw it down the well, where it splashed into the water and sank from sight.

But that night, while he was trying vainly to sleep, there came such a rattling and clattering that Maibon clapped his hands over his ears, jumped out of bed, and went stumbling into the yard. At the well, the bucket was jiggling back and forth and up and down at the end of the rope; and in the bottom of the bucket was the stone.

Reading Strategy
Drawing Inferences What inference can you make about the stone's effects based on these details?

Literary Analysis
Theme What clue to the story's message is provided by Maibon's inability to get rid of the stone?

Now Maibon began to be truly distressed, not only for the toothless baby, the calfless cow, the fruitless tree, and the hen sitting desperately on her eggs, but for himself as well.

"Nothing's moving along as it should," he groaned. "I can't tell one day from another. Nothing changes, there's nothing to look forward to, nothing to show for my work. Why sow if the seeds don't sprout? Why plant if there's never a harvest? Why eat if I don't get hungry? Why go to bed at night, or get up in the morning, or do anything at all? And the way it looks, so it will stay for ever and ever! I'll shrivel from boredom if nothing else!"

"Maibon," pleaded his wife, "for all our sakes, destroy the dreadful thing!"

Maibon tried now to pound the stone to dust with his heaviest mallet;◆ but he could not so much as knock a chip from it. He put it against his grindstone without so much as scratching it. He set it on his anvil and belabored it with hammer and tongs, all to no avail.

At last he decided to bury the stone again, this time deeper than before. Picking up his shovel, he hurried to the field. But he suddenly halted and the shovel dropped from his hands. There, sitting cross-legged on a stump, was the dwarf.

"You!" shouted Maibon, shaking his fist. "Cheat! Villain! Trickster! I did you a good turn, and see how you've repaid it!"

The dwarf blinked at the furious Maibon. "You mortals are an ungrateful crew. I gave you what you wanted."

"You should have warned me!" burst out Maibon.

"I did," Doli snapped back. "You wouldn't listen. No, you yapped and yammered, bound to have your way. I told you we didn't like to give away those stones. When you mortals get hold of one, you stay just as you are—but so does everything around you. Before you know it, you're mired in time like a rock in the mud. You take my advice. Get rid of that stone as fast as you can."

"What do you think I've been trying to do?" blurted Maibon. "I've buried it, thrown it down the well, pounded it with a hammer—it keeps coming back to me!"

"That's because you really didn't want to give it up," Doli said. "In the back of your mind and the bottom of your heart, you didn't want to change along with the rest of the world. So long as you feel that way, the stone is yours."

"No, no!" cried Maibon. "I want no more of it. Whatever may happen, let it happen. That's better than nothing happening at all.

Literature in context Vocabulary Connection

◆ **Mallet**

The word *mallet* comes from the Old French word *maillet*. A mallet is a kind of hammer that usually has a heavy wooden head and a short handle. Mallets are used for driving things, such as chisels to shape wood. In the days before electricity and power tools, a mallet would have had a lot of uses, especially in a rural life like Maibon's.

✔Reading Check

What is the stone doing to everything on Maibon's farm?

I've had my share of being young, I'll take my share of being old. And when I come to the end of my days, at least I can say I've lived each one of them."

"If you mean that," answered Doli, "toss the stone onto the ground, right there at the stump. Then get home and be about your business."

Maibon flung down the stone, spun around, and set off as fast as he could. When he dared at last to glance back over his shoulder, fearful the stone might be bouncing along at his heels, he saw no sign of it, nor of the redheaded dwarf.

Maibon gave a joyful cry, for at that same instant the <u>fallow</u> field was covered with green blades of wheat, the branches of the apple tree bent to the ground, so laden they were with fruit. He ran to the cottage, threw his arms around his wife and children, and told them the good news. The hen hatched her chicks, the cow bore her calf. And Maibon laughed with glee when he saw the first tooth in the baby's mouth.

Never again did Maibon meet any of the Fair Folk, and he was just as glad of it. He and his wife and children and grandchildren lived many years, and Maibon was proud of his white hair and long beard as he had been of his sturdy arms and legs.

"Stones are all right, in their way," said Maibon. "But the trouble with them is, they don't grow."

fallow (fal´ ō) *adj.* inactive; unproductive

Review and Assess

Thinking About the Selection
1. **Respond:** Would you have given up the stone? Explain.
2. **(a) Recall:** Describe how Maibon gets the stone.
   (b) Infer: Why does Maibon choose the stone over all the other gifts that Doli suggests?
3. **(a) Recall:** How does the stone cause problems for Maibon, his family, and his farm? **(b) Analyze:** Why does Maibon say he will "shrivel from boredom"? **(c) Compare and Contrast:** How does this remark suggest that Maibon's opinion of the stone is different from his initial opinion of it?
4. **(a) Recall:** What happens when Maibon tries to get rid of the stone? **(b) Interpret:** Why can't Maibon get rid of the stone? **(c) Analyze:** What new belief does Maibon have that finally allows him to get rid of the stone?
5. **(a) Infer:** How does Maibon feel when the stone is gone? **(b) Draw Conclusions:** How has the stone changed Maibon's feelings about growing old?

Lloyd Alexander

(b. 1924)

Lloyd Alexander has written stories and novels about an imaginary kingdom called Prydain. Alexander found in creating this kingdom that "a writer could know and love a fantasy world as much as his real one."

Perhaps the best-known Prydain novel is *The High King* (1968), winner of a Newbery medal. "The Stone" also takes place in Prydain, where fantastic happenings are a part of everyday life.

Review and Assess

Literary Analysis
Theme

1. Provide three specific actions in "The All-American Slurp" that reveal the story's **theme.** Use a graphic organizer like the one here to organize your thoughts.

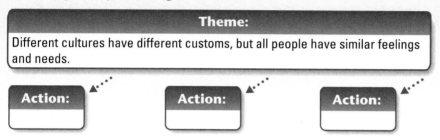

Theme:

Different cultures have different customs, but all people have similar feelings and needs.

Action:

Action:

Action:

2. What is the theme of "The Stone"?

Comparing Literary Works

3. Make a chart like the one here to show how the main characters of both stories change.

"The All-American Slurp"	"The Stone"
At the beginning, the narrator • • By the end, the narrator • •	At the beginning, Maibon • • By the end, Maibon • •

4. What does each story say about change?
5. **(a)** What themes do these stories share? **(b)** What themes are unique to each story?

Reading Strategy
Drawing Inferences

6. In "The All-American Slurp," what is one thing you can infer about the narrator from her way of getting jeans?
7. Based on Maibon's wish, what can you infer about how he feels about aging?

Extend Understanding

8. **Cultural Connection:** What agencies or services are available in your area to help recent immigrants?

Quick Review

A **theme** is the central message of a literary work and often is an insight about life. To review theme, see page 495.
A **stated theme** is expressed directly.
An **implied theme** is suggested, or stated indirectly.

Drawing inferences means reaching conclusions about something based on evidence and your own thoughts.

 Take It to the Net
www.phschool.com
Take the interactive self-test online to check your understanding of these selections.

Integrate Language Skills

Vocabulary Development Lesson

Word Analysis: Forms of *migrate*

Some forms of the word *migrate*, "to travel from one place to another," have to do with settling in a new land. For example, *emigrated* means "left one country to settle in another." Explain the meaning of each italicized word.

1. The Lins *emigrated* from China.
2. They *immigrated* to their new home, the United States.
3. Here, they were known as *immigrants*.

Spelling Strategy

In some words, the *k* sound is spelled *qu*, as in *plaque* and *etiquette*. On your paper, select the words that reflect this rule.

1. cost 2. racquet 3. ache 4. kin 5. physique

Concept Development: True or False

On your paper, answer each question **true** or **false.** Then, explain your answer.

1. People settle in the country from which they *emigrated*.
2. Different countries have different rules of *etiquette*.
3. Your food *consumption* affects your weight.
4. A *plight* is something you would enjoy.
5. Winning a prize inspires people with *jubilation*.
6. People *rue* great achievements.
7. A *fallow* field is ready to be harvested.

Grammar Lesson

Compound and Complex Sentences

A **compound sentence** is made of two or more independent clauses. The clauses are joined by a semicolon or by a comma and a coordinating conjunction, such as *and, but, for, or, yet,* or *so.*

Ind. Clause
Example: [Mother picked up one of the green
Ind. Clause
stalks], and [Father followed suit].

A **complex sentence** consists of one independent clause and one or more subordinate clauses.

Ind. Clause
Example: [That is the first dinner party] [that
Sub. Clause
she attends in the story].

▶ *For more practice, see page R29, Exercise F.*
Practice Write the following sentences. Underline independent clauses once and subordinate clauses twice. Label each sentence *compound* or *complex.*

1. The old man refused, so Maibon left.
2. Maibon saw that wheat grew.
3. We had a hard time with manners when we arrived in the U.S.
4. The table was covered, but we couldn't see chairs around it.
5. In China, we never ate celery; we never ate any kinds of raw vegetables.

Writing Application Write two compound and two complex sentences about American eating habits.

W͞G Prentice Hall Writing and Grammar Connection: Chapter 20, Section 2

Writing Lesson

Story Plot

One theme or message can be communicated by a variety of events. Write a plot proposal—a plan of story events—that illustrates the theme of one of these selections.

Prewriting   Write a statement of the theme. Then, identify the problem and the resolution that will show the message.

Model: Identify the Problem and the Resolution

Main Character	What Main Character Wants	Who or What Gets in the Way
Twyla	Wants to fit in at a new school	She has trouble meeting other students who share her interests.

Drafting   Tell the basic events and explain what the character learns.

Revising   If necessary, add a sentence or two that explains how events illustrate the theme.

Prentice Hall Writing and Grammar Connection: Chapter 5, Section 2

Extension Activities

Listening and Speaking Present an **oral response** to the theme of one of the stories.

1. Clearly state the story's theme.
2. Explain how you came to this conclusion.
3. Support your interpretation of the theme with details from the text.
4. Use examples from other literature and from your own experience to explain whether you agree or disagree with the message of the story.

Rehearse your presentation after you have prepared it. Make sure to organize your ideas logically and speak in a slow, clear manner.

Research and Technology "The Stone" concerns human aging. With a group, use technology resources to prepare a written and visual **report** on human growth. Prepare charts and diagrams that share exciting facts about these and other topics:

- how many cells are in a human body
- how often in a lifetime cells change
- what happens to skin as we age

When you finish, present your findings to your class. **[Group Activity]**

 **Take It to the Net**   www.phschool.com

Go online for an additional research activity using the Internet.

Book Reviews

About Book Reviews

If you want to learn more about a book before you decide whether to read it, you can find useful information in a *book review*. A book review is an article which gives you a brief summary of a book, tells you about its author, and sometimes presents a short excerpt. Reading the excerpt gives you a chance to see if you would enjoy the style and content of the book. If you like the excerpt and want to read more, you can locate the book in a bookstore or library.

Most book reviews include

- an opening paragraph introducing the book, including title and author.
- a brief summary of the book.
- a description of the background of the author or authors.
- an opinion about the quality of the book.
- an excerpt from the book.

Reading Strategy

Reading to Take Action

When you read to take action, you focus on finding specific information in order to help you do something. This is especially important if the activity is unfamiliar to you. To help guide your reading, begin by asking one or two questions. Then, look for answers as you read. For example, if you were planning a snorkeling trip, you might ask, "How can I protect the wildlife I encounter?" As you read to take action, take notes on the information that answers your question. Then organize the information in a graphic organizer like the one shown.

Read to Take Action

Questions	Facts That Answer Questions
1.	a. _____
	b. _____
	c. _____
2.	a. _____
	b. _____

Snorkeling Tips

Daniel Lenihan and John D. Brooks

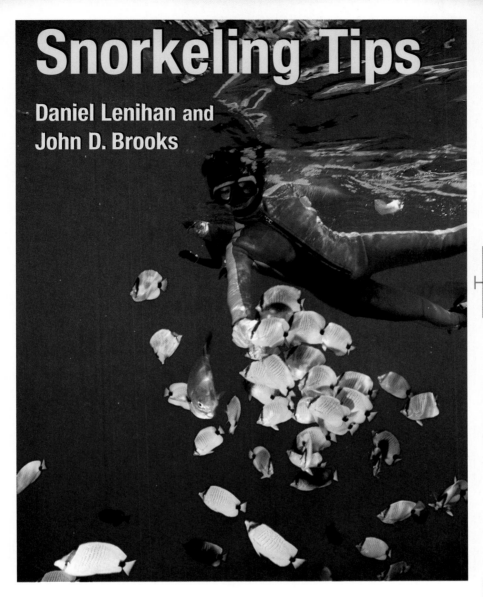

This picture makes snorkeling look like an interesting thing to do.

Underwater Wonders of the National Parks, published last year, is an indispensable resource for anyone considering a snorkeling trip. Written by Daniel Lenihan, director of the NPS Submerged Cultural Resource Unit, and John D. Brooks, an underwater photographer with the unit, the book details the watery wonders of the park system, from the coral reefs of the Caribbean to the icebergs in Alaska.

The two have gone snorkeling and scuba diving at every park mentioned in the book and include detailed suggestions on where to go, how to get there, and what you might find. They also have some sound advice for making your snorkeling excursion more enjoyable and helping to protect the fragile reef environment, including these tips:

This paragraph provides the title and authors of the book. It also includes a brief summary.

This paragraph discusses the authors' backgrounds.

- Do not touch the animals. Even a gentle caress can disturb the mucous coating that helps protect fish from disease.

- Do not feed the fish. If fed by humans, after a while they become dependent on handouts and lose the ability to forage. Also, they lose their natural wariness, which makes them easy prey for poachers. Even though harvesting fish for tropical collectors is illegal in the national parks, it still goes on.

- Do not touch the coral. The tiny jelly-like polyps that live inside the hard calcium casing are fragile. One swipe of the hand can kill hundreds of them. Many popular shallow reefs have been decimated by careless swimmers who stand on them when they get tired.

- Swim gently and avoid kicking up a lot of sand when near a reef. The sediment can eventually smother the coral and block vital sunlight.

- Wear a liberal coating of waterproof sunscreen on your back and the backs of your legs. The thin film of water over you acts as a magnifier, and because the water keeps your skin cool, you may not realize your skin is burning until it is too late. People who are especially sun-sensitive should wear a covering.

This excerpt from the book gives some tips for enjoying the reef.

- Keep an eye out for stinging organisms like jellyfish and fire coral.

- Do not reach into holes or crevices in the reef. They could turn out to be the lair of a moray eel.

- Take off your jewelry. While barracuda attacks are almost unheard of, the toothy fish are attracted to shiny objects.

- Shark spottings are rare on the shallow reefs that snorkelers frequent, but if you see a shark, do not panic. Most reef sharks are passive types, not man-eaters, and they usually ignore swimmers. If one acts aggressively or pays undue attention to you, calmly and slowly leave the water.

- Do not walk in shallow water near the reef; sea urchin spines can cause nasty puncture wounds to the bottom of your feet.

- Shuffle your feet across the bottom as you wade through the shallow sandy areas on your way to and from the reef. Stingrays lying on the bottom will swim off if you bump into them, but sometimes sting when they are stepped on.

- Be aware of currents. Unless you plan to do a "drift dive" where you start in one spot and let the current carry you to an exit point, it's usually best to swim into the current first and then let it carry you back at the end of your dive when you are most tired.

Check Your Comprehension

1. Why are the authors of this book well qualified to write about snorkeling?
2. Who might find this book useful?
3. What type of information could a reader find in this book?
4. Why do the authors advise snorkelers not to touch the coral?
5. Why should you shuffle your feet when you are walking in shallow water?

Applying the Reading Strategy

Reading to Take Action

6. How can you protect the wildlife you encounter when snorkeling?
7. What can you do to protect your skin?
8. What measures can you take to avoid a dangerous encounter with a jellyfish, moray eel, or barracuda?
9. Why should you avoid walking in shallow water near the reef without anything protecting your feet?
10. What steps can you take to avoid being carried off by ocean currents?

Activity

Write a Book Review

Select a book you have read and enjoyed. Write a book review to persuade others to read the book. Introduce the book and identify the intended audience. Include an excerpt that is interesting.

To learn more about writing about literature, see the Writing Workshop: Response to Literature on page 694.

Comparing Informational Texts

Positive and Negative Book Reviews

Look in newspapers, magazines, or online to find two book reviews by different people on the same book. The book reviews should express different opinions of the book. Read the reviews and fill out a chart like the one shown. Then, answer the questions.

Comparing Book Reviews	Book Review 1	Book Review 2
Title		
Author		
Summary		
Opinion		
Excerpt		

1. (a) Which book review is more complete?
   (b) What information is missing from the less complete review?
2. (a) Which book review is more effective? Why?
   (b) Do you want to read the book? Why or why not?

Writing WORKSHOP

Narration: Short Story

A **short story** is a brief, fictional account of an event or series of events with a beginning, middle, and end. In this workshop, you will write a short story.

Assignment Criteria. Your short story should have the following characteristics:

- One or more well-drawn **characters**
- An interesting **conflict** or problem
- A **plot**, or series of events that move toward the resolution of the conflict
- A consistent **point of view**, or perspective
- Sensory details and concrete language that establish the **setting**, the time and place
- **Dialogue**; conversations between characters

See the Rubric on page 523 for criteria on which your short story may be assessed.

Prewriting

Choose a topic. Set a timer and freewrite for five minutes. Start with an image—a bus, a snowshoe, a bank robber—or an idea—*jealousy* or *a lie*. During freewriting, focus more on the flow of ideas than on spelling, grammar, or punctuation. After five minutes, go back and circle ideas to use in your story.

Identify conflict. Establish **conflict**—a struggle between opposing forces. To identify the conflict, ask yourself these questions.

- What does your main character want?
- Who or what is getting in the way?
- What will the main character do to overcome the person or thing getting in the way?

Consider your purpose. Some short story writers want to make readers laugh. Others want to give their readers goosebumps. Still others want to deliver an important message about life. Decide your purpose for writing a short story.

Student Model

Before you begin drafting your short story, read this portion of the student model and review the characteristics of a successful short story. To read the full short story, visit www.phschool.com.

Jocelyn Meyer
St. Leon, IN

Pharaoh's Peak

Terri looked around as she knocked on the door of her best friend Sara's house. Sara's mom opened the door.

"Well, hello, Terri," Mrs. Duncan said.

"Hello, Mrs. Duncan. Is Sara ready yet?" Terri asked.

"She will be down in a minute. So where are you two going riding today?" Mrs. Duncan asked.

"Maybe up to Pharaoh's Peak."

"Oh, well, be careful. Make sure you both wear your riding helmets."

*   *   *

It was a beautiful summer day. The sun was hot on the dusty trail, but the temperature cooled off suddenly as the girls turned the horses onto the trail that entered the cool darkness of the pine woods. The girls were about to the top of the hill when both horses stopped. As Terri tried to nudge Cajun along, Sara asked, "Terri, what's wrong?"

"I don't know. Maybe they heard some . . ." Before she could finish, there was a movement in the bushes and a mountain lion stepped out.

"Terri," Sara said in a whisper, "what should we do?"

"I don't know," Terri replied. "Just don't move and scare the horses more."

But it was too late. . . . She hit the ground with a thud as O.T. galloped off down the trail.

"Sara, Sara! Are you all right?" Terri cried.

There was no reply. Through tears, Terri turned Cajun and charged the mountain lion. The suddenness of this attack sent the mountain lion running into the bushes. Terri looked around. Sara was still breathing, but she was not moving. . . .

*   *   *

Three days later, Terri walked into a hospital room. . . .

"Sara, are you awake?" she whispered into the darkness.

"Terri, is that you?" said a faint voice. . . .

Jocelyn introduces her main characters in the first sentence.

Sensory details describe the setting.

The writer introduces a problem.

The plot moves forward toward the climax.

The writer includes an exciting climax.

Drafting

Develop a plot. Organize the plot—the arrangement of events in sequence in a short story. Plot often follows this pattern:

- **Exposition** introduces characters and their situation, including the central conflict.
- The **conflict** develops during the **rising action,** which leads to the climax of the story
- The **climax,** or point of greatest tension, is when the story turns out one way or another.
- In the **falling action,** events and emotions wind down.
- In the **resolution,** the conflict is resolved and loose ends are tied up.

Build suspense. Writers build suspense by creating uncertainty about future events and developing tension about how a problem will be resolved. On your plot diagram, make notes about how you can raise questions that build suspense into the story's rising action.

Establish setting with sensory details. Use each of the five senses (taste, touch, smell, sight, and hearing) to describe details of the setting. For example, instead of just saying "It's a cold day," use sensory images to show your reader how cold it is.

Write from a specific point of view. Tell your story from a single point of view, either as a participant or an observer.

> **First-person point of view**: participant
>
> **Example:** I stood by the door, wondering how long I should wait.

> **Third-person point of view**: observer
>
> **Example:** Matt stood by the door checking his watch and looking uncertain.

Revising

Revise to add dialogue. You can bring your story to life by using dialogue. Review your draft for places to add characters speaking to each other.

> We were near the top of the hill when both horses
>
> *"What do you think they see?" I asked. "Who knows. . ." said Sarah.*
>
> stopped. ∧ Then we saw a movement in the trees.

Revise to strengthen setting. You can make your story more realistic by adding sensory details to the description of the setting.

Compare the model and nonmodel. Why is the model more interesting than the nonmodel?

Nonmodel	Model
It was a beautiful summer day. The girls rode up the trail then took the turnoff into the woods. They were about to the top of the hill when both horses stopped.	It was a beautiful summer day. The sun was hot on the dusty trail, but the temperature cooled off suddenly as the girls turned the horses onto the trail that entered the cool darkness of the pine woods. The girls were about to the top of the hill when both horses stopped.

Publishing and Presenting

Choose one of these ways to share your writing with classmates or a larger audience.

Storytelling. Perform your story as a live reading. Use gestures and tone of voice to give it pizzazz. If possible, tape record or videotape your storytelling.

Submit your story to a magazine. Send your story to a school or local literary magazine that publishes student writing.

 Prentice Hall Writing and Grammar Connection: Chapter 5

 **Speaking Connection**

For instruction about narrative presentations, see the **Listening and Speaking Workshop,** p. 94.

Rubric for Self-Assessment

Evaluate your short story using the following criteria and rating scale:

Criteria	Rating Scale Not very				Very
How well drawn are the characters?	1	2	3	4	5
Is the conflict interesting?	1	2	3	4	5
How well does the plot move toward resolving the conflict?	1	2	3	4	5
How consistent is the point of view?	1	2	3	4	5
How effectively are sensory details used to describe setting?	1	2	3	4	5
How often is dialogue used?	1	2	3	4	5

Listening and Speaking WORKSHOP

Identifying Tone, Mood, and Emotion

Understanding oral communication involves more than just listening to the speaker's words. It means being able to identify the tone, mood, and emotion.

- **Tone:** the speaker's attitude toward the subject and the listeners

- **Mood:** the overall feeling of the presentation

- **Emotion:** the speaker's feelings

Using Verbal Clues

The way a person speaks is closely connected with the words he or she chooses. Verbal clues are the spoken indications of tone, mood, and emotion.

Listen to tone of voice. In an oral presentation, a speaker conveys his or her attitude through tone of voice as well as through words. A serious speaker might speak slowly and deliberately in a quiet voice. A speaker who is enthusiastically trying to persuade you might use a high-pitched voice and talk faster than in normal speech.

Consider content. The mood of a presentation is often a result of *what* is said in addition to *how* it is said. The feeling the audience gets from a presentation will be influenced by the subject.

Notice word choice. The specific words a speaker uses can indicate attitude and emotion. The intensity of a word is a clue to the speaker's emotion. The connotations, or associations, of a word can indicate attitude.

Using Nonverbal Clues

Motion. A speaker who moves with energy and purpose has a positive attitude toward his or her subject and listeners. Watch how a speaker stands, gestures, and leans to get a sense of the feelings they have and the feelings they want listeners to have.

Expression. Facial expressions are a clear clue to emotions. Smiles, frowns, and thoughtful looks are meant to communicate feelings. Watch expressions to connect the speaker's feelings with the words being spoken.

Activity: Speech Watching
Watch a news interview program in which one or two people speak for at least five minutes. Keep a chart like the one shown here to record verbal and nonverbal clues to the speakers' tone, mood, and emotion.

	Verbal	Nonverbal
Tone		
Mood		
Emotion		

Assessment WORKSHOP

Describing Plot, Setting, Character, and Mood

The reading sections of some tests require you to read a passage and answer multiple-choice questions about such literary elements as plot, setting, character, and mood. Use the following strategies to help you answer such questions:

- When you are asked about plot, choose the answer that most accurately tells what happens.
- You may have to infer the time and place based on information in the story.
- You may have to draw inferences about character based on words and actions.
- You can identify the mood based on your feelings and descriptive details.

Test-Taking Strategies

- Read the questions first to focus your attention on the most important elements of the passage.
- Before answering, scan the passage (run your eyes quickly over the text to find specific details) to find the correct answer.

Sample Test Item

Use the strategies you have learned to answer the question on the passage.

With a deep sigh, Dulcie drifted toward the window. In the fading light, she could barely see the figure riding up the path. As soon as he sprang from his horse and strode to the front door, Dulcie knew it was Lance. Quickly, she thrust the letter she had been reading into her dress pocket. The door to the drawing room swung open.

"What have you done with our son?" Lance bellowed, his face distorted with rage.

"He is in a safe place," Dulcie replied, and with a sudden movement, she yanked at the bell cord to summon the servant.

1. Before Lance arrived, Dulcie had been—

   A waiting for him

   B saying good-bye to their son

   C reading a letter

   D staring out the window

Answer and Explanation

The text supports choice **C.** The text does not say that Dulcie was doing **A, B,** or **D.**

▶ Practice

Use the strategies you have learned to answer these questions on the passage.

1. Dulcie and Lance are in conflict over—

   A their home

   B their son

   C the servant

   D money

2. The story takes place in—

   A a foreign country

   B the United States

   C the past

   D the present

3. Lance can be described as—

   A angry

   B unhappy

   C supportive

   D distant

4. At the beginning of the passage, the mood is—

   A eerie

   B energetic

   C quiet

   D romantic

UNIT 7 Nonfiction

Desk Set, 1972, Wayne Thiebaud, Courtesy of the artist

Exploring the Genre

You will discover in this unit that nonfiction tells true stories that are as interesting and unique as any you will find in fiction. Nonfiction is about real people and real events. In this unit, you will read the following types of nonfiction:

- **Letters and journals** contain personal thoughts and reflections.

- **Biographies and autobiographies** are life stories. A biography is the life story of someone written by someone else. An autobiography is a writer's own life story.

- **Media accounts** are nonfiction works written for newspapers, magazines, television, or radio.

- **Essays** are short nonfiction works about a particular subject. Types of essays include historical essays, persuasive essays, informational essays, narrative essays, and visual essays.

As you read the nonfiction works in this unit, you will learn the characteristics of this genre, meet a variety of authors and styles, and learn facts and other information on a variety of subjects.

◀ **Critical Viewing** What details of this picture suggest factual details and accuracy? [Analyze]

Why Read Literature?

This unit presents a variety of material called nonfiction. Your purpose for reading each selection may be different, depending on the type of nonfiction and the content. You might want to read for information, read to be entertained, or read for the love of literature. Preview the three purposes you might set before reading the works in this unit.

1

Read for the love of literature.

Francis Scott Key Fitzgerald began writing at an early age. One of his teachers at St. Paul Academy encouraged him to write because he "did not shine in his other subjects." During his life, he was not highly regarded by critics, but since his death, he is considered one of this country's most important writers. Enjoy Fitzgerald's letter to his daughter in **"Letter to Scottie,"** page 542.

2

Read to be entertained.

As a Mexican American from a working-class family, Gary Soto understands and connects with the emotions and experiences of Latino teenagers. His poetry and stories depict the world of young people learning, growing, and changing with humor and sensitivity, for which his works are admired. Read Soto's **"The Drive-In Movies,"** page 558, to get a glimpse of life during the 1950s.

3

Read for information.

Textbooks provide in-depth material on many topics. In "Populations," a section from a science textbook on page 592, you will read about environmental issues and how they affect humans and animals in different parts of the globe.

Patricia and Frederick McKissack have written many books individually and together and won many awards for their children's books. Frederick McKissack was a general contractor but found writing more satisfying because he met wonderful children. The McKissacks' books cover a range of topics, including a **"Great African Americans"** series. Read **"The Shutout"** for information about the origins of baseball.

 Take It to the Net

Visit the Web site for online instruction and activities related to each selection in this unit.

www.phschool.com

How to Read Literature

Strategies for Reading Nonfiction

Nonfiction writing, such as biographies and encyclopedia articles, gives you facts and explanations concerning real people, places, and events. When you read nonfiction, choose the facts you need and judge the connections between them. The following strategies, which you will learn in this unit, will help you read nonfiction.

1. Understand the author's purpose.

A nonfiction writer gives facts about a subject. What the writer does with the facts depends on his or her purpose. For example, a writer may present facts to provide information, to entertain you, or perhaps to persuade you of a particular viewpoint. In this unit, you will learn to recognize an author's purpose and how it is presented.

> "It is papa I am writing about, and I shall have no trouble in not knowing what to say about him, as he is a *very* striking character."

The author's purpose is to inform.

2. Use context to determine meaning.

In nonfiction works, the author often includes vocabulary that is specialized, or specific to the topic of the work, and therefore unfamiliar to readers. Context—the situation in which the word is used—can help you get an idea of the word's meaning.

3. Clarify the author's meaning.

Sometimes, you need to clarify, or make clear to yourself, what the author's statements mean. Read the following statements from Amanda Borden's "Olympic Diary."

"I look back now and the injuries seem so small. When I had to deal with them, I felt like I was holding the world. After I competed, I felt I was on top of it."

She follows with examples of situations that will help you clarify what she means.

4. Identify the author's evidence.

The author should give evidence—facts or arguments—supporting the statements he or she makes. In this unit, you will practice identifying and evaluating evidence.

As you read the selections in this unit, review the reading strategies and look at the notes in the side columns. Use the suggestions to help you apply strategies for reading nonfiction.

Identify the Author's Evidence

Statement: Baseball was invented before 1839.
Evidence: A diary reports George Washington's troops batting balls.

Prepare to Read

The Shutout

Take It to the Net

Visit www.phschool.com
for interactive activities
and instruction related to
"The Shutout," including

- background
- graphic organizers
- literary elements
- reading strategies

Preview

Connecting to the Literature

You have probably used the expression "That's not fair!" when you feel you are being unjustly punished or made to follow a rule with which you do not agree. In "The Shutout," authors Patricia C. and Frederick McKissack describe an unfair situation that African American ballplayers faced in the early days of major league baseball.

Background

In the earliest days of baseball, African Americans played alongside white players. Eventually, however, baseball was segregated, or separated, into teams of "blacks" and teams of "whites." As this essay shows, though, segregation could not shut out African Americans from playing the game and creating baseball legends as amazing as those of their white counterparts.

Literary Analysis

Historical Essay

An essay is a short nonfiction work about a particular subject. A **historical essay** gives facts, explanations, and interpretations of historical events. For example, in "The Shutout," the authors provide facts about a variety of stick-and-ball games from different cultures. They interpret these facts by stating:

> Although baseball is a uniquely American sport, it was not invented by a single person.

As you read "The Shutout," use a graphic organizer like the one shown to take notes on the facts, explanations, and interpretations you find in the essay.

Connecting Literary Elements

The **author's purpose** is his or her reason for writing. In a historical essay, the author's general purpose is to give information about events from history. The author's more specific purpose is often to show the significance or effects of the events. To achieve this purpose, an author may draw conclusions. Read critically to determine whether facts in the essay support the conclusions. Begin with the following focus questions.

1. What conclusion does the author draw about the origins of baseball?
2. Which facts in the essay support this conclusion?

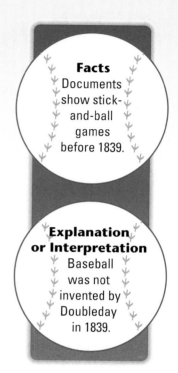

Facts
Documents show stick-and-ball games before 1839.

Explanation or Interpretation
Baseball was not invented by Doubleday in 1839.

Reading Strategy

Clarifying the Author's Meaning

Often a nonfiction writer will state a conclusion or offer an opinion or interpretation. This general statement will be followed by details, examples, and explanations that will help you **clarify the author's meaning,** that is, make the author's meaning clear. As you read "The Shutout," notice general statements made by the authors. Then, look for details that explain, elaborate on, or support these statements.

Vocabulary Development

anecdotes (an´ ik dōts´) *n.* short, entertaining tales (p. 532)

evolved (ē vôlvd´) *v.* grew gradually; developed (p. 533)

diverse (də vʉrs´) *adj.* various; with differing characteristics (p. 533)

composed (kəm pōzd´) *adj.* made up (of) (p. 535)

irrational (ir rash´ ə nəl) *adj.* unreasonable; not making sense (p. 535)

The Shutout

Patricia C. McKissack and Frederick McKissack, Jr.

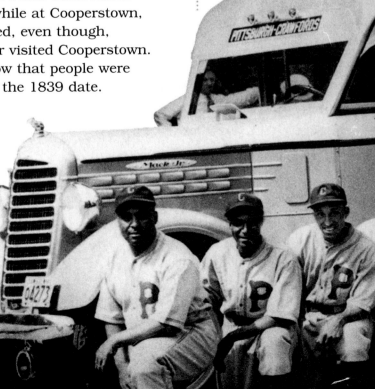

The history of baseball is difficult to trace because it is embroidered with wonderful <u>anecdotes</u> that are fun but not necessarily supported by fact. There are a lot of myths that persist about baseball—the games, the players, the owners, and the fans—in spite of contemporary research that disproves most of them. For example, the story that West Point cadet Abner Doubleday "invented" baseball in 1839 while at Cooperstown, New York, continues to be widely accepted, even though, according to his diaries, Doubleday never visited Cooperstown. A number of records and documents show that people were playing stick-and-ball games long before the 1839 date.

Albigence Waldo, a surgeon with George Washington's troops at Valley Forge, wrote in his diary that soldiers were "batting balls and running bases" in their free time. Samuel Hopkins Adams (1871–1958), an American historical novelist, stated that his grandfather "played baseball on Mr. Mumford's pasture" in the 1820's.

anecdotes (an´ ik dōts´) *n.* short, entertaining tales

Although baseball is a uniquely American sport, it was not invented by a single person. Probably the game <u>evolved</u> from a variety of stick-and-ball games that were played in Europe, Asia, Africa, and the Americas for centuries and brought to the colonies by the most <u>diverse</u> group of people ever to populate a continent. More specifically, some historians believe baseball is an outgrowth of its first cousin, *rounders*, an English game. Robin Carver wrote in his *Book of Sports* (1834) that "an American version of rounders called *goal ball* was rivaling cricket in popularity."

It is generally accepted that by 1845, baseball, as it is recognized today, was becoming popular, especially in New York. In that year a group of baseball enthusiasts organized the New York Knickerbocker Club. They tried to standardize the game by establishing guidelines for "proper play."

The Knickerbockers' rules set the playing field—a diamond-shaped infield with four bases (first, second, third, and home) placed ninety feet apart. At that time, the pitching distance was forty-five feet from home base and the "pitch" was thrown underhanded. The three-strikes-out rule, the three-out inning, and the ways in which a player could be called out were also specified. However, the nine-man team and nine-inning game were not established until later. Over the years, the Knickerbockers' basic rules of play haven't changed much.

evolved (ē vôlvd´) *v.* grew gradually; developed

diverse (də vʉrs´) *adj.* various; with differing characteristics

✔ Reading Check

Why is the history of baseball difficult to trace?

In 1857–1858, the newly organized National Association of Base Ball Players was formed, and baseball became a business. Twenty-five clubs—mostly from eastern states—formed the Association for the purpose of setting rules and guidelines for club and team competition. The Association defined a professional player as a person who "played for money, place or emolument (profit)." The Association also authorized an admission fee for one of the first "all-star" games between Brooklyn and New York. Fifteen hundred people paid fifty cents to see that game. Baseball was on its way to becoming the nation's number-one sport.

By 1860, the same year South Carolina seceded from the Union, there were about sixty teams in the Association. For obvious reasons none of them were from the South. Baseball's development was slow during the Civil War years, but teams continued to compete, and military records show that, sometimes between battles, Union solders chose up teams and played baseball games. It was during this time that records began mentioning African-American players. One war journalist noted that black players were "sought after as teammates because of their skill as ball handlers."

Information about the role of African Americans in the early stages of baseball development is slight. Several West African cultures had stick-and-ball and running games, so at least some blacks were familiar with the concept of baseball. Baseball, however, was not a popular southern sport, never equal to boxing, wrestling, footracing, or horse racing among the privileged landowners.

Slave owners preferred these individual sports because they could enter their slaves in competitions, watch the event from a safe distance, pocket the winnings, and personally never raise a sweat. There are documents to show that slave masters made a great deal of money from the athletic skills of their slaves.

Free blacks, on the other hand, played on and against integrated[1] teams in large eastern cities and in small midwestern hamlets. It is believed that some of the emancipated[2] slaves and runaways who served in the Union Army learned how to play baseball from northern blacks and whites who had been playing together for years.

After the Civil War, returning soldiers helped to inspire a new interest in baseball all over the country. Teams sprung up in northern and midwestern cities, and naturally African Americans

---

1. **integrated** (in´ tə grā tid) *adj.* open to both African Americans and whites.
2. **emancipated** (ē man´ sə pā´ tid) *adj.* freed from slavery.

Literary Analysis
Historical Essay
What are two facts in this paragraph that can be proven true?

Reading Strategy
Clarify the Author's Meaning What details clarify the meaning of the statement that slave owners preferred individual sports?

Union Prisoners at Salisbury, N.C., National Baseball Library and Archive, Cooperstown, NY

were interested in joining some of these clubs. But the National Association of Base Ball Players had other ideas. They voted in December 1867 not to admit any team for membership that "may be <u>composed</u> of one or more colored persons." Their reasoning was as <u>irrational</u> as the racism that shaped it: "If colored clubs were admitted," the Association stated, "there would be in all probability some division of feeling whereas, by excluding them no injury could result to anyone . . . and [we wish] to keep out of the convention the discussion of any subjects having a political bearing as this [admission of blacks on the Association teams] undoubtedly would."

So, from the start, organized baseball tried to limit or exclude African-American participation. In the early days a few black ball players managed to play on integrated minor league teams. A few even made it to the majors, but by the turn of the century, black players were shut out of the major leagues until after World War II. That doesn't mean African Americans didn't play the game. They did.

composed (kəm pōzd´) v. made up (of)

irrational (ir rash´ ə nəl) *adj.* unreasonable; not making sense

✔**Reading Check**

What was the National Association of Baseball Players rule about African American players?

Black people organized their own teams, formed leagues, and competed for championships. The history of the old "Negro Leagues" and the players who barnstormed[3] on black diamonds is one of baseball's most interesting chapters, but the story is a researcher's nightmare. Black baseball was outside the mainstream of the major leagues, so team and player records weren't well kept, and for the most part, the white press ignored black clubs or portrayed them as clowns. And for a long time the Baseball Hall of Fame didn't recognize any of the Negro League players. Because of the lack of documentation, many people thought the Negro Leagues' stories were nothing more than myths and yarns, but that is not the case. The history of the Negro Leagues is a patchwork of human drama and comedy, filled with legendary heroes, infamous owners, triple-headers, low pay, and long bus rides home—not unlike the majors.

---

3. **barnstormed** v. went from one small town to another, putting on an exhibition.

Review and Assess
Thinking About the Selection

1. **Respond:** How might you have felt as an African American baseball player who was denied the chance to play in the major leagues?
2. **(a) Recall:** When did baseball probably begin? **(b) Connect:** From what English game did baseball probably grow?
3. **(a) Recall:** When did baseball become popular, and who created the playing rules? **(b) Analyze:** Give specific examples of the changes that occurred following the creation of baseball as a professional sport. **(c) Generalize:** What is one reason that rules and regulations were created as baseball moved from an informal game to a professional sport?
4. **(a) Identify Cause and Effect:** What effect did the Civil War have on baseball? **(b) Infer:** In what way did the end of the Civil War help the growth of baseball?
5. **(a) Recall:** What were the team owners' reasons for not letting African Americans play? **(b) Identify Cause and Effect:** What effect did this exclusion have on the history of baseball? **(c) Connect:** What attitudes and conditions contributed to this exclusion?
6. **(a) Make a Judgment:** Do you think that sports today are segregated in any way? **(b) Take a Position:** Do you think there are any sports from which girls and women should be excluded? Why or why not?

**Patricia C. McKissack
Frederick McKissack, Jr.**

Patricia McKissack (b. 1944) and Frederick McKissack (b. 1939) are husband and wife. Both were born in Nashville, Tennessee, and they have been writing books since 1984. Their works, including *Christmas in the Big House*, *Christmas in the Quarters*, honor the struggles of African Americans. The McKissacks try to "build bridges with books." By showing young readers the sometimes "forgotten" parts of history, they hope to encourage understanding between different groups. As a team and individually, the McKissacks have written more than 100 books.

Review and Assess

Literary Analysis

Historical Essay

1. Explain why researchers are not completely sure about the origins of baseball.
2. One insight the authors offer is that the Negro leagues were filled with "drama and comedy." What historical evidence is provided to support this insight?

Connecting Literary Elements

3. Make an organizer like the one below to record facts and conclusions about the conditions faced by African American ball players.

Facts	Conclusions

4. Do the facts provide adequate evidence for the authors' conclusions?

Reading Strategy

Clarifying the Author's Meaning

5. In your own words, explain the meaning of the statement "The history of baseball is difficult to trace because it is embroidered with wonderful anecdotes that are fun, but not necessarily supported by fact."
6. What details are grouped together to communicate this meaning?
7. On an organizer like the one below, list details from the selection that help you clarify the meaning of the statement given. In the last box, explain the meaning.

Statement	Details used to clarify	Meaning
From the start, organized baseball tried to limit or exclude African American participation		

Extending Understanding

8. **Take a Position:** Do you think that baseball is truly "the great American pastime"? Explain.

Quick Review

Nonfiction explains ideas or tells about real people, places, or events. A **historical essay** is nonfiction that gives facts, explanations, and interpretations of historical events. To review nonfiction and historical essays, see p. 531.

When you **clarify the author's meaning**, you look for details that make clear the writer's point. To review clarifying the author's meaning, see p. 531.

 Take It to the Net
www.phschool.com
Take the interactive self-test online to check your understanding of the selection.

Integrate Language Skills

Vocabulary Development Lesson

Word Analysis: Latin Prefix *ir-*

The Latin prefix *ir-*, as in the word *irrational*, turns a word meaning into its opposite. Define each italicized word:

1. You broke an *irreplaceable* vase!
2. I find chocolate *irresistible*.
3. The lost money is *irrecoverable*.

Spelling Strategy

The prefix *ir-* is used only with words that begin with *r*. When adding the prefix *ir-*, keep both *r*'s. For example: *ir- + rational = irrational.*

Write the word for each numbered definition. Underline the base word before *ir-* is added. Then, use each word in a complete sentence.

1. not regular
2. not relevant
3. not responsible

Concept Development: Definitions

For each numbered item below, match the word with its meaning.

1. anecdote   a. unreasonable
2. evolved   b. varied
3. irrational   c. grew gradually
4. diverse   d. tale
5. composed   e. made up

Use each vocabulary word in a sentence that restates its meaning.

Examples: The anecdote she told was an amusing tale of camping.

The diverse species of the rain forest are more varied than most ecosystems.

Grammar Lesson

Compound and Complex Sentences

A **compound sentence** consists of two or more independent clauses. In most cases, the independent clauses are joined by a comma and a coordinating conjunction such as *and, but, for, nor, or, so,* or *yet.*

> ——— IND ———   ——— IND ———
> I wanted to go to the game, but I had the flu.

A **complex sentence** consists of one independent clause—called the main clause—and one or more subordinate clauses. The subordinate clause can appear at the beginning or end of the sentence.

> —— IND ——   —— SUB ——
> They left when the game ended.

> —— SUB ——   —— IND ——
> When the game ended, they left.

Practice Copy the sentences below. Label each sentence as compound or complex.

1. Bring your glove to the picnic because we might play ball.
2. Brad is a great pitcher, but he can't field the ball.
3. Since Nolan gave his report, everyone is interested in the Negro leagues.
4. Maya signed up for the baseball clinic, and Ashley signed up for gymnastics.
5. Put your cap on sideways when you want your team to rally.

Writing Application Write two compound sentences and two complex sentences about baseball.

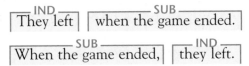 *Prentice Hall Writing and Grammar Connection: Chapter 20, Section 2*

Writing Lesson

Researched Response

"The Shutout" ends with the statement beginning "The history of the Negro Leagues is a patchwork of human drama and comedy . . ." Conduct research on the Negro Leagues and use the information you find in a response to that statement.

Prewriting   Identify questions that you will investigate during your research. For example, who were some of the heroes of the league? What legends and anecdotes are told about players and games?

Drafting   In your introduction, cite the quotation by the McKissacks. In the body of your essay, organize details around each part of the quotation: heroes, owners, games, and so on.

Model: Crediting a Quotation

In "The Shutout," Patricia and Frederick McKissack explain the circumstances leading to the formation of the Negro Leagues. With the following comment, they leave readers wanting to learn more. "The history of the Negro Leagues is a patchwork of human drama and comedy, filled with legendary heroes, infamous owners, triple-headers, low pay, and long bus rides home—not unlike the majors." (McKissack 10)

> After giving the quotation, the writer cites the author of the source and the page number. Complete information about sources is given in a "Works Cited" list at the end of the essay.

Revising   Check that you have correctly punctuated and credited any quotations you have used. Use quotation marks before and after each quotation. In parentheses, give the author of the source and the page number.

*W*G *Prentice Hall Writing and Grammar Connection: Chapter 11, Section 2*

Extension Activities

Listening and Speaking Plan and deliver a brief **presentation** about the origins of baseball.

1. Review the general information provided in "The Shutout."
2. List questions you will research when looking for additional details.
3. Use a variety of resources to find answers to your questions.
4. Deliver your presentation to the class.

Research and Technology With a small group, create a **timeline** on a specific era in the history of baseball.

Writing Write a **summary** of "The Shutout." Identify and explain the main events and ideas.

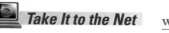 **Take It to the Net**   www.phschool.com

Go online for an additional research activity using the Internet.

Prepare to Read

Letter to Scottie ◆ Olympic Diary

 Take It to the Net

Visit www.phschool.com for interactive activities and instruction related to these selections, including
- background
- graphic organizers
- literary elements
- reading strategies

Preview

Connecting to the Literature

The letter and journal entries in this group capture the personal side—the thoughts and feelings—of two famous people, in this case, a well-known author and an athlete. While reading, look for ways in which the cares and concerns of these famous people are similar to those of "ordinary" people.

Background

Letters and journals are not usually written for a public audience. Sometimes, however, a person may keep a journal when traveling or during an interesting time period with the intention of allowing others to read it. Letters of historical or literary figures are sometimes published (with permission) to give personal insights into the person's life.

Literary Analysis

Letters and Journals

A **letter** is a written communication, usually from one person to another. In personal letters, the writer shares information, thoughts, and feelings with one other person. A **journal** is a daily account of events and the writer's thoughts and feelings about those events. As you read these two works, notice that the language is less formal than in most other kinds of writing.

Comparing Literary Works

The letter and the journal in this group are both examples of personal writing—they include details about the writers' thoughts and feelings. However, the works are intended for different **audiences,** or readers. Although now published, "Letter to Scottie" was originally written by F. Scott Fitzgerald to his daughter. Amanda Borden's Olympic Diary was written for a wider audience. She kept a record of her experiences to publish and share with the general public. Compare and contrast the letter and the journal by answering the following focus questions:

1. How much or how little background information does each writer give about his or her experiences?
2. In what way might the difference in the amount of background material be related to the intended audience for each work?

Reading Strategy

Understanding the Author's Purpose

An **author's purpose** is his or her reason for writing. Fitzgerald's purposes in writing his letter to his daughter, Scottie, are to encourage her to do her best and also to show his affection. The following example includes details and language that indicate his purpose of encouraging his daughter to do her best.

> **Example:** I feel very strongly about you doing [your] duty. Would you give me a little more documentation about your reading in French?

Use an organizer like the one shown here to record details that will help you understand each author's purpose.

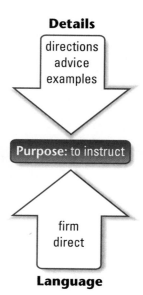

Details

directions
advice
examples

Purpose: to instruct

firm
direct

Language

Vocabulary Development

documentation (däk´ yoo mən tā´ shən) *n.* supporting evidence (p. 543)

intrigued (in trēgd´) *adj.* fascinated (p. 545)

compulsory (kəm pul´ sə rē) *adj.* must be done; having specific requirements (p. 546)

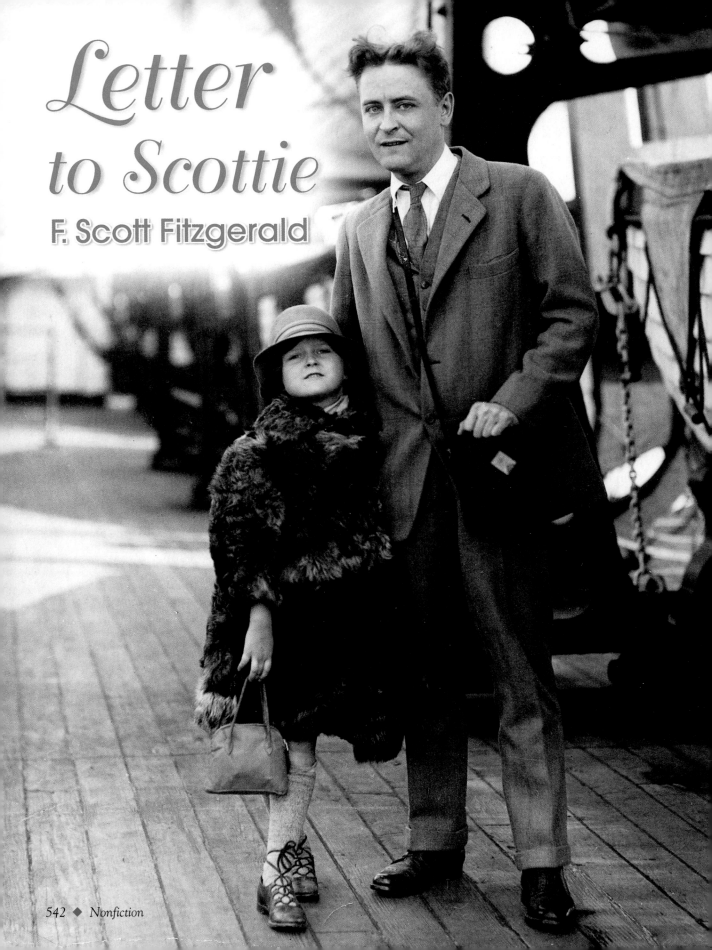

Letter
to Scottie
F. Scott Fitzgerald

La Paix, Rodgers' Forge
Towson, Maryland
August 8, 1933

Dear Pie:[1]

I feel very strongly about you doing [your] duty. Would you give me a little more <u>documentation</u> about your reading in French? I am glad you are happy—but I never believe much in happiness. I never believe in misery either. Those are things you see on the stage or the screen or the printed page, they never really happen to you in life.

All I believe in in life is the rewards for virtue (according to your talents) and the *punishments* for not fulfilling your duties, which are doubly costly. If there is such a volume in the camp library, will you ask Mrs. Tyson to let you look up a sonnet of Shakespeare's in which the line occurs *"Lilies that fester smell far worse than weeds."*

Have had no thoughts today, life seems composed of getting up a *Saturday Evening Post*[2] story. I think of you, and always pleasantly; but if you call me "Pappy" again I am going to take the White Cat out and beat his bottom *hard, six times for every time you are impertinent.* Do you react to that?

I will arrange the camp bill.

Halfwit, I will conclude.

Things to worry about:

Worry about courage
Worry about cleanliness
Worry about efficiency
Worry about horsemanship
Worry about . . .

Things not to worry about:

Don't worry about popular opinion
Don't worry about dolls
Don't worry about the past
Don't worry about the future
Don't worry about growing up
Don't worry about anybody getting ahead of you
Don't worry about triumph
Don't worry about failure unless it comes through your own fault
Don't worry about mosquitoes
Don't worry about flies
Don't worry about insects in general

---

1. Pie affectionate nickname for his daughter, Frances Scott Fitzgerald, also known as Scottie, who was away at summer camp.
2. Saturday Evening Post a weekly magazine.

◀ **Critical Viewing** What details in the letter indicate the affection that is shown between Fitzgerald and his daughter in this picture? **[Support]**

documentation
(däk´ yo͞o mən tā´ shən) *n.* supporting evidence

Reading Strategy
Understanding the Author's Purpose
How does the first sentence of the letter establish the author's purpose for writing the letter?

☑**Reading Check**
Who is writing to whom?

Don't worry about parents
Don't worry about boys
Don't worry about disappointments
Don't worry about pleasures
Don't worry about satisfactions
Things to think about:
What am I really aiming at?
How good am I really in comparison to my contemporaries
in regard to:
(a) Scholarship
(b) Do I really understand about people and am I able to get
along with them?
(c) Am I trying to make my body a useful instrument or am I
neglecting it?

With dearest love,
[Daddy]

P.S. My come-back to your calling me Pappy is christening you by the word Egg, which implies that you belong to a very rudimentary state of life and that I could break you up and crack you open at my will and I think it would be a word that would hang on if I ever told it to your contemporaries. "Egg Fitzgerald." How would you like that to go through life with—"Eggie Fitzgerald" or "Bad Egg Fitzgerald" or any form that might occur to fertile minds? Try it once more and I swear I will hang it on you and it will be up to you to shake it off. Why borrow trouble?

Love anyhow.

Review and Assess

Thinking About the Selections

1. **Respond:** How would you react if you received this letter?
2. **(a) Recall:** What is Scottie's nickname for her father?
   (b) Infer: How does he feel about this, and how do you know?
   (c) Speculate: What kind of relationship do you think Fitzgerald had with his daughter?
3. **(a) Recall:** What is Fitzgerald's main message to Scottie?
   (b) Infer: What qualities does Fitzgerald indicate are important? **(c) Speculate:** How do you think Scottie would respond to this letter? Why?
4. **Evaluate:** Which item on Fitzgerald's list of things to worry about do you think is most important? Explain.

F. Scott Fitzgerald

(1896–1940)

A descendant of the author of "The Star-Spangled Banner," Francis Scott Key Fitzgerald was born in Minnesota, educated at Princeton University, and served in the army. At the age of twenty-three, he published his first novel, *This Side of Paradise*. Fitzgerald married and had a daughter, Scottie. Frances (Scottie) spent much of her childhood in boarding schools and at camps. F. Scott Fitzgerald died at the age of forty-four.

OLYMPIC DIARY

Amanda Borden

March 22, 1996

Growing up, I couldn't decide which sport I liked the best. My first sport was T-ball. I wasn't very good. I had trouble hitting the ball and even more trouble catching it. So I moved on to soccer. I was pretty good at that, but I got bored when I didn't have the ball. Then came ballet. When I saw the girls leaping and jumping in beautiful tutus, I fell in love. I really enjoyed dancing and performing. But after many recitals and shows, I was ready for a new challenge.

A friend of the family suggested gymnastics. Wow, did my life change! I was 7 years old when I started and absolutely <u>intrigued</u> with Mary Lou Retton. I watched her in the 1984 Olympics and thought she was amazing. I never really thought I could do the things she did or even have a chance to be in the Olympics like she was. All I knew is that it looked like a lot of fun.

intrigued (in trēgd') *adj.* fascinated

☑ **Reading Check**

What is Amanda Borden's sport?

▼ **Critical Viewing** What qualities do you think these gymnasts share that helped them become Olympic gold medalists? **[Speculate]**

In the beginning, I practiced one hour, one day a week. That lasted one week. My coaches moved me up to training two hours a day, three days a week. I was in the Junior Elite Testing program, where they measured physical strength and flexibility as well as basic gymnastics skills. If your scores were high enough, you qualified for a national-level training camp.

I went to Tennessee for a week. It was my first time away from home and I didn't like it.

By the time I was 10, gymnastics had become a part of me. I was in the gym 12 hours a week—and loving every minute of it. I began competing at the <u>compulsory</u> level, traveling around my home state of Ohio as well as Kentucky, Indiana and Michigan. My family went along. My older brother Bryan usually brought a friend to play in the hotel.

[Amanda began training with a new coach, and soon qualified for the USA Championships.]

I was training really hard for the biggest competition of the year. But 12 weeks before the meet, I broke my elbow. The doctors said I could compete as long as I let it heal, so I had my arm in a cast for six weeks. But when the doctor gave me the OK to start again, I pulled my hamstring. I know, it sounds like bad luck. I couldn't compete, so I began to get my body healthy again for the next year.

I was now 15 and had to compete at the Senior Elite level. That meant going up against all the big guys like Kim Zmeskal. I made the U.S. Championships and did great—finishing fifth. That qualified me for the 1992 Olympic Trials.♦ It wasn't until that point that I realized I really had a chance to make the Olympic team. I had a really good competition and finished seventh. Seven girls make the Olympic team. So you would've thought I'd have been in Barcelona.

Well, I wasn't. There were a lot of politics involved, but to make it short and sweet they put two injured athletes, who didn't compete at the trials, on the team, and bumped Kim, Kelly and me off. It was disappointing, but life goes on. I didn't quit.

[At the end of 1995, Amanda broke her toe and her hand. Once again, she had to stop training and competing to allow her body to heal.]

♦ **Qualifying for the Olympics**
In competition for gymnastics, the sessions are given numbers, and each session is judged by different rules. The sessions, in order, are the Team compulsories, Team optionals, All-around finals, and Event finals. A gymnast is required to do more difficult exercises in the last competitions to achieve the "start value" of 10.0. A start value is the maximum score that a gymnast can receive for a routine before any deductions are taken for errors.

In the Olympic Games, the top 36 gymnasts qualify for all-around finals with three gymnasts per country. In the event finals, the top eight qualify on each apparatus, with a maximum of two gymnasts per country. In the all-around and event finals, the gymnasts start over with a score of zero.

compulsory (kəm pul′ sə rē) *adj.* must be done; having specific requirements

April 12, 1996

Four weeks ago, I got the go-ahead to start practicing again and, let me tell you, I was more than ready to get back on the mat. I began training and—slowly—I got everything back. Two weeks later, I was able to compete at the Budget Gymnastics Invitational (United States vs. France). It was going to be my first competition in a year. I was so excited I could not wait!

I flew to Miami and had a wonderful time. The women only were able to compete on bars, beam and floor—and you didn't have to compete in every event if you didn't want to.

We had four people on the team, and three had to compete in each event. I had planned on competing on the beam and floor.

The day before the competition, I was asked to compete on bars. I had only been practicing for two weeks, but I was honored to compete for the USA.

The competition was great! On bars, I got a 9.725. I had to water down my routine a little because I had not been training for my full routine, so I was pleased with that score—even with an easy dismount.

We then went to the beam. I was second up and extremely confident. I went up and rocked a set—my score was 9.775.

Our next event was the floor. I have a new routine and was excited to let everybody see it. I had to water down my tumbling passes, too, because I did not have enough time to get them ready. My first pass was a double Arabian, which is two flips in the air with a half-twist on the first flip. I had a little too much energy and ran out of bounds—but I was happy to be on my feet. My second pass was a two-and-a-half twist. That went great! I finished with a front full punch front, and that was good, too. I received a 9.512, which isn't the best score I've ever received, but I was happy to be back in competition.

I did it! I had a great meet! I felt so good! I was back, the people still remembered me and I did wonderfully!

I look back now and the injuries seem so small. When I had to deal with them, I felt like I was holding the world. After I competed, I felt I was on top of it.

Unfortunately, everyone goes through tough times, but those tough times only make the good times even better. You may think I have had my share of bad luck. I have thought that at some times, too. But when I look back on my gymnastics career, the places I've been, the people I've met and the things I've learned—the good far outweighs the bad.

Reading Strategy
Understand the Author's Purpose What was the author's purpose in recording these entries?

Literary Analysis
Letters and Journals and Author's Style What word choices and expressions give Amanda's journal a style that reflects her personality?

✔**Reading Check**

What prevents Amanda from doing her full routine at the meet in Miami?

Of course, I would like to never have to deal with problems, but I know that it will only make me a better person.

[Amanda's Olympic dream finally came true. In 1996, at the Olympic trials in Boston, Amanda claimed one of seven spots on the women's gymnastic team.]

July 21, 1996

What a whirlwind I've been on since the Olympic trials! We arrived in Atlanta at 1:30 P.M. and had processing, which took seven hours. We received lots of great clothes and other goodies. We were also measured for Olympic uniforms, which we will receive later. We finally got to our home at Emory University at 9 P.M. We're staying in a fraternity house until we are competing and then can move into the Olympic Village after that. Jaycie and I are rooming together, sharing a bathroom with Shannon Miller. We decorated our room to make it a little more "homey."

Training is going very well. We train at a private club, except when we have podium training. Tuesday, we had 22,000 cheering fans at our training. I was totally overwhelmed. You just can't imagine the feeling.

Here we are in the Georgia Dome and the Dream Team will be using the other side. I'm hoping to meet some of them. Too bad Michael Jordan isn't here. Oh well.

I was honored by being named captain of our team. I think we will do just great—everyone gets along so well and supports each other. Here's hoping we bring home the gold!

[Amanda Borden and her teammates did bring home the gold medal in 1996. The picture on page 545 shows the 1996 women's team after receiving their gold medals.]

Amanda Borden

(b. 1977)

At age seven, this Olympic-gymnast-to-be was training two hours a day, three days a week. By age ten, Borden spent twelve hours a week in the gym. By nineteen, she was the captain of the gold-medal-winning 1996 U.S. Olympic gymnastic team.

Review and Assess

Thinking About the Selections

1. **Respond:** Would you enjoy gymnastic competition? Why or why not?

2. **(a) Recall:** What sport did Amanda Borden play? **(b) Infer:** How did bad luck play a role in her career? **(c) Support:** In what two ways did Amanda show her determination to succeed?

3. **(a) Recall:** What is Amanda's reaction to being bumped from the 1992 Olympic team? **(b) Infer:** Why does she react as she does?

4. **Make a Judgment:** Do you think becoming an Olympic gymnast is worth the effort? Why or why not?

Review and Assess

Literary Analysis

Letters and Journals

1. How can a **letter** or a **journal** be personal in ways that other kinds of writing cannot?

2. Identify examples of the language in "Letter to Scottie" and "Olympic Diary" that distinguish letters and journals from other kinds of writing.

Examples of Language	"Letter to Scottie"	"Olympic Diary"
informal		
humorous		
personal		

Comparing Literary Works

3. What is the difference between the **audiences** for which the works were written?

4. On a Venn diagram, show similarities and differences in the types of details Fitzgerald and Borden include. Consider background information, thoughts and feelings, and factual details.

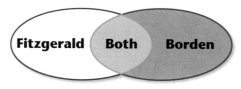

5. How do the different audiences affect the details included in each work?

Reading Strategy

Understanding the Author's Purpose

6. Explain the **purpose** for the "Letter to Scottie." Do you think Fitzgerald achieves his purpose? What details does he include to achieve that purpose?

7. What are two purposes Amanda Borden may have for writing her "Olympic Diary"? What does she include in her diary to achieve the purpose?

Extending Understanding

8. **Take a Position:** Do you think professional athletes should be allowed to compete in the Olympics? Why or why not?

Quick Review

Letters and journals are forms of communication that a writer uses to share information, thoughts, and feelings with another person. To review letters and journals, see p. 541.

Audience is the readers for whom a work is intended.

To **understand an author's purpose,** notice the language and details supported by quotes or cited material.

 Take It to the Net

www.phschool.com

Take the interactive self-test online to check your understanding of these selections.

Integrate Language Skills

Vocabulary Development Lesson

Word Analysis: Forms of *document*

Words that are related to *document*, such as *documentary* and *documentation*, usually have something to do with a record, or proof. Write the form of *document* that fits each description.

1. A piece of written proof
2. A visual record of an event or time period
3. A collection of evidence

Spelling Strategy

In some words, like *intrigue*, the g sound is spelled *gue*. On your paper, unscramble the letters to make words that end with *gue*.

1. disease: gluape
2. unclear: vugae

Concept Development: Synonyms

Synonyms are words that have almost the same meaning. On your paper, write the synonym of the vocabulary word.

1. documentation: **(a)** paper, **(b)** interest, **(c)** proof
2. compulsory: **(a)** suggested, **(b)** interesting, **(c)** required
3. intrigued: **(a)** curious, **(b)** disgusted, **(c)** confused

Rewrite each sentence, replacing the underlined word with a synonym from the vocabulary words.

1. We need <u>records</u> of her scores.
2. They were <u>fascinated</u> by her story.
3. The <u>mandatory</u> exercises are difficult.

Grammar Lesson

Subject and Object Pronouns

To name or rename the subject of a sentence, use a **subject pronoun**. The subject pronouns are *I, you, he, she, it, we, you,* and *they*. The object pronouns are *me, you, him, her, them,* and *us*.

> **Subject:** *They* tried to standardize the game.
> **Rename Subject:** It was *I* who batted last.
> **Direct Object:** That qualified *her* for the Olympics.
> **Indirect Object:** The doctor gave *her* the okay to start again.

Use an **object pronoun** for a **direct object** (receives the action of the verb) or an **indirect object** (person or thing to which or for which an action is performed).

Practice Copy the following sentences. Circle each subject pronoun. Underline each object pronoun. Then, tell how each pronoun is used.

1. Despite setbacks, I continued to compete in the trials.
2. They bumped Kim, Kelly, and me off.
3. The doctor told her the news.
4. Would you give me more documentation?
5. Is it she the crowd wants to see perform?

Writing Application Write a brief journal entry that uses at least four subject and object pronouns. Use the object pronouns as direct and indirect objects. State how each pronoun is used.

W_G *Prentice Hall Writing and Grammar Connection: Chapter 23*

Writing Lesson

Letter to an Author

One way to respond to literature is to write a letter to an author. Even if you never mail your letter, the form allows you to express your reactions in a direct way. Write a letter to F. Scott Fitzgerald in which you respond to the letter he wrote to his daughter. Tell whether or not you find his advice useful for students your age.

Prewriting   On a photocopy of Fitzgerald's letter, mark parts you will use as examples of advice that is or is not useful.

Drafting   Begin with a sentence that states your overall reaction. Do not use the words "I am writing to you because . . ." In the body of your letter, develop the reasons for your overall reaction and give examples.

Model: Appropriate Beginnings

Dear Mr. Fitzgerald,

  Your advice to your daughter may have been useful in the 1930s, but some of your ideas just don't apply in the twenty-first century.

> In the first sentence, the writer directly states the overall reaction. In later sentences and paragraphs she will support her response with examples from the work.

Revising   Look for statements that are not supported by examples, and revise by adding an example.

*W*_G *Prentice Hall Writing and Grammar Connection: Chapter 12, Section 2*

Extension Activities

Listening and Speaking   The list of things to worry about and not worry about identifies potential problems F. Scott Fitzgerald's daughter, Scottie, may be trying to solve. Identify one of the problems and give an **oral presentation** on how she or another student her age might solve the problem.

Writing   As Amanda Borden, write a **journal entry** about how you feel after your team wins the gold medal. Include details about how you, as Amanda, have worked to achieve this goal.

Research and Technology   With a group, prepare a **presentation** on the Olympics. Group members can choose from the following tasks:

- research the history of the Olympics
- create a map of Olympic sites
- prepare posters showing athletic events
- research new sports and future changes

Use a variety of electronic resources, such as the library card catalog, CD-ROMs, and the Internet, to conduct research.

 **Take It to the Net**   www.phschool.com

Go online for an additional research activity using the Internet.

Prepare to Read

My Papa, Mark Twain ◆ The Drive-In Movies
Space Shuttle *Challenger*

El Auto Cinema, Roberto Gil de Montes, Jan Baum Gallery

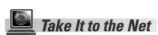 **Take It to the Net**

Visit www.phschool.com
for interactive activities
and instruction related to
these selections, including

- background
- graphic organizers
- literary elements
- reading strategies

Preview

Connecting to the Literature

In these three works, the writers share important experiences from childhood and adult life. As you read, use the author's experiences and your own to think about what makes a moment or experience memorable.

Background

In the 1950s and 1960s, many people saw movies at the "drive-in," where people parked in front of a large, outdoor screen, hooked up to a listening box, and enjoyed the show. The drive-in movie was an economical way for an entire family to see a movie.

Literary Analysis

Biography and Autobiography

A **biography** is the story of all or part of someone's life. An **autobiography** is a person's account of his or her own life and experiences. In a biography, the subject is shown from the perspective of an observer, someone who can report only how the subject acts, looks, and speaks. In autobiographical writing, the subject writes about himself or herself. The Venn diagram shows the main similarity and difference between biographical and autobiographical writing.

Comparing Literary Works

Both of these works are written in the **first-person point of view**—by a narrator who participates in the action. Compare the two works by answering the following focus questions.

1. How is the amount you learn influenced by who the first-person narrator is in each work?
2. How is the first-person narrator in a biography different from the first-person narrator of an autobiography?

Reading Strategy

Identifying Author's Evidence

When you read a general statement by the author of a biography, autobiography, or other work of nonfiction, decide whether or not you accept the statement as true. Make your decision based on examples, observations, or details that show the truth of the statement. In "My Papa, Mark Twain," Susy Clemens writes that her father is "a *very* striking character." The following example shows some of the evidence she provides for that general statement.

> He has beautiful gray hair, not any too thick or any too long, but just right; a Roman nose which greatly improves the beauty of his features; . . .

Vocabulary Development

incessantly (in ses´ ənt lē) *adv.* never ceasing (p. 555)

consequently (kän´ si kwent´ lē) *adv.* as a result (p. 555)

monitoring (män´ i tər iŋ) *v.* watching or listening to (p. 563)

accumulations (ə kyo͞om´ yo͞o lā´ shənz) *n.* buildups over a period of time (p. 564)

moot (mo͞ot) *adj.* not worthy of thought or discussion because it has already been resolved (p. 564)

peripheral (pə rif´ ər əl) *adj.* lying on the outside edge (p. 565)

catastrophic (kat´ ə sträf´ ik) *adj.* causing a complete disaster (p. 565)

Biography

The writer observes the subject

Both
Narrative writing tells part of the subject's (person's) life.

The writer is the subject

Autobiography

My Papa, Mark Twain

Susy Clemens

◀ **Critical Viewing**
What details in the picture show that the Clemens family enjoys spending time together? **[Analyze]**

We are a very happy family. We consist of Papa, Mamma, Jean, Clara and me. It is papa I am writing about, and I shall have no trouble in not knowing what to say about him, as he is a *very* striking character.

Papa's appearance has been described many times, but very incorrectly. He has beautiful gray hair, not any too thick or any too long, but just right; a Roman nose which greatly improves the beauty of his features; kind blue eyes and a small mustache. He has a wonderfully shaped head and profile. He has a very good figure—in short, he is an extrodinarily fine looking man. All his features are perfect except that he hasn't extrodinary teeth. His complexion is very fair, and he doesn't ware a beard. He is a very good man and a very funny one. He has got a temper, but we all of us have in this family. He is the loveliest man I ever saw or ever hope to see—and oh, so absentminded.

Papa's favorite game is billiards, and when he is tired and wishes to rest himself he stays up all night and plays billiards, it seems to rest his head. He smokes a great deal almost <u>incessantly</u>. He has the mind of an author exactly, some of the simplest things he can't understand. Our burglar alarm is often out of order, and papa had been obliged to take the mahogany room off from the alarm altogether for a time, because the burglar alarm had been in the habit of ringing even when the mahogany-room window was closed. At length he thought that perhaps the burglar alarm might be in order, and he decided to try and see; accordingly he put it on and then went down and opened the window; <u>consequently</u> the alarm bell rang, it would even if the alarm had been in order. Papa went despairingly upstairs and said to mamma, "Livy the mahogany room won't go on. I have just opened the window to see."

"Why, Youth," mamma replied. "If you've opened the window, why of course the alarm will ring!"

"That's what I've opened it for, why I just went down to see if it would ring!"

Mamma tried to explain to papa that when he wanted to go and see whether the alarm would ring while the window was closed he *mustn't go* and open the window—but in vain, papa couldn't understand, and got very impatient with mamma for trying to make him believe an impossible thing true.

Papa has a peculiar gait we like, it seems just to suit him, but most people do not; he always walks up and down the room while thinking and between each coarse at meals.

Papa is very fond of animals particularly of cats, we had a dear little gray kitten once that he named "Lazy" (papa always wears gray to match his hair and eyes) and he would carry him around on his shoulder, it was a mighty pretty sight! the gray cat sound asleep against papa's gray coat and hair. The names that he has give our different cats are really remarkably funny, they are named Stray Kit, Abner, Motley, Fraeulein, Lazy, Buffalo Bill, Soapy Sall, Cleveland, Sour Mash, and Pestilence and Famine.

Papa uses very strong language, but I have an idea not nearly so strong as when he first married mamma. A lady acquaintance of his is rather apt to interrupt what one is saying, and papa told mamma he thought he should say to the lady's husband "I am glad your wife wasn't present when the Deity said Let there be light."

Papa said the other day, "I am a mugwump[1] and a mugwump is pure from the marrow out." (Papa knows that I am writing this biography of him, and he said this for it.) He doesn't like to go to

---

1. mugwump (mug´ wump´) *n.* a Republican who refused to support the candidates of the party in the 1884 election.

incessantly (in ses´ ənt lē) *adv.* never ceasing

consequently (kän´ si kwent´ lē) *adv.* as a result

Literary Analysis
Biography and Autobiography
What details make Susy's account different from one Mark Twain himself may have given?

**Reading Check**

What is the relationship between the writer and the subject?

▲ **Critical Viewing**
Susy is observing her two sisters in this picture. What do you think she might write about them in her journal? **[Speculate]**

church at all, why I never understood, until just now, he told us the other day that he couldn't bear to hear anyone talk but himself, but that he could listen to himself talk for hours without getting tired, of course he said this in joke, but I've no dought it was founded on truth.

One of papa's latest books is "The Prince and the Pauper" and it is unquestionably the best book he has ever written, some people want him to keep to his old style, some gentleman wrote him, "I enjoyed Huckleberry Finn immensely and am glad to see that you have returned to your old style." That enoyed me, that enoyed me greatly, because it trobles me to have so few people know papa, I mean realy know him, they think of Mark Twain as a humorist joking at everything; "And with a mop of reddish brown hair which sorely needs the barbar brush, a roman nose, short stubby mustache, a sad care-worn face, with maney crows' feet" etc. That is the way people picture papa, I have wanted papa to write a book that would reveal something of his kind sympathetic nature, and "The Prince and the Pauper" partly does it. The book is full of lovely charming ideas, and oh the language! It is perfect. I think that one of the most touching scenes in it is where the pauper is riding on horseback with his nobles in the "recognition procession" and he

Literary Analysis
Biography and Autobiography
What details on this page show how the writer's role of daughter helps her as a biographer?

sees his mother oh and then what followed! How she runs to his side, when she sees him throw up his hand palm outward, and is rudely pushed off by one of the King's officers, and then how the little pauper's conscience troubles him when he remembers the shameful words that were falling from his lips when she was turned from his side "I know you not woman" and how his grandeurs were stricken valueless and his pride consumed to ashes. It is a wonderfully beautiful and touching little scene, and papa has described it so wonderfully. I never saw a man with so much variety of feeling as papa has; now the "Prince and the Pauper" is full of touching places, but there is always a streak of humor in them somewhere. Papa very seldom writes a passage without some humor in it somewhere and I don't think he ever will.

Clara and I are sure that papa played the trick on Grandma about the whipping that is related in "The Adventures of Tom Sawyer": "Hand me that switch." The switch hovered in the air, the peril was desperate—"My, look behind you Aunt!" The old lady whirled around and snatched her skirts out of danger. The lad fled on the instant, scrambling up the high board fence and disappeared over it.

We know papa played "Hookey" all the time. And how readily would papa pretend to be dying so as not to have to go to school! Grandma wouldn't make papa go to school, so she let him go into a printing office to learn the trade. He did so, and gradually picked up enough education to enable him to do about as well as those who were more studious in early life.

Review and Assess

Thinking About the Selection

1. **Respond:** What questions do you have about Mark Twain after reading Susy Clemens's account?

2. **(a) Recall:** What does Susy think of her father's appearance? **(b) Infer:** If Susy Clemens were to use three words to describe her father, what would they be? **(c) Synthesize:** What three words would you use to describe Mark Twain?

3. **(a) Recall:** What details does the author give about her father's education? **(b) Deduce:** Explain how you think she feels about her father's lack of formal education. **(c) Support:** What do you think Susy Clemens feels about her father's books? What details does the account provide?

4. **Speculate:** This essay contains many misspelled words. Why do you think it was published without correcting the errors?

Susy Clemens

(1872–1896)

The oldest of Mark Twain's three daughters, Susy Clemens grew up in a luxurious home in Hartford, Connecticut, where her parents entertained some of the most prominent people of the time. As a girl, Susy adored her father; as she grew older, she began to resent his showy public image. She died at the age of twenty-four.

The Drive-In Movies

GARY SOTO

For our family, moviegoing was rare. But if our mom, tired from a week of candling eggs,[1] woke up happy on a Saturday morning, there was a chance we might later scramble to our blue Chevy and beat nightfall to the Starlight Drive-In. My brother and sister knew this. I knew this. So on Saturday we tried to be good. We sat in the cool shadows of the TV with the volume low and watched cartoons, a prelude of what was to come.

One Saturday I decided to be extra good. When she came out of the bedroom tying her robe, she yawned a hat-sized yawn and blinked red eyes at the weak brew of coffee I had fixed for her. I made her toast with strawberry jam spread to all the corners and set the three boxes of cereal in front of her. If she didn't care to eat cereal, she could always look at the back of the boxes as she drank her coffee.

I went outside. The lawn was tall but too wet with dew to mow. I picked up a trowel and began to weed the flower bed. The weeds were really bermuda grass, long stringers that ran finger-deep in the ground. I got to work quickly and in no time crescents of earth began rising under my fingernails. I was sweaty hot. My knees hurt from kneeling, and my brain was dull from making the trowel go up and down, dribbling crumbs of earth. I dug for half an hour, then stopped to play with the neighbor's dog and pop ticks from his poor snout.

I then mowed the lawn, which was still beaded with dew and noisy with bees hovering over clover. This job was less dull because as I pushed the mower over the shaggy lawn, I could see it looked tidier. My brother and sister watched from the window. Their faces

---

1. candling eggs examining uncooked eggs for freshness by placing them in front of a candle.

◀ Critical Viewing What are some reasons people might enjoy watching a movie from their car? **[Speculate]**

✔ Reading Check

Why is the narrator being extra good?

were fat with cereal, a third helping. I made a face at them when they asked how come I was working. Rick pointed to part of the lawn. "You missed some over there." I ignored him and kept my attention on the windmill of grassy blades.

While I was emptying the catcher, a bee stung the bottom of my foot. I danced on one leg and was ready to cry when Mother showed her face at the window. I sat down on the grass and examined my foot: the stinger was pulsating. I pulled it out quickly, ran water over the sting and packed it with mud, Grandmother's remedy.

Hobbling, I returned to the flower bed where I pulled more stringers and again played with the dog. More ticks had migrated to his snout. I swept the front steps, took out the garbage, cleaned the lint filter to the dryer (easy), plucked hair from the industrial wash basin in the garage (also easy), hosed off the patio, smashed three snails sucking paint from the house (disgusting but fun), tied a bundle of newspapers, put away toys, and, finally, seeing that almost everything was done and the sun was not too high, started waxing the car.

My brother joined me with an old gym sock, and our sister watched us while sucking on a cherry Kool-Aid ice cube. The liquid wax drooled onto the sock, and we began to swirl the white slop on the chrome. My arms ached from buffing, which though less boring than weeding, was harder. But the beauty was evident. The shine, hurting our eyes and glinting like an armful of dimes, brought Mother out. She looked around the yard and said, "Pretty good." She winced[2] at the grille and returned inside the house.

We began to wax the paint. My brother applied the liquid and I followed him rubbing hard in wide circles as we moved around the car. I began to hurry because my arms were hurting and my stung foot looked like a water balloon. We were working around the trunk when Rick pounded on the bottle of wax. He squeezed the bottle and it sneezed a few more white drops.

We looked at each other. "There's some on the sock," I said. "Let's keep going."

We polished and buffed, sweat weeping on our brows. We got scared when we noticed that the gym sock was now blue. The paint was coming off. Our sister fit ice cubes into our mouths and we worked harder, more intently, more dedicated to the car and our mother. We ran the sock over the chrome, trying to pick up extra wax. But there wasn't enough to cover the entire car. Only half got waxed, but we thought it was better than nothing and went inside for lunch. After lunch, we returned outside with tasty sandwiches.

---

2. **winced** (winst) *v.* drew back slightly, as if in pain.

Literary Analysis
Biography and Autobiography
What autobiographical details would only the writer know about his own childhood?

Literary Analysis
Autobiography and First-Person Narrator
What different details might be included if the first-person narrator were Soto's mother?

Rick and I nearly jumped. The waxed side of the car was foggy white. We took a rag and began to polish vigorously and nearly in tears, but the fog wouldn't come off. I blamed Rick and he blamed me. Debra stood at the window, not wanting to get involved. Now, not only would we not go to the movies, but Mom would surely snap a branch from the plum tree and chase us around the yard.

Mom came out and looked at us with hands on her aproned hips. Finally, she said, "You boys worked so hard." She turned on the garden hose and washed the car. That night we did go to the drive-in. The first feature was about nothing, and the second feature, starring Jerry Lewis,[3] was *Cinderfella*. I tried to stay awake. I kept a wad of homemade popcorn in my cheek and laughed when Jerry Lewis fit golf tees in his nose. I rubbed my watery eyes. I laughed and looked at my mom. I promised myself I would remember that scene with the golf tees and promised myself not to work so hard the coming Saturday. Twenty minutes into the movie, I fell asleep with one hand in the popcorn.

---

3. **Jerry Lewis** comedian who starred in many movies during the 1950s and 1960s.

Gary Soto

(b. 1952) This popular writer of poetry and prose was once a farm worker in California's San Joaquin Valley. Some of his work—including the poetry collection *The Elements of San Joaquin*—explores the lives of migrant farm workers. Other books—such as the collection of essays *Living Up the Street* and *Baseball in April and Other Stories*—focus on the large and small events in the lives of family and friends. Today, Gary Soto lives and teaches in Berkeley, California.

Review and Assess
Thinking About the Selections

1. **Respond:** How would you have felt if you had worked so hard and had then fallen asleep at the movies?

2. **(a) Recall:** How does Soto convince his mother to take the family to the drive-in movies? **(b) Draw Conclusions:** Why do you think the boys' mother does not get angry with them for making a mess of the car with the wax? **(c) Relate:** Do you think it was worth the hard work? Why or why not?

3. **Deduce:** Do you think the narrator is older or younger than his brother and sister? Use evidence from the story to support your answer.

4. **(a) Recall:** What two things does the narrator promise himself to remember? **(b) Assess:** As an adult, do you think he still has fond memories about that day and night? Why or why not?

5. **Speculate:** Do you think children should have to work hard on chores before their parents allow them to do something enjoyable? Why or why not?

SPACE SHUTTLE
Challenger
William Harwood

I witnessed the launch from the Kennedy Space Center press site just 4.2 miles from pad 39B. It was my 19th shuttle launch but my first without the comforting presence of UPI Science Editor Al Rossiter Jr., a space veteran with all of the experience I lacked. He was in Pasadena, California, at the Jet Propulsion Laboratory covering *Voyager 2*'s flyby of Uranus.

I arrived at the UPI trailer around 11:30 P.M. Monday night, January 27. I always came to work before the start of fueling on the theory that anytime anyone loaded a half-million gallons of liquid oxygen and liquid hydrogen into anything it was an event worth staffing.

It was bitterly cold that night. I remember cranking up the drafty UPI trailer's baseboard heaters in a futile attempt to warm up while I started banging out copy. I was writing for afternoon, or PM, newspapers that would hit the streets the following afternoon. Because *Challenger*'s launch was scheduled for that morning, the PM cycle was where the action was, the closest thing to "live" reporting that print journalists ever experience. . . . I had written my launch copy the day before and as usual, I spent most of the early morning hours tweaking the story, checking in periodically with NASA public affairs and monitoring the chatter on the bureau's radio scanner. I would occasionally glance toward the launch pad where *Challenger* stood bathed in high power spotlights, clearly visible for dozens of miles around. Off to the side, a brilliant tongue of orange

Literary Analysis
Biography and Autobiography
What details about the author's experience of preparing for the launch do you learn about in this section?

monitoring (män´ i tər iŋ) *v.* watching or listening to

✔**Reading Check**

What is the narrator's job?

flame periodically flared in the night as excess hydrogen was vented harmlessly into the atmosphere. Back in the UPI trailer, radio reporter Rob Navias rolled in around 4 A.M. A veteran shuttle reporter with an encyclopedic memory for space trivia, Rob and I had covered 14 straight missions together. In keeping with long-standing launch-day tradition, Rob's first comment after stomping into the trailer was "Will it go?" to which I would respond: "Or will it blow?" It was a grim little charade we carried out to mask our constant fear of catastrophe.

As night gave way to day, the launch team was struggling to keep the countdown on track. Problems had delayed fueling and launch—originally scheduled for 9:38 A.M.—for two hours to make sure no dangerous <u>accumulations</u> of ice had built up on *Challenger*'s huge external tank. Finally, all systems were "go" and the countdown resumed at the T-minus nine-minute mark for a liftoff at 11:38 A.M. Battling my usual pre-launch jitters, I called UPI national desk editor Bill Trott in Washington about three minutes before launch. I had already filed the PM launch story to UPI's computer and Trott now called it up on his screen. We shot the breeze. I reminded him not to push the send button until I confirmed vertical motion; two previous launches were aborted at the last second and we didn't want to accidentally "launch" a shuttle on the wire when it was still firmly on the ground. But there were no such problems today. *Challenger*'s three main engines thundered to life on schedule, belching blue-white fire and billowing clouds of steam. Less than seven seconds later, the shuttle's twin boosters ignited with a ground-shaking roar and the spacecraft vaulted skyward.

"And liftoff . . . liftoff of the 25th space shuttle mission, and it has cleared the tower!" said NASA commentator Hugh Harris.

"OK, let it go," I told Trott when Harris started talking. He pushed the SEND button and my story winged away on the A-wire.

Four miles away, *Challenger* was climbing majestically into a cloudless blue sky. We could not see the initial puffs of smoke indicating a fatal booster flaw. A few seconds later, the crackling roar of those boosters swept over the press site and the UPI trailer started shaking and rattling as the ground shock arrived. I marveled at the view, describing it to Trott in Washington. We always kept the line open for the full eight-and-a-half minutes it took for a shuttle to reach orbit; should disaster strike, the plan went, I would start dictating and Trott would start filing raw copy to the wire.

But for the first few seconds, it was a <u>moot</u> point. The roar was so loud we couldn't hear each other anyway. But the sound quickly faded to a dull rumble as *Challenger* wheeled about and arced over behind its booster exhaust plume, disappearing from view. NASA television, of course, carried the now-familiar closeups of the

accumulations
(ə kyo͞om′ yo͞o lā′ shənz) *n.* buildups occurring over a period of time

Reading Strategy
Author's Evidence
What details does the author provide as evidence that his view of the launch was marvelous?

moot (mo͞ot) *adj.* not worthy of thought or discussion because it has already been resolved

orbiter, but I wasn't watching television. I was looking out the window at the exhaust cloud towering into the morning sky.

"Incredible," I murmured.

And then, in the blink of an eye, the exhaust plume seemed to balloon outward, to somehow thicken. I recall a fleeting <u>peripheral</u> impression of fragments, of debris flying about, sparkling in the morning sunlight. And then, in that pregnant instant before the knowledge that something terrible has happened settled in, a single booster emerged from the cloud, corkscrewing madly through the sky.

I sat stunned. I couldn't understand what I was seeing.

"Wait a minute . . . something's happened . . ." I told Trott. A booster? Flying on its own? "They're in trouble," I said, my heart pounding. "Lemme dictate something!"

"OK, OK, hang on," Trott said. He quickly started punching in the header material of a one-paragraph "story" that would interrupt the normal flow of copy over the wire and alert editors to breaking news.

I still didn't realize *Challenger* had actually exploded. I didn't know what had happened. For a few heartbeats, I desperately reviewed the crew's options: Could the shuttle somehow have pulled free? Could the crew somehow still be alive? Had I been watching television, I would have known the truth immediately and my copy would have been more final.

But I wasn't watching television.

"Ready," Trott said.

The lead went something like this: "The space shuttle *Challenger* apparently exploded about two minutes after launch today (pause for Trott to catch up) and veered wildly out of control. (pause) The fate of the crew was not known."

"Got it . . ." Trott said, typing as I talked. Bells went off seconds later as the story started clattering out on the bureau's A-wire printer behind me.

Out in Pasadena, Rossiter had watched the launch on NASA television. He ran to his computer, checked the wire and urgently called the bureau. He wanted to know why we had "apparently" blown up the shuttle in the precede. On television, there was no "apparently" about it.

Trott and I quickly corrected the time of the accident (my sense of time was distorted all day) and clarified that *Challenger* had, in fact, suffered a <u>catastrophic</u> failure. While we did not yet know what had happened to the crew, we all knew the chances for survival were virtually zero and the story began reflecting that belief.

For the next half hour or so, I simply dictated my impressions and background to Trott, who would file three or four paragraphs

peripheral (pə rif′ ər əl)
adj. lying on the outside edge

Literary Analysis
Autobiography and First-Person Narrator
How do the narrator's thoughts and feelings appear in this account?

catastrophic (kat′ ə sträf′ ik)
adj. causing a complete disaster

**Reading Check**

What happens to the shuttle?

of "running copy" to the wire at a time. At one point, I remember yelling "Obits! Tell somebody to refile the obits!" Before every shuttle mission, I wrote detailed profiles of each crew member. No one actually printed these stories; they were written to serve as instant obits in the event of a disaster. Now, I wanted to refile my profiles for clients who had not saved them earlier. At some point—I have no idea when—I put the phone down and started typing again, filing the copy to Washington where Trott assembled all the pieces into a more-or-less coherent narrative. Dozens of UPI reporters swung into action around the world, later funneling reaction and quotes into the evolving story.

For the next two hours or so I don't remember anything but the mad rush of reporting. Subconsciously, I held the enormity of the disaster at bay; I knew if I relaxed my guard for an instant it could paralyze me. I was flying on some kind of mental autopilot. And then, around 2 P.M. or so, I recall a momentary lull. My fingers dropped to the keyboard and I stared blankly out the window toward the launch pad. I saw those seven astronauts. I saw them waving to the photographers as they headed for the launch pad. I remembered Christa McAuliffe's smile and Judy Resnik's flashing eyes. Tears welled up. I shook my head, blinked rapidly and turned back to my computer. I'll think about it all later, I told myself. I was right. I think about it every launch.

Review and Assess

Thinking About the Selections

1. (a) **Recall:** What kinds of activities does Harwood describe taking place before the launch? (b) **Describe:** How would you describe the mood, or feeling, of the reporters before the launch?

2. (a) **Recall:** What nervous joke do Harwood and another reporter make before every launch? (b) **Analyze:** What details reveal that the reporters know the launch could go either way? (c) **Deduce:** Why does Harwood write detailed biographies of the astronauts before every launch?

3. (a) **Recall:** How far away is *Challenger* from Harwood's observation post? (b) **Contrast:** How is the view on television different from Harwood's eyewitness view? (c) **Evaluate:** Which view gives a more reliable view of events?

4. (a) **Speculate:** What do you think Harwood felt when he saw the booster come out of the cloud from the explosion? (b) **Synthesize:** Why does Harwood have difficulty understanding what has happened?

William Harwood

(b. 1952)
William Harwood's first article about the space program was written for his school newspaper at the University of Tennessee. Since then, he has covered more than eighty-five shuttle flights, working for United Press International, CBS News, and the *Washington Post*. In addition to writing about the space program, Harwood has written astronomy articles for *Ciel et Espace* (a French astronomy magazine) and *Astronomy Now*.

Review and Assess

Literary Analysis

Biography and Autobiography

1. Identify two details that Susy Clemens includes in her **biography** "My Papa, Mark Twain" that Twain might not tell about himself.
2. Name three details in "The Drive-In Movies" that an author besides Soto would not know or include.
3. What would be different about "Space Shuttle *Challenger*" if it were narrated by someone who did not actually witness the event?

Comparing Literary Works

4. Complete an organizer like the one here to compare these works.

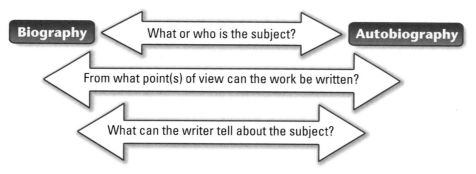

5. How is the **first-person narrator** in a biography different from the first-person narrator of an autobiography?
6. How is the amount you learn about the thoughts and feelings of each subject influenced by who the first-person narrator is in each work?

Reading Strategy

Identifying Author's Evidence

7. Make a chart like the one shown to record author's evidence for each statement.

Selection	Statement	Evidence
"My Papa, Mark Twain	"We are a happy family."	
"The Drive-In Movies"	"So on Saturday we tried to be good."	
"Space Shuttle *Challenger*"	"I couldn't understand what I was seeing."	

Extending Understanding

8. **Take a Position:** How much or how little personal information should the media publish about celebrities' lives?

Quick Review

A **biography** is the story of someone's life written by another person. An **autobiography** is a person's own account of his or her life. To review biography and autobiography, see p. 553.

A **first-person narrator** participates in the events being narrated. To review first-person narrator, see p. 553.

Author's evidence is details and information that support the author's statements.

 Take It to the Net
www.phschool.com
Take the interactive self-test online to check your understanding of these selections.

Integrate Language Skills

Vocabulary Development Lesson

Word Analysis: Latin Root -sequi-

When you see the Latin root -sequi-, as in the word *consequently* found in "My Papa, Mark Twain," remember that *sequi* means "follow." Thus, a word with this root means "following" or "coming after."

On your paper, explain the meaning of each italicized word.

1. The alarm didn't ring; *consequently*, I was late.
2. We liked the *sequel* to the movie more than the first one because it was funnier and more action-packed.
3. In the *sequence* for this pattern, a blue dot follows three red dots.

Concept Development: Synonyms

On your paper, write the vocabulary word that could be used as a synonym for each word below.

1. steadily
2. on the edge
3. watching
4. disastrous
5. unimportant
6. therefore
7. buildups

Spelling Strategy

Words with several syllables may have more letters than you expect. Copy the sentences below, completing each one with the words provided. Pronounce each syllable of the word before writing.

ac•cum•u•la•tions   vig•or•ous•ly
per•i•pher•al   in•cess•ant•ly

1. There were large _____ of snow.
2. The rain drummed _____ on the roof.
3. They exercised _____.
4. The _____ colors are fading.

Grammar Lesson

Writing Proper Nouns

In the selections you have just read, there are many kinds of proper nouns. All proper nouns begin with a capital letter. Titles are proper nouns. Each word in a title, unless it is an article or a preposition with fewer than four letters, begins with a capital letter. In addition, titles have special punctuation and formatting. Short works are set off by quotation marks. Full-length works are italicized.

Titles of short works, such as stories and essays: "My Papa, Mark Twain," "The Drive-In Movies," "The Circuit"
Titles of full-length works, such as novels, plays, and movies: *Cinderfella*, *The Adventures of Tom Sawyer*

Practice Copy each sentence, and use capital letters and quotation marks where needed. Then, underline any words that should be printed in italics.

1. The article was written by William Harwood.
2. We read the prince and the pauper.
3. The film starred jerry lewis.
4. We watched the launch at the kennedy space center.
5. The science editor was in pasadena, california, covering voyager 2.

Writing Application Write three sentences using proper nouns.

WG Prentice Hall Writing and Grammar Connection: Chapter 27

Writing Lesson

Autobiographical Narrative

Gary Soto wrote an autobiographical account to share his memories of going to drive-in movies. Write an autobiographical narrative to tell about an event, period, or person in your life.

Prewriting Brainstorm for ideas from your life experience. Then, narrow your topic to a single event or experience you can thoroughly cover.

Drafting Write your draft, putting the details and events together as you remember them. Then, put the paragraphs in order to create a story with a beginning, middle, and end.

Revising Revise your draft, using concrete language—language that names or describes things that can be perceived through the senses. Where possible, replace words with ones that give a more specific sensory impression.

> ### Model: Concrete Language
>
> *clanging, yapping, and howling*
> As we drove up to the shelter, we heard ~~a lot of noise.~~ Inside
>
> *squirming bundle of brown fur that barked.*
> the volunteer handed me a ~~puppy.~~

W̶G Prentice Hall Writing and Grammar Connection: Chapter 5, Section 3

Extension Activities

Listening and Speaking William Harwood, as a newspaper reporter, communicates through words only. In contrast, television newscasters use their voices and expressions as well as words. In a small group, watch a newscast and observe the reporter. In an **informal presentation,** share your observations in the following areas:

- **Tone of voice:** Is the reporter sympathetic, concerned, unconcerned, objective?

- **Mood or atmosphere:** Do the descriptions, examples, and quotations create a positive or negative feeling?

Research and Technology With a partner, research some of Mark Twain's characters. Make a **poster** or chart that shows some of Twain's best known works and characters.

Writing Write a **response** in which you explain which of these nonfiction works you found most realistic. Give examples from the work to support your answer.

 **Take It to the Net**   www.phschool.com

Go online for an additional research activity using the Internet.

Prepare to Read

Restoring the Circle ◆ How the Internet Works
Turkeys

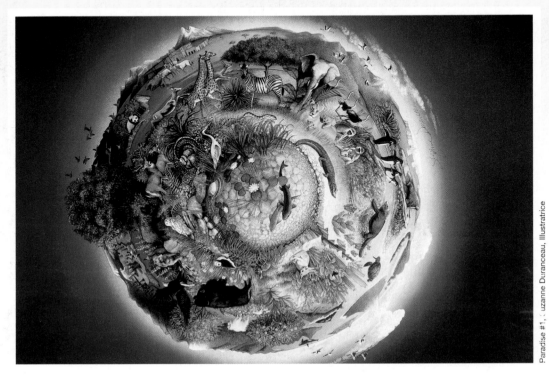

Paradise #1, Suzanne Duranceau, Illustratrice

Take It to the Net

Visit www.phschool.com
for interactive activities
and instruction related to
these selections, including
- background
- graphic organizers
- literary elements
- reading strategies

Preview

Connecting to the Literature

"Restoring the Circle" by Joseph Bruchac, "How the Internet Works" by Kerry Cochrane, and "Turkeys" by Bailey White are all essays in this grouping. Each essay shows how people make connections between themselves and the world around them. As you read, think about where you find connections between your own experience and the rest of the world.

Background

"Turkeys" tells of the efforts of conservationists to preserve a population of wild turkeys. Conservation became an issue in the United States in the early 1900s. President Theodore Roosevelt established the first federal wildlife refuge at Pelican Island in Florida and set aside more than 140 million acres to be national forest reserves.

Literary Analysis

Types of Essays

An **essay** is a nonfiction work about a particular subject.

- "Restoring the Circle" is a **persuasive essay:** it presents reasons or arguments in favor of something and provides supporting evidence.
- "How the Internet Works" is an **informational essay:** it presents facts, information, and explanations about a topic.
- "Turkeys" is a **narrative essay:** it tells about real-life experiences using the elements of storytelling.

Comparing Literary Works

An informational essay and a persuasive essay both provide facts. However, because the two types of essays have different **purposes,** or goals, different types of facts may be used or the facts may be presented in different ways. Compare and contrast the essays in this group by thinking about the following focus questions.

1. What characteristics do all essays share?
2. How do the different purposes of essays influence the kinds of details they include?

Reading Strategy

Using Context to Determine Meaning

Nonfiction works often include words that are unfamiliar or that are used in a way that is specific to the topic of the work. Use **context**—the situation in which the word is used—to help determine the meaning. Look for clues in the surrounding words, sentences, and paragraphs. The chart at right shows clues from the selection that can help you figure out the meaning of the word *ornithologist*. As you read, use a chart like it to record unfamiliar words and clues to their meanings.

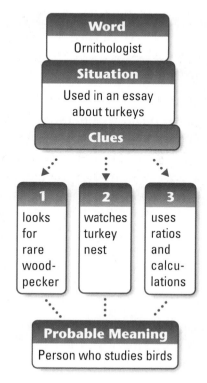

Vocabulary Development

tolerance (tälʹ ər əns) *n.* respect for something different (p. 575)

detrimental (deʹ trə mentʹ əl) *adj.* harmful (p. 575)

dilution (di lōōʹ shən) *n.* weakening by mixing with something else (p. 582)

vigilance (vijʹ ə ləns) *n.* watchfulness (p. 584)

Restoring The Circle

Native American Literature as a Means of Preserving Cultural Traditions

Joseph Bruchac

In many Native American traditions life is seen as a circle. We enter that circle when we are born and as we travel around that circle we come back, as elders, to the place where we began. The elders, who have spent a lifetime learning their cultural traditions, are the ones who are supposed to be the closest to the children, passing on their traditions through the teaching to be found in stories. As long as that circle remains unbroken, the people will survive.

Imagine what it would be like if someone who never met you and knew nothing about the circle of your life wrote a story about you. Even if that person was a good writer, you probably would not agree with what he wrote. As interesting as imagination may be, it cannot take the place of experience and firsthand knowledge. In a similar way, imaginative portrayals of Native American people and Native American cultures became painful stereotypes and distorted history. Native American men were pictured as savage and dangerous people who were aggressive for no good reason. Yet it is historically true that none of America's so-called "Indian wars" were ever begun by the Indians. Native American women were pictured as nothing more than

beasts of burden. Yet in many Native American cultures, such as that of the Iroquois, the women were the heads of families, the owners of the houses, and the ones who chose the chiefs. Details of Native cultures were badly confused. For example, the famous poem *Hiawatha* by Henry Wadsworth Longfellow actually tells the story of Managozho, a trickster hero of the Chippewa people. The real Hiawatha was a political leader of the Iroquois people. It would be like calling the hero of the Anglo-Saxon epic *Beowulf* Julius Caesar. More than 400 different languages are spoken by the various Native American nations of North America, but instead of showing the complexity and variety of Native American cultures, much of the literature by non-Native people made all Indians look and sound alike.

Many Native Americans chose to become writers because they wanted to restore the circle through more accurate portrayals of themselves and their people. In many cases, too, they hoped to restore a sense of pride in their own heritage. Because of the inaccurate and unpleasant ways Native Americans have been portrayed in books by non-Indian authors, Native children have

▲ **Critical Viewing** In what two ways does the picture reflect the title? **[Identify]**

**Reading Check**

What problem bothers the writer?

Restoring the Circle ◆ 573

sometimes felt ashamed of themselves and decided that it would be better for them to forget their own cultures and try to be "just like everyone else." Today, because of the writing of such Native American authors as Michael Dorris or Linda Hogan, young Native people can read stories and poems in which Native Americans are presented as fully-rounded characters from accurately described tribal traditions. As portrayed by Native American authors, Indians are sometimes good, sometimes not so good, but no longer one-dimensional stereotypes.

In the period between 1850 and 1950, many Native American children were sent away to Indian boarding schools where they were not allowed to speak their own Native languages. Whether they wanted to or not, they were expected to no longer "be Indian" and, removed completely from the circle of their families, denied contact with their elders. It was felt by many well-meaning people in the United States government that the only way to "help the Indians" was by making them be more like European Americans. Today, of course, we see things differently. In a multicultural world we understand how important cultural traditions are in maintaining a sense of self-worth. It is now believed that whoever you are, whether you are Jewish American, African American, Italian American, or Native American, knowing about your own history and culture can make you a stronger person. Today, many Native American people are discovering that Native American literature can help them find their way back to that old circle of knowledge. In some cases, people who were not taught their tribal languages as children are learning those languages again through literature. In Arizona, a successful project helped Pima and Papago children learn their native O'odham language by reading traditional songs in O'odham and then writing poems in O'odham. Those songs, which had been preserved as literature, and the new poems worked together to help strengthen traditions.

One of the most prominent Native American writers is N. Scott Momaday, who is of Kiowa Indian ancestry. His first novel, *House Made of Dawn*, tells the story of a young Native American man who returns home after fighting as an American soldier in a foreign war. He feels divided between the white world and the Indian world, and that division in himself makes him sick. It is only by understanding his own traditions and returning to them that he is able to restore his health and self-respect. That novel, which won a Pulitzer Prize in 1969, is a good example of the kind of Native American writing which helps preserve cultural traditions. It contains authentic and very well-written descriptions of Native American life around the time of the late 1940's and early

Literary Analysis
Types and Purposes of Essays How does the detail about native languages add to the persuasive power of the essay?

▼ Critical Viewing Based on the essay and this picture of Bruchac, explain whether you think Bruchac enjoys nature. **[Speculate]**

1950's. Many Native Americans who have read this book have felt deeply inspired by it because its main character, caught between the white and Indian worlds, experiences some of the confusion and pain which they have also felt. It is hard to be a stranger in your own country, but that is the way many Native Americans sometimes feel. By reading Momaday's novel, they gained a better understanding of their own feelings, and it strengthened their convictions about the importance of preserving their own traditions.

Native American literature, like all literatures, is also a way to speak to the world. In some cases, novels by Native American writers are now being used as textbooks in college courses in history and sociology. Writing can become a window into another reality, offering to non-Natives the opportunity to authentically experience something of Native American culture. If you read a book about another culture, you may be more likely to have understanding and <u>tolerance</u> for that culture. When you have respect for another culture, then you are much less likely to do things which will be <u>detrimental</u> to that culture and to the people of that culture. Perhaps, because of the cultural understanding offered through Native American literature, the circle of Native American cultural traditions will be less threatened in the generations to come.

tolerance (täl′ ər əns) *n.* respect for something different

detrimental (de′ trə ment′ əl) *adj.* harmful

Review and Assess

Thinking About the Selection

1. **Respond:** What questions would you like to ask Joseph Bruchac about his heritage?

2. **(a) Recall:** Describe how some Native Americans use a circle to explain life. **(b) Interpret:** Explain the title "Restoring the Circle." **(c) Support:** In what ways do Native American writers help to restore the circle?

3. **(a) Recall:** What are two examples of ways in which Native American people have been misunderstood by those who are not Native American? **(b) Generalize:** Why is it important to Bruchac that Native American culture be portrayed accurately and sensitively?

4. **(a) Recall:** What does Bruchac say happens when people read about another culture? **(b) Apply:** How do writers of all cultures help to build people's understanding of a multicultural world?

5. **Make a Judgment:** Do you think an understanding of one's heritage makes a person stronger? Explain why.

Joseph Bruchac

(b. 1942)
A writing instructor once said to Joseph Bruchac, "Give it up. You'll never write a good poem." Since that awful prediction, Bruchac has written and edited many collections of poetry, winning numerous writing awards. His poems, stories, and essays have been translated into Russian, Italian, Polish, German, and many other languages. Among many other things, Bruchac is committed to preserving and celebrating his Native American heritage.

How the Internet Works

Kerry Cochrane

The central problem in designing the Internet was finding a way for different kinds of computers all over the country to talk to one another. ARPA solved this problem with Internet protocols. Protocols are sets of rules that standardize how something is done, so that everyone knows what to expect. For example, think of any game you've played and the rules that went with that game. The rules of the game tell you how many players you can have, what order you play in, what's allowed and what's not allowed, and how to keep score. Once you know the rules, you can play with people very different from you. Internet protocols are like game rules: they set up standard procedures for computers to follow so that they can communicate with each other.

The Internet is often compared to the postal service. They both seem to work like one big organization, but are actually made up of smaller parts that work together. There are local post offices in small towns, regional postal systems in big cities, and national postal services for countries. They all use different machinery to handle the mail, and different equipment to deliver it, from bicycles to trucks to airplanes. Postal workers all over the world speak hundreds of different languages. But they all manage to work together because of certain rules, or protocols. Postal protocols say that mail must be in envelopes or packages, there must be postage, and every piece of mail must have an address. As long as you know these rules, you can send mail to anyone in the world.

The Internet works in a similar way. As long as everyone knows the protocols, information can travel easily between machines and the people using them worldwide. The basic group of protocols that governs the Internet is the TCP/IP set of protocols. This stands for Transmission Control Protocol (TCP)

Literary Analysis
Types of Essays How does this comparison to the post office help you learn about the Internet?

and Internet Protocol (IP). Internet Protocol says that every computer connected to the Internet must have a unique address. These addresses consist of four sets of numbers separated by periods. For example, the IP address for one of the computers at the University of Illinois at Urbana-Champaign is **128.174.5.49**. Once you have the IP address of a computer, you know where to send messages or other information. Transmission Control Protocol manages the information you send out by computer. TCP breaks each message into manageable chunks and numbers each chunk in order. Then the numbered groups of information are marked with the IP address of the other computer and are sent out to it. When they arrive on the other end, TCP software checks to see that all the pieces are there and puts them back in order, ready to use.

When you drop a letter into a mailbox, it gets collected and sorted with hundreds of other pieces of mail. Your local post office sorts and routes the mail according to its destination and then sends it on to the next post office. Information is sorted and routed on the Internet in the same way. Computers on the Internet called routers, or packet switchers, read the IP addresses on each packet of information, and direct the packets to their destination. The information can be sent from one computer to another on phone lines, by satellite networks, on fiber-optic cables, or even through radio transmissions.

IP addresses are made up of numbers, which can be hard to remember and use. So computers usually have alphabetical addresses as well. Like IP addresses, these alphabetical addresses have several parts separated by periods, although they may have fewer or more than four parts. So a computer at the University of Iowa with the IP address **128.255.40.201** also has the alphabetical address **panda.uiowa.edu**, which is easier to remember. The first part of this address, **panda**, is the name of the *host* computer. The rest of this address, **uiowa.edu**, is called a domain name, because each part of the name refers to a domain. Each domain gives information about the Internet site, such as where it's located, who's responsible for the computer, and what kind of institution it's connected to. Moving from right to left, the domains give more specific information about the location of the host computer. In the domain name **uiowa.edu**, for example, the domain **edu** tells you that the host computer is run by an educational institution, because **edu** is the domain attached to all United States educational sites. The domain **uiowa** stands for the University of Iowa, which is the specific educational institution where the host computer named **panda** is located.

Reading Check

To what does the writer compare the Internet?

In the United States, there are six domains that are used at the end of domain names, and each one refers to the type of site that's running the computer.

Countries outside the United States do not use these domains. Instead, they have two-letter country domains at the end of their names, such as **nz** for New Zealand, **br** for Brazil, or **ca** for Canada.

Every person with an Internet *account* has a personal address, too. Individual Internet addresses are made up of a unique *user ID* (sometimes called a user name) for each person, which is attached to an alphabetical address by an "at" symbol (@). User IDs are usually taken from your name. My full Internet address is **kcochra@orion.it.luc.edu.** Reading this address from left to right, you see that my user ID is **kcochra** (from Kerry Cochrane), and I'm at the address **orion.it.luc.edu. Orion** is the name of the host machine running this account. The office of Information Technologies runs the computer named orion, so the first domain is called **it.** Information Technologies is an office of Loyola University Chicago, so the next domain is **luc.** Because this is an educational institution, the final domain is **edu.** The President of the United States even has an Internet address at the White House: **president@ whitehouse.gov.** Although they may seem complicated at first, Internet addresses make sense when you know how they work.

A few years ago the Internet was not available to the general public. Most people with Internet accounts got them through universities or companies where they were students or employees. As interest in the Internet has grown, however, ways to connect have increased, and they are improving all the time. One of the fastest-growing groups of Internet users is students and teachers in kindergarten through 12th grade. Schools around the world are getting access to the Internet so children can benefit from the immense resources available on-line.

There are several ways for schools to connect to the Internet. Many states or regions have developed their own networks to link schools together and get them on-line. Some universities and colleges provide guest accounts for local schools. Also, companies called Internet providers have begun to market Internet accounts to schools, companies, and private individuals. Your school may already be connected to the Internet, or someone in your family may have an account at work or at home.

Reading Strategy
Using Context Clues
Which context clues help you understand the term *user ID*?

Review and Assess
Thinking About the Selection

1. **Respond:** Did the comparison to a post office help you understand how the Internet works?
2. **(a) Recall:** What are Internet protocols?
   (b) Compare and Contrast: How does the Internet operate in a way that is similar to and different from the postal service?
   (c) Generalize: What makes the Internet different from anything that has come before it?
3. **(a) Recall:** What parts does an Internet address contain?
   (b) Draw Conclusions: What do you know about this person from this Internet address: chairman@computerinc.br?
4. **(a) Apply:** Explain how your life would or would not be different if there were no Internet. **(b) Take a Position:** What government regulation or rule regarding Internet use would you make more or less strict?

Kerry Cochrane

(b. 1956)

Kerry Cochrane has taught classes and written books on using the Internet. Her first book, *The Internet*, provides an introduction to the Internet and the many ways it can be used. Cochrane is Head of Reference and Development Librarian at Loyola University's Cudahy Library.

Turkeys

Bailey White

▲ **Critical Viewing** Why would scientists be interested in saving this species of bird? **[Speculate]**

Something about my mother attracts ornithologists. It all started years ago when a couple of them discovered she had a rare species of woodpecker coming to her bird feeder. They came in the house and sat around the window, exclaiming and taking pictures with big fancy cameras. But long after the red cockaded woodpeckers had gone to roost, the ornithologists were still there. There always seemed to be three or four of them wandering around our place and staying for supper.

Reading Strategy
Using Context What does an ornithologist study?

In those days, during the 1950's, the big concern of ornithologists in our area was the wild turkey. They were rare, and the pure-strain wild turkeys had begun to interbreed with farmers' domestic stock. The species was being degraded. It was extinction by <u>dilution</u>, and to the ornithologists it was just as tragic as the more dramatic demise of the passenger pigeon or the Carolina parakeet.

One ornithologist had devised a formula to compute the ratio of domestic to pure-strain wild turkey in an individual bird by comparing the angle of flight at takeoff and the rate of acceleration. And in those sad days, the turkeys were flying low and slow.

It was during that time, the spring when I was six years old, that I caught the measles. I had a high fever, and my mother was worried about me. She kept the house quiet and dark and crept around silently, trying different methods of cooling me down.

Even the ornithologists stayed away—but not out of fear of the measles or respect for a household with sickness. The fact was, they had discovered a wild turkey nest. According to the formula, the hen was pure-strain wild—not a taint of the sluggish domestic bird in her blood—and the ornithologists were camping in the woods, protecting her nest from predators and taking pictures.

One night our phone rang. It was one of the ornithologists. "Does your little girl still have measles?" he asked.

"Yes," said my mother. "She's very sick. Her temperature is 102."

"I'll be right over," said the ornithologist.

In five minutes a whole carload of them arrived. They marched solemnly into the house, carrying a cardboard box. "A hundred and two, did you say? Where is she?" they asked my mother.

They crept into my room and set the box down on the bed. I was barely conscious, and when I opened my eyes, their worried faces hovering over me seemed to float out of the darkness like giant, glowing eggs. They snatched the covers off me and felt me all over. They consulted in whispers.

"Feels just right, I'd say."

"A hundred two—can't miss if we tuck them up close and she lies still."

dilution (di lōō′ shən) *n.* process of weakening by mixing with something else

Reading Strategy
Using Context How do the clues *extinction* and *tragic* help you determine the meaning of *demise*?

Literary Analysis
Types of Essays How are these details different from the details in "How the Internet Works"?

I closed my eyes then, and after a while the ornithologists drifted away, their pale faces bobbing up and down on the black wave of fever.

The next morning I was better. For the first time in days I could think. The memory of the ornithologists with their whispered voices was like a dream from another life. But when I pulled down the covers, there staring up at me with googly eyes and wide mouths were six-teen fuzzy baby turkeys, and the cracked chips and caps of sixteen brown speckled eggs.

I was a sensible child. I gently stretched myself out. The eggshells crackled, and the turkey babies fluttered and cheeped and snuggled against me. I laid my aching head back on the pillow and closed my eyes. "The ornithologists," I whispered. "The ornithologists have been here."

It seems the turkey hen had been so dis-turbed by the elaborate protective measures that had been undertaken on her behalf that she had abandoned her nest on the night the eggs were due to hatch. It was a cold night. The ornithologists, not having an incubator on hand, used their heads and came up with the next best thing.

The baby turkeys and I gained our strength together. When I was finally able to get out of bed and feebly creep around the house, the turkeys peeped and cheeped around my ankles, scrambling to keep up with me and tripping over their own big spraddle-toed feet. When I went outside for the first time, the turkeys tumbled after me

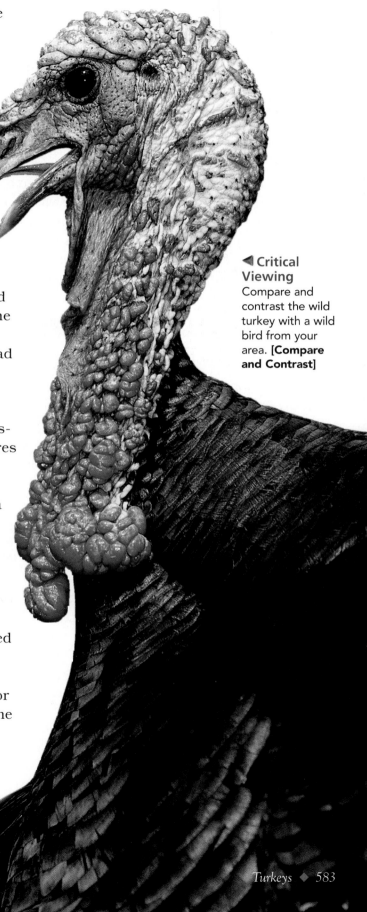

◀ **Critical Viewing** Compare and contrast the wild turkey with a wild bird from your area. **[Compare and Contrast]**

☑ **Reading Check**

What do the ornithologists do to keep the chicks warm?

down the steps and scratched around in the yard while I sat in the sun.

Finally, in late summer, the day came when they were ready to fly for the first time as adult birds. The ornithologists gathered. I ran down the hill, and the turkeys ran too. Then, one by one, they took off. They flew high and fast. The ornithologists made Vs with their thumbs and forefingers, measuring angles. They consulted their stopwatches and paced off distances. They scribbled in their tiny notebooks. Finally they looked at each other. They sighed. They smiled. They jumped up and down and hugged each other. "One hundred percent pure wild turkey!" they said.

Nearly forty years have passed since then. Now there's a vaccine for measles. And the woods where I live are full of pure wild turkeys. I like to think they are all descendants of those sixteen birds I saved from the <u>vigilance</u> of the ornithologists.

vigilance (vij´ ə ləns) *n.* watchfulness

Review and Assess

Thinking About the Selection

1. **Respond:** How would you have reacted if you woke up surrounded by newly hatched turkeys?

2. **(a) Recall:** What is the setting of "Turkeys"? **(b) Analyze:** What problem threatens the wild turkey at this time? **(c) Interpret:** How do you know the author is concerned about this problem?

3. **(a) Recall:** Why are the ornithologists around the author's home? **(b) Interpret:** At the beginning of the essay, what is the relationship between the author and the ornithologists?

4. **(a) Recall:** What event brings the wild turkeys and the author together? **(b) Connect:** Why is the author's fever important to the ornithologists? **(c) Analyze:** What is comical about the solution to the ornithologists' problem?

5. **(a) Recall:** How do the scientists determine how much domestic turkey is mixed into the wild turkey population? **(b) Analyze:** How do the ornithologists know that the turkeys that hatched are 100 percent wild?

6. **(a) Make a Judgment:** Do you think the actions of the ornithologists in this narrative are important? Why or why not? **(b) Speculate:** How do you think White feels when she watches the turkeys take off?

Bailey White

(b. 1950)

As a first-grade teacher in the town where she was born and raised, Bailey White didn't expect to become famous. Radio, though, brought her voice and observations into homes across the country. Although she is now a best-selling author, she continues to live a simple life in the pine woods of Georgia.

Review and Assess

Literary Analysis

Types of Essays

1. What is the main point of each **essay?**
2. Make an organizer like this one to show the type of each essay in this group.

	Type	Characteristics
"Restoring the Circle"		
"How the Internet Works"		
"Turkeys"		

Comparing Literary Works

3. What characteristics do all essays share?
4. What is the unique purpose of each essay in the group?
5. How do the different purposes of essays influence the kinds of details they include?
6. Choose two works and show the similarities and differences in purpose and types of details.

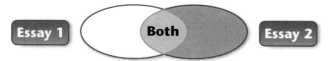

Reading Strategy

Using Context Clues

7. In the second paragraph of "Restoring the Circle," Bruchac uses the word *stereotypes*. What clues in the sentences that follow help you determine the word's meaning?
8. "How the Internet Works" uses the word *domain* in a way that may be new to you. What context clues can help you figure out the meaning of *domain* as it relates to the Internet?
9. What are two possible meanings for the word *formula*? What is its meaning in "Turkeys"?

Extending Understanding

10. **Math Connection:** In what ways does a good understanding of math help you use and work with a computer?

Quick Review

A **persuasive essay** attempts to convince a reader to think or act in a certain way.

An **informational essay** explains or informs.

A **narrative essay** tells a story about a real-life experience. To review the types of essays, see p. 571.

Context clues are the words and phrases surrounding an unfamiliar word that help you figure out the meaning of the word. To review context clues, see p. 571.

 Take It to the Net
www.phschool.com
Take the interactive self-test online to check your understanding of these essays.

Integrate Language Skills

Vocabulary Development Lesson

Word Analysis: Forms of *tolerate*

In "Restoring the Circle," Joseph Bruchac encourages *tolerance*, which is a form of *tolerate*; it means "the action of respecting something you do not necessarily agree with."

On your paper, copy each sentence and complete it with one of these words: *tolerated, tolerance, tolerant, tolerable*.

1. The baby turkeys were ____?____ of the sick little girl.
2. White's mother ____?____ the unusual habits of the scientists.
3. Bruchac's ____?____ makes him open to many ideas.
4. The baby turkeys find a very limited range of temperatures ____?____ .

Concept Development: Antonyms

An **antonym** is a word with an opposite meaning. Copy each numbered word and write its antonym from the list of vocabulary words.

1. concentration
2. rejection
3. carelessness
4. helpful

a. tolerance
b. detrimental
c. dilution
d. vigilance

Spelling Strategy

When adding suffixes -*ance*, -*ant*, -*ence*, or -*ent*, there is no sound clue to help you decide whether to use *a* or *e*. Practice the spellings of the following words by rewriting them in two columns—an "a" column and an "e" column. Use each word marked by an asterisk in a sentence.

* descendant   * tolerant   resistant
* vigilance   resident   * importance
* defiant   insistent

Grammar Lesson

Punctuation and Capitalization in Dialogue

Dialogue is speech that is presented exactly as a character utters it. Quotation marks are used to enclose the exact words of a speaker. A comma, question mark, or exclamation point separates the speaker's words from the words that indicate who said them. Punctuation marks at the end of a quotation go inside the closing quotation marks. The comma at the end of the introductory words comes before the opening quotation marks.

Examples: "I'll be right over," said the ornithologist.
"Look!" I yelled.
She asked, "Why do you want to know?"

Practice Copy each sentence. Insert the quotation marks and all other punctuation in each sentence.

1. feels just right the scientists said
2. what do you want my mother asked
3. does your little girl have measles he asked
4. she thought why are all these turkeys here
5. the scientists called out one hundred percent

Writing Application Write a conversation between you and a friend. Use quotation marks and punctuation in your dialogue.

Writing Lesson

Compare-and-Contrast Composition

In "How to Use the Internet," Kerry Cochrane compares the postal service to the Internet. Write a composition comparing and contrasting two Internet sites.

Prewriting Choose a topic and find two Web sites with information on the topic. Use an organizer like this one to gather details.

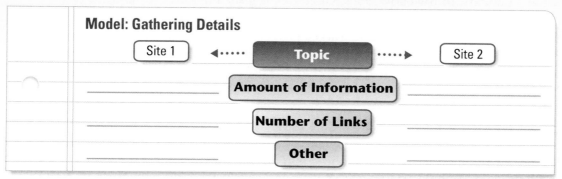

Model: Gathering Details

Site 1 ◄••••• **Topic** •••••► Site 2

Amount of Information

Number of Links

Other

Drafting Begin with an introductory paragraph in which you identify your two sites. Then, organize paragraphs around the categories on the chart.

Revising Highlight all the details about the first site in one color. Highlight all the details about the second site in a second color. If there are many more details in one color than in the other, add details that will improve the balance.

𝒲𝒢 Prentice Hall Writing and Grammar Connection: Chapter 8, Section 3

Extension Activities

Listening and Speaking Deliver **oral directions** to the class for starting a computer, logging on to e-mail, or doing an Internet search.

1. Present the steps in order.
2. Be clear and specific in identifying each part of the computer for each step of the directions.
3. Define any terms that may be unfamiliar.
4. Speak clearly, and pause after explaining each step so that listeners can remember what you have said.

Research and Technology Joseph Bruchac calls for respect and honor for Native American cultures through literature that develops understanding and tolerance. Compile a list of Native American authors and works that students your age might enjoy. Share your list with the class.

Writing Write a letter to one of the authors. Tell the author what you think are the strengths and weaknesses of the work. Use examples from the text.

 **Take It to the Net**   www.phschool.com

Go online for an additional research activity using the Internet.

CONNECTIONS
Literature and Science

Environmental Emergencies

In "Turkeys," Bailey White gives a personal account of her experience with efforts to save populations of wild turkeys. At the turn of the twentieth century, wild turkeys had disappeared from 18 of the 39 states they had inhabited. In 1937, the Federal Aid in Wildlife Restoration Act began funding the acquisition of wildlife habitats. In the early 1950s, wildlife biologists in South Carolina trapped healthy wild turkeys and released them in habitats where there were few wild turkeys. When the National Wild Turkey Federation was founded in 1973, the restoration of wild turkeys was underway in many states. Today, more than five million wild turkeys roam the fields and forests of North America.

This article discusses another wildlife "emergency." Saving the many species of migrating birds and fish from the increasingly polluted Salton Sea is a challenge facing engineers and scientists. The Salton Sea is a landlocked lake in Southern California's Imperial Valley. This popular, 360-mile-square saltwater lake has become polluted by agricultural runoff, including chemicals and silt. Lacking a steady supply of fresh water, it is becoming more salty and polluted every day and increasingly dangerous for wildlife.

California's Much-Maligned Salton Sea— Is a Desert Oasis for Wildlife

National Wildlife
August–Sept. 2000

Joby Warrick

To appreciate the beauty of the Salton Sea you first have to look past some very big warts. Dennis Imhoff, state park ranger and booster for California's biggest inland lake, is trying to steer a visitor away from the sea's gnarliest features but they keep popping up, like the dying fish now floating in clumps near the shoreline.

The midday heat is ferocious, a blistering 100 degrees F. The sand whines with millions of insects. The public beach is deserted, except for a few dozen black cormorants keeping sullen watch over the rotting fish. As Imhoff watches, a young couple in a Volvo cruises slowly through the parking lot and then drives away without even cracking a window. . . .

Yet this ugly duckling of a lake harbors surprises, some of which are only now becoming fully appreciated. Recent biological surveys of this much-maligned water body have revealed an astonishing richness in wildlife. The 90-degree water churns with fish in such abundance that some locals describe scooping them up in trash bags. The fish in turn attract birds by the millions. Indeed, this unusual lake attracts more species of migrating birds than any other location in the contiguous United States, except for the Texas coastline.

That's why, say the lake's supporters, the Salton Sea has become a natural wonder. The problem is convincing government officials and a less-than-eager public that it is a treasure worth saving.

"That smell—it's the smell of life," says Steven Horvitz, superintendent of the state's Salton Sea Recreation Area. With nearly 95 percent of California's inland wetlands lost to development in the past 150 years, the sea has taken on critical importance as a feeding ground for birds migrating north along the Pacific flyway, he says. "If the sea can no longer support the bird population," he adds, "many of the birds that use the lake as a feeding ground will no longer be able to survive."

The lake itself is a tear-shaped body of water that lies 227 feet below sea level, in a natural and utterly barren depression that

---

Thematic Connection
Why is the Salton Sea worth saving?

Spanish explorers once called "the palm of the hand of God." To the east and west are rugged hills; to the south is one of California's most productive agricultural regions, a former desert that exploded to life at the turn of the last century with the arrival of irrigated water from the Colorado River.

It was an irrigation accident that brought the Salton Sea into existence. In 1905, a flood-swollen Colorado River crashed through a poorly made dike, sending billions of gallons of water surging into the Imperial Valley. The flow continued unchecked for 18 months, creating a new freshwater sea larger than Lake Tahoe.

Stocked with game fish in the 1950s, the sea's shores sprouted fish clubs and motels that drew hundreds of thousands of visitors a year. But ultimately the sea was doomed by its own geography. Lacking an outlet, the lake became increasingly salty, with each day bringing new deposits of minerals and silt in the form of farm runoff. Slowly, many of the businesses in the new area dried up. In the former resort known as Salton Sea, a dilapidated yacht club and a few rusted trailers are all that's left of a bustling waterfront that once was the stomping ground of the Beach Boys and Hollywood's infamous Rat Pack.

Despite the sea's odd origins and seemingly harsh environment, birds are continually drawn to the area. "It is a crown jewel of avian biodiversity," says Milton Friend, executive director of the Salton Sea Science Subcommittee, a multiagency task force.

Science Subcommittee researchers recently completed the most comprehensive survey ever of the sea's biological assets, and pronounced it "incredibly rich" with life in all its variety. The study found 200 new species of plants, animals and microbes that previously had not been recorded at Salton Sea. In addition, it reported that more than 400 kinds of birds—nearly half the total number of known species in North America—have been spotted around the lake, drawn by prey both large and small. And the fish population, widely believed to be in decline, is actually vibrant. Highly prized game fish such as corvina and other species such as croaker and tilapia are not only plentiful, but apparently also safe to eat. "The Salton Sea," the report noted, "may be the most productive fishery in the world."

But it also may be doomed. Eventually, the rising salt levels could destroy the fish—and that's only if farm chemicals fail to do the job first. Nutrients from fertilizers accelerate the life cycle of tiny plants called algae, and the runaway growth strips the water of the oxygen fish need to live. Last year, eight million fish died of asphyxiation on a single day.

Reversing the sea's decline will require major feats in both engineering and public relations. "It represents one of the greatest challenges I've seen in 40 years of studying damaged ecosystems, says

Thematic Connection
Are the environmental problems that are dooming the Salton Sea similar to those facing the wild turkey? Explain.

Friend. Several proposals are being studied that would reverse the rising salt levels, but launching any of them would require generating large amounts of money and equally large amounts of political capital—a not-so-easy feat for supporters of a lake that generates relatively little income and doesn't always put on its best face for visitors.

But with the arrival of fall the sea turns into a different place. Daytime temperatures drop into the 60s and 70s. The algal blooms cease, the fish stop dying and the birds begin to arrive-by the millions. Egrets, herons, ducks and pelicans feed and roost along the shores, along with such rarely seen creatures as the frigate bird and booby. The annual migrations draw serious birders from across the West to Sonny Bono National Wildlife Refuge, a reserve recently renamed to honor the former California congressman who led efforts to restore the sea before his death in a Sierra Nevada skiing accident.

Some who visit never leave and grow to love the place, warts and all. The beauty of the desert sunsets and the endless variety of wildlife convinced Los Angeles bartender John White to trade his city apartment eight years ago for a small bungalow in Bombay Beach, one of the largest of a half-dozen villages of trailers and cottages scattered along the 60 miles of waterfront. As he fishes from the town pier, his head wrapped in a sweaty bandana to muffle the sun's intensity, a pair of large pelicans take flight behind him with a great whooshing sound like a helicopter's rotor.

"Sometimes when I come here early in the morning, there will be hundreds of birds scattered out in the weeds," White says. "I like to just sit here and listen to the noises they make."

The chattering of birds is getting fainter, and Imhoff, the park ranger, worries that it may eventually disappear. If the Salton Sea goes, the birds go, too.

"Only now, we've destroyed so many wetlands there's no place else for them to go," he says. "There won't be anything left when this is gone."

Joby Warrick, a staff writer for The Washington Post, *visited the Salton Sea while reporting for this article.*

Thematic Connection

What challenges face scientists working to preserve the Salton Sea habitat? How are these challenges similar to and different from those that scientists working with wild turkey habitats?

Connecting Literature and Science

1. Compare the conditions for saving the wild turkey with the conditions for saving the birds and fish that inhabit the Salton Sea. Why would it be more difficult to save the wildlife at the Salton Sea?

2. If the turkey hen abandoned her eggs today rather than in 1950, how would the ornithologists save the eggs? What measures or procedures do scientists and conservationists have today to save other kinds of wildlife?

Textbooks

About Textbooks

Since you first started school, you have read and used many textbooks. Though they covered different topics, they were alike in some ways.

- A textbook gives information about a particular subject, such as literature, math, science, geography, or American history.
- The purpose of a textbook is to help students learn new materials. The material is divided into units, chapters, and sections, usually by topic. Within the text, boldface heads, color, and other graphic devices highlight important ideas. Questions at the end of a unit or section help you review what you have read.
- Textbooks also include visual aids such as photos, graphs, charts, and fine art. Visuals work with the text by illustrating concepts, showing examples, or summarizing information.

Reading Strategy

Making an Outline

An outline is an organized list of main ideas and significant details. Its organization shows the relationship between ideas and information. Outlines can be used to take notes on informational materials.

Outlines usually follow a form like the one shown here. Each main heading is listed under a Roman numeral: I, II, III, and so on. Each subhead is identified by a capital letter: A, B, C. Supporting details are numbered: 1, 2, 3. In a formal outline structure, there must be at least two of each type of head. For example, if you have a subhead A, you must also have a subhead B.

In a textbook, the organization of the material itself helps shape your outline. Boldface heads and subheads point out the main ideas. These heads are the "skeleton" of your outline.

Model: Outline

I. First main topic or idea

  A. Subheading #1

  B. Subheading #2

    1. Supporting detail 1

      (a) smaller detail

      (b) smaller detail

    2. Supporting detail 2

    3. Supporting detail 3

II. Second main topic or idea

  A. Subheading #1

  B. Subheading #2

  C. Subheading #3

Populations and Communities

The section head states the topic of this section of the textbook.

Populations

In 1900, travelers saw a prairie dog town in Texas covering an area twice the size of the city of Dallas. The sprawling town contained more than 400 million prairie dogs! These prairie dogs were all members of one species, or single kind, of organism. A **species** (SPEE sheez) is a group of organisms that are physically similar and can reproduce with each other to produce fertile offspring.

New terms are defined and their pronunciation given.

All the members of one species in a particular area are referred to as a **population**. The 400 million prairie dogs in the Texas town are one example of a population. All the pigeons in New York City make up a population, as do all the daisies in a field. In contrast, all the trees in a forest do not make up a population, because they do not all belong to the same species. There may be pines, maples, birches, and many other tree species in the forest.

A different style or size of the type indicates an important idea or term.

The area in which a population lives can be as small as a single blade of grass or as large as the whole planet. Scientists studying a type of organism usually limit their study to a population in a defined area. For example, they might study the population of bluegill fish in a pond, or the population of alligators in the Florida Everglades.

Some populations, however, do not stay in a contained area. For example, to study the population of finback whales, a scientist might need to use the entire ocean.

☑ **CHECKPOINT** *What is the difference between a species and a population?*

Questions in the text make sure the student is learning the most important ideas.

Figure 1
A single organism

Figure 2
A population

Figure 3
A community

Communities

Of course, most ecosystems contain more than one type of organism. The prairie, for instance, includes prairie dogs, hawks, grasses, badgers, and snakes, along with many other organisms. All the different populations that live together in an area make up a **community**.

The smallest unit of organization is a single **organism** (*figure 1*). The organism belongs to a **population** of other members of its species (*figure 2*). The population belongs to a **community** of different species (*figure 3*). The community and abiotic factors together form an **ecosystem** (*figure 4*).

To be considered a community, the different populations must live close enough together to interact. One way the populations in a community may interact is by using the same resources, such as food and shelter. For example, the tunnels dug by the prairie dogs also serve as homes for burrowing owls and black-footed ferrets. The prairie dogs share the grass with other animals. Meanwhile, prairie dogs themselves serve as food for many species.

☑ **CHECKPOINT** *What is a community? How is it different from an ecosystem?*

References to pictures, charts, and photographs give you another way to look at concepts described or explained in the text.

Figure 4
An ecosystem

Check Your Comprehension

1. What is an example of a population?
2. Where could you go to study an alligator habitat?
3. What is one way that populations in a community interact?

Applying the Reading Strategy

Creating an Outline

4. What two terms or concepts would you assign to Roman numerals in an outline of this section?
5. How do the section title and subheads help you decide what the main categories on your outline will be?
6. Make an outline of this textbook section that you could keep in your notebook for study.

Activity

Identify Features of Textbooks

In addition to headings, visual aids, and formatting, textbooks include other features that help readers find and organize information.

- The table of contents provides a quick reference to locate each topic.
- The index is a kind of outline of all the smaller categories of information listed alphabetically with page numbers.
- A glossary defines specialized vocabulary at the end of the book. Choose a textbook you use in any class. Identify as many features as you can using this checklist and include an example or description of each feature.

Feature	Example
Photos, fine art, charts, graphs, tables, other visuals	
Chapter, unit, or section titles	
Subheads	
Color bars with type	
Word definitions at page bottom	
Table of contents	
Index	
Glossary	

Contrasting Informational Materials

Textbooks and Magazines

Using library resources, find a magazine article related to environmental issues. Look in magazines such as *National Geographic World* and *National Wildlife*. Compare the article with this textbook section in terms of **(a)** text organization, **(b)** text features such as boldface heads and vocabulary, **(c)** use of graphics like photographs and graphs or charts. Write a brief explanation of the similarities and differences in each category.

READING INFORMATIONAL MATERIALS

Research Reports

About Research Reports

A research report presents detailed factual information about a subject. There are many reasons people use research reports. A heart surgeon might turn to a research report to learn about new surgical techniques. A new parent might turn to research to find out about good methods for raising children. As a student, you might use a research report to increase your level of knowledge about an interesting subject. Most research reports have the following characteristics:

- a well-defined topic
- a clear organization
- information from a variety of sources
- facts and details supporting each main point

Reading Strategy

Asking Questions

To understand a research report better, ask questions *before*, *while*, and *after* you read:

Before you read, you may not know very much about the subject. Your questions will be very general. For instance, you might ask, "What types of sharks are there?"

While you read, your questions should be geared toward understanding the information the author is presenting. If the author has just claimed that sharks have more to fear from people than the reverse, you might reasonably ask, "Why is that?" These questions can usually be answered by reading further.

After you read, you might ask two types of questions, "What did I just learn?" and "What more do I still want to know?" For the first type of question, go back to the reading material. For the second question, choose another book or article on the subject to find out more. Use the Works Cited list or the Bibliography to find additional resources.

Research Phase	General Questions You Can Ask
Before you read . . .	What do I already know about a subject? What would I like to learn?
While you read . . .	What is the main point the author is making? How does the author support the main point with evidence?
After you read . . .	What new information did I learn? Do I agree with the author's conclusions? Do I have additional questions that this research report does not answer?

Check Your Comprehension

1. Why does the author say that sharks have more to fear from humans than the reverse?
2. Approximately how many species of sharks exist?
3. What are two reasons sharks are killed?

Applying the Reading Strategy

Asking Questions

4. What views and knowledge did you have of sharks before reading this article?
5. What questions occurred to you as you read? Why?
6. What are the main questions McGrath poses in this article?
7. What information would you like to know about sharks that is not included in this article?

Activity

Problem Investigation

In the article on sharks, the author mentions the problem of overfishing of ocean species. This is a problem with many other fish species as well, including salmon, cod, and bluefin tuna. Research and write a report on the problem of overfishing. Be sure to ask yourself questions as you prepare. Consult multiple sources in your research and cite them appropriately in your report. To learn more about how to write a research report, use the Writing Workshop on page 600 to guide you.

Comparing Informational Texts

Research Reports and Newspaper Articles

Research reports follow a specific format for citing information from sources and providing information to help readers find the source materials. Newspaper articles, while often research based, do not follow a set format for crediting sources. In fact, newspaper articles sometimes do not tell source information at all.

Find two newspaper articles about sharks, shark populations, or shark hunting. Use a chart like the one shown to compare and contrast the characteristics of the two informational materials.

	Research	Newspaper
Main Ideas		
Number of Sources Created		
Similar Facts		
Different Facts		

Writing WORKSHOP

Research: Research Report

A **research report** presents facts and information gathered from several credible sources, such as public records, reference books, and periodicals. In this workshop, you will choose a subject, gather information, and write a report, citing your sources in a bibliography.

Assignment Criteria Your research report should have the following characteristics:

- A topic that is narrow enough in scope to thoroughly cover in the course of the report
- Facts, details, examples, and explanations from multiple authoritative sources to support the main ideas
- A clear method of organization
- Accurate and complete citations identifying sources
- A complete and accurate bibliography

See the Rubric on page 605 for the criteria on which your research report may be assessed.

Prewriting

Choose and narrow a topic. Browse through reference sources or magazines at the library to find topics you are interested in. Narrow broad topics by asking questions about particular areas of your topic. Then, circle parts of your answers to consider as possibilities for the focus of your research report.

- What are the causes or effects?
- Who is the most important or influential person?
- How is it similar to something else?

Locate authoritative sources. Use a variety of sources to find information about your topic: speeches, periodicals, newspapers, online information, videotapes, interviews, books, and brochures. Keep careful track of the source you use for each piece of information. Write down title, author, publication date, and place. You'll need this information to write your bibliography.

Take notes. Take careful notes about information you can use. Use quotation marks when you copy words directly. Otherwise, use your own words.

Sample Source Card

Connolly, Peter, and Hazel Dodge. *The Ancient City.*
New York: Oxford University Press, 1998. p. 28

Sample Note Card

Connolly, 28   Construction

Colosseum construction begins — A. D. 75

Student Model

Before you begin drafting your research report, read this portion of a student model and review the characteristics of a successful research report. To read the full report, see www.phschool.com.

Elizabeth Cleary,
Maplewood, New Jersey

Ice Ages

Ice ages occur every two hundred million years or so. An ice age is defined as a long period of cold where large amounts of water are trapped under ice. Although ice ages happened long ago, studing their causes and effects helps contemporary scientists understand geological conditions of the world today.

When an ice age does occur, ice covers much of the Earth. This ice forms when the climate changes. The polar regions become very cold and the temperatures drop everywhere else. The ice is trapped in enormous mountains of ice called glaciers. Glaciers can be as large as a continent in size. When the Earth's temperature warms up, the glaciers start to melt, forming rivers and lakes. Glaciers' tremendous weight and size can actually wear away mountains and valleys as the glaciers melt and move. The melting ice also raises ocean levels.

There are many different theories to explain why ice ages occur, but no one knows for sure. Many scientists agree that it is probably due to a combination of causes, including changes in the sun's intensity, the distance of the Earth from the sun, changes in ocean currents, the continental plates rubbing up against each other, and the varying amounts of carbon dioxide in the atmosphere (*PBS Nova* Web site "The Big Chill").

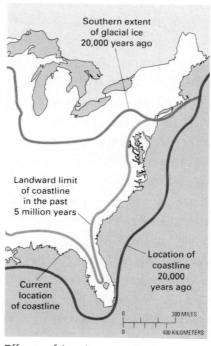

Southern extent of glacial ice 20,000 years ago

Landward limit of coastline in the past 5 million years

Location of coastline 20,000 years ago

Current location of coastline

300 MILES

400 KILOMETERS

Effects of Ice Ages on Eastern Coastline of United States

The author defines her topic clearly in this sentence.

This map illustrates the writer's point that ice ages caused current conditions.

Here the author presents factual information related to the possible causes of ice ages.

During the last ice age, or the Wisconsin Ice Age, people lived on the Earth. These people saw ice and snow all the time. It was never warm enough for it to melt, so it piled up. In the summertime, women fished in chilly streams. The men hunted year-round.

The skeleton of one person who lived and hunted during this time was found by some hikers in 1901 in the European Alps. He had been buried in the ice for nearly 5,000 years. Nicknamed "The Iceman," scientists believe that perhaps he was suddenly caught by a blizzard or that he possibly ran out of food, became weak, and died.

Scientists were able to learn a lot about this ancient period from the leather clothes and animal skins he was wearing and the tools he was carrying (Roberts, p. 38).

Ice ages also affect our life today. The ice sheets that formed weighed a huge amount. When the ice retreated, it left behind large rocks and other debris which otherwise would not be there. Also, without ice ages, large bodies of water like the Great Lakes simply wouldn't exist. We depend on these bodies of water every day for fresh drinking water, recreation, and shipping large quantities of materials.

Scientists discovered ice ages because of Louis Agassiz, a nineteenth-century scientist who is sometimes called the "Father of Glaciology." In Switzerland, he saw boulders or granite far from where any granite should be. He also noticed scrapes and grooves, or striae. He theorized that glaciers had caused all of these geologic features (University of California Museum of Paleontology Web page).

Many animals that are extinct now lived during the Ice Age. The saber-toothed tiger and the mastodon, an elephantlike animal, formerly lived in North America. They became extinct because of climate change and hunting. Other animals became extinct as well because they could not adapt to the way the Earth was changing.

Baron Gerard de Geer, a Swedish geologist, did pioneering work which estimated the end of the last Ice Age. In a similar way to the way we count

Elizabeth clearly and accurately cites her sources to show where she obtained a set of specific details.

In each section, Elizabeth explores a different aspect of the ice ages. Here she is explaining scientific discovery.

tree rings to estimate a tree's age, De Geer used layers of sediment left by glaciers' summer melts to calculate the history of the Ice Age. He did much of his work in Sweden, but he also visited areas that had been affected by glaciers in New England.

Thanks to scientists like De Geer and Agassiz, we know a great deal about that remote age when glaciers roamed the Earth. We can now estimate the history of ice ages and determine what features—valleys, inland seas, mountains, lakes, rocks—were caused by glaciers. We are even able to determine where the large glaciers were, as you can see by the map displayed here of the Eastern United States. There is still a lot more to be discovered about the causes of ice ages, but one thing is clear: Glaciers had a powerful effect on the world as we know it today.

> The author restates the main idea that she presented in the introduction and supported in the body of the paper.

Bibliography

Department of Geosciences, University of Arizona. 10 Nov. 2000.
    <http://www.geo.arizona.edu/Antevs/degeer.html>
History of the Universe. 11 Nov. 2000.
    <http://www.historyoftheuniverse.com/iceage.html>
Ice Age. Compton's Interactive Encyclopedia © The Learning
    Company, Inc. [CD-ROM] (1998).
Roberts, David. "The Iceman." *National Geographic Magazine,*
    June 1993: 37–49
University of California Museum of Paleontology. 11 Nov. 2000
    <http://www.ucmp.berkeley.edu/history/aggassiz.html>
PBS Nova "The Big Chill." 10 Nov. 2000.
    <http://www.pbs.org/wgbh/nova/ice/chill.html>

> In her bibliography, Elizabeth cites all the sources used to research her paper.

Drafting

Organize your research report. Group your notes by categories that break your topic into subtopics. For example, if you are writing about the Colosseum, you might use these topics in your notes:

- architecture of Colosseum
- construction of Colosseum
- events held in Colosseum
- spectators at Colosseum

Use Roman numerals (I, II, III) to number topics and A, B, C to indicate subtopics, as in the outline shown here.

Match your draft to your outline. A solid, detailed outline will guide you through writing your draft. The headings with Roman numerals indicate sections of your report. You will need to write several paragraphs to fully cover each Roman numeral. Organize your paragraphs around the topics with capital letters. You can even include headings in your draft if you want to guide your reader through complex subjects.

Support main ideas with facts. Using your outline, jot down sentences about each of the main ideas in your report. Leave spaces between sentences, and add wide margins. Then, fill in supporting facts, details, examples, and explanations drawn from your reference sources.

Prepare to cite sources. Part of "drafting" a research report is making a bibliography or Works Cited list.

I. Introduction
II. Architecture of Colosseum
A. measurements
B. building material
III. Construction of Colosseum
A. beginning date
B. workers

Model: Making a Bibliography

1. Organize your source cards in alphabetical order by author's or editor's last name. If the work has no author or editor, use the first word of the entry to alphabetize.
2. Write or keyboard information on a separate page.
3. Refer to Citing Sources and Preparing Manuscripts, page R12, to check styles of different kinds of entries.

Revising

Revise for effective paragraph structure. In a research report, most paragraphs will be built like this:

- a **topic sentence** (T) stating the paragraph's main idea
- a **restatement** or elaboration (R) of the topic sentence
- **illustrations** (I), facts, examples, or details about the main idea

Review your draft. Label each of your sentences with *T*, *R*, or *I*. If you find a group of *I*'s, make sure there is a *T* they support. If you find a *T* by itself, add *I*'s to support it.

Model: Balancing Your Paragraphs

R
These people saw ice and snow all the time. *R* **It was never warm enough for it to melt, so it piled up.**

T During the last ice age, or the Wisconsin Ice Age, people lived on the Earth. *I* In the summertime, women fished in chilly streams. *I* The men hunted year-round.

> Elizabeth adds sentences that restate her topic sentence to achieve balance in the paragraph.

Publishing and Presenting

Use the following suggestion to share your writing with classmates or a larger audience.

Present a Mini-Lesson Use your report as the basis for an oral presentation on your topic for your classmates. Make a poster announcing your presentation.

WG *Prentice Hall Writing and Grammar Connection: Chapter 11*

Speaking Connection
To learn more about delivering a research report as a speech, see the **Listening and Speaking Workshop: Delivering a Research Presentation**, page 606.

Rubric for Self-Assessment

Evaluate your research report using the following criteria and rating scale:

Criteria	Rating Scale				
	Not very				Very
How well defined is the topic?	1	2	3	4	5
How well do facts, details, examples, and explanations support the main ideas?	1	2	3	4	5
How well does the writer use a variety of credible sources?	1	2	3	4	5
How clear is the method of organization?	1	2	3	4	5
How accurate and complete are citations in the bibliography?	1	2	3	4	5

Listening and Speaking WORKSHOP

Delivering a Research Presentation

Delivering an effective **research presentation** has many of the same characteristics as preparing a research report. (To review the characteristics of a successful research report, see the Writing Workshop, pp. 600–605.) For hints on preparing and delivering a research report, use some of the strategies suggested here.

Effective Preparation

Before giving a research presentation, take time to go over your material and organize your notes and any visual aids you plan to use. Have on hand a list of reliable sources, including Web site addresses that you used.

Draw from multiple sources. Make the audience aware that your information is drawn from a number of reliable sources, such as expert interviews, books, newspapers, videotapes, periodicals, and online sites. Keep in mind that some sources, such as government Web sites, are more reliable than others.

Support your topic. Develop your topic so that you introduce your main ideas and then support them with interesting facts, details, and explanations from a variety of sources. Providing examples will further enhance your presentation.

Use visual aids. As often as possible, present photographs, charts, and diagrams. Use slides and videotapes when appropriate. These aids will give your presentation variety.

Effective Delivery

Before giving a research presentation, take time to rehearse, practicing ways to use your voice for emphasis. Be sure that your topic is not so broad that you cannot adequately cover it in the allotted time.

Pose relevant questions. It's a good idea to begin your presentation with a few good questions, sufficiently narrow in scope to be completely and thoroughly answered in your presentation. This technique will let your audience know exactly what you will cover.

Slow down; take your time. Sometimes, presenters speak too quickly because they are nervous. Pause for a moment before you begin and take a deep breath.

Using Visual Aids

- **Maps**

  Use **maps** when presenting a report on a country or region.

- **Charts and Graphs**

  Use **charts and graphs** to show statistics or changes in amount.

- **Diagrams**

  Use **diagrams** with explanations of parts or processes.

Activity:
Presentation

Choose a subject related to a current event in the news. Research the background, as well as the importance of the event, using newspapers, magazines, and Web sites. Prepare and deliver a research presentation on your topic.

Assessment WORKSHOP

Distinguishing Fact From Opinion

The reading sections of some tests require you to read a passage and answer multiple-choice questions about distinguishing fact from opinion. Use the following strategies to help you answer such questions:

- A *fact* is a statement that can be proved by consulting a reliable source, such as a book or an expert on the topic. When you are asked to identify a statement as a fact, ask yourself, "Could this statement be proved?"

- An *opinion* may sound like a fact but cannot be proved. To determine if a statement is an opinion, ask yourself if it reflects the writer's belief and whether it can be proved.

Test-Taking Strategies

- Look for certain words that signal an opinion, such as "think" or "believe."

- Ask yourself if the statement could be seen from another point of view. If so, it is probably an opinion.

Sample Test Item

Directions: Read the following passage, and then choose the letter of the best possible answer.

"Be careful," warned the dealer. "That's the most valuable stamp in the shop. It's the prettiest, too. You'll never see another one of those. There are only five in the world. I never get tired of telling the story of how I found that stamp. It happened when I was traveling in North Africa. Stamp collecting is a hobby for the adventurous."

1. Which of these is a FACT from the passage?
   A You'll never see another one of those.
   B That's the most valuable stamp in the shop.
   C It's the prettiest one, too.
   D Stamp collecting is for the adventurous.

Answer and Explanation

The correct answer is *B*. Answers *A*, *C*, and *D* cannot be proved. An exact value can be found for the stamp.

▶ Practice

Directions: Read the following passage, and then choose the letter of the best possible answer.

It is illegal to hunt and sell wild chimpanzees. Captured chimps often get sick in captivity. Then, their owners give them up. Concerned people have set up sanctuaries to shelter chimps who cannot be returned to the wild. Some wildlife experts think the money used to run the sanctuaries should be spent on enforcing the hunting laws instead. Famous chimpanzee specialist Jane Goodall says, "I cannot turn my back on an individual."

1. Which of these statements is an OPINION?
   A It is illegal to hunt chimpanzees.
   B Chimps often get sick in captivity.
   C Money spent on sanctuaries should be used to enforce the hunting laws.
   D Goodall cannot turn her back on chimps.

Drama

Theatre Scene, Edgar Degas

Exploring the Genre

Drama is different from other forms of literature—it is written to be performed. When you
read a drama, you should imagine that you see
and hear the action of the performance. The following elements help readers and performers
create the magic of drama:

- **Dialogue** is the conversation among characters.

- **Stage directions** are the words that tell readers and performers about the action, the
  sets, and the way in which the dialogue
  should be spoken.

- Scenery, costumes, props, sound effects, and
  lighting help create the world in which the
  actors perform. Playwrights usually give
  directions about these elements in the stage
  directions.

As you read the dramas in this unit, notice
these features that make drama a unique form of
literature.

◀ **Critical Viewing** What elements of drama are
captured in the picture? **[Connect]**

Why Read Literature?

As you read drama, visualize how the words and actions might be performed on a stage or onscreen. To help you understand and remember dramatic works, set different purposes for your reading. Preview three purposes you might set before reading the works in this unit.

1

Read for the love of literature.

Renowned American playwright Arthur Miller was an impressionable teenager in 1929 when the New York Stock Exchange crashed and the Great Depression began. His family was forced to sell off their home and all their possessions to pay the bills. The experience deeply affected Miller, leading him to question what things in life have lasting value and permanence. Read **"Grandpa and the Statue,"** page 666, in which a stingy grandfather resists seeing any lasting value in the Statue of Liberty.

2

Read to be entertained.

Norton Juster started out as an architect but ended up as a writer. Unlike his character Milo, who says, "It seems to me that almost everything is a waste of time," Juster pursued many interests. Enjoy the humor in Juster's ingenious fantasy **"The Phantom Tollbooth,"** page 614. Step into Milo's car and ride through the secret tollbooth into the Land Beyond.

3

Read for information.

Known as the Ellis Island of the West, Angel Island in San Francisco Bay, California, opened in 1910 as an immigration station. Thousands of Chinese immigrants were detained and processed at Angel Island. Today, it is a National Historic Landmark. Read **"Chinese Immigrants Remember Detention at Angel Island,"** page 687, for personal accounts of some who were held there.

Take It to the Net

Visit the Web site for online instruction and activities related to each selection in this unit.

www.phschool.com

How to Read Literature

Strategies for Reading Drama

The story of a drama is told mostly through performance—what actors say and what they do. Stage directions in the script give other helpful information about the setting and about how actors should move and speak. When you read a drama, keep in mind that it is written to be performed. The following strategies will help you as you read a drama.

1. Summarize.

Dramas are frequently broken into parts called acts, which may be broken into smaller parts called scenes. To clarify your understanding of the drama, pause at the end of an act or a scene to summarize what has happened so far—restate what you have read briefly in your own words.

- If the play is not broken into acts or scenes, pause to summarize when an episode or event is over.

- Include main events of the scene or episode expressed in the order in which they occurred.

Use an organizer like the one shown to summarize in notes that you can use to review the play.

Summarizing a Scene

1. Name the characters.

2. Identify the key events.

3. Explain the meaning or significance.

Act	Scene	Known Characters	New Characters	Main Events
I	1	none	Milo Clock	Milo is bored until he gets the tollbooth
II	2	Milo	Dischord Dynne Dodecahedron	

2. Distinguish fact from fantasy.

Sometimes writers combine imaginary characters, situations, and events with real-life elements. In this passage, Grandpa and his dialogue are fantasy—made-up details—but the Statue of Liberty and the inscription on it are factual—details that can be proved true.

> MONAGHAN. . . . I'll try it with me spectacles, just a minute. Why, it's a poem, I believe. . . . "Give me your tired, your poor, your huddled masses yearning to breathe free, the wretched refuse of your teeming shore. . . ."

In this unit, you will learn strategies for distinguishing fact from fantasy.

As you read the plays in this unit, review the reading strategies and look at the notes in the side columns. Use the suggestions to apply the strategies for reading drama.

Prepare to Read

The Phantom Tollbooth, Act I

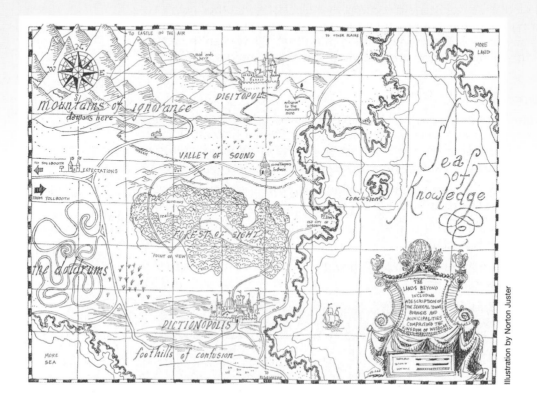

Illustration by Norton Juster

 Take It to the Net

Visit www.phschool.com for interactive activities and instruction related to *The Phantom Tollbooth*, including

- background
- graphic organizers
- literary elements
- reading strategies

Preview

Connecting to the Literature

Milo, the main character in *The Phantom Tollbooth*, suffers from boredom and sets off to find adventure. As you read, identify with the character by thinking of things that cause—and things that cure—boredom.

Background

The names of some of the people and places in *The Phantom Tollbooth* describe their qualities. The roots of two of the names are explained below.

Lethargarians (leth´ ər jer´ ē ənz) From *lethargy*, which means "sluggish; without energy."

Digitopolis (di´ ji täp´ ə ləs) From *digit*, any numeral from 0 to 9, and from *polis* (pä´ lis), a word from the ancient Greek that means "city-state."

Literary Analysis

Elements of Drama

A **drama** is a story that is written to be performed. Like short stories, dramas have characters, people or animals that take part in the action; setting, the time and place of the action; and plot, the sequence of events. In drama, these elements are developed mainly through dialogue, the words spoken by characters. Notice how the characters' names appear before their words.

> **WATCHDOG.** Dictionopolis, here we come.
>
> **MILO.** Hey, Watchdog, are you coming along?

Connecting Literary Elements

Stage directions are unique to drama. They tell performers how to move and speak, and they help readers envision the action and scenes. Stage directions are not spoken. They are usually printed in italics between brackets. Look at the stage directions in the following example.

> **AZAZ AND THE MATHEMAGICIAN.** [*To the* PRINCESSES.] You are hereby banished from this land to the Castle-in-the-Air. [*To each other.*] And as for you, KEEP OUT OF MY WAY! [*They stalk off in opposite directions.*]

As you read, use these focus questions to help you analyze the stage directions and other elements of drama:

1. What do you learn about the characters and setting through dialogue?
2. What details are provided through the stage directions?

Reading Strategy

Summarizing

To **summarize** is to restate something briefly in your own words. A good summary

- includes all the important events and details.
- makes clear the order in which the events occurred.
- groups related details and indicates connections among them.

Copy the timeline at right. As you read, pause at the points shown and summarize events and connections up to that point.

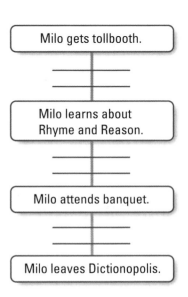

Vocabulary Development

ignorance (ig´ ner ens) *n.* lack of knowledge, education, or experience (p. 615)

precautionary (prē kô´ shən er´ ē) *adj.* done to prevent danger (p. 616)

misapprehension (mis´ ap rē hen´ shən) *n.* misunderstanding (p. 625)

The Phantom Tollbooth

Based on the book by Norton Juster
Susan Nanus

CAST (in order of appearance)

- THE CLOCK
- MILO, a boy
- THE WHETHER MAN
- SIX LETHARGARIANS
- TOCK, THE WATCHDOG
  (same as the clock)
- AZAZ THE UNABRIDGED,
  KING OF DICTIONOPOLIS
- THE MATHEMAGICIAN,
  KING OF DIGITOPOLIS
- PRINCESS SWEET RHYME
- PRINCESS PURE REASON

- GATEKEEPER OF DICTIONOPOLIS
- THREE WORD MERCHANTS
- THE LETTERMAN
  (fourth word merchant)
- SPELLING BEE
- THE HUMBUG
- THE DUKE OF DEFINITION
- THE MINISTER OF MEANING
- THE EARL OF ESSENCE
- THE COUNT OF CONNOTATION
- THE UNDERSECRETARY OF
  UNDERSTANDING

- A PAGE
- KAKAFONOUS A. DISCHORD,
  DOCTOR OF DISSONANCE
- THE AWFUL DYNNE
- THE DODECAHEDRON
- MINERS OF THE NUMBERS MINE
- THE EVERPRESENT
  WORDSNATCHER
- THE TERRIBLE TRIVIUM
- THE DEMON OF INSINCERITY
- SENSES TAKER

THE SETS

1. MILO'S BEDROOM — WITH SHELVES, PENNANTS, PICTURES ON THE WALL, AS WELL AS SUGGESTIONS OF THE CHARACTERS OF THE LAND OF WISDOM.

2. THE ROAD TO THE LAND OF WISDOM — A FOREST, FROM WHICH THE WHETHER MAN AND THE LETHARGARIANS EMERGE.

3. DICTIONOPOLIS — A MARKETPLACE FULL OF OPEN AIR STALLS AS WELL AS LITTLE SHOPS. LETTERS AND SIGNS SHOULD ABOUND.

4. DIGITOPOLIS — A DARK, GLITTERING PLACE WITHOUT TREES OR GREENERY, BUT FULL OF SHINING ROCKS AND CLIFFS, WITH HUNDREDS OF NUMBERS SHINING EVERYWHERE.

5. THE LAND OF IGNORANCE — A GRAY, GLOOMY PLACE FULL OF CLIFFS AND CAVES, WITH FRIGHTENING FACES. DIFFERENT LEVELS AND HEIGHTS SHOULD BE SUGGESTED THROUGH ONE OR TWO PLATFORMS OR RISERS, WITH A SET OF STAIRS THAT LEAD TO THE CASTLE IN THE AIR.

Act I

Scene i

[The stage is completely dark and silent. Suddenly the sound of someone winding an alarm clock is heard, and after that, the sound of loud ticking is heard.]

[LIGHTS UP on the CLOCK, a huge alarm clock. The CLOCK reads 4:00. The lighting should make it appear that the CLOCK is suspended in mid-air (if possible). The CLOCK ticks for 30 seconds.]

CLOCK. See that! Half a minute gone by. Seems like a long time when you're waiting for something to happen, doesn't it? Funny thing is, time can pass very slowly or very fast, and sometimes even both at once. The time now? Oh, a little after four, but what that means should depend on you. Too often, we do something simply because time tells us to. Time for school, time for bed, whoops, 12:00, time to be hungry. It can get a little silly, don't you think? Time is important, but it's what you do with it that makes it so. So my advice to you is to use it. Keep your eyes open and your ears perked. Otherwise it will pass before you know it, and you'll certainly have missed something!

Things have a habit of doing that, you know. Being here one minute and gone the next.
In the twinkling of an eye.
In a jiffy.
In a flash!

I know a girl who yawned and missed a whole summer vacation. And what about that caveman who took a nap one afternoon, and woke up to find himself completely alone. You see, while he was sleeping, someone had invented the wheel and everyone had moved to the suburbs. And then of course, there is Milo. *[LIGHTS UP to reveal MILO's Bedroom. The CLOCK appears to be on a shelf in the room of a young boy—a room filled with books, toys, games, maps, papers, pencils, a bed, a desk. There is a dartboard with numbers and the face of the MATHEMAGICIAN, a bedspread made from KING AZAZ'S cloak, a kite looking like the SPELLING BEE, a punching bag with the HUMBUG'S face, as well as records, a television, a toy car, and a large box that is wrapped and has an envelope taped to the top. The sound of FOOTSTEPS is heard, and then enter MILO dejectedly. He throws down his books and coat, flops into a chair, and sighs loudly.]* Who never knows what to do with himself—not just sometimes, but always. When he's in school, he wants to be out, and when he's out, he wants to be in. *[During the following speech, MILO examines the*

ignorance (ig′ ner ens) *n.* lack of knowledge, education, or experience

**Literary Analysis
Elements of Drama** What are four parts of the setting described in the stage directions?

**Reading Check**

What is wrong with Milo?

The Phantom Tollbooth, Act I ◆ 615

various toys, tools, and other possessions in the room, trying them out and rejecting them.] Wherever he is, he wants to be somewhere else—and when he gets there, so what. Everything is too much trouble or a waste of time. Books—he's already read them. Games—boring. T.V.—dumb. So what's left? Another long, boring afternoon. Unless he bothers to notice a very large package that happened to arrive today.

MILO. [*Suddenly notices the package. He drags himself over to it, and disinterestedly reads the label.*] "For Milo, who has plenty of time." Well, that's true. [*Sighs and looks at it.*] No. [*Walks away.*] Well . . . [*Comes back. Rips open envelope and reads.*]

A VOICE. "One genuine turnpike tollbooth,♦ easily assembled at home for use by those who have never traveled in lands beyond."

MILO. Beyond what? [*Continues reading.*]

A VOICE. "This package contains the following items:" [MILO *pulls the items out of the box and sets them up as they are mentioned.*] "One (1) genuine turnpike tollbooth to be erected according to directions. Three (3) <u>precautionary</u> signs to be used in a precautionary fashion. Assorted coins for paying tolls. One (1) map, strictly up to date, showing how to get from here to there. One (1) book of rules and traffic regulations which may not be bent or broken. Warning! Results are not guaranteed. If not perfectly satisfied, your wasted time will be refunded."

MILO. [*Skeptically.*] Come off it, who do you think you're kidding? [*Walks around and examines tollbooth.*] What am I supposed to do with this? [*The ticking of the* CLOCK *grows loud and impatient.*] Well . . . what else do I have to do. [MILO *gets into his toy car and drives up to the first sign.*]

VOICE. "HAVE YOUR DESTINATION IN MIND."

MILO. [*Pulls out the map.*] Now, let's see. That's funny. I never heard of any of these places. Well, it doesn't matter anyway. Dictionopolis. That's a weird name. I might as well go there. [*Begins to move, following map. Drives off.*]

CLOCK. See what I mean? You never know how things are going to get started. But when you're bored, what you need more than anything is a rude awakening.

♦*Turnpike Tollbooth*

A *turnpike* is a road that people pay a fee, or toll, to use. Long ago, long spears called pikes barred the road. The pikes were turned aside only after travelers paid the toll to use the road. A *tollbooth* is the booth or gate at which tolls are collected. The first record of tolls being collected dates from about 2000 B.C., when tolls were collected on a Persian military road between Babylon and Syria. It's not surprising that such an unusual surprise gift like a turnpike tollbooth slowly pulls Milo out of his bored state of mind.

precautionary
(prē kô´ shən er´ ē) *adj.*
done to prevent danger

[*The ALARM goes off very loudly as the stage darkens. The sound of the alarm is transformed into the honking of a car horn, and is then joined by the blasts, bleeps, roars and growls of heavy highway traffic. When the lights come up, MILO's bedroom is gone and we see a lonely road in the middle of nowhere.*]

Scene ii *The Road to Dictionopolis.*

[*ENTER* MILO *in his car.*]

MILO. This is weird! I don't recognize any of this scenery at all. [*A SIGN is held up before* MILO, *startling him.*] Huh? [*Reads.*] WELCOME TO EXPECTATIONS. INFORMATION, PREDICTIONS AND ADVICE CHEERFULLY OFFERED. PARK HERE AND BLOW HORN. [MILO *blows horn.*]

WHETHER MAN. [*A little man wearing a long coat and carrying an umbrella pops up from behind the sign that he was holding. He speaks very fast and excitedly.*] My, my, my, my, my, welcome, welcome, welcome, welcome to the Land of Expectations, Expectations, Expectations! We don't get many travelers these days; we certainly don't get many travelers. Now what can I do for you? I'm the Whether Man.

MILO. [*Referring to map.*] Uh . . . is this the right road to Dictionopolis?

WHETHER MAN. Well now, well now, well now, I don't know of any *wrong* road to Dictionopolis, so if this road goes to Dictionopolis at all, it must be the right road, and if it doesn't, it must be the right road to somewhere else, because there are no wrong roads to anywhere. Do you think it will rain?

MILO. I thought you were the Weather Man.

WHETHER MAN. Oh, no, I'm the Whether Man, not the weather man. [*Pulls out a SIGN or opens a FLAP of his coat, which reads: "WHETHER."*] After all, it's more important to know whether there will be weather than what the weather will be.

MILO. What kind of place is Expectations?

WHETHER MAN. Good question, good question! Expectations is the place you must always go to before you get to where you are going. Of course, some people never go beyond Expectations, but my job is to hurry them along whether they like it or not. Now what else can I do for you? [*Opens his umbrella.*]

MILO. I think I can find my own way.

WHETHER MAN. Splendid, splendid, splendid! Whether or not you find your own way, you're bound to find some way. If you happen to find my way, please return it. I lost it years ago. I imagine by now it must be quite rusty. You did say it was going to rain, didn't you?

Reading Strategy
Summarizing Why would you include the change of place in your summary?

✓Reading Check

What is in the package Milo opens?

The Phantom Tollbooth, Act I ◆ 617

[*Escorts* MILO *to the car under the open umbrella.*] I'm glad you made your own decision. I do so hate to make up my mind about anything, whether it's good or bad, up or down, rain or shine. Expect everything, I always say, and the unexpected never happens. Goodbye, goodbye, goodbye, good . . .

[*A loud CLAP of THUNDER is heard.*] Oh dear! [*He looks up at the sky, puts out his hand to feel for rain, and RUNS AWAY.* MILO *watches puzzledly and drives on.*]

MILO. I'd better get out of Expectations, but fast. Talking to a guy like that all day would get me nowhere for sure. [*He tries to speed up, but finds instead that he is moving slower and slower.*] Oh, oh, now what? [*He can barely move. Behind* MILO, *the* LETHARGARIANS *begin to enter from all parts of the stage. They are dressed to blend in with the scenery and carry small pillows that look like rocks. Whenever they fall asleep, they rest on the pillows.*] Now I really am getting nowhere. I hope I didn't take a wrong turn. [*The car stops. He tries to start it. It won't move. He gets out and begins to tinker with it.*] I wonder where I am.

LETHARGARIAN 1. You're . . . in . . . the . . . Dol . . . drums . . . [MILO *looks around.*]

LETHARGARIAN 2. Yes . . . the . . . Dol . . . drums . . . [*A YAWN is heard.*]

MILO. [*Yelling.*] WHAT ARE THE DOLDRUMS?

LETHARGARIAN 3. The Doldrums, my friend, are where nothing ever happens and nothing ever changes. [*Parts of the Scenery stand up or Six People come out of the scenery colored in the same colors of the trees or the road. They move very slowly and as soon as they move, they stop to rest again.*] Allow me to introduce all of us. We are the Lethargarians at your service.

MILO. [*Uncertainly.*] Very pleased to meet you. I think I'm lost. Can you help me?

LETHARGARIAN 4. Don't say think. [*He yawns.*] It's against the law.

LETHARGARIAN 1. No one's allowed to think in the Doldrums. [*He falls asleep.*]

LETHARGARIAN 2. Don't you have a rule book? It's local ordinance 175389-J. [*He falls asleep.*]

MILO. [*Pulls out rule book and reads.*] Ordinance 175389-J: "It shall be unlawful, illegal and unethical to think, think of thinking, surmise, presume, reason, meditate or speculate while in the Doldrums. Anyone breaking this law shall be severely punished." That's a ridiculous law! Everybody thinks.

ALL THE LETHARGARIANS. We don't!

Literary Analysis
Elements of Drama What important information is revealed in the stage directions?

Reading Strategy
Summarizing How would you describe what has happened since Milo left Expectations?

◀ **Critical Viewing**
Which details in the picture give clues to the characteristics of the Lethargarians? **[Analyze]**

LETHARGARIAN 2. And most of the time, you don't, that's why you're here. You weren't thinking and you weren't paying attention either. People who don't pay attention often get stuck in the Doldrums. Face it, most of the time, you're just like us. [*Falls, snoring, to the ground.* MILO *laughs.*]

LETHARGARIAN 5. Stop that at once. Laughing is against the law. Don't you have a rule book? It's local ordinance 574381-W.

MILO. [*Opens rule book and reads.*] "In the Doldrums, laughter is frowned upon and smiling is permitted only on alternate Thursdays." Well, if you can't laugh or think, what can you do?

LETHARGARIAN 6. Anything as long as it's nothing, and everything as long as it isn't anything. There's lots to do. We have a very busy schedule . . .

LETHARGARIAN 1. At 8:00 we get up and then we spend from 8 to 9 daydreaming.

✔Reading Check

Why does Milo get stuck in the Doldrums?

LETHARGARIAN 2. From 9:00 to 9:30 we take our early midmorning nap . . .

LETHARGARIAN 3. From 9:30 to 10:30 we dawdle and delay . . .

LETHARGARIAN 4. From 10:30 to 11:30 we take our late early morning nap . . .

LETHARGARIAN 5. From 11:30 to 12:00 we bide our time and then we eat our lunch.

LETHARGARIAN 6. From 1:00 to 2:00 we linger and loiter . . .

LETHARGARIAN 1. From 2:00 to 2:30 we take our early afternoon nap. . .

LETHARGARIAN 2. From 2:30 to 3:30 we put off for tomorrow what we could have done today . . .

LETHARGARIAN 3. From 3:30 to 4:00 we take our early late afternoon nap . . .

LETHARGARIAN 4. From 4:00 to 5:00 we loaf and lounge until dinner . . .

LETHARGARIAN 5. From 6:00 to 7:00 we dilly-dally . . .

LETHARGARIAN 6. From 7:00 to 8:00 we take our early evening nap and then for an hour before we go to bed, we waste time.

LETHARGARIAN 1. [*Yawning.*] You see, it's really quite strenuous doing nothing all day long, and so once a week, we take a holiday and go nowhere.

LETHARGARIAN 5. Which is just where we were going when you came along. Would you care to join us?

MILO. [*Yawning.*] That's where I seem to be going, anyway. [*Stretching.*] Tell me, does everyone here do nothing?

LETHARGARIAN 3. Everyone but the terrible watchdog. He's always sniffing around to see that nobody wastes time. A most unpleasant character.

MILO. The Watchdog?

LETHARGARIAN 6. THE WATCHDOG!

ALL THE LETHARGARIANS. [*Yelling at once.*] RUN! WAKE UP! RUN! HERE HE COMES! THE WATCHDOG! [*They all run off and ENTER a large dog with the head, feet, and tail of a dog, and the body of a clock, having the same face as the character* THE CLOCK.]

WATCHDOG. What are you doing here?

MILO. Nothing much. Just killing time. You see . . .

WATCHDOG. KILLING TIME! [*His ALARM RINGS in fury.*] It's bad enough wasting time without killing it. What are you doing in the Doldrums, anyway? Don't you have anywhere to go?

Literary Analysis
Elements of Drama What does the dialogue by the Lethargarians reveal about their lives?

Literary Analysis
Elements of Drama What do you learn from the stage directions here?

MILO. I think I was on my way to Dictionopolis when I got stuck here. Can you help me?

WATCHDOG. Help you! You've got to help yourself. I suppose you know why you got stuck.

MILO. I guess I just wasn't thinking.

WATCHDOG. Precisely. Now you're on your way.

MILO. I am?

Reading Strategy
Summarizing Will you include the arrival of the Watchdog in your summary? Why or why not?

WATCHDOG. Of course. Since you got here by not thinking, it seems reasonable that in order to get out, you must *start* thinking. Do you mind if I get in? I love automobile rides. [*He gets in. They wait.*] Well?

MILO. All right. I'll try. [*Screws up his face and thinks.*] Are we moving?

WATCHDOG. Not yet. Think harder.

MILO. I'm thinking as hard as I can.

WATCHDOG. Well, think just a little harder than that. Come on, you can do it.

MILO. All right, all right. . . . I'm thinking of all the planets in the solar system, and why water expands when it turns to ice, and all the words that begin with "q," and . . . [*The wheels begin to move.*] We're moving! We're moving!

WATCHDOG. Keep thinking.

MILO. [*Thinking.*] How a steam engine works and how to bake a pie and the difference between Fahrenheit and Centigrade. . .

WATCHDOG. Dictionopolis, here we come.

MILO. Hey, Watchdog, are you coming along?

TOCK. You can call me Tock, and keep your eyes on the road.

MILO. What kind of place is Dictionopolis, anyway?

TOCK. It's where all the words in the world come from. It used to be a marvelous place, but ever since Rhyme and Reason left, it hasn't been the same.

MILO. Rhyme and Reason?

TOCK. The two princesses. They used to settle all the arguments between their two brothers who rule over the Land of Wisdom. You see, Azaz is the king of Dictionopolis and the Mathemagician is the king of Digitopolis and they almost never see eye to eye on anything. It was the job of the Princesses Sweet Rhyme and Pure Reason to solve the differences between the two kings, and

Reading Check

How does Milo get out of Doldrums?

they always did so well that both sides usually went home feeling very satisfied. But then, one day, the kings had an argument to end all arguments. . . .

[*The LIGHTS DIM on* TOCK *and* MILO, *and come up on* KING AZAZ *of Dictionopolis on another part of the stage.* AZAZ *has a great stomach, a grey beard reaching to his waist, a small crown and a long robe with the letters of the alphabet written all over it.*]

AZAZ. Of course, I'll abide by the decision of Rhyme and Reason, though I have no doubt as to what it will be. They will choose *words*, of course. Everyone knows that words are more important than numbers any day of the week.

[*The* MATHEMAGICIAN *appears opposite* AZAZ. *The* MATHEMAGICIAN *wears a long flowing robe covered entirely with complex mathematical equations, and a tall pointed hat. He carries a long staff with a pencil point at one end and a large rubber eraser at the other.*]

MATHEMAGICIAN. That's what you think, Azaz. People wouldn't even know what day of the week it is without *numbers*. Haven't you ever looked at a calendar? Face it, Azaz. It's numbers that count.

Reading Strategy
Summarizing Briefly explain the argument between Azaz and Mathemagician.

AZAZ. Don't be ridiculous. [*To audience, as if leading a cheer.*] Let's hear it for WORDS!

MATHEMAGICIAN. [*To audience, in the same manner.*] Cast your vote for NUMBERS!

AZAZ. A, B, C's!

MATHEMAGICIAN. 1, 2, 3's! [*A FANFARE is heard.*]

AZAZ AND MATHEMAGICIAN. [*To each other.*] Quiet! Rhyme and Reason are about to announce their decision.

[RHYME *and* REASON *appear.*]

RHYME. Ladies and gentlemen, letters and numerals, fractions and punctuation marks—may we have your attention, please. After careful consideration of the problem set before us by King Azaz of Dictionopolis [AZAZ *bows.*] and the Mathemagician of Digitopolis [MATHEMAGICIAN *raises his hands in a victory salute.*] we have come to the following conclusion:

REASON. Words and numbers are of equal value, for in the cloak of knowledge, one is the warp and the other is the woof.

RHYME. It is no more important to count the sands than it is to name the stars.

RHYME AND REASON. Therefore, let both kingdoms, Dictionopolis and Digitopolis, live in peace.

[*The sound of CHEERING is heard.*]

AZAZ. Boo! is what I say. Boo and Bah and Hiss!

MATHEMAGICIAN. What good are these girls if they can't even settle an argument in anyone's favor? I think I have come to a decision of my own.

AZAZ. So have I.

AZAZ AND MATHEMAGICIAN. [*To the* PRINCESSES.] You are hereby banished from this land to the Castle-in-the-Air. [*To each other.*] And as for you, KEEP OUT OF MY WAY! [*They stalk off in opposite directions.*]

[*During this time, the set has been changed to the Market Square of Dictionopolis. LIGHTS come UP on the deserted square.*]

TOCK. And ever since then, there has been neither Rhyme nor Reason in this kingdom. Words are misused and numbers are mismanaged. The argument between the two kings has divided everyone and the real value of both words and numbers has been forgotten. What a waste!

MILO. Why doesn't somebody rescue the Princesses and set everything straight again?

TOCK. That is easier said than done. The Castle-in-the-Air is very far from here, and the one path which leads to it is guarded by ferocious demons. But hold on, here we are. [*A Man appears, carrying a Gate and a small Tollbooth.*]

GATEKEEPER. AHHHHREMMMM! This is Dictionopolis, a happy kingdom, advantageously located in the foothills of Confusion and caressed by gentle breezes from the Sea of Knowledge. Today, by royal proclamation, is Market Day. Have you come to buy or sell?

MILO. I beg your pardon?

GATEKEEPER. Buy or sell, buy or sell. Which is it? You must have come here for a reason.

MILO. Well, I . . .

GATEKEEPER. Come now, if you don't have a reason, you must at least have an explanation or certainly an excuse.

Reading Strategy
Summarizing How would you summarize events up to this point?

▲ **Critical Viewing**
Why is a clock part of this character's body? **[Connect]**

✔**Reading Check**
What does Milo learn about the Princesses?

The Phantom Tollbooth, Act I ◆ **623**

MILO. [*Meekly.*] Uh . . . no.

GATEKEEPER. [*Shaking his head.*] Very serious. You can't get in without a reason. [*Thoughtfully.*] Wait a minute. Maybe I have an old one you can use. [*Pulls out an old suitcase from the tollbooth and rummages through it.*] No . . . no . . . no . . . this won't do . . . hmmm . . .

MILO. [*To* TOCK.] What's he looking for? [TOCK *shrugs.*]

GATEKEEPER. Ah! This is fine. [*Pulls out a Medallion on a chain. Engraved in the Medallion is: "WHY NOT?"*] Why not. That's a good reason for almost anything . . . a bit used, perhaps, but still quite serviceable. There you are, sir. Now I can truly say: Welcome to Dictionopolis.

[*He opens the Gate and walks off.* CITIZENS *and* MERCHANTS *appear on all levels of the stage, and* MILO *and* TOCK *find themselves in the middle of a noisy marketplace. As some people buy and sell their wares, others hang a large banner which reads: WELCOME TO THE WORD MARKET.*]

MILO. Tock! Look!

MERCHANT 1. Hey-ya, hey-ya, hey-ya, step right up and take your pick. Juicy tempting words for sale. Get your fresh-picked "if's," "and's" and "but's!" Just take a look at these nice ripe "where's" and "when's."

MERCHANT 2. Step right up, step right up, fancy, best-quality words here for sale. Enrich your vocabulary and expand your speech with such elegant items as "quagmire," "flabbergast," or "upholstery."

MERCHANT 3. Words by the bag, buy them over here. Words by the bag for the more talkative customer. A pound of "happy's" at a very reasonable price . . . very useful for "Happy Birthday," "Happy New Year," "happy days," or "happy-go-lucky." Or how about a package of "good's," always handy for "good morning," "good afternoon," "good evening," and "goodbye."

MILO. I can't believe it. Did you ever see so many words?

TOCK. They're fine if you have something to say. [*They come to a Do-It-Yourself Bin.*]

MILO. [*To* MERCHANT 4 *at the bin.*] Excuse me, but what are these?

MERCHANT 4. These are for people who like to make up their own words. You can pick any assortment you like or buy a special box complete with all the letters and a book of instructions. Here, taste an "A." They're very good. [*He pops one into* MILO'S *mouth.*]

MILO. [*Tastes it hesitantly.*] It's sweet! [*He eats it.*]

Literary Analysis
Elements of Drama What details about the new setting are given in the stage directions?

MERCHANT 4. I knew you'd like it. "A" is one of our best-sellers. All of them aren't that good, you know. The "Z," for instance—very dry and sawdusty. And the "X"? Tastes like a trunkful of stale air. But most of the others aren't bad at all. Here, try the "I."

MILO. [*Tasting.*] Cool! It tastes icy.

MERCHANT 4. [*To* TOCK.] How about the "C" for you? It's as crunchy as a bone. Most people are just too lazy to make their own words, but take it from me, not only is it more fun, but it's also *de*-lightful, [*Holds up a "D."*] e-lating, [*Holds up an "E."*] and extremely *u*seful! [*Holds up a "U."*]

MILO. But isn't it difficult? I'm not very good at making words.

[*The* SPELLING BEE, *a large colorful bee, comes up from behind.*]

SPELLING BEE. Perhaps I can be of some assistance . . . a-s-s-i-s-t-a-n-c-e. [*The Three turn around and see him.*] Don't be alarmed . . . a-l-a-r-m-e-d. I am the Spelling Bee. I can spell anything. Anything. A-n-y-t-h-i-n-g. Try me. Try me.

MILO. [*Backing off,* TOCK *on his guard.*] Can you spell goodbye?

SPELLING BEE. Perhaps you are under the <u>misapprehension</u> . . . m-i-s-a-p-p-r-e-h-e-n-s-i-o-n that I am dangerous. Let me assure you that I am quite peaceful. Now, think of the most difficult word you can, and I'll spell it.

MILO. Uh . . . o.k. [*At this point,* MILO *may turn to the audience and ask them to help him choose a word or he may think of one on his own.*] How about . . . "Curiosity"?

SPELLING BEE. [*Winking.*] Let's see now . . . uh . . . how much time do I have?

MILO. Just ten seconds. Count them off, Tock.

SPELLING BEE. [*As* TOCK *counts.*] Oh dear, oh dear. [*Just at the last moment, quickly.*] C-u-r-i-o-s-i-t-y.

MERCHANT 4. Correct! [ALL *Cheer.*]

MILO. Can you spell anything?

SPELLING BEE. [*Proudly.*] Just about. You see, years ago, I was an ordinary bee minding my own business, smelling flowers all day, occasionally picking up part-time work in people's bonnets. Then one day, I realized that I'd never amount to anything without an education, so I decided that . . .

HUMBUG. [*Coming up in a booming voice.*] BALDERDASH! [*He wears a lavish coat, striped pants, checked vest, spats and a derby*

misapprehension
(mis´ ap rē hen´ shən) *n.* misunderstanding

Literary Analysis
Elements of Drama What do the dialogue and the stage directions reveal about Spelling Bee?

Reading Check

What is sold in the marketplace of Dictionopolis?

hat.] Let me repeat . . . BALDER-DASH! [*Swings his cane and clicks his heels in the air.*] Well, well, what have we here? Isn't someone going to intro-duce me to the little boy?

SPELLING BEE. [*Disdainfully.*] This is the Humbug. You can't trust a word he says.

HUMBUG. NONSENSE! Everyone can trust a Humbug. As I was saying to the king just the other day . . .

SPELLING BEE. You've never met the king. [*To* MILO.] Don't believe a thing he tells you.

HUMBUG. Bosh, my boy, pure bosh. The Humbugs are an old and noble family, honorable to the core. Why, we fought in the Crusades with Richard the Lionhearted, crossed the Atlantic with Columbus, blazed trails with the pioneers. History is full of Humbugs.

SPELLING BEE. A very pretty speech . . . s-p-e-e-c-h. Now, why don't you go away? I was just advising the lad of the importance of proper spelling.

HUMBUG. BAH! As soon as you learn to spell one word, they ask you to spell another. You can never catch up, so why bother? [*Puts his arm around* MILO.] Take my advice, boy, and forget about it. As my great-great-great-grandfather George Washington Humbug used to say. . .

SPELLING BEE. You, sir, are an impostor i-m-p-o-s-t-o-r who can't even spell his own name!

HUMBUG. What? You dare to doubt my word? The word of a Humbug? The word of a Humbug who has direct access to the ear of a King? And the king shall hear of this, I promise you . . .

VOICE 1. Did someone call for the King?

VOICE 2. Did you mention the monarch?

VOICE 3. Speak of the sovereign?

VOICE 4. Entreat the Emperor?

VOICE 5. Hail his highness?

▲ **Critical Viewing**
How does this picture of Spelling Bee compare to the description of him in the play? (Compare)

Literary Analysis
Elements of Drama In what one way are the characters of Humbug and Spelling Bee similar to their names?

[*Five tall, thin gentlemen regally dressed in silks and satins, plumed hats and buckled shoes appear as they speak.*]

MILO. Who are they?

SPELLING BEE. The King's advisors. Or in more formal terms, his cabinet.

MINISTER 1. Greetings!

MINISTER 2. Salutations!

MINISTER 3. Welcome!

MINISTER 4. Good Afternoon!

MINISTER 5. Hello!

MILO. Uh . . . Hi.

[*All the* MINISTERS, *from here on called by their numbers, unfold their scrolls and read in order.*]

MINISTER 1. By the order of Azaz the Unabridged . . .

MINISTER 2. King of Dictionopolis . . .

MINISTER 3. Monarch of letters . . .

MINISTER 4. Emperor of phrases, sentences, and miscellaneous figures of speech . . .

MINISTER 5. We offer you the hospitality of our kingdom . . .

MINISTER 1. Country

MINISTER 2. Nation

MINISTER 3. State

MINISTER 4. Commonwealth

MINISTER 5. Realm

MINISTER 1. Empire

MINISTER 2. Palatinate

MINISTER 3. Principality.

MILO. Do all those words mean the same thing?

MINISTER 1. Of course.

MINISTER 2. Certainly.

MINISTER 3. Precisely.

MINISTER 4. Exactly.

MINISTER 5. Yes.

MILO. Then why don't you use just one? Wouldn't that make a lot more sense?

Literary Analysis
Elements of Drama How do the characters' words indicate the importance of words in the kingdom of Dictionopolis?

Reading Check

Which characters does Milo meet in Dictionopolis?

MINISTER 1. Nonsense!

MINISTER 2. Ridiculous!

MINISTER 3. Fantastic!

MINISTER 4. Absurd!

MINISTER 5. Bosh!

MINISTER 1. We're not interested in making sense. It's not our job.

MINISTER 2. Besides, one word is as good as another, so why not use them all?

MINISTER 3. Then you don't have to choose which one is right.

MINISTER 4. Besides, if one is right, then ten are ten times as right.

MINISTER 5. Obviously, you don't know who we are. [*Each presents himself and* MILO *acknowledges the introduction.*]

MINISTER 1. The Duke of Definition.

MINISTER 2. The Minister of Meaning.

MINISTER 3. The Earl of Essence.

MINISTER 4. The Count of Connotation.

MINISTER 5. The Undersecretary of Understanding.

ALL FIVE. And we have come to invite you to the Royal Banquet.

SPELLING BEE. The banquet! That's quite an honor, my boy. A real h-o-n-o-r.

HUMBUG. DON'T BE RIDICULOUS! Everybody goes to the Royal Banquet these days.

SPELLING BEE. [*To the* HUMBUG.] True, everybody does go. But some people are invited and others simply push their way in where they aren't wanted.

HUMBUG. HOW DARE YOU? You buzzing little upstart, I'll show you who's not wanted . . . [*Raises his cane threateningly.*]

SPELLING BEE. You just watch it! I'm warning w-a-r-n-i-n-g you! [*At that moment, an ear-shattering blast of* TRUMPETS, *entirely off-key, is heard, and a* PAGE *appears.*]

PAGE. King Azaz the Unabridged is about to begin the Royal banquet. All guests who do not appear promptly at the table will automatically lose their place. [*A huge Table is carried out with* KING AZAZ *sitting in a large chair, carried out at the head of the table.*]

AZAZ. Places. Everyone take your places. [*All the characters, including the* HUMBUG *and the* SPELLING BEE, *who forget their quarrel,*

Literary Analysis
Elements of Drama
Which characters' actions are described in the stage directions?

Reading Strategy
Summarizing What are the most significant events that have occurred since Milo learned about Rhyme and Reason?

rush to take their places at the table. MILO *and* TOCK *sit near the king.* AZAZ *looks at* MILO.] And just who is this?

MILO. Your Highness, my name is Milo and this is Tock. Thank you very much for inviting us to your banquet, and I think your palace is beautiful!

MINISTER 1. Exquisite.

MINISTER 2. Lovely.

MINISTER 3. Handsome.

MINISTER 4. Pretty.

MINISTER 5. Charming.

AZAZ. SILENCE! Now tell me, young man, what can you do to entertain us? Sing songs? Tell stories? Juggle plates? Do tumbling tricks? Which is it?

MILO. I can't do any of those things.

AZAZ. What an ordinary little boy. Can't you do anything at all?

MILO. Well . . . I can count to a thousand.

AZAZ. AARGH, numbers! Never mention numbers here. Only use them when we absolutely have to. Now, why don't we change the subject and have some dinner? Since you are the guest of honor, you may pick the menu.

MILO. Me? Well, uh . . . I'm not very hungry. Can we just have a light snack?

AZAZ. A light snack it shall be!

[AZAZ *claps his hands. Waiters rush in with covered trays. When they are uncovered, Shafts of Light pour out. The light may be created through the use of battery-operated flashlights which are secured in the trays and covered with a false bottom. The Guests help themselves.*]

HUMBUG. Not a very substantial meal. Maybe you can suggest something a little more filling.

MILO. Well, in that case, I think we ought to have a square meal . . .

AZAZ. [*Claps his hands.*] A square meal it is! [*Waiters serve trays of Colored Squares of all sizes. People serve themselves.*]

SPELLING BEE. These are awful. [HUMBUG *Coughs and all the Guests do not care for the food.*]

AZAZ. [*Claps his hands and the trays are removed.*] Time for speeches. [*To* MILO.] You first.

Literary Analysis
Elements of Drama
What do Azaz's words contribute to the development of the plot?

Literary Analysis
Elements of Drama How do the stage directions help you realize that Milo's light snack is something unusual?

**Reading Check**
What does the king forbid Milo to talk about?

MILO. [*Hesitantly.*] Your Majesty, ladies and gentlemen, I would like to take this opportunity to say that . . .

AZAZ. That's quite enough. Mustn't talk all day.

MILO. But I just started to . . .

AZAZ. NEXT!

HUMBUG. [*Quickly.*] Roast turkey, mashed potatoes, vanilla ice cream.

SPELLING BEE. Hamburgers, corn on the cob, chocolate pudding p-u-d-d-i-n-g. [*Each Guest names two dishes and a dessert.*]

AZAZ. [*The last.*] Pâté de foie gras, soupe à l'oignon, salade endives, fromage et fruits et demi-tasse. [*He claps his hands. Waiters serve each Guest his Words.*] Dig on. [*To* MILO.] Though I can't say I think much of your choice.

MILO. I didn't know I was going to have to eat my words.

AZAZ. Of course, of course, everybody here does. Your speech should have been in better taste.

MINISTER 1. Here, try some somersault. It improves the flavor.

MINISTER 2. Have a rigamarole. [*Offers breadbasket.*]

MINISTER 3. Or a ragamuffin.

MINISTER 4. Perhaps you'd care for a synonym bun.

MINISTER 5. Why not wait for your just desserts?

AZAZ. Ah yes, the dessert. We're having a special treat today . . . freshly made at the half-bakery.

MILO. The half-bakery?

AZAZ. Of course, the half-bakery! Where do you think half-baked ideas come from? Now, please don't interrupt. By royal command, the pastry chefs have . . .

MILO. What's a half-baked idea?

[AZAZ *gives up the idea of speaking as a cart is wheeled in and the Guests help themselves.*]

HUMBUG. They're very tasty, but they don't always agree with you. Here's a good one. [HUMBUG *hands one to* MILO.]

MILO. [*Reads.*] "The earth is flat."

SPELLING BEE. People swallowed that one for years. [*Picks up one and reads.*] "The moon is made of green cheese." Now, there's a half-baked idea.

[*Everyone chooses one and eats. They include: "It Never Rains But*

Literary Analysis
Elements of Drama
What happens to Milo each time he tries to talk? How does this relate to the action that follows?

Reading Strategy
Summarizing How would you summarize the events at the banquet so far?

Pours," "Night Air Is Bad Air," "Everything Happens for the Best," "Coffee Stunts Your Growth."]

AZAZ. And now for a few closing words. Attention! Let me have your attention! [*Everyone leaps up and Exits, except for* MILO, TOCK, *and the* HUMBUG.] Loyal subjects and friends, once again on this gala occasion, we have . . .

MILO. Excuse me, but everybody left.

AZAZ. [*Sadly.*] I was hoping no one would notice. It happens every time.

HUMBUG. They're gone to dinner, and as soon as I finish this last bite, I shall join them.

MILO. That's ridiculous. How can they eat dinner right after a banquet?

AZAZ. SCANDALOUS! We'll put a stop to it at once. From now on, by royal command, everyone must eat dinner before the banquet.

MILO. But that's just as bad.

HUMBUG. Or just as good. Things which are equally bad are also equally good. Try to look at the bright side of things.

MILO. I don't know which side of anything to look at. Everything is so confusing, and all your words only make things worse.

AZAZ. How true. There must be something we can do about it.

HUMBUG. Pass a law.

AZAZ. We have almost as many laws as words.

HUMBUG. Offer a reward. [AZAZ *shakes his head and looks madder at each suggestion.*] Send for help? Drive a bargain? Pull the switch? Lower the boom? Toe the line?

[*As* AZAZ *continues to scowl, the* HUMBUG *loses confidence and finally gives up.*]

MILO. Maybe you should let Rhyme and Reason return.

AZAZ. How nice that would be. Even if they were a bother at times, things always went so well when they were here. But I'm afraid it can't be done.

HUMBUG. Certainly not. Can't be done.

MILO. Why not?

HUMBUG. [*Now siding with* MILO.] Why not, indeed?

AZAZ. Much too difficult.

HUMBUG. Of course, much too difficult.

Literary Analysis
Elements of Drama What is the problem that must be settled as the plot unfolds?

Reading Check

What does Milo suggest Azaz should do to solve his problems?

MILO. You could, if you really wanted to.

HUMBUG. By all means, if you really wanted to, you could.

AZAZ. [*To* HUMBUG.] How?

MILO. [*Also to* HUMBUG.] Yeah, how?

HUMBUG. Why . . . uh, it's a simple task for a brave boy with a stout heart, a steadfast dog and a serviceable small automobile.

AZAZ. Go on.

HUMBUG. Well, all that he would have to do is cross the dangerous, unknown countryside between here and Digitopolis, where he would have to persuade the Mathemagician to release the Princesses, which we know to be impossible because the Mathemagician will never agree with Azaz about anything. Once achieving that, it's a simple matter of entering the Mountains of Ignorance from where no one has ever returned alive, an effortless climb up a two thousand foot stairway without railings in a high wind at night to the Castle-in-the-Air. After a pleasant chat with the Princesses, all that remains is a leisurely ride back through those chaotic crags where the frightening fiends have sworn to tear any intruder from limb to limb and devour him down to his belt buckle. And finally after doing all that, a triumphal parade! If, of course, there is anything left to parade . . . followed by hot chocolate and cookies for everyone.

AZAZ. I never realized it would be so simple.

MILO. It sounds dangerous to me.

TOCK. And just who is supposed to make that journey?

AZAZ. A very good question. But there is one far more serious problem.

MILO. What's that?

AZAZ. I'm afraid I can't tell you that until you return.

MILO. But wait a minute, I didn't . . .

AZAZ. Dictionopolis will always be grateful to you, my boy, and your dog. [AZAZ *pats* TOCK *and* MILO.]

TOCK. Now, just one moment, sire . . .

AZAZ. You will face many dangers on your journey, but fear not, for I can give you something for your protection. [AZAZ *gives* MILO *a box*.] In this box are the letters of the alphabet. With them you can form all the words you will ever need to help you overcome

Literary Analysis
Elements of Drama
What problem does Milo have to solve? What difficulties will he face as the plot unfolds?

Reading Strategy
Summarizing What are the main events of the first act?

the obstacles that may stand in your path. All you must do is use them well and in the right places.

MILO. [*Miserably.*] Thanks a lot.

AZAZ. You will need a guide, of course, and since he knows the obstacles so well, the Humbug has cheerfully volunteered to accompany you.

HUMBUG. Now, see here . . . !

AZAZ. You will find him dependable, brave, resourceful and loyal.

HUMBUG. [*Flattered.*] Oh, your Majesty.

MILO. I'm sure he'll be a great help. [*They approach the car.*]

TOCK. I hope so. It looks like we're going to need it.

[*The lights darken and the* KING *fades from view.*]

AZAZ. Good luck! Drive carefully! [*The three get into the car and begin to move. Suddenly a thunderously loud NOISE is heard. They slow down the car.*]

MILO. What was that?

TOCK. It came from up ahead.

HUMBUG. It's something terrible, I just know it. Oh, no. Something dreadful is going to happen to us. I can feel it in my bones. [*The NOISE is repeated. They all look at each other fearfully as the lights fade.*]

Review and Assess

Thinking About the Selection

1. **Respond:** Which character would you most like to meet?
2. **(a) Recall:** Who are Rhyme and Reason? **(b) Identify Cause and Effect:** What effect does their absence have on Dictionopolis?
3. **(a) Recall:** Why were Rhyme and Reason banished?
   (b) Infer: Why do you think Milo is chosen to rescue them?
4. **(a) Recall:** How does the Humbug describe the journey Milo must make? **(b) Speculate:** Describe what you think Milo's journey will be like, and give three details from the story to support your answer.
5. **(a) Recall:** What gift does King Azaz give Milo?
   (b) Hypothesize: Describe a situation in which the gift might help Milo.

Review and Assess

Literary Analysis

Elements of Drama

1. How does the dialogue in the play show you what kind of people the characters are? Copy and complete a chart like the one below to track how the dialogue shows a character's qualities.

Dialogue	Shows about the character
Milo: Well, it doesn't matter anyway. Dictionopolis. That's a weird name. I might as well go there.	He is a bored and indifferent person.
Tock:	
The Humbug:	

2. **(a)** Which character explains the problem in the play? **(b)** What is the effect of this character explaining the problem?

Connecting Literary Elements

3. What details of each setting do you learn in the stage directions? Record them on a chart like the one below.

Places	Details
Expectations	
The Doldrums	
Dictionopolis	

4. **(a)** Describe one place in the play where stage directions were necessary to understanding the events. **(b)** Find one place in the play that has no stage direction. Using your imagination, write your own stage directions for that scene.

Reading Strategy

Summarizing

5. **(a)** What are the most important events in Act I? **(b)** Why do you think they are the most important events?

6. Use the most important events to **summarize** Act I.

Extending Understanding

7. **Study Skills Connection:** What are three strategies for using time well?

Quick Review

The elements of drama—characters, setting, and plot—are developed mainly through dialogue. To review elements of drama, see page 613.

Stage directions are the explanations of how the characters move, look and talk and how the setting looks. To review setting, see page 613.

Summarizing is restating key events or ideas in your own words. To review summarizing, see page 613.

 Take It to the Net
www.phschool.com
Take the interactive self-test online to check your understanding of the selection.

Integrate Language Skills

Vocabulary Development Lesson

Word Analysis: Latin Prefix *pre-*

The Latin prefix *pre-* means "before." Using the meaning of *pre-*, write a definition for each italicized word.

1. I wonder if Milo's trip was *prearranged?*
2. None of the food at the banquet was *precooked.*
3. I want to *preview* the next act.

Fluency: Sentence Completions

Fill in each blank with a vocabulary word.

The ___?___ directions helped Milo avoid danger. He had the ___?___ that the Humbug could be trusted. He soon regretted his ___?___ .

Spelling Strategy

Some of the words below are misspelled. On your paper, correctly spell the misspelled words.

1. quotation
2. discussion
3. subtracsion
4. tention

Grammar Lesson

Subject and Verb Agreement

The verb in a sentence must **agree** in number with the subject. A singular subject is one person, place, or thing. A plural subject is more than one. Verbs in the present tense change form to agree with a singular or plural subject. Singular verbs add an *s*, while plural verbs do not.

The chart shows rules for **compound subjects**—subjects with two or more nouns.

▶ *For more practice, see page R30, Exercise D.*
Practice Write the verb to agree with the subject.

1. A tollbooth (is, are) in the package.
2. The Lethargarians (is, are) sleepy.
3. A word or number (means, mean) a lot.
4. The ministers (say, says), "Hello!"
5. Milo and Tock (is, are) learning.

Rules	Examples
Parts of a compound subject joined by *and* usually take a plural verb.	<u>Milo</u> and <u>Tock</u> <u>drive</u> to Dictionopolis.
Singular subjects joined by *or* or *nor* use a singular verb.	Neither <u>Reason</u> **nor** <u>Rhyme</u> <u>lives</u> in Dictionopolis.
Plural subjects joined by *or* or *nor* use a plural verb.	Neither <u>words</u> **nor** <u>numbers</u> <u>are</u> superior.
When a compound subject is made up of one singular subject and one plural subject joined by *or* or *nor,* the verb agrees with the subject closer to it.	Neither <u>Milo</u> **nor** his <u>friends</u> <u>are</u> fearless. Neither his <u>friends</u> **nor** <u>Milo</u> <u>is</u> fearless.

𝒲_G *Prentice Hall Writing and Grammar Connection: Chapter 6, Section 3*

Extension Activities

Listening and Speaking Write and deliver to classmates a brief **speech** that Milo might have given at the banquet about his experiences so far. Rehearse the speech before presenting it to the class, using gestures and tone of voice to reinforce the feeling and meaning of your words.

Writing As Milo, write a **letter** to friends at home. In the letter, describe your experiences so far. Include details about the thoughts and feelings that you, as Milo, have about events. End your letter with a prediction about the adventure you are about to begin with Tock and Humbug.

Prepare to Read

The Phantom Tollbooth, Act II

Reading 3.6 Identify and analyze themes. (*Developed in the Literary Analysis*)

Writing 2.4 Write a response to literature. (*Developed in the Writing Lesson*)

Language Conventions 1.2 Identify and use indefinite pronouns. (*Concluded in the Grammar Lesson*)

Listening and Speaking 1.6 Support opinions with evidence. (*Developed in the Listening and Speaking activity*)

Literary Analysis

Theme

The **theme**, or central idea, of a literary work is the idea or insight about life that the events in the work suggest. The lessons Milo learns from his experiences are clues to the theme of *The Phantom Tollbooth*. As you read, think about these focus questions:

1. What are two lessons Milo learns on his travels?
2. How can these lessons be applied in real life?

Connecting Literary Elements

Images are the "word pictures" created by language that appeals to the senses—sight, sound, smell, taste, touch. They can be used to reinforce the author's theme, or message. For example, at the opening of Act II, images are used to reinforce the message that Milo should be using his imagination or powers of observation.

> VOICE: Have you ever heard a whole set of dishes dropped from the ceiling onto a hard stone floor? [. . . MILO *shakes his head.* VOICE *happily.*] Have you ever heard an ant wearing fur slippers walk across a thick wool carpet? [MILO *shakes his head again.*] . . . Just as I expected . . . You're all suffering from a severe lack of noise.

Reading Strategy

Recognizing Wordplay

In addition to mental pictures, this play provides mental exercise. Through **wordplay**, the author calls readers' attention to the richness of language by playing with several meanings of the same word. In the example, notice that the two meanings of *fork* lead to a shift in the conversation.

> MILO. But wait! The fork in the road . . . You didn't tell us where it is . . .
>
> HUMBUG. I could use a fork of my own at the moment . . . All of a sudden I feel very hungry.

Vocabulary Development

dissonance (dis′ ə nəns) *n.* harsh combination of sounds (p. 637)

admonishing (ad män′ ish iŋ) *adj.* disapproving (p. 642)

iridescent (ir′ ə des′ ənt) *adj.* showing different colors when seen from different angles (p. 644)

malicious (mə lish′ əs) *adj.* showing evil intentions (p. 651)

Review and Anticipate

In Act I, Milo is lifted from his boredom into a strange kingdom in conflict over the importance of letters and numbers. After traveling through Dictionopolis, he agrees to rescue the princesses who can settle the conflict. As Act II opens, Milo enters Digitopolis with Tock and Humbug—characters who will help him rescue the princesses.

Act II

Scene i

The set of Digitopolis glitters in the background, while Upstage Right near the road, a small colorful Wagon sits, looking quite deserted. On its side in large letters, a sign reads:
"KAKAFONOUS A. DISCHORD Doctor of <u>Dissonance</u>"
Enter MILO, TOCK *and* HUMBUG, *fearfully. They look at the wagon.*

TOCK. There's no doubt about it. That's where the noise was coming from.

HUMBUG. [*To* MILO.] Well, go on.

MILO. Go on what?

HUMBUG. Go on and see who's making all that noise in there. We can't just ignore a creature like that.

MILO. Creature? What kind of creature? Do you think he's dangerous?

HUMBUG. Go on, Milo. Knock on the door. We'll be right behind you.

MILO. O.K. Maybe he can tell us how much further it is to Digitopolis.

[MILO *tiptoes up to the wagon door and* KNOCKS *timidly. The moment he knocks, a terrible* CRASH *is heard inside the wagon, and* MILO *and the others jump back in fright. At the same time, the Door Flies Open, and from the dark interior, a Hoarse* VOICE *inquires.*]

VOICE. Have you ever heard a whole set of dishes dropped from the ceiling onto a hard stone floor? [*The Others are speechless with fright.* MILO *shakes his head.* VOICE *happily.*] Have you ever heard an ant wearing fur slippers walk across a thick wool carpet? [MILO *shakes his head again.*] Have you ever heard a blindfolded octopus unwrap a cellophane-covered bathtub? [MILO *shakes his*

▼ **Critical Viewing**
How do you think a character like the one shown will fit into Milo's adventures? **[Speculate]**

dissonance (dis´ ə nəns) *n.* harsh combination of sounds

☑ **Reading Check**

Where do Milo, Tock, and Humbug find themselves?

head a third time.] Ha! I knew it. [*He hops out, a little man, wearing a white coat, with a stethoscope around his neck, and a small mirror attached to his forehead, and with very huge ears, and a mortar and pestle in his hands. He stares at* MILO, TOCK *and* HUMBUG.] None of you looks well at all! Tsk, tsk, not at all. [*He opens the top or side of his Wagon, revealing a dusty interior resembling an old apothecary shop, with shelves lined with jars and boxes, a table, books, test tubes and bottles and measuring spoons.*]

MILO. [*Timidly.*] Are you a doctor?

DISCHORD. [VOICE.] I am KAKAFONOUS A. DISCHORD, DOCTOR OF DISSONANCE! [*Several small explosions and a grinding crash are heard.*]

HUMBUG. [*Stuttering with fear.*] What does the "A" stand for?

DISCHORD. AS LOUD AS POSSIBLE! [*Two screeches and a bump are heard.*] Now, step a little closer and stick out your tongues. [DISCHORD *examines them.*] Just as I expected. [*He opens a large dusty book and thumbs through the pages.*] You're all suffering from a severe lack of noise. [DISCHORD *begins running around, collecting bottles, reading the labels to himself as he goes along.*] "Loud Cries." "Soft Cries." "Bangs, Bongs, Swishes. Swooshes." "Snaps and Crackles." "Whistles and Gongs." "Squeeks, Squacks, and Miscellaneous Uproar." [*As he reads them off, he pours a little of each into a large glass beaker and stirs the mixture with a wooden spoon. The concoction smokes and bubbles.*] Be ready in just a moment.

MILO. [*Suspiciously.*] Just what kind of doctor are you?

DISCHORD. Well, you might say, I'm a specialist. I specialize in noises, from the loudest to the softest, and from the slightly annoying to the terribly unpleasant. For instance, have you ever heard a square-wheeled steamroller ride over a street full of hard-boiled eggs? [*Very loud CRUNCHING SOUNDS are heard.*]

MILO. [*Holding his ears.*] But who would want all those terrible noises?

DISCHORD. [*Surprised at the question.*] Everybody does. Why, I'm so busy I can hardly fill all the orders for noise pills, racket lotion, clamor salve and hubbub tonic. That's all people seem to want these days. Years ago, everyone wanted pleasant sounds and business was terrible. But then the cities were built and there was a great need for honking horns, screeching trains, clanging bells and all the rest of those wonderfully unpleasant sounds we use so much today. I've been working overtime ever since and my medicine here is in great demand. All you have to do is

Literary Analysis
Theme and Images What images come to mind as you read Dischord's words?

Literary Analysis
Theme What message about noise is suggested by Dischord's speech?

take one spoonful every day, and you'll never have to hear another beautiful sound again. Here, try some.

HUMBUG. [*Backing away.*] If it's all the same to you, I'd rather not.

MILO. I don't want to be cured of beautiful sounds.

TOCK. Besides, there's no such sickness as a lack of noise.

DISCHORD. How true. That's what makes it so difficult to cure. [*Takes a large glass bottle from the shelf.*] Very well, if you want to go all through life suffering from a noise deficiency, I'll just give this to Dynne for his lunch. [*Uncorks the bottle and pours the liquid into it. There is a rumbling and then a loud explosion accompanied by smoke, out of which* DYNNE, *a smog-like creature with yellow eyes and a frowning mouth, appears.*]

DYNNE. [*Smacking his lips.*] Ahhh, that was good, Master. I thought you'd never let me out. It was really cramped in there.

DISCHORD. This is my assistant, the awful Dynne. You must forgive his appearance, for he really doesn't have any.

MILO. What is a Dynne?

DISCHORD. You mean you've never heard of the awful Dynne? When you're playing in your room and making a great amount of noise, what do they tell you to stop?

MILO. That awful din.

DISCHORD. When the neighbors are playing their radio too loud late at night, what do you wish they'd turn down?

TOCK. That awful din.

DISCHORD. And when the street on your block is being repaired and the drills are working all day, what does everyone complain of?

HUMBUG. [*Brightly.*] The dreadful row.

DYNNE. The Dreadful Rauw was my grandfather. He perished in the great silence epidemic of 1712. I certainly can't understand why you don't like noise. Why, I heard an explosion last week that was so lovely, I groaned with appreciation for two days. [*He gives a loud groan at the memory.*]

DISCORD. He's right, you know! Noise is the most valuable thing in the world.

MILO. King Azaz says words are.

DISCHORD. NONSENSE! Why, when a baby wants food, how does he ask?

DYNNE. [*Happily.*] He screams!

DISCHORD. And when a racing car wants gas?

Literary Analysis
Theme What is the meaning of the name *Dynne?*

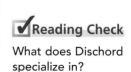
Reading Check

What does Dischord specialize in?

DYNNE. [*Jumping for joy.*] It chokes!

DISCHORD. And what happens to the dawn when a new day begins?

DYNNE. [*Delighted.*] It breaks!

DISCHORD. You see how simple it is? [*To* DYNNE.] Isn't it time for us
to go?

MILO. Where to? Maybe we're going the same way.

DYNNE. I doubt it. [*Picking up empty sacks from the table.*] We're
going on our collection rounds. Once a day, I travel throughout
the kingdom and collect all the wonderfully horrible and beautifully unpleasant sounds I can find and bring them back to the
doctor to use in his medicine.

DISCHORD. Where are you going?

MILO. To Digitopolis.

DISCHORD. Oh, there are a number of ways to get to Digitopolis, if
you know how to follow directions. Just take a look at the sign
at the fork in the road. Though why you'd ever want to go there,
I'll never know.

MILO. We want to talk to the Mathemagician.

HUMBUG. About the release of the Princesses Rhyme and Reason.

DISCHORD. Rhyme and Reason? I remember them. Very nice girls,
but a little too quiet for my taste. In fact, I've been meaning to
send them something that Dynne brought home by mistake and
which I have absolutely no use for. [*He rummages through the
wagon.*] Ah, here it is . . . or maybe you'd like it for yourself.
[*Hands* MILO *a Package.*]

MILO. What is it?

DISCHORD. The sounds of laughter. They're so unpleasant to hear, it's
almost unbearable. All those giggles and snickers and happy
shouts of joy, I don't know what Dynne was thinking of when he
collected them. Here, take them to the Princesses or keep them for
yourselves, I don't care. Well, time to move on. Goodbye now and
good luck! [*He has shut the wagon by now and gets in. LOUD
NOISES begin to erupt as* DYNNE *pulls the wagon offstage.*]

MILO. [*Calling after them.*] But wait! The fork in the road . . . you
didn't tell us where it is . . .

TOCK. It's too late. He can't hear a thing.

HUMBUG. I could use a fork of my own, at the moment. And a knife
and a spoon to go with it. All of a sudden, I feel very hungry.

MILO. So do I, but it's no use thinking about it. There won't be

Literary Analysis
Theme and Images
Do you think the author
wants you to agree with
Dischord about the sound
of laughter?

anything to eat until we reach Digitopolis. [*They get into the car.*]

HUMBUG. [*Rubbing his stomach.*] Well, the sooner the better is what I say. [*A SIGN suddenly appears.*]

VOICE. [*A strange voice from nowhere.*] But which way will get you there sooner? That is the question.

TOCK. Did you hear something?

MILO. Look! The fork in the road and a signpost to Digitopolis! [*They read the Sign.*]

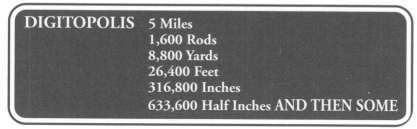

DIGITOPOLIS 5 Miles
1,600 Rods
8,800 Yards
26,400 Feet
316,800 Inches
633,600 Half Inches AND THEN SOME

HUMBUG. Let's travel by miles, it's shorter.

MILO. Let's travel by half inches. It's quicker.

TOCK. But which road should we take? It must make a difference.

MILO. Do you think so?

TOCK. Well, I'm not sure, but . . .

HUMBUG. He could be right. On the other hand, he could also be wrong. Does it make a difference or not?

VOICE. Yes, indeed, indeed it does, certainly, my yes, it does make a difference.

[*The DODECAHEDRON Appears, a 12-sided figure with a different face on each side, and with all the edges labeled with a small letter and all the angles labeled with a large letter. He wears a beret and peers at the others with a serious face. He doffs his cap and recites:*]

DODECAHEDRON.
> *My angles are many.*
> *My sides are not few.*
> *I'm the Dodecahedron.*
> *Who are you?*

MILO. What's a Dodecahedron?

DODECAHEDRON. [*Turning around slowly.*] See for yourself. A Dodecahedron is a mathematical shape with 12 faces. [*All his faces appear as he turns, each face with a different expression. He points to them.*] I usually use one at a time. It saves wear and tear. What are you called?

MILO. Milo.

Literary Analysis
Theme What message about making choices is suggested by the characters' questions?

Reading Check

What does Dischord give Milo to take with him?

DODECAHEDRON. That's an odd name. [*Changing his smiling face to a frowning one.*] And you have only one face.

MILO. [*Making sure it is still there.*] Is that bad?

DODECAHEDRON. You'll soon wear it out using it for everything. Is everyone with one face called Milo?

MILO. Oh, no. Some are called Billy or Jeffery or Sally or Lisa or lots of other things.

DODECAHEDRON. How confusing. Here everything is called exactly what it is. The triangles are called triangles, the circles are called circles, and even the same numbers have the same name. Can you imagine what would happen if we named all the twos Billy or Jeffery or Sally or Lisa or lots of other things? You'd have to say Robert plus John equals four, and if the fours were named Albert, things would be hopeless.

MILO. I never thought of it that way.

DODECAHEDRON. [*With an admonishing face.*] Then I suggest you begin at once, for in Digitopolis, everything is quite precise.

MILO. Then perhaps you can help us decide which road we should take.

DODECAHEDRON. [*Happily.*] By all means. There's nothing to it. [*As he talks, the three others try to solve the problem on a Large Blackboard that is wheeled onstage for the occasion.*] Now, if a small car carrying three people at 30 miles an hour for 10 minutes along a road 5 miles long at 11:35 in the morning starts at the same time as 3 people who have been traveling in a little automobile at 20 miles an hour for 15 minutes on another road exactly twice as long as half the distance of the other, while a dog, a bug, and a boy travel an equal distance in the same time or the same distance in an equal time along a third road in mid-October, then which one arrives first and which is the best way to go?

HUMBUG. Seventeen!

MILO. [*Still figuring frantically.*] I'm not sure, but . . .

DODECAHEDRON. You'll have to do better than that.

MILO. I'm not very good at problems.

DODECAHEDRON. What a shame. They're so very useful. Why, did you know that if a beaver 2 feet long with a tail a foot and a half long can build a dam 12 feet high and 6 feet wide in 2 days, all you would need to build Boulder Dam is a beaver 68 feet long with a 51 foot tail?

HUMBUG. [*Grumbling as his pencil snaps.*] Where would you find a beaver that big?

admonishing
(ad män´ ish iŋ) *adj.*
disapproving

Literary Analysis
Theme Why should the characters bother to solve such a difficult problem?

DODECAHEDRON. I don't know, but if you did, you'd certainly know what to do with him.

MILO. That's crazy.

DODECAHEDRON. That may be true, but it's completely accurate, and as long as the answer is right, who cares if the question is wrong?

TOCK. [*Who has been patiently doing the first problem.*] All three roads arrive at the same place at the same time.

DODECAHEDRON. Correct! And I'll take you there myself. [*The blackboard rolls off, and all four get into the car and drive off.*] Now you see how important problems are. If you hadn't done this one properly, you might have gone the wrong way.

MILO. But if all the roads arrive at the same place at the same time, then aren't they all the right road?

DODECAHEDRON. [*Glaring from his upset face.*] Certainly not! They're all the wrong way! Just because you have a choice, it doesn't mean that any of them has to be right. [*Pointing in another direction.*] That's the way to Digitopolis and we'll be there any moment. [*Suddenly the lighting grows dimmer.*] In fact, we're here. Welcome to the Land of Numbers.

HUMBUG. [*Looking around at the barren landscape.*] It doesn't look very inviting.

MILO. Is this the place where numbers are made?

DODECAHEDRON. They're not made. You have to dig for them. Don't you know anything at all about numbers?

MILO. Well, I never really thought they were very important.

DODECAHEDRON. NOT IMPORTANT! Could you have tea for two without the 2? Or three blind mice without the 3? And how would you sail the seven seas without the 7?

MILO. All I meant was . . .

DODECAHEDRON. [*Continues shouting angrily.*] If you had high hopes, how would you know how high they were? And did you know that narrow escapes come in different widths? Would you travel the whole world wide without ever knowing how wide it was? And how could you do anything at long last without knowing how long the last was? Why numbers are the most beautiful and valuable things in the world. Just follow me and I'll show you. [*He motions to them and pantomimes walking through rocky terrain with the others in tow. A Doorway similar to the Tollbooth appears and the DODECAHEDRON opens it and motions the others to follow him through.*] Come along, come along. I can't wait for you all day. [*They enter the doorway and the lights are dimmed*

Literary Analysis
Theme To what situation outside the play could you apply this statement: "Just because you have a choice, it doesn't mean that any of them has to be right"?

Reading Strategy
Recognizing Wordplay How does Dodecahedron twist the literal meanings of words in these expressions?

**Reading Check**

What important fact does Dodecahedron give about Digitopolis?

very low, as to simulate the interior of a cave. The SOUNDS of scrapings and tapping, scuffling and digging are heard all around them. He hands them Helmets with flashlights attached.] Put these on.

MILO. [Whispering.] Where are we going?

DODECAHEDRON. We're here. This is the numbers mine. [LIGHTS UP A LITTLE, revealing Little Men digging and chopping, shoveling and scraping.] Right this way and watch your step. [His voice echoes and reverberates. Iridescent and glittery numbers seem to sparkle from everywhere.]

MILO. [Awed.] Whose mine is it?

VOICE OF MATHEMAGICIAN. By the four million eight hundred and twenty-seven thousand six hundred and fifty-nine hairs on my head, it's mine, of course! [ENTER the MATHEMAGICIAN, carrying his long staff which looks like a giant pencil.]

HUMBUG. [Already intimidated.] It's a lovely mine, really it is.

MATHEMAGICIAN. [Proudly.] The biggest number mine in the kingdom.

MILO. [Excitedly.] Are there any precious stones in it?

MATHEMAGICIAN. Precious stones! [Then softly.] By the eight million two hundred and forty-seven thousand three hundred and twelve threads in my robe, I'll say there are. Look here. [Reaches in a cart, pulls out a small object, polishes it vigorously and holds it to the light, where it sparkles.]

MILO. But that's a five.

MATHEMAGICIAN. Exactly. As valuable a jewel as you'll find anywhere. Look at some of the others. [Scoops up others and pours them into MILO's arms. They include all numbers from 1 to 9 and an assortment of zeros.]

DODECAHEDRON. We dig them and polish them right here, and then send them all over the world. Marvelous, aren't they?

TOCK. They are beautiful. [He holds them up to compare them to the numbers on his clock body.]

iridescent (ir´ ə des´ ənt) adj. showing different colors when seen from different angles

▲ **Critical Viewing**
Which details of Dodecahedron are the most interesting to you? Why?

MILO. So that's where they come from. [*Looks at them and carefully hands them back, but drops a few which smash and break in half.*] Oh, I'm sorry!

MATHEMAGICIAN. [*Scooping them up.*] Oh, don't worry about that. We use the broken ones for fractions. How about some lunch? [*Takes out a little whistle and blows it. Two miners rush in carrying an immense cauldron which is bubbling and steaming. The workers put down their tools and gather around to eat.*]

HUMBUG. That looks delicious! [TOCK *and* MILO *also look hungrily at the pot.*]

MATHEMAGICIAN. Perhaps you'd care for something to eat?

MILO. Oh, yes, sir!

TOCK. Thank you.

HUMBUG. [*Already eating.*] Ummm . . . delicious! [*All finish their bowls immediately.*]

MATHEMAGICIAN. Please have another portion. [*They eat and finish.* MATHEMAGICIAN *serves them again.*] Don't stop now. [*They finish.*] Come on, no need to be bashful. [*Serves them again.*]

MILO. [*To* TOCK *and* HUMBUG *as he finishes again.*] Do you want to hear something strange? Each one I eat makes me a little hungrier than before.

MATHEMAGICIAN. Do have some more. [*He serves them again. They eat frantically, until the* MATHEMAGICIAN *blows his whistle again and the pot is removed.*]

HUMBUG. [*Holding his stomach.*] Uggghhh! I think I'm starving.

MILO. Me, too, and I ate so much.

DODECAHEDRON. [*Wiping the gravy from several of his mouths.*] Yes, it was delicious, wasn't it? It's the specialty of the kingdom . . . subtraction stew.

TOCK. [*Weak from hunger.*] I have more of an appetite than when I began.

MATHEMAGICIAN. Certainly, what did you expect? The more you eat, the hungrier you get, everyone knows that.

MILO. They do? Then how do you get enough?

MATHEMAGICIAN. Enough? Here in Digitopolis, we have our meals when we're full and eat until we're hungry. That way, when you don't have anything at all, you have more than enough. It's a very economical system. You must have been stuffed to have eaten so much.

Reading Strategy
Recognizing Wordplay
Explain why broken numbers are an accurate description of a fraction.

Reading Strategy
Recognizing Wordplay
How does the name of the stew reveal why the characters are hungrier than they were before they ate?

**Reading Check**

To what topic does everything in Digitopolis relate?

DODECAHEDRON. It's completely logical. The more you want, the less you get, and the less you get, the more you have. Simple arithmetic, that's all. [TOCK, MILO *and* HUMBUG *look at him blankly.*] Now, look, suppose you had something and added nothing to it. What would you have?

MILO. The same.

DODECAHEDRON. Splendid! And suppose you had something and added less than nothing to it? What would you have then?

HUMBUG. Starvation! Oh, I'm so hungry.

DODECAHEDRON. Now, now, it's not as bad as all that. In a few hours, you'll be nice and full again . . . just in time for dinner.

MILO. But I only eat when I'm hungry.

MATHEMAGICIAN. [*Waving the eraser of his staff.*] What a curious idea. The next thing you'll have us believe is that you only sleep when you're tired.

[*The mine has disappeared as well as the Miners.*]

HUMBUG. Where did everyone go?

MATHEMAGICIAN. Oh, they're still in the mine. I often find that the best way to get from one place to another is to erase everything and start again. Please make yourself at home.

[*They find themselves in a unique room, in which all the walls, tables, chairs, desks, cabinets and blackboards are labeled to show their heights, widths, depths and distances to and from each other. To one side is a gigantic notepad on an artist's easel, and from hooks and strings hang a collection of rulers, measures, weights and tapes, and all other measuring devices.*]

MILO. Do you always travel that way? [*He looks around in wonder.*]

MATHEMAGICIAN. No, indeed! [*He pulls a plumb line♦ from a hook and walks.*] Most of the time I take the shortest distance between any two points. And of course, when I have to be in several places at once . . . [*He writes 3 × 1 = 3 on the notepad with his staff.*] I simply multiply. [THREE FIGURES *looking like the* MATHEMAGICIAN *appear on a platform above.*]

MILO. How did you do that?

MATHEMAGICIAN AND THE THREE. There's nothing to it, if you have a magic staff. [THE THREE FIGURES *cancel themselves out and disappear.*]

♦*Plumb Line*

A **plumb line** is a cord that has a weight, often called a *plumb* or *plumb bob*, at one end. The word *plumb* comes from the Old French word *plomb*, which means "lead." Not surprisingly, the weight on a plumb line is frequently made of lead. The weight keeps the line straight and makes it a useful tool for measuring heights and straight lines. In *The Phantom Tollbooth*, the Mathemagician uses the plumb line to show the shortest distance between any two points.

HUMBUG. That's nothing but a big pencil.

MATHEMAGICIAN. True enough, but once you learn to use it, there's no end to what you can do.

MILO. Can you make things disappear?

MATHEMAGICIAN. Just step a little closer and watch this. [*Shows them that there is nothing up his sleeve or in his hat. He writes:*]

$4 + 9 - 2 \times 16 + 1 = 3 \times 6 - 67 + 8 \times 2 - 3 + 26 - 1 - 34 + 3 - 7 + 2 - 5 =$ [*He looks up expectantly.*]

HUMBUG. Seventeen?

MILO. It all comes to zero.

MATHEMAGICIAN. Precisely. [*Makes a theatrical bow and rips off paper from notepad.*] Now, is there anything else you'd like to see? [*At this point, an appeal to the audience to see if anyone would like a problem solved.*]

MILO. Well . . . can you show me the biggest number there is?

MATHEMAGICIAN. Why, I'd be delighted. [*Opening a closet door.*] We keep it right here. It took four miners to dig it out. [*He shows them a huge "3" twice as high as the* MATHEMAGICIAN.]

MILO. No, that's not what I mean. Can you show me the longest number there is?

MATHEMAGICIAN. Sure. [*Opens another door.*] Here it is. It took three carts to carry it here. [*Door reveals an "8" that is as wide as the "3" was high.*]

MILO. No, no, that's not what I meant either. [*Looks helplessly at* TOCK.]

TOCK. I think what you would like to see is the number of the greatest possible magnitude.

MATHEMAGICIAN. Well, why didn't you say so? [*He busily measures them and all other things as he speaks, and marks it down.*] What's the greatest number you can think of? [*Here, an appeal can also be made to the audience or* MILO *may think of his own answers.*]

MILO. Uh . . . nine trillion, nine hundred and ninety-nine billion, nine hundred ninety-nine million, nine-hundred ninety-nine thousand, nine hundred and ninety-nine [*He puffs.*]

MATHEMAGICIAN. [*Writes that on the pad.*] Very good. Now add one to it. [MILO *or audience does.*] Now add one again. [MILO *or audience does so.*] Now add one again. Now add one again. Now add . . .

MILO. But when can I stop?

Literary Analysis
Theme What message about life is suggested by the Mathemagician's statement?

Reading Strategy
Recognizing Wordplay Explain how the meanings of *biggest* and *longest* lead to the Mathemagician's misunderstanding.

Reading Check
What does the Mathemagician teach Milo about numbers?

MATHEMAGICIAN. Never. Because the number you want is always at least one more than the number you have, and it's so large that if you started saying it yesterday, you wouldn't finish tomorrow.

HUMBUG. Where could you ever find a number so big?

MATHEMAGICIAN. In the same place they have the smallest number there is, and you know what that is?

MILO. The smallest number . . . let's see . . . one one-millionth?

MATHEMAGICIAN. Almost. Now all you have to do is divide that in half and then divide that in half and then divide that in half and then divide that . . .

MILO. Doesn't that ever stop either?

MATHEMAGICIAN. How can it when you can always take half of what you have and divide it in half again? Look. [*Pointing offstage.*] You see that line?

MILO. You mean that long one out there?

MATHEMAGICIAN. That's it. Now, if you just follow that line forever, and when you reach the end, turn left, you will find the Land of Infinity. That's where the tallest, the shortest, the biggest, the smallest and the most and the least of everything are kept.

MILO. But how can you follow anything forever? You know, I get the feeling that everything in Digitopolis is very difficult.

MATHEMAGICIAN. But on the other hand, I think you'll find that the only thing you can do easily is be wrong, and that's hardly worth the effort.

MILO. But . . . what bothers me is . . . well, why is it that even when things are correct, they don't really seem to be right?

MATHEMAGICIAN. [*Grows sad and quiet.*] How true. It's been that way ever since Rhyme and Reason were banished. [*Sadness turns to fury.*] *And all because of that stubborn wretch Azaz!* It's all his fault.

▲ **Critical Viewing**
Which details in this picture best represent Mathemagician? Why?

MILO. Maybe if you discussed it with him . . .

MATHEMAGICIAN. He's just too unreasonable! Why just last month, I sent him a very friendly letter, which he never had the courtesy to answer. See for yourself. [*Puts the letter on the easel. The letter reads:*]

4738 1919,

667 394107 5841 62589 85371 14

39588 7190434 203 27689 57131 481206.

5864 98053,

62179875073

MILO. But maybe he doesn't understand numbers.

MATHEMAGICIAN. Nonsense! Everybody understands numbers. No matter what language you speak, they always mean the same thing. A seven is a seven everywhere in the world.

MILO. [*To* TOCK *and* HUMBUG.] Everyone is so sensitive about what he knows best.

TOCK. With your permission, sir, we'd like to rescue Rhyme and Reason.

MATHEMAGICIAN. Has Azaz agreed to it?

TOCK. Yes, sir.

MATHEMAGICIAN. THEN I DON'T! Ever since they've been banished, we've never agreed on anything, and we never will.

MILO. Never?

MATHEMAGICIAN. NEVER! And if you can prove otherwise, you have my permission to go.

MILO. Well then, with whatever Azaz agrees, you disagree.

MATHEMAGICIAN. Correct.

MILO. And with whatever Azaz disagrees, you agree.

MATHEMAGICIAN. [*Yawning, cleaning his nails.*] Also correct.

MILO. Then, each of you agrees that he will disagree with whatever each of you agrees with, and if you both disagree with the same thing, aren't you really in agreement?

MATHEMAGICIAN. I'VE BEEN TRICKED! [*Figures it over, but comes up with the same answer.*]

TOCK. And now may we go?

MATHEMAGICIAN. [*Nods weakly.*] It's a long and dangerous journey. Long before you find them, the demons will know you're there.

Literary Analysis
Theme What real-life situations support the Mathemagician's statement?

Reading Strategy
Recognizing Wordplay How does Milo use words and logic to get the Mathemagician to agree to the rescue?

**Reading Check**
To what does Milo get the Mathemagician to agree?

Watch out for them, because if you ever come face to face, it will be too late. But there is one other obstacle even more serious than that.

MILO. [*Terrified.*] What is it?

MATHEMAGICIAN. I'm afraid I can't tell you until you return. But maybe I can give you something to help you out. [*Claps hands. ENTER the* DODECAHEDRON, *carrying something on a pillow. The* MATHEMAGICIAN *takes it.*] Here is your own magic staff. Use it well and there is nothing it can't do for you. [*Puts a small, gleaming pencil in* MILO's *breast pocket.*]

HUMBUG. Are you sure you can't tell about that serious obstacle?

MATHEMAGICIAN. Only when you return. And now the Dodecahedron will escort you to the road that leads to the Castle-in-the-Air. Farewell, my friends, and good luck to you. [*They shake hands, say goodbye, and the* DODECAHEDRON *leads them off.*] Good luck to you! [*To himself.*] Because you're sure going to need it. [*He watches them through a telescope and marks down the calculations.*]

DODECAHEDRON. [*He re-enters.*] Well, they're on their way.

MATHEMAGICIAN. So I see. . . [DODECAHEDRON *stands waiting.*] Well, what is it?

DODECAHEDRON. I was just wondering myself, your Numbership. What actually *is* the serious obstacle you were talking about?

MATHEMAGICIAN. [*Looks at him in surprise.*] You mean you really don't know?

BLACKOUT

Scene ii

The Land of Ignorance

LIGHTS UP on RHYME *and* REASON, *in their castle, looking out two windows.*

RHYME. *I'm worried sick, I must confess*
    I wonder if they'll have success
    All the others tried in vain,
    And were never seen or heard again.

REASON. Now, Rhyme, there's no need to be so pessimistic. Milo, Tock, and Humbug have just as much chance of succeeding as they do of failing.

Literary Analysis
Theme What can Milo do with the Mathemagician's gift?

RHYME. *But the demons are so deadly smart*
They'll stuff your brain and fill your heart
With petty thoughts and selfish dreams
And trap you with their nasty schemes.

REASON. Now, Rhyme, be reasonable, won't you? And calm down, you always talk in couplets when you get nervous. Milo has learned a lot from his journey. I think he's a match for the demons and that he might soon be knocking at our door. Now come on, cheer up, won't you?

RHYME. I'll try.

[*LIGHTS FADE on the* PRINCESSES *and COME UP on the little Car, traveling slowly.*]

MILO. So this is the Land of Ignorance. It's so dark. I can hardly see a thing. Maybe we should wait until morning.

VOICE. They'll be mourning for you soon enough. [*They look up and see a large, soiled, ugly* BIRD *with a dangerous beak and a malicious expression.*]

MILO. I don't think you understand. We're looking for a place to spend the night.

BIRD. [*Shrieking.*] It's not yours to spend!

MILO. That doesn't make any sense, you see . . .

BIRD. Dollars or cents, it's still not yours to spend.

MILO. But I don't mean . . .

BIRD. Of course you're mean. Anybody who'd spend a night that doesn't belong to him is very mean.

TOCK. Must you interrupt like that?

BIRD. Naturally, it's my job. I take the words right out of your mouth. Haven't we met before? I'm the Everpresent Wordsnatcher.

MILO. Are you a demon?

BIRD. I'm afraid not. I've tried, but the best I can manage to be is a nuisance. [*Suddenly gets nervous as he looks beyond the three.*] And I don't have time to waste with you. [*Starts to leave.*]

TOCK. What is it? What's the matter?

MILO. Hey, don't leave. I wanted to ask you some questions. . . . Wait!

Literary Analysis
Theme How can the princess's rhyme be applied to real life?

malicious (mə lish′ əs) *adj.* showing evil intentions

Literary Analysis
Theme and Images What message is suggested by the image of a loud, annoying, unattractive bird that interrupts?

Reading Check

What are the princesses worried about?

BIRD. Weight? Twenty-seven pounds. Bye-bye. [*Disappears.*]

MILO. Well, he was no help.

MAN. Perhaps I can be of some assistance to you? [*There appears a beautifully dressed man, very polished and clean.*] Hello, little boy. [*Shakes* MILO'S *hand.*] And how's the faithful dog? [*Pats* TOCK.] And who is this handsome creature? [*Tips his hat to* HUMBUG.]

HUMBUG. [*To others.*] What a pleasant surprise to meet someone so nice in a place like this.

MAN. But before I help you out, I wonder if first you could spare me a little of your time, and help me with a few small jobs?

HUMBUG. Why, certainly.

TOCK. Gladly.

MILO. Sure, we'd be happy to.

MAN. Splendid, for there are just three tasks. First, I would like to move this pile of sand from here to there. [*Indicates through pantomime a large pile of sand.*] But I'm afraid that all I have is this tiny tweezers. [*Hands it to* MILO, *who begins moving the sand one grain at a time.*] Second, I would like to empty this well and fill that other, but I have no bucket, so you'll have to use this eyedropper. [*Hands it to* TOCK, *who begins to work.*] And finally, I must have a hole in this cliff, and here is a needle to dig it. [HUMBUG *eagerly begins. The man leans against a tree and stares vacantly off into space. The LIGHTS indicate the passage of time.*]

MILO. You know something? I've been working steadily for a long time, now, and I don't feel the least bit tired or hungry. I could go right on the same way forever.

MAN. Maybe you will. [*He yawns.*]

MILO. [*Whispers to* TOCK.] Well, I wish I knew how long it was going to take.

TOCK. Why don't you use your magic staff and find out?

MILO. [*Takes out pencil and calculates. To* MAN.] Pardon me, sir, but it's going to take 837 years to finish these jobs.

MAN. Is that so? What a shame. Well then you'd better get on with them.

MILO. But . . . it hardly seems worthwhile.

MAN. WORTHWHILE! Of course they're not worthwhile. I wouldn't ask you to do anything that was worthwhile.

Reading Strategy
Recognizing Wordplay
What is the wordplay used with the words "wait" and "weight"?

Literary Analysis
Theme How would you describe the work the man is asking them to do? How might it relate to a theme in the play?

TOCK. Then why bother?

MAN. Because, my friends, what could be more important than doing unimportant things? If you stop to do enough of them, you'll never get where you are going. [*Laughs villainously.*]

MILO. [*Gasps.*] Oh, no, you must be . . .

MAN. Quite correct! I am the Terrible Trivium, demon of petty tasks and worthless jobs, ogre of wasted effort and monster of habit. [*They start to back away from him.*] Don't try to leave, there's so much to do, and you still have 837 years to go on the first job.

MILO. But why do unimportant things?

MAN. Think of all the trouble it saves. If you spend all your time doing only the easy and useless jobs, you'll never have time to worry about the important ones which are so difficult. [*Walks toward them whispering.*] Now do come and stay with me. We'll have such fun together. There are things to fill and things to empty, things to take away and things to bring back, things to pick up and things to put down . . . [*They are transfixed by his soothing voice. He is about to embrace them when a* VOICE *screams.*]

VOICE. Run! Run! [*They all wake up and run with the Trivium behind. As the* VOICE *continues to call out directions, they follow until they lose the Trivium.*] RUN! RUN! This way! This way! Over here! Over here! Up here! Down there! Quick, hurry up!

TOCK. [*Panting.*] I think we lost him.

VOICE. Keep going straight! Keep going straight! Now step up! Now step up!

MILO. Look out! [*They all fall into a Trap.*] But he said "up!"

VOICE. Well, I hope you didn't expect to get anywhere by listening to me.

HUMBUG. We're in a deep pit! We'll never get out of here.

VOICE. That is quite an accurate evaluation of the situation.

MILO. [*Shouting angrily.*] Then why did you help us at all?

VOICE. Oh, I'd do as much for anybody. Bad advice is my specialty. [*A Little Furry Creature appears.*] I'm the demon of Insincerity. I don't mean what I say; I don't mean what I do; and I don't mean what I am.

MILO. Then why don't you go away and leave us alone!

INSINCERITY. (VOICE) Now, there's no need to get angry. You're a very clever boy and I have complete confidence in you. You can certainly climb out of that pit . . . come on, try. . .

Literary Analysis
Theme What message about laziness is revealed through Terrible Trivium's words?

Literary Analysis
Theme What lesson have Milo and the others learned?

**Reading Check**

Where are Milo and the others stuck, and how did they get there?

MILO. I'm not listening to one word you say! You're just telling me what you think I'd like to hear, and not what is important.

INSINCERITY. Well, if that's the way you feel about it . . .

MILO. That's the way I feel about it. We will manage by ourselves without any unnecessary advice from you.

INSINCERITY. [*Stamping his foot.*] Well, all right for you! Most people listen to what I say, but if that's the way you feel, then I'll just go home. [*Exits in a huff.*]

HUMBUG. [*Who has been quivering with fright.*] And don't you ever come back! Well, I guess we showed him, didn't we?

MILO. You know something? This place is a lot more dangerous than I ever imagined.

TOCK. [*Who's been surveying the situation.*] I think I figured a way to get out. Here, hop on my back. [MILO *does so.*] Now, you, Humbug, on top of Milo. [*He does so.*] Now hook your umbrella onto that tree and hold on. [*They climb over* HUMBUG, *then pull him up.*]

HUMBUG. [*As they climb.*] Watch it! Watch it, now. Ow, be careful of my back! My back! Easy, easy . . . oh, this is so difficult. Aren't you finished yet?

TOCK. [*As he pulls up* HUMBUG.] There. Now, I'll lead for a while. Follow me, and we'll stay out of trouble. [*They walk and climb higher and higher.*]

HUMBUG. Can't we slow down a little?

TOCK. Something tells me we better reach the Castle-in-the-Air as soon as possible, and not stop to rest for a single moment. [*They speed up.*]

MILO. What is it, Tock? Did you see something?

TOCK. Just keep walking and don't look back.

MILO. You *did* see something!

▲ **Critical Viewing**
How does this image show that Milo, Tock and Humbug need each other to succeed?

HUMBUG. What is it? Another demon?

TOCK. Not just one, I'm afraid. If you want to see what I'm talking about, then turn around. [*They turn around. The stage darkens and hundreds of Yellow Gleaming Eyes can be seen.*]

HUMBUG. Good grief! Do you see how many there are? Hundreds! The Overbearing Know-it-all, the Gross Exaggeration, the Horrible Hopping Hindsight, . . . and look over there! The Triple Demons of Compromise! Let's get out of here! [*Starts to scurry.*] Hurry up, you two! Must you be so slow about everything?

MILO. Look! There it is, up ahead! The Castle-in-the-Air! [*They all run.*]

HUMBUG. They're gaining!

MILO. But there it is!

HUMBUG. I see it! I see it!

[*They reach the first step and are stopped by a little man in a frock coat, sleeping on a worn ledger. He has a long quill pen and a bottle of ink at his side. He is covered with ink stains over his clothes and wears spectacles.*]

TOCK. Shh! Be very careful. [*They try to step over him, but he wakes up.*]

SENSES TAKER. [*From sleeping position.*] Names? [*He sits up.*]

HUMBUG. Well, I . . .

SENSES TAKER. *NAMES?* [*He opens book and begins to write, splattering himself with ink.*]

HUMBUG. Uh . . . Humbug, Tock and this is Milo.

SENSES TAKER. Splendid, splendid. I haven't had an "M" in ages.

MILO. What do you want our names for? We're sort of in a hurry.

SENSES TAKER. Oh, this won't take long. I'm the official Senses Taker and I must have some information before I can take your sense. Now if you'll just tell me: [*Handing them a form to fill. Speaking slowly and deliberately.*] When you were born, where you were born, why you were born, how old you are now, how old you were then, how old you'll be in a little while . . .

MILO. I wish he'd hurry up. At this rate, the demons will be here before we know it!

SENSES TAKER. . . . Your mother's name, your father's name, where you live, how long you've lived there, the schools you've attended, the schools you haven't attended . . .

HUMBUG. I'm getting writer's cramp.

Literary Analysis
Theme and Images Why are these qualities shown as scary creatures that cannot be completely seen?

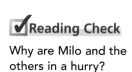**Reading Check**

Why are Milo and the others in a hurry?

TOCK. I smell something very evil and it's getting stronger every second. [*To* SENSES TAKER.] May we go now?

SENSES TAKER. Just as soon as you tell me your height, your weight, the number of books you've read this year . . .

MILO. We have to go!

SENSES TAKER. All right, all right, I'll give you the short form. [*Pulls out a small piece of paper.*] Destination?

MILO. But we have to . . .

SENSES TAKER. *DESTINATION?*

MILO, TOCK AND HUMBUG. The Castle-in-the-Air! [*They throw down their papers and run past him up the first few stairs.*]

SENSES TAKER. Stop! I'm sure you'd rather see what I have to show you. [*Snaps his fingers; they freeze.*] A circus of your very own. [CIRCUS MUSIC *is heard.* MILO *seems to go into a trance.*] And wouldn't you enjoy this most wonderful smell? [TOCK *sniffs and goes into a trance.*] And here's something I know you'll enjoy hearing . . . [*To* HUMBUG. *The sound of CHEERS and APPLAUSE for* HUMBUG *is heard, and he goes into a trance.*] There we are. And now, I'll just sit back and let the demons catch up with you.

[MILO *accidentally drops his package of gifts. The Package of Laughter from* DR. DISCHORD *opens and the Sounds of Laughter are heard. After a moment,* MILO, TOCK *and* HUMBUG *join in laughing and the spells are broken.*]

MILO. There was no circus.

TOCK. There were no smells.

HUMBUG. The applause is gone.

SENSES TAKER. I warned you I was the Senses Taker. I'll steal your sense of Purpose, your sense of Duty, destroy your sense of Proportion—and but for one thing, you'd be helpless yet.

▲ Critical Viewing
Does this picture of Senses Taker look similar to the image of him you had in your mind when you read his description?

MILO. What's that?

SENSES TAKER. As long as you have the sound of laughter, I cannot take your sense of Humor. Agh! That horrible sense of humor.

HUMBUG. HERE THEY COME! LET'S GET OUT OF HERE!

[*The demons appear in nasty slithering hordes, running through the audience and up onto the stage, trying to attack* TOCK, MILO *and* HUMBUG. *The three heroes run past the* SENSES TAKER *up the stairs toward the Castle-in-the-Air with the demons snarling behind them.*]

MILO. Don't look back! Just keep going! [*They reach the castle. The two* PRINCESSES *appear in the windows.*]

PRINCESSES. Hurry! Hurry! We've been expecting you.

MILO. You must be the Princesses. We've come to rescue you.

HUMBUG. And the demons are close behind!

TOCK. We should leave right away.

PRINCESSES. We're ready anytime you are.

MILO. Good, now if you'll just come out. But wait a minute—there's no door! How can we rescue you from the Castle-in-the-Air if there's no way to get in or out?

HUMBUG. Hurry, Milo! They're gaining on us.

REASON. Take your time, Milo, and think about it.

MILO. Ummm, all right . . . just give me a second or two. [*He thinks hard.*]

HUMBUG. I think I feel sick.

MILO. I've got it! Where's that package of presents? [*Opens the package of letters.*] Ah, here it is. [*Takes out the letters and sticks them on the door, spelling:*] E-N-T-R-A-N-C-E. Entrance. Now, let's see. [*Rummages through and spells in smaller letters:*] P-u-s-h. Push. [*He pushes and a door opens. The* PRINCESSES *come out of the castle. Slowly, the demons ascend the stairway.*]

HUMBUG. Oh, it's too late. They're coming up and there's no other way down!

MILO. Unless . . . [*Looks at* TOCK.] Well . . . Time flies, doesn't it?

TOCK. Quite often. Hold on, everyone, and I'll take you down.

HUMBUG. Can you carry us all?

TOCK. We'll soon find out. Ready or not, here we go! [*His alarm begins to ring. They jump off the platform and disappear. The demons, howling with rage, reach the top and find no one there. They see the* PRINCESSES *and the heroes running across the stage*

Reading Check

What prevents Senses Taker from taking Milo's sense of humor?

and bound down the stairs after them and into the audience. There is a mad chase scene until they reach the stage again.]

HUMBUG. I'm exhausted! I can't run another step.

MILO. We can't stop now . . .

TOCK. Milo! Look out there! [*The armies of* AZAZ *and* MATHEMAGICIAN *appear at the back of the theater, with the Kings at their heads.*]

AZAZ. [*As they march toward the stage.*] Don't worry, Milo, we'll take over now.

MATHEMAGICIAN. Those demons may not know it, but their days are numbered!

SPELLING BEE. Charge! C-H-A-R-G-E! Charge! [*They rush at the demons and battle until the demons run off howling. Everyone cheers. The* FIVE MINISTERS *of* AZAZ *appear and shake* MILO'S *hand.*]

MINISTER 1. Well done.

MINISTER 2. Fine job.

MINISTER 3. Good work!

MINISTER 4. Congratulations!

MINISTER 5. CHEERS! [*Everyone cheers again. A fanfare interrupts. A* PAGE *steps forward and reads from a large scroll:*]

PAGE.

> Henceforth, and forthwith,
> Let it be known by one and all,
> That Rhyme and Reason
> Reign once more in Wisdom.

[*The* PRINCESSES *bow gratefully and kiss their brothers, the Kings.*]

> And furthermore,
> The boy named Milo,
> The dog known as Tock,
> And the insect hereinafter referred to as the Humbug
> Are hereby declared to be Heroes of the Realm.

[*All bow and salute the heroes.*]

MILO. But we never could have done it without a lot of help.

REASON. That may be true, but you had the courage to try, and what you can do is often a matter of what you *will* do.

AZAZ. That's why there was one very important thing about your quest we couldn't discuss until you returned.

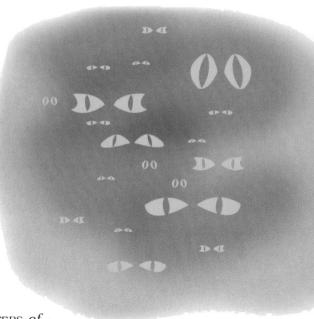

Reading Strategy
Recognizing Wordplay
What wordplay is used when Mathemagician says "their days are numbered"?

Literary Analysis
Theme What does Reason mean by "what you can do is often what you will do"?

MILO. I remember. What was it?

AZAZ. Very simple. It was impossible!

MATHEMAGICIAN. *Completely* impossible!

HUMBUG. Do you mean . . . ? [*Feeling faint.*] Oh . . . I think I need to sit down.

AZAZ. Yes, indeed, but if we'd told you then, you might not have gone.

MATHEMAGICIAN. And, as you discovered, many things are possible just as long as you don't know they're impossible.

MILO. I think I understand.

RHYME. I'm afraid it's time to go now.

REASON. And you must say goodbye.

MILO. To everyone? [*Looks around at the crowd. To* TOCK *and* HUMBUG.] Can't you two come with me?

HUMBUG. I'm afraid not, old man. I'd like to, but I've arranged for a lecture tour which will keep me occupied for years.

TOCK. And they do need a watchdog here.

MILO. Well, O.K., then. [MILO *hugs the* HUMBUG.]

HUMBUG. [*Sadly.*] Oh, bah.

MILO. [*He hugs* TOCK, *and then faces everyone.*] Well, goodbye. We all spent so much time together, I know I'm going to miss you. [*To the* PRINCESSES.] I guess we would have reached you a lot sooner if I hadn't made so many mistakes.

REASON. You must never feel badly about making mistakes, Milo, as long as you take the trouble to learn from them. Very often you learn more by being wrong for the right reasons than you do by being right for the wrong ones.

MILO. But there's so much to learn.

RHYME. That's true, but it's not just learning that's important. It's learning what to do with what you learn and learning why you learn things that matters.

MILO. I think I know what you mean, Princess. At least, I hope I do. [*The car is rolled forward and* MILO *climbs in.*] Goodbye! Goodbye! I'll be back someday! I will! Anyway, I'll try. [*As* MILO *drives the set of the Land of Ignorance begins to move offstage.*]

AZAZ. Goodbye! Always remember. Words! Words! Words!

MATHEMAGICIAN. And numbers!

AZAZ. Now, don't tell me you think numbers are as important as words?

Literary Analysis
Theme Do you agree with Mathemagician's statement?

**Reading Check**

How do they get rid of the demons?

MATHEMAGICIAN. Is that so? Why I'll have you know . . . [*The set disappears, and* MILO'S *Room is seen onstage.*]

MILO. [*As he drives on.*] Oh, oh, I hope they don't start all over again. Because I don't think I'll have much time in the near future to help them out. [*The sound of loud ticking is heard.* MILO *finds himself in his room. He gets out of the car and looks around.*]

THE CLOCK. Did someone mention time?

MILO. Boy, I must have been gone for an awful long time. I wonder what time it is. [*Looks at clock.*] Five o'clock. I wonder what day it is. [*Looks at calendar.*] It's still today! I've only been gone for an hour! [*He continues to look at his calendar, and then begins to look at his books and toys and maps and chemistry set with great interest.*]

CLOCK. An hour. Sixty minutes. How long it really lasts depends on what you do with it. For some people, an hour seems to last forever. For others, just a moment, and so full of things to do.

MILO. [*Looks at clock.*] Six o'clock already?

CLOCK. In an instant. In a trice. Before you have time to blink. [*The stage goes black in less than no time at all.*]

Review and Assess

Thinking About the Selection

1. **Respond:** Of all the senses that the Senses Taker wants to steal, which do you think is most important? Why?

2. **(a) Recall:** What kind of knowledge is important to the Mathemagician? **(b) Compare and Contrast:** Do you think the Mathemagician is similar to Azaz? Why or why not?

3. **(a) Recall:** What does the Terrible Trivium want Milo, Tock, and the Humbug to do? **(b) Deduce:** What will be the result if they follow his instructions? **(c) Interpret:** What lesson does Milo learn as a result of their meeting?

4. **(a) Recall:** How is the Senses Taker's spell broken? **(b) Draw Conclusions:** What does Milo learn about humor from his encounter with the Senses Taker?

5. **(a) Recall:** How is Milo different when he returns to his own room? **(b) Evaluate:** Do you agree that how time passes depends on what you are doing? **(c) Support:** Support your answer with examples from the play or from your own experience.

Susan Nanus

Susan Nanus has won several awards for her scripts. Like other screenwriters, she sometimes adapts novels to create screenplays for movies and scripts for stage plays. Her script for *The Phantom Tollbooth* is an adaptation of Norton Juster's novel.

Norton Juster

(b. 1929)

Norton Juster's first career was as an architect, designing buildings and other structures. He took up creative writing in his spare time "as a relaxation" from architecture. He began writing what he thought was just a short story for his own pleasure. Yet before long, Juster says, "it had created its own life and I was hooked." As a writer and as an architect, he puts words and ideas together in creative ways, as in *The Phantom Tollbooth*, the novel on which this play is based.

Review and Assess

Literary Analysis

Theme

1. What message does the author suggest by having demons run through the audience to reach the stage?
2. What theme is expressed in Milo's farewell to Rhyme and Reason at the end of the play?

Connecting Literary Elements

3. Make a chart like the one shown to analyze the images associated with each character and the message suggested by each character's qualities.

Character	Quality Represented	Images Associated	Suggested Message
Trivium	Doing meaningless tasks	Well-dressed, soothing voice	Some bad habits can sneak up on you
Word Snatcher			
Insincerity			

Reading Strategy

Recognizing Wordplay

4. Review the scene with the Bird in Act II, Scene ii. Use an organizer like the one below to show the two meanings used for each word (or pair of words that sound the same).

Word(s)	Milo's Meaning	Bird's Meaning
morning/mourning		
spend		
sense/cents		
mean		
wait/weight		

5. The Dodecahedron asks Milo, "And did you know that narrow escapes come in different widths?" How does the wordplay lead you to recognize the bigger message behind the statement?

Extending Understanding

6. **Social Studies Connection:** Name two examples from history that show that "many things are possible just as long as you don't know they're impossible."

Quick Review

The **theme** of a work is the central idea or message about life. To review theme, see p. 636.

Images are word pictures made by language that appeals to the senses.

Through **wordplay,** the author calls readers' attention to the richness of language by playing with several meanings of the same word. To review wordplay, see p. 636.

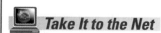 **Take It to the Net**
www.phschool.com
Take the interactive self-test online to check your understanding of the selection.

Integrate Language Skills

Vocabulary Development Lesson

Word Analysis: Latin Root -son-

Words with the Latin root -son- include the idea of sound in their meaning. *Dissonance* means "a harsh or disagreeable combination of sounds."

On your paper, fill in the blanks to match each definition. Hint: The root -son- is in each word.

1. A letter that is not a vowel:
   c _____ nt
2. Vibrate with sound: re _____ te
3. Sounding harsh: dis _____ a __ t

Spelling Strategy

The sound *shus* at the end of a word is often spelled *cious*, as in *malicious*. On your paper, add *cious* to make a word that matches the definition.

1. Valuable: pre
2. Well-mannered: gra
3. Roomy: spa
4. Tasty: deli

Fluency: Sentence Completions

On your paper, write out this paragraph. Choose from the following vocabulary words to fill in the blanks.

dissonance   admonishing
iridescent   malicious

Though the peacock's ___?___ tail feathers are beautiful, its song is of unbelievable ___?___. When the seemingly ___?___ bird wakes you up at night, your lecture to the bird's owner is likely to be ___?___.

Replace the underlined word in each sentence with a vocabulary word that is the same part of speech. Explain how the meaning of the sentence changes. Use each word only once.

1. The singers' <u>harmony</u> was unbelievable.
2. The color was <u>dull</u>.
3. He spoke with an <u>appreciative</u> tone.
4. The <u>helpful</u> act did not go unnoticed.

Grammar Lesson

Indefinite Pronouns

An **indefinite pronoun** is a word that refers to a person, place, or thing in a general way. Use singular verbs with singular indefinite pronouns. Use plural verbs with plural indefinite pronouns.

Indefinite Pronouns	Examples
Singular: each, everyone, everything, much, nobody, somebody	Somebody <u>has</u> the answer.
Plural: both, few, many, others, several	Others <u>have</u> <u>tried</u> to rescue the princesses.

Practice On your paper, write the indefinite pronoun that correctly completes each sentence.

1. (Each, Many) agrees to disagree.
2. (Few, Nobody) understands the king.
3. Is (everyone, others) called Milo?
4. Here (everything, both) is called what it is.
5. (Several, Somebody) help Milo.

Writing Application On your paper, write three sentences describing the inhabitants of Digitopolis. Use an indefinite pronoun in each.

W͞G Prentice Hall Writing and Grammar Connection: Chapter 24, Section 2

Writing Lesson

Drama Review

Be a drama critic and share your opinions with others! Write a review of *The Phantom Tollbooth*, explaining whether or not the play is well written and entertaining.

Prewriting   Use a graphic organizer such as the one shown to help you gather details about what happened in the act you are reviewing.

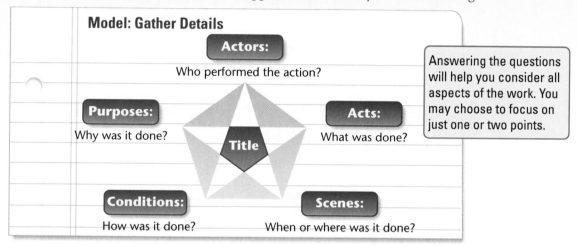

Model: Gather Details

Actors: Who performed the action?

Purposes: Why was it done?

Acts: What was done?

Title

Conditions: How was it done?

Scenes: When or where was it done?

Answering the questions will help you consider all aspects of the work. You may choose to focus on just one or two points.

Drafting   Begin by stating your overall impression. Then, organize your review around several clear premises, or statements about the work. With each statement you write, ask yourself "What is my evidence?" Add supporting details to answer the question.

Revising   Reread your review. Be sure you support your opinions with examples and textual evidence such as quotations or descriptions of settings.

WG Prentice Hall Writing and Grammar Connection: Chapter 12, Section 2

Extension Activities

Listening and Speaking As part of a group, **debate** the following: Numbers are more important and more fun than words. Divide into two teams, one speaking for numbers and one for words. In the debate, use details and examples in the play and in your experience that support your points.

Writing Write a **summary** of Act II. Identify the key events, and retell them, in order, in your own words. ¨

Research and Technology Use print and electronic resources to **research** the ideas of infinity and of the biggest and smallest numbers. Display your findings in a chart or other visual. Prepare a written summary to accompany your visual.

 ***Take It to the Net***   www.phschool.com

Go online for an additional research activity using the Internet.

Prepare to Read

Grandpa and the Statue

 Take It to the Net

Visit www.phschool.com
for interactive activities
and instruction related to
"Grandpa and the Statue,"
including

- background
- graphic organizers
- literary elements
- reading strategies

Literature in Your Life

Connecting to the Literature

This play tells a story from the Statue of Liberty's early days. The only way to see the statue then was "in person." Even if you've never visited the Statue of Liberty, you've probably seen it in a movie, a book, or on television. What thoughts or feelings do you have when you see it?

Background

The Statue of Liberty was dedicated in 1886. Although the statue itself was a gift from France, money for the pedestal on which it stands was raised in the United States. It was placed on a small island in New York Harbor, and, at the time, stood taller than any building in New York City.

Literary Analysis

Dialogue

Grandpa and the Statue was written in 1945 as a radio play—a play to be listened to, not watched. (At the time, radios were very popular, and few people had television sets or could afford to see a play on Broadway.) In a radio play, most of the action must be conveyed through dialogue—the conversations among characters—because the audience cannot view what the characters are doing.

Connecting Literary Elements

In radio plays as well as stage plays, much of the **characterization**—how the characters' personalities are revealed—occurs through dialogue. The audience learns about a character through what the character says, the way in which he or she says it, and what other characters say about him or her. The characters' words also reveal the **plot**—the set of events that move the story forward.

As you read, pay attention to what the dialogue reveals about the characters and the plot. Think about whether these elements seem realistic or believable. Use these focus questions to guide you:

1. Do the characters act like real people? (Keep in mind that the play is set in the 1800s.)
2. How well-developed and realistic are the characters' personalities?

Reading Strategy

Distinguishing Fact From Fantasy

This play is an example of historical fiction—literature set in a specific period in history. It deals with the building of the Statue of Liberty in the 1800s. Like other works of historical literature, it includes factual as well as made-up details.

- **Facts** are true details that can often be found through research in an encyclopedia or other reference work.
- **Fantasy** is made up of details that are fictional and do not exist in real life.

Use a chart like the one here to track details from the play as you read, and record whether or not you find that they are factual.

Detail	Fact or Fiction?
People collected dimes and nickels	**Fact:** Even school children made contributions

Vocabulary Development

subscribed (səb skrībd´) *adj.* signed up to give money (p. 669)

peeved (pēvd) *adj.* bad-tempered or annoyed (p. 670)

uncomprehending (ən cäm prē hend´ iŋ) *adj.* not understanding (p. 673)

tempest (tem´ pist) *n.* violent storm with high winds (p. 679)

GRANDPA AND THE STATUE

ARTHUR MILLER

CHARACTERS

CHARACTERS IN THE PRESENT TIME OF THE PLAY

*   ANNOUNCER
*   AUGUST
*   MONAGHAN *(Young Monaghan, a soldier)*

CHARACTERS FROM THE PAST
(Heard in the flashback scenes that Young Monaghan remembers)

*   SHEEAN
*   MONAGHAN
    (Grandfather of Young Monaghan)
*   CHILD MONAGHAN
    (Young Monaghan himself, as a child)
*   GEORGE
*   CHARLEY
*   JACK   } *(Neighborhood children, Child Monaghan's friends)*
*   MIKE
*   JOE

*   ALF
*   GIRL   } *(Passengers on the Statue of Liberty boat)*
*   YOUNG MAN
*   MEGAPHONE VOICE
*   VETERAN
    (Visitor to the statue)

[*Music: Theme*]

ANNOUNCER. The scene is the fourth floor of a giant army hospital overlooking New York Harbor. A young man sitting in a wheel chair is looking out a window—just looking. After a while another young man in another wheel chair rolls over to him and they both look.

[*Music out*]

AUGUST. You want to play some checkers with me, Monaghan?

MONAGHAN. Not right now.

AUGUST. Okay. [*Slight pause*] You don't want to go feeling blue, Monaghan.

MONAGHAN. I'm not blue.

AUGUST. All you do most days is sit here looking out this window.

MONAGHAN. What do you want me to do, jump rope?

Reading Check

Where are these characters?

◀ **Critical Viewing** In what way does the angle of this picture make the statue look very impressive? [**Analyze**]

AUGUST. No, but what do you get out of it?

MONAGHAN. It's a beautiful view. Some companies make millions of dollars just printing that view on postcards.

AUGUST. Yeh, but nobody keeps looking at a postcard six, seven hours a day.

MONAGHAN. I come from around here, it reminds me of things. My young days.

AUGUST. That's right, you're from Brooklyn, aren't you?

MONAGHAN. My house is only about a mile away.

AUGUST. That so. Tell me, are you looking at just the water all the time? I'm curious. I don't get a kick out of this view.

MONAGHAN. There's the Statue of Liberty out there. Don't you see it?

AUGUST. Oh, that's it. Yeh, that's nice to look at.

MONAGHAN. I like it. Reminds me of a lot of laughs.

AUGUST. Laughs? The Statue of Liberty?

MONAGHAN. Yeh, my grandfather. He got all twisted up with the Statue of Liberty.

AUGUST. [*Laughs a little*] That so? What happened?

MONAGHAN. Well. My grandfather was the stingiest man in Brooklyn. "Mercyless" Monaghan, they used to call him. He even used to save umbrella handles.

AUGUST. What for?

MONAGHAN. Just couldn't stand seeing anything go to waste. After a big windstorm there'd be a lot of broken umbrellas laying around in the streets.

AUGUST. Yeh?

MONAGHAN. He'd go around picking them up. In our house the closets were always full of umbrella handles. My grandma used to say that he would go across the Brooklyn Bridge on the trolley just because he could come back on the same nickel. See, if you stayed on the trolley they'd let you come back for the same nickel.

AUGUST. What'd he do, just go over and come back?

MONAGHAN. Yeh, it made him feel good. Savin' money. Two and a half cents.

AUGUST. So how'd he get twisted up with the Statue of Liberty?

MONAGHAN. Well, way back in 1887 around there they were living on Butler Street. Butler Street, Brooklyn, practically runs right down to the river. One day he's sitting on the front porch, reading

Literary Analysis
Dialogue What does the dialogue on this page reveal about the time and place of the play's beginning?

Reading Strategy
Distinguishing Fact and Fantasy Which part of Monaghan's explanation is a fact about the time period?

a paper he borrowed from the neighbors, when along comes this man Jack Sheean who lived up the block.

[*Music: Sneak into above speech, then bridge, then out*]

SHEEAN. [*Slight brogue¹*] A good afternoon to you, Monaghan.

MONAGHAN. [*Grandfather*] How're you, Sheean, how're ya?

SHEEAN. Fair, fair. And how's Mrs. Monaghan these days?

MONAGHAN. Warm. Same as everybody else in summer.

SHEEAN. I've come to talk to you about the fund, Monaghan.

MONAGHAN. What fund is that?

SHEEAN. The Statue of Liberty fund.

MONAGHAN. Oh, that.

SHEEAN. It's time we come to grips with the subject, Monaghan.

MONAGHAN. I'm not interested, Sheean.

SHEEAN. Now hold up on that a minute. Let me tell you the facts. This here Frenchman has gone and built a fine statue of Liberty. It costs who knows how many millions to build. All they're askin' us to do is contribute enough to put up a base for the statue to stand on.

MONAGHAN. I'm not . . . !

SHEEAN. Before you answer me. People all over the whole United States are puttin' in for it. Butler Street is doin' the same. We'd like to hang up a flag on the corner saying—"Butler Street, Brooklyn, is one hundred per cent behind the Statue of Liberty." And Butler Street *is* a hundred per cent <u>subscribed</u> except for you. Now will you give us a dime, Monaghan? One dime and we can put up the flag. Now what do you say to that?

MONAGHAN. I'm not throwin' me good money away for somethin' I don't even know exists.

SHEEAN. Now what do you mean by that?

MONAGHAN. Have you seen this statue?

SHEEAN. No, but it's in a warehouse. And as soon as we get the money to build the pedestal they'll take it and put it up on that island in the river, and all the boats comin' in from the old country will see it there and it'll raise the hearts of the poor immigrants to see such a fine sight on their first look at this country.

MONAGHAN. And how do I know it's in this here warehouse at all?

SHEEAN. You read your paper, don't you? It's been in all the papers for the past year.

---

1. brogue (brōg) *n.* Irish accent.

Literary Analysis
Dialogue What action does the dialogue here reveal?

Literary Analysis
Dialogue and Characterization Are Monaghan's and Sheean's different reactions realistic for the situation? Explain.

subscribed (səb skrībd′) *adj.* signed up to give money

Reading Check

What does Sheean want Monaghan to do?

MONAGHAN. Ha, the papers! Last year I read in the paper that they were about to pave Butler Street and take out all the holes. Turn around and look at Butler Street, Mr. Sheean.

SHEEAN. All right. I'll do this: I'll take you to the warehouse and show you the statue. Will you give me a dime then?

MONAGHAN. Well . . . I'm not sayin' I would, and I'm not sayin' I wouldn't. But I'd be more *likely* if I saw the thing large as life, I would.

SHEEAN. [*Peeved*] All right, then. Come along.

[*Music up and down and out*]

[*Footsteps, in a warehouse . . . echo . . . they come to a halt.*]

Now then. Do you see the Statue of Liberty or don't you see it?

MONAGHAN. I see it all right, but it's all broke!

SHEEAN. *Broke!* They brought it from France on a boat. They had to take it apart, didn't they?

MONAGHAN. You got a secondhand statue, that's what you got, and I'm not payin' for new when they've shipped us something that's all smashed to pieces.

SHEEAN. Now just a minute, just a minute. Visualize what I'm about to tell you, Monaghan, get the picture of it. When this statue is

peeved (pēvd) *adj.* bad-tempered or annoyed

Literary Analysis
Dialogue and Characterization Is Grandpa's reaction to what he sees believable?

▼ **Critical Viewing** Why might Grandpa be unwilling to contribute after seeing these pieces of the statue? **[Infer]**

put together it's going to stand ten stories high. Could they get a thing ten stories high into a four-story building such as this is? Use your good sense, now, Monaghan.

MONAGHAN. What's that over there?

SHEEAN. Where?

MONAGHAN. That tablet there in her hand. What's it say? July Eye Vee (IV) MDCCLXXVI . . . what . . . what's all that?

SHEEAN. That means July 4, 1776. It's in Roman numbers. Very high class.

MONAGHAN. What's the good of it? If they're going to put a sign on her they ought to put it: Welcome All. That's it. Welcome All.

SHEEAN. They decided July 4, 1776, and July 4, 1776, it's going to be!

MONAGHAN. All right, then let them get their dime from somebody else!

SHEEAN. Monaghan!

MONAGHAN. No, sir! I'll tell you something. I didn't think there was a statue but there is. She's all broke, it's true, but she's here and maybe they can get her together. But even if they do, will you tell me what sort of a welcome to immigrants it'll be, to have a gigantic thing like that in the middle of the river and in her hand is July Eye Vee MCDVC . . . whatever it is?

SHEEAN. That's the date the country was made!

MONAGHAN. The divil with the date! A man comin' in from the sea wants a place to stay, not a date. When I come from the old country I git off at the dock and there's a feller says to me, "Would you care for a room for the night?" "I would that," I sez, and he sez, "All right then, follow me." He takes me to a rooming house. I no sooner sign me name on the register—which I was able to do even at that time—when I look around and the feller is gone clear away and took my valise[2] in the bargain. A statue anyway can't move off so fast, but if she's going to welcome let her say welcome, not this MCDC. . . .

SHEEAN. All right, then, Monaghan. But all I can say is, you've laid a disgrace on the name of Butler Street. I'll put the dime in for ya.

MONAGHAN. Don't connect me with it! It's a swindle, is all it is. In the first place, it's broke; in the second place, if they do put it up it'll come down with the first high wind that strikes it.

SHEEAN. The engineers say it'll last forever!

MONAGHAN. And I say it'll topple into the river in a high wind! Look at the inside of her. She's all hollow!

Literary Analysis
Dialogue What does this speech suggest about Grandpa's character?

✔Reading Check

What condition is the statue in when Sheean and Monaghan see it in the warehouse?

---

2. valise (və lēs´) *n.* small suitcase.

SHEEAN. I've heard everything now, Monaghan. Just about every-thing. Good-bye.

MONAGHAN. What do you mean, good-bye? How am I to get back to Butler Street from here?

SHEEAN. You've got legs to walk.

MONAGHAN. I'll remind you that I come on the trolley.

SHEEAN. And I'll remind you that I paid your fare and I'm not repeating the kindness.

MONAGHAN. Sheean? You've stranded me!

[*Music up and down*]

YOUNG MONAGHAN. That was Grandpa. That's why I have to laugh every time I look at the statue now.

AUGUST. Did he ever put the dime in?

YOUNG MONAGHAN. Well—in a way. What happened was this: His daughters got married and finally my mom . . . put *me* out on Butler Street. I got to be pretty attached to Grandpa. He'd even give me an umbrella handle and make a sword out of it for me. Naturally, I wasn't very old before he began working on me about the statue.

[*High wind*]

CHILD MONAGHAN. [*Softly, as though* GRANDPA *is in bed*] Grampa?

MONAGHAN. [*Awakened*] Heh? What are you doin' up?

CHILD MONAGHAN. Ssssh! Listen!

[*Wind rising up and fading. Rising higher and fading*]

MONAGHAN. [*Gleefully*] Aaaaaaaah! Yes, yes. This'll do it, boy. This'll do it! First thing in the morning we'll go down to the docks and I'll bet you me life that Mr. Sheean's statue is smashed down and layin' on the bottom of the bay. Go to sleep now, we'll have a look first thing.

[*Music up and down*]

[*Footsteps*]

CHILD MONAGHAN. If it fell down, all the people will get their dimes back, won't they, Grampa? Slow down, I can't walk so fast.

MONAGHAN. Not only will they get their dimes back, but Mr. Sheean and the whole crew that engineered the collection are going to rot in jail. Now mark my words. Here, now, we'll take a short cut around this shed . . .

[*Footsteps continue a moment, then gradually . . . disappointedly they come to a halt.*]

Literary Analysis
Dialogue How does the dialogue here convey the relationship that young Monaghan had with his grandfather?

Literary Analysis
Dialogue and Characterization Why do you think people in the 1880s might have said and believed what Grandpa says here?

CHILD MONAGHAN. She's . . . she's still standing, Grampa.

MONAGHAN She is that. [*Uncomprehending*] I don't understand it. That was a terrible wind last night. Terrible.

CHILD MONAGHAN. Maybe she's weaker though. Heh?

MONAGHAN. Why . . . sure, that must be it. I'll wager she's hangin' by a thread. [*Realizing*] Of course! That's why they put her out there in the water so when she falls down she won't be flattening out a lot of poor innocent people. Hey—feel that?

CHILD MONAGHAN. The wind! It's starting to blow again!

MONAGHAN. Sure, and look at the sky blackening over!

[*Wind rising*]

Feel it comin' up! Take your last look at the statue, boy. If I don't mistake me eyes she's takin' a small list[3] to Jersey already!

[*Music up and down*]

YOUNG MONAGHAN. It was getting embarrassing for me on the block. I kept promising the other kids that when the next wind came the statue would come down. We even had a game. Four or five kids would stand in a semicircle around one kid who was the statue. The statue kid had to stand on his heels and look right in our eyes. Then we'd all take a deep breath and blow in his face. He'd fall down like a stick of wood. They all believed me and Grampa . . . until one day. We were standing around throwing rocks at an old milk can . . .

[*Banging of rocks against milk can*]

GEORGE. [*Kid*] What're you doin'?

CHILD MONAGHAN. What do we look like we're doin'?

GEORGE. I'm going someplace tomorrow.

CHARLEY. [*Kid*] I know, church. Watch out, I'm throwin'.

[*Can being hit*]

GEORGE. I mean after church.

JACK. Where?

GEORGE. My old man's going to take me out on the Statue of Liberty boat.

[*Banging against can abruptly stops.*]

---

3. list (list) *n.* lean; tilt.

uncomprehending
(ən käm prē hend´ iŋ) *adj.*
not understanding

Reading Strategy
Distinguishing Fact From Fantasy Do you think this is a factual or a made-up detail?

**Reading Check**

What does Grandpa expect the statue to do?

CHILD MONAGHAN. You're not going out on the statue, though, are you?

GEORGE. Sure, that's where we're going.

CHILD MONAGHAN. But you're liable to get killed. Supposing there's a high wind tomorrow?

GEORGE. My old man says that statue couldn't fall down if all the wind in the world and John L. Sullivan[4] hit it at the same time.

CHILD MONAGHAN. Is that so?

GEORGE. Yeh, that's so. My old man says that the only reason your grandfather's saying that it's going to fall down is that he's ashamed he didn't put a dime in for the pedestal.

CHILD MONAGHAN. Is that so?

GEORGE. Yeh, that's so.

CHILD MONAGHAN. Well, you tell your old man that if he gets killed tomorrow not to come around to my grandfather and say he didn't warn him!

---

4. **John L. Sullivan** American prizefighter at the time of the play's action.

▲ **Critical Viewing**
What tools and equipment might be needed to reassemble the statue? **[Draw Conclusions]**

Reading Strategy
Distinguishing Fact and Fantasy Is John Sullivan a real person or a made-up character?

JACK. Hey, George, would your father take me along?

GEORGE. I'll ask him, maybe he—

CHILD MONAGHAN. What, are you crazy, Jack?

MIKE. Ask him if he'd take me too, will ya, George?

CHILD MONAGHAN. Mike, what's the matter with you?

JOE. Me too, George, I'll ask my mother for money.

CHILD MONAGHAN. Joe! Didn't you hear what my grampa said?

JOE. Well . . . I don't really believe that any more.

CHILD MONAGHAN. You don't be . . .

MIKE. Me neither.

JACK. I don't really think your grampa knows what he's talkin' about.

CHILD MONAGHAN. He don't, heh? [*Ready to weep*] Okay . . . Okay. [*Bursting out*] I just hope that wind blows tomorrow, boy! I just hope that wind blows!

[*Music up and down*]
[*Creaking of a rocking chair*]

Grampa . . . ?

MONAGHAN. Huh?

CHILD MONAGHAN. Can you stop rocking for a minute?

[*Rocking stops*]

Can you put down your paper?

[*Rustle of paper*]

I—I read the weather report for tomorrow.

MONAGHAN. The weather report . . .

CHILD MONAGHAN. Yeh. It says fair and cool.

MONAGHAN. What of it?

CHILD MONAGHAN. I was wondering. Supposing you and me we went on a boat tomorrow. You know, I see the water every day when I go down to the docks to play, but I never sat on it. I mean in a boat.

MONAGHAN. Oh. Well, we might take the ferry on the Jersey side. We might do that.

CHILD MONAGHAN. Yeh, but there's nothing to see in Jersey.

MONAGHAN. You can't go to Europe tomorrow.

CHILD MONAGHAN. No, but couldn't we go *toward* the ocean? Just . . . *toward* it?

MONAGHAN. Toward it. What—what is it on your mind, boy? What is it now?

Literary Analysis
Dialogue What does the conversation reveal about the characters' changing attitudes?

Literary Analysis
Dialogue How does the child bring up the subject of going out to see the statue?

**Reading Check**

How do Child Monaghan's friends react to Grandpa's predictions about the statue?

CHILD MONAGHAN. Well, I . . .

MONAGHAN. Oh, you want to take the Staten Island ferry. Sure, that's in the direction of the sea.

CHILD MONAGHAN. No, Grampa, not the Staten Island ferry.

MONAGHAN. You don't mean—[*Breaks off*] Boy!

CHILD MONAGHAN. All the kids are going tomorrow with Georgie's old man.

MONAGHAN. You don't believe me any more.

CHILD MONAGHAN. I do, Grampa, but . . .

MONAGHAN. You don't. If you did you'd stay clear of the Statue of Liberty for love of your life!

CHILD MONAGHAN. But, Grampa, when is it going to fall down? All I do is wait and wait.

MONAGHAN. [*With some uncertainty*] You've got to have faith.

CHILD MONAGHAN. But every kid in my class went to see it and now the ones that didn't are going tomorrow. And they all keep talking about it and all I do . . . Well, I can't keep telling them it's a swindle. I—I wish we could see it, Grampa. It don't cost so much to go.

MONAGHAN. As long as you put it that way I'll have to admit I'm a bit curious meself as to how it's managed to stand upright so long. Tell you what I'll do. Barrin' wind, we'll chance it tomorrow!

CHILD MONAGHAN. Oh, Gramp!

MONAGHAN. But! If anyone should ask you where we went you'll say—Staten Island. Are y' on?

CHILD MONAGHAN. Okay, sure. Staten Island.

MONAGHAN. [*Secretively*] We'll take the early boat, then. Mum's the word, now. For if old man Sheean hears that I went out there I'll have no peace from the thief the rest of m' life.

[*Music up and down*]

[*Boat whistles*]

CHILD MONAGHAN. Gee, it's nice ridin' on a boat, ain't it, Grampa?

MONAGHAN. Never said there was anything wrong with the boat. Boat's all right. You're sure now that Georgie's father is takin' the kids in the afternoon.

CHILD MONAGHAN. Yeh, that's when they're going. Gee, look at those two sea gulls. Wee!—look at them swoop! They caught a fish!

MONAGHAN. What I can't understand is what all these people see in that statue that they'll keep a boat like this full makin' the trip, year in year out. To hear the newspapers talk, if the statue was

Literary Analysis
Dialogue What words and expressions are different from the way people speak today?

gone we'd be at war with the nation that stole her the followin' mornin' early. All it is is a big high pile of French copper.

CHILD MONAGHAN. The teacher says it shows us that we got liberty.

MONAGHAN. Bah! If you've got liberty you don't need a statue to tell you you got it; and if you haven't got liberty no statue's going to do you any good tellin' you you got it. It was a criminal waste of the people's money. [*Quietly*] And just to prove it to you I'll ask this feller sitting right over there what he sees in it. You'll see what a madness the whole thing was. Say, mister?

ALF. Hey?

MONAGHAN. I beg your pardon. I'm a little strange here, and curious. Could you tell me why you're going to the Statue of Liberty?

ALF. Me? Well, I tell ya. I always wanted to take an ocean voyage. This is a pretty big boat—bigger than the ferries—so on Sundays, sometimes, I take the trip. It's better than nothing.

MONAGHAN. Thank you. [*To the kid*] So much for the great meaning of that statue, me boy. We'll talk to this lady standing at the rail. I just want you to understand why I didn't give Sheean me dime. Madam, would you be good enough to . . . Oh pardon me. [*To the kid*] Better pass her by, she don't look so good. We'll ask that girl there. Young lady, if you'll pardon the curiosity of an old man . . . could you tell me in a few good words what it is about that statue that brings you out here?

GIRL. What statue?

MONAGHAN. Why, the Statue of Liberty up 'head. We're coming up to it.

GIRL. Statue of Liberty! Is this the Statue of Liberty boat?

MONAGHAN. Well, what'd you think it was?

GIRL. Oh, my! I'm supposed to be on the Staten Island ferry! Where's the ticket man? [*Going away*] Ticket man! Where's the ticket man?

CHILD MONAGHAN. Gee whiz, nobody seems to want to see the statue.

MONAGHAN. Just to prove it, let's see this fellow sitting on this bench here. Young man, say . . .

YOUNG MAN. I can tell you in one word. For four days I haven't had a minute's peace. My kids are screaming, my wife is yelling, upstairs they play the piano all day long. The only place I can find that's quiet is a statue. That statue is my sweetheart. Every Sunday I beat it out to the island and sit next to her, and she don't talk.

CHILD MONAGHAN. I guess you were right, Grampa. Nobody seems to think it means anything.

MONAGHAN. Not only doesn't mean anything, but if they'd used the

Literary Analysis
Dialogue How does the author use this speech to reveal actions and characters that listeners cannot see?

Reading Check

What do the passengers on the boat think about visiting the Statue of Liberty?

money to build an honest roomin' house on that island, the immigrants would have a place to spend the night, their valises wouldn't get robbed, and they—

MEGAPHONE VOICE. *Please keep your seats while the boat is docking. Statue of Liberty—all out in five minutes!*

CHILD MONAGHAN. Look down there, Gramp! There's a peanut stand! Could I have some?

MONAGHAN. I feel the wind comin' up. I don't think we dare take the time.

[*Music up and down*]

CHILD MONAGHAN. Sssssseuuuuuww! Look how far you can see! Look at that ship way out in the ocean!

MONAGHAN. It is, it's quite a view. Don't let go of me hand now.

CHILD MONAGHAN. I betcha we could almost see California.

MONAGHAN. It's probably that grove of trees way out over there. They do say it's beyond Jersey.

CHILD MONAGHAN. Feels funny. We're standing right inside her head. Is that what you meant . . . July IV, MCD . . . ?

MONAGHAN. That's it. That tablet in her hand. Now shouldn't they have put Welcome All on it instead of that foreign language? Say! Do you feel her rockin'?

CHILD MONAGHAN. Yeah, she's moving a little bit. Listen, the wind!

[*Whistling of wind*]

MONAGHAN. We better get down, come on! This way!

CHILD MONAGHAN. No, the stairs are this way! Come on!

[*Running in echo. Then quick stop*]

MONAGHAN. No, I told you they're the other way! Come!

VETERAN. [*Calm, quiet voice*] Don't get excited, pop. She'll stand.

MONAGHAN. She's swayin' awful.

VETERAN. That's all right. I been up here thirty, forty times. She gives with the wind, flexible. Enjoy the view, go on.

▶ **Critical Viewing** Using details from this picture, explain whether or not you think this statue is a good symbol of liberty. **[Assess]**

MONAGHAN. Did you say you've been up here forty times?

VETERAN. About that many.

MONAGHAN. What do you find here that's so interesting?

VETERAN. It calms my nerves.

MONAGHAN. Ah. It seems to me it would make you more nervous than you were.

VETERAN. No, not me. It kinda means something to me.

MONAGHAN. Might I ask what?

VETERAN. Well . . . I was in the Philippine War . . . back in '98.[5] Left my brother back there.

MONAGHAN. Oh, yes. Sorry I am to hear it. Young man, I suppose, eh?

VETERAN. Yeh. We were both young. This is his birthday today.

MONAGHAN. Oh, I understand.

VETERAN. Yeh, this statue is about the only stone he's got. In my mind I feel it is anyway. This statue kinda looks like what we believe. You know what I mean?

MONAGHAN. Looks like what we believe . . . I . . . I never thought of it that way. I . . . I see what you mean. It does look that way. [*Angrily*] See now, boy? If Sheean had put it that way I'd a give him me dime. [*Hurt*] Now, why do you suppose he didn't tell me that! Come down now. I'm sorry, sir, we've got to get out of here.

[*Music up and down*]

[*Footsteps under*]

Hurry now, I want to get out of here. I feel terrible. I do, boy. That Sheean, that fool. Why didn't he tell me that? You'd think . . .

CHILD MONAGHAN. What does this say?

[*Footsteps halt*]

MONAGHAN. Why, it's just a tablet, I suppose. I'll try it with me spectacles, just a minute. Why, it's a poem, I believe . . . "Give me your tired, your poor, your huddled masses yearning to breathe free, the wretched refuse of your teeming[6] shore. Send these, the homeless, <u>tempest</u>-tost to me, I lift . . . my lamp beside . . . the golden door!" Oh, dear. [*Ready to weep*] It had Welcome All on it all the time. Why didn't Sheean tell me? I'd a given him a quarter! Boy . . . go over there and here's a nickel and buy yourself a bag of them peanuts.

CHILD MONAGHAN. [*Astonished*] Gramp!

---

5. **back in '98** 1898.
6. **teeming** (tēm´ iŋ) *adj.* swarming with life.

Reading Strategy

Distinguishing Fact and Fantasy Do you think the veteran is a real person? Does he refer to real events?

tempest (tem´ pist) *n.* violent storm with high winds

**Reading Check**

What are the words on the Statue of Liberty's base?

MONAGHAN. Go on now, I want to study this a minute. And be sure the man gives you full count.

CHILD MONAGHAN. I'll be right back.

[*Footsteps running away*]

MONAGHAN. [*To himself*] "Give me your tired, your poor, your huddled masses . . ."

[*Music swells from a sneak to full, then under to background*]

YOUNG MONAGHAN. [*Soldier*] I ran over and got my peanuts and stood there cracking them open, looking around. And I happened to glance over to Grampa. He had his nose right up to that bronze tablet, reading it. And then he reached into his pocket and kinda spied around over his eyeglasses to see if anybody was looking, and then he took out a coin and stuck it in a crack of cement over the tablet.

[*Coin falling onto concrete*]

It fell out and before he could pick it up I got a look at it. It was a half a buck. He picked it up and pressed it into the crack so it stuck. And then he came over to me and we went home.

[*Music: Change to stronger, more forceful theme*]

That's why, when I look at her now through this window, I remember that time and that poem, and she really seems to say, Whoever you are, wherever you come from, Welcome All. Welcome Home.

[*Music: Flare up to finish*]

Review and Assess

Thinking About the Selection

1. **(a) Respond:** What does the Statue of Liberty mean to you?

2. **(a) Recall:** Where is Monaghan when the play opens?
   (b) Deduce: What makes him think of his grandfather?

3. **(a) Recall:** What does Sheean want Grandpa to do?
   (b) Support: Explain why Grandpa is called "stingy."

4. **(a) Recall:** At first, what is Grandpa's attitude about the Statue of Liberty? **(b) Connect:** What problem does this cause for his grandson? **(c) Compare and Contrast:** How do Grandpa's feelings change during the play?

5. **(a) Recall:** What words does Grandpa read at the base of the Statue of Liberty? **(b) Apply:** Why do you think these words are powerful and moving for so many people?

Arthur Miller

(b. 1915)

Arthur Miller has known good times and bad. Today, he is one of the most respected and influential of American playwrights. In 1932, Miller graduated from high school, but was rejected by the University of Michigan. However, Miller's own life "script" did not include failure or defeat. In 1934, Miller convinced the University of Michigan to accept him as a student. In college, he began to write—which he continued to do after graduation, even while he worked at a variety of other jobs. In 1949, he won a Pulitzer Prize for his play *Death of a Salesman*. Other works include *A View From the Bridge* and *The Crucible*.

Review and Assess

Literary Analysis

Dialogue

1. Using a chart like the one below, record at least one example of dialogue that fits each category.

Shows action	Shows thoughts and feelings	Shows setting
	And I say it'll topple into the river in a high wind! Look at the inside of her. She's all hollow!	

2. Identify two examples of actions that are revealed through **dialogue** and explain how the words tell you what is happening.

Connecting Literary Elements

3. Make an organizer like the one shown. Answer the questions to help you evaluate the credibility, or believability, of characterization and plot.

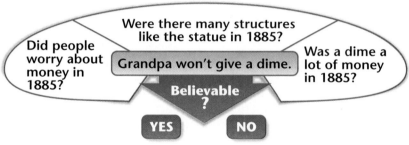

4. Do the characters act like real people? Explain.
5. How well developed and realistic are the characters' personalities?
6. In the situation of the play, do the events of the plot seem believable? Explain.

Reading Strategy

Distinguishing Fact From Fantasy

7. When Monaghan tells his grandson that the statue was placed in the bay to avoid crushing people when it falls, did you believe that statement to be factual? Why or why not?
8. Were there parts of the drama that you could not identify as being either fact or fantasy? Explain.

Extending Understanding

9. **Take a Position:** Do you think Grandpa's reaction to the Latin inscription that says "July 4, 1776" is fair? Why or why not?

Quick Review

Dialogue is conversation between characters. To review dialogue, see page 665.

Characterization is the way the characters' personalities are developed and revealed.

A **fact** is true information about a real person, situation, or event. **Fantasy** is made up from the writer's imagination. To review **fact** and **fantasy**, see page 665.

 Take It to the Net

www.phschool.com

Take the interactive self-test online to check your understanding of the selection.

Integrate Language Skills

Vocabulary Development Lesson

Word Analysis: Latin Root -scrib-

The Latin roots -scrib- and -scrip- come from the Latin word *scribere*, which means "to write." Explain the way *writing* contributes to the meaning of each numbered item.

1. A child's *scribble*
2. The *script* for a play
3. Initials *inscribed* on a locket

Spelling Strategy

When adding *er* or *est* to an adjective that ends in y, change the y to *i* before adding the ending: *stingy* + *est* = *stingiest*. Add the ending indicated to each word.

1. happy (er)   3. mighty (est)
2. silly (est)   4. dingy (er)

Fluency: Sentence Completions

Review the vocabulary list on page 665. On your paper, complete each sentence with a vocabulary word.

1. Rewards are pleasing, but a disappointment can make a person ____?____.
2. We joined the club, and we ____?____ to the magazine.
3. We picnicked in the sunshine, but we took shelter when the ____?____ began.
4. A scientist would enjoy a lecture on physics, but a toddler would be ____?____.

Grammar Lesson

Pronoun and Antecedent Agreement

Pronouns help writers avoid repeating the same nouns over and over. For a pronoun to make sense, however, it must agree with its **antecedent** (the noun or pronoun it replaces) in gender (masculine, feminine, or neuter) and in number (singular or plural).

> **Example:** My grandfather was the stingiest man. . . . *He* even used to save umbrella handles.

The singular masculine pronoun *he* agrees with its antecedent, *grandfather*, which is also masculine and singular.

Practice On your paper, fill in each blank with a pronoun that agrees with its antecedent.

1. All the kids said that ____?____ believed me.
2. Each man must make ____?____ own decision.
3. The island now had ____?____ own attraction.
4. My sister said ____?____ might go with us.
5. All the visitors felt the statue belonged to them; it was ____?____.

Writing Application Write five sentences about famous people. Use a pronoun and an antecedent in each sentence.

W̶G̶ Prentice Hall Writing and Grammar Connection: Chapter 24, Section 2

Writing Lesson

Position Paper

Write a position paper from Grandpa's or Sheean's viewpoint at the beginning of the play—either for or against the statue.

Prewriting Find details in the play related to your character's position. Evaluate whether these are convincing facts or details. Add more supporting evidence to your notes, as needed.

Drafting Begin by stating your position. Then, give your reasons. Follow each of your reasons with examples and details that support your position. Remember to speak in the voice of your character. Conclude with a summary that reemphasizes your position.

Model: Supporting Evidence

People all over the whole United States are puttin' in for it. Butler Street is doin' the same. We'd like to hang a flag on the corner saying—"Butler Street, Brooklyn, is one hundred percent behind the Statue of Liberty."

> Sheean provides supporting evidence for his position. He gives examples (people contributing to the fund) and a reason (putting up a flag) to persuade Grandpa.

Revising Ask a partner to review your draft. Add more examples and details if your reviewer is unconvinced of one of your points.

W̶G̶ Prentice Hall Writing and Grammar Connection: Chapter 7, Section 3

Extension Activities

Listening and Speaking In a group, plan a **reader's theater** production of *Grandpa and the Statue*, or of an excerpt from the play.

- Assign parts.
- Practice the reading.
- After each rehearsal, provide feedback for each other on how well you have interpreted the characters' speech and actions.

When you are satisfied with the reading, perform it for the class.

Writing Write a brief **explanation** of Grandpa's change of heart. Use examples of his actions and words as well as your own inferences.

Research and Technology With a group, create a **Liberty Island Fair** in your classroom. Use the Internet and other sources to gather information, then write overviews and create visuals on the computer. Group members can choose to make diagrams of the island, describe its history, prepare factual charts, or make posters that show the Statue and display facts about it. **[Group Activity]**

 **Take It to the Net**   www.phschool.com

Go online for an additional research activity using the Internet.

Both Julia Alvarez's essay from her book *Something to Declare* and Arthur Miller's drama *Grandpa and the Statue* explore the theme of having something to say, a statement to make, something to declare. Grandpa's "statement" changes after he finds out what the Statue of Liberty "says" or declares to immigrants entering the United States. Julia Alvarez explains that she has many statements to make, many things to declare. As you read Alvarez's essay, which is the introduction to her book *Something to Declare*, think about the statements each writer is making. Ask yourself why each writer connects his or her theme to the idea of immigration. Identify ways in which the writers' ideas are connected to each other.

from
Something to Declare
Julia Alvarez

The title of Julia Alvarez's book Something to Declare *is based on a question that travelers entering the United States are asked, whether they are coming to live or to visit. The question is "Do you have anything to declare?" The literal meaning of the question is "Do you have any statement to make about taxable items or other things you are bringing into the country?" Alvarez recalls being asked that question when she entered the United States. Since much of what Alvarez has to say is related to her experience as an immigrant, she uses the question to make a connection between her life and her work.*

The first time I received a letter from one of my readers, I was surprised. I had just published my first book of poems, *Homecoming*, which concludes with a sonnet sequence titled "33." My reader wanted to know why I had included forty-one sonnets when the title of the sequence was "33."

I considered not answering. Often, it is the little perplexities and curiosities and quandaries that remain after I have finished reading a book that send me to buy another book by that author. If I want to know more, the best way to find out is to read all the books that the author has written.

In the end, though, I couldn't resist. I wrote back, explaining how thirty-three represented my age at the time I wrote the sequence, how I had meant to include only thirty-three sonnets but I kept writing them and writing them, how the sonnets were not sonnets in the traditional sense. . . . Before I knew it, I had written my reader not just a note on my sonnet sequence but a short essay.

Many of the essays in this book began in just that way—as answers to such queries. Jessica Peet, a high-school student, read my first novel, *How the García Girls Lost Their Accents*, in her Vermont Authors class and wanted to know if I considered myself a Vermonter. The Lane Series, our local arts and entertainment series, wanted to know what I might have to say about opera. Share Our Strength was putting together a fund-raising anthology. Did I have anything at all to declare about food?

I could not really say to any of them, "Read my novels or my poems or my stories." These folks wanted what my boarding-school housemother used to call a straight answer. Which is where essays start. Not that they obey housemothers. Not that they list everything you are supposed to list on that Customs Declaration form. (How could the wild, multitudinous, daily things in anyone's head be inventoried in a form?) But that is the pretext of essays: *we have something to declare.*

And so this essay book is dedicated to you, my readers, who have asked me so many good questions and who want to know more than I have told you in my novels and poems. About my experience of immigration, about switching languages, about the writing life, the teaching life, the family life, about all of those combined.

Your many questions boil down finally to this one question: Do you have anything more to declare?

Yes, I do.

Thematic Connection
Why can't Julia resist answering questions from her readers?

Julia Alvarez

(b. 1950)

Julia Alvarez was born in New York City, but raised until the age of ten in the Dominican Republic. She is the author of three critically acclaimed novels: *¡Yo!*, *In the Time of the Butterflies*, and *How the García Girls Lost Their Accents*. She is also the author of four books of poetry, including *The Other Side/El Otro Lado* and *Homecoming*.

Connecting Drama and Nonfiction

1. What theme or message about making statements do Arthur Miller and Julia Alvarez communicate in their works?
2. Explain how the message is revealed in each work.
3. Do you find the theme of Alvarez's nonfiction or Miller's drama easier to understand? Why?

Newspaper Feature Articles

About Newspaper Feature Articles

Most of a newspaper is news articles about very recent events. However, articles that are on topics or issues of current *interest* may or may not be on current *events*. These are called feature articles. The list shows a few types of feature articles you will encounter in newspapers.

At the time this article was written, Angel Island had recently been declared a National Landmark, and money was being assigned to restore the buildings. These events stirred public interest in the topic of the article.

Reading Strategy

Making Assertions About the Text

An assertion is a statement of opinion. When you make an assertion about a text, you give an opinion. For example, when you say "The article was interesting," you are making an assertion. However, the statement "The article is 2,000 words long" is simply a statement of fact. It is not an assertion. When you make an assertion about a text, you should be prepared to support it by citing evidence from the text.

In the model, two assertions are underlined in blue. The assertions are supported by a quotation from the text, underlined in red.

A Few Types of Feature Articles

- Historical articles on the anniversary of an event

- Articles on education at the beginning of a school year

- Biographical articles on a famous person's birthday

Model: Citing Evidence From Text

The article highlights the difficulties faced by Chinese immigrants who were processed through Angel Island. The details are specific and vivid, giving readers a clear understanding of the conditions. For example, the situation of Dale Ching shows how trivial the reasons were that people were detained. "Days after he arrived on the island, Ching learned that he could not leave because his description of his family's house in China did not match what his uncle had told immigration authorities."

The title of a feature article identifies the subject of the article. The title is always worded in the present tense.

from Chinese Immigrants Remember Detention at Angel Island

Newspaper articles often begin with a label telling you where the article was written.

The writer uses the experiences of one man to personalize the situation she will analyze.

By Esther Wu
The Dallas Morning News,
May 19, 2000

ANGEL ISLAND, Calif. Dale Ching was a teenager in 1937 when he rode on a steamer bound for America from China. For 22 days, he dreamed about San Francisco, fortified by the knowledge that his father was waiting for him there.

But when his boat docked in San Francisco's bay, he didn't see his father. Instead, his welcoming committee was a group of armed guards who ordered him and other Chinese immigrants to board a boat bound for Angel Island, where he was detained.

Ching was one of 175,000 Chinese immigrants who entered this country between 1910 and 1940 through the Angel Island Immigration Station, often called the Ellis Island of the West. They came to escape war and famine in their homeland. But once in America, they were subjected to interrogations, and some were held for as long as three to four years.

"Life here was harsh," Ching said recently during a tour of the immigration station.

"When we landed at Angel Island, the guards took away our suitcases. We were allowed the clothes we had on and one change of underwear."

Days after he arrived on the island, Ching learned that he could not leave because his description of his family's house in China did not match what his uncle had told immigration authorities. Officials, suspicious of immigrants entering the United States using false identity papers, detained Ching for three months before his father successfully petitioned officials for his release.

While immigrants coming to America through Ellis Island were welcomed by the Statue of Liberty, Chinese immigrants here had no such symbol, and many felt the sting of scorn and discrimination.

"The stories of Angel Island are not as welcoming, obviously, as it is on the East Coast," said Nick Franco, Angel Island park superintendent. "But it is still a symbolic place, and the stories need to be preserved. It's uncomfortable, but that's all the more why they need to be told."

Today, visitors to the island can experience the immigrants' despair in poems written and carved on barracks walls. More than 135 poems from the barracks have been recorded, most undated and unsigned.

Some voice resentment at being confined and bitterness over the political process that imprisoned the immigrants on the island. Most simply record a writer's anguish. Others reflect on being homesick and longing for freedom.

Some of the immigrants' despair can be traced to the early history of Chinese immigration to this country.

Long before the Angel Island Immigration Station was opened in 1910, officials tried to stem the flow of Chinese immigration to America.

The Chinese Exclusion Act of 1882 barred immigration of Chinese laborers to the United States and prohibited Chinese immigrants from becoming naturalized U.S. citizens. The National Origins Act of 1924 banned all Chinese from coming to America but was later amended to allow a small number, determined by the number of immigrants already in the United States.

The Exclusion Act was the first and only time the United States restricted immigration by ethnicity. It was not repealed until 1943, when China was a U.S. ally in World War II, and Congress established a set quota of 105 Chinese immigrants into the country annually. The quota system was banned in 1965.

Outcry for Preservation

Angel Island, in the western part of San Francisco Bay a few miles beyond the Golden Gate Bridge and Alcatraz, served as a military base as early as the Civil War. The base was active during World War II, when the threat of a West Coast invasion by the Japanese was a possibility. After the war, however, the hilly island was deserted and became covered with lush vegetation.

U.S. officials closed the island's immigration station in 1940 after a fire destroyed the administration building. And in 1962, the abandoned island was given to California's state park system. The barracks were about to be demolished in 1970 when a park ranger discovered the poems on the walls.

Public outcry persuaded state officials to preserve what was left of the immigration station, and it became a National Historic Landmark in 1997. Last year, the National Trust named it one of 11 endangered historic sites.

In March, Californians approved a $15 million bond issue that will help restore some of the buildings and preserve the writings. Preliminary renovation studies are being done, and work may start as early as 2001 and take as long as eight years to complete.

What's left of the immigration station is basically the hospital and barracks. What remained of a two-story administration building, kitchen and dining hall has been demolished.

A few small houses that were once used as officers' private quarters have been refurbished as offices for park officials.

Public tours have been conducted since 1982, and schoolchildren take field trips here. Groups often come to boat, hike or camp overnight. An estimated 200,000 people visit the island each year.

Quotations may be used to give individual viewpoints or expert opinions.

Feature articles often link historical information to current-day information.

Check Your Comprehension

1. Where is Angel Island?
2. Why is Angel Island called the Ellis Island of the West?
3. Why did thousands of people leave China for the United States between 1910 and 1940?
4. Why were Chinese immigrants detained at Angel Island?
5. What happened in 1970 to change plans to demolish the barracks on Angel Island?

Applying the Reading Strategy

Making Assertions About the Text

6. Make an assertion about the writer's position regarding the problems of the Chinese immigrants. Cite two details that support your assertion.
7. Which of the following is an assertion?
   - Preserving the immigration station on Angel Island is important to Californians.
   - Ching is one of 175,000 Chinese immigrants.
8. What assertion can you make about the balance of fact and opinion in this text? Cite one example of a fact and one of an opinion.

Activity

Media Investigation

Find two media sources that give an update on the plans to restore the buildings and preserve the writings at Angel Island. Give an oral summary of the information you find.

Comparing Informational Materials

Characteristics of Newspaper Feature Articles

Compare feature articles in newspapers to special features on television newscasts. Watch a special-interest or feature story on a newscast. Then, read a newspaper feature article on the same or a closely related topic. Use a chart like the one shown to record similarities and differences.

	Newspaper	Television
Uses facts?		
Includes opinions?		
Connects to a current event or issue?		
Uses images?		
Other?		

READING INFORMATIONAL MATERIALS

How-to Essay

About How-to Essays

A how-to essay presents a step-by-step process for completing a certain task. Examples of how-to writing include directions for how to build and fly a model airplane or how to get a short story published. How-to essays teach you how to do or make something new, how to improve a skill, or how to achieve a desired result.

The elements of a how-to essay include

- a specific result that the reader can accomplish by following the directions or explanation.
- a list of the materials needed.
- a series of steps explained in logical order.
- details that tell when, how much, how often, or to what extent.

Reading Strategy

Identifying Cause-and-Effect Relationships

When a baseball hits a glass window, everyone knows what happens. The glass breaks. This is an example of a simple cause-and-effect relationship. The ball hitting the window is the cause, or reason. The glass breaking is the effect, or result.

In a how-to essay or a set of instructions, each step is a cause that, if the step is performed correctly, results in a particular effect. In the following example, the fold is the cause, the legs are the effect.

Cause	Effect
Step 1	
Step 2	
Step 3	
Step 4	
Step 5	
Step 6	
Step 7	
Step 8	

Example: Fold the long bubble over again and twist against the two new bubbles (another locking twist). Now you have two front legs.

Identify the cause-and-effect relationships in "Twist and Shout" by completing a chart like the one shown here.

Twist and Shout

K. Wayne Wincey

The essay begins by identifying the final, specific result that the essay will help the reader accomplish.

A pinch here, a twist there, and you've made a balloon animal! Creating balloon animals is easy. All you need is a bag of balloons and the desire to have some fun. You can usually master the basics in about a week.

The best part of balloon twisting is that most animal sculptures follow the same 10-step order: nose, ear, ear, neck, leg, leg, body, leg, leg, and tail. What varies is the size of the bubbles and the amount of uninflated balloon (tail) that you start with.

Here, the writer identifies the materials.

Supplies are cheap. A gross of animal balloons, that's 144 of 'em, costs about $10. Find the balloons (also called 260's, twisties, or pencil balloons) at party supply stores or magic shops. While there, consider paying about $4 for a palm pump that helps blow up the balloons. (It'll save time and heavy breathing.)

Start with an easy balloon animal, like the dog shown here. Experiment a little, and you'll soon have a whole zoo of critters!

Numbered steps create a logical order.

1. Blow up a balloon, leaving about three inches uninflated. This is called the tail; the open end is the nozzle. Tie off the nozzle in an overhand knot. Note: The more twists in your sculpture, the more uninflated the balloon must be.

Details in the directions identify how much balloon to pinch and how many times to pinch and how many times to twist.

2. Using your thumb and forefinger, pinch or squeeze off three inches of the balloon from the nozzle for the dog's nose. Twist the body of the balloon around at least three times. Don't worry about pops—they happen, but not often with this type of balloon.

3. Pinch off another three inches of balloon and twist. This will be one ear of your dog.

The writer identifies the effect of not completing the step correctly.

4. Fold the first two bubbles against the rest of the balloon. Squeeze the long segment against the twist of the two shorter segments. Keep a firm grip on all the bubbles at this point or they'll come undone. Twist the long bubble and the two short bubbles together. Now your critter has two ears and a nose.

5. Pinch off and twist three more inches for the neck, followed by three additional inches for one front leg.

6. Fold the long bubble over again and twist against the two new bubbles (another locking twist). Now you have two front legs.

7. Another three inches and a twist gives your dog a body. Squeeze and twist off three more.

8. Now give your canine one last locking twist with the rest of the balloon. You've got two hind legs, a tail, and finally, a dog!

Check Your Comprehension

1. Which materials does Wincey suggest for creating your own balloon animals?
2. Why does the author say it is easy to create other balloon animals once you have completed one?
3. Why does the author include the note about making sure your balloons are uninflated?
4. What is a split or locking twist?

Applying the Reading Strategy

Identifying Cause-and-Effect Relationships

5. If you did not let air out of the balloon and you twisted it several times, what might be the effect?
6. What would be the effect of pinching off ten inches instead of three in Step 3?
7. Why do the steps have to be performed in order?

Activity

Balloon Animal Demonstration

Use what you have learned in the essay to give a demonstration in which you orally explain how to make balloon animals while you make one.

Comparing Informational Texts

How-to Essays and User's Guides

A user's guide is like a how-to essay for a specific product or piece of equipment. Find a user's guide and compare its format and contents to this how-to essay.

	How-to Essay	User's Guide
Purpose		
Contents		
Format or Presentation		

Writing WORKSHOP
Response to Literature

A **response to literature** is a work that expresses the writer's feelings and thoughts about what he or she has read—a book, short story, essay, article, or poem. Using examples from the literature, you can explain why you reacted to the work as you did. In this workshop, you will choose a piece of literature and write a response to it.

Assignment Criteria. Your response to literature should have the following characteristics:

- A clear organization, based on several clear ideas, premises, or images
- Your interpretation, based on careful reading, understanding, and insight
- Relevant examples and textual evidence that support and justify your interpretation
- A brief summary of important features of the literature
- Your own feelings or judgments about the literature

To see the criteria on which your response to literature may be assessed, see the Rubric on page 697.

Prewriting

Choose a topic. With a small group of readers, hold a round-table discussion of literary works you all have enjoyed. Each member should offer the title, author, and special qualities of a work. Jot down titles. Choose one of these works that you had a strong reaction to as the subject for your writing.

Use a pentad. To help you focus your topic, fill in a pentad like the one shown by answering these questions:

- **Actors:** Who performs the action?
- **Acts:** What is done?
- **Scenes:** When or where is it done?
- **Conditions:** How is it done?
- **Purposes:** Why is it done?

After answering the questions, highlight the most interesting points and choose your specific topic.

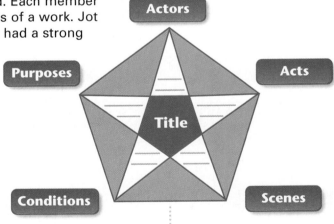

Student Model

Before you begin drafting your response to literature, read this student model and review the characteristics of a successful response to literature.

Chris Harshfield
Louisville, Kentucky

Response to *Tuck Everlasting*

Imagine finding a way to stay young forever! That's what the characters in *Tuck Everlasting*, a novel by Natalie Babbit, do. The novel makes the idea especially interesting by presenting it in a story that makes a realistic situation out of a very unrealistic idea.

Winnie, the main character, meets a strange family, the Tucks. She soon discovers that they have a secret: All of them have drunk from a spring of water that makes them live forever. Because Winnie has a crush on Jesse, one of the Tucks, she is tempted to drink from the spring, too, when she is old enough to marry him. Based on things the characters say and do, we know that this will not be an easy decision for Winnie.

The theme of this story is not a new one, but the way it is presented is better than in other stories. Like most of the other writers, Babbit suggests that living forever is not a good idea. Unlike other stories I have read about this theme, however, *Tuck Everlasting* really convinced me by showing examples I could understand and by doing it with characters who seem like real people. Even though I know there is no spring like the one in the book, the book made it seem real enough to get me thinking about the problem Winnie faces.

The final outcome of the story settles the question as far as Winnie is concerned. When Jesse returns years later, he finds her marker in the cemetery. Because she is dead, we know that she decided to not drink from the spring. The words on her marker suggest that she had a happy life, and that she got over Jesse. For Winnie, in any case, Mr. Tuck's words prove true: ". . .the stream keeps moving on, taking it all back again" (Babbit 31).

The questions that do not get answered left me a little disappointed. I would have preferred to know how Winnie reached her decision, not just what she decided. Overall, though, *Tuck Everlasting* tells a good story and raises interesting questions. In the end, Tuck gives the answer, "Life. Moving, growing, changing, never the same two minutes together" (Babbit 30).

Sidebar notes:

In the introduction, the writer indicates what the focus of his response will be.

Enough of a summary is given so that readers can understand the response that follows.

As identified in the introduction, the response is organized mainly around the theme.

Here, the writer gives his interpretation of the theme and supports it with an example from the novel.

In the conclusion, the writer shares his own feelings and judgments. He finishes with a general impression and a quotation from the novel. The page number where the quotation is found is given in parentheses after the author's name.

Drafting

Organize your interpretation. Your draft should develop around several clearly expressed ideas, premises, or images. A well-organized draft has these connected parts:

- **Introduction** that includes your brief summary and states your main idea about the literature
- **Body** that offers a variety of supporting evidence, including quotations, examples, and specific references to the text
- **Conclusion** that restates your interpretation and may include feelings or opinions about what you have read

Justify your interpretation. Elaborate on your general ideas by pushing yourself to go deeper to reach new insights. A sentence such as "This story is full of suspense" needs details to support it. Ask, "*Why* is it suspenseful?" or "*In what way* is it suspenseful?"

Revising

Revise your draft to make sure your ideas will be clearly organized.

Color-code related details. Reread what you have written. Circle each of your main points in a different color. Underline the sentences supporting each main point in the same color as the main point. Use the following suggestions for revision.

1. If a paragraph contains marks of a few different colors, revise by moving sentences to the paragraph they support.

2. If a sentence is neither circled nor underlined, delete it or use it in a new paragraph.

Model: Color-coding Details

The theme of this story is not a new one, but the way it is presented is better than in other stories. Many stories, folk tales, and books have been written about characters who want to live forever or end up living forever. Like most of the other writers, Babbit suggests that living forever is not a good idea. ~~Although at the end, we find out whether Winnie agrees, I was disappointed that some questions were not answered.~~ Unlike other stories I have read about this theme, however, *Tuck Everlasting* really convinced me by showing examples I could understand and by doing it with characters who seem like real people.

> The sentence underlined in red was deleted here because it did not relate to the main point of the paragraph.

Add a quotation—or two. Go back to the text as you revise. Now that you have written your response, find quotations that leap out as good examples. Using the writer's exact words will strengthen your interpretation of the work.

Example: "The Geese" is an uplifting poem. When I read it, I felt my "earthbound soul take flight."

Compare the model and nonmodel. Why is the model more effective than the nonmodel?

Nonmodel	Model
Because she is dead, we know that she decided to not drink from the spring. The words on her marker suggest that she had a happy life, and that she got over Jesse.	Because she is dead, we know that she decided to not drink from the spring. The words on her marker suggest that she had a happy life, and that she got over Jesse. For Winnie, in any case, Mr. Tuck's words prove true: ". . .the stream keeps moving on, taking it all back again" (Babbit 31).

Publishing and Presenting

Choose one of these ways to share your writing with classmates or a larger audience.

Organize a Book Day. Arrange a day on which you and your classmates present your responses to literature and hold discussions about the works you have enjoyed.

Write a letter to an author. Turn your written response to a work into a letter to the author. Share your letter and any response you get to it with your classmates.

WG *Prentice Hall Writing and Grammar Connection: Chapter 12.*

Speaking Connection
To learn more about delivering a response to literature, see the **Listening and Speaking Workshop: Delivering an Oral Response to Literature, p. 698.**

Rubric for Self-Assessment

Evaluate your response to literature, using the following criteria and rating scale:

Criteria	Rating Scale				
	Not very				Very
How clearly and logically organized is the response?	1	2	3	4	5
How well does the response express understanding and insight into the work?	1	2	3	4	5
How relevant and effective are the examples?	1	2	3	4	5
How well are the necessary points summarized?	1	2	3	4	5
How well does the response express the writer's feelings or judgments about the work?	1	2	3	4	5

Listening and Speaking WORKSHOP

Delivering an Oral Response to Literature

After you have read a literary work, you may be asked to deliver an **oral response to literature**. An oral response includes many of the characteristics of a successful written response. (To review response to literature, see the Writing Workshop, pp. 694–697.) The speaking strategies that follow will help you develop and deliver an organized response that your audience will appreciate. Use the checklist on this page to improve your performance.

Develop an Interpretation

The first step toward a successful oral response is to read carefully and thoughtfully to develop an interpretation.

Organize around clear ideas. Organize your response around a number of clear ideas, premises, or images. Do not try to cover everything. Your introduction should include your interpretation of the work. The body of the speech should support those ideas with good reasons. Conclude by restating your interpretation and voicing your opinion.

Use examples and textual evidence. To give your oral response credibility, pull out quotations and examples from the literature to support your response. Keep yourself focused on what the text has to say.

Deliver with Confidence

To deliver an effective response to literature, use speaking techniques such as tone, volume, and pacing to engage the audience and win them over to your interpretation of the literature.

Use a strong speaking voice. Speak clearly, confidently, and loudly enough to be heard by everyone. Include the title and author and mention where the work can be found in case your audience wants to read it, too.

Speak slowly. Too many speakers rush through their presentations because they are nervous and want the presentation to be over! Do not make this mistake. Speak slowly and enunciate clearly. You want your audience to hear every word. Do not be afraid to pause before reading a quotation or starting a new thought.

(Activity: Videotape a review**)** Suppose you have been asked to deliver a two- to three-minute review of a piece of literature to be broadcast on your local television station. With a partner, prepare and rehearse your review. While one of you speaks, the other should videotape. Then, exchange roles. Share your videotapes with your classmates.

Tips for Engaging the Audience

Show the work

Hold up the novel or the collection in which you read the work.

Read from the work

When reading a quotation or passage, read directly from the work. Use sticky notes to mark pages before the presentation.

Use props

Hold up an object mentioned in your presentation.

Assessment WORKSHOP

Sentence Construction

The writing sections of some tests require you to read a passage and answer multiple-choice questions about sentence construction. Use the following strategies to help you answer such questions:

- **Recognize incomplete sentences and run-on sentences**. An incomplete sentence is lacking a subject or a predicate or both. It is not a complete thought. Run-on sentences are two or more sentences without the correct punctuation.

- **Combine sentences**. Sometimes two short, closely related sentences can be combined into one sentence. When you are given this option as a test-answer choice, make sure the answer you choose is a complete sentence. Look at the following sample test item:

Test-Taking Strategies

- Identify the problem in the underlined section before choosing a replacement.
- Proofread the replacement you choose to make sure new errors are not introduced.

Sample Test Item

Directions: Choose the best way to write the underlined section. If it needs no change, choose "Correct as is."

According to Thomas Edison, genius is one percent inspiration and ninety-nine percent perspiration. (1) By his own definition, he certainly qualified during his lifetime he patented 1,093 inventions.

A He certainly qualified by his own definition during his lifetime he patented 1,093 inventions.

B By his own definition, he certainly qualified. During his lifetime, he patented 1,093 inventions.

C By his own definition. He certainly qualified during his lifetime he patented 1,093 inventions.

D Correct as is

Answer and Explanation

A is a run-on sentence. **C** contains an incomplete sentence and a run-on sentence. **B** is correct. It turns a run-on sentence into two complete sentences.

▶ Practice

Directions: Choose the best way to write the underlined section. If it needs no change, choose "Correct as is."

(1) Scientists have been studying bubbles. The bubbles were trapped in the Antarctic ice for thousands of years. Studies show a connection between the amount of carbon dioxide in the air and the temperature. (2) This is important for people today. Because the amount of carbon dioxide in the air is increasing yearly.

1. **A** Scientists have been studying Antarctic ice for thousands of years.

   B Scientists have been in Antarctic ice for thousands of years.

   C Bubbles were trapped in Antarctic ice.

   D Correct as is

2. **A** This is important for people today because the amount of carbon dioxide in the air is increasing yearly.

   B This is important. For people today because carbon dioxide is increasing yearly.

   C This is important for people today the amount of carbon dioxide in the air increasing yearly.

   D Correct as is

UNIT
9

Poetry

Waves of Matsushima, Endo period, early 18th century, six-panel folding screen, Korin Ogata, Courtesy, Museum of Fine Arts, Boston, MA

Exploring the Genre

Poems can tell stories, describe natural events, and express feelings. Some poems are shaped to look like their subjects, and others follow strict patterns of rhyme, rhythm, or syllables. Through the use of images, or word pictures, poets paint vivid pictures for readers to see with their minds as well as their eyes. By reading poems, you can learn a new way to see something that you have looked at hundreds of times before.

As you read the poems in this unit, notice how the poets blend language and feeling to convey new ideas to you.

◀ **Critical Viewing** Which details in the painting seem poetic? **[Connect]**

Why Read Literature?

When you read poems, make sure you put your mind, your voice, and all of your senses to work to get the full meaning. Often, how words sound and look is just as important as what they mean. To help you understand and remember poems, set different purposes for your reading. Review the three purposes you might set before reading the poems in this unit.

1

Read for the love of literature.

Did you know that an adult walrus eats about 6,000 clams per day? For a humorous and imaginative spin on a scientific fact, read **"The Walrus and the Carpenter,"** page 708.

Some people think that the ginkgo is the hardest tree to destroy. In fact, a 350-year-old ginkgo survived the atom bomb that was dropped on Hiroshima, Japan, in 1945. Note the special qualities that poet Eve Merriam sees in the ginkgo when you read **"Simile: Willow and Ginkgo,"** page 740.

Imagine a poem that looks like a skateboard and makes you feel as if you are skateboarding on an "asphalt sea." Read Lillian Morrison's **"The Sidewalk Racer"** for its look and its feeling, page 718.

2

Read to be entertained.

The first limericks, written in the 1820s, were part of a collection called *Book of Nonsense.* It was a perfect name, since limericks are supposed to be fun and even silly. Read **"Limerick"** to see how the poet mixes funny ideas with plays on words, page 720.

Did you know that your brain is more active when it is asleep than when it is awake but watching television? It's true! Read how TV affects a little boy in **"Jimmy Jet and His TV Set,"** page 707.

3

Read for information.

Shakespeare lived in a world of danger, excitement, and change. Learn details about Shakespeare's world when you read **"Shakespeare's London,"** page 735.

You may think from its name that the Dead Sea is a sea, but did you know that it is actually a lake? To learn more about the Dead Sea, read **"More Than a Pinch,"** page 749.

Take It to the Net

Visit the Web site for online instruction and activities related to each selection in this unit.

www.phschool.com

How to Read Literature

Strategies for Reading Poetry

In a poem, even plain, everyday words seem to stand out and mean more than they usually do in other types of writing. The unique arrangements and combinations of words can, at times, seem like unfamiliar territory. The following strategies that you will learn in this unit will help you understand the poetry you read.

1. Identify the speaker.

The voice that "says" a poem is its speaker, but the speaker is not necessarily the poet. Sometimes, the poet takes on an imaginary voice to describe what is going on. In this unit, you will learn to recognize the speaker of a poem.

2. Use your senses.

Poets often include details that appeal to your five senses—sight, hearing, smell, touch, or taste. To get the full meaning of a poem, put all of your senses to work to help you paint a mental picture of what the poet is describing. To which of your senses do the following lines appeal?

> A frog jumps into the pond,
> Splash! Silence again.
> —from "Haiku"

> **Poet's words**
>
> The willow is sleek as a velvet-nosed calf;
>
> The ginkgo is leathery as an old bull.
>
> —from "Simile: Willow and Ginkgo"

> **My words**
>
> A willow is smooth and soft to the touch.
>
> A ginkgo is tough and rough feeling.

3. Read lines according to punctuation.

Do not sound like a stiff computer voice by automatically stopping after each line. Keep going when a line has no punctuation mark at the end. Pause at commas and semicolons; stop longer at end marks. In this unit, you will practice using reading clues provided by punctuation. Look at the punctuation in the lines to the right:

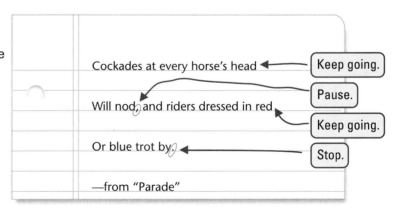

Cockades at every horse's head ← Keep going.

Will nod, and riders dressed in red ← Pause.

← Keep going.

Or blue trot by, ← Stop.

—from "Parade"

4. Paraphrase the lines.

If you are unsure of a poem's meaning, you may want to restate a line or a passage in your own words to help you understand it. Notice the example above.

As you read the selections in this unit, review the strategies for reading poetry and look at the examples. Use the suggestions to help you understand the text.

Prepare to Read

The Geese ◆ Jimmy Jet and His TV Set ◆ The Walrus and the Carpenter

 Take It to the Net

Visit www.phschool.com
for interactive activities
and instruction related to
these selections, including
- background
- graphic organizers
- literary elements
- reading strategies

Preview

Connecting to the Literature

You probably use different tones of voice to express humor, sadness, and other thoughts and feelings. The poems in this section have distinctly different voices too. In "The Walrus and the Carpenter" and "Jimmy Jet and His TV Set," the poets Lewis Carroll and Shel Silverstein sound like stand-up comics. In "The Geese," Richard Peck sounds more like the singer of a sad ballad. Listen to these different voices as you read.

Background

The poem "The Geese" is a lyric poem. The word *lyric* comes from the word *lyre*, the name of a stringed instrument. This instrument was used in ancient Greece to accompany poets as they performed their poetry.

Literary Analysis

Narrative and Lyric Poetry

Narrative poetry tells a story in verse. "The Walrus and the Carpenter" and "Jimmy Jet and His TV Set" are narrative poems. Notice how the following lines from "The Walrus and the Carpenter" suggest the beginning of a story.

> "O Oysters, come and walk with us!"
> The Walrus did beseech.

In contrast, **lyric poetry** is highly musical verse that expresses a speaker's personal thoughts and feelings. A lyric poem usually focuses on a single powerful emotion, event, or image. "The Geese" is a lyric poem.

Comparing Literary Works

Each of these poems has a regular **rhythm,** or pattern of beats. The chart shows how to mark accented and unaccented syllables to discover the pattern of beats. Although all three of the poems have a regular rhythm, the rhythm is not the same in all three poems. Compare and contrast the rhythms of the poems by answering the following focus questions:

Accented ´	Unaccented ˘
Ŏ Óystĕrs cŏme aňd wálk wĭth ús (4)	
Thĕ Wálrŭs dĭd bĕsééch. (3)	

1. In which two poems does the rhythm go back and forth between a line with four beats and a line with three beats?
2. In what three ways are these two poems different from the third poem in the group?

Reading Strategy

Identifying the Speaker

The imaginary voice you hear when you read a poem is the **speaker.** The speaker can be, but is not always, the same "person" as the poet. When you read a poem, think about what the word choice, details, and language level suggest about the age, personality, and outlook of the speaker.

Vocabulary Development

lean (lēn) *adj.* thin (p. 707)

antennae (an ten´ ē) *n.* metal rods that receive TV or radio signals (p. 707)

beseech (bi sēch´) *v.* beg (p. 709)

The Geese

Richard Peck

▲ **Critical Viewing**
Why might a sight like this one cause someone to think of the past or the future? **[Infer]**

My father was the first to hear
The passage of the geese each fall,
Passing above the house so near
He'd hear within his heart their call.

5   And then at breakfast time he'd say:
"The geese were heading south last night,"
For he had lain awake till day,
Feeling his earthbound soul take flight.

Knowing that winter's wind comes soon
10   After the rushing of those wings,
Seeing them pass before the moon,
Recalling the lure of faroff things.

Richard Peck

(b. 1934)
Born in Illinois, Richard Peck grew up listening to dramas and stories presented on the radio, which stimulated his imagination. Peck has written poetry and won awards for some of his many young-adult novels, which include *Ghosts I Have Been*, *Secrets of the Shopping Mall*, and *The Last Safe Place on Earth*.

Jimmy Jet and His TV Set

SHEL SILVERSTEIN

I'll tell you the story of Jimmy Jet—
And you know what I tell you is true.
He loved to watch his TV set
Almost as much as you.

5 He watched all day, he watched all night
Till he grew pale and <u>lean</u>,
From *The Early Show* to *The Late Late Show*
And all the shows between.

He watched till his eyes were frozen wide,
10 And his bottom grew into his chair.
And his chin turned into a tuning dial,
And <u>antennae</u> grew out of his hair.

And his brains turned into TV tubes,
And his face to a TV screen.
15 And two knobs saying "VERT." and "HORIZ."
Grew where his ears had been.

And he grew a plug that looked like a tail
So we plugged in little Jim.
And now instead of him watching TV
20 We all sit around and watch him.

lean (lēn) *adj.* thin

antennae (an ten´ ē) *n.* metal rods that receive TV or radio signals

Shel Silverstein

(1932–1999)

Chicago-born Shel Silverstein was a talented poet, cartoonist, playwright, and songwriter. His tremendously popular poetry collections, *Where the Sidewalk Ends* and *A Light in the Attic*, show Silverstein's imaginative sense of humor, which both children and adults enjoy. He also wrote the classic children's book *The Giving Tree*.

Review and Assess

Thinking About the Selections

1. **Respond:** Have you ever felt "the lure of faroff things"? Explain your answer.
2. **(a) Recall:** Why does the father lie awake all night in "The Geese"? **(b) Infer:** Why do the sounds of geese going south have a strong effect on him? **(c) Relate:** Describe something in the change of seasons that, for you, brings certain memories or feelings.
3. **(a) Recall:** Describe Jimmy's TV-watching habits.
   (b) Interpret: What is funny about what happens to Jimmy?
   (c) Draw Conclusions: What is the poet saying about the effects of watching television?

The Walrus
and the
Carpenter

Lewis Carroll

From *Alice Through the Looking Glass* by Lewis Carroll, Illustration by John Tenniel

▲ **Critical Viewing** How does the picture help you predict that this poem will be funny? **[Connect]**

The sun was shining on the sea,
　　Shining with all his might:
He did his very best to make
　　The billows smooth and bright—
5　And this was odd, because it was
　　The middle of the night.

The moon was shining sulkily,
　　Because she thought the sun
Had got no business to be there
10　　After the day was done—
"It's very rude of him," she said,
　　"To come and spoil the fun!"

The sea was wet as wet could be,
　　The sands were dry as dry.
15　You could not see a cloud, because
　　No cloud was in the sky:
No birds were flying overhead—
　　There were no birds to fly.

The Walrus and the Carpenter
20　　Were walking close at hand:
They wept like anything to see
　　Such quantities of sand:
"If this were only cleared away,"
　　They said, "it would be grand!"

25　"If seven maids with seven mops
　　Swept it for half a year,
Do you suppose," the Walrus said,
　　"That they could get it clear?"
"I doubt it," said the Carpenter,
30　　And shed a bitter tear.

"O Oysters, come and walk with us!"
　　The Walrus did beseech.
"A pleasant walk, a pleasant talk,
　　Along the briny beach:
35　We cannot do with more than four,
　　To give a hand to each."

Literary Analysis
Narrative and Lyric Poetry, Rhyme, and Rhythm
How many lines in each stanza, or group of lines, rhyme with one another?

beseech (bi sēch´) v. beg

Reading Check

With whom do the Walrus and Carpenter want to walk?

The Walrus and the Carpenter ◆ 709

From *Alice Through the Looking Glass* by Lewis Carroll, Illustration by John Tenniel

▲ **Critical Viewing** Explain how this picture tells a story by itself. **[Interpret]**

The eldest Oyster looked at him,
　　But never a word he said:
The eldest Oyster winked his eye,
40　　And shook his heavy head—
Meaning to say he did not choose
　　To leave the oyster-bed.

But four young Oysters hurried up,
　　All eager for this treat:
45　Their coats were brushed, their faces
　　　washed,
　　Their shoes were clean and neat—
And this was odd, because, you know,
　　They hadn't any feet.

Four other Oysters followed them,
50　　And yet another four;
And thick and fast they came at last,
　　And more, and more, and more—
All hopping through the frothy waves,
　　And scrambling to the shore.

**Reading Strategy
Identifying the Speaker**
What does this humorous comment reveal about the speaker's personality?

55 The Walrus and the Carpenter
        Walked on a mile or so,
    And then they rested on a rock
        Conveniently low:
    And all the little Oysters stood
60   And waited in a row.

    "The time has come," the Walrus said,
        "To talk of many things:
    Of shoes—and ships—and sealing wax—
        Of cabbages—and kings—
65 And why the sea is boiling hot—
        And whether pigs have wings."

    "But wait a bit," the Oysters cried,
        "Before we have our chat;
    For some of us are out of breath,
70   And all of us are fat!"
    "No hurry!" said the Carpenter.
        They thanked him much for that.

    "A loaf of bread," the Walrus said,
        "Is what we chiefly need:
75 Pepper and vinegar besides
        Are very good indeed—
    Now, if you're ready, Oysters dear,
        We can begin to feed."

    "But not on us!" the Oysters cried,
80   Turning a little blue.
    "After such kindness, that would be
        A dismal thing to do!"
    "The night is fine," the Walrus said.
        "Do you admire the view?"

85 "It was so kind of you to come!
        And you are very nice!"
    The Carpenter said nothing but
        "Cut us another slice.

Literary Analysis
Narrative and Lyric Poetry, Rhyme, and Rhythm. How many syllables should you pronounce in *conveniently* to maintain the poem's regular rhythm?

✓ **Reading Check**

What are the Walrus and Carpenter going to do with the Oysters?

The Walrus and the Carpenter ◆ 711

I wish you were not quite so deaf—
90   I've had to ask you twice!"

"It seems a shame," the Walrus said,
    "To play them such a trick.
After we've brought them out so far,
    And made them trot so quick!"
95 The Carpenter said nothing but
    "The butter's spread too thick!"

"I weep for you," the Walrus said:
    "I deeply sympathize."
With sobs and tears he sorted out
100   Those of the largest size,
Holding his pocket-handkerchief
    Before his streaming eyes.

"O Oysters," said the Carpenter,
    "You've had a pleasant run!
105 Shall we be trotting home again?"
    But answer came there none—
And this was scarcely odd, because
    They'd eaten every one.

Review and Assess

Thinking About the Selection

1. **Respond:** What passage in the poem seems silliest to you? Why?

2. **(a) Recall:** Why is it odd that the sun is shining in the poem? **(b) Analyze:** Give two other examples of ridiculous happenings. **(c) Generalize:** What is the overall effect of these details?

3. **(a) Recall:** How does the "eldest Oyster" react to the Walrus and the Carpenter? **(b) Infer:** What might this oyster think of the Walrus and the Carpenter? **(c) Predict:** What does this oyster's reaction hint about the events to come?

4. **(a) Recall:** Where is it clear that the oysters are in trouble? **(b) Analyze:** How is this poem both funny and sad?

5. **(a) Define:** Lewis Carroll is known for "nonsense verse." Based on your reading of the poem, how would you define nonsense verse? **(b) Evaluate:** Is nonsense verse worth reading? Why or why not? Use examples from the poem in your answer.

Lewis Carroll

(1832–1898)

Lewis Carroll is the pen name of Englishman Charles Lutwidge Dodgson, a math professor. He began writing as a youth, compiling family magazines with his siblings. Later he wrote two children's classics, *Alice's Adventures in Wonderland* and *Through the Looking Glass*, which contains "The Walrus and the Carpenter." These works sprang from stories he told to a real-life Alice, the child of one of Carroll's friends. As you'll see from the poem, Carroll's work sparkles with imagination and wordplay.

Review and Assess

Literary Analysis

Narrative and Lyric Poetry

1. List the main **narrative** events in "The Walrus and the Carpenter." Use a chart like this one. (Add boxes as needed.)

2. What qualities make "The Geese" an example of **lyric** poetry?
3. Describe the character Jimmy Jet, noting both the funny and sad aspects of him.

Comparing Literary Works

4. Which two poems have a four-beat line alternating with a three-beat line?
5. How does this alternating pattern affect the way you read the poems?
6. Make a chart like the one shown to compare and contrast the lyric poem with one of the narrative poems in this group.

Reading Strategy

Identifying the Speaker in a Poem

7. Could the **speaker** of "The Walrus and the Carpenter" be the poet? Explain.
8. Do you think the speaker of "Jimmy Jet" likes television? Explain.
9. In "The Geese," what can you infer about where the speaker lives?

Extending Understanding

10. **Science Connection:** Some animal behavior, such as the migration of geese, occurs in predictable seasonal cycles. Find the names of some animals, birds, and fish that migrate and explain the reason for their migration.

Quick Review

Narrative poetry tells a story in verse. **Lyric poetry** is verse that focuses on the speaker's personal thoughts and feelings, using musical language. To review these two types of poetry, see page 705.

Rhythm refers to the pattern of stressed and unstressed beats in a poem. To review rhythm, see page 705.

The **speaker** is the imaginary voice that a poet uses when writing a poem. To review speaker, see page 705.

 Take It to the Net
www.phschool.com
Take the interactive self-test online to check your understanding of these selections.

Integrate Language Skills

Vocabulary Development Lesson

Concept Development: Using Multiple Meanings

A number of words, like *lean* found in "Jimmy Jet and His TV Set," have more than one meaning.

Explain the two different meanings of *lean*, *might*, and *bright* in the following sentences.

1. The lean Carpenter stopped to lean on the rock.
2. You might discover that his might is greater than yours.
3. The sun was bright, but the Oysters were not bright.

Fluency: Word Choice

Respond to each numbered item by writing a sentence that includes a vocabulary word.

1. How do Oysters speak to the Walrus to spare them?
2. Why will Jimmy Jet have trouble with haircuts?
3. Describe Jimmy Jet's appearance.

Spelling Strategy

The long *e* sound can be spelled *ie*, *ei*, *ee*, and *ea*. Write the vocabulary words that relate to the clues below.

1. This word and *need* are both spelled with *ee*.
2. This word, *team*, and *mean* are all spelled with *ea*.

Grammar Lesson

Comparisons With Adjectives and Adverbs

Most adjectives and adverbs have different forms—the **positive** (*large*), the **comparative** (*larger*), and the **superlative** (*largest*). In the following example, Carroll uses the superlative form to describe the size of the Oysters:

> "With sobs and tears he sorted out / Those of the *largest* size."

With short adjectives and adverbs,

- form the comparative by adding *-er* to the positive.
- form the superlative by adding *-est*.

Use the comparative form when comparing two items and the superlative form when comparing more than two.

Practice Change the word in parentheses from the positive to the comparative form.

1. Could seven maids make the beach (clean) than it is now?
2. The Oysters looked (neat) than the Walrus and the Carpenter did.
3. The sun is (bright) than the moon.
4. Who is (rude), the Walrus or the Carpenter?
5. The Walrus talked (long) than the Carpenter did.

Writing Application Using the comparative forms of one adjective and one adverb, compare the behavior of the "eldest Oyster" with that of the young Oysters.

WG *Prentice Hall Writing and Grammar Connection: Chapter 25, Section 1*

Writing Lesson

Story with Dialogue

The two narrative poems you have read each tell a story. Now retell the story in "Jimmy Jet and His TV Set" as a prose narrative, a narrative not written in verse.

Prewriting   List each important event in the story. Then, imagine details not mentioned in the poem (for example, how Jimmy's family reacts), and write them next to each event. You might include people in Jimmy's family, what Jimmy looks like, and what people say.

Drafting   Draft your story, using your own words rather than those in the poem. Use dialogue to bring the characters to life.

Model: Adding Dialogue

Jimmy's sister Minnie gasped. "Jimmy, what's that on your head?"

"Quiet down," mumbled Jimmy. "I don't want to miss any of this game show."

"I'm serious, Jimmy," Minnie continued. "It looks like—can you believe it?—it looks like an antenna!"

> Dialogue can show characters' personalities and give information about what is happening in the story.

Revising   Highlight all the places you used dialogue and check that you punctuated it correctly. Add dialogue if you find you need more.

W͜G Prentice Hall Writing and Grammar Connection: Chapter 5, Section 3

Extension Activities

Listening and Speaking   After reading "Jimmy Jet and His TV Set," prepare a **persuasive presentation,** commenting on the quality of current television programming. Suggest two ways in which it might be improved. Include the following:

- Your viewpoint and two strong reasons for the viewpoint
- An example to support each reason
- Two precise ideas for improvement

Organize your ideas clearly, expressing your main point at the beginning and again at the end of your presentation.

Research and Technology   Shel Silverstein pokes fun at TV watching. In a group, conduct research on the history of television. Write a brief **report** about when TV was invented and how much television use has increased since then.

Writing   Write a brief literary response in which you explain which of the three poems you liked best. In your response, discuss the mood or feeling of each poem, the subject, and the word choice.

Take It to the Net   www.phschool.com

Go online for an additional research activity using the Internet.

Prepare to Read

The Sidewalk Racer ◆ Haiku ◆ Limerick

 Take It to the Net

Visit www.phschool.com
for interactive activities
and instruction related to
these selections, including
- background
- graphic organizers
- literary elements
- reading strategies

Preview

Connecting to the Literature

In poetry, everyday actions, scenes, and words are revealed in a fresh new way. In "The Sidewalk Racer," Lillian Morrison captures the zest of skateboarding. Bashō's haiku brings one moment in nature into sharp focus. A limerick twists simple words into hilarious knots. As you read, think about times when you found a whole new way of looking at something.

Background

"The Sidewalk Racer" is a poem shaped like a skateboard. Scientists design vehicles such as airplanes, speedboats, and skateboards to be streamlined so they can cut through air or water smoothly. Objects can move faster when shaped with a narrow, rounded front and a body that widens as it curves back.

Literary Analysis

Special Forms of Poetry

Poets use **special forms of poetry** suited to the ideas, images, and feelings they want to express. Here are just a few of the many forms available to poets.

- In a **concrete poem**, words are arranged in a shape that reflects the subject of the poem.
- A **haiku** is a Japanese verse form with three lines. Line 1 has five syllables, line 2 has seven, and line 3 has five. Haiku often focus on nature.
- A **limerick** is a short, funny poem of five lines. The first, second, and fifth lines rhyme and have three beats, or stressed syllables. The third and fourth lines rhyme and have two strong beats.

Look carefully at the examples of concrete poem, haiku, and limerick in this section.

Comparing Literary Works

The different forms of poetry you will read in this section will vary in length and deal with very different topics. Compare and contrast the poems based on line length, the way sentences are written, and topic. Keep the following focus questions in mind:

1. **(a)** Which poem has the shortest lines? **(b)** What is the effect created by the short lines?
2. What are the similarities and differences in the ways the ideas of the poems are organized into sentences?

Reading Strategy

Using Your Senses

Poems speak to the mind, the heart, and also to the senses. You will get more from a poem if you **use your senses** to experience it. Look at its visual shape on the page. Also, imagine seeing, hearing, tasting, smelling, and touching what the words describe. As you read each poem, fill in a chart like this one to jot down words and images that appeal to the senses.

Sight
Hearing
Smell
Touch
Taste

Vocabulary Development

skimming (skim´ iŋ) *adj.* gliding; moving swiftly and lightly over a surface. (p. 719)

flue (floo) *n.* a tube for the passage of smoke, as in a chimney. (p. 720)

flee (flē) *v.* to run or escape from danger. (p. 720)

flaw (flô) *n.* break; crack. (p. 720)

The Sidewalk Racer

or
On the Skateboard

Lillian Morrison

Skimming
an asphalt sea
I swerve, I curve, I
sway; I speed to whirring
5   sound an inch above the
ground; I'm the sailor
and the sail, I'm the
driver and the wheel
I'm the one and only
10   single engine
human auto
mobile.

skimming (skim´ iŋ) *adj.*
gliding; moving swiftly
and lightly over a surface

◀ **Critical Viewing**
How does this
photograph compare
with the image of the
skateboarder described
in the poem?

Lillian Morrison

(b. 1917)
Lillian Morrison
spent nearly forty
years working in
the New York
Public Library.
She has written
several books of
poetry, including *The Sidewalk Racer and Other Poems of Sports and Motion.* Morrison says, "I love rhythms, the body movement implicit in poetry, explicit in sports." Many of her poems, such as "The Sidewalk Racer," celebrate the human body in motion.

Review and Assess

Thinking About the Selections

1. **Respond:** Do you, or would you, enjoy skateboarding? Why or why not?

2. **(a) Recall:** What images help show motion in "The Sidewalk Racer"? **(b) Interpret:** How can the speaker be both "the sailor / and the sail"? **(c) Draw Conclusions:** Which image most successfully conveys the sense of being on a skateboard? Explain your answer.

3. **(a) Infer:** How does the speaker feel about skateboarding? **(b) Support:** On what details do you base your answer? **(c) Extend:** What word would you use to describe the speaker's personality?

4. **Speculate:** What other sports or activities could the words from this poem describe? Explain.

Haiku
Bashō

An old silent pond . . .
A frog jumps into the pond,
 splash! Silence again.

Limerick
Anonymous

A flea and a fly in a <u>flue</u>
Were caught, so what could they do?
 Said the fly, "Let us <u>flee</u>."
 "Let us fly," said the flea.
5 So they flew through a <u>flaw</u> in the flue.

flue (flōō) *n.* a tube for the passage of smoke, as in a chimney

flee (flē) *v.* to run or escape from danger

flaw (flô) *n.* break; crack

Matsuo Bashō

(1644–1694)

Bashō was born into a land-owning Japanese family, but his father died when Bashō was only twelve. Bashō then entered the service of a local lord and began to write poetry. He was an important developer of the haiku form and one of its greatest masters. He wrote "An old silent pond" in the spring of 1686. The Japanese have erected a monument in the place where people believe he wrote it. Bashō revised the poem several times, changing it from the past to the present tense, for example. Bashō also wrote fascinating descriptions of his travels.

Review and Assess

Thinking About the Selections

1. **Respond:** Do you think the limerick is funny? Why or why not?
2. **(a) Recall:** Describe the setting of the haiku. **(b) Speculate:** Why might the poet have chosen present tense for the poem? **(c) Generalize:** Describe the overall feeling that the haiku portrays.
3. **(a) Recall:** What consonant sound is repeated in the limerick? **(b) Analyze:** How does this sound contribute to the humor in the poem?
4. **(a) Recall:** Which words with double meanings are used in the limerick? **(b) Interpret:** Explain what is funny about the double meanings.

Review and Assess

Literary Analysis

Special Forms of Poetry

1. Would "The Sidewalk Racer" be more or less effective if it were written in a different shape? Explain your answer.
2. What image is presented in each line of the haiku? Use a web like this one to record your answer.

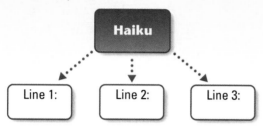

Haiku

Line 1:   Line 2:   Line 3:

3. Would it be possible to write a serious limerick? Explain.

Comparing Literary Works

4. **(a)** Which poem has the shortest lines? **(b)** What is the effect created by the short lines?
5. What are the similarities and differences in the ways the poems organize ideas into sentences?

Poem	Line Length	Sentences	Effect
"The Sidewalk Racer"	Short	All ideas in poem expressed in one long sentence	Captures the effect of continuous motion
"Haiku"			
"Limerick"			

Reading Strategy

Using Your Senses

6. Which two senses does the haiku appeal to?
7. Which three senses help you experience "The Sidewalk Racer"?
8. Which senses does the limerick engage?

Extending Understanding

9. **Extend:** Why do you think there are many different forms of poetry?

Quick Review

In a **concrete poem,** words take the shape of the poem's subject. A **haiku** is a three-line poem in which line 1 has five syllables, line 2 has seven, and line 3 has five. A **limerick** is a short, funny poem of five lines with a distinct pattern of rhyme and rhythm.
To review each form of poetry, see page 717.

Using your senses while reading a poem will help you imagine seeing, hearing, tasting, smelling, and touching what the words describe.

 Take It to the Net
www.phschool.com
Take the interactive self-test online to check your understanding of these selections.

Integrate Language Skills

Vocabulary Development Lesson

Concept Development: Homophones

Homophones are words that sound the same but have different meanings and that may be spelled differently. For example, *their*, *there*, and *they're* are homophones.

On your paper, choose the homophone that best completes each sentence.

1. Pursued by a (flee, flea), he had to (flea, flee) the room.
2. The fly and the flea (flue, flew) speedily.
3. Those two creatures went up the (flue, flew).
4. We went to (there, their) house.
5. Over (there, their) is the park.
6. (They're Their) my friends.
7. When you (see, sea) him on the skateboard, he sails so high you think he could fly over the (see, sea).

Fluency: Word Replacement

On your paper, replace each italicized word or phrase with a vocabulary word.

> A fly and a flea were *gliding* along when a frog jumped out of a pond to chase them. The fly said to the flea, "We don't have to *escape* from the *chimney-tube* to get away from this beast." Turning to the frog, the fly said calmly, "There's a *mistake* in your thinking. You're in the wrong poem!"

Spelling Strategy

The *oo* sound in words can be spelled in different ways. For each word, write a rhyming word that uses the same spelling for the *oo* sound.

1. flue
2. do
3. new
4. assume

Grammar Lesson

Irregular Comparisons

Depending on your opinion, you might say the first limerick is *good*, but the second one is *better*. A few modifiers, such as *good* and *bad*, are irregular. You must memorize their comparative and superlative forms.

Positive	Comparative	Superlative
good	better	best
bad	worse	worst
well	better	best
little	less	least
many	more	most

Practice On your paper, change the positive form of the modifier to the correct comparative or superlative form.

1. Sarita is (good) at skateboarding than Sasha is.
2. Of my three tries at skateboarding, the second was the (bad) one.
3. My stunts are (little) dramatic than hers.
4. She is the (good) skateboarder in our class.
5. She has practiced for (many) hours than I have.

Writing Application Write a series of sentences in which you use three irregular modifiers to compare the poems in this section.

 Prentice Hall Writing and Grammar Connection: Chapter 25, Section 1

Writing Lesson

Limerick

Now that you have read a limerick—a five-line poem with a comical twist at the end—try writing your own limerick.

Prewriting   Brainstorm for a list of possible topics, which might include silly animals or unusual people. Think of rhyming words to go with each one. Then, choose the funniest character as your topic.

Drafting   In the first line, introduce the character. Then, describe the situation, and in the last line or two, add a twist of humor. Follow the pattern of rhyme and rhythm that characterizes a limerick.

Model: Rhyme and Rhythm in a Limerick

Line 1: 3 beats	There was a young fellow named Hall,	a
Line 2: 3 beats	Who fell in the spring in the fall;	a
Line 3: 2 beats	'Twould have been a sad thing	b
Line 4: 2 beats	If he'd died in the spring	b
Line 5: 3 beats	But he didn't—he died in the fall.	a

> To write a limerick, follow the rhyme scheme (shown by letters), and provide the correct number of beats (stressed syllables) in each line.

Revising   Read your limerick aloud to check for the correct rhyme scheme and rhythm. Tap the beat as you go. Mark lines where there are too many or too few syllables or beats, or where the beats fall in the wrong place. Rewrite marked lines.

*W*G *Prentice Hall Writing and Grammar Connection: Chapter 5, Section 2*

Extension Activities

Listening and Speaking Prepare and deliver an **oral response** to one of the poems in this section. Include the following in your response.

- a clear, careful oral reading of the poem
- your interpretation of the poem's meaning
- examples and clear ideas to support your interpretation
- selected images that support your interpretation
- your opinion of how successful the poem is

After you deliver your response, ask your classmates for feedback.

Research and Technology Choose one of the poems to format. On the computer, develop a well-designed presentation of a poem. Since lines of poetry must break as they are originally written, set wide enough margins. Choose a font that will make the poem easy to read. Use tabs to set off indented lines, and set the title in larger type. Use spacing to enhance the appearance of the poem.

 **Take It to the Net**   www.phschool.com

Go online for an additional research activity using the Internet.

Prepare to Read

Wind and water and stone ◆ February Twilight ◆ The Fairies' Lullaby ◆ Cynthia in the Snow ◆ Parade

 Take It to the Net

Visit www.phschool.com for interactive activities and instruction related to these selections, including

- background
- graphic organizers
- literary elements
- reading strategies

Preview

Connecting to the Literature

The poets who wrote the next five poems stopped to listen to the world's music. They captured what they saw and heard and stored it up in words on the silent page. What words would you use to describe the music around you—a cough, the squeak of a chair, or the ticking of a clock?

Background

"Parade" describes a circus tradition more than 100 years old—the circus parade. In the days before television and radio, a parade down the main street of town was the best way to advertise the performances to come: clowns on stilts, cages of wild animals, and a giant musical instrument called the calliope.

Literary Analysis

Sound Devices

Poets use the **sound** of words—the musical quality of words—to express images and feelings in poetry. In addition to rhyme, poets use the following sound devices.

- **Onomatopoeia:** The use of words to imitate sounds, such as *clash*.
- **Alliteration:** The repetition of initial consonant sounds, as in the *wh* sound in "whitely whirs."
- **Repetition:** The use, more than once, of any element of language, such as a sound, word, phrase, or sentence. A **refrain** is a line or group of lines that is repeated at regular intervals.

Comparing Literary Works

Whether they are impressions of magic and mystery or natural beauty, the sounds created by the words in a poem form various impressions and impact the reader in different ways. Compare and contrast the use of sound in these poems by answering the following focus questions:

1. Which poem uses the greatest variety of sound devices?
2. Which poem makes the strongest impression through sound?

Reading Strategy

Reading According to Punctuation

In reading poetry, read according to **punctuation**—follow the set of instructions to stop or pause or read on. The punctuation groups words to reflect a specific meaning or sound. Notice in the example how changing the punctuation would change the meaning of the words, as well as the sound of how they are read.

As written:	With different punctuation:
It hushes	It hushes.
The loudness in the road.	The loudness in the road—
It flitter-twitters . . .	It flitter-twitters!

Punctuation Guide

STOP after
periods (.)
question marks (?)
exclamation marks (!)

PAUSE after
commas (,)
semicolons (;)
dashes (—)

Use the punctuation guide at right to review how you should use punctuation when reading.

Vocabulary Development

nigh (nī) *adv.* near (p. 728)

offense (ə fens´) *n.* harmful act (p. 728)

hence (hens) *adv.* away (p. 728)

gilded (gild´ id) *adj.* coated with a thin layer of gold (p. 730)

leisurely (lē´ zhər lē) *adv.* in an unhurried way (p. 730)

Wind and water and stone

Octavio Paz

The water hollowed the stone,
the wind dispersed the water,
the stone stopped the wind.
Water and wind and stone.

5 The wind sculpted the stone,
the stone is a cup of water,
the water runs off and is wind.
Stone and wind and water.

The wind sings in its turnings,
10 the water murmurs as it goes,
the motionless stone is quiet.
Wind and water and stone.

One is the other, and is neither:
among their empty names
15 they pass and disappear,
water and stone and wind.

Octavio Paz

(1914–1998)
Mexican poet Octavio Paz (ok täv´yó päs) traveled widely and used his experiences and memories in his poetry.

Although he lived in and visited many countries, he remained deeply committed to his Mexican heritage. In "Wind and water and stone," he captures the beauty of a Mexican landscape and uses it to suggest how a culture changes and yet stays the same. In 1990, Paz received the Nobel Prize for Literature.

February Twilight

Sara Teasdale

I stood beside a hill
  Smooth with new-laid snow,
A single star looked out
  From the cold evening glow.

5   There was no other creature
  That saw what I could see—
I stood and watched the evening star
  As long as it watched me.

Review and Assess

Thinking About the Selections

1. Which poem gives a view of nature that is more familiar to you?
2. **(a) Recall:** What does each natural element named in the title of "Wind and water and stone" do? **(b) Relate:** How do these activities make the elements related to one another? **(c) Interpret:** Explain the meaning of the last stanza.
3. **(a) Recall:** Where is the speaker of "February Twilight"? **(b) Speculate:** Why do you think the speaker is there? **(c) Infer:** Does the speaker enjoy the experience he or she describes?

Sara Teasdale

(1884–1933)
Teasdale had a very protected childhood in St. Louis, Missouri. Perhaps that's why her highly musical poems seem so delicate. Her book *Love Songs* (1917) received a Columbia Poetry Prize, now known as the Pulitzer Prize.

The Fairies' Lullaby
from A Midsummer Night's Dream

William Shakespeare

Fairies. You spotted snakes with double tongue,
    Thorny hedgehogs, be not seen.
    Newts and blindworms,[1] do no wrong,
    Come not near our fairy Queen.

5   **Chorus.** Philomel,[2] with melody
    Sing in our sweet lullaby;
    Lulla, lulla, lullaby, lulla, lulla, lullaby.
    Never harm,
    Nor spell, nor charm,
10   Come our lovely lady <u>nigh</u>.
    So, good night, with lullaby.

Fairies. Weaving spiders, come not here.
    <u>Hence</u>, you long-legged spinners, hence!
    Beetles black, approach not near.
15   Worm nor snail do no <u>offense</u>.

Chorus. Philomel, with melody
    Sing in our sweet lullaby;
    Lulla, lulla, lullaby, lulla, lulla, lullaby.
    Never harm,
20   Nor spell, nor charm,
    Come our lovely lady nigh.
    So, good night, with lullaby.

nigh (nī) *adv.* near

hence (hens) *adv.* away

offense (ə fens′) *n.* harmful act

William Shakespeare

(1564–1616)

William Shakespeare is the most highly regarded poet and playwright in the English language. He was born in the English town of Stratford-on-Avon and went to London when he was a young man. There, he began writing and acting in plays. Shakespeare wrote at least thirty-seven plays, as well as several long, narrative poems and more than one hundred and fifty shorter poems called sonnets.

"The Fairies' Lullaby" appears in *A Midsummer Night's Dream*, a comedy written around 1600.

---

1. newts (no͞ots) **and blindworms** *n.* newts are salamanders, animals that look like lizards but are related to frogs. Blindworms are legless lizards.
2. Philomel (fil′ ō mel′) *n.* nightingale.

Cynthia in the Snow

Gwendolyn Brooks

It SUSHES.
It hushes
The loudness in the road.
It flitter-twitters,
5 And laughs away from me.
It laughs a lovely whiteness,
And whitely whirs away,
To be
Some otherwhere,
10 Still white as milk or shirts.
So beautiful it hurts.

Review and Assess

Thinking About the Selections

1. **Respond:** Which poem presents a scene that is more appealing to you? Why?
2. **(a) Recall:** What do the fairies tell the snakes and hedgehogs to do? **(b) Infer:** What tone of voice do you think the fairies would use?
3. **(a) Recall:** Name all the creatures the fairies address. **(b) Classify:** What do all these creatures have in common?
4. **(a) Recall:** Whom does the chorus ask to join them? **(b) Contrast:** How is this creature different from the others? **(c) Infer:** Why do you think they ask this creature to sing with them?
5. **(a) Recall:** In "Cynthia in the Snow," what five things does the snow do? **(b) Analyze:** How is the snow something that the speaker cannot hold or keep?
6. **Assess:** What is unusual about the speaker's description of the snow?

Gwendolyn Brooks

(1917–2000)
Gwendolyn Brooks wrote many poems about her neighbors in Chicago, the city she lived in most of her life. She included "Cynthia in the Snow" in a book titled *Bronzeville Boys and Girls* (1956). Bronzeville refers to an African American community in Chicago.

When she was only seven, Brooks started writing poetry. As a teenager, her poetry was published in a well-known magazine. Her poems were also published in a local newspaper, the *Chicago Defender*. Brooks became a well-respected poet who received the Pulitzer Prize for *Annie Allen* (1949).

PARADE

RACHEL FIELD

This is the day the circus comes
With blare of brass, with beating drums,
And clashing cymbals, and with roar
Of wild beasts never heard before
5 Within town limits. Spick and span
Will shine each <u>gilded</u> cage and van;
Cockades at every horse's head
Will nod, and riders dressed in red
Or blue trot by. There will be floats
10 In shapes like dragons, thrones and boats,
And clowns on stilts; freaks big and small,
Till <u>leisurely</u> and last of all
Camels and elephants will pass
Beneath our elms, along our grass.

▲ **Critical Viewing**
To which senses do sights
like this one appeal?
[Analyze]

gilded (gild´ id) *adj.*
coated with a thin layer
of gold

leisurely (lē´ zhər lē) *adv.* in
an unhurried way

Review and Assess

Thinking About the Selections

1. **Respond:** Does "Parade" remind you of any procession that you have seen? Explain why or why not.
2. **(a) Recall:** What are four attractions you would see if you were watching the circus procession in "Parade"? **(b) Infer:** Which details suggest that the speaker is excited? **(c) Infer:** Is the speaker in "Parade" an adult or a child? Explain.
3. **(a) Recall:** Which details in "Parade" describe the town? **(b) Infer:** In what way is the procession an extraordinary event in ordinary surroundings?
4. **(a) Compare:** What contemporary event generates the excitement in a community that a circus parade once did? **(b) Contrast:** In what ways have communities changed to make holding a circus parade more difficult than it once was?

Rachel Field

(1894–1942)

Rachel Field could not read until she was ten. However, this late reader became a well-known writer of books for adults and children. She also became the first woman to receive the Newbery medal for children's literature. One reason for her success as a writer was her "camera memory," which stored up details such as those described in "Parade."

Review and Assess

Literary Analysis

Sound Devices

1. On a chart like this one, record examples of sound devices in the poems and categories indicated.

Onomatopoeia	Alliteration	Repetition
"Parade"	"Cynthia in the Snow"	"Wind and water and stone"
"Cynthia in the Snow"		"The Fairies' Lullaby"

2. Which poems could be listed under more than one column in the chart? Why?

Comparing Literary Works

3. Which poem uses the greatest variety of sound devices? Explain.
4. Which poem makes the strongest impression through sound? Explain.
5. Which poems have the most similar effects based on their use of sound? Explain and give examples.

Reading Strategy

Reading According to Punctuation

6. In what way do the commas in lines 1–3 of "The Fairies' Lullaby" help you understand the meaning?
7. Read aloud "Parade." How does the punctuation affect the pace of the poem?
8. Read aloud "Cynthia in the Snow." How does the punctuation affect the pace and meaning of this poem?

Extending Understanding

9. **Science Connection:** "The Fairies' Lullaby" mentions four classes of vertebrates—animals that have a backbone. Identify one example of a reptile, a mammal, a bird, and an amphibian in the poem. Which vertebrate class is missing from this list?

Quick Review

Onomatopoeia is the use of words to imitate sounds. **Alliteration** is the repetition of initial consonant sounds. **Repetition** is the use, more than once, of any element of language—a sound, word, phrase, or sentence. To review sound devices, see page 725.

Punctuation is the set of symbols that give specific directions to the reader, such as when to pause or stop.

 Take It to the Net
www.phschool.com
Take the interactive self-test online to check your understanding of these selections.

Integrate Language Skills

Vocabulary Development Lesson

Word Analysis: Suffix -ly

The suffix -ly often turns adjectives into adverbs that tell *when*, *how*, or *in what way* an action happens. Add -ly to each adjective. Use each new word in a sentence.

1. clever
2. stubborn
3. affectionate
4. sly

Spelling Strategy

When you spell a word that has the letters *i* and *e* next to each other, you can often follow this rule: *i* before *e* except after *c* (*ceiling*) and in words with a long *a* sound (*weigh*). Among the exceptions to the rule are *leisure*, *weird*, *seize*, *height*, and *neither*. Write the word that is spelled correctly in each pair.

1. freight, frieght
2. weird, wierd
3. wieght, weight
4. receive, recieve

Concept Development: Analogies

An **analogy** makes a comparison between two or more things that are similar in some ways but otherwise unalike.

Write the vocabulary word that best completes each analogy. To help you, review the vocabulary list on page 725.

1. *Solid* is to *soft* as *plain* is to ____?____.
2. *Anxiously* is to *uneasily* as *unhurriedly* is to ____?____.
3. *Enormous* is to *miniature* as *far* is to ____?____.
4. *Generosity* is to *kindness* as *insult* is to ____?____.
5. *Forward* is to *backward* as *come* is to ____?____.

Grammar Lesson

Commas and Semicolons

The clauses in a compound sentence can be connected in one of two ways—with a comma or with a semicolon. Use a **comma** to separate two independent clauses that are linked by a conjunction, such as *and*, *or*, *yet*, or *but*. Add the comma before the conjunction. Use a **semicolon** to link two independent clauses that are closely connected in meaning.

Examples:
Cynthia has seen snow before, yet she is dazzled by its whiteness.
Cynthia has never seen snow before; she is dazzled by its whiteness.

Practice On your paper, write each sentence with the correct punctuation.

1. The spiders weave webs but they do not draw near.
2. The nightingale sings and the fairy queen sleeps.
3. The snowstorm was blinding she could not see the road.
4. The band and floats are in view everyone starts to clap.
5. The band blares and the trumpets blast.

Writing Application On your paper, write two compound sentences, one connected by a comma and the other connected by a semicolon.

W͜G Prentice Hall Writing and Grammar Connection: Chapter 26, Sections 2 and 3

Writing Lesson

Response to a Poem

Write an essay in which you respond to one of the poems you just read. Choose a poem that you had a strong response to, either positive or negative.

Prewriting Jot down reasons why you respond to the poem as you do. For example, you may have a negative response because you think the images or comparisons are too far outside your experience. Identify specific examples that illustrate your point. Find examples that support your response.

Drafting As you draft, pause at the end of each paragraph. Circle the main point. If necessary, add supporting details that answer the question.

Model: Justify Interpretation with Examples and Textual Evidence

> Writer circles main point of paragraph.

Rachel Field's "Parade" is a masterful poem that brings a parade to life. You can hear the band and animals as you read. The poet uses onomatopoeic words such as *blare, beating, clashing,* and *roar.*

> Writer adds an example (in blue) as support.

Revising Reread your draft. Strengthen support for your points by adding specific quotations from the poem.

WG Prentice Hall Writing and Grammar Connection: Chapter 12, Section 4

Extension Activities

Listening and Speaking With a small group, **respond to an oral presentation** of a poem or character's speech from Shakespeare. Listen carefully to a recording of the poem or speech. Notice especially the sound devices used.

- Explain which sound devices are used and provide examples of each.
- Describe the effect created by the sound devices.

After working in your small groups, share your response with your class. **[Group Activity]**

Research and Technology A **résumé** is a summary that includes important information about a person's career and education. Prepare a résumé for your favorite poet! Go online to find examples of résumés and to collect important facts about the poet you choose, such as

- schools attended
- awards received.
- books and poems written

Turn these facts into a "résumé" for your poet.

 **Take It to the Net**   www.phschool.com

Go online for an additional research activity using the Internet.

READING INFORMATIONAL MATERIALS

Literary Backgrounds

About Literary Backgrounds

The background information given in the introduction to a text is an important type of informational material. It can provide information about the author, the setting, or even the history of the time when the text was written. Literary backgrounds include facts, statistics, and interesting or unusual information that enriches your understanding and appreciation by providing details that put the work in context. When reading literary backgrounds, pay attention to important details.

Reading Strategy

Taking Notes

Taking notes is one of the best ways to remember what you have read. Everyone takes notes differently. There are a variety of note-taking methods, including the following:

- Outlines
- Highlighted photocopies
- Summaries

When you use an outline, you should break down the information into the main points followed by the major and supporting details. The outline shown gives you the basic structure you can use to take notes on almost any topic.

Highlighting a photocopy is also an effective note-taking tool. After highlighting sentences that state main ideas, you can underline or circle supporting details.

Another way to take notes is to summarize. Summaries are an excellent tool to help you review the stories or information you have read. Summaries are created by stating in your own words the main ideas and major details of what you have read.

Outline
1. Sentence about first main idea
• Sentence or phrase about major detail
Words and phrases related to
supporting details
• Sentence or phrase about major detail
Words and phrases related to
supporting details
2. Sentence about second main idea
• Sentence or phrase about major detail
• Sentence or phrase about major detail

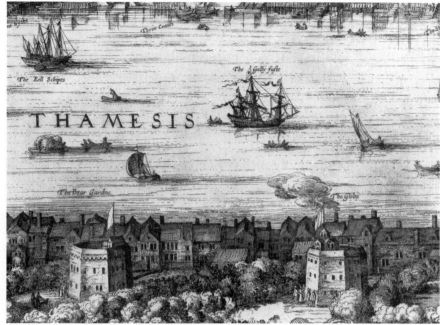
The Globe Theater is shown in the lower right corner of the picture.

Pictures can help you envision places and people.

Shakespeare's London

Anna Claibourne and Rebecca Treays

Shakespeare's poem "The Fairies' Lullaby" comes from his play
A Midsummer Night's Dream. *In Shakespeare's time, most
people believed that fairies and goblins lived among the humans.
The following background gives more information about
the times in which Shakespeare lived.*

"All the World's a Stage"

The world Shakespeare knew was full of danger,
excitement and change. Elizabethan London was
filthy, crowded, crime-ridden, hazardous, thrilling and
inspiring. The theatres, situated in the seedier parts of
town, were among the most popular places of entertainment, and the best plays to see were
Shakespeare's. . . .

By the early 1590s, Shakespeare had arrived in London, England's capital city. It was a thriving port with an expanding population. His first impressions would have been of teeming crowds, the squalor of poverty, and the extravagance of the wealthy. Although none of Shakespeare's plays is set wholly in London, the city must have had a great influence on him. He would have attended lectures on new scientific discoveries, discussed the latest trends in playwriting, listened to tales of foreign lands from merchants and enjoyed the lively night life.

This section of the background gives information on details that affect Shakespeare's writing.

"From Tower to Temple"

The City of London was said to stretch "from Tower to Temple" – from the Tower of London in the east, to the Temple Bar (the buildings where young men trained to be lawyers) about a mile away in the west. It was bordered to the north by a wall about two miles long, and to the south by the River Thames. Beyond these boundaries were London's suburbs, areas outside the strict control of the City authorities.

There was no shortage of entertainment in London. Apart from the attractions of inns and taverns, cockfighting and bear-baiting were popular sports, and many people enjoyed watching public beatings and executions.

The dangers of Shakespeare's time help you understand why audiences would appreciate a song or poem that criticizes bugs, snakes, and other "pest" animals such as "The Fairies' Lullaby."

Plague

Crowded conditions and poor sanitation made London an ideal breeding ground for plague, a fatal disease carried by fleas on rats. In 1592-4, 1603-4 and 1623 London was devastated by the disease. Over 100,000 people died.

Check Your Comprehension

1. What would Shakespeare's first impressions have been of London?
2. How would London have influenced Shakespeare?
3. What kinds of entertainment could be found in London?

Applying the Reading Strategy

Taking Notes

4. What three main ideas would you include in an **outline** of this background?
5. Which sentences would you **highlight** or **underline** on a photocopy?
6. Write a **summary** of the background.

Activity

Build a Background

"Shakespeare's London" provides information about London during the time when Shakespeare was writing his plays. It helps the reader get a better understanding of the time and setting of England before reading the works of Shakespeare. Choose a story that you have recently read. Find information about the author and the time that the story was written. Then, write a brief background for the story.

Comparing and Contrasting Informational Materials

Background and Biography

Both literary backgrounds and author biographies give factual information about the author of a piece of literature. A literary background provides information on all or some of the following:

- the time and place
- the customs
- the politics
- the problems

Information in an author biography is more focused on the author only. It will include dates, places, and details specific to the author. Compare and contrast background and biography by making a chart like the one shown. Use the author biography on page 728 and the background in this feature to complete the chart.

What information do you find in each source?

	Background	Biography
Shakespeare's occupations	playwright	writer and actor
Birth and death	None	
London	• England's capital • a port city • poor and rich	Shakespeare
Entertainment		

Prepare to Read

Simile: Willow and Ginkgo ◆ Fame Is a Bee ◆ April Rain Song

 Take It to the Net

Visit www.phschool.com
for interactive activities
and instruction related to
these selections, including
• background
• graphic organizers
• literary elements
• reading strategies

Preview

Connecting to the Literature

Poets may write about ordinary subjects—trees, bees, or rain—but they use imagination to surprise you into seeing things in a new way. As you read, ask yourself what words you would use to make an ordinary object unique.

Background

Willow trees and ginkgo trees are very different from each other. A willow tree has long, slender branches with long, narrow leaves. The ginkgo, on the other hand, is a large tree with fan-shaped leaves.

Literary Analysis

Figurative Language

Figurative language is language that uses comparisons to help you see or feel things in a new way.

- **Simile** uses *like* or *as* to make a direct comparison between unlike things, as in "The willow is like an etching."
- **Metaphor** compares unlike things by describing one as if it were the other, without using *like* or *as*. An example is "peace is a dove," which means "peace is like a dove."
- **Personification** gives human characteristics to a nonhuman subject as if it were human, as in "Let the rain kiss you."

As you read, find examples of figurative language, and record and analyze each in an organizer like the one shown.

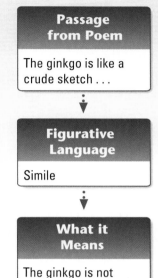

Comparing Literary Works

All of these poems use figurative language. The things being compared, however, are very different and give each poem a distinct mood or feeling. Compare and contrast the poems by answering the following focus questions:

1. Which two poems make comparisons that emphasize grace or beauty?
2. How does the comparison in "Fame Is a Bee" make its mood different from that of the other poems? What other characteristics set it apart from the other two poems?

Reading Strategy

Paraphrasing

Paraphrasing is restating an author's words in your own words. Paraphrasing difficult or confusing passages in a poem helps you clarify the meaning. Look at the following example from "The Fairies' Lullaby," and notice how it can be paraphrased.

Example: Beetles black, approach not near.
Worm nor snail do no offense.

Paraphrased: Don't come near, you black beetles; don't do any harm, you worm and snail.

As you read confusing or difficult lines, paraphrase them in your own words.

Vocabulary Development

soprano (sə pran′ ō) *n.* the highest singing voice of women, girls, or young boys (p. 740)

chorus (kôr′ əs) *n.* the part of a song sung by many voices at once (p. 740)

Simile: *Willow* *and* *Ginkgo*

Eve Merriam

The willow is like an etching,[1]
Fine-lined against the sky.
The ginkgo is like a crude sketch,
Hardly worthy to be signed.

5 The willow's music is like a <u>soprano</u>,
Delicate and thin.
The ginkgo's tune is like a <u>chorus</u>
With everyone joining in.

The willow is sleek as a velvet-nosed calf;
10 The ginkgo is leathery as an old bull.
The willow's branches are like silken thread;
The ginkgo's like stubby rough wool.

The willow is like a nymph[2] with streaming hair;
Wherever it grows, there is green and gold and fair.
15 The willow dips to the water,
Protected and precious, like the king's favorite daughter.

The ginkgo forces its way through gray concrete;
Like a city child, it grows up in the street.
Thrust against the metal sky,
20 Somehow it survives and even thrives.

My eyes feast upon the willow,
But my heart goes to the ginkgo.

---

1. etching (ech´ in) *n.* a print of a drawing or design made on metal, glass, or wood.
2. nymph (nimf) *n.* goddess of nature thought of as a beautiful maiden.

soprano (sə pran´ ō) *n.* the highest singing voice of women, girls, or young boys

chorus (kôr´ əs) *n.* the part of a song sung by many voices at once

Eve Merriam

(1916–1992)

Eve Merriam was bitten by the word bug early in life, falling in love with the music of language. Among her many books of poems is the award-winning *Family Circle*.

Fame Is a Bee

Emily Dickinson

Fame is a bee.
It has a song—
It has a sting—
Ah, too, it has a wing.

Reading Strategy
Paraphrasing State the third line in your own words.

Review and Assess

Thinking About the Selections

1. **Respond:** Which poem do you think makes the most powerful comparison? Why?
2. **(a) Recall:** To what three things are the willow and ginkgo compared in "Simile: Willow and Ginkgo"? **(b) Compare and Contrast:** Contrast the general impression you get of the willow and the ginkgo. **(c) Interpret:** Explain the meaning of the last two lines in the poem. **(d) Assess:** Based on the rest of the poem, is the last line surprising?
3. **(a) Recall:** What three things does Fame have in "Fame Is a Bee"? **(b) Interpret:** What is Fame's song? **(c) Assess:** Is a bee a good image to suggest fame? Explain.
4. **Take a Position:** Celebrities often have details of their private lives analyzed in the media. What is your stand on the following questions **(a)** At what point, if any, is publishing information on a celebrity's life an invasion of privacy? **(b)** What strategies, if any, should reporters be prohibited from using when gathering information?

Emily Dickinson

(1830–1886)

Only a handful of Dickinson's poems appeared in print during her lifetime. However, together with Walt Whitman, she is considered a founder of American poetry. Her poems are a kind of lifelong diary of her deepest guesses and wonderings. The daughter of a lawyer in Amherst, Massachusetts, Emily Dickinson lived quietly in her family's home all her life. All the while, she was writing and saving away over 1,700 of her brief lyrics.

April Rain Song

Langston Hughes

◄ **Critical Viewing**
Which line from the poem
would you use as a
caption for this picture?
[Connect]

Let the rain kiss you.
Let the rain beat upon your head with silver liquid drops.
Let the rain sing you a lullaby.

The rain makes still pools on the sidewalk.
5   The rain makes running pools in the gutter.
The rain plays a little sleep-song on our roof at night—

And I love the rain.

Langston Hughes

(1902–1967)
Langston Hughes
brought the
rhythms of
African American
music and speech
to American poetry.
Raised in the
Midwest, Hughes trav-
eled as a young man before
settling in New York City's
African American commu-
nity of Harlem. There he
felt the influence of musical
styles such as jazz and the
blues. Among his best-
known collections of poetry
are *The Weary Blues* (1926)
and *The Dream Keeper and
Other Poems* (1932).

Review and Assess
Thinking About the Selections

1. **Respond:** Do you share the speaker's feelings about rain? Why
   or why not?
2. **(a) Recall:** In "April Rain Song," what kind of songs does the
   rain sing? **(b) Infer:** What is revealed about the poet's
   thoughts about rain? **(c) Evaluate:** How would the poem be
   different if it were about a late autumn rain in a cold climate?
3. **(a) Recall:** What three things does the speaker tell the reader
   to let the rain do? **(b) Apply:** What would be the positive
   aspects of experiencing these three things?

Review and Assess

Literary Analysis

Figurative Language

1. **(a)** What is being compared in lines 5–8 in "Simile: Willow and Ginkgo"? **(b)** What is meant by this comparison?
2. What type of figurative language is used in "Fame Is a Bee"?
3. Explain the figurative language in line 2 of "April Rain Song."

Comparing Literary Works

4. **(a)** Using a chart like this one, compare the animal comparisons used in "Simile: Willow and Ginkgo" and "Fame Is a Bee." **(b)** Have both poems used effective comparisons? Explain.

"Simile: Willow and Ginkgo"	"Fame Is a Bee"
Line: Type of Figurative Language:	Line: Type of Figurative Language:

5. What types of figurative language does each poet use?
6. Which poem uses figurative language most effectively to help convey the meaning of the poem?

Reading Strategy

Paraphrasing

7. Restate lines 9–10 of "Simile: Willow and Ginkgo" in your own words. Record your answer in a graphic organizer like the one shown.

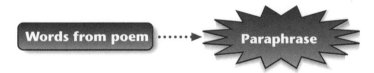

Words from poem ·····▶ Paraphrase

8. Restate "Fame Is a Bee" in your own words.
9. How would you paraphrase line 2 of "April Rain Song"?

Extending Understanding

10. **Cultural Connection:** Langston Hughes was part of an African American cultural movement in the 1920s called the Harlem Renaissance, which included aspiring writers, artists, and musicians. Find out what Hughes contributed to the movement.

Quick Review

Figurative language is language that uses comparisons to help you see or feel things in a new way. A **simile** uses *like* or *as* to compare two apparently unlike items.
A **metaphor** compares one thing to another without using *like* or *as*.
Personification gives human characteristics to a nonhuman subject. To review figurative language, see page 739.

Paraphrasing is restating an author's words in your own words.

 Take It to the Net
www.phschool.com
Take the interactive self-test online to check your understanding of these selections.

Integrate Language Skills

Vocabulary Development Lesson

Concept Development: Musical Words

"Simile: Willow and Ginkgo" uses words from the world of music. One of these is *soprano*, which means "the highest singing voice." Another music term is *chorus*, which means "a singing group."

Write these terms for the singers in a chorus in order. List the highest voice first and the lowest voice last. Use a dictionary to check definitions as needed.

bass   soprano

alto   tenor

Word Analysis: Special Terms

Explain your answer to each question.

1. Would you cast a woman or a man to sing a *soprano* part?
2. Would a *soloist*, a *chorus*, or a *songbird* sing the loudest?

Spelling Strategy

When a consonant precedes a final *o*, you usually add *es* to the end of the word to form the plural. Exceptions include all musical terms, such as *sopranos*. Correctly write the italicized words that are misspelled:

The *altoes* and *sopranoes* sang to the accompaniment of *banjoes*, *celloes*, and *pianos*.

Grammar Lesson

Colons

A **colon** (:) is a punctuation mark with a number of uses. The chart shown here explains how to use colons and gives examples.

Use Colons	Examples
After the salutation, or greeting, in a business letter	Dear Ms. Tang: Gentlemen:
To introduce an example or illustration	Simile: Willow and Ginkgo
After an independent clause to introduce a list of items. (Note: An independent clause that comes before a colon often includes *the following, as follows, these*, or *those*.)	The following trees grow in the park: maples, oaks and elms. These are my favorite kinds of weather: snowstorms and gentle rain.
To separate hours and minutes	3:15 P.M.
On warnings and labels	Warning: Thin ice

Practice Rewrite each item below, adding colons where necessary. If the item is correct as is, write *Correct*.

1. To whom it may concern
2. Bees do things such as the following sing, sting, and fly away.
3. Jed eats lunch at 12:30 P.M.
4. Dear Sir
5. Warning Keep Out of Reach of Children

Writing Application Write a three-sentence business letter to request information about ordering books from a publisher. Correctly use two colons in your letter.

WG Prentice Hall Writing and Grammar Connection: Chapter 26, Section 3

Writing Lesson

Description

The writers in this group describe their topics largely through figurative language. The effect of the figurative language is a fanciful picture that focuses on a mood or feeling. Choose one of the topics from the poems and write a practical description.

Prewriting Choose the poem and topic you will re-describe. Identify the main qualities on which the poet focuses. Then make a list of qualities you will describe in your more practical description. Some may be the same as those in the poem, with a different emphasis.

Model: Identifying Qualities

In poem	In my description
• like an etching	• brittle, thin, easily broken branches
• fine-lined	

Drafting Begin by identifying the topic you are describing. In the body of your description, develop the description with details that show the "reality" of your subject. Refer to the qualities mentioned in the poem and give your own description of these qualities.

Revising Add detail to your description by elaborating on statements with examples.

*W*_G *Prentice Hall Writing and Grammar Connection: Chapter 6, Section 2*

Extension Activities

Research and Technology Work with a small group to conduct research and prepare a **multimedia report** on trees. Prepare the following to accompany your report:

- Printouts, slides, photos, or drawings of trees
- Leaves mounted on posterboard
- Labeled diagram showing the parts of a tree

Present your report to the class. **[Group Activity]**

Writing Write a poem of your own about a topic from nature. Choose one of the poems in this group as a model of figurative language. For example, you might use personification in your poem as Langston Hughes does in his.

Listening and Speaking Prepare and give a **speech** to explain to classmates how advertisers and the media use famous people to promote products in print and on television. Identify persuasive techniques used in ads, such as presenting a celebrity's image to give false or misleading information on a product.

 **Take It to the Net** www.phschool.com

Go online for an additional research activity using the Internet.

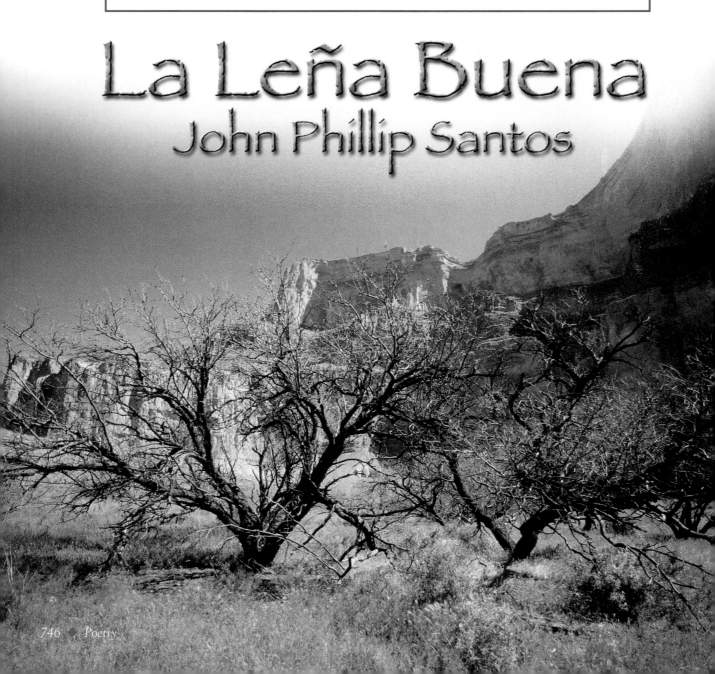

CONNECTIONS
Poetry and Prose
Comparisons from Nature

Both Eve Merriam and John Phillip Santos compare and contrast trees. Merriam writes in poetry, focusing mostly on the appearance of the trees. Santos writes in prose, writing that is not in verse. He considers the function as well as the appearance. As you read, notice that the writing is organized to emphasize the similarities and differences. Think about the point Santos is making when he compares and contrasts the qualities of the trees.

La Leña Buena
John Phillip Santos

Good wood is like a jewel, Tío Abrán, my great-grandfather Jacobo's twin brother, used to say. Huisache burns fast, in twisting yellow flames, engulfing the log in a cocoon of fire. It burns brightly, so it is sought after for Easter bonfires. But it does not burn hot, so it's poor wood for home fires. On a cold morning in the sierra, you can burn a whole tree by noon. Mesquite, and even better, cedar—these are noble, hard woods. They burn hot and long. Their smoke is fragrant. And if you know how to do it, they make exquisite charcoal.

"La leña buena es como una joya"

Good wood is like a jewel. And old Tío Abrán knew wood the way a jeweler knows stones, and in northern Coahuila, from Múzquiz to Rosita, his charcoal was highly regarded for its sweet, long-burning fire.

Abrán was one of the last of the Garcias to come north. Somewhere around 1920, he finally had to come across the border with his family. He was weary of the treacheries along the roads that had become a part of life in the sierra towns since the beginning of the revolution ten years earlier. Most of the land near town had been deforested and the only wood he could find around Palaú was huisache. To find any of the few pastures left with arbors of mesquite trees, he had to take the unpaved mountain road west from Múzquiz, along a route where many of the militantes had their camps. Out by the old Villa las Rusias, in a valley far off the road, there were mesquite trees in every direction as far as you could see. He made an arrangement with the owner of the villa to give him a cut from the sale of charcoal he made from the mesquite. But many times, the revolucionarios confiscated his day's load of wood, leaving him to return home, humiliated, with an empty wagon.

Aside from Tía Pepa and Tío Anacleto, who had returned to Mexico by then, he had been the last of the Garcias left in Mexico, and he had left reluctantly. On the day he arrived in San Antonio with his family, he had told his brother Abuelo Jacobo, "If there was still any mesquite that was easy to get to, we would've stayed."

◀ **Critical Viewing** What details from Santos's description can you identify in this picture of mesquite trees? [**Compare**]

John Phillip Santos

Author John Phillip Santos was the first Mexican American Rhodes Scholar. He has won numerous awards for his writing. His works include reviews, opinion pieces, and features for magazines and newspapers such as the *New York Times* and the *Los Angeles Times*. He has also written and produced more than forty television documentaries. Santos has received Emmy nominations for two of his films. He currently works for the Ford Foundation.

Connecting Poetry and Prose

1. Why does Santos think mesquite or cedar trees are "noble"?
2. What tree does Merriam use to represent noble qualities?
3. What role did trees play in Santos's family immigrating to the United States?
4. What are two reasons Santos and Merriam might have picked the trees they compared?
5. Explain how each author's comparisons and contrasts are developed either through poetry or prose.

Comparison-and-Contrast Articles

About Comparison-and-Contrast Articles

A comparison-and-contrast article uses factual details to analyze the similarities and differences between two or more persons, places, or things. For example, a newspaper might feature a comparison-and-contrast article about the policies of two presidential candidates or the talents of two sports teams. Comparison-and-contrast articles include

- a topic involving two or more things that are similar in some ways and different in other ways.
- an organized presentation of details that illustrate similarities and differences.

Reading Strategy

Identify Main Points

In a comparison-and-contrast article, the main points are the main similarities and differences that the writer examines. By identifying the writer's main points, you can more easily grasp the information he or she provides. For instance, in "More Than a Pinch: Two Salt Lakes," the first main idea is a similarity—the Dead Sea and the Great Salt Lake have similar percentages of salt.

As you identify each main point, decide whether it is a similarity or a difference. Record these main points on a Venn diagram.

Paragraph	Main Point
1	Both the Dead Sea and the Great Salt Lake contain uncommonly high percentages of salt.
2	
3	
4	
5	

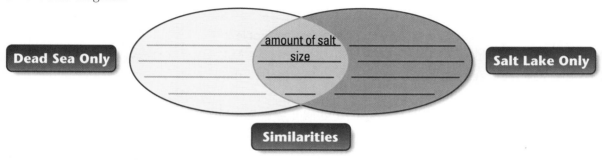

Dead Sea Only

amount of salt
size

Salt Lake Only

Similarities

More Than a Pinch: Two Salt Lakes

Douglas Armine

Holidaymakers on a first visit to the Dead Sea are invariably in for a surprise: those who enjoy swimming underwater in town pools at home have great difficulty in just staying below the surface. This is because the Dead Sea contains 25 to 30 percent salt, compared to 4 to 6 percent in ocean water. Similar readings have been recorded at Utah's Great Salt Lake in the United States, where it is equally difficult to sink.

The two salt lakes have very different histories. The spectacular trench occupied by the Dead Sea

> In the first paragraph, the writer introduces two things to be compared: the Dead Sea and the Great Salt Lake.

Travel Section

and the Jordan River, which flows into it, was created some 26 million years ago by an upheaval on the seabed at a time when the Mediterranean covered the Holy Land. At 1300 feet below sea level, the Dead Sea is the lowest body of water on Earth.

The Great Salt Lake is of more recent origin, being the remnant of the glacial Lake Bonneville which came into existence 18,000 to 25,000 years ago. Having shrunk, through evaporation, to one-twentieth of its original size, it now, like the Dead Sea, has no outlet. But rivers still feed the lake, bearing minerals dissolved from surrounding rocks. As the water evaporates, the minerals remain–66 million tons of them, including magnesium, lithium, boron, and potash.

> At 1300 feet below sea level, the Dead Sea is the lowest body of water on Earth.

Salt lakes are conventionally seen as barren, because they support no fish, but the Dead Sea is not completely dead: certain algae and bacteria are adapted to its salt-rich environment. The Great Salt Lake, too, has its single-cell organisms, most noticeably the algae that color the northern part of the lake pink. There are also larger life forms: brine shrimps and flies, whose larvae develop in the water. The shrimps are eaten by gulls, and shrimp eggs are harvested for sale as tropical fish food.

This business is miniscule compared to trade in the lake's great mineral wealth, such as the valuable potash used for fertilizer. The Dead Sea also yields potash, and the Israelis run health spas where tourists can coat themselves in rich, black mineral mud.

Here the writer identifies and explains a main difference—age.

A significant similarity is that the lakes have similar life forms.

Check Your Comprehension

1. Why do swimmers in the Dead Sea have difficulty staying below the surface?
2. How was the trench occupied by the Dead Sea created?
3. How and when did Lake Bonneville become the Great Salt Lake?
4. What are two life forms that exist in the Great Salt Lake?
5. In what ways do the lakes contribute to the mineral trade?

Applying the Reading Strategy

Identify Main Points

6. What are the main points about similarities between the Dead Sea and the Salt Lake?
7. Name two ways in which the lakes' histories are different.
8. Why do you think the writer organized the article point by point rather than writing all about one lake and then all about the other?

Activity

Travel Brochures

Choose two vacation spots that have something in common, such as two beaches or ski lodges. On the Internet or in the library, find a brochure for each destination. Read the brochures and then compare and contrast the two destinations in a chart like the one shown here. Make sure to focus on main points that would be helpful to someone planning a trip.

	Destination A:	Destination B:
Activities Available		
Where to Stay		
Cost		
Distance		

Contrasting Informational Materials

Comparison-and-Contrast Articles and Consumer Reports

Consumer reports offer information on different brands of a single product, such as cars or computers. Consumers often use these reports to compare and contrast products or services before deciding which one to purchase. Examine a consumer report and contrast it with the comparison-and-contrast article you read here. Answer the following questions:

1. What is the purpose of each document?
2. How does its purpose affect what information is included?
3. How does its purpose affect the way the information is organized and presented?

Exposition: Comparison-and-Contrast Essay

A **comparison-and-contrast essay** is a work in which a writer uses factual details to analyze similarities and differences between two or more persons, places, or things. In this workshop, you will choose a topic involving two related things and discuss each one by considering how it is like and unlike the other.

Assignment Criteria. Your comparison-and-contrast essay should have the following characteristics:

● A **thesis** or purpose that states how two or more things are alike and different

● An **organizational pattern** appropriate for a comparison-contrast composition

● Specific and **concrete details** to support each main point

See the rubric on page 755 for the criteria on which your comparison-and-contrast essay may be assessed.

Prewriting

Choose a topic. To write a comparison-and-contrast essay, choose two things that have noticeable similarities and differences. Choose two subjects for which there is a reason to make a comparison, such as

● to show benefits.

● to make a choice.

● to persuade.

Gather Details. Gather facts, descriptions, and examples that you can use to make comparisons and contrasts. Organize your details in a Venn diagram like the one shown here. In the two outside sections, write details about how each is different. In the overlapping middle section, write details about how the subjects are alike.

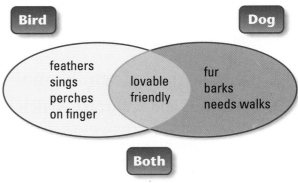

Different Kinds of Pets

Bird: feathers, sings, perches on finger

Both: lovable, friendly

Dog: fur, barks, needs walks

State a thesis. Review your notes and thoughts, and write one good sentence that states the purpose of your essay. Consider this a "working thesis" that may change.

> **Example:** Birds and dogs are very different animals, but both make lovable pets.

Student Model

Before you begin drafting your comparison-and-contrast essay, read this student model and review the characteristics of a successful comparison-and-contrast essay.

Elizabeth Leanard
Fort Wayne, Indiana

Which Instrument Is Better for You?

Have you ever wanted to play a musical instrument? Children all over the United States learn to play musical instruments in the band. Here is a look at the similarities and differences of two of the most popular instruments children play—trumpets and clarinets. Trumpets and clarinets are similar in cost and function, but they differ in their sound and the way they are played. Each of these facts will help in making a decision about which instrument to play.

The trumpet is part of the brass family, while the clarinet belongs to the woodwinds. However, although they are from different musical families, clarinets and trumpets are similar in that they both use the treble scale. This similarity also makes them quite different from other brass and woodwind instruments, which play only the bass scale. This means that they can share the same sheet music. It also means that clarinets and trumpets have the same pitch.

Another way clarinets and trumpets are similar is in their cost. The cost of a basic clarinet is around four hundred eighty-five dollars. An average trumpet costs a little more, usually around five hundred ninety-five dollars. If cost is an important factor, then clarinets are less costly.

Another difference is the way in which each instrument is played. With trumpets, you must change your lips to play each note. This is called buzzing. For clarinets, you simply change your key position. Trumpets are played this way because they have only three valves, while clarinets have seventeen buttons.

Clarinets and trumpets also sound quite different. Clarinets can sound serious or happy. For example, the low notes sound grim, while the higher notes sound happy and bubbly. Trumpets may sound military or festive, but they can also show a range of moods.

In conclusion, based on these facts, I would pick the clarinet over the trumpet. The clarinet is less costly, easier to play, and I like the way it sounds better than the trumpet. However, whichever instrument you choose, I'm sure you will enjoy it.

> The thesis states how a clarinet and a trumpet are similar and different.

> The essay is organized point by point—each point of similarity or difference is explained for each instrument.

> The writer states how the trumpet and clarinet are different and then follows with supporting details.

Drafting

Follow an organizational pattern. Develop a draft that organizes information logically so the reader clearly understands similarities and differences. Use the point-by-point method in which you discuss each aspect of your subject in turn.

- First, discuss one aspect of both subjects.
- Next, discuss another aspect of both subjects.

For example, first compare and contrast physical characteristics of birds and dogs; then compare and contrast the personalities of each.

Organizational Pattern for Compare/Contrast
Introduce the subjects you are comparing.
Identify a feature or aspect you are comparing and contrasting.
Provide specific details that support similarities and differences.
Identify another feature you are comparing and contrasting.
Provide specific details that support similarities and differences.
State your conclusion about your subjects.

State your thesis. Draft an introductory paragraph that clearly states the subject and the aspects of two things that you plan to compare and contrast.

Use specific details. The more specific and concrete your examples, the better your reader will understand your comparisons and contrasts. As you draft, review what you have written and add concrete details wherever possible.

Revising

Check organizational pattern and balance. Your essay should give equal space to each thing being compared. Reread your essay. Use one color to highlight the details about one of your subjects. Use another color to highlight details about the other subject. Check the balance.

1. If you find more highlight of one color than another, add more details to the subject with fewer highlights.

2. If you find large chunks of a color and places where colors alternate, revise to follow the point-by-point method of organization.

Check subject-verb agreement. Look over your draft for agreement between subjects and verbs. Check to see that sentences with singular subjects have the singular form of the verb. Check that plural subjects have plural verbs.

> **Example:** Both football and hockey *are* fast-paced.
> Hockey *is* played both indoors and outdoors.

Compare the model and nonmodel. Why is the model correct?

Nonmodel	Model
What do you notice about these sentences? It also means that clarinets and trumpets has the same pitch. The clarinet are less costly.	*Read these sentences aloud. What do you notice about the revisions that were made?* It also means that clarinets and trumpets have the same pitch. The clarinet is less costly.

Publishing and Presenting

Choose one of these ways to share your writing with classmates or a larger audience.

Make an audiotape. Practice reading your essay aloud several times. Then, record it using a tape recorder. Play the recording for your classmates. Have them evaluate its effectiveness.

Make a two-part poster. Turn your essay into a poster that compares and contrasts two subjects. Provide illustrations, photographs, or drawings. Use your main points to write captions that state similarities and differences. Display your poster in your classroom.

𝒲𝒢 *Prentice Hall Writing and Grammar Connection: Chapter 8*

Speaking Connection

To learn tips for engaging listeners during a reading or presentation, see the **Listening and Speaking Workshop,** Engaging Listeners, p. 756.

Rubric for Self-Assessment

Evaluate your comparison-and-contrast essay using the following criteria and rating scale:

Criteria	Rating Scale				
	Not very				Very
How clearly does the thesis state how two or more subjects are similar and different?	1	2	3	4	5
How consistent and appropriate is the organizational pattern?	1	2	3	4	5
How effectively are concrete details used to illustrate similarities and differences?	1	2	3	4	5
How balanced is the support of both subjects?	1	2	3	4	5

Listening and Speaking WORKSHOP

Engaging Listeners

Being a good speaker in an empty room is easy. Being an effective, persuasive speaker in front of an audience is a challenge. In delivering a persuasive presentation, you want to **engage the listener**—grab and hold the attention of the audience from your first words to your closing statement. If you can keep your listeners interested, you have a good chance of convincing them to accept your opinion or proposal. Use some of the strategies suggested here. Practice your speech, using the Self-Evaluation Form to assess your performance.

Engage the Audience

Identify your audience. If you want to convince your listeners, you must determine who they are—classmates, the whole student body, or teachers and students. Once you know your audience, you can tailor what you say to their interests. Lead off with a target statement that you know will hook them—a surprising fact, an amusing statement, or an opening that will touch them personally.

Address your audience. Speak directly to your audience by saying "you." For example, when you say, "You might be wondering why a gecko makes a better pet than a hamster," you make listeners feel that you are speaking directly to them.

Build Acceptance for Your Proposal

To convince your listeners to accept your idea or proposal, you need to use more than just persuasive language. You also need to win them over by using nonverbal techniques—your voice, posture, facial expressions, body movements, and gestures. Here are some tips.

Use body language. Your body language—posture, movement, and gestures—should send the same message that your words convey. When you deliver a powerful message, stand up straight and look confident.

Vary the pitch and pace of your voice. Speak in a strong voice so you appear sure of yourself. It will help to keep your audience engaged if you vary the pitch and volume of your voice to emphasize important points. Speak clearly so you will be understood.

> **Self-Evaluation Form for Engaging Listeners**
>
> **Self-Rating System:**
> + = Very well ✔ = Needs improvement
> – = Not very well
>
> **How well did I . . .**
> • identify my audience? _____
> • hook the audience in my introduction? _____
> • speak directly to my audience? _____
> • use appropriate gestures and movements? _____
> • vary my voice pitch and pace? _____

Activity: Presentation Choose a topic on which you have an opinion. For example, paper bags are better than plastic bags, or vice versa. Develop a proposal and deliver a presentation that is engaging and persuasive. Rehearse your persuasive presentation and evaluate your performance using the checklist shown here.

Assessment WORKSHOP

Identifying Appropriate Usage

The writing sections of some tests require you to read a passage and answer multiple-choice questions about appropriate usage. Use the following strategies to help you answer such questions:

Use the Correct Form of a Word Some test questions ask you to choose the correct part of speech, the appropriate form of an adjective or adverb, the correct pronoun, or the correct form of a negative. Use what you have learned about usage to answer these questions.

Test-Taking Strategy

After selecting an answer, read the sentence with your selected answer in place. If it does not seem correct in context, read the sentence with the other choices in place.

Sample Test Items

1. Get the teacher's _____ for your topic.
   - **A** approve
   - **B** approving
   - **C** approval
   - **D** approved

2. The first problem is _____ than the second.
   - **A** simple
   - **B** simply
   - **C** more simpler
   - **D** simpler

Answers and Explanations

1. A noun is needed, so **C** is correct.

2. Two things are compared, so the comparative form of the adjective is needed. **D** is correct.

Practice

Read the passage and choose the word or words that belong in each space.

Christopher Wolfe __(1)__ believe his eyes. Sticking out of a hillside __(2)__ dinosaur horns! Chris and his dad, who is a paleontologist, __(3)__ up the fossils and took __(4)__ to a museum. Imagine their excitement when they learned that the fossils were a ninety-million-year-old dinosaur!

1. **A** couldn't hardly
   - **B** could hardly
   - **C** could never hardly
   - **D** didn't hardly
2. **A** has been
   - **B** was
   - **C** were
   - **D** is
3. **A** dug
   - **B** dugged
   - **C** had digged
   - **D** digged
4. **A** it
   - **B** him
   - **C** themselves
   - **D** them

UNIT 10 The Oral Tradition

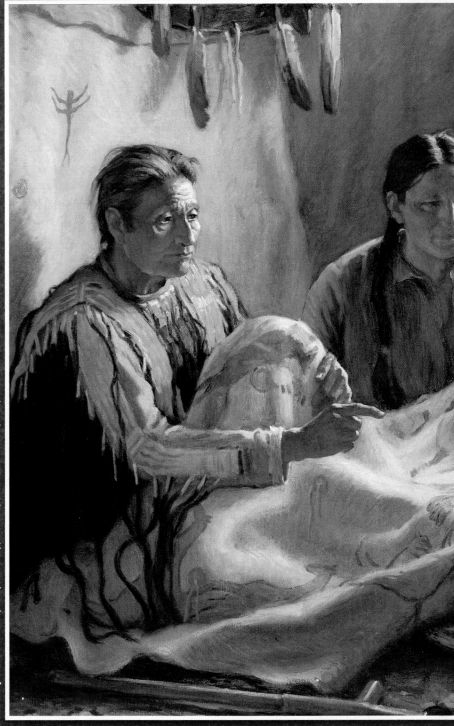

The Story of the War Robe, Joseph H. Sharp, 0137.37.321, ©Gilcrease Museum, Tulsa, Oklahoma

Exploring the Genre

Long before there were books, there were stories—stories that were passed along from one generation to the next by storytellers. These word-of-mouth tales make up what is called an oral tradition. The oral tradition includes folk tales, myths, and fables. An oral tradition is found in every culture. Stories are told to teach important lessons and to explain the way the world works, as well as to entertain.

◀ **Critical Viewing** Who do you think is telling the story of the war robe in this picture? Why? **[Analyze]**

Why Read Literature?

Whenever you read a folk tale, you have a purpose, or reason. You might read a folk tale for enjoyment or to learn something new about a different culture. Preview the following specific purposes you might choose for reading the works in this unit.

1 Read for the love of literature.

Lions roar for a variety of reasons, but the main reason is to announce "Here I am." That announcement can be heard by a lot of animals, because the sound of a lion's roar can be heard from five miles away! Read an entertaining tale in which a rabbit teaches a lion to tone down his roar, **"He Lion, Bruh Bear, and Bruh Rabbit,"** page 765.

The "heroes" of folk literature are usually—but not always—strong and powerful. Read a folk tale with two unlikely heroes, **"The Ant and the Dove,"** page 764.

2 Read to appreciate connections between past and present.

Comparatively speaking, a spider's "silk" is five times as strong as steel and twice as elastic as nylon. Scientists study spiders and their webs in hopes of learning how to make synthetic spider silk. Read the ancient Greek explanation of spiders and their silk in **"Arachne,"** page 784.

The idea of citizenship was first explained, not at a political gathering, but at a funeral. Read **"Pericles' Funeral Oration,"** page 796, the speech that historians believe contains the first definition of citizenship.

3 Read for information.

Dogs don't sweat. Instead, they regulate their body temperature by panting. Find out why this fact helped decide the outcome of the race to the South Pole when you read **"Race to the End of the Earth,"** page 799.

Elephants can make a sound that other elephants can hear miles away. You might think that such a sound would be loud enough to hurt your ears. In fact, the sound can't be heard by human ears at all. Learn how technology has helped scientists discover this and other interesting animal facts when you read **"High-Tech Windows to the Animal Kingdom,"** page 804.

 Take It to the Net

Visit the Web site for online instruction and activities related to each selection in this unit.

www.phschool.com

How to Read Literature

Strategies for Reading Folk Literature

Every culture in every country around the world has its own folk literature. Folk literature can take the form of a myth, a legend, a fairy tale, a folk tale, or a tall tale. In this unit, you will learn the following strategies that will help you understand and appreciate the different types of folk literature.

1. Understand oral tradition.

The oral tradition refers to songs, stories, and poems that were originally composed and passed along orally—in speech rather than in print. Every culture has an oral tradition: a body of literature passed down from ancient times. In contemporary times, writers have set down many of these traditional tales in writing. In this unit, you will read works from a variety of countries and cultures.

2. Predict.

Stories from the oral tradition are usually very predictable. Good behavior is rewarded; bad behavior has serious consequences. Predicting what will happen leads you to analyze characters' actions and think about the lesson being taught.

Clue: Arachne challenges the goddess Athene by saying: "If Athene herself were to come down and compete with me, she could do no better than I."

Prediction: Something bad will happen to Arachne, and she will be humbled.

Evidence: In other Greek myths, whenever a human is disrespectful to a god, he or she suffers negative consequences.

3. Recognize the storyteller's purpose.

As you read folk literature, look for the reason, or reasons, the storyteller is sharing the story. The notebook shows two purposes the tellers of "He Lion" may have had. As you read the tales in this unit, jot down notes like these about the storytellers' purposes.

As you read the selections in this unit, review the reading strategies and look at the notes in the side column. Use the suggestions to interact with the text.

– Purpose –

"He Lion, Bruh Bear, and Bruh Rabbit" is a folk tale that teaches and entertains.

- It teaches a lesson about humility.
- It entertains because its characters are funny.

Prepare to Read

The Ant and the Dove ◆ He Lion, Bruh Bear, and Bruh Rabbit ◆ Señor Coyote and the Tricked Trickster

Coyote at Sunset, detail from painting on wood, Maureen Mahoney-Barraclough

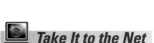 **Take It to the Net**

Visit www.phschool.com for interactive activities and instruction related to these selections, including

- background
- graphic organizers
- literary elements
- reading strategies

Preview

Connecting to the Literature

Like cartoons, "The Ant and the Dove" by Leo Tolstoy, "He Lion, Bruh Bear, and Bruh Rabbit" by Virginia Hamilton, and "Señor Coyote and the Tricked Trickster" by I. G. Edmonds use animal characters that seem like people. How do these animals and their problems remind you of real people and problems?

Background

"Señor Coyote and the Tricked Trickster" is, as the title suggests, a trickster tale. Many cultures contain trickster tales—folk stories about a clever character who outwits others through sly thinking and tricky maneuvering. Often, tricksters rely on cleverness to outsmart bigger, more powerful opponents.

Literary Analysis

Folk Tales

Folk tales are stories shared by a people—the "folk." The tales usually do not originate from a single author; they are passed down from generation to generation. Often, the details of a folk tale reveal elements of the culture from which the folk tale comes. A folk tale may contain cultural details such as

- **dialect:** The characters' speech reflects the way a language is spoken in a particular region or by a particular group.
- **values:** The actions and abilities of the characters show what actions and abilities the culture admired in people.
- **geography:** The landscape, animals, and climate are ones that would have been familiar to the storytellers.

Today, many authors write down folk tales for all to enjoy. Besides entertaining, folk tales may teach a lesson or explain something in nature.

Comparing Literary Works

Folk tales often teach a lesson related to the qualities, abilities, and behavior that the people of a culture value or admire. The chart shows three general topics or subjects about which all three folk tales have something to say. Copy the chart, and complete it by explaining the specific lesson each tale teaches about one or all of the topics. Compare and contrast the lessons.

Reading Strategy

Recognizing the Storyteller's Purpose

You will better understand a folk tale if you recognize the **storyteller's purpose** or reason for telling the story. Many folk tales have a combination of purposes. For example, the purpose of these folk tales is to teach lessons, but they also entertain while they teach. As you read, ask yourself the following focus questions.

1. What part of each story teaches a lesson?
2. Which parts entertain?

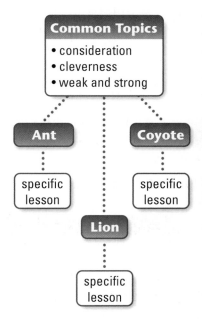

Vocabulary Development

startled (stärt′ əld) *adj.* surprised (p. 764)

lair (lār) *n.* cave or den (p. 767)

cordial (kôr′ jəl) *adj.* warm and friendly (p. 767)

ungrateful (un grāt′ fəl) *adj.* not thankful (p. 771)

reproachfully (ri prōch′ fəl lē) *adv.* with blame (p. 771)

indignantly (in dig′ nənt lē) *adv.* angrily (p. 772)

The Ant and the Dove

Russian Folk Tale

Leo Tolstoy

A thirsty ant went to the stream to drink. Suddenly it got caught in a whirlpool and was almost carried away.

At that moment a dove was passing by with a twig in its beak. The dove dropped the twig for the tiny insect to grab hold of. So it was that the ant was saved.

A few days later a hunter was about to catch the dove in his net. When the ant saw what was happening, it walked right up to the man and bit him on the foot. <u>Startled</u>, the man dropped the net. And the dove, thinking that you never can tell how or when a kindness may be repaid, flew away.

startled (stärt´ əld) *adj.* surprised

Leo Tolstoy

(1828–1910)

Leo Tolstoy was born into a wealthy family, and he inherited his family estate at the age of nineteen. Yet, by the time he was fifty and the author of some of the most famous novels in the world, *Anna Karenina* and *War and Peace,* he began to reject his life of luxury. He surrendered the rights to many of his works and gave his property to his family. This world-famous writer died alone in an obscure train station in Russia.

Review and Assess
Thinking About the Selection
1. **Respond:** What other story or stories does this tale remind you of? Explain.
2. **(a) Recall:** What does the dove do for the ant? **(b) Speculate:** Why does the dove help the ant, even when she does not think the ant can ever repay her?
3. **(a) Recall:** How does the ant repay the dove? **(b) Interpret:** What does the dove mean when she thinks, "you can never tell how or when a kindness may be repaid"? **(c) Draw Conclusions:** What lesson does this story appear to teach?

He Lion, Bruh Bear, and Bruh Rabbit

African American Folk Tale

Virginia Hamilton

◀ **Critical Viewing** Why do you think a lion might be used to represent someone who has a high opinion of himself or herself? **[Draw Conclusions]**

Say that he Lion would get up each and every mornin. Stretch and walk around. He'd roar, ME AND MYSELF, ME AND MYSELF, like that. Scare all the little animals so they were afraid to come outside in the sunshine. Afraid to go huntin or fishin or whatever the little animals wanted to do.

"What we gone do about it?" they asked one another. Squirrel leapin from branch to branch, just scared. Possum[1] playin dead, couldn't hardly move him.

He Lion just went on, stickin out his chest and roarin, "ME AND MYSELF, ME AND MYSELF."

✔ **Reading Check**

In what way does the lion frighten the other animals?

---

1. Possum (päs´ əm) colloquial for "opossum," a small tree-dwelling mammal that pretends to be dead when it is trapped.
2. Bruh (bru) early African American dialect for "brother."

The little animals held a sit-down talk, and one by one and two by two and all by all, they decide to go see Bruh[2] Bear and Bruh Rabbit. For they know that Bruh Bear been around. And Bruh Rabbit say he has, too.

So they went to Bruh Bear and Bruh Rabbit. Said, "We have some trouble. Old he Lion, him scarin everybody, roarin every mornin and all day, ME AND MYSELF, ME AND MYSELF, like that.

"Why he Lion want to do that?" Bruh Bear said.

"Is that all he Lion have to say?" Bruh Rabbit asked.

"We don't know why, but that's all he Lion can tell us and we didn't ask him to tell us that," said the little animals. "And him scarin the children with it. And we wish him to stop it."

"Well, I'll go see him, talk to him. I've known he Lion a long kind of time," Bruh Bear said.

"I'll go with you," said Bruh Rabbit. "I've known he Lion most long as you."

That bear and that rabbit went off through the forest. They kept hearin somethin. Mumble, mumble. Couldn't make it out. They got farther in the forest. They heard it plain now. "ME AND MYSELF. ME AND MYSELF."

▶ **Critical Viewing** How well does this bear fit the image of Bruh Bear? [**Assess**]

"Well, well, well," said Bruh Bear. He wasn't scared. He'd been around the whole forest, seen a lot.

"My, my, my," said Bruh Rabbit. He'd seen enough to know not to be afraid of an old he lion. Now old he lions could be dangerous, but you had to know how to handle them.

The bear and the rabbit climbed up and up the cliff where he Lion had his <u>lair</u>. They found him. Kept their distance. He watchin them and they watchin him. Everybody actin <u>cordial</u>.

"Hear tell you are scarin everybody, all the little animals, with your roarin all the time," Bruh Rabbit said.

"I roars when I pleases," he Lion said.

"Well, might could you leave off the noise first thing in the mornin, so the little animals can get what they want to eat and drink?" asked Bruh Bear.

"Listen," said he Lion, and then he roared: "ME AND MYSELF. ME AND MYSELF. Nobody tell me what not to do," he said. "I'm the king of the forest, *me and myself.*"

"Better had let me tell you something," Bruh Rabbit said, "for I've seen Man, and I know him the real king of the forest."

He Lion was quiet awhile. He looked straight through that scrawny lil Rabbit like he was nothin atall. He looked at Bruh Bear and figured he'd talk to him.

"You, Bear, you been around," he Lion said.

"That's true," said old Bruh Bear. "I been about everywhere. I've been around the whole forest."

"Then you must know something," he Lion said.

"I know lots," said Bruh Bear, slow and quiet-like.

"Tell me what you know about Man," he Lion said. "He think him the king of the forest?"

"Well, now, I'll tell you," said Bruh Bear, "I been around, but I haven't ever come across Man that I know of. Couldn't tell you nothin about him."

So he Lion had to turn back to Bruh Rabbit. He didn't want to but he had to. "So what?" he said to that lil scrawny hare.

"Well, you got to come down from there if you want to see Man," Bruh Rabbit said. "Come down from there and I'll show you him."

lair (lār) *n.* cave or den

cordial (kôr´ jəl) *adj.* warm and friendly

✔**Reading Check**

What does Bruh Rabbit tell the Lion?

► **Critical Viewing**
In what ways does Bruh Rabbit represent opposite qualities from Bruh Bear's?
[Compare and Contrast]

He Lion thought a minute, an hour, and a whole day. Then, the next day, he came on down.

He roared just once, "ME AND MYSELF. ME AND MYSELF. Now," he said, "come show me Man."

So they set out. He Lion, Bruh Bear, and Bruh Rabbit. They go along and they go along, rangin the forest. Pretty soon, they come to a clearin. And playin in it is a little fellow about nine years old.

"Is that there Man?" asked he Lion.

"Why no, that one is called Will Be, but it sure is not Man," said Bruh Rabbit.

So they went along and they went along. Pretty soon, they come upon a shade tree. And sleepin under it is an old, olden fellow, about ninety years olden.

"There must lie Man," spoke he Lion. "I knew him wasn't gone be much."

"That's not Man," said Bruh Rabbit. "That fellow is Was Once. You'll know it when you see Man."

So they went on along. He Lion is gettin tired of strollin. So he roars, "ME AND MYSELF. ME AND MYSELF." Upsets Bear so that Bear doubles over and runs and climbs a tree.

"Come down from there," Bruh Rabbit tellin him. So after a while Bear comes down. He keepin his distance from he Lion, anyhow. And they set out some more. Goin along quiet and slow.

In a little while they come to a road. And comin on way down the road, Bruh Rabbit sees Man comin. Man about twenty-one years old. Big and strong, with a big gun over his shoulder.

"There!" Bruh Rabbit says. "See there, he Lion? There's Man. You better go meet him."

"I will," says he Lion. And he sticks out his chest and he roars, "ME AND MYSELF. ME AND MYSELF." All the way to Man he's roarin proud, "ME AND MYSELF. ME AND MYSELF!"

"Come on, Bruh Bear, let's go!" Bruh Rabbit says.

"What for?" Bruh Bear wants to know.

"You better come on!" And Bruh Rabbit takes ahold of Bruh Bear and half drags him to a thicket. And there he makin the Bear hide with him.

For here comes Man. He sees old he Lion real good now. He drops to one knee and he takes aim with his big gun.

Old he Lion is roarin his head off: "ME AND MYSELF. ME AND MYSELF!"

The big gun goes off: PA-LOOOM!

He Lion falls back hard on his tail.

The gun goes off again. PA-LOOOM!

Literary Analysis
Folk Tales What quality or qualities does Bruh Rabbit represent?

Literary Analysis
Folk Tales What details give this narrative the quality of being told aloud?

He Lion is flyin through the air. He lands in the thicket.

"Well, did you see Man?" asked Bruh Bear.

"I seen him," said he Lion. "Man spoken to me unkind, and got a great long stick him keepin on his shoulder. Then Man taken that stick down and him speakin real mean. Thunderin at me and lightnin comin from that stick, awful bad. Made me sick. I had to turn around. And Man pointin that stick again and thunderin at me some more. So I come in here, cause it seem like him throwed some stickers at me each time it thunder, too."

"So you've met Man, and you know zactly what that kind of him is," says Bruh Rabbit.

"I surely do know that," he Lion said back.

Awhile after he Lion met Man, things were some better in the forest. Bruh Bear knew what Man looked like so he could keep out of his way. That rabbit always did know to keep out of Man's way. The little animals could go out in the mornin because he Lion was more peaceable. He didn't walk around roarin at the top of his voice all the time. And when he Lion did lift that voice of his, it was like, "Me and Myself and Man. Me and Myself and Man." Like that.

Wasn't too loud at all.

Reading Strategy
Recognizing the Storyteller's Purpose
What is the purpose of showing that he Lion becomes humble?

Review and Assess

Thinking About the Selection

1. **Respond:** Which character in "He Lion, Bruh Bear, and Bruh Rabbit" do you think is most amusing? Why?

2. **(a) Recall:** In "He Lion, Bruh Bear, and Bruh Rabbit," why do the little animals seek help from Bruh Bear and Bruh Rabbit? **(b) Infer:** What do Bruh Bear and Bruh Rabbit think of he Lion? **(c) Analyze:** Why isn't Bruh Rabbit scared of he Lion?

3. **(a) Recall:** Why does he Lion want to see Man, and what happens when he sees him? **(b) Compare and Contrast:** Describe he Lion before and after he meets Man. **(c) Analyze Cause and Effect:** What causes the change in he Lion's attitude?

4. **(a) Draw Conclusions:** Based on he Lion's behavior, what lesson does this story appear to teach? **(b) Evaluate:** Is the lesson one that applies in modern life? Explain.

5. **Take a Position:** What responsibility do individuals have to other members of a community?

Virginia Hamilton

(1936–2002)

Virginia Hamilton came from Yellow Springs, Ohio, a town famous as a stop on the Underground Railroad before the Civil War. Hamilton was lucky to come from a family of storytellers who passed along tales of their family experience and heritage. Although she focused her writing mainly on African American subjects and characters, the themes in her books are meaningful to all people.

Señor Coyote and the Tricked Trickster

Mexican Folk Tale   **I.G. Edmonds**

Coyotes, detail from painting on wood, Maureen Mahoney-Barraclough

▲ **Critical Viewing** What qualities does folk art share with folk tales? **[Connect]**

One day long ago in Mexico's land of sand and giant cactus *Señor* Coyote and Señor Mouse had a quarrel.

None now alive can remember why, but recalling what spirited *caballeros*[1] these two were, I suspect that it was some small thing that meant little.

Be that as it may, these two took their quarrels seriously and for a long time would not speak to each other.

Then one day Mouse found Señor Coyote caught in a trap. He howled and twisted and fought, but he could not get out. He had just about given up when he saw Señor Mouse grinning at him.

"Mouse! *Mi viejo amigo*◆—my old friend!" he cried. "Please gnaw this leather strap in two and get me out of this trap."

---

1. *caballeros* (kä bä yer´ ôs) Spanish for "gentlemen."

"But we are no longer friends," Mouse said. "We have quarreled, remember?"

"Nonsense!" Señor Coyote cried. "Why I love you better than I do Rattlesnake, Owl, or anybody in the desert. You must gnaw me loose. And please hurry for if the *peon*[2] catches me I will wind up a fur rug on his wife's kitchen floor."

Mouse remembered how mean Señor Coyote had been to him. He was always playing tricks on Mouse and his friends. They were very funny to Señor Coyote for he was a great trickster, but often they hurt little Mouse.

"I'd like to gnaw you free," he said, "but I am old and my teeth tire easily."

"Really, Señor Mouse, you are <u>ungrateful</u>," said Señor Coyote <u>reproachfully</u>. "Remember all the nice things I have done for you."

"What were they?"

"Why—" Coyote began and stopped. He was unable to think of a single thing. There was a good reason for this. He had done nothing for Mouse but trick him.

But Señor Coyote is a sly fellow. He said quickly, "Oh, why remind you of them. You remember them all."

"I fear my memory of yesterday is too dim," Mouse said, "but I could remember very well what you could do for me tomorrow."

"Tomorrow?" Coyote asked.

"Yes, tomorrow. If I gnaw away the leather rope holding you in the trap, what will you do for me tomorrow, and the day after tomorrow and the day after the day after tomorrow and the day—"

"Stop!" Señor Coyote cried. "How long is this going on?"

"A life is worth a life. If I save your life, you should work for me for a lifetime. That is the only fair thing to do."

"But everyone would laugh at a big, brave, smart fellow like me working as a slave for a mere mouse!" Señor Coyote cried.

"Is that worse than feeling sad for you because your hide is a rug in the peon's kitchen?"

Señor Coyote groaned and cried and argued, but finally agreed when he saw that Mouse would not help him otherwise.

"Very well," he said tearfully, "I agree to work for you until either of us dies or until I have a chance to get even by saving your life."

Mouse said with a sly grin, "That is very fine, but I remember what a great trickster you are. So you must also promise that as

Literature **in context** Vocabulary Connection

♦ **Spanish Words and Expressions**

Señor Coyote uses the expression *mi viejo amigo* [mē vē ā′ hō ä mē′ gō], which means *my old friend*. The word *amigo* has come to be commonly understood and used by many speakers of English. Other commonly used Spanish words and expressions include

• *Señor* Mr. (p. 770)

• *Señora* Mrs.

• *amigo* friend (p. 770)

• *mamacita* "mommy" (p. 773)

• *adiós* goodbye

• *hasta la vista* until we meet again

• *mañana* tomorrow

ungrateful (un grāt′ fəl) *adj.* not thankful

reproachfully (ri prōch′ fəl lē) *adv.* with blame

✔**Reading Check**

What does Señor Coyote want Señor Mouse to do?

---

2. *peon* (pē′ ən) Spanish for "worker"—an unskilled laborer.

soon as I free you that you will not jump on me, threaten to kill me, and then save my life by letting me go!"

"Why, how can you suggest such a thing!" Coyote cried <u>indignantly</u>. And then to himself he added, "This mouse is getting *too* smart!"

"Very well, promise," Mouse said.

"But I am not made for work," Señor Coyote said tearfully. "I live by being sly."

"Then be sly and get out of the trap yourself," Mouse retorted.

"Very well," Señor Coyote said sadly. "I will work for you until I can pay back the debt of my life."

And so Mouse gnawed the leather strap in two and Coyote was saved. Then for many days thereafter Señor Coyote worked for Mouse. Mouse was very proud to have the famous Señor Coyote for a servant. Señor Coyote was greatly embarrassed since he did not like being a servant and disliked working even more.

There was nothing he could do since he had given his promise. He worked all day and dreamed all night of how he could trick his way out of his troubles. He could think of nothing.

Then one day Baby Mouse came running to him. "My father has been caught by Señor Snake!" he cried. "Please come and save him."

"Hooray!" cried Coyote. "If I save him, I will be released from my promise to work for him."

He went out to the desert rocks and found Señor Rattlesnake with his coils around Señor Mouse.

"Please let him go and I will catch you two more mice," Coyote said.

indignantly (in dig′ nənt lē) *adv.* angrily

Literary Analysis
Folk Tales What landscape is familiar to the original tellers of this folk tale?

▼ **Critical Viewing**
What do you think Mouse is telling Owl about Coyote? **[Speculate]**

Mouse and Owl, detail from painting on wood, Maureen Mahoney-Barraclough

"My wise old mother used to tell me that a bird in the hand is worth two in the bush," Snake replied. "By the same reasoning, one mouse in Snake's stomach is worth two in Coyote's mind."

"Well, I tried, Mouse," Coyote said. "I'm sorry you must be eaten."

"But you must save me, then you will be free from your promise to me," Mouse said.

"If you're eaten, I'll be free anyway," Coyote said.

"Then everyone will say that Coyote was not smart enough to trick Snake," Mouse said quickly. "And I think they will be right. It makes me very sad for I always thought Señor Coyote the greatest trickster in the world."

This made Coyote's face turn red. He was very proud that everyone thought him so clever. Now he just *had* to save Mouse.

So he said to Snake, "How did you catch Mouse anyway?"

"A rock rolled on top of him and he was trapped," Mouse said. "He asked me to help him roll it off. When I did he jumped on me before I could run away."

"That is not true," Snake said. "How could a little mouse have the strength to roll away a big rock. There is the rock. Now you tell me if you think Mouse could roll it."

It was a very big rock and Coyote admitted that Mouse could not possibly have budged it.

"But it is like the story *Mamacita* tells her children at bedtime," Mouse said quickly. "Once there was a poor burro who had a load of hay just as large as he could carry. His master added just one more straw and the poor burro fell in the dirt. Snake did not have quite enough strength to push the rock off himself. I came along and was like that last straw on the burro's back and together we rolled the rock away."

Literary Analysis
Folk Tales What lesson is taught by the folk tale that Mouse tells?

"Maybe that is true," Snake said, "but by Mouse's own words, he did only a very little of the work. So I owe him only a very little thanks. That is not enough to keep me from eating him."

"Hmmm," said Coyote. "Now you understand, Snake, that I do not care what happens myself. If Mouse is eaten, I will be free of my bargain anyway. I am only thinking of your own welfare, Snake."

"Thank you," said Señor Rattlesnake, "but I do enough thinking about my welfare for both of us. I don't need your thoughts."

"Nevertheless," Coyote insisted, "everyone is going to say that you ate Mouse after he was kind enough to help you."

"I don't care," Snake said. "Nobody says anything good of me anyway."

"Well," said Coyote, "I'll tell you what we should do. We should put everything back as it was. Then I will see for myself if Mouse was as much help as he said he was or as little as you claim. Then I can tell everyone that you were right, Snake."

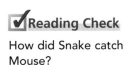

Reading Check

How did Snake catch Mouse?

"Very well," said Señor Snake. "I was lying like this and the rock was on me—"

"Like this?" Coyote said, quickly rolling the rock across Snake's body.

"Ouch!" said Snake. "That is right."

"Can you get out?" Coyote asked.

"No," said Snake.

"Then turn Mouse loose and let him push," said Coyote.

This Snake did, but before Mouse could push, Coyote said, "But on second thought if Mouse pushes, you would then grab him again and we'd be back arguing. Since you are both as you were before the argument started, let us leave it at that and all be friends again!"

Then Coyote turned to Mouse. "So, my friend, I have now saved your life. We are now even and my debt to you is paid."

"But mine is such a *little* life," Mouse protested. "And yours is so much *larger*. I don't think they balance. You should still pay me part."

"This is ridiculous!" Coyote cried. "I—"

"Wait!" Snake put in hopefully. "Let me settle the quarrel. Now you roll the rock away. I'll take Mouse in my coils just the way we were when Coyote came up. We'll be then in a position to decide if—"

"Thank you," said Mouse. "It isn't necessary to trouble everyone again. Señor Coyote, we are even."

Reading Strategy
Recognizing the Storyteller's Purpose In what ways is this folk tale entertaining?

Review and Assess

Thinking About the Selection

1. **Respond:** Which character do you think is the most clever? Why?
2. **(a) Recall:** Describe the relationship between Coyote and Mouse at the time the story begins. **(b) Infer:** Why is Mouse reluctant to help the trapped Coyote?
3. **(a) Recall:** Why does Coyote work as Mouse's servant? **(b) Interpret:** What does Mouse mean when he tells Coyote "a life is worth a life"?
4. **(a) Recall:** For what reason does Mouse need Coyote's help? **(b) Draw Conclusions:** To which of Coyote's characteristics does Mouse appeal in persuading Coyote to save him?
5. **(a) Distinguish:** In this situation, who is tricked, and who is the trickster? **(b) Compare and Contrast:** What common failing do Snake and Coyote share that makes them easy to trick?
6. **Make a Judgment:** Which character, if any, owes something to another character?

I. G. Edmonds

(b. 1917)

I. G. Edmonds is a collector of folk tales. As a soldier in the South Pacific during World War II, Edmonds decided to collect folk tales after he heard a native chief's story about how his island was created. The tales Edmonds collected are published in his book *Trickster Tales.* Other folk tales are collected in his anthology, *Ooka the Wise: Tales of Old Japan.*

Another of Edmonds's interests, communications, led to the writing of a nonfiction book, *Broadcasting for Beginners.*

Review and Assess

Literary Analysis

Folk Tales

1. Record examples of the types of cultural details in "Señor Coyote and the Tricked Trickster."

language ← — → geography

Culture

values ← — → [ ]

2. In "He Lion, Bruh Bear, and Bruh Rabbit," how does Virginia Hamilton preserve the feeling that this is a story being told aloud?

3. Why do you think several cultures have a folk tale similar to the one taught in "The Ant and the Dove"?

Comparing Literary Works

4. Use a chart like this one to show the qualities that the different characters represent.

Character	Quality	Examples
Señor Coyote	Cleverness	He talks Snake into being trapped.

5. What is one common or shared point in the lessons of the folk tales? Explain.

6. In what ways are the lessons different from one another?

Reading Strategy

Recognizing the Storyteller's Purpose

7. What are two details in "The Ant and the Dove" that indicate that its purpose is to teach?

8. Identify one detail that entertains and one that is meant to teach in "He Lion, Bruh Bear, and Bruh Rabbit."

9. Identify three details that indicate that one purpose of "Señor Coyote and the Tricked Trickster" is to entertain.

Extending Understanding

10. **Science Connection:** Explain how prey animals (animals that are hunted) such as mice protect themselves in the wild.

Quick Review

Folk tales are stories that were composed orally and then passed down by word of mouth. They often reflect the time and place in which they were told. To review folk tales, see page 763.

The **storyteller's purpose** is his or her reason for telling the story.

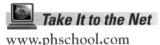 **Take It to the Net**

www.phschool.com
Take the interactive self-test online to check your understanding of these selections.

The Ant and the Dove/He Lion, Bruh Bear, and Bruh Rabbit/Señor Coyote and the Tricked Trickster ◆ 775

Integrate Language Skills

Vocabulary Development Lesson

Word Analysis: Forms of *Dignity*

In "Señor Coyote and the Tricked Trickster," Coyote responds *indignantly* to Mouse's accusations. He thinks that they are unfair or not respectful. The word *indignantly* is the opposite of *dignity*, which means "being worthy of respect."

Match each form of *dignity* with its definition.

1. dignity
2. dignitary
3. indignity
4. indignantly

   a. angrily
   b. something that insults one's worth
   c. a person worthy of respect
   d. the quality of being worthy

Fluency: Definitions

Write the vocabulary word that matches each definition:

1. in an insulted way
2. surprised
3. cave or den
4. friendly
5. as if blaming
6. not thankful

Spelling Strategy

Some words, such as *gnaw*, have unexpected silent letters. Practice spelling the following words.

hour   stomach   debt

Copy the sentences and fill in the blank with one of the words above.

1. A _____ ache hurts.
2. Borrowing builds a _____.
3. Hold still for half an _____.

Identify the words in each sentence that begin with the silent letter in the word you supplied.

Grammar Lesson

Using Capitals for Titles of People

Whether or not a person's title is capitalized depends on how it is used. Most titles, whether social, professional, or family titles, are capitalized when they are used as part of a name or in place of a name. They are not capitalized when preceded by an article or a possessive pronoun.

Examples: Have you met Aunt Bridget?
Meet my aunt, Bridget Donato.

Call Dr. Cushwa.
Call the doctor.

We're meeting Dad later.
Our dad will drive us.

Practice Copy the sentences below, and add capital letters where necessary.

1. I told my grandpa about the folk tale.
2. What was your favorite part of the story, mom?
3. I liked how señor Coyote tricked Snake.
4. She saw her doctor.
5. Do you think uncle Al would like to hear a trickster story?

Writing Application Write an alternative ending for "Señor Coyote and the Tricked Trickster." Use at least three capitals in titles.

*W*G *Prentice Hall Writing and Grammar Connection: Chapter 27*

Writing Lesson

Folk Tale

Most folk tale characters appear in more than one folk tale in the culture from which they come. Write your own folk tale using the characters from one of the tales in this group. First, identify the point of your folk tale, such as the value of friendship or the importance of teamwork. Make a list of several problems or conflicts that will help you illustrate the point. For example, Bruh Bear and Bruh Rabbit may need to combine forces to escape from a hunter.

Prewriting   Decide on a conflict, or problem, for your characters to solve. Then, review the original folk tale, and gather details about how your characters think, act, and talk.

Drafting   Develop some of the action through dialogue—the conversations between characters—to show the characters' personalities.

Model: Show Action Character With Dialogue

"Quick! Follow me into this cave!" cried Bruh Rabbit.

"Hold on. I'll go first to make sure it's safe." said Bruh Bear.

> The dialogue shows what they are doing and suggests how they are doing it.

Revising   Be sure you have used quotation marks to show the beginning and the ending of each character's words. Each time the speaker changes, you must start a new paragraph.

WG *Prentice Hall Writing and Grammar Connection: Chapter 5, Section 5*

Extension Activities

Research and Technology Using the Internet, prepare a **display** about folk art from various cultures. Include the following in your display:

- A caption identifying the work and where it was created
- A brief explanation of what the art shows and what is interesting and unique about the design, colors, or materials used to create it

Writing Choose one of the folk tales and write an **explanation** of the tale's message.

Listening and Speaking "Señor Coyote and the Tricked Trickster" is one of many folk tales in which a coyote appears as a trickster. In a small group, research another character that recurs in many folk tales. Then, prepare an **oral presentation** that offers the following information:

1. The qualities that the character represents
2. Summaries of two or three folk tales in which the character appears

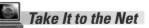 **Take It to the Net**   www.phschool.com

Go online for an additional research activity using the Internet.

Prepare to Read

Why Monkeys Live in Trees ◆ Arachne ◆ The Three Wishes ◆ A Crippled Boy

 Take It to the Net

Visit www.phschool.com for interactive activities and instruction related to these selections, including
- background
- graphic organizers
- literary elements
- reading strategies

Preview

Connecting to the Literature

The characters in these stories show varying degrees of self-confidence. For some of them self-confidence becomes overconfidence. Before reading, think about what your own experience and observations have shown about the positive and negative sides of confidence.

Background

Different versions of "The Three Wishes" exist in cultures around the world. Because folk tales are passed on orally, they can "migrate" from one place to another. Each storyteller adds details based on personal experience or culture. After a number of tellings, a new version of the tale emerges.

Literary Analysis

Oral Tradition

The **oral tradition** is the passing of songs, stories, and poems from generation to generation by word of mouth. There are several types of stories in the oral tradition.

- **Myths** tell stories of gods and goddesses. They may also explain something in nature or teach a lesson.
- **Folk tales** feature heroes, adventure, magic, and romance. They often entertain while teaching a lesson.

These works reflect the traditions, beliefs, and values of the common people. As you read, think about the following focus questions:

1. What cultural traditions are reflected in this story?
2. What beliefs and values does it reveal?

Comparing Literary Works

A story's **theme** is its central insight into life or human nature. As you read, determine the theme or message of each work by thinking about how the characters change or grow or what they learn during the course of the story. Compare the themes of these works and how they are presented.

Reading Strategy

Making Predictions

A **prediction** is an educated guess about future events in a story. To make a prediction, use what you already know from your experiences in reading and in life.

Myths and folk tales are often predictable. Cleverness and bravery are usually rewarded, but undesirable qualities, such as pride, are punished.

On an organizer like this one, predict the outcome of each story as soon as you think you know what will happen. Later, record the actual outcome of the folk tale or myth.

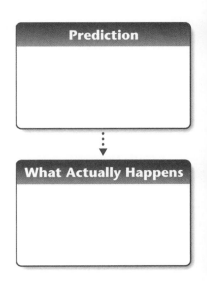

Vocabulary Development

obscure (əb skyoor´) *adj.* not well known (p. 785)

mortal (môr´ təl) *adj.* referring to humans, who must eventually die (p. 786)

obstinacy (äb´ stə nə sē) *n.* stubbornness (p. 786)

embraced (em brāsd´) *v.* clasped in the arms, usually as an expression of affection (p. 789)

covetousness (kuv´ ət əs nəs) *n.* envy; wanting what another person has (p. 790)

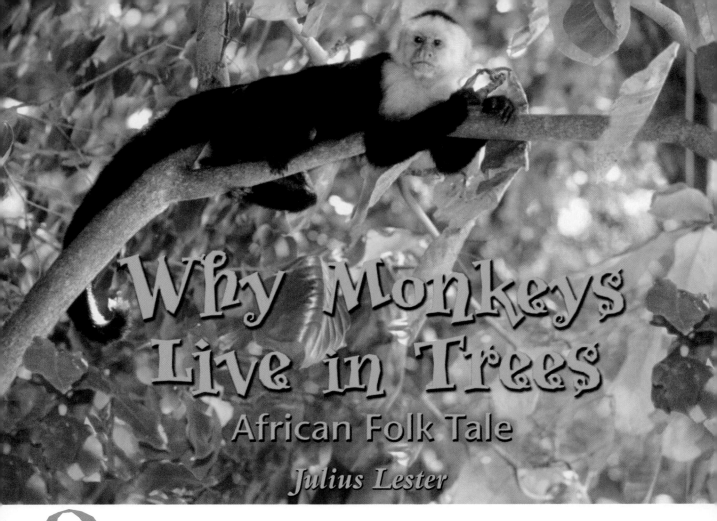

Why Monkeys Live in Trees

African Folk Tale

Julius Lester

One day Leopard was looking at his reflection in a pool of water. Looking at himself was Leopard's favorite thing in the world to do. Leopard gazed, wanting to be sure that every hair was straight and that all his spots were where they were supposed to be. This took many hours of looking at his reflection, which Leopard did not mind at all.

Finally he was satisfied that nothing was disturbing his handsomeness, and he turned away from the pool of water. At that exact moment, one of Leopard's children ran up to him.

"Daddy! Daddy! Are you going to be in the contest?"

"What contest?" Leopard wanted to know. If it was a beauty contest, of course he was going to be in it.

"I don't know. Crow the Messenger just flew by. She said that King Gorilla said there was going to be a contest."

Without another word, Leopard set off. He went north-by-northeast, made a right turn at the mulberry bush and traveled east-by-south-by-west until he came to a hole in the ground. He went around in a circle five times, and headed north-by-somersault

▲ **Critical Viewing**
Based on details in this picture, why would a story-teller choose to use monkeys as characters in a tale meant to entertain?
[Analyze]

until he came to a big clearing in the middle of the jungle and that's where King Gorilla was.

King Gorilla sat at one end of the clearing on his throne. Opposite him, at the other side of the clearing, all the animals sat in a semicircle. In the middle, between King Gorilla and the animals, was a huge mound of what looked like black dust.

Leopard looked around with calm dignity. Then he strode regally over to his friend, Lion.

"What's that?" he asked, pointing to the mound of black dust.

"Don't know," Lion replied. "King Gorilla said he will give a pot of gold to whoever can eat it in one day. I can eat it in an hour."

Leopard laughed. "I'll eat it in a half hour."

It was Hippopotamus's turn to laugh. "As big as my mouth is, I'll eat that mound in one gulp."

The time came for the contest. King Gorilla had the animals pick numbers to see who would go in what order. To everybody's dismay, Hippopotamus drew Number 1.

Hippopotamus walked over to the mound of black dust. It was

☑**Reading Check**

What does an animal have to do to win the contest?

Why Monkeys Live in Trees ◆ 781

bigger than he had thought. It was much too big to eat in one gulp. Nonetheless, Hippopotamus opened his mouth as wide as he could, and that was very wide indeed, and took a mouthful of the black dust.

He started chewing. Suddenly he leaped straight into the air and screamed. He screamed so loudly that it knocked the ears off the chickens and that's why to this day chickens don't have ears.

Hippopotamus screamed and Hippopotamus yelled. Hippopotamus roared and Hippopotamus bellowed. Then he started sneezing and crying and tears rolled down his face like he was standing in the shower. Hippopotamus ran to the river and drank as much water as he could, and that was very much, indeed, to cool his mouth and tongue and throat.

The animals didn't understand what had happened to Hippopotamus, but they didn't care. They were happy because they still had a chance to win the pot of gold. Of course, if they had known that the mound of black dust was really a mound of black pepper, maybe they wouldn't have wanted the gold.

Nobody was more happy than Leopard because he had drawn Number 2. He walked up to the black mound and sniffed at it.

"AAAAAAAACHOOOOOOO!" Leopard didn't like that but then he remembered the pot of gold. He opened his mouth wide, took a mouthful and started chewing and swallowing.

Leopard leaped straight into the air, did a back double flip and screamed. He yelled and he roared and he bellowed and, finally, he started sneezing and crying, tears rolling down his face like a waterfall. Leopard ran to the river and washed out his mouth and throat and tongue.

Lion was next, and the same thing happened to him as it did to all the animals. Finally only Monkey remained.

Monkey approached King Gorilla. "I know I can eat all of whatever that is, but after each mouthful, I'll need to lie down in the tall grasses and rest."

King Gorilla said that was okay.

Monkey went to the mound, took a tiny bit of pepper on his tongue, swallowed, and went into the tall grasses. A few minutes

▲ **Critical Viewing**
For what reason might monkeys need extraordinary climbing ability? **[Deduce]**

later, Monkey came out, took a little more, swallowed it, and went into the tall grasses.

Soon the pile was almost gone. The animals were astonished to see Monkey doing what they had not been able to do. Leopard couldn't believe it either. He climbed a tree and stretched out on a sturdy limb to get a better view. From his limb high in the tree Leopard could see into the tall grasses where Monkey went to rest. Wait a minute! Leopard thought something was suddenly wrong with his eyes because he thought he saw a hundred monkeys hiding in the tall grasses.

He rubbed his eyes and looked another look. There wasn't anything wrong with his eyes. There were a hundred monkeys in the tall grasses and they all looked alike!

Just then, there was the sound of loud applause. King Gorilla announced that Monkey had won the contest and the pot of gold.

Leopard growled a growl so scary that even King Gorilla was frightened. Leopard wasn't thinking about anybody except the monkeys. He took a long and beautiful leap from the tree right smack into the middle of the tall grasses where the monkeys were hiding.

The monkeys ran in all directions. When the other animals saw monkeys running from the grasses, they realized that the monkeys had tricked them and started chasing them. Even King Gorilla joined in the chase. He wanted his gold back.

The only way the monkeys could escape was to climb to the very tops of the tallest trees where no one else, not even Leopard, could climb.

And that's why monkeys live in trees to this very day.

Literary Analysis
Oral Tradition and Theme
What theme do the monkeys' actions reveal?

Review and Assess

Thinking About the Selections

1. **Respond:** Which character or characters in this story do you find most entertaining?
2. **(a) Recall:** What contest does King Gorilla hold? **(b) Infer:** Why do the animals think it will be easy to win the contest? **(c) Support:** Explain why it will not be easy for animals to win the contest.
3. **(a) Recall:** What does the monkey do between bites of pepper? **(b) Connect:** What does Leopard see in the tall grass? **(c) Deduce:** Why is the monkey able to eat all the pepper?
4. **(a) Assess:** Is the contest a fair one? **(b) Make a Judgment:** Do the monkeys deserve to win the contest?

Julius Lester

(b. 1939)
Julius Lester had a successful career in music when he turned to writing books on subjects related to his African American background. He has been a runner-up for the Newbery Medal and a finalist for the National Book Award.

Arachne (detail), Arvis Stewart, Reprinted with the permission of Macmillan Publishing Company from The Macmillan Book of Greek Gods and Heroes by Arvis Stewart, illustrated by Alice Low, Copyright © 1985 by Macmillan Publishing Company

GREEK MYTH

OLIVIA E. COOLIDGE

Arachne [ä räk´ nē] was a maiden who became famous throughout Greece, though she was neither wellborn nor beautiful and came from no great city. She lived in an <u>obscure</u> little village, and her father was a humble dyer of wool. In this he was very skillful, producing many varied shades, while above all he was famous for the clear, bright scarlet which is made from shellfish, and which was the most glorious of all the colors used in ancient Greece. Even more skillful than her father was Arachne. It was her task to spin the fleecy wool into a fine, soft thread and to weave it into cloth on the high, standing loom within the cottage. Arachne was small and pale from much working. Her eyes were light and her hair was a dusty brown, yet she was quick and graceful, and her fingers, roughened as they were, went so fast that it was hard to follow their flickering movements. So soft and even was her thread, so fine her cloth, so gorgeous her embroidery, that soon her products were known all over Greece. No one had ever seen the like of them before.

At last Arachne's fame became so great that people used to come from far and wide to watch her working. Even the graceful nymphs[1] would steal in from stream or forest and peep shyly through the dark doorway, watching in wonder the white arms of Arachne as she stood at the loom and threw the shuttle from hand to hand between the hanging threads, or drew out the long wool,

obscure (əb skyoor´) *adj.* not well known

☑**Reading Check**

What is Arachne's special skill?

---

1. nymphs (nimfz) *n.* minor nature goddesses, thought of as beautiful maidens living in rivers, trees, and so on.

◀ **Critical Viewing** How can you tell that the characters in this picture are in conflict? [**Draw Conclusions**]

fine as a hair, from the distaff[2] as she sat spinning. "Surely Athene[3] herself must have taught her," people would murmur to one another. "Who else could know the secret of such marvelous skill?"

Arachne was used to being wondered at, and she was immensely proud of the skill that had brought so many to look on her. Praise was all she lived for, and it displeased her greatly that people should think anyone, even a goddess, could teach her anything. Therefore when she heard them murmur, she would stop her work and turn round indignantly to say, "With my own ten fingers I gained this skill, and by hard practice from early morning till night. I never had time to stand looking as you people do while another maiden worked. Nor if I had, would I give Athene credit because the girl was more skillful than I. As for Athene's weaving, how could there be finer cloth or more beautiful embroidery than mine? If Athene herself were to come down and compete with me, she could do no better than I."

Reading Strategy
Making Predictions What do you think will be the result of this bragging?

One day when Arachne turned round with such words, an old woman answered her, a gray old woman, bent and very poor, who stood leaning on a staff and peering at Arachne amid the crowd of onlookers. "Reckless girl," she said, "how dare you claim to be equal to the immortal gods themselves? I am an old woman and have seen much. Take my advice and ask pardon of Athene for your words. Rest content with your fame of being the best spinner and weaver that <u>mortal</u> eyes have ever beheld."

mortal (môr′ təl) *adj.* referring to humans, who must eventually die

"Stupid old woman," said Arachne indignantly, "who gave you a right to speak in this way to me? It is easy to see that you were never good for anything in your day, or you would not come here in poverty and rags to gaze at my skill. If Athene resents my words, let her answer them herself. I have challenged her to a contest, but she, of course, will not come. It is easy for the gods to avoid matching their skill with that of men."

At these words the old woman threw down her staff and stood erect. The wondering onlookers saw her grow tall and fair and stand clad in long robes of dazzling white. They were terribly afraid as they realized that they stood in the presence of Athene. Arachne herself flushed red for a moment, for she had never really believed that the goddess would hear her. Before the group that was gathered there she would not give in; so pressing her pale lips together in <u>obstinacy</u> and pride, she led the goddess to one of the great looms and set herself before the other. Without a word both began

obstinacy (äb′ stə nə sē) *n.* stubbornness

---

2. **distaff** (dis′ taf) *n.* a stick on which flax or wool is wound for use in spinning.
3. **Athene** (ə thē′ nə) Greek goddess of wisdom, skills, and warfare.

to thread the long woolen strands that hang from the rollers, and between which the shuttle[4] moves back and forth. Many skeins lay heaped beside them to use, bleached white, and gold, and scarlet, and other shades, varied as the rainbow. Arachne had never thought of giving credit for her success to her father's skill in dyeing, though in actual truth the colors were as remarkable as the cloth itself.

Soon there was no sound in the room but the breathing of the onlookers, the whirring of the shuttles, and the creaking of the wooden frames as each pressed the thread up into place or tightened the pegs by which the whole was held straight. The excited crowd in the doorway began to see that the skill of both in truth was very nearly equal, but that, however the cloth might turn out, the goddess was the quicker of the two. A pattern of many pictures was growing on her loom. There was a border of twined branches of the olive, Athene's favorite tree, while in the middle, figures began to appear. As they looked at the glowing colors, the spectators realized that Athene was weaving into her pattern a last warning to Arachne. The central figure was the goddess herself competing with Poseidon[5] for possession of the city of Athens; but in the four corners were mortals who had tried to strive with gods and pictures of the awful fate that had overtaken them. The goddess ended a little before Arachne and stood back from her marvelous work to see what the maiden was doing.

Never before had Arachne been matched against anyone whose skill was equal, or even nearly equal to her own. As she stole glances from time to time at Athene and saw the goddess working swiftly, calmly, and always a little faster than herself, she became angry instead of frightened, and an evil thought came into her head. Thus as Athene stepped back a pace to watch Arachne

---

4. shuttle (shut´ əl) *n.* an instrument used in weaving to carry the thread back and forth.
5. Poseidon (pō sī´ dən) Greek god of the seas and of horses.

Literary Analysis
Oral Tradition and Theme
What lesson is suggested here?

Reading Check

Who is Athene and why is she competing with Arachne?

finishing her work, she saw that the maiden had taken for her design a pattern of scenes which showed evil or unworthy actions of the gods, how they had deceived fair maidens, resorted to trickery, and appeared on earth from time to time in the form of poor and humble people. When the goddess saw this insult glowing in bright colors on Arachne's loom, she did not wait while the cloth was judged, but stepped forward, her gray eyes blazing with anger, and tore Arachne's work across. Then she struck Arachne across the face. Arachne stood there a moment, struggling with anger, fear, and pride. "I will not live under this insult," she cried, and seizing a rope from the wall, she made a noose and would have hanged herself.

The goddess touched the rope and touched the maiden. "Live on, wicked girl," she said. "Live on and spin, both you and your descendants. When men look at you they may remember that it is not wise to strive with Athene." At that the body of Arachne shriveled up, and her legs grew tiny, spindly, and distorted. There before the eyes of the spectators hung a little dusty brown spider on a slender thread.

All spiders descend from Arachne, and as the Greeks watched them spinning their thread wonderfully fine, they remembered the contest with Athene and thought that it was not right for even the best of men to claim equality with the gods.

Review and Assess

Thinking About the Selections

1. **Respond:** If you were Arachne, would you have challenged the goddess Athene? Why or why not?
2. **(a) Recall:** Describe Arachne's skills. **(b) Interpret:** Why does Arachne refuse to accept advice from the old woman? **(c) Analyze:** What character traits are revealed through her behavior?
3. **Recall:** What design does Athene weave? **(b) Infer:** What is her original intention toward Arachne? **(c) Deduce:** What makes Athene angry?
4. **(a) Recall:** What does Athene do to Arachne? **(b) Interpret:** What lesson might the Greeks have learned from this myth? **(c) Extend:** What does this show about both the benefits and the drawbacks of confidence and pride?
5. **Extend:** Explain the connection between a spider and Arachne's skill. **(b) Connect:** Why do you think spiders are also called *arachnids*?

Olivia E. Coolidge

(b. 1908)

Working as a teacher of English, Latin, and Greek, as well as a writer, Olivia E. Coolidge has lived in both the United States and Europe. She has written many stories, myths, and biographical sketches for young readers. She writes about legends because she feels that the tales express timeless values still relevant today.

In addition to writing about subjects from classical mythology, such as the Trojan War, she has also written about colonial times in American history.

The Three Wishes

PUERTO RICAN FOLK TALE   Ricardo E. Alegría

Many years ago, there lived a woodsman and his wife. They were very poor but very happy in their little house in the forest. Poor as they were, they were always ready to share what little they had with anyone who came to their door. They loved each other very much and were quite content with their life together. Each evening, before eating, they gave thanks to God for their happiness.

One day, while the husband was working far off in the woods, an old man came to the little house and said that he had lost his way in the forest and had eaten nothing for many days. The woodsman's wife had little to eat herself, but, as was her custom, she gave a large portion of it to the old man. After he had eaten everything she gave him, he told the woman that he had been sent to test her and that, as a reward for the kindness she and her husband showed to all who came to their house, they would be granted a special grace. This pleased the woman, and she asked what the special grace was.

The old man answered, "Beginning immediately, any three wishes you or your husband may wish will come true."

When she heard these words, the woman was overjoyed and exclaimed, "Oh, if my husband were only here to hear what you say!"

The last word had scarcely left her lips when the woodsman appeared in the little house with the ax still in his hands. The first wish had come true.

The woodsman couldn't understand it at all. How did it happen that he, who had been cutting wood in the forest, found himself here in his house? His wife explained it all as she <u>embraced</u> him. The woodsman just stood there, thinking over what his wife had said. He looked at the old man who stood quietly, too, saying nothing.

Suddenly he realized that his wife, without stopping to think, had used one of the three wishes, and he became very annoyed when he remembered all of the useful things she might have asked for with the first wish. For the first time, he became angry with his wife. The desire for riches had turned his head, and he scolded his wife, shouting at her, among other things, "It doesn't seem possible that you could be so stupid! You've wasted one of our wishes, and now we have only two left! May you grow ears of a donkey!"

He had no sooner said the words than his wife's ears began to grow, and they continued to grow until they changed into the pointed, furry ears of a donkey.

Reading Strategy
Making Predictions How will the wishes turn out?

embraced (em brāsd´) v. clasped in the arms, usually as an expression of affection

✔**Reading Check**
What is the first wish the woman makes?

When the woman put her hand up and felt them, she knew what had happened and began to cry. Her husband was very ashamed and sorry, indeed, for what he had done in his temper, and he went to his wife to comfort her.

The old man, who had stood by silently, now came to them and said, "Until now, you have known happiness together and have never quarreled with each other. Nevertheless, the mere knowledge that you could have riches and power has changed you both. Remember, you have only one wish left. What do you want? Riches? Beautiful clothes? Servants? Power?"

The woodsman tightened his arm about his wife, looked at the old man, and said, "We want only the happiness and joy we knew before my wife grew donkey's ears."

No sooner had he said these words than the donkey ears disappeared. The woodsman and his wife fell upon their knees to ask forgiveness for having acted, if only for a moment, out of <u>covetousness</u> and greed. Then they gave thanks for all their happiness.

The old man left, but before going, he told them that they had undergone this test in order to learn that there can be happiness in poverty just as there can be unhappiness in riches. As a reward for their repentance, the old man said that he would bestow upon them the greatest happiness a married couple could know. Months later, a son was born to them. The family lived happily all the rest of their lives.

covetousness
(kuv´ ət əs nəs) *n.* envy; wanting what another person has

Review and Assess

Thinking About the Selections

1. **Respond:** Do you think the woodsman and his wife made a good third wish? Explain your answer.

2. **(a) Recall:** Describe the life of the woodsman and his wife before they make the three wishes. **(b) Interpret:** How does the couple earn the chance to make three wishes? **(c) Interpret:** What does this reveal about the values of the old man?

3. **(a) Recall:** How does the couple use the first two wishes? **(b) Compare and Contrast:** How does the behavior of the couple change after they are given the opportunity to make wishes? **(c) Analyze:** What does this say about the consequences of greed?

4. **(a) Interpret:** How does the saying "Be careful what you wish for" apply to the woodsman and his wife? **(b) Distinguish:** What is the difference between "having a dream" and "being dissatisfied with your life"?

Ricardo E. Alegría

(b. 1921)

A native of San Juan, Ricardo Alegría has held many important positions in education, archaeology, and culture in Puerto Rico. He has served as the director of the Center for Advanced Studies of Puerto Rico and the Caribbean.

Alegría has written nonfiction books on excavations of archaeological sites in Puerto Rico and on customs and ceremonies in the West Indies. He has said, "Culture is the way mankind expresses itself to live and live collectively."

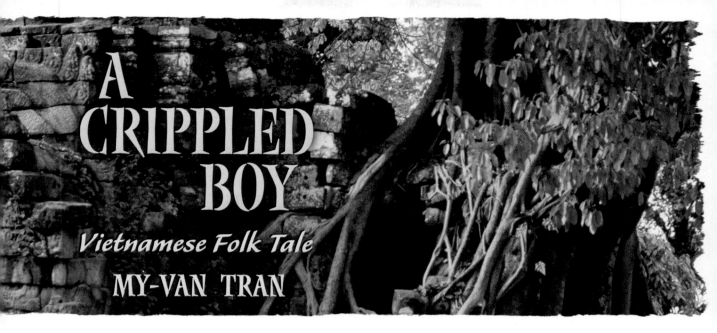

A CRIPPLED BOY

Vietnamese Folk Tale

MY-VAN TRAN

Long, long ago there was a boy called Theo. He was crippled in both legs and could hardly walk. Since he could not work, he had no choice but to live on rice and vegetables which kind people gave him.

Often he sat watching other children play and run about. Unable to join them, he felt very miserable. To amuse himself Theo practiced throwing pebbles at targets. Hour after hour he would spend practicing his aim. Having nothing else to do he soon learned to hit all his targets. Other children took pity on him and gave him more pebbles to throw. Besides this, Theo could also make all sorts of shapes with stones on the ground.

One hot day Theo sat under a big banyan tree[1] which provided him with a delightful, cool shade under its thick leaves. He aimed stones at the thick foliage and managed to cut it into the outlines of animal forms. He was very pleased at what he could do and soon forgot his loneliness.

One day Theo was under his favorite banyan tree. To his surprise, he heard a drumbeat. Soon he saw many men in official clothes. It happened that the King was out for a country walk with some of his officials and was passing by Theo's tree.

The King's attention was caught by the unusual shadow of the tree. He stopped and was very surprised to see little crippled Theo sitting there all alone.

Theo was very frightened and tried to get away; but he could not crawl very far. The King asked Theo what he had been doing. Theo told the King his story.

Then the King asked Theo to demonstrate his skill at pebble throwing. Theo was happy to do so. The King was impressed and

▲ **Critical Viewing**
Why might Theo enjoy sitting under a banyan tree like the one in the picture? **[Speculate]**

✔**Reading Check**

What is Theo's special skill?

---

1. banyan tree a tropical fig tree.

asked Theo to return with him to the palace where the King said:

"I have a little job for you to do."

The following day, before the King had a meeting with his mandarins,[2] he ordered Theo to sit quietly behind a curtain. The King had ordered a few holes to be made in the curtain so that Theo could see what was going on.

"Most of my mandarins talk too much," the King explained. "They never bother to listen to me or let me finish my sentence. So if anybody opens his mouth to speak while I am talking, just throw a pebble into his mouth. This will teach him to shut up."

Sure enough, just as the meeting was about to start one mandarin opened his big mouth, ready to speak.

Oops! Something got into his mouth and he quickly closed it.

Another mandarin opened his mouth to speak but strangely enough he, too, shut his mouth without saying a word.

A miracle had happened. Throughout the whole meeting all the mandarins kept their silence.

For once the King could speak as much as he wanted without being interrupted. The King was extremely pleased with his success and the help that Theo had given him.

After that he always treasured Theo's presence and service. So Theo remained happily at the palace, no longer needing to beg for food and no longer always sitting alone under the banyan tree.

---

2. **mandarins** (man´ də rinz) *n.* high-ranking officials and counselors.

Review and Assess

Thinking About the Selections

1. **Respond:** What do you think of the king's solution to his problem?

2. **(a) Recall:** Why does Theo begin to throw stones? **(b) Analyze:** Name two ways in which Theo benefits from developing his talent.

3. **(a) Recall:** How does the King meet Theo, and what does he ask Theo to do? **(b) Distinguish:** How is Theo different from the mandarins in the king's court? **(c) Draw Conclusions:** How do both Theo and the king benefit from their plan?

4. **(a) Interpret:** What message does this story offer about skill and practice? **(b) Make a Judgment:** When developing a skill, is talent or practice a bigger factor? Support your answer with details from the story and from life.

My-Van Tran

My-Van Tran left her native land, Vietnam, and moved to Australia because of the Vietnam War. However, she never abandoned her cultural heritage. She received a medal for her service in fostering Australian-Asian relations.

One of the ways she celebrates her Vietnamese heritage is by collecting and recording folk tales from her homeland. Literature is an important part of Vietnamese history and culture; poets are highly respected.

Review and Assess

Literary Analysis

Oral Tradition

1. What does the African folk tale "Why Monkeys Live in Trees" suggest about the value ancient African cultures placed on working as a group?
2. What beliefs about gods, godesses, and humans are reflected in "Arachne"?
3. What values are reflected in "The Three Wishes" and "A Crippled Boy"?
4. How are stories from the **oral tradition** similar to and different from other stories?

Comparing Literary Works

5. For each work, complete an organizer like the one shown here.

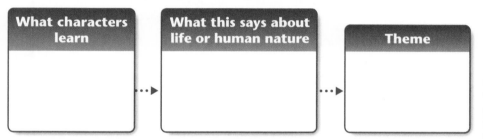

6. Which two **themes** are most similar?
7. In which stories is the theme mostly revealed by characters' actions?
8. In which stories is the theme mostly revealed by what characters learn?

Reading Strategy

Making Predictions

9. Explain why the outcome of "The Three Wishes" is predictable.
10. What did you **predict** about the outcome of "Why Monkeys Live in Trees"? Why?
11. For which story was it most difficult to predict the outcome? Why?

Extending Understanding

12. **Cultural Connection:** Would you consider some or all of these tales as good tools for teaching about a culture's values and beliefs? Explain.

Quick Review

Oral tradition is the handing down of tales and myths through oral storytelling. To review oral tradition, see page 779.

Theme is a story's central insight into life or human nature. To review theme, see page 779.

To **predict** is to make an educated guess about future events in a story.

 Take It to the Net

www.phschool.com

Take the interactive self-test online to check your understanding of these selections.

Integrate Language Skills

Vocabulary Development Lesson

Word Analysis: Latin Root -mort-

The myth "Arachne" tells about mortals and immortals. The Latin root -mort-, which means "death," appears in both words.

On your paper, write the meaning of the words containing the root -mort-.

1. The *mortician* prepared the body for burial.
2. The *mortality* rate drops when the sick receive good medical treatment and live longer.
3. Folk tales that are passed along from one generation to the next achieve a kind of *immortality*.

Concept Development: Context

Complete the paragraph with the vocabulary word that makes the most sense in each blank.

Some rarely told, ___?___ folk tales are among the most entertaining. They may tell tales of those who are immortal or ___?___. Some characters are punished for their flaws, such as ___?___ and ___?___. Others are ___?___ by good fortune.

Spelling Strategy

The letter pairs *cy* and *sy* have the same pronunciation. Remember that -*cy* is a suffix that creates nouns meaning "the quality or state of." The suffix -*sy* forms other kinds of nouns and adjectives. Complete the word in each sentence with the letters *cy* or *sy*.

1. Arachne's obstina ___?___ caused problems.
2. Arachne needs to learn courte ___?___.

Grammar Lesson

Sentence Structure and Style

A **compound-complex sentence** consists of two or more independent clauses and one or more subordinate clauses.

Independent Clauses
Arachne could weave skillfully.
She was very proud of this.

Subordinate Clause
because she had practiced hard

Compound-Complex Sentence
Because she had practiced hard, Arachne could weave skillfully, and she was very proud of this.

When you write, use a variety of sentence types, including compound-complex sentences, to make your work lively and engaging.

Practice Use each of the following groups of clauses to make a compound-complex sentence.

1. after Athene heard Arachne's words
   Athene became angry
   she accepted Arachne's challenge
2. since they had never seen a goddess
   the people were amazed
   they watched with wonder
3. because Arachne insulted the gods
   Athene turned her into a spider
   all people remember Arachne's story

Writing Application Summarize one of the stories in this section. Use at least two compound-complex sentences.

WG Prentice Hall Writing and Grammar Connection: Chapter 20, Section 2

Writing Lesson

Ancient Theme in a Modern Setting

Folk tales present timeless themes. Pick one theme from a tale in this section, and write a new tale that coveys the same theme.

Prewriting With a group, brainstorm for a conflict, problem, or situation that could be used to teach the lesson or demonstrate the theme. Identify the actions and events that will lead to the problem being solved. Arrange events on a plot diagram like the one shown here.

Model: Plot Diagram

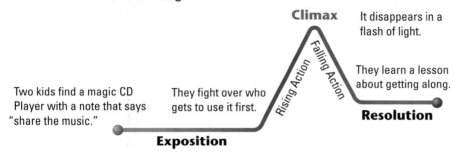

Drafting Tell events in the order in which you have organized them on your plot diagram. Add details about the time and place to make clear that the tale has a modern setting.

Revising Ask a classmate to read your story and try to determine the theme. If he or she has trouble, revise your story by adding events or dialogue.

*W*_G *Prentice Hall Writing and Grammar Connection: Chapter 5, Sections 1–7*

Extension Activities

Speaking and Listening Prepare an **oral report** of scientific information about either monkeys or spiders. Conduct research about them in the following areas.

- appearance
- habitat
- diet

In your presentation, compare and contrast the kinds of information you find through research with the type of details you find in the story. Show some information with visual aids such as photographs, drawings, and charts.

Research and Technology With a small group, use the Internet, CD-ROMs, and other library resources to research folk takes from a particular culture. Together, produce a **collection of folk tales** that represents some of the important traditions, values, and beliefs of that culture. Write a brief introduction for each folk tale in the collection. [Group Activity]

 **Take It to the Net** www.phschool.com

Go online for an additional research activity using the Internet.

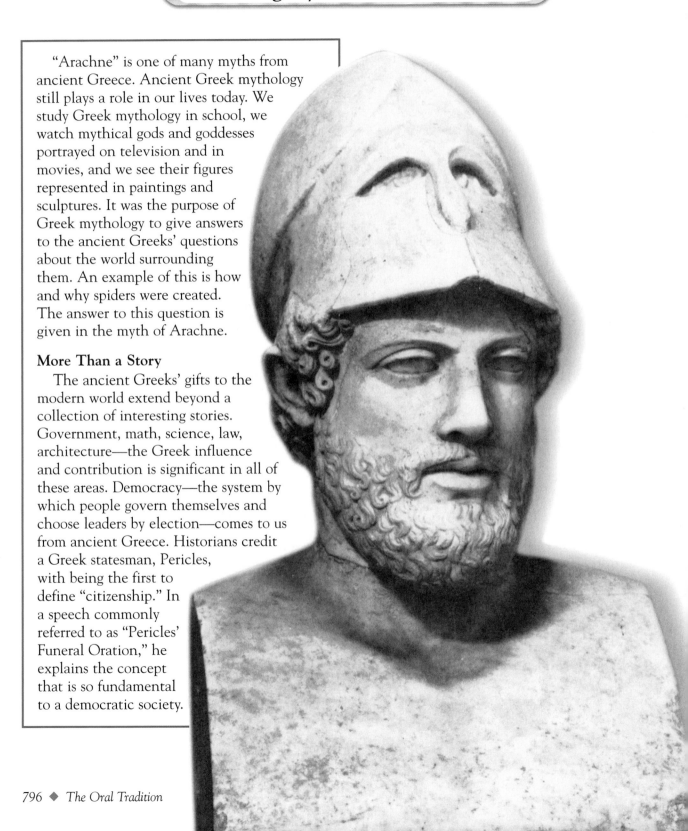

"Arachne" is one of many myths from ancient Greece. Ancient Greek mythology still plays a role in our lives today. We study Greek mythology in school, we watch mythical gods and goddesses portrayed on television and in movies, and we see their figures represented in paintings and sculptures. It was the purpose of Greek mythology to give answers to the ancient Greeks' questions about the world surrounding them. An example of this is how and why spiders were created. The answer to this question is given in the myth of Arachne.

More Than a Story

The ancient Greeks' gifts to the modern world extend beyond a collection of interesting stories. Government, math, science, law, architecture—the Greek influence and contribution is significant in all of these areas. Democracy—the system by which people govern themselves and choose leaders by election—comes to us from ancient Greece. Historians credit a Greek statesman, Pericles, with being the first to define "citizenship." In a speech commonly referred to as "Pericles' Funeral Oration," he explains the concept that is so fundamental to a democratic society.

from Pericles' Funeral Oration

Pericles began his speech by praising past generations for building a culturally rich and well-governed society. In the portion of the speech presented here, he analyzes the principles of the society.

But what was the road by which we reached our position, what the form of government under which our greatness grew, what the national habits out of which it sprang; these are questions which I may try to solve before I proceed to by panegyric upon these men; since I think this to be a subject upon which on the present occasion a speaker may properly dwell, and to which the whole assemblage, whether citizens or foreigners, may listen with advantage.

Our constitution does not copy the laws of neighboring states; we are rather a pattern to others than imitators ourselves. Its administration favors the many instead of the few; this is why it is called a democracy. If we look to the laws, they afford equal justice to all in their private differences; if no social standing, advancement in public life falls to reputation for capacity, class considerations not being allowed to interfere with merit; nor again does poverty bar the way, if a man is able to serve the state, he is not hindered by the obscurity of his condition. The freedom which we enjoy in our government extends also to our ordinary life. There, far from exercising a jealous surveillance over each other, we do not feel called upon to be angry with our neighbor for doing what he likes, or even to indulge in those injurious looks which cannot fail to be offensive, although they inflict no positive penalty. But all this ease in our private relations does not make us lawless as citizens. Against this fear is our chief safeguard, teaching us to obey the magistrates and the laws, particularly such as regard the protection of the injured, whether they are actually on the statute book, or belong to that code which, although unwritten, yet cannot be broken without acknowledged disgrace.

Connecting Literature and Social Studies

1. What are three qualities of citizenship that Pericles lists in his speech?
2. How is Pericles' definition of citizenship similar to and different from the way the word is defined in today's world?
3. How do you know that ancestors were important in ancient Greek culture?

Comparison-and-Contrast Articles

About Comparison-and-Contrast Articles

Comparison-and-contrast articles are expository writing in which the writer identifies and examines similarities and differences. There are two common organizations for writing that compares and contrasts.

- **Block** method presents all details about one subject, then presents all details about the next subject.
- **Point-by-point** method presents one point about all the subjects, then presents another point about all the subjects.

Your purpose for reading a comparison-and-contrast article may be to evaluate, to clarify details, or to make a decision.

Reading Strategy

Analyzing Compare-and-Contrast Text

In the magazine article on the next three pages, the writer uses a comparison-and-contrast pattern to describe two men who raced each other to the South Pole. The article compares and contrasts the men's backgrounds, how they prepared for the trip, and their strategies to reach their goals.

As you read the article, fill in a diagram like the one shown with details showing the men's similarities and differences.

When reading materials that make comparisons and contrasts, read critically. **Analyze** the information presented—break it down into parts or categories. Then, evaluate the comparison by asking yourself the following questions:

1. Are the same categories covered for each half of the comparison?
2. Is an approximately equal number of details in each category supplied for each half of the comparison?

Finally, evaluate whether the writer supports statements that compare and contrast with examples and facts.

Scott

- Background
- Preparations
- Strategies

- Shared Goal
- Adventurous
- Brave

- Background
- Preparations
- Strategies

Amundsen

Race to the End of the Earth

William G. Scheller

Amundsen's team proving South Pole location

Two explorers competed against each other and a brutal environment to reach the South Pole.

The drifts were so deep and the snow was falling so heavily that the team of five Norwegian explorers could hardly see their sled dogs a few feet ahead of them. Behind rose a monstrous mountain barrier. The men had been the first to cross it. But now they and their dogs were stumbling toward a stark and desolate plateau continually blasted by blizzards. The landscape was broken only by the towering peaks of mountains that lay buried beneath a mile of ancient ice. Led by Roald Amundsen, the men were still 300 miles from their goal: the South Pole.

On that same day, a party of 14 British explorers was also struggling across a similarly terrifying landscape toward the same destination. But they were almost twice as far from success. Their commander was Capt. Robert Falcon Scott, a naval officer. Amundsen was Scott's rival.

Exploration Preparation Both expedition leaders had long been preparing for their race to the South Pole. Amundsen came from a family of hardy sailors, and he had decided at the age of 15 to become a polar explorer. He conditioned himself by taking long ski trips across the Norwegian countryside and by sleeping with his windows open in winter.

By the time of his South Pole attempt, Amundsen was an experienced explorer. He had sailed as a naval officer on an expedition in 1897 that charted sections of the Antarctic coast. Between 1903 and 1906 he commanded the ship that made the first voyage through the Northwest Passage, the icy route that threads its way through the Canadian islands separating the Atlantic and Pacific Oceans. During that long journey Amundsen learned how the native people of the Arctic dress and eat to survive in extreme cold. He also learned that the dogsled was the most efficient method of polar transportation. These lessons would serve him well at Earth's frozen southern end.

Robert Scott was an officer in the British Navy. He had decided that leading a daring expedition of discovery would be an immediate route to higher rank. He heard that Great Britain's Royal Geographical Society was organizing such an exploration, and he volunteered in 1899 to be its commander. Now he was in command again.

The two expedition leaders had different styles. Scott followed a British tradition of brave sacrifice. He felt that he and his men should be able to reach the South Pole with as little help as possible from sled dogs and special equipment. He did bring dogs to Antarctica, as

Here, the differences that affected the outcome of the race are analyzed.

well as 19 ponies and three gasoline-powered sledges, or sturdy sleds. But his plan was for his team to "man-haul," or carry, all of their own supplies along the final portion of the route.

Roald Amundsen had spent much time in the far north, and he was a practical man. He'd seen how useful dogs were to Arctic inhabitants. He would be traveling in one of the most dangerous places on Earth, and he knew that sled dogs would be able to get his party all the way to the South Pole and make a safe return. Amundsen also placed great faith in skis, which he and his Norwegian team members had used since childhood. The British explorers had rarely used skis before this expedition and did not understand their great value.

The two leaders even had different ideas about diet. Scott's

Scott's ill-fated team

men would rely on canned meat. But Amundsen's plan made more sense. He and his men would eat plenty of fresh seal meat. Amundsen may not have fully understood the importance of vitamins, but fresh meat is a better source of vitamin C, which prevents scurvy, a painful and sometimes deadly disease.

The Race Is On! After making long sea voyages from Europe, Scott and Amundsen set up base camps in January on opposite edges of the Ross Ice Shelf. Each team spent the dark winter months making preparations to push on to the Pole when spring would arrive in Antarctica. Amundsen left base camp on October 20, 1911, with a party of four. Scott, accompanied by nine men, set off from his camp 11 days later. Four others had already gone ahead on the motorized sledges.

Scott's final diary entry Things went wrong for Scott from the beginning. The sledges broke down and had to be abandoned. Scott and his men soon met up with the drivers, who were traveling on foot. Blizzards then struck and lasted several weeks into December. Scott's ponies were proving to be a poor choice for Antarctic travel as well. Their hooves sank deep into the snow, and their perspiration froze on their bodies, forming sheets of ice. (Dogs do not perspire; they pant.) On December 9, the men shot the last of the surviving weak and frozen ponies. Two days later Scott sent his remaining dogs back to base camp along with several members of the expedition. Over the next month, most of the men returned to the camp. Scott's plan from here on was for the five men remaining to man-haul supplies the rest of the way to the Pole and back.

For Scott and his men, the journey was long and brutal. To cover only ten miles each day, the team toiled like dogs—like the dogs they no longer had. Food and fuel were in short supply, so the men lacked the energy they needed for such a crushing task.

Roald Amundsen's careful planning and Arctic experience were paying off. Even so, there's no such thing as easy travel by land in Antarctica. To the men who had just crossed those terrible mountains, the Polar Plateau might have looked easy. But Amundsen's team still had to cross a long stretch they later named the "Devil's Ballroom." It was a thin crust of ice that concealed crevasses, or deep gaps, that could swallow men, sleds, and dogs. Stumbling into one crevasse, a team of dogs dangled by their harnesses until the men could pull them up to safety.

Reaching the Goal On skis, with the "ballroom" behind them and well-fed dogs pulling their supply sleds, Amundsen and his men swept across the ice. The going was smooth for them, and the weather was fine. The Norwegian's only worry was that they'd find Scott had gotten to the Pole first. On the afternoon of December 14, 1911, it was plain that no one was ahead of them. At three o'clock, Amundsen skied in front of the team's sleds, then stopped to look at his navigation instruments. There was no point further south. He was at the South Pole!

Each section of the article highlights additional similarities and differences between Scott and Amundsen.

Check Your Comprehension

1. How did Amundsen condition himself for the expedition?
2. Why did Scott plan for his team to man-haul their supplies along the final portion of their route?
3. Why was fresh seal meat a better food source than canned meat?
4. What went wrong for Scott?
5. Who reached the South Pole first?

Applying the Reading Strategy
Analyzing Compare-and-Contrast Text

6. Describe similarities and differences in the backgrounds of Amundsen and Scott.
7. The author contrasts Amundsen's and Scott's food plan by saying "Amundsen's plan made more sense." What details are supplied to support this contrast?
8. Explain the different strategies of each team during the race.

Activity
Oral Presentation

Speaking as one of the explorers, give a presentation on the conditions you and your crew faced on your expedition. Include information in the following categories:

- food
- weather
- traveling

If possible, conduct research to add details to your presentation.

Comparing Informational Materials
Articles and Encyclopedias

Locate an encyclopedia article about the 1911 race to the South Pole. Fill in a chart like the one shown, listing the details about the journey from each source. Explain your observations about the depth and kind of information provided in each source.

	The Men's Backgrounds	Preparations for the Expedition	Strategies for Success
Magazine Article			
Encyclopedia Article			

READING INFORMATIONAL MATERIALS

Web Sites

About Web Sites

A Web site is a collection of Web pages linked for posting on the World Wide Web. A Web site may be created by an organization or an individual. The type and reliability of the information supplied on a Web site depend on the provider. You can usually identify the type of provider by the last three letters of the URL, or address.

- Sites ending in .edu are maintained by educational institutions.
- Sites ending in .gov are maintained by government agencies.
- Sites ending in .org are usually maintained by nonprofit organizations and agencies.
- Sites ending in .com are commercially or personally maintained.

Just as you would evaluate the quality, bias, and validity of any other research material, judge Web site information based on the reliability and authority of the source.

Reading Strategy

Forming Questions for Investigation

The key to finding useful information efficiently is to have a focus. Whether you are searching print or electronic resources, having questions in mind will help you quickly identify information that is relevant to your investigation and skip over information that is not.

As you read the information on the Web site here, jot down questions for investigation. Circle the key words in each question. Look for these words in the alphabetically organized print listings of periodical indexes or card catalogs. Use them as the key word search terms for electronic catalogs. The notepad shows how questions and key words can be used to conduct an Internet search.

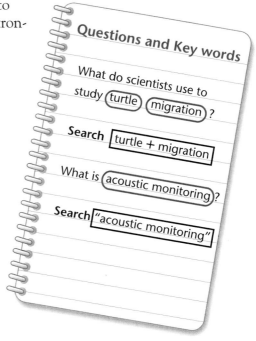

Questions and Key words

What do scientists use to study turtle migration?

Search turtle + migration

What is acoustic monitoring?

Search "acoustic monitoring"

- Use a plus sign between words to retrieve documents containing all terms connected by the sign in any order.
- Use quotation marks around words to retrieve documents containing terms in specific order.

Links to other pages can help you find additional related information and resources.

The last three letters of the URL show that this Web site is commercially maintained.

http://www.nationalgeographic.com

nationalgeographic.com/NEWS Friday, Oct. 22, 1999

High-Tech Windows to the Animal Kingdom

NGNews Home
Today's Story
Archive
Search
Toolbox
Instant Delivery

Click here!

First Finds and
Special Reports

Press Releases
and Events

national
geographic
.com

enn.com

Elephants like these will be acoustically monitored in Africa next year.

By Robinson Shaw

Many exciting discoveries in the animal kingdom are a result of advances in technology. Scientists plot the migration routes of sea turtles over thousands of miles. Undersea acoustical studies reveal that different whales sing different tunes. And scientists recently discovered that elephants communicate with each other in a range undetectable by humans. Today s technology has opened a sophisticated window on the world of animals.

To search for information about migration routes of turtles, you could use *migration* and *turtles* as key words.

Check Your Comprehension

1. According to the information next to the elephant photograph, how are elephants going to be monitored?
2. In what country will the elephants be monitored?
3. What do undersea acoustical studies reveal about whales?
4. What have scientists recently learned about how elephants communicate?

Applying the Reading Strategy

Forming Questions for Investigation

5. What are two questions you will investigate about the topic?
6. What two questions might the author have investigated to write this National Geographic article?

Activity

Web Site Investigation

Find other Web sites related to the technology used to study animals. Locate at least two sites from different types of sources. With a partner evaluate the information provided on each site, based on the source.

Comparing and Contrasting Informational Materials

Web Sites and Encyclopedias

Compare and contrast a Web site and an encyclopedia article on African elephants. Make a chart like the one shown.

	Web Site	Encyclopedia
Easy/hard to find information		
Amount of information		
Suggestions for other sources		

Writing WORKSHOP

Research: Multimedia Report

A **multimedia report** presents information through a variety of media, including text, slides, videos, music, maps, charts, and art. In this workshop, you will learn to prepare a multimedia report that incorporates some or all of these media as appropriate.

Assignment Criteria. Your multimedia report should have the following characteristics:

- A topic that can be thoroughly covered in the time and space allotted
- Supportive facts, details, examples, and explanations
- Appropriate formatting using a word-processor and principles of design
- Appropriate and effective media elements

To see the criteria on which your multimedia research report will be assessed, see the Rubric on page 809.

Prewriting

Choose a topic. Conduct a self-interview to come up with possible topics. Ask yourself the following questions:

- What topics in other classes interest me?
- What subjects do I know a lot about?
- What topic do I want to learn more about?

Plan ahead. Once you have chosen your topic, consider how you will effectively incorporate media. If you are explaining a process, models and props will help make actions in the process clear. Ask yourself the following questions:

- What sound effects or pieces of music will enhance and support this topic?
- What visuals would dramatize my report?
- What special equipment will I need?

Conduct Research. Do research to find information on your topic and to find different ways of presenting the information. Use the ideas on the chart to get you started.

General Topic	Media Possibilities
Person	• Photos • Audio or video of interview
Event	• Video of eyewitness account

Student Model

Before you begin drafting your multimedia report, read this portion of a student model and review the characteristics of a successful multimedia report. To see the full multimedia report, visit www.phschool.com.

David Papineau
Chris Casey
Indianapolis, Indiana

The Power of Numbers

Slide 1

Script: In this presentation, you will be shown the various uses of mathematics in a wide range of careers. You will also see some prime examples of what would happen if people did not know the fundamentals of mathematics in a real-life situation. So sit back and prepare to be amazed by . . .
The Power of Numbers.

Visual: Blank screen (blues and greens). As the presentation begins, the following words appear line by line.
Sound: Typewriter
Sound: Explosion

> Math would be too broad a topic, but the writers have narrowed it to focus on how math is used in a variety of careers. Each slide will provide an example.

Slide 4

Script: A word of advice: Never go to a concert where the musicians can't add the fractions of the notes to get the correct beat count. If you do, though, you'd better have earplugs!

Visual: Violinist

Sound: Music played off tempo

> The best way to show the problems a "mathless musician" would have is to let the audience hear the results. The writers chose to include music that is played out of rhythm to support their point.

Slide 5

Script: The picture says it all. If you have a pilot who can't read graphs or make course calculations, you might find the plane way off course.

Visual: Snow-covered mountaintop with an airplane flying near it

Sound: Airplane flying

> The formatting of the text and the use of a visual emphasize the disastrous effects of a pilot's not knowing math.

Drafting

Write a script. Plan every word and action in your multimedia presentation by writing a script. Include any words that you will speak and any stage directions that make actions and effects clear. Fold a paper lengthwise. In the left column, write the words of the script. In the right column, indicate sound effects, visuals, etc.

Evaluate media needs. Read through your draft, making notes of media cited in the script that you need to find or prepare. Leave time during your drafting stage to do the following:

Model: Multimedia Script

Erosion—it creates amazing natural sculptures And terrible damage	**Visual:** of Bryce Canyon **Sound:** gently flowing water
Although it usually occurs over thousands or millions of years, erosion is sometimes speeded up by human activity, such as mining, farming, or developing for construction.	**Visual:** Image of creek bed washed away, barn tilting into creek **Sound:** Roaring water
	Visual: bare field with no plants, dust blowing away **Sound:** Heavy equipment like a tractor or cement truck.

- Draw pictures, make slides, or edit video
- Edit audiotape or tape sound effects
- Make charts or graphs
- Copy or scan documents

Revising

Evaluate media. Look for places where adding media will improve the audience's understanding. Consider whether sound will emphasize an impression you want to give or whether a diagram will make a comparison clearer.

Model:

Script: A word of advice: Never go to a concert where the musicians can't add the fractions of the notes to get the correct beat count. If you do, though, you'd better have earplugs!

Sound: Music played off tempo

> The writers realized that sound effects would illustrate their point about the effect of math mistakes in music better than any description could.

Fine-tune the presentation. Rehearse with any equipment used in your presentation.

- Identify the on, off, fast-forward, and rewind switches on audio or video recorders.
- Adjust volume for the size of the room and the audience.

Proofread. Mistakes in spelling, grammar, or capitalization will look twice as bad if they are projected on a screen. Proofread slides, posters, and other visuals. Check especially for homophones—words that sound the same but have different spellings and meanings (*their, they're, there*). Remember that the spell-check feature of a word-processing program will not report the misuse of a homophone as a misspelling.

Publishing and Presenting

Choose one of these ways to share your writing with classmates or a larger audience.

Report to a small audience. In a small group, take turns presenting your multimedia presentations and giving feedback.

Take it on the road. Take your report "on the road" outside your school. Contact a local library or club that might be interested in your report.

 Speaking Connection

To learn more about delivering effective multimedia reports, see the **Listening and Speaking Workshops: Delivering a Research Presentation**, p. 606, and **Using Visual Aids**, p. 810.

 Prentice Hall Writing and Grammar Connection: Chapter 28, Section 2

Rubric for Self-Assessment

Evaluate your multimedia research report using the following criteria and rating scale:

Criteria	Rating Scale Not very				Very
How appropriate and clear is the main idea of this report?	1	2	3	4	5
How well does the writer use supportive facts, details, examples, and explanations?	1	2	3	4	5
How appropriate is the formatting?	1	2	3	4	5
How well does the writer use visuals?	1	2	3	4	5
How well does the writer use sound?	1	2	3	4	5

Using Visual Aids

Visual Aids can effectively enhance and dramatize an oral presentation. You may want to use visual aids to show detailed evidence that backs your opinions in a persuasive presentation. You might also use visual aids to reinforce statements in a research report. (To review the characteristics of a successful multimedia report, see the Writing Workshop, pp. 806–809; to review delivering a persuasive presentation, see the Writing Workshop, pp. 340–343.) Visual aids can take many forms. Use some of the strategies suggested here when choosing visual aids.

Show and Tell

You have probably heard the saying "A picture is worth a thousand words." Look for appropriate visual aids that will enhance and dramatize your statements and opinions. Try experimenting with both high-tech and low-tech displays.

Display key terms. Keep your audience's attention focused by showing them important words and new terms. It can be as simple as writing them on a chalkboard or as high-tech as using a colorful display on a monitor or a wall.

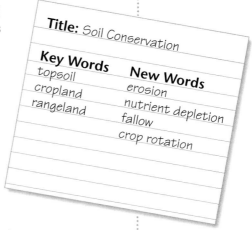

Title: Soil Conservation

Key Words
topsoil
cropland
rangeland

New Words
erosion
nutrient depletion
fallow
crop rotation

Engage your listeners. Alternating between having your audience look at images and listen to you speak will hold their attention and keep them interested. Use visual aids that are clear, informative, and dramatic.

Provide detailed evidence. By showing your listeners a photograph, drawing, graph, or chart, you can visually represent facts and opinions. A few well-chosen images in a persuasive presentation can effectively drive home your point.

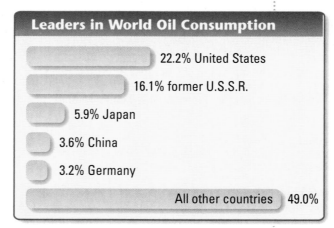

Leaders in World Oil Consumption

22.2% United States
16.1% former U.S.S.R.
5.9% Japan
3.6% China
3.2% Germany
All other countries 49.0%

Activity:
Brainstorm for Visual Aids

Choose a topic you are studying or have studied in science, math, or social studies. Identify three points related to the topic that are appropriately and effectively supported or illustrated with visual aids. Make the visual aids.

Assessment WORKSHOP

Spelling, Capitalization, Punctuation

The writing sections of some tests require you to read a passage and answer multiple-choice questions about spelling, capitalization, and punctuation. Use what you have learned in this unit about proofreading and punctuation to answer these types of questions.

Test-Taking Strategies

Check especially for spelling errors in

- homophones
- words with suffixes
- words with two vowels in the middle.

Sample Test Item

Directions: Read the passage and decide which type of error, if any, appears.

(1) If you think relay races are fun imagine one on horseback! (2) At United States Pony club rallies, (3) horses and there riders compete in ten different relay races.

1. A Spelling error
   B Capitalization error
   C Punctuation error
   D No error

2. A Spelling error
   B Capitalization error
   C Punctuation error
   D No error

3. A Spelling error
   B Capitalization error
   C Punctuation error
   D No error

Answers and Explanations

1. Use a comma after an introductory adverb clause (*fun,*). ***C*** is correct.

2. *United States Pony Club* is a compound proper noun. ***B*** is correct.

3. *There* is a homophone for *their.* ***A*** is correct.

▶ Practice

Directions: Read the passage and decide which type of error, if any, appears.

(1) While Rick set the table, Carol strung the streamers over the dining room table (2) Suddenly, they herd a click at the door. The children quickly assembled in the dining room. (3) their parents walked in. "Happy Anniversary!" the children shouted.

1. A Spelling error
   B Capitalization error
   C Punctuation error
   D No error

2. A Spelling error
   B Capitalization error
   C Punctuation error
   D No error

3. A Spelling error
   B Capitalization error
   C Punctuation error
   D No error

RESOURCES

Suggestions for Sustained Reading R1
Glossary R7

Handbooks

Tips for Improving Reading Fluency R9
High-Frequency Words R11
Literary Terms Handbook R12
Rubric Handbook. R18
Writing Handbook. R22
Citing Sources and Preparing Manuscript R24
MLA Style for Listing Sources R25
Formatting Business Letters. R26
Writing Friendly Letters R27
Internet Guide R28
Spelling Handbook R29
Commonly Misspelled Words. R32
Grammar, Usage, and Mechanics Handbook R33
Grammar, Usage, and Mechanics Exercises R39
Speaking, Listening, and Viewing Handbook R47

Indexes

Index of Authors and Titles R49
Index of Skills. R50
Index of Features. R54
Acknowledgments *(continued)* R56
Credits. R59

Following are some suggestions for longer works that will give you the opportunity to experience the fun of sustained reading. Each of the suggestions further explores one of the themes in this book. All of the titles are included in the **Prentice Hall Literature Library**, featuring the **Penguin Literature Library**.

You may want to consult your teacher before choosing one of these longer works.

Unit 1:
Growing and Changing

Searching for Candlestick Park
Peg Kehret
Puffin Books, 1997

In this novel, twelve-year-old Spencer Atwood leaves his home in Seattle, Washington, to look for his father in San Francisco's Candlestick Park. This famous stadium was home to the San Francisco Giants baseball team for almost 40 years. With his cat Foxey, Spencer travels by bike about 800 miles from the state of Washington through Oregon to California. Along the way, he learns a lot about himself and about being responsible for someone else.

Going Home
Nicholasa Mohr
Puffin Books, 1986

Felita, a young girl from New York City, gets the opportunity to spend a summer with her extended family in Puerto Rico. She is excited to see the land her grandmother has so often described. She is also glad to escape the strict supervision of her family. Felita's summer, however, is not quite as she had imagined. Her Puerto Rican relatives are as strict as her parents. Her uncle, Tio Jorge, seems to spend most of his time mourning the passing of old ways. Some of the kids in Tio Jorge's small village resent her as an outsider. Felita must find a way to blend both parts of her background into her emerging identity.

Park's Quest
Katherine Paterson
Puffin Books, 1988

Eleven-year-old Parkington Waddell Broughton V is on a quest to "find" his father. His mother has told Park that his father was killed in Vietnam during a second tour of duty, but that is all she will say. After finding his father's books and reading them, Park begins his quest. In this book, the author poses important questions about war and the wreckage it leaves behind, both in lives lost and in lives that are forever changed.

Bluestem
Frances Arrington
Puffin Books, 2000

For pioneers on the American prairie in the nineteenth century, life was uncertain. They had to worry about disease and possible starvation as well as unpredictable weather—including droughts, floods, blizzards, and extreme temperatures. Many of those who arrived in the United States from Scandinavia or other parts of Europe journeyed to the wide prairies of the Midwest and the plains of the West. Most pioneers, like the families in *Bluestem,* tried to make their living by farming. In this story, two young pioneer girls, Polly and Jessie, must take care of themselves and make difficult decisions when their mother becomes seriously ill.

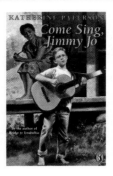

Come Sing, Jimmy Jo
Katherine Paterson
Puffin Books, 1985

The Johnsons are becoming country music stars. They are on television and the radio—and it is all because of James. His voice and his guitar playing bring the songs to life and make audiences beg for more. Most kids would love this life of stardom, but James does not. He has had to change his name to "Jimmy Jo," dress in clothes he hates, and pretend he is someone else. During the course of the story, James comes to terms with his gift and what it means for his own future and the future of his family.

Unit 2:
Reaching Out

The Secret Garden
Frances Hodgson Burnett
Signet Classic, 1986

Orphaned Mary Lennox, lonely and sad, is sent to live at her uncle's house on the Yorkshire moors in England. Mary finds the huge house full of secrets. At night, she hears the sound of crying down one of the long corridors. Outside, she meets Dickon, a magical boy who can charm and talk to animals. Then, one day, with the help of a friendly robin, Mary discovers the most mysterious wonder of all—a secret garden, walled and locked, which has been completely forgotten for many years.

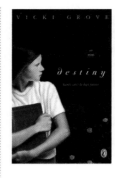

Destiny
Vicki Grove
Puffin Books, 2000

Life is complicated for twelve-year-old Destiny Louise Capperson. She has three younger siblings and a mother whose plans for the future focus solely on winning the lottery. Because she needs a job, Destiny begins reading to the mysterious Mrs. Peck, a former Latin teacher who is losing her eyesight. Through Mrs. Peck's books, Destiny discovers Greek mythology, fictional tales that tell about the causes of natural events or about the actions of gods and goddesses. Through the mythical story of a woman named Pandora, Destiny learns the importance of hope and finds the courage to solve her problems.

Letters from Rifka with Connected Readings
Karen Hesse
Pearson Prentice Hall, 2000

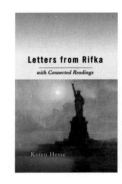

This novel, written in the form of letters, traces the experiences of a Russian Jewish girl named Rifka. Modeled on the author's great-aunt, Rifka overcomes one obstacle after another in this gripping story. In 1919, Rifka and her family flee Russia's brutal treatment of Jews for a new life in the United States. The path to freedom is a difficult one, but the family pushes bravely forward. At last, when it seems that Rifka's family has triumphed over every possible hardship, the doctors refuse to let Rifka board the ship to the United States—and her family must leave without her. Through her "letters," Rifka brings the immigrant experience to life for readers.

Flip-Flop Girl
Katherine Paterson
Puffin Books, 1994

After her father's death, Vinnie Matthews needs a real lifesaver—one that will let her family go home. Living with Grandma means having to be responsible for her little brother, Mason, who refuses to speak. It also means ignoring the kids who make fun of Mason. Vinnie is thrust into a new school, without friends or the right clothes and with rumors about her troubled brother wafting around her. Then, Vinnie meets Lupe, the mysterious "flip-flop girl." Lupe might just be the friend she needs, if Vinnie can only ignore the rumors about her past.

The Heart of a Chief
Joseph Bruchac
Puffin Books, 1998

Eleven-year-old Chris Nicola is a member of the Penacook nation, which is part of the Western Abaneki nation. Chris lives on the Penacook Indian Reservation and goes to school in town. At school, things are going well—he has been selected to lead a group project on using Indian names for sports teams. However, at home there is controversy. The Penacook are divided over whether or not to build a casino on a beautiful island Chris thinks of as his own. In *The Heart of a Chief,* Chris takes on two controversial subjects. One is casino gambling, and the other is the naming of sports teams. Readers of this novel will be moved by Chris's pride in his culture and his simple message of respect.

Unit 3: Proving Yourself

Amelia Earhart: Courage in the Sky
Mona Kerby, illustrated by Eileen McKeating
Puffin Books, 1990

As a child, Amelia Earhart wondered why there were no heroines in her favorite adventure stories. She resolved to change that when she grew up. This is a biography of a female adventurer, a woman who was years ahead of her time. It is also about the people who touched her life. Amelia Earhart's family background might have pointed her in a different direction, but she had the determination and purpose to achieve her goals. She also was lucky to know wealthy, powerful people who supported her during critical times and helped her achieve the goals she set for herself.

Eagle Song
Joseph Bruchac, illustrated by Dan Andreasen
Puffin Books, 1997

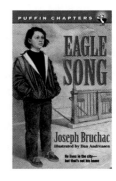

Danny Bigtree's family has moved to a new city, and no matter how hard he tries, Danny cannot seem to fit in. He is homesick for the Mohawk reservation where he used to live. The kids in his class call him "Chief" and tease him about being an Indian. Things finally begin to change when Danny's father visits the class to talk about the Iroquois Confederacy. However, Danny must still decide if he is up to the challenge of turning the school bully into a friend.

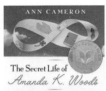

The Secret Life of Amanda K. Woods

Ann Cameron
Puffin Books, 1998

Growing up in 1950s rural Wisconsin, Amanda Woods feels isolated and lonely. Her older sister is too smart and pretty for Amanda to feel close to her, and her parents are distant. When her best friend moves away, Amanda decides to create a new version of herself. She transforms herself from bland Amanda Woods to Amanda K. Woods—someone who is proud and strong and sure of herself. This touching coming-of-age novel was a National Book Award Finalist.

Brady

Jean Fritz, illustrated by Lynd Ward
Puffin Books, 1960

This story takes place during the period before the U.S. Civil War, when tensions were heating up about the subject of slavery. Brady Minton, the main character, has never been able to keep a secret. Then one day, he discovers an Underground Railroad Station near his family's farm. Suddenly, Brady realizes that some secrets must never be revealed—and this realization sets him on the path to manhood.

Moki

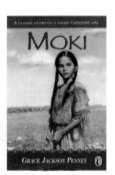

Grace Jackson Penney
Puffin Books, 1960

Moki is a young Cheyenne girl. The Cheyenne are a Native American people who once lived in the region that is now called the Great Lakes. At the time of Moki's story, however, the Cheyenne lived on the Great Plains. As the story begins, Moki is tired of merely watching while all the boys her age learn to fish and hunt and have adventures. She wants to do something important, too. Even though her friends do not understand, Moki has made up her mind to do something so important, the whole camp will take notice.

Unit 4: Seeing It Through

Boy of the Painted Cave

Justin Denzel
PaperStar Book, 1988

This novel is set in the Dordogne Valley, in what is now France, during the Paleolithic period. This period, which is sometimes called the Old Stone Age, included the earliest stages of human development as well as the greatest portion of human history. Experts date the era from about 2 million years ago to between 40,000 and 10,000 years ago. The book tells the story of a boy named Tao who longs to be a cave painter. He is forbidden from fulfilling his dream, however, because he is not a Chosen One. Instead, he is a tribal outcast with a crippled foot and no father to claim him. Forced into isolation by the superstitious leader of his tribe, Tao befriends a wolf dog, Ram, and the shaman, Greybeard, who teaches him to paint.

Johnny Tremain

Esther Forbes
Laurel-Leaf, 1971

This historical novel is set in pre-Revolutionary New England. Following a serious accident, a young apprentice silversmith, Johnny Tremain, is swept up into the colonists' rebellion against the British. Johnny participates in the Boston Tea Party and the Battle of Lexington—events that prompted the Revolutionary War. During his escapades, Johnny meets such notable figures as Paul Revere, Samuel Adams, and John Hancock.

Amistad: A Long Road to Freedom
Walter Dean Myers
Puffin Books, 1998

In 1839, a young man named Sengbe Pieh led a group of illegally enslaved Africans to revolt against their captors aboard the slave ship *Amistad*. The Africans landed in the United States, where they were imprisoned and charged with murder. The *Amistad* captives faced several court battles. Some of the arguments were simply over which court had the authority to make decisions about the case. Slavery was legal in some states and illegal in others. The court battles went through the federal court system, from the Connecticut district court to the circuit court and, finally, to the Supreme Court, where the final decision was made.

My Side of the Mountain
Written and illustrated by Jean Craighead George
Puffin Books, 1988

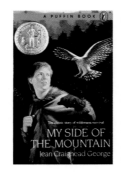

Sam Gribley is tired of living in a crowded New York City apartment, so, with his parents' permission, he runs away to the Catskill Mountain wilderness to make a life of his own. No one takes his plans seriously—except Sam himself. With only a penknife, a ball of cord, an ax, forty dollars, and some flint and steel, he must rely on his intelligence and the resources of the land to survive. He sets up a house in a hollowed-out tree with a falcon and a weasel for companions. Sam learns about courage, danger, and independence during his year in the wilderness, a year that changes his life forever.

Lyddie
Katherine Paterson
Puffin Books, 1991

Lyddie is set in the mid-1800s, a time when much of American culture was undergoing tremendous change. As the nation moved from a largely agricultural society to a more industrial one, families had to make adjustments that sometimes ripped apart the stability of their lives. The character of Lyddie is a victim of this societal change. Her parents are gone, and her brother and sisters have been sent to live with other people. Lyddie is on her own. When she hears that jobs are available in the textile mills of Lowell, Massachusetts, she heads there with the goal of earning enough money to reunite her family.

Unit 5:
Mysterious Worlds

Secret of the Andes
Ann Nolan Clark
Puffin Books, 1980

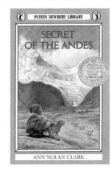

High up in the Andes there is a beautiful mountain valley, hidden away from the rest of the world. There, a young boy named Cusi helps an old Incan llama herder guard his precious flock. Cusi is an Incan Indian whose ancestors founded the great Incan Empire. The Incas built the capital city of Cuzco, in present-day Peru, which Cusi visits in the story. Accompanied by his pet llama, Cusi leaves the valley to go down to the "world of people" in order to search for his heart's desire. Cusi soon learns to understand the ancient Incan saying, "Grieve not if your searching circles."

James and the Giant Peach

Roald Dahl, illustrated by Lane Smith
Puffin Books, 1961, 1996

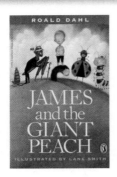

After his parents are eaten by an angry rhinoceros, James Trotter is sent to live with his two horrible aunts. James is miserable until he meets an old man in the woods who gives him a bag of magic crystals. When James accidentally drops some crystals by an old peach tree, strange things begin to happen. One peach at the tip of the tree grows larger and larger until it is as big as a house. When James crawls inside, he meets a roomful of oversized insects—Grasshopper, Centipede, Earthworm, and more. With a snap of the stem, the peach starts rolling away, and the adventure begins.

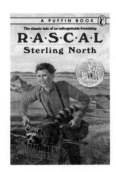

Rascal

Sterling North, illustrated by John Schoenherr
Puffin Books, 1963

Having lost his mother at the age of seven, Sterling North is a very independent eleven-year-old boy. One day, he finds a baby raccoon and decides to call him Rascal. Sterling watches in amazement as this baby raccoon, barely the size of his hand, instinctively washes everything before eating it. Sterling knows that every night Rascal will sneak into the house by hooking his claws onto the back screen door and head straight for Sterling's bed! Virtually everywhere Sterling goes, Rascal is there, and life is filled with one adventure after another.

Charlie and the Chocolate Factory

Roald Dahl, illustrated by Quentin Blake
Puffin Books, 1964, 1998

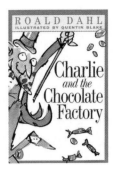

Willy Wonka, the strange and solitary chocolate maker, is opening his doors to the public. Five lucky people who find a Golden Ticket in their Wonka chocolate bars will receive a private tour of the factory, given by Mr. Wonka himself. For young Charlie Bucket, this is a dream come true. When he finds a dollar bill in the street, he cannot help but buy two Wonka candy bars—even though his family could certainly use the extra money for food. As Charlie unwraps the second chocolate bar, he sees the glimmer of gold just under the wrapper! The very next day, Charlie and his fellow winners step through the factory gates to discover whether or not the rumors surrounding the Chocolate Factory and its mysterious owner are true.

The Little White Horse

Elizabeth Goudge
Puffin Books, 1974

When young orphan Maria Merryweather arrives at Moonacre Manor, she feels as if she has entered Paradise. Her new guardian, her uncle Sir Benjamin, is kind and funny. The Manor itself feels like home right away. Every person and animal she meets is like an old friend. However, there is something incredibly sad beneath all of this beauty and comfort—a tragedy that happened years ago, shadowing Moonacre Manor and the town around it. Maria is determined to learn about the tragedy, change it, and give her own life story a happy ending.

abundant (ə bun´ dənt) *adj.* plentiful

accumulations (ə kyo̅o̅m´ yo̅o̅ lā´ shənz) *n.* buildup occurring over a period of time

adamant (ad´ ə mənt´) *adj.* not flexible; not willing to give in; stubborn; unyielding

aggrieved (ə grēvd´) *adj.* offended; wronged

anecdotes (an´ ik dōts´) *n.* short, entertaining tales

anonymity (an´ ə nim´ ə tē) *n.* the condition of being a stranger, of not being known by name

antennae (an ten´ ē) *n.* metal rods that receive TV or radio signals

aptitude (ap´ tə to̅o̅d´) *n.* natural ability

atone (a tōn´) *v.* make up for a wrong

becoming (bē kum´ iŋ) *adj.* suitable to the wearer

beseech (bi sēch´) *v.* beg

bough (bou) *n.* branch of a tree

bound (bound) *v.* tied

calculated (kal´ kyo̅o̅ lāt´ id) *v.* determined by using math

catastrophic (kat´ ə sträf´ ik) *adj.* causing a complete disaster

cavernous (kav´ ər nəs) *adj.* deep and empty

ceased (sēsd) *v.* stopped

chaotic (kā ät´ ik) *adj.* completely confused

chorus (kôr´ əs) *n.* the part of a song sung by many voices at once

clamor (klam´ ər) *n.* loud demand

coaxed (kōkst) *v.* tried to persuade

collision (kə lizh´ ən) *n.* coming together with a sudden violent force; a crash

composed (kəm pōzd´) *adj.* made up (of)

compulsory (kəm pul´ sə rē) *adj.* must be done; having specific requirements

conclusion (kən klo̅o̅´ zhən) *n.* belief or decision reached by reasoning

condemnation (kän´ dem nā´ shən) *n.* extreme disapproval; harsh judgment

confidence (kän´ fi dəns´) *n.* belief in one's own abilities

consequently (kän´ si kwent´ lē) *adj.* as a result

consoled (kən sōld´) *v.* comforted

consumed (kən so̅o̅md´) *v.* destroyed

consumption (kən sump´ shən) *n.* eating; drinking; using up

cordial (kôr´ jəl) *adj.* warm and friendly

covetousness (kuv´ ət əs nəs) *n.* envy

craned (krānd) *v.* stretched out (one's neck) for a better view

crescent (kres´ ənt) *n.* anything shaped like the moon in its first or last quarter

cudgel (kuj´ əl) *n.* short, thick stick or club

decisively (di sī´ siv lē) *adv.* with determination

declined (di klīnd´) *v.* refused

deem (dēm) *v.* judge

demise (dē mīz´) *n.* death

dense (dens) *adj.* tightly packed

detrimental (de´ trə ment´ əl) *adj.* harmful

devours (di vourz´) *v.* swallows whole

diagnosis (dī əg nō´ sis) *n.* explanation of or prediction about a person's medical condition

dilution (di lo̅o̅´ shən) *n.* process of weakening by mixing with something else

diminutive (də min´ yo̅o̅ tiv) *adj.* very small

disinfect (dis´ in fekt´) *n.* dialect for disinfectant, a substance that kills germs

dispute (di spyo̅o̅t´) *n.* argument; debate

dissonance (dis´ ə nəns) *n.* harsh combination of sounds

distorted (di stôr´ tid) *adj.* twisted out of the normal shape

diverse (də vurs´) *adj.* various; with differing characteristics

documentation (däk´ yo̅o̅ mən tā´ shən) *n.* supporting evidence

drawbacks (drô´ baks´) *n.* disadvantages

drawing (drô´ iŋ) *v.* bringing forth

drone (drōn) *n.* continuous humming sound

eased (ēzd) *v.* comforted; freed from pain

eloquent (el´ ə kwint) *adj.* persuasive and expressive

elusive (ē lo̅o̅´ siv) *adj.* always escaping

emaciated (ē mā´ shē āt id) *adj.* thin and bony as a result of starvation or disease

embedded (em bed´ əd) *adj.* firmly fixed in a surrounding material

embraced (em brāsd´) *v.* clasped in the arms, usually as an expression of affection

emerged (ē merjd´) *v.* came out from

emigrated (em´ i grāt´ id) *v.* left one country to settle in another

endured (en do̅o̅rd´) *v.* suffered through

episode (ep´ ə sōd´) *n.* one in a series of related events

etiquette (et´ i ket) *n.* acceptable social manners

evaporate (i vap´ ə rāt´) *v.* disappear like vapor

evolved (ē vôlvd´) *v.* grew gradually

exact (eg zakt´) *v.* take using force or authority

executioner (ek´ si kyo̅o̅´ shən ər) *n.* one who carries out a death penalty

exhaust (ig zôst´) *v.* use up

exhausted (eg zôs´ tid) *adj.* tired out

expend (ek spend´) *v.* spend

exuded (eg zyo̅o̅d´ əd) *v.* gave off; oozed

fallow (fal´ ō) *adj.* inactive; unproductive

famine (fa´ min) *n.* shortage of food

feats (fēts) *n.* remarkable deeds or acts

flaw (flô) *n.* break; crack

flee (flē) *v.* run or escape from danger

flue (flo̅o̅) *n.* a tube for the passage of smoke, as in a chimney

foliage (fō´ lē ij) *n.* leaves of trees and bushes

foresee (fôr sē´) *v.* know beforehand

fostering (fôs´ tər iŋ) *n.* taking care of

frenzied (fren´ zēd) *adj.* wild; frantic

fusing (fyo̅o̅´ ziŋ) *v.* joining permanently

gilded (gild´ id) *adj.* coated with a thin layer of gold

gnashes (nash´ iz) *v.* bites with grinding teeth

gnaw (nô) *v.* bite and wear away bit by bit with the teeth

goading (gō´ diŋ) *v.* pushing a person into acting, especially by using pain or insults

grant (grant) *v.* admit

grief (grēf) *n.* deep sadness

groveled (grä´ vəld) *v.* lay or crawled about before someone in hope of mercy

grudgingly (gruj´ iŋ lē) *adv.* in an unenthusiastic or resentful way

heathen (hē´ *th*ən) *adj.* uncivilized

hence (hens) *adv.* away

henceforth (hens fôrth´) *adv.* from now on

ignorance (ig´ nər əns) *n.* lack of knowledge, education, or experience

ignore (ig nôr´) *v.* pay no attention to

immense (i mens´) *adj.* huge

immortal (i môr´ təl) *adj.* living forever

incessantly (in ses´ ənt lē) *adj.* never ceasing

inconsistent (in´ kən sis´ tənt) *adj.* contradictory; not making sense

indignantly (in dig´ nənt lē) *adv.* angrily

inedible (in ed´ ə bəl) *adj.* not fit to be eaten

inevitably (in ev´ i tə blē) *adv.* unavoidably

initial (i nish´ əl) *adj.* original

inscribed (in skrībd´) *adj.* written on

instinctively (in stiŋk´ tiv lē) *adv.* done by instinct, without thinking

integrate (in´ tə grāt´) *v.* remove barriers and allow access to all

intimated (in´ tə māt´ id) *v.* hinted

intrigued (in trēgd´) *v.* fascinated

irrational (ir rash´ ə nəl) *adj.* unreasonable

jubilation (jōō′ bə lā′ shən) *n.* great joy

lair (lār) *n.* cave or den

lean (lēn) *adj.* thin

leisurely (lē′ zhər lē) *adj.* in an unhurried way

liable (lī′ ə bəl) *adj.* likely (to do something or have something happen to one)

loftily (lof′ tə lē) *adv.* in a superior way

majestically (mə jes′ tik lē) *adv.* grandly

malicious (mə lish′ əs) *adj.* showing evil intentions

mascot (mas′ kät) *n.* any person, animal, or thing adopted by a group for good luck

massive (mass′ iv) *adj.* huge; large

meanderings (mē an′ dər iŋz) *n.* aimless wanderings

meditated (med′ ə tāt id) *v.* thought deeply

melancholy (mel′ ən käl′ ē) *adj.* sad; gloomy

membranes (mem′ brānz) *n.* thin, flexible layers of tissue

menace (men′ əs) *n.* threat; a troublesome or annoying person

misapprehension (mis′ ap rē hen′ shən) *n.* misunderstanding

monotonous (mə nät′ ən əs′) *adj.* tiresome because it does not vary

monitoring (män′ i tər iŋ) *v.* watching or listening to

moot (mōōt) *adj.* not worthy of thought or discussion because it has been resolved

mortal (môr′ təl) *adj.* referring to humans, who must eventually die

mortified (môrt′ ə fīd′) *adj.* ashamed

nigh (nī) *adv.* near

nonchalantly (nän′ shə länt′ lē) *adv.* without concern or interest

novelty (näv′ əl tē) *n.* something new or unusual

obligatory (əb lig′ ə tôr′ ē) *adj.* required

obscure (əb skyoor′) *adj.* not well known

obstacle (äb′ stə kəl) *n.* something that stands in the way

obstinacy (äb′ stə nə sē) *n.* stubbornness

obstructed (əb strukt′ id) *adj.* blocked

occasionally (ō kā′ zhən əl ē) *adv.* now and then

offense (ə fens′) *n.* harmful act

opposition (äp′ ə zish′ ən) *n.* here, the other team

orator (ôr′ ə tər) *n.* speaker

peeved (pēvd) *v.* made bad-tempered or annoyed

peripheral (pə rif′ ər əl) *adj.* lying on the outside edge

piers (pirz) *n.* heavy structures supporting the sections of a bridge.

plagued (plāgd) *v.* tormented

plight (plīt) *n.* sad or dangerous situation

poising (poiz′ iŋ) *v.* balancing

precautionary (prē kô′ shən er′ ē) *adj.* taking care beforehand to prevent danger

prelude (prel′ yōōd′) *n.* an introduction to a main event or action coming later

prey (prā) *n.* animals hunted or killed for food by other animals

prolonged (prō lôŋd′) *adj.* long and drawn out

prospectors (prä′ spekt′ erz) *n.* people who search for valuable ores, such as gold

prowled (prould) *v.* crawled quietly and secretly

pulsating (pul′ sāt iŋ) *v.* beating or throbbing in rhythm

quarry (kwôr′ ē) *n.* prey

querulous (kwer′ yōō ləs) *adj.* inclined to find mistakes; complaining

rancor (raŋ′ kər) *n.* bitter hate or ill will

rapidly (rap′ id lē) *adv.* quickly

raucous (rô′ kəs) *adj.* loud and rowdy

ravaged (rav′ ijd) *v.* violently destroyed

ravenous (rav′ ə nəs′) *adj.* greedily hungry

reckless (rek′ lis) *adj.* not careful; taking chances

reflecting (ri flekt′ iŋ) *adj.* thinking seriously

regulation (reg′ yə lā′ shən) *n.* rule

reproachfully (ri prōch′ fəl lē) *adv.* with blame

repulse (ri puls′) *v.* drive back; repel an attack

resolutions (rez′ ə lōō′ shənz) *n.* intentions

retaliated (ri tal′ ē at′ id) *v.* harmed or did wrong to someone in return for an injury or wrong he or she has done

rue (rōō) *v.* regret

savoring (sā′ ver iŋ) *v.* enjoying with appreciation; tasting; relishing

scarce (skers) *adj.* few in number or infrequent; not common

scuttled (skut′ əld) *v.* scurried; scampered

sheared (shird) *v.* cut off sharply

sibling (sib′ liŋ) *n.* brother or sister

skimming (skim′ iŋ) *v.* gliding; moving swiftly and lightly over a surface

slanderous (slan′ der əs′) *adj.* untrue and damaging

slough (sluf) *v.* cast off; get rid of

soprano (sə pran′ ō) *n.* the highest singing voice of women, girls, or young boys

startled (stärt′ əld) *adj.* surprised

stingiest (stin′ jē əst) *adj.* most unwilling to spend money; cheapest

stoic (stō′ ik) *adj.* showing no reaction to good or bad events; unaffected by hardship

sublime (sə blīm′) *adj.* majestic; causing awe

subscribed (səb skrībd′) *adj.* signed up to give money

sufficient (sə fish′ ənt) *adj.* enough

summit (sum′ it) *n.* highest part

suspended (sə spend′ id) *v.* stopped for a time

swiftest (swift′ est) *adj.* the most rapid; the fastest

tableaus (ta blōz′) *n.* dramatic scenes or pictures

tactics (tak′ tiks) *n.* methods used for a particular purpose; tricks

tempest (tem′ pist) *n.* violent storm with high winds

timidly (tim′ id lē) *adv.* in a way that shows fear or shyness

toil (toil) *n.* hard work

tolerance (täl′ ər əns) *n.* respect for something different

trace (trās) *n.* mark left behind by something

transport (trans pôrt′) *v.* carry from one place to another

treacherous (trech′ ər əs) *adj.* dangerous

trudged (trujd) *v.* walked as if tired or with effort

tyrant (tī′ rənt) *n.* cruel, unjust ruler

uncomprehending (ən cäm prē hend′ iŋ) *adj.* not understanding

undulating (un′ dyōō lā′ tiŋ) *adj.* moving in waves, like a snake

ungrateful (un grāt′ fəl) *adj.* not thankful

variegated (ver′ ē ə gāt′ id) *adj.* marked with different colors in spots or streaks

veranda (və ran′ də) *n.* open porch, usually with a roof, along the outside of a building

veterans (vet′ ər ənz′) *n.* those having experience

vigilance (vij′ ə ləns) *n.* watchfulness

vigorously (vig′ ər əs lē) *adv.* forcefully; powerfully

wallowed (wäl′ ōd) *v.* rolled and tilted

TIPS FOR IMPROVING READING FLUENCY

When you were younger, you learned to read. Then, you read to expand your experiences or for pure enjoyment. Now, you are expected to read to learn. As you progress in school, you are given more and more material to read. The tips on these pages will help you improve your reading fluency, or your ability to read easily, smoothly, and expressively.

Keeping Your Concentration

One common problem that readers face is the loss of concentration. When you are reading an assignment, you might find yourself rereading the same sentence several times without really understanding it. The first step in changing this behavior is to notice that you do it. Becoming an active, aware reader will help you get the most from your assignments. Practice using these strategies:

- Cover what you have already read with a note card as you go along. Then, you will not be able to reread without noticing that you are doing it.
- Set a purpose for reading beyond just completing the assignment. Then, read actively by pausing to ask yourself questions about the material as you read.
- Use the Reading Strategy instruction and notes that appear with each selection in this textbook.
- Stop reading after a specified period of time (for example, 5 minutes) and summarize what you have read. To help you with this strategy, use the Reading Check questions that appear with each selection in this textbook. Reread to find any answers you do not know.

Reading Check
What common problem do many readers face?

Reading Phrases

Fluent readers read phrases rather than individual words. Reading this way will speed up your reading and improve your comprehension. Here are some useful ideas:

- Experts recommend rereading as a strategy to increase fluency. Choose a passage of text that is neither too hard nor too easy. Read the same passage aloud several times until you can read it smoothly. When you can read the passage fluently, pick another passage and keep practicing.
- Read aloud into a tape recorder. Then, listen to the recording, noting your accuracy, pacing, and expression. You can also read aloud and share feedback with a partner.
- Use the *Prentice Hall Listening to Literature* audiotapes or CDs to hear the selections read aloud. Read along silently in your textbook, noticing how the reader uses his or her voice and emphasizes certain words and phrases.

Reading Check
In what ways will reading phrases rather than individual words affect your reading?

Understanding Key Vocabulary

If you do not understand some of the words in an assignment, you may miss out on important concepts. Therefore, it is helpful to keep a dictionary nearby when you are reading. Follow these steps:

- Before you begin reading, scan the text for unfamiliar words or terms. Find out what those words mean before you begin reading.
- Use context—the surrounding words, phrases, and sentences—to help you determine the meanings of unfamiliar words.
- If you are unable to understand the meaning through context, refer to the dictionary.

☑ **Reading Check**

Why should you look up words you do not know when reading an assignment?

Paying Attention to Punctuation

When you read, pay attention to punctuation. Commas, periods, exclamation points, semicolons, and colons tell you when to pause or stop. They also indicate relationships between groups of words. When you recognize these relationships you will read with greater understanding and expression. Look at the chart below.

Punctuation Mark	Meaning
comma	brief pause
period	pause at the end of a thought
exclamation point	pause that indicates emphasis
semicolon	pause between related but distinct thoughts
colon	pause before giving explanation or examples

Using the Reading Fluency Checklist

Use the checklist below each time you read a selection in this textbook. In your Language Arts journal or notebook, note which skills you need to work on and chart your progress each week.

Reading Fluency Checklist

- ❏ Preview the text to check for difficult or unfamiliar words.
- ❏ Practice reading aloud.
- ❏ Read according to punctuation.
- ❏ Break down long sentences into the subject and its meaning.
- ❏ Read groups of words for meaning rather than reading single words.
- ❏ Read with expression (change your tone of voice to add meaning to the word).

Reading is a skill that can be improved with practice. The key to improving your fluency is to read. The more you read, the better your reading will become.

HIGH-FREQUENCY WORDS

Approximately fifty percent of the words you read will be the same one hundred words. Learning to instantly recognize **high-frequency words**—words that are used often in print—will greatly improve your reading fluency. Learn to instantly recognize the words on this page. Practice any that give you trouble.

the	said	could	things	large	still	seemed	second
of	there	people	our	must	learn	next	later
and	use	my	just	big	should	hard	miss
a	an	than	name	even	American	open	idea
to	each	first	good	such	world	example	enough
in	which	water	sentence	because	high	beginning	eat
is	she	been	man	turned	ever	life	face
you	do	called	think	here	near	always	watch
that	how	who	say	why	add	those	far
it	their	oil	great	asked	food	both	Indians
he	if	sit	where	went	between	paper	rally
was	will	now	help	men	own	together	almost
for	up	find	through	read	below	got	let
on	other	long	much	need	country	group	above
are	about	down	before	land	plants	often	girl
as	out	day	line	different	last	run	sometimes
with	many	did	right	home	school	important	mountains
his	then	get	too	us	father	until	cut
they	them	come	means	move	keep	children	young
I	these	made	old	try	trees	side	talk
at	so	may	any	kind	never	feet	soon
be	some	part	same	hand	started	car	list
this	her	over	tell	picture	city	miles	song
have	would	new	boy	again	earth	night	being
from	make	sound	following	change	eyes	walked	leave
or	like	take	came	off	light	white	family
one	him	only	want	play	thought	sea	it's
had	into	little	show	spell	head	began	
by	time	work	also	air	under	grow	
words	has	know	around	away	story	took	
but	look	place	form	animals	saw	river	
not	two	years	three	house	left	four	
what	more	live	small	point	don't	carry	
all	write	me	set	page	few	state	
were	go	back	put	letters	while	once	
we	see	give	end	mother	along	book	
when	number	most	does	answer	might	hear	
your	no	very	another	found	close	stop	
can	way	after	well	study	something	without	

ALLITERATION *Alliteration* is the repetition of initial conso-nant sounds. Writers use alliteration to draw attention to certain words or ideas, to imitate sounds, and to create musical effects.

ANALOGY An *analogy* makes a comparison between two or more things that are similar in some ways but otherwise unalike.

ANECDOTE An *anecdote* is a brief story about an interest-ing, amusing, or strange event. Writers tell anecdotes to enter-tain or to make a point.

ANTAGONIST An *antagonist* is a character or a force in conflict with a main character, or protagonist.

See *Conflict* and *Protagonist.*

ATMOSPHERE *Atmosphere,* or *mood,* is the feeling created in the reader by a literary work or passage.

AUTOBIOGRAPHY An *autobiography* is the story of the writer's own life, told by the writer. Autobiographical writing may tell about the person's whole life or only a part of it.

Because autobiographies are about real people and events, they are a form of nonfiction. Most autobiographies are written in the first person.

See *Biography, Nonfiction,* and *Point of View.*

BIOGRAPHY A *biography* is a form of nonfiction in which a writer tells the life story of another person. Most biographies are written about famous or admirable people. Although biographies are nonfiction, the most effective ones share the qualities of good narrative writing.

See *Autobiography* and *Nonfiction.*

CHARACTER A *character* is a person or an animal that takes part in the action of a literary work. The main, or *major,* character is the most important character in a story, poem, or play. A *minor* character is one who takes part in the action but is not the focus of attention.

Characters are sometimes classified as flat or round. A *flat character* is one-sided and often stereotypical. A *round charac-ter,* on the other hand, is fully developed and exhibits many traits—often both faults and virtues. Characters can also be classified as dynamic or static. A *dynamic character* is one who changes or grows during the course of the work. A *static char-acter* is one who does not change.

See *Characterization, Hero/Heroine,* and *Motive.*

CHARACTERIZATION *Characterization* is the act of creat-ing and developing a character. Authors use two major methods of characterization—*direct* and *indirect.* When using *direct* characterization, a writer states the *characters' traits,* or characteristics.

When describing a character indirectly, a writer depends on the reader to draw conclusions about the character's traits. Sometimes the writer tells what other participants in the story say and think about the character.

See *Character* and *Motive.*

CLIMAX The climax, also called the turning point, is the high point in the action of the plot. It is the moment of greatest ten-sion, when the outcome of the plot hangs in the balance.

See *Plot.*

COMEDY A *comedy* is a literary work, especially a play, which is light, often humorous or satirical, and ends happily. Comedies frequently depict ordinary characters faced with tem-porary difficulties and conflicts. Types of comedy include *romantic comedy,* which involves problems among lovers, and the *comedy of manners,* which satirically challenges social cus-toms of a society.

CONCRETE POEM A *concrete poem* is one with a shape that suggests its subject. The poet arranges the letters, punctu-ation, and lines to create an image, or picture, on the page.

CONFLICT A *conflict* is a struggle between opposing forces. Conflict is one of the most important elements of stories, novels, and plays because it causes the action. There are two kinds of conflict: external and internal. An *external conflict* is one in which a character struggles against some outside force, such as another person. Another kind of external conflict may occur between a character and some force in nature.

An *internal conflict* takes place within the mind of a charac-ter. The character struggles to make a decision, take an action, or overcome a feeling.

See *Plot.*

CONNOTATIONS The *connotation* of a word is the set of ideas associated with it in addition to its explicit meaning. The connotation of a word can be personal, based on individual expe-riences. More often, cultural connotations—those recognizable by most people in a group—determine a writer's word choices.

See also *Denotation.*

DENOTATION The *denotation* of a word is its dictionary meaning, independent of other associations that the word may have. The denotation of the word *lake,* for example, is "an inland body of water." "Vacation spot" and "place where the fishing is good" are connotations of the word *lake.*

See also *Connotation.*

DESCRIPTION A *description* is a portrait, in words, of a person, place, or object. Descriptive writing uses images that appeal to the five senses—sight, hearing, touch, taste, and smell.

See *Image.*

DEVELOPMENT See *Plot.*

DIALECT *Dialect* is the form of a language spoken by people in a particular region or group. Dialects differ in pronunciation, grammar, and word choice. The English language is divided into many dialects. British English differs from American English.

DIALOGUE A *dialogue* is a conversation between characters. In poems, novels, and short stories, dialogue is usually set off by quotation marks to indicate a speaker's exact words.

In a play, dialogue follows the names of the characters, and no quotation marks are used.

DRAMA A *drama* is a story written to be performed by actors. Although a drama is meant to be performed, one can also read the script, or written version, and imagine the action. The *script* of a drama is made up of dialogue and stage directions. The *dialogue* is the words spoken by the actors. The *stage directions,* usually printed in italics, tell how the actors should look, move, and speak. They also describe the setting, sound effects, and lighting.

Dramas are often divided into parts called *acts.* The acts are often divided into smaller parts called *scenes.*

DYNAMIC CHARACTER See *Character.*

ESSAY An *essay* is a short nonfiction work about a particular subject. Most essays have a single major focus and a clear introduction, body, and conclusion.

There are many types of essays. An *informal essay* uses casual, conversational language. A *historical essay* gives facts, explanations, and insights about historical events. An *expository essay* explains an idea by breaking it down. A *narrative essay* tells a story about a real-life experience. An *informational essay* explains a process. A *persuasive essay* offers an opinion and supports it.

See *Exposition, Narration,* and *Persuasion.*

EXPOSITION In the plot of a story or a drama, the *exposition,* or introduction, is the part of the work that introduces the characters, setting, and basic situation.

See *Plot.*

EXPOSITORY WRITING *Expository writing* is writing that explains or informs.

EXTENDED METAPHOR In an *extended metaphor,* as in a regular metaphor, a subject is spoken or written of as though it were something else. However, extended metaphor differs from regular metaphor in that several connected comparisons are made.

See *Metaphor.*

EXTERNAL CONFLICT See *Conflict.*

FABLE A *fable* is a brief story or poem, usually with animal characters, that teaches a lesson, or moral. The moral is usually stated at the end of the fable.

See *Irony* and *Moral.*

FANTASY A *fantasy* is highly imaginative writing that contains elements not found in real life. Examples of fantasy include stories that involve supernatural elements, stories that resemble fairy tales, stories that deal with imaginary places and creatures, and science-fiction stories.

See *Science Fiction.*

FICTION *Fiction* is prose writing that tells about imaginary characters and events. Short stories and novels are works of fiction. Some writers base their fiction on actual events and people, adding invented characters, dialogue, settings, and plots. Other writers rely on imagination alone.

See *Narration, Nonfiction,* and *Prose.*

FIGURATIVE LANGUAGE *Figurative language* is writing or speech that is not meant to be taken literally. The many types of figurative language are known as *figures of speech.* Common figures of speech include metaphor, personification, and simile. Writers use figurative language to state ideas in vivid and imaginative ways.

See *Metaphor, Personification, Simile,* and *Symbol.*

FIGURE OF SPEECH See *Figurative Language.*

FLASHBACK A *flashback* is a scene within a story that interrupts the sequence of events to relate events that occurred in the past.

FLAT CHARACTER See *Character.*

FOLK TALE A *folk tale* is a story composed orally and then passed from person to person by word of mouth. Folk tales originated among people who could neither read nor write. These people entertained one another by telling stories aloud—often dealing with heroes, adventure, magic, or romance. Eventually, modern scholars collected these stories and wrote them down.

Folk tales reflect the cultural beliefs and environments from which they come.

See *Fable, Legend, Myth,* and *Oral Tradition.*

FOOT See *Meter.*

FORESHADOWING *Foreshadowing* is the author's use of clues to hint at what might happen later in the story. Writers use foreshadowing to build their readers' expectations and to create suspense.

FREE VERSE *Free verse* is poetry not written in a regular, rhythmical pattern, or meter. The poet is free to write lines of any length or with any number of stresses, or beats. Free verse is therefore less constraining than *metrical verse,* in which every line must have a certain length and a certain number of stresses.

See *Meter.*

GENRE A *genre* is a division or type of literature. Literature is commonly divided into three major genres: poetry, prose, and drama. Each major genre is, in turn, divided into lesser genres, as follows:

1. *Poetry:* lyric poetry, concrete poetry, dramatic poetry, narrative poetry, epic poetry
2. *Prose:* fiction (novels and short stories) and nonfiction (biography, autobiography, letters, essays, and reports)
3. *Drama:* serious drama and tragedy, comic drama, melodrama, and farce

See *Drama, Poetry,* and *Prose.*

HAIKU The *haiku* is a three-line Japanese verse form. The first and third lines of a haiku each have five syllables. The second line has seven syllables. A writer of haiku uses images to create a single, vivid picture, generally of a scene from nature.

HERO/HEROINE A *hero* or *heroine* is a character whose actions are inspiring, or noble. Often heroes and heroines struggle to overcome the obstacles and problems that stand in their way. Note that the term *hero* was originally used only for male characters, while heroic female characters were always called *heroines.* However, it is now acceptable to use *hero* to refer to females as well as to males.

HISTORICAL FICTION In *historical fiction* real events, places, or people are incorporated into a fictional or made-up story.

IMAGES *Images* are words or phrases that appeal to one or more of the five senses. Writers use images to describe how their subjects look, sound, feel, taste, and smell. Poets often paint images, or word pictures, that appeal to your senses. These pictures help you to experience the poem fully.

IMAGERY See *Image.*

INTERNAL CONFLICT See *Conflict.*

IRONY *Irony* is the general name given to literary techniques that involve surprising, interesting, or amusing contradictions.

JOURNAL A *journal* is a daily, or periodic, account of events and the writer's thoughts and feelings about those events. Personal journals are not normally written for publication, but sometimes they do get published later with permission from the author or the author's family.

LEGEND A *legend* is a widely told story about the past—one that may or may not have a foundation in fact. Every culture has its own legends—its familiar, traditional stories.

See *Folk Tale, Myth,* and *Oral Tradition.*

LETTERS A *letter* is a written communication from one person to another. In personal letters, the writer shares information and his or her thoughts and feelings with one other person or group. Although letters are not normally written for publication, they sometimes do get published later with the permission of the author or the author's family.

LIMERICK A *limerick* is a humorous, rhyming, five-line poem with a specific meter and rhyme scheme. Most limericks have three strong stresses in lines 1, 2, and 5 and two strong stresses in lines 3 and 4. Most follow the rhyme scheme *aabba.*

LYRIC POEM A *lyric poem* is a highly musical verse that expresses the observations and feelings of a single speaker. It creates a single, unified impression.

MAIN CHARACTER See *Character.*

MEDIA ACCOUNTS *Media Accounts* are reports, explanations, opinions, or descriptions written for television, radio, newspapers, and magazines. While some media accounts report only facts, others include the writer's thoughts and reflections.

METAPHOR A *metaphor* is a figure of speech in which something is described as though it were something else. A metaphor, like a simile, works by pointing out a similarity between two unlike things.

See *Extended Metaphor* and *Simile.*

METER The *meter* of a poem is its rhythmical pattern. This pattern is determined by the number of *stresses,* or beats, in each line. To describe the meter of a poem, read it emphasizing the beats in each line. Then, mark the stressed and unstressed syllables, as follows:

My fath | er was | the first | to hear |

As you can see, each strong stress is marked with a slanted line (´) and each unstressed syllable with a horseshoe symbol (˘). The weak and strong stresses are then divided by vertical lines (|) into groups called *feet*.

MINOR CHARACTER See *Character.*

MOOD See *Atmosphere.*

MORAL A *moral* is a lesson taught by a literary work. A fable usually ends with a moral that is directly stated. A poem, novel, short story, or essay often suggests a moral that is not directly stated. The moral must be drawn by the reader, based on other elements in the work.

See *Fable.*

MOTIVATION See *Motive.*

MOTIVE A *motive* is a reason that explains or partially explains a character's thoughts, feelings, actions, or speech. Writers try to make their characters' motives, or motivations, as clear as possible. If the motives of a main character are not clear, then the character will not be believable.

Characters are often motivated by needs, such as food and shelter. They are also motivated by feelings, such as fear, love, and pride. Motives may be obvious or hidden.

MYTH A *myth* is a fictional tale that explains the actions of gods or heroes or the origins of elements of nature. Myths are part of the oral tradition. They are composed orally and then passed from generation to generation by word of mouth. Every ancient culture has its own mythology, or collection of myths. Greek and Roman myths are known collectively as *classical mythology.*

See *Oral Tradition.*

NARRATION *Narration* is writing that tells a story. The act of telling a story is also called narration. Each piece is a *narrative.* A story told in fiction, nonfiction, poetry, or even in drama is called a narrative.

See *Narrative, Narrative Poem,* and *Narrator.*

NARRATIVE A *narrative* is a story. A narrative can be either fiction or nonfiction. Novels and short stories are types of fictional narratives. Biographies and autobiographies are nonfiction narratives. Poems that tell stories are also narratives.

See *Narration* and *Narrative Poem.*

NARRATIVE POEM A *narrative poem* is a story told in verse. Narrative poems often have all the elements of short stories, including characters, conflict, and plot.

NARRATOR A *narrator* is a speaker or a character who tells a story. The narrator's perspective is the way he or she sees things. A *third-person narrator* is one who stands outside the action and speaks about it. A *first-person narrator* is one who tells a story and participates in its action.

See *Point of View.*

NONFICTION *Nonfiction* is prose writing that presents and explains ideas or that tells about real people, places, objects, or events. Autobiographies, biographies, essays, reports, letters, memos, and newspaper articles are all types of nonfiction.

See *Fiction.*

NOVEL A *novel* is a long work of fiction. Novels contain such elements as characters, plot, conflict, and setting. The writer of novels, or novelist, develops these elements. In addition to its main plot, a novel may contain one or more subplots, or independent, related stories. A novel may also have several themes. See *Fiction* and *Short Story.*

NOVELLA A fiction work that is longer than a short story but shorter than a novel.

ONOMATOPOEIA *Onomatopoeia* is the use of words that imitate sounds. *Crash, buzz, screech, hiss, neigh, jingle,* and *cluck* are examples of onomatopoeia. *Chickadee, towhee,* and *whippoorwill* are onomatopoeic names of birds.

Onomatopoeia can help put the reader in the activity of a poem.

ORAL TRADITION *Oral tradition* is the passing of songs, stories, and poems from generation to generation by word of mouth. Folk songs, folk tales, legends, and myths all come from the oral tradition. No one knows who first created these stories and poems.

See *Folk Tale, Legend,* and *Myth.*

PERSONIFICATION *Personification* is a type of figurative language in which a nonhuman subject is given human characteristics.

PERSPECTIVE See *Narrator* and *Point of View.*

PERSUASION *Persuasion* is used in writing or speech that attempts to convince the reader or listener to adopt a particular opinion or course of action. Newspaper editorials and letters to the editor use persuasion. So do advertisements and campaign speeches given by political candidates.

See *Essay.*

PLAYWRIGHT A *playwright* is a person who writes plays. William Shakespeare is regarded as the greatest playwright in English literature.

PLOT *Plot* is the sequence of events in which each event results from a previous one and causes the next. In most novels, dramas, short stories, and narrative poems, the plot involves both characters and a central conflict. The plot usually begins with an *exposition* that introduces the setting, the characters, and the basic situation. This is followed by the *inciting incident,* which introduces the central conflict. The conflict then increases during the *development* until it reaches a high point of interest or suspense, the *climax*. The climax is followed by the *falling action,* or end, of the central conflict. Any events that occur during the falling action make up the *resolution* or *denouement*.

Some plots do not have all of these parts. Some stories begin with the inciting incident and end with the resolution.

See *Conflict*.

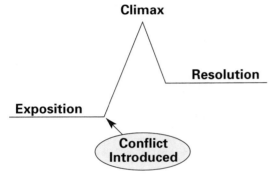

POETRY *Poetry* is one of the three major types of literature, the others being prose and drama. Most poems make use of highly concise, musical, and emotionally charged language. Many also make use of imagery, figurative language, and special devices of sound such as rhyme. Major types of poetry include *lyric poetry, narrative poetry,* and *concrete poetry.*

See *Concrete Poem, Genre, Lyric Poem,* and *Narrative Poem*.

POINT OF VIEW Point of view is the perspective, or vantage point, from which a story is told. It is either a narrator outside the story or a character in the story. *First-person point of view* is told by a character who uses the first-person pronoun "I."

The two kinds of *third-person point of view,* limited and omniscient, are called "third person" because the narrator uses third-person pronouns such as *he* and *she* to refer to the characters. There is no "I" telling the story.

In stories told from the *omniscient third-person point of view,* the narrator knows and tells about what each character feels and thinks.

In stories told from the *limited third-person point of view,* the narrator relates the inner thoughts and feelings of only one character, and everything is viewed from this character's perspective.

See *Narrator*.

PROBLEM See *Conflict*.

PROSE *Prose* is the ordinary form of written language. Most writing that is not poetry, drama, or song is considered prose. Prose is one of the major genres of literature and occurs in two forms—fiction and nonfiction.

See *Fiction, Genre,* and *Nonfiction*.

PROTAGONIST The *protagonist* is the main character in a literary work. Often, the protagonist is a person, but sometimes it can be an animal.

See *Antagonist* and *Character*.

REFRAIN A *refrain* is a regularly repeated line or group of lines in a poem or a song.

REPETITION *Repetition* is the use, more than once, of any element of language—a sound, word, phrase, clause, or sentence. Repetition is used in both prose and poetry.

See *Alliteration, Meter, Plot, Rhyme,* and *Rhyme Scheme*.

RESOLUTION The *resolution* is the outcome of the conflict in a plot.

See *Plot*.

RHYME *Rhyme* is the repetition of sounds at the ends of words. Poets use rhyme to lend a songlike quality to their verses and to emphasize certain words and ideas. Many traditional poems contain *end rhymes,* or rhyming words at the ends of lines.

Another common device is the use of *internal rhymes,* or rhyming words within lines. Internal rhyme also emphasizes the flowing nature of a poem.

See *Rhyme Scheme*.

RHYME SCHEME A *rhyme scheme* is a regular pattern of rhyming words in a poem. To indicate the rhyme scheme of a poem, one uses lowercase letters. Each rhyme is assigned a different letter, as follows in the first stanza of "Dust of Snow," by Robert Frost:

The way a crow	*a*
Shook down on me	*b*
The dust of snow	*a*
From a hemlock tree	*b*

Thus, the stanza has the rhyme scheme *abab*.

RHYTHM *Rhythm* is the pattern of stressed and unstressed syllables in spoken or written language.

See *Meter*.

ROUND CHARACTER See *Character*.

SCENE A *scene* is a section of uninterrupted action in the act of a drama.

See *Drama.*

SCIENCE FICTION *Science fiction* combines elements of fiction and fantasy with scientific fact. Many science-fiction stories are set in the future.

SENSORY LANGUAGE *Sensory language* is writing or speech that appeals to one or more of the five senses.

See *Image.*

SETTING The *setting* of a literary work is the time and place of the action. The setting includes all the details of a place and time—the year, the time of day, even the weather. The place may be a specific country, state, region, community, neighborhood, building, institution, or home. Details such as dialects, clothing, customs, and modes of transportation are often used to establish setting. In most stories, the setting serves as a backdrop—a context in which the characters interact. Setting can also help to create a feeling, or atmosphere.

See *Atmosphere.*

SHORT STORY A *short story* is a brief work of fiction. Like a novel, a short story presents a sequence of events, or plot. The plot usually deals with a central conflict faced by a main character, or protagonist. The events in a short story usually communicate a message about life or human nature. This message, or central idea, is the story's theme.

See *Conflict, Plot,* and *Theme.*

SIMILE A *simile* is a figure of speech that uses *like* or *as* to make a direct comparison between two unlike ideas. Everyday speech often contains similes, such as "pale as a ghost," "good as gold," "spread like wildfire," and "clever as a fox."

SPEAKER The *speaker* is the imaginary voice a poet uses when writing a poem. The speaker is the character who tells the poem. This character, or voice, often is not identified by name. There can be important differences between the poet and the poem's speaker.

See *Narrator.*

STAGE DIRECTIONS *Stage directions* are notes included in a drama to describe how the work is to be performed or staged. Stage directions are usually printed in italics and enclosed within parentheses or brackets. Some stage directions describe the movements, costumes, emotional states, and ways of speaking of the characters.

STAGING *Staging* includes the setting, the lighting, the costumes, special effects, music, dance, and so on that go into putting on a stage performance of a drama.

See *Drama.*

STANZA A *stanza* is a group of lines of poetry that are usually similar in length and pattern and are separated by spaces. A stanza is like a paragraph of poetry—it states and develops a single main idea.

STATIC CHARACTER See *Character.*

SURPRISE ENDING A *surprise ending* is a conclusion that is unexpected. The reader has certain expectations about the ending based on details in the story. Often, a surprise ending is *foreshadowed,* or subtly hinted at, in the course of the work.

See *Foreshadowing* and *Plot.*

SUSPENSE *Suspense* is a feeling of anxious uncertainty about the outcome of events in a literary work. Writers create suspense by raising questions in the minds of their readers.

SYMBOL A *symbol* is anything that stands for or represents something else. Symbols are common in everyday life. A dove with an olive branch in its beak is a symbol of peace. A blindfolded woman holding a balanced scale is a symbol of justice. A crown is a symbol of a king's status and authority.

THEME The *theme* is a central message, concern, or purpose in a literary work. A theme can usually be expressed as a generalization, or a general statement, about human beings or about life. The theme of a work is not a summary of its plot. The theme is the writer's central idea.

Although a theme may be stated directly in the text, it is more often presented indirectly. When the theme is stated indirectly, or implied, the reader must figure out what the theme is by looking carefully at what the work reveals about people or about life.

TONE The *tone* of a literary work is the writer's attitude toward his or her audience and subject. The tone can often be described by a single adjective, such as *formal* or *informal, serious* or *playful, bitter,* or *ironic.* Factors that contribute to the tone are word choice, sentence structure, line length, rhyme, rhythm, and repetition.

TRAGEDY A *tragedy* is a work of literature, especially a play, that results in a catastrophe for the main character. In ancient Greek drama, the main character is always a significant person—a king or a hero—and the cause of the tragedy is a tragic flaw, or weakness, in his or her character. In modern drama, the main character can be an ordinary person, and the cause of the tragedy can be some evil in society itself. The purpose of tragedy is not only to arouse fear and pity in the audience, but also, in some cases, to convey a sense of the grandeur and nobility of the human spirit.

TURNING POINT See *Climax.*

RUBRICS

What is a rubric?

A rubric is a tool, often in the form of a chart or a grid, that helps you assess your work. Rubrics are particularly helpful for writing and speaking assignments.

To help you or others assess, or evaluate, your work, a rubric offers several specific criteria to be applied to your work. Then the rubric helps you or an evaluator indicate your range of success or failure according to those specific criteria. Rubrics are often used to evaluate writing for standardized tests.

Using a rubric will save you time, focus your learning, and improve the work you do. When you know what the rubric will be before you begin writing a persuasive essay, for example, as you write you will be aware of specific criteria that are important in that kind of an essay. As you evaluate the essay before giving it to your teacher, you will focus on the specific areas that your teacher wants you to master— or on areas that you know present challenges for you. Instead of searching through your work randomly for any way to improve it or correct its errors, you will have a clear and helpful focus on specific criteria.

How are rubrics constructed?

Rubrics can be constructed in several different ways.
- Your teacher may assign a rubric for a specific assignment.
- Your teacher may direct you to a rubric in your textbook.
- Your teacher and your class may construct a rubric for a particular assignment together.
- You and your classmates may construct a rubric together.
- You may create your own rubric with criteria you want to evaluate in your work.

How will a rubric help me?

A rubric will help you assess your work on a scale. Scales vary from rubric to rubric but usually range from 6 to 1, 5 to 1, or 4 to 1, with 6, 5, or 4 being the highest score and 1 being the lowest. If someone else is using the rubric to assess your work, the rubric will give your evaluator a clear range within which to place your work. If you are using the rubric yourself, it will help you make improvements to your work.

What are the types of rubrics?

- A **holistic rubric** has general criteria that can apply to a variety of assignments. See p. R20 for an example of a holistic rubric.
- An **analytic rubric** is specific to a particular assignment. The criteria for evaluation address the specific issues important in that assignment. See p. R19 for examples of analytic rubrics.

SAMPLE ANALYTIC RUBRICS

Rubric With a 4-point Scale

The following analytic rubric is an example of a rubric to assess a persuasive essay.
It will help you evaluate audience and purpose, organization, elaboration, and use of language.

	Audience/Purpose	Organization	Elaboration	Use of Language
4	Demonstrates highly effective word choice; clearly focused on task.	Uses clear, consistent organizational strategy.	Provides convincing, well-elaborated reasons to support the position.	Incorporates transitions; includes very few mechanical errors.
3	Demonstrates good word choice; states focus on persuasive task.	Uses clear organizational strategy with occasional inconsistencies.	Provides two or more moderately elaborated reasons to support the position.	Incorporates some transitions; includes few mechanical errors.
2	Shows some good word choices; minimally states focus on persuasive task.	Uses inconsistent organizational strategy; presentation is not logical.	Provides several reasons but few are elaborated; only one elaborated reason.	Incorporates few transitions; includes many mechanical errors.
1	Shows lack of attention to persuasive task.	Demonstrates lack of organizational strategy.	Provides no specific reasons or does not elaborate.	Does not connect ideas; includes many mechanical errors.

Rubric With a 6-point Scale

The following analytic rubric is an example of a rubric to assess a persuasive essay.
It will help you evaluate presentation, position, evidence, and arguments.

	Presentation	Position	Evidence	Arguments
6	Essay clearly and effectively addresses an issue with more than one side.	Essay clearly states a supportable position on the issue.	All evidence is logically organized, well presented, and supports the position.	All reader concerns and counterarguments are presented effectively.
5	Most of essay addresses an issue that has more than one side.	Essay clearly states a position on the issue.	Most evidence is logically organized, well presented, and supports the position.	Most reader concerns and counterarguments are presented effectively.
4	Essay adequately addresses issue that has more than one side.	Essay adequately states a position on the issue.	Many parts of evidence support the position; some evidence is out of order.	Many reader concerns and counterarguments are presented adequately.
3	Essay addresses issue with two sides but does not present second side clearly.	Essay states a position on the issue, but the position is difficult to support.	Some evidence supports the position, but some evidence is out of order.	Some reader concerns and counterarguments are presented.
2	Essay addresses issue with two sides but does not present second side.	Essay states a position on the issue, but the position is not supportable.	Not much evidence supports the position, and what is included is out of order.	A few reader concerns and counterarguments are presented.
1	Essay does not address issue with more than one side.	Essay does not state a position on the issue.	No evidence supports the position.	No reader concerns or counterarguments are presented.

SAMPLE HOLISTIC RUBRIC

Holistic rubrics such as this one are sometimes used to assess writing assignments on standardized tests. Notice that the criteria for evaluation are focus, organization, support, and use of conventions.

Points	Criteria
6 Points	• The writing is strongly focused and shows fresh insight into the writing task. • The writing is marked by a sense of completeness and coherence and is organized with a logical progression of ideas. • A main idea is fully developed, and support is specific and substantial. • A mature command of the language is in evidence, and the writing may employ characteristic creative writing strategies. • Sentence structure is varied, and writing is free of all but purposefully used fragments. • Virtually no errors in writing conventions appear.
5 Points	• The writing is clearly focused on the task. • The writing is well organized and has a logical progression of ideas, though there may be occasional lapses. • A main idea is well developed and supported with relevant details. • Command of the language is mature. • Sentence structure is varied, and the writing is free of fragments, except when used purposefully. • Writing conventions are followed correctly.
4 Points	• The writing is clearly focused on the task, but extraneous material may intrude at times. • A clear organizational pattern is present, though lapses may occur. • A main idea is adequately supported, but development may be uneven. • Sentence structure is generally free of fragments but shows little variation. • Writing conventions are generally followed correctly.
3 Points	• Writing is generally focused on the task, but extraneous material may intrude at times. • An organizational pattern is evident, but writing may lack a logical progression of ideas. • Support for the main idea is generally present but is sometimes illogical. • Sentence structure is generally free of fragments, but there is almost no variation. • The work generally demonstrates a knowledge of writing conventions, with occasional misspellings.
2 Points	• The writing is related to the task but generally lacks focus. • There is little evidence of organizational pattern, and there is little sense of cohesion. • Support for the main idea is generally inadequate, illogical, or absent. • Sentence structure is unvaried, and serious errors may occur. • Errors in writing conventions and spelling are frequent.
1 Point	• The writing may have little connection to the task and is generally unfocused. • There has been little attempt at organization or development. • The paper seems fragmented, with no clear main idea. • Sentence structure is unvaried, and serious errors appear. • Poor word choice and poor command of the language obscure meaning. • Errors in writing conventions and spelling are frequent.
Unscorable	The paper is considered unscorable if: • The response is unrelated to the task or is simply a rewording of the prompt. • The response has been copied from a published work. • The student did not write a response. • The response is illegible. • The words in the response are arranged with no meaning. • There is an insufficient amount of writing to score.

STUDENT MODEL

Persuasive Writing

This persuasive essay, which would receive a top score according to a persuasive rubric, is a response to the following writing prompt, or assignment:

Most young people today spend more than 5 hours a day watching television. Many adults worry about the effects on youth of seeing too much television violence. Write a persuasive piece in which you argue against or defend the effects of television watching on young people. Be sure to include examples to support your views.

Until the television was invented, families spent their time doing different activities. Now most families stay home and watch TV. Watching TV risks the family's health, reduces the children's study time, and is a bad influence on young minds. Watching television can be harmful.

> The writer clearly states a position in the first paragraph.

The most important reason why watching TV is bad is that the viewers get less exercise. For example, instead of watching their favorite show, people could exercise for 30 minutes. If people spent less time watching TV and more time exercising, then they could have healthier bodies. My mother told me a story about a man who died of a heart attack because he was out of shape from watching television all the time. Obviously, watching TV can put a person's health in danger.

> Each paragraph provides details that support the writer's main points.

Furthermore, watching television reduces children's study time. For example, children would spend more time studying if they didn't watch television. If students spent more time studying at home, then they would make better grades at school. Last week I had a major test in science, but I didn't study because I started watching a movie. I was not prepared for the test and my grade reflected my lack of studying. Indeed, watching television is bad because it can hurt a student's grades.

Finally, watching TV can be a bad influence on children. For example, some TV shows have inappropriate language and too much violence. If children watch programs that use bad language and show violence, then they may start repeating these actions because they think the behavior is "cool." In fact, it has been proven that children copy what they see on TV. Clearly, watching TV is bad for children and it affects children's behavior.

In conclusion, watching television is a bad influence for these reasons: It reduces people's exercise time and students' study time and it shows children inappropriate behavior. Therefore, people should take control of their lives and stop allowing television to harm them.

> The conclusion restates the writer's position.

TYPES OF WRITING

NARRATION

Whenever writers tell any type of story, they are using **narration.** While there are many kinds of narration, most narratives share certain elements, such as characters, a setting, a sequence of events, and, often, a theme.

Autobiographical writing tells the story of an event or person in the writer's life.

Biographical writing is a writer's account of another person's life.

Short story A short story is a brief, creative narrative—a retelling of events arranged to hold a reader's attention.

A few types of short stories are realistic stories, fantasy, science-fiction stories, and adventure stories.

DESCRIPTION

Descriptive writing is writing that creates a vivid picture of a person, place, thing, or event. Descriptive writing can stand on its own or be part of a longer work, such as a short story.

Descriptive writing includes descriptions of people or places, remembrances, observations, vignettes, and character profiles.

PERSUASION

Persuasion is writing or speaking that attempts to convince people to accept a position or take a desired action. When used effectively, persuasive writing has the power to change people's lives. As a reader and a writer, you will find yourself engaged in many forms of persuasion.

Forms of persuasive writing include persuasive essays, advertisements, persuasive letters, editorials, persuasive speeches, and public-service announcements.

EXPOSITORY WRITING

Expository writing is writing that informs or explains. The information you include in expository writing is factual or based on fact. Effective expository writing reflects a well-thought-out organization—one that includes a clear introduction, body, and conclusion. The organization should be appropriate for the type of exposition you are writing. Here are some types of exposition.

Comparison-and-Contrast essay A comparison-and-contrast essay analyzes the similarities and differences between two or more things.

Cause-and-Effect essay A cause-and-effect essay is expository writing that explains the reasons why something happened or the results an event or situation will probably produce. You may examine several causes of a single effect or several effects of a single cause.

Problem-and-Solution essay The purpose of a problem-and-solution essay is to describe a problem and offer one or more solutions to it. It describes a clear set of steps to achieve a result.

How-to essay A how-to essay explains how to do or make something. You break the process down into a series of logical steps and explain the steps in order.

Summary A summary is a brief statement of the main ideas and significant supporting details presented in a piece of writing. A summary should include

- main events, ideas, or images.
- connections among significant details.
- your own words.
- underlying meaning rather than superficial details.
- background information, such as setting or characters.

RESEARCH WRITING

Writers often use outside research to gather information and explore subjects of interest. The product of that research is called **research writing.** Good research writing does not simply repeat information. It guides readers through a topic, showing them why each fact matters and creating an overall picture of the subject. Here are some types of research writing.

Research report A research report presents information gathered from reference books, observations, interviews, or other sources.

Biographical report A biographical report examines the high points and achievements in the life of a notable person. It includes dates, details, and main events in the person's life as well as background on the period in which the person lived. The writer may also make educated guesses about the reasons behind events in the person's life.

Multimedia report A multimedia report presents information gathered from a variety of reliable sources, both print and nonprint. A wide range of materials are available, such as tape recorders, videocameras, slides, photographs, overhead projectors, prerecorded music and sound effects, digital imaging, graphics software, computers, spreadsheets, data bases, electronic resources, and Web sites.

I-Search report An I-Search report begins with a topic of immediate concern to you and provides well-researched information on that topic. Unlike a research report, it tells the story of your exploration of the topic, using the pronoun *I*. It explains

- your purpose in learning about the topic.
- the story of how you researched it.
- an account of what you learned.

RESPONSE TO LITERATURE

A **response to literature** is an essay or other type of writing that discusses and interprets what is of value in a book, short story, essay, article, or poem. You take a careful, critical look at various important elements in the work.

In addition to the standard literary essay, here are some other types of responses to literature.

Literary criticism Literary criticism is the result of literary analysis—the examination of a literary work or a body of literature. In literary criticism, you make a judgment or evaluation by looking carefully and critically at various important elements in the work. You then attempt to explain how the author has used those elements and how effectively they work together to convey the author's message.

Book or movie reviews A book review gives readers an impression of a book, encouraging them either to read it or to avoid reading it. A movie review begins with a basic response to whether or not you enjoyed the movie, and then explains the reasons why or why not.

Letter to an author People sometimes respond to a work of literature by writing a letter to the writer. It lets the writer know what a reader found enjoyable or disappointing in a work. You can praise the work, ask questions, or offer constructive criticism.

Comparisons of works A comparison of works highlights specific features of two or more works by comparing them.

CREATIVE WRITING

Creative writing blends imagination, ideas, and emotions, and allows you to present your own unique view of the world. Poems, plays, short stories, dramas, and even some cartoons are examples of creative writing. Here are some types of creative writing.

Lyric poem A lyric poem uses sensory images, figurative language, and sound devices to express deep thoughts and feelings about a subject. Writers give lyric poems a musical quality by employing sound devices, such as rhyme, rhythm, alliteration, and onomatopoeia.

Narrative poem A narrative poem is similar to a short story in that it has a plot, characters, and a theme. However, a writer divides a narrative poem into stanzas, usually composed of rhyming lines that have a definite rhythm, or beat.

Song lyrics Song lyrics, or words to accompany a song contain many elements of poetry—rhyme, rhythm, repetition, and imagery. In addition, song lyrics convey emotions, as well as interesting ideas.

Drama A drama or a dramatic scene is a story that is intended to be performed. The story is told mostly through what the actors say (dialogue) and what they do (action).

PRACTICAL AND TECHNICAL DOCUMENTS

Practical writing is fact-based writing that people do in the workplace or in their day-to-day lives. A business letter, memorandum, school form, job application, and a letter of inquiry are a few examples of practical writing.

Technical documents are fact-based documents that identify the sequence of activities needed to design a system, operate a tool, follow a procedure, or explain the bylaws of an organization. You encounter technical writing every time you read a manual or a set of instructions.

In the following descriptions, you'll find tips for tackling several types of practical and technical writing.

Business letter A formal letter that follows one of several specific formats. (See page R26.)

News release A news release, also called a press release, announces factual information about upcoming events. A writer might send a news release to a local newspaper, local radio station, TV station, or other media that will publicize the information.

Guidelines Guidelines give information about how people should act or provide tips on how to do something.

Process explanation A process explanation is a step-by-step explanation of how to do something. The explanation should be clear and specific and might include diagrams or other illustrations to further clarify the process.

Proofreading and Preparing Manuscript

Before preparing a final copy, proofread your manuscript. The chart shows the standard symbols for marking corrections to be made.

Proofreading Symbols	
insert	∧
delete	⤺
close space	⌒
new paragraph	¶
add comma	⋏
add period	⊙
transpose (switch)	∼
change to cap	⎁
change to lowercase	ⱻ

- Choose a standard, easy-to-read font.
- Type or print on one side of unlined 8 1/2" x 11" paper.
- Set the margins for the side, top, and bottom of your paper at approximately one inch. Most word-processing programs have a default setting that is appropriate.
- Double-space the document.
- Indent the first line of each paragraph.
- Number the pages in the upper right corner.

Follow your teacher's directions for formatting formal research papers. Most papers will have the following features:

- Title page
- Table of Contents or Outline
- Works-Cited List

Avoiding Plagiarism

Whether you are presenting a formal research paper or an opinion paper on a current event, you must be careful to give credit for any ideas or opinions that are not your own. Presenting someone else's ideas, research, or opinion as your own—even if you have phrased it in different words—is *plagiarism*, the equivalent of academic stealing, or fraud.

Do not use the ideas or research of others in place of your own. Read from several sources to draw your own conclusions and form your own opinions. Incorporate the ideas and research of others to support your points. Credit the source of the following types of support:

- Statistics
- Direct quotations
- Indirectly quoted statements of opinions
- Conclusions presented by an expert
- Facts available in only one or two sources

Crediting Sources

When you credit a source, you acknowledge where you found your information and you give your readers the details necessary for locating the source themselves. Within the body of the paper, you provide a short citation, a footnote number linked to a footnote, or an endnote number linked to an endnote reference. These brief references show the page numbers on which you found the information. Prepare a reference list at the end of the paper to provide full bibliographic information on your sources. These are two common types of reference lists:

- A **bibliography** provides a listing of all the resources you consulted during your research.
- A **works-cited list** indicates the works you have referenced in your paper.

The chart on the next page shows the Modern Language Association format for crediting sources. This is the most common format for papers written in the content areas in middle school and high school. Unless instructed otherwise by your teacher, use this format for crediting sources.

MLA Style for Listing Sources

Book with one author	Pyles, Thomas. *The Origins and Development of the English Language.* 2nd ed. New York: Harcourt Brace Jovanovich, Inc., 1971.
Book with two or three authors	McCrum, Robert, William Cran, and Robert MacNeil. *The Story of English.* New York: Penguin Books, 1987.
Book with an editor	Truth, Sojourner. *Narrative of Sojourner Truth.* Ed. Margaret Washington. New York: Vintage Books, 1993.
Book with more than three authors or editors	Donald, Robert B., et al. *Writing Clear Essays.* Upper Saddle River, NJ: Prentice-Hall, Inc., 1996.
A single work from an anthology	Hawthorne, Nathaniel. "Young Goodman Brown." *Literature: An Introduction to Reading and Writing.* Ed. Edgar V. Roberts and Henry E. Jacobs. Upper Saddle River, NJ: Prentice-Hall, Inc., 1998. 376–385. [Indicate pages for the entire selection.]
Introduction in a published edition	Washington, Margaret. Introduction. *Narrative of Sojourner Truth.* By Sojourner Truth. New York: Vintage Books, 1993. v–xi.
Signed article in a weekly magazine	Wallace, Charles. "A Vodacious Deal." *Time* 14 Feb. 2000: 63.
Signed article in a monthly magazine	Gustaitis, Joseph. "The Sticky History of Chewing Gum." *American History* Oct. 1998: 30–38.
Unsigned editorial or story	"Selective Silence." Editorial. *Wall Street Journal* 11 Feb. 2000: A14. [If the editorial or story is signed, begin with the author's name.]
Signed pamphlet	[Treat the pamphlet as though it were a book.]
Pamphlet with no author, publisher, or date	*Are You at Risk of Heart Attack?* n.p. n.d. [n.p. n.d. indicates that there is no known publisher or date]
Filmstrip, slide program, or videotape	*The Diary of Anne Frank.* Dir. George Stevens. Perf. Millie Perkins, Shelley Winters, Joseph Schildkraut, Lou Jacobi, and Richard Beymer. Twentieth Century Fox, 1959.
Radio or television program transcript	"Nobel for Literature." Narr. Rick Karr. *All Things Considered.* National Public Radio. WNYC, New York. 10 Oct. 2002. Transcript.
Internet	*National Association of Chewing Gum Manufacturers.* 19 Dec. 1999 <http://www.nacgm.org/consumer/funfacts.html> [Indicate the date you accessed the information. Content and addresses at Web sites change frequently.]
Newspaper article	Thurow, Roger. "South Africans Who Fought for Sanctions Now Scrap for Investors." *Wall Street Journal* 11 Feb. 2000: A1+ [For a multipage article, write only the first page number on which it appears, followed by a plus sign.]
Personal interview	Smith, Jane. Personal interview. 10 Feb. 2000.
CD (with multiple publishers)	Simms, James, ed. *Romeo and Juliet.* By William Shakespeare. CD-ROM. Oxford: Attica Cybernetics Ltd.; London: BBC Education; London: HarperCollins Publishers, 1995.
Article from an encyclopedia	Askeland, Donald R. "Welding." *World Book Encyclopedia.* 1991 ed.

Formatting Business Letters

Business letters follow one of several acceptable formats. In **block format,** each part of the letter begins at the left margin. A double space is used between paragraphs. In **modified block format,** some parts of the letter are indented to the center of the page. No matter which format is used, all letters in business format have a heading, an inside address, a salutation or greeting, a body, a closing, and a signature. These parts are shown and annotated on the model business letter below, formatted in modified block style.

Model Business Letter

In this letter, Yolanda Dodson uses modified block format to request information.

The **inside address** indicates where the letter will be sent.

The **salutation** is punctuated by a colon. When the specific addressee is not known, use a general greeting, such as "To whom it may concern:"

The **body** of the letter states the writer's purpose. In this case, the writer requests information.

The **closing** "Sincerely" is common, but "Yours truly" or "Respectfully yours" are also acceptable. To end the letter, the writer types her name and provides a **signature.**

Students for a Cleaner Planet
c/o Memorial High School
333 Veterans' Drive
Denver, Colorado 80211

January 25, 20--

Steven Wilson, Director
Resource Recovery Really Works
300 Oak Street
Denver, Colorado 80216

Dear Mr. Wilson:

Memorial High School would like to start a branch of your successful recycling program. We share your commitment to reclaiming as much reusable material as we can. Because your program has been successful in other neighborhoods, we're sure that it can work in our community. Our school includes grades 9–12 and has about 800 students.

Would you send us some information about your community recycling program? For example, we need to know what materials can be recycled and how we can implement the program.

At least fifty students have already expressed an interest in getting involved, so I know we'll have the people power to make the program work. Please help us get started.

Thank you in advance for your time and consideration.

Sincerely,

Yolanda Dodson

Yolanda Dodson

Writing Friendly Letters

A friendly letter is much less formal than a business letter. It is a letter to a friend, a family member, or anyone with whom the writer wants to communicate in a personal, friendly way. Most friendly letters are made up of five parts:

- the heading
- the salutation, or greeting
- the body
- the closing
- the signature

The purpose of a friendly letter is often one of the following:

- to share personal news and feelings
- to send or to answer an invitation
- to express thanks

Model Friendly Letter

In this friendly letter, Betsy thanks her grandparents for a birthday present and gives them some news about her life.

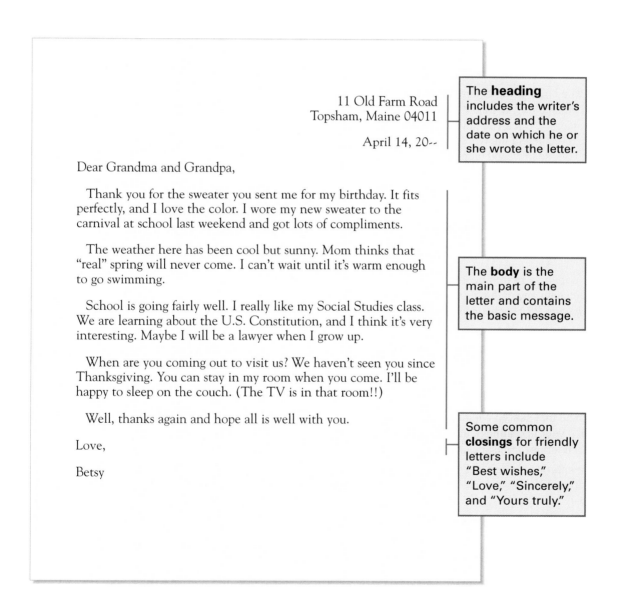

11 Old Farm Road
Topsham, Maine 04011

April 14, 20--

The **heading** includes the writer's address and the date on which he or she wrote the letter.

Dear Grandma and Grandpa,

Thank you for the sweater you sent me for my birthday. It fits perfectly, and I love the color. I wore my new sweater to the carnival at school last weekend and got lots of compliments.

The weather here has been cool but sunny. Mom thinks that "real" spring will never come. I can't wait until it's warm enough to go swimming.

School is going fairly well. I really like my Social Studies class. We are learning about the U.S. Constitution, and I think it's very interesting. Maybe I will be a lawyer when I grow up.

When are you coming out to visit us? We haven't seen you since Thanksgiving. You can stay in my room when you come. I'll be happy to sleep on the couch. (The TV is in that room!!)

Well, thanks again and hope all is well with you.

Love,

Betsy

The **body** is the main part of the letter and contains the basic message.

Some common **closings** for friendly letters include "Best wishes," "Love," "Sincerely," and "Yours truly."

Key Word Search

Before you begin a search, you should identify your specific topic. To make searching easier, narrow your subject to a key word or a group of **key words.** These are your search terms, and they should be as specific as possible. For example, if you are looking for information about your favorite musical group, you might use the band's name as a key word. You might locate such information as band member biographies, the group's history, fan reviews of concerts, and hundreds of sites with related names containing information that is irrelevant to your search. Depending on your research needs you might need to narrow your search.

How to Narrow Your Search

If you have a large group of key words and still don't know which ones to use, write out a list of all the words you are considering. Once you have completed the list, scrutinize it. Then, delete the words that are least important to your search, and highlight those that are most important.

These **key search connectors** can help you fine-tune your search:

AND: narrows a search by retrieving documents that include both terms. For example: *baseball AND playoffs*

OR: broadens a search by retrieving documents including any of the terms. For example: *playoffs OR championships*

NOT: narrows a search by excluding documents containing certain words. For example: *baseball NOT history*

Tips for an Effective Search

1. Keep in mind that search engines can be case-sensitive. If your first attempt at searching fails, check your search terms for misspellings and try again.

2. If you are entering a group of key words, present them in order, from the most important to the least important key word.

3. Avoid opening the link to every single page in your results list. Search engines present pages in descending order of relevancy. The most useful pages will be located at the top of the list. However, read the description of each link before you open the page.

4. When you use some search engines, you can find helpful tips for specializing your search. Take the opportunity to learn more about effective searching.

Tips for Evaluating Internet Sources

Consider who constructed and who now maintains the Web page. Determine whether this author is a reputable source. Often, the URL endings indicate a source.

- Sites ending in *.edu* are maintained by educational institutions.
- Sites ending in *.gov* are maintained by government agencies (federal, state, or local).
- Sites ending in *.org* are normally maintained by nonprofit organizations and agencies.
- Sites with a *.com* ending are commercially or personally maintained.

Other Ways to Search

How you search should be tailored to what you are hoping to find. If you are looking for data and facts, use reference sites before you jump onto a simple search engine. For example, you can find reference sites to provide definitions of words, statistics about almost any subject, biographies, maps, and concise information on many topics. Some useful online reference sites:

Online libraries

Online periodicals

Almanacs

Encyclopedias

You can also use other electronic sources such as CD-ROMs. Ask a reference librarian to help you locate and use the full range of electronic resources.

Respecting Copyrighted Material

Because the Internet is a relatively new and quickly growing medium, issues of copyright and ownership arise almost daily. As laws begin to govern the use and reuse of material posted online, they may change the way that people can access or reprint material.

Text, photographs, music, and fine art printed online may not be reproduced without acknowledged permission of the copyright owner.

Applying Spelling Rules

Choosing Between *ie* and *ei*

When a word has a long *e* sound, use *ie*. When a word has a long *a* sound, use *ei*. When a word has a long *e* sound preceded by the letter *c*, use *ei*.

Long *e* Sound	Long *a* Sound	Long *e* Sound Preceded by *c*
believe	freight	deceive
grief	reign	receive

Exceptions: either, neither, seize, weird

Choosing the Ending *-cede*, *-ceed*, or *-sede*

There are ten words that end with this sound. You will need to memorize their spellings.

-cede Words	*-ceed* Words	*-sede* Words
accede	exceed	supersede
concede	proceed	
intercede	succeed	
precede		
recede		
secede		

Adding Prefixes

A *prefix* is one or more syllables added at the beginning of a word to form a new word. Adding a prefix to a word does not usually change the spelling of the original word.

re- + place = replace

un- + fair = unfair

mis- + spell = misspell

dis- + appear = disappear

il- + legal = illegal

Adding Suffixes

A *suffix* is one or more syllables added at the end of a word to form a new word. Adding a suffix often involves a spelling change in the original word.

Adding Suffixes That Begin With a Consonant

When adding a suffix that begins with a consonant—such as *-ly, -ness, -less, -ment,* and *-ful*—you usually do not change the spelling of the original word.

calm + *-ly* = calmly

open + *-ness* = openness

time + *-less* = timeless

employ + *-ment* = employment

help + *-ful* = helpful

Except for *truly, argument, judgment, daily*

Exceptions: If a word ends in *y* preceded by a consonant, change the *y* to *i* before adding these suffixes:

ready + *-ly* = readily

busy + *-ness* = business

Except for *shyness, slyly, spryness*

Adding Suffixes to Words That End in Silent *e*

If a word ends in a silent *e*, drop the *e* before adding a suffix that begins with a vowel.

love + *-able* = lovable

Except for *changeable, agreeable, useable*

Adding Suffixes That Begin With a Vowel to Words That End in *y*

When adding a suffix that begins with a vowel to a word that ends in *y* preceded by a consonant, change the *y* to *i* before adding the suffix.

greedy + *-er* = greedier

worry + *-ed* = worried

Exceptions: Do not change the *y* to *i* if the suffix begins with *i*—*carrying, babyish*

When adding a suffix that begins with a vowel to a word that ends in *y* preceded by a vowel, keep the *y* before adding the suffix.

portray + *-al* = portrayal

obey + *-ed* = obeyed

Exceptions: paid (not *payed*), said (not *sayed*), laid (not *layed*), gaiety (not *gayety*)

Doubling the Final Consonant Before Adding a Suffix

If a one-syllable word ends in a single consonant preceded by a single vowel, double the final consonant before adding a suffix that begins with a vowel.

stop + -*ed* = stopped

dim + -*ing* = dimming

Exceptions: Words that end in *x, y,* or *w* (*mixer, prayed, flowing*)

If a word of more than one syllable ends in a single consonant preceded by a single vowel and the accent is on the final syllable, double the final consonant before adding a suffix that begins with a vowel.

omit + -*ed* = omitted

occur + -*ence* = occurrence

Exceptions: Words in which the accent shifts when the suffix is added (*prefer—preference*)

Do not double the final consonant if the accent is not on the last syllable.

travel + -*ing* = traveling

endanger + -*ed* = endangered

Forming the Plurals of Nouns

Forming Regular Plurals The rules below apply to most nouns whose plurals are formed in regular ways.

Noun Ending	Rule	Examples
s, ss, x, z, zz, sh, ch	Add -*es*	circus, circuses
		lass, lasses
		fox, foxes
		waltz, waltzes
		buzz, buzzes
		bush, bushes
		church, churches
o preceded by a consonant	Add -*es*	potato, potatoes
		hero, heroes
		Exceptions:
		Musical terms—
		solo, solos
		piano, pianos

Noun Ending	Rule	Examples
o preceded by a vowel	Add -*s*	radio, radios
		patio, patios
y preceded by a consonant	Change *y* to *i* and add -*es*	party, parties
		enemy, enemies
y preceded by a vowel	Add -*s*	key, keys
		convoy, convoys
ff	Add -*s*	staff, staffs
		sheriff, sheriffs
fe	Change *f* to *v* and add -*es*	life, lives
		knife, knives
f	Add -*s*	chief, chiefs
		roof, roofs
	OR	
	Change *f* to *v* and add -*es*	leaf, leaves
		shelf, shelves

Forming Irregular Plurals The plurals of some nouns are formed in irregular ways. You will need to memorize these:

goose, geese   foot, feet

man, men   woman, women

ox, oxen   child, children

tooth, teeth   mouse, mice

deer, deer   sheep, sheep

Forming Plurals of Compound Nouns Most one-word compound nouns have regular plural forms. If one part of a compound word is irregular, the plural form will also be irregular.

flashlight, flashlights (regular)

handful, handfuls (regular)

stepchild, stepchildren (irregular)

The plurals of most compound nouns written with hyphens or as separate words are formed by making the modified word—the word being described—plural.

mother-in-law, mothers-in-law

Web site, Web sites

Forming Plurals of Proper Nouns To form the plurals of proper nouns, follow the same rules as with common nouns. In most cases, simply add -s to the proper noun. Add -es if the name ends in *s, ss, x, z, sh,* or *ch.*

> There are two Anns in our class.
>
> All of the Coxes arrived in one car.

For proper nouns ending in *y,* just add -s. Do not change the *y* to *i* and add -es.

> The Kennedys live in the house on the corner.
>
> There are two Kansas Citys; one in Missouri and one in Kansas.

Forming Plurals of Signs and Symbols Use an apostrophe and an -s to write the plurals of numbers, symbols, letters, and words used to name themselves.

> Business names often include &'s.
>
> All of the 6's were written as 9's.
>
> She received only *A*'s and *B*'s.
>
> You used too many *and*'s in this sentence.

Writing Numbers

Spelling Out Numbers If a number begins a sentence, spell it out.

> *Twenty-two* players are on the field during a football game.

Within a sentence, spell out numbers that can be written in one or two words.

> There are *fifty-two* weeks in a year.

Spell out numbers used to indicate place or order.

> Shelley came in *second* in the race.
>
> This is the *fifth* day in a row that it has rained.

Using Numerals Use numerals for longer numbers that come within a sentence.

> Approximately *875* people attended the game.

If you include both small and large numbers in the same sentence, write them in the same way. It is best to use numerals.

> During a *12*-hour period, we counted *680* cars crossing the intersection.

Suggestions for Improving Your Spelling

Start a Personal Spelling List

Select the words that you have difficulty spelling, enter them in a special area in your notebook, and study them regularly. Add new words to your list, and cross out words you have mastered. You may find many of the words on your list among the Commonly Misspelled Words on the next page of this textbook.

Sound Out Difficult Words

Say the words aloud. Then, sound them out syllable by syllable as you study how to spell them.

Devise Memory Aids

Underline the part of a word that gives you the most trouble. Then, develop a memory device to help you remember the correct spelling.

Word	Memory Aid
des<u>s</u>ert	My des<u>s</u>ert is me<u>ss</u>y.
lib<u>r</u>ary	library <u>br</u>anch
ne<u>c</u>essary	Only one <u>c</u> is ne<u>c</u>essary.

Look for Roots and Derivatives

Many words have common *roots.* Look for the root inside a word to help you focus on its spelling. Then, use the root to help you spell related words.

> bene<u>f</u>it, bene<u>f</u>icial, bene<u>f</u>actor
>
> pre<u>ferr</u>ed, re<u>ferr</u>ed, in<u>ferr</u>ed
>
> de<u>c</u>ide, in<u>c</u>ident, ac<u>c</u>ident
>
> trans<u>mit</u>, trans<u>mission</u>, ad<u>mit</u>, ad<u>mission</u>

A *derivative* is a word that is formed from another word. Once you know how to spell a base word—the word from which the others are formed—you can more easily learn to spell its derivatives.

> de<u>c</u>ide, de<u>c</u>ision, de<u>c</u>isive
>
> <u>c</u>aution, <u>c</u>autious, pre<u>c</u>aution
>
> regu<u>l</u>ar, regu<u>l</u>ation, regu<u>l</u>ate
>
> stron<u>g</u>, stren<u>g</u>th, stren<u>g</u>then

Commonly Misspelled Words

The words on this page are ones that cause spelling problems for many people. As you review the list, check to see how many of the words give you trouble in your own writing. Then, try some of the suggestions for improving your spelling discussed on the previous page.

abbreviate	bicycle	criticize	grammar	naturally	realize
absence	bookkeeper	cylinder	grievance	necessary	really
absolutely	boulevard	deceive	guarantee	negotiate	receipt
accelerate	brief	decision	guard	neighbor	recipe
accidentally	brilliant	defendant	guidance	neutral	recognize
accurate	bruise	definitely	handkerchief	nickel	recommend
ache	bulletin	delinquent	harass	niece	rehearse
achievement	buoy	dependent	height	ninety	relevant
acquaintance	bureau	descendant	humorous	noticeable	reminiscence
adequate	bury	description	hygiene	nuclear	renowned
advertisement	buses	desirable	immediately	nuisance	repetition
aerial	business	dessert	immigrant	obstacle	restaurant
aggravate	cafeteria	dining	independent	occasion	rhythm
agreeable	calendar	disappoint	individual	occurrence	ridiculous
aisle	campaign	disastrous	inflammable	omitted	sandwich
all right	canceled	discipline	interfere	opinion	satellite
aluminum	candidate	eighth	irritable	opportunity	schedule
amateur	captain	eligible	jewelry	optimistic	scissors
analysis	career	embarrass	judgment	outrageous	secretary
analyze	carriage	enthusiastic	knowledge	pamphlet	siege
ancient	cashier	entrepreneur	laboratory	parallel	sincerely
anecdote	category	envelope	lawyer	paralyze	solely
anniversary	ceiling	environment	legible	parentheses	sponsor
anonymous	cemetery	equipped	legislature	particularly	subtle
answer	census	equivalent	leisure	patience	superintendent
anxiety	certain	especially	liable	permanent	surveillance
apologize	characteristic	exaggerate	library	permissible	susceptible
appall	chauffeur	excel	license	perseverance	tariff
appearance	clothes	excellent	lieutenant	persistent	temperamental
appreciate	colonel	exercise	lightning	perspiration	theater
appropriate	column	existence	likable	persuade	threshold
architecture	commercial	extraordinary	liquefy	phenomenon	truly
argument	commitment	familiar	literature	physician	unmanageable
associate	committee	fascinating	maintenance	pneumonia	unwieldy
athletic	competitor	February	marriage	possession	usage
attendance	condemn	fiery	mathematics	prairie	usually
awkward	congratulate	financial	maximum	preferable	valuable
banquet	conscience	fluorescent	meanness	prejudice	various
bargain	conscious	foreign	mediocre	prerogative	vegetable
barrel	convenience	forfeit	mileage	privilege	voluntary
battery	cooperate	fourth	millionaire	probably	volunteer
beautiful	correspondence	fragile	minuscule	procedure	weight
beggar	counterfeit	gauge	miscellaneous	pronunciation	weird
beginning	courageous	genius	mischievous	psychology	whale
behavior	courteous	genuine	misspell	pursue	wield
benefit	criticism	government	mortgage	questionnaire	yield

Parts of Speech

Nouns A **noun** is the name of a person, place, or thing. A **common noun** names any one of a class of people, places, or things. A **proper noun** names a specific person, place, or thing.

Common Nouns	Proper Nouns
writer	Francisco Jiménez
city	Los Angeles

Pronouns A **pronoun** is a word that stands for a noun or for a word that takes the place of a noun.

A **personal pronoun** refers to (1) the person speaking, (2) the person spoken to, or (3) the person, place, or thing spoken about.

	Singular	Plural
First Person	I, me, my, mine	we, us, our, ours
Second Person	you, your, yours	you, your, yours
Third Person	he, him, his, she, her, hers, it, its	they, them, their, theirs

A **demonstrative pronoun** directs attention to a specific person, place, or thing.

These are the juiciest pears I have ever tasted.

An **interrogative pronoun** is used to begin a question.

Who is the author of "Jeremiah's Song"?

An **indefinite pronoun** refers to a person, place, or thing, often without specifying which one.

Many of the players were tired.

Everyone bought something.

Verbs A **verb** is a word that expresses time while showing an action, a condition, or the fact that something exists.

An **action verb** indicates the action of someone or something.

A **linking verb** connects the subject of a sentence with a noun or a pronoun that renames or describes the subject.

A **helping verb** can be added to another verb to make a single verb phrase.

Adjectives An **adjective** describes a noun or a pronoun or gives a noun or a pronoun a more specific meaning. Adjectives answer the questions *what kind, which one, how many, how much.*

The articles *the, a,* and *an* are adjectives. *An* is used before a word beginning with a vowel sound.

A noun may sometimes be used as an adjective.

family home   *science* fiction

Adverbs An **adverb** modifies a verb, an adjective, or another adverb. Adverbs answer the questions *where, when, in what way,* or *to what extent.*

Prepositions A **preposition** relates a noun or a pronoun following it to another word in the sentence.

Conjunctions A **conjunction** connects other words or groups of words.

A **coordinating conjunction** connects similar kinds or groups of words.

Correlative conjunctions are used in pairs to connect similar words or groups of words.

both Grandpa *and* Dad   *neither* they *nor* I

Interjections An **interjection** is a word that expresses feeling or emotion and functions independently of a sentence.

"Ah!" says he—

Phrases, Clauses, and Sentences

Sentences A **sentence** is a group of words with two main parts: a complete subject and a complete predicate. Together, these parts express a complete thought.

We read that story last year.

A **fragment** is a group of words that does not express a complete thought.

"Not right away."

Subject The **subject** of a sentence is the word or group of words that tells whom or what the sentence is about. The **simple subject** is the essential noun, pronoun, or group of words acting as a noun that cannot be left out of the complete subject. A **complete subject** is the simple subject plus any modifiers. In the following example, the complete subject is underlined. The simple subject is italicized.

<u>Pony express *riders*</u> carried packages more than 2,000 miles.

A **compound subject** is two or more subjects that have the same verb and are joined by a conjunction.

> Neither the *horse nor the driver* looked tired.

Predicate The **predicate** of a sentence is the verb or verb phrase that tells what the complete subject of the sentence does or is. The **simple predicate** is the essential verb or verb phrase that cannot be left out of the complete predicate. A **complete predicate** is the simple predicate plus any modifiers or complements. In the following example, the complete predicate is underlined. The simple predicate is italicized.

> Pony express riders *carried* packages more than 2,000 miles.

A **compound predicate** is two or more verbs that have the same subject and are joined by a conjunction.

> She *sneezed and coughed* throughout the trip.

Complement A **complement** is a word or group of words that completes the meaning of the predicate of a sentence. Five different kinds of complements can be found in English sentences: *direct objects, indirect objects, objective complements, predicate nominatives* and *predicate adjectives.*

A **direct object** is a noun, pronoun, or group of words acting as a noun that receives the action of a transitive verb.

> We watched the *liftoff.*

An **indirect object** is a noun, pronoun, or group of words that appears with a direct object and names the person or thing that something is given to or done for.

> He sold the *family* a mirror.

An **objective complement** is an adjective or noun that appears with a direct object and describes or renames it.

> I called Meg my *friend.*

A **subject complement** is a noun, pronoun, or adjective that appears with a linking verb and tells something about the subject. A subject complement may be a *predicate nominative* or a *predicate adjective.*

A **predicate nominative** is a noun or pronoun that appears with a linking verb and renames, identifies, or explains the subject.

> Kiglo was the *leader.*

A **predicate adjective** is an adjective that appears with a linking verb and describes the subject of a sentence.

> Roko became *tired.*

Simple Sentence A **simple sentence** consists of a single independent clause.

Compound Sentence A **compound sentence** consists of two or more independent clauses joined by a comma and a coordinating conjunction or by a semicolon.

Complex Sentence A **complex sentence** consists of one independent clause and one or more subordinate clauses.

Compound-Complex Sentence A **compound-complex sentence** consists of two or more independent clauses and one or more subordinate clauses.

Declarative Sentence A **declarative sentence** states an idea and ends with a period.

Interrogative Sentence An **interrogative sentence** asks a question and ends with a question mark.

Imperative Sentence An **imperative sentence** gives an order or a direction and ends with either a period or an exclamation mark.

Exclamatory Sentence An **exclamatory sentence** conveys a strong emotion and ends with an exclamation mark.

Phrases A **phrase** is a group of words, without a subject and a verb, that functions in a sentence as one part of speech.

A **prepositional phrase** is a group of words that includes a preposition and a noun or a pronoun that is the object of the preposition.

> near the town   with them

An **adjective phrase** is a prepositional phrase that modifies a noun or a pronoun by telling *what kind* or *which one*.

> Mr. Sanderson brushed his hands over the shoes in the window . . . .

An **adverb phrase** is a prepositional phrase that modifies a verb, an adjective, or an adverb by pointing out *where, when, in what manner,* or *to what extent.*

> The trees were black where the bark was wet.

An **appositive phrase** is a noun or a pronoun with modifiers, placed next to a noun or a pronoun to add information and details.

> The story, *a tale of adventure,* takes place in the Yukon.

A **participial phrase** is a participle modified by an adjective or an adverb phrase or accompanied by a complement. The entire phrase acts as an adjective.

> *Running at top speed,* he soon caught up with them.

An **infinitive phrase** is an infinitive with modifiers, complements, or a subject, all acting together as a single part of speech.

> At first I was too busy enjoying my food *to notice how the guests were doing.*

Clauses

A **clause** is a group of words with its own subject and verb.

An **independent clause** can stand by itself as a complete sentence.

> "I think it belongs to Rachel."

A **subordinate clause** has a subject and a verb but cannot stand by itself as a complete sentence; it can only be part of a sentence.

> "Although it was late"

Using Verbs and Pronouns

Principal Parts

A verb has four **principal parts**: the *present,* the *present participle,* the *past,* and the *past participle.*

Regular verbs form the past and past participle by adding *-ed* to the present form.

Present: walk
Present Participle: (am) walking
Past: walked
Past Participle: (have) walked

Irregular verbs form the past and past participle by changing form rather than by adding *-ed.*

Present: go
Present Participle: (am) going
Past: went
Past Participle: (have) gone

Verb Tense

A **verb tense** tells whether the time of an action or condition is in the past, the present, or the future. Every verb has six tenses: *present, past, future, present perfect, past perfect,* and *future perfect.*

The **present tense** shows actions that happen in the present.

The **past tense** shows actions that have already happened.

The **future tense** shows actions that will happen.

The **present perfect tense** shows actions that begin in the past and continue to the present.

The **past perfect tense** shows a past action or condition that ended before another past action.

The **future perfect tense** shows a future action or condition that will have ended before another begins.

Pronoun Case

The **case** of a pronoun is the form it takes to show its use in a sentence. There are three pronoun cases: *nominative, objective,* and *possessive.*

The **nominative case** is used to name or rename the subject of the sentence. The nominative case pronouns are *I, you, he, she, it, we, you, they.*

> **As the subject:** *She* is brave.
> **Renaming the subject:** The leader is *she.*

The **objective case** is used as the direct object, indirect object, or object of a preposition. The objective case pronouns are *me, you, him, her, it, us, you, them.*

> **As a direct object:** Tom called *me.*
> **As an indirect object:** My friend gave *me* advice.
> **As an object of a preposition:** The coach gave pointers to *me.*

The **possessive case** is used to show ownership. The possessive pronouns are *my, your, his, her, its, our, their, mine, yours, his, hers, its, ours, theirs.*

Subject-Verb Agreement

To make a subject and a verb agree, make sure that both are singular or both are plural. Two or more singular subjects joined by *or* or *nor* must have a singular verb. When singular and plural subjects are joined by *or* or *nor,* the verb must agree with the closest subject.

> *He is* at the door.
> *They drive* home every day.
> Both *pets are* hungry.
> Either the *chairs* or the *table is* on sale.

Pronoun-Antecedent Agreement

Pronouns must agree with their antecedents in number and gender. Use singular pronouns with singular antecedents and plural pronouns with plural antecedents. Many errors in pronoun-antecedent agreement occur when a plural pronoun is used to refer to a singular antecedent for which the gender is not specified.

> Incorrect: Everyone did their best.
> Correct: Everyone did his or her best.

The following indefinite pronouns are singular: *anybody, anyone, each, either, everybody, everyone, neither, nobody, no one, one, somebody, someone.*

The following indefinite pronouns are plural: *both, few, many, several.*

The following indefinite pronouns may be either singular or plural: *all, any, most, none, some.*

Glossary of Common Usage

accept, except *Accept* is a verb that means "to receive" or "to agree to." *Except* is a preposition that means "other than" or "leaving out." Do not confuse these two words.

> Aaron sadly *accepted* his father's decision to sell Zlateh.

> Everyone *except* the fisherman and his wife had children.

affect, effect *Affect* is normally a verb meaning "to influence" or "to bring about a change in." *Effect* is usually a noun, meaning "result."

among, between *Among* is usually used with three or more items. *Between* is generally used with only two items.

bad, badly Use the predicate adjective *bad* after linking verbs such as *feel, look,* and *seem.* Use *badly* whenever an adverb is required.

> Mouse does not feel *bad* about tricking Coyote.

> In the myth, Athene treats Arachne *badly.*

beside, besides *Beside* means "at the side of" or "close to." *Besides* means "in addition to."

can, may The verb *can* generally refers to the ability to do something. The verb *may* generally refers to permission to do something.

different from, different than *Different from* is generally preferred over *different than.*

farther, further Use *farther* when you refer to distance. Use *further* when you mean "to a greater degree or extent" or "additional."

fewer, less Use *fewer* for things that can be counted. Use *less* for amounts or quantities that cannot be counted.

good, well Use the predicate adjective *good* after linking verbs such as *feel, look, smell, taste,* and *seem.* Use *well* whenever you need an adverb.

hopefully You should not loosely attach this adverb to a sentence, as in "*Hopefully*, the rain will stop by noon." Rewrite the sentence so *hopefully* modifies a specific verb. Other possible ways of revising such sentences include using the adjective *hopeful* or a phrase like "everyone *hopes* that."

its, it's The word *its* with no apostrophe is a possessive pronoun. The word *it's* is a contraction for *it is*. Do not confuse the possessive pronoun *its* with the contraction *it's*, standing for "it is" or "it has."

lay, lie Do not confuse these verbs. *Lay* is a transitive verb meaning "to set or put something down." Its principal parts are *lay, laying, laid, laid. Lie* is an intransitive verb meaning "to recline." Its principal parts are *lie, lying, lay, lain.*

leave, let Be careful not to confuse these verbs. *Leave* means "to go away" or "to allow to remain." *Let* means "to permit."

like, as *Like* is a preposition that usually means "similar to" or "in the same way as." *Like* should always be followed by an object. Do not use *like* before a subject and a verb. Use *as* or *that* instead.

loose, lose *Loose* can be either an adjective (meaning "unattached") or a verb (meaning "to untie"). *Lose* is always a verb (meaning "to fail to keep, have, or win").

many, much Use *many* to refer to a specific quantity. Use *much* for an indefinite amount or for an abstract concept.

of, have Do not use *of* in place of *have* after auxiliary verbs like *would, could, should, may, might,* or *must.*

raise, rise *Raise* is a transitive verb that usually takes a direct object. *Rise* is intransitive and never takes a direct object.

set, sit *Set* is a transitive verb meaning "to put (something) in a certain place." Its principal parts are *set, setting, set, set*. *Sit* is an intransitive verb meaning "to be seated." Its principal parts are *sit, sitting, sat, sat*.

than, then The conjunction *than* is used to connect the two parts of a comparison. Do not confuse *than* with the adverb *then,* which usually refers to time.

that, which, who Use the relative pronoun *that* to refer to things or people. Use *which* only for things and *who* only for people.

their, there, they're *Their* is a possessive adjective and always modifies a noun. *There* is usually used either at the beginning of a sentence or as an adverb. *They're* is a contraction for "they are."

to, too, two *To* is a preposition that begins a prepositional phrase or an infinitive. *Too*, with two *o*'s, is an adverb and modifies adjectives and other adverbs. *Two* is a number.

when, where, why Do not use *when, where,* or *why* directly after a linking verb such as *is*. Reword the sentence.

Faulty:	Suspense is *when* an author increases the reader's tension.
Revised:	An author uses suspense to increase the reader's tension.
Faulty:	A biography is *where* a writer tells the life story of another person.
Revised:	In a biography, a writer tells the life story of another person.

who, whom In formal writing, remember to use *who* only as a subject in clauses and sentences and *whom* only as an object.

Capitalization and Punctuation Rules

Capitalization

1. Capitalize the first word of a sentence.
   Young Roko glances down the valley.
2. Capitalize all proper nouns and adjectives.

Mark Twain	Amazon River	Thanksgiving Day
Montana	October	Italian

3. Capitalize a person's title when it is followed by the person's name or when it is used in direct address.

Doctor	General Khokhotov	Mrs. Price

4. Capitalize titles showing family relationships when they refer to a specific person, unless they are preceded by a possessive noun or pronoun.

Granny-Liz	Margie's mother

5. Capitalize the first word and all other key words in the titles of books, periodicals, poems, stories, plays, paintings, and other works of art.

from *Tom Sawyer*	"Grandpa and the Statue"
"Breaker's Bridge"	"The Spring and the Fall"

6. Capitalize the first word and all nouns in letter salutations and the first word in letter closings.

Dear Willis,	Yours truly,

Punctuation

End Marks

1. Use a **period** to end a declarative sentence, an imperative sentence, and most abbreviations.
2. Use a **question mark** to end a direct question or an incomplete question in which the rest of the question is understood.
3. Use an **exclamation mark** after a statement showing strong emotion, an urgent imperative sentence, or an interjection expressing strong emotion.

Commas

1. Use a comma before the conjunction to separate two independent clauses in a compound sentence.
2. Use commas to separate three or more words, phrases, or clauses in a series.
3. Use commas to separate adjectives of equal rank. Do not use commas to separate adjectives that must stay in a specific order.
4. Use a comma after an introductory word, phrase, or clause.
5. Use commas to set off parenthetical and nonessential expressions.
6. Use commas with places and dates made up of two or more parts.
7. Use commas after items in addresses, after the salutation in a personal letter, after the closing in all letters, and in numbers of more than three digits.

Semicolons

1. Use a semicolon to join independent clauses that are not already joined by a conjunction.

2. Use a semicolon to join independent clauses or items in a series that already contain commas.

  The Pengelly family had no say in the choosing of Lob; he came to them in the second way. . . .

Colons

1. Use a colon before a list of items following an independent clause.
2. Use a colon in numbers giving the time, in salutations in business letters, and in labels used to signal important ideas.

Quotation Marks

1. A direct quotation represents a person's exact speech or thoughts and is enclosed in quotation marks.
2. An **indirect quotation** reports only the general meaning of what a person said or thought and does not require quotation marks.
3. Always place a comma or a period inside the final quotation mark of a direct quotation.
4. Place a question mark or an exclamation mark inside the final quotation mark if the end mark is part of the quotation; if it is not part of the quotation, place it outside the final quotation mark.

Titles

1. Underline or italicize the titles of long written works, movies, television and radio shows, lengthy works of music, paintings, and sculptures.
2. Use quotation marks around the titles of short written works, episodes in a series, songs, and titles of works mentioned as parts of collections.

Hyphens

1. Use a **hyphen** with certain numbers, after certain prefixes, with two or more words used as one word, and with a compound modifier that comes before a noun.

Apostrophes

1. Add an **apostrophe** and *s* to show the possessive case of most singular nouns.
2. Add an apostrophe to show the possessive case of plural nouns ending in *s* and *es*.
3. Add an apostrophe and *s* to show the possessive case of plural nouns that do not end in *s* or *es*.
4. Use an apostrophe in a contraction to indicate the position of the missing letter or letters.

Parts of Speech

> **Exercise A** Classifying Nouns and Pronouns Identify the nouns and pronouns in the following sentences. Label each noun *compound*, *common*, or *proper*, and *singular* or *plural*. Label each pronoun *personal* or *demonstrative*.

1. One element of the weather is temperature.
2. Every day is warmest during the middle of the afternoon.
3. It is usually warmer in the Tropics.
4. The North Pole and the South Pole have the lowest temperatures.
5. Temperature varies with latitude, elevation, and season.
6. This means temperature can change suddenly.
7. These are the scales used for measuring temperature.
8. Scientists use Kelvin, or they use Celsius.
9. That is used in many countries.
10. The United States continues to use Fahrenheit.

> **Exercise B** Classifying Verbs Write the verbs in the following sentences, and label each *action* or *linking*. Include and underline all helping verbs.

1. Wind moves horizontally through the atmosphere.
2. Some winds are called "prevailing."
3. The trade winds are included in the prevailing winds category.
4. The doldrums lie within 10 degrees of the equator.
5. The horse latitudes, 30 degrees from the equator, consist of calm, light winds.
6. Surface air travels from the horse latitudes to the equator.
7. Those are the trade winds.
8. Seasonal winds are determined by air temperature.

9. The air over the continents is warmer in the summer than the air over the oceans.
10. Then, winds from the colder ocean blow inland.

> **Exercise C** Recognizing Adjectives and Adverbs Label each underlined word in the following sentences as *adjective* or *adverb*. Then, write the word each one modifies.

1. Clouds are composed of small water droplets or <u>tiny</u> ice crystals.
2. They are <u>usually</u> divided into four families.
3. Cirrus clouds rise <u>higher</u> above the Earth.
4. They consist <u>mainly</u> of ice particles.
5. These feathery clouds are <u>commonly</u> arranged in bands.
6. <u>Thick</u> altostratus clouds may obscure the sun or moon.
7. Light <u>barely</u> filters through the bluish veil.
8. Altocumulus clouds resemble <u>dense</u> puffs.
9. Low clouds are <u>generally</u> less than one mile high.
10. Like <u>middle</u> clouds, they are composed of water droplets.

> **Exercise D** Recognizing Prepositions, Conjunctions, and Interjections Identify the underlined words in the following sentences as *prepositions*, *conjunctions*, or *interjections*. Write the object of each preposition. Label the conjunctions *coordinating* or *correlative*.

1. <u>Wow</u>! Did you see the hail falling <u>to</u> the ground?
2. It looks like a combination of <u>both</u> ice <u>and</u> snow.
3. Raindrops <u>or</u> snow pellets become hailstones as they collide with each other.
4. <u>Gee</u>, that requires the wind characteristic of thunderstorms.
5. They travel through the clouds <u>but</u> become too heavy.

> **Exercise E** Supplying Interjections In the following sentences, write an interjection that expresses the feeling shown in parentheses.

1. (surprise) Did you see that meteor shower last night?
2. (hesitation) I was not sure what that was.
3. (disappointment) did that happen while I was sleeping?
4. (amazement) I could not believe my eyes.
5. (agreement) it is a natural event.

> **Exercise F** Identifying All the Parts of Speech Write the part of speech of each underlined word in the following paragraph. Be as specific as possible.

Hey, those rainbows are an interesting sight. They can be seen after a shower or near a waterfall. The brightest rainbows show the spectrum colors with red on the outside. When the sun is low in the sky, rainbows appear relatively high.

> **Exercise G** Supplying the Correct Part of Speech In the following sentences, supply the part of speech indicated in parentheses.

1. Thunderstorms can be very (adjective).
2. Not only is there a lot of noise, (correlative conjunction) the lightning can be dangerous.
3. You should not stand under a (noun) during a thunderstorm.
4. The best place to be is (preposition) your house away from the windows.
5. (verb) not talk on the telephone during a storm.
6. Some thunderstorms also have (adverb) high winds.
7. Wind, rain, thunder, (conjunction) lightning are all elements of a storm.
8. Most thunderstorms (verb) in the spring and summer months.
9. (Adjective) tornadoes can accompany these storms.
10. (Interjection) It seems that every season has its (adjective) weather.

> **Exercise H** Revising With Adjectives and Adverbs Revise the following passage by adding adjectives and adverbs to modify nouns, verbs, and adjectives.

Some people enjoy winter. They like snow and cold winds. Snow covers everything and makes it look clean. There are a lot of outdoor activities that people enjoy in the winter: skiing, ice skating, and sledding. Some people just like to sit by a fire and watch through the window as the snow falls.

> **Exercise I** Writing Application Write a short narrative about a weather event that you have witnessed or learned about. Underline at least one noun, pronoun, verb, adjective, adverb, preposition, conjunction, and interjection. Then, label each word's part of speech as specifically as possible.

Phrases, Clauses, and Sentences

> **Exercise A** Recognizing Basic Sentence
Parts Copy the following sentences, underlining each simple subject once and each simple predicate twice. Circle the complements, and label each one *direct object, indirect object, predicate nominative,* or *predicate adjective.* Then, identify each sentence as *declarative, imperative, interrogative,* or *exclamatory.*

1. Does Matt or Jeremy enjoy figure skating or speed skating?
2. Speed skating is good exercise.
3. There are races against the clock and against other skaters.
4. Speed skaters use skates with long straight edges.
5. Wow! The blades are so long and look so sharp!
6. Try that pair of skates.
7. I gave Danielle figure-skating lessons.
8. She and Hannah were eager and attentive.
9. We practiced cross-overs and snowplow stops.
10. Can you do any jumps?

> **Exercise B** Using Basic Sentence Parts
Rewrite the following sentences according to the directions in parentheses. In your new sentences, underline each simple subject once and each simple predicate twice. Circle each complement.

1. Ice hockey is a winter sport. It is a rough game. (Combine by creating a compound predicate nominative.)
2. Hockey-playing countries include Canada. Hockey is a big sport in Russia. (Combine by creating a compound direct object.)
3. Defense is an important part of the game, and so is offense. (Rewrite by creating a compound subject.)
4. The players use hockey sticks. They wear protective pads. (Rewrite by creating a compound predicate.)

5. Goaltenders wear face masks. They wear other protective equipment. (Combine by creating a compound direct object.)
6. One area on the ice is the neutral zone. Another is the attacking zone. (Combine by creating a compound predicate nominative.)
7. Substitution of players is frequent. It occurs during the game. (Combine by creating a compound predicate.)
8. Hockey skate blades are thin. They are also short. (Combine by creating a compound predicate adjective.)
9. Teams pass the puck, shooting it with their sticks. (Rewrite by creating a compound predicate.)
10. Ancient Egyptians played games similar to hockey, and so did the Persians. (Rewrite by creating a compound subject.)

> **Exercise C** Identifying Phrases and
Clauses Label each phrase in the following sentences as an *adjective prepositional phrase,* an *adverb prepositional phrase,* or an *appositive phrase.* Identify and label each clause.

1. Skiing is a popular winter sport in many countries.
2. Boots, flexible or rigid, are important pieces of equipment.
3. Ski poles that vary in length are used for balance.
4. There are three kinds of skiing that have been developed.
5. One type, Alpine skiing, involves racing down steep, snow-covered slopes.
6. Skiers descend in the fastest time possible.
7. A course is defined by a series of gates, which are made of poles and flag markers.
8. The racer passes through these gates.
9. This downhill racing includes the slalom, in which the course is made of many turns.
10. The super giant slalom, a combination of downhill and slalom, is decided after one run.

Exercise D Using Phrases and Clauses

Rewrite the following sentences according to the instructions in parentheses.

1. Cross-country skiing is called Nordic skiing and is practiced in many parts of the world. (Rewrite by creating an appositive phrase.)
2. It is performed on longer courses. These courses are also flatter than downhill courses. (Combine by creating a clause.)
3. Nordic skiing emphasizes two things. Those are endurance and strength. (Combine by creating a clause.)
4. A side-to-side motion is the way cross-country skiers move. (Rewrite by creating an adverb prepositional phrase.)
5. Cross-country skiing developed to fill a need. That need was for transportation. (Combine by creating an adjective prepositional phrase.)

Exercise E Revising Sentences to Eliminate Errors and Create Variety

Rewrite the following sentences according to the instructions in parentheses.

1. Bobsledding was first developed in Saint Moritz, Switzerland, the first competition was held there. (Correct the run-on sentence.)
2. Teams of two or four people descend an icy run in bobsledding. (Vary the sentence by beginning with a prepositional phrase.)
3. The part of a bobsled run most critical is its start. (Correct the misplaced modifier.)
4. The captain occupies the front position in the sled. This person is also called the driver. (Combine the sentences by creating a phrase.)
5. The crew members lean backward and forward in unison and accelerate the speed of the sled. (Vary the sentence by beginning with a participial phrase.)
6. Bobsledding is different than the luge. (Correct the common usage problem.)

7. Lie on their backs with their feet at the front of the luge sled. (Correct the sentence fragment.)
8. Luge courses are not constructed for nothing other than this sport. (Correct the double negative.)
9. These courses feature turns. Courses also feature straight stretches. (Combine by creating a compound direct object.)
10. The reason it looks dangerous is because luges travel at high speeds. (Correct the common usage problem.)

Exercise F Revision Practice: Sentence Combining

Rewrite the following passage, combining sentences where appropriate.

Most children are delighted when it snows. They wake up early. They listen for school cancellations on the radio. If school is cancelled, the children are excited. The parents say "Oh, no!" It means the schedule is off. The day has to be rearranged. They get out the boots and warm clothes. They get out the sleds. An unexpected vacation day.

Exercise G Writing Application

Write a description of a winter activity that you enjoy. Vary the lengths and beginnings of your sentences. Underline each simple subject once and each simple verb twice. Then, circle at least three phrases and three clauses. Avoid fragments, run-ons, double negatives, misplaced modifiers, and common usage problems.

Usage

Exercise A Using Verbs Choose the correct verb or verb phrase in parentheses to complete each sentence below. Identify its principal part and tense.

1. Several Native American groups (brung, brought) their culture to what is now Texas.
2. The foundations of early dwellings were found where they were (lain, laid).
3. The Karankawa (did, done) a great deal of fishing in the Gulf of Mexico.
4. The Apache and the Comanche (caught, catched) and (eat, ate) the buffalo.
5. Alonzo Álvarez de Piñeda (set, sat) foot in Texas in 1519.
6. He was (leading, led) a group around the mouth of the Rio Grande.
7. Cabeza de Vaca (began, begun) to explore more of inland Texas.
8. In 1682, the Spanish (built, builded) the first mission in Texas.
9. That was near the site where present-day El Paso (is, was).
10. Spain (knew, known) that France was claiming the area.

Exercise B Identifying the Case of Pronouns Identify the case of each pronoun in the following sentences as *nominative*, *objective*, or *possessive*.

1. One French explorer was La Salle. He built a fort near Matagorda Bay.
2. La Salle named it Fort Saint Louis.
3. France claimed the Mississippi River and its tributaries.
4. In 1716, the Spanish established missions, founding them throughout the territory.
5. They include the city of San Antonio.
6. However, the Spanish found that their hold on the province of Texas was weak.
7. Expeditions of adventurers from the United States had been traveling through it.
8. Philip Nolan led one invasion, but the Spanish captured him.

9. In 1820, Moses Austin, a United States citizen, made his request to settle in Texas.
10. His son, Stephen F. Austin, carried out the plan.

Exercise C Using Agreement Fill in each blank below with a pronoun that agrees with its antecedent.

1. In our social studies class, __?__ are studying Texas and __?__ fight for independence.
2. Texans decided that they wanted to make __?__ own laws.
3. The Mexican government wanted settlers in Texas to obey __?__ laws.
4. General Santa Anna gathered __?__ troops together to crush the rebellious Texans.
5. Texans declared __?__ independence from Mexico on March 2, 1836, in the town of Washington-on-the-Brazos.
6. Either Oleg or Sam will give __?__ report on the Alamo today.
7. Fewer than 200 Texans tried to defend __?__ territory against Santa Anna's army there.
8. Jim Bowie, Davey Crockett, and William B. Travis lost __?__ lives at the Alamo.
9. I hope that I will do well on __?__ test about the Alamo.
10. Texans captured Santa Anna and forced __?__ to sign a treaty.

Exercise D Using Verb Agreement Write the form of the verb in parentheses that agrees with the subject of each sentence below.

1. All of our reports (be) about the settling of the West.
2. Many students (want) to write about California.
3. No one (know) more about the early days in California than Rudy.
4. Everybody in our class (love) to look at the maps of the trails heading west.
5. Each of the students (have) to pick a trail to report on.

6. Julie and Thomas (ask) to read about the Oregon Trail.
7. Neither Sam nor Randy (have) picked a topic yet.
8. Tanya and I (hope) to do our report on the Santa Fe Trail.
9. Either the Santa Fe Trail or the Oregon Trail (be) interesting.
10. According to the map, each of the trails (appear) to begin in Independence, Missouri.

▶ **Exercise E** Using Modifiers In the sentences below, write the form of the adjective or adverb indicated in parentheses.

1. A Texan army gathered (quickly—comparative) than expected.
2. After taking San Antonio, (many—superlative) soldiers left the city.
3. They believed that Santa Anna, the Mexican dictator, would wait until (late—positive) spring.
4. Santa Anna's army was (large—comparative) than that of the settlers.
5. The (small—superlative) of all Texan forces withdrew to the Alamo.
6. (Brave—comparative) than expected, the Texans fought for thirteen days.
7. (Many—superlative) of the Texan forces were defeated in other battles.
8. Then, a group of Texans declared independence (cautiously—comparative) than they had earlier.
9. They attacked, (probably—superlative) surprising the Mexican Army.
10. Santa Anna (soon—positive) recognized Texas's independence.

▶ **Exercise F** Correcting Usage Mistakes Rewrite the following sentences, correcting any errors in usage.

1. The Republic of Texas continued their existence for almost ten years.
2. The more prominent of all Texas's problems was finances.
3. There was disputes about the new country's boundaries.
4. More immigrants came to Texas, and the troubles did not prevent they from settling.
5. Sam Houston will be one who wanted the United States to annex the republic.
6. After Sam Houston wins in the battle of San Jacinto, Texas had become independent.
7. These two groups, the Cherokee and the Mexicans, brought its concerns into battle.
8. However, the Cherokee and them were arrested by the Texas army.
9. A new president of Texas, Mirabeau Lamar, were elected in 1838.
10. The Cherokee resist his orders, but they were defeated and moved to what is now Oklahoma.

▶ **Exercise G** Writing Application Write a short description of the state in which you live or one that you have visited. Be sure that the words in your sentences follow the rules of agreement and that your modifiers are used correctly. Then, list the verbs and verb phrases, identifying their tenses. Make a list of pronouns, and identify their case.

Mechanics

> **Exercise A** Using End Marks Copy the following sentences, inserting the appropriate end marks.

1. What was your favorite toy when you were young
2. My little brother has a rattle and a teething ring
3. Hey, I *really* miss my baby toys
4. Do you still sleep with a favorite stuffed animal
5. Maybe they will be collectible items one day

> **Exercise B** Using Commas, Semicolons, and Colons Copy the following sentences, inserting the appropriate commas, semicolons, and colons.

1. Every summer at the beach we make sand castles using sand seashells and water.
2. I play catch with my cousins who visit us for several weeks each year.
3. Last summer I learned a new sport volleyball.
4. When we first started playing the net seemed so high.
5. Then I learned how to hit the ball it was not very difficult.
6. I enjoyed volleyball in fact we played from noon until about 530 p.m.
7. Some people do not play sports at the beach They read listen to music or just lie in the sun.
8. After a full enjoyable day we like to have a barbecue.
9. We cook many of my favorite foods hamburgers hot dogs and corn on the cob.
10. When the sun sets the temperature drops but we still stay outside.

> **Exercise C** Using All the Rules of Punctuation Copy the following sentences, inserting the appropriate end marks, commas, semicolons, colons, quotation marks, underlining, hyphens, and apostrophes.

1. Did you know that there are three types of kites
2. The most well known type is the diamond shaped kite
3. There are also box kites delta kites and bowed kites
4. Paper or cloth is used for the kite however the frame can be wood or metal
5. During the 1800s kites served an important purpose weather forecasting
6. When Benjamin Franklin flew a kite he proved his theory about electricity
7. Alexander Graham Bell the inventor of the telephone also created kites
8. Let's Go Fly a Kite is a great song
9. Remember the line Lets go fly a kite up to the highest height
10. It is from a famous movie Mary Poppins

> **Exercise D** Using All the Rules of Capitalization Copy the following sentences, inserting the appropriate capital letters.

1. people throughout north america, south america, and europe ride bicycles.
2. around 1790, count divrac of france invented a wooden scooter.
3. a german inventor, baron drais, improved upon that model.
4. his version had a steering bar attached to the front wheel.
5. then, a scottish blacksmith, kirkpatrick macmillan, added foot pedals.
6. in 1866, pierre lallement, a french carriage maker, took out the first u.s. patent on a pedal bicycle.
7. mr. j. k. starley of england produced the first commercially successful bicycle.
8. by 1897, more than four million americans were riding bikes.
9. there are many road races like the tour de france.
10. other races, called bmx, are held on bumpy dirt tracks.

Exercise E Proofreading Dialogue for Punctuation and Capitalization Copy the following dialogue, adding the proper punctuation and capitalization.

1. is that a new yo-yo asked pam i have never seen it before
2. no i have had it awhile replied joe i found it underneath my bed
3. i bet you do not know how yo-yos were invented
4. joe answered sure i do they are toys for children
5. no pam said they originated in the philippines
6. right as toys joe insisted
7. they were weapons and toys pam corrected
8. ok well i know what the word yo-yo means
9. pam said so do i tell me and i will see if you are correct
10. well joe said i am pretty sure it means come back
11. that is right pam said
12. it is a toy that has been around for more than 3,000 years joe continued
13. it was not until the 1920s pam added that they were developed in the united states
14. who was donald duncan asked joe
15. he was the man who improved upon the design of the yo-yo and made it a popular toy in the united states

► **Exercise F** Writing Sentences With Correct Punctuation and Capitalization Write five sentences following the instructions given below. Be sure to punctuate and capitalize correctly.

1. Write a sentence about your favorite board game or video game.
2. Describe what you like about it.
3. Write a sentence about a favorite outdoor game.
4. Tell what time of year you play it, and name some of the friends who join in.
5. Write an exclamatory sentence about a great play in a game.

► **Exercise G** Proofreading Paragraphs for Punctuation and Capitalization Proofread the following paragraphs, copying them into your notebook and adding punctuation and capitalization as needed.

Do children still play board games I wonder. perhaps tv and video games have begun to replace checkers and chess.

There was a time you know when i excitedly hoped for board games as gifts on certain special occasions birthdays and holidays. one birthday when my twin sister, lily, and i received our first checkers set we were thrilled we could not wait to begin playing i think we played for hours. when aunt dotti and uncle larry came over with our cousins joanie and mark we all took turns playing. wow what a great time we had.

► **Exercise H** Writing Application Write a brief dialogue between you and a friend about your favorite toy from childhood. Be sure to include proper punctuation, capitalization, and indentation.

You use communication every day in writing, speaking, listening, and viewing. Having strong communication skills will benefit you both in and out of school. Many of the assignments accompanying the literature in this textbook involve speaking, listening, and viewing. This handbook identifies some of the terminology related to the oral and visual communication you experience every day and the assignments you may do in conjunction with the literature in this book.

Communication

You use speaking and listening skills everyday. When you talk with your friends, teachers, or parents, or when you interact with store clerks, you are communicating orally. In addition to everyday conversation, oral communication includes class discussions, speeches, interviews, presentations, debates, and performances. When you communicate, you usually use more than your voice to get your message across. For example, you use one set of skills in face-to-face communication and another set of skills in a telephone conversation.

The following terms will give you a better understanding of the many elements that are part of communication:

BODY LANGUAGE refers to the use of facial expressions, eye contact, gestures, posture, and movement to communicate a feeling or an idea.

CONNOTATION is the set of associations a word calls to mind. The connotations of the words you choose influence the message you send. For example, most people respond more favorably to being described as "slim" rather than as "skinny." The connotation of *slim* is more appealing than that of *skinny.*

EYE CONTACT is direct visual contact with another person's eyes.

FEEDBACK is the set of verbal and nonverbal reactions that indicate to a speaker that a message has been received and understood.

GESTURES are the movements made with arms, hands, face, and fingers to communicate.

LISTENING is understanding and interpreting sound in a meaningful way. You listen differently for different purposes.

Listening for key information: For example, when a teacher gives an assignment, or when someone gives you directions to a place, you listen for key information.

Listening for main points: In a classroom exchange of ideas or information, or while watching a television documentary, you listen for main points.

Listening critically: When you evaluate a performance, song, or a persuasive or political speech, you listen critically, questioning and judging the speaker's message.

MEDIUM is the material or technique used to present a visual image. Common media include paint, clay, and film.

NONVERBAL COMMUNICATION is communication without the use of words. People communicate nonverbally through gestures, facial expressions, posture, and body movements. Sign language is an entire language based on nonverbal communication.

PROJECTION is speaking in such a way that the voice carries clearly to an audience. It's important to project your voice when speaking in a large space like a classroom or an auditorium.

VIEWING is observing, understanding, analyzing, and evaluating information presented through visual means. You might use the following questions to help you interpret what you view:

- What subject is presented?
- What is communicated about the subject?
- Which parts are factual? Which are opinion?
- What mood, attitude, or opinion is conveyed?
- What is your emotional response?

VOCAL DELIVERY is the way in which you present a message. Your vocal delivery involves all of the following elements:

Volume: the loudness or quietness of your voice

Pitch: the high or low quality of your voice

Rate: the speed at which you speak; also called pace

Stress: the amount of emphasis placed on different syllables in a word or on different words in a sentence

All of these elements individually, and the way in which they are combined, contribute to the meaning of a spoken message.

Speaking, Listening, and Viewing Situations

Here are some of the many types of situations in which you apply speaking, listening, and viewing skills:

AUDIENCE Your audience in any situation refers to the person or people to whom you direct your message. An audience can be a group of people observing a performance or just one person. When preparing for any speaking situation, it's useful to analyze your audience, so that you can tailor your message to them.

CHARTS AND GRAPHS are visual representations of statistical information. For example, a pie chart might indicate how the average dollar is spent by government, and a bar graph might compare populations in cities over time.

DEBATE A debate is a formal public-speaking situation in which participants prepare and present arguments on opposing sides of a question, stated as a **proposition.**

The two sides in a debate are the *affirmative* (pro) and the *negative* (con). The affirmative side argues in favor of the proposition, while the negative side argues against it. Each side has an opportunity for *rebuttal,* in which they may challenge or question the other side's argument.

DOCUMENTARIES are nonfiction films that analyze news events or other focused subjects. You can watch a documentary for the information on its subject.

GRAPHIC ORGANIZERS summarize and present information in ways that can help you understand the information. Graphic organizers include charts, outlines, webs, maps, lists, and diagrams. For example, a graphic organizer for a history chapter might be an outline. A Venn diagram is intersecting circles that display information showing how concepts are alike and different.

GROUP DISCUSSION results when three or more people meet to solve a common problem, arrive at a decision, or answer a question of mutual interest. Group discussion is one of the most widely used forms of interpersonal communication in modern society.

INTERVIEW An interview is a form of interaction in which one person, the interviewer, asks questions of another person, the interviewee. Interviews may take place for many purposes: to obtain information, to discover a person's suitability for a job or a college, or to inform the public of a notable person's opinions.

MAPS are visual representations of Earth's surface. Maps may show political boundaries and physical features and provide information on a variety of other topics. A map's title and its key identify the content of the map.

ORAL INTERPRETATION is the reading or speaking of a work of literature aloud for an audience. Oral interpretation involves giving expression to the ideas, meaning, or even the structure of a work of literature. The speaker interprets the work through his or her vocal delivery. **Storytelling,** in which a speaker reads or tells a story expressively, is a form of oral interpretation.

PANEL DISCUSSION is a group discussion on a topic of interest common to all members of a panel and to a listening audience. A panel is usually composed of four to six experts on a particular topic who are brought together to share information and opinions.

PANTOMIME is a form of nonverbal communication in which an idea or a story is communicated completely through the use of gesture, body language, and facial expressions, without any words at all.

POLITICAL CARTOONS are drawings that comment on important political or social issues. Often, these cartoons use humor to convey a message about their subject. Viewers use their own knowledge of events to evaluate the cartoonist's opinion.

READERS THEATRE is a dramatic reading of a work of literature in which participants take parts from a story or play and read them aloud in expressive voices. Unlike a play, however, sets and costumes are not part of the performance, and the participants remain seated as they deliver their lines.

ROLE PLAY To role-play is to take the role of a person or character and act out a given situation, speaking, acting, and responding in the manner of the character.

SPEECH A speech is a talk or address given to an audience. A speech may be **impromptu**—delivered on the spur of the moment with no preparation—or formally prepared and delivered for a specific purpose or occasion.

- *Purposes:* The most common purposes of speeches are to persuade, to entertain, to explain, and to inform.
- *Occasions:* Different occasions call for different types of speeches. Speeches given on these occasions could be persuasive, entertaining, or informative, as appropriate.

VISUAL REPRESENTATION refers to informative texts, such as newspapers and advertisements, and entertaining texts, such as magazines. Visual representations use elements of design—such as texture and color, shapes, drawings, and photographs—to convey the meaning, message, or theme.

Index of Authors and Titles

Page numbers in *italics* refer to biographical information.

A

Aaron's Gift, 112
Abuelito Who, 300
Achebe, Chinua, 411, *414*
Adoff, Arnold, 232, *234*
Adventures of Isabel, 246
Aesop, 284, *284*
Aiken, Joan, 270, *281*
Alegría, Ricardo E., 789, *790*
Alexander, Lloyd, 505, *512*
All-American Slurp, The, 496
Alone in the Nets, 232
Alvarez, Julia, 224, *228*, 684
Angelou, Maya, 304, *305*
Ankylosaurus, 370
Ant and the Dove, The, 764
April Rain Song, 742
Arachne, 785
Armine, Douglas, 749
Asimov, Isaac, 352, *356*
Astronaut's Answers, An, 87

B

Backwoods Boy, A, 316
Baker, Russell, 72, *78*
Ballard, Robert D., 380, *386*
Bankson, Ross, 255
Bashō, Matsuo, 720, *720*
Becky and the Wheel-and-Brake Boys, 448
Benét, Rosemary and Stephen Vincent, 248, *249*
Berry, James, 448, *454*
Borden, Amanda, 545, *548*
Borzoi Young Reader, The, 150
Bradbury, Ray, 6, *12*
Breaker's Bridge, 393
Brooks, Gwendolyn, 247, *247*, 729, *729*
Bruchac, Joseph, 572, *575*
Bud, Not Buddy, from, 310
Burns, Ken, 325, *328*

C

"California's Much-Maligned Salton Sea," 588
"Can Oiled Seabirds Be Rescued?", 491
Carroll, Lewis, 708, *712*
Chang, Diana, 32, *32*
Chekhov, Anton, 460, *464*
Circuit, The, 66
Cisneros, Sandra, 300, *301*, 465, *468*
Clarke, Arthur C., 159, *162*
Clemens, Susy, 554, *557*
Close As We Can Get, As, 167
Cochrane, Kerry, 576, *579*
Coolidge, Olivia E., 785, *788*
Count That Day Lost, 141
Crippled Boy, A, 791
Cummings, E. E., 306, *306*
Curtis, Christopher Paul, 310, *313*
Cynthia in the Snow, 729

D

Dickens, Charles, 478, *481*
Dickinson, Emily, 741, *741*
Door Number Four, 140
Dragon, Dragon, 434
Dream Dust, 250
Dream Within a Dream, A, 366
Drive-In Movies, The, 558
Durbin, Richard, 337
Dust of Snow, 30

E

Edmonds, I. G., 770, *774*
Eleven, 465
Eliot, George, 141, *141*
Esperanza Rising, from, 361
Exploring the Titanic, from, 380

F

Fairies' Lullaby, The, 728
Fame Is a Bee, 741
Feathered Friend, 159
February Twilight, 727
Field, Rachel, 730, *730*
Fitzgerald, F. Scott, 542, *544*
Freedman, Russell, 316, *324*
Frost, Robert, 30, *30*
Fun They Had, The, 352

G

Gardner, John, 434, *442*
Geese, The, 706
Gentle Giants in Trouble, 255
George, Jean Craighead, 482, *486*
Giovanni, Nikki, 142, *142*
Glenn, John, 87
Grandpa and the Statue, 666
Greyling, 290

H

Haiku, 720
Hamilton, Virginia, 765, *769*
Hard as Nails, 72
Harrington, Spencer P.M., 419
Harwood, William, 562, *566*
He Lion, Bruh Bear, and Bruh Rabbit, 765
"High-Tech Windows to the Animal Kingdom" from the *National Geographic* Web site, 804
How the Internet Works, 576
How to Write a Letter, 102
How to Write a Poem About the Sky, 106
Hughes, Langston, 250, *250*, 742, *742*
Human Footprints at Chauvet Cave, 419

I

I'll Stay, 247

J

Jackie Robinson: Justice at Last, 325
Jeremiah's Song, 38
"Jerry Spinelli" Interview, 150
Jiménez, Francisco, 66, *71*
Jimmy Jet and His TV Set, 707

K

Keillor, Garrison, 102, *105*
Keller, Helen, 120, *122*
King of Mazy May, The, 52
Kipling, Rudyard, 210, *218*

L

La Leña Buena, 746
Lawyer and the Ghost, The, 478
Laycock, George, 406, *410*
Lenihan, Daniel, 517
Lester, Julius, 780, *783*
Letter to Scottie, 542
Levoy, Myron, 112, *119*
Levy, Sharon, 491
"Life and Times of Sue Web Pages" from *The Field Museum* Web site, 375

Life Doesn't Frighten Me, 304
Limerick, 720
Lindgren, Amy, 83
Lion and the Bulls, The, 284
Lob's Girl, 270
Loch Ness Monster, The, 406
London, Jack, 52, *60*

M

McGrath, Susan, 597
McKissack, Frederick Jr., 532, *536*
McKissack, Patricia C., 532, *536*
Merriam, Eve, 740, *740*
Meyers, Walter Dean, 38, *46*
Millay, Edna St. Vincent, 369, *369*
Miller, Arthur, 666, *680*
More Than a Pinch, 749
Morrison, Lillian, 718, *719*
Mowgli's Brothers, 210
My Papa, Mark Twain, 554
My Picture-Gallery, 31
My-Van, Tran, 791, *792*

N

Names/Nombres, 224
Namioka, Lensey, 496, *504*
Nanus, Susan, 614, *633*
Nash, Ogden, 246, *246*

O

Obie's Gift, from, 472
Old Ben, 154
Olympic Diary, 545
Open Road, The, 302
Overdoing It, 460

P

Parade, 730
Paz, Octavio, 726, *726*
Peck, Richard, 706, *706*
"Pericles' Funeral Oration," 796
Phantom Tollbooth, The, 614
Pigman and Me, The, from 182
Poe, Edgar Allan, 366, *367*
Pomerantz, Charlotte, 140, *140*
"Populations and Ecosystems," 597
Prelutsky, Jack, 370, *370*
Preserving a Great American Symbol, 337

R

Race to the End of the Earth, 799
Restoring the Circle, 572
Ryan, Pam Muñoz, 361, *363*
Rylant, Cynthia, 18, *22*

S

Santos, John Phillip, 746, *747*
Saying Yes, 32
Seibel, Deborah Starr, 26, *27*
Señor Coyote and the Tricked Trickster, 770
Shakespeare, William, 728, *728*
Shakespeare's London, 735
Sharks, 597
Shutout, The, 532
Sidewalk Racer, The, 718
Silko, Leslie Marmon, 106, *106*
Silverstein, Shel, 707, *707*
Simile: Willow and Ginkgo, 740
Singer, Isaac Bashevis, 128, *134*
Sneve, Virginia Driving Hawk, 194, *204*

Snorkeling Tips, 517
Something to Declare, from, 684
Soto, Gary, 558, *561*
Sound of Summer Running, The, 6
Southpaw, The, 229
Space Shuttle Challenger, 562
Spinelli, Jerry, 146, *148*
Spring and the Fall, The, 369
Stargirl, from, 146
Stone, The, 505
Stray, 18
Stuart, Jesse, 154, *158*
Summer Hats, 83

T

Teasdale, Sara, 727, *727*
Three Wishes, The, 789
"Throw and Tell" from *People Weekly*, 333

Thunder Butte, 194
Thurber, James, 282, *283*
Tiger Who Would Be King, The, 282
Tolstoy, Leo, 764, *764*
Turkeys, 580
"TV's Top Dogs" from *TV Guide*, 26
Twist and Shout, 690

V

Viorst, Judith, 229, *231*

W

Waddell, Martin, 472, *475*
Walrus and the Carpenter, The, 708
Ward, Geoffrey C., 325, *328*
Warrick, Joby, 588
Water, 120
White, Bailey, 580, *584*

Whitman, Walt, 31, *31*, 302, *303*
who knows if the moon's, 306
Why Monkeys Live in Trees, 780
Why the Tortoise's Shell Is Not Smooth, 411
Wilbur Wright and Orville Wright, 248
Wind and water and stone, 726
World Is Not a Pleasant Place to Be, The, 142
Wounded Wolf, The, 482

Y

Yep, Laurence, 393, *400*
Yolen, Jane, 290, *294*

Z

Zebrowski, Carl, 167
Zindel, Paul, 182, *188*
Zlateh the Goat, 128

Index of Skills

LITERARY ANALYSIS
Alliteration, 725, 731, R12
Animal characters, personification of
  defined, 209, 219
  examples of, 211, 213, 215, 217
  in folk tales, 763
Atmosphere
  defined, 193, 205, R12
  details of, 199, 203
  examples of, 196
  setting and, 198
  suspense and, 379, 387
Author's style, 547
Autobiographical narrative, 90, 569
Autobiography
  defined, 553, 567, R12
  examples of, 555, 556, 563, 565
  as nonfiction, 527
Biography
  defined, 553, 567, R12
  examples of, 555, 556, 563
  as nonfiction, 527
Character traits
  conflict and, 289, 295
  examples of, 393, 397, 399
  theme and, 391, 401
Characterization
  defined, 459, 469, R12
  direct and indirect, 459, 469
  examples of, 462, 467
Characters
  conflict between, 51, 61
  in drama, 626, 627
  in short story, 357
Characters' motives
  defined, 5, 13
  examples of, 7, 8
Character's qualities
  conflict and, 289, 295
  defined, 5, 13
  examples of, 9, 10
Climax, narrative
  defined, 111, 123, R12
  examples of, 113, 117, 118, 121
Conflict
  character's qualities and, 289, 292
  climax and, 111, 118, 123
  resolution and, 295
  setting and, 477, 487
Conflict, between characters
  defined, 51, 61, R12
  examples of, 54, 57, 59

Conflict, between opposing forces
  defined, 447, 455, R12
  examples of, 449, 453
Conflict, external
  defined, 181, 189, R12
Conflict, internal
  defined, 181, 189, R12
  example of, 186
Conflict, with nature
  defined, 127, 135
  examples of, 129, 132
Dialogue, in drama
  defined, 665, 681, R13
  examples of, 620, 625, 668, 669, 670, 671, 672, 675, 676, 677
Dialogue, in poetry, 29
Distinguishing Fact From Fantasy
  defined, 665, 681
  examples of, 668, 673, 674, 679
Drama
  defined, IN1, IN6–IN7, 613, 634, R13
  examples of, 615, 618, 620, 622, 624, 625, 626, 627, 628, 629, 630, 631, 632
Essay, as nonfiction, 527
Fiction
  forms of, 153, 351, 357, 405, 472, 763
  narrative, 153, 163
  theme in, 65
Figurative language
  defined, 739, 743, R13
Folk tales
  defined, IN1, IN10–11, 763, 775, R13
  examples of, 768, 772, 773
Foreshadowing
  defined, 269, 285, R14
  examples of, 271, 273, 277, 279, 280, 282
Free verse, in poetry, 299, 307
Genre, defined, xxvi, R14
Haiku, 719, 721
Historical account
  defined, 315, 329
  examples of, 318, 319, 323
Historical essay
  defined, 531, 537
  examples of, 534
Images, in drama
  defined, 636, 661, R14
  examples of, 640, 651
Images, in poetry, 29, 33
Informal essay
  defined, 101, 107
  examples of, 102

Informational essay
  defined, 571, 585
  examples of, 576
Journals
  defined, 541, 549, R14
  examples of, 547
  as nonfiction, 527
Languages, non-English, in poetry, 139
Letters
  business, R26
  defined, 541, 549, R14
  examples of, 547
  friendly, R27
  as nonfiction, 527
Limerick poetry, 721
Line, in poetry, 717, 721
Line length, in poetry, 251
Media accounts, as nonfiction, 527
Metaphor, in poetry, 33, 739, 743
Narrative
  climax and conflict in, 111, 123
  defined, 153, 163, R15
  examples of, 154, 157
Narrative essay, 571, 585
Narrator
  comparing, in different works, 223
  oral tradition and, 405, 412, 415
Narrator or speaker
  defined, 223, 235, R15
  examples of, 225, 227, 229, 231
Narrator, first-person
  autobiography and, 560, 565
  defined, 37, 47, R15
  examples of, 42
Narrator, third-person
  defined, 37, 47, R15
Nonfiction
  defined, xxvi, IN4–IN5, R15
  essay, 107
  narrative, 153, 157, 163
  theme in, 65
Onomatopoeia, 725, 731
Oral tradition
  defined, IN1, IN10–IN11, 405, 415, 779, 793, R15
  examples of, 407, 413, 780, 783, 787
Personification, in poetry, 739
Personification, of animal characters
  defined, 209, 219, R15
  examples of, 213, 217
Persuasive essay, 571, 585

Plot
  defined, 17, 23
  in drama, 631, 632
  and surprise ending, 17
Plot, short story
  defined, 357, 433, 443, R16
  examples of, 438, 441
Poetry
  concrete, 721
  dialogue in, 29
  figurative language in, 739, 743
  free verse in, 299, 307
  haiku, 721
  images in, 29, 33
  limerick, 721
  line in, 717, 721
  line length of, 251
  metaphors in, 33
  non-English language in, 139
  rhyme in, 365, 371, 713
  rhyme scheme in, 371
  rhythm in, 713
  speaker in, 139, 143, 223, 235
  special forms of, 717, 721
  stanzas in, 245, 248, 251
  tone of, 299, 307
Poetry, lyric
  defined, IN8, 705, 713
Poetry, narrative
  defined, IN8, 705, 713
Point of view, first-person
  in biographies, 553
  defined, 37, 47, R16
  examples of, 38, 40, 42, 45
Point of view, third-person
  defined, 37, 47, R16
  examples of, 45
Repetition, 725, 731
Resolution
  between characters, 51, 59, 61
  and character's qualities, 289, 292, 295
  between opposing forces, 447, 453, 455
  and setting, 477, 487
Rhyme, in poetry, 365, 371
Rhyme scheme, in poetry, 365, 371
Rhythm, in poetry, 705, 709, 711, 713
Science fiction
  defined, 351, 357, R17
  examples of, 354, 355
Setting
  atmosphere and, 198
  defined, 193, 205, 477, 487, R17
  examples of, 481, 483, 485, 624
  nature, 127, 135
  short story, 357
Short story, elements of, IN2–IN3, 357
Simile, in poetry, 739
Sound devices, in poetry, 725, 731
Speaker or narrator
  defined, 223, 235, R17
  examples of, 225, 227, 229, 231
Speaker, in poetry, 139, 143
Stage directions
  defined, 613, 634, R17
  examples of, 618, 620, 624, 625
Stanzas, in poetry
  defined, 245, 251, R17
  examples of, 248
Surprise ending
  defined, 17, 23, R17
  examples of, 20
Suspense
  defined, 379, 387, R17
  examples of, 382, 385

Theme
  character traits and, 391, 401
  clues to, 67, 70, 73, 74, 76
  defined, 65, 79, 495, 513, R17
  examples of, 499, 503, 507, 510
  images and, 655
  implied, 495, 513
  short story and, 357
  stated, 495, 513
Theme, in drama
  defined, 636, 661
  examples of, 638, 639, 640, 641, 642, 643,
    647, 649, 650, 651, 652, 653, 655, 659
Theme, in oral tradition
  defined, 779, 793
  examples of, 783, 787
Theme, plot and
  defined, 433, 443
  examples of, 438, 441
Tone, of poetry, 299, 307, 365, 371

READING STRATEGIES
Action, taking, 516, 519
Applications, completing, 239, 243
Assertions, making, 686, 689
Author's conclusions, evaluating evidence for,
  332, 335
Author's evidence, identifying
  examples of, 564
  explained, 529, 553, 567
Author's meaning, clarifying
  example of, 534
  explained, 529, 531, 537
Author's message, evaluating, 349, 351, 357
Author's purpose, understanding
  examples of, 543, 547
  explained, 529, 541, 549
Author's style, appreciating, 98
Capitalization errors, recognizing, 811
Cause and effect
  analyzing, 254, 256
  identifying, on tests, 345
Cause and effect, determining
  examples of, 395, 396
  explained, 349, 391, 401
Cause-and-effect relationships, identifying,
  690, 693
Character, describing, 525
Characters' actions, predicting
  examples of, 212, 215
  explained, 179, 209, 219
Characters, comparing and contrasting
  examples of, 274, 275, 278, 437, 440
  explained, 267, 269, 285, 433, 443
Claims, evaluating, 490, 493
Clarification, rereading for, 3, 29, 33
Compare-and-contrast text, analyzing, 748,
  751, 798, 802
Conclusions
  drawing, from test questions, 427
  evaluating author's, 332, 335
Context clues, using
  examples of, 155, 156, 160, 578
  explained, 153, 163, 571, 585
Context, to clarify meaning
  examples of, 113, 115
  explained, 99, 111, 123
  for pronunciation, 118
Context, to determine meaning
  examples of, 39, 42, 44, 581
  explained, 3, 37, 47, 529, 571, 585
  in test questions, 95
Details, identifying supporting, 175
Directions, following multiple-step, 239, 243

Drama, reading, 611
Entertainment
  drama, 610
  literature, 348
  nonfiction, 528
  poem, 702
Evidence, evaluating author's
  examples of, 564
  explained, 332, 529, 553, 567
Expression, reading aloud with, 65, 67, 68,
  74, 76, 79, 101, 103, 107
Fact, distinguishing
  examples of, 668, 674, 679
  explained, 611, 665, 681
Fact vs. opinion, distinguishing
  examples of, 385
  explained, 349, 379, 387
  on tests, 607
Fallacious reasoning, recognizing, 405, 415
Fantasy, distinguishing
  examples of, 668, 674, 679
  explained, 611, 665, 681
Fiction, reading, 431
Figurative language, interpreting, 245, 251
Folk literature, 761
Foreign words, recognizing origins and
  meanings, 139, 143, 145, 181, 189, 459, 469
Inferences, drawing
  explained, 267, 299, 307, 365, 371
  from test questions, 427
Inferences, drawing, from fiction
  examples of, 497, 503, 506, 510
  explained, 431, 495, 513
Inferences, identifying unsupported, 405, 415
Information, reading for
  in drama, 610
  in folk tales, 760
  in literature, 2, 98, 178, 266, 348
  in nonfiction, 528
  in poetry, 702
  in short stories, 430
Information, to find
  using newspapers, 82
  using text features, 85
  using Web-site features, 374, 377
Inspiration, reading for, 266
Instructions, following, 239, 243
Interactive, 179
Intonation, varying, 101, 107
Investigation, forming questions for, 803
Language
  interpreting another, 179, 183
  interpreting figurative, 251
Link, using Web site, 374
Literal comprehension, using, 3, 99
Logic and reasoning, evaluating
  examples of, 408, 409
  explained, 349, 405, 415
Love of literature, for, 2, 98, 178, 266, 348
  in drama, 610
  in folk tales, 760
  in nonfiction, 528
  in poetry, 702
  in short stories, 430
Magazine articles, reading, 490, 493
Main ideas, connecting and clarifying, 149, 151
Main ideas, determining
  examples of, 317, 319, 322, 327
  explained, 267, 315, 329
Main ideas, identifying, 263
Main points, identifying, 748, 751
Meaning, clarifying author's
  examples of, 534
  explained, 529, 531, 537
Meaning, to construct, 267. see also Context

Mood, describing, 525
Multiple meanings, identifying and
    interpreting, 29, 33, 37, 47, 111, 123, 245,
    251
Newspapers, reading, 82, 85, 149, 151
Nonfiction, for reading, 529
Notes, taking, 734, 737
Novel meanings, words with, 37, 47, 111, 123
Opinion vs. fact, distinguishing
    examples of, 385
    explained, 349, 379, 387
Outline, making, 592, 595
On-line information, 86, 87, 88, 89, 374, 375
Pacing, 101, 107
Paraphrasing
    explained, 99, 139, 143
    in poetry, 739, 741, 743
Persuasion, recognizing, 490
Plot, describing, 525
Poetry, for reading, 703
Predicting, in oral tradition
    examples of, 786, 789
    explained, 761, 779, 793
Predicting, in short stories
    examples of, 450, 452
    explained, 431, 447, 455
Predictions, making
    examples of, 293
    explained, 267, 289, 295
Prior knowledge, using, 86, 89
Pronunciation, using context for, 118
Punctuation errors, recognizing, 811
Punctuation, reading according to, 703, 725,
    731
Purpose
    analyzing writer's, 339
    establishing a, 418, 421
    understanding writer's, 336
Purpose, recognizing storyteller's
    examples of, 769, 774
    explained, 761, 763, 775
Purpose, setting a
    examples of, 225
    explained, 179, 223, 235
Purpose, understanding author's
    examples of, 543
    explained, 529, 541, 549
Questions
    asking, 596, 599
    forming, 803, 805
Reading accurately explained, 3, 166, 169
Reading aloud, with expression
    examples of, 67, 68, 74, 76, 103
    explained, 65, 79, 101, 107
Reading critically, 349
Reading fluently
    examples of, 8, 10
    explained, 3, 5, 13
Reasoning
    evaluating logic and, 349
    recognizing faulty, 405, 415
Rereading, 3, 29, 33
Senses, using your, 703, 717, 721
Setting, describing, 525
Setting, picturing the
    examples of, 479
    explained, 431, 477, 487
Shades of meaning, distinguishing, 17, 18,
    23, 193, 205
Signal words, recognizing
    examples of, 56, 58
    explained, 3, 51, 61
    on tests, 345
Speaker, identifying
    examples of, 710

explained, 703, 705, 713
Speed, pacing, 101, 107
Spelling errors, recognizing, 811
Storyteller's purpose, recognizing
    examples of, 769, 774
    explained, 761, 763, 775
Summarizing
    examples of, 131, 133, 134
    explained, 99, 127, 135, 611
Summarizing drama
    examples of, 617, 621, 622, 623, 628, 632
    explained, 613, 634
Text features
    identifying, in textbooks, 595
    using, in newspapers, 82, 85
Text, making assertions about, 686, 689
Usage, identifying appropriate, 757
Venn diagram, using, 553
Viewpoint, for another, 2, 430
Web-site features, using, 374
Word forms, identifying correct, 757
Word groups, reading, 99
Word meanings. see also Context
    distinguishing multiple, 95
    interpreting, 179, 245, 249, 251
Word meanings, understanding shades of
    examples of, 195, 197, 199, 201
    explained, 179, 193, 205
Word origins, recognizing
    examples of, 184, 186, 463
    explained, 181, 189, 469
Wordplay, recognizing
    examples of, 643, 645, 647, 649, 652
    explained, 636, 661
Writer's purpose
    analyzing, 339
    understanding, 336

GRAMMAR, USAGE, AND MECHANICS

Adjectives, 190, R33
    adverbs modifying, 236
    adverbs vs., 252, 714
    comparative, 714
    irregular, 722
    positive, 714
    possessive, 206
    superlative, 714
Adverbs, 220, R33
    adjectives vs., 252, 714
    comparative, 714
    modifying adjectives/adverbs, 236
    positive, 714
    superlative, 714
Antecedents
    agreement with pronouns, 80, 682, R35
    of pronouns, 62
Articles, 190
Capitalization, R37
    of dialogue, 586
    of titles of people, 776
Clauses
    compound, 456
    independent, 444, 456, 794
    subordinate, 444, 470, 794
Colons, 744
Commas, 732
Comparisons, irregular, 722
Conjunctions, 330, R33
    coordinating, 308
    subordinating, 308
Dialogue
    capitalization of, 586
    punctuation of, 586
Interjections, 296, R33
Modifiers, irregular, 722

Nouns, 14, R33
    common, 34
    compound, 24
    proper, 34, 568
Objects
    direct, 402, 550, R34
    indirect, 402, 550, R34
Predicates, simple, 358
Prepositional phrases, 286, R34
Prepositions, 286, R33
Pronouns, 48, R33
    antecedent agreement with, 80, 682, R35
    antecedents of, 62
    indefinite, 48, 662
    interrogative, 48
    object, 550
    personal, 48
    possessive, 206
    subject, 550
Punctuation, R37
    colons, 744
    commas, 732
    of dialogue, 586
    semicolons, 732
Semicolons, 732
Sentence structure, 794
Sentence style, 794
Sentences, R33, R34
    complete, 372
    complex, 514, 538, 794
    compound, 488, 514, 538, 794
    declarative, 388
    exclamatory, 388
    imperative, 388
    interrogative, 388
    simple, 456, 488
Subject and verb agreement, 635, R35
Subject complements, 416
Subjects, R33
    compound, 488
    simple, 358
Verb phrases, 124
Verb tenses, 144, R35
    future perfect, 164
    past perfect, 164
    present perfect, 164
    principle parts and, 136
Verbs
    base (present), 136
    compound, 488
    defined, 108, 144, R33
    past, 136
    past participle, 136

VOCABULARY

Adjectives, compound, 388
Analogies, 144, 456
Antonyms, 144
Connotations, 24, 190
Foreign words, 470
Homophones, 34, 722
Language, non-English, 470
Meanings, using multiple, 714
Musical words, 744
Nouns, compound, 80
Prefixes:
    Greek
        mono-, 220
    Latin
        dis-, 48
        ex-, 136
        in-, 372, 488
        ir-, 538
        non-, 358
        pre-, 635

Prefixes, Latin (continued)
  re-, 330
  trans-, 236
Regional synonyms, 456
Suffixes:
  Latin
    -or, 62
    -ory, 108
    -ous, 252
    -tion, 190
  Other
    -ly, 24, 732
Synonyms, 80, 144, 220, 456
Transition words, compound, 308
Word forms
  of console, 124
  of decide, 286
  of dignity, 776
  of document, 550
  of execute, 402
  of grief, 296
  of migrate, 514
  of orate, 416
  of regulate, 164
  of tolerate, 586
  of tyrant, 444
  of vary, 206
Word roots:
  Greek
    -meter-, 14
  Latin
    -mort-, 794
    -scrib-, 682
    -sequi-, 568
    -son-, 662

CRITICAL THINKING AND VIEWING

Analyze, 12, 21, 22, 43, 71, 105, 120, 142,
  182, 188, 196, 203, 204, 218, 228, 229,
  265, 272, 281, 284, 301, 305, 324, 325,
  326, 327, 328, 347, 353, 367, 370, 381,
  395, 400, 414, 429, 442, 449, 468, 472,
  481, 482, 512, 527, 532, 536, 554, 566,
  584, 619, 710, 720, 758, 769, 788, 790
Analyze cause and effect, 22, 105, 119, 158,
  162, 228, 301, 303, 386, 468
Apply, 134, 141, 162, 188, 249, 250, 283,
  284, 305, 356, 410, 414, 468, 472, 575,
  579, 742
Assess, 97, 228, 234, 247, 284, 356, 369,
  386, 400, 468, 472, 678, 741, 766, 783
Classify, 31, 324, 728
Compare, 218, 730
Compare and contrast, 60, 78, 112, 119, 122,
  142, 162, 218, 247, 248, 301, 304, 305,
  306, 356, 386, 436, 480, 481, 486, 504,
  512, 579, 583, 660, 680, 729, 741, 767,
  769, 774, 790
Connect, 44, 55, 60, 130, 214, 228, 271, 283,
  291, 294, 300, 324, 328, 367, 369, 384,
  411, 468, 472, 584, 609, 623, 680, 701,
  706, 742, 770, 783
Contrast, 12, 105, 188, 204, 218, 566, 728,
  730
Deduce, 12, 105, 134, 158, 188, 204, 303,
  305, 414, 442, 468, 557, 561, 566, 660,
  680, 782, 783, 788
Define, 710
Describe, 407, 442, 468, 472, 481, 566
Distinguish, 105, 410, 442, 468, 472, 774,
  790
Draw conclusions, 9, 22, 31, 46, 60, 71, 78,
  105, 106, 119, 122, 134, 158, 204, 228,
  294, 301, 316, 356, 369, 386, 481, 486,

512, 561, 566, 579, 660, 674, 712, 719,
  765, 769, 774, 785
Evaluate, 12, 22, 31, 32, 46, 60, 78, 105, 106,
  119, 122, 162, 188, 218, 228, 234, 247,
  249, 281, 303, 305, 439, 468, 486, 504,
  544, 566, 660, 742
Extend, 12, 31, 32, 60, 71, 142, 158, 301,
  306, 414, 719, 788
Generalize, 31, 52, 71, 249, 281, 324, 486,
  536, 575, 579, 710, 720
Hypothesize, 162, 370, 633
Identify, 573
Identify cause and effect, 536, 633
Infer, 12, 32, 46, 60, 71, 75, 78, 119, 122,
  128, 141, 158, 161, 162, 188, 204, 218,
  247, 249, 250, 281, 283, 284, 305, 306,
  328, 356, 369, 386, 400, 414, 468, 472,
  481, 484, 486, 504, 512, 536, 544, 548,
  557, 633, 670, 710, 711, 712, 719, 727,
  728, 730, 742, 769, 774, 788, 790
Interpret, 7, 22, 46, 71, 106, 114, 119, 141,
  185, 218, 228, 247, 250, 281, 283, 284,
  301, 303, 305, 306, 324, 367, 369, 400,
  414, 442, 468, 472, 486, 504, 512, 575,
  584, 660, 680, 708, 712, 719, 720, 727,
  741, 769, 774, 788, 790
Make a judgment, 141, 162, 283, 294, 305,
  354, 356, 386, 410, 414, 468, 472, 536,
  548, 575, 584, 783
Predict, 234, 410, 414, 710
Recall, 12, 22, 31, 32, 46, 60, 71, 78, 105,
  106, 119, 122, 134, 141, 142, 158, 162,
  188, 204, 218, 228, 234, 247, 249, 250,
  281, 283, 284, 294, 301, 303, 305, 306,
  324, 356, 369, 370, 386, 400, 410,
  414, 442, 468, 472, 481, 486, 504, 512,
  536, 544, 548, 557, 561, 566, 575, 579,
  584, 633, 660, 680, 710, 712, 719, 720,
  727, 728, 729, 730, 741, 742, 769, 774,
  783, 788, 790
Relate, 56, 140, 561, 712, 727
Respond, 12, 22, 31, 32, 46, 60, 71, 78, 105,
  106, 119, 122, 134, 141, 142, 158, 162,
  188, 204, 218, 228, 234, 247, 249, 250,
  281, 283, 294, 301, 306, 324, 328, 356,
  367, 369, 370, 386, 400, 410, 414, 442,
  454, 468, 472, 481, 486, 504, 512, 536,
  544, 548, 557, 561, 575, 579, 584, 633,
  660, 680, 710, 712, 719, 720, 729, 730,
  741, 742, 769, 774, 783, 788, 790
Speculate, 12, 22, 46, 78, 104, 119, 132, 141,
  162, 188, 211, 249, 281, 284, 294, 303,
  324, 328, 356, 370, 412, 414, 451, 468,
  470, 544, 556, 557, 558, 566, 574, 581,
  584, 633, 720, 727, 769, 772, 791
Support, 31, 72, 78, 142, 158, 218, 234, 249,
  294, 301, 400, 468, 479, 505, 509, 543,
  557, 575, 660, 680, 719, 783
Synthesize, 12, 60, 71, 106, 134, 162, 188,
  218, 228, 250, 410, 486, 557, 566
Take a position, 22, 46, 134, 188, 204, 410,
  536, 579, 741

WRITING

Writing Applications
Ad, help-wanted, formatting key points in,
  445
Ancient theme, in modern setting, 795
Autobiographical narrative, 90, 569
Bibliography, annotated, 489
Cause-and-effect essay, 422
Characters
  comparison and contrast of, 221
  description of, 49

letter to, 81
  qualities of, in folk tale, 777
Compare-and-contrast composition, 587
Comparison-and-contrast essay, 359, 752
Description
  of character, 49, 471
  of dinosaur, 373
  of scene, 35
Descriptive essay, 170
Drama review, 663
Fable, to teach a lesson, 287
Feature story, 165
Figurative descriptions, 745
Folk tale
  choosing characters for, 777
  modernizing, 795
Interview, organizing, 125
Invitation to the feast, identifying details of,
  417
Journal entry, including thoughts and
  feelings, 457
Letter
  to an author, 551
  to a character, 81
  from a character, 297
  to family or a friend, 145, 635
Limerick, 723
List of rules, using imperative sentences, 191
News report, 25
Opinion paper, 207
Personal narrative, 63
Persuasive composition, 340
Plot proposal, using theme, 515
Portrait, using precise words, 309
Position paper, supporting evidence in, 683
Problem-solution, 258
Proposal for research, 403
Prose narrative, adding dialogue to, 715
Report
  investigative, 389
  multimedia, 806
  research, 600
Researched response, 539
Response
  to literature, 694
  to poem, 253, 733
Sensory details, for description, 35
Short story, using elements of, 520
Sneaker advertisement, 15
Speech, persuasive, 137
Sports Scene, rewriting, with new purpose, 237
Writer's choice, for historical account, 331

Writing Strategies
Audience, considering, 253
Balance, revising for, 359
Bibliography, formatting, 489
Categories, organizing, 125, 145
Characters, comparing and contrasting, 221
Character's traits, supporting, 475
Chronological order, organizing for, 172, 389
Concrete language, using, in
  autobiographical narrative, 569
Conflict, focusing on, 92
Details
  eliminating unnecessary, 297
  gathering, 663
Dialogue, adding
  to folk tale, 777
  to prose narrative, 715
Evidence
  supporting, 683, 733
Ideas, organizing paragraph, 389
Illustrations, using, 605

Interpretation
  justifying, 733
  organizing, 696
Interview questions, organizing, 125
Invitation, identifying parts of, 417
Language, using concrete, in
    autobiographical narrative, 569
Lead
  beginning with effective, 25
  strengthening, 92
Letter, beginning appropriately, 551
Limerick, using rhyme and rhythm in, 723
Morals, illustrating, 287
Order of importance, organizing, 172
Order, organizing
  chronologically, 172, 389
  spatially, 172
Paragraphs
  organizing ideas in, 389
  structuring, 604
Pentad, summarizing literary works with, 694
Plot, organizing
  in short story, 522
  using diagram, 795
Point of view, using, in short story, 522
Problem/resolution, identifying, 515
Purpose
  choosing form to convey, 331
  establishing clear, 137
  matching form to, 373
  writing with different, 237
Quicklist, using, 90
Restatement, using, 605
Revising, for clarity, 109
Sentence construction, recognizing, 699
Sentence structure, revising, 260
Sentences
  organizing, 604
  recognizing incomplete, 699
  recognizing run-on, 699
Spatial order, organizing, 172
Thoughts and feelings, including, 457
Trigger words, using, 170
Words, using precise, 309

LISTENING AND SPEAKING
Advertisements, evaluating, 389
Choral reading, with rhyme and rhythm, 373
Debate, supporting details of, 663
Delivery techniques, 94
Directions
  following oral, 426
  presenting oral, 457, 581
Discussion, of propaganda, 475
Drama, to convey speaker's feelings, 35

Dramatic reading
  to communicate feelings, 445
  to communicate meaning, 15
Dramatization, to convey mood, 403
Emotion, identifying, 524
Emotional appeals, identifying, 191
Fact vs. opinion, distinguishing, 174
Gestures, using, 94
Interview
  for point of view, 253
  for research of theme, 81
Listener, engaging, 756
Monologue, delivering humorous, 137
Mood, identifying, 524
Multimedia presentation, narrative, 165
Opinion vs. fact, distinguishing, 174
Persuasive message, 174
Pitch of voice, varying, 94
Presentation
  with folk tale character, 777
  historical, 539
  informal, 569
  informative, 25, 125, 207, 417
  instructional, 145, 237
  narrative, 94, 165
  persuasive, 489, 551, 715
  problem-solution, 262
  research, 606
Propaganda, recognizing, 174, 475
Proposal, presenting problem-solution, 262
Reader's theater, interpreting characters of, 683
Report, informative oral, 795
Response, oral
  to literary work, 698
  to oral presentation, 733
  to poem, 723
  to theme, 515
Role-play
  characters' dialogue, 221
  characters' emotions, 331
  for point of view, 49
  using body language, 297
Source, identifying, 174
Speech
  acceptance, 63
  comparison, 359
  descriptive, 635
  informal, 109
  persuasive, 344, 745
Speed, pacing, 94
Television advertisement, analyzing images of, 309
Television news feature, planning focus of, 287

Tone, identifying, 524
Visual aids, using, 810

RESEARCH AND TECHNOLOGY
Annotations, to compare and contrast, 309
Chart
  to compare and contrast, 445, 457, 475
  for historical account, 715
  illustrating research, 663
  to inform, 25, 515, 569, 683
  using keyword search, 137
Diagram
  of history, 715
  to inform, 35, 515
Diorama, using keyword search, 137
Display
  of folk art, 777
  of information, 15
Fact sheets, using research, 165
Fair, creating, to inform, 683
Folk tale collection, 795
Keyword search, 63, 297
List, to compare, 581
Map, detail, to inform, 35
Poster, to inform, 569, 683
Presentation
  of poem, 723
  using keyword search, 63
  using research, 125, 221, 237, 551
Report
  on historical setting, 489
  using keyword search, 81
Report, multimedia
  for comparison, 359
  to inform, 515, 745
Research, illustrating, 663, 715
Research tools, using, 191
Résumé, of favorite poet, 733
Search, multi-reference
  to compare and contrast, 287
  for source of opinion, 207
  for word origins, 145
Search, text, using keywords, 63, 297
Summary
  of comparisons, 581
  of description, 373
  of electronic research, 417, 663
Timeline
  for comparison, 389
  for description, 49
  for historical account, 539, 715
  for informal essay, 109
  for presentation, 253
  visual, for historical account, 331

Index of Features

HOW TO READ LITERATURE
Clarifying author's meaning, 529
Comparing and contrasting characters, 267, 431
Context, 3, 99, 529
Determining cause and effect, 349
Determining main ideas, 267
Distinguishing fact, 349, 611
Drama, 611
Drawing inferences, 267, 431
Evaluating author's message, 349
Evaluating logic and reasoning, 349
Fiction, 431
Folk literature, 761

Identifying author's evidence, 529
Identifying speaker in poetry, 703
Interpreting meaning, 179
Making predictions, 267, 431, 761
Nonfiction, 529
Paraphrasing, 99, 703
Picturing setting, 431
Poetry, 703
Predicting characters' actions, 179
Purpose
  recognizing storyteller's, 761
  setting, 179
  understanding author's, 529
Reading according to punctuation, 703

Reading accurately, 3
Reading fluently, 3
Reading words in groups, 99
Recognizing signal words, 3
Recognizing storyteller's purpose, 761
Rereading, 3
Summarizing, 611
Understanding author's purpose, 529
Using interactive reading strategies, 179
Using literal comprehension strategies, 3, 99
Using your senses, 703
Word meanings
  shades of, 179
  using context for, 3, 99
  using rereading for, 3

LITERATURE IN CONTEXT

Agricultural Seasons, 69
Cossacks, 116
Coup, 200
Eight Immortals, The, 399
Journalism, 77
Mallet, 511
Piers and Bridges, 396
Plesiosaurs, 409
Plumb Line, 646
Qualifying for the Olympics, 546
Spanish Words and Expressions, 771
Traditional Dragon Stories, 436
Turnpike Tollbooth, 616

READING INFORMATIONAL MATERIALS

Advertisements, comparing with political
  speeches, 339
Applications, 239, 243
Autobiographies, contrasting with magazine
  articles, 335
Background information, literary, 734, 737
Biographies, comparing with interviews, 151
Book reviews
  comparing, 519
  reading, to take action, 516
  writing, 519
Cause-and-effect articles, 254, 257
Cause-and-effect relationships, identifying,
  690, 693
Citations, accurate supporting, 686
Comparison-and-contrast articles, 748, 751
Consumer reports, 751
Directions, following multiple-step
  on applications, 239
Directions, writing multiple-step
  in how-to essay, 690
Encyclopedia articles, comparing magazine
  articles with, 802
Encyclopedias vs. Web sites, comparing, 377
Evidence, evaluating author's
  in magazine articles, 332
How-to essay
  comparing user's guides with, 693
  identifying cause and effect in, 690
  writing steps of, 690
Interviews
  clarifying main ideas in, 149, 151
  comparing biographies with, 151
  contrasting news articles with, 89
  using prior knowledge for, 86, 89
  writing questions for, 89, 151
Investigation, forming questions for, 803, 805
Literary backgrounds, 734
Magazine articles, 798, 802
Main points, identifying, in comparison-and-
  contrast articles, 748, 751
Music reviews, 166, 169

Newspaper articles
  comparing different, 85
  contrasting interviews with, 89
  finding information in, 82
  using text features in, 82, 85
Newspaper feature articles
  comparing characteristics of, 689
  making assertions about, 686, 689
Notes, taking, 734, 737
Persuasive speeches
  analyzing writer's purpose in, 339
  comparing with advertisements, 339
  understanding writer's purpose in, 336
Political speeches vs. advertisements,
  comparing, 339
Product descriptions vs. music reviews,
  contrasting, 169
Questions, forming, for investigation, 803, 805
Research report
  asking questions for, 596, 599
  comparing newspaper articles with, 599
Social studies articles, identifying purpose for
  reading, 418, 421
Textbooks
  contrasting magazines with, 595
  identifying features of, 595
  outlining material in, 592, 595
Travel brochures
  comparing and contrasting, 751
  contrasting biographies with, 737
User's guides, comparing how-to essay with,
  693
Web sites
  comparing with encyclopedias, 377, 805
  forming questions for investigation, 803,
    805
  using features of, 374, 377
  using information from, 377, 421

CONNECTIONS

Literature and Culture, 238
Literature and the Media, 26
Literature Past and Present, 146, 310
Literature and Science, 588
Literature and Social Studies, 796
Poetry and Prose, 746
Science Fiction and Historical Fiction, 360
Short Stories and Novels, 472
Themes in Drama and Nonfiction, 684

WRITING WORKSHOPS

Autobiographical writing, 90
Cause-and-effect essay, 422
Chronological order, organizing, 172
Comparison-and-contrast essay, 752
Conflict, establishing, 520
Conflict, focusing on, 92
Descriptive essay, 170
Illustrations, using, 604
Lead, strengthening narrative, 92
Multimedia report, 806

Order of importance, organizing, 172
Order, organizing
  chronologically, 172
  spatially, 172
Paragraph structure, revising, 605
Pentad, using, to summarize literary works,
  694
Persuasive composition, 340
Problem-solution essay, 258
Quicklist, using, to choose topic, 90
Research report, 600
Response to literature, 694
Restatement, using, 605
Run-on sentences, revising, 260
Short story, using elements of, 520, 522
Spatial order, organizing, 172
Trigger words, using, 170

LISTENING AND SPEAKING WORKSHOPS

Delivery techniques, using, 94
Directions, following multiple-step, 426
Directions, following oral, 426
Emotion, identifying, 524
Fact vs. opinion, distinguishing, 174
Listeners, engaging, 756
Mood, identifying, 524
Narrative presentation, organizing and
  giving, 94
Opinion vs. fact, recognizing, 174
Persuasive messages, evaluating, 174
Persuasive speech, delivering, 344
Problem-solution proposal, presenting, 262
Propaganda, recognizing, 174
Research presentation, delivering, 606
Response to literature, delivering oral, 698
Sources, evaluating, 174
Tone, identifying, 524
Visual aids, using, 810

ASSESSMENT WORKSHOPS

Capitalization errors, recognizing, 811
Cause and effect, identifying, 345
Character, describing, 525
Conclusions, drawing, 427
Context, using, 95
Details, identifying supporting, 175
Fact from opinion, distinguishing, 607
Inferences, drawing, 427
Main idea, identifying, 175, 263
Mood, describing, 525
Multiple meanings, distinguishing, 95
Plot, describing, 525
Punctuation errors, recognizing, 811
Sentence construction, recognizing, 699
Setting, describing, 525
Signal words, recognizing, 345
Spelling errors, recognizing, 811
Usage, identifying appropriate, 757
Word forms, identifying correct, 757

Cleveland.com "An Astronaut's Answers" by John Glenn, from *Snappy,* published online on Cleveland Live. Copyright © 1998 by Cleveland Live. Reprint permission given by Cleveland.com, formerly Cleveland Live. All rights reserved.

Ruth Cohen Literary Agency, Inc. "The All-American Slurp," by Lensey Namioka, copyright © 1987, from *Visions,* ed. by Donald R. Gallo. Reprinted by permission of Lensey Namioka. All rights reserved by the author.

Don Congdon Associates, Inc. "The Sound of Summer Running" by Ray Bradbury. Published in *The Saturday Evening Post,* 2/18/56. Copyright © 1956 by the Curtis Publishing Co., renewed 1984 by Ray Bradbury. "Hard As Nails" from *The Good Times* by Russell Baker. Copyright © 1989 by Russell Baker. Used by permission.

Curtis Brown, Ltd. From "Adventures of Isabel" by Ogden Nash. Copyright © 1951 by Ogden Nash. First appeared in *Parents Keep Out,* published by Little, Brown & Co. Reprinted by permission.

Dell Publishing, a division of Random House, Inc., and Sheldon Fogelman Agency, Inc. "The Geese" by Richard Peck, from *Sounds and Silences: Poetry for Now* by Richard Peck, Editor, copyright © 1970, 1990 by Richard Peck. Used by permission.

Dell Publishing, a division of Random House, Inc., and Walter Dean Myers "Jeremiah's Song" by Walter Dean Myers, copyright © 1987 by Donald R. Gallo from *Visions* by Donald R. Gallo, Editor.

Doubleday, a division of Random House, Inc. "The Fun They Had" from *Earth Is Room Enough* by Isaac Asimov, copyright © 1957 by Isaac Asimov. Used by permission of Doubleday, a division of Random House, Inc.

Paul Eriksson "My Papa Mark Twain" by Susy Clemens from *Small Voices* by Josef and Dorothy Berger. © Copyright 1966 by Josef and Dorothy Berger. Reproduced by permission of Paul S. Eriksson, Publisher.

Everyman Publishers PLC From "Funeral Oration of Pericles" by Thucydides, from *The History of the Peloponnesian War.* New Introduction, copyright © 1950, by E. P. Dutton & Co., Inc. The new American edition published 1950 by E. P. Dutton & Co., Inc. All rights reserved. Reprinted by permission of Everyman Publishers PLC, Glouster Mansions, 140A Shaftesbury Avenue, London WC2H 8HD.

The Field Museum "Life and Times of Sue," from *www.fieldmuseum.org.* Copyright © 1999 by The Field Museum. Used by permission.

Fodors Travel Publications, a division of Random House, Inc. "Snorkeling Tips" from *Compass American Guides: Underwater Wonders of the National Parks* by Daniel J. Lenihan and John D. Brooks, Copyright © 1998 by Fodors LLC. Used by permission of Fodors Travel Publications, a division of Random House, Inc.

Samuel French, Inc. "The Phantom Tollbooth" by Susan Nanus from *The Phantom Tollbooth: A Children's Play in Two Acts* by Susan Nanus and Norton Juster. Copyright © 1977 by Susan Nanus and Norton Juster. Reprinted by permission of Samuel French, Inc. All rights reserved. *Caution:* Professionals and amateurs are hereby warned that "The Phantom Tollbooth," being fully protected under the copyright laws of the United States of America, the British Commonwealth countries, including Canada, and the other countries of the Copyright Union, is subject to royalty. All rights, including professional, amateur, motion picture, recitation, lecturing, public reading, radio, television and cable broadcasting, and the rights of translation into foreign languages, are strictly reserved. In its present form the play is dedicated to the reading public only. The amateur live performance rights are controlled exclusively by Samuel French, Inc. Any inquiry regarding the availability of performance rights, or the purchase of individual copies of the authorized acting edition, must be directed to Samuel French, Inc., 45 West 25th Street, NY, NY 10010 with other locations in Hollywood and Toronto, Canada.

Jean Grasso Fitzpatrick c/o Sandford J. Greenberger Associates "The Ant and the Dove" by Leo Tolstoy from *Fables and Folktales Adapted from Tolstoy,* translation by Jean Grasso Fitzpatrick. Published in 1986. Copyright © 1985 by Barrons. Used by permission.

Greenwillow Books, an imprint of HarperCollins Publishers, Inc. "Ankylosaurus" from *Tyrannosaurus Was a Beast* by Jack Prelutsky. Text copyright © 1988 by Jack Prelutsky. Used by permission.

Grolier Incorporated "How the Internet Works" from *The Internet* by Kerry Cochrane. Copyright © 1995 by Kerry Cochrane. All rights reserved. Used by permission.

Harcourt, Inc. "The Fairies' Lullaby" from *A Midsummer Night's Dream* from *Shakespeare: Major Plays and the Sonnets,* by G. B. Harrison. Published by Harcourt, Inc.

HarperCollins Publishers, Inc. "Zlateh the Goat" by Isaac Bashevis Singer from *Zlateh the Goat and Other Stories.* Text copyright © 1966 by Isaac Bashevis Singer. Illustrations copyright © 1966 by Maurice Sendak, copyright © renewed 1944 by Maurice Sendak. "Aaron's Gift" from *The Witch of Fourth Street and Other Stories* by Myron Levoy. Text copyright © 1972 by Myron Levoy. "Jimmy Jet and His TV Set" from *Where the Sidewalk Ends* by Shel Silverstein. Copyright © 1974 by Evil Eye Music, Inc. "Breaker's Bridge" from *The Rainbow People* by Laurence Yep. Text copyright © 1989 by Laurence Yep. "Señor Coyote and the Tricked Trickster" from *Trickster Tales* by I. G. Edmonds. Copyright © 1966 by I. G. Edmonds. "Limerick" (Originally titled "A flea and a fly in a flue") by Anonymous, from *Laughable Limericks.* Copyright © by Sara and John E. Brewton.

HarperCollins Publishers, Inc., and Curtis Brown Ltd. From *The Wounded Wolf* by Jean Craighead George. Text copyright © 1978 by Jean Craighead George. Reprinted by permission of HarperCollins Publishers, Inc. From *The Pigman and Me* (pp. 97–100) by Paul Zindel. Copyright © 1991 by Paul Zindel. "Alone in the Nets" from *Sports Pages* by Arnold Adoff. Text copyright © 1986 by Arnold Adoff.

Harper's Magazine "Preserving the Great American Symbol" (originally titled "Desecrating America") by Richard Durbin from *Harper's Magazine,* October 1989, p. 32. Copyright © 1989 by Harper's Magazine. All rights reserved. Used by permission.

William Harwood "Space Shuttle *Challenger*" (Challenger Remembered) by William Harwood from AOL News, online service (Vienna, VA: American Online, 1996). Reprinted by permission of the author.

Harvard University Press "Fame Is a Bee" (#1763) is reprinted by permission of the publishers and the Trustees of Amherst College from *The Poems of Emily Dickinson,* Thomas H. Johnson, editor, Cambridge, Mass.: The Belknap Press of Harvard University Press, Copyright © 1951, 1955, 1979 by the President and Fellows of Harvard College. Used by permission.

Heinemann Educational Publishers "Why the Tortoise's Shell Is Not Smooth" from *Things Fall Apart* by Chinua Achebe. Copyright © 1959 by Chinua Achebe. Reprinted by permission of Heinemann Educational Publishers.

Henry Holt and Company, Inc. "Dust of Snow" by Robert Frost from *The Poetry of Robert Frost* edited by Edward Connery Lathem. Copyright 1923, © 1969 by Henry Holt & Co., copyright © 1951 by Robert Frost. Reprinted by permission of Henry Holt and Company, LLC. From *The Walrus and the Carpenter,* by Lewis Carroll (108 lines), Illustrations by Jane Breskin Zalben, with annotations by Tweedledee and Tweedledum. Published by Henry Holt and Company.

Henry Holt and Company, Inc., and Brandt and Hochman Literary Agents, Inc. "The Stone" from *The Foundling and Other Stories of Prydain* by Lloyd Alexander, © 1973 by Lloyd Alexander. Used by permission.

Houghton Mifflin Company "Arachne," from *Greek Myths.* Copyright © 1949 by Olivia E. Coolidge; copyright renewed © 1977 by Olivia E.

Coolidge. Reprinted by permission of Houghton Mifflin Company. All rights reserved.

International Creative Management, Inc. *Grandpa and the Statue* by Arthur Miller. Copyright © 1945 by Arthur Miller. Reprinted by permission.

IpswichBank Corp. "Ipswich Bank Savings Account Application" from www.ipswichbank.com by IpswichBank Corp., Ipswich, MA. Ipswich Bank is a publicly traded company symbol IPSQ on NASDAQ. Used by permission.

Dr. Francisco Jiménez "The Circuit" by Francisco Jiménez from *America Street: A Multicultural Anthology of Stories.* Copyright © 1993 by Anne Mazer. Reprinted with permission of the author Francisco Jiménez.

Alfred A. Knopf, a division of Random House, Inc. "Dream Dust" from *The Collected Poems of Langston Hughes* by Langston Hughes. Copyright © 1994 by The Estate of Langston Hughes. "April Rain Song" from *The Collected Poems of Langston Hughes* by Langston Hughes. Copyright © 1994 by The Estate of Langston Hughes. Used by permission of Alfred A. Knopf, a division of Random House, Inc.

Alfred A. Knopf Children's Books, a division of Random House, Inc. From "Stargirl" by Jerry Spinelli, copyright © 2000 by Jerry Spinelli. "Jackie Robinson: Justice at Last" from *25 Great Moments* by Geoffrey C. Ward and Ken Burns with Jim O'Connor, copyright © 1994 by Baseball Licensing International, Inc. "He Lion, Bruh Bear, and Bruh Rabbit" from *The People Could Fly: AMERICAN BLACK FOLKTALES* by Virginia Hamilton, and Leo and Diane Dillon. Copyright © 1985 by Virginia Hamilton. From "Jerry Spinelli" from *The Borzoi Young Reader*, 1998, copyright © 1998 by Alfred A. Knopf, a division of Random House, Inc. Used by permission of Alfred A. Knopf Children's Books, a division of Random House, Inc.

George Laycock "The Loch Ness Monster" from *Mysteries, Monsters and Untold Secrets* by George Laycock. Copyright © 1978 by George Laycock. All rights reserved. Used by permission.

The Lazear Literary Agency "Turkeys" from *Mama Makes Up Her Mind* (Addison-Wesley, 1993), reprinted by permission of the author.

Lescher & Lescher Ltd. "The Southpaw" by Judith Viorst. Copyright © 1974 by Judith Viorst. From *Free to Be...You and Me.* This usage granted by permission of Lescher & Lescher, Ltd. All rights reserved.

Ellen Levine Literary Agency, Inc. "How to Write A Letter" by Garrison Keillor. Copyright © 1987 by International Paper Company. From *We Are Still Married*, published by Viking Penguin Inc. Reprinted by permission International Paper Company. (Originally titled "How to Write a Personal Letter")

Liveright Publishing Corporation, an imprint of W. W. Norton & Company "who knows if the moon's," copyright 1923, 1925, 1951, 1953, © 1991 by the Trustees for the E. E. Cummings Trust. Copyright © 1976 by George James Firmage, from *Complete Poems: 1904–1962* by E. E. Cummings, edited by George J. Firmage. Used by permission of Liveright Publishing Corporation.

Los Angeles Times Syndicate "TV's Top Dogs" by Deborah Starr Seibel, published in *TV Guide*, June 18, 1994. Used by permission of the Los Angeles Times Syndicate.

Madison Press Books and Penguin Canada Text © 1988 Odyssey Corporation from *Exploring the* Titanic by Robert D. Ballard, a Scholastic Inc./Madison Press Book. Used by permission.

McIntosh and Otis, Inc. "Overdoing It" from *Shadows and Light: Nine Stories* by Anton Chekhov, edited and translated by Miriam Morton, originally published by Doubleday & Company. Reprinted with the permission of McIntosh and Otis, Inc.

William Morrow & Company, Inc., a division of Harper-Collins Publishers, Inc. "The World Is Not a Pleasant Place to Be" from *My House* by Nikki Giovanni. Copyright © 1972 by Nikki Giovanni.

Reprinted by permission of William Morrow, a division of HarperCollins Publishers, Inc.

National Geographic World From "Race to the End of the Earth" by William G. Scheller from *National Geographic World*, Number 294, February 2000. Copyright © 2000 by National Geographic Society. "Sharks" by Susan McGrath from *National Geographic World*, Number 222, February 1994. Copyright © 1994 by National Geographic Society. All rights reserved. "National Geographic Website" (featuring "High Tech Windows to the Animal Kingdom" by Robinson Shaw) from www.nationalgeographic.com. "Gentle Giants in Trouble" (originally titled "Gentle Giants in Trouble: Manatees") by Ross Bankson, from *National Geographic World*, Number 199, March 1992. Used by permission.

National Wildlife Federation From "Can Oiled Seabirds Be Rescued, or Are We Just Fooling Ourselves?" by Sharon Levy from *National Wildlife*, February/March 1999. Copyright © 1999 by National Wildlife Federation. From "California's Much-Maligned Salton Sea is a Desert Oasis for Wildlife" by Joby Warrick, from *National Wildlife*, August/September 2000. Copyright © 2000 by National Wildlife Federation. Used by permission.

New Directions Publishing Corp. "Wind and water and stone" by Octavio Paz, translation by Mark Strand, from *Collected Poems 1957–1987.* Copyright © 1979 by The New Yorker Magazine. Reprinted by permission of New Directions Publishing.

Orchard Books, an imprint of Scholastic, Inc. "Becky and the Wheels-and-Brake Boys" from *A Thief in the Village and Other Stories* by James Berry. Published by Orchard Books, an imprint of Scholastic, Inc. Copyright © 1987 by James Berry. Reprinted by permission.

Richard Orlikoff for The Estate of Gwendolyn Brooks "Cynthia in the Snow" from *Bronzeville Boys and Girls* by Gwendolyn Brooks. Copyright © 1956 by Gwendolyn Brooks Blakely.

Pasadena Youth Roller Hockey League "Pasadena Youth Roller Hockey Registration Form" from the Pasadena Youth Roller Hockey League, Pasadena, TX.

Penguin Putnam, Inc. "La leña buena" from *Places Left Unfinished at the Time of Creation* by John Phillip Santos. Copyright © John Phillip Santos, 1999. Used by permission.

Curtis Brown Ltd. "Greyling" from *Greyling: A Picture Story from the Islands* by Jane Yolen. Text copyright © 1968 by Jane Yolen. Used by permission. All rights reserved.

People Weekly "Throw and Tell" from *People Weekly*, October 11, 1999, VOLUME 52. Copyright © 1999 Time, Inc. Used by permission.

Philomel Books From *Greyling* by Jane Yolen, published by Philomel Books. Text copyright © 1968 and 1991, renewed 1996 by Jane Yolen. Used by permission of Philomel Books, an imprint of Penguin Putnam Books for Young Readers, a division of Penguin Putnam, Inc.

Charlotte Pomerantz c/o Writers House LLC "Door Number Four" from *If I Had a Paka* by Charlotte Pomerantz. Copyright © 1982 by Charlotte Pomerantz. Reprinted by arrangement with the author, c/o Writers House as agent to the author.

Prentice-Hall, Inc., a division of Pearson Education. "Restoring the Circle" by Joseph Bruchac, from *The Writer's Solution Sourcebook, Bronze*, copyright © 1996 by Prentice Hall, Inc. Used by permission of the publisher.

PRIMEDIA Special Interest Publications (History Group) "As Close As We Can Get" by Carl Zebrowski. This article is reprinted from the Volume XXXVIII, Number 5 issue of *Civil War Times Illustrated* with the permission of *Primedia* Special Interest Publications (History Group), copyright Civil War Times Illustrated. Used by permission.

Random House, Inc. "Life Doesn't Frighten Me," copyright © 1978 by Maya Angelou, from *And Still I Rise* by Maya Angelou. Used by permission of Random House, Inc.

Random House Children's Books, a division of Random House, Inc. "Lob's Girl," from *A Whisper in the Night* by Joan Aiken, copyright © 1984 by Joan Aiken. "Bud, Not Buddy" from *Bud, Not Buddy* by Christopher Paul Curtis, copyright © 1999 by Christopher Paul Curtis. Used by permission of Random House Children's Books, a division of Random House, Inc.

The Reader's Digest Association Limited, London "More Than a Pinch" (originally titled "More Than A Pinch of Salt") from *Did You Know?* Copyright © 1990 by The Reader's Digest Association Limited. Used by permission of The Reader's Digest Association Limited.

Marian Reiner, Literary Agent "Haiku" by Bashō from *Cricket Songs: Japanese Haiku*, translated by Harry Behn, © 1964 by Harry Behn; © Renewed 1992 Prescott Behn, Pamela Behn Adam and Peter Behn. Reprinted by permission of Marian Reiner. All rights reserved.

Marian Reiner, Literary Agent for Eve Merriam "Simile: Willow and Ginkgo" by Eve Merriam, from *A Sky Full of Poems*. Copyright © 1964, 1970, 1973 by Eve Merriam; © renewed 1992 Eve Merriam. Reprinted by permission of Marian Reiner, Literary Agent for the author. All rights reserved.

Marian Reiner, Literary Agent for Lillian Morrison "The Sidewalk Racer or On the Skateboard" by Lillian Morrison, from *The Sidewalk Racer and Other Poems of Sports and Motion* by Lillian Morrison. Copyright © 1968, 1977 by Lillian Morrison. Reprinted by permission of Marian Reiner for the author.

Marian Reiner, Literary Agent for The Jesse Stuart Foundation "Old Ben" from *Dawn of Remembered Spring* by Jesse Stuart. Copyright © 1955, 1972 Jesse Stuart. © Renewed 1983 Jesse Stuart Foundation. Reprinted by permission of Marian Reiner for The Jesse Stuart Foundation.

Scholastic, Inc. "Why Monkeys Live in Trees" from *How Many Spots Does a Leopard Have? and Other Tales* by Julius Lester. Copyright © 1989 by Julius Lester. "The Shutout" from *Black Diamond: The Story of the Negro Baseball Leagues* by Patricia C. McKissack and Frederick McKissack, Jr. Copyright © 1994 by Patricia C. McKissack and Frederick McKissack, Jr. Reproduced by permission of Scholastic Inc. From *Exploring the Titanic* by Robert D. Ballard. Copyright © 1988 by Ballard & Family; Copyright © 1988 by The Madison Press Ltd.

Scholastic Press, a division of Scholastic, Inc. From *Esperanza Rising* by Pam Muñoz Ryan. Published by Scholastic Press, a division of Scholastic, Inc. Copyright © 2000 by Pam Muñoz Ryan. Reprinted by permission.

Scovil Chichak Galen Literary Agency, Inc. "Feathered Friend" from *The Other Side of the Sky* by Arthur C. Clarke. Copyright © 1958 by Arthur C. Clarke. Used by permission of the author and the author's agents, Scovil Chichak Galen Literary Agency, Inc.

Scribner, a division of Simon & Schuster, Inc., and Harold Ober Associates, Inc. "Letter to Scottie" reprinted with permission of Scribner, a division of Simon & Schuster, Inc., and Harold Ober Associates, Inc., from *F. Scott Fitzgerald: A Life in Letters*, edited by Matthew J. Bruccoli. Copyright © 1994 by The Trustees Under Agreement Dated July 3, 1975, Created by Frances Scott Fitzgerald Smith.

Simon & Schuster, Inc. "February Twilight" from *The Collected Poems of Sara Teasdale*. Copyright © 1926 by Macmillan Publishing Company, renewed 1954 by Mamie T. Wheless. Used by permission.

Simon & Schuster Books for Young Readers, an imprint of Simon & Schuster Children's Publishing Division "Stray" from *Every Living Thing* by Cynthia Rylant. Copyright © 1985 by Cynthia Rylant. "Parade" from *Branches Green* by Rachel Field. Copyright © 1934 Macmillan Publishing Company; copyright renewed © 1962 by Arthur S. Pederson. Reprinted with the permission of Simon & Schuster Books for Young Readers, an imprint of Simon & Schuster Children's Publishing Division.

Virginia Driving Hawk Sneve "Thunder Butte" by Virginia Driving Hawk Sneve, from *When Thunders Spoke*. Copyright © 1974 by Virginia Driving Hawk Sneve. Reprinted by permission of the author.

St. Paul Pioneer Press "Summer Hats" by Amy Lindgren from *Saint Paul Pioneer*, Sunday 6/13/99. St. Paul, Minn.: Northwest Publications, Inc., 1990. Used by permission.

Rosemary A. Thurber and the Barbara Hogenson Agency "The Tiger Who Would Be King" by James Thurber, from *Further Fables for Our Time*, published by Simon & Schuster. Copyright © 1956 by James Thurber. Copyright © 1984 by Helen Thurber and Rosemary A. Thurber. Used by permission of Rosemary A. Thurber and the Barbara Hogenson Agency.

Edna St. Vincent Millay Society c/o Elizabeth Barnett "The Spring and the Fall" by Edna St. Vincent Millay. From *Collected Poems*, HarperCollins. Copyright 1923, 1951 by Edna St. Vincent Millay and Norma Millay Ellis. All rights reserved. Reprinted by permission of Elizabeth Barnett, literary executor.

Third Woman Press and Susan Bergholz Literary Services "Abuelito Who" from *My Wicked Wicked Ways* by Sandra Cisneros. Copyright © 1987 by Sandra Cisneros, published by Third Woman Press and in hardcover by Alfred A. Knopf. Used by permission of Susan Bergholz Literary Services, New York, and Third Woman Press. All rights reserved.

Dr. My-Van Tran "A Crippled Boy" from *Folk Tales from Indochina* by My-Van Tran. First published in 1987. Copyright © Vietnamese Language and Culture Publications and My-Van Tran. Used by permission.

University Press of New England and Gary Soto Gary Soto, "The Drive-In Movies," from *A Summer Life* © 1990 by University Press of New England. Used by permission.

Usborne Publishing Ltd. "Shakespeare's London" from *The World of Shakespeare* (originally titled "London Life") by Anna Claybourne and Rebecca Treays. Copyright © Usborne Publishing Ltd 1996. Used by permission.

Villa Park Public Library "Villa Park Public Library Card Application" from the Villa Park Public Library, 305 South Ardmore Avenue, Villa Park, Illinois 60181. Used by permission.

K. Wayne Wincey "Twist and Shout" by K. Wayne Wincey, from *Boys Life*, August 1999. By permission of K. Wayne Wincey and *Boys Life*, August 1999, published by the Boy Scouts of America.

The Wylie Agency, Inc. "How to Write a Poem About the Sky" from *Storyteller* by Leslie Marmon Silko. Copyright © 1981 by Leslie Marmon Silko, reprinted by permission of the Wylie Agency, Inc.

Note: Every effort has been made to locate the copyright owner of material reprinted in this book. Omissions brought to our attention will be corrected in subsequent printings.

CREDITS

Art Credits

Cover and Title Page *The Haystacks*, oil on canvas, Vincent van Gogh/ Nationalmuseum, Stockholm, Sweden/Bridgeman Art Library, London/New York **vii** (b.) © Dorling Kindersley/Tim Ridley **vii** (t.) David Macias/Photo Researchers, Inc. **viii** M.P. Kahl/Photo Researchers, Inc. **ix** AP/Wide World Photos **x** *Ezra Davenport*, 1929, Clarence Holbrook Carter, Oil on canvas, Courtesy of the artist **xi** (t.) *The Immortal*, 1990, Chi-Fong Lei, Courtesy of the artist; **xi** (b.) Frans Lanting/Photo Researchers, Inc. **xii** (t.) ©Stone **xii** (b.) Animals Animals/©James Watt **xiii** AP/Wide World Photos **xiv** Grace Davies/Omni-Photo Communications, Inc. **xv** © Mike & Elvan Habicht/Animals Animals **xvi** (t.) Steve Satushek/The Image Bank **xvi** (m.) Bettmann/ CORBIS **xvi–xvii** (b.) ©Richard Hamilton Smith/CORBIS **xvii** (t.) Courtesy of the Library of Congress **xviii–xix** Corel Professional Photos CD-ROM™ **xx** Philip van den Berg/HPH Photography **xxi** David Stover, Stock South/PictureQuest **1** *In the Garden*, Joseph Raphael, The Redfern Gallery **2** (t.) The Granger Collection, New York **2** (b.), **4, 6** Silverstre Machado/Tony Stone Images **9** *New Shoes for H*, 1973–1974, Don Eddy, The Cleveland Museum of Art, Acrylic on canvas, 111.7 x 121.9 cm © The Cleveland Museum of Art, 1998, Purchase with a grant from the National Endowment for the Arts and matched by gifts from members of The Cleveland Society for Contemporary Art, 1974.53 **12** Thomas Victor **16**, **18–19** ©Zig Leszczynski/Animals Animals **21** ©Margot Conte/Animals Animals **26** Everett Collection **27** ©1996 Paramount Pictures. All Rights Reserved. **28** University of Washington Press, Photo by Gordon Robotham **30** (t.) David Macias/Photo Researchers, Inc. **30** (b.) Dimitri Kessel/Life Magazine; **31** Courtesy of the Library of Congress **32** (b.) Rollie McKenna **32** (t.) University of Washington Press, Photo by Gordon Robotham **36** Frank Orel/Tony Stone Images **38** Pictor International/PictureQuest **40** Corel Professional Photos CD-ROM™ **43** *Harmonizing*, 1979, Robert Gwathmey, Courtesy Terry Dintenfass Gallery, © Estate of Robert Gwathmey/Licensed by VAGA, New York, NY **44** *Springtime Rain*, 1975, Ogden M. Pleissner, Ogden M. Pleissner Estate Marion G. Pleissner Trust, Bankers Trust Company. Photo by Grace Davies/Omni-Photo Communications, Inc. **46** John Craig Photo **50** Special Collections Division, University of Washington Libraries, E.A. Hegg, 181 **52** The Granger Collection, New York **53** ©Colin Hawkins /Stone **56** *After Dinner Music*, 1988, Scott Kennedy, © 1988, Greenwich Workshop Inc. Courtesy of the Greenwich Workshop Inc. **58** Digital Imagery ©Copyright 2001 PhotoDisc, Inc. **60** CORBIS-Bettmann **64** Marc Solomon/The Image Bank **66** *My Brother*, 1942, Guayasamin (Oswaldo Guayasamin Calero), Oil on wood, 15 7/8 x 12 3/4", Collection, The Museum of Modern Art, New York, Inter-American Fund **69** Walter Choroszewski/Stock Connection/PictureQuest **71** Charles G. Barry **72** ©Anthony Potter Collections/Archive Photos **75** ©Levick/Archive Photos **77** AP/Wide World Photos **78** CORBIS-Bettmann **83** ©Mary Kay Denny/PhotoEdit **87** AP/Wide World Photos **90** David Young-Wolff/PhotoEdit **96–97** Gogh, Vincent van (1853– 1890). *First Steps, after Millet*. Oil on canvas, 72.4 x 91.2 cm. The Metropolitan Museum of Art, Gift of George N. and Helen M. Richard. (64.165.2) **98** (b.) M.P. Kahl/Photo Researchers, Inc. **98** (m.) *The Calm After the Storm*, Edward Moran, Private Collection/SuperStock **98** (t.) © William J. Jahoda/Photo Researchers, Inc. **100** *The Calm After the Storm*, Edward Moran, Private Collection/SuperStock **102** Richard Hutchings/Photo Researchers, Inc. **104** ©Jim Cummings/FPG International Corp. **105** Minnesota Public Radio, photo by Carmen Quesada **106** (b.) Thomas Victor **106** (t.) Silver Burdett Ginn **110** ©The Stock Market/Marco Cristofori **112** Jane Burton/Bruce Coleman, Inc. **114** *Pigeons*, John Sloan, Oil on canvas, 26 x 32", The Hayden Collection, Courtesy, Museum of Fine Arts, Boston, Massachusetts **116** Steve Raymer/CORBIS **120** Photofest **122** American Foundation for the Blind **126** ©The Stock Market/Frank P. Rossotto **128, 130, 132** from "Zlateh the Goat and Other Stories" by Isaac Bashevis Singer, illustrations by Maurice Sendak © 1966, HarperCollins Publishers, Inc. **134** Thomas Victor **138** Michelle Bridwell/PhotoEdit **140** (t.) *One Child Between Doors* (Seorang Anak di Antara Pintu Ruang), 1984, Dede Eri Supria, Courtesy of Joseph Fischer **140** (b.) Hearst Books, Photo by Daniel Pomerantz. **141** Hulton Getty Images/Tony Stone Images **142** (b.) Courtesy of the author **142** (t.) NASA **146** Jacket Illustration copyright ©2000 by Alfred A. Knopf **152** ©William J. Jahoda/Photo Researchers, Inc. **154** M.P. Kahl/Photo Researchers, Inc. **157** Corel Professional Photos CD-ROM™ **158** Jesse Stuart Foundation **159** © William J. Jahoda/Photo Researchers, Inc. **161** NASA **162** CORBIS-Bettmann **167, 168** *The Banjo Lesson*, 1893, Henry Ossawa Tanner, Hampton University Museum, Hampton, Virginia **170** David Young-Wolff/PhotoEdit **176– 177** ©Paul Schulenburg/Stock Illustration Source, Inc. **178** (t.) ©Tom McHugh/Photo Researchers, Inc. **178** (b.) Lou Jones/The Image Bank **182** Mary Kate Denny/PhotoEdit **185** *Elephant Tree*, ©1996 Robert Vickrey/ Licensed by VAGA, New York NY **188** Harper Collins **192, 194–195** Corel Professional Photos CD-ROM™ **196** ©The Stock Market/Bob Shaw **200** ©British Museum **203** Corel Professional Photos CD-ROM™ **204** Courtesy of the author **208** ©Tom McHugh/Photo Researchers, Inc. **210** Renne Lynn/Tony Stone Images **214** ©Tom McHugh/Photo Researchers, Inc. **216** Corel Professional Photos CD-ROM™ **218** By Courtesy of the National Portrait Gallery, London **222** Rhoda Sidney/Stock, Boston **224** © Pete Seaward/Stone **226** *Collage* (detail), 1992, Juan Sanchez, Courtesy of Juan Sanchez and Guarighen, Inc., NYC **228** Prentice Hall **229, 230** Lou Jones/The Image Bank **231** Atheneum Books, photo by Didi Cutler **232** (t.) David Young-Wolff/PhotoEdit **232** (b.) Digital Imagery ©Copyright 2001 PhotoDisc, Inc. **234** Virginia Hamilton **238** (l., r.) AP/Wide World Photos **244** The Granger Collection, New York **246** UPI/CORBIS-Bettmann **247** CORBIS-Bettmann **248** The Granger Collection, New York **249** Courtesy of Thomas Benét **250** (b.) New York Public Library **250** (t.) Jon Sanford/Photo Network/PictureQuest **255** ©The Stock Market/Kennan Ward **258** Bill Bachmann/Stock, Boston Inc. /PictureQuest **264–265** *Emigrants Crossing the Plains, 1867*, Albert Bierstadt, oil on canvas, 60 x 96 in., A.011.1T, National Cowboy Hall of Fame, Oklahoma City **266** (l.) National Baseball Library and Archive, Cooperstown, N.Y. **266** (t.) David Stover, Stock South/PictureQuest **266** (b.) National Baseball Library and Archive, Cooperstown, N.Y. **268** Renee Lynn/Photo Researchers, Inc. **270** Corel Professional Photos CD-ROM™ **272** *That's My Dog* (German Shepherd), Jim Killen, Voyageur Art **276** Brian Yarvin/Photo Researchers, Inc. **282** Renee Lynn/Photo Researchers, Inc. **283** CORBIS-Bettmann **284** The Granger Collection, New York **288** *One*, 1986, April Gornik, Edward Thorp Gallery **290** Jeremy Walker/Tony Stone Images **291, 292** Corel Professional Photos CD-ROM™ **294** Prentice Hall **298** Corel Professional Photos CD-ROM™ **300** *Ezra Davenport*, 1929, Clarence Holbrook Carter, Oil on canvas, Courtesy of the artist **301** AP/Wide World Photos **302–303** David Stover, Stock South/PictureQuest **303** Courtesy of the Library of Congress **305** (t.) ©Jeffery A. Salter **305** (b.) Henry McGee/Globe Photos **306** (t.) Digital Imagery ©Copyright 2001 PhotoDisc, Inc. **306** (b.) *Self-Portrait* (detail), 1958, E. E. Cummings, The National Portrait Gallery, Smithsonian Institution, Washington, D.C./Art Resource, New York; **310** Cover illustration ©1999 by Ernie Norcia. Cover design by Vikki Sheatsley **312, 313** AP/Wide World Photos **314** UPI/CORBIS-Bettmann **316** Courtesy of the Illinois State Historical Library **320** Lincoln Boyhood National Memorial, Photo by John Lei/Omni-Photo Communications, Inc. **324** Russell Freedman, Photograph by Charles Osgood, Copyrighted 5/23/88, Chicago Tribune Company, All rights reserved, Used with permission **325, 326** UPI/CORBIS-Bettmann **328** (t.) Villard Books, photo © John Isaac **328** (b.) Florentine Films. Photo by Pam Tubridy Baucom **333, 337** AP/Wide World Photos **340** Myrleen/PhotoEdit **346–347** *This, That, There*, 1993, Pat Adams, Courtesy of the Eleanor Munro Collection/Zabriskie Gallery **348** (b.) Corel Professional Photos CD-ROM™ **348** (t.) Frans Lanting/Photo Researchers, Inc. **350** David Crosier/Tony Stone Images **352** ©1997, Michael Simpson/FPG International Corp. **354** Benelux Press/H. Armstrong Roberts **356** Thomas Victor **360** Jacket Art ©2000 by Joe Cepeda. Jacket Design by Marijka Kostiw **362** Laurie Platt Winfrey, Inc. **363** Scholastic Art and Writing Awards **364** Maurice Huser/Tony Stone Images **366** Digital Imagery ©Copyright 2001 PhotoDisc, Inc. **367** CORBIS-Bettmann **368** Digital Imagery ©Copyright 2001 PhotoDisc, Inc. **369** Nationwide News Service **378, 380–381** Corel Professional Photos CD-ROM™ **382** (l.) Courtesy of the Library of Congress **382** (r.) Courtesy of Ken Marschall **383** (l.) Photo by Brown Bros./Ken Marschall **383** (r.) Courtesy Madison Press, Illustrated by Pronk and Associates **384** Courtesy Madison Press, Illustrated by Pronk and Associates **386** Woods Hole Oceanographic Institution **390** *The Kintai Bridge in Springtime* (detail), Kawase Hasui, Private Collection/Bridgeman Art Library, London/New York **392** *The Immortal*, 1990, Chi-Fong Lei, Courtesy of the artist; **394–395, 396** Corel Professional Photos CD-ROM™ **399** *The Eight Immortals Crossing the Sea*, illustration from "Myths and Legends of China" by Edward T.C. Werner, pub. by George G. Harrap & Co., 1922, Private Collection/Bridgeman Art Library, London/New York **400** Permission granted by Troll Communications, LLC

404 ©Popperfoto/Archive Photos **406** (b.) ©Susan Greenspan/Archive Photos **406** (t.), **409** ©Popperfoto/Archive Photos **410** Photo by Darr Bass **411** Frans Lanting/Photo Researchers, Inc. **412** M & E Bernheim/Woodfin Camp & Associates **414** AP/Wide World Photos **419** Peter H. Buckley/Pearson Education/PH College **420** Ministère de la Culture et des Communications, Paris, France **422** J. Nouvok/PhotoEdit **428–429** *The Storyteller*, Adolphe Tidemand, Christie's, London/SuperStock **430** (t.) Hulton Getty/Tony Stone Images **430** (b.) Tom and Pat Leeson/Photo Researchers, Inc. **432** ©Stone **434** Courtesy of J. Alimena **436** Reprinted with the permission of Atheneum Books for Young Readers, an imprint of Simon & Schuster Children's Publishing Division, from THE BOY'S KING ARTHUR by Sidney Lanier, illustrated by N.C. Wyeth. Copyright © 1917 Charles Scribner's Sons; copyrights renewed 1945 N.C. Wyeth and 1952 John Lanier, David Lanier and Sterling Lanier. **439** *Dick Whittington on his way to London* from "My Nursery Story Book", published by Blackie and Son (book illustration) by Frank Adams, Private Collection/ The Bridgeman Art Library, London **442** ©1979 R.E. Potter III **446** *Biking for Fun*, 1992, Carlton Murrell, Courtesy of the artist, photo by John Lei/Omni-Photo Communications, Inc.; **448** *Daddy's Girl*, 1992, Carlton Murrell, Courtesy of the artist, photo by John Lei/Omni-Photo Communications, Inc.; **451** *Mother, I Love to Ride*, 1992, Carlton Murrell, Courtesy of the artist, photo by John Lei/Omni-Photo Communications, Inc.; **454** Camera Press/Globe Photos **458** ©Elizabeth Simpson/FPG International Corp. **460** Corel Professional Photos CD-ROM™ **460** (inset) *Old Man's Head, Study*, 1955, Yuri Alexeevich Dryakhlov, Courtesy of Overland Gallery of Fine Art, Scottsdale, AZ **464** CORBIS-Bettmann **465** *Orange Sweater*, 1955, Elmer Bischoff, San Francisco Museum of Modern Art, Gift of Mr. and Mrs. Mark Schorer **466** *Portrait, From the Estate of Eloy Blanco*, Collection of El Museo del Barrio, New York, NY **468** AP/Wide World Photos **473** Jacket illustration copyright ©1991 by Elsie Lennox **474** CORBIS **476** UPI/CORBIS-Bettmann **478** Hulton Getty/Tony Stone Images **480** UPI/CORBIS-Bettmann **481** CORBIS-Bettmann **482** ©Stephen J. Krasemann/Peter Arnold, Inc. **484** Tom and Pat Leeson/Photo Researchers, Inc. **486** Prentice Hall **491** Ron Levy/Liaison Agency **494** © Stone **497** Corel Professional Photos CD-ROM™ **498, 500** Digital Imagery ©Copyright 2001 PhotoDisc, Inc. **503** David Young-Wolff/Tony Stone Images **504** Courtesy of the author. Photo by Don Perkins. **505** *Walk in the Country*, Javran, Superstock; **509** *Harvesting the Fruit Crop*, Javran, Superstock **511** Digital Imagery ©Copyright 2001 PhotoDisc, Inc. **512** Alexander Limont **517** ©Stone **520** David Young-Wolff/PhotoEdit **526–527** *Desk Set*, 1972, Wayne Thiebaud, Courtesy of the artist, Collection of The Southland Corporation **528** (t.) Culver Pictures, Inc. **528** (b.) Ebbets Field Flannels **528** (m.) Bettmann/CORBIS **530, 532–533, 535** National Baseball Library and Archive, Cooperstown, N.Y. **536** Scholastic, Inc **540** Steven E. Sutton/Duomo Photography, Inc. **542** Culver Pictures, Inc. **544** *F. Scott Fitzgerald,* David Silvette, The National Portrait Gallery, Smithsonian Institution, Washington, DC/Art Resource, New York; **545** Steven E. Sutton/Duomo Photography, Inc. **546** Jan Butchofsky-Houser/CORBIS **548** William Sallaz/Duomo Photography, Inc. **552** *El Auto Cinema*, 1985, Roberto Gil de Montes, Oil on wood, Courtesy of Jan Baum Gallery, Collection of Patricia Storace; **554, 556, 557** The Mark Twain House, Hartford, CT **558** Bettmann/CORBIS **561** Dianne Trejo **562** AP/Wide World Photos **570** *Paradise #1*, Suzanne Duranceau, Illustratrice **573** Jerry Jacka Photography **574, 575** Prentice Hall **579** Digital Imagery ©Copyright 2001 PhotoDisc, Inc. **580–581** Leonard Le Rue III/Tony Stone Images

583 Animals Animals **584** Spencer **588** Richard Cummins/CORBIS **597** Animals Animals/ ©James Watt **600** Esbin/Anderson/Omni-Photo Communications, Inc. **601** U.S. Department of the Interior, U.S. Geological Survey **608–609** *Theatre Scene*, Edgar Degas/Private Collection/Bridgeman Art Library, London/New York **610** Grace Davies/Omni-Photo Communications, Inc. **612** Illustration by Norton Juster **616** ©Robert Holmes/CORBIS **646** Digital Imagery ©Copyright 2001 PhotoDisc, Inc. **660** Photo, John Martin **664** Jon Ortner/Tony Stone Images **666** Grace Davies/Omni-Photo Communications, Inc. **670** Courtesy of the Library of Congress **674** Musée Bartholdi, Colmar, France **678** Ron Watts/Black Star **680** Garcia/Stills/ Retna, LTD **684** Penguin **685** Prentice Hall **687** David Ryan/Photo 20-20/PictureQuest **691** Wolfgang Kaehler/CORBIS **700–701** *Waves of Matsushima*, Edo period, early 18th century, six-panel folding screen, Korin Ogata, Courtesy, Museum of Fine Arts, Boston, Fenollosa-Weld Collection **702** (b.) Dave G. Houser/CORBIS **702** (m.) © Mike & Elvan Habicht/Animals Animals **702** (t.) Illustration from *Alice Through the Looking Glass* by Lewis Carroll, John Tenniel, Photography by John Lei/Omni-Photo Communications, Inc. **704, 706** (t.) Corel Professional Photos CD-ROM™ **706** (b.) Don Lewis Photography **707** AP/Wide World Photos **708, 709, 710, 711** Illustration from *Alice Through the Looking Glass* by Lewis Carroll, John Tenniel, Photography by John Lei/Omni-Photo Communications, Inc. **712** New York Public Library Picture Collection **716, 718** © Mike & Elvan Habicht/Animals Animals **719** Photo by Isidro Rodriguez **720** The Granger Collection, New York **724** Vicki Silbert/PhotoEdit **726–727** ©Richard Hamilton Smith/CORBIS **726** (b.) AP/Wide World Photos **727** (b.) CORBIS-Bettmann **728** (b.) William Shakespeare (detail), Artist unknown, by courtesy of the National Portrait Gallery, London **728–729** © Ron Dahlquist/Stone **729** (b.) CORBIS-Bettmann **730** (t.) Corel Professional Photos CD-ROM™ **730** (b.) Courtesy of Simon & Schuster, Children's Publishing Division **735** Bettmann/CORBIS **738** Debra P. Hershkowitz/Bruce Coleman, Inc. **740–741** ©Richard Hamilton Smith/CORBIS **740** (b.) Photo by Bachrach **741** (b.) The Granger Collection, New York **742** (b.) New York Public Library **742** (t.) Steve Satushek/The Image Bank **746** Digital Imagery ©Copyright 2001 PhotoDisc, Inc. **747** Courtesy of Dana Gluckstein **749** ©Carl Purcell/Photo Researchers, Inc. **760** (t.l.) ©John Gerlach/Animals Animals **760** (t.r.) Myrleen Ferguson/CORBIS **760** (b.) Courtesy of the Library of Congress **762** *Coyote at Sunset*: detail from hand-painted wood bird house, Maureen Mahoney-Barraclough **764** L. N. Tolstoi, I. E. Repin, Sovfoto/Eastfoto; **765, 766** Corel Professional Photos CD-ROM™ **767** ©John Gerlach/Animals Animals **769** Prentice Hall **770** *Coyotes*: detail from hand-painted wood desk, Maureen Mahoney Barraclough **772** *Mouse and Owl*: detail from hand-painted wood desk, Maureen Mahoney Barraclough **778** Nigel Dennis/Photo Researchers, Inc. **780** Wolfgang Kaehler/Liaison Agency **781** JC Carton/Bruce Coleman, Inc./PictureQuest **782** Philip van den Berg/HPH Photography **783** Scholastic Art and Writing Awards **784** *Arachne* (detail), Arvis Stewart, Reprinted with the permission of Macmillan Publishing Company from *The Macmillan Book of Greek Gods and Heroes* by Alice Low, illustrated by Arvis Stewart, Copyright © 1985 by Macmillan Publishing Company; **787** Myrleen Ferguson/PhotoEdit **788** (b.) Courtesy, Houghton Mifflin Company **788** (t.) Digital Imagery ©Copyright 2001 PhotoDisc, Inc. **791** Michael Freeman/CORBIS **796** Courtesy of the Library of Congress **799, 800** ©Bettmann/CORBIS **804** Corel Professional Photos CD-ROM™ **806** David Young-Wolff/PhotoEdit **812** Brand X Pictures/Media Bakery

Staff Credits

The people who made up the *Prentice Hall Literature: Timeless Voices, Timeless Themes* team—representing design services, editorial, editorial services, market research, marketing services, media resources, online services & multimedia development, production services, project office, and publishing processes—are listed below. Bold type denotes the core team members.

Susan Andariese, Rosalyn Arcilla, Laura Jane Bird, Betsy Bostwick, **Anne M. Bray,** Evonne Burgess, **Louise B. Capuano, Pam Cardiff,** Megan Chill, Ed Cordero, Laura Dershewitz, Philip Fried, **Elaine Goldman,** Barbara Goodchild, Barbara Grant, **Rebecca Z. Graziano, Doreen Graizzaro,** Dennis Higbee, **Leanne Korszoloski,** Ellen Lees, David Liston, **Mary Luthi, George Lychock,** Gregory Lynch, Sue Lyons, **William McAllister,** Frances Medico, Gail Meyer, Jessica S. Paladini, Wendy Perri, Carolyn Carty Sapontzis, **Melissa Shustyk, Annette Simmons, Alicia Solis,** Robin Sullivan, Cynthia Sosland Summers, Lois Teesdale, **Elizabeth Torjussen, Doug Utigard,** Bernadette Walsh, Helen Young

The following persons provided invaluable assistance and support during the production of this program.

Gregory Abrom, Robert Aleman, Diane Alimena, Michele Angelucci, Gabriella Apolito, Penny Baker, Sharyn Banks, Anthony Barone, Barbara Blecher, Helen Byers, Rui Camarinha, Lorelee J. Campbell, John Carle, Cynthia Clampitt, Jaime L. Cohen, Martha Conway, Dina Curro, Nancy Dredge, Johanna Ehrmann, Josie K. Fixler, Steve Frankel, Kathy Gavilanes, Allen Gold, Michael E. Goodman, Diana Hahn, Kerry L. Harrigan, Jacki Hasko, Evan Holstrom, Beth Hyslip, Helen Issackedes, Cathy Johnson, Susan Karpin, Raegan Keida, Stephanie Kota, Mary Sue Langan, Elizabeth Letizia, Christine Mann, Vickie Menanteaux, Kathleen Mercandetti, Art Mkrtchyan, Karyl Murray, Kenneth Myett, Stefano Nese, Kim Ortell, Lissette Quiñones, Erin Rehill-Seker, Patricia Rodriguez, Mildred Schulte, Adam Sherman, Mary Siener, Jan K. Singh, Diane Smith, Barbara Stufflebeem, Louis Suffredini, Lois Tatarian, Tom Thompkins, Lisa Valente, Ryan Vaarsi, Linda Westerhoff, Jeff Zoda

Prentice Hall gratefully acknowledges the following teachers who provided student models for consideration in the program.

Barbara Abel, Dawn Akuna, Kathy Allen, Joan Anderson, Amy Bales, Lisa Cobb, Ann Collier-Buchanan, Janice Crews, Denise Donahue, Becky Dressler, Nicci Durban, Nancy Fahner, Margo Graf, Jan Graham, Carleen Hemric, Karen Hurley, Max Hutto, Lenore Hynes, Kim Johnson, Gail Kidd, Ashley MacDonald, Maureen Macdonald, Akiko Morimoto, Judy Plouff, Charlene Revels, Lynn Richter, Kathleen Riley, Sandy Shannon, Marilyn Shaw, Cheryl Spivak, Lynn Striepe, John Tierney, Vanna Turner, Pam Walden, Holly Ward, Jennifer Watson, Joan West, Virginia Wong